The Legal Environment of Business and Online Commerce

Fourth Edition

Henry R. Cheeseman

Clinical Professor of Business Law
Director of the Legal Studies Program
Marshall School of Business
University of Southern California

Upper Saddle River, New Jersey 07458

Library of Congress Cataloging-in-Publication Data

Cheeseman, Henry R.
The legal environment of business and online commerce / Henry R. Cheeseman.—4th ed.
p. cm.
Rev. ed. of: The legal and regulatory environment. 3rd ed. c2002.
Includes index.
ISBN 0-13-146533-3
1. Business law—United States. I. Cheeseman, Henry R. Legal and regulatory environment. II. Title.
KF888.C464 2004
346.7307—dc22
2003070745

Editorial Director: Jeff Shelstad
Senior Managing Editor (Editorial): Alana Bradley
Assistant Editor: Sam Goffinet
Senior Editorial Assistant: Jane Avery
Senior Media Project Manager: Nancy Welcher
Executive Marketing Manager: Beth Toland
Marketing Assistant: Melissa Owens
Managing Editor (Production): Cynthia Regan
Production Editor: Michael Reynolds
Production Assistant: Joe DeProspero
Manufacturing Buyer: Diane Peirano
Design Director: Maria Lange
Art Director: Kevin Kall
Interior Design: Jill Little
Cover Design: Karen Quigley
Cover Illustration/Photo: Superstock 55
Illustrator (Interior): GGS Book Services, Atlantic Highlands
Image Permission Coordinator: Debbie Hewitson
Manager, Print Production: Christy Mahon
Print Production Liaison: Suzanne Duda
Composition/Full-Service Project Management: GGS Book Services, Atlantic Highlands
Printer/Binder: Von Hoffmann

Credits and acknowledgments borrowed from other sources and reproduced, with permission, in this textbook appear on appropriate page within text. All interior photos © Henry R. Cheeseman.

Pearson Education LTD.
Pearson Education Singapore, Pte. Ltd
Pearson Education, Canada, Ltd
Pearson Education–Japan
Pearson Education Australia PTY, Limited
Pearson Education North Asia Ltd
Pearson Educación de Mexico, S.A. de C.V.
Pearson Education Malaysia, Pte. Ltd

10 9 8 7 6 5 4 3 2 1
0-13-146533-3

Business Ethics

Contemporary Business Environment

Entrepreneur and the Law

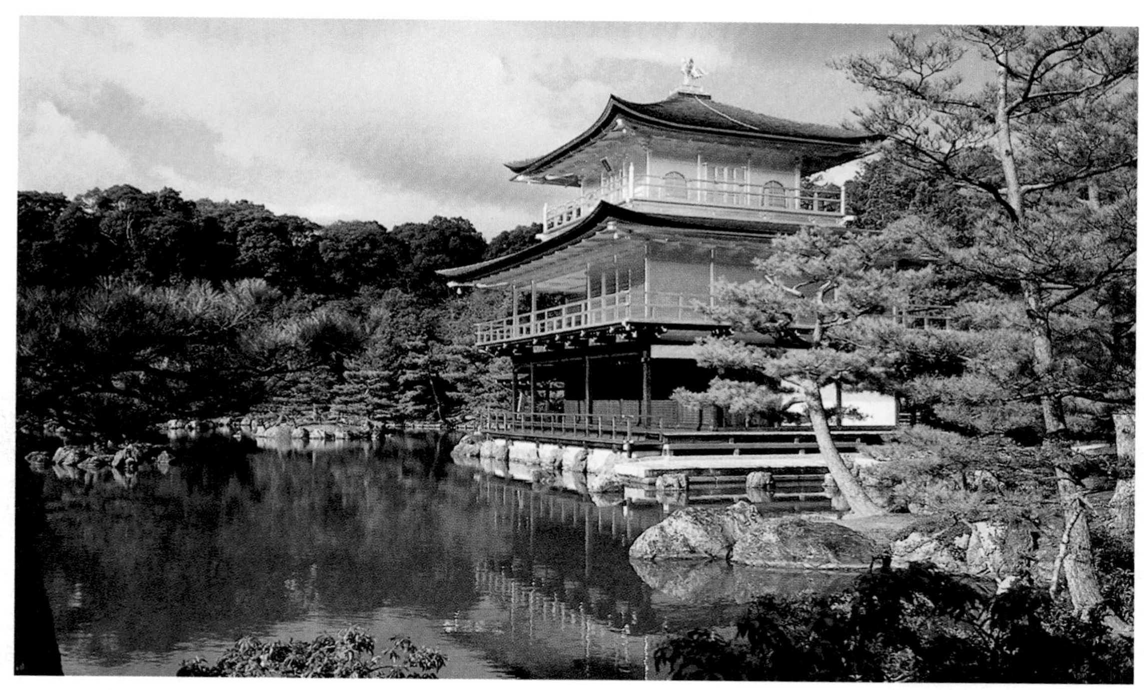

Cherry blossom,
          appearing as mysterious
as a white peasant,
          I sat as still
as a Zen garden
          when your color
announced the season.

Your delicate petals
          swept across time
and ocean,
          lost in the setting sun.
I laid to rest
          on my Samurai sword.
This life is winter.

As Buddhists, death is life,
          and in the next
we will meet
          in the shadow
of Mount Fuji.
          I will not sit zazen
when you blossom.

Contents in Brief

Contents

Preface

To the Students

Each semester, as I stand up in front of a new group of business majors in my business law class I am struck by the thought that, cases and statutes aside, I know two very important things that they have yet to learn. The first is that I draw as much from them as they do from me. Their youth, enthusiasm, questions, and even the doubts a few of them hold about the relevance of law to their futures, fuel my teaching. They don't know that every time they open their minds to look at a point from a new perspective or critically question something they have taken for granted, I get a wonderful reward for the work that I do.

The other thing I know is that both teaching and learning the legal and ethical environment are all about stories. The stories I tell provide the framework on which students will hang everything they learn about the law in my class. It is my hope that long after the facts about the specific language of the statutes have faded, they will retain that framework. Several years from now, "unintentional torts" may draw only a glimmer of recognition with business managers who learn about them as students in my class this year. However, they will likely recall the story of the woman who sued McDonalds for serving her coffee that was too hot and caused her injuries. The story sticks and gives students the hook on which to hang the concepts.

I remind myself of these two facts every time I sit down to work on writing and revising *The Legal Environment and Online Commerce* as well. My goal is to present law and ethics in a way that will spur students to ask questions, to go beyond rote memorization. Business law is an evolving outgrowth of its environment, and that environment keeps changing. In addition to the social, ethical, and international contexts I have incorporated in previous editions of *The Legal Environment and Online Commerce*, this fourth edition emphasizes coverage of e-commerce and the Internet as two vital catalysts to the law and a key part of its environment.

It is my wish that my commitment to these goals shines through in this labor of love, and I hope you have as much pleasure in using it as I have had in creating it for you.

Henry Cheeseman

Making the Most of the Fourth Edition

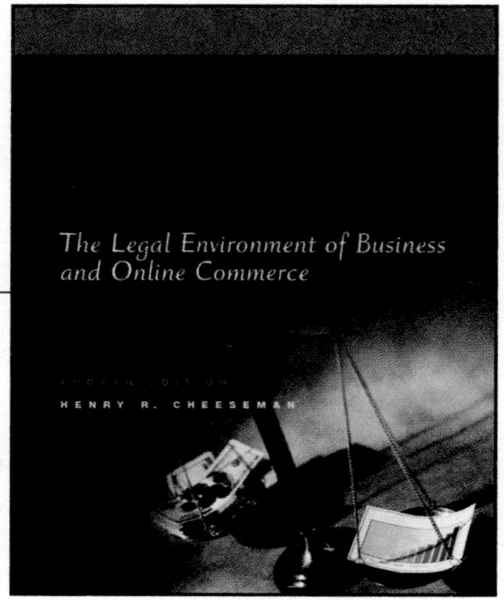

The Legal Environment of Business and Online Commerce
HENRY R. CHEESEMAN

These cases and boxes focus on the legal and ethical issues businesses, managers, and entrepreneurs face as they start businesses, operate existing enterprises, launch new Internet ventures, and incorporate on-line technologies into their current businesses.

Cases

Cases—Over *70 new cases* have been added to the Fourth Edition. Each chapter includes 3 to 6 interesting and lively cases presented in an edited format, retaining the language of the court for the "Reasoning of the Court" portion of the case. The format of each case: Background and Facts, Issue, Language of the Court, Decision and Remedy. Three questions follow each case to promote active learning.

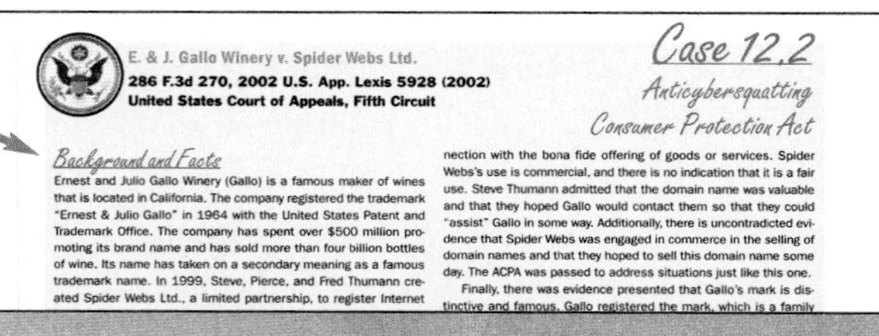

E. & J. Gallo Winery v. Spider Webs Ltd.
286 F.3d 270, 2002 U.S. App. Lexis 5928 (2002)
United States Court of Appeals, Fifth Circuit

Case 12.2
Anticybersquatting Consumer Protection Act

Background and Facts

Ernest and Julio Gallo Winery (Gallo) is a famous maker of wines that is located in California. The company registered the trademark "Ernest & Julio Gallo" in 1964 with the United States Patent and Trademark Office. The company has spent over $500 million promoting its brand name and has sold more than four billion bottles of wine. Its name has taken on a secondary meaning as a famous trademark name. In 1999, Steve, Pierce, and Fred Thumann created Spider Webs Ltd., a limited partnership, to register Internet nection with the bona fide offering of goods or services. Spider Webs's use is commercial, and there is no indication that it is a fair use. Steve Thumann admitted that the domain name was valuable and that they hoped Gallo would contact them so that they could "assist" Gallo in some way. Additionally, there is uncontradicted evidence that Spider Webs was engaged in commerce in the selling of domain names and that they hoped to sell this domain name some day. The ACPA was passed to address situations just like this one.

Finally, there was evidence presented that Gallo's mark is distinctive and famous. Gallo registered the mark, which is a family

U.S. SUPREME COURT CASE
Grutter v. Bollinger and the University of Michigan Law School
123 S.Ct. 2325, 2003 U.S. Lexis 4800 (2003)
Supreme Court of the United States

Case 1.2
Affirmative Action

Background and Facts

Barbara Grutter, a Caucasian resident of the state of Michigan, applied to the Law School of the University of Michigan, a state government–supported institution, in 1996 with a 3.8 undergraduate grade point average and a 161 LSAT score. The Law School rejected her application. The Law School received 3,500 applications for a class of 350 students. The Law School used race as one of the factors in considering applicants for admission to law school. The race of minority applicants, defined as blacks, Hispanics, and Native Americans, was considered as a "plus factor" in considering their applications to law school. Caucasians and Asians were not given such a plus factor. The Law School stated that it used race as a plus factor to obtain a critical mass of underrepresented minority students in order to create diversity at the school.

Grutter brought a class action lawsuit against the Law School of the University of Michigan, alleging that its use of a minority's race as a plus factor in admissions violated the Equal Protection Clause of the Fourteenth Amendment to the U.S. Constitution. The district court held that the Law School's use of race as a factor in admissions violated the Equal Protection Clause. The court of appeals reversed. The U.S. Supreme Court granted certiorari to hear the appeal.

Supreme Court Issue

Does the University of Michigan Law School's use of race as a plus factor in accepting minority applicants for admission to the Law School violate the Equal Protection Clause of the Fourteenth Amendment to the U.S. Constitution?

In The Language of The U.S. Supreme Court

O'Connor, Justice The Equal Protection Clause provides that no State shall "deny to any person within its jurisdiction the equal protection of the laws." Racial classifications imposed by government must be analyzed by a reviewing court under strict scrutiny. When race-based action is necessary to further a compelling governmental interest, such action does not violate the constitutional guarantee of equal protection so long as the narrow-tailoring requirement is also satisfied. Universities occupy a special niche in our constitutional tradition. In order to cultivate a set of leaders with legitimacy in the eyes of the citizenry, it is necessary that the path to leadership be visibly open to talented and qualified individuals of every race and ethnicity.

To be narrowly tailored, a race-conscious admissions program cannot use a quota system. Instead, a university may consider race or ethnicity only as a "plus" in a particular applicant's file. We find that the Law School's admissions program bears the hallmarks of a narrowly tailored plan. Universities cannot establish quotas for members of certain racial groups or put members of those groups on separate admissions tracks. Nor can universities insulate applicants who belong to certain racial or ethnic groups from the competition for admission. Universities can, however, consider race or ethnicity more flexibly as a "plus" factor in the context of individualized consideration of each and every applicant.

The Law School's goal of attaining a critical mass of underrepresented minority students does not transform its program into a quota. Here, the Law School engages in a highly individualized, holistic review of each applicant's file, giving serious consideration to all the ways an applicant might contribute to a diverse educational environment. The Law School affords this individualized consideration to applicants of all races. We agree that, in the context of its individualized inquiry into the possible diversity contributions of all applicants, the Law School's race conscious admissions program does not unduly harm nonminority applicants.

We take the Law School at its word that it would like nothing better than to find a race-neutral admissions formula and will terminate its race-conscious admissions program as soon as practicable. We expect that 25 years from now, the use of racial preferences will no longer be necessary to further the interest approved today.

Decision and Remedy

The U.S. Supreme Court held that the University of Michigan Law School's policy of using race as a plus factor in admitting minority applicants furthers a compelling state interest and is narrowly tailored to accomplish that interest. The Supreme Court held that the Law School's race-conscious admissions policy does not violate the Equal Protection Clause of the Fourteenth Amendment to the U.S. Constitution.

Case Questions

Critical Legal Thinking What does the Equal Protection Clause provide? Should the government ever be allowed to treat persons differently because of their race? Explain.

Business Ethics Is it socially responsible for the University of Michigan Law School to consider a minority applicant's race as a plus factor in its admissions decisions?

Contemporary Business Is anyone hurt by the University of Michigan Law School's race-conscious admissions policy? Explain.

United States Supreme Court Cases—Over 70 cases of the United States Supreme Court are presented throughout the book. These are the most important and modern cases affecting business that have been decided by the Supreme Court.

Business Ethics

The *ethical environment* of business is covered in many ways in the Fourth Edition. **Chapter 4 Ethics and Social Responsibility of Business,** is just the beginning of the ethics coverage in the fourth edition.

4

Ethics and Social Responsibility of Business

"Ethical considerations can no more be excluded from the administration of justice, which is the end and purpose of all civil laws, than one can exclude the vital air from his room and live."

—John F. Dillon
Laws and Jurisprudence of England and America Lecture I (1894)

Chapter Objectives

After studying this chapter, you should be able to:

1. Describe morality.

Business Ethics

Sarbanes-Oxley Act Prompts Public Companies to Adopt Code of Ethics

In the late 1990s and early 2000s, many large corporations in the United States were found to have engaged in massive financial frauds. Many of these frauds were perpetrated by the chief executive officer and other senior officers of the companies. Financial officers, such as the chief financial officer and controller, were also found to have been instrumental in creating these frauds. In response, Congress enacted the **Sarbanes-Oxley Act of 2002**, which makes certain conduct illegal and establishes criminal penalties for violations.

In addition, the Sarbanes-Oxley Act prompts companies to encourage senior officers of public companies to act ethically in their dealings with shareholders, employees, and other constituents. **Section 406** of the Sarbanes-Oxley Act requires a public company to disclose whether it has adopted a **Code of Ethics** for senior financial officers, including its principal financial officer and principal accounting officer. In response, public companies have adopted codes of ethics for their senior financial officers. Many public companies have included all officers and employees in the coverage of their codes of ethics.

A typical code of ethics follows.

Big Cheese Corporation
Code of Ethics

Big Cheese Corporation's mission includes the promotion of professional conduct in the practice of general management worldwide. Big Cheese's Chief Executive Officer (CEO), Chief Financial Officer (CFO), corporate Controller, and other employees of the finance organization and other employees of the corporation hold an important and elevated role in the corporate governance of the corporation. They are empowered and uniquely capable to ensure that all constituents' interests are appropriately balanced, protected, and preserved.

This Code of Ethics embodies principles to which we are expected to adhere and advocate. The CEO, CFO, finance organization employees, and other employees of the corporation are expected to abide by this Code of Ethics and all business conduct standards of the corporation relating to areas covered by this Code of Ethics. Any violation of the Code of Ethics may result in disciplinary action, up to and including termination of employment. All employees will:

- Act with honesty and integrity, avoiding actual or apparent conflicts of interest in their personal and professional relations.
- Provide stakeholders with information that is accurate, fair, complete, timely, objective, relevant, and understandable, including in our filings with and other submissions to the U.S. Securities and Exchange Commission.
- Comply with rules and regulations of federal, state, provincial, and local governments and other appropriate private and public regulatory agencies.

More than 30 **"Business Ethics" boxes** use issues from real companies to highlight the importance of ethics in making business decisions.

Trademark Act. Although not finding that Samara's clothes had acquired a secondary meaning in the minds of the public, the district court held in favor of Samara and awarded damages. The court of appeals affirmed. Wal-Mart appealed to the U.S. Supreme Court.

Supreme Court Issue

Must a product's design have acquired a secondary meaning before it is protected as trade dress under Section 43(a) of the Lanham Trademark Act?

In The Language of The U.S. Supreme Court

Scalia, Justice In addition to protecting registered marks, the Lanham Act, in Section 43(a), gives a producer a cause of action for the use by any person of "any word, term, name, symbol, or device, or any combination thereof . . . which . . . is likely to cause confusion . . . as to the origin, sponsorship, or approval of his or her goods. . . ." It is this provision that is at issue in this case. The text of Section 43(a) provides little guidance as to the

Decision and Remedy

The U.S. Supreme Court held that a product's design has to have acquired a secondary meaning in the public's eye before it is protected as trade dress under Section 43(a) of the Lanham Trademark Act. The Supreme Court reversed the decision of the court of appeals.

Case Questions

Critical Legal Thinking What is trade dress? What is secondary meaning? Can this case be reconciled with the previous case, Two Pesos, Inc. v. Taco Cabana, Inc., which held that no secondary meaning had to be shown to protect trade dress in product packaging?

Business Ethics Was it ethical for Wal-Mart to copy Samara Brothers' design for children's clothing? What was Wal-Mart's motive?

Contemporary Business What were the economic consequences of the U.S. Supreme Court's decision? Who are the winners? Who are the losers?

Every case in the text ends with an *ethics question* for discussion.

Business Ethics Cases

4.1 Business Ethics The A. H. Robins Company manufactured the Dalkon Shield, an intrauterine device used by more than 2 million women for contraception during the early 1970s. The device was defectively designed and caused women problems of infection, pelvic inflammatory disease, infertility, and spontaneous abortion, as well as health defects in their children. Thousands of product liability lawsuits were filed against the company by the women and children who were injured by the Dalkon Shield. The company and its insurers chose to fight these cases aggressively and spent many dollars in legal fees.

U.S. District Court Judge Miles Lord handled many of these cases. He called the Dalkon Shield an "instrument of death, mutilation, and disease" and chastised the executives of the company for violating "every ethical precept" of the Hippocratic oath, the medical profession's promise to save lives. Judge Lord stated,

> *Your company in the face of overwhelming evidence denies its guilt and continues its monstrous mischief. You have taken the bottom line as your guiding beacon and the low road as your route. This is corporate irresponsibility at its meanest.*

The company eventually filed for bankruptcy. The U.S. court of appeals censored Judge Lord for being too vocal. Is it ethical for a company to aggressively contest lawsuits that are filed against it even if it knows that it is responsible for the injury?

In 1972, the FTC filed a complaint against Warner-Lambert, alleging that the company engaged in false advertising in violation of federal law. Four months of hearings held before an administrative law judge produced an evidentiary record of more than 4,000 pages of documents from witnesses. In 1975, after examining the evidence, the FTC issued an opinion that held that the company's representations that Listerine prevented and cured colds and sore throats were false. The U.S. court of appeals affirmed.

Did Warner-Lambert act ethically in making its claims for Listerine? What remedy should the court impose on the company? Would making Warner-Lambert cease such advertising be sufficient? [*Warner-Lambert Company v. Federal Trade Commission*, 562 F.2d 749, 1977 U.S. App. Lexis 11599 (D.C. Cir. 1977)]

4.3 Business Ethics Stanford University is one of the premier research universities in the country. Stanford has an operating budget of approximately $400 million a year and receives about $175 million a year in direct research funding from the federal government. In addition, the government reimburses the university for certain overhead and indirect costs associated with the research. This amounts to about $85 million a year.

In 1990, a navy accountant took a close look at Stanford's books and alleged that the university may have overstated overhead and indirect costs associated with research by as much as $200 million during the 1980s. The university provides a house

Each chapter ends with additional business ethics case questions.

E-Commerce & Information Technology

Two chapters dedicated to coverage of Intellectual Property, the Internet and E-Commerce Law.

- **Chapter 8 "Intellectual Property and Information Technology"**
- **Chapter 12 "Internet Law and Electronic Commerce"**

8

Intellectual Property and Information Technology

"The Congress shall have the power . . . to promote the Progress of Science and useful Arts, by securing for limited Times to Authors

12

Internet Law and Electronic Commerce

"Through the use of chat rooms, any person with a phone line can become a town crier with a voice that resonates farther than it could from any soapbox. Through the use of Web pages, mail exploders, and newsgroups, the same individual can become a pamphleteer."

—Justice Stevens

Over 45 **E-Commerce** and **Information Technology boxes** focus on the legal issues businesses face as they either launch new Internet ventures or rise to the challenge of incorporating on-line technologies into their existing business models.

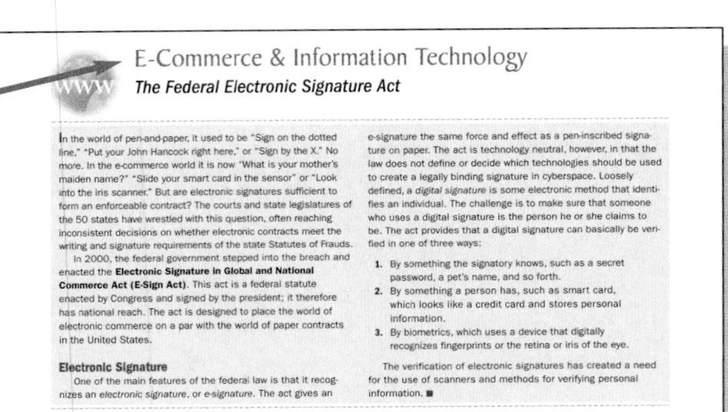

E-Commerce & Information Technology

The Federal Electronic Signature Act

In the world of pen-and-paper, it used to be "Sign on the dotted line," "Put your John Hancock right here," or "Sign by the X." No more. In the e-commerce world it is now "What is your mother's maiden name?" "Slide your smart card in the sensor" or "Look into the iris scanner." But are electronic signatures sufficient to form an enforceable contract? The courts and state legislatures of the 50 states have wrestled with this question, often reaching inconsistent decisions on whether electronic contracts meet the writing and signature requirements of the state Statutes of Frauds.

In 2000, the federal government stepped into the breach and enacted the **Electronic Signature in Global and National Commerce Act (E-Sign Act)**. This act is a federal statute enacted by Congress and signed by the president; it therefore has national reach. The act is designed to place the world of electronic commerce on a par with the world of paper contracts in the United States.

Electronic Signature

One of the main features of the federal law is that it recognizes an *electronic signature*, or *e-signature*. The act gives an e-signature the same force and effect as a pen-inscribed signature on paper. The act is technology neutral, however, in that the law does not define or decide which technologies should be used to create a legally binding signature in cyberspace. Loosely defined, a *digital signature* is some electronic method that identifies an individual. The challenge is to make sure that someone who uses a digital signature is the person he or she claims to be. The act provides that a digital signature can basically be verified in one of three ways:

1. By something the signatory knows, such as a secret password, a pet's name, and so forth.
2. By something a person has, such as smart card, which looks like a credit card and stores personal information.
3. By biometrics, which uses a device that digitally recognizes fingerprints or the retina or iris of the eye.

The verification of electronic signatures has created a need for the use of scanners and methods for verifying personal information. ■

Contemporary Business Environment

The 70-plus **"Contemporary Business Environment" boxes** recognize that not all of the modern challenges facing businesses are Internet-related. These boxes explore other types of legal issues currently confronting businesses.

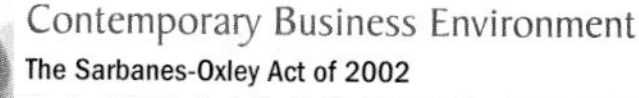

Contemporary Business Environment

The Sarbanes-Oxley Act of 2002

During the late 1990s and early 2000s, the U.S. economy was wracked by a number of business and accounting scandals. Companies such as Enron, Tyco, and Worldcom engaged in fraudulent conduct, leading to the conviction of many corporate officers of financial crimes. Many of these companies went bankrupt, causing huge losses to their shareholders, employees, and creditors. Accounting firms were caught conspiring to conceal this fraudulent conduct, and one of them, the prior Big 5 accounting firm Arthur Andersen, went under. Boards of directors were also complacent, not keeping a watchful eye over the conduct of their officers and employees.

In response, Congress enacted the federal **Sarbanes-Oxley Act of 2002**. This act established far-reaching new rules regarding corporate governance, established independence between public accounting firms and the public companies they audit, and created new government oversight over public corporations and their officers and the public accountants that audit public companies. The act also created new criminal penalties for violations of its provisions and other federal criminal laws. The provisions of the act apply to public companies.

The goals of the Sarbanes-Oxley Act are to improve corporate governance rules, eliminate conflicts of interest, and instill confidence in investors and the public that management will run public companies in the best interests of all constituents. Although the Sarbanes-Oxley Act applies only to public companies, private companies and nonprofit organizations will be influenced by the act's accounting and corporate governance rules.

A summary of important provisions of the Sarbanes-Oxley Act follows.

Separation of Audit and Nonaudit Services

The act makes it unlawful for a registered public accounting firm to simultaneously provide audit and certain nonaudit services to a public company. If a public accounting firm audits a public company, the accounting firm may not provide the following nonaudit services to the client: (1) bookkeeping services; (2) financial information systems; (3) appraisal or valuation services; (4) internal audit services; (5) management functions; (6) human resources; (7) broker, dealer, or investment services; (8) investment banking services; (9) legal services; (10) or any other services the Board determines. A certified public accounting firm may provide tax services to audit clients if such tax services are preapproved by the audit committee of the client.

Audit Reports Sign-Offs

Each audit by a certified public accounting firm is assigned an audit partner of the firm to supervise the audit and approve the audit report. The act requires that a second partner of the accounting firm review and approve audit reports prepared by the firm. All audit papers must be retained for at least seven years. The lead audit partner and reviewing partner must rotate off an audit every five years.

Prohibited Employment

Any person who is employed by a public accounting firm that audits a client cannot be employed by that client as the chief executive officer (CEO), chief financial officer (CFO), controller, chief accounting officer, or equivalent position for a period of one year following the audit.

International Law

Chapter 9 "International and Comparative Law," is devoted exclusively to coverage of international laws, courts, organizations, dispute resolution, and regional trade agreements.

"International law, or the law that governs between nations, has at times, been like the common law within states, a twilight existence during which it is hardly distinguishable from morality or justice, till at length the imprimatur of a court attests its jural quality."

—Justice Cardozo
New Jersey v. Delaware, 291 U.S. 361, 54 S.Ct. 407, 78 L.Ed. 847 (1934)

Chapter Objectives

After studying this chapter, you should be able to:

1. Describe the federal government's power under the Foreign Commerce and Treaty Clauses of the U.S. Constitution.
2. List and describe the sources of international law.
3. Describe the functions and governance of the United Nations.

International Law

China Joins the WTO

For the past 50 years, China and the United States have pursued divergent paths. China became the world's largest communist country and the United States the leading democracy. China maintained its agricultural base, while the United States pursued industrialization. China's businesses were state owned, while those in the United States were privately owned under a capitalist system. So what do these countries have in common? A new landmark trade pact. For over a decade, these two countries engaged in on-again, off-again trade negotiations. Then in November 1999 they formed a landmark trade pact.

In exchange for being granted the right to import most goods and services into the United States, China, which had substantially restricted imports into its country, agreed to open its markets to foreign goods and services in the following ways:

- ***Telecommunications*** Foreign telephone companies may own up to 50 percent of Chinese telephone companies.
- ***Entertainment*** China will double the number of U.S. films that can be imported into the country to 20 annually; the content of these films must be approved by the Chinese government.
- ***Banking and Financial Services*** Foreign banks may offer financial services to Chinese customers. China will allow foreign companies to own up to 49 percent of banks, insurance companies, and other financial-service companies.
- ***Distribution*** Foreigners may establish their own product distribution systems and sell directly to Chinese customers.
- ***Services*** Foreigners may establish their own repair and maintenance service businesses in China.
- ***Vehicle Sales*** China will permit foreign automobile manufacturers to sell and finance sales to Chinese customers.
- ***Farm Products*** China will eliminate subsidies of Chinese exports.
- ***Internet*** Foreign investors may own up to 50 percent of Chinese Internet businesses.

The China–U.S. trade agreement was a prelude to China's application to join the WTO. In 2002, China became a member of the WTO. China's entry into the WTO makes it a full partner in the world's trading system. The landmark China–U.S. trade pact is only one of many agreements that underscore the importance that trade and commerce now play in international politics.

The China–U.S. trade agreement is not without its critics. In the United States, labor unions criticize the agreement for its potential to ship U.S. manufacturing jobs to China, while environmentalists complain that little is being done to protect the environment from an industrialized economy the size of China. In China, workers at state-owned enterprises might lose their jobs to foreign capitalist companies that can produce goods and services more efficiently, and China's already impoverished farmers may be harmed by cheap farm products imported from other countries. But leaders from both countries thought the entry of China as a full member of the international trading community was worth these risks. ■

More than 50 **International Law boxes** provide students the opportunity to draw comparisons between the American system of justice and various other systems abroad.

Entrepreneur and the Law

Chapter 14 "Entrepreneurship, Sole Proprietorships and Franchising," recognizes the explosion of entrepreneurial ventures as an important factor in contemporary American business and investigates the legal issues unique to them.

14

Entrepreneurships, Sole Proprietorships, and Franchising

"Commerce never really flourishes so much, as when it is delivered from the guardianship of legislators and ministers."

—William Godwin
Enquiry Concerning Political Justice (1798)

Entrepreneur and the Law

Management of a Limited Liability Company

In a member-managed LLC, each member has equal rights in the management of the business of the LLC, irrespective of the size of his or her capital contribution. Any matter relating to the business of the LLC is decided by a majority vote of the members [ULLCA § 404(a)].

Consider This Example Allison, Jaeson, Stacy, Lan-Wei, and Ivy form NorthWest.com, LLC. Allison contributes $100,000 capital, and each of the other four members contributes $25,000 capital. When deciding whether to add another line of products to the business, Stacy, Lan-Wei, and Ivy vote to add the line, and Allison and Jaeson vote against it. The line of new products is added to the LLC's business because three members voted yes while two members voted no. It does not matter that the two members who voted no contributed $125,000 in capital collectively versus $75,000 in capital contributed by the three members who voted yes.

In a manager-managed LLC, the members and nonmembers who are designated managers control the management of the LLC. The members who are not managers have no rights to manage the LLC unless otherwise provided in the operating agreement. A manager must be appointed by a vote of a majority of the members; managers may also be removed by a vote of the majority of the members [ULLCA § 404(b)(3)]. In a manager-managed LLC, each manager has equal rights in the management and conduct of the company's business. Any matter relating to the business of the LLC may be exclusively decided by the managers by a majority vote of the managers [ULLCA § 403(b)].

Certain actions cannot be delegated to managers but must be voted on by all members of the LLC. These include (1) amending the articles of organization, (2) amending the operating agreement, (3) admitting new members, (4) consenting to dissolve the LLC, (5) consenting to merge the LLC with another entity, and (6) selling, leasing, or disposing of all or substantially all of the LLC's property [ULLCA § 404(c)].

A member or manager may appoint a proxy to vote or otherwise act for him or her by signing an appropriate proxy card [ULLCA § 404(e)]. ■

Over 40 **"Entrepreneur and the Law" boxes** examine the legal implications of entrepreneurial successes and failures.

Landmark Law

Landmark Law—More than 30 **"Landmark Law" boxes** highlight the most important cases and statutes that have shaped the law in the United States.

Landmark Law

Family and Medical Leave Act

In February 1993, Congress enacted the **Family and Medical Leave Act**. The act guarantees workers unpaid time off from work for medical emergencies. The act, which applies to companies with 50 or more workers as well as federal, state, and local governments, covers about half of the nation's workforce. To be covered by the act, an employee must have worked for the employer for at least one year and have performed more than 1,250 hours of service during the previous 12-month period.

Covered employers are required to provide up to 12 weeks of unpaid leave during any 12-month period due to the

1. Birth of, and care for, a child.
2. Placement of a child for adoption or in foster care.
3. Serious health condition that makes the employee unable to perform his or her duties.
4. Care for a spouse, child, or parent with a serious health problem.

Leave because of the birth of a child or the placement of a child for adoption or foster care cannot be taken intermittently unless the employer agrees. Other leaves may be taken on an intermittent basis. The employer may require medical proof of claimed serious health conditions.

An eligible employee who takes leave must, upon returning to work, be restored to either the same or an equivalent position with equivalent employment benefits and pay. The restored employee is not entitled to the accrual of seniority during the leave period, however. A covered employer may deny restoration to a salaried employee who is among the highest-paid 10 percent of that employer's employees if the denial is necessary to prevent "substantial and grievous economic injury" to the employer's operations. ■

Additional Features

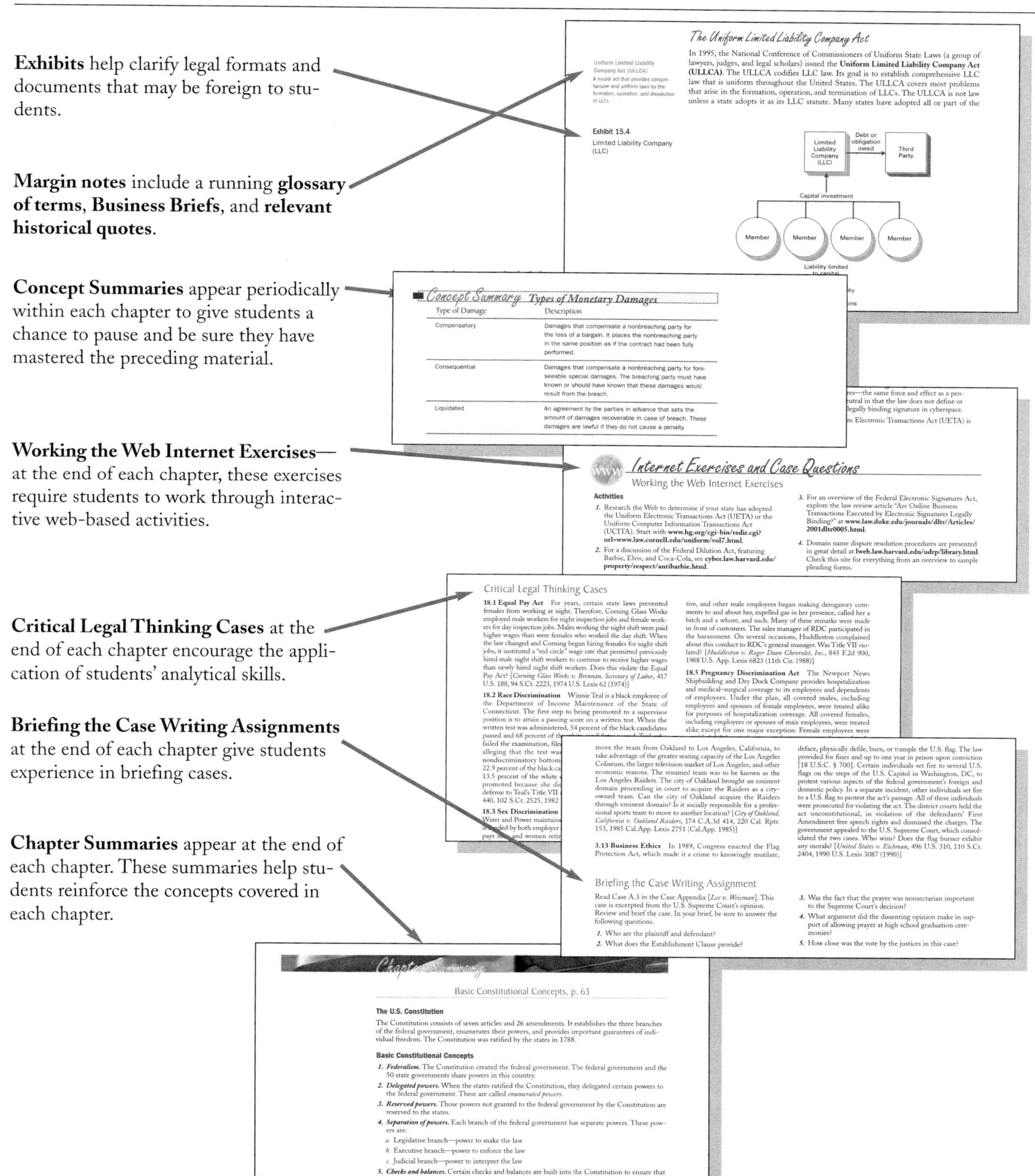

Exhibits help clarify legal formats and documents that may be foreign to students.

Margin notes include a running **glossary of terms, Business Briefs**, and **relevant historical quotes**.

Concept Summaries appear periodically within each chapter to give students a chance to pause and be sure they have mastered the preceding material.

Working the Web Internet Exercises—at the end of each chapter, these exercises require students to work through interactive web-based activities.

Critical Legal Thinking Cases at the end of each chapter encourage the application of students' analytical skills.

Briefing the Case Writing Assignments at the end of each chapter give students experience in briefing cases.

Chapter Summaries appear at the end of each chapter. These summaries help students reinforce the concepts covered in each chapter.

An Integrated Supplements Package

To ensure consistency of style, approach, and coverage among the key *print* and *online supplements*, these critical pieces were created by an author team working in conjunction with Henry Cheeseman. The supplements include:

Companion Web site Access at **www.prenhall.com/cheeseman**. This Web site will contain an Online Study Guide, including true/false and multiple choice questions, as well as PowerPoint presentations for each chapter. Also available is the **Business Law Case Library**, featuring regularly updated cases covering the key topics in most business law courses, including consumer protection, cyberlaw, and securities. Cases include actual legal decisions as well as hypothetical legal situations with questions for students. Answers to the hypothetical cases are provided. In addition, the business law timeline places all of the significant legal decisions, legislation, and other legal events on an easy-to-use interface.

Instructor's Manual A comprehensive outline of each text chapter. Also included are terms with definitions, chapter objectives, a key questions checklist, and sample syllabi.

Test Item File A bank of questions specially designed to aid in the preparation of tests. Each question includes a corresponding difficulty level, enabling the easy creation of tailor-made testing material.

TestGen Test management software containing all the material from the Test Item File. This software is completely user-friendly and allows instructors to view, edit, and add test questions with a few clicks of the mouse.

PowerPoints A ready-to-use PowerPoint slideshow, designed for classroom presentation. Use "as-is," or edit content to fit your individual class needs.

Study Guide A student aid designed to facilitate learning by enforcing key concepts. Each chapter contains a chapter overview, a list of objectives, and an explanation of the practical applications of each chapter. Also included is a "helpful hints" section and a sample quiz in addition to several exercises.

Instructor's Resource Center on CD A compilation of instructor's tools, including the Instructor's Manual, PowerPoints, Test Item File, and TestGen.

Enron Case Study This brief case explores the Enron debacle and the legal implications that are surrounding the case. It can be packaged with the text at no additional cost.

Acknowledgments

When I first began writing this book, I was a solitary figure researching cases and statutes in the law library and online, and writing text at my desk. As time passed, others entered upon the scene—editors, research assistants, reviewers, production personnel—and touched the project and made it better. Although my name appears on the cover of this book, it is no longer mine alone. I humbly thank the following persons for their contributions to this project.

The Professionals at Prentice Hall

For this fourth edition of *The Legal Environment of Business and Online Commerce* a special group of people from Prentice Hall have come together: Alana Bradley, acquisitions editor, who brought wonderful new ideas to revision who was the guiding light during the entire production, and whose imprint is everywhere in the new edition; Sandra Krausman, production coordinator, who was a joy to work with through the patient task of shepherding the manuscript from first manuscript pages to the final bound book; Beth Toland, executive marketing manager, who conducted marketing surveys to assure the fourth edition served the needs of its users and helped implement those suggestions; P. J. Boardman, vice president/editorial director, who authorized all the resources necessary to make this fourth edition possible; and Jerome Grant, president of Prentice Hall Business Publishing.

The Supplements Team

Sam Goffinet, supplements editor, is in charge of producing the extensive supplements that support this fourth edition of *The Legal Environment of Business and Online Commerce.* The supplements have been produced by a remarkable team of authors: Rhonda Carlson; Ed Gac, University of Colorado; Gloria Walker, Fayetteville Tech; Gregory Cermingnano, Widener University; Jimidene Murphey, Clandon College. I have worked closely with this team in producing the *Instructors Manual, Study Guide, Test Item File, PowerPoint slides*, and *web support* for this edition.

The Prentice Hall "family" has come together and produced a book and supplement package that I believe is the best available. My success is theirs, and theirs' mine. They are my friends.

Reviews

I would like to personally thank the following reviewers, who have spent considerable time and effort reviewing the manuscripts for *The Legal Environment of Business and Online Commerce*, and whose comments, suggestions, and criticisms are seen in the final project.

David Austill	Union University
Eli C. Bortman	Babson College
Thomas D. Cavenagh	North Central College
Gregory P. Cermignano	Widener University
Ed Gac	University of Colorado
Gamewell Gantt	Idaho State University
Duane R. Lambert	California State University, Hayward
William Maakestad	Western Illinois University
Gregory McCann	Stetson University
Neal A. Phillips	University of Delaware

James Rittenbaum	St. Louis University
Scott Sandstrom	College of the Holy Cross
Allen Simonson	Montclair State University
S. Jay Sklar	Temple University
Joanie Sompayrac	University of Tennessee-Chattanooga
John A. Wrieden	Florida International University

Personal Acknowledgments

My family: My wife Shou-Yi Kang; my parents—Henry B. and Florence, deceased; my twin brother Gregory and his wife Lana; my sister Marcia; my nephew Gregory and niece Nikki, and the two new additions to the family, my great nieces Lauren and Addison.

The students at the Marshall School of Business at the University of Southern California. Their spirit, energy, and joy is contagious, and I love teaching them (and as important, they teaching me).

While writing this Preface and Acknowledgment, I have thought about the thousands of hours I have spent researching, writing, and preparing this manuscript. I loved every minute, and the knowledge gained has been sufficient reward for the endeavor.

I hope this book and its supplementary materials will serve you as well as they have served me.

Personal Note

With joy and sadness,
emptiness and fullness,
honor and humility,
I surrender the fruits of this labor

Henry R. Cheeseman

1

Nature of Law and Critical Legal Thinking

"Where there is no law, there is no freedom."

—John Locke
Second Treatise of Government, Sec. 57

Chapter Objectives

After studying this chapter, you should be able to:

1. Define law and describe the functions of law.
2. Explain the development of the U.S. legal system.
3. List and describe the sources of law in the United States.
4. Describe the international civil law legal system used in some other countries.
5. Apply critical legal thinking in analyzing judicial decisions.

Chapter Contents

- What Is Law?
- Schools of Jurisprudential Thought
- History of American Law
- Sources of Law in the United States
- Critical Legal Thinking

Management Decision Nature of Law and Critical Legal Thinking

You are the only female security guard employed by Carson Security Agency, a family-owned business that has 50 employees. You have worked for the company for six years and have an exemplary work record. However, your new supervisor has asked you on several occasions to go out on dates. You have rejected his advances. The supervisor has begun to belittle you in the presence of your co-workers and has sent you several sexually explicit e-mail messages. Your work schedule now consists of the most undesirable hours to work. Recently, your supervisor has offered you a job as a dispatcher, with an increase in pay. If you accept the dispatcher job, you will work in the office with your supervisor.

1. Have any laws been broken by the actions of your supervisor?
2. Should you inform the owner, Mr. Carson, about this situation?
3. What should Mr. Carson do to make sure that a similar situation does not occur?

Let every American, every lover of liberty, every well-wisher to his posterity, swear by the blood of the Revolution never to violate in the least particular the laws of the country, and never to tolerate their violation by others.

Abraham Lincoln Speech
January 27, 1837

Every society makes and enforces laws that govern the conduct of the individuals, businesses, and other organizations that function within it. In the words of Judge Learned Hand, "Without law we cannot live; only with it can we insure the future which by right is ours. The best of men's hopes are enmeshed in its success."[1]

Although the law of this country is primarily based on English common law, other legal systems, such as Spanish and French civil law, also influenced it. The sources of law in this country are the U.S. Constitution, state constitutions, federal and state statutes, ordinances, administrative agency rules and regulations, executive orders, and judicial decisions by federal and state courts.

Businesses that are organized in the United States are subject to its laws. They are also subject to the laws of other countries in which they operate. Businesses organized in other

Statue of Liberty, New York City, New York. The United States is the world's leading democracy. Peoples from around the world immigrate to the United States to seek the protection of its Constitution and laws.

countries must obey the laws of the United States when doing business here. In addition, businesspeople owe a duty to act ethically in the conduct of their affairs, and businesses owe a responsibility not to harm society.

This chapter discusses the nature and definition of law, the history and sources of law, and "critical legal thinking" as applied by the U.S. Supreme Court in deciding an actual case.

What Is Law?

The law consists of rules that regulate the conduct of individuals, businesses, and other organizations within society. It is intended to protect persons and their property against unwanted interference from others. In other words, the law forbids persons from engaging in certain undesirable activities.

Consider the following passage:

> Hardly anyone living in a civilized society has not at some time been told to do something or to refrain from doing something, because there is a law requiring it, or because it is against the law. What do we mean when we say such things? Most generally, how are we to understand statements of the form "x is law"? This is an ancient question. In his Memorabilia (I, ii), Xenophon reports a statement of the young Alcibiades, companion of Socrates, who in conversation with the great Pericles remarked that "no one can really deserve praise unless he knows what a law is."
>
> At the end of the 18th century, Immanuel Kant wrote of the question "What is law?" that it "may be said to be about as embarrassing to the jurist as the well-known question 'What is truth?' is to the logician."[2]

A lawyer without history or literature is a mechanic, a mere working mason: if he possesses some knowledge of these, he may venture to call himself an architect.

Sir Walter Scott
Guy Mannering, Ch. 37 (1815)

E-Commerce & Information Technology

Students Plug into the Internet and the Law

Every year millions of students arrive on college campuses and unpack an array of items—clothes, books, furniture, decorations, and their computers. College students used to be judged by the size of their stereo speakers; today it is their computers and their Internet savvy. Ninety percent of college students now own personal computers.

The Internet has revolutionized campus life. Computer kiosks abound around college campuses, occupying more space in libraries, dorm rooms, and hallways of athletic departments. Traditional libraries have become obsolete for many students as they conduct almost all of their research online. More than 70 percent of college students check out the Web daily, while others communicate through e-mail, pick up course assignments, download course notes, and socialize online. Current university and college students are wired to modern technology and will lead their parents, employers, and sometimes even their professors into the new world of high technology. Today's college students are the leaders of the e-generation.

Universities and colleges are now rated on not only how well they are connected with alumni but also on how well they are connected to computer technology. Some universities have installed software that allows their students to sit anywhere on campus with their laptops and "plug" into the school's computers. The computer is no longer just a study tool; it has become totally integrated into the lives of college students. The new generation of students study online, shop online, and even date online.

With this new technology comes one other thing that a student should know about: e-commerce and Internet law. The use of new computer technology has developed rapidly. For example, purchase of goods and items over the Internet is exploding. How is the contract formed? What about signatures? Is a purchaser's credit card information protected? What laws protect privacy over the Internet? Can an Internet user crack a wrapper and use certain software? What criminal laws apply to fraud over the Internet? The number of legal questions pertaining to this new technology is endless.

To help the student understand his or her legal rights and duties, this business law book fully integrates e-commerce and Internet law. Through this total integration of e-commerce and Internet law, a student will not only learn traditional business law topics, but will also be well versed in his or her legal rights while using the Internet. ■

Definition of Law

law
That which must be obeyed and followed by citizens subject to sanctions or legal consequences; a body of rules of action or conduct prescribed by controlling authority and having binding legal force.

The concept of **law** is very broad. Although it is difficult to state a precise definition, *Black's Law Dictionary* gives one that is sufficient for this text:

> Law, in its generic sense, is a body of rules of action or conduct prescribed by controlling authority, and having binding legal force. That which must be obeyed and followed by citizens subject to sanctions or legal consequences is a law.[3]

Functions of the Law

Commercial law lies within a narrow compass, and is far purer and freer from defects than any other part of the system.

Henry Peter Brougham
House of Commons, February 7, 1828

The law is often described by the function it serves within a society. The primary *functions* served by the law in this country are:

1. Keeping the peace, which includes making certain activities crimes.
2. Shaping moral standards (e.g., enacting laws that discourage drug and alcohol abuse).
3. Promoting social justice (e.g., enacting statutes that prohibit discrimination in employment).
4. Maintaining the status quo (e.g., passing laws preventing the forceful overthrow of the government).
5. Facilitating orderly change (e.g., passing statutes only after considerable study, debate, and public input).
6. Facilitating planning (e.g., well-designed commercial laws allow businesses to plan their activities, allocate their productive resources, and assess the risks they take).
7. Providing a basis for compromise (approximately 90 percent of all lawsuits are settled prior to trial).
8. Maximizing individual freedom (e.g., the rights of freedom of speech, religion, and association granted by the First Amendment to the U.S. Constitution).

Nepal. Each country has developed its own laws. A company conducting business in a foreign country is subject to that country's laws.

Landmark Law

Brown v. Board of Education

One of the main attributes of American law is its *flexibility*. It is generally responsive to cultural, technological, economic, and social changes. For example, laws that are no longer viable—such as those that restricted the property rights of women—are often repealed.

Sometimes it takes years before the law reflects the norms of society. Other times, society is led by the law. The Supreme Court's landmark decision in *Brown v. Board of Education* (347 U.S. 483, 74 S.Ct. 686, 1954 U.S. Lexis 2094 (1954)) is an example of the law leading the people. The Court's decision overturned the old "separate but equal" doctrine that condoned separate schools for black children and white children. ■

Fairness of the Law

On the whole, the American legal system is one of the most comprehensive, fair, and democratic systems of law ever developed and enforced. Nevertheless, some misuses and oversights of our legal system—including abuses of discretion and mistakes by judges and juries, unequal applications of the law, and procedural mishaps—allow some guilty parties to go unpunished.

In *Standefer v. United States*[4] the Supreme Court *affirmed* (let stand) the criminal conviction of a Gulf Oil Corporation executive for aiding and abetting the bribery of an Internal Revenue Service agent. The agent had been acquitted in a separate trial. In writing the opinion of the Court, Chief Justice Burger stated, "This case does no more than manifest the simple, if discomforting, reality that different juries may reach different results under any criminal statute. That is one of the consequences we accept under our jury system."

The law, in its majestic equality, forbids the rich as well as the poor to sleep under bridges.

Anatole France

Flexibility of the Law

U.S. law evolves and changes along with the norms of society, technology, and the growth and expansion of commerce in the United States and the world. The following quote by Judge Jerome Frank discusses the value of the adaptability of law:

> The law always has been, is now, and will ever continue to be, largely vague and variable. And how could this be otherwise? The law deals with human relations in their most complicated aspects. The whole confused, shifting helter-skelter of life parades before it—more confused than ever, in our kaleidoscopic age.
>
> Men have never been able to construct a comprehensive, eternalized set of rules anticipating all possible legal disputes and formulating in advance the rules which would apply to them. Situations are bound to occur which were never contemplated when the original rules were made. How much less is such a frozen legal system possible in modern times?
>
> The constant development of unprecedented problems requires a legal system capable of fluidity and pliancy. Our society would be straightjacketed were not the courts, with the able assistance of the lawyers, constantly overhauling the law and adapting it to the realities of ever-changing social, industrial, and political conditions; although changes cannot be made lightly, yet rules of law must be more or less impermanent, experimental and therefore not nicely calculable.
>
> Much of the uncertainty of law is not an unfortunate accident; it is of immense social value.[5]

The following case demonstrates how the original constitutional protection of freedom of speech is applied by the U.S. Supreme Court in examining a contemporary issue.

Business Brief

Laws cannot be written in advance to anticipate every dispute that could arise in the future. Therefore, general principles are developed to be applied by courts and juries to individual disputes. This flexibility in the law leads to some uncertainty in predicting results of lawsuits.

Two things most people should never see made: sausages and laws.

An old saying

Case 1.1 Flexibility of the Law

U.S. SUPREME COURT CASE

Ashcroft, Attorney General v. The Free Speech Coalition

535 U.S. 234, 122 S.Ct. 1389, 2002 U.S. Lexis 2789 (2002)

Supreme Court of the United States

Background and Facts

In 1996, Congress enacted the Child Pornography Prevention Act (CPPA). Section 2256(8)(B) of the act prohibits "any visual depiction, including any photograph, film, video, picture, or computer-generated image or picture" that "is, or appears to be, of a minor engaging in sexually explicit conduct." This section includes computer-generated images known as "virtual child pornography." A first-time offender may be imprisoned for 15 years; repeat offenders face prison sentences up to 30 years. The Free Speech Coalition, a trade association for the adult-entertainment industry, sued the United States, alleging that Section 2256(8)(B) violated their constitutional free speech rights. The district court granted summary judgment to the United States government, but the court of appeals reversed. The U.S. Supreme Court granted certiorari.

Supreme Court Issue

Does Section 2256(8)(B), which criminalizes virtual child pornography, violate the Freedom of Speech Clause of the First Amendment to the U.S. Constitution?

In The Language of The U.S. Supreme Court

Kennedy, Justice This case provides a textbook example of why we permit facial challenges to statutes that burden expression. With these severe penalties in force, few legitimate movie producers or book publishers, or few other speakers in any capacity, would risk distributing images in or near the uncertain reach of this law. The Constitution gives significant protection from overbroad laws that chill speech within the First Amendment's vast and privileged sphere. Under this principle, the CPPA is unconstitutional on its face if it prohibits a substantial amount of protected expression.

The Government submits that virtual child pornography whets the appetites of pedophiles and encourages them to engage in illegal conduct. This rationale cannot sustain the provision in question. The mere tendency of speech to encourage unlawful acts is not a sufficient reason for banning it. The government cannot constitutionally premise legislation on the desirability of controlling a person's private thoughts. First Amendment freedoms are most in danger when the government seeks to control thought or to justify its laws for that impermissible end. The right to think is the beginning of freedom, and speech must be protected from the government because speech is the beginning of thought. The government may not prohibit speech because it increases the chance an unlawful act will be committed at some indefinite future time.

Finally, the Government says that the possibility of producing images by using computer imaging makes it very difficult for it to prosecute those who produce pornography by using real children. Experts, we are told, may have difficulty in saying whether the pictures were made by using real children or by using computer imaging. The necessary solution, the argument runs, is to prohibit both kinds of images. The argument, in essence, is that protected speech may be banned as a means to ban unprotected speech. This analysis turns the First Amendment upside down. The Government may not suppress lawful speech as the means to suppress unlawful speech.

Decision and Remedy

The U.S. Supreme Court held that Section 2256(8)(B), which criminalizes virtual child pornography, violates the plaintiffs' free speech rights under the First Amendment to the U.S. Constitution. The Supreme Court affirmed the judgment of the court of appeals and remanded the case for further proceedings, consistent with its opinion.

Case Questions

Critical Legal Thinking What reasoning did the U.S. Supreme Court use in holding that the federal statute at issue was unconstitutional?

Business Ethics Is it ethical for an industry to make profits from virtual child pornography? Explain.

Contemporary Business Does this decision have any far-reaching economic effects? How big do you think the virtual child pornography market is?

Contemporary Business Environment

Feminist Legal Theory

In the past, the law treated men and women unequally. For example, women were denied the right to vote, could not own property if they were married, were unable to have legal abortions, and could not hold the same jobs as men. The enactment of statutes and the interpretation of constitutional provisions by the courts have changed all of these things. The Nineteenth Amendment gave women the right to vote. States have repealed constraints on the ability of women to own property. The famous U.S. Supreme Court decision in *Roe v. Wade*, 410 U.S. 959 (1973), gave women the constitutional right to an abortion.

Title VII of the Civil Rights Act of 1964 prohibits employment discrimination based on sex. In addition, the Equal Protection Clause of the U.S. and state constitutions provides that women cannot be treated differently from men (and vice versa) by the government unless some imperative reason warrants different treatment.

But is it enough for women to be treated like men? Should the female perspective be taken into account when legislators and judges develop, interpret, and apply the law? A growing body of scholarship known as **feminist legal theory** or **feminist jurisprudence** is being created around just such a theory.

The so-called "battered woman's syndrome" illustrates how this type of theory works. It has been introduced into evidence to prove self-defense in homicide cases where a woman is accused of killing her husband or another male. This defense asserts that sustained domestic violence against a woman may justify such a murder. Although this defense has been rejected by many courts, some courts have recognized battered woman's syndrome as a justifiable defense.

Some other areas of the law where a woman's perspective might differ from a man's include male-only combat rules in the military, rights to privacy, family law, child custody, surrogate motherhood, job security for pregnant women, rape, sexual assault, abortion, and sexual harassment. Even the traditional "reasonable man standard," so prevalent in American law, is being attacked as being gender biased. ■

Schools of Jurisprudential Thought

The philosophy or science of the law is referred to as **jurisprudence**. There are several different philosophies about how the law developed. They range from the classical natural theory to modern theories of law and economics and critical legal studies. Legal philosophers can generally be grouped into the major categories discussed in the paragraphs that follow.

jurisprudence
The philosophy or science of law.

The Natural Law School

The **Natural Law School** of jurisprudence postulates that the law is based on what is "correct." Natural law philosophers emphasize a **moral theory of law**—that is, law should be based on morality and ethics. Natural law is "discovered" by humans through the use of reason and choosing between good and evil. Documents such as the U.S. Constitution, the Magna Carta, and the United Nations Charter reflect this theory.

The Historical School

The **Historical School** of jurisprudence believes that the law is an aggregate of social traditions and customs that have developed over the centuries. It believes that changes in the norms of society will gradually be reflected in the law. To these legal philosophers, the law is an evolutionary process. Thus, historical legal scholars look to past legal decisions (precedent) to solve contemporary problems.

Human beings do not ever make laws; it is the accidents and catastrophes of all kinds happening in every conceivable way that make law for us.

Plato Laws IV.709

The Analytical School

The **Analytical School** of jurisprudence maintains that the law is shaped by logic. Analytical philosophers believe results are reached by applying principles of logic to the specific facts of the case. The emphasis is on the logic of the result rather than on how the result is reached.

The Sociological School

The **Sociological School** of jurisprudence asserts that the law is a means of achieving and advancing certain sociological goals. The followers of this philosophy, who are known as *realists*, believe that the purpose of law is to shape social behavior. Sociological philosophers are unlikely to adhere to past law as precedent.

Law must be stable and yet it cannot stand still.

Roscoe Pound
Interpretations of Legal History (1923)

The Command School

The philosophers of the **Command School** of jurisprudence believe that the law is a set of rules developed, communicated, and enforced by the ruling party rather than a reflection of the society's morality, history, logic, or sociology. This school maintains that the law changes when the ruling class changes.

The Critical Legal Studies School

> The law is not a series of calculating machines where definitions and answers come tumbling out when the right levers are pushed.
>
> William O. Douglas
> *The Dissent, A Safeguard of Democracy (1948)*

The **Critical Legal Studies School** proposes that legal rules are unnecessary and are used as an obstacle by the powerful to maintain the status quo. Critical legal theorists (the "*Crits*") argue that legal disputes should be solved by applying arbitrary rules that are based on broad notions of what is "fair" in each circumstance. Under this theory, subjective decision making by judges would be permitted.

Contemporary Business Environment

The Law and Economics School of Jurisprudential Thought

Should free-market principles, like the supply-and-demand and cost–benefit theories, determine the outcome of lawsuits and legislation? U.S. Court of Appeals Judge Richard Posner thinks so, and so do a growing number of other judges and legal theorists. These people are members of the **Law and Economics School** (or the "Chicago School") of jurisprudence, which began at the University of Chicago.

According to the Law and Economics School, which is unofficially headed by Judge Posner, promoting market efficiency should be the central goal of legal decision making. In the area of antitrust law, for example, law and economics theorists would not find corporate mergers and takeovers to be illegal simply because they resulted in market domination. Instead, they would find this practice to be illegal only if it rendered the overall market less efficient.

Focusing on cold economic categories like market efficiency may seem appropriate when making decisions in cases that involve businesses. However, proponents of law and economics theory use this type of analysis in cases involving everything from freedom of religion to civil rights. For example, in a 1983 dissenting opinion, Judge Posner suggested that the practice of appointing counsel, free of charge, to prisoners who bring civil rights cases should be abolished. If a prisoner cannot find a lawyer who will take the case on a contingency fee basis, it probably means that the case is not worth bringing. Naysayers warn that the morality of certain rights and liberties must be safeguarded even if it is unpopular or costly from an economic point of view. ■

Concept Summary Schools of Jurisprudential Thought

School	Philosophy
Natural Law	Postulates that law is based on what is "correct." It emphasizes a moral theory of law—that is, law should be based on morality and ethics.
Historical	Believes that law is an aggregate of social traditions and customs.
Analytical	Maintains that law is shaped by logic.
Sociological	Asserts that the law is a means of achieving and advancing certain sociological goals.
Command	Believes that the law is a set of rules developed, communicated, and enforced by the ruling party.
Critical Legal Studies	Maintains that legal rules are unnecessary and that legal disputes should be solved by applying arbitrary rules based on fairness.
Law and Economics	Believes that promoting market efficiency should be the central concern of legal decision making.

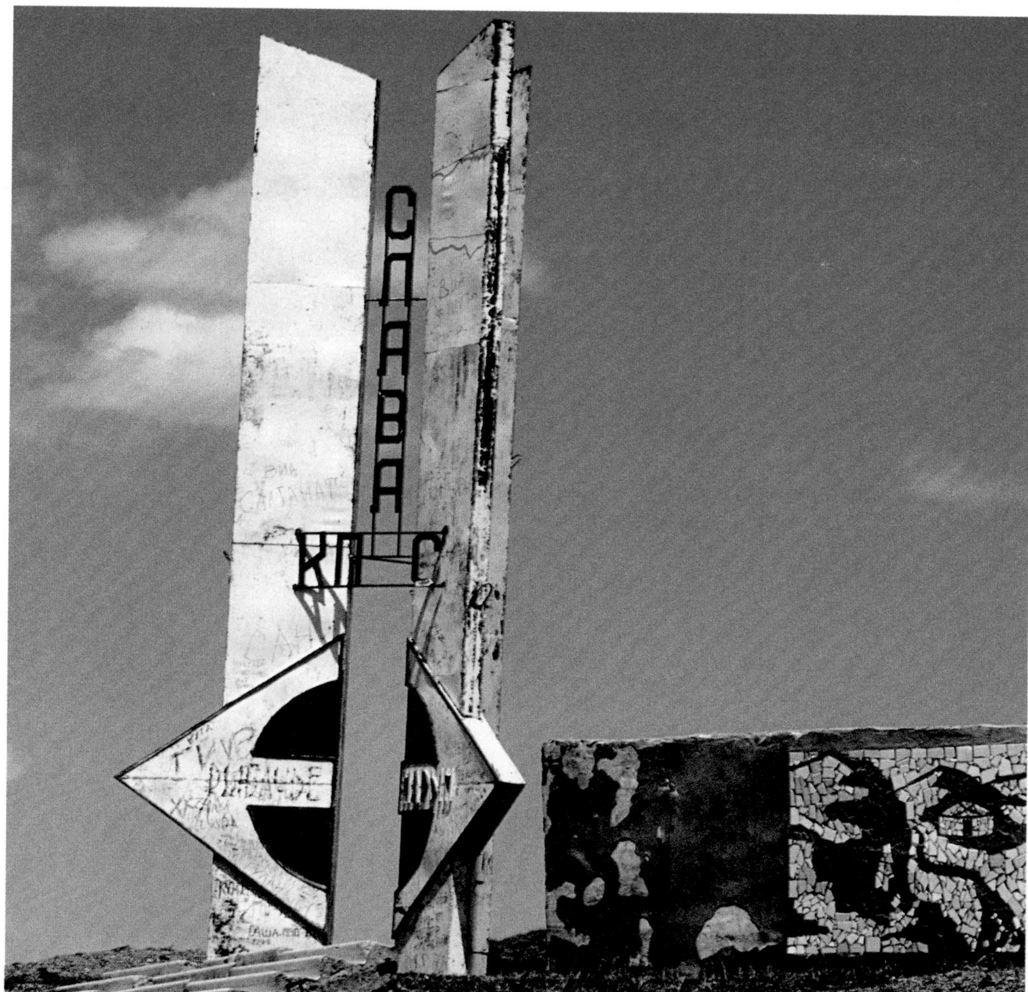

Kazakhstan. Many of the republics of the now-dismantled Soviet Union are giving up their prior command school system of law and replacing it with systems of law based on morality, history, logic, and sociology.

History of American Law

When the American colonies were first settled, the English system of law was generally adopted as the system of jurisprudence. This was the foundation from which American judges developed a common law in America.

English Common Law

English **common law** was law developed by judges who issued their opinions when deciding a case. The principles announced in these cases became *precedent* for later judges deciding similar cases. The English common law can be divided into cases decided by the law courts, equity courts, and merchant courts.

common law
Law developed by judges who issued their opinions when deciding a case. The principles announced in these cases became precedent for later judges deciding similar cases.

Law Courts Prior to the Norman Conquest of England in 1066, each locality in England was subject to local laws as established by the lord or chieftain in control of the local area. There was no countrywide system of law. After 1066, William the Conqueror and his successors to the throne of England began to replace the various local laws with one uniform system of law. To accomplish this, the king or queen appointed loyal followers as judges in all local areas. These judges were charged with administering the law in a uniform manner

law court
A court that developed and administered a uniform set of laws decreed by the kings and queens after William the Conqueror; legal procedure was emphasized over merits at that time.

Court of Chancery
A court that granted relief based on fairness. Also called equity court.

in courts that were called **law courts**. Law at that time tended to emphasize form (legal procedure) over the substance (merit) of the case. The only relief available at law courts was a monetary award for damages.

Chancery (Equity) Courts Because of the unfair results and the limited remedy available in the law courts, a second set of courts—the **Court of Chancery** (or **equity court**)—was established. These courts were under the authority of the Lord Chancellor. Persons who believed that the decision of the law court was unfair or that the law court could not grant an appropriate remedy could seek relief in the Court of Chancery. The Chancery Court inquired into the merits of the case, rather than emphasizing legal procedure. The Chancellor's remedies were called *equitable remedies* because they were shaped to fit each situation. Equitable order and remedies of the Court of Chancery took precedence over the legal decisions and remedies of the law courts.

Merchant Court
The separate set of courts established to administer the "law of merchants."

Merchant Courts As trade developed in the Middle Ages, the merchants who traveled about England and Europe developed certain rules to solve their commercial disputes. These rules, known as the "law of merchants" or the **Law Merchant,** were based upon common trade practices and usage. Eventually, a separate set of courts was established to administer these rules. This court was called the **Merchant Court**. In the early 1900s, the Merchant Court was absorbed into the regular law court system of England.

International Law

Adoption of English Common Law in America

All the states except Louisiana base their legal systems primarily on the English *common law*. Because of its French heritage, Louisiana bases its law on the *civil law* (see discussion of international legal systems later in this chapter). Elements of California and Texas law, as well as other southwestern states, are rooted in civil law.

In the United States, the law, equity, and merchant courts have been merged. Thus, most U.S. courts permit the aggrieved party to seek both law and equitable orders and remedies.

The importance of common law to the American legal system is described in the following excerpt from Justice Douglas's opinion in the 1841 case of *Penny v. Little* [4 Ill. 301 (IL 1841)]

The common law is a beautiful system, containing the wisdom and experiences of ages. Like the people it ruled and protected, it was simple and crude in its infancy and became enlarged, improved, and polished as the nation advanced in civilization, virtue, and intelligence. Adapting itself to the conditions and circumstances of the people and relying upon them for its administration, it necessarily improved as the condition of the people was elevated. The inhabitants of this country always claimed the common law as their birthright, and at an early period established it as the basis of their jurisprudence. ■

International Law

The Civil Law System

One of the major legal systems that has developed in the world in addition to the Anglo-American common law system is the **Romano-Germanic civil law system**. This legal system, which is commonly called the **civil law**, dates to 450 B.C., when Rome adopted the Twelve Tables, a code of laws applicable to the Romans. A compilation of Roman law, called the *Corpus Juris Civilis* (the Body of Civil Law), was completed in A.D. 534. Later, two national codes—the French Civil Code of 1804 (the Napoleonic Code) and the German Civil Code of 1896—became models for countries that adopted civil codes.

In contrast to the Anglo-American common law, where laws are created by the judicial system as well as by congressional legislation, the Civil Code and the parliamentary statutes that expand and interpret it are the sole sources of the law in most civil law countries. Thus, the adjudication of a case is simply the application of the code or the statutes to a particular set of facts. In some civil law countries, court decisions do not have the force of law.

Today, Austria, Belgium, Greece, Indonesia, Japan, Latin America, the Netherlands, Poland, Portugal, South Korea, Spain, Sub-Saharan Africa, Switzerland, and Turkey follow the civil law. ■

Red bus, London. The legal system of most states in the United States is primarily based on the English common law. Some state legal systems, because of their French and Spanish heritage, reflect the European civil law as well.

Sources of Law in the United States

In the more than 200 years since the founding of this country and the adoption of the English common law, American lawmakers have developed a substantial body of law. The *sources of modern law* in the United States are discussed in the paragraphs that follow.

Constitutions

The **Constitution of the United States of America** is the *supreme law of the land.* This means that any law—whether federal, state, or local—that conflicts with the U.S. Constitution is unconstitutional and, therefore, unenforceable.

The principles enumerated in the Constitution are extremely broad because the founding fathers intended them to be applied to evolving social, technological, and economic conditions. The U.S. Constitution is often referred to as a "living document" because it is so adaptable.

The U.S. Constitution established the structure of the federal government. It created the following three branches of government and gave them the following powers:

- ***Legislative (Congress)*** Power to make (enact) the law.
- ***Executive (president)*** Power to enforce the law.
- ***Judicial (courts)*** Power to interpret and determine the validity of the law.

Powers not given to the federal government by the Constitution are reserved for the states. States also have their own constitutions. These are often patterned after the U.S. Constitution, although many are more detailed. State constitutions establish the

Constitution of the United States of America
The supreme law of the United States.

The Constitution of the United States is not a mere lawyers' document: it is a vehicle of life, and its spirit is always the spirit of age.

Woodrow Wilson
Constitutional Government in the United States 69 (1927)

Web Site

U.S. Judicial Branch Resources
Hundreds of links that allow you to access pertinent information regarding the executive, legislative, and judicial branches of government are available on this site. Federal decisions can be found, and many federal public laws are searchable through this site. Visit at **www.lcweb.loc.gov/globaljudiciary.html**.

legislative, executive, and judicial branches of state government and establish the powers of each branch. Provisions of state constitutions are valid unless they conflict with the U.S. Constitution or any valid federal law.

Treaties

treaty
A compact made between two or more nations.

The U.S. Constitution provides that the president, with the advice and consent of the Senate, may enter into **treaties** with foreign governments. Treaties become part of the supreme law of the land. With increasing international economic relations among nations, treaties will become an even more important source of law that will affect business in the future.

Codified Law

statute
Written law enacted by the legislative branch of the federal and state governments that establishes certain courses of conduct that must be adhered to by covered parties.

Statutes are written laws that establish certain courses of conduct that must be adhered to by covered parties. The U.S. Congress is empowered by the Commerce Clause and other provisions of the U.S. Constitution to enact *federal statutes* to regulate foreign and interstate commerce. Federal statutes include antitrust laws, securities laws, bankruptcy laws, labor laws, equal employment opportunity laws, environmental protection laws, consumer protection laws, and such. State legislatures enact *state statutes*. State statutes include corporation laws, partnership laws, workers' compensation laws, the Uniform Commercial Code, and the like. The statutes enacted by the legislative branches of the federal and state governments are organized by topic into code books. This is often called *codified law*.

ordinances
Laws enacted by local government bodies such as cities and municipalities, countries, school districts, and water districts.

State legislatures often delegate lawmaking authority to local government bodies, including cities and municipalities, countries, school districts, water districts, and such. These governmental units are empowered to adopt **ordinances**. Examples of ordinances are traffic laws, local building codes, and zoning laws. Ordinances are also codified.

The Great Wall, China. The United States has entered into treaties with other countries of the world.

Contemporary Business Environment

American Indian Gambling Regulatory Statute

The Commerce Clause in the U.S. Constitution grants the federal government the power to deal with the American Indian tribes. Pursuant to this power, the federal government has enacted many statutes granting rights to and regulating commerce with the American Indian nations.

In 1988, Congress enacted the **Indian Gaming Regulatory Act (IGRA)** [25 U.S.C. 2701]. The IGRA is a federal statute that authorizes Native American Indian tribes to conduct various gambling operations—including casino-style gambling—if the state permits such gambling. Most states have entered into compacts that permit American Indian tribes to conduct gambling on Indian reservation lands. American Indian gambling casinos have been erected in most states and now provide a substantial income to members of the tribes that operate them. ■

Contemporary Business Environment

Regulations and Order of Administrative Agencies

The legislative and executive branches of federal and state governments are empowered to establish **administrative agencies** to enforce and interpret statutes enacted by Congress and state legislatures. Many of these agencies regulate business. For example, Congress has created the Securities and Exchange Commission (SEC) and the Federal Trade Commission (FTC), among others.

Congress or the state legislatures usually empower these agencies to adopt **administrative rules and regulations** to interpret the statutes that the agency is authorized to enforce. These rules and regulations have the force of law. Administrative agencies usually have the power to hear and decide disputes. Their decisions are called *orders*. Because of their power, administrative agencies are often informally referred to as the "fourth branch" of government. ■

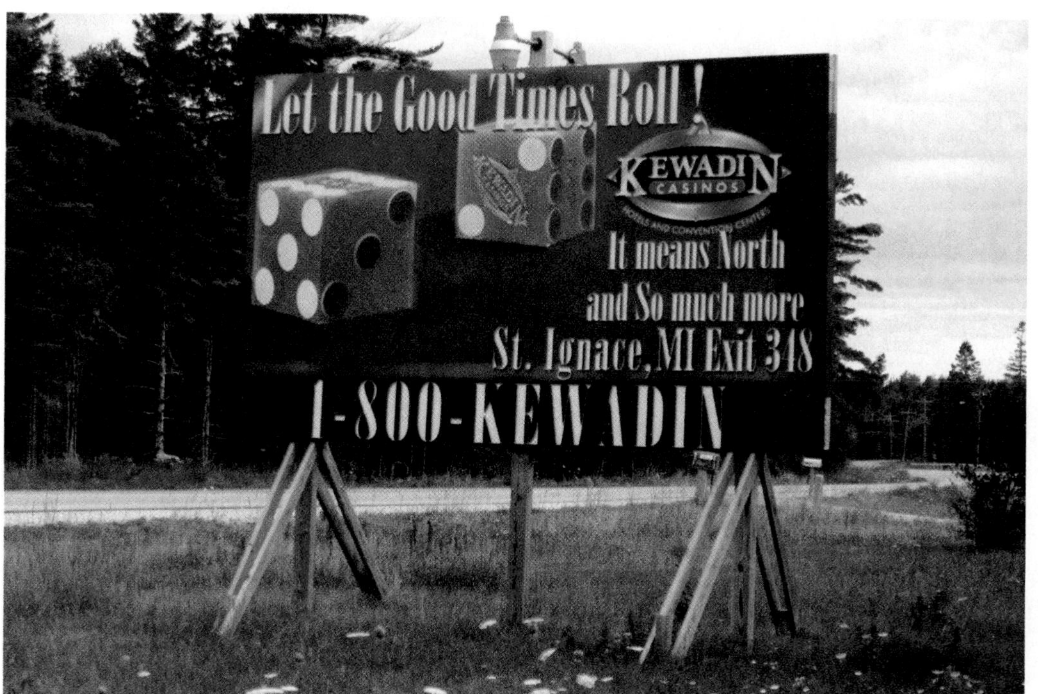

Lawful Gambling. Federal law permits lawful gambling on American Indian reservation land if the state permits such gambling.

Executive Orders

executive order
An order issued by a member of the executive branch of the government.

The executive branch of government, which includes the president of the United States and state governors, is empowered to issue **executive orders**. This power is derived from express delegation from the legislative branch and is implied from the U.S. Constitution and state constitutions.

E-Commerce & Information Technology

Executive Order Protects Encryption Technology

Encryption technology permits a computer user to basically put a lock around its computer information to protect it from being discovered by others. Encryption technology is like a lock on a house: Without the lock in place, unwanted persons can easily enter the house and steal its contents; with the lock in place, it is more difficult to enter. Encryption software serves a similar function in that it lets a computer user scramble information so that only those who have the encryption code can enter the database and find the information.

Software companies in the United States led the development of encryption technology. For years, however, the U.S. government permitted U.S. software companies to sell encryption software domestically but prohibited the export of the most powerful encryption technology to foreigners. The U.S. government worried that powerful encryption and data-scrambling technology would fall into the hands of criminals and terrorists who would use it to protect their illegal and clandestine activities. Based on this fear, the Clinton administration issued an executive order that prohibited the export of much of the most powerful encryption technology developed in the United States, to Iran, Iraq, Syria, Sudan, North Korea, and Cuba, countries that have a history of terrorist activities. ■

Judicial Decisions

judicial decision
A decision about an individual lawsuit issued by federal or state courts.

When deciding individual lawsuits, federal and state courts issue **judicial decisions**. In these written opinions, the judge or justice usually explains the legal reasoning used to decide the case. These opinions often include interpretations of statutes, ordinances,

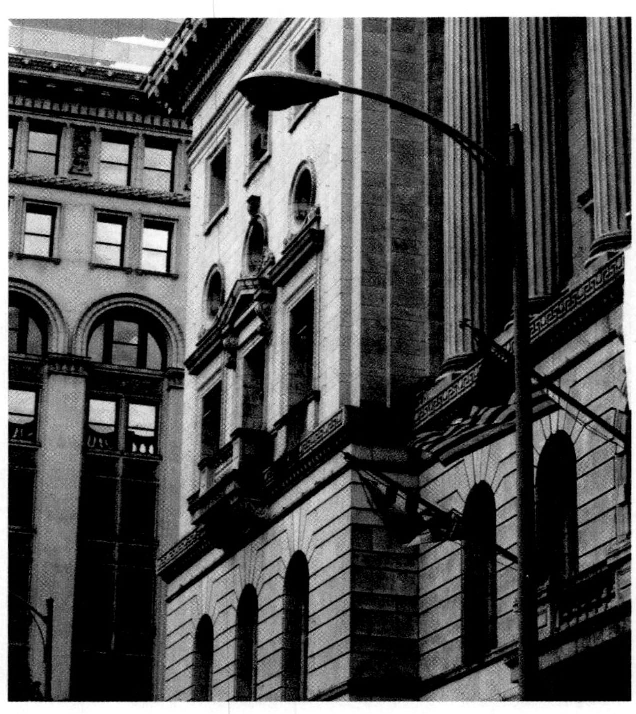

Courthouse, Baltimore, Maryland. Courts are often called upon to decide lawsuits between disputing parties.

administrative regulations, and the announcement of legal principles used to decide the case. Many court decisions are printed (reported) in books that are available in law libraries.

The Doctrine of Stare Decisis Based on the common law tradition, past court decisions become **precedent** for deciding future cases. Lower courts must follow the precedent established by higher courts. That is why all federal and state courts in the United States must follow the precedents established by U.S. Supreme Court decisions.

precedent
A rule of law established in a court decision. Lower courts must follow the precedent established by higher courts.

The courts of one jurisdiction are not bound by the precedent established by the courts of another jurisdiction, although they may look to each other for guidance. For example, state courts of one state are not required to follow the legal precedent established by the courts of another state.

Adherence to precedent is called **stare decisis** ("to stand by the decision"). The doctrine of *stare decisis* promotes uniformity of law within a jurisdiction, makes the court system more efficient, and makes the law more predictable for individuals and businesses. A court may later change or reverse its legal reasoning if a new case is presented to it and change is warranted. The doctrine of *state decisis* is discussed in the following excerpt from Justice Musmanno's decision in *Flagiello v. Pennsylvania*:[6]

stare decisis
Latin: "to stand by the decision." Adherence to precedent.

> Without stare decisis, there would be no stability in our system of jurisprudence. Stare decisis channels the law. It erects lighthouses and flies the signal of safety. The ships of jurisprudence must follow that well-defined channel which, over the years, has been proved to be secure and worthy.

The following are two judicial decisions of the Supreme Court of the United States.

U.S. SUPREME COURT CASE

Grutter v. Bollinger and the University of Michigan Law School

123 S.Ct. 2325, 2003 U.S. Lexis 4800 (2003)
Supreme Court of the United States

Case 1.2
Affirmative Action

Background and Facts

Barbara Grutter, a Caucasian resident of the state of Michigan, applied to the Law School of the University of Michigan, a state government–supported institution, in 1996 with a 3.8 undergraduate grade point average and a 161 LSAT score. The Law School rejected her application. The Law School received 3,500 applications for a class of 350 students. The Law School used race as one of the factors in considering applicants for admission to law school. The race of minority applicants, defined as blacks, Hispanics, and Native Americans, was considered as a "plus factor" in considering their applications to law school. Caucasians and Asians were not given such a plus factor. The Law School stated that it used race as a plus factor to obtain a critical mass of underrepresented minority students in order to create diversity at the school.

Grutter brought a class action lawsuit against the Law School of the University of Michigan, alleging that its use of a minority's race as a plus factor in admissions violated the Equal Protection Clause of the Fourteenth Amendment to the U.S. Constitution. The district court held that the Law School's use of race as a factor in admissions violated the Equal Protection Clause. The court of appeals reversed. The U.S. Supreme Court granted certiorari to hear the appeal.

Supreme Court Issue

Does the University of Michigan Law School's use of race as a plus factor in accepting minority applicants for admission to the Law School violate the Equal Protection Clause of the Fourteenth Amendment to the U.S. Constitution?

In The Language of The U.S. Supreme Court

O'Connor, Justice The Equal Protection Clause provides that no State shall "deny to any person within its jurisdiction the equal protection of the laws." Racial classifications imposed by government must be analyzed by a reviewing court under strict scrutiny. When race-based action is necessary to further a compelling governmental interest, such action does not violate the constitutional guarantee of equal protection so long as the narrow-tailoring requirement is also satisfied. Universities occupy a special niche in our constitutional tradition. In order to cultivate a set of leaders with legitimacy in the eyes of the citizenry, it is necessary that the path to leadership be visibly open to talented and qualified individuals of every race and ethnicity.

To be narrowly tailored, a race-conscious admissions program cannot use a quota system. Instead, a university may consider race or ethnicity only as a "plus" in a particular applicant's file. We find that the Law School's admissions program bears the hallmarks of a narrowly tailored plan. Universities cannot establish quotas for

Grutter v. Bollinger and the University of Michigan Law School

123 S.Ct. 2325, 2003 U.S. Lexis 4800 (2003)
Supreme Court of the United States
(continued)

members of certain racial groups or put members of those groups on separate admissions tracks. Nor can universities insulate applicants who belong to certain racial or ethnic groups from the competition for admission. Universities can, however, consider race or ethnicity more flexibly as a "plus" factor in the context of individualized consideration of each and every applicant.

The Law School's goal of attaining a critical mass of underrepresented minority students does not transform its program into a quota. Here, the Law School engages in a highly individualized, holistic review of each applicant's file, giving serious consideration to all the ways an applicant might contribute to a diverse educational environment. The Law School affords this individualized consideration to applicants of all races. We agree that, in the context of its individualized inquiry into the possible diversity contributions of all applicants, the Law School's race conscious admissions program does not unduly harm nonminority applicants.

We take the Law School at its word that it would like nothing better than to find a race-neutral admissions formula and will terminate its race-conscious admissions program as soon as practicable. We expect that 25 years from now, the use of racial preferences will no longer be necessary to further the interest approved today.

Decision and Remedy

The U.S. Supreme Court held that the University of Michigan Law School's policy of using race as a plus factor in admitting minority applicants furthers a compelling state interest and is narrowly tailored to accomplish that interest. The Supreme Court held that the Law School's race-conscious admissions policy does not violate the Equal Protection Clause of the Fourteenth Amendment to the U.S. Constitution.

Case Questions

Critical Legal Thinking What does the Equal Protection Clause provide? Should the government ever be allowed to treat persons differently because of their race? Explain.

Business Ethics Is it socially responsible for the University of Michigan Law School to consider a minority applicant's race as a plus factor in its admissions decisions?

Contemporary Business Is anyone hurt by the University of Michigan Law School's race-conscious admissions policy? Explain.

Case 1.3 Affirmative Action

U.S. SUPREME COURT CASE

Gratz v. Bollinger and the Regents of the University of Michigan

123 S.Ct. 2411, 2003 U.S. Lexis 4801 (2003)
Supreme Court of the United States

Background and Facts

Jennifer Gratz, a Caucasian resident of the state of Michigan, applied for admission to the College of Literature, Science, and the Arts at the University of Michigan, a state government–supported university. In its review of applicants, the University of Michigan considered high school grade point average; standardized test scores (i.e., SAT, ACT); high school quality, curriculum strength, geography, and alumni relationships; and leadership. Each item was assigned a certain number of points for each applicant. If an applicant received 100 points, he or she would be guaranteed admission to the university. Minority applicants, defined as blacks, Hispanics, and Native Americans, were automatically given 20 points, or one-fifth of the points needed to guarantee admission. Gratz was originally placed in a postponed decision category, but was ultimately rejected for admission. A minority applicant with Gratz's score, with the extra 20 points, would have been admitted.

Gratz brought a class action lawsuit against the University of Michigan, alleging that the University violated the Equal Protection Clause of the Fourteenth Amendment to the U.S. Constitution. Plaintiff Gratz sought damages for past violations and an injunction prohibiting the university from continuing to discriminate on the basis of race in violation of the Fourteenth Amendment. The district court granted the university's motion for summary judgment and upheld the university's policy of adding 20 points to minority applicants' applications for admission. The U.S. Supreme Court granted certiorari to hear the appeal of this issue.

Issue

Does the University of Michigan's automatic award of 20 points to minority applicants for admission to the university's undergraduate College of Literature, Sciences, and the Arts violate the Equal Protection Clause of the Fourteenth Amendment to the U.S. Constitution?

In The Language of The U.S. Supreme Court

Rehnquist, Chief Justice Each applicant received points based on high school grade point average, standardized test scores, academic quality of an applicant's high school, strength or weakness of high school curriculum, in-state residency, alumni relationships, personal essay, and personal achievement or leadership. Of particular significance here, under a "miscellaneous" category, an applicant was entitled to 20 points based upon his or her membership in an underrepresented racial or ethnic minority group. During all periods relevant to this litigation, the University has considered African-Americans, Hispanics, and Native Americans to be underrepresented minorities, and it is undisputed that the University admits virtually every qualified applicant from these groups.

We granted certiorari in this case to decide whether the University of Michigan's use of racial preferences in undergraduate admissions violates the Equal Protection Clause. All racial classifications reviewable under the Equal Protection Clause must be strictly scrutinized. To withstand our strict scrutiny analysis, respondents must demonstrate that the University's use of race in its current admission program employs narrowly tailored measures that further compelling governmental interests. We find that the University's policy, which automatically distributes 20 points, or one-fifth of the points needed to guarantee admission, to every single underrepresented minority applicant solely because of race, is not narrowly tailored to achieve the interest in educational diversity that respondents claim justify their program.

Respondents contend that the volume of applications and the presentation of applicant information make it impractical to use the admissions system upheld by the U.S. Supreme Court in *Grutter v. Bollinger*, 123 S.Ct. 2325, 2003 U.S. Lexis 4800 (2003). But the fact that the implementation of a program capable of providing individualized consideration might present administrative challenges does not render constitutional an otherwise problematic system.

Decision and Remedy

The U.S. Supreme Court held that the University of Michigan's undergraduate admission policy that automatically assigned 20 points, or one-fifth of the points needed to guarantee admission, to minority applicants did not pass the strict scrutiny test and was not narrowly tailored to accomplish the compelling state interest of obtaining a diverse student population. The Supreme Court held that the University of Michigan had violated the Equal Protection Clause of the Fourteenth Amendment. The Supreme Court reversed and remanded the case for further proceedings.

Case Questions

Critical Legal Thinking What is the difference between the Supreme Court's decision in this case and its decision in the *Grutter v. Bollinger* case? Explain.

Business Ethics Did the University of Michigan act socially responsible by using the plus 20-point program for minority applicants?

Contemporary Business After this decision, can race still be used in university admissions decisions? Explain.

Priority of Law in the United States

As mentioned previously, the U.S. Constitution and treaties take precedence over all other laws. Federal statutes take precedence over federal regulations. Valid federal law takes precedence over any conflicting state or local law. State constitutions rank as the highest state law. State statutes take precedence over state regulations. Valid state law takes precedence over local laws.

Web Site

Dumb Laws Very often, laws are passed that serve a particular purpose but either become obsolete or simply don't make any sense because the original purpose is abandoned or forgotten. This site is a compilation of state, federal, and foreign laws that often cannot be explained. Visit at **www.dumblaws.com**.

Concept Summary Sources of Law in the United States

Source of Law	Description
Constitutions	The U.S. Constitution establishes the federal government and enumerates its powers. Powers not given to the federal government are reserved to the states. State constitutions establish state governments and enumerate their powers.
Treaties	The president, with the advice and consent of the Senate, may enter into treaties with foreign countries.
Codified law: Statutes and ordinances	Statutes are enacted by Congress and state legislatures. Ordinances are enacted by municipalities and local government agencies. They establish courses of conduct that must be followed by covered parties.
Administrative agency rules and regulations	Administrative agencies are created by the legislative and executive branches of government. They may adopt rules and regulations that regulate the conduct of covered parties.
Executive orders	Issued by the president and governors of states, executive orders regulate the conduct of covered parties.
Judicial decisions	Courts decide controversies. In doing so, a court issues decisions that state the holding of the case and the rationale used by the court in reaching that decision.

Critical Legal Thinking

Judges apply *legal reasoning* in reaching a decision in a case. That is, the judge must specify the issue presented by the case, identify the key facts in the case and the applicable law, and then apply the law to the facts to come to a conclusion that answers the issue presented. This process is called **critical legal thinking**. Skills of analysis and interpretation are important in deciding legal cases.

critical legal thinking
The process of specifying the issue presented by a case, identifying the key facts in the case and applicable law, and then applying the law to the facts to come to a conclusion that answers the issue presented.

Key Terms

Before you embark upon the study of law, you should know the following key legal terms:

- ***Plaintiff*** The party who originally brought the lawsuit.
- ***Defendant*** The party against whom the lawsuit has been brought.
- ***Petitioner*** or ***Appellant*** The party who has appealed the decision of the trial court or lower court. The petitioner may be either the plaintiff or defendant, depending on who lost the case at the trial court or lower court level.
- ***Respondent*** or ***Appellee*** The party who must answer the petitioner's appeal. The respondent may be either the plaintiff or defendant, depending on which party is the petitioner. In some cases, both the plaintiff *and* the defendant may disagree with the trial court's or lower court's decision, and both parties may appeal the decision.

Briefing a Case

It is often helpful for a student to "brief" a case in order to clarify the legal issues involved and to gain a better understanding of the case.

The procedure for briefing a case is as follows. The student must summarize, or brief, the court's decision in no more than 400 words (some professors may shorten or lengthen this limit). The assignment's format is highly structured, consisting of five parts, each of which is numbered and labeled:

case brief
A summary of each of the following items of a case:
1. Case name and citation
2. Key facts
3. Issue presented
4. Holding of the court
5. Court's reasoning

Part	Maximum Words
1. Case name and citation	25
2. A summary of the key facts in the case	125
3. The issue presented by the case, stated as a one-sentence question answerable only by *yes* or *no*	25
4. The court's resolution of the issue (the "holding")	25
5. A summary of the court's reasoning justifying the holding	200
Total words	400

Briefing a case consists of making a summary of each of the following items of the case.

1. ***Case Name and Citation*** The name of the case should be placed at the beginning of each briefed case. The case name usually contains the names of the parties to the lawsuit. Where there are multiple plaintiffs or defendants, however, some of the names of the parties may be omitted from the case name. Abbreviations are also often used in case names.

   The case citation, which consists of a number plus the year in which the case was decided, such as "532 U.S. 661, 121 S.Ct. 1879, 2001 U.S. Lexis 4115," is set forth below the case name. The case citation identifies the book in the law library or the Internet site where the case may be found. For example, the case in the above citation may be found in volume 532 of the *United States Reports*, page 661, in volume 121 of the *Supreme Court Reporter*, page 1879, and on the Lexis Web site at 2001 U.S. Lexis 4115. The name of the court that decided the case should be set forth below the case name for the case.

2. ***Summary of the Key Facts in the Case*** The important facts of a case should be stated briefly. Extraneous facts and facts of minor importance should be omitted from the brief. The facts of the case can usually be found at the beginning of the case, but not necessarily. Important facts may be found throughout the case.
3. ***Issue Presented by the Case*** It is crucial in the briefing of a case to identify the issue presented to the court to decide. The issue on appeal is most often a legal question, although questions of fact are sometimes the subject of an appeal. The issue presented in each case is usually quite specific and should be asked in a one-sentence question that is answerable only by a *yes* or *no*. For example, the issue statement, "Is Mary liable?" is too broad. A more proper statement of the issue would be, "Is Mary liable to Joe for breach of the contract made between them based on her refusal to make the payment due on September 30?"
4. ***Holding*** The *holding* is the decision reached by the present court. It should be *yes* or *no*. The holding should also state which party won.
5. ***Summary of the Court's Reasoning*** When an appellate court or supreme court issues a decision, which is often called an *opinion*, the court will normally state the reasoning it used in reaching its decision. The rationale for the decision may be based on the specific facts of the case, public policy, prior law, or other matters. In stating the reasoning of the court, the student should reword the court's language into his or her own language. This summary of the court's reasoning should pick out the meat of the opinions and weed out the nonessentials.

Critical Legal Thinking Example Writing Assignments

The following cases are excerpted decisions by the Supreme Court of the United States. The cases are presented in the language of the Supreme Court. Following each case is a *Brief of the Case*, using the preceding "Briefing a Case" model.

Case Writing Example 1

U.S. SUPREME COURT CASE

Americans with Disabilities Act

Case name, Citation, and Court	**PGA TOUR, Inc. v. Martin, 532 U.S. 661, 121 S.Ct. 1879, 2001 U.S. Lexis 4115 (2001) U.S. Supreme Court**
Opinion of the Court **Issue**	***OPINION, STEVENS, JUSTICE*** *This case raises two questions concerning the application of the Americans with Disabilites Act of 1990 [42 U.S.C. § 12101 et seq.] to a gifted athlete: first, whether the Act protects access to professional golf tournaments by a qualified entrant with a disability; and second, whether a disabled contestant may be denied the use of a golf cart because it would "fundamentally alter the nature" of the tournaments to allow him to ride when all other contestants must walk.*
Facts **Petitioner: PGA TOUR Inc.**	*Petitioner PGA TOUR, Inc., a nonprofit entity formed in 1968, sponsors and cosponsors professional golf tournaments conducted on three annual tours. About 200 golfers participate in the PGA TOUR; about 170 in the NIKE TOUR; and about 100 in the SENIOR PGA TOUR. PGA TOUR and NIKE TOUR tournaments typically are four-day events, played on courses leased and operated by petitioner. The revenues generated by television, admissions, concessions, and contributions from cosponsors amount to about $300 million a year, much of which is distributed in prize money. The "Conditions of Competition and Local Rules," often described as the "hard card," apply specifically to petitioner's professional tours. The hard cards for the PGA TOUR and NIKE TOUR required players to walk the golf course during tournaments, but not during open qualifying rounds. On the SENIOR PGA TOUR, which is limited to golfers age 50 and older, the contestants may use golf carts. Most seniors, however, prefer to walk.*
Respondent: Casey Martin	*Casey Martin is a talented golfer. As an amateur, he won 17 Oregon Golf Association junior events before he was 15, and he won the state championship as a high school senior. He played on the Stanford University golf team that won the 1994 National Collegiate Athletic Association (NCAA) championship. As a professional, Martin qualified for the NIKE TOUR in 1998 and 1999, and based on his 1999 performance, qualified for the PGA TOUR in 2000. In the 1999 season, he entered 24 events, made the cut 13 times, and had six top-10 finishes, coming in second twice and third once.*

Martin is also an individual with a disability, as defined in the Americans with Disabilities Act of 1990 (ADA or Act). Since birth he has been afflicted with Klippel-Trenaunay-Weber Syndrome, a degenerative circulatory disorder that obstructs the flow of blood from his right leg back to his heart. The disease is progressive; it causes severe pain and has atrophied his right leg. During the latter part of his college career, because of the progress of the disease, Martin could no longer walk an 18-hole golf course. Walking not only caused him pain, fatigue, and anxiety, but also created a significant risk of hemorrhaging, developing blood clots, and fracturing his tibia so badly that an amputation might be required.

When Martin turned pro and entered petitioner's Qualifying-School, the hard card permitted him to use a cart during his successful progress through the first two stages. He made a request, supported by detailed medical records, for permission to use a golf cart during the third stage. Petitioner refused to review those records or to waive its walking rule for the third stage. Martin therefore filed this action.

District Court's Decision
994 F. Supp. 1242, 1998
U.S Dist. Lexis 1980
[District: Oregon (1998)]

At trial, petitioner PGA TOUR did not contest the conclusion that Martin has a disability covered by the ADA, or the fact that his disability prevents him from walking the course during a round of golf. Rather, petitioner asserted that the condition of walking is a substantive rule of competition and that waiving it as to any individual for any reason would fundamentally alter the nature of the competition. Petitioner's evidence included the testimony of a number of experts, among them some of the greatest golfers in history. Arnold Palmer, Jack Nicklaus, and Ken Venturi explained that fatigue can be a critical factor in a tournament, particularly on the last day, when psychological pressure is at a maximum. Their testimony makes it clear that, in their view, permission to use a cart might well give some players a competitive advantage over other players who must walk.

The judge found that the purpose of the rule was to inject fatigue into the skill of shot-making, but that the fatigue injected "by walking the course cannot be deemed significant under normal circumstances." Furthermore, Martin presented evidence, and the judge found, that even with the use of a cart, Martin must walk over a mile during an 18-hole round, and that the fatigue he suffers from coping with his disability is "undeniably greater" than the fatigue his able-bodied competitors endure from walking the course. As a result, the judge concluded that it would "not fundamentally alter the nature of the PGA Tour's game to accommodate him with a cart." The judge accordingly entered a permanent injunction requiring petitioner to permit Martin to use a cart in tour and qualifying events.

Court of Appeals Decision
204 F.3d 994, 2000 U.S. App.
Lexis 3376
[9th Circuit (2000)]

The Court of Appeals concluded that golf courses remain places of public accommodation during PGA tournaments. On the merits, because there was no serious dispute about the fact that permitting Martin to use a golf cart was both a reasonable and a necessary solution to the problem of providing him access to the tournaments, the Court of Appeals regarded the central dispute as whether such permission would "fundamentally alter" the nature of the PGA TOUR or NIKE TOUR. Like the District Court, the Court of Appeals viewed the issue not as "whether use of carts generally would fundamentally alter the competition, but whether the use of a cart by Martin would do so." That issue turned on "an intensively fact-based inquiry," and, the court concluded, had been correctly resolved by the trial judge. In its words, "all that the cart does is permit Martin access to a type of competition in which he otherwise could not engage because of his disability."

Federal Statute
Being Interpreted

Congress enacted the ADA in 1990 to remedy widespread discrimination against disabled individuals. To effectuate its sweeping purpose, the ADA forbids discrimination against disabled individuals in major areas of public life, among them employment (Title I of the Act), public services (Title II), and public accommodations (Title III). At issue now is the applicability of Title III to petitioner's golf tours and qualifying rounds, in particular to petitioner's treatment of a qualified disabled golfer wishing to compete in those events

U.S. Supreme Court's
Reasoning

It seems apparent, from both the general rule and the comprehensive definition of "public accommodation," that petitioner's golf tours and their qualifying rounds fit comfortably within the coverage of Title III, and Martin within its protection. The events occur on "golf courses," a type of place specifically identified by the Act as a public accommodation [Section 12181(7)(L)]. In this case, the narrow dispute is whether allowing Martin to use a golf cart, despite the walking requirement that applies to the PGA TOUR, the NIKE TOUR, and the third stage of the Qualifying-School, is a modification that would "fundamentally alter the nature" of those events.

As an initial matter, we observe that the use of carts is not itself inconsistent with the fundamental character of the game of golf. From early on, the essence of the game has been shot-making—using clubs to cause a ball to progress from the teeing ground to a hole some distance away with as few strokes as possible. Golf carts started appearing with increasing regularity on American golf courses in the 1950s. Today they are everywhere. And they are encouraged. For one thing, they often speed up play, and for another, they are great revenue producers. There is nothing in the rules of golf that either forbids the use of carts or penalizes a player for using a cart.

Petitioner, however, distinguishes the game of golf as it is generally played from the game that it sponsors in the PGA TOUR, NIKE TOUR, and the last stage of the Qualifying-School—golf at the "highest level." According to petitioner, "the goal of the highest-level competitive athletics is to assess and compare the performance of different competitors, a task that is meaningful only if the competitors are subject to identical substantive rules." The waiver of any possibly "outcome-affecting" rule for a contestant would violate this principle and therefore, in petitioner's view, fundamentally alter the nature of the highest-level athletic event. The walking rule is one such rule, petitioner submits, because its purpose is "to inject the element of fatigue into the skill of shot-making," and thus its effect may be the critical loss of a stroke. As a consequence, the reasonable modification Martin seeks would fundamentally alter the nature of petitioner's highest-level tournaments.

The force of petitioner's argument is, first of all, mitigated by the fact that golf is a game in which it is impossible to guarantee that all competitors will play under exactly the same conditions or that an individual's ability will be the sole determinant of the outcome. For example, changes in the weather may produce harder greens and more head winds for the tournament leader than for his closest pursuers. A lucky bounce may save a shot or two. Whether such happenstance events are more or less probable than the likelihood that a golfer afflicted with Klippel-Trenaunay-Weber Syndrome would one day qualify for the NIKE TOUR and PGA TOUR, they at least demonstrate that pure chance may have a greater impact on the outcome of elite golf tournaments than the fatigue resulting from the enforcement of the walking rule.

Further, the factual basis of petitioner's argument is undermined by the District Court's finding that the fatigue from walking during one of petitioner's 4-day tournaments cannot be deemed significant. The District Court credited the testimony of a professor in physiology and expert on fatigue, who calculated the calories expended in walking a golf course (about five miles) to be approximately 500 calories—"nutritionally less than a Big Mac." What is more, that energy is expended over a 5-hour period, during which golfers have numerous intervals for rest and refreshment. In fact, the expert concluded, because golf is a low-intensity activity, fatigue from the game is primarily a psychological phenomenon in which stress and motivation are the key ingredients. And even under conditions of severe heat and humidity, the critical factor in fatigue is fluid loss rather than exercise from walking. Moreover, when given the option of using a cart, the majority of golfers in petitioner's tournaments have chosen to walk, often to relieve stress or for other strategic reasons. As NIKE TOUR member Eric Johnson testified, walking allows him to keep in rhythm, stay warmer when it is chilly, and develop a better sense of the elements and the course than riding a cart. As we have demonstrated, the walking rule is at best peripheral to the nature of petitioner's athletic events, and thus it might be waived in individual cases without working a fundamental alteration.

Holding and Remedy

Under the ADA's basic requirement that the need of a disabled person be evaluated on an individual basis, we have no doubt that allowing Martin to use a golf cart would not fundamentally alter the nature of petitioner's tournaments. As we have discussed, the purpose of the walking rule is to subject players to fatigue, which in turn may influence the outcome of tournaments. Even if the rule does serve that purpose, it is an uncontested finding of the District Court that Martin "easily endures greater fatigue even with a cart than his able-bodied competitors do by walking." The purpose of the walking rule is therefore not compromised in the slightest by allowing Martin to use a cart. A modification that provides an exception to a peripheral tournament rule without impairing its purpose cannot be said to "fundamentally alter" the tournament. What it can be said to do, on the other hand, is to allow Martin the chance to qualify for and compete in the athletic events petitioner offers to those members of the public who have the skill and desire to enter. That is exactly what the ADA requires. As a result, Martin's request for a waiver of the walking rule should have been granted.

Dissenting Opinion

The judgment of the Court of Appeals is affirmed. It is so ordered.

DISSENTING OPINION, SCALIA, JUSTICE *In my view today's opinion exercises a benevolent compassion that the law does not place it within our power to impose. The judgment distorts the text of Title III, the structure of the ADA, and common sense. I respectfully dissent.*

The Court, for its part, assumes that conclusion for the sake of argument, but pronounces respondent to be a "customer" of the PGA TOUR or of the golf courses on which it is played. That seems to me quite incredible. The PGA TOUR is a professional sporting event, staged for the entertainment of a live and TV audience. The professional golfers on the tour are no more "enjoying" (the statutory term) the entertainment that the tour provides, or the facilities of the golf courses on which it is held, than professional baseball players "enjoy" the baseball games in which they play or the facilities of Yankee Stadium. To be sure, professional ballplayers participate *in the games, and* use *the ball fields, but no one in his right mind would think that they are* customers *of the American League or of Yankee Stadium. They are themselves the entertainment that the customers pay to watch. And professional golfers are no different. A professional golfer's practicing his profession is not comparable to John Q. Public's frequenting "a 232-acre amusement area with swimming, boating, sunbathing, picnicking, miniature golf, dancing facilities, and a snack bar."*

Having erroneously held that Title III applies to the "customers" of professional golf who consist of its practitioners, the Court then erroneously answers—or to be accurate simply ignores—a second question. The ADA requires covered businesses to make such reasonable modifications of "policies, practices, or procedures" as are necessary to "afford" goods, services, and privileges to individuals with disabilities; but it explicitly does not require "modifications that would fundamentally alter the nature" of the goods, services, and privileges [Section 12182(b)(2)(A)(ii)]. In other words, disabled individuals must be given access to the same goods, services, and privileges that others enjoy.

A camera store may not refuse to sell cameras to a disabled person, but it is not required to stock cameras specially designed for such persons. It is hardly a feasible judicial function to decide whether shoe stores should sell single shoes to one-legged persons and if so at what price, or how many braille books the Borders or Barnes and Noble bookstore chains should stock in each of their stores. Eighteen-hole golf courses, 10-foot-high basketball hoops, 90-foot baselines, 100-yard football fields—all are arbitrary and none is essential. The only support for any of them is tradition and (in more modern times) insistence by what has come to be regarded as the ruling body of the sport—both of which factors support the PGA TOUR's position in the present case. One can envision the parents of a Little League player with attention deficit disorder trying to convince a judge that their son's disability makes it at least 25 percent more difficult to hit a pitched ball. (If they are successful, the only thing that could prevent a court order giving the kid four strikes would be a judicial determination that, in baseball, three strikes are metaphysically necessary, which is quite absurd.)

Agility, strength, speed, balance, quickness of mind, steadiness of nerves, intensity of concentration —these talents are not evenly distributed. No wild-eyed dreamer has ever suggested that the managing bodies of the competitive sports that test precisely these qualities should try to take account of the uneven distribution of God-given gifts when writing and enforcing the rules of competition. And I have no doubt Congress did not authorize misty-eyed judicial supervision of such a revolution. The year was 2001, and "everybody was finally equal." K. Vonnegut, Harrison Bergeron, in Animal Farm and Related Readings *129 (1997).*

Brief of the Case

1. **PGA TOUR, Inc. v Martin**
   532 U.S. 661, 121 S.Ct. 1879, 2001 Lexis 415 (2001)
   U.S. Supreme Court
2. **Key Facts**
   A. PGA TOUR, Inc., is a nonprofit organization that sponsors professional golf tournaments.
   B. The PGA establishes rules for its golf tournaments. A PGA rule requires golfers to walk the golf course and not use golf carts.
   C. Casey Martin is a professional golfer who suffers from Klippel-Trenaunay-Weber Syndrome, a degenerative circulatory disorder that atrophied Martin's right leg and causes him pain, fatigue, and anxiety when walking.
   D. When Martin petitioned the PGA to use a golf cart during golf tournaments, the PGA refused.
   E. Martin sued the PGA, alleging discrimination against a disabled individual in violation of the Americans with Disabilities Act of 1990, a federal statute.
3. **Issue**
   Does the Americans with Disabilities Act require the PGA to accommodate Martin by permitting him to use a golf cart while playing in PGA tournaments?
4. **Holding**
   Yes. The Supreme Court held that the PGA must allow Martin to use a golf cart when competing in PGA golf tournaments. Affirmed.
5. **Court's Reasoning**
   The Supreme Court held that:
   A. Martin was disabled and covered by the act.
   B. Golf courses are "public accommodations" covered by the act.
   C. The use of golf carts is not a fundamental character of the game of golf.
   D. Other than the PGA rule, there is no rule of golf that forbids the use of golf carts.
   E. It is impossible to guarantee all players in golf will play under the exact same conditions, so allowing Martin to use a golf cart gives him no advantage over other golfers.
   F. Martin, because of his disease, will probably suffer more fatigue playing golf using a golf cart than other golfers will suffer without using a cart.
   G. The PGA's "walking rule" is only peripheral to the game of golf and not a fundamental part of golf.
   H. Allowing Martin to use a golf cart will not fundamentally alter the PGA's highest-level professional golf tournaments.

Case Writing Example II

U.S. SUPREME COURT CASE

Sexual Harassment

Case name, Citation, and Court

Harris v. Forklift Systems, Inc., 510 U.S. 17, 114 S.Ct. 367, 1993 U.S. Lexis 7155 (1993)
United States Supreme Court

Opinion of the Court

OPINION, O'CONNOR, JUSTICE *Teresa Harris worked as a manager at Forklift Systems, Inc., an equipment rental company, from April 1985 until October 1987. Charles Hardy was Forklift's president. Throughout Harris's time at Forklift, Hardy often insulted her because of her gender and often made her the target of unwanted sexual innuendos. Hardy told Harris on several occasions, in the presence of other employees, "You're a woman, what do you know" and "We need a man as the rental manager"; at least once, he told her she was "a dumb-ass woman." Again in front of others, he suggested that the two of them "go to the Holiday Inn to negotiate Harris's raise." Hardy occasionally asked Harris and other female employees to get coins from his front pants pocket. He threw objects on the ground in front of Harris and other women, and asked them to pick the objects up. He made sexual innuendos about Harris's and other women 's clothing.*

Facts

In mid-August 1987, Harris complained to Hardy about his conduct. Hardy said he was surprised that Harris was offended, claimed he was only joking, and apologized. He also promised he would stop and based on this assurance, Harris stayed on the job. But in early September, Hardy began anew: While Harris was arranging a deal with one of Forklift's customers, he asked her, again in front of other employees, "What did you do, promise the guy some sex Saturday night?" On October 1, Harris collected her paycheck and quit.

Lower Courts' Opinions

Harris then sued Forklift, claiming that Hardy's conduct had created an abusive work environment for her because of her gender. The United States District Court for the Middle District of Tennessee found this to be "a close case," but held that Hardy's conduct did not create an abusive environment. The court found that some of Hardy's comments "offended Harris, and would offend the reasonable woman," but that they were not "so severe as to be expected to seriously affect Harris's psychological well-being." A reasonable woman manager under like circumstances would have been offended by Hardy, but his conduct would not have risen to the level of interfering with that person's work performance. The United States Court of Appeals for the Sixth Circuit affirmed in a brief unpublished decision.

Issue

We granted certiorari to resolve a conflict among the Circuits on whether conduct, to be actionable as "abusive work environment" harassment, must "seriously affect an employee's psychological well-being" or lead the plaintiff to "suffer injury."

Statute Being Interpreted

Title VII of the Civil Rights Act of 1964 makes it "an unlawful employment practice for an employer . . . to discriminate against any individual with respect to his compensation, terms, conditions, or privileges of employment, because of such individual's race, color, religion, sex, or national origin" [42 U.S.C. §2000e-2(a)(1)].

U.S. Supreme Court's Reasoning

When the workplace is permeated with discriminatory intimidation, ridicule, and insult that is sufficiently severe or pervasive to alter the conditions of the victim's employment and create an abusive working environment, Title VII is violated. This standard takes a middle path between making actionable any conduct that is merely offensive and requiring the conduct to cause a tangible psychological injury. Mere utterance of an epithet which engenders offensive feelings in an employee does not sufficiently affect the conditions of employment to implicate Title VII. Conduct that is not severe or pervasive enough to create an objectively hostile or abusive work environment—an environment that a reasonable person would find hostile or abusive—is beyond Title VII's purview. Likewise, if the victim does not subjectively perceive the environment to be abusive, the conduct has not actually altered the conditions of the victim's employment, and there is no Title VII violation.

But Title VII comes into play before the harassing conduct leads to a nervous breakdown. A discriminatorily abusive work environment, even one that does not seriously affect employees' psychological well-being, can and often will detract from employees' job performance, discourage employees from remaining on the job, or keep them from advancing in their careers. Moreover, even without regard to these tangible effects, the very fact that the discriminatory conduct was so severe or pervasive that it created a work environment abusive to employees because of their race, gender, religion, or national origin offends Title VII's broad rule of workplace equality.

Holding

We therefore believe the district court erred in relying on whether the conduct "seriously affected plaintiff's psychological well-being" or led her to "suffer injury." Such an inquiry may needlessly focus the factfinder's attention on concrete psychological harm, an element Title VII does not require. So long as the environment would reasonably be perceived, and is perceived, as hostile or abusive, there is no need for it also to be psychologically injurious. This is not, and by its nature cannot be, a mathematically precise test. But we can say that whether an environment is "hostile" or "abusive" can be determined only by looking at all the circumstances.

We therefore reverse the judgment of the Court of Appeals, and remand the case for further proceedings consistent with this opinion.

Concurring Opinion

CONCURRING OPINION, GINSBURG, JUSTICE *The critical issue, Title VII's text indicates, is whether members of one sex are exposed to disadvantageous terms or conditions of employment to which members of the other sex are not exposed. The adjudicator's inquiry should center, dominantly, on whether the discriminatory conduct has unreasonably interfered with the plaintiff's work performance. To show such interference, the plaintiff need not prove that his or her tangible productivity has declined as a result of the harassment.*

Brief of the Case

1. **Case Name, Citation, and Court**
   Harris v. Forklift Systems, Inc.
   510 U.S. 17, 114 S.Ct. 367, 1993 U.S. Lexis 7155 (1993)
   United States Supreme Court
2. **Summary of the Key Facts**
   A. Teresa Harris worked as a manager at Forklift Systems, Inc. (Forklift). Charles Hardy was Forklift's president.
   B. While Harris worked at Forklift, Hardy continually insulted her because of her gender and made her the target of unwanted sexual innuendos.
   C. This conduct created an abusive and hostile work environment, causing Harris to terminate her employment.
   D. Harris sued Forklift, alleging sexual harassment in violation of Title VII of the Civil Rights Act of 1964, which makes it an unlawful employment practice for an employer to discriminate in employment because of an individual's sex.
3. **The Issue**
   Must an employee prove that she suffered severe psychological injury before she can prove a Title VII claim for sexual harassment against her employer?
4. **The Holding**
   No. The Supreme Court remanded the case for further proceedings, consistent with its opinion.
5. **Summary of the Court's Reasoning**
   The Supreme Court held that a workplace that is permeated with discriminatory intimidation, ridicule, and insult so severe that it alters the conditions of the victim's employment creates an abusive and hostile work environment that violates Title VII. The Court held that the victim is not required to prove that she suffered tangible psychological injury to prove her Title VII claim. The Court noted that Title VII comes into play before the harassing conduct leads the victim to have a nervous breakdown.

Chapter Summary

What Is Law? p. 3

Law

Law is a body of rules of action or conduct that has binding legal force. Laws must be obeyed by citizens subject to sanction or legal consequences.

Functions of the Law

1. Keep the peace
2. Shape moral standards
3. Promote social justice
4. Maintain the status quo
5. Facilitate orderly change
6. Facilitate planning
7. Provide a basis for compromise
8. Maximize individual freedom

Flexibility and Fairness of the Law

1. ***Flexibility.*** The law must be flexible to meet social, technological, and economic changes in the United States and the world.
2. ***Fairness.*** Although the American legal system is one of the fairest and most democratic systems of law, abuses of process and mistakes in the application of the law do occur.

Schools of Jurisprudential Thought, p. 7

Schools of Jurisprudential Thought

1. ***Natural Law School.*** Postulates that law is based on what is "correct." It emphasizes a moral theory of law—that is, law should be based on morality and ethics.
2. ***Historical School.*** Believes that law is an aggregate of social traditions and customs.
3. ***Analytical School.*** Maintains that law is shaped by logic.
4. ***Sociological School.*** Asserts that the law is a means of achieving and advancing certain sociological goals.
5. ***Command School.*** Believes that the law is a set of rules developed, communicated, and enforced by the ruling party.
6. ***Critical Legal Studies School* (the Crits).** Maintains that legal rules are unnecessary and that legal disputes should be solved by applying arbitrary rules based on fairness.
7. ***Law and Economics School.*** Believes that promoting market efficiency should be the central concern of legal decision making.

History of American Law, p. 9

Foundation of American Law

The English common law (judge-made law) forms the basis of the legal systems of most states in this country. Louisiana bases its law on the French civil code.

Sources of Law in the United States, p. 11

Sources of Law in the United States

1. ***Constitutions.*** The U.S. Constitution establishes the federal government and enumerates its powers. Powers not given to the federal government are reserved to the states. State constitutions establish state governments and enumerate their powers.
2. ***Treaties.*** The president, with the advice and consent of the Senate, may enter into treaties with foreign countries.
3. ***Codified law.*** *Statutes* are enacted by the federal Congress and state legislatures. *Ordinances* are passed by municipalities and local government bodies. They establish courses of conduct that must be followed by covered parties.
4. ***Administrative agency regulations and orders.*** Administrative agencies are created by the legislative and executive branches of government. They may adopt administrative regulations and issue orders.
5. ***Executive orders.*** Issued by the president and governors of states, they regulate the conduct of covered parties.
6. ***Judicial decisions.*** Federal and state courts decide controversies. In doing so, they issue decisions that state the holding of each case and the reasoning used by the court in reaching its decision.

Doctrine of *Stare Decisis*

Stare decisis. This doctrine provides for the adherence to precedent. *Stare decisis* means "to stand by the decision."

Internet Exercises and Case Questions

Working the Web Internet Exercises

Activities

Visit the Web sites listed below for more information about the topics covered in this chapter:

1. For a broad overview of legal history visit **jurist.law.pitt.edu/sg_hist.htm**.
2. To better understand the conceptual differences between law and equity see **www.law.cornell.edu/topics/equity.html**.
3. For a working definition of basic legal categories, visit *The Columbia Encyclopedia*, Sixth Edition, 2001, at **www.bartleby.com/65/co/commonla.html**.
4. The Law, Commerce & Technology Center, University of Washington Law, provides online information about Internet issues, biotechnology, electronic commerce, and technology news in the northwest. Visit **www.law.washington.edu/lct**.
5. Check out the latest developments at the Business Law—Committee on Cyberspace Law home page, **www.abanet.org/buslaw/cyber/home.html**.
6. An ongoing series of publications and seminars can be found at the Online Education—Berkman Center for Internet and Society, **cyber.harvard.edu/online**.

Critical Legal Thinking Cases

1.1 Fairness of the Law In 1909, the state legislature of Illinois enacted a statute called the "Woman's 10-Hour Law." The law prohibited women who were employed in factories and other manufacturing facilities from working more than 10 hours per day. The law did not apply to men. W. C. Ritchie & Co., an employer, brought a lawsuit that challenged the statute as being unconstitutional in violation of the Equal Protection Clause of the Illinois constitution. In upholding the statute, the Illinois Supreme Court stated,

> *It is known to all men (and what we know as men we cannot profess to be ignorant of as judges) that woman's physical structure and the performance of maternal functions place her at a great disadvantage in the battle of life; that while a man can work for more than 10 hours a day without injury to himself, a woman, especially when the burdens of motherhood are upon her, cannot; that while a man can work standing upon his feet for more than 10 hours a day, day after day, without injury to himself, a woman cannot; and that to require a woman to stand upon her feet for more than 10 hours in any one day and perform severe manual labor while thus standing, day after day, has the effect to impair her health, and that as weakly and sickly women cannot be mothers of vigorous children.*
>
> *We think the general consensus of opinion, not only in this country but in the civilized countries of Europe, is, that a working day of not more than 10 hours for women is justified for the following reasons: (1) the physical organization of women, (2) her maternal function, (3) the rearing and education of children, (4) the maintenance of the home; and these conditions are, so far, matters of general knowledge that the courts will take judicial cognizance of their existence.*
>
> *Surrounded as women are by changing conditions of society, and the evolution of employment which environs them, we agree fully with what is said by the Supreme Court of Washington in the Buchanan case; "law is, or ought to be, a progressive science."*

Is the statute fair? Would the statute be lawful today? Should the law be a "progressive science"? [*W. C. Ritchie & Co. v. Wayman, Attorney for Cook County, Illinois*, 91 N.E. 695 (IL 1910)]

Business Ethics Cases

1.2 Business Ethics In 1975, after the war in Vietnam, the U.S. government discontinued draft registration for men in this country. In 1980, after the Soviet Union invaded Afghanistan, President Jimmy Carter asked Congress for funds to reactivate draft registration. President Carter suggested that both males and females be required to register. Congress allocated funds only for the registration of males. Several men who were subject to draft registration brought a lawsuit that challenged the law as being unconstitutional in violation of the Equal Protection Clause of the U.S. Constitution. The U.S. Supreme Court upheld the constitutionality of the draft registration law, reasoning as follows:

> *The question of registering women for the draft not only received considerable national attention and was the subject of wide-ranging public debate, but also was extensively considered by Congress in hearings, floor debate, and in committee. The foregoing clearly establishes that the decision to exempt women from registration was not the "accidental by-product of a traditional way of thinking about women."*
>
> *This is not a case of Congress arbitrarily choosing to burden one of two similarly situated groups, such as would be the case with an all-black or all-white, or an all-Catholic or all-Lutheran, or an all-Republican or all-Democratic registration. Men and women are simply not similarly situated for purposes of a draft or registration for a draft.*

Justice Marshall dissented, stating that "The Court today places its imprimatur on one of the most potent remaining public expressions of 'ancient canards about the proper role of women.' It upholds a statute that requires males but not females to register for the draft, and which thereby categorically excludes women from a fundamental civil obligation. I dissent."

Was the decision fair? Has the law been a "progressive science" in this case? Is it ethical for males, but not females, to have to register for the draft? [*Rostker, Director of the Selective Service v. Goldberg*, 453 U.S. 57, 101 S.Ct. 2646, 69 L.Ed.2d 478 (1981)]

Briefing the Case Writing Assignment

Read Case A.1 in the Case Appendix [*Anheuser-Busch Incorporated v. Schmoke Mayor of Baltimore City*]. This case is excerpted from the court of appeals opinion. Review and brief the case. In your brief, be sure to answer the following questions.

1. What law was at issue in this case and what was the source of the law?
2. Who challenged the law? On what grounds did the plaintiff challenge the law?
3. Do you think the challenged law was fair? Explain.
4. How did the court of appeals decide the case? Was this an easy case for the court to decide?

Answers to Management Decision Questions

1. Females have long been discriminated against in employment. **Title IV of the Civil Rights Act of 1964**, a federal statute, prohibits sex discrimination in employment. In addition, most states have enacted laws that prohibit sexual harassment in the workplace. Title VII applies to employers with 15 or more employees and prohibits discrimination in hiring, decisions regarding promotion or demotion, payment of compensation and fringe benefits, availability of job training, and . . . any other "terms, condition, or privilege." More than likely, the actions on the part of the supervisor are actionable under both federal and state laws.
2. Mr. Carson should be informed of the actions of the supervisor. As the owner of the company, he is responsible for the actions of the supervisor and has an ethical responsibility to maintain a nondiscriminatory work environment.
3. Mr. Carson should severely discipline the supervisor or fire the supervisor. In addition, Mr. Carson should investigate and seek comments from employees in order to determine whether additional forms of discrimination are occurring at Carson Security Agency. Policies should be immediately formulated and implemented to prohibit discrimination on the job. Most importantly, he should make sure that no retaliatory actions are taken against the victim of this wrongful behavior.

Endnotes

1. *The Spirit of Liberty*, 3d ed. (New York: Alfred A. Knopf, 1960).
2. "Introduction," *The Nature of Law: Readings in Legal Philosophy*, ed. M. P. Golding (New York: Random House, 1966).
3. *Black's Law Dictionary*, 5th ed. (St. Paul, MN: West, 1979).
4. 447 U.S. 10, 100 S.Ct. 1999, 1980 U.S. Lexis 127 (1980).
5. *Law and the Modern Mind* (New York: Brentano's, 1930).
6. 208 A.2d 193, 1965 Pa. Lexis 442 (PA 1965).

2

Judicial and Alternative Dispute Resolution

"I was never ruined but twice; once when I lost a lawsuit, and once when I won one."

—Voltaire

Chapter Objectives

After studying this chapter, you should be able to:

1. Describe and compare the state court systems and the federal court system.
2. Explains subject matter jurisdiction and venue of federal and state courts.
3. Describe the pretrial litigation process.
4. Describe how a case proceeds through trial and how a trial court decision is appealed.
5. Explain the use of arbitration and other nonjudicial methods of alternative dispute resolution.

Chapter Contents

- The State Court Systems
- The Federal Court System
- The Jurisdiction of Courts
- The Pretrial Litigation Process
- The Trial
- The Appeal
- Alternative Dispute Resolution

Management Decision Judicial and Alternative Dispute Resolution

As the national president of Beta Sigma Theta fraternity, you have learned of several alleged incidents of hazing of pledgees by the collegiate chapter at Smith College in North Carolina. The fraternity is incorporated and headquartered in Illinois. The pledgees are not residents of North Carolina or Illinois. Two of the alleged victims were hospitalized with severe physical injuries. Their parents are threatening to file a lawsuit seeking hundreds of thousands of dollars in damages for physical abuse and mental anguish against the chapter members involved, the local chapter, and the national fraternity.

1. If a lawsuit is filed, where will the trial take place?
2. Are there methods of alternative dispute resolution that you can propose to the executive board of Beta Sigma Theta fraternity to settle this issue?
3. Are there criminal statutes that deal with hazing?

There are two major court systems in the United States: (1) the federal court system and (2) the court systems of the 50 states and the District of Columbia. Each of these systems has jurisdiction to hear different types of lawsuits. The process of bringing, maintaining, and defending a lawsuit is called **litigation**. Litigation is a difficult, time-consuming, and costly process that must comply with complex procedural rules. Although it is not required, most parties employ a lawyer to represent them when they are involved in a lawsuit.

Several forms of *nonjudicial* dispute resolution have developed in response to the expense and difficulty of bringing a lawsuit. These methods, collectively called **alternative dispute resolution**, are being used more and more often to resolve commercial disputes.

This chapter discusses the various court systems, the jurisdiction of courts to hear and decide cases, the litigation process, and alternative dispute resolution.

> The law, wherein, as in a magic mirror, we see reflected, not only our own lives, but the lives of all men that have been! When I think on this majestic theme, my eyes dazzle.
>
> Oliver Wendell Holmes
> *The Law, Speeches 17 (1913)*

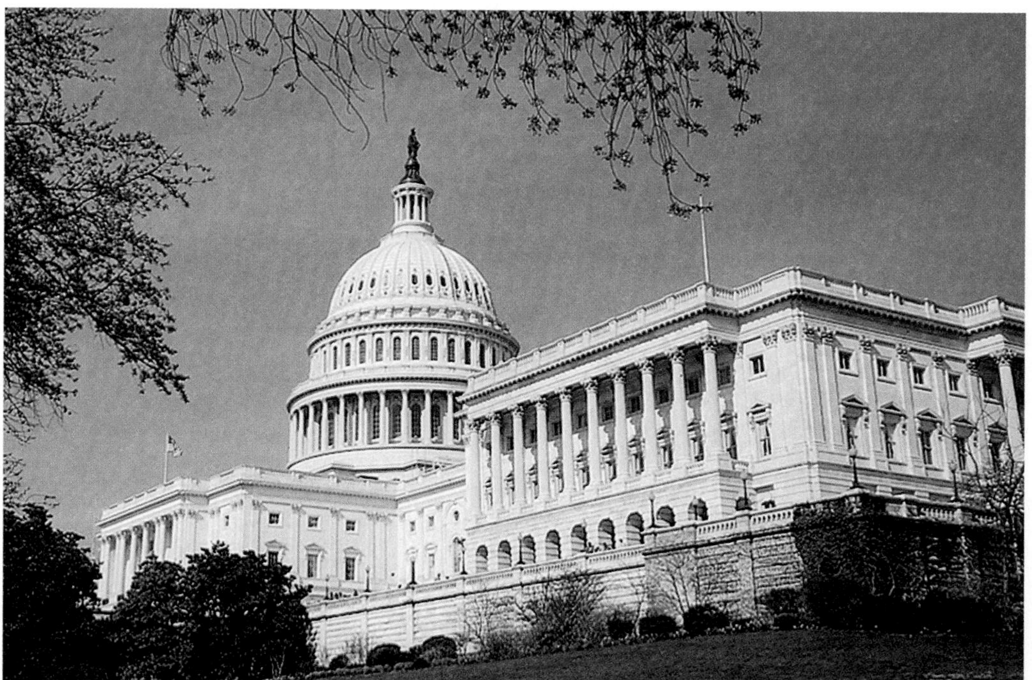

U.S. Congress, Washington, DC. The U.S. Congress, which is a bicameral system made up of the U.S. Senate and the U.S. House of Representatives, creates federal law by enacting statutes. Each state has two senators and is allocated a certain number of representatives based on population.

The State Court Systems

> We're the jury, dread our fury!
> William S. Gilbert
> *Trial by Jury*

Each state and the District of Columbia has a separate court system. Most state court systems include the following: *limited-jurisdiction trial courts*, *general-jurisdiction trial courts*, *intermediate appellate courts*, and a *supreme court*.

Limited Jurisdiction Trial Court

limited-jurisdiction trial court
A court that hears matters of a specialized or limited nature.

State **limited-jurisdiction trial courts**, which are sometimes referred to as **inferior trial courts**, hear matters of a specialized or limited nature. In many states, traffic courts, juvenile courts, justice-of-the-peace courts, probate courts, family law courts, and courts that hear misdemeanor criminal law cases and civil cases involving lawsuits under a certain dollar amount are examples of such courts. Because these courts are trial courts, evidence can be introduced and testimony given. Most limited-jurisdiction courts keep a record of their proceedings. Their decisions usually can be appealed to a general-jurisdiction court or an appellate court.

small claims court
A court that hears civil cases involving small dollar amounts.

Many states have also created **small claims courts** to hear civil cases involving small dollar amounts (e.g., $5,000 or less). Generally, the parties must appear individually and cannot have lawyers represent them. The decision of small claims courts are often appealable to general-jurisdiction trial courts or appellate courts.

general-jurisdiction trial court
A court that hears cases of a general nature that are not within the jurisdiction of limited-jurisdiction trial courts. Testimony and evidence at trial are recorded and stored for future reference.

General-Jurisdiction Trial Court Every state has a **general-jurisdiction trial court**. These courts are often referred to as **courts of record** because the testimony and evidence at trial are recorded and stored for future reference. They hear cases that are not within the jurisdiction of limited-jurisdiction trial courts, such as felonies, civil cases over a certain dollar amount, and so on. Some states divide their general-jurisdiction courts into two divisions, one for criminal cases and another for civil cases. Evidence and testimony are given at general-jurisdiction trial courts. The decisions handed down by these courts are appealable to an intermediate appellate court or the state supreme court, depending on the circumstances.

Courthouse, St. Louis Missouri. State Courts hear and decide the majority of cases in this country.

Intermediate Appellate Court

In many states, **intermediate appellate courts** (also called **appellate courts** or **courts of appeal**) hear appeals from trial courts. They review the trail court record to determine if there have been any errors at trial that would require reversal or modification of the trial court's decision. Thus, the appellate court reviews either pertinent parts or the whole trial court record from the lower court. No new evidence or testimony is permitted. The parties usually file legal *briefs* with the appellate court, stating the law and facts that support their positions. Appellate courts usually grant a brief oral hearing to the parties. Appellate court decisions are appealable to the state's highest court. In sparsely populated states that do not have an intermediate appellate court, trial court decisions can be appealed directly to the state's highest court.

intermediate appellate court
An intermediate court that hears appeals from trial courts.

Highest State Court

Each state has a highest court in its court system. Most states call this highest court the **supreme court**. The function of a state supreme court is to hear appeals from intermediate state courts and certain trial courts. No new evidence or testimony is heard. The parties usually submit pertinent parts of or the entire lower court record for review. The parties also submit legal briefs to the court and are usually granted a brief oral hearing. Decisions of state supreme courts are final, unless a question of law is involved that is appealable to the U.S. Supreme Court.

state supreme court
The highest court in a state court system; it hears appeals from intermediate state courts and certain trial courts.

Exhibit 2.1 portrays a typical state court system.

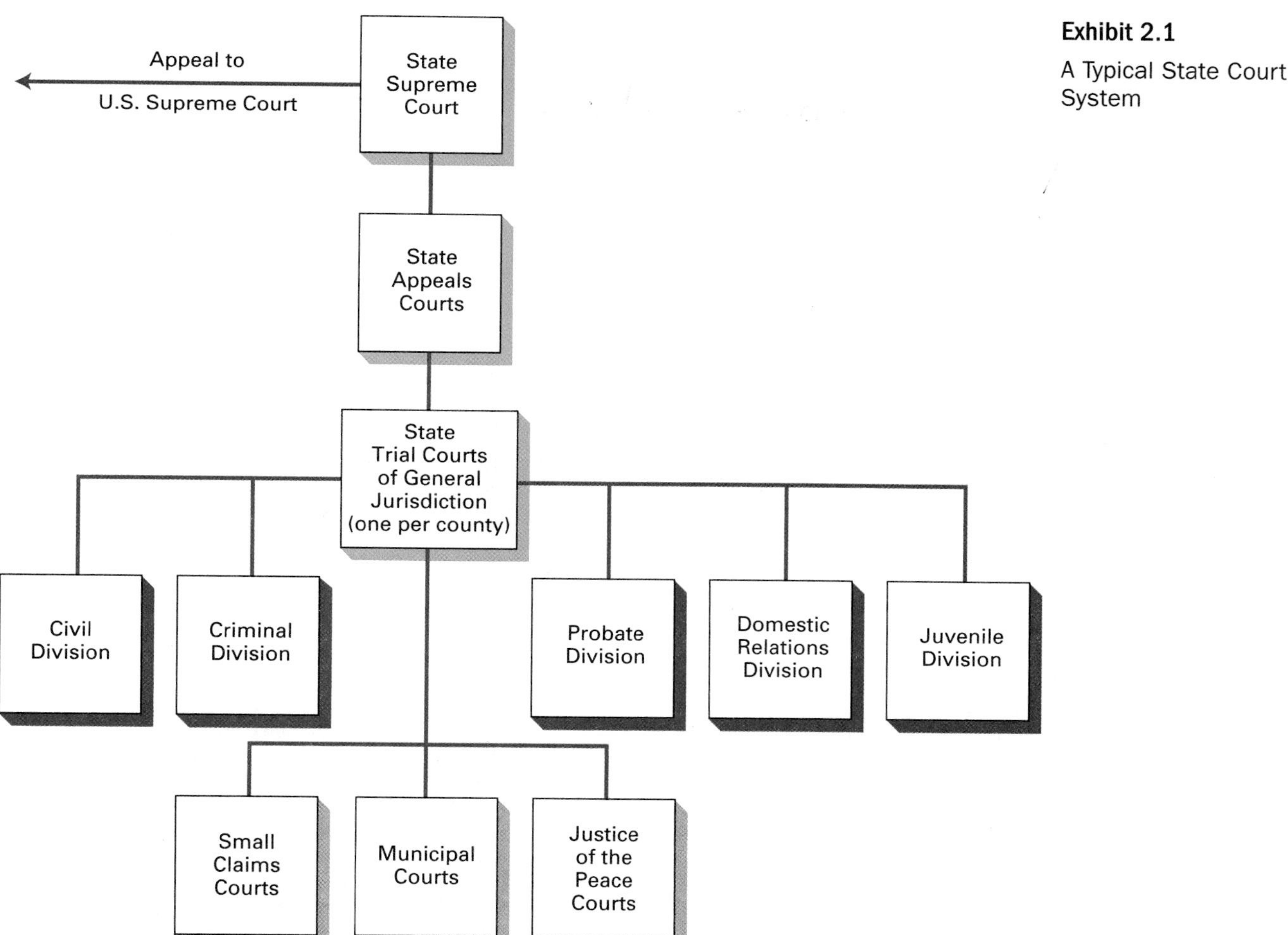

Exhibit 2.1
A Typical State Court System

Entrepreneur and the Law

Specialized Courts Hear Commercial Disputes

In most states, business and commercial disputes are heard by the same judges who hear and decide criminal, landlord–tenant, matrimonial, medical malpractice, and other non-business-related cases. The one major exception to this standard has been the state of Delaware, where a special Chancery Court hears and decides business litigation. The court, which deals mainly with cases involving corporate government disputes, has earned a reputation for its expertise in handling and deciding corporate matters. Perhaps the existence of this special court and a corporation code that tends to favor corporate management are the primary reasons that more than 60 percent of the corporations listed on the New York Stock Exchange are incorporated in Delaware.

New York is one state that is following Delaware's lead in this area. New York has designated four courts within its general court system to hear commercial disputes. These courts, which began operating in 1993, hear contract, sales, insurance, unfair competition, libel, and slander, shareholder, business-related torts, and other commercial cases. Other states are expected to establish courts that specialize in commercial matters in the near future.

Businesses tend to favor special commercial courts because the judges presiding over them are expected to have the expertise to handle complex commercial lawsuits. The courts are also expected to be more efficient in deciding business-related cases, thus saving time and money for the parties. ■

The Federal Court System

> Pieces of evidence, each by itself insufficient, may together constitute a significant whole and justify by their combined effect a conclusion.
>
> Lord Wright
> *Grant v. Australian Knitting Mills, Ltd.* (1936)

Article III of the U.S. Constitution provides that the federal government's judicial power is vested in one "Supreme Court." This court is the **U.S. Supreme Court**. The Constitution also authorizes Congress to establish "inferior" federal courts. Pursuant to this power, Congress has established special federal courts, the U.S. district courts, and the U.S. courts of appeal. Federal judges are appointed for life by the president, with the advice and consent of the Senate (except bankruptcy court judges, who are appointed for 14-year terms).

Special Federal Courts

special federal courts Federal courts that hear matters of specialized or limited jurisdiction.

The **special federal courts** established by Congress have limited jurisdiction. They include the following:

- ***U.S. tax court*** Hears cases involving federal tax laws.
- ***U.S. claims court*** Hears cases brought against the United States.
- ***U.S. Court of International Trade*** Hears cases involving tariffs and international commercial disputes.
- ***U.S. bankruptcy court*** Hears cases involving federal bankruptcy laws.

U.S. District Courts

U.S. district courts The federal court system's trial courts of general jurisdiction.

The **U.S. district courts** are the federal court system's trial courts of general jurisdiction. There is at least one federal district court in each state and the District of Columbia, although heavily populated states have more than one district court. The geographical area served by each court is referred to as a *district*. There are presently 96 federal district courts. The federal district courts are empowered to impanel juries, receive evidence, hear testimony, and decide cases. Most federal cases originate in federal district courts.

U.S. Courts of Appeal

The **U.S. courts of appeals** are the federal court system's intermediate appellate courts. There are 13 circuits in the federal court system. The first 12 are geographical. Eleven are designated by a number, such as the "First Circuit," "Second Circuit," and so on. The geographical area served by each court is referred to as a *circuit*. The twelfth circuit court is located in Washington, DC, and is called the "District of Columbia Circuit."

U.S. courts of appeals
The federal court system's intermediate appellate courts.

As appellate courts, each of these courts hears appeals from the district courts located in its circuit as well as from certain special courts and federal administrative agencies. The court reviews the record of the lower court or administrative agency proceedings to determine if there has been any error that would warrant reversal or modification of the lower court decision. No new evidence or testimony is heard. The parties file legal briefs with the court and are given a short oral hearing. Appeals are usually heard by a three-judge panel. After a decision is rendered by the three-judge panel, a petitioner can request a review *en banc* by the full court.

The thirteenth court of appeals was created by Congress in 1982. It is called the **Court of Appeals for the Federal Circuit** and is located in Washington, DC.[1] This court has special appellate jurisdiction to review the decisions of the Claims Court, the Patent and Trademark Office, and the Court of International Trade. This court was created to provide uniformity in the application of federal law in certain areas, particularly patent law.

Exhibit 2.2 shows the 13 federal circuit courts of appeals.

Web Site
U.S. Court of Appeals The Villanova Center for Information Law and Policy is your gateway to various circuit courts whose Web sites are located at different universities. Visit at **www.vcilp.org/Fed-Ct/fedcourt.html**.

Court of Appeals for the Federal Circuit
A court of appeals in Washington, DC, that has special appellate jurisdiction to review the decisions of the Claims Court, the Patent and Trademark Office, and the Court of International Trade.

The U.S. Supreme Court

The highest court in the land is the **Supreme Court of the United States**, located in Washington, DC. The Court is composed of nine justices who are nominated by the president and confirmed by the Senate. The president appoints one justice as *chief justice*, responsible for the administration of the Supreme Court. The other eight justices are *associate justices*.

Supreme Court of the United States
The Supreme Court was created by Article III of the U.S. Constitution. The Supreme Court is the highest court in the land. It is located in Washington, DC.

Exhibit 2.2
The Thirteen Federal Judicial Circuits

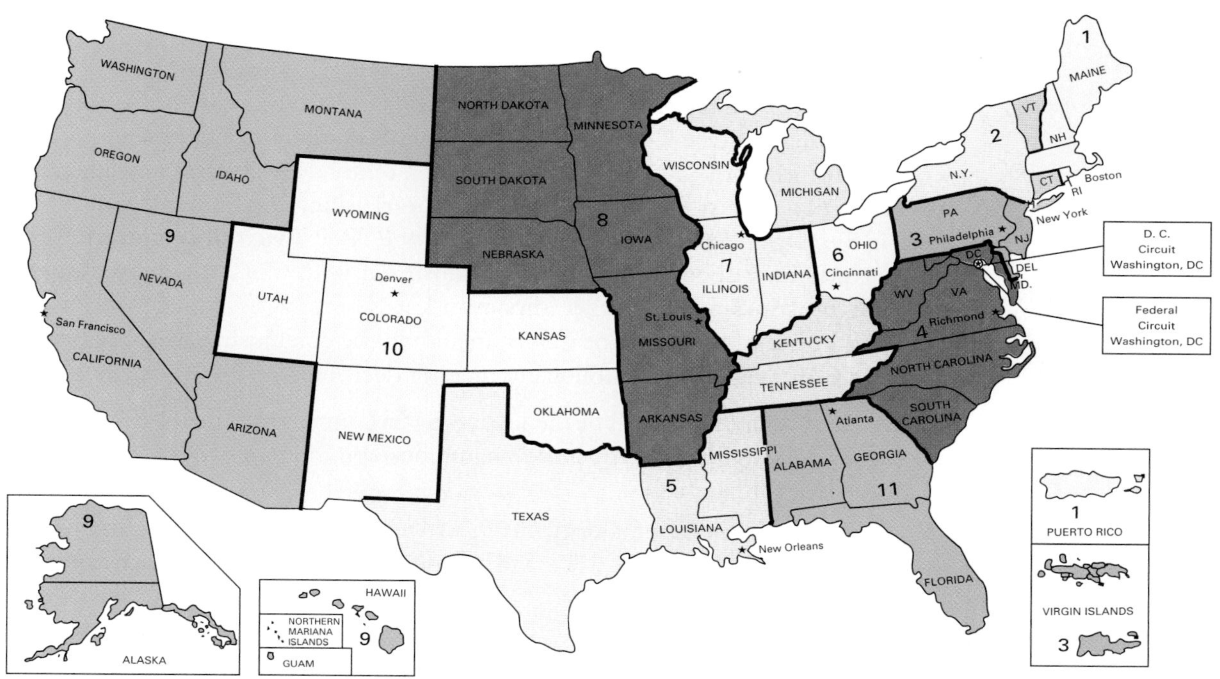

Exhibit 2.3

The Federal Court System

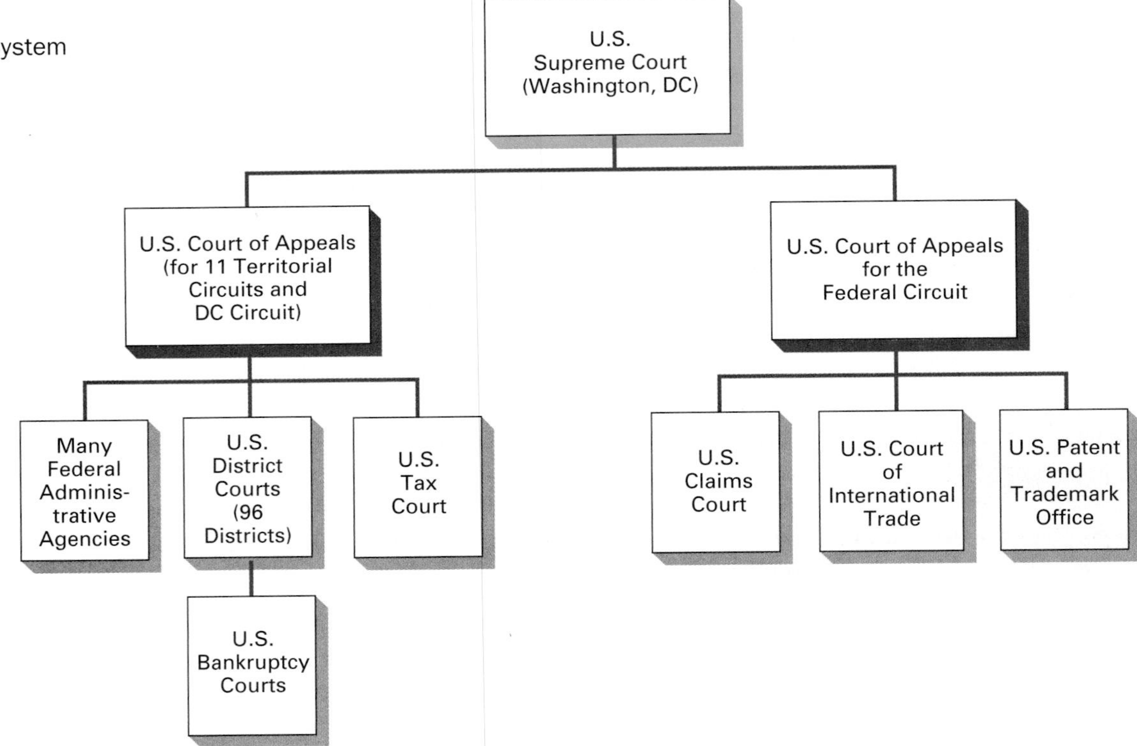

Web Site

U.S. Supreme Court Cornell University maintains a site that features recent decisions and selected historic decisions of the U.S. Supreme Court. You can search for decisions by date, by party, and by subject. Visit at **supct.law.cornell.edu/supct/index/html**.

The Supreme Court, which is an appellate court, hears appeals from federal circuit courts of appeals and, under certain circumstances, from federal district courts, special federal courts, and the highest state courts. No new evidence or testimony is heard. As with other appellate courts, the lower court record is reviewed to determine whether there has been an error that warrants a reversal or modification of the decision. Legal briefs are filed, and the parties are granted a brief oral hearing. The Supreme Court's decision is final.

The federal court system is illustrated in Exhibit 2.3.

Decisions by the U.S. Supreme Court

Web Site

The Supreme Court of the United States maintains a Web site. Visit at **www.supremecourtus.gov**.

petition for certiorari

A petition asking the Supreme Court to hear one's case.

writ of certiorari

An official notice that the Supreme Court will review one's case.

The U.S. Constitution gives Congress the authority to establish rules for the appellate review of cases by the Supreme Court, except in the rare case where mandatory review is required. Congress has given the Supreme Court discretion to decide what cases it will hear.[2]

A petitioner must file a **petition for certiorari** asking the Supreme Court to hear the case. If the Court decides to review a case, it will issue a **writ of certiorari**. Because the Court issues only about 150 to 200 opinions each year, writs are granted only in cases involving constitutional and other important issues.

Each justice of the Supreme Court, including the chief justice, has an equal vote. The Supreme Court can issue the following types of decisions:

- ***Unanimous decision*** If all of the justices voting agree as to the outcome and reasoning used to decide the case, it is a unanimous opinion. Unanimous decisions are precedent for later cases.
- ***Majority decision*** If a majority of the justices agree to the outcome and reasoning used to decide the case, it is a majority opinion. Majority decisions are precedent for later cases.
- ***Plurality decision*** If a majority of the justices agree to the outcome of the case, but not as to the reasoning for the reaching outcome, it is a plurality opinion. A plurality decision settles the case but is not precedent for later cases.

- ***Tie decision*** Sometimes the Supreme Court sits without all nine justices being present. This could happen because of illness, conflict of interest, or a justice not having been confirmed to fill a vacant seat on the Court. If there is a tie vote, the lower court decision is affirmed. Such votes are not precedent for later cases.

A justice who agrees with the outcome of a case, but not the reason proffered by other justices, can issue a *concurring opinion* that sets forth his or her reasons for deciding the case. A justice who does not agree with a decision can file a *dissenting opinion* that sets forth the reasons for his or her dissent.

Sancho: But if this is hell, why do we see no lawyers?

Clarindo: They won't receive them, lest they bring lawsuits here.

Sancho: If there are no lawsuits here, hell's not so bad.

Lope de Vega
The Star of Seville, Act 3, Scene 2

Contemporary Business Environment

I'll Take You to the U.S. Supreme Court!—Not!

As textbooks say, in the United States you can appeal your legal case all the way to the U.S. Supreme Court. In reality, however, the chance of ever having your case heard by the highest court is slim to none.

Each year, more than 7,000 petitioners ask the Supreme Court to hear their cases. These petitioners usually pay big law firms from $30,000 to $100,000 or more to write the appeal petition. In recent years, the Supreme Court has accepted only fewer than 100 of these cases for full review each term.

Each of the nine Supreme Court justices has three law clerks—recent law school graduates usually chosen from the elite law schools across the country—who assist them. The justices rarely read the appellate petitions but instead delegate this task to their law clerks. A clerk then writes a short memorandum, discussing the key issues raised by the appeal, and recommends to the justices whether they should grant or deny a review. The justices meet once a week to discuss what cases merit review. The votes of four justices are necessary to grant an appeal and schedule an oral argument before the Court ("rule of four"). Written opinions by the justices are usually issued many months later.

So what does it take to win a review by the Supreme Court? The U.S. Supreme Court usually decides to hear cases involving major constitutional questions such as freedom of speech, freedom of religion, and due process. The Court, therefore, rarely decides day-to-day legal issues such as breach of contract, tort liability, or corporations law unless they involve more important constitutional or federal law questions. Often a case is not heard unless there was a "split" in the circuit courts of appeal, that is, several circuit courts have decided the legal issue differently. The Supreme Court's ruling resolves the split among the circuit courts.

So the next time you hear someone say, "I'll take you to the U.S. Supreme Court!" just say, "Not!" ■

Supreme Court of the United States. The highest court in the land is the Supreme Court of the United States, located in Washington, DC. The Supreme Court's decisions establish precedent for all the other courts in the country.

Jurisdiction of Federal and State Courts

Article III, Section 2 of the U.S. Constitution sets forth the jurisdiction of federal courts. Federal courts have *limited jurisdiction* to hear cases involving:

federal question
A case arising under the U.S. Constitution, treaties, or federal statutes and regulations.

diversity of citizenship
A case between (1) citizens of different states, (2) a citizen of a state and a citizen or subject of a foreign country, and (3) a citizen of a state and a foreign country where a foreign country is the plaintiff.

1. ***Federal questions*** Cases arising under the U.S. Constitution, treaties, and federal statutes and regulations. There is no dollar-amount limit on federal question cases that can be brought in federal court.[3]
2. ***Diversity of citizenship*** Cases between (a) citizens of different states, and (b) a citizen of a state and a citizen or subject of a foreign country. A corporation is considered to be a citizen of the state in which it is incorporated and in which it has its principal place of business. The reason for providing diversity of citizenship jurisdiction was to prevent state court bias against nonresidents. The federal court must apply the appropriate state's law in deciding the case. The dollar amount of the controversy must exceed $75,000.[4] If this requirement is not met, action must be brought in the appropriate state court.

exclusive jurisdiction
Jurisdiction held by only one court.

Federal courts have **exclusive jurisdiction** to hear cases involving federal crimes, antitrust, bankruptcy, patent and copyright cases, suits against the United States, and most admiralty cases. State courts cannot hear these cases.

concurrent jurisdiction
Jurisdiction shared by two or more courts.

State and federal courts have **concurrent jurisdiction** to hear cases involving diversity of citizenship and federal questions over which federal courts do not have exclusive jurisdiction (e.g., cases involving federal securities laws). If a case involving concurrent jurisdiction is brought by a plaintiff in state court, the defendant can remove the case to federal court. If a case does not qualify to be brought in federal court, it must be brought in the appropriate state court.

Exhibit 2.4 illustrates the jurisdiction of federal and state courts.

Landmark Law

The Process of Choosing a Supreme Court Justice

In an effort to strike a balance of power between the executive and legislative branches of government, Article II, Section 2 of the U.S. Constitution gives the president the power to appoint Supreme Court justices "with the advice and consent of the Senate." In recent years, however, many conservative and liberal critics have charged that this process has become nothing more than a political tennis match in which the hapless nominee is the ball.

Some of the most notorious fights over Supreme Court nominations in U.S. history took place during the Reagan administration. President George Bush was given the chance to cast a conservative shadow over the Court's decisions when Justice Thurgood Marshall retired in 1991. Marshall, who served 24 years, was one of the most liberal members of the Court. Also, he had been the only black person to serve on the Supreme Court. In 1991, Bush nominated Clarence Thomas, a black conservative serving as a judge of the U.S. Court of Appeals in the District of Columbia, to replace Marshall. Thomas grew up in rural Georgia and graduated from Yale Law School. After a heated political debate, Clarence Thomas was confirmed by the U.S. Senate with a 52–48 vote in October 1991.

The election of Bill Clinton as president swung the pendulum back to the Democrats. President Clinton got an early opportunity to nominate a candidate when Justice Byron R. White, a Democrat-appointed member of the Court, retired.

President Clinton nominated Judge Ruth Bader Ginsburg to serve on the Supreme Court. Justice Ginsburg was considered a moderate liberal. Ginsburg was approved by a bipartisan vote of the Senate and took office for the Supreme Court's 1993–1994 term. She is the second woman to serve on the Court, joining Sandra Day O'Connor, who was nominated by President Ronald Reagan. Ginsburg is also the first Jewish person to serve on the Court since Justice Abe Fortas resigned in 1969. ■

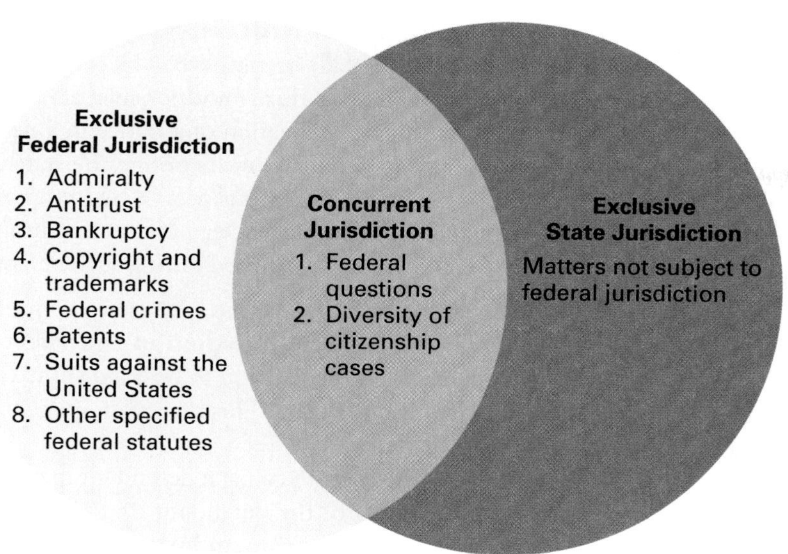

Exhibit 2.4

Jurisdiction of Federal and State Courts

The Jurisdiction of Courts

Not every court has the authority to hear all types of cases. First, to bring a lawsuit in a court the plaintiff must have *standing to sue*. In addition, the court must have *jurisdiction* to hear the case, and the case must be brought in the proper *venue*. These topics are discussed in the following paragraphs.

Standing to Sue

To bring a lawsuit, a plaintiff must have **standing to sue**. This means the plaintiff must have some stake in the outcome of the lawsuit.

standing to sue
The plaintiff must have some stake in the outcome of the lawsuit.

Consider This Example Linda's friend Jon is injured in an accident caused by Emily. Jon refuses to sue. Linda cannot sue Emily on Jon's behalf because she does not have an interest in the result of the case.

A few states now permit investors to invest money in a lawsuit for a percentage return of any award of judgment. Courts hear and decide actual disputes involving specific controversies. Hypothetical questions will not be heard, and trivial lawsuits will be dismissed.

Jurisdiction

A court must have **jurisdiction** to hear and decide a case. There are two types of jurisdiction: (1) subject matter jurisdiction and (2) in personam, in rem, or quasi in rem jurisdiction.

jurisdiction
The authority of a court to hear a case.

subject matter jurisdiction
Jurisdiction over the subject matter of a lawsuit.

1. ***Subject Matter Jurisdiction*** To hear and decide a case, a court must have **subject matter jurisdiction** over the subject matter of the case. Some courts have only limited jurisdiction. For example, federal courts have jurisdiction to hear only certain types of cases (discussed later in this chapter). Certain state courts, such as probate courts and small claims courts, can hear only designated types of cases. If a court does not have subject matter jurisdiction, it cannot hear the case.
2. ***In Personam, in Rem, and Quasi in Rem Jurisdiction*** Jurisdiction over the person is called **in personam jurisdiction**, or **personal jurisdiction**. A *plaintiff*, by filing a lawsuit with a court, gives the court in personam jurisdiction over themselves. The court must also have in personam jurisdiction over the *defendant*, which is usually obtained by hav-

in personam jurisdiction
Jurisdiction over the parties to a lawsuit.

ing that person served a summons within the territorial boundaries of the state (i.e., **service of process**). Service of process is usually accomplished by personal service of the summons and complaint on the defendant. If this is not possible, alternative forms of notice, such as mailing of the summons or publication of a notice in a newspaper, may be permitted. A corporation is subject to personal jurisdiction in the state in which it is incorporated, has its principal office, and is doing business. A party who disputes the jurisdiction of a court can make a *special appearance* in that court to argue against imposition of jurisdiction. Service of process is not permitted during such an appearance.

service of process
A summons being served on the defendant to obtain personal jurisdiction over him or her.

A court may have jurisdiction to hear and decide a case because it has jurisdiction over the property of the lawsuit. This is called **in rem jurisdiction** ("jurisdiction over the thing"). For example, a state court would have jurisdiction to hear a dispute over the ownership of a piece of real estate located within the state. This is so even if one or more of the disputing parties live in another state or states.

in rem jurisdiction
Jurisdiction to hear a case because of jurisdiction over the property of the lawsuit.

Sometimes a plaintiff who obtains a judgment against a defendant in one state will try to collect the judgment by attaching property of the defendant that is located in another state. This is permitted under **quasi in rem**, or **attachment jurisdiction**.[5]

quasi in rem jurisdiction
Jurisdiction allowed a plaintiff who obtains a judgment in one state to try to collect the judgment by attaching property of the defendant located in another state.

Long-Arm Statutes In most states, a state court can obtain jurisdiction over persons and businesses located in another state or country through the state's **long-arm statute**. These statutes extend a state's jurisdiction to nonresidents who were not served a summons within the state. The nonresident must have had some *minimum contact* with the state.[6] In addition, the maintenance of the suit must uphold the traditional notions of fair play and substantial justice.

long-arm statute
A statute that extends a state's jurisdiction to nonresidents who were not served a summons within the state.

The exercise of long-arm jurisdiction is generally permitted over nonresidents who have (1) committed torts within the state (e.g., caused an automobile accident in the state), (2) entered into a contract either in the state or that affects the state (and allegedly breached the contract), or (3) transacted other business in the state that allegedly caused injury to another person.

Parties to a contract may include a **forum-selection clause** that designates a certain court to hear any dispute concerning nonperformance of the contract. The following case illustrates the application of a forum-selection clause.

forum-selection clause
A contract provision that designates a certain court to hear any dispute concerning nonperformance of the contract.

Case 2.1 Forum-Selection Clause

U.S. SUPREME COURT CASE
Carnival Cruise Lines, Inc. v. Shute
499 U.S. 585, 111 S.Ct. 1522, 1991 U.S. Lexis 2221 (1991)
Supreme Court of the United States

Background and Facts

Mr. and Mrs. Shute, residents of the State of Washington, purchased passage for a seven-day cruise on the *Tropicale*, a cruise ship operated by the Carnival Cruise Lines, Inc. (Carnival). They paid the fare to the travel agent, who forwarded the payment to Carnival's headquarters in Miami, Florida. Carnival prepared the tickets and sent them to the Shutes. Each ticket consisted of five pages, including contract terms. The ticket contained a forum-selection clause that designated the state of Florida as the forum for any lawsuits arising under or in connection with the ticket and cruise. The Shutes boarded the *Tropicale* in Los Angeles, which set sail for Puerto Vallarta, Mexico. While the ship was on its return voyage and in international waters off the Mexican coast, Mrs. Shute was injured when she slipped on a deck mat during a guided tour of the ship's galley. Upon return to Washington, she filed a negligence lawsuit against Carnival in U.S. district court in Washington seeking damages. Carnival filed a motion for summary judgment, contending that the lawsuit could be brought only in a court located in the state of Florida. The district court granted Carnival's motion. The court of appeals reversed, holding that Mrs. Shute could sue Carnival in Washington. Carnival appealed to the U.S. Supreme Court.

Supreme Court Issue

Is the forum-selection clause in the Carnival Cruise Lines ticket enforceable?

In The Language of The U.S. Supreme Court

Blackmun, Justice As an initial matter, we do not adopt the court of appeals' determination that a nonnegotiated forum-selection clause in a form ticket contract is never enforceable simply because it is not the subject of bargaining. Including a reasonable forum clause in form contract of this kind may well be permissible for several reasons: First, a cruise line has a special interest in limiting the fora in which it potentially could be subject to suit. Because a cruise ship typically carries passengers from many locales, it is not unlikely that a mishap on a cruise could subject the cruise line to litigation in several different fora.

Additionally, a clause establishing the forum for dispute resolution has the salutary effect of dispelling any confusion where suits arising from the contract must be brought and defended, sparing litigants the time and expense of pretrial motions to determine the correct forum, and conserving judicial resources that otherwise would be devoted to deciding those motions. Finally, it stands to reason that passengers who purchase tickets containing a forum clause like that at issue in this case benefit in form of reduced fares reflecting the savings that the cruise line enjoys by limiting the fora in which it may be sued.

Decision and Remedy

The forum-selection clause in Carnival's ticket is fair and reasonable and therefore enforceable against Mrs. Shute. If she wishes to sue Carnival, she must do so in a court in the state of Florida, not in a court in the state of Washington. The U.S. Supreme Court reversed the decision of the court of appeals.

Case Questions

Critical Legal Thinking Should forum-selection clauses be enforced? Why or why not?

Business Ethics Did Carnival Cruise Lines act ethically by placing the forum-selection clause in its tickets?

Contemporary Business Do forum-selection clauses serve any legitimate business purpose? Explain.

Venue

Venue requires lawsuits to be heard by the court with jurisdiction nearest the location in which the incident occurred or where the parties reside.

venue
A concept that requires lawsuits to be heard by the court with jurisdiction that is nearest the location in which the incident occurred or where the parties reside.

Consider This Example Harry, a Georgia resident, commits a felony crime in Los Angeles County, California. The California Superior Court located in Los Angeles is the proper venue because the crime was committed there, the witnesses are probably from the area, and so on.

Occasionally, pretrial publicity may prejudice jurors located in the proper venue. In such cases, a *change of venue* may be requested so that a more impartial jury can be found. The courts generally frown upon *forum shopping* (i.e., looking for a favorable court without a valid reason).

E-Commerce & Information Technology

Obtaining Personal Jurisdiction in Cyberspace

Obtaining personal jurisdiction over a defendant located in another state has always been a difficult issue for the courts. To make sure this is not overly burdensome, the U.S. Supreme Court has held that out-of-state defendants must have had certain "minimum contacts" with the state before they are made to answer to a lawsuit there [*International Shoe Co. v. Washington*, 326 U.S. 310, 66 S.Ct. 154 (1945)]. Today, with the advent of the Internet and the ability of persons and businesses to reach millions of people in other states electronically, the application of the *International Shoe* minimum contacts standard is even more difficult.

Several courts have decided cases involving the reach of a state's long-arm statute to obtain jurisdiction over someone in another state because of his or her Internet activities. In one case, Zippo Manufacturing Company (Zippo) sued Zippo Dot Com, Inc., in federal district court in Pennsylvania. Zippo manufactures its well-known line of Zippo tobacco lighters in Bradford, Pennsylvania, and sells them worldwide. Zippo Dot Com, a California corporation with its principal place of business and its servers located in Sunnyvale, California, operates an Internet Web site that transmits information and sexually explicit material to its subscribers. Three thousand of Zippo Dot Com's 140,000 paying subscribers worldwide are located in Pennsylvania. Zippo sued Zippo Dot Com in federal district court in Pennsylvania for trademark infringement. Zippo Dot Com alleged that it was not subject to personal jurisdiction in Pennsylvania. The district court applied the *International Shoe* "minimum contacts" standard and held that Zippo Dot Com was subject of personal jurisdiction under the Pennsylvania long-arm statute and ordered it to defend itself there. [*Zippo Manufacturing Company v. Zippo Dot Com, Inc.*, 952 F.Supp. 1119 (W.D.Pa. 1997)]

Courts will be faced with thousands of lawsuits that involve the issue of when a state's long-arm statute can reach into cyberspace and make an out-of-state Web site owner respond to a lawsuit in that state. The *International Shoe* "minimum contacts" standard is in for a whole new application. ■

Entrepreneur and the Law

Cost–Benefit Analysis of a Lawsuit

In most civil lawsuits each party is responsible for paying its own attorneys' fees, whether the party wins or loses. This is called the "American rule." The court can award lawyers' fees to the winning party if a statute so provides, the parties have so agreed (e.g., in a contract), or the losing party has acted maliciously or pursued a frivolous case.

An attorney in a civil lawsuit can represent the plaintiff on an hourly, project, or contingency fee basis. Hourly fees usually range from $75 to $500 per hour, depending on the type of case, the expertise of the lawyer, and the locality of the lawsuit. Under a *contingency fee arrangement*, the lawyer receives a percentage of the amount recovered for the plaintiff upon winning or settling the case. Contingency fees normally range from 20 to 50 percent of the award or settlement, with the average being about 35 percent. Lawyers for defendants in lawsuits are normally paid on an hourly basis.

The choice of whether to bring or defend a lawsuit should be analyzed like any other business decision. This includes performing a **cost–benefit analysis** of the lawsuit. For the plaintiff, it may be wise not to sue. For the defendant, it may be wise to settle. The following factors should be considered in deciding whether to bring or settle a lawsuit:

- The probability of winning or losing.
- The amount of money to be won or lost.
- Lawyers' fees and other costs of litigation.
- Loss of time by managers and other personnel.
- The long-term effects on the relationship and reputation of the parties.
- The amount of prejudgment interest provided by law.
- The aggravation and psychological costs associated with a lawsuit.
- The unpredictability of the legal system and the possibility of error.
- Other factors peculiar to the parties and lawsuit. ■

The Pretrial Litigation Process

litigation
The process of bringing, maintaining, and defending a lawsuit.

The bringing, maintaining, and defense of a lawsuit are generally referred to as the *litigation process*, or **litigation**. The pretrial litigation process can be divided into the following major phases: *pleadings*, *discovery*, *dismissals and pretrial judgments*, and *settlement conference*. Each of these phases is discussed in the paragraphs that follow.

The White House, Washington, DC. The White House, located in Washington, DC, is the home of the president of the United States. The U.S. Department of Justice, which is part of the executive branch of the federal government, prosecutes federal crimes.

The Pleadings

The paperwork that is filed with the court to initiate and respond to a lawsuit is referred to as the **pleadings**. The major pleadings are the *complaint*, the *answer*, the *cross-complaint*, and the *reply*.

pleadings
The paperwork that is filed with the court to initiate and respond to a lawsuit.

Complaint and Summons To initiate a lawsuit, the party who is suing (the **plaintiff**) must file a **complaint** with the proper court. The complaint must name the parties to the lawsuit, allege the ultimate facts and law violated, and contain a "prayer for relief" for a remedy to be awarded by the court. The complaint can be as long as necessary, depending on the case's complexity. A sample complaint appears in Exhibit 2.5.

plaintiff
The party who files the complaint.

complaint
The document the plaintiff files with the court and serves on the defendant to initiate a lawsuit.

Once a complaint has been filed with the court, the court issues a **summons**. A summons is a court order directing the defendant to appear in court and answer the complaint. The complaint and summons are served on the defendant by a sheriff, another government official, or a private process server.

summons
A court order directing the defendant to appear in court and answer the complaint.

Answer The defendant must file an **answer** to the plaintiff's complaint. The defendant's answer is filed with the court and served on the plaintiff. In the answer, the defendant admits or denies the allegations contained in the plaintiff's complaint. A judgment will be entered against a defendant who admits all of the allegations in the complaint. The case will proceed if the defendant denies all or some of the allegations. If the defendant does not answer the complaint, a *default judgment* is entered against him or her. A default judgment establishes the defendant's liability. The plaintiff then has only to prove damages.

answer
The defendant's written response to the plaintiff's complaint, which is filed with the court and served on the plaintiff.

Exhibit 2.5

A Sample Complaint

In the United States District Court for the District of Idaho

John Doe
Plaintiff

v.

Jane Roe

Defendant

Civil No. 2-1001

COMPLAINT

The plaintiff, by and through his attorney, alleges:

1. The plaintiff is a resident of the State of Idaho, the defendant is a resident of the State of Washington, and there is diversity of citizenship between the parties.
2. The amount in controversy exceeds the sum of $75,000, exclusive of interest and costs.
3. On January 10, 2004, plaintiff was exercising reasonable care while walking across the intersection of Sun Valley Road and Main Street, Ketchum, Idaho, when defendant negligently drove her car through a red light at the intersection and struck plaintiff.
4. As a result of the defendant's negligence, plaintiff has incurred medical expenses of $104,000 and suffered severe physical injury and mental distress.

WHEREFORE, plaintiff claims judgment in the amount of $1,000,000, interest at the maximum legal rate, and costs of this action.

By ______________________
Edward Lawson
Attorney for Plaintiff
100 Main Street
Ketchum, Idaho

Business Brief

Some complaints in complicated cases exceed 100 pages.

In addition to answering the complaint, a defendant's answer can assert *affirmative defenses*. For example, if a complaint alleges that the plaintiff was personally injured by the defendant, the defendant's answer could state that he or she acted in self-defense. Another affirmative defense would be an assertion that the plaintiff's lawsuit is barred because the *statute of limitations* (time within which to bring the lawsuit) has expired.

cross-complaint

A document filed by the defendant against the plaintiff to seek damages or some other remedy.

reply

A document filed by the original plaintiff to answer the defendant's cross-complaint.

Cross-Complaint and Reply A defendant who believes that he or she has been injured by the plaintiff can file a **cross-complaint** against the plaintiff in addition to an answer. In the cross-complaint, the defendant (now the *cross-complainant*) sues the plaintiff (now the *cross-defendant*) for damages or some other remedy. The original plaintiff must file a **reply** (answer) to the cross-complaint. The reply, which can include affirmative defenses, must be filed with the court and served on the original defendant.

intervention

The act of others joining as parties to an existing lawsuit.

consolidation

The act of a court to combine two or more separate lawsuits into one lawsuit.

Intervention and Consolidation If other persons have an interest in a lawsuit, they may **intervene** and become parties to the lawsuit. For instance, a bank that has made a secured loan on a piece of real estate can intervene in a lawsuit between parties who are litigating ownership of the property.

If several plaintiffs have filed separate lawsuits stemming from the same fact situation against the same defendant, the court can **consolidate** the cases into one case if it would not cause undue prejudice to the parties. Suppose, for example, that a commercial airplane crashes, killing and injuring many people. The court could consolidate all of the lawsuits against the defendant airplane company.

Case 2.2
Notice Pleading

U.S. SUPREME COURT CASE

Swierkiewicz v. Sorema N.A.

534 U.S. 506, 122 S.Ct. 992, 2002 U.S. Lexis 1374 (2002)

Supreme Court of the United States

Background and Facts

In April 1989, Akos Swierkiewicz, a native of Hungary, began working for Sorema N.A., a reinsurance company headquartered in New York. Swierkiewicz was initially employed as senior vice president and chief underwriting officer. Nearly six years later the chief executive officer of the company demoted Swierkiewicz to a marketing position, and he was removed of his underwriting responsibilities. Swierkiewicz's underwriting responsibilities were transferred to a 32-year-old employee with less than 1 year of underwriting experience. Swierkiewicz, who was 53 years old at the time and had 26 years of experience in the insurance industry, was dismissed by Sorema. Swierkiewicz sued Sorema to recover monetary damages for alleged age and national origin discrimination in violation of federal antidiscrimination laws. Sorema moved to have Swierkiewicz's complaint dismissed. The district court dismissed Swierkiewicz's complaint for not being specific enough, and the court of appeals affirmed. Swierkiewicz appealed to the U.S. Supreme Court.

Supreme Court Issue

Under the notice pleading system, was plaintiff Swierkiewicz's complaint sufficiently stated to permit the case to go to trial?

In The Language of The U.S. Supreme Court

Thomas, Justice When a federal court reviews the sufficiency of a complaint, before the reception of any evidence either by affidavit or admissions, its task is necessarily a limited one. The issue is not whether a plaintiff will ultimately prevail but whether the claimant is entitled to offer evidence to support the claims.

In addition, under a notice pleading system, it is not appropriate to require a plaintiff to plead facts establishing a prima facie case.

Furthermore, imposing the Court of Appeals' heightened pleading standard in employment discrimination cases conflicts with Federal Rule of Civil Procedure 8(a)(2), which provides that a complaint must include only "a short and plain statement of the claim showing that the pleader is entitled to relief." Such a statement must simply give the defendant fair notice of what the plaintiff's claim is and the grounds upon which it rests. Thus, complaints must satisfy only the simple requirements of Rule 8(a). For example, Form 9 sets forth a complaint for negligence in which plaintiff simply states in relevant part: "On June 1, 1936, in a public highway called Boylston Street in Boston, Massachusetts, defendant negligently drove a motor vehicle against plaintiff who was then crossing said highway."

The Federal Rules reject the approach that pleading is a game of skill in which one misstep by counsel may be decisive to the outcome and accept the principle that the purpose of pleading is to facilitate a proper decision on the merits. Applying the relevant standard, petitioner Swierkiewicz's complaint easily satisfies the requirements of Rule 8(a) because it gives respondent Sorema N.A. fair notice of the basis for petitioner's claims. Petitioner alleged that he had been terminated on account of his national origin in violation of Title VII and on account of his age in violation of the Age Discrimination in Employment Act.

Decision and Remedy

The U.S. Supreme Court held that plaintiff Swierkiewicz's complaint met the requirements of notice pleading and was sufficient to withstand Sorema's motion to dismiss. The Supreme Court reversed the judgment of the court of appeals and remanded the case for further proceedings.

Case Questions

Critical Legal Thinking Describe "notice pleading." What is the public policy supporting notice pleading?

Business Ethics Did Sorema act ethically in trying to dismiss plaintiff Swierkiewicz's complaint? Explain.

Contemporary Business Does notice pleading cause any problems for either of the parties to a lawsuit? Is the defendant put on sufficient notice of the charges against it by notice pleading?

E-Commerce & Information Technology

E-Filings in Court

When litigation ensues, the clients, lawyers, and judges involved in the case are usually buried in papers. These papers include pleadings, interrogatories, documents, motions to the court, briefs, and memorandums; the list goes on and on. By the time a case is over, reams of paper are stored in dozens, if not hundreds, of boxes. In addition, court appearances, for no matter how small the matter, must be made in person. For example, lawyers often wait hours for a 10-minute scheduling or other conference with the judge. The time it takes to drive to and from court also has to be taken into account, which in an urban area may amount to hours.

Some forward-thinking judges and lawyers envision a day when the paperwork and hassle are reduced or eliminated in a "virtual courthouse." The technology is currently available for implementing electronic filing—**e-filing**—of pleadings, briefs, and other documents related to a lawsuit. E-filing would include using CD-ROMs for briefs, scanning evidence and documents into a computer for storage and retrieval, and e-mailing correspondence and documents to the court and the opposing counsel. Scheduling and other conferences with the judge or opposing counsel could be held via telephone conferences and e-mail.

Some courts have instituted e-filing. For example, in the Manhattan bankruptcy court, e-filing is now mandatory. Other courts around the world are doing the same. Companies such as Microsoft, West Group, and LexisNexis have developed systems, to manage e-filings of court documents. ■

Statute of Limitations

A **statute of limitations** establishes the period during which a plaintiff must bring a lawsuit against a defendant. If a lawsuit is not filed within this time period, the plaintiff loses his or her right to sue. A statute of limitations begins to "run" at the time the plaintiff first has the right to sue the defendant (e.g., when the accident happens or when the breach of contract occurs).

statute of limitations
A statute that establishes the period during which a plaintiff must bring a lawsuit against a defendant.

Federal and state governments have established statutes of limitations for each type of lawsuit. Most are from one to four years, depending on the type of lawsuit. For example, a one-year statute of limitation is common for ordinary negligence actions. Thus, if on July 1, 2004, Otis negligently causes an automobile accident in which Cha-Yen is injured, Cha-Yen has until July 1, 2005, to bring a negligence lawsuit against Otis. If she waits longer than that, she loses her right to sue him.

Case 2.3

Statue of Limitations

Norgart v. The Upjohn Company

21 Cal.4th 383, 87 Cal.Rpt. 2nd 453, 1999 Cal. Lexis 5308 (1999)

Supreme Court of California

Facts and Background

Kristi Norgart McBride lived with her husband in Santa Rosa, California. Kristi suffered from manic-depressive mental illness (now called bipolar disorder). In this disease, the person cycles between manic (ultrahappy, expansive, extrovert) episodes to depressive episodes. The disease is often treated with prescription drugs. In April 1984, Kristi attempted suicide. A psychiatrist prescribed an antianxiety drug. In May 1985, Kristi attempted suicide again by overdosing on drugs. The doctor prescribed Halcion, a hypnotic drug, and added Darvocet-N, a mild narcotic analgesic. On October 16, 1985, after descending into a severe depression, Kristi committed suicide by overdosing on Halcion and Darvocet-N. On October 16, 1991, exactly six years after Kristi's death, Leo and Phyllis Norgart, Kristi's parents, filed a lawsuit against the Upjohn Company, the maker of Halcion, for wrongful death based on Upjohn's alleged failure to warn of the unreasonable dangers of taking Halcion. The trial court granted Upjohn's motion for summary judgment based on the fact that the one-year statute of limitations for wrongful death actions had run. The court of appeals reversed, and Upjohn appealed to the supreme court of California.

Issue

Is the plaintiff's action for wrongful death barred by the one-year statute of limitations?

In The Language of The Court

Mosk, Justice Statute of limitations is the collective term commonly applied to a great number of acts that prescribe the periods beyond which a plaintiff may not bring a cause of action. It has a purpose to protect defendants from the stale claims of dilatory plaintiffs. It has as a related purpose to stimulate plaintiffs to assert fresh claims against defendants in a diligent fashion. Inasmuch as it necessarily fixes a definite period of time, it operates conclusively across the board and not flexibly on a case-by-case basis.

Under the statute of limitations, a plaintiff must bring a cause of action from wrongful death within one year of accrual. The limitations period is thus defined by the Legislature. That means that the date of accrual of a cause of action for wrongful death is the date of death. Under the statute of limitations, the Norgarts had to bring the cause of action for wrongful death within one year of accrual. They did not do so. Pursuant to this rule, the Norgarts were too late, exactly five years too late.

Decision and Remedy

The supreme court of California held that the defendant, the Upjohn Company, was entitled to judgment as a matter of law based on the fact that the one-year statute of limitations for wrongful death actions had run out, thus barring the plaintiff's lawsuit. Reversed.

Case Questions

Critical Legal Thinking What is the public policy behind having statues of limitations? What is the public policy against having such statutes? Which policy should dominate and why?

Business Ethics Was it ethical for the Upjohn Company to avoid facing the merits of the lawsuit by asserting the one-year statute of limitations?

Contemporary Business What are the business implications for having statutes of limitations?

Discovery

discovery

A legal process during which both parties engage in various activities to discover facts of the case from the other party and witnesses prior to trial.

deposition

The oral testimony given by a party or witness prior to trial. The testimony is given under oath and is transcribed.

deponent

The party who gives his or her deposition.

The legal process provides for a detailed pretrial procedure called **discovery**. During discovery, both parties engage in various activities to discover facts of the case from the other party and witnesses prior to trial. Discovery serves several functions, including preventing surprise, allowing parties to thoroughly prepare for trial, preserving evidence, saving court time, and promoting the settlement of cases. The major forms of discovery are as follows:

1. ***Depositions*** A **deposition** is the oral testimony given by a party or witness prior to trial. The person giving the deposition is called the **deponent**. The *parties* to the lawsuit must give their depositions, if called upon by the other party to do so. The deposition of a *witness* can be given voluntarily or pursuant to a subpoena (court order). The deponent can be required to bring documents to the deposition. Most depositions are taken at the office of one of the attorneys. The deponent is placed under oath

and then asked oral questions by one or both of the attorneys. The questions and answers are recorded in written form by a court reporter. Depositions can also be videotaped. The deponent is given an opportunity to correct his or her answers prior to signing the deposition. Depositions are used to preserve evidence (e.g., if the deponent is deceased, ill, or not otherwise available at trial) and impeach testimony given by witnesses at trial.

2. ***Interrogatories*** **Interrogatories** are written questions submitted by one party to a lawsuit to another party. The questions can be very detailed. In addition, it might be necessary to attach certain documents to the answers. A party is required to answer the interrogatories in writing within a specified time period (e.g., 60 to 90 days). An attorney usually helps with the preparation of the answers. The answers are signed under oath.

interrogatories
Written questions submitted by one party to another party. The questions must be answered in writing within a stipulated time.

3. ***Production of Documents*** Often, particularly in complex business cases, a substantial portion of the lawsuit may be based on information contained in documents (e.g., memorandums, correspondence, company records, and such). One party to a lawsuit may request that the other party produce all documents that are relevant to the case prior to trial. This is called **production of documents**. If the documents sought are too voluminous to be moved, are in permanent storage, or would disrupt the ongoing business of the party who is to produce them, the requesting party may be required to examine the documents at the other party's premises.

production of documents
A request by one party to another party to produce all documents relevant to the case prior to the trial.

4. ***Physical and Mental Examination*** In cases that concern the physical or mental condition of a party, a court can order the party to submit to certain **physical or mental examinations** to determine the extent of the alleged injuries. This would occur, for example, where the plaintiff has been injured in an accident and is seeking damages for physical injury and mental distress.

physical or mental examination
Examinations that may be ordered by a court to determine the extent of a defendant's alleged injuries.

Business Ethics

Calendars Ordered into the Daylight

Most executives keep some form of calendar that contains lists of things to do, where to be, and "what I've done" notes. If a calendar contains business-related information exclusively, it is discoverable by the prosecution in a criminal case. If the calendar is personal in nature, its owner can shield it from discovery under the Fifth Amendment's self-incrimination privilege. What if an executive's calendar contains both business and personal information? Is it discoverable or not? The court had to decide that issue in the following case.

John Doe I and John Doe II are two executives of a company that is the subject of an ongoing grand jury investigation into possible illegal price fixing in a certain industry. Both executives kept calendars that contained both business and personal notes. The grand jury sought production of the calendars, but the executives refused to produce them, alleging Fifth Amendment protection. After examining the evidence, the district court determined that the calendars were corporate in nature and ordered them to be disclosed. The court also issued an order, holding the executive in contempt for their failure to turn over their calendars. The executives appealed.

The court of appeals decided that where a calendar contains a mixture of business and personal notes, a multifactor approach should be applied to determine if it is discoverable. The court will look at ownership, preparation, access, content, purpose, and ratio of business to personal entries in determining whether a document is corporate or personal in nature. This balancing test asks What is the essential nature of the document? No single factor is dispositive, and the final determination of whether the calendar is business or personal in nature is a question of fact.

Applying this multifactor approach to the present case, the court found that the executives' calendars contained a majority of business-related entries. The court held that the executives' calendars were discoverable and were not protected by the Fifth Amendment's privilege against self-incrimination. [*In Re Grand Jury Proceedings*, 55 F3d. 1012 (1995)]

1. Is asserting the Fifth Amendment privilege against self-incrimination an ethical act? Explain.
2. Why do you think the executives asserted the Fifth Amendment privilege in this case? ■

Dismissals and Pretrial Judgments

pretrial motion

A motion a party can make to try to dispose of all or part of a lawsuit prior to trial.

motion for judgment on the pleadings

A motion that alleges that if all the facts presented in the pleadings are taken as true, the party making the motion would win the lawsuit when the proper law is applied to these asserted facts.

motion for summary judgment

A motion that asserts that there are no factual disputes to be decided by the jury; in this case, the judge can apply the proper law to the undisputed facts and decide the case without a jury. These motions are supported by affidavits, documents, and deposition testimony.

There are several **pretrial motions** that parties to a lawsuit can make to try to dispose of all or part of a lawsuit prior to trial. The two major pretrial motions are:

1. ***Motion for Judgment on the Pleadings*** A **motion for judgment on the pleadings** can be made by either party once the pleadings are complete. This motion alleges that if all of the facts presented in the pleadings are true, the party making the motion would win the lawsuit when the proper law is applied to these facts. In deciding this motion, the judge cannot consider any facts outside the pleadings.
2. ***Motion for Summary Judgment*** The trier of fact (i.e., the jury, or, if there is no jury, the judge) determine factual issues. A **motion for summary judgment** asserts that there are no factual disputes to be decided by the jury and that the judge should apply the relevant law to the undisputed facts to decide the case. Motions for summary judgment, which can be made by either party, are supported by evidence outside the pleadings. Affidavits from the parties and witnesses, documents (e.g., a written contract between the parties), depositions, and such are common forms of evidence. If, after examining the evidence, the court finds no factual dispute, it can decide the issue or issues raised in the summary judgment motion. This may dispense with the entire case or with part of the case. If the judge finds that a factual dispute exists, the motion will be denied, and the case will go to trial.

Settlement Conference

pretrial hearing

A hearing before the trial in order to facilitate the settlement of a case. Also called a *settlement conference*.

Federal court rules and most state court rules permit the court to direct the attorneys or parties to appear before the court for a **pretrial hearing**, or **settlement conference**. One of the major purposes of such hearings is to facilitate the settlement of the case. Pretrial conferences are often held informally in the judge's chambers. If no settlement is reached, the pretrial hearing is used to identify the major trial issues and other relevant factors. More than 90 percent of all cases are settled before they go to trial.

Contemporary Business Environment

Ford Explorer SUV Rollover Lawsuit Settled for $22 Million

Approximately 90 percent of civil lawsuits are settled prior to trial. Settlements are reached when both parties believe that a trial provides too much risk of loss and the amount of the settlement is reasonable in light of that risk. Consider the settlement in the following case. On June 23, 1992, Nabil Boury was driving a 1992 Ford Explorer SUV on the Eisenhower Expressway in Chicago, with five passengers in the vehicle. When another car clipped the Explorer on the driver's-side rear wheel well, the Explorer immediately rolled over. By the time it came to rest, the Explorer had rolled over three times, ejecting several of the passengers. Boury's sister and another teenager were killed, Boury's cousin lost vision in one eye, and another passenger was rendered a quadriplegic; Boury and his mother suffered minor injuries.

After the accident, the injured persons and the estates of the two deceased teenagers sued Ford Motor Company in a product liability lawsuit, alleging that there was a defect in the design of the Explorer SUV that caused it to roll over. The plaintiffs sued Packey Webb Ford, the car dealer that sold the Explorer, for putting Michelin tires on the SUV in a size and type specifically contrary to the warnings in the Ford owner's manual. The plaintiffs also sued Cassidy Tire Company, the distributor of the Michelin tires.

Several months before the case was to proceed to trial in the fall of 2001, the parties reached settlement. Ford agreed to pay $8 million, Packey Webb $10.5 million, Cassidy Tire $3 million, and Michelin Tire $500,000. The plaintiffs reached a separate agreement as to how to divide the settlement proceeds. This is just one example of the hundreds of thousands of lawsuits that are settled every year. [*Boury v. Ford Motor Company*, Cook County Circuit Court, Illinois (2001)] ■

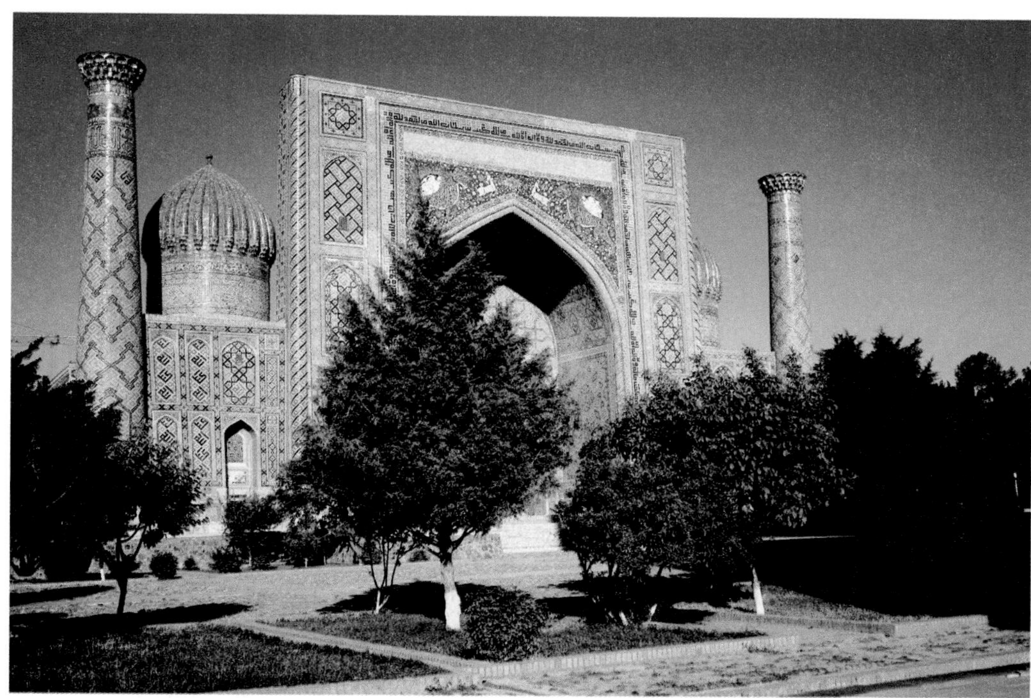

Samarkan, Uzbekistan. Each country has its own national courts that hear and decide legal disputes in that country.

The Trial

Pursuant to the Seventh Amendment to the U.S. Constitution, a party to an action at law is guaranteed the right to a *jury trial* in cases in federal court.[7] Most state constitutions contain a similar guarantee for state court actions. If either party requests a jury, the trial will be by jury. If both parties waive their right to a jury, the trial will occur without a jury. The judge sits as the **trier of fact** in nonjury trials. At the time of trial, each party usually submits to the judge a **trial brief** that contains legal support for its side of the case.

trier of fact
The jury in a jury trial; the judge where there is not a jury trial.

trial briefs
Documents submitted by the parties' attorneys to the judge that contain legal support for their sides of the case.

Phases of a Trial

Trials are usually divided into the following phases:

1. ***Jury Selection*** The pool of the potential jurors is usually selected from voter or automobile registration lists. Individuals are selected to hear specific cases through the process called **voir dire** ("to speak the truth"). Lawyers for each party and the judge can ask prospective jurors questions to determine if they would be biased in their decisions. Biased jurors can be prevented from sitting on a particular case. Once the appropriate number of jurors is selected (usually 6 to 12 jurors), they are *impaneled* to hear the case and are sworn in. The trial is ready to begin. A jury can be *sequestered* (i.e., separated from family, etc.) in important cases. Jurors are paid minimum fees for the service.
2. ***Opening Statements*** Each party's attorney is allowed to make an **opening statement** to the jury. In opening statements, an attorney usually summarizes the main factual and legal issues of the case and describes why he or she believes the client's position is valid. The information given in this statement is not considered as evidence.

voir dire
A process whereby prospective jurors are asked questions by the judge and attorneys to determine if they would be biased in their decisions.

opening statements
Statements made by the attorneys to the jury in which they summarize the factual and legal issues of the case.

burden of proof
A burden that the plaintiff bears to prove the allegations made in his or her complaint.

plaintiff's case
The process by which the plaintiff introduces evidence to prove the allegations contained in his or her complaint.

3. ***The Plaintiff's Case*** Plaintiffs bear the **burden of proof** to persuade the trier of fact of the merits of their case. This is called the **plaintiff's case**. The plaintiff's attorney will call witnesses to give testimony. After a witness has been sworn in, the plaintiff's attorney examines (i.e., questions) the witness. This is called *direct examination*. Documents and other evidence can be introduced through each witness. After the plaintiff's attorney has completed his or her questions, the defendant's attorney can question the witness. This is called *cross-examination*. The defendant's attorney can ask questions only about the subjects that were brought up during the direct examination. After the defendant's attorney completes his or her questions, the plaintiff's attorney can ask questions of the witness. This is called *redirect examination*.

defendant's case
The process by which the defendant (1) rebuts the plaintiff's evidence, (2) proves affirmative defenses, and (3) proves allegations made in a cross-complaint.

4. ***The Defendant's Case*** The **defendant's case** proceeds after the plaintiff has concluded his or her case. The defendant's case must (1) rebut the plaintiff's evidence, (2) prove any affirmative defenses asserted by the defendant, and (3) prove any allegations contained in the defendant's cross-complaint. The defendant's witnesses are examined in much the same way as the plaintiff's attorney cross-examines each witness. This is followed by redirect and recross-examination.
5. ***Rebuttal and Rejoinder*** After the defendant's attorney has completed calling witnesses, the plaintiff's attorney can call witnesses and put forth evidence to rebut the defendant's case. This is called a *rebuttal*. The defendant's attorney can call additional witnesses and introduce other evidence to counter the rebuttal. This is called the *rejoinder*.

closing arguments
Statements made by the attorneys to the jury at the end of the trial to try to convince the jury to render a verdict for their clients.

jury instructions
Instructions given by the judge to the jury that informs the jurors of the law to be applied in the case.

6. ***Closing Arguments*** At the conclusion of the evidence, each party's attorney is allowed to make a **closing argument** to the jury. Both attorneys try to convince the jury to render a verdict for their clients by pointing out the strengths in the client's case and the weaknesses in the other side's case. Information given by the attorneys in their closing statements is not evidence.
7. ***Jury Instructions*** One the closing arguments are completed, the judge reads **jury instructions** (or **charges**) to the jury. These instructions inform the jury about what law to apply when they decide the case. For example, in a criminal trial, the judge will read the jury the statutory definition of the crime charged. In an accident case, the judge will read the jury the legal definition of *negligence*.
8. ***Jury Deliberation*** The jury then retires to the jury room to deliberate its findings. This can take from a few minutes to many weeks. After deliberation, the jury assesses penalties in criminal cases.

verdict
The decision reached by the jury.

judgment
The official decision of the court.

judgment notwithstanding the verdict (j.n.o.v.)
In a civil case, the overturning of the jury's verdict by the judge if he or she finds bias or jury misconduct.

9. ***Entry of Judgment*** After the jury has returned its **verdict**, in most cases the judge will enter **judgment** to the successful party based on the verdict. This is the official decision of the court. The court may, however, overturn the verdict if it finds bias or jury misconduct. This is called a **judgment notwithstanding the verdict** or **judgment n.o.v.** or **j.n.o.v.** In a civil case, the judge may reduce the amount of monetary damages awarded by the jury if he or she finds the jury to have been biased, emotional, or inflamed. This is called *remittitur*. The trial court usually issues a *written memorandum* setting forth the reasons for the judgment. This memorandum, together with the trial transcript and evidence introduced at trial, constitutes the permanent *record* of the trial court proceeding.

The Appeal

appeal
The act of asking an appellate court to overturn a decision after the trial court's final judgment has been entered.

In a civil case, either party can **appeal** the trial court's decision once a *final judgment* is entered. Only the defendant can appeal in a criminal case. The appeal is made to the appropriate appellate court. A *notice of appeal* must be filed within a prescribed time after judgment is entered (usually within 60 or 90 days). The appealing party is called the **appellant**, or **petitioner**. The responding party is called the **appellee**, or the **respondent**. The appellant is often required to post a bond (e.g., one-and-one-half times the judgment) on appeal.

appellant
The appealing party in an appeal. Also known as *petitioner*.

apellee
The responding party in an appeal. Also known as *respondent*.

The parties may designate all or relevant portions of the trial record to be submitted to the appellate court for review. The appellant's attorney may file an *opening brief* with the court that sets forth legal research and other information to support his or her contentions on appeal. The appellee can file a *responding brief* answering the appellant's contentions. Appellate courts usually permit a brief oral argument at which each party's attorney is heard.

An appellate court will reverse a lower court decision if it finds an *error of law* in the record. An error of law occurs if the jury was improperly instructed by the trial court judge, prejudicial evidence was admitted at trial when it should have been excluded, prejudicial evidence was obtained through an unconstitutional search and seizure, and the like. An appellate court will not reverse a *finding of fact* unless such finding is unsupported by the evidence or is contradicted by the evidence.

Business Brief
Trial court decisions are overturned on appeal only if there has been an error of law or the decision is not supported by the evidence.

U.S. SUPREME COURT CASE
Weisgram v. Marley Company

528 U.S. 440, 120 S.Ct. 1011, 2000 U.S. Lexis 1011 (2000)
Supreme Court of the United States

Case 2.4
Appeal

Background and Facts

On December 30, 1993, Bonnie Weisgram died from carbon monoxide poisoning from a fire at her home. Her son, Chad Weisgram, brought a wrongful death tort action against Marley Company to recover damages, alleging that a defect in the electric baseboard heater manufactured by Marley had caused the fire and his mother's death. At trial, over Marley's objections, Weisgram introduced the evidence from three expert (paid-for) witnesses. The jury returned a verdict against Marley. Marley requested judgment as a matter of law, asserting that the expert testimony was unreliable and therefore inadmissible. The court of appeals agreed with Marley, finding that the expert witnesses' testimony was speculative and not scientifically sound. The court of appeals granted judgment as a matter of law for Marley and refused to grant Weisgram's motion for a new trial. Weisgram appealed to the U.S. Supreme Court.

Supreme Court Issue

Can an appellate court enter judgment as a matter of law against a jury-verdict winner if it determines on appeal that evidence was erroneously admitted at trial and concludes that the other properly admitted evidence is not sufficient to constitute a submissible case?

In The Language of The U.S. Supreme Court

Ginsburg, Justice Our decision is guided by Federal Rule of Civil Procedure 50, which governs the entry of judgment as a matter of law. Courts of appeals should be constantly alert to the trial judge's firsthand knowledge of witnesses, testimony, and issues; in other words, appellate courts should give due consideration to the first-instance decision maker's "feel" for the overall case. But the court of appeals has authority to render the final decision. If, in the particular case, the appellate tribunal determines that the district court is better positioned to decide whether a new trial, rather than judgment for defendant, should be ordered, the court of appeals should return the case to the trial court for such an assessment. But if, as in the instant case, the court of appeals concludes that further proceedings are unwarranted because the loser on appeal has had a full and fair opportunity to present the case, including arguments for a new trial, the appellate court may appropriately instruct the district court to enter judgment against the jury-verdict winner.

Decision and Remedy

The U.S. Supreme Court held that an appellate court may enter judgment as a matter of law against a jury-verdict winner if it determines that evidence was erroneously admitted at trial and that other properly admitted evidence is not sufficient to remand the case for a new trial.

Case Questions

Critical Legal Thinking Is the testimony of expert witnesses important at many types of trials? Give some examples.

Business Ethics Can an expert witness be found to testify for almost anyone, plaintiff or defendant, at trial? Why or why not?

Contemporary Business What implications does the Supreme Court's opinion in this case have for business?

Mountain, China. The settlement of claims varies in different countries. In some countries parties try to settle claims privately, while parties in other countries, such as the United States, are more prone to use an adversarial legal process.

Alternative Dispute Resolution

The use of the court system to resolve business and other disputes can take years and cost thousands, if not millions, of dollars in legal fees and expenses. In commercial litigation, the normal business operations of the parties are often disrupted. To avoid or lessen these problems, businesses are increasingly turning to methods of **alternative dispute resolution (ADR)** and other aids to resolving disputes. The most common form of ADR is *arbitration*. Other forms of ADR are *mediation*, *conciliation*, *minitrial*, *fact-finding*, and using a *judicial referee*.

alternative dispute resolution (ADR)
Methods other than litigation of resolving disputes.

Arbitration

In **arbitration**, the parties choose an impartial third party to hear and decide the dispute. This neutral party is called the *arbitrator*. Arbitrators are usually selected from members of the American Arbitration Association (AAA) or another arbitration association. Labor union agreements, franchise agreements, leases, and other commercial contracts often contain **arbitration clauses** that require disputes arising out of the contract to be submitted to arbitration. If there is no arbitration clause, the parties can enter into a *submission agreement* whereby they agree to submit a dispute to arbitration after the dispute arises.

arbitration
A form of ADR in which the parties choose an impartial third party to hear and decide the dispute.

arbitration clause
A clause in contracts that requires disputes arising out of the contract to be submitted to arbitration.

Evidence and testimony are presented to the arbitrator at a hearing held for this purpose. Less formal evidentiary rules are usually applied in arbitration hearings than at court. After the hearing, the arbitrator reaches a decision and enters an *award*. The parties often agree in advance to be bound by the arbitrator's decision and award. If the parties have not so agreed, the arbitrator's award can be appealed to court. The court gives great deference to the arbitrator's decision.

Congress enacted the **Federal Arbitration Act** to promote the arbitration of disputes.[8] About half of the states have adopted the **Uniform Arbitration Act**. This act promotes the arbitration of disputes at the state level. Many federal and state courts have instituted programs to refer legal disputes to arbitration or another form of ADR.

Business Brief
Litigation is expensive and time-consuming. Businesses should consider ADR to solve their disputes.

Landmark Law

The Federal Arbitration Act

The **Federal Arbitration Act (FAA)** was originally enacted in 1925 to reverse the long-standing judicial hostility to arbitration agreements that had existed as English common law and had been adopted by American courts. The act provides that arbitration agreements involving commerce are valid, irrevocable, and enforceable contracts, unless some grounds exist at law or equity (e.g., fraud, duress) to revoke them. The FAA permits one party to obtain a court order to compel arbitration if the other party has failed, neglected, or refused to comply with an arbitration agreement.

Since the FAA's enactment, the courts have wrestled with the problem of which types of disputes should be arbitrated. Breach of contract cases, tort claims, and such are clearly candidates for arbitration if there is a valid arbitration agreement. In addition, the U.S. Supreme court has enforced arbitration agreements that call for the resolution of disputes arising under federal statutes. For example, in *Shearson/American Express Inc. v. McMahon*, 482 U.S. 220, 107 S.Ct. 2332, 1987 U.S. Lexis 2478 (1987), *Rodriquez de Quijas v. Shearson/American Express, Inc.*, 490 U.S. 4777 (1990), the Court held that certain civil claims arising under federal securities laws and the Racketeer Influenced and Corrupt Organizations Act (RICO) were arbitrative. In these cases, the Court enforced arbitration clauses contained in customer agreements with the securities firm.

In another case, *Gilmer v. Interstate/Johnson Lane Corporation*, 500 U.S. 20, 111 S.Ct. 1647, 1991 U.S. Lexis 2529 (1991), the supreme court upheld an arbitration clause in an employment contract. In that case, a 62-year-old employee who was dismissed from his job sued his employer for alleged age discrimination in violation of the federal Age Discrimination in Employment Act (ADEA). The employer countered with a motion to compel arbitration. The supreme court upheld the motion and stated, "By agreeing to arbitrate a statutory claim, a party does not forgo the substantive rights afforded by the statute, it only submits to their resolution in an arbitral, rather than a judicial, forum."

The court did not find any reason to revoke the contract. There was no indication that the employee was coerced or defrauded into agreeing to the arbitration clause at issue in the case.

Because the U.S. Supreme Court has placed its imprimatur on the use of arbitration to solve employment disputes, it is likely that such clauses will appear in more employment contracts. Critics contend that this gives the advantage to employers. Employers argue that arbitration is the only way to combat skyrocketing jury verdicts. In the following case, the U.S. Supreme Court upheld arbitration in a case. ■

U.S. SUPREME COURT CASE

Circuit City Stores, Inc. v. Adams

532 U.S. 105, 121 S.Ct. 1302, 2001 U.S. Lexis 2459 (2001)

Supreme Court of the United States

Case 2.5

Arbitration

Background and Facts

In October 1995, Saint Clair Adams was hired as a sales counselor by Circuit City Stores, Inc., a national retailer of consumer electronics. Adams signed an employment contract that included the following arbitration clause:

> I agree that I will settle any and all previously unasserted claims, disputes or controversies arising out of or relating to my application or candidacy for employment, employment and/or cessation of employment with Circuit City, *exclusively* by final and binding *arbitration* before a neutral Arbitrator. By way of example only, such claims include claims under federal, state, and local statutory or common law, such as the Age Discrimination in Employment Act, Title VII of the Civil Rights Act of 1964, the Americans with Disabilities Act, the law of contract and the law of tort.

Two years later Adams filed an employment discrimination lawsuit against Circuit City in court. Circuit City sought to enjoin the court proceeding and to compel arbitration, pursuant to the Federal Arbitration Act (FAA). The district court granted Circuit City's request. The court of appeals reversed, holding that employment contracts are not subject to arbitration. The U.S. Supreme Court granted certiorari to hear the appeal.

Supreme Court Issue

Are employment contracts, other than those of exempted transportation workers, subject to arbitration if a valid arbitration agreement has been entered into between the parties?

In The Language of The U.S. Supreme Court

Kennedy, Justice Congress enacted the FAA in 1925. As the Court has explained, the FAA was a response to hostility of American courts to the enforcement of arbitration agreements, a judicial disposition inherited from then-long-standing English practice. To give effect to this purpose, the FAA compels judicial enforcement of a wide range of written arbitration agreements. The FAA's coverage provision, Section 2, provides that "a written provision in any contract evidencing a transaction involving commerce to settle by

Circuit City Stores, Inc. v. Adams

532 U.S. 105, 121 S.Ct. 1302, 2001 U.S. Lexis 2459 (2001)

Supreme Court of the United States

(continued)

arbitration a controversy thereafter arising out of such contract or transaction, or the refusal to perform the whole or any part thereof, shall be valid, irrevocable, and enforceable, save upon such grounds as exist at law or in equity for the revocation of any contract."

The instant case, of course, involves not the basic coverage authorization under Section 2 of the Act, but the exemption from coverage under Section 1. The exemption clause provides the Act shall not apply to contracts of employment of seamen, railroad employees, or any other class of workers engaged in foreign or interstate commerce. In sum, the text of the FAA forecloses the construction of Section 1 followed by the Court of Appeals in the case under review, a construction which would exclude all employment contracts from the FAA. The text of Section 1 precludes interpreting the exclusion provision to defeat the language of Section 2 as to all employment contracts. Section 1 exempts from the FAA only contract of employment of transportation workers.

Decision and Remedy

The U.S. Supreme Court held that the exemption of Section 1 of the Federal Arbitration Act only exempts employment contracts of transportation workers from arbitration. All other employment contracts, including the one in this case between Circuit City and Adams, are subject to arbitration if a valid arbitration agreement has been executed. Reversed and remanded.

Case Questions

Critical Legal Thinking How do you think transportation workers became exempted from arbitration under the Federal Arbitration Act?

Business Ethics Is it ethical for employers to include arbitration clauses in employment contracts?

Contemporary Business Who do you think benefits most from arbitration clauses in employment contracts, employers or employees? Why?

Mediation and Conciliation

mediation
A form of ADR in which the parties choose a *neutral* third party to act as the mediator of the dispute.

conciliation
A form of mediation in which the parties choose an *interested* third party to act as the mediator.

In **mediation**, the parties choose a neutral third party to act as the mediator of the dispute. Unlike an arbitrator, a mediator does not make a decision or an award. Instead, the mediator acts as a conveyor of information between the parties and assists them in trying to reach a settlement of the dispute. A mediator often meets separately with each of the parties. A settlement agreement is reached if the mediator is successful. If not, the case proceeds to trial. In a **conciliation**, the parties choose an interested third party, the *conciliator*, to act as the mediator.

Minitrial

A *minitrial* is a session, usually lasting a day or less, in which the lawyers for each side present their cases to representatives of each party who have authority to settle the dispute. In many cases, the parties hire a neutral person (e.g., a retired judge) to preside over the minitrial. Following the presentations, the parties meet to try to negotiate a settlement.

Fact-Finding

Fact-finding is a process whereby the parties hire a neutral person to investigate the dispute. The *fact-finder* reports his or her findings to the adversaries and may recommend a basis for settlement.

Judicial Referee

If the parties agree, the court may appoint a *judicial referee* to conduct a private trial and render a judgment. Referees, who are often retired judges, have most of the powers of a trial judge, and their decisions stand as a judgment of the court. The parties usually reserve their right to appeal.

International Law

Comparison of the Japanese and American Legal Systems

Businesses often complain that there are too many lawyers and too much litigation in the United States. There are currently more than 900,000 lawyers and more than 20 million lawsuits per year in this country. On the other hand, in Japan, a country with about half the population, there are only 20,000 lawyers and little litigation. Why the difference?

Much of the difference is cultural: Japan nurtures the attitude that confrontation should be avoided. Litigious persons in Japan are looked down upon. Thus, companies rarely do battle in court. Instead, they opt for private arbitration of most of their disputes. Other differences are built into the legal system itself. For example, there is only one place to go to become a *bengoshi*, or lawyer, in Japan—the government-operated National Institute for Legal Training. Only 2 percent of 35,000 applicants are accepted annually, and only 400 new *bengoshi* are admitted to Japan's exclusive legal club per year.

There are other obstacles, too. For example, no class actions or contingency fee arrangements are allowed. Plaintiffs must pay their lawyers a front fee of up to 8 percent of the damages sought, plus a nonrefundable filing fee to the court of one-half of 1 percent of the damages. To make matters even more difficult, no discovery is permitted. Thus, plaintiffs are denied access before trial to an opponent's potential evidence, and even if the plaintiff wins the lawsuit, damage awards are low.

Kyoto, Japan. The laws of different countries vary.

Some experts argue that Japan has more legal practitioners than statistics reveal. For example, there are approximately 5,000 non-*bengoshi* patent specialists who perform services similar to U.S. patent attorneys. Another 50,000 licensed tax practitioners offer services similar to U.S. tax attorneys. Many non-*bengoshi* legal experts handle tasks such as contract negotiation and drafting. In addition, sales personnel and frontline managers often act as problem solvers.

The Japanese bias against courtroom solutions remains strong. The current system is designed to save time and money and to preserve long-term relationships. ■

Chapter Summary

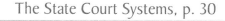

The State Court Systems, p. 30

State Court Systems

1. ***Limited-jurisdiction trial court.*** State courts that hear matters of a specialized or limited nature (e.g., misdemeanor criminal matters, traffic tickets, civil matters under a certain dollar amount). Many states have created small claims courts that hear small-dollar-amount civil cases (e.g., under $5,000) where the parties cannot be represented by lawyers.
2. ***General-jurisdiction trial court.*** State courts that hear cases of a general nature that are not within the jurisdiction of limited-jurisdiction trial courts.
3. ***Intermediate appellate court.*** State courts that hear appeals from state trial courts. The appellate court reviews the trial court record in making its decision. No new evidence is introduced at this level.
4. ***Highest state court.*** Each state has a highest court in its court system. This court hears appeals from appellate courts and, where appropriate, trial courts. This court reviews the record in making its decision. No new evidence is introduced at this level. Most states call this court the supreme court.

The Federal Court System, p. 32

Federal Court System

1. ***Special federal courts.*** Federal courts that have specialized or limited jurisdiction. They include:
   a. *U.S. tax court.* Hears cases involving federal tax laws.
   b. *U.S. claims court.* Hears cases brought against the United States.
   c. *U.S. Court of International Trade.* Hears cases involving tariffs and international commercial disputes.
   d. *U.S. bankruptcy courts.* Hear cases involving federal bankruptcy law.
2. ***U.S. district courts.*** Federal trial courts of general jurisdiction that hear cases not within the jurisdiction of specialized courts. There is at least one U.S. district court per state; more populated states have several district courts. The area served by one of these courts is called a *district.*
3. ***U.S. courts of appeals.*** Intermediate federal appellate courts that hear appeals from district courts located in their circuit, and in certain instances from special federal courts and federal administrative agencies. There are 12 geographical *circuits* in this country. Eleven serve areas that are comprised of several states, while another is located in Washington, DC. A thirteenth circuit court—the *Court of Appeals for the Federal Circuit*—is located in Washington, DC, and reviews patent, trademark, and international trade cases.
4. ***U.S. Supreme Court.*** Highest court of the federal court system. It hears appeals from the circuit courts and, in some instances, from special courts and U.S. district courts. The Court, which is located in Washington, DC, is composed of nine justices, one of whom is named chief justice.
5. ***Decisions by the U.S. Supreme Court.***
   a. *Writ of certiorari.* To have a case heard by the U.S. Supreme Court, a petitioner must file a *petition for certiorari* with the Court. If the Court decides to hear the case, it will issue a *writ of certiorari.*
   b. Voting by the U.S. Supreme Court:
      i. *Unanimous decision.* All of the justices agree as to the outcome and reasoning used to decide the case. The decision becomes precedent.
      ii. *Majority decision.* A majority of the justices agrees as to the outcome and reasoning used to decide the case. The decision becomes precedent.
      iii. *Plurality decision.* A majority of the justices agrees to the outcome but not to the reasoning. The decision is not precedent.
      iv. *Tie decision.* If there is a tie vote, the lower court's decision stands. The decision is not precedent.
      v. *Concurring opinion.* A justice who agrees as to the outcome of the case but not the reasoning used by other justices may write a concurring opinion, setting forth his or her reasoning.
      vi. *Dissenting opinion.* A justice who disagrees with the outcome of a case may write a dissenting opinion setting forth his or her reasoning for dissenting.

Jurisdiction of Federal and State Courts

1. ***Jurisdiction of federal courts.*** Federal courts may hear the following cases:
   a. *Federal question.* Cases arising under the U.S. Constitution, treaties, and federal statutes and regulations. There is no dollar-amount limit in federal question cases.
   b. *Diversity of citizenship.* Cases between (i) citizens of different states and (ii) citizens of a state and a citizen or subject of a foreign country. Federal courts must apply the appropriate state law in such cases. The controversy must exceed $50,000 for the federal court to hear the case.
2. ***Jurisdiction of state courts.*** State courts hear some cases that may be heard by federal courts.
   a. *Exclusive jurisdiction.* Federal courts have exclusive jurisdiction to hear cases involving federal crimes, antitrust, and bankruptcy, patent and copyright cases, suits against the United States, and most admiralty cases. State courts may not hear these matters.
   b. *Concurrent jurisdiction.* State courts have concurrent jurisdiction to hear cases involving diversity of citizenship cases and federal question cases over which the federal courts do not have exclusive jurisdiction. The defendant may have the case removed to federal court.

The Jurisdiction of Courts, p. 37

Standing to Sue, Jurisdiction and Venue

1. ***Standing to sue.*** To bring a lawsuit, the plaintiff must have some stake in the outcome of the lawsuit.
2. ***Subject matter jurisdiction.*** The court must have jurisdiction over the subject matter of the lawsuit. Each court has limited jurisdiction to hear only certain types of cases.
3. ***In personam jurisdiction* (or *personal jurisdiction*).** The court must have jurisdiction over the parties to a lawsuit. The plaintiff submits to the jurisdiction of the court by filing the lawsuit there. Personal jurisdiction is obtained over the defendant by serving that person *service of process*.
4. ***In rem jurisdiction.*** A court may have jurisdiction to hear and decide a case because it has jurisdiction over the property at issue in the lawsuit (e.g., real property located in the state).
5. ***Quasi in rem jurisdiction* (or *attachment jurisdiction*).** A plaintiff who obtains a judgment against a defendant in one state may utilize the court system of another state to attach property of the defendant's located in the second state.
6. ***Long-arm statutes.*** These statutes permit a state to obtain personal jurisdiction over an out-of-state defendant as long as the defendant had the requisite minimum contact with the state. The out-of-state defendant may be served process outside the state in which the lawsuit has been brought.
7. ***Venue.*** A case must be heard by the court that has jurisdiction nearest to where the incident at issue occurred or where the parties reside. A *change of venue* will be granted if prejudice would occur because of pretrial publicity or another reason.
8. ***Forum-selection clause.*** A clause in a contract that designates the court that will hear any dispute that arises out of the contract.

The Pretrial Litigation Process, p. 40

Pleadings

Paperwork that initiates and responds to a lawsuit. Pleadings include:

1. ***Complaint.*** Filed by the plaintiff with the court and served with a *summons* on the defendant. It sets forth the basis of the lawsuit.
2. ***Answer.*** Filed by the defendant with the court and served on the plaintiff. It usually denies most allegations of the complaint.
3. ***Cross-complaint.*** Filed and served by the defendant if he or she countersues the plaintiff. The defendant is the *cross-complainant* and the plaintiff is the *cross-defendant*. The cross-defendant must file and serve a *reply* (answer).
4. ***Intervention.*** A person who has an interest in a lawsuit may intervene and become a party to the lawsuit.
5. ***Consolidation.*** Separate cases against the same defendant arising from the same incident may be consolidated by the court into one case if it would not cause prejudice to the parties.

Discovery

The pretrial litigation process for discovering facts of the case from the other party and witnesses. Discovery consists of:

1. ***Depositions.*** Oral testimony given by a *deponent*, either a party or witness. Depositions are transcribed.
2. ***Interrogatories.*** Written questions submitted by one party to the other party. They must be answered within a specified period of time.
3. ***Production of documents.*** A party to a lawsuit may obtain copies of all relevant documents from the other party.
4. ***Physical and mental examination.*** These examinations of a party are permitted upon order of the court where injuries are alleged that could be verified or disputed by such examination.

Dismissals and Pretrial Judgments

1. ***Motion for judgment on the pleadings.*** Alleges that if all facts as pleaded are true, the moving party would win the lawsuit. No facts outside the pleadings may be considered.
2. ***Motion for summary judgment.*** Alleges that there are no factual disputes, so the judge may apply the law and decide the case without a jury. Evidence outside the pleadings may be considered (e.g., affidavits, documents, depositions).

Settlement Conference

Conference prior to trial between the parties in front of the judge to facilitate the settlement of the case. Also called *pretrial hearing*. If a settlement is not reached, the case proceeds to trial.

The Trial, p. 47

Phases of a Trial

1. ***Jury selection.*** Done through a process called *voir dire*. Biased jurors are dismissed and replaced.
2. ***Opening statements.*** Made by the parties' lawyers. Are not evidence.
3. ***The plaintiff's case.*** The plaintiff bears the burden of proof. The plaintiff calls witnesses and introduces evidence to try to prove his or her case.
4. ***The defendant's case.*** The defendant calls witnesses and introduces evidence to rebut the plaintiff's case and to prove affirmative defenses and cross-complaints.
5. ***Rebuttal and rejoinder.*** The plaintiff and defendant may call additional witnesses and introduce additional evidence.
6. ***Closing arguments.*** Made by the parties' lawyers. Are not evidence.
7. ***Jury instructions.*** Judge reads instructions to the jury as to what law they are to apply to the case.
8. ***Jury deliberation.*** Jury retires to the jury room and deliberates until it reaches a *verdict*.
9. ***Entry of judgment.*** The judge may:
   a. Enter the verdict reached by the jury as the court's *judgment*.
   b. Grant a motion for *judgment n.o.v.* if the judge finds the jury was biased. This means that the jury's verdict does not stand.
   c. Order *remittitur* (reduction) of any damages awarded if the judge finds the jury to have been biased or emotional.

The Appeal, p. 48

Appeal

Both parties in a civil suit and the defendant in a criminal trial may appeal the decision of the trial court. *Notice of appeal* must be filed within a specified period of time. The appeal must be made to the appropriate appellate court.

Alternative Dispute Resolution, p. 50

Alternative Dispute Resolution (ADR)

Nonjudicial means of solving legal disputes. ADR usually saves time and money of costly litigation.

Types of ADR

1. ***Arbitration.*** An impartial third party, called the *arbitrator* hears and decides the dispute. The arbitrator makes an award. The award is appealable to a court if the parties have not given up this right. Arbitration is designated by the parties pursuant to:
   a. Arbitration clause. Agreement contained in a contract stipulating that any dispute arising out of the contract will be arbitrated.
   b. Submission agreement. Agreement to submit a dispute to arbitration after the dispute arises.

2. ***Mediation.*** A neutral third party, called a *mediator*, assists the parties in trying to reach a settlement of their dispute. The mediator does not make an award.
3. ***Conciliation.*** An interested third party, called a *conciliator*, assists the parties in trying to reach a settlement of their dispute. The conciliator does not make an award.
4. ***Minitrial.*** A short session in which the lawyers for each side present their cases to representatives of each party who have the authority to settle the dispute.
5. ***Fact-finding.*** The parties hire a neutral third person, called a *fact-finder*, to investigate the dispute and report his or her findings to the adversaries.
6. ***Judicial referee.*** With the consent of the parties, the court appoints a judicial referee (usually a retired judge or lawyer) to conduct a private trial and render a judgment. The judgment stands as the judgment of the court and may be appealed to the appropriate appellate court.

Internet Exercises and Case Questions

Working the Web Internet Exercises

Activities

1. At the International Chamber of Commerce (ICC) Web site, **www.iccwbo.org/court/english/news_archives/2001/adr.asp**, you will find information about rules and procedures for settlement of international commercial disputes. Under what circumstances would you advise a client to elect ICC arbitration rules as compared with AAA rules?
2. Go to the U.S. Supreme Court site, **www.supremecourtus.gov**. Find a case from your state that recently has been appealed to the court. Outline the procedural steps involved in the process.
3. The site **guide.lp.findlaw.com/10fedgov/judicial/appeals_courts.html** contains links to each of the federal judicial circuits. Find your jurisdiction and review the cases available there. What is the oldest case you can find? the most recent? Compare your search results with the same two questions, looking at state court cases available in your state.

Critical Legal Thinking Cases

2.1 Federal Question Nutrilab, Inc., manufactures and markets a product known as "Starch Blockers." The purpose of the product is to block the human body's digestion of starch as an aid in controlling weight. On July 1, 1982, the U.S. FDA classified Starch Blockers as a drug and requested that it be removed from the market until the FDA approved of its use. The FDA claimed that it had the right to classify new products as drugs and prevent their distribution until their safety is determined. Nutrilab disputes the FDA's decision and wants to bring suit to halt the FDA's actions. Do the federal courts have jurisdiction to hear this case? [*Nutrilab, Inc. v. Schweiker*, 713 F.2d 335, 1983 U.S. App. Lexis 25121 (7th Cir. 1983)]

2.2 Diversity of Citizenship James Clayton Allison, a resident of the state of Mississippi, was employed by the Tru-Amp Corporation as a circuit breaker tester. As part of his employment, Allison was sent to inspect, clean, and test a switch gear located at the South Central Bell Telephone Facility in Brentwood, Tennessee. On August 26, 1988, he attempted to remove a circuit breaker manufactured by ITE Corporation (ITE) from a bank of breakers, when a portion of the breaker fell off. The broken piece fell behind a switching bank and, according to Allison, caused an electrical fire and explosion. Allison was severely burned in the accident. Allison brought suit against ITE in a Mississippi state court, claiming more than $50,000 in damages. Can this suit be removed to federal court? [*Allison v. ITE Imperial Corp.*, 729 F.Supp. 45, 1990 U.S. Dist. Lexis 607 (S.D. Miss. 1990)]

2.3 In Personam Jurisdiction Saul and Elaine Kozuck borrowed money from the Peoples Trust Company of Bergen County, New Jersey, and cosigned a promissory note promising to repay the money. When Peoples Trust contacted the Kozucks about payment, they denied liability on the ground that the bank improperly filled in the due date on the note. Peoples Trust filed suit against the Kozucks in a New Jersey state court. A process server went to the Kozucks' home in New Jersey to serve the summons. The process server rang the bell at the home and a woman appeared at the upstairs window. The process server asked her if she was Mrs. Kozuck, and the woman replied in the affirmative. When the process server identified himself, the woman denied that she was Mrs. Kozuck and refused to come out of the house. The process server told the woman that he would leave the papers in the mailbox if she refused to open the door. When the woman did not reappear, the process server placed the summons in the mailbox and left. Is the service of process good? [*Peoples Trust Co. v. Kozuck*, 236 A.2d 630, 1967 N.J.Super. Lexis 389 (N.J.Super. 1967)]

2.4 Long-Arm Statute Sean O'Grady, a professional boxer, was managed by his father, Pat. Sean was a contender for the world featherweight title. On January 30, 1978, Pat entered into a contract with Magna Verde Corporation, a Los Angeles–based business, to copromote a fight between Sean and the current featherweight champion. The fight was scheduled to take place on February 5, 1978, in Oklahoma City, Oklahoma. To promote the fight, Pat O'Grady scheduled a press conference for January 30, 1978. At the conference, Pat was involved in a confrontation with a sportswriter named Brooks. He allegedly struck Brooks in the face. Brooks brought suit against Pat O'Grady and Magna Verde Corporation in an Oklahoma state court. Court records showed that the only contact Magna Verde had with Oklahoma was that a few of its employees had taken several trips to Oklahoma in January 1978 to plan the title fight. The fight was never held. Oklahoma has a long-arm statute. Magna Verde was served by mail and made a special appearance in Oklahoma state court to argue that Oklahoma does not have personal jurisdiction over it. Does Oklahoma have jurisdiction over Magna Verde Corporation? [*Brooks v. Magna Verde Corp.*, 619 P.2d 1271, 1980 Okla. Civ. App. Lexis 118 (Okla.App. 1980)]

2.5 Minimum Contacts The National Enquirer, Inc., is a Florida corporation with its principal place of business in Florida. It publishes the *National Enquirer*, a national weekly newspaper with a total circulation of more than 5 million copies. About 600,000 copies, almost twice the level in the next highest state, are sold in California. On October 9, 1979, the *Enquirer* published an article about Shirley Jones, an entertainer. Jones, a California resident, filed a lawsuit in California state court against the *Enquirer* and its president, who was a resident of Florida. The suit sought damages for alleged defamation, invasion of privacy, and intentional infliction of emotional distress. Are the defendants subject to suit in California? [*Calder v. Jones*, 465 U.S. 783, 104 S.Ct. 1482, 1984 U.S. Lexis 41 (1984)]

2.6 Service of Process On May 9, 1983, attorneys for Ronald Schiavone filed a lawsuit against *Fortune* magazine in U.S. district court in New Jersey. The complaint claimed that *Fortune* had defamed Schiavone in a cover story titled "The Charges against Reagan's Labor Secretary," which appeared in the May 31, 1982, issue of the magazine. The complaint named *Fortune* as the defendant. *Fortune*, however, is only a trademark owned by Time, Incorporated, a New York corporation. Time, Incorporated, refused to accept service of the complaint because it had not been named as a defendant. Has there been proper service of process? [*Schiavone v. Fortune*, 477 U.S. 21, 106 S.Ct. 2379, 1986 U.S. Lexis 106 (1986)]

2.7 Summary Judgment Captain Conrad was a pilot for Delta Airlines. In 1970, the airline forced Conrad to resign. He sued, alleging that he was discharged due to his prounion activities and not because of poor job performance, as claimed by Delta. During discovery, a report written by a Delta flight operations manager was produced that stated: "More than a few crew members claimed that Conrad professed to being a leftist-activist. His overactivity with the local pilots' union, coupled with inquiries regarding company files to our secretary, lead to the conclusion that potential trouble will be avoided by acceptance of his resignation." Conrad claims that the report is evidence of the antiunion motivation for his discharge. Delta made a summary judgment motion to the trial court. Should its summary judgment motion be granted? [*Conrad v. Delta Airlines, Inc.*, 494 F.2d 914, 1974 U.S. App. Lexis 9186 (7th Cir. 1974)]

2.8 Physical Examination Robert Schlagenhauf worked as a bus driver for the Greyhound Corporation. One night the bus he was driving rear-ended a tractor-trailer. Seven passengers on the bus who were injured sued Schlagenhauf and Greyhound for damages. The complaint alleged that Greyhound was negligent for allowing Schlagenhauf to drive a bus when it knew that his eyes and vision "were impaired and deficient." The plaintiffs petitioned the court to order Schlagenhauf to be medically examined concerning these allegations. Schlagenhauf objected to the examination. Who wins? [*Schlagenhauf v. Holder*, 379 U.S. 104, 85 S.Ct. 234, 1964 U.S. Lexis 152 (1964)]

2.9 Deposition Haviland & Company filed suit against Montgomery Ward & Company in U.S. district court, claiming that Ward used the trademark "Haviland" on millions of dollars worth of merchandise. As the owner of the mark, Haviland & Company sought compensation from Ward. Ward served notice to take the deposition of Haviland & Company's president, William D. Haviland. The attorneys for Haviland told the court that Haviland was 80 years old, lived in France, and was too ill to travel to the United States for the deposition. Haviland's physician submitted an affidavit confirming these facts. Must Haviland give his deposition? [*Haviland & Co. v. Montgomery Ward & Co.*, 31 F.R.D. 578, 1962 U.S. Dist. Lexis 5964 (S.D.N.Y. 1962)]

2.10 Interrogatories Cine Forty-Second Street Theatre Corporation operates a movie theater in New York City's Times Square area. Cine filed a lawsuit against Allied Artists Pictures Corporation, alleging that Allied Artists and local theater owners illegally attempted to prevent Cine from opening its theater in violation of federal antitrust law. The suit also alleged that once Cine opened the theater, the defendants conspired with motion picture distributors to prevent Cine from exhibiting first-run, quality films. Attorneys for Allied Artists served a set of written questions concerning the lawsuit on Cine. Does Cine have to answer these questions? [*Cine Forty-Second Street Theatre Corp. v. Allied Artists Pictures Corp.*, 602 F.2d 1062, 1979 U.S. App. Lexis 13586 (2d Cir. 1979)]

2.11 Judgment n.o.v. On November 9, 1965, Mr. Simblest was driving a car that collided with a fire engine at an intersection in Burlington, Vermont. The accident occurred on a night on which a power blackout left most of the state without lights. Mr. Simblest, who was injured in the accident, sued the driver of the fire truck for damages. During the trial, Simblest testified that when he entered the intersection, the traffic light was green in his favor. All of the other witnesses testified that the traffic light had gone dark at least 10 minutes before the accident. Simblest testified that the accident was caused by the fire truck's failure to use any warning lights or sirens. Simblest's testimony was contradicted by four witnesses, who testified that the fire truck had used both its lights and sirens. The jury found that the driver of the fire truck had been negligent and rendered a verdict for Simblest. The defense made a motion for judgment n.o.v. Who wins? [*Simblest v. Maynard*, 427 F.2d 1, 1970 U.S. App. Lexis 9265 (2d Cir. 1970)]

2.12 Arbitration AMF Incorporated and Brunswick Corporation both manufacture electric and automatic bowling center equipment. In 1983 the two companies became involved in a dispute over whether Brunswick had advertised certain automatic scoring devices in a false and deceptive manner. The two parties settled the dispute by signing an agreement that any future problems between them involving advertising claims would be submitted to the National Advertising Council for arbitration. In March 1985, Brunswick advertised a new product, Armor Plate 3000, a synthetic laminated material used to make bowling lanes. Armor Plate 3000 competed with wooden lanes produced by AMF. Brunswick's advertisements claimed that bowling centers could save up to $500 per lane per year in maintenance and repair costs if they switched to Armor Plate 3000 from wooden lanes. AMF disputed this claim and requested arbitration. Is the arbitration agreement enforceable? [*AMF Incorporated v. Brunswick Corp.*, 621 F.Supp. 456, 1985 U.S. Dist. Lexis 14205 (E.D.N.Y. 1985)]

2.13 Delegation Doctrine The Federal Communications Commission (FCC) is a federal administrative agency that is empowered to enforce the federal Communications Act of 1934. This act, as amended, gives the FCC power to regulate broadcasting on radio and television. In *United States v. Midwest Video Corporation*, 406 U.S. 649 (1972), the U.S. Supreme Court held that the FCC also has the power to regulate cable television. In May 1976, the FCC promulgated rules requiring cable television operators that have 3,500 or more subscribers to (1) develop a 20-channel capacity; (2) make 4 channels available for use by public, educational, local, government, and leased-access users; (3) make equipment available for those utilizing these public-access channels; and (4) limit the fees cable operators could charge for their services. Do these rules exceed the statutory authority of the FCC? [*Federal Communications Commission v. Midwest Video Corporation*, 440 U.S. 689, 99 S.Ct. 1435, 1979 U.S. Lexis 82 (1979)]

Business Ethics Cases

2.14 Business Ethics One day Joshua Gnaizda, a three-year-old, received what he (or his mother) thought was a tantalizing offer in the mail from Time, Inc. The front of the envelope contained a see-through window that revealed the following statement: "Joshua Gnaizda, I'll give you this versatile new calculator watch free just for opening this envelope before Feb. 15, 1985." Beneath the offer was a picture of the calculator watch itself. When Joshua's mother opened the envelope, she realized that the see-through window had not revealed the full text of Time's offer. Not viewable through the see-through window were the following words: "And mailing this Certificate today." The certificate required Joshua to purchase a subscription to *Fortune* magazine in order to receive the free calculator watch. Joshua (through his father, a lawyer) sued Time in a class action, seeking compensatory damages in an amount equal to the value of the calculator watch and $15 million in punitive damages. The trial court dismissed the lawsuit as being too trivial for the court to hear. Joshua appealed. Should Joshua be permitted to maintain his lawsuit against Time, Inc.? Did Time act ethically? Should Joshua's father have sued for $15 million? [*Harris v. Time, Inc.*, 191 C.A.3d 449, 237 Cal. Rptr. 584, 1987 Cal. App. Lexis 1617 (Cal. App. 1987)]

2.15 Business Ethics Dennis and Francis Burnham were married in 1976 in West Virginia. In 1977, the couple moved to New Jersey, where their two children were born. In July 1987, the Burnhams decided to separate. Mrs. Burnham, who intended to move to California, was to have custody of the children. Mr. Burnham agreed to file for divorce on grounds of "irreconcilable differences." In October 1987, Mr. Burnham threatened to file for divorce in New Jersey on grounds of "desertion." After unsuccessfully demanding that Mr. Burnham adhere to the prior agreement, Mrs. Burnham brought suit for divorce in California state court in early January 1988. In late January, Mr. Burnham visited California on a business trip. He then visited his children in the San Francisco Bay area, where his wife resided. He took the older child to San Francisco for the weekend. Upon returning the child to Mrs. Burnham's home, he was served with a California court summons and a copy of Mrs. Burnham's divorce petition. He then returned to New Jersey. Mr. Burnham made a special appearance in the California court and moved to quash the service of process. Did Mr. Burnham act ethically in trying to quash the service of process? Did Mrs. Burnham act ethically in having Mr. Burnham served on his visit to California? Is the service of process good? [*Burnham v. Superior Court of California*, 495 U.S. 604, 110 S.Ct. 2105, 1990 U.S. Lexis 2700 (1990)]

Briefing the Case Writing Assignment

Read Case A.2 in the Case Appendix [*Gnazzo v. G.D. Searle & Co.*]. This case is excerpted from the court of appeals opinion. Review and brief the case. In your brief, be sure to answer the following questions.

1. What is a statute of limitations? What purposes are served by such a statute?
2. What was the Connecticut statute of limitations for the injury alleged by the plaintiff?
3. What is summary judgment? When will it be granted?
4. What was the decision of the trial court? of the court of appeals?
5. Was the decision fair? Should the plaintiff have been granted her day in court against the defendant?

Answers to Management Decision Questions

1. In order for a court to hear a lawsuit, the court must have both jurisdiction over the subject matter of the lawsuit and personal jurisdiction over the litigants. The suit can be initiated in the appropriate state court of general trial jurisdiction in North Carolina, where the incident took place, or in Illinois. The suit can also be held in a federal district court located in one of these states. A state court has jurisdiction over torts committed in the state and has jurisdiction over

its citizens. The plaintiffs, by filing a lawsuit with a court, give the court personal jurisdiction over themselves. A corporation is subject to personal jurisdiction in the state in which it is incorporated, has its principal office, and is doing business. The lawsuits can also be filed in the appropriate federal courts because there is a diversity of citizenship between the plaintiffs and the defendants. Article II, Section 2 of the U.S. Constitution sets forth the jurisdiction of federal courts. Federal courts have limited jurisdiction to hear cases involving diversity of citizenship. For diversity purposes, a corporation is a citizen of the state in which it is incorporated and in which it has its principal place of business. The federal court must apply the appropriate state's law in deciding the case. The dollar amount must exceed $75,000.

2. The most common form of alternative dispute resolution (ADR) is arbitration. Other forms of ADR that may be proposed are mediation, conciliation, minitrial, fact-finding, and using a judicial referee.

3. North Carolina has enacted criminal laws against hazing. The definition of hazing and the associated penalty are spelled out in Article 9, section 14.35 of the General Statutes of North Carolina. Other states have similar statutes. The following definition and associated penalties for hazing come from the North Carolina General Statutes:

> It shall be unlawful for any student in any college or school in this state to engage in what is known as hazing, or to aid or abet any other student in the commission of this offense. For purposes of this section hazing is defined as follows: "to annoy any student by playing abusive or ridiculous tricks upon him, to frighten, scold, beat or harass him, or to subject him to personal indignity." Any violation of this section shall constitute a misdemeanor punishable by a fine not to exceed five hundred dollars ($500.00), imprisonment for not more than six months, or both.

Endnotes

1. Federal Courts Improvement Act of 1982. Pub. L. 97–164, 96 Stat. 25, 28 U.S.C. § 1292 and § 1295.
2. Effective September 25, 1988, mandatory appeals were all but eliminated, except for reapportionment cases and cases brought under the Civil Rights and Voting Rights Acts, antitrust laws, and the Presidential Election Campaign Fund Act.
3. Prior to 1980, there was a minimum dollar amount controversy requirement of $10,000 to bring a federal question action in federal court. This minimum amount was eliminated by the Federal Question Jurisdictional Amendment Act of 1980, Public Law 96–486.
4. The amount was raised from $50,000 to $75,000 by the 1996 Federal Courts Improvement Act.
5. Under the Full Faith and Credit Clause of the U.S. Constitution, a judgment of a court in one state must be given "full faith and credit" by the courts of another state. (Article IV, Section 1.)
6. *International Shoe Co. v. Washington*, 326 U.S. 310, 66 S.Ct. 154, 1945 U.S. Lexis 1447 (1945).
7. There is no right to a jury trial for actions in equity (e.g., injunctions, specific performance).
8. 9 U.S.C. §§ 1 et seq.

3

Constitutional Authority to Regulate Business

"The nation's armour of defence against the passions of men is the Constitution. Take that away, and the nation goes down into the field of its conflicts like a warrior without armour."

—Henry Ward Beecher
Proverbs from Plymouth Pulpit, 1887

Chapter Objectives

After studying this chapter, you should be able to:

1. Describe the concept of federalism and the doctrine of separation of powers.
2. Define and apply the Supremacy Clause of the U.S. Constitution.
3. Explain the federal government's authority to regulate foreign commerce and interstate commerce.
4. Explain how speech is protected by the First Amendment.
5. Explain the doctrines of equal protection and due process.

Chapter Contents

- Basic Constitutional Concepts
- The Supremacy Clause
- The Commerce Clause
- The Bill of Rights and Business
- Other Constitutional Clauses and Business

Management Decision Constitutional Authority to Regulate Business

You are planning to establish a Web site on the Internet to sell X-rated books, videos, and other adult paraphernalia. Citizens for Decency in Communications, a nonprofit consumer group, was founded in order to lobby for federal legislation to prevent children and adults from being exposed to obscene and pornographic communications. Congress enacts a federal statute that prohibits "pornographic" communications over the Internet. Citizens for Decency in Communications learns of your intentions and threatens to sue you in federal court to block the establishment of your e-commerce site. Your financial backers are concerned about the threatened lawsuit and are reconsidering the wisdom of entering into this business venture with you.

1. What is the probable legal outcome of such a lawsuit by Citizens for Decency in Communication?
2. Would it make a difference if this suit were initiated in an appropriate state court?

> The Constitution of the United States is not a mere lawyers' document: It is a vehicle of life, and its spirit is always the spirits of the age.
>
> Woodrow Wilson
> *Constitutional Government in the United States 69 (1927)*

Prior to the American Revolution, each of the 13 original colonies operated as a separate sovereignty under the rule of England. In September 1774, representatives of the colonies met as a Continental Congress. In 1776, the colonies declared independence from England, and the American Revolution ensued.

This chapter examines the major provisions of the U.S. Constitution and the amendments that have been adopted to the Constitution. Of particular importance, this chapter discusses how these provisions affect the operations of business in this country. The Constitution, with amendments, is set forth as Appendix B to this book.

New York, New York. The Constitution of the United States of America establishes the structure of the federal government, delegates powers to the federal government, and guarantees certain fundamental rights.

Basic Constitutional Concepts

The **U.S. Constitution** is a unique document that provides rights and protections to individuals and businesses. Some important constitutional concepts are discussed in the following paragraphs.

U.S. Constitution
The fundamental law of the United States of America. It was ratified by the states in 1788.

Landmark Law

The Constitution of the United States of America

In 1778, the Continental Congress formed a *federal government* and adopted the **Articles of Confederation**. The Articles of Confederation created a federal Congress composed of representatives of the 13 new states. The Articles of Confederation was a particularly weak document that gave limited power to the newly created federal government. For example, it did not provide Congress with the power to levy and collect taxes, to regulate commerce with foreign countries, or to regulate interstate commerce among the states.

The **Constitutional Convention** was convened in Philadelphia in May 1787. The primary purpose of the Convention was to strengthen the federal government. After substantial debate, the delegates agreed to a new **U.S. Constitution**. The constitution was reported to Congress in September 1787. State ratification of the Constitution was completed in 1788. Many amendments, including the **Bill of Rights**, have been added to the Constitution since that time.

The U.S. Constitution serves two major functions:

1. It creates the three branches of the federal government (i.e., the executive, legislative, and judicial branches) and allocates powers to these branches.
2. It protects individual rights by limiting the government's ability to restrict those rights.

The Constitution itself provides that it may be amended to address social and economic changes. ■

Federalism and Delegated Powers

Our country's form of government is referred to as **federalism**. That means that the federal government and the 50 state governments share powers.

When the states ratified the Constitution, they *delegated* certain powers to the federal government. They are called **enumerated powers**. The federal government is authorized to deal with national and international affairs. Any powers that are not specifically delegated to the federal government by the Constitution are reserved to the state governments. State governments are empowered to deal with local affairs.

federalism
The U.S. form of government; the federal government and the 50 state governments share powers.

enumerated powers
Certain powers delegated to the federal government by the states.

The Doctrine of Separation Powers

As mentioned previously, the federal government is divided into three branches:

1. Article I of the Constitution established the **legislative branch** of government. This branch is bicameral; that is, it consists of the Senate and the House of Representatives. Collectively, they are referred to as *Congress*.[1] Each state has two senators. The number of representatives to the House of Representatives is determined according to the population of each state. The current number of representatives is determined from the 2000 census.
2. Article II of the Constitution establishes the **executive branch** of government by providing for the election of the president and vice president. The president is not elected by popular vote but instead is selected by the *electoral college*, whose representatives are appointed by state delegations.[2]
3. Article III establishes the **judicial branch** of the government by establishing the Supreme Court and providing for the creation of other federal courts by Congress.[3]

legislative branch
The part of the government that consists of Congress (the Senate and the House of Representatives).

executive branch
The part of the government that consists of the president and vice president.

judicial branch
The part of the government that consists of the Supreme Court and other federal courts.

United States Post Office, Alhambra, California. The United States is the world's leading democracy. The country, however, has had many blemishes on its citizens' constitutional rights. For example, during World War II Japanese Americans were involuntarily placed in camps. During the McCarthy hearings of the 1950s, citizens who were communists or associated with communists were "blackballed" from their occupations, most notably in the film industry. It was not until the mid-1960s that equal opportunity laws outlawed discrimination in the workplace based on race and sex.

Checks and Balances

Business Brief

Checks and balances is the way the U.S. Constitution prevents any one of the three branches of the government from becoming too powerful.

Certain **checks and balances** are built into the Constitution to ensure that no one branch of the federal government becomes too powerful. Some of the checks and balances in our system of government are as follows:

1. The judicial branch has authority to examine the acts of the other two branches of government and determine whether those acts are constitutional.[4]
2. The executive branch can enter into treaties with foreign governments only with the advice and consent of the Senate.
3. The legislative branch is authorized to create federal courts and determine their jurisdiction and to enact statutes that change judicially made law.

"Just once, before I retire from the bench, I'd like to make a landmark decision."
Reproduced by permission of James Estes.

The Supremacy Clause

The **Supremacy Clause** establishes that the federal Constitution, treaties, federal laws, and federal regulations are the supreme law of the land.[5] State and local laws that conflict with valid federal law are unconstitutional. The concept of federal law taking precedence over state or local law is commonly called the **preemption doctrine**.

Congress may expressly provide that a particular federal statute *exclusively* regulates a specific area or activity. No state or local law regulating the area or activity is valid if there is such a statute. More often, though, federal statutes do not expressly provide for exclusive jurisdiction. In these instances, state and local governments have *concurrent jurisdiction* to regulate the area or activity. However, any state or local law that "directly and substantially" conflicts with valid federal law is preempted under the Supremacy Clause. The following case applies the Supremacy Clause.

Supremacy Clause
A clause of the U.S. Constitution that establishes that the federal Constitution, treaties, federal laws, and federal regulations are the supreme law of the land.

preemption doctrine
The concept that federal law takes precedence over state or local law.

U.S. SUPREME COURT CASE

Geier v. American Honda Motor Company, Inc.

529 U.S. 861, 120 S.Ct. 1913, 2000 U.S. Lexis 3425 (2000)
Supreme Court of the United States

Case 3.1 The Supremacy Clause

Background and Facts

The United States Department of Transportation is the federal administrative agency responsible for administering and enforcing federal traffic safety laws, including the National Traffic and Motor Vehicle Safety Act of 1966. Pursuant to this act, in 1987 the Department of Transportation adopted a Federal Motor Vehicle Safety Standard that required automobile manufacturers to equip 10 percent of their 1987 vehicles with passive restraints, including automatic seat belts or air bags.

In 1992, Alexis Geier, driving a 1987 Honda Accord automobile in the District of Columbia, collided with a tree and was seriously injured. The car was equipped with manual shoulder and lap belts that were buckled up at the time of the accident; the car was not equipped with air bags, however. Geier sued the car's manufacturer, the American Honda Motor Company, Inc., alleging that American Honda had negligently and defectively designed the car because it lacked a driver's side air bag, thus violating the District of Columbia's tort law. The trial court dismissed Geier's lawsuit, finding that the District of Columbia's tort law conflicted with the federal passive restraint safety standard and was therefore preempted under the Supremacy Clause of the U.S. Constitution. The court of appeals affirmed. Geier appealed to the U.S. Supreme Court, which granted review.

Supreme Court Issue

Does the federal passive restraint safety standard preempt the District of Columbia's common law tort action in which the plaintiff claims that the defendant, American Honda, which was in compliance with the federal standard, should nonetheless have equipped the 1987 automobile with air bags?

In The Language of The U.S. Supreme Court

Breyer, Justice In effect, the petitioner Geier's tort action depends upon his claim that the manufacturer had a duty to install an air bag when it manufactured the 1987 Honda Accord. Such a state law—i.e., a rule of state tort law imposing such a duty—by its terms would have required manufacturers of all similar cars to install air bags rather than other passive restraint systems, such as automatic belts or passive interiors. It would have required all manufacturers to have installed air bags in respect to the entire District of Columbia–related portion of their 1987 new car fleet, even though the federal safety standard at that time required only 10 percent of a manufacturer's nationwide fleet be equipped with any passive restraint device at all. Regardless, the language of the federal passive restraint standard is clear enough: The Federal standard sought a gradually developing mix of alternative passive restraint devices for safety-related reasons. The rule of state tort law for which petitioner Geier argues would stand as an "obstacle" to the accomplishment of that objective. And the federal statute foresees the application of ordinary principles of preemption in cases of actual conflict. Hence the tort action is preempted.

Decision and Remedy

The U.S. Supreme Court held that the federal passive restraint safety standard preempted petitioner Geier's tort lawsuit under the District of Columbia's law against American Honda.

Case Questions

Critical Legal Thinking What would be the consequences if there were no Supremacy Clause? Explain.

Business Ethics Do you think American Honda owed a duty to equip all of its 1987 vehicles with air bags even though federal law did not require this?

Contemporary Business Do laws ever protect—rather than harm—businesses? Do you think defendant American Honda would say "There are too many laws" in this case?

Business Ethics

Cigarette Companies Assert Supremacy Clause

Business people often complain that there are too many laws. In some cases business executives actually like a law because it works in their favor, however. Consider the following case.

Rose Cipollone began smoking cigarettes in 1942, when she was 17 years old. She continued to smoke between one and two packs of cigarettes per day until the early 1980s.

Cipollone first smoked Chesterfield cigarettes, manufactured by Liggett Group, Inc. She then switched to L&M filter cigarettes, also made by Liggett Group. Cipollone subsequently switched to Virginia Slims cigarettes, manufactured by Phillip Morris, Inc. Finally, she smoked Parliament cigarettes, also made by Phillip Morris.

In 1981, Cipollone was diagnosed with lung cancer. Even though her doctor advised her to quit smoking, she was unable to do so. Cipollone continued to smoke heavily until June 1982 when her lung was removed, but even after that she smoked in secret. She only stopped smoking in 1983, after she had become terminally ill with cancer. On August 1, 1983, she sued those cigarette manufacturers for personal injuries. Cipollone died on October 21, 1984, but her heir continued to prosecute the case.

In 1965 the Congress enacted the Federal Cigarette Labeling and Advertising Act, which required cigarette manufacturers to place on cigarette packages a warning of the dangers of smoking. The act requires one of the following warning labels, which must be rotated every quarter, to be placed on each cigarette package after the words "SURGEON GENERAL'S WARNING":

1. Smoking Causes Lung Cancer, Heart Disease, Emphysema, and May Complicate Pregnancy.
2. Cigarette Smoke Contains Carbon Monoxide.
3. Quitting Smoking Now Greatly Reduces Serious Risks to Your Health.
4. Smoking by Pregnant Women May Result in Fetal Injury, Premature Birth, and Low Birth Weight.

The cigarette company defendants argued that the warnings on cigarette packages—which are mandated by the Federal Cigarette Labeling and Advertising Act—preempted Cipollone's state tort action against them.

The U.S. Supreme Court held that the federal act preempted Cipollone's state law claims based on failure to warn of the dangers of smoking. The Court held that the Federal Cigarette Labeling and Advertising Act was a valid federal law that, under the Supremacy Clause of the U.S. Constitution, took precedence over conflicting state law failure to warn claims.

The Supreme Court did, however, rule that the act did not bar lawsuits against cigarette companies for claims based on fraudulent misrepresentation or conspiracy among cigarette companies to misrepresent or conceal material facts about the dangers of cigarette smoking. Therefore, if they can prove fraud—that is, intentional conduct whereby the cigarette companies knew of the dangers of cigarette smoking and either lied to the public or concealed this information—smokers can win against cigarette companies. The Supreme Court reversed the court of appeals and allowed Cipollone's heirs to proceed against the defendants on this issue. Worn down, Cipollone's heirs dropped the lawsuit after this U.S. Supreme Court ruling. [*Cipollone v. Liggett Group, Inc.*, 112 S.Ct. 2608 (1992)]

1. Do you think cigarette companies knew of the dangers of smoking during the period that Cipollone smoked? Did they conceal this information from her?
2. What would be the economic consequences if courts held cigarette companies liable to injured smokers? Who would gain? Who would suffer? ■

The Commerce Clause

Commerce Clause
A clause of the U.S. Constitution that grants Congress the power "to regulate commerce with foreign nations, and among the several states, and with Indian tribes."

The **Commerce Clause** of the U.S. Constitution grants Congress the power "to regulate commerce with foreign nations, and among the several states, and with Indian tribes."[6] Because this clause authorizes the federal government to regulate commerce, it has a greater impact on business than any other provision in the Constitution. Among other things, this clause is intended to foster the development of a national market and free trade among the states.

In the following case, the U.S. Supreme Court upheld a treaty between the United States and an Indian nation.

U.S. SUPREME COURT CASE

Minnesota v. Mille Lacs Band of Chippewa Indians

526 U.S. 172, 119 S.Ct. 1187, 1999 U.S. Lexis 2190 (1999)

Supreme Court of the United States

Case 3.2

Treaty with an Indian Tribe

Background and Facts

When the Constitution was ratified by the original 13 colonies in 1788, it delegated to the federal government the exclusive power to regulate commerce with Indian tribes. At that time, the area making up the United States of America was substantially occupied by dozens of American Indian nations. During the next one hundred years, as the colonists migrated westward, the federal government represented the United States in dealing with the American Indians and entered into many treaties with Indian nations. One such treaty was with the Chippewa Indians in 1837 whereby they sold land located in the Minnesota Territory to the United States. The treaty provided: "The privilege of hunting, fishing, and gathering wild rice, upon the lands, the rivers and the lakes included in the territory ceded, is guaranteed to the Indians." The state of Minnesota was admitted to the Union in 1858.

In 1990, the Mille Lacs Band of the Chippewa nation of American Indians sued the state of Minnesota, seeking declaratory judgment that they retained the hunting, fishing, and gathering rights provided in the 1837 treaty and an injunction to prevent Minnesota from interfering with those rights. The state of Minnesota argued that its admission to the Union in 1858 extinguished those rights. The district court and court of appeals held in favor of the Chippewa Indians. The U.S. Supreme Court agreed to hear the appeal.

Supreme Court Issue

Are the hunting, fishing, and gathering rights guaranteed to the Chippewa Indians in the 1837 treaty still valid and enforceable?

In The Language of The U.S. Supreme Court

The state of Minnesota argues that the Chippewa's rights under the 1837 treaty were extinguished when Minnesota was admitted to the Union in 1958. In making this argument, the state faces an uphill battle. Congress may abrogate Indian treaty rights, but it must clearly express its intent to do so. There is no such clear evidence of congressional intent to abrogate the Chippewa Treaty rights here. The relevant statute—Minnesota's enabling act—provides in relevant part: "The state of Minnesota shall be one, and is hereby declared to be one, of the United States of America, and admitted into the Union on an equal footing with the original states in all respects whatever."

This language, like the rest of the act, makes no mention of Indian treaty rights.

Decision and Remedy

The U.S. Supreme Court held that the hunting, fishing, and gathering rights provided to the Chippewa Indians in the 1837 treaty with the United States of America were valid and enforceable and had not been extinguished when Minnesota was admitted to the union.

Case Questions

Critical Legal Thinking Do the American Indians have any legal claim to the lands that now comprise the United States of America? Discuss.

Business Ethics Did the state of Minnesota act ethically in arguing that the Chippewa Indians' hunting, fishing, and gathering rights had been extinguished? Why do you think the state argued this?

Contemporary Business Does the Supreme Court's decision have any effects on either American Indian or non-Indian businesses located in Minnesota? Explain.

Federal Regulation of Interstate Commerce

The Commerce Clause also gives the federal government the authority to regulate **interstate commerce**. Originally, the courts interpreted this clause to mean that the federal government could only regulate commerce that moved *in* interstate commerce. The modern rule, however, allows the federal government to regulate activities that *affect* interstate commerce.

interstate commerce
Commerce that moves between states or that affects commerce between states.

Under the **effects on interstate commerce test**, the regulated activity does not itself have to be in interstate commerce. Thus, any local (*intrastate*) activity that has an effect on interstate commerce is subject to federal regulation. Theoretically, this test subjects a substantial amount of business activity in the United States to federal regulation.

Business Brief
The federal government may regulate:

1. *Interstate* commerce that crosses state borders.
2. *Intrastate* commerce that affects interstate commerce.

For example, in the famous case *Wickard, Secretary of Agriculture v. Filburn*,[7] a federal statute limited the amount of wheat that a farmer could plant and harvest for home consumption. Filburn, a farmer, violated the law. The U.S. Supreme Court upheld the statute on the grounds that it prevented nationwide surpluses and shortages of wheat. The Court reasoned that wheat grown for home consumption would affect the supply of wheat available in interstate commerce.

> The American Constitution is, so far as I can see, the most wonderful work ever struck off at a given time by the brain and purpose of man.
>
> W. E. Glastone
> *Kin Beyond Sea (1878)*

In several recent cases, the U.S. Supreme Court held that the federal government had enacted statutes beyond its interstate commerce clause powers. For example, in *United States v. Lopez*, the Supreme Court invalidated the Gun-Free School Zone Act, a federal statute that made it a crime to knowingly possess a firearm in a school zone.[8] The Court found that there was no commercial activity that was being regulated.

The federal government's authority to enact federal statutes pursuant to the Interstate Commerce Clause was at issue in the following two cases.

Case 3.3 The Commerce Clause

U.S. SUPREME COURT CASE

Reno, Attorney General of the United States v. Condon, Attorney General of South Carolina

528 U.S. 141, 120 S.Ct. 666, 2000 U.S. Lexis 503 (2000)
Supreme Court of the United States

Background and Facts

State departments of motor vehicles (DMVs) register automobiles and issue drivers' licenses. State DMVs require automobile owners and drivers to provide personal information, which includes a person's name, address, telephone number, vehicle description, Social Security number, medical information, and a photograph, as a condition for registering an automobile or obtaining a driver's license. Many states DMVs sold this personal information to individuals, advertisers, and businesses. These sales generated significant revenues for the states.

After receiving thousands of complaints from individuals whose personal information had been sold, the Congress of the United States enacted the Driver's Privacy Protection Act of 1994 (DPPA) [18 U.S.C. §§ 2721–2775]. This federal statute prohibits a state from selling the personal information of a person unless the state obtains that person's affirmative consent to do so. South Carolina sued the United States, alleging that the Commerce Clause was violated by the federal government by adopting the DPPA. The district court and the court of appeals held for South Carolina. The U.S. Supreme Court granted review.

Supreme Court Issue

Was the Driver's Privacy Protection Act properly enacted pursuant to the interstate commerce clause power granted to the federal government by the U.S. Constitution?

In The Language of The U.S. Supreme Court

Rehnquist, Chief Justice The United States asserts that the DPPA is a proper exercise of Congress's authority to regulate interstate commerce under the Commerce Clause. The United States bases its Commerce Clause argument on the fact that the personal, identifying information that the DPPA regulates is a thing in interstate commerce, and that the sale or release of that information in interstate commerce is therefore a proper subject of congressional regulation. We agree with the United States' contention.

The motor vehicle information which the States have historically sold is used by insurers, manufacturers, direct marketers, and others engaged in interstate commerce to contact drivers with customized solicitations. The information is also used in the stream of interstate commerce by various public and private entities for matters related to interstate motoring. Because drivers' information is, in this context, an article of commerce, its sale or release into the interstate stream of business is sufficient to support congressional regulation.

Decision and Remedy

The U.S. Supreme Court held that Congress had the authority under the Commerce Clause to enact the federal Driver's Privacy Protection Act.

Case Questions

Critical Legal Thinking How often do you think one government (the federal government) saves people from the intrusiveness of another government (state or local government)?

Business Ethics Was it ethical for the states to sell the personal information of automobile owners and drivers?

Contemporary Business Who were the winners from this decision? Who were the losers?

Case 3.4 The Commerce Clause

U.S. SUPREME COURT CASE

United States v. Morrison

529 U.S. 598, 120 S.Ct. 1740, 2000 U.S. Lexis 3422 (2000)

Supreme Court of the United States

Background and Facts

Christy Brzonkala enrolled at Virginia Polytechnic Institute (Virginia Tech) in the fall of 1994. In September 1994, Brzonkala met Antonio Morrison and James Crawford, who were both students at Virginia Tech and members of the varsity football team. Brzonkala alleges that, within 30 minutes of meeting Morrison and Crawford, they assaulted and repeatedly raped her. Brzonkala alleges that this attack caused her to become severely emotionally disturbed and depressed, and she withdrew from the university. In December 1995, Brzonkala brought a civil lawsuit in district court to recover damages against Morrison and Crawford, as provided in Section 13981 of the Violence Against Women Act of 1994, a federal statute. In the statute, Congress stated that it had enacted the statute pursuant to the power granted it by the Commerce Clause of the U.S. Constitution. The defendants alleged that Section 13981 was invalid because the activity it regulated did not involve interstate commerce, and therefore Congress lacked the authority to enact the statute. The district court and court of appeals agreed with the defendants and dismissed the case. The U.S. Supreme Court accepted the appeal of the case.

Supreme Court Issue

Is Section 13981 of the Violence Against Women Act of 1994 which provides a civil cause of action to recover damages valid as a proper exercise of Congress's Commerce Clause power?

In The Language of The U.S. Supreme Court

Every law enacted by Congress must be based on one or more of its powers enumerated in the Constitution. Due respect for the decisions of a coordinate branch of Government demands that we invalidate a congressional enactment only upon a plan showing that Congress has exceeded its constitutional bounds. The proper resolution of the present case is clear. Gender-motivated crimes of violence are not, in any sense of the phrase, economic activity. While we need not adopt a categorical rule against aggregating the effects of any noneconomic activity in order to decide this case, thus far in our nation's history our cases have upheld Commerce Clause regulation of intrastate activity only where that activity is economic in nature.

Decision and Remedy

The U.S. Supreme Court held that Congress lacked constitutional authority under the Commerce Clause to enact Section 13981 of the Violence Against Women Act because the activity it regulated did not constitute interstate commerce. The judgment of the court of appeals was affirmed.

Case Questions

Critical Legal Thinking Do you agree with the reasoning of the Supreme Court that there was no intrastate commerce regulated in this case?

Business Ethics What state law civil and criminal remedies does Brzonkala have against the defendants?

State and Local Government Regulation of Business—State "Police Power"

The states did not delegate all power to regulate business to the federal government. They retained the power to regulate *intrastate* and much interstate business activity that occurs within their borders. This is commonly referred to as states' **police power**.

Police power permits states (and, by delegation, local governments) to enact laws to protect or promote the *public health, safety, morals, and general welfare*. This includes the authority to enact laws that regulate the conduct of business. Zoning ordinances, state environmental laws, corporation and partnership laws, and property laws are enacted under this power.

State and local laws cannot **unduly burden interstate commerce**. If they do, they are unconstitutional because they violate the Commerce Clause. For example, if the federal government has chosen not to regulate an area that it has the power to regulate (*dormant Commerce Clause*), but the state does regulate it, the state law cannot unduly burden interstate commerce. A state was found to have violated the dormant Commerce Clause in the following case.

police power
The power of states to regulate private and business activity within their borders.

Business Brief
States may enact laws that protect or promote the public health, safety, morals, and general welfare, as long as the law does not unduly burden interstate commerce.

Business Brief
State and local governments may regulate:

1. *Interstate* commerce.
2. *Intrastate* commerce not exclusively regulated by the federal government.

U.S. SUPREME COURT CASE

Fort Gratiot Sanitary Landfill, Inc. v. Michigan Department of Natural Resources

504 U.S. 353, 112 S.Ct. 2019, 1992 U.S. Lexis 3252 (1992)
Supreme Court of the United States

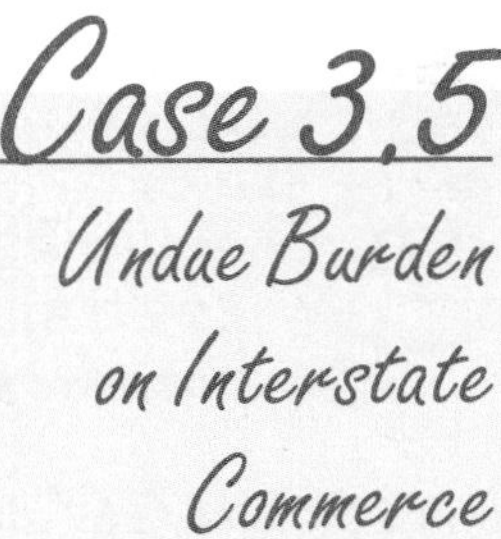

Background and Facts

In 1988, the state of Michigan added the Waste Import Restrictions to its Solid Waste Management Act. These restrictions prohibited privately owned landfills in the state from accepting solid wastes (e.g., garbage, rubbish, sludges, and industrial waste) from any source outside the county in which the landfill was located unless the county expressly permitted it. Fort Gratiot Sanitary Landfill, Inc. (Fort Gratiot), submitted an application to the county government to allow it to accept up to 1,750 tons per day of out-of-state solid waste. The county rejected the application. Fort Gratiot sued the county and state, alleging that the Waste Import Restrictions created an undue burden on interstate commerce in violation of the Commerce Clause of the U.S. Constitution. The U.S. district court concluded that the restrictions did not create an undue burden on interstate commerce. The U.S. court of appeals agreed. The U.S. Supreme Court granted review.

Supreme Court Issue

Do Michigan's Waste Import Restrictions violate the Commerce Clause?

In The Language of The U.S. Supreme Court

Stevens, Justice Solid waste, even if it has no value, is an article of commerce. The Commerce Clause thus imposes some constraints on Michigan's ability to regulate these transactions. The "negative" or "dormant" aspect of the Commerce Clause prohibits states from advancing their own commercial interests by curtailing the movement of articles of commerce, either into or out of the state.

Michigan and St. Clair County assert that the Waste Import Restrictions are necessary because they enable individual counties to make adequate plans for the safe disposal of future waste. Although accurate forecasts about the volume and compositions of future waste flows may be an indispensable part of a comprehensive waste disposal plan, Michigan could attain that objective without discriminating between in- and out-of-state waste. Michigan could, for example, limit the amount of waste that landfill operators may accept each year.

The Waste Import Restrictions enacted by Michigan authorize each of its 83 counties to isolate itself from the national economy. The Court has consistently found parochial legislation of this kind to be constitutionally invalid.

Decision and Remedy

The Supreme Court held that the Waste Import Restrictions created an undue burden on interstate commerce in violation of the Commerce Clause of the U.S. Constitution.

Case Questions

Critical Legal Thinking Do you think some states will "export" their wastes to other states rather than provide landfills within their own boundaries?

Business Ethics Is it ethical for a state to prohibit wastes from other states to be dumped within its boundaries? Was the state of Michigan acting in "good faith"?

Contemporary Business What effect will the Supreme Court's ruling have on landfill operators? Would your answer be different if the restriction had been found constitutional?

E-Commerce & Information Technology

Federal Telecommunications Act Preempts State and Local Laws

Congress enacted the **Federal Telecommunications Act of 1996 (FTA)** to increase competition within the telecommunications industry. In addition to deregulating the telephone industry, the FTA prohibits state and local governments from blocking freedom of entry into the burgeoning telecommunications industry. To accomplish this goal, **Section 253** of the FTA prohibits any state or local government laws that "prohibit or have the effect of prohibiting the ability of any entity to provide any interstate or intrastate telecommunications service."

Because the FTA is federal law, under the Supremacy Clause of the U.S. Constitution, it preempts any state or local law that conflicts with its provisions. Consider the following case.

Prince George's County, Maryland, enacted a county ordinance that required telecommunications firms to obtain a franchise from the county to use its rights-of-way, imposed a $5,000 application fee, charged 3 percent of the franchisee's gross revenues, and gave the county sole discretion to deny the franchise. Bell Atlantic–Maryland, Inc. (Bell Atlantic), a telecommunications company, sued Prince George's County in federal district court, alleging that the county ordinance violated the FTA and was preempted by the Supremacy Clause.

The court agreed with plaintiff Bell Atlantic. The court held that the county's ordinance went way beyond the county's authority to recover legitimate costs of maintaining the county's rights-of-way and instead was a general revenue-raising tax statute. The court also determined that the local government did not have the authority to keep out telecommunications companies because that authority was granted by Congress to the Federal Communications Commission (FCC), a federal administrative agency that oversees telecommunications for the nation. The Supreme Court concluded that the county's ordinance was preempted by FTA. [*Bell Atlantic–Maryland, Inc. v. Prince George's County, Maryland*, 49 F.Supp.2d 805 (D.Md. 1999)] ■

International Law

Foreign Commerce Clause

The Commerce Clause of the U.S. Constitution gives the federal government the exclusive power to regulate commerce with foreign nations. Direct and indirect regulation of *foreign commerce* by state or local governments that discriminates against foreign commerce violates the Foreign Commerce Clause and is therefore unconstitutional.

Consider the Following Examples The state of Michigan is the home of General Motors Corporation, Ford Motor Company, and Chrysler Corporation, the three largest automobile manufacturers in the United States. Suppose the Michigan state legislature enacts a law that imposes a 100 percent tax on any automobile imported from a foreign country that is sold in Michigan but does not impose the same tax on domestic automobiles sold in Michigan. The Michigan tax violates Foreign Commerce Clause and is therefore unconstitutional and void. If, on the other hand, Michigan enacts a law that imposes a 100 percent tax on all automobiles sold in Michigan, domestic and foreign, the law does not discriminate against foreign commerce and therefore does not violate the Foreign Commerce Clause. The federal government could enact a 100 percent tax on all foreign automobiles but not domestic automobiles sold in the United States, and that law would be valid, however. ■

The Bill of Rights and Business

The Bill of Rights provides certain freedoms and protections to individuals and businesses. The most important of these rights are discussed in the following paragraphs.

Business Brief

The first 10 amendments to the Constitution are called the Bill of Rights. They were added to the U.S. Constitution in 1791.

Nepal. Many countries of the world are not democracies like the United States. The Kingdom of Nepal, for example, is a monarchy.

Landmark Law

The Bill of Rights

In 1791, the 10 amendments that are commonly referred to as the **Bill of Rights** were approved by the states and became part of the U.S. Constitution. The Bill of Rights guarantees certain fundamental rights to natural persons and protects these rights from intrusive government action. Most of these rights have also been found applicable to so-called artificial persons (i.e., corporations).

In addition to the Bill of Rights, 17 other amendments have been added to the Constitution. These amendments cover a variety of things. For instance, they have abolished slavery, prohibited discrimination, authorized a federal income tax, given women the right to vote, and specifically recognized that persons 18 years of age and older have the right to vote.

Originally, the Bill of Rights limited intrusive action by the *federal government* only. Intrusive actions by state and local governments were not limited until the **Due Process Clause of the Fourteenth Amendment** was added to the Constitution in 1868. The Supreme Court has applied the **incorporation doctrine** and held that most of the fundamental guarantees contained in the Bill of Rights are applicable to state and local government action. The amendments to the Constitution that are most applicable to business are discussed in the paragraphs that follow. ■

Freedom of Speech

freedom of speech
The right to engage in oral, written, and symbolic speech protected by the First Amendment.

One of the most honored freedoms guaranteed by the Bill of Rights is the **freedom of speech** of the First Amendment. Many other constitutional freedoms would be meaningless without it. The First Amendment's Freedom of Speech Clause protects speech only, not conduct. The U.S. Supreme Court places speech into three categories: (1) *fully protected*, (2) *limited protected*, and (3) *unprotected speech*.

> I disapprove of what you say, but I will defend to the death your right to say it.
>
> Voltaire

Fully Protected Speech Fully protected speech is speech that the government cannot prohibit or regulate. Political speech is an example of such speech. For example, the government could not enact a law that forbids citizens from criticizing the current administration. The First Amendment protects oral, written, and symbolic speech.

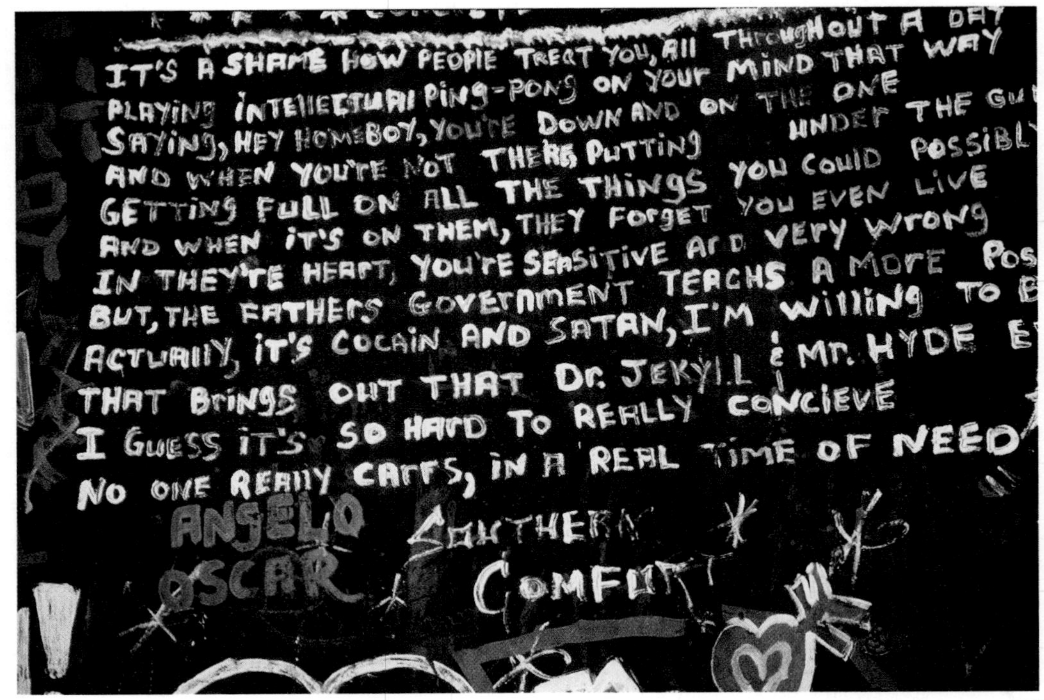

Homeless Poets' Wall, Downtown Los Angeles. The Freedom of Speech Clause of the First Amendment to the Constitution of the United Sates of America guarantees free speech rights. These rights have been defined by decisions of the Supreme Court of the United States.

Protest, Los Angeles. The Freedom of Speech Clause of the First Amendment to the U.S. Constitution protects the right to engage in political speech.

Limited Protected Speech The Supreme Court has held that certain types of speech have only *limited protection* under the First Amendment. The government cannot forbid this type of speech, but it can subject this speech to **time**, **place**, and **manner restrictions**. The following types of speech are accorded limited protection:

1. ***Offensive Speech*** **Offensive speech** is a speech that offends many members of society. (It is not the same as obscene speech, however.) The Supreme Court has held that offensive speech may be restricted by the government under time, place, and manner restrictions. For example, the Federal Communications Commission (FCC) can regulate the use of offensive language on television by limiting such language to time periods when children would be unlikely to be watching (e.g., late at night).
2. ***Commercial Speech*** **Commercial speech**, such as advertising, was once considered unprotected by the First Amendment. The Supreme Court's landmark decision in *Virginia State Board of Pharmacy v. Virginia Citizens Consumer Council, Inc.*[9] changed this rule. In that case, the Supreme Court held that a state statute prohibiting a pharmacist from advertising the price of prescription drugs was unconstitutional because it violated the Freedom of Speech Clause. However, the Supreme Court held that commercial speech is subject to proper time, place, and manner restrictions. For example, a city could prohibit billboards along its highways for safety and aesthetic reasons as long as other forms of advertising (e.g., print media) were available.

offensive speech
Speech that is offensive to many members of society. It is subject to time, place, and manner restrictions.

commercial speech
Speech used by businesses, such as advertising. It is subject to time, place, and manner restrictions.

Web Site
The executive branch of the United States government has its own Web site. Visit at **www.whitehouse.gov**.

Unprotected Speech The Supreme Court has held that the following types of speech are **unprotected speech**; they are not protected by the First Amendment and may be totally forbidden by the government:

1. Dangerous speech (including such things as yelling "fire" in a crowded theater when there is no fire)
2. Fighting words that are likely to provoke a hostile or violent response from an average person[10]
3. Speech that incites the violent or revolutionary overthrow of the government; the mere abstract teaching of the morality and consequences of such action is protected[11]

unprotected speech
Speech that is not protected by the First Amendment and may be forbidden by the government.

Web Site
Each house of the legislative branch of the United States government has its own Web site. Visit the U.S. House of Representatives at **www.house.gov**. Visit the U.S. Senate at **www.senate.gov**.

4. Defamatory language[12]
5. Child pornography[13]
6. Obscene speech[14]

obscene speech
Speech that (1) appeals to the prurient interest, (2) depicts sexual conduct in a patently offensive way, and (3) lacks serious literary, artistic, political, or scientific value.

The definition of **obscene speech** is quite subjective. One Supreme Court justice stated, "I know it when I see it."[15] In *Miller v. California*, the Supreme Court determined that speech is obscene when

1. The average person, applying contemporary community standards, would find that the work, taken as a whole, appeals to the prurient interest.
2. The work depicts or describes, in a patently offensive way, sexual conduct specifically defined by the applicable state law.
3. The work, taken as a whole, lacks serious literary, artistic, political, or scientific value.[16]

States are free to define what constitutes obscene speech. Movie theaters, magazine publishers, and so on are often subject to challenges that the materials they display or sell are obscene and therefore not protected by the First Amendment.

The following cases demonstrate the application of the Freedom of Speech Clause.

Case 3.6
Free Speech

U.S. SUPREME COURT CASE
United States v. Playboy Entertainment Group, Inc.
529 U.S. 803, 120 S.Ct. 1878, 2000 U.S. Lexis 3427 (2000)
Supreme Court of the United States

Background and Facts

Many entertainment companies, including Playboy Entertainment Group, Inc., produce and distribute sexually explicit adult entertainment features for transmission over cable television stations. These shows are usually offered on a pay-per-view subscription service. Cable operators provide viewers with a converter box that attaches to the television set that scrambles these sexually explicit materials so they can only be viewed by subscribers who pay the subscription fee. However, with analog television sets, there often occurs "signal bleed" of either a blurred visual image or muted audio transmission of these materials. Digital television eliminates the signal bleed problem.

To address the signal bleed problem, Congress enacted Section 505 of the Telecommunications Act of 1996, which requires cable operators not to transmit sexually explicit materials during the hours from 6:00 A.M. to 10:00 P.M. if the signal bleed problem can occur.

Playboy Entertainment Group, Inc., a cable operator of Playboy Television and Spice, two adult entertainment cable television networks, sued the federal government, alleging that Section 505 violated its free speech rights guaranteed by the U.S. Constitution. The district court declared Section 505 unconstitutional. The court found it feasible to allow cable operators to block individual cable boxes in the home, and therefore Section 505 was an overly broad restriction on content-based speech. The U.S. Supreme Court agreed to hear the case on direct appeal.

Supreme Court Issue

Is Section 505 an overly broad restriction on content-based speech that violates the free speech rights of Playboy Entertainment Group, Inc.?

In The Language of The U.S. Supreme Court

Kennedy, Justice As this case has been litigated, the programming is not alleged to be obscene; adults have a constitutional right to view it.

The effect of the federal statute on the protected speech is now apparent. It is evident that the only reasonable way for a substantial number of cable operators to comply with the letter of Section 505 is to "time channel," which silences the protected speech for two-thirds of the day in every home in a cable service area, regardless of the presence or likely presence of children or of the wishes of the viewers. According to the District Court, 30 to 50 percent of all adult programming is viewed by households prior to 10 P.M., when the safeharbor period begins. To prohibit this much speech is a significant restriction of communication between speakers and willing adult listeners, communication which enjoys First Amendment protection.

Cable systems have the capacity to block unwanted channels on a household-by-household basis. Simply put, targeted blocking is less restrictive than banning, and the Government cannot ban speech if targeted blocking is a feasible and effective means of furthering its compelling interests. If a less restrictive means is available for the Government to achieve its goals, the Government must use it.

Decision and Remedy

The U.S. Supreme Court held that Section 505 was an overly broad restriction on legal content-based speech and was therefore an unconstitutional violation of free speech rights. The judgment of the district court was affirmed.

Case Questions

Critical Legal Thinking Do you think that Section 505 was an overly broad restriction on free speech rights? Why or why not?

Business Ethics Why do you think Congress enacted Section 505 rather than require each home to choose to individually block the challenged programming?

Contemporary Business What economic consequences did the Supreme Court's ruling have for Playboy Entertainment and other adult entertainment cable companies?

U.S. SUPREME COURT CASE

Greater New Orleans Broadcasting Association, Inc. v. United States

527 U.S. 173, 119 S.Ct. 1923, 1999 U.S. Lexis 4010 (1999)
Supreme Court of the United States

Case 3.7 Commercial Speech

Background and Facts

The state of Louisiana permits licensed gambling casinos. Section 1304 of the Federal Communications Act, a federal statute, and Federal Communication Commission (FCC) rules, prohibit the broadcast of gambling and lottery information and advertisements over radio and television. The Greater New Orleans Broadcasting Association, Inc., an association of radio and television station owners, sued the federal government, alleging that Section 1304 and the FCC rules violated their commercial free speech rights as guaranteed by the First Amendment to the U.S. Constitution. The district court and the court of appeals sided with the federal government. The U.S. Supreme Court agreed to hear the appeal.

Supreme Court Issue

Do Section 1304 and the FCC rules violate the petitioner association members' commercial free speech rights?

In The Language of The U.S. Supreme Court

Stevens, Justice All parties to this case agree that the messages petitioners wish to broadcast constitute commercial speech. Their content is not misleading and concerns lawful activities, private casino gambling in Louisiana. In addition, petitioners' broadcasts presumably would disseminate accurate information as to the operation of market competitors, such as pay-out ratios, which can benefit listeners by informing their consumption choices and fostering price competition. Thus, even if the broadcasters' interest in conveying these messages is entirely pecuniary, the interests of, and benefits to, the audience may be broader.

Decision and Remedy

The U.S. Supreme Court held that Section 1304 and the FCC rules, restricting the broadcast of casino gambling information and advertisements on radio and television violate the petitioner association members' commercial free speech rights as guaranteed by the First Amendment to the U.S. Constitution.

Case Questions

Critical Legal Thinking What was the federal government's purpose in restricting casino advertising on radio and television? Explain.

Business Ethics What are the social implications of gambling? Should all gambling be outlawed? Should all forms of gambling be legal?

Contemporary Business What are the economic implications of the U.S. Supreme Court's ruling? Explain.

U.S. SUPREME COURT CASE

United States Department of Agriculture v. United Foods, Inc.

533 U.S. 405, 121 S.Ct. 2334, 2001 U.S. Lexis 4904 (2001)
Supreme Court of the United States

Case 3.8 The Free Speech Clause

Background and Facts

In 1990, Congress enacted the Mushroom Promotion, Research, and Consumer Information Act. This federal statute authorizes the U.S. Department of Agriculture, a federal administrative agency, to impose, through representatives, a mandatory financial assessment on the handlers and sellers of fresh mushrooms in an amount not to exceed one cent (1¢) per pound of mushrooms produced or imported. The assessment is used to pay for generic advertising to promote mushroom sales. In 1996, United Foods, Inc., a mushroom producer and importer,

United States Department of Agriculture v. United Foods, Inc.

533 U.S. 405, 121 S.Ct. 2334, 2001 U.S. Lexis 4904 (2001)
Supreme Court of the United States
(continued)

refused to pay its mandatory assessment as required by the statute, arguing that the forced subsidy for generic advertising violated its First Amendment free speech rights. The administrative law judge (ALJ) at the U.S. Department of Agriculture and the district court held against United Foods. The court of appeals reversed, and the U.S. Supreme Court granted review to hear the case.

Supreme Court Issue

Does the forced subsidy for generic advertising of mushrooms mandated by the federal Mushroom Promotion, Research, and Consumer Information Act violate the Free Speech Clause of the First Amendment to the Constitution?

In The Language of The U.S. Supreme Court

A quarter of a century ago, the Court held that commercial speech, usually defined as speech that does no more than propose a commercial transaction, is protected by the First Amendment. The question is whether the government may underwrite and sponsor speech with a certain viewpoint using special subsidies exacted from a designated class of persons, some of whom object to the idea being advanced. Just as the First Amendment may prevent the government from prohibiting speech, the Amendment may prevent the government from compelling individuals to express certain views, or from compelling certain individuals to pay subsidies for speech to which they object. The fact that the speech is in aid of a commercial purpose does not deprive United Foods, Inc. of all First Amendment protection. First Amendment concerns apply here because of the requirement that producers subsidize speech with which they disagree.

It is true that the party who protests the assessment here is required simply to support speech by others, not to utter the speech itself. We conclude, however, that the mandated support is contrary to the First Amendment principles.

Decision and Remedy

The U.S. Supreme Court held that the federal Mushroom Promotion, Research, and Consumer Information Act that requires mushroom handlers to pay a mandatory assessment for the generic advertising of mushrooms violates the commerce speech rights of United Foods, Inc., and is therefore unconstitutional.

Case Questions

Critical Legal Thinking In its opinion, the U.S. Supreme Court stated: "Just as the First Amendment may prevent the government from prohibiting speech, the Amendment may prevent the government from compelling individuals to express certain views." Is one violation as bad as the other? Comment.

Business Ethics Was it ethical for United Foods, Inc., to refuse to pay its assessment? Why do you think United Foods refused to pay its assessment?

Contemporary Business What are the business and economic consequences of the U.S. Supreme Court's decision? What would be the consequences if the Supreme Court had ruled in favor of the government?

E-Commerce & Information Technology

Broad Free Speech Rights Granted in Cyberspace

Once or twice a century a new medium comes along that presents new problems for applying freedom of speech rights. This time it is the Internet. In 1996 Congress enacted the **Telecommunications Act** to regulate telecommunications, including the Internet. Two provisions of this federal statute restricted the ability of cyberspace operators from transmitting certain images. These two provisions were:

- ***Computer Decency Act*** This part of the statute made it a felony to knowingly make "indecent" or "patently offensive" materials available on computer systems, including the Internet, to persons under 18 years of age.
- ***Signal Bleed Provision*** This provision of the statute required cable operators to either limit programming on cable channels to the hours between 10:00 P.M. and 6:00 A.M. or to scramble sexually explicit channels in full.

The act provided for fines, prison terms, and loss of licenses for anyone convicted of violating the terms of these provisions. Immediately, cyberspace providers and users filed lawsuits challenging these provisions of the act as violating their free speech rights granted under the First Amendment to the Constitution. Proponents of the act countered that these provisions were necessary to protect children from indecent materials. The plaintiffs won both cases at trial, and the U.S. Supreme Court granted review to decide the free speech issues.

The Supreme Court also came down on the plaintiffs' side in each case. The Court overturned the Computer Decency Act, finding that the terms *indecent* and *patently offensive* were too vague to define and criminally enforce. The Court decided that the signal bleed provisions imposed an overly broad illegal content-based restriction on speech. In both cases, the Supreme Court reasoned that limiting the content on the Internet to what is suitable for a child resulted in unconstitutional limiting of adult speech. The Court noted that children are far less likely to trip over indecent material on the Internet than on TV or radio because the information must be actively sought out on the Internet. The Court also stated that parents can regulate their children's access to the Internet and can install blocking and filtering software programs to protect their children from seeing adult materials.

The Supreme Court declared emphatically that the Internet must be given the highest possible level of First Amendment free speech protection, greater than that accorded to TV and radio. The Court concluded that the Internet allows an individual to reach an audience of millions at almost no cost, setting it apart from TV, radio, and print media, which are prohibitively expensive to use. The Supreme Court stated, "As the most participatory form of mass speech yet developed, the Internet deserves the highest protection from government intrusion." The Court also reasoned that because the Internet is a global medium, even if the challenged provisions of the act were upheld, there would be no way to prevent indecent material from flowing over the Internet from abroad. [*Reno v. American Civil Liberties Union*, 117 S.Ct. 2329 (1997); *United States v. Playboy Entertainment Group, Inc.*, 120 S.Ct. 1878 (2000)] ■

Freedom of Religion

The U.S. Constitution requires federal, state, and local governments to be neutral toward religion. The First Amendment actually contains two separate religion clauses. They are:

1. ***The Establishment Clause*** The **Establishment Clause** prohibits the government from either establishing a state religion or promoting one religion over another. Thus, it guarantees that there will be no state-sponsored religion. The Supreme Court used this clause as its reason for ruling that an Alabama statute that authorized a one-minute period of silence in school for "meditation or voluntary prayer" was invalid.[17] The Court held that the statute endorsed religion.

Establishment Clause
A clause to the First Amendment that prohibits the government from either establishing a state religion or promoting one religion over another.

2. ***The Free Exercise Clause*** The **Free Exercise Clause** prohibits the government from interfering with the free exercise of religion in the United States. Generally, this clause prevents the government from enacting laws that either prohibit or inhibit individuals from participating in or practicing their chosen religion. For example, in *Church of Lukumi Babalu Aye, Inc. v. City of Hialeah, Florida*,[18] the U.S. Supreme Court held that a city ordinance that prohibited ritual sacrifices of animals (chickens) during church services violated the Free Exercise Clause. Of course, this right to be free from government intervention in the practice of religion is not absolute. For example, human sacrifices are unlawful and are not protected by the First Amendment.

Free Exercise Clause
A clause to the First Amendment that prohibits the government from interfering with the free exercise of religion in the United States.

In the following case, the U.S. Supreme Court held that the Establishment Clause had been violated.

U.S. SUPREME COURT CASE

Case 3.9
The Establishment Clause

Santa Fe Independent School District v. Jane and John Doe
530 U.S. 290, 120 S.Ct. 2266, 2000 U.S. Lexis 4154 (2000)
United States Supreme Court

Background and Facts

The Santa Fe Independent School District is a political subdivision of the state of Texas that operates the Santa Fe High School, a public high school. The school district adopted a policy that permitted the students of the high school to elect a student who would give invocations over the public loud speaker system at all football games during the football season. The invocations were religious in nature, invoking Jesus Christ and the Lord, as well as Christian beliefs. Several students (designated the Does so that their identity would be kept secret) sued the school district, alleging that this football game policy violated the Establishment Clause of the U.S. Constitution and was therefore unconstitutional. The district court upheld the school district's policy if it only permitted nonproselytizing prayer. The court of appeals held that the football prayer policy was unconstitutional. The U.S. Supreme Court granted review.

Supreme Court Issue

Does the school district's policy permitting student-led prayer at football games violate the Establishment Clause?

Santa Fe Independent School District v. Jane and John Doe

530 U.S. 290, 120 S.Ct. 2266, 2000 U.S. Lexis 4154 (2000)
United States Supreme Court
(continued)

In The Language of The U.S. Supreme Court

Stevens, Justice The first Clause in the First Amendment to the Federal Constitution provides that "Congress shall make no law respecting an establishment of religion, or prohibiting the free exercise thereof." The Fourteenth Amendment imposes those substantive limitations on the legislative power of the States and their political sub-divisions. In this case the School District first argues that this principle is inapplicable to its October policy because the messages are private student speech, not public speech. We are not persuaded that the pregame invocations should be regarded as "private speech."

Granting only one student access to the stage at a time does not, of course, necessarily preclude a finding that a school has created a limited public forum. Here, Santa Fe's student election system ensures that only those messages deemed "appropriate" under the School District's policy may be delivered. That is, the majoritarian process implemented by the School District guarantees, by definition, that minority candidates will never prevail and that their views will be effectively silenced. This student election does nothing to protect minority views but rather places the students who hold such views at the mercy of the majority.

The choice between whether to attend these games or to risk facing a personally offensive religious ritual is in no practical sense an easy one. The Constitution, moreover, demands that the school may not force this difficult choice upon these students. Thus, nothing in the Constitution as interpreted by this Court prohibits any public school student from voluntarily praying at any time before, during, or after the schoolday. But the religious liberty protected by the Constitution is abridged when the State affirmatively sponsors the particular religious practice of prayer.

Decision and Remedy

The U.S. Supreme Court held that the school district's policy permitting student-led prayer at high school football games violated the Establishment Clause of the U.S. Constitution and therefore must be struck down as unconstitutional.

Case Questions

Critical Legal Thinking What is the purpose of the Establishment Clause? Explain.

Business Ethics Do you think that the school district was attempting to force the majority of the students' religious beliefs on other students?

Mackinac Island, Michigan/Freedom of Religion. The **Establishment Clause** prohibits the government from establishing a state religion or promoting one religion over another; the **Free Exercise Clause** prohibits the government from interfering with the free exercise of religion.

Contemporary Business Environment

High Court Upholds School Voucher Program

For decades there has been a crisis of failure in many public school systems in America. One such program was Cleveland, Ohio's public school system, where fewer than one-third of high school students graduated. Cleveland's public school system was in such a woeful state that a federal court judge ordered the federal government to take it over.

In response, the Ohio legislature enacted a program whereby the state issued vouchers to parents of inner-city school children to enroll their children in private schools. The program offered vouchers that paid up to 90 percent of the annual tuition—up to $2,250 per year. The parents who used the vouchers to send their children to private schools selected religious private schools 96 percent of the time.

Opponents of the Cleveland voucher system attacked the system in court, alleging that it violated the Establishment Clause of the U.S. Constitution, which separates church and state. The federal circuit court of appeals agreed and struck down the voucher system. The U.S. Supreme Court decided to hear the appeal. In a 5–4 decision in 2002, the U.S. Supreme Court held that the Cleveland voucher system did not violate the Establishment Clause and was, therefore, constitutional. The majority wrote that the Cleveland voucher system was *neutral* on its face because parents could send their children to either secular or religious private schools. The Supreme Court also cited the fact that many parents choose to send their children, even without vouchers, to public schools outside their inner-city neighborhood—to suburban or magnet schools.

Now that the U.S. Supreme Court has held that voucher systems are constitutional, state legislatures will have to grapple with the decision to adopt voucher systems or reject the idea. A rather rare coalition of conservatives and inner-city parents will fight for the voucher system, while public school teacher unions and some liberal groups will fight against the adoption of such voucher programs [*Zelman v. Simmons-Harris*]. ■

Concept Summary Freedom of Religion

Clause	Description
Establishment Clause	Prohibits the government from either establishing a government-sponsored religion or promoting one religion over other religions.
Free Exercise Clause	Prohibits the government from enacting laws that either prohibit or inhibit individuals from participating in or practicing their chosen religion.

Other Constitutional Clauses and Business

The **Fourteenth Amendment** was added to the U.S. Constitution in 1868. Its original purpose was to guarantee equal rights to all persons after the Civil War. The provisions of the Fourteenth Amendment prohibit discriminatory and unfair action by the government. Several of these provisions—namely, the *Equal Protection Clause*, the *Due Process Clause*, and the *Privileges and Immunities Clause*—have important implications for business.

Fourteenth Amendment
An amendment that was added to the U.S. Constitution in 1868. It contains the Due Process, Equal Protection, and Privileges and Immunities Clauses.

The Equal Protection Clause

The **Equal Protection Clause** provides that a state cannot "deny to any person within its jurisdiction the equal protection of the laws." Although this clause expressly applies to state and local government action, the Supreme Court has held that it also applies to federal government action.

Equal Protection Clause
A clause that provides that a state cannot "deny to any person within its jurisdiction the equal protection of the laws."

Laos. People in other countries of the world seek religious freedom.

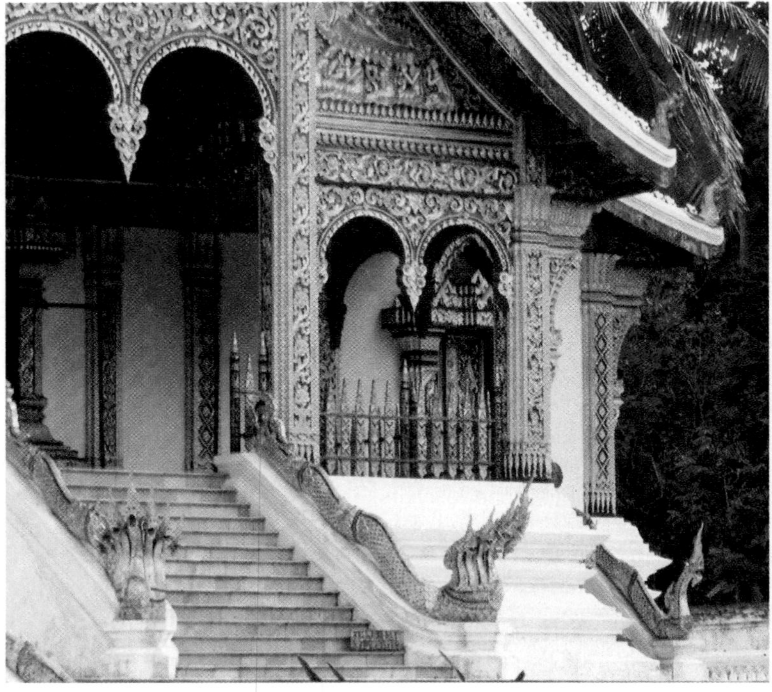

This clause prohibits state, local, and federal governments from enacting laws that classify and treat "similarly situated" persons differently. Artificial persons, such as corporations, are also protected. Note that this clause is designed to prohibit invidious discrimination: it does not make the classification of individuals unlawful per se.

The Supreme Court has adopted three different standards for reviewing equal protection cases. They are:

strict scrutiny test
A test that is applied to classifications based on race.

intermediate scrutiny test
A test that is applied to classifications based on protected classes other than race (e.g., sex or age).

rational basis test
A test that is applied to classifications not involving a suspect or protected class.

1. ***Strict Scrutiny Test*** Any government activity or regulation that classifies persons based on a *suspect class* (i.e., **race**) is reviewed for lawfulness using a **strict scrutiny test**. Under this standard, most government classifications of persons based on race are found to be unconstitutional. For example, a government rule that permitted persons of one race, but not of another race, to receive government benefits would violate this test.
2. ***Intermediate Scrutiny Test*** The lawfulness of government classifications based on *protected classes* other than race (such as **sex** or **age**) are examined using an **intermediate scrutiny test**. Under this standard, the courts determine whether the government classification is "reasonably related" to a legitimate government purpose. For example, a rule prohibiting persons over a certain age from military combat would be lawful, but a rule prohibiting persons over a certain age from acting as government engineers would not be.
3. ***Rational Basis Test*** The lawfulness of all government classifications that do not involve suspect or protected classes is examined using a **rational basis test**. Under this test, the courts will uphold government regulation as long as there is a justifiable reason for the law. This standard permits much of the government regulation of business. For example, providing government subsidies to farmers but not to those in other occupations is permissible.

The Equal Protection Clause was at issue in the following case.

U.S. SUPREME COURT CASE

Village of Willowbrook v. Olech

528 U.S. 562, 120 S.Ct. 1073, 2000 U.S. Lexis 1540 (2000), Supreme Court of the United States

Case 3.10

The Equal Protection Clause

Background and Facts

Grace Olech, who owned real property in the Village of Willowbrook, Illinois, asked the Village to connect her property to the municipal water supply. The Village conditioned the connection, requiring Olech to grant the Village a 33-foot easement across her property. Olech cited evidence that the Village required only a 15-foot easement from other real property owners seeking access to the Village's water supply. Olech claimed that the Village's demand for an additional 18-foot easement from her was irrational and arbitrary, and was actually motivated by ill will resulting from her previous filing of an unrelated, successful lawsuit against the Village. Olech sued the Village, claiming that the Village's action violated the Equal Protection Clause of the U.S. Constitution. The district court dismissed the lawsuit, but the court of appeals reversed, allowing Olech to sue. The U.S. Supreme Court granted certiorari to hear the case.

Supreme Court Issue

Can a party of one qualify as a "class" to bring a lawsuit alleging a violation of the Equal Protection Clause of the U.S. Constitution?

In The Language of The U.S. Supreme Court

Our cases have recognized successful Equal Protection Clause claims brought by a "class of one," where the plaintiff alleges that she has been intentionally treated differently from others similarly situated and that there is no rational basis for the difference in treatment. We have explained that the purpose of the Equal Protection Clause of the Fourteenth Amendment is to secure every person within the State's jurisdiction against intentional and arbitrary discrimination, whether occasioned by express terms of a statute or by its improper execution through duly constituted agents. That reasoning is applicable to this case. Olech's complaint can fairly be construed as alleging that the Village intentionally demanded a 33-foot easement as a condition of connecting her property to the municipal water supply where the Village required only a 15-foot easement from other similarly situated property owners.

Decision and Remedy

The U.S. Supreme Court held that Olech, a "class of one," may pursue an Equal Protection Clause claim against the Village of Willowbrook.

Case Questions

Critical Legal Thinking What does the Equal Protection Clause protect persons from? Which one of the following tests would be applied in analyzing the legality of the Village of Willowbrook's action?

1. Strict scrutiny test
2. Intermediate scrutiny test
3. Rational basis test

Business Ethics Do you think Olech was discriminated against by the Village? Was this case a violation of the Equal Protection Clause?

Contemporary Business Can government laws or decisions treat classes of businesses or industries differently without violating the Equal Protection Clause? If so, give an example.

Due Process Clause

The Fifth and Fourteenth Amendments to the U.S. Constitution both contain **Due Process Clauses**. These clauses provide that no person shall be deprived of "life, liberty, or property" without due process of the law. The Due Process Clause of the Fifth Amendment applied to federal government action; that of the Fourteenth Amendment applies to state and local government action. It is important to understand that the government is not prohibited from taking a person's life, liberty, or property. However, the government must follow due process to do so. There are two categories of due process: *substantive* and *procedural.*

Due Process Clause A clause that provides that no person shall be deprived of "life, liberty, or property" without due process of the law.

Substantive Due Process This category of due process requires that government statutes, ordinances, regulations, or other laws be clear on their face and not overly broad in scope. The test of whether substantive due process is met is whether a "reasonable person" could understand the law to be able to comply with it. Laws that do not meet this test are declared *void for vagueness.* Suppose, for example, that a city ordinance made it illegal for persons to wear "clothes of the opposite sex." Such an ordinance would be held unconsti-

substantive due process A category of due process that requires that government statutes, ordinances, regulations, or other laws be clear on their face and not overly broad in scope.

tutional as void for vagueness because a reasonable person could not clearly determine whether his or her conduct violates the law.

procedural due process
A category of due process that requires that the government give a person proper notice and hearing of the legal action before that person is deprived of his or her life, liberty, or property.

Procedural Due Process This form of due process requires that the government must give a person proper *notice* and *hearing* of the legal action before that person is deprived of his or her life, liberty, or property. The government action must be fair. For example, if the government wants to take a person's home by eminent domain to build a highway, the government must (1) give the homeowner sufficient notice of its intention and (2) provide a hearing. Under the **Just Compensation Clause** of the Fifth Amendment, the government must pay the owner just compensation for taking the property.

Concept Summary Due Process

Type of Due Process	Description
Substantive due process	Requires government laws to be clear and not overly broad. The test is whether a reasonable person could understand the law.
Procedural due process	Requires the government to give a person proper notice and hearing before depriving that person of his or her life, liberty, or property.

Business Ethics

When Are Punitive Damages Too Big?

Punitive damages are damages that can be awarded to plaintiffs in civil cases. These damages are assessed against defendants who have engaged in fraud, intentional misconduct, or other egregious conduct. They are intended to (1) punish the defendant, (2) deter the defendant from similar conduct in the future, and (3) set an example for others. Punitive damages are awarded in addition to actual damages.

U.S. businesses have argued for years that the award of punitive damages has gotten out of hand. They point to hundreds of multimillion-dollar punitive damage awards to back up their claim. Plaintiffs, on the other hand, argue that punitive damages serve a useful purpose and that without them businesses could engage in reprehensible conduct with impunity.

The U.S. Supreme Court addressed the issue of punitive damages in *BMW of North America, Inc. v. Gore* [517 U.S. 559, 116 S.Ct. 1589 (U.S.)]. In that case, Dr. Ira Gore, Jr., purchased a black BMW sports sedan for $40,470 from an authorized BMW dealer. Later, Dr. Gore discovered that several panels on the car had been repainted by BMW because of damage suffered while the car was being transported from Germany to the United States. BMW failed to disclose this fact to Dr. Gore when he purchased the car.

Dr. Gore sued BMW for fraud. The jury found BMW liable and awarded Dr. Gore $4,000 in compensatory damages and $4 million in punitive damages. The Alabama Supreme Court reduced the punitive damages to $2 million. BMW appealed to the U.S. Supreme Court.

In a 5–4 decision, the Supreme Court found that the punitive damage was "grossly excessive" and therefore violated the Due Process Clause of the U.S. Constitution. The Court based its determination on the fact that the harm was purely economic, the repainting had no effect on the car's performance, BMW's conduct evinced no reckless disregard for the health and safety of others, and the amount of the punitive damages—500 times actual damages—was excessive. The Supreme Court remanded the case to the Alabama supreme court for a determination of reasonably punitive damages. On remand, the award was reduced to $50,000 by the Alabama court.

The business community hailed the *BMW v. Gore* decision as a necessary limitation on oppressive and excessive awards of punitive damages by juries. Plaintiffs' lawyers and consumer groups argue that the case reduces an important lever against businesses that engage in unethical and illegal conduct.

1. What purposes are served by the award of punitive damages?
2. Do you think that the specter of punitive damage awards forces companies to act more ethically?
3. Should punitive damages be awarded to charities or other worthy causes rather than to the plaintiff? ■

The Privileges and Immunities Clause

The purpose of the U.S. Constitution is to promote nationalism. If the states were permitted to enact laws that favored their residents over out-of-state residents, the concept of nationalism would be defeated. Both Article IV of the Constitution and the Fourteenth Amendment contain **Privileges and Immunities Clauses** that prohibit states from enacting laws that unduly discriminate in favor of their residents. For example, a state cannot enact a law that prevents residents of other states from owning property or businesses in that state. Only invidious discrimination is prohibited. Thus, state universities are permitted to charge out-of-state residents higher tuition than in-state residents. Note that this clause applies only to citizens; it does not protect corporations.

Privileges and Immunities Clause
A clause that prohibits states from enacting laws that unduly discriminate in favor of their residents.

International Law

Constitution of the People's Republic of China

Chapter Two

The Fundamental Rights and Duties of Citizens [Selected Provisions]

Article 33

All citizens of the People's Republic of China are equal before the law.

Article 34

All citizens of the People's Republic of China who have reached the age of 18 have the right to vote and stand for election, regardless of ethnic status, race, sex, occupation, family background, religious belief, education, property status or length of residence, except persons deprived of political rights according to law.

Article 35

Citizens of the People's Republic of China enjoy freedom of speech, of the press, of assembly, of association, of procession and of demonstration.

Article 36

Citizens of the People's Republic of China enjoy freedom of religious belief. No state organ, public organization or individual may compel citizens to believe in, or not to believe in, any religion; nor may they discriminate against citizens who believe in, or do not believe in, any religion.

Article 40

Freedom and privacy of correspondence of citizens of the People's Republic of China are protected by law. No organization or individual may, on any ground, infringe upon citizens' freedom and privacy of correspondence, except in cases where, to meet the needs of state security or of

criminal investigation, public security or procuratorial organs are permitted to censor correspondence in accordance with procedures prescribed by law.

Article 41

Citizens of the People's Republic of China have the right to criticize and make suggestions regarding any state organ or functionary.

Article 48

Women in the People's Republic of China enjoy equal rights with men in all spheres of life, in political, economic, cultural, social and family life.

Article 54

It is the duty of citizens of the People's Republic of China to safeguard the security, honor and interests of the motherland; they must not commit acts detrimental to the security, honor and interests of the motherland. ■

Chapter Summary

Basic Constitutional Concepts, p. 63

The U.S. Constitution

The Constitution consists of seven articles and 26 amendments. It establishes the three branches of the federal government, enumerates their powers, and provides important guarantees of individual freedom. The Constitution was ratified by the states in 1788.

Basic Constitutional Concepts

1. ***Federalism.*** The Constitution created the federal government. The federal government and the 50 state governments share powers in this country.
2. ***Delegated powers.*** When the states ratified the Constitution, they delegated certain powers to the federal government. These are called *enumerated powers*.
3. ***Reserved powers.*** Those powers not granted to the federal government by the Constitution are reserved to the states.
4. ***Separation of powers.*** Each branch of the federal government has separate powers. These powers are:
   - *a.* Legislative branch—power to make the law
   - *b.* Executive branch—power to enforce the law
   - *c.* Judicial branch—power to interpret the law
5. ***Checks and balances.*** Certain checks and balances are built into the Constitution to ensure that no one branch of the Federal government becomes too powerful.

The Supremacy Clause, p. 65

The Supremacy Clause

Stipulates that the U.S. Constitution, treaties, and federal law (statutes and regulations) are the *supreme law of the land*. State or local laws that conflict with valid federal law are unconstitutional. This is called the *preemption doctrine*.

The Commerce Clause, p. 66

The Commerce Clause

1. ***Commerce Clause.*** Authorizes the federal government to regulate commerce with foreign nations, among the states, and with Indian tribes.
2. ***Interstate commerce.*** Under the broad *effects test*, the federal government may regulate any activity (even intrastate commerce) that *affects* interstate commerce.
3. ***Undue burden on interstate commerce.*** Any state or local law that cause an undue burden on interstate commerce is unconstitutional as a violation of the Commerce Clause.

The Bill of Rights and Business, p. 71

The Bill of Rights

The Bill of Rights consists of the first 10 amendments to the Constitution, which establish basic individual rights. The Bill of Rights was ratified in 1791.

Freedom of Speech

1. ***Freedom of Speech Clause.*** Clause of the First Amendment that guarantees that the government shall not infringe on a person's right to speak. Protects oral, written, and symbolic

speech. This right is not absolute—that is, some speech is not protected and other speech is granted only limited protection.

2. ***Fully protected speech.*** Speech that cannot be prohibited or regulated by the government.
3. ***Limited protected speech.*** The following types of speech are granted only limited protection under the Freedom of Speech Clause—that is, they are subject to governmental *time, place, and manner restrictions*:
   a. Offensive speech
   b. Commercial speech
4. ***Unprotected speech.*** The following speech is not protected by the Freedom of Speech Clause:
   a. Dangerous speech
   b. Fighting words
   c. Speech that advocates the violent overthrow of the government
   d. Defamatory language
   e. Child pornography
   f. Obscene speech

Freedom of Religion

There are two religion clauses in the First Amendment. They are:

1. ***Establishment Clause.*** Prohibits the government from establishing a state religion or promoting religion.
2. ***Free Exercise Clause.*** Prohibits the government from interfering with the free exercise of religion. This right is not absolute; for example, human sacrifices are forbidden.

Other Constitutional Clauses and Business, p. 79

Equal Protection Clause

Equal Protection Clause. Prohibits the government from enacting laws that classify and treat "similarly situated" persons differently. This standard is not absolute. The U.S. Supreme Court has applied the following tests to determine if the Equal Protection Clause has been violated:

1. ***Strict scrutiny test.*** Applies to *suspect classes* (e.g., race and national origin).
2. ***Intermediate scrutiny test.*** Applies to other *protected classes* (e.g., sex and age).
3. ***Rational basis test.*** Applies to government classifications that do not involve a suspect or protected class.

Due Process Clause

Due Process Clause. Provides that no person shall be deprived of "life, liberty, or property" without due process. There are two categories of due process:

1. ***Substantive due process.*** Requires that laws be clear on their face and not overly broad in scope. Laws that do not meet this test are *void for vagueness.*
2. ***Procedural due process.*** Requires that the government give a person proper *notice* and *hearing* before that person is deprived of his or her life, liberty, or property. An owner must be paid *just compensation* if the government takes his or her property.

Privileges and Immunities Clause

Prohibits states from enacting laws that unduly discriminate in favor of their residents over residents of other states.

Internet Exercises and Case Questions

Working the Web Internet Exercises

Activities

Visit **www.infoctr.edu/fwl**, the Web site for the Federal Law Locator. Try the following:

1. Check on the product safety record for selected products at the U.S. Consumer Product Safety Commission site. For example, "CPSC, Burger King Corporation Announce Voluntary Recall of Pokemon Ball."

2. Find and compare the U.S. Constitution to the Washington State Constitution, at **www.access.wa.gov**. How are they similar? How are they different?

3. Locate the Municipal Code for your city. Find the law on loitering in public places. Is it constitutional?

4. Find and review the USA Patriot Act of 2001. Is it constitutional?

Critical Legal Thinking Cases

3.1 Separation of Powers In 1951, a dispute arose between steel companies and their employees about the terms and conditions that should be included in a new labor contract. At the time, the United States was engaged in a military conflict in Korea that required substantial steel resources from which to make weapons and other military goods. On April 4, 1952, the steelworkers' union gave notice of a nationwide strike called to begin at 12:01 A.M. on April 9. The indispensability of steel as a component in weapons and other war materials led President Dwight D. Eisenhower to believe that the proposed strike would jeopardize the national defense and that governmental seizure of the steel mills was necessary in order to ensure the continued availability of steel. Therefore, a few hours before the strike was to begin, the president issued Executive Order 10340, which directed the secretary of commerce to take possession of most of the steel mills and keep them running. The steel companies obeyed the order under protest and brought proceedings against the president. Was the seizure of the steel mills constitutional? [*Youngstown Co. v. Sawyer, Secretary of Commerce*, 343 U.S. 579, 72 S.Ct. 863, 1952 U.S. Lexis 2625 (1952)]

3.2 Preemption Doctrine Article 1, Section 8, Clause 8 of the U.S. Constitution grants Congress the power to enact laws to give inventors the exclusive right to their discoveries. Pursuant to this power, Congress enacted federal patent laws that establish the requirements to obtain a patent. Once a patent is granted, the patent holder has exclusive rights to use the patent. Bonito Boats, Inc., developed a hull design for a fiberglass recreational boat that it marketed under the trade name Bonito Boats Model 5VBR. The manufacturing process involved creating a hardwood model that was sprayed with fiberglass to create a mold. The mold then served to produce the finished fiberglass boats for sale. Bonito did not file a patent application to protect the utilitarian or design aspects of the hull or the manufacturing process. After the Bonito 5VBR was on the market for six years, the Florida legislature enacted a statute prohibiting the use of a direct molding process to duplicate unpatented boat hulls and forbid the knowing sale of hulls so duplicated. The protection afforded under the state statute was broader than that provided for under the federal patent statute. Subsequently, Thunder Craft Boats, Inc., produced and sold boats made by the direct molding process. Bonito sued Thunder Craft under Florida law. Is the Florida statute valid? [*Bonito Boats, Inc. v. Thunder Craft Boats, Inc.*, 489 U.S. 141, 109 S.Ct. 971, 1989 U.S. Lexis 629 (1989)]

3.3 Commerce Clause The Heart of Atlanta Motel, located in the state of Georgia, has 216 rooms available to guests. The motel is readily accessible to interstate highways 75 and 85 and to state highways 23 and 41. The motel solicits patronage from outside the state of Georgia through various national advertising media, including magazines of national circulation, and it maintains more than 50 billboards and highway signs within the state. Approximately 75 percent of the motel's registered guests are from out of state. Congress enacted the Civil Rights Act of 1964, which made it illegal for public accommodations to discriminate against guests based on their race. Prior to that, the Heart of Atlanta Motel had refused to rent rooms to blacks. After the act was passed, it alleged that it intended to continue not to rent rooms to blacks. The owner of the motel brought an action to have the Civil Rights Act of 1964 declared unconstitutional, alleging that Congress, in passing the act, had exceeded its powers to regulate commerce under the Commerce Clause of the U.S. Constitution. Who wins? [*Heart of Atlanta Motel v. United States*, 379 U.S. 241, 85 S.Ct. 348, 1964 U.S. Lexis 2187 (1964)]

3.4 Commerce and Supremacy Clauses In 1972, Congress enacted a federal statute, called the Ports and Waterways Safety Act, that established uniform standards for the operation of boats on inland waterways in the United States. The act coordinated its provisions with those of foreign countries so that there was a uniform body of international rules that applied to vessels that traveled between countries. Pursuant to the act, a federal rule was adopted that regulated the design, length, and size of oil tankers, some of which traveled the waters of the Puget Sound area in the state of Washington. Oil tankers from various places entered Puget Sound to bring crude oil to refineries located in Washington. In 1975, the state of Washington enacted a statute that established different designs, smaller lengths, and smaller sizes for oil tankers serving Puget Sound than allowed by the federal law. Oil tankers used by the Atlantic Richfield Company (ARCO) to bring oil into Puget Sound met the federal standards but not the state standards. ARCO sued to have the state statute declared unconstitutional. Who wins? [*Ray, Governor of Washington v. Atlantic Richfield Co.*, 435 U.S. 151, 98 S.Ct. 988, 1978 U.S. Lexis 18 (1978)]

3.5 Undue Burden on Interstate Commerce Most trucking firms, including Consolidated Freightways Corporation, use 65-foot-long "double" trailer trucks to ship commodities on the highway system across the United States. Almost all states permit these vehicles on their highways. The federal government does not regulate the length of trucks that can use the nation's highways. The state of Iowa enacted a statute that restricts the length of trucks that can use highways in the state to 55 feet. This means that if Consolidated wants to move goods through Iowa it must either use smaller trucks or detach the double trailers and shuttle them through the state separately. Its only other alternative is to divert its 65-foot doubles around Iowa. Consolidated filed suit against Iowa, alleging that the state statute is unconstitutional. Is it? [*Kassel v. Consolidated Freightways Corporation*, 450 U.S. 662, 101 S.Ct. 1309, 1981 U.S. Lexis 17 (1981)]

3.6 Privileges and Immunities Clause During the 1970s, a period of a booming economy in Alaska, many residents of other states moved there in search of work. Construction work on the Trans-Alaska Pipeline was a major source of employment. In 1972, the Alaska legislature enacted an act entitled the "Local Hire" Statute. This act required employers to hire Alaska residents in preference to nonresidents. Is this statute constitutional? [*Hicklin v. Orbeck, Commissioner of the Department of Labor of Alaska,* 437 U.S. 518, 98 S.Ct. 2482, 1978 U.S. Lexis 36 (1978)]

3.7 Offensive Speech Satiric humorist George Carlin recorded a 12-minute monologue entitled "Filthy Words" before a live audience in a California theater. He began referring to "the words you couldn't say on the public airwaves—the ones you definitely couldn't say, ever." He proceeded to list those words and repeat them over and over again in a variety of colloquialisms. At about 2:00 P.M. on October 30, 1973, a New York radio station owned by Pacifica Foundation broadcast the "Filthy Words" monologue. A man who heard the broadcast while driving with his young son complained to the FCC, the federal administrative agency in charge of granting radio licenses and regulating radio broadcasts. The FCC administers a statute that forbids the use of any offensive language on the radio. The FCC found that Carlin's monologue violated this law and censured the Pacifica Foundation for playing the monologue. Can the FCC prohibit Pacifica Foundation from playing the Carlin monologue on the radio? [*Federal Communications Commission v. Pacifica Foundation,* 438 U.S. 726, 98 S.Ct. 3026, 1978 U.S. Lexis 135 (1978)]

3.8 Commercial Speech The city of San Diego, California, enacted a city zoning ordinance that prohibited outdoor advertising display signs—including billboards. On-site signs at a business location were exempted from this rule. The city based the restriction on traffic safety and esthetics. Metromedia, Inc., a company that is in the business of leasing commercial billboards to advertisers, sued the city of San Diego, alleging that the zoning ordinance is unconstitutional. Is it? [*Metromedia, Inc. v. City of San Diego*, 453 U.S. 490, 101 S.Ct. 2882, 1981 U.S. Lexis 50 (1981)]

3.9 Freedom of Religion Eddie C. Thomas, a Jehovah's Witness, was initially hired to work in a roll factory at Blaw-Knox Company. The function of the department was to fabricate sheet steel for a variety of industrial uses. On his application, Thomas listed that he was a Jehovah's Witness. Approximately one year later, the roll foundry closed and Blaw-Knox transferred Thomas to a department that fabricated turrets for military tanks. On the first day at this new job, Thomas realized that the work he was doing violated his religious beliefs because it was weapon related. Because there were no other jobs available, Thomas quit and filed for unemployment compensation. The state of Indiana denied his claim on the ground that Thomas quit his job for personal reasons. Thomas sued, alleging that the government's denial of unemployment benefits violated his right to freedom of religion. Who wins? [*Thomas v. Review Board of the Indiana Employment Security Division*, 450 U.S. 707, 101 S.Ct. 1425, 1981 U.S. Lexis 11 (1981)]

3.10 Substantive Due Process On February 20, 1978, the village of Hoffman Estates, Illinois, enacted an ordinance regulating drug paraphernalia. The ordinance made it unlawful for any person "to sell any items, effect, paraphernalia, accessory or thing which is designed or marketed for use with illegal cannabis or drugs as defined by Illinois Revised Statutes, without obtaining a license therefore." The license fee was $150. A violation was subject to a fine of not more than $500. The Flipside, a retail store located in the village, sold a variety of merchandise, including smoking accessories, clamps, roach clips, scales, water pipes, vials, cigarette rolling papers, and other items. On May 30, 1978, instead of applying for a license, Flipside filed a lawsuit against the village, alleging that the ordinance was unconstitutional as a violation of substantive due process because it was overly broad and vague. Who wins? [*Village of Hoffman Estates v. Flipside, Hoffman Estates, Inc.*, 455 U.S. 489, 102 S.Ct. 1186, 1982 U.S. Lexis 78 (1982)]

3.11 Equal Protection Clause The state of Alabama enacted a statute that imposed a tax on premiums earned by insurance companies. The statute imposed a 1 percent tax on domestic insurance companies (i.e., insurance companies that were incorporated in Alabama and had their principal office in the state). The statute imposed a 4 percent tax on the premiums earned by out-of-state insurance companies that sold insurance in Alabama. Out-of-state insurance companies could reduce the premium tax by 1 percent by investing at least 10 percent of their assets in Alabama. Domestic insurance companies did not have to invest any of their assets in Alabama. Metropolitan Life Insurance Company, an out-of-state insurance company, sued the state of Alabama, alleging that the Alabama statute violated the Equal Protection Clause of the U.S. Constitution. Who wins? [*Metropolitan Life Insurance Co. v. Ward, Commissioner of Insurance of Alabama*, 470 U.S. 869, 105 S.Ct. 1676, 1985 U.S. Lexis 80 (1985)]

Business Ethics Cases

3.12 Business Ethics The Raiders are a professional football team and a National Football League (NFL) franchise. Each NFL franchise is independently owned. Al Davis is an owner and the managing general partner of the Raiders. The NFL establishes schedules, negotiates television contracts, and otherwise promotes NFL football, including conducting the Super Bowl each year. The Raiders play home and away games against other NFL teams.

Up until 1982, the Raiders played their home games in Oakland, California. The owners of the Raiders decided to move the team from Oakland to Los Angeles, California, to take advantage of the greater seating capacity of the Los Angeles Coliseum, the larger television market of Los Angeles, and other economic reasons. The renamed team was to be known as the Los Angeles Raiders. The city of Oakland brought an eminent domain proceeding in court to acquire the Raiders as a city-owned team. Can the city of Oakland acquire the Raiders through eminent domain? Is it socially responsible for a professional sports team to move to another location? [*City of Oakland, California v. Oakland Raiders*, 174 C.A.3d 414, 220 Cal. Rptr. 153, 1985 Cal.App. Lexis 2751 (Cal.App. 1985)]

3.13 Business Ethics In 1989, Congress enacted the Flag Protection Act, which made it a crime to knowingly mutilate, deface, physically defile, burn, or trample the U.S. flag. The law provided for fines and up to one year in prison upon conviction [18 U.S.C. § 700]. Certain individuals set fire to several U.S. flags on the steps of the U.S. Capitol in Washington, DC, to protest various aspects of the federal government's foreign and domestic policy. In a separate incident, other individuals set fire to a U.S. flag to protest the act's passage. All of these individuals were prosecuted for violating the act. The district courts held the act unconstitutional, in violation of the defendants' First Amendment free speech rights and dismissed the charges. The government appealed to the U.S. Supreme Court, which consolidated the two cases. Who wins? Does the flag burner exhibit any morals? [*United States v. Eichman*, 496 U.S. 310, 110 S.Ct. 2404, 1990 U.S. Lexis 3087 (1990)]

Briefing the Case Writing Assignment

Read Case A.3 in the Case Appendix [*Lee v. Weisman*]. This case is excerpted from the U.S. Supreme Court's opinion. Review and brief the case. In your brief, be sure to answer the following questions.

1. Who are the plaintiff and defendant?
2. What does the Establishment Clause provide?
3. Was the fact that the prayer was nonsectarian important to the Supreme Court's decision?
4. What argument did the dissenting opinion make in support of allowing prayer at high school graduation ceremonies?
5. How close was the vote by the justices in this case?

Answers to Management Decision Questions

1. **The lawsuit will likely fail in court.** The Supreme Court of the United States found provisions of Congress's first attempt to protect children from exposure to pornographic material on the Internet unconstitutional in two separate rulings. In 1996, Congress enacted the Telecommunication Act to regulate telecommunications, including the Internet. According to the text of the U.S. Supreme Court ruling in *Reno v. American Civil Liberties Union* (1997), the Communications Decency Act of 1996 ran afoul of the First Amendment in its regulation of indecent transmissions and the display of patently offensive material. The terms *indecent* and *patently offensive* were too vague to define and criminally enforce. The Supreme Court decided that the signal bleed provisions imposed an overly broad illegal content-based restriction on speech. In addition to the above-mentioned case, in *United States v. Playboy Entertainment Group, Inc.* (2000), the Supreme Court reasoned that limiting the content of the Internet to what is suitable for a child would result in unconstitutional limitation of adult speech. All federal courts must follow the precedents set by the U.S. Supreme Court.
2. The lawsuit would also likely fail if the lawsuit were initiated in an appropriate state court. When the states ratified the Constitution, they delegated certain power to the federal government. The federal government is authorized to deal with national and international affairs. The Supremacy Clause of the Constitution establishes that the federal Constitution, treaties, federal law, and federal regulations are the supreme law of the land. The rulings of the Supreme Court are part of the federal law; thus, all state courts must follow the precedents set by the Supreme Court.

Endnotes

1. To be elected to Congress, an individual must be a U.S. citizen, either naturally born or granted citizenship. To serve in the Senate, a person must be 30 years of age or older. To serve in the House of Representatives, a person must be 25 years of age or older.
2. To be president, a person must be 35 years of age or older and a natural citizen of the United States. By amendment to the Constitution (Amendment XXII), a person can serve only two full terms as president.
3. Federal court judges and justices are appointed by the president with the consent of the Senate.
4. The principle that the U.S. Supreme Court is the final arbiter of the U.S. Constitution evolved from *Marbury v. Madison*, 1 Cranch 137 (1803). In that case, the Supreme Court held that a judiciary statute enacted by Congress was unconstitutional.
5. Article VI, Section 2.
6. Article I, Section 8, clause 3.
7. 317 U.S. III., 63 S.Ct. 82, 1942 U.S. Lexis 1046 (1942).
8. 514 U.S. 549, 115 S.Ct. 1624, 1995 U.S. Lexis 3039 (1995).
9. 425 U.S. 748, 96 S.Ct. 1817, 1976 U.S. Lexis 55 (1976).

10. *Chaplinsky v. New Hampshire*, 315 U.S. 568, 62 S.Ct. 766, 1942 U.S. Lexis 851 (1942).
11. *Brandenburg v. Ohio*, 395 U.S. 444, 89 S.Ct. 1827, 1969 U.S. Lexis 1367 (1969).
12. *Beauharnais v. Illinois*, 343 U.S. 250, 72 S.Ct. 725, 1952 U.S. Lexis 2799 (1952).
13. *New York v. Ferber*, 458 U.S. 747, 102 S.Ct. 3348, 1982 U.S. Lexis 12 (1982).
14. *Roth v. United States*, 354 U.S. 476, 77 S.Ct. 1304, 1957 U.S. Lexis 587 (1957).
15. Justice Stewart in *Jacobellis v. Ohio*, 378 U.S. 184, 84 S.Ct. 1676, 1964 U.S. Lexis 822 (1963).
16. 413 U.S. 15, 93 S.Ct. 2607, 1973 U.S. Lexis 149 (1973).
17. *Wallace v. Jaffree*, 472 U.S. 38, 105 S.Ct. 2479, 1985 U.S. Lexis 91 (1985).
18. 508 U.S. 520, 113 S.Ct. 2217, 1993 U.S. Lexis 4022 (1993).

4

Ethics and Social Responsibility of Business

"Ethical considerations can no more be excluded from the administration of justice, which is the end and purpose of all civil laws, than one can exclude the vital air from his room and live."

—John F. Dillon
Laws and Jurisprudence of England and America Lecture I (1894)

Chapter Objectives

After studying this chapter, you should be able to:

1. Describe morality.
2. Describe ethical theories and their applications to decision-making in business.
3. Describe theories of social responsibility and their application to business.

Chapter Contents

- Law and Ethics
- Moral Theories and Business Ethics
- The Social Responsibility of Business

Management Decision Ethics and Social Responsibility of Business

You are the executive secretary to the senior vice president in charge of government contracts at Spaulding Aeronautical Corp. (Spaulding), a major supplier of navigational equipment to the U.S. Air Force. Congress is planning to convene committee hearings on possible overbilling and substandard equipment supplied to the government by Spaulding. The Federal Bureau of Investigation (FBI) is also investigating allegations of wrongdoing by former employees of the company. Your boss has asked you to destroy various documents associated with several government contracts. You suspect that these documents contain information that can be used by the government in a criminal prosecution of Spaulding. You are torn between your loyalty to your company and your possible criminal wrongdoing on the part of Spaulding.

1. What should you do?
2. Did your boss act ethically in requesting that you destroy the documents in question?

Businesses organized in the United States are subject to its laws. They are also subject to the laws of other countries in which they operate. In addition, businesspersons owe a duty to act ethically in the conduct of their affairs, and businesses owe a social responsibility not to harm society.

Although much of the law is based on ethical standards, not all ethical standards have been enacted as law. The law establishes a minimum degree of conduct expected by persons and businesses in society. Ethics demands more. This chapter discusses business ethics and the social responsibility of business.

Ethics precede laws as man precedes society.

Jason Alexander
Philosophy for Investors (1979)

Beijing, China. Ethics is a function of history, culture, religion, and other factors. Therefore, ethical standards vary from country to country.

Myanmar (Burma). Some companies refuse to do business with Myanmar because of allegations that its military-led government engages in humanitarian violations.

Law and Ethics

Sometimes the rule of law and the golden rule of **ethics** demand the same response by the person confronted with a problem. For example, federal and state laws make bribery unlawful. A person violates the law if he or she bribes a judge for a favorable decision in a case. Ethics would also prohibit this conduct.

ethics

A set of moral principles or values that governs the conduct of an individual or a group.

The law may permit something that would be ethically wrong.

Business Brief

What is lawful conduct is not always ethical conduct.

Consider This Example Occupational safety laws set standards for emissions of dust from toxic chemicals in the workplace. Suppose a company can reduce the emissions below the legal standard by spending additional money. The only benefit from the expenditure would be better employee health. Ethics would require the extra expenditure; the law would not.

Another alternative occurs where the law demands certain conduct but a person's ethical standards are contrary.

International Brief

Corruption by government officials and the influence of criminal mafias are the largest impediments to the growth of the economies of several countries. Can such corruption be contained?

Consider This Example Federal law prohibits employees from hiring certain illegal alien workers. Suppose an employer advertises the availability of a job and receives no response except from a person who cannot prove he or she is a citizen of this country or does not possess a required visa. The worker and his or her family are destitute. Should the employer hire him or her? The law says no, but ethics says yes (see Exhibit 4.1).

Exhibit 4.1

Law and Ethics

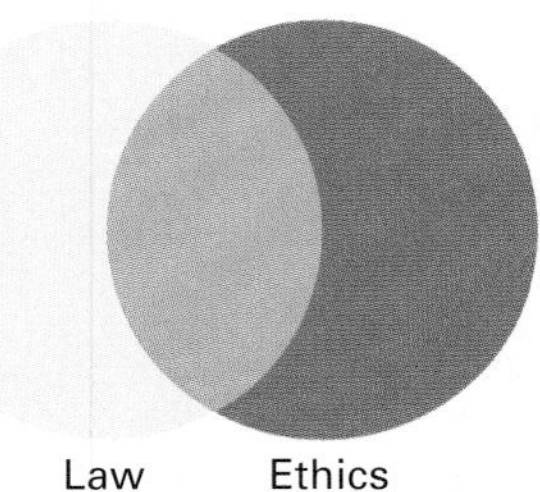

Moral Theories and Business Ethics

How can ethics be measured? The answer is very personal: What is considered ethical by one person may be considered unethical by another. However, there do seem to be some universal rules about what conduct is ethical and what conduct is not. The following discussion highlights five major theories of ethics.

> He who seeks equality must do equity.
>
> Joseph Story
> *Equity Jurisprudence (1836)*

Ethical Fundamentalism

Under **ethical fundamentalism** a person looks to an *outside source* for ethical rules or commands. This may be a book (e.g., the Bible or the Koran) or a person (e.g., Karl Marx). Critics argue that ethical fundamentalism does not permit people to determine right and wrong for themselves. Taken to an extreme, the result could be considered unethical under most other moral theories. For example, a literal interpretation of the maxim "an eye for an eye" would permit retaliation.

ethical fundamentalism
A moral theory in which a person looks to an outside source for ethical rules or commands.

Business Ethics

Enron Corporation Plunges into Bankruptcy

By the year 2000, the Enron Corporation, a Houston-based energy company, had become the sixth-largest corporation in America. Its rise to this status was meteoric, and the company's stock was trading at over $90 per share. The company's main business was brokering energy between buyers and sellers. It also engaged in building huge energy projects worldwide, as well as speculating in oil and gas futures on the world's commodities markets. Enron spread its money around by making large political campaign donations to presidential candidates and members of the U.S. Congress.

But all was not well with the corporation. Enron had created hundreds of partnerships, many located in off-shore tax havens. These partnerships were used to borrow money from banks and other creditors and to engage in speculative business dealings. Enron booked its investments and money from these partnerships as assets, but the debts of these partnerships and much of the self-dealing with and among them were not reported on Enron's consolidated financial statements. Enron executives purposefully created this maze of entities to perpetrate accounting fraud. Thus, the company looked profitable when in fact it was not. Enron was able to run this charade for years before the bubble finally burst.

In 2002, reporters and securities analysts began investigating Enron's financial empire. As rumors of Enron's "creative accounting" reached the public, the price of its stock began to fall. Many of its top executives sold their Enron shares before the

Business Ethics

(continued)

stock price plummeted. Investors who did not have inside information were not so lucky and lost their investments as the price of Enron stock tumbled to less than 50 cents per share.

The Securities and Exchange Commission (SEC), a federal government agency, announced it was investigating the Enron affair. Officers and employees at Enron began to shred thousands of documents relevant to the investigation. Andersen LLP, one of the "Big Five" accounting firms in the United States, had been Enron's auditor for years. Andersen was making between $2 million and $4 million per month, providing auditing and other services to Enron. Andersen's malpractice or fraud contributed to Enron's being able to conceal its fraud from the investing public. Several of Andersen's partners in the Houston office who were responsible for auditing Enron also shredded thousands of documents pertaining to the Enron audits. Once alerted, the court issued an injunction prohibiting the destruction of any more documents by Enron or Andersen.

In late 2002, Enron Corporation filed for Chapter 11 bankruptcy. By that time, billions of dollars of shareholder wealth had been wiped out. Enron's employees, who had their pension funds invested in Enron stock, saw their dreams of a comfortable retirement evaporate. And bondholders, banks, suppliers, and other creditors lost billions of dollars in unpaid debts. Enron was the largest company in America ever to file for bankruptcy. Some parts of it were sold to other energy companies, but the majority of its businesses were worthless. Andersen LLP unraveled, was sued criminally by the U.S. government, and eventually went out of business.

The Enron debacle is one of the grossest examples of corporate greed and fraud in America. The positive effects of the Enron fraud are that many U.S. firms cleaned up their accounting practices, shareholders and creditors became more demanding of financial data before committing funds to corporations, and the SEC became a fiercer watchdog of corporate activities. This has diminished, but not eliminated, the ability of large corporations to engage in similar fraudulent activities.

1. Did the Enron executives act ethically when they sold their stock before the Enron collapse?
2. Did the Enron executives and Andersen partners act ethically in shredding documents? ■

Utilitarianism

utilitarianism
A moral theory that dictates that people must choose the action or follow the rule that provides the greatest good to society.

The ultimate justification of the law is to be found, and can only be found, in moral considerations.

Lord MacMillan
Law and Other Things (1937)

Utilitarianism is a moral theory with origins in the works of Jeremy Bentham (1748–1832) and John Stuart Mill (1806–1873). This moral theory dictates that people must choose the actions or follow the rule that provides the *greatest good to society*. This does not mean the greatest good for the greatest number of people. For instance, if one action would increase the good of 25 people by one unit each, and an alternative action would increase the good of one person 26 units, the latter action should be taken.

Utilitarianism has been criticized because it is difficult to estimate the "good" that will result from different actions, it is hard to apply in an imperfect world, and it treats morality as if it were an impersonal mathematical calculation.

Consider This Example A company is trying to determine whether it should close an unprofitable plant located in a small community. Utilitarianism would require that the benefits to shareholders from closing the plant be compared to the benefits to employees, their families, and others in the community in keeping it open. The following special feature, "General Motors Skips Town," is such a real-life example.

Business Ethics

General Motors Skips Town

For decades, job-hungry communities have offered tax abatements, low-interest loans, and other financial incentives to induce companies to locate in their communities. Some companies take these incentives but then leave town when the incentives run out. Cities are fighting back, and many are bringing lawsuits.

Consider the case of Ypsilanti, Michigan. From 1984 to 1988, Ypsilanti gave General Motors Corporation (GM) $13 million in tax abatements to keep its Willow Run plant, which produced Chevrolet automobiles, in the city. In 1991, GM announced that it was going to close the Willow Run plant and move the work being done there to its Arlington, Texas, plant. The closure meant the loss of thousands of jobs in a city already suffering severe unemployment and financial difficulties.

Ypsilanti sued GM for reneging on its implied promise to stay put in return for the tax breaks. The trial court judge invoked a doctrine of promissory estoppel and enjoined GM from closing its plant in Ypsilanti.

The trial court judge stated, "There would be a gross inequity and patent unfairness if General Motors, having lulled the people of the Ypsilanti area into giving up millions of tax dollars which they desperately need to educate their children and provide basic governmental services, is allowed to simply decide it will desert 4,500 workers and their families because it thinks it can make these same cars cheaper somewhere else."

The Michigan court of appeals reversed, however. The appeals court held that GM made no promise to stay put in Ypsilanti as a quid pro quo for the tax abatements. The court held that any statements made by GM concerning maintaining continuous employment at the Willow Run plant were merely expressions of hope or expectation but did not amount to a promise. The court's decision permitted GM to transfer production from the Michigan plant to Texas. [*Charter Township of Ypsilanti, Michigan v. General Motors Corporation*, 506 N.W.2d 556, 1993 Mich. App. Lexis 300 (Mich. App. 1993)].

1. Did GM act ethically by attempting to close its plant in Ypsilanti? Would your answer be different if GM were losing money at the plant?
2. Which court do you think was correct, the trial court or the court of appeals?

Kantian Ethics

Immanuel Kant (1724–1804) is the best-known proponent of **duty ethics**, or **deontology** (from the Greek word *deon*, meaning duty). Kant believed that people owe moral duties that are based on *universal* rules. For example, keeping a promise to abide by a contract is a moral duty, even if that contract turns out to be detrimental to the obligated party. Kant's philosophy is based on the premise that people can use reasoning to reach ethical decisions. His ethical theory would have people behave according to the *categorical imperative* "Do unto others as you would have them do unto you."

Kantian or duty ethics
A moral theory that says that people owe moral duties that are based on universal rules, such as the categorical imperative "do unto others as you would have them do unto you."

Deontology's universal rules are based on two important principles: (1) consistency, that is, all cases are treated alike, with no exceptions, and (2) reversibility, that is, the actor must abide by the rule he or she uses to judge the morality of someone else's conduct. Thus, if you are going to make an exception for yourself, that exception becomes a universal rule that applies to all others. For example, if you rationalize that it is all right for you to engage in deceptive practices, it is all right for competitors to do so also. A criticism of Kantian ethics is that it is hard to reach a consensus as to what the universal rules should be.

Web Site
KPMG US—Business Ethics Practice This site aims to provide a place where businesspeople can turn for guidance on ethical problems that threaten their progress as well as the prosperity of their organization. Visit at **www.us.kpmg.com/ethics**.

Business Ethics

Toy Sales Not Child's Play

When a child opens a new toy, there is a 20 percent probability that the toy was purchased at a Toys "R" Us retail store; the company controls that much of the retail toy market in the United States. But Toys "R" Us did not gain this 20 percent market share by being a stuffed animal on a shelf. In fact, the Federal Trade Commission (FTC), the federal government agency empowered to protect consumers, decided that Toys "R" Us needed to be disciplined for its unruly behavior on the playground.

This company, the nation's largest toy retailer, built a reputation for being a low-cost toy seller, but it now faces price competition from warehouse clubs such as Costco and Wal-Mart. Not liking this competition, Toys "R" Us decided to bully its suppliers, the toy manufacturers. It used its dominance as a toy distributor to extract agreements from toy manufacturers to *boycott*—not sell—toys to warehouse clubs. The manufacturers that were "persuaded" to join the Toys "R" Us–sponsored boycott accounted for 40 percent of the toys sold in the United States. To police its policy, Toys "R" Us threatened to stop buying from any toy manufacturer that violated this vertical boycott. In addition, the company used its muscle to orchestrate a horizontal boycott agreement among most of these manufacturers to adhere to the restriction on toy sales to warehouse clubs and to "tattle" on one another for any violations.

The FTC investigated and found that Toys "R" Us and its reluctant collaborators unfairly stifled competition in the marketplace. The FTC held that the Toys "R" Us boycott was an unreasonable restraint of trade in violation of the federal Sherman Antitrust Act. It also ruled that the boycott caused harmful effects to consumers and to the warehouse clubs and that there was no legal business justification for this conduct. The FTC issued a *cease and desist order* that barred Toys "R" Us from entering into any agreement

Business Ethics

(continued)

with toy manufacturers to limit the supply of toys that can be sold to discount warehouse stores, and it prohibited Toys "R" Us from attempting to facilitate any agreement among its suppliers regarding the sale of toys to any retailer. [*Federal Trade Commission v. Toys "R" Us*, 221 F.3d 928, 2000 U.S. App. Lexis 18304 (7th Cir. 2000)]

1. Why did Toys "R" Us engage in such conduct? Explain.
2. Did Toys "R" Us act unfairly, or was this just good, clean competition? Did Toys "R" Us misuse its market power?
3. What would be the consequences if Toys "R" Us had gotten away with what it was doing?

Rawls's Social Justice Theory

Rawls's social justice theory
A moral theory that says each person is presumed to have entered into a social contract with all others in society to obey moral rules that are necessary for people to live in peace and harmony.

John Locke (1632–1704) and Jean-Jacques Rousseau (1712–1778) proposed a **social justice theory** of morality. Under this theory, each person is presumed to have entered into a social contract with all others in society to obey moral rules that are necessary for people to live in peace and harmony. This implied contract states, "I will keep the rules if everyone else does." These moral rules are then used to solve conflicting interests in society.

The leading proponent of the modern social justice theory is John Rawls, a contemporary philosopher at Harvard University. Under Rawls's *social justice theory*, fairness is considered the essence of justice. The principles of justice should be chosen by persons who do not yet know their station in society—thus, their "veil of ignorance" would permit the fairest possible principles to be selected. For example, the principle of equal opportunity would be promulgated by people who would not yet know if they were in a favored class. As a caveat, Rawls also proposes that the least advantaged in society must receive special assistance to allow them to realize their potential.

Rawls's theory of distributive justice is criticized for two reasons. First, establishing the blind "original position" for choosing moral principles is impossible in the real world. Second, many persons in society would choose not to maximize the benefit to the least advantaged persons in society.

Web Site

Students for Responsible Business
SRB has established a communications network that facilitates the exchange of ideas, information, and experiences both within SRB and beyond to the community at large. Visit at **www.srb.org**.

Louang-Phrabang, Laos. Under the ethical theory *ethical relativism*, individuals decide what is ethical based on their own feelings as to what is right or wrong. This differs from country to country.

Business Ethics

Sears Auto Repair Centers: Who Got the Lube Job?

Sears Roebuck & Co. is a venerable retailer at which generations of Americans have shopped for clothes, tools, appliances, and other goods and services. For years the company billed itself as the place "where Americans shop." Today, Sears auto repair centers, which generate more than $3 billion in annual sales, have been charged with being the place where Americans get robbed.

Spurred by a 50 percent increase in consumer complaints over a three-year period, several states conducted undercover investigations to determine the legitimacy of those complaints. The New Jersey Division of Consumer Affairs found that all six Sears Auto Centers visited by undercover agents recommended unnecessary repairs. The California Department of Consumer Affairs found that Sears—the largest provider of auto services in the state—had systematically overcharged an average of $223 for repairs and routinely billed for work that was not done. Forty-one other states lodged similar complaints.

The "bait-and-rip-off" scheme worked as follows: Sears would send consumers coupons advertising discounts on brake jobs. When consumers came in to redeem their coupons, the sales staff would convince them to authorize additional repairs. Sears also established quotas for repair services that its employees had to meet.

California officials got the company's attention when the state started proceedings to revoke Sears's auto repair license. Sears quickly agreed to settle all lawsuits against it. As part of the settlement, Sears agreed to distribute $50 worth of coupons to almost 1 million customers nationwide who obtained one of five specific repair services from Sears between August 1, 1990, and January 31, 1992. The coupons could be redeemed for merchandise and services at Sears stores. In addition, Sears agreed to pay $3.5 million to cover the costs of various government investigations, to contribute $1.5 million to community colleges to conduct auto mechanic training programs, and to abandon its repair service quotas. The settlement cost Sears $30 million.

In agreeing to the settlement, Sears denied any wrong-doing, simply stating that "mistakes were made." It said that it agreed to the settlement to avoid the burden, expenses, and uncertainty of prolonged litigation.

1. Did Sears act ethically in this case? Should it have admitted culpability?
2. Why do you think Sears chose to settle the cases instead of defending itself in court?
3. Do you think Sears let the "profit motive" overshadow its ethics?

Ethical Relativism

Ethical relativism holds that individuals must decide what is ethical based on their own feelings as to what is right or wrong. Under this moral theory, if a person meets his or her own moral standard in making a decision, no one can criticize him or her for it. Thus, there are no universal ethical rules to guide a person's conduct. This theory has been criticized because action that is usually thought to be unethical (e.g., committing fraud) would not be unethical if the perpetrator thought it was in fact ethical. Few philosophers advocate ethical relativism as an acceptable moral theory.

ethical relativism
A moral theory that holds that individuals must decide what is ethical based on their own feelings as to what is right or wrong.

The ethics of both the defendant and plaintiff are raised in the following case.

Case 4.1 Ethics

Bradley v. McDonald's Corporation

2003 U.S. Dist. Lexis 15202 (2003)
United States District Court, Southern District of New York

Background and Facts

McDonald's Corporation operates the largest fast food restaurant chain in the United States and the world. It produces such famous foods as the Big Mac hamburger, Chicken McNuggets, the egg McMuffin, French fries, shakes, and other foods. A McDonald's survey showed that 22% of its customers are "super heavy users," meaning that they eat at McDonald's at least 10 times or more per month. Super heavy users make up approximately 75% of McDonald's sales. The survey also found that 72% of McDonald's customers were "heavy users," meaning they ate at McDonald's at least once a week.

Jazlyn Bradley, a minor, through her father, sued McDonald's Corporation for causing her obesity and health problems associated with obesity. The complaint alleged that Bradley "consumed

Bradley v. McDonald's Corporation

2003 U.S. Dist. Lexis 15202 (2003)

United States District Court, Southern District of New York

(continued)

McDonald's foods her entire life . . . during school lunch breaks and before and after school, approximately five times per week, ordering two meals per day." Bradley was 19 years old when this case was heard by the district court.

Plaintiff Bradley sued McDonald's for violating the New York Consumer Protection Act, which prohibits deceptive and unfair acts and practices. The plaintiff alleged in Count I of her complaint that McDonald's mislead her, through its advertising campaigns and other publicity, that its food products were nutritious, of a beneficial nutritional nature, and easily part of a healthy lifestyle if consumed on a daily basis. Count II alleged that McDonald's failed to adequately disclose the fact that certain of its foods were substantially less healthy, as a result of processing and ingredient additives, than represented by McDonald's in its advertising campaigns and other publicity. The plaintiff sued on behalf of herself and a class of minors residing in New York State who purchased and consumed McDonald's products. McDonald's filed a motion with the district court to dismiss the plaintiff's complaint.

Issue

Did the plaintiff state a case against McDonald's for deceptive and unfair acts and practices in violation of the New York Consumer Protection Act?

In The Language of The Court

Sweet, District Judge It is well-known that fast food in general, and McDonald's products in particular, contain high levels of cholesterol, fat, salt and sugar, and that such attributes are bad for one. The plaintiff therefore either knew or should have known enough of the critical facts of her injury that her claims accrued upon being injured. The complaint does specify how often the plaintiff ate at McDonald's. Jazlyn Bradley is alleged to have "consumed McDonald's foods her entire life during school lunch breaks and before and after school, approximately five times per week, ordering two meals per day."

What the plaintiff has not done, however, is to address the role that a number of other factors other than diet may come to play in obesity and the health problems of which the plaintiff complains. In order to allege that McDonald's products were a significant factor in the plaintiff's obesity and health problems, the complaint must address these other variables and, if possible, eliminate them or show that a McDiet is a substantial factor despite these other variables. Similarly, with regards to plaintiff's health problems that she claims resulted from her obesity, it would be necessary to allege that such diseases were not merely hereditary or caused by environmental or other factors. Without this additional information, McDonald's does not have sufficient information to determine if its foods are the cause of the plaintiff's obesity, or if instead McDonald's foods are only a contributing factor.

Decision and Remedy

The district court granted defendant McDonald's motion to dismiss the plaintiff's complaint.

Case Questions

Critical Legal Thinking What is the purpose of consumer protection laws?

Business Ethics Do you think McDonald's has a duty to warn consumers of the dangers of eating its fast food? Do parents owe a duty to their children not to let them eat fast food too often?

Contemporary Business What would have been the effect on McDonald's and other fast food companies if the plaintiff had won her lawsuit against McDonald's? Explain.

Concept Summary Theories of Ethics

Theory	Description
Ethical fundamentalism	Persons look to an outside source (e.g., Bible or Koran) or central figure for ethical guidelines.
Utilitarianism	Persons choose the alternative that would provide the greatest good to society.
Kantian ethics	A set of universal rules establishes ethical duties. The rules are based on reasoning and require (1) consistency in application and (2) reversibility.
Rawls's social justice theory	Moral duties are based on an implied social contract. Fairness is justice. The rules are established from an original position of a "veil of ignorance."
Ethical relativism	Individuals decide what is ethical based on their own feelings as to what is right or wrong.

Business Ethics

Sarbanes-Oxley Act Prompts Public Companies to Adopt Code of Ethics

In the late 1990s and early 2000s, many large corporations in the United States were found to have engaged in massive financial frauds. Many of these frauds were perpetrated by the chief executive officer and other senior officers of the companies. Financial officers, such as the chief financial officer and controller, were also found to have been instrumental in creating these frauds. In response, Congress enacted the **Sarbanes-Oxley Act of 2002**, which makes certain conduct illegal and establishes criminal penalties for violations.

In addition, the Sarbanes-Oxley Act prompts companies to encourage senior officers of public companies to act ethically in their dealings with shareholders, employees, and other constituents. **Section 406** of the Sarbanes-Oxley Act requires a public company to disclose whether it has adopted a **Code of Ethics** for senior financial officers, including its principal financial officer and principal accounting officer. In response, public companies have adopted codes of ethics for their senior financial officers. Many public companies have included all officers and employees in the coverage of their codes of ethics.

A typical code of ethics follows.

Big Cheese Corporation
Code of Ethics

Big Cheese Corporation's mission includes the promotion of professional conduct in the practice of general management worldwide. Big Cheese's Chief Executive Officer (CEO), Chief Financial Officer (CFO), corporate Controller, and other employees of the finance organization and other employees of the corporation hold an important and elevated role in the corporate governance of the corporation. They are empowered and uniquely capable to ensure that all constituents' interests are appropriately balanced, protected, and preserved.

This Code of Ethics embodies principles to which we are expected to adhere and advocate. The CEO, CFO, finance organization employees, and other employees of the corporation are expected to abide by this Code of Ethics and all business conduct standards of the corporation relating to areas covered by this Code of Ethics. Any violatioin of the Code of Ethics may result in disciplinary action, up to and including termination of employment. All employees will:

- Act with honesty and integrity, avoiding actual or apparent conflicts of interest in their personal and professional relations.
- Provide stakeholders with information that is accurate, fair, complete, timely, objective, relevant, and understandable, including in our filings with and other submissions to the U.S. Securities and Exchange Commission.
- Comply with rules and regulations of federal, state, provincial, and local governments and other appropriate private and public regulatory agencies.
- Act in good faith, responsibly, with due care, competence, and diligence, without misrepresent-ing materials facts or allowing one's independent judgment to be subordinated.
- Respect the confidentiality of information acquired in the course of one's work, except when authorized or otherwise legally obligated to disclose. Confidential information acquired in the course of one's work will not be used for personal advantage.
- Share knowledge and maintain professional skills important and relevant to stakeholders' needs.
- Proactively promote and be an example of ethical behavior as a responsible partner among peers, in the work environment and the community.
- Achieve responsible use, control, and stewardship over all Big Cheese's assets and resources that are employed or entrusted to us.
- Not unduly or fraudulently influence, coerce, manipulate, or mislead any authorized audit or interfere with any auditor engaged in the performance of an internal or independent audit of Big Cheese's financial statements or accounting books and records.

If you are aware of any suspected or known violations of this Code of Ethics or other Big Cheese policies or guidelines, you have a duty to promptly report such concerns either to your manager, another responsible member of management, a Human Resources representative, or the Director of Compliance or the 24-hour Business Conduct Line.

If you have a concern about a questionable accounting or auditing matter and wish to submit the concern confidentially or anonymously, you may do so by sending an e-mail to (bc.codeofethics@bigcheese.cc) or calling the Business Conduct Line 24-hour number at 1-888-666-BIGC (2442).

Big Cheese will handle all inquiries discretely and make every effort to maintain, within the limits allowed by law, the confidentiality of anyone requesting guidence or reporting questionable behavior and/or a compliance concern.

It is Big Cheese's intention that this Code of Ethics to be its written code of ethics under Section 406 of the Sarbaines-Oxley Act of 2002 complying with the standards set forth in Securities and Ex-change Commission Regulation S-K Item 406.

1. Do you think the Sarbanes-Oxley Act will be effective in promoting ethical conduct by officers and directors? Explain.
2. Can ethics be mandated? In other words, will crooks still be crooks? ■

The Social Responsibility of Business

Ethics Brief

Corporations that conduct social audits will be more apt to prevent unethical and illegal conduct by managers, employees, and agents.

Business does not operate in a vacuum. Decisions made by businesses have far-reaching effects on society. In the past, many business decisions were based solely on a cost–benefit analysis and how they affected the "bottom line." Such decisions, however, may cause negative externalities for others. For example, the dumping of hazardous wastes from a manufacturing plant into a river affects the homeowners, farmers, and others who use the river's waters. Thus, corporations are considered to owe some degree of **social responsibility** for their actions. Four theories of the social responsibility of business are discussed in the following paragraphs.

International Law

Caux Round Table Principles for International Business

Recognizing that laws are necessary but insufficient guides for conduct, a group called the Caux Round Table—a collaboration of leaders from various multinational corporations—promulgated an international ethics code called the *Principles for International Business*. These principles are unique because they are based on transnational values from the East and the West: the Japanese concept of *kyosei* (living and working together for the common good) and the Western concept of the dignity of the human being. Since they were first introduced in 1994, the *Principles* have been adopted by many multinational corporations around the world.

The Caux Round Table *Principles* are:

- ***Principle 1*** *The Responsibilities of Business Beyond Shareholders Toward Stakeholders.* The value of business to society is the wealth and employment it creates and the marketable products and services it provides to consumers at a reasonable price, commensurate with quality. To create such value, a business must maintain its own economic health and viability, but survival is not a sufficient goal.

  Businesses have a role to play in improving the lives of all their customers, employees, and shareholders by sharing with them the wealth they have created. Suppliers and competitors as well should expect businesses to honor their obligations in a spirit of honesty and fairness. As responsible citizens of the local, national, regional, and global communities in which they operate, businesses share a part in shaping the future of those communities.
- ***Principle 2*** *The Economic and Social Impact of Business: Toward Innovation, Justice, and World Community.* Businesses established in foreign countries to develop, produce, or sell should also contribute to the social advancement of those countries by creating productive employment and helping to raise the purchasing power of their citizens. Businesses should also contribute to human rights, education, welfare, and vitalization of the countries in which they operate.

  Businesses should contribute to economic and social development not only in the countries in which they operate but also in the world community at large, through effective and prudent use of resources, free and fair competition, and emphasis upon innovation in technology, production methods, marketing, and communications.
- ***Principle 3*** *Business Behavior: Beyond the Letter of Law Toward a Spirit of Trust.* While accepting the legitimacy of trade secrets, businesses should recognize that sincerity, candor, truthfulness, the keeping of promises, and transparency contribute not only to their own credibility and stability but also to the smoothness and efficiency of business transactions, particularly on the international level.
- ***Principle 4*** *Respect for Rules.* To avoid trade frictions and to promote freer trade, equal conditions for competition, and fair and equitable treatment for all participants, businesses should respect international and domestic rules. In addition, they should recognize that some behavior, although legal, may still have adverse consequences.
- ***Principle 5*** *Support for Multilateral Trade.* Businesses should support the multilateral trade systems of the GATT/World Trade Organization and similar international agreements. They should cooperate in efforts to promote the progressive and judicious liberalization of trade and to relax those domestic measures that unreasonably hinder global commerce, while giving due respect to national policy objectives.
- ***Principle 6*** *Respect for the Environment.* A business should protect and, where possible, improve the environment, promote sustainable development, and prevent the wasteful use of natural resources.
- ***Principle 7*** *Avoidance of Illicit Operations.* A business should not participate in or condone bribery, money laundering, or other corrupt practices; indeed, it should seek cooperation with others to eliminate them. It should not trade in arms or other materials used for terrorist activities, drug traffic, or other organized crime. ■

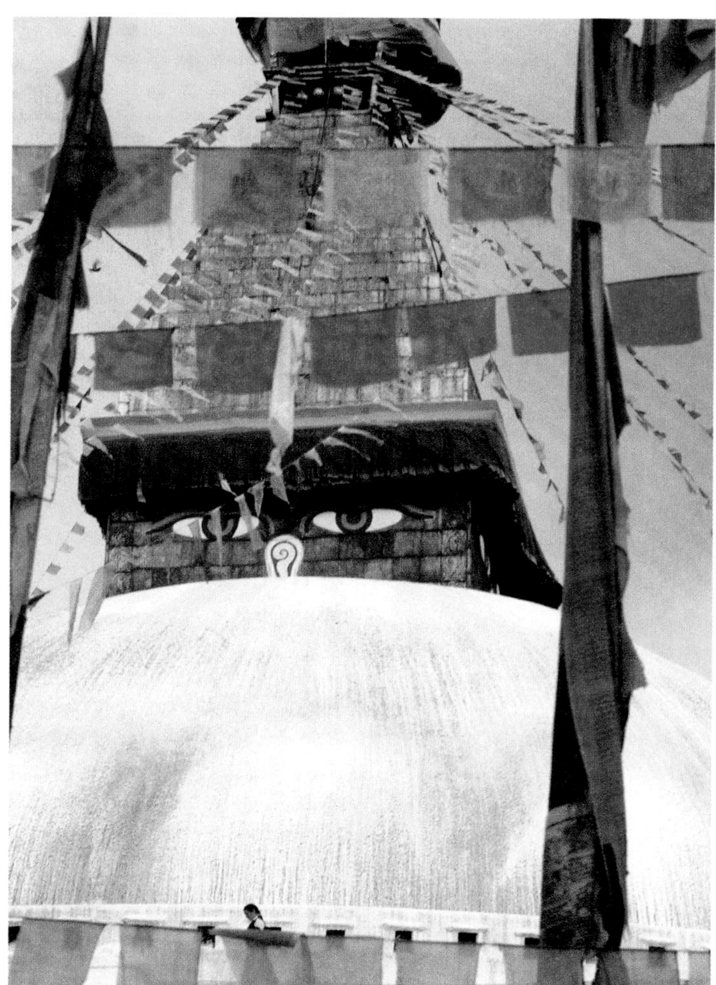

Kathmandu, Nepal. Religious principles often help shape the moral beliefs of the residents of a country.

Maximizing Profits

The traditional view of the social responsibility of business is that business should **maximize profits** for shareholders. This view, which dominated business and the law during the nineteenth century, holds that the interests of other constituencies (e.g., employees, suppliers, residents of the communities in which businesses are located) are not important in and of themselves.

maximizing profits
A theory of social responsibility that says a corporation owes a duty to take actions that maximize profits for shareholders.

In the famous case of *Dodge v. Ford Motor Company*[1] a shareholder sued the car company when Henry Ford introduced a plan to reduce the price of cars so that more people would be put to work and more people could own cars. The shareholders alleged that such a plan would not increase dividends. Mr. Ford testified, "My ambition is to employ still more men, to spread the benefits of this industrial system to the greatest number, to help them build up their lives and their homes." The court sided with the shareholders and stated that

> [Mr. Ford's] testimony creates the impression that he thinks the Ford Motor company has made too much money, has had too large profits and that, although large profits might still be earned, a sharing of them with the public, by reducing the price of the output of the company, ought to be undertaken.
>
> There should be no confusion of the duties which Mr. Ford conceives that he and the stockholders owe to the general public and the duties which in law he and his codirectors owe to protesting, minority stockholders. A business corporation is organized and carried on primarily for the profit of the stockholders. The powers

Public policy: That principle of the law which holds that no subject can lawfully do that which has a tendency to be injurious to the public or against the public good.

Lord Truro
Egerton v. Brownlow (1853)

> of the directors are to be employed for that end. The discretion of directors is to be exercised in the choice of means to attain that end and does not extend to a change in the end itself, to the reduction of profits, or to the nondistribution of profits among stockholders in order to devote them to other purposes.

Milton Friedman, who won the Nobel Prize in economics when he taught at the University of Chicago, advocated this theory. Friedman asserted that in a free society, "there is one and only one social responsibility of business—to use its resources and engage in activities designed to increase its profits as long as it stays within the rules of the game, which is to say, engages in open and free competition without deception and fraud."[2]

Business Ethics

Joe Camel Exhales

From his introduction in 1988, Joe Camel was a cartoon icon. R.J. Reynolds Tobacco Company splashed the cool camel on billboards, in magazines, and in other media across the country. Joe Camel could be seen riding motorcycles, playing pool, jamming with a jazz band, and hanging out with his female comrade, Josephine Camel. Joe and his buddies were used to promote R.J. Reynolds's Camel cigarettes.

Why would a cigarette company choose a cartoon character to advertise its cigarettes? In December 1991, San Francisco attorney Janet Mangini thought she knew when she read results of three studies that were published by the *Journal of the American Medical Association (JAMA)*. These studies concluded that the popularity of Camel cigarettes had increased 66-fold with teen smokers in the three years following the introduction of Joe Camel. Joe Camel was right up there with Mickey Mouse in recognition by children. Mangini concluded that R.J. Reynolds had gone after children and teens to promote cigarette smoking, so she decided to go after Joe Camel.

But how do you successfully sue a monolith like R.J. Reynolds? Mangini enlisted the lawyers at the five-attorney firm of Bushnell, Caplan & Fielding in San Francisco to help brainstorm the attack on R.J. Reynolds. They were aware that traditional personal-injury lawsuits against cigarette companies had not been successful, so they turned to California Business and Professional Code Section 17200 et seq., also known as the Unfair Business Practices Act. This act permits any individual to act as a private attorney general for the state of California and to file a suit against a company to halt a harmful or unfair business practice. Mangini and the small law firm knew they were in over their heads in taking on R.J. Reynolds, so they sought the help of Milberg Weiss, a large law firm in San Diego known for filing shareholder class-action lawsuits. Patrick J. Coughlin, a partner at the firm whose father was a smoker who had died of lung cancer, became interested. Milberg Weiss joined the team and agreed to shoulder 80 percent of the work. Mangini became the plaintiff. The law firms filed an unfair business practice lawsuit against R.J. Reynolds to try to eliminate Joe Camel and his cohorts.

R.J. Reynolds's first action was to try to get the case thrown out of court. The company argued that Joe Camel was protected by the Freedom of Speech Clause of the First Amendment of the U.S. Constitution and that the state law claims were preempted by the Federal Cigarette Labeling and Advertising Act, the act that requires warnings on cigarette packages. The trial court threw the case out of court, but the California supreme court reinstated the case, stating

> The targeting of minors is oppressive and unscrupulous, in that it exploits minors by luring them into an unhealthy and potentially life-threatening addiction before they have achieved the maturity necessary to make an informed decision whether to take up smoking despite its health risks.

R.J. Reynolds appealed to the U.S. Supreme Court, which declined to hear the case. With the courtroom door finally open, the real work began. The plaintiff's attorneys reviewed more than 30 million pages of documents over a five-year period. The evidence showed that R.J. Reynolds's advertising was aimed at the "youth market." Company reports outlined the importance of attracting "presmokers," aged 12 to 24, and stated that "young adult smokers are the only source of replacement smokers." R.J. Reynolds's market research reported: "Less than one third of smokers start after age 18. Only 5 percent of smokers start after age 24."

Twenty states, the U.S. Surgeon General, the American Lung Association, the American Cancer Society, and the American Heart Association backed Mangini's claim against R.J. Reynolds. Eventually, the parties entered into settlement negotiations. The plaintiff and her lawyers agreed that there was no amount of money they would accept to settle the case; Joe Camel must go! With mounting pressure and facing trial, in July 1997, R.J. Reynolds formally agreed to terminate the Joe Camel campaign across the nation. [*Mangini v. R.J. Reynolds Tobacco Company*]

1. Do you think that the Joe Camel advertising campaign was aimed at children and teenagers? Did R.J. Reynolds make a profit from children and teenage smokers? Explain.
2. Do you believe that there was a link between the advertising campaign and smoking? If there was no link, do you think that R.J. Reynolds would have spent millions of dollars on the advertising campaign?
3. Should R.J. Reynolds have been permitted to continue the Joe Camel advertising campaign under free-speech rights of the First Amendment of the U.S. Constitution? Why or why not?

Moral Minimum

Some proponents of corporate social responsibility argue that a corporation's duty is to make a profit while avoiding causing harm to others. This theory of social responsibility is called the **moral minimum**. Under this theory, as long as business avoids or corrects the social injury it causes, it has met its duty of social responsibility. For instance, a corporation that pollutes the waters and then compensates those whom it injures has met its moral minimum duty of social responsibility.

moral minimum
A theory of social responsibility that says a corporation's duty is to make a profit while avoiding harm to others.

Ethics Brief
Many people do not buy tuna because the tuna nets also catch dolphins. Is this socially responsible behavior? Should someone care about the dolphins?

The legislative and judicial branches of government have established laws that enforce the moral minimum of social responsibility on corporations. For example, occupational safety laws establish minimum safety standards for protecting employees from injuries in the workplace. Consumer protection laws establish safety requirements for products and make manufacturers and sellers liable for injuries caused by defective products. Other laws establish similar minimum standards for conduct for business in other areas.

Business Ethics

The Bhopal Disaster

On the night of December 2–3, 1984, the most tragic industrial disaster in history occurred in the city of Bhopal, state of Madhya Pradesh, Union of India. Located there was a chemical plant owned and operated by Union Carbide India Limited (UCIL), an Indian company. Most of UCIL's stock (50.9 percent) was owned by Union Carbide Corporation, a New York corporation; 22 percent was owned by the government of India; and the remainder was held by more than 23,000 Indian citizens.

The plant manufactured the pesticides Sevin and Temik. Methyl isocyanate (MIC), a highly toxic gas, is an ingredient in the production of both pesticides. On the night of the tragedy, MIC leaked from the plant in substantial quantities. The prevailing winds blew the deadly gas into the overpopulated residential areas adjacent to the plant and one of the most densely occupied areas of the city. The results were horrendous: More than 3,000 people died and more than 200,000 people suffered injuries—some serious and permanent. Livestock were killed and crops damaged. Businesses were interrupted.

The Union of India filed a consolidated complaint on behalf of all Indian claimants in the U.S. district courts in the United States. Union Carbide filed a motion with the district courts seeking dismissal of the consolidated action on the grounds of *forum non conveniens*. Union Carbide argued that the action should be transferred to a more convenient judicial forum within the Union of India pursuant to this doctrine. India opposed the motion. The court had to decide whether U.S. courts or Indian courts should hear the cases.

After permitting and reviewing extensive discovery on the issue, the district court held that the United States was a *forum non conveniens* for the purpose of suits arising from the Bhopal disaster. The court stated, "This court is firmly convinced that the Indian legal system is in a far better position than the American courts to determine the cause of the tragic event and thereby fix liability."

Litigation continued in India for more than two years. On February 14, 1989, the Supreme Court of India entered an order settling all civil claims and criminal charges arising out of the Bhopal disaster upon payment by UCIL and Union Carbide of $470 million to a fund to be administered on behalf of the claimants. The companies, declaring the settlement "just and reasonable," agreed to the terms. The Indian Parliament established a procedure for claimants to submit their claims for payment. Critics argued that the amount of the settlement was too low—less than $1,000 per claimant. [*In re Union Carbide Corporation Gas Plant Disaster at Bhopal, India, in December, 1984*, 634 F.Supp. 842, 1986 U.S. Dist. Lexis 25624 (S.D.N.Y. 1986); 809 F.2d 195, 1987 U.S. App. Lexis 1186 (2d Cir. 1987); cert. denied, 484 U.S. 871 (1987)]

1. Did Union Carbide act responsibly in fighting so hard to get the case removed from the United States?
2. Why did the Indian plaintiffs want their case heard in the United States rather than India? Is "forum-shopping" ethical conduct? ■

Stakeholder Interest

Businesses have relationships with all sorts of people other than their stockholders, including employees, suppliers, customers, creditors, and the local community. Under the **stakeholder interest** theory of social responsibility, a corporation must consider the effects its actions have on these *other stakeholders*. For example, a corporation would violate the stakeholder interest theory if it viewed employees solely as a means of maximizing stockholder wealth.

stakeholder interest
A theory of social responsibility that says a corporation must consider the effects its actions have on persons other than its stockholders.

Web Site

Business for Social Responsibility
BSR is an organization that believes that member companies can achieve long-term success by implementing policies and practices that honor high ethical standards and meet their responsibilities to all who are affected by their decisions. Visit at **www.bsr.org**.

This theory is criticized because it is difficult to harmonize the conflicting interests of stakeholders. For example, in deciding whether to close a plant, certain stakeholders may benefit (e.g., stockholders and creditors) while other stakeholders may not (e.g., current employees and the local community).

In the following case, the U.S. Supreme Court examined an award of punitive damages to punish a corporate defendant.

Case 4.2
Punitive Damages

U.S. SUPREME COURT CASE

State Farm Mutual Automobile Insurance Company v. Campbell

123 S.Ct. 1513, 2003 U.S. Lexis 2713 (2003)
Supreme Court of the United States

Background and Facts

In 1981, Curtis Campbell was driving with his wife in Utah when he decided to pass six vans traveling ahead of him on a two-lane highway. Todd Ospital, who was driving on the opposite side of the road toward Campbell, swerved to avoid a collision with Campbell and collided with an automobile driven by Robert Slusher. Ospital was killed; Slusher was rendered permanently disabled; the Campbells escaped unscathed. Early investigations determined that Campbell made an unsafe pass and had caused the crash. Ospital's heirs and Slusher sued Campbell for wrongful death and injuries, respectively. Campbell's insurance company, State Farm Mutual Automobile Insurance Company (State Farm) declined offers by Ospital's estate and Slusher to settle their claims for the insurance policy limit of $50,000 and took the case to trial. The jury determined that Campbell was 100 percent at fault and returned a judgment for $185,000.

Campbell reached a settlement with Ospital's and Slusher's attorneys whereby Campbell agreed to pursue a bad faith tort action against State Farm, and Ospital's estate and Slusher would receive 90 percent of any verdict against State Farm. One and one-half years after the initial judgment, State Farm paid all of the $185,000 judgment against Campbell, even though it exceeded the $50,000 policy limit. The bad faith tort case went to trial against State Farm in Utah trial court. At trial, evidence was introduced that State Farm had a policy to take many cases to trial even though they could be settled within the insurance policy limits. The jury held against State Farm and awarded Campbell $2.6 million in compensatory damages and $145 million in punitive damages. The trial court judge reduced compensatory damages to $1 million and punitive damages to $25 million. The Utah Supreme Court reinstated the $145 million punitive damage award. State Farm appealed to the U.S. Supreme Court.

Supreme Court Issue

Is an award of $145 million in punitive damages, where compensatory damages are $1 million, excessive and a violation of the Due Process Clause of the Fourteenth Amendment to the Constitution of the United States?

In The Language of The U.S. Supreme Court

Kennedy, Justice While States possess discretion over the imposition of punitive damages, it is well established that there are procedural and substantive constitutional limitations on these awards. The Due Process Clause of the Fourteenth Amendment prohibits the imposition of grossly excessive or arbitrary punishments on a tortfeasor. To the extent an award is grossly excessive, it furthers no legitimate purpose and constitutes an arbitrary deprivation of property. This case is neither close nor difficult. It was error to reinstate the jury's $145 million punitive damages award.

This case was used as a platform to expose, and punish, the perceived deficiencies of State Farm's operations throughout the country. The Utah Supreme Court's opinion makes explicit that State Farm was being condemned for its nationwide policies rather than for the conduct directed toward the Campbells. The Utah court awarded punitive damages to punish and deter conduct that bore no relation to the Campbells' harm. A defendant's dissimilar acts, independent from the acts upon which liability was premised, may not serve as the basis for punitive damages. A defendant should be punished for the conduct that harmed the plaintiff, not for being an unsavory individual or business. Due process does not permit courts, in the calculation of punitive damages, to adjudicate the merits of other parties' hypothetical claims against a defendant under the guise of the reprehensibility analysis, but we have no doubt the Utah Supreme Court did that here.

We have been reluctant to identify concrete constitutional limits on the ratio between harm, or potential harm, to the plaintiff and the punitive damages award. Our jurisprudence and the principles it has now established demonstrate, however, that, in practice, few awards exceeding a single-digit ratio between punitive and compensatory damages, to a significant degree, will satisfy due process. In *Pacific Mutual Life Insurance Company v. Haslip*, 499 U.S. 1, 111 S.Ct. 1032, 1991 U.S. Lexis 1306 (1991), in upholding a punitive damages award, we concluded that an award of more than four times the amount of compensatory damages might be close to the line of constitutional impropriety. We cited that 4-to-1 ratio again in *BMW of North America, Inc. v. Gore*, 517 U.S. 559, 116 S.Ct. 1589, 1996 U.S. Lexis 3390 (1996). While these ratios are not binding, they are instructive. They demonstrate what should be obvious: Single-digit multipliers are more likely to comport with due process, while still achieving the State's goals of deterrence and retribution, than awards with ratios in range of 500 to 1, or, in this case, of 145 to 1.

Nonetheless, because there are no rigid benchmarks that a punitive damages award may not surpass, ratios greater than those we have previously upheld may comport with due process where a particularly egregious act has resulted in only a small amount of economic damages. The converse is also true, however. When compensatory damages are substantial, then a lesser ratio, perhaps only equal to compensatory damages, can reach the outermost limit of the due process guarantee. The precise award in any case, of course, must be based upon the facts and circumstances of the defendant's conduct and the harm to the plaintiff.

Decision and Remedy

The U.S. Supreme Court held that an award of $145 million in punitive damages where compensatory damages were $1 million was excessive and violated the Due Process Clause of the Fourteenth Amendment to the U.S. Constitution. The U.S. Supreme Court reversed the decision of the Utah supreme court and remanded the case for proceedings consistent with the U.S. Supreme Court's opinion.

Case Questions

Critical Legal Thinking What is the purpose of punitive damages? What is the protection afforded by the Due Process Clause? Explain.

Business Ethics Did Campbell act ethically in this case? Did State Farm act ethically in this case?

Contemporary Business How important is this case for businesses? Explain.

Corporate Citizenship

The **corporate citizenship** theory of social responsibility argues that business has a *responsibility to do good.* That is, business is responsible for helping to solve social problems that it did little, if anything, to cause. For example, under this theory corporations owe a duty to subsidize schools and help educate children.

corporate citizenship
A theory of responsibility that says a business has a responsibility to do good.

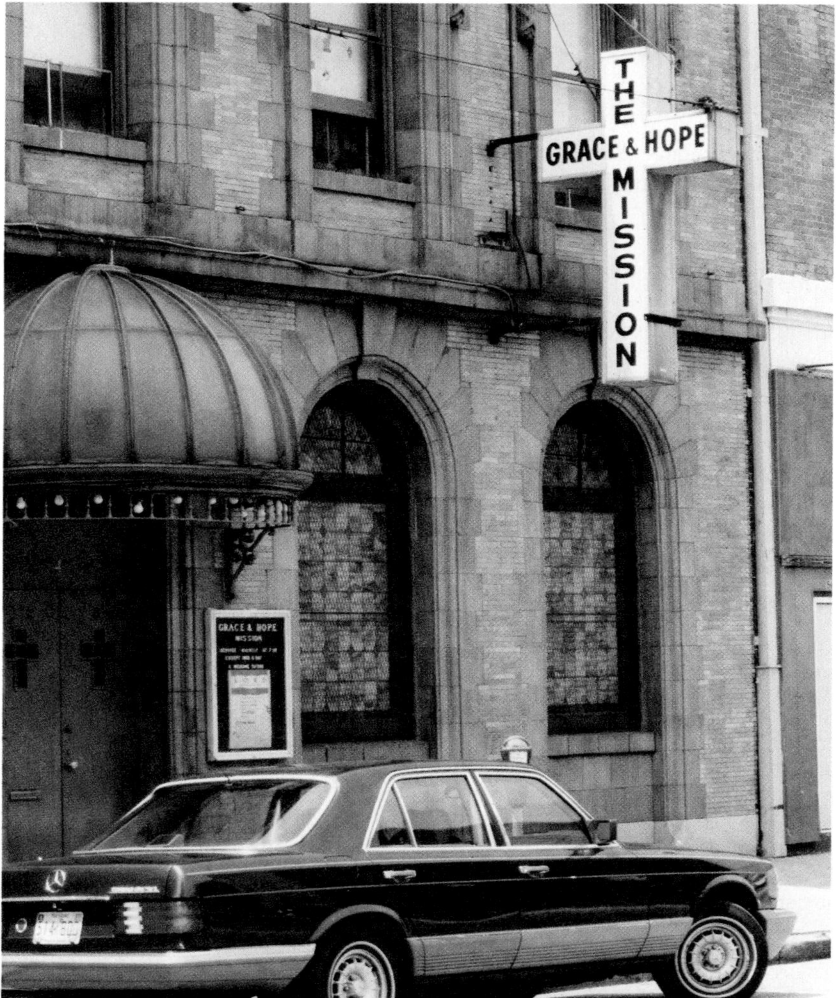

St. Louis, Missouri. The corporate citizenship theory of social responsibility states that businesses have the responsibility to do good for society.

> The notion that a business is clothed with a public interest and has been devoted to the public use is little more than a fiction intended to beautify what is disagreeable to the sufferers.
>
> Justice Holmes
> *Tyson & Bro-United Theatre Ticket Officers v. Banton (1927)*

This theory contends that corporations owe a duty to promote the same social goals as do individual members of society. Proponents of the "do good" theory argue that corporations owe a debt to society to make it a better place and that this duty arises because of the social power bestowed on them. That is, this social power is a gift from society and should be used to good ends.

A major criticism of this theory is that the duty of a corporation to do good cannot be expanded beyond certain limits. There is always some social problem that needs to be addressed, and corporate funds are limited. Further, if this theory were taken to its maximum limit, potential shareholders might be reluctant to invest in corporations.

Business Ethics

The Corporate Social Audit

It has been suggested that corporate audits should be extended to include audits of not only the financial health of a corporation but also its moral health. Corporations that conduct social audits will be more apt to prevent unethical and illegal conduct by managers, employees, and agents. The audit would examine how well employees have adhered to the company's code of ethics and how well the corporation has met its duty of social responsibility. Such audits would focus on the corporation's efforts to promote employment opportunities for members of protected classes, worker safety, environmental protection, consumer protection, and the like. Social audits are not easy. First, it may be hard to conceptualize just what is being audited. Second, it may be difficult to measure results. Despite these factors, more companies are expected to undertake social audits.

Companies should institute the following procedures when conducting a social audit:

- An independent consulting firm should be hired to conduct the social audit. This will ensure autonomy and objectivity in conducting the audit.
- The company's personnel should cooperate fully with the auditing firm while the social audit is being conducted.
- The auditing firm should report its findings directly to the company's board of directors.
- The results of the social audit should be reviewed by the board of directors.
- The board of directors should determine how the company can better meet its duty of social responsibility and can use the social audit to implement a program to correct any deficiencies it finds.

1. What are the purposes of conducting a social audit of a business?
2. Do you think that requiring social audits of businesses will increase ethical responsible behavior by those businesses?

Concept Summary *Theories of Social Responsibility*

Theory	Social Responsibility
Maximizing profits	To maximize profits for stockholders.
Moral minimum	To avoid causing harm and to compensate for harm caused.
Stakeholder interest	To consider the interests of all stakeholders, including stockholders, employees, customers, suppliers, creditors, and the local community.
Corporate citizenship	To do good and solve social problems.

Business Ethics

Nike Cleans Up Its Act in Vietnam

Nike produces basketball, running, and other athletic shoes that it sells in the United States and worldwide. For over 40 percent of the athletic shoe market, Nike has basketball great Michael Jordan as its pitchman. The majority of Nike's shoes are produced by subcontractors located in some of the poorest countries of the world. In 1997, Nike faced a public relations and ethical nightmare: It was being charged with selling shoes made by slave and child laborers who worked in horrid conditions.

In Vietnam, where Nike has 12 percent of its shoes manufactured, subcontractors worked employees eight hours per day, six days per week, and paid them as little as $40 per month in wages. These workers, who were mostly women in their twenties, worked under terrible conditions. They were subjected to hot and noisy working environments, exposed to toxic chemicals and fumes, and were mistreated by the managers. Workers were hit for not working fast enough or for talking, were made to run in stifling heat or lick the factory floor if they did not do what the managers told them to do, and were subject to sexual harassment. These conditions were brought to light not by Nike but by humanitarian organizations. After first vehemently denying the allegations, Nike backed down and agreed to improve the working conditions at the factories of its subcontractors in Vietnam.

Nike took the following steps:

- Required many managers at the subcontractors' factories to be fired for their abusive conduct.
- Reduced toxic petroleum-based compounds used in making Nike shoes.
- Banned its subcontractors from paying below Vietnam's minimum wage of $45 per month.
- Installed Nike managers in the subcontractors' plants to monitor working conditions.
- Opened the manufacturing plants to outside inspectors.

Nike states that it has taken the necessary steps to prohibit and prevent abuses by its subcontractors in Vietnam and that its decision to have its shoes made in Vietnam is an economic one. Critics contend that Nike is outsourcing the production of its shoes to workers in poor countries that do not have the same worker protections as provided in the United States. They cite the fact that Michael Jordan's payment of $25 million from Nike exceeds the wages of all 35,000 persons who work for Nike's subcontractors in Vietnam.

1. Was Nike breaching its ethical duty before instituting the work condition changes?
2. Why does Nike have its shoes manufactured in Vietnam rather than the United States?

Hue, Vietnam. Companies such as Nike have instituted inspection programs to prevent labor and employment abuses by subcontractors in foreign countries.

International Law

United Nations Code of Conduct for Transnational Corporations

Respect for National Sovereignty

Transnational corporations shall respect the national sovereignty of the countries in which they operate and the right of each state to exercise its permanent sovereignty over its natural wealth and resources. Transnational corporations should carry out their activities in conformity with the development policies, objectives and priorities set out by the governments of the countries in which they operate and work seriously toward making a positive contribution to the achievement of such goals at the national and, as appropriate, the regional level, within the framework of regional integration programs. Transnational corporations should cooperate with the governments of the countries in which they operate with a view to contributing to the development process and should be responsive to requests for consultation in this respect, thereby establishing mutually beneficial relations with these countries.

Adherence to Socio-Cultural Objectives and Values

Transnational corporations should respect the social and cultural objectives, values, and traditions of the countries in which they operate. While economic and technological development is normally accompanied by social change, transnational corporations should avoid practices, products or services which cause detrimental effects on cultural patterns and socio-cultural objectives as determined by governments. For this purpose, transnational corporations should respond positively to requests for consultations from governments concerned.

Respect for Human Rights and Fundamental Freedoms

Transnational corporations shall respect human rights and fundamental freedoms in the countries in which they operate. In their social and industrial relations, transnational corporations shall not discriminate on the basis of race, color, sex, religion, language, social, national and ethnic origin or political or other opinion. Transnational corporations shall conform to government policies designed to extend quality of opportunity and treatment.

Abstention from Corrupt Practices

Transnational corporations shall refrain, in their transactions, from the offering, promising or giving of any payment, gift or other advantage to or for the benefit of a public official as consideration for performing or refraining from the performance of his duties in connection with those transactions. ■

Chapter Summary

Moral Theories and Business Ethics, p. 93

Moral Theories

1. ***Ethical fundamentalism.*** Persons look to an outside source (e.g., Bible or Koran) or central figure to set ethical guidelines.
2. ***Utilitarianism.*** Persons choose the alternative that would provide the greatest good to society.
3. ***Kantian ethics.*** A set of universal rules establishes ethical duties. The rules are based on reasoning and require (1) consistency in application and (2) reversibility.
4. ***Rawls's social justice theory.*** Moral duties are based on an implied social contract. Fairness is justice. The rules are established from an original position of a "veil of ignorance."
5. ***Ethical relativism.*** Individuals decide what is ethical based on their own feelings of what is right or wrong.

The Social Responsibility of Business, p. 100

Theories of Social Responsibility

1. ***Maximizing profits.*** To maximize profits for shareholders.
2. ***Moral minimum.*** To make a profit and avoid harm and to compensate for harm caused.
3. ***Stakeholder interests.*** To consider the interests of stakeholders other than stockholders, such as employees, suppliers, customers, creditors, and the local community.
4. ***Corporate citizenship.*** To do good and help solve social problems.

Corporate Social Audit

Audit of a corporation by independent auditors that examines how well employees have adhered to the company's code of ethics and how well the company has met its duty of social responsibility.

Internet Exercises and Case Questions

Working the Web Internet Exercises

Activities

1. Find the list titled Baby Boomer Sports Injuries at **www.cpsc.gov**. What is the ethical duty of the companies who sell sports equipment to consumers in this age bracket?
2. Locate the Drudge Report at **www.drudgereport.com**. What is the ethical basis for the press to report on topics such as consumer fraud, arrests and trials of notorious criminals, questionable tax policies, and so on?
3. Locate and review the story on the use of torture and drugs to interrogate captured suspected terrorists at **www.alchemind.org/news/narcointerrogation1.html**. Is it constitutional? Is it ethical?

Business Ethics Cases

4.1 Business Ethics The A. H. Robins Company manufactured the Dalkon Shield, an intrauterine device used by more than 2 million women for contraception during the early 1970s. The device was defectively designed and caused women problems of infection, pelvic inflammatory disease, infertility, and spontaneous abortion, as well as health defects in their children. Thousands of product liability lawsuits were filed against the company by the women and children who were injured by the Dalkon Shield. The company and its insurers chose to fight these cases aggressively and spent many dollars in legal fees.

U.S. District Court Judge Miles Lord handled many of these cases. He called the Dalkon Shield an "instrument of death, mutilation, and disease" and chastised the executives of the company for violating "every ethical precept" of the Hippocratic oath, the medical profession's promise to save lives. Judge Lord stated,

> *Your company in the face of overwhelming evidence denies its guilt and continues its monstrous mischief. You have taken the bottom line as your guiding beacon and the low road as your route. This is corporate irresponsibility at its meanest.*

The company eventually filed for bankruptcy. The U.S. court of appeals censored Judge Lord for being too vocal. Is it ethical for a company to aggressively contest lawsuits that are filed against it even if it knows that it is responsible for the injury?

4.2 Business Ethics The Warner-Lambert company has manufactured and distributed Listerine antiseptic mouthwash since 1879. Its formula has never changed. Ever since Listerine's introduction, the company has represented it as being beneficial in preventing and curing colds and soar throats. Direct advertising of these claims to consumers began in 1921. In 1971, Warner-Lambert spent $10 million advertising these claims in print media and in television commercials.

In 1972, the FTC filed a complaint against Warner-Lambert, alleging that the company engaged in false advertising in violation of federal law. Four months of hearings held before an administrative law judge produced an evidentiary record of more than 4,000 pages of documents from 46 witnesses. In 1975, after examining the evidence, the FTC issued an opinion that held that the company's representations that Listerine prevented and cured colds and sore throats were false. The U.S. court of appeals affirmed.

Did Warner-Lambert act ethically in making its claims for Listerine? What remedy should the court impose on the company? Would making Warner-Lambert cease such advertising be sufficient? [*Warner-Lambert Company v. Federal Trade Commission*, 562 F.2d 749, 1977 U.S. App. Lexis 11599 (D.C. Cir. 1977)]

4.3 Business Ethics Stanford University is one of the premier research universities in the country. Stanford has an operating budget of approximately $400 million a year and receives about $175 million a year in direct research funding from the federal government. In addition, the government reimburses the university for certain overhead and indirect costs associated with the research. This amounts to about $85 million a year.

In 1990, a navy accountant took a close look at Stanford's books and alleged that the university may have overstated overhead and indirect costs associated with research by as much as $200 million during the 1980s. The university provides a house for its president, Donald Kennedy. Some of the expenses charged against overhead for research were (a) $3,000 for a cedar-lined closet at the president's home, (b) $4,000 for the president's 1987 wedding reception, (c) $7,000 in bed sheets and table linens, and (d) $184,000 in depreciation on a yacht donated to Stanford's sailing program. Did the administration of Stanford act ethically in charging these expenditures as overhead against research? What penalty should be assessed?

4.4 Business Ethics The Johns-Manville Corporation was a profitable company that made a variety of building and other products. It was a major producer of asbestos, which was used for insulation in buildings and for a variety of other uses. It has been medically proven that excessive exposure to asbestos causes asbestosis, a fatal lung disease. Thousands of employees of the company and consumers who were exposed to asbestos and contracted this fatal disease sued the company for damages. In 1983, the lawsuits were being filed at a rate of more than 400 per week.

As a response, the company filed for reorganization bankruptcy. It argued that if it did not, an otherwise viable company that provides thousands of jobs and serves a useful purpose in this country would be destroyed and that without the declaration of bankruptcy a few of the plaintiffs who first filed their lawsuits would win awards of hundreds of millions of dollars, leaving nothing for the remainder of the plaintiffs. Under the bankruptcy court's protection, the company was restructured to survive. As part of the release from bankruptcy, the company contributed money to a fund to pay current and future claimants. The fund is not large enough to pay all injured persons the full amount of their claims.

Was it ethical for Johns-Manville to declare bankruptcy? Did the company meet its duty of social responsibility in this case? If you were a member of the board of directors of the company, would you have voted to place the company in bankruptcy? Why or why not? [*In re Johns-Manville Corporation*, 36 B.R. 727, 1984 Bankr. Lexis 6384 (B.C. S.D.N.Y. 1984)]

4.5 Business Ethics In 1977, Reverend Leon H. Sullivan, a Baptist minister from Philadelphia who was also a member of the board of directors of General Motors Corporation, proposed a set of rules to guide American-owned companies doing business in the Republic of South Africa. The *Sullivan Principles*, as they became known, call for the nonsegregation of races in South Africa. They call for employers to (a) provide equal and fair employment practices for all employees and (b) improve the quality of employees' lives outside the work environment in such areas as housing, schooling, transportation, recreation, and health facilities. The principles also require signatory companies to report regularly and be graded on their conduct in South Africa.

Eventually, the *Sullivan Principles* were subscribed to by several hundred U.S. corporations with affiliates doing business in South Africa. Which of the following theories of social responsibility are the companies that have subscribed to the *Sullivan Principles* following?

1. Maximizing profits
2. Moral minimum
3. Stakeholder interest
4. Corporate citizenship

To put additional pressure on the government of the Republic of South Africa to end apartheid, in 1987, Reverend Sullivan called for the complete withdrawal of all U.S. companies from doing business in or with South Africa. After some companies agreed to do so, the South African government took steps to reduce and eliminate apartheid in the country. Because of these efforts, more international companies operate businesses in South Africa today. Do companies owe a social duty to withdraw from South Africa? Should universities divest themselves of investments in companies that do not withdraw from South Africa?

4.6 Business Ethics In 1974, Kaiser Aluminum & Chemical Corporation entered into a collective bargaining agreement with the United Steelworkers of America, a union that represented employees at Kaiser's plants. The agreement contained an affirmative action program to increase the representation of minorities in craft jobs. To enable plants to meet these goals, on-the-job training programs were established to teach unskilled production workers the skills necessary to become craft workers. Assignment to the training program was based on seniority, except the plan reserved 50 percent of the openings for black employees.

In 1974, 13 craft trainees were selected from Kaiser's Gramercy plant for the training program. Of these, seven were black and six white. The most senior black selected had less seniority than several white production workers who had applied for the positions but were rejected. Brian Webster, one of the rejected white employees, instituted a class action lawsuit, alleging that the affirmative action plan violated Title VII of the Civil Rights Act of 1964, which made it "unlawful to discriminate because of race" in hiring and selecting apprentices for training programs. The U.S. Supreme Court upheld the affirmative action plan in this case. The decision stated,

> *We therefore hold that Title VII's prohibition against racial discrimination does not condemn all private, voluntary, race-conscious affirmative action plans. At the same time, the plan does not unnecessarily trammel the interests of the white employees. Moreover, the plan is a temporary measure; it is not intended to maintain racial balance, but simply to eliminate a manifest racial imbalance.*

Do companies owe a duty of social responsibility to provide affirmative action programs? [*Steelworkers v. Weber*, 443 U.S. 193, 99 S.Ct. 2721, 1979 U.S. Lexis 40 (1979)]

4.7 Business Ethics Iroquois Brands, Ltd., is a Delaware corporation that had $78 million in assets, $141 million in sales, and $6 million in profits in 1984. As part of its business, Iroquois imports pâté de foie gras (goose pâté) from France and sells it in the United States. Iroquois derived only $79,000 in revenues from sales of such pâté. The French producer force-feeds the geese from which the pâté is made. Peter C. Lovenheim, who owns 200 shares of Iroquois common stock, proposed to include a shareholder proposal in Iroquois's annual proxy materials to be sent to shareholders. His proposal criticized the company because the force-feeding caused "undue stress, pain and suffering" to the geese and requested that shareholders vote to have Iroquois discontinue importing and selling pâté produced by this method.

Iroquois refused to allow the information to be included in its proxy materials. Iroquois asserted that its refusal was based on the fact that Lovenheim's proposal was "not economically significant" and had only "ethical and social" significance. The company reasoned that because corporations are economic entities, only an economic test would apply to its activities, and it was not subject to an ethical or social responsibility test. Is the company correct; that is, should only an economic test be applied in judging the activities of a corporation? Or should a corporation also be subject to an ethical or social responsibility test? [*Lovenheim v. Iroquois Brands, Ltd.*, 618 F.Supp. 554, 1985 U.S. Dist. Lexis 21259 (D.C. 1985)]

Briefing the Case Writing Assignment

Read Case A.4 in the Case Appendix [*Ramirez v. Plough, Inc.*]. This case is excerpted from the court of appeals opinion. Review and brief the case. In your brief, be sure to answer the following questions.

1. Did Plough, Inc., act ethically in participating in efforts to influence the government to reject mandatory warning labels?

2. Did the company act ethically in voluntarily providing the warning labels? How "voluntary" was its decision?

3. Does a company owe a duty of social responsibility to provide warning labels in foreign languages? If so, under what circumstances?

4. If a causal connection is shown between the use of aspirin and Reye's syndrome, would you find Plough liable for the death of the child? If so, what amount of damages would you award?

Answers to Management Decision Questions

1. You should not destroy the documents. The Sarbanes-Oxley Act of 2002 strengthened existing criminal laws relating to acts that obstruct justice, by prohibiting the destruction, mutilation, or concealment of documents in order to impede any federal investigation or proceeding—whether formal or informal, current or impending. Individuals who wrongfully destroy corporate documents face stiff fines and possible imprisonment for up to 20 years. If the defendant has reason to know an action is under consideration, liability exists, even before a federal agency has commenced a formal proceeding or investigation. State statutes also prohibit such action.

Also, it is your public duty as a citizen of the United States to refrain from the aiding and abetting of criminal activity. Criminal violations should be reported to the proper government officials.

2. A corporation acts through its board, officers, and employees. As a corporate officer, your boss has a moral obligation to act in a socially responsible manner. To expose a subordinate to possible criminal prosecution and to subject Spaulding to public ridicule and financial collapse is a violation of the fiduciary duty owed his employer and corporate stockholders. Corporations are considered to owe some degree of social responsibility for their actions. Several theories of social responsibility have developed to address this issue. They range from the maximizing profits theory, which stresses maximizing profits as the main social responsibility of corporate management, to a corporate citizenship theory of corporate responsibility that argues that business has a responsibility to do good and solve social problems.

Endnotes

1. 170 N.W. 668, 1919 Mich. Lexis 720 (MI 1919).
2. Milton Friedman, "The Social Responsibility of Business Is to Increase Its Profits," *New York Times Magazine*, September 13, 1970.

5

Negligence and Intentional Torts

"Negligence is not actionable unless it involves the invasion of a legally protected interest, the violation of a right. Proof of negligence in the air, so to speak, will not do."

—C. J. Cardozo
Palsgraf v. Long Island Railroad Co. (1928)

Chapter Objectives

After studying this chapter, you should be able to:

1. List and describe intentional torts against persons and against property.
2. List and explain the elements necessary to prove negligence.
3. Apply special negligence doctrines such as negligence per se, negligent infliction of emotional distress, and res ipsa loquitur.
4. Describe the business torts of fraud, unfair competition, and disparagement.
5. Describe and apply the doctrine of strict liability.

Chapter Contents

Management Decision Negligence and Intentional Torts

Daisy Foxx, a well-known computer programmer, designed a simulation program named Bringing Down the Big Game. The program demonstrates the procedure for choosing a high-powered rifle or gun that fits your needs and demonstrates the proper technique for using these weapons. The program is distributed by Foxx & Foxx, Inc. Charles, an acquaintance of your teenage son, purchased this program. Six months later, Charles and your son got into an argument at school. Charles, using a gun owned by his father and following the instructions shown in Bringing Down the Big Game, killed your son. You are considering filing a wrongful death lawsuit based on negligence against Daisy Foxx and Foxx & Foxx, Inc.

1. Is there any legal precedence for bringing a negligence lawsuit against Daisy Foxx and Foxx & Foxx, Inc.?
2. What legal defenses may be raised by the defendants in such a lawsuit?

Tort is the French word for a "wrong." Tort law protects a variety of injuries and provides remedies for them. Under tort law, an injured party can bring a *civil lawsuit* to seek compensation for a wrong done to the party or to the party's property. Many torts have their origin in common law. The courts and legislatures have extended tort law to reflect changes in modern society.

tort
A wrong. There are three categories of torts. (1) intentional torts, (2) unintentional torts (negligence), and (3) strict liability.

Tort damages are monetary damages that are sought from the offending party. They are intended to compensate the injured party for the injury suffered. They may consist of past and future medical expenses, loss of wages, pain and suffering, mental distress, and other damages caused by the defendant's tortious conduct. If the victim of a tort dies, his or her beneficiaries can bring a *wrongful death action* to recover damages from the defendant. *Punitive damages*, which are awarded to punish the defendant, may be recovered in intentional tort and strict liability cases. Other remedies, such as injunctions, may be available, too.

This chapter discusses various tort laws, including intentional torts, negligence, and strict liability.

Ethics Brief
Tort law imposes a duty on persons and business agents not to intentionally or negligently injure others in society.

Thoughts much too deep for tears subdue the Court When I assumpsit bring, and godlike waive a tort.

J. L. Adolphus
The Circuiteers (1885)

Pier, Santa Monica, California. Who would be liable if the roller-coaster broke, causing injury to a rider?

Intentional Torts Against Persons

The law protects a person from unauthorized touching, restraint, or other contact. In addition, the law protects a person's reputation and privacy. Violations of these rights are actionable as torts. **Intentional torts** against persons are discussed in the paragraphs that follow.

intentional tort
A category of torts that requires that the defendant possessed the intent to do the act that caused the plaintiff's injuries.

assault
(1) The threat of immediate harm or offensive contact or (2) any action that arouses reasonable apprehension of imminent harm. Actual physical contact is unnecessary.

Assault

Assault is (1) the threat of immediate harm or offensive contact or (2) any action that arouses reasonable apprehension of imminent harm. Actual physical contact is unnecessary. Threats of future harm are not actionable. For example, suppose a 6-foot-5-inch, 250-pound male makes a fist and threatens to punch a 5-foot, 100-pound woman. If the woman is afraid that the man will physically harm her, she can sue him for assault. If she is a black-belt karate champion and laughs at the threat, there is no assault because the threat does not cause any apprehension.

Battery

battery
Unauthorized and harmful or offensive physical contact with another person. Direct physical contact is not necessary.

Business Brief
Civil lawsuits allow injured victims to recover dollar damages from the responsible parties.

Battery is unauthorized and harmful or offensive physical contact with another person. Basically, the interest protected here is each person's reasonable sense of dignity and safety. For example, intentionally hitting someone is considered battery because it is harmful. Note that there does not have to be direct physical contact between the victim and the perpetrator. If an injury results, throwing a rock, shooting an arrow or a bullet, knocking off a hat, pulling a chair out from under someone, and poisoning a drink are all instances of actionable battery. The victim need not be aware of the harmful or offensive contact (e.g., it may take place while the victim is asleep). Assault and battery often occur together, although they do not have to (e.g., the perpetrator hits the victim on the back of the head without any warning).

Transferred Intent Doctrine Sometimes a person acts with the intent to injure one person but actually injures another. The *doctrine of transferred intent* applies to these situations. Under this doctrine, the law transfers the perpetrator's intent from the target to the actual victim of the act. The victim can then sue the defendant.

False Imprisonment

false imprisonment
The intentional confinement or restraint of another person without authority or justification and without that person's consent.

Business Brief
Merchant protection statutes allow merchants to stop, detain, and investigate suspected shoplifters without being held liable for false imprisonment if (1) there are reasonable grounds for the suspicion, (2) suspects are detained for only a reasonable time, and (3) investigations are conducted in a reasonable manner.

The international confinement or restraint of another person without authority or justification and without that person's consent constitutes **false imprisonment**. The victim may be restrained or confined by physical force, barriers, threats of physical harm, or the perpetrator's false assertion of legal authority (i.e., *false arrest*). A threat of future harm or moral pressure is not considered false imprisonment. The false imprisonment must be complete. For example, merely locking one door to a building when other exits are not locked is not false imprisonment. A person is not obliged to risk danger or an affront to his or her dignity by attempting to escape.

Merchant Protection Statutes Shoplifting causes substantial losses to merchants each year. Almost all states have enacted **merchant protection statutes**, also known as the **shopkeeper's privilege**. These statutes allow merchants to stop, detain, and investigate suspected shoplifters without being held liable for false imprisonment if

1. There are reasonable grounds for the suspicion.
2. Suspects are detained for only a reasonable time.
3. Investigations are conducted in a reasonable manner.

Contemporary Business Environment

Wal-Mart Shopper Wins $3.2 Million

On Christmas Eve 1995, LaShawna Goodman went to a local Wal-Mart store in Opelika, Alabama, to do some last-minute holiday shopping. She brought along her two young daughters and telephone she had purchased earlier at Wal-Mart to exchange. She presented the telephone and receipt to a Wal-Mart employee, who took the telephone. Unable to find another telephone she wanted, Goodman retrieved the previously purchased telephone from the employee, bought another item, and left. Outside, Ms. Goodman was stopped by Wal-Mart security personnel and was accused of stealing the phone. Goodman offered to show the Wal-Mart employees the original receipt, but the Wal-Mart employees detained her and called the police. Ms. Goodman was handcuffed in front of her children. Wal-Mart filed criminal charges against Ms. Goodman.

At the criminal trial, Ms. Goodman was acquitted of all charges. Now it was Ms. Goodman's turn: She filed a civil lawsuit against Wal-Mart Stores, Inc., to recover damages for falsely accusing her of stealing the telephone. She presented evidence as outlined above. Wal-Mart asserted the defense that it was within its rights to detain Ms. Goodman as it did and to prosecute Ms. Goodman based on its investigation. Wal-Mart asserted that the merchant protection statutes protected its actions in this case. Wal-Mart alleged that it had reasonable grounds to suspect Ms. Goodman of shoplifting, that it conducted the investigation in a reasonable manner, and that it had sufficient grounds to have Ms. Goodman prosecuted criminally based on its investigation.

But the jury did not accept Wal-Mart's plea that it had acted reasonably. The jury rejected Wal-Mart's defenses. The jury determined that Ms. Goodman should be awarded $200,000 in compensatory damages for her suffering. The jury then decided that Wal-Mart had acted so badly in this case that it tacked on $3 million in punitive damages in its award to Ms. Goodman just to teach Wal-Mart a lesson. The Alabama Supreme Court reduced the award of punitive damages to $600,000. [*Wal-Mart v. Goodman*, 789 So.2d 166, 2000 Ala. Lexis 548 (AL 2000)] ■

Defamation of Character

A person's reputation is a valuable asset. Therefore, every person is protected from false statements made by others during his or her lifetime. This protection ends upon a person's death. The tort of **defamation of character** requires a plaintiff to prove that (1) the defendant made an *untrue statement of fact* about the plaintiff and (2) the statement was intentionally or accidentally *published* to a third party. In this context, *publication* simply means that a third person heard or saw the untrue statement. It does not just mean appearance in newspapers, magazines, or books.

defamation of character
False statement(s) made by one person about another. In court, the plaintiff must prove that (1) the defendant made an untrue statement of fact about the plaintiff and (2) the statement was intentionally or accidentally published to a third party.

slander
Oral defamation of character.

libel
A false statement that appears in a letter, newspaper, magazine, book, photograph, movie, video, and so on.

The name for an oral defamatory statement is **slander**. A false statement that appears in a letter, newspaper, magazine, book, photograph, movie, video, and the like is called **libel**. Most courts hold that defamatory statements in radio and television broadcasts are considered libel because of the permanency of the media.

The publication of an untrue statement of fact is not the same as the publication of an opinion. The publication of opinions is usually not actionable. For example, the statement "My lawyer is lousy" is an opinion. Because defamation is defined as an untrue statement of fact, truth is an absolute defense to a charge of defamation.

Public Figures as Plaintiffs In *New York Times Co. v. Sullivan*,[1] the U.S. Supreme Court held that *public officials* cannot recover for defamation unless they can prove that the defendant acted with "actual malice." *Actual malice* means that the defendant made the false statement knowingly or with reckless disregard of its falsity. This requirement has since been extended to *public figure* plaintiffs such as movie stars, sports personalities, and other celebrities.

Landmark Law
In *New York Times Co. v. Sullivan*, the U.S. Supreme Court held that public officials cannot recover for defamation unless they can prove that the defendant acted with *actual malice*.

Misappropriation of the Right to Publicity

Each person has the exclusive legal right to control and profit from the commercial use of his or her name and personality during his or her lifetime. This is a valuable right, particularly to well-known persons such as sports figures and movie stars. Any attempt by

tort of misappropriation of the right to publicity
An attempt by another person to appropriate a living (and in some states dead) person's name or identity for commercial purposes.

another person to appropriate a living person's name or identify for commercial purposes is actionable. The wrongdoer is liable for the **tort of misappropriation of the right to publicity** (also called the **tort of appropriation**). For example, if a sportswear company were to use a picture of a star professional basketball player without his permission, this would constitute the misappropriation of the basketball star's right to publicity. In such cases, the plaintiff can (1) recover the unauthorized profits made by the offending party and (2) obtain an injunction against further unauthorized use of his or her name or identity. Many states provide that the right to publicity survives a person's death and may be enforced by the deceased's heirs.

Contemporary Business Environment

Sound-Alike Commits Tort of Misappropriation of Publicity

Tom Waits is a professional singer, songwriter, and actor of some renown. He has a raspy, gravelly singing voice, described by one fan as "like how you'd sound if you drank a quart of bourbon, smoked a pack of cigarettes, and swallowed a pack of razor blades." Waits has recorded more than 17 albums and has played to sold-out audiences throughout the United States, Canada, Europe, Japan, and Australia. Waits follows a strict personal policy against doing commercials.

When Frito-Lay, Inc., which is in the business of manufacturing, distributing, and selling prepared and packaged food products, decided to introduce a new product, SalsaRio Doritos corn chips, it hired Tracy-Locke, Inc., an advertising agency, to help develop a marketing campaign. Tracy-Locke found inspiration in a 1976 Waits song "Step Right Up." The agency wrote a commercial that echoed the rhyming word play of the Waits song. Only one problem remained: Since Waits refused to do commercials, who would sing the song in the commercial?

Tracy-Locke auditioned many singers, but none could imitate Waits's gravelly style. Finally, the agency found Stephen Carter, a professional musician who did Tom Waits imitations. Carter had performed Waits's songs as part of his band's repertoire for over 10 years, and he had perfected an imitation of Waits's voice.

The commercial, which was recorded with Frito-Lay's authorization, was broadcast on more than 250 radio stations located in 61 markets nationwide. After Waits heard the commercial during an appearance on a Los Angeles radio station, he sued Frito-Lay and Tracy-Locke. Waits claimed misappropriation of the right to publicity. The jury found in Waits's favor and awarded him $375,000 in compensatory damages and $2 million in punitive damages. The defendants appealed.

The court of appeals affirmed the judgment, holding that voice misappropriation is a form of the tort of misappropriation of the right to publicity. The court stated, "We recognize that when voice is a sufficient indicia of a celebrity's identity, the right to publicity protects against its imitation for commercial purposes without the celebrity's consent." The court found that the award of punitive damages was warranted because the defendants acted with malice and conscious disregard toward Waits by recording and broadcasting the commercial that pirated his voice.

Waits's victory made advertisers and their agencies think twice before producing "sound-alike" commercials that misappropriate a celebrity's vocal style. [*Waits v. Frito-Lay, Inc.*, 978 F.2d 1093, 1992 U.S. App. Lexis 24838 (9th Cir. 1992)] ■

Invasion of the Right to Privacy

invasion of the right to privacy
A tort that constitutes the violation of a person's right to live his or her life without being subjected to unwarranted and undesired publicity.

The law recognizes each person's right to live his or her life without being subjected to unwarranted and undesired publicity. A violation of this right constitutes the tort of **invasion of the right to privacy**. Examples of this tort include reading someone else's mail, wiretapping, and such. In contrast to defamation, the fact does not have to be untrue. Therefore, truth is not a defense to a charge of invasion of privacy. If the fact is public information, there is no claim to privacy. However, a fact that was once public (e.g., the commission of a crime) may become private after the passage of time.

Placing someone in a "false light" constitutes an invasion of privacy. For example, sending an objectionable telegram to a third party and signing another's name would place the purported sender in a false light in the eyes of the receiver. Falsely attributing beliefs or acts to another can also form the basis of a lawsuit.

Intentional Infliction of Emotional Distress

In some situations, a victim may suffer mental or emotional distress without first being physically harmed. The *Restatement (Second) of Torts* provides that a person whose *extreme and outrageous* conduct intentionally or recklessly causes severe emotional distress to another is liable for that emotional distress.[2] This is called the tort of **intentional infliction of emotional distress**, or the **tort of outrage**. The plaintiff must prove that the defendant's conduct was "so outrageous in character and so extreme in degree as to go beyond all possible bounds of decency, and to be regarded as atrocious and utterly intolerable in a civilized society."[3] An indignity, an annoyance, rough language, or an occasional inconsiderate or unkind act does not constitute outrageous behavior. However, repeated annoyances or harassment coupled with threats are considered "outrageous."

intentional infliction of emotional distress
A tort that says that a person whose extreme and outrageous conduct intentionally or recklessly causes severe emotional distress to another person is liable for that emotional distress. Also known as the *tort of outrage*.

This tort does not require any publication to a third party or physical contact between the plaintiff and defendant. For example, a credit collection agency making harassing telephone calls to a debtor every morning between 1:00 and 5:00 A.M. is outrageous conduct.

The mental distress suffered by the plaintiff must be severe. Many states require that this mental distress be manifested by some form of physical injury, discomfort, or illness, such as nausea, ulcers, headaches, or miscarriage. This requirement is intended to prevent false claims. Some states have abandoned this requirement. The courts have held that shame, humiliation, embarrassment, anger, fear, and worry constitute severe mental distress. The tort of intentional infliction of emotional distress was asserted in the following case.

Case 5.1
Intentional Infliction of Emotional Distress

Roach v. Stern
675 N.Y.S.2d 133, 1998 N.Y.App.Div. Lexis 7998 (1998)
Supreme Court, Appellate Division, New York

Background and Facts

Howard Stern is a famous television talk-show host who emcees an irreverent daily show on the radio. The show is syndicated by Infinity Broadcasting, Inc. (Infinity), and is listened to by millions of people across the country. Deborah Roach, a self-described topless dancer and cable-access television host, was a perennial guest on the Howard Stern radio show. She was famous for her stories about encounters with aliens. Roach died of a drug overdose at the age of 27. Roach's sister, Melissa Driscoll, had Roach's body cremated and gave a portion of the remains to Roach's close friend Chaunce Hayden. Driscoll said she did so with the understanding that Hayden would "preserve and honor said remains in an appropriate and private manner."

On July 18, 1995, Hayden brought a box containing Roach's cremated remains to Stern's radio show. Hayden said she did so as a memorial to Roach because "the only happiness Debbie had was the Howard Stern show." Thereafter, Stern, Hayden, and other participants in the broadcast played with Roach's ashes and made crude comments about the remains. The radio show was videotaped and later broadcast on a national cable television station. Roach's sister and brother sued Stern, Infinity, and Hayden to recover damages for intentional infliction of emotional distress. The trial court dismissed the complaint. The plaintiffs appealed.

Issue

Did the plaintiffs sufficiently plead a cause of action to cover damages for the intentional infliction of emotional distress?

In The Language of The Court

Memorandum by the Court Upon our review of the allegations in the case at bar, we conclude that the supreme court erred in determining that the element of outrageous conduct was not satisfied as a matter of law. Although the defendants contend that the conduct at issue was not particularly shocking, in light of Stern's reputation for vulgar humor and Roach's actions during her guest appearances on his program, a jury might reasonably conclude that the manner in which Roach's remains were handled, for entertainment purposes and against the express wishes of her family, went beyond the bounds of decent behavior.

Roach v. Stern

675 N.Y.S.2d 133, 1998 N.Y.App.Div. Lexis 7998 (1998)
Supreme Court, Appellate Division, New York
(continued)

Decision and Remedy

The court held that the complaint and the facts of the case as pleaded sufficiently stated a cause of action to recover damages for intentional infliction of emotional distress. Reversed.

Case Questions

Critical Legal Thinking Should the tort of intentional infliction of emotional distress be recognized by the law? What difficulties arise in trying to apply this tort?

Business Ethics Was Stern's and the other participants' conduct on the radio show tasteless? Did it amount to "outrageous conduct" for which legal damages should be awarded?

Contemporary Business If Stern and Infinity are found liable, will a chilling effect on future broadcasts result?

Entrepreneur and the Law

Liability for Frivolous Lawsuits

Entrepreneurs and others often believe they have a reason to sue someone to recover damages or other remedies. If the plaintiff has a reason to bring a lawsuit and does so, but the plaintiff does not win the lawsuit, he or she does not have to worry about being sued by the person whom he or she sued. A losing plaintiff does have to worry about being sued by the defendant in a second lawsuit for **malicious prosecution** if certain elements are met, however.

In a lawsuit for malicious prosecution, the original defendant sues the original plaintiff. In this second lawsuit, which is a *civil* action for damages, the original defendant is the plaintiff and the original plaintiff is the defendant. The courts do not look favorably on malicious prosecution lawsuits because they feel they inhibit the original plaintiff's incentive to sue. Thus, to succeed in a malicious prosecution lawsuit, the courts require the plaintiff to prove all of the following:

- The plaintiff in the original lawsuit (now the defendant) instituted or was responsible for instituting the original lawsuit.
- There was no *probable cause* for the first lawsuit; that is, it was a frivolous lawsuit.
- The plaintiff in the original action brought it with *malice*. (Caution: This is a very difficult element to prove.)
- The original lawsuit was terminated in favor of the original defendant (now the plaintiff).
- The current plaintiff suffered injury as a result of the original lawsuit.

A successful case of malicious prosecution involves proof of malicious conduct, which is an intentional tort. Therefore, punitive damages can be awarded in a malicious prosecution case. The moral of the story is simple: Make sure you have probable cause for instituting an action before bringing a lawsuit. ■

Intentional Torts Against Property

Law must be stable and yet it cannot stand still.

Roscoe Pour
Interpretations of Legal History (1929)

There are two general categories of property: real property and personal property. *Real property* consists of land and anything permanently attached to that land. *Personal property* consist of things that are movable, such as automobiles, books, clothes, pets, and such. The law recognizes certain torts against real and personal property. These torts are discussed in the paragraphs that follow.

Trespass to Land

trespass to land
A tort in which a person interferes with an owner's right to exclusive possession of land.

Interference with an owner's right to exclusive possession of land constitutes the tort of **trespass to land**. There does not have to be any interference with the owner's use or enjoyment of the land; the ownership itself is what counts. Thus, unauthorized use of another person's land is trespass, even if the owner is not using it. Actual harm to the property is not necessary.

Gitchie Manitou Shores, Upper Michigan. Trespass to land is a tort that interferes with an owner's right to exclusive possession of land. Some state laws require landowners to allow the public access to beaches.

Examples of trespass to land include entering another person's land without permission, remaining on the land of another after permission to do so has expired (e.g., a guest refuses to leave), and causing something or someone to enter another's land (e.g., one person builds a dam that causes another person's land to flood). A person who is pushed onto another's land or enters that land with good reason is not liable for trespass. For example, a person may enter onto another person's land to save a child or a pet from harm.

Trespass to and Conversion of Personal Property

The tort of **trespass to personal property** occurs whenever one person injures another person's personal property or interferes with that person's enjoyment of his or her personal property. The injured party can sue for damages. For example, breaking another's car window is trespass to personal property.

trespass to personal property
A tort that occurs whenever one person injures another person's personal property or interferes with that person's enjoyment of his or her personal property.

Depriving a true owner of the use and enjoyment of his or her personal property by taking over such property and exercising ownership rights over it constitutes the tort of **conversion of personal property**. Conversion also occurs when someone who originally is given possession of personal property fails to return it (e.g., fails to return a borrowed car). The rightful owner can sue to recover the property. If the property was lost or destroyed, the owner can sue to recover its value.

Unintentional Torts (Negligence)

Under the doctrine of **unintentional tort**, commonly referred to as **negligence**, a person is liable for harm that is the *foreseeable consequence* of his or her actions. Negligence is defined as "the omission to do something which a reasonable man would do, or doing something which a prudent and reasonable man would not do."[4]

unintentional tort or negligence
A doctrine that says a person is liable for harm that is the foreseeable consequence of his or her actions.

Consider This Example A driver who causes an automobile accident because he or she fell asleep at the wheel is liable for any resulting injuries caused by his or her negligence.

Sawtooth Mountains, Idaho. Few of us can pass one of these familiar roadside markers without thinking about the pain and suffering of the occupants of the vehicle and their surviving loved ones.

Elements of Negligence

Negligence is the omission to do something which a reasonable man would do, or doing something which a prudent and reasonable man would not do.

B. Alderson Blyth v. Brimingham Waterworks Co. *(1856)*

To be successful in a negligence lawsuit, the plaintiff must prove that (1) the defendant owed a *duty of care* to the plaintiff, (2) the defendant *breached* this duty of care, (3) the plaintiff suffered *injury*, and (4) the defendant's negligent act *caused* the plaintiff's injury. These elements are discussed in the paragraphs that follow.

duty of care
The obligation we all owe each other not to cause any unreasonable harm or risk of harm.

Duty of Care To determine whether a defendant is liable for negligence, it must first be ascertained whether the defendant owed a **duty of care** to the plaintiff. Duty of care refers to the obligation we all owe each other—that is, the duty not to cause any unreasonable harm or risk of harm. For example, each person owes a duty to drive his or her car carefully, not to push or shove on escalators, not to leave skateboards on the sidewalk, and the like. Businesses owe a duty to make safe products, not to cause accidents, and so on.

Business Brief
Domino's Pizza canceled its 30-minute delivery guarantee after juries concluded in several cases that Domino's drivers, trying to meet this deadline, negligently caused accidents.

The courts decide whether a duty of care is owed in specific cases by applying a *reasonable person standard*. Under this test, the courts attempt to determine how an *objective, careful, and conscientious person would have acted in the same circumstances* and then measure the defendant's conduct against this standard. The defendant's subjective intent ("I did not mean to do it") is immaterial in assessing liability. Certain impairments do not affect the reasonable person standard. For example, there is no reasonable alcoholic standard.

Defendants with a particular expertise or competence are measured against a *reasonable professional standard*. This standard is applied in much the same way as the reasonable person standard. For example, a brain surgeon is measured against a reasonable brain surgeon standard rather than a lower reasonable doctor standard. A child is generally required to act as a *reasonable child* of similar age and experience would act.

breach of the duty of care
A failure to exercise care or to act as a reasonable person would act.

Breach of Duty Once a court finds that the defendant actually owed the plaintiff a duty of care, it must determine whether the defendant breached his duty. A **breach of the duty of care** is the failure to exercise care. In other words, it is the failure to act as a reasonable person would act. A breach of this duty may consist of either an action (e.g., throwing a lit match on the ground in the forest and causing a fire) or a failure to act when there is a duty to act (e.g., a firefighter refusing to put out a fire). Generally, passersby are not expected to rescue others gratuitously to save them from harm.

In the following case, the court had to decide whether the defendants owed and breached a duty of care to the plaintiffs.

James v. Meow Media, Inc.

300 F.3d 683, 2002 U.S.App. Lexis 16185 (2002)
United States Court of Appeals, Sixth Circuit

Case 5.2
Duty of Care

Background and Facts

Michael Carneal was a 14-year-old freshman student at Heath High School in Paducah, Kentucky. Carneal regularly played the violent interactive video and computer games *Doom*, *Quake*, *Castle Wolfenstein*, *Rampage*, *Nightmare Creatures*, *Mech Warrior*, *Resident Evil*, and *Final Fantasy*. These games involved the player shooting virtual opponents with computer guns and other weapons. Carneal also watched videotaped movies, including one called *The Basketball Diaries* in which a high-school-student protagonist dreams of killing his teacher and several of his fellow classmates. On December 1, 1997, Carneal brought a .22-caliber pistol and five shotguns to the lobby of Heath High School and shot several of his fellow students, killing three and wounding many others. The three students killed were Jessica James, Kayce Steger, and Nicole Hadley.

The parents of the three dead children ("James") sued the producers and distributors of the violent video games and movies that Carneal had watched previous to the shooting. The parents sued to recover damages for wrongful death, alleging that the defendants were negligent in producing and distributing such games and movies to Carneal. The U.S. district court applied Kentucky law and held that the defendants did not owe or breach a duty to the plaintiffs and therefore were not liable for negligence. The plaintiffs appealed.

Issue

Did the defendant video and movie producers and distributors owe a duty of care to the plaintiffs by selling and licensing violent video games and movies to Carneal, who killed the three students?

In The Language of The Court

Boggs, Judge Kentucky courts have held that the determination of whether a duty of care exists is whether the harm to the plaintiff resulting from the defendant's negligence was "foreseeable." Kentucky courts have struggled with the formless nature of this inquiry. At bottom, Kentucky courts have conceded, deciding the existence of a duty of care is essentially a policy determination. Thus, we are called, as best we can, to implement Kentucky's duty of care analysis in this case. Our inquiry is whether the deaths of James, Steger, and Hadley were the reasonably foreseeable result of the defendants' creation and distribution of their games, movie, and Internet sites.

It appears simply impossible to predict that these games, movie, and Internet sites (alone, or in what combinations) would incite a young person to violence. Carneal's reaction to the games and movies at issue here, assuming that his violent actions were such a reaction, was simply too idiosyncratic to expect the defendants to have anticipated it. We find that it is simply too far a leap from shooting characters on a video screen (an activity undertaken by millions) to shooting people in a classroom (an activity undertaken by a handful, at most) for Carneal's actions to have been reasonably foreseeable to the manufacturers of the media that Carneal played and viewed. Carneal's reaction was not a normal reaction. Indeed, Carneal is not a normal person, but it is not utter craziness to predict that someone like Carneal is out there. Individuals are generally entitled to assume that third parties will not commit intentional criminal acts. The defendants in this case had no idea Carneal even existed, much less the particular idiosyncrasies of Carneal that made their products particularly dangerous in his hands.

Decision and Remedy

The court of appeals held that the defendant video game and movie producers and distributors did not owe a duty of care to the plaintiffs by selling and licensing violent video games and movies to Carneal, who murdered the three students.

Case Questions

Critical Legal Thinking How does the court define *foreseeability*? Did the court use a narrow, middle, or broad interpretation of foreseeability in deciding this case? Explain.

Business Ethics Do producers and distributors of video games and movies owe a duty to society not to produce and distribute violent games and movies?

Contemporary Business What would have been the consequences for the video game and movie industries if the court had held in favor of the plaintiffs? Explain.

Contemporary Business Environment

Ouch! The Coffee's Too Hot!

Studies have shown that people care less about how good their coffee tastes than whether it is hot. So restaurants, coffee shops, and other sellers make their coffee hot. McDonald's, however, discovered that it was in hot water for making its coffee *too* hot. Consider this case.

Stella Liebeck, an 81-year-old resident of Albuquerque, New Mexico, visited a drive-through window of a McDonald's restaurant with her grandson. Her grandson, the driver of the vehicle, placed the order. When it came, he handed a hot cup of coffee to Liebeck. As her grandson drove away from the drive-through

Contemporary Business Environment (continued)

window, Liebeck took the lid off the coffee cup she held in her lap. The coffee spilled all over Liebeck, who suffered third-degree burns on her legs, groin, and buttocks. She required medical treatment, was hospitalized, and suffers permanent scars from the incident.

Liebeck sued McDonald's for selling coffee that was too hot and for failing to warn her of the danger of the hot coffee it served. McDonald's rejected Liebeck's pretrial offer to settle the case for $300,000. At trial, McDonald's denied that it had been negligent and asserted that Liebeck's own negligence—opening a hot coffee cup on her lap—caused her injuries. The jury heard evidence that McDonald's enforces a quality-control rule that requires its restaurants and franchises to serve coffee at 180 to 190 degrees Fahrenheit. Evidence showed that this was 10 to 30 degrees hotter than coffee served by competing restaurant chains and approximately 40 to 50 degrees hotter than normal house-brewed coffee.

Based on this evidence, the jury concluded that McDonald's acted recklessly and awarded Liebeck $200,000 compensatory damages (reduced by $40,000 for her own negligence) and $2.7 million punitive damages. After the trial court judge reduced the amount of punitive damages to $480,000, the parties reached an out-of-court settlement for an undisclosed amount. Because of this case, McDonald's and other purveyors of coffee have reduced the temperature at which they sell coffee and have placed warnings on their coffee cups. ■

injury
Personal injury or damage that a plaintiff suffers to his or her property to recover monetary damages for the defendant's negligence.

Injury to Plaintiff Even though a defendant's act may have breached a duty of care owed to the plaintiff, this breach is not actionable unless the plaintiff suffers **injury**. For example, a business's negligence causes an explosion and fire to occur at its factory at night. No one is injured, and there is no damage to the neighbors' property. The negligence is not actionable.

The damages that are recoverable depend on the effect of the injury on the plaintiff's life or profession. Suppose two men injure their hands when a train door malfunctions. The first man is a professional basketball player. The second is a college professor. The first man can recover greater damages than the second.

In the first case that follows, the court found negligence. In the second case, the court did not find negligence.

Case 5.3 Negligence

Wal-Mart Stores, Inc. v. Frierson
818 So.2d 1135, 2002 Miss. Lexis 191 (2002)
Supreme Court of Mississippi

Background and Facts

Turner Frierson and his wife, Pinkie Mae Frierson, went to a Wal-Mart Store in Indianola, Mississippi. As the Friersons were leaving the store, Mr. Frierson slipped and fell in the vestibule of the store. Evidence showed that it had rained that afternoon and that Wal-Mart employees had left open an outside door that led to the vestibule so that Wal-Mart employees could return shopping carts to the inside of the store. Rain blew through the open door and into the vestibule, and water dripped off the shopping carts, making the tile floor slippery. Mr. Frierson sued Wal-Mart Stores, Inc., for negligence to recover injuries he suffered from the slip and fall. Mrs. Frierson sued Wal-Mart for loss of consortium caused to her because of Mr. Frierson's injuries. The jury returned a verdict awarding $100,000 to Mr. Frierson and $25,000 to Mrs. Frierson, and the court entered judgment. Wal-Mart Stores appealed, alleging that the jury's verdict was based on bias, passion, and prejudice.

Issue

Was the jury verdict in favor of the Friersons the result of the jury's bias, passion, or prejudice?

In The Language of The Court

We will first address the verdict for Pinkie Mae Frierson. Mrs. Frierson filed a claim against Wal-Mart for loss of consortium. The Legislature has provided for such a claim by statute, which reads: "A married woman shall have a cause of action for loss of consortium through negligent injury of her husband." She is entitled to society, companionship, love, affection, aid, services, support, sexual relations and the comfort of her husband as special rights and duties growing out of the marriage covenant. All of these are included in the broad term "conjugal rights." Mr. Frierson testified that he is in such pain that he sometimes watches television all night, that he cannot do things he used to be able to do, that he is in pain most of the time. Mrs. Frierson corroborated Mr. Frierson's testimony that he is in much pain and added that the pain causes him to be very irritable and that he takes it out on her. The jury could and did infer that Mr. Frierson's pain and suffering adversely affected their relationship. We affirm the verdict in favor of Mrs. Frierson, finding it was not against the overwhelming weight of the evidence or the result of bias, passion, or prejudice.

Wal-Mart asserts the $100,000 verdict in favor of Turner Frierson was against the overwhelming weight of the evidence or the result of bias, prejudice, or passion. Wal-Mart claims this is supported by the fact that Frierson's medical expenses totaled $16,574, and the jury's award is more than six times that amount. There is no fixed rule for determining damages for personal injuries. We will not disturb a jury's award of damages unless its size, in comparison to the actual amount of damages, "shocks the conscience." Frierson testified that he could not get around as much as he used to and that the pain in his back was more severe than what it was prior to the fall. He also testified that he wakes up at night. Pinkie Mae Frierson's testimony contains descriptions of Frierson's pain and suffering. The $100,000 verdict in this case does not shock the conscience of the court. We cannot say that the verdict in favor of Frierson was against the overwhelming weight of the evidence or the result of bias, passion, or prejudice.

Decision and Remedy

The Supreme Court of Mississippi found no jury bias, passion, or prejudice in reaching its verdicts, and upheld the monetary awards to both Mr. and Mrs. Frierson. Affirmed.

Case Questions

Critical Legal Thinking What are the elements of negligence? Were they found in this case? Explain.

Business Ethics Did Wal-Mart act ethically in alleging that the jury had acted with bias, passion, or prejudice?

Contemporary Business Do you think retail stores face many faked slip-and-fall cases? Is this easy to do?

Case 5.4 Negligence

Ferlito v. Johnson & Johnson Products, Inc.

771 F.Supp. 196, 1991 U.S. Dist. Lexis 11747 (1991)
U.S. District Court, E.D. Michigan

Background and Facts

Susan and Frank Ferlito were invited to a Halloween party. They decided to attend as Mary (Mrs. Ferlito) and her little lamb (Mr. Ferlito). Mrs. Ferlito constructed a lamb costume for her husband by gluing cotton batting manufactured by Johnson & Johnson Products, Inc. (JJP), to a suit of long underwear. She used the same cotton batting to fashion a headpiece, complete with ears. The costume covered Mr. Ferlito from his head to his ankles, except for his face and hands, which were blackened with paint. At the party, Mr. Ferlito attempted to light a cigarette with a butane lighter. The flame passed close to his left arm, and the cotton batting ignited. He suffered burns over one-third of his body. The Ferlitos sued JJP to recover damages, alleging that JJP failed to warn them of the ignitability of cotton batting. The jury returned a verdict for Mr. Ferlito in the amount of $555,000 and for Mrs. Ferlito in the amount of $70,000. JJP filed a motion for judgment notwithstanding the verdict (j.n.o.v.).

Issue

Should defendant JJP's motion for j.n.o.v. be granted?

In The Language of The Court

Gadola, District Judge If after reviewing the evidence, however, the trial court is of the opinion that reasonable minds could not come to the result reached by the jury, then the motion for j.n.o.v. should be granted. In this action no reasonable jury could find that JJP's failure to warn of the flammability of cotton batting was a proximate cause of plaintiffs' injuries because plaintiffs failed to offer any evidence to establish that a flammability warning on JJP's cotton batting would have dissuaded them from using the product in the manner that they did. In addition, both plaintiffs testified that they knew that cotton batting burns when it is exposed to flame.

Susan Ferlito testified that the idea for the costume was hers alone. As described on the product's package, its intended uses are for cleansing, applying medications, and infant care. Plaintiffs' showing that the product may be used on occasion in classrooms for decorative purposes failed to demonstrate the foreseeability of an adult male encapsulating himself from head to toe in cotton batting and then lighting up a cigarette.

Decision and Remedy

The trial court granted defendant JJP's motion for j.n.o.v. By doing so, the court vacated the verdict entered by the jury in favor of Mr. and Mrs. Ferlito.

Case Questions

Critical Legal Thinking Should trial courts have the authority to enter j.n.o.v., or should jury verdicts always be allowed to stand? Explain your answer.

Business Ethics Did the Ferlitos act ethically in suing JJP in this case? Were they responsible for their own injuries?

Business Applications What would have been the business implications had JJP been found liable?

causation
The act or process of causing. A person who commits a negligent act is not liable unless his or her act was the cause of the plaintiff's injuries. The two types of causation that must be proven are (1) causation in fact (actual cause) and (2) proximate cause (legal cause).

causation in fact, or actual cause
The actual cause of negligence. A person who commits a negligent act is not liable unless causation in fact can be proven.

Causation A person who commits a negligent act is not liable unless this act was the cause of the plaintiff's injuries. Courts have divided **causation** into two categories—*causation in fact* and *proximate cause*—and require each to be shown before the plaintiff may recover damages.

1. ***Causation in Fact*** The defendant's negligent act must be the **causation in fact** (or **actual cause**) of the plaintiff's injuries. For example, suppose a corporation negligently pollutes the plaintiff's drinking water. The plaintiff dies of a heart attack unrelated to the polluted water. Although the corporation has acted negligently, it is not liable for the plaintiff's death. There were a negligent act and an injury, but there was no cause-and-effect relationship between them. If, instead, the plaintiff had died from the pollution, there would have been causation in fact, and the polluting corporation would have been liable. If two (or more) persons are liable for negligently causing the plaintiff's injuries, both (or all) can be held liable to the plaintiff if each of their acts is a substantial factor in causing the plaintiff's injuries.
2. ***Proximate Cause*** Under the law, a negligent party is not necessarily liable for all damages set in motion by his or her negligent act. Based on public policy, the law establishes a point along the damage chain after which the negligent party is no longer responsible for the consequences of his or her actions. This limitation on liability is referred to as **proximate cause** (or **legal cause**). The general test of proximate cause is *foreseeability*. A negligent party who is found to be the actual cause—but not the proximate cause—of the plaintiff's injuries is not liable to the plaintiff. Situations are examined on a case-by-case basis.

proximate cause, or legal cause
A point along a chain of events caused by a negligent party after which this party is no longer legally responsible for the consequences of his or her actions.

Ethics Brief
A negligent party who is found to be the actual cause but not the proximate cause of the plaintiff's injuries is not liable.

Landmark Law
The doctrine of proximate cause was defined in the *Palsgraf v. Long Island Railroad Company* case.

The landmark case establishing the doctrine of proximate cause is *Palsgraf v. Long Island Railroad Company*.[5] Helen Palsgraf was standing on a platform, waiting for a passenger train. The Long Island Railroad Company owned and operated the trains and employed the station guards. As a man carrying a package wrapped in a newspaper tried to board the moving train, railroad guards tried to help him. In doing so, the package was dislodged from the man's arm, fell to the railroad tracks, and exploded. The package contained hidden fireworks. The explosion shook the railroad platform, causing a scale located on the platform to fall on Palsgraf, injuring her. She sued the railroad for negligence. Justice Cardoza denied her recovery, finding that the railroad was not the proximate cause of her injuries.

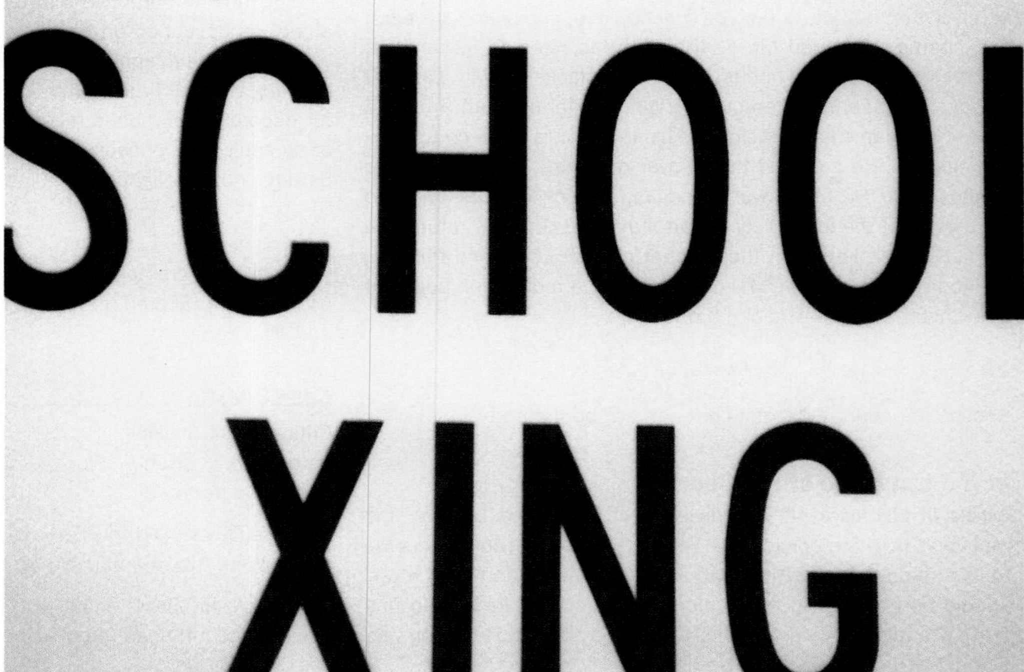

Montecito, California. Local laws reduce speed limits, and drivers owe a heightened duty of care in school zones.

Contemporary Business Environment

Is a Singer Liable When Someone Acts on His Lyrics?

Many people, particularly youths, are influenced by singers, musicians, sports figures, movie stars, and other celebrities. Some listeners, readers, or watchers will be moved to love; others to tears; some to creativity, spirituality, or fear. But what happens when a person is so moved by a song, a movie, or a book that he or she commits a crime or engages in other dangerous conduct? Is the songwriter, singer, author, scriptwriter, or movie company liable for this conduct? This question was posed to the court in *McCollum v. CBS, Inc., and Osbourne*.

John "Ozzie" Osbourne is a well-known singer of rock-and-roll music and has become a cult figure. The words and music of his songs demonstrate a preoccupation with unusual, antisocial, and even bizarre attitudes and beliefs, often emphasizing such things as satanic worship, the mocking of religious beliefs, death, and suicide. CBS Records (CBS) produced and distributed Osbourne's albums.

On Friday night, October 26, 1984, John Daniel McCollum (John) listened over and over again to certain music recorded by Osbourne. He was a 19-year-old youth who had a problem with alcohol abuse as well as serious emotional problems. John was in his bedroom, using headphones to listen to the final side of Osbourne's two-record album *Speak to the Devil* when he placed a .22 caliber handgun next to his right temple and took his own life.

One of the songs that John had been listening to was called "Suicide Solution." Three of the verses of the song stated:

> Wine is fine but whiskey's quicker
> Suicide is slow with liquor
> Take a bottle drown your sorrows
> Then it floods away tomorrows
>
> Made your bed, rest your head
> But you lie there and moan
> Suicide is the only way out
> Don't you know what it's really about
>
> Ah know people
> You really know where it's at
> You got it
> Why try, why try
> Get the gun and try it
> Shoot, shoot, shoot

John's relative, Jack McCollum, and John's estate sued Ozzie Osbourne and CBS for negligence, alleging that the lyrics of Osbourne's music incited John to commit suicide. When the trial court dismissed the action, the plaintiffs appealed. The appellate court held that although Osbourne's lyrics might have been an actual cause of John's suicide, they were not the proximate cause of the suicide. The court stated:

> John's tragic self-destruction, while listening to Osbourne's music, was not a reasonably foreseeable risk or consequence of defendant's remote artistic activities. It is simply not acceptable to a free and democratic society to impose a duty upon performing artists to limit and restrict their creativity in order to avoid the dissemination of ideas in artistic speech that may adversely affect emotionally troubled individuals. Such a burden would quickly have the effect of reducing and limiting artistic expression to only the broadest standard of taste and acceptance and the lowest level of offense, provocation, and controversy. [*McCollum v. CBS, Inc., and Osbourne*, 202 Cal.App.3d 989, 249 Cal.Rptr. 187, 1988 Cal.App. Lexis 909 (Cal.App. 1988)] ■

Negligent Infliction of Emotional Distress

Some jurisdictions have extended the tort of emotional distress to include the **negligent infliction of emotional distress.** The most common examples of this involve bystanders who witness the injury or death of a loved one that is caused by another's negligent conduct. The bystander, even though not personally physically injured, can sue the negligent party for his or her own mental suffering under this tort.

negligent infliction of emotional distress
A tort that permits a person to recover for emotional distress caused by the defendant's negligent conduct.

Generally, to be successful in this type of case, the plaintiff must prove that (1) a relative was killed or injured by the defendant, (2) the plaintiff suffered severe emotional distress, and (3) the plaintiff's mental distress resulted from a sensory and contemporaneous observance of the accident. Some states require that the plaintiff's mental distress be manifested by some physical injury; other states have eliminated this requirement.

> No court has ever given, nor do we think ever can give, a definition of what constitutes a reasonable or an average man.
>
> Lord Goddard C.J.R. v. McCarthy *(1954)*

In the following case, the plaintiff recovered damages for negligent infliction of emotional distress.

Case 5.5 Negligent Infliction of Emotional Distress

Estrada v. Aeronaves de Mexico, S.A.

967 F.2d 1421, 1992 U.S.App. Lexis 14722 (1992)

United States Court of Appeals, Ninth Circuit

Background and Facts

On the morning of August 31, 1986, Theresa Estrada left her home near Cerritos, California, to go shopping at a nearby grocery store. She left her husband at home reading the newspaper, and her three children were still in bed. Returning from the store, Estrada saw, heard, and felt a big explosion. Within minutes, she maneuvered her way through burning homes, cars, and debris to find her home engulfed in flames. Her husband and children died in the house. Although she did not know it at the time, an Aeromexico passenger airplane had crashed into her home after colliding with a privately owned plane. Estrada suffered severe emotional distress from the incident. She sued Aeromexico, the owner of the private plane, and the U.S. government for the wrongful deaths of her family members. Aeromexico was found not responsible for the accident. The jury found the private pilot 50 percent liable and the United States 50 percent liable because air traffic controllers had failed to detect the private plane's intrusion into commercial airspace and to give a traffic advisory to the Aeromexico flight. The jury awarded Estrada $5.5 million for the death of her family and $1 million for negligent infliction of emotional distress. The U.S. government appealed the $500,000 judgment against it for negligent infliction of emotional distress.

Issue

Was Estrada entitled under the law to recover damages for negligent infliction of emotional distress?

In The Language of The Court

Hug, Circuit Judge A plaintiff may recover damages for emotional distress caused by observing the negligently inflicted injury of a third person if, but only if, said plaintiff: (1) is closely related to the injury victim; (2) is present at the scene of the injury-producing event at the time it occurs and is then aware that it is causing injury to the victim; and (3) as a result suffers serious emotional distress—a reaction beyond that which would be anticipated in a disinterested witness and which is not an abnormal response to the circumstances.

Estrada clearly satisfies the first and third requirements. The second requirement is the one at issue here. The Government argues that Estrada was neither present at the scene of the injury-producing event nor aware that it was causing injury to her family. The plaintiff need not visually perceive the injury while it is being inflicted. The district court concluded that the disaster was still occurring while Mrs. Estrada was driving to her home and after she arrived to see her house in flames. The injury-producing event was the fire. The district court correctly found that Estrada knew her husband and children were being injured by the fire. Estrada understandably experienced great emotional distress as a result of watching helplessly as flames engulfed her home and burned her family to death.

Decision and Remedy

The court of appeals held that Estrada had established the elements necessary to recover damages for the negligent infliction of emotional distress.

Case Questions

Critical Legal Thinking Should the law recognize the doctrine of negligent infliction of emotional distress? Should the elements be expanded so that they are easier to meet?

Business Ethics Did the U.S. government act ethically in arguing against paying Mrs. Estrada the award assessed by the jury?

Contemporary Business What economic effects does the doctrine of negligent infliction of emotional distress have on businesses?

Professional Malpractice

professional malpractice
The liability of a professional who breaches his or her duty of ordinary care.

Professionals, such as doctors, lawyers, architects, accountants, and others, owe a duty of ordinary care in providing their services. This duty is known as the *reasonable professional standard*. A professional who breaches this duty of care is liable for the injury his or her negligence causes. This liability is commonly referred to as **professional malpractice**. For example, a doctor who amputates a wrong leg is liable for *medical malpractice*. A lawyer who fails to file a document with the court on time, causing a client's case to be dismissed, is liable for *legal malpractice*. An accountant who fails to use reasonable care, knowledge, skill, and judgment when providing auditing and other accounting services to a client is liable for *accounting malpractice*.

Professionals who breach this duty are liable to their patients or clients. They may also be liable to some third parties.

Special Negligence Doctrines

The courts have developed many *special negligence doctrines*. The most important of these are discussed in the paragraphs that follow.

> Every unjust decision is a reproach to the law or the judge who administers it. If the law should be in danger of doing injustice, then equity should be called in to remedy it. Equity was introduced to mitigate the rigour of the law.
>
> Lord Denning
> *M. R. Re Vandervell's Trusts (1974)*

Negligence Per Se

Statutes often establish duties owed by one person to another. The violation of a statute that proximately causes an injury is **negligence per se**. The plaintiff in such an action must prove that (1) a statute existed, (2) the statute was enacted to prevent the type of injury suffered, and (3) the plaintiff was within a class of persons meant to be protected by the statute.

negligence per se
A tort in which the violation of a statute or an ordinance constitutes the breach of the duty of care.

Consider This Example Most cities have an ordinance that places the responsibility for fixing public sidewalks in residential areas on the homeowners whose homes front the sidewalk. A homeowner is liable if he or she fails to repair a damaged sidewalk in front of his or her home and a pedestrian trips and is injured because of the damage. The injured party does not have to prove that the homeowner owed the duty because the statute establishes that.

Res Ipsa Loquitur

If a defendant is in control of a situation where a plaintiff has been injured and has superior knowledge of the circumstances surrounding the injury, the plaintiff might have difficulty proving the defendant's negligence. In such a situation, the law applies the doctrine of **res ipsa loquitur** (Latin for "the thing speaks for itself"). This doctrine raises a presumption of negligence and switches the burden to the defendant to prove that he or she was not negligent. *Res ipsa loquitur* applies in cases where the following elements are met:

1. The defendant had exclusive control of the instrumentality or situation that caused the plaintiff's injury.
2. The injury would not have ordinarily occurred but for someone's negligence.

res ipsa loquitur
A tort in which the presumption of negligence arises because (1) the defendant was in exclusive control of the situation and (2) the plaintiff would not have suffered injury but for someone's negligence. The burden switches to the defendant to prove that he or she was not negligent.

Consider These Examples Haeran goes in for major surgery and is given anesthesia to put her to sleep during the operation. Sometime after the operation, it is discovered that a surgical instrument was left in Haeran during the operation. She suffers severe injury because of the left-in instrument. Haeran would be hard-pressed to identify which doctor or nurse was careless and left the instrument in her body. In this case, the court can apply the doctrine of *res ipsa loquitur* and place the presumption of negligence on the defendants. Any defendant who can prove he or she did not leave the instrument in Haeran escapes liability; any defendant who does not disprove his or her negligence is liable. Other typical *res ipsa loquitur* cases involve commercial airplane crashes, falling elevators, and the like.

Good Samaritan Laws

In the past, liability exposure made many doctors, nurses, and other medical professionals reluctant to stop and render aid to victims in emergency situations, such as highway accidents. Almost all states have enacted **Good Samaritan laws** that relieve medical

Good Samaritan law
A statute that relieves medical professionals from liability for ordinary negligence when they stop and render aid to victims in emergency situations.

professionals from liability for injury caused by their ordinary negligence in such circumstances. Good Samaritan laws protect medical professionals only from liability for their *ordinary negligence*, not for injuries caused by their gross negligence or reckless or intentional conduct. Most Good Samaritan laws protect licensed doctors and nurses and laypersons who have been certified in CPR. Laypersons not trained in CPR are not generally protected by Good Samaritan statutes—that is, they are liable for injuries caused by their ordinary negligence in rendering aid.

Consider This Example Sam is injured in an automobile accident and is unconscious in his automobile alongside the road. Dr. Pamela Heathcoat, who is driving by the scene of the accident, stops, pulls Sam from the burning wreckage, and administers first aid. In doing so, Pamela negligently breaks Sam's shoulder. If Pamela's negligence is ordinary negligence, she is not liable to Sam because the Good Samaritan law protects her from liability; if Pamela was grossly negligent or reckless in administering aid to Sam, she is liable to him for the injuries she caused. It is a question of fact for the jury to decide whether a doctor's conduct was ordinary negligence or gross negligence or recklessness. If Cathy, a layperson not trained in CPR, had rendered aid to Sam and caused Sam injury because of her ordinary negligence, the Good Samaritan law would not protect her, and she would be liable to Sam.

Dram Shop Acts

Dram Shop Act
A statute that makes taverns and bartenders liable for injuries caused to or by patrons who are served too much alcohol.

Many states have enacted **Dram Shop Acts** that make a tavern and bartender civilly liable for injuries caused to or by patrons who are served too much alcohol. The alcohol must be either served in sufficient quantity to make the patron intoxicated or served to an already intoxicated person. Both the tavern and the bartender are liable to third persons injured by the patron and for injuries suffered by the patron. They are also liable for injuries caused by or to minors served by the tavern, regardless of whether the minor is intoxicated.

Guest Statutes

guest statute
A statute that provides that if a driver of a vehicle voluntarily and without compensation gives a ride to another person, the driver is not liable to the passenger for injuries caused by the driver's ordinary negligence.

Many states have enacted **guest statutes** that provide that if a driver voluntarily and without compensation gives a ride in a vehicle to another person (e.g., a hitchhiker), the driver is not liable to the passenger for injuries caused by the driver's ordinary negligence. However, if the passenger pays compensation to the driver, the driver owes a duty of ordinary care to the passenger and will be held liable. The driver is always liable to the passenger for wanton and gross negligences—for example, injuries caused because of excessive speed.

Fireman's Rule

Under the **fireman's rule**, a firefighter who is injured while putting out a fire may not sue the party whose negligence caused the fire. This rule has been extended to police officers and other government workers. The bases for this rule are (1) people might not help if they could be held liable; (2) firefighters, police officers, and other such workers receive special training for their jobs; and (3) these workers have special medical and retirement programs paid for by the public.

"Danger Invites Rescue" Doctrine

The law recognizes a **"danger invites rescue" doctrine**. Under this doctrine, a rescuer who is injured while going to someone's rescue can sue the person who caused the dangerous situation. For example, a passerby who is injured while trying to rescue children from a fire set by an arsonist can bring a civil suit against the arsonist.

"danger invites rescue" doctrine
A doctrine that provides that a rescuer who is injured while going to someone's rescue can sue the person who caused the dangerous situation.

Social Host Liability Rule

Several states have adopted the **social host liability rule**. This rule provides that a social host is liable for injuries caused by guests who are served alcohol at a social function (e.g., a birthday party, a wedding reception) and later cause injury because they are intoxicated. The injury may be to a third person or to the guest himself or herself. The alcohol served at the social function must be the cause of the injury. A few states have adopted statutes that relieve social hosts from such liability.[6]

social host liability rule
A rule that provides that social hosts are liable for injuries caused by guests who become intoxicated at a social function. States vary as to whether they have this rule in effect.

Liability of Landowners

Owners and renters of real property owe certain duties to protect visitors from injury while on the property. A landowner's and tenant's liability generally depends on the status of the visitor. Visitors fall into the following categories:

1. ***Invites and Licensees*** An *invitee* is a person who has been expressly or impliedly invited onto the owner's premises for the *mutual benefit* of both parties (e.g., guests invited for dinner, the mail carrier, customers of a business). A licensee is a person who, *for his or her own benefit*, enters onto the premises, with the express or implied consent of the owner (e.g., the Avon representative, encyclopedia salesperson, Seventh-Day Adventists). An owner owes a **duty of ordinary care** to invitees and licensees. An owner is liable if he or she negligently causes injury to an invitee or a licensee. For example, a homeowner is liable if she leaves a garden hose across the walkway on which an invitee or a licensee trips and is injured.
2. ***Trespassers*** A *trespasser* is a person who has no invitation, permission, or right to be on another's property. Burglars are a common type of trespasser. Generally, an owner does not owe a duty of ordinary care to a trespasser. For example, if a trespasser trips and injures himself on a bicycle the owner negligently left out, the owner is not liable. An owner does owe a **duty not to willfully or wantonly injure a trespasser**. Thus, an owner cannot set traps to injure trespassers.

duty of ordinary care
The duty an owner owes an invitee or a licensee to prevent injury or harm when the invitee or licensee steps on the owner's premises.

duty not to willfully or wantonly injure
The duty an owner owes a trespasser to prevent intentional injury or harm to the trespasser when the trespasser is on his or her premises.

A few states have eliminated the invitee-licensee-trespasser distinction. These states hold that owners and renters owe a duty of ordinary care to all persons who enter upon the property.

Liability of Common Carriers and Innkeepers

The common law holds common carriers and innkeepers to a higher standard of care than most other businesses. Common carriers and innkeepers owe a **duty of utmost care**—rather than a duty of ordinary care—to their passengers and guests. For example, innkeepers must provide security for their guests. The concept of utmost care is applied on a case-by-case basis. Obviously, a large hotel must provide greater security to guests than a "mom-and-pop" motel. Some states and cities have adopted specific statutes and ordinances relating to this duty.

duty of utmost care
A duty of care that goes beyond ordinary care and that says common carriers and innkeepers have a responsibility to provide security to their passengers or guests.

Grand Hotel, Mackinac Island, Michigan. An innkeeper owes a duty of utmost care to his or her guests.

Defenses Against Negligence

A defendant in a negligence lawsuit may raise several defenses to the imposition of liability. These defenses are discussed in the following paragraphs.

Superseding or Intervening Event

superseding event
An intervening event for which a defendant is not responsible.

Under negligence, a person is liable only for foreseeable events. Therefore, an original negligent party can raise a **superseding** (or **intervening**) **event** as a defense to liability. For example, assume that an avid golfer negligently hits a spectator with a golf ball, knocking the spectator unconscious. While lying on the ground waiting for an ambulance to come, the spectator is struck by a bolt of lightning and killed. The golfer is liable for the injuries caused by the golf ball. He is not liable for the death of the spectator, however, because the lightning bolt was an unforeseen intervening event.

Assumption of the Risk

assumption of the risk
A defense that a defendant can use against a plaintiff who knowingly and voluntarily enters into or participates in a risky activity that results in injury.

If a plaintiff knows of and voluntarily enters into or participates in a risky activity that results in injury, the law recognizes that the plaintiff assumed, or took on, the risk involved. Thus, the defendant can raise the defense of **assumption of the risk** against the plaintiff. This defense assumes that the plaintiff (1) had knowledge of the specific risk and (2) voluntarily assumed that risk. For example, under this theory, a race-car driver assumes the risk of being injured or killed in a crash. Assumption of the risk was raised as a defense in the following case.

Cheong v. Antablin

16 Cal. 4th 1063, 68 Cal.Rptr.2d 859, 1997 Cal. Lexis 7662 (1997)

Supreme Court of California

Case 5.6

Assumption of Risk

Background and Facts

On April 11, 1991, Wilkie Cheong and Drew R. Antablin, longtime friends and experienced skiers, skied together at Alpine Meadows, a resort near Tahoe City, California. While skiing, Antablin accidentally collided with Cheong, causing injury to him. Cheong sued Antablin to recover damages for negligent skiing. The trial court granted Antablin's motion for summary judgment, holding that the doctrine of assumption of risk barred Cheong's claim and dismissed the lawsuit. The court of appeals affirmed. Cheong appealed to the California supreme court.

Issue

Does the doctrine of assumption of risk bar recovery?

In The Language of The Court

As a general rule, persons have a duty to use due care to avoid injuring others. This general rule, however, does not apply to coparticipants in a sport, where conditions or conduct that otherwise might be viewed as dangerous often are an integral part of the sport itself. Courts should not hold a sports participant liable to a coparticipant for ordinary careless conduct committed during the sport because in the heat of an active sporting event a participant's normal energetic conduct often includes accidentally careless behavior. Vigorous participation in such sporting events likely would be chilled if legal liability were to be imposed on a participant on the basis of his or her ordinary careless conduct.

For these reasons, the general test is that a participant in an active sport breaches a legal duty of care to other participants—i.e., engages in conduct that properly may subject him or her to financial liability—only if the participant intentionally injures another player or engages in conduct that is so reckless as to be totally outside the range of the ordinary activity involved in the sport.

Decision and Remedy

The state supreme court held that the doctrine of assumption of risk barred recovery in this case.

Case Questions

Critical Legal Thinking Do you think the law should recognize the doctrine of assumption of risk: Why or why not?

Business Ethics Should Cheong have sued Antablin? Discuss.

Contemporary Business Should the doctrine of assumption of risk be applied as a defense when spectators are injured at professional sports events? Explain.

Contributory Negligence

Under the common law doctrine of **contributory negligence**, a plaintiff who is partially at fault for his or her own injury cannot recover against the negligent defendant. For example, suppose a driver who is driving over the speed limit negligently hits and injures a pedestrian who is jaywalking. Suppose the jury finds that the driver is 80 percent responsible for the accident and the jaywalker is 20 percent responsible. The pedestrian suffered $100,000 in injuries. Under the doctrine of contributory negligence, the pedestrian cannot recover any damages from the driver.

contributory negligence
A doctrine that says a plaintiff who is partially at fault for his or her own injury cannot recover against the negligent defendant.

There is one major exception to the doctrine of contributory negligence: The defendant has a duty under the law to avoid the accident if at all possible. This rule is known as the *last clear chance rule*. For example, a driver who sees a pedestrian walking across the street against a "Don't Walk" sign must avoid hitting him or her if possible. When deciding cases involving this rule, the courts consider the attentiveness of the parties and the amount of time each has to respond to the situation.

Comparative Negligence

As seen, the application of the doctrine of contributory negligence could reach an unfair result where a party only slightly at fault for his or her injuries could not recover from an otherwise negligent defendant. Many states have replaced the doctrine of contributory negligence with the doctrine of **comparative negligence**. Under this doctrine, damages are apportioned according to fault. When the comparative negligence rule is applied to the previous example, the result is much fairer. The plaintiff–pedestrian can recover 80 percent

comparative negligence
A doctrine under which damages are apportioned according to fault.

of his damages (or $80,000) from the defendant–driver. This is an example of *pure comparative negligence*. Several states have adopted *partial comparative negligence*, which provides that a plaintiff must be less than 50 percent responsible for causing his or her own injuries to recover under comparative negligence; otherwise, contributory negligence applies.

Concept Summary Contributory and Comparative Negligence Compared

Situation	Doctrine	Liability of the Defendant
Defendant liable for causing injury to plaintiff, but plaintiff partially at fault for causing his own injuries	Contributory negligence	Defendant not liable exception: Last clear chance rule
	Comparative negligence	
	1. Pure comparative negligence	Defendant liable for plaintiff's injuries according to fault
	2. Partial comparative negligence	
	a. Plaintiff less than 50 percent responsible	Defendant liable for plaintiff's injuries according to fault
	b. Plaintiff 50 percent or more responsible	Defendant not liable

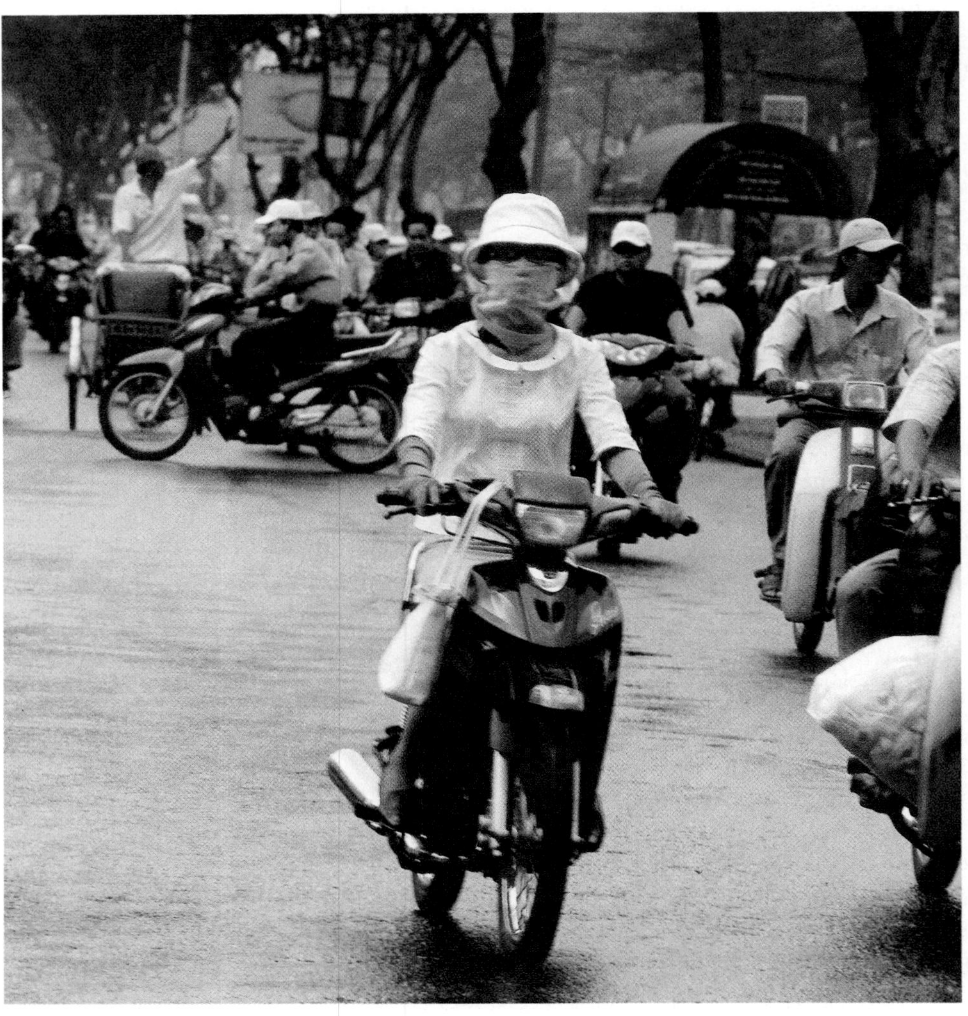

Vietnam. The tort laws of countries differ.

Special Business Torts

Although many of the torts previously discussed are committed by or against businesses, certain other torts commonly involve businesses. Several of these torts are discussed in the following paragraphs.

He that's cheated twice by the same man, is an accomplice with the Cheater.

Thomas Fuller
Gnomologia (1732)

Entering Certain Businesses and Professions Without a License

There are government restrictions and prohibitions on the freedom of entry into certain businesses and professions. These restrictions are intended to protect the public from unqualified practitioners and to promote the efficient operation of the economy.

Business Brief
A license must be obtained from the government to enter certain industries, such as banking and broadcasting, and to practice certain professions, such as law and medicine.

For example, a person cannot simply erect a television or radio transmitter and start broadcasting: The Federal Communications Commission grants television and radio station licenses for assigned frequencies. In addition, those in many occupations, such as lawyers, physicians, dentists, real estate brokers, hairdressers, and the like, must have state licenses. In some states, even palm readers and astrologists must be licensed. To obtain the necessary license, an applicant must (1) meet certain educational requirements and (2) demonstrate a certain level of proficiency in the subject matter through examination, experience, or both. Entry into these industries or professions without permission subjects the violator to various civil and criminal penalties. In many states, a licensed professional can bring an action to prevent an unlicensed person from practicing.

Unfair Competition

In most situations, competitors are free to compete vigorously, even if that means that someone is driven out of business or sustains severe losses. However, competitors may not engage in illegal **unfair competition** or **predatory practices**.

unfair competition
Competition that violates the law.

palming off
Unfair competition that occurs when a company tries to pass off one of its products as that of a rival.

The common law tort of **palming off** is one of the oldest forms of unfair competition. This tort usually occurs when one company tries to palm off its products as those of a rival. For example, if a company implied that it was affiliated with International Business Machines (IBM) by selling computers under the IBM label, it would be liable for the business tort of palming off.

To prove the tort of palming off, the plaintiff must prove that (1) the defendant used the plaintiff's logo, symbol, mark, and so on and (2) there is a likelihood of confusion as to the source of the product. Actual consumer confusion need not be shown. The key element is whether consumers are likely to be confused as to the origin of the copied product.

Disparagement

Business firms rely on their reputation and the quality of their products and services to attract and keep customers. That is why state unfair-competition laws protect businesses from disparaging statements made by competitors or others. A disparaging statement is an untrue statement made by one person or business about the products, services, property, or reputation of another business.

To prove **disparagement**, which is also called **product disparagement**, **trade libel**, or **slander of title**, the plaintiff must show that the defendant (1) made an untrue statement about the plaintiff's products, services, property, or business reputation; (2) published this untrue statement to a third party; (3) knew the statement was not true; and (4) made the statement maliciously (i.e., with intent to injure the plaintiff).

disparagement
False statements about a competitor's products, services, property, or business reputation.

The court had to decide if disparagement had occurred in the following case.

Case 5.7
Appeal

Engler v. Winfrey
201 F.3d 680, 200 U.S.App. Lexis 1723 (2000)
United States Court of Appeals, Fifth Circuit

Background and Facts

In early 1996, a disease called Mad Cow Disease was diagnosed in Britain. The disease triggers a deadly brain condition in cattle, which in turn causes degeneration and fatal brain disease in humans who eat beef from infected cattle. Oprah Winfrey hosts a popular television show in the United States, which is produced by Harpo Productions Inc., a company wholly owned by Winfrey. Producers, editors, and other employees of the Oprah Winfrey Show researched the Mad Cow Disease topic as part of a "Dangerous Foods" episode of the Oprah Winfrey Show. Guests on the show included Dr. Gary Weber, who holds a Ph.D. in animal science and represented the National Cattlemen's Beef Association; Dr. Will Hueston from the U.S. Department of Agriculture and a leading expert on Mad Cow Disease; Dr. James Miller, a physician with experience in treating individuals inflicted with the disease; and Howard Lyman, a former cattle rancher turned vegetarian and an activist for the Humane Society.

On the show, which was aired April 16, 1996, Lyman made several statements regarding the threat that Mad Cow Disease posed to people in the United States. The experts on the show countered that no case of Mad Cow Disease had been reported in the United States and explained the extensive animal testing and oversight employed by the U.S. Department of Agriculture and cattle producers to prevent Mad Cow Disease in the United States. Following the broadcast of Oprah Winfrey's "Dangerous Foods" show, the cattle market in Texas dropped drastically. In the week before the show aired, finished cattle sold for approximately $61.90 per hundredweight; After the show, the price dropped to the mid-$50s. The live cattle futures market on the Chicago Mercantile Exchange dropped within an hour of the airing of the Oprah Winfrey Show. The depressed market for finished cattle continued its slump for approximately three months after the show.

Plaintiffs Paul Engler and Cattle Feeders, Inc., filed a lawsuit against defendants Oprah Winfrey and Harpo Productions, Inc., alleging that the defendants had engaged in the intentional tort of business disparagement of the product cattle. After testimony was heard from both sides, the trial court judge submitted the following question to the jury:

> Did a named defendant publish a false, disparaging statement that was of and concerning the cattle of a plaintiff?

The trial court jury returned the answer "no" to this question, and the trial court judge entered judgment in favor of the defendants Oprah Winfrey and Harpo Productions, Inc. The plaintiffs appealed this decision to the U.S. Court of Appeals arguing that the trial court judge's business disparagement instruction was in error.

Issue

Was the trial court judge's business disparagement instruction to the jury an error that requires the case to be reversed on this issue on appeal?

In The Language of The Court

The district court submitted the plaintiffs' business disparagement claim to the jury. The jury was charged as follows:

> To recover on a claim of business disparagement, a plaintiff must prove the following:
>
> 1. That the defendant published a false, disparaging statement;
> 2. That the statement was "of and concerning" a plaintiff's specific property;
> 3. That the statement was made with knowledge of the falsity of the disparaging statement or with reckless disregard concerning its falsity, or with spite, ill will, and evil motive, or intending to interfere in the economic interests of the plaintiff in an unprivileged fashion; and
> 4. That the disparaging statement played a substantial and direct part in inducing specific damage to the business interests of the plaintiff in question.

The cattlemen challenge the district court's business disparagement instruction. This court can find no plain error in the district court's instructions regarding the business disparagement claim.

Case Questions

Critical Legal Thinking What are the elements of the doctrine of disparagement?

Business Ethics Did appellee Oprah Winfrey act ethically in airing her TV show that discussed Mad Cow Disease? Did the appellants Engler and Cattle Feeders, Inc., act ethically in suing Oprah Winfrey and her company?

Contemporary Business In reading the jury instructions, do you find them clear or confusing? Would you have been able to apply these jury instructions to decide this case?

False Advertising

Business Brief

Companies that engage in comparative advertising must be able to substantiate their claims of superiority over a rival's products or services.

Companies often engage in comparative advertising in which they compare the qualities of their products to those of competitors. Truthful comparative advertising is lawful. However, untruthful comparative advertising constitutes disparagement of product and false and misleading advertising in violation of **Section 43(a) of the Lanham Act,**[7] a federal statute.

Section 43(a) prohibits false and misleading advertising. Under this act, private parties may obtain injunctions and recover damages from competitors who make disparaging or false or misleading statements about the plaintiff's products. In the following case, the court addressed the issue of false advertising.

Case 5.8

Appeal

Pizza Hut, Inc. v. Papa John's International, Inc.

227 F.3d 489, 2000 U.S.App. Lexis 23444 (2000)

United States Court of Appeals, Fifth Circuit

Background and Facts

Pizza Hut, Inc., the largest pizza chain in the United States, operates more than 7,000 restaurants. Papa John's International, Inc., is the third-largest pizza chain in the United States, with more than 2,050 locations. In May 1995, Papa John's adopted a new slogan, "Better Ingredients. Better Pizza," and applied for and received a federal trademark for this slogan. Papa John's spent over $300 million building customer recognition and goodwill for this slogan. The slogan has appeared on millions of signs, shirts, menus, pizza boxes, napkins, and other items and has regularly appeared as the tag line at the end of Papa John's radio and television advertisements.

On May 1, 1997, Pizza Hut launched a new advertising campaign in which it declared "war" on poor-quality pizza. The advertisements touted the "better taste" of Pizza Hut's pizza and "dared" anyone to find a better pizza. A few weeks later, Papa John's launched a comparative advertising campaign that touted the superiority of Papa John's pizza over Pizza Hut's pizza. Papa John's claimed it had superior sauce and dough to Pizza Hut. Many of these advertisements were accompanied by Papa John's slogan "Better Ingredients. Better Pizza."

In 1998, Pizza Hut filed a civil action in federal district court, charging Papa John's with false advertising in violation of Section 43(a) of the federal Lanham Act. The district court found that Papa John's slogan "Better Ingredients. Better Pizza," standing alone, was mere puffery and did not constitute false advertising. The district court found, however, that Papa John's claims of superior sauce and dough were misleading and that Papa John's slogan "Better Ingredients. Better Pizza" became tainted because it was associated with these misleading statements. The district court enjoined Papa John's from using the slogan "Better Ingredients. Better Pizza." Papa John's appealed.

Issue

Is Papa John's slogan "Better Ingredients. Better Pizza" false advertising in violation of Section 43(a) of the Lanham Act?

In The Language of The Court

Essential to any claim under Section 43(a) of the Lanham Act is a determination whether the challenged statement is one of fact—actionable under Section 43(a)—or one of general opinion—not actionable under Section 43(a). One form of non-actionable statements of general opinion under Section 43(a) of the Lanham Act has been referred to as "puffery." We think that non-actionable "puffery" comes in at least two possible forms: (1) an exaggerated, blustering, and boasting statement upon which no reasonable buyer would be justified in relying; or (2) a general claim of superiority over comparable products that is so vague that it can be understood as nothing more than a mere expression of opinion. Prosser and Keeton on the *Law of Torts* (5th edition) defines "puffing" as "a seller's privilege to lie his head off, so long as he says nothing specific, on the theory that no reasonable man would believe him, or that no reasonable man would be influenced by such talk."

We turn now to consider the case before us. Reduced to its essence, the question is whether the evidence established that Papa John's slogan "Better Ingredients. Better Pizza." is misleading and violative of Section 43(a) of the Lanham Act. Bisecting the slogan "Better Ingredients. Better Pizza.," it is clear that the assertion by Papa John's that it makes a "Better Pizza." is a general statement of opinion regarding the superiority of its product over all others This simple statement, "Better Pizza.," epitomizes the exaggerated advertising, blustering and boasting by a manufacturer upon which no consumer would reasonably rely. Consequently, it appears indisputable that Papa John's assertion "Better Pizza." is non-actionable puffery.

Moving next to consider the phrase "Better Ingredients.," the same conclusion holds true. Like "Better Pizza.," it is typical puffery. The word "better," when used in this context is unquantifiable. What makes one food ingredient "better" than another comparable ingredient, without further description, is wholly a matter of individual taste or preference not subject to scientific quantification. Indeed, it is difficult to think of any product, or any component of any product, to which the term "better," without more quantifiable. Thus, it is equally clear that Papa John's assertion that it uses "Better Ingredients." is one of opinion not actionable under the Lanham Act.

Finally, turning to the combination of the two non-actionable phrases as the slogan "Better Ingredients. Better Pizza.," we fail to see how the mere joining of these two statements of opinion could create an actionable statement of fact. Each half of the slogan amounts to little more than an exaggerated opinion of superiority that no consumer would be justified in relying upon. Consequently, the slogan as a whole is a statement of non-actionable opinion. Thus, there is no legally sufficient basis to support the jury's finding that the slogan is a "false or misleading" statement of fact.

Decision and Remedy

The court of appeals held that Papa John's trademarked slogan "Better Ingredients. Better Pizza" was mere puffery and a statement of opinion that did not violate Section 43(a) of the Landham

Pizza Hut, Inc. v. Papa John's International, Inc.

227 F.3d 489, 2000 U.S.App. Lexis 23444 (2000)

United States Court of Appeals, Fifth Circuit

(continued)

Act. The court of appeals reversed the judgment of the district court and remanded the case to the district court for entry of judgment for Papa John's.

Case Questions

Critical Legal Thinking What are the elements needed to prove false advertising? Explain.

Business Ethics Do businesses sometimes make exaggerated claims about their products? Are consumers smart enough to "see through" companies' "puffery"?

Contemporary Business If the court of appeals had found in favor of Pizza Hut, what would have been the effect on advertising in this country? Explain.

Intentional Misrepresentation (Fraud)

intentional misrepresentation
The intentional deception of another person out of money, property, or something else of value.

One of the most pervasive business torts is **intentional misrepresentation.** This tort is also known as **fraud** or **deceit.** It occurs when a wrongdoer deceives another person out of money, property, or something else of value. A person who has been injured by an intentional misrepresentation can recover damages from the wrongdoer. The elements required to find fraud are

1. The wrongdoer made a false representation of material fact.
2. The wrongdoer had knowledge that the representation was false and intended to deceive the innocent party.
3. The innocent party justifiably relied on the misrepresentation.
4. The innocent party was injured.

There are some frauds so well conducted that it would be stupidity not to be deceived by them.

C. C. Colton
Lacon Vol. 1 (1820)

Item 2 above, which is called **scienter**, includes situations in which the wrongdoer recklessly disregards the truth in making a representation that is false. Intent or recklessness can be inferred from the circumstances.

Business Ethics

Used-Car Dealer Punished for Fraud

On December 11, 1992, Charles Forshey did what millions of people in this country have done—bought a used vehicle from a used-car dealership. Forshey brought two older vehicles he owned, traded them in for a value of $3,100, added some cash, and purchased a used 1983 three-quarter-ton Chevrolet Suburban truck for $5,995 from Carr Chevrolet, Inc., in Oregon. Forshey bought the vehicle "as-is," which means that the dealership disclaimed any warranties as to quality.

Shortly after the purchase, Forshey noticed that the Suburban was missing all of its emission control equipment. Through library research, he learned that the engine had a distributor coil that did not belong to the year and engine he thought he had bought. He learned later that the 1983 suburban had a 1981 engine. He also noticed that the vehicle identification number (VIN) was not on the door, transmission, or glove box. Forshey took the vehicle to an environmental agency and was told that it did not have the required smog control equipment and that the vehicle could not be brought into compliance because of the difference in age between the vehicle and the engine. Forshey conducted his own title search and found that the truck had been stolen at some previous time in California and stripped of its parts.

After discovering this information, Forshey tried to return the truck to the dealer and recover his two vehicles and the cash he paid. The dealer told Forshey that he had purchased the Suburban "as-is" and it was his problem. The dealer told Forshey that he could not have his trade-in vehicles back because they had been sold (they had not) and he could not get a refund of the

$3,100 trade-in value because the dealer would not reimburse him. Exasperated, Forshey sued the dealership for fraud.

At trial, evidence proved that the vehicle had had a rear-wheel alignment; the driver's door was misaligned, was a different color, and had been replaced; the dashboard came from a different vehicle; the VIN had been cut out of the glove box and the door; the VIN had been ground off the transmission; the engine was not the original; the odometer had been tampered with; and the truck had been heavily reconditioned. The dealership denied any knowledge of these facts, however. The trial court disagreed. The jury returned a verdict in favor of Forshey, awarded him $11,496 in compensatory damages and $1 million in punitive damages.

On appeal, the dealership argued that the "as-is" clause saved it from liability. The court of appeals rejected this argument, stating that an "as-is" clause saves a seller from being liable for normal features—that is, the engine fails because of honestly disclosed miles—but does not save a seller who concealed facts from the buyer and who has engaged in fraud. The court of appeals changed the award of punitive damages to $300,000 and awarded the plaintiff $55,468 to cover his attorney's fees. The court stated that this award would "accomplish the legitimate state interest in punishing the defendant and deterring its future misconduct." [*Forshey v. Carr Chevrolet, Inc.*, 965 P.2d 440, 1998 Ore.App. Lexis 1560 (OR 1998)]

1. How reprehensible was the dealership's conduct? Was this conduct ethical?
2. Should an "as-is" clause shield the seller from liability? Why or why not?
3. Was the award of punitive damages sufficient in this case?

Intentional Interference with Contractual Relations

A party to a contract may sue any third person who intentionally interferes with the contract and causes that party injury. The third party does not have to have acted with malice or bad faith. This tort, which is known as the tort of **intentional interference with contractual relations**, usually arises when a third party induces a contracting party to breach the contract with another party. The following elements must be shown:

intentional interference with contractual relations
A tort that arises when a third party induces a contracting party to breach the contract with another party.

1. A valid, enforceable contract between the contracting parties
2. Third-party knowledge of this contract
3. Third-party inducement to breach the contract

A third party can contract with the breaching party without becoming liable for this tort if a contracting party has already breached the contract. This is because the third party cannot be held to have induced a preexisting breach.

Breach of the Implied Covenant of Good Faith and Fair Dealing

Several states have held that a **covenant of good faith and fair dealing** is implied in certain types of contracts. Under this covenant, the parties to a contract not only are held to the express terms of the contract but also are required to act in "good faith" and deal fairly in all respects in obtaining the objective of the contract. A breach of this implied covenant is a tort for which tort damages are recoverable. This tort, which is sometimes referred to as the **tort of "bad faith"** is an evolving area of the law.

covenant of good faith and fair dealing
Under this implied covenant, the parties to a contract not only are held to the express terms of the contract but also are required to act in "good faith" and deal fairly in all respects in obtaining the objective of the contract.

Punitive Damages

Generally, **punitive damages** are not recoverable for breach of contract. They are recoverable, however, for certain *tortious* conduct. This includes fraud, intentional conduct, and other egregious conduct. Punitive damages are in addition to actual damages and may be kept by the plaintiff. Punitive damages are awarded to punish the defendant, to deter the defendant from similar conduct in the future, and to set an example for others.

punitive damages
Damages that are awarded to punish the defendant, to deter the defendant from similar conduct in the future, and to set an example for others.

The court found interference with a contract in the following case and awarded punitive damages.

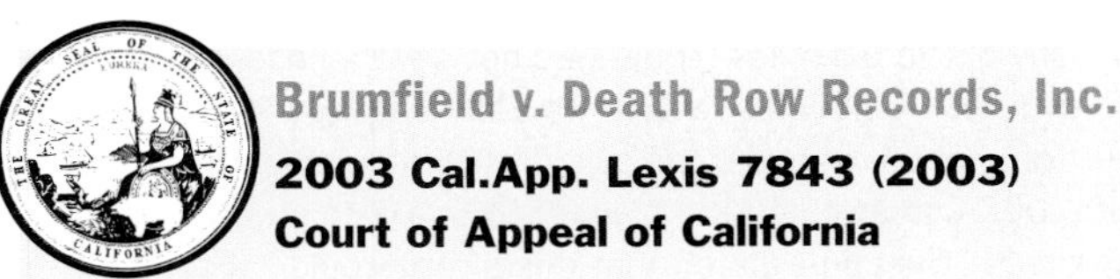

Brumfield v. Death Row Records, Inc.

2003 Cal.App. Lexis 7843 (2003)

Court of Appeal of California

Case 5.9

Intentional Interference with a Contract

Background and Facts

Ricardo E. Brown, Jr., known as "Kurupt," was an unknown teenage rap singer who lived with his father. In 1989, Lamont Brumfield, a promoter of young rappers, "discovered" Kurupt. Lamont introduced his brother Kenneth Brumfield, who owned a music publishing business, to Kurupt. Beginning in 1990, Lamont produced demos for Kurupt, set up photo shoots, booked him to sing at many clubs, and paid for Kurupt's clothing and personal and living expenses. Kurupt lived with Lamont after Kurupt's father kicked him out of the house. In 1991, Lamont obtained recording work for Kurupt with the rap group SOS. In November 1991, Kurupt signed an exclusive recording agreement with Lamont's company, an exclusive publishing agreement with Kenneth's company, and a management agreement with Kenneth for an initial term of three years with an additional option term. These contracts gave Kurupt 7% royalties on sales. The Brumfields spent at least $65,000 to support and promote Kurupt, often borrowing money from family and friends to do so.

Andre Young, known as Dr. Dre, invited Lamont, Kenneth, and Kurupt to a picnic where he introduced them to Marion Knight, the owner of Death Row Records, Inc. The Brumfields and Kurupt made it clear to Dr. Dre and Knight that the Brumfields had exclusive contracts with Kurupt. After Kurupt performed at the picnic, Dr. Dre invited Kurupt to his house to record songs for Dr. Dre's album *Chronic*. In December 1992, *Chronic* was released by Death Row Records, Inc. and sold millions of albums. The Brumfields continued to promote Kurupt and to take care of his living expenses. When Dr. Dre invited Kurupt to go on tour to promote the *Chronic* album, Kurupt told the Brumfields that he was going to visit family in Philadelphia but instead went on tour for four weeks. In 1993, Kurupt worked on another Death Row Records album. In May 1994, Kenneth exercised his option and renewed his management agreement with Kurupt. Despite the multimillion-dollar profit of the *Chronic* album, the Brumfields were aid nothing by Death Row Records. At the end of 1994, Death Row moved Kurupt out of the condominium he shared with Lamont and into a house. While cleaning out the condominium, Lamont found papers showing that Death Row Records had paid Kurupt advances commencing in April 1993.

The Brumfields sued Death Row Records, Inc., for damages for the tort of intentional interference with their contracts with Kurupt. The jury found in favor of the Brumfields and awarded them $14,344,000 in compensatory and punitive damages. The trial court judge reduced the award to $5,519,000, including $1.5 million in punitive damages to Lamont and $1 million in punitive damages to Kenneth. Defendant Death Row Records appealed this decision.

Issue

Did defendant Death Row Records, Inc., engage in the tort of intentional interference with the contracts that plaintiffs Lamont and Kenneth Brumfield had with rapper Kurupt?

In The Language of The Court

The evidence shows that Kurupt was in material breach of the agreements by signing contracts with Death Row, contrary to the terms of his exclusive contracts with the Brumfields, and that he earned approximately $1.5 million in royalties from his Death Row work. However, the Brumfields were never paid pursuant to their agreements. Despite Death Row's claims that there was no direct evidence, and that therefore there was no interference with the contract, circumstantial evidence shows interference. The evidence shows that Death Row was informed early on by both the Brumfields and Kurupt that the Brumfields had exclusive contracts with Kurupt. Despite this knowledge, Death Row induced Kurupt to execute written contracts with Death Row Records, depriving the Brumfields of their contractual rights with Kurupt.

Decision and Remedy

The court of appeal held that defendant Death Row Records, Inc., had committed the tort of intentionally interfering with the contracts that the Brumfields had with rapper Kurupt. The court of appeal upheld the award of $5,519,000 to the Brumfields, including $1.5 million in punitive damages to Lamont and $1 million punitive damages to Kenneth. Affirmed.

Case Questions

Critical Legal Thinking Should there be a tort of intentional interference with a contract? Why or why not? What public policy is served by this tort?

Business Ethics Did Marion Knight and Dr. Dre act ethically in this case? Did Kurupt act ethically in this case?

Contemporary Business Will this decision make parties more apt to not interfere with other parties' contracts?

strict liability
Liability without fault.

Business Brief
Whereas intentional torts and negligence require the defendant to have been at fault, strict liability imposes liability without the defendant's having been at fault.

Strict Liability

Strict liability is another category of torts. Strict liability is *liability without fault*. That is, a participant in a covered activity will be held liable for any injuries caused by the activity even if he or she was not negligent. This doctrine holds that (1) there are certain activities that can place the public at risk of injury even if reasonable care is taken and (2) the public should have some means of compensation if such injury occurs.

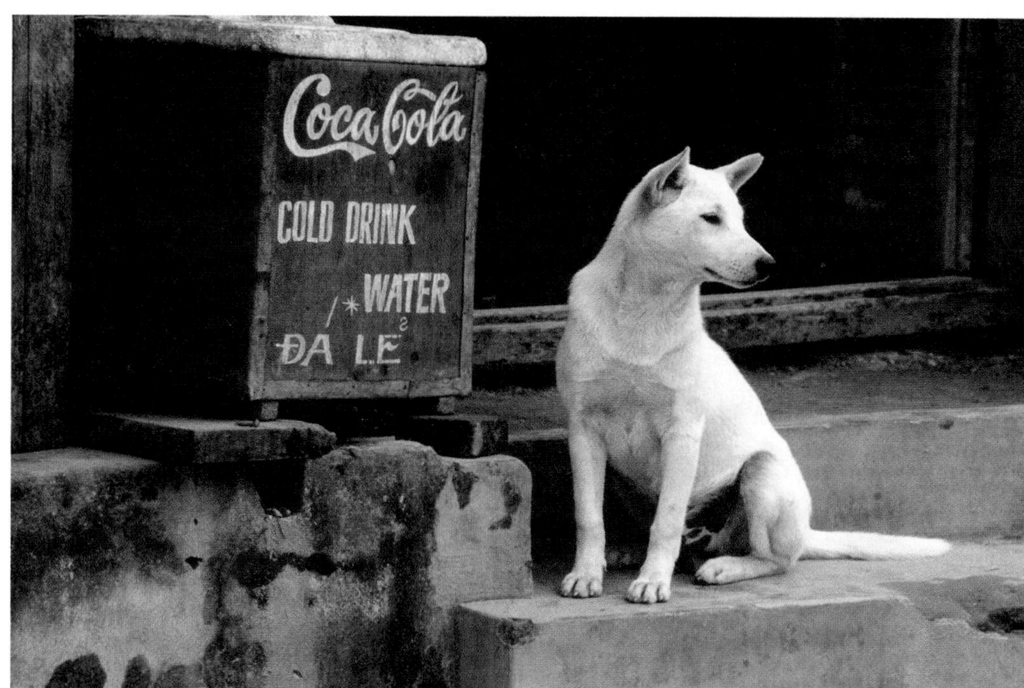

Domestic Animal. Owners of domestic animals are strictly liable for injuries caused by their animals.

Strict liability was first imposed for *abnormally dangerous activities*, such as crop dusting, blasting, fumigation, burning fields, storage of explosives, and keeping wild animals as pets.

Consider This Example Suppose Offshore Fireworks Company, which is located in a foreign country, manufactures fireworks. Iowa Fireworks Display Corporation, a fireworks display company, purchases fireworks from Offshore. The city of Ames, Iowa, hires Iowa Fireworks to shoot off fireworks at the city's Fourth of July celebration. When the fireworks are shot off, one of them explodes too soon, injuring several spectators. Evidence shows that Offshore was negligent and made the defective fireworks and that Iowa Fireworks was not at fault. The injured persons could sue Offshore for producing defective fireworks, but doing so and collecting damages could be difficult. Because shooting off fireworks is an abnormally dangerous activity, the injured persons can sue and recover from Iowa Fireworks under the doctrine of strict liability even though Iowa Fireworks did nothing wrong.

International Law

Israeli Tort Law

David Ben Gurion proclaimed the establishment of the State of Israel on May 14, 1948. Historically, the Jewish people have been governed by biblical law. With the advent of a national state, secular laws were developed and coexist with religious law. One of the laws developed by the State of Israel was tort law. Israeli tort law is based on the theory that monetary compensation is awarded to promote justice and to ensure fair compensation when a tort occurs.

American tort law allows juries almost unlimited discretion to evaluate injuries and award damages. Under Israeli tort law, there is no right to trial by jury. Instead, all actions are tried by a panel of three judges or three laypeople who decide both questions of fact and law. In essence, they are closer to arbitrators than judges.

Also, under Israeli tort law, all damages awarded must be assessed under one of these categories of damages:

1. ***Medical expenses (ripui)*** actually incurred and those expected to be incurred in order to cure the victim or return him or her to as close as possible to a preinjury state.
2. ***Loss of earnings (shevet)*** incurred during the time of the victim's injury and recovery.
3. ***Loss of income (nezek)*** for the long-term decrease in the victim's market value as a worker and skills he or she will never recover.

International Law

(continued)

4. ***Pain and suffering (tza'ar)*** for short-term pain and suffering incurred at the time of the injury and their immediate consequences.
5. ***Embarrassment (boshet)*** for long-term pain and suffering caused by such things as permanent disfigurement, emotional distress, and such.

Israeli law limits the assessment of noneconomic damages (categories 4 and 5) to cases of willful, intentional, or grossly negligent infliction of harm.

Medical malpractice is one area of tort law where the U.S. and Israeli systems differ. Under U.S. law, doctors are liable for their negligent conduct unless a Good Samaritan law relieves them of liability. Jewish law goes one step further. It excuses doctors from liability for their negligence in most situations. This is based on the public policy that the fear of such liability would otherwise discourage people from going into the medical profession. ■

Intentional Torts Against Persons, p. 114

Intentional Torts Against Persons

1. ***Assault.*** Threat of immediate harm or offensive contact, or any action that arouses reasonable apprehension of imminent harm.
2. ***Battery.*** Unauthorized and harmful or offensive physical contact with another person.
   a. *Transferred intent doctrine.* If a person intends to injure one person but actually harms another person, the law transfers the perpetrator's intent from the target to the actual victim.
3. ***False imprisonment.*** Intentional confinement or restraint of another person without authority or justification and without that person's consent.
   a. *Merchant protection statutes.* Statutes that permit businesses to stop, detain, and investigate suspected shoplifters (and not be held liable for false imprisonment) if the following requirements are met:
      i. There are reasonable grounds for the suspicion.
      ii. Suspects are detained for only a reasonable time.
      iii. Investigations are conducted in a reasonable manner.
4. ***Defamation of character.*** A defendant making an untrue statement of fact about the plaintiff that is published to a third party. Truth is an absolute defense.
   a. Types of defamation:
      i. *Slander.* Oral defamation
      ii. *Libel.* Written defamation
   b. *Public figure plaintiffs.* Such plaintiffs must prove the additional element of *malice.*
5. ***Misappropriation of the right to publicity.*** Appropriating another person's name or identity for commercial purposes without that person's consent. Also called the *tort of appropriation.*
6. ***Invasion of privacy.*** Unwarranted and undesired publicity of a private fact about a person. The fact does not have to be untrue. Truth is not a defense.
7. ***Intentional infliction of emotional distress.*** Extreme and outrageous conduct intentionally or recklessly done that causes severe emotional distress. Some states require that the mental distress be manifested by physical injury. Also known as the *tort of outrage.*
8. ***Malicious prosecution.*** A successful defendant in a prior lawsuit suing the plaintiff if the first lawsuit was frivolous.

Intentional Torts Against Property, p. 118

Intentional Torts Against Property

1. ***Trespass to land.*** Interference with a landowner's right to exclusive possession of his or her land.
2. ***Trespass to personal property.*** A person injures another person's personal property or interferes with that person's enjoyment of his or her property.
3. ***Conversion of personal property.*** Taking over another person's personal property and depriving him or her of the use and enjoyment of the property.

Unintentional Torts (Negligence), p. 119

Negligence

"The omission to do something which a reasonable man would do, or doing something which a prudent and reasonable man would not do."

Elements of Negligence

To establish negligence, the plaintiff must prove:

1. The defendant owed a *duty of care* to the plaintiff.
2. The defendant *breached this duty.*
3. The plaintiff suffered *injury.*
4. The defendant's negligent act *caused* the plaintiff's injury. Two types of causation must be shown:
    a. *Causation in fact (or actual cause).* The defendant's negligent act was the actual cause of the plaintiff's injury.
    b. *Proximate cause (or legal cause).* The defendant is liable only for the *foreseeable* consequences of his or her negligent act.

Negligent Infliction of Emotional Distress

Negligent infliction of emotional distress. A person who witnesses a close relative's injury or death may sue the negligent party who caused the accident to recover damages for any emotional distress suffered by the bystander. To recover for *negligent infliction of emotional distress*, the plaintiff must prove:

1. A relative was killed or injured by the defendant.
2. The plaintiff suffered severe emotional distress.
3. The plaintiff's mental distress resulted from a sensory and contemporaneous observance of the accident.

Some states require that the mental distress be manifested by physical injury.

Professional Malpractice

Doctors, lawyers, architects, accountants, and other professionals owe a duty of ordinary care in providing their services. They are judged by a *reasonable professional standard.* Professionals who breach this duty are liable to clients and some third parties for *professional malpractice.*

Special Negligence Doctrines, p. 127

Special Negligence Doctrines

1. ***Negligence per se.*** A statute or an ordinance establishes the duty of care. A violation of the statute or ordinance constitutes a breach of this duty of care.
2. ***Res ipsa loquitur.*** A presumption of negligence is established if the defendant had exclusive control of the instrumentality or situation that caused the plaintiff's injury and the injury would not have ordinarily occurred but for someone's negligence. The defendant may rebut this presumption.

3. ***Good Samaritan laws.*** Laws that relieve doctors and other medical professionals from liability for ordinary negligence when rendering medical aid in emergency situations.
4. ***Dram Shop Acts.*** State statutes that make taverns and bartenders liable for injuries caused to or by patrons who are served too much alcohol and cause injury to themselves or others.
5. ***Guest statutes.*** Statutes that provide that a driver of a vehicle is not liable for ordinary negligence to passengers he or she gratuitously transports. The driver is liable for gross negligence.
6. ***Fireman's rule.*** Firefighters, police officers, and other government employees who are injured in the performance of their duties cannot sue the person who negligently caused the dangerous situation that caused the injury.
7. ***"Danger invites rescue" doctrine.*** A person who is injured while going to someone's rescue may sue the person who caused the dangerous situation.
8. ***Social host liability.*** Some states make social hosts liable for injuries caused by guests who are served alcohol at a social function and later cause injury because they are intoxicated.
9. ***Liability of landowners.*** Landowners (and tenants) owe the following duties to persons who come upon their property:
   a. *Invitees.* Duty of ordinary care.
   b. *Licensees.* Duty of ordinary care.
   c. *Trespassers.* Duty not to willfully and wantonly injure trespassers.
10. ***Liability of common carriers and innkeepers.*** Such individuals owe a *duty of utmost care*, rather than a duty of ordinary care, to protect their passengers and patrons from injury.

Defenses Against Negligence, p. 130

Defenses Against Negligence

1. ***Superseding event.*** An intervening event caused by another person that caused the plaintiff's injuries and relieves the defendant from liability.
2. ***Assumption of the risk.*** A defendant is not liable for the plaintiff's injuries if the plaintiff had knowledge of a specific risk and voluntarily assumed that risk.
3. ***Plaintiff partially at fault.*** States have adopted one of the following two rules that affect a defendant's liability if the plaintiff had been partially at fault for causing his or her own injuries:
   a. *Contributory negligence.* A plaintiff cannot recover anything from the defendant.
   b. *Comparative negligence.* Damages are apportioned according to the parties' fault. Also called *comparative fault.*

Special Business Torts, p. 133

Business Torts

1. ***Entering business without a license.*** The law requires that persons obtain licenses from the government prior to entering certain businesses or professions.
2. ***Palming off.*** A company passes off its products or services as those of another company.
3. ***Disparagement.*** An untrue statement about the products, services, property, or reputation of a business. Also called *product disparagement*, *trade libel*, or *slander of title.*
4. ***False advertising.*** Section 43(a) of the Lanham Act, a federal law, prohibits false and misleading advertising. State laws also prohibit false and misleading advertising.
5. ***Intentional misrepresentation.*** A wrongdoer defrauds another person out of money, property, or something else of value. Also known as *fraud* or *deceit*. The following elements must be shown:
   a. The wrongdoer made a false representation of material fact.
   b. The wrongdoer had knowledge that the representation was false and intended to deceive the innocent party.
   c. The innocent party justifiably relied on the misrepresentation.
   d. The innocent party was injured.

6. ***Intentional interference with contractual relations.*** A third party intentionally interferes with another party's contract and induces the other party to that contract to breach it, causing the nonbreaching party injury.
7. ***Breach of the implied covenant of good faith and fair dealing.*** A party to a contract does not act in good faith or fails to deal fairly in achieving the object of the contract. This duty is only implied in certain contracts (e.g., insurance contracts). Also called *tort of bad faith.*

Tort Damages

1. ***Actual damages.*** Include compensation for personal injury, pain and suffering, emotional distress, and other injuries caused by the defendant's tortious conduct.
2. ***Punitive damages.*** Recoverable against a defendant for intentional or egregious conduct. Awarded to punish the defendant, to deter the defendant from similar conduct in the future, and to set an example for others. The plaintiff may keep these damages.

Strict Liability, p. 138

Strict Liability

Liability is assessed on defendants without regard to fault. Applies to *abnormally dangerous activities* and certain products.

Internet Exercises and Case Questions

Working the Web Internet Exercises

Activities

1. Find a state court case opinion relating to intentional torts. See for example, a state-based plaintiffs' trial lawyers association site (**www.wstla.org**) or, at the national level, The Association of Trial Lawyers of America site (**www.atla.org**), or the ABA Tort and Insurance Practice Section site (**www.abanet.org/tips/thebrief.html**).
2. Find a medical malpractice case. For the viewpoint of the defense, see **www.dri.org**. For the insurance industry's view, see **www.ircweb.org**.

Check the following site as a starting point for the questions below: **www.law.cornell.edu/topics/torts.html**.

3. Find a state court case that establishes the rule in your jurisdiction on social host liability.
4. Find the statute in your jurisdiction that contains the Good Samaritan law.
5. Finds the statute in your jurisdiction that contains the innkeepers' liability law.

Critical Legal Thinking Cases

5.1 Intentional Tort On September 16, 1975, the Baltimore Orioles professional baseball team was at Boston's Fenway Park to play the Boston Red Sox. Ross Grimsley was a pitcher for the visiting Baltimore club. During one period of the game, Grimsley was warming up in the bullpen, throwing pitches to a catcher. During this warmup, Boston spectators in the stands heckled Grimsley. After Grimsley had completed warming up and the catcher had left from behind the plate in the bullpen, Grimsley wound up as if he were going to throw the ball in his hand at the plate, then turned and threw the ball at one of the hecklers in the stand. The ball traveled at about 80 miles an hour, passed through a wire fence protecting the spectators, missed the heckler that Grimsley was aiming at, and hit another spectator, David Manning, Jr., causing injury. Manning sued Grimsley and the Baltimore Orioles. Are the defendants liable? [*Manning v. Grimsley*, 643 F.2d 20, 1981 U.S.App. Lexis 19782 (1st Cir. 1981)]

5.2 Merchant Protection Statute At about 7:30 P.M. on September 8, 1976, Deborah A. Johnson entered a Kmart store located in Madison, Wisconsin, to purchase some diapers and several cans of motor oil. She took her small child along to enable her to purchase the correct size diapers, carrying the child in an infant seat that she had purchased at Kmart two or three weeks previously. A large Kmart price tag was still attached to the infant seat. Johnson purchased the diapers and oil and some children's clothes. She was in a hurry to leave because it was 8:00 P.M., her child's feeding time, and she hurried through the checkout lane. She paid for the diapers, the oil, and the clothing. Just after leaving the store she heard someone ask her to stop. She turned around and saw a Kmart security officer. He showed her a badge and asked her to come back into the store, which she did. The man stated, "I have reason to believe that you have stolen this car seat." Johnson explained that she had purchased the seat previously. She demanded to see the manager, who was called to the scene. When

Johnson pointed out that the seat had cat hairs, food crumbs, and milk stains on it, the man said, "I'm really sorry, there's been a terrible mistake. You can go." Johnson looked at the clock, which read 8:20 P.M., when she left. Johnson sued Kmart for false imprisonment. Is Kmart liable? [*Johnson v. Kmart Enterprises, Inc.*, 297 N.W.2d 74, 1980 Wisc.App. Lexis 3197 (Wis.App. 1980)]

5.3 Defamation Dorchen Leidholdt is a New Yorker who is a vigorous opponent of pornography. She is a founding member of the organization Women Against Pornography, has given public speeches against pornography, and has debated opponents in the national media. Larry Flynt Publications is a California corporation that owns *Hustler* magazine. *Hustler* regularly includes a monthly column in which some personage whose activities *Hustler* opposes is vilified in graphic terms. *Hustler's* June 1985 issue featured Leidholdt in the column. The article criticizes Leidholdt and her fellow antipornographers in scatological terms, employing such phrases as a "pus bloated walking sphincter," "sexually repressed," "hating men, hating sex, and hating themselves," and "this frustrated group of sexual fascists." The article was accompanied by a small photograph of Leidholdt's face superimposed over the buttocks of a bent-over naked man. Leidholdt sued *Hustler* for defamation. Who wins? [*Leidholdt v. Larry Flynt Publications*, 860 F.2d 890, 1988 U.S.App. Lexis 14439 (9th Cir. 1988)]

5.4 Right to Privacy On December 15, 1956, Marvin Briscoe and another man hijacked a truck in Danville, Kentucky. They were caught and convicted, and Briscoe served a term in prison. After release from prison, Briscoe established a life of respectability. In 1967, *Reader's Digest* published an article titled "The Big Business of Hijacking," stating that the looting of trucks had reached a rate of more than $100 million per year. Without indicating that the Briscoe hijacking had occurred 11 years earlier, the article contained the following sentence: "Typical of many beginners, Marvin Briscoe and another man stole a 'valuable-looking' truck in Danville, Ky., and then fought a gun battle with the local police, only to learn that they had hijacked four bowling pin spotters." After publication of the article, Briscoe brought an action for damages against Reader's Digest Association, Inc., for the intentional tort of invasion of the right of privacy. The complaint alleged that as a result of the *Reader's Digest* publication, the plaintiff's 11-year-old daughter, as well as the plaintiff's friends, learned of his criminal record for the first time and thereafter scorned and abandoned him. Did Briscoe's complaint state a cause of action for invasion of the right to privacy? [*Briscoe v. Reader's Digest Association, Inc.*, 4 Cal.3d 529, 93 Cal.Rptr. 866, 1971 Cal. Lexis 338 (Cal. 1971)]

5.5 Trespass A. C. Wade operated a liquor store in Cordele, Georgia. Because the store had been burglarized on several occasions and money had been stolen from a cigarette vending machine, Wade booby-trapped the machine with dynamite, with the intent to scare away thieves when they tried to steal money from the vending machine. Robert McKinsey, a 16-year-old, was killed when the dynamite attached to the vending machine exploded while McKinsey was burglarizing the liquor store. Mrs. Ella McKinsey, Robert's mother, although admitting her son was committing a crime at the time he was killed, brought action for damages against Wade for the wrongful death of her son. Who wins? [*McKinsey v. Wade*, 220 SE.2d 30, 1975 Ga.App. Lexis 1264 (Ga. 1975)]

5.6 Negligence In January 1984, George Yanase was a paying guest at the Royal Lodge-Downtown Motel in San Diego, California. Yanase was a member of the Automobile Club of Southern California. The Auto Club publishes a "Tourbook" in which it lists hotels and motels and rates the quality of their services, including the cleanliness of rooms, quality of the restaurant, level of personal service, and the like. Yanase had selected the Royal from the Tourbook. On the night of his stay at the Royal, Yanase was shot in the parking lot adjacent to the motel and died as a result of his injuries. Yanase's widow sued Auto Club for negligence. Is the Auto Club liable? [*Yanase v. Automobile Club of Southern California*, 212 Cal.App.3d 468, 260 Cal.Rptr. 513, 1989 Cal.App. Lexis 746 (Cal.App. 1989)]

5.7 Causation In February 1973, W. L. Brown purchased a new large Chevrolet truck from Days Chevrolet. The truck had been manufactured by General Motors Corporation. On March 1, 1973, an employee of Brown's was operating the truck when it ceased to function in rush-hour traffic on Interstate Highway 75 in the Atlanta suburbs. A defect within the alternator caused a complete failure of the truck's electrical system. The defect was caused by General Motors's negligence in manufacturing the truck. When the alternator failed to operate, the truck came to rest in the right-hand lane of two north-bound lanes of freeway traffic. Because of the electrical failure, no blinking lights could be used to warn traffic of the danger. The driver, however, tried to motion traffic around the truck. Some time later, when the freeway traffic had returned to normal, the large Chevrolet truck was still motionless on the freeway. At approximately 6:00 P.M. a panel truck approached the stalled truck in the right-hand lane of traffic at freeway speed. Immediately behind the panel truck, Mr. Davis, driving a Volkswagen fastback, was unable to see the stalled truck. At the last moment the driver of the panel truck saw the stalled truck and swerved into another lane to avoid it. Mr. Davis drove his Volkswagen into the stalled truck at freeway speed, causing his death. Mr. Davis's wife brought a wrongful death action based on negligence against General Motors. Was there causation linking the negligence of the defendant to the fatal accident? [*General Motors Corporation v. Davis*, 233 S.E.2d 825, 1977 Ga.App. Lexis 1961 (Ga.App. 1977)]

5.8 Negligence Per Se On March 21, 1980, Julius Ebanks set out from his home in East Elmhurst, Queens, New York, en route to his employment in the downtown district of Manhattan. When Ebanks reached the Bowling Green subway station, he boarded an escalator owned and operated by the New York City Transit Authority. While the escalator was ascending, Ebanks's left foot became caught in a two-inch gap between the escalator step on which he was standing and the side wall of the escalator. Ebanks was unable to free himself. When he reached the top of the escalator he was thrown to the ground, fracturing his hip and causing other serious injuries. The two-inch gap exceeded the three-eighths-inch standard required by the city's building code. Ebanks sued the Transit Authority to recover damages for his injuries. Who wins? [*Ebanks v. New York City Transit Authority*, 70 N.Y.2d 621, 518 N.Y.S.2d 776, 1987 N.Y. Lexis 17294 (N.Y.App. 1986)]

5.9 Res Ipsa Loquitur Elsie Mack was admitted as a patient to the Lydia E. Hall Hospital for a surgical procedure for the treatment of rectal cancer. Dr. Joseph Jahr was the surgeon in charge of the operation. An anesthesiologist, nurses, and other hospital personnel assisted with the operation. An electrical instrument called an electrocoagulator was used during the surgery to coagulate Mack's blood vessels and stop the bleeding. A component part of the electrocoagulator known as a grounding pad was placed on Mack's left thigh and remained there throughout the surgery. While under anesthesia, Mack sustained third-degree burns on the side of her left thigh during the course of surgery. This was because the pad came in full contact with Mack's skin tissue. When the grounding pad was removed at the conclusion of the operation, a burn more than ½ inch deep and over 2 inches in diameter was discovered where the pad had been. The burn was excised, along with the nerves, and a 2¾-inch scar remains. Mack sued the hospital, Dr. Jahr, and other medical personnel to recover damages caused by their negligence. Does the doctrine of *res ipsa loquitur* apply to this lawsuit? [*Mack v. Lydia E. Hall Hospital*, 503 N.Y.S.2d 131, 1986 N.Y.App.Div. Lexis 58398 (N.Y.Sup.Ct. 1986)]

5.10 Liability of Landowners George and Beverly Wagner own a 1.6-acre parcel of land on which they operate "Bowag Kennels," which caters to training, boarding, and caring for show dogs. The property is entirely surrounded by land owned by Reuben Shiling and W. Dale Hess. In August 1964, Shiling and Hess granted the Wagners an easement right-of-way over their land that connected the kennel to Singer Road, a public road. Singer Road is a rural, unlit two-lane road running through a wooded area. The right-of-way is an unpaved, unlit, narrow road that crosses an uninhabited wooded area leading to Bowag Kennels. On numerous occasions, unauthorized motorcyclists drove on the right-of-way. On several occasions, the bikers had loud parties along the right-of-way. In September 1982, the Wagners stretched a large metal chain between two poles at the entrance of the right-of-way. The Wagners testified that they marked the chain with reflectors and signs. Just before midnight on October 2, 1982, William E. Doehring, Jr., and his passenger, Kelvin Henderson, drove their motorcycle off Singer Road and turned on to the right-of-way. The motorcycle they were riding was not equipped with a headlight, and the riders were not wearing helmets. Doehring and Henderson had not been granted permission by the Wagners or Shiling or Hess to use the right-of-way. The motorcycle struck the chain, and the riders were thrown off. Doehring died several hours later at a hospital. Doehring's father filed a wrongful death and survival action against the Wagners. Who wins? [*Wagner v. Doehring*, 553 A.2d 684, 1989 Md. Lexis 29 (Md.App. 1089)]

5.11 Social Host Liability David Andres was a 19-year-old student at Northeast Missouri State University. He was a member of Alpha Kappa Lambda Fraternity and lived in the fraternity house. During the evening of December 11, 1979, and the early morning hours of December 12, 1979, the fraternity sponsored a mixer at its house with the Delta Zeta Sorority at which alcoholic beverages were furnished without restriction as to age. Missouri's lawful age for drinking alcoholic beverages was 21. Andres was observed drinking before, during, and following the mixer. During the early morning hours of December 12, he was sitting at the bar in the fraternity house, matching straight shots of whiskey with a fraternity brother. After watching them for some time, another fraternity brother took the bottle from them. Several fraternity brothers helped Andres into the television room, where a pillow and blanket were obtained for him. He was left to "sleep it off" on the television room floor. At about 10:00 A.M. on December 12, when Andres could not be wakened, he was taken to a local hospital but could not be revived. The autopsy showed Andres's blood level measured 0.43 percent, and the cause of death was acute alcohol intoxication with aspiration. Andres' parents brought a wrongful death action against the fraternity. Who wins? [*Andres v. Alpha Kappa Lambda Fraternity*, 730 S.W.2d 547, 1987 Mo. Lexis 296 (Mo. 1987)]

5.12 Liability of Common Carrier The Southern California Rapid Transit District (RTD) is a public common carrier that operates public buses throughout the Los Angeles area. Carmen and Carla Lopez were fare-paying passengers on an RTD bus when a group of juveniles began harassing them and other passengers. When the bus driver was notified of this problem, he failed to take any precautionary measures and continued to operate the bus. The juveniles eventually physically assaulted Carmen and Carla, who were injured. The RTD was aware of a history of violent attacks on its bus line. Carmen and Carla sued the RTD to recover damages for their injuries. Who wins? [*Lopez v. Southern California Rapid Transit District*, 40 Cal.3d 780, 221 Cal.Rptr. 840, 1985 Cal. Lexis 434 (Cal. 1985)]

5.13 Emotional Distress Virginia Rulon-Miller began working for IBM in 1967. Over the course of several years, she was promoted to a marketing-representative position, selling typewriters and office equipment in San Francisco's financial district. She became one of the most successful salespersons in the office and received money prizes and awards for her work. She also received the highest merit rating an employee could receive under the IBM rating system. In 1976, Rulon-Miller met Matt Blum, who was an account manager for IBM. They began dating shortly thereafter and became involved in a romantic relationship. This fact was widely known at IBM. In 1977, Blum left IBM to work at QXY, a competitor of IBM. Rulon-Miller and Blum continued their relationship. About one year later, Phillip Callahan, who was Rulon-Miller's immediate manager, called her into his office. He told her that her dating Blum constituted a "conflict of interest," told her to stop dating Blum, and told her he would give her a "couple of days to a week" to think about it. The next day, however, Callahan called Rulon-Miller in again and told her he had "made up her mind for her" and dismissed her. Rulon-Miller suffered severe emotional distress because of this incident. She sued IBM for intentional infliction of emotional distress. Who wins? [*Rulon-Miller v. International Business Machines Corporation*, 162 Cal.App.3d 241, 208 Cal.Rptr. 524, 1984 Cal.App. Lexis 2732 (Cal. App. 1985)]

5.14 Emotional Distress On August 10, 1983, Gregory and Demetria James, brother and sister, were riding their bicycles north on 50th Street in Omaha, Nebraska. Spaulding Street intersects 50th Street. A garbage truck owned by Watts Trucking Service, Inc., and driven by its employee, John Milton Lieb, was backing up into the intersection of 50th and Spaulding Streets. The truck backed into the intersection, through a stop sign, and hit and ran over Demetria, killing her. Gregory helplessly watched the entire accident but was not in danger himself. As a result of watching his sister's peril, Gregory suffered severe emotional distress. Gregory sued Watts and Lieb to recover damages for his emotional distress. Who wins? [*James v. Watts Trucking Service, Inc.*, 375 N.W.2d 109, 1985 Neb. Lexis 1209 (Neb. 1985)]

5.15 Defense On the night of June 13, 1975, the New York Yankees professional baseball team played the Chicago White Sox at Shea Stadium, New York. Elliot Maddox played center field for the Yankees that night. It had rained the day before, and the previous night's game had been canceled because of bad weather. On the evening of June 13 the playing field was still wet, and Maddox commented on this fact several times to the club's manager but continued to play. In the ninth inning, when Maddox was attempting to field a ball in center field, he slipped on a wet spot, fell, and injured his right knee. Maddox sued the City of New York, which owned Shea Stadium; the Metropolitan Baseball Club, Inc., as lessee; the architect; the consulting engineer; and the American League. Maddox alleged that the parties were negligent in causing the field to be wet and that the injury ended his professional career. Who wins? [*Maddox v. City of New York*, 496 N.Y.S.2d 726, 1985 N.Y. Lexis 17254 (N.Y.App. 1985)]

5.16 Palming Off Stiffel Company designed a pole lamp (a vertical tube that can stand upright between the floor and ceiling of a room with several lamp fixtures along the outside of it). Pole lamps proved to be a decided commercial success. Soon after Stiffel brought them on the market, Sears, Roebuck & Company put a substantially identical pole lamp on the market. The Sears retail price was about the same as Stiffel's wholesale price. Sears used its own name on the lamps it sold. Stiffel sued Sears for unfair competition, alleging that Sears had engaged in the tort of palming off. Is Sears liable for palming off? [*Sears, Roebuck & Co. v. Stiffel Co.*, 376 U.S. 225, 84 S.Ct. 784, 1964 U.S. Lexis 2365 (1964)]

5.17 Disparagement Robin Williams, a comedian, did a comedy performance at the Great American Music Hall, a San Francisco nightclub. During the performance he told a joke that contained the following words: "Whoa—White Wine. This is a little wine here. If it's not wine it's been through somebody already. Oh—There are White wines, there are Red Wines, but why are there no Black wines like: Rege. It goes with fish, meat, any damn thing it wants to. I like my wine like I like my women, ready to pass out." Audio versions of the performance were distributed by Polygram Records, Inc., and a video version was shown on Home Box Office (HBO). David H. Rege, who sells and distributes assorted varieties of "Rege" brand wines from his San Francisco store, Rege Cellars, sued Williams, Polygram, and HBO for disparagement of his products and business (trade libel). Are the defendants liable for disparagement? [*Polygram Records, Inc. v. Superior Court*, 170 Cal.App.3d 543, 216 Cal.Rptr. 252, 1985 Cal.App. Lexis 2260 (Cal.App. 1985)]

Business Ethics Cases

5.18 Business Ethics Radio station KHJ was a successful Los Angeles broadcaster of rock music that commanded a 48 percent market share of the teenage audience in the Los Angeles area. KHJ was owned and operated by RKO General, Inc. In July 1973, KHJ inaugurated a promotion titled "The Super Summer Spectacular." As part of this promotion, KHJ had a disc jockey known as "The Real Don Steele" ride around the Los Angeles area in a conspicuous red automobile. Periodically KHJ would announce to its radio audience Steele's location. The first listener to thereafter locate Steele and answer a question received a cash prize and participated in a brief interview on the air with Steele. On July 16, 1973, one KHJ broadcast identified Steele's next destination as Canoga Park. Robert Sentner, 17 years old, heard the broadcast and immediately drove to Canoga Park. Marsha Baime, 19 years old, also heard the broadcast and drove to Canoga Park. By the time Sentner and Baime located Steele, someone else had already claimed the prize. Without the knowledge of the other, Sentner and Baime each decided to follow Steele to the next destination and to be first to "find" him.

Steele proceeded onto the freeway. For the next few miles Sentner and Baime tried to jockey for position closest to the Steele vehicle, reaching speeds of up to 80 miles per hour. There is no evidence that the Steele vehicle exceeded the speed limit. When Steele left the freeway at the Westlake off ramp, Sentner and Baime tried to follow. In their attempts to do so, they knocked another vehicle, driven by Mr. Weirum, into the center divider of the freeway, where it overturned. Mr. Weirum died in the accident. Baime stopped to report the accident. Sentner, after pausing momentarily to relate the tragedy to a passing police officer, got back into his car, pursued and successfully located Steele, and collected the cash prize. The wife and children of Mr. Weirum brought a wrongful death negligence action against Sentner, Baime, and RKO General. Who wins? Did RKO General, Inc., act responsibly in this case? [*Weirum v. RKO General, Inc.*, 15 Cal.3d 40, 123 Cal.Rptr. 468, 175 Cal. Lexis 220 (Cal. 1975)]

5.19 Business Ethics Guy Portee, a seven-year-old resided with his mother in an apartment building in Newark, New Jersey. Edith and Nathan Jaffee owned and operated the building. On the afternoon of May 22, 1976, Guy became trapped in the building's elevator, between its outer door and the wall of the elevator shaft. When someone activated the elevator, he boy was dragged up to the third floor. Another child who saw the accident ran to seek help. Soon afterward, Renee Portee, the boy's mother, and officers at the Newark Police Department arrived. The officers worked for 4½ hours, trying to release the boy, during which time the mother watched as her son moaned, cried out, and flailed his arms. The police contacted the Atlantic Elevator Company, which was responsible for the installation and maintenance of the elevator, and requested that the company send a mechanic to assist in the effort to free the boy. Apparently no one came. The boy suffered multiple bone fractures and massive internal hemorrhaging. He died while still trapped, his mother a helpless observer.

After her son's death, Renee became severely distressed and seriously self-destructive. On March 24, 1979, she attempted to take her own life. She survived, and the wound was repaired by surgery, but she has since required considerable physical therapy. She had received extensive counseling and psychotherapy to help overcome the mental and emotional problems associated with her son's death. Renee sued the Jaffees and Atlantic to recover damages for her emotional distress. Who wins? Did either of the defendants act unethically in this case? [*Portee v. Jaffee*, 417, A.2d 521, 1980 N.J. Lexis 1387 (N.J. 1980)]

5.20 Business Ethics Rosina Crisci owned an apartment building in which Mrs. DiMare was a tenant. One day while Mrs. DiMare was descending a wooden staircase on the outside of the apartment building, she fell through the staircase and was left hanging 15 feet above the ground until she was saved. Crisci had a $10,000 liability insurance policy on the building from the Security Insurance Company of New Haven, Connecticut. Mrs. DiMare sued Crisci and Security for $400,000 for physical injuries and psychosis suffered from the fall. Prior to trial, Mrs. DiMare agreed to take $10,000 in settlement of the case. Security refused this settlement offer. Mrs. DiMare reduced her settlement offer to $9,000, of which Crisci offered to pay $2,500. Security again refused to settle the case. The case proceeded to trial, and the jury awarded Mrs. DiMare and her husband $110,000. Security paid $10,000 pursuant to the insurance contract, and Crisci had to pay the difference. Crisci, a widow of 70 years of age, had to sell her assets, became dependent on her relatives, declined in physical health, and suffered from hysteria and suicide attempts. Crisci sued Security for tort damages for breach of the implied covenant of good faith and fair dealing. Who wins? Did Security Insurance Company act ethically in this case? [*Crisci v. Security Insurance Company of New Haven, Connecticut*, 426 P.2d 173, 66 Cal.App.2d 425, 58 Cal.Rptr. 13, 1967 Cal. Lexis 313 (Cal.App. 1967)]

Briefing the Case Writing Assignment

Read Case A.5 in the Case Appendix [*Braun v. Soldier of Fortune Magazine, Inc.*]. This case is excerpted from the court of appeals opinion. Review and brief the case. In your brief, be sure to answer the following questions.

1. Who are the plaintiffs? What are they suing for?
2. When does a magazine owe a duty to refrain from publishing an advertisement?
3. Was the advertisement the proximate cause of the plaintiff's injuries?
4. Should the award of punitive damages have been reduced?

Answers to Management Decision Questions

1. A parent generally is allowed to bring a wrongful death lawsuit based on the wrongful death of a child. Damages may be awarded to compensate for the mental anguish, lost income, and lost companionship suffered by the parent. Most wrongful death lawsuits are based on negligence. Film, television, and multimedia producers have been subject to lawsuits for copycat crimes and negligence based on violence depicted in movies, songs, and computer-generated games.

   Negligence is the failure to do something that a reasonable person would do or the act of doing something that a prudent and reasonable person would not do. Under tort law, anyone in the marketing distribution chain can be sued. To be successful in a negligence lawsuit, the plaintiff must prove that (1) the defendant owed a duty of care to the plaintiff, (2) the defendant breached this duty of care, (3) the plaintiff suffered injury, and (4) the defendant's negligent act caused the plaintiff's loss.
2. In the beginning, these lawsuits were dismissed because of legal defenses such as the First Amendment protection of free speech and the negligence defense of lack of proximate cause. Proximate cause is difficult to show in these lawsuits. A person who commits a negligent act is not liable unless his or her act was the cause of the plaintiff's injuries. One of the types of causation that must be proven is proximate cause. Under the law, even if you prove that **Bringing Down the Big Game** was the actual cause of Charles's knowledge of the use of high-powered rifles and this led to the death of your son, the court may rule that proximate causation is missing.

   Proximate cause is usually defined as the initial act that sets off a natural and continuous sequence of events that produces an injury. Based on public policy, the law establishes a point along the damage chain after which the negligent party is no longer responsible for the consequences of his or her actions. This limitation on liability is referred to as proximate cause. The general test of proximate cause is foreseeability. The defendant successfully argued that the use of the software "was not a reasonably foreseeable risk or consequence of defendant's remote artistic activities."

Endnotes

1. 376 U.S. 254, 84 S.Ct. 710 (1964).
2. *Restatement (Second) of Torts*, Section 46.
3. *Restatement (Second) of Torts*, Section 46, comment d.
4. Justice B. Anderson, *Blyth v. Birmingham Waterworks Co.*, 11 Exch. 781, 784 (1856).
5. 248 N.Y. 339, 162 N.E. 99 (1928).
6. For example, see Cal. Civil Code, Section 1714(c).
7. 15 U.S.C. § 1125(a).

6

Product and Strict Liability

"A manufacturer is strictly liable in tort when an article he places on the market, knowing that it is to be used without inspection for defects, proves to have a defect that causes injury to a human being."

—Greenmun v. Yuba Power Products, Inc.,
59 Cal.2d 57, 27 Cal.Rptr. 697, 1963 Cal. Lexis 140 (1963)

Chapter Objectives

After studying the chapter, you should be able to:

1. Identify and describe express warranties.
2. Describe the implied warranties of merchantability and fitness for a particular purpose.
3. Define the doctrine of strict liability.
4. Identify examples of defects in manufacture, design, packaging, failure to warn, and failure to provide adequate instructions.
5. List and describe the damages that are recoverable in a product liability action.

Chapter Contents

- Warranties of Quality
- Product Liability Based on Fault
- The Doctrine of Strict Liability
- The Concept of Defect
- Defenses to Product Liability

Management Decision Product and Strict Liability

You are the parent of a four-year-old girl. Last year, you painted your daughter's bedroom with paint manufactured by Colorful Paint Company. Recently, your daughter became sluggish and complained of headaches and stomach cramps. Upon testing, it was determined that her blood contained high levels of volatile organic compounds that have been found in paint and finishes. She was hospitalized for several weeks and may have permanent damage to her digestive tract. There were no warnings on the paint bucket to indicate that the paint should not be applied on walls where children could come in contact with it.

1. What legal action can you take to compensate for the harm caused to your daughter? Who can be sued?
2. What possible defenses can a defendant in such a lawsuit assert?

The doctrine of *caveat emptor*—let the buyer beware—governed the law of sales and leases for centuries. Finally, the law recognized that consumers and other purchasers and lessees of goods needed greater protection. Article 2 of the Uniform Commercial Code (UCC), which has been adopted in whole or in part by all 50 states, establishes certain **warranties** that apply to the sale of goods. Article 2A of the UCC, which many states have adopted, establishes warranties that apply in lease transactions. Consumers and others can sue to recover damages caused by breach of warranty.

warranty
A buyer's or lessee's assurance that the goods meet certain standards.

In addition, if a product defect causes injury to purchasers, lessees, users, or bystanders, the injured party may be able to recover for his or her injuries under certain tort theories, including negligence, misrepresentation, and the modern theory of strict liability. The liability of manufacturers, sellers, lessors, and others for injuries caused by defective products is commonly referred to as **products liability**.

products liability
The liability of manufacturers, sellers, and others for the injuries caused by defective products.

The various warranty and tort principles that permit injured parties to recover damages caused by defective products are discussed in this chapter.

Beverly Hills, California. The crashworthiness doctrine requires automobile manufacturers that design automobiles to take into account the possibility of harm from a person's body striking something inside the automobile in case of a car accident.

Warranties of Quality

warranties of quality
Seller's or lessor's assurance to the buyer or lessee that the goods meet certain standards of quality. Warranties may be expressed or implied.

Warranties are the buyer's or lessee's assurance that the goods they sell or lease meet certain standards of quality. **Warranties of quality**, which are based on contract law, may be either expressly stated or implied by law. If the goods fail to meet a warranty, the buyer or lessee can sue the seller or lessor for breach of warranty. Warranties are discussed in the following paragraphs.

Express Warranties

express warranty
A warranty that is created when a seller or lessor makes an affirmation that the goods he or she is selling or leasing meet certain standards of quality, description, performance, or condition.

When a manufacturer engages in advertising in order to bring his goods and their quality to the attention of the public and thus to create consumer demand, the representations made constitute an express warranty running directly to a buyer who purchases in reliance thereon. The fact that the sale is consummated with an independent dealer does not obviate the warranty.

Justice Francis Henningsen v. Bloomfield Motors, Inc.
161 A.2d 69 (NJ 1960)

Express warranties, which are the oldest form of warranty, are created when a seller or lessor affirms that the goods he or she is selling or leasing meet certain standards of quality, description, performance, or condition [UCC 2-313(1); UCC 2A-210(1)]. Express warranties can be either written, oral, or inferred from the seller's conduct.

It is not necessary to use formal words such as *warrant* or *guarantee* to create an express warranty. Express warranties can be made by mistake because the seller or lessor does not have to specifically intend to make the warranty [UCC 2-313(2); UCC 2A-210(2)].

Sellers and lessors are not required to make such warranties. Generally, such warranties are made to entice consumers and others to buy or lease their products. That is why these warranties often are in the form of advertisements, brochures, catalogs, pictures, illustrations, diagrams, blueprints, and so on.

Express warranties are created when the seller or lessor indicates that the goods will conform to

1. All *affirmations of fact or promise* made about them (e.g., statements such as "This car will go 100 miles per hour" or "This house paint will last at least five years").
2. Any *description* of them (e.g., terms such as *Idaho potatoes* and *Michigan cherries*).
3. Any *model* or *sample* of them (e.g., a model oil drilling rig or a sample of wheat taken from a silo).

Business Brief
Sellers and lessors of goods do not have to make express warranties concerning the quality of their goods. They often make such warranties to convince people or businesses to purchase or lease goods from them.

Basis of the Bargain Buyers and lessees can recover for breach of an express warranty if the warranty was a contributing factor—not necessarily the sole factor—that induced the buyer to purchase the product or the lessee to lease the product. This is known as the **basis of the bargain** [UCC 2-313(1); UCC 2A-210(1)]. The UCC does not define the term *basis of the bargain*, so this test is broadly applied by the courts. Generally, all statements by the seller or lessor prior to or at the time of contracting are presumed to be part of the basis of the bargain unless good reason is shown to the contrary. Postsale statements that modify the contract are part of the basis of the bargain.

Generally, a retailer is liable for the express warranties made by manufacturers of goods it sells. A manufacturer is not liable for express warranties made by wholesalers and retailers unless the manufacturer authorizes or ratifies such a warranty.

Business Brief
Sales "puffing" by salespersons usually does not create a warranty; it is merely a statement of opinion.

Statements of Opinion Many express warranties arise during the course of negotiations between the buyer and the seller (or lessor and lessee). The seller's or lessor's **statements of opinion** (i.e., **puffing**) or commendation of the goods do not create an express warranty [UCC 2-313(2)]. Therefore, a used-car salesperson's statement that "This is the best used car available in town" does not create an express warranty. However, a statement such as "This car has been driven only 20,000 miles" is an express warranty. It is often difficult to determine whether the seller's statement is an affirmation of fact (which creates an express warranty) or a statement of opinion (which does not create a warranty).

An affirmation of the *value* of goods does not create an express warranty [UCC 2-313(2)]. For example, statements such as "This painting is worth a fortune" or "Others would gladly pay $20,000 for this car" do not create an express warranty.

In the following case, the court had to decide whether an express warranty had been created.

Case 6.1
Express Warranty

Daughtrey v. Ashe
413 S.E.2d 336, 1992 Va. Lexis 152 (1992)
Supreme Court of Virginia

Background and Facts
In October 1985, W. Hayes Daughtrey consulted Sidney Ashe, a jeweler, about the purchase of a diamond bracelet as a Christmas present for his wife. Ashe showed Daughtrey a diamond bracelet that he had for sale for $15,000. When Daughtrey decided to purchase the bracelet, Ashe completed and signed an appraisal form that stated that the diamonds were "H color and v.v.s. quality." (v.v.s. is one of the highest ratings in a quality classification employed by jewelers.) After Daughtrey paid for the bracelet, Ashe put the bracelet and the appraisal form in a box. Daughtrey gave the bracelet to his wife as a Christmas present. In February 1987, when another jeweler looked at the bracelet, Daughtrey discovered that the diamonds were of substantially lower grade than v.v.s. Daughtrey filed a specific performance suit against Ashe to compel him to replace the bracelet with one mounted with v.v.s. diamonds or pay appropriate damages. The trial court denied relief for breach of warranty. Daughtrey appealed.

Issue
Was an express warranty made by Ashe regarding the quality of the diamonds in the bracelet?

In The Language of The Court
Whiting, Justice We consider whether Ashe's statement of the grade of the diamonds was an express warranty. The Ashes contend that Ashe's statement of the grade of the diamonds is a mere opinion and, thus, cannot qualify as an express warranty.

It is not necessary to the creation of an express warranty that the seller use formal words such as "warrant" or "guarantee" or that he have a specific intention to make a warranty. Here, Ashe did more than give a mere opinion of the value of the goods; he specifically described them as diamonds of "H color and v.v.s. quality." Ashe did not qualify his statement as a mere opinion. And, if one who has superior knowledge makes a statement about the goods sold and does not qualify the statement as his opinion, the statement will be treated as a statement of fact. The trial judge found that the diamonds were of a grade substantially less than v.v.s.

Given these considerations, we conclude that Ashe's description of the goods was more than his opinion; rather, he intended it to be a statement of a fact. Therefore, the court erred in holding that the description was not an express warranty.

Decision and Remedy
The appellate court held that an express warranty had been created. The trial court's decision was reversed, and the case was remanded for a determination of appropriate damages to be awarded to Daughtrey.

Case Questions
Critical Legal Thinking What is the remedy when an express warranty has been breached? Is the remedy sufficient?

Business Ethics Did Ashe act ethically in denying that his statement created an express warranty?

Contemporary Business Do businesses have to make express warranties? Why do businesses make warranties about the quality of their products?

Implied Warranty of Merchantability

If the seller or lessor of a good is a merchant with respect to goods of that kind, the sales contract contains an **implied warranty of merchantability** unless it is properly disclaimed [UCC 2-314(1), UCC 2A-212(1)]. This requires the following standards to be met:

implied warranty of merchantability
Unless properly disclosed, a warranty that is implied that sold or leased goods are fit for the ordinary purpose for which they are sold or leased, and other assurances.

- ***The goods must be fit for the ordinary purposes for which they are used.*** For example, a chair must be able to safely perform the function of a chair. Thus, if a normal-sized person sits in a chair that has not been tampered with, and the chair collapses, there has been a breach of the implied warranty of merchantability. If, however, the same person is injured because he or she used the chair as a ladder and it tips over, there is no breach of implied warranty because serving as a ladder is not the ordinary purpose of a chair.

- ***The goods must be adequately contained, packaged, and labeled.*** Thus, the implied warranty of merchantability applies to the milk bottle as well as to the milk inside the bottle.
- ***The goods must be of an even kind, quality, and quantity within each unit.*** For example, all of the goods in a carton, package, or box must be consistent.
- ***The goods must conform to any promise or affirmation of fact made on the container or label.*** For example, the goods can be used safely in accordance with the instructions on the package or label.
- ***The quality of the goods must pass without objection in the trade.*** That is, other users of the goods would not object to their quality.
- ***Fungible goods must meet a fair average or middle range of quality.*** For example, to be classified as a certain grade, grain or ore must meet the average range of quality of that grade.

Business Brief
The implied warranty of merchantability does not apply to sales or leases by nonmerchants or casual sales.

Warranties are favored in law, being a part of a man's assurance.
Coke First Institute

Note that the implied warranty of merchantability does not apply to sales or leases by nonmerchants or casual sales. For example, the implied warranty of merchantability applies to the sale of a lawn mower that is sold by a merchant who is in the business of selling lawn mowers. It does not apply when one neighbor sells a lawn mower to another neighbor. The following case raises the issue of implied warranty of merchantability.

Case 6.2

Implied Warranty of Merchantability

Denny v. Ford Motor Company

639 N.Y.S.2d 250, 87 N.Y.2d 248, 1995 N.Y. Lexis 4445 (1995)
Court of Appeals of New York

Background and Facts

Nancy Denny purchased a Bronco II, a small utility vehicle that was manufactured by Ford Motor Company. Denny testified that she purchased the Bronco for use on paved city and suburban streets and not for off-road use. On June 9, 1986, when Denny was driving the vehicle on a paved road, she slammed on the brakes in an effort to avoid a deer that had walked directly into her motor vehicle's path. The Bronco II rolled over, and Denny was severely injured. Denny sued Ford Motor Company to recover damages for breach of the implied warranty of merchantability.

Denny alleged that the Bronco II presented a significantly higher risk of occurrence of rollover accidents than did ordinary passenger vehicles. Denny introduced evidence at trial that showed that the Bronco II had a low stability index because of its high center of gravity, narrow tracks, and short wheel base, and because of the design of its suspension system. Ford countered that the Bronco II was intended as an off-road vehicle and was not designed to be used as a conventional passenger automobile on paved streets. The trial court found Ford liable and awarded Denny $1.2 million in damages. Ford appealed.

Issue

Did Ford Motor Company breach the implied warranty of merchantability?

In The Language of The Court

Titone, Judge Plaintiff introduced a Ford marketing manual that predicted many buyers would be attracted to the Bronco II because utility vehicles were suitable to "contemporary lifestyles" and were "considered fashionable" in some suburban areas. According to this manual, the sales presentation of the Bronco II should take into account the vehicle's "suitability for commuting and for suburban and city driving." Additionally, the vehicle's ability to switch between two-wheel and four-wheel drive would "be particularly appealing to women who may be concerned about driving in snow and ice with their children." Plaintiff testified that the perceived safety benefits of its four-wheel drive capacity was what attracted her to the Bronco II. She was not at all interested in its off-road use.

The law implies a warranty by a manufacturer that places its product on the market that the product is reasonably fit for the ordinary purpose for which it was intended. If it is, in fact, defective and not reasonably fit to be used for its intended purpose, the warranty is breached. Plaintiff's proof focused on the sale of the Bronco II for suburban driving and everyday road travel. Plaintiff also adduced proof that the Bronco II's design characteristics made it unusually susceptible to rollover accidents when used on paved roads. All of this evidence was useful in showing that routine highway and street driving was the "ordinary purpose" for which the Bronco II was sold and that it was not "fit"—or safe—for that purpose. Thus, under the evidence in this case, a rational fact finder could have concluded that the vehicle was not safe for the "ordinary purpose" of daily driving for which it was marketed and sold.

Decision and Remedy

The court of appeals held that Ford had breached the implied warranty of merchantability and upheld the jury award for the plaintiff.

Case Questions

Critical Legal Thinking Should the law impose an *implied* warranty of merchantability in the sale of goods? What is the public policy underlying this implied warranty?

Business Ethics Did Ford act ethically in defending that the Bronco II was sold only as an off-road vehicle? Was this argument persuasive?

Contemporary Business What are the business implications of this decision? Do you think that utility vehicles such as the Bronco II have a higher rollover danger than normal passenger automobiles?

Implied Warranty of Fitness for Human Consumption The common law implied a special warranty—the **implied warranty of fitness for human consumption**—to food products. The UCC incorporates this warranty, which applies to food and drink consumed on or off the premises, within the implied warranty of merchantability. Restaurants, grocery stores, fast-food outlets, and vending-machine operators are all subject to this warranty.

implied warranty of fitness for human consumption
A warranty that applies to food or drink consumed on or off the premises of restaurants, grocery stores, fast-food outlets, and vending machines.

Some states apply a *foreign substance test* to determine whether food products are unmerchantable. Under this test, a food product is unmerchantable if a foreign object in that product causes injury to a person. For example, the warranty would be breached if an injury were caused by a nail in a cherry pie. If the same injury were caused by a cherry pit in the pie, the pie would not be unmerchantable.

Business Brief
The consumer expectation test is the modern test adopted by the majority of states to determine merchantability based on what the average consumer would expect to find in food products.

The majority of states have adopted the modern *consumer expectation test* to determine the merchantability of food products. Under this implied warranty, if a person is injured by a chicken bone while eating fried chicken, the injury is not actionable. However, the warranty would be breached if a person is injured by a chicken bone while eating a chicken salad sandwich. This is because a consumer would expect that the chicken salad preparer would have removed all bones from the chicken.

The majority of states have adopted the modern consumer expectation test to determine the merchantability of food products.

Implied Warranty of Fitness for a Particular Purpose

The UCC contains an implied **warranty of fitness for a particular purpose**. This implied warranty is breached if the goods do not meet the buyer's or lessee's expressed needs. The warranty applies to both merchant and nonmerchant sellers and lessors.

The warranty of fitness for a particular purpose is implied at the time of contracting if

1. The seller or lessor has reason to know the particular purpose for which the buyer is purchasing the goods or the lessee is leasing the goods.
2. The seller or lessor makes a statement that the goods will serve this purpose.
3. The buyer or lessee relies on the seller's or lessor's skill and judgment and purchases or leases the goods [UCC 2-315, UCC 2A-213].

Consider This Example Susan Logan wants to buy lumber to build a house, so she goes to Winter's lumber yard. Logan describes the house she intends to build to Winter. She also tells Winter that she is relying on him to select the right lumber. Winter selects the lumber, and Logan buys it and builds the house. Unfortunately, the house collapses because the lumber was not strong enough to support it. Logan can sue Winter for breach of the implied warranty of fitness for a particular purpose.

Concept Summary *Express and Implied Warranties of Quality*

Type of Warranty	How Created	Description
Express warranty	Made by seller or lessor.	Affirmation that the goods meet certain standards of quality, description, performance, or condition [UCC 2-313(1), UCC 2A-210(1)].
Implied warranty of merchantability	Implied by law if the seller or lessor is a merchant.	Implied that the goods 1. Are fit for the ordinary purposes for which they are used. 2. Are adequately contained, packaged, and labeled. 3. Are of an even kind, quality, and quantity within each unit. 4. Conform to any promise or affirmation of fact made on the container or label. 5. Pass without objection in the trade. 6. Meet a fair average or middle range of quality for fungible goods [UCC 2-314(1), UCC 2A-212(1)].
Implied warranty for fitness for a particular purpose	Implied by law.	Implied that the goods are fit for the purpose for which the buyer or lessee acquires the goods if (1) the seller or lessor has reason to know the particular purpose for which the goods will be used, (2) the seller or lessor makes a statement that the goods will serve that purpose, and (3) the buyer or lessee relies on the statement and buys or leases the goods [UCC 2-315, UCC 2A-213].

Landmark Law

Magnuson–Moss Warranty Act

In 1975, Congress enacted the **Magnuson–Moss Warranty Act** (the act), which covers written warranties relating to *consumer* products. The act is administered by the Federal Trade Commission (FTC) [15 U.S.C. § 2301–2312].

Commercial and industrial transactions are not governed by the act. The act does not require a seller or lessor to make express written warranties. However, persons who do make such warranties are subject to the provisions of the act.

Full and Limited Warranties

If the cost of the good is more than $10 and the warrantor chooses to make an express warranty, the Magnuson–Moss Warranty Act requires that the warranty be labeled as either "full" or "limited."

For the warranty to qualify as a **full warranty**, the warrantor must guarantee free repair or replacement of the defective product. The warrantor must indicate whether there is a time limit on the full warranty (e.g., "full 36-month warranty").

In a **limited warranty**, the warrantor limits the scope of a full warranty in some way (e.g., to return of the purchase price or replacement or such). The fact that the warranty is full or limited must be conspicuously displayed. The disclosures must be in "understandable language."

Limitation on Disclaiming Implied Warranties

The act does not create any implied warranties. It does, however, modify the state law of implied warranties in one crucial respect: Sellers or lessors who make express written warranties are forbidden from disclaiming or modifying the implied warranties of merchantability and fitness for a particular purpose. A seller or lessor may set a time limit on implied warranties, but this time limit must correspond to the duration of any express warranty. ■

E-Commerce & Information Technology

Warranty Disclaimers in Software Licenses

Most software companies license their software to users. The software license is a complex contract that contains the terms of the license. Most software licenses contain warranty disclaimer and limitation on liability clauses that limit the licensor's liability if the software malfunctions. Disclaimer of warranty and limitation on liability clauses that are included in a typical software license appear below. ■

SOFTWARE.COM, INC.
LIMITATION AND WAIVERS OF WARRANTIES,
REMEDIES, AND CONSEQUENTIAL DAMAGES

Limited Warranty. Software.com, Inc. warrants that (a) the software will perform substantially in accordance with the accompanying written materials for a period of 90 days from the date of receipt, and (b) any hardware accompanying the software will be free from defects in materials and workmanship under normal use and service for a period of one year from the date of the receipt. Any implied warranties on the software and hardware are limited to 90 days and one (1) year, respectively. Some states do not allow limitations on duration of an implied warranty, so the above limitation may not apply to you.

Customer Remedies. Software.com, Inc.'s entire liability and your exclusive remedy shall be, at Software.com, Inc.'s option, either (a) return of the price paid or (b) repair or replacement of the software or hardware that does not meet Software.com, Inc.'s Limited Warranty and that is returned to Software.com, Inc. with a copy of your receipt. This Limited Warranty is void if failure of the software or hardware has resulted from accident, abuse, or misapplication. Any replacement software will be warranted for the remainder of the original warranty or 30 days, whichever is longer. These remedies are not available outside the United States of America.

No Other Warranties. Software.com, Inc. disclaims all other warranties, either express or implied, including but not limited to implied warranties of merchantability and fitness for a particular purpose, with respect to the software, the accompanying written materials, and any accompanying hardware. This Limited Warranty gives you specific legal rights. You may have others, which vary from state to state.

No Liability for Consequential Damages. In no event shall Software.com, Inc. or its suppliers be liable for any damages whatsoever (including, without limitation, damages for loss of business profits, business interruption, loss of business information, or other pecuniary loss) arising out of the use of or inability to use this Software.com, Inc. product, even if Software.com, Inc. has been advised of the possibility of such damages. Because some states do not allow the exclusion or limitation of liability for consequential or incidental damages, the above limitation may not apply to you.

Product Liability Based on Fault

Depending on the circumstances of the case, persons who are injured by defective products may be able to recover damages under the tort theories of *negligence* and *misrepresentation*. Both theories require the defendant to be *at fault* for causing the plaintiff's injuries. These theories are discussed in the paragraphs that follow.

Negligence

negligence
A tort related to defective products in which the defendant has breached a duty of due care and caused harm to the plaintiff.

A person injured by a defective product may bring an action for **negligence** against the negligent party. To be successful, the plaintiff must prove that the defendant breached a duty of due care to the plaintiff that caused the plaintiff's injuries. Failure to exercise due care includes failing to assemble the product carefully, negligent product design, negligent inspection or testing of the product, negligent packaging, failure to warn of the dangerous propensities of the product, and such. It is important to note that in a negligence lawsuit, only a party who was actually negligent is liable to the plaintiff.

Landmark Law
In *MacPherson v. Buick Motor Co.*, the court held that an injured consumer could recover damages from the manufacturer of a product even though he or she was only in privity of contract with the retailer from whom he or she had purchased the product.

The plaintiff and the defendant do not have to be in privity of contract.[1] For example, in the landmark case *MacPherson v. Buick Motor Co.*,[2] the court held that an injured consumer could recover damages from the manufacturer of a product even though the consumer was only in privity of the contract with the retailer from whom he had purchased the product. The plaintiff generally bears the difficult burden of proving that the defendant was negligent.

Consider This Example Assume that the purchaser of a motorcycle is injured in an accident. The accident occurred because a screw was missing from the motorcycle. How does the buyer prove who was negligent? Was it the manufacturer who left the screw out during the assembly of the motorcycle? Was it the retailer who negligently failed to discover the missing screw while preparing the motorcycle for sale? Was it the mechanic who failed to replace the screw after repairing the motorcycle? Negligence remains a viable, yet difficult, theory upon which to base a product liability action.

Misrepresentation

intentional misrepresentation
A seller or lessor fraudulently misrepresenting the quality of a product and a buyer being injured thereby.

A buyer or lessee who is injured because a seller or lessor fraudulently misrepresented the quality of a product can sue the seller for the tort of **intentional misrepresentation**, or **fraud**. Recovery is limited to persons who were injured because they relied on the misrepresentation.

Intentional misrepresentation occurs where a seller or lessor either (1) affirmatively misrepresents the quality of a product or (2) conceals a defect in it. Because most reputable manufacturers, sellers, and lessors do not intentionally misrepresent the quality of their products, fraud is not often used as the basis for product liability actions.

In the following case, the court held a defendant manufacturer liable for negligence in a product liability lawsuit.

Benedi v. McNeil-P.P.C., Incorporated
66 F.3d 1378, 1995 U.S. App. Lexis 28061 (1995)
United States Court of Appeals, Fourth Circuit

Case 6.3
Negligence

Background and Facts

Antonio Benedi consumed three to four glasses of wine a night during the week and sometimes more on the weekend. On February 5, 1993, Benedi began taking Extra-Strength Tylenol in normal doses for flu-like aches. On February 10, 1993, Benedi was admitted to the hospital in a coma and near death due to liver and kidney failure. On the night of February 12, 1993, Benedi underwent an emergency liver transplant. Because of the transplant, Benedi will have to undergo kidney dialysis in the future. Blood tests performed shortly after Benedi's admission to the hospital revealed that he suffered from acetaminophen (Tylenol) toxicity, which is caused by the combination of Tylenol and too much alcohol. The bottle from which Benedi took the Tylenol did not contain a warning of the dangers of the combination of Tylenol and excessive alcohol consumption. Benedi sued McNeil-P.P.C., Incorporated (McNeil), the manufacturer of Tylenol, for negligent failure to warn. The jury found McNeil negligent and awarded Benedi $7,850,000 in compensatory damages. McNeil appealed.

Issue

Is McNeil liable for negligent failure to warn?

In The Language of The Court

Anderson, District Judge At trial, Benedi called two liver disease specialists who both testified that a warning of the possible danger to heavy drinkers from combining alcohol and acetaminophen should have been placed on the Tylenol label since the mid-1980s. These experts described exactly how the alcohol–acetaminophen mixture can become a toxin in the liver. They cited numerous treatises and articles published in medical journals prior to 1993 that described the increased risk of liver injury when acetaminophen is combined with alcohol. One of plaintiff's experts referred to sixty reports that McNeil had received by the end of 1992 documenting cases of liver injury associated with combining therapeutic doses of Tylenol with alcohol. Because Benedi's experts presented sufficient evidence on the issue of causation, the district judge properly submitted that issue to the jury. It was the jury's role to assess the weight and credibility of the evidence, and the jury found that Benedi proved causation. We find that ample evidence existed from which a reasonable jury could find for Benedi.

Decision and Remedy

The court of appeals affirmed the jury's verdict awarding plaintiff Benedi $7,850,000 against McNeil for negligent failure to warn.

Note: In the summer of 1993 (after Benedi's injury), McNeil included a warning on Tylenol that persons who regularly consume three or more alcoholic drinks a day should consult a physician before using Tylenol.

Case Questions

Critical Legal Thinking What elements are necessary to prove negligence? Do you think that McNeil was negligent in this case? Do you think jurors are sophisticated enough to evaluate and judge scientific evidence?

Business Ethics Did McNeil act ethically in failing to put a warning on Tylenol? Do you think a warning was warranted?

Contemporary Business What will be the implication of this case to manufacturers of pain-killing drugs? Will consumers be better off because of this decision? Explain.

The Doctrine of Strict Liability

In the landmark case *Greenmun v. Yuba Power Products, Inc.*,[3] the California supreme court adopted the **doctrine of strict liability in tort** as a basis for product liability actions. Most states have now adopted this doctrine as a basis for product liability actions. The doctrine of strict liability removes many of the difficulties for the plaintiff associated with other theories of product liability. The remainder of this chapter examines the scope of the strict liability doctrine.

Landmark Law

In *Greenmun v. Yuba Power Products Inc.*, the California supreme court adopted the doctrine of strict liability in tort for product liability actions.

doctrine of strict liability in tort

A tort doctrine that makes manufacturers, distributors, wholesalers, retailers, and others in the chain of distribution of a defective product liable for the damages caused by the defect, irrespective of fault.

Landmark Law

Strict Liability in Tort

The most widely recognized articulation of the doctrine of strict liability in tort is found in **Section 402A** of the **Restatement (Second) of Torts**, which provides

1. One who sells any product in a defective condition unreasonably dangerous to the user or consumer or to his property is subject to liability for physical harm thereby caused to the ultimate user or consumer, or to his property, if
   a. the seller is engaged in the business of selling such a product, and
   b. it is expected to and does reach the user or consumer without substantial change in the condition in which it is sold.
2. The rule stated in Subsection (1) applies although
   a. the seller has exercised all possible care in the preparation and sale of his product, and
   b. the user or consumer has not bought the product from or entered into any contractual relation with the seller.

In 1997, the American Law Institute (ALI) adopted the **Restatement (Third) of Torts: Product Liability**. This new Restatement includes the following definition of *defect*:

> A product is defective when, at the time of sale or distribution, contains a manufacturing defect, is defective in design, or is defective because of inadequate instructions or warnings.

Landmark Law
(continued)

A product:

a. contains a manufacturing defect when the product departs from its intended design even though all possible care was exercised in the preparation and marketing of the product;
b. is defective in design when the foreseeable risks of harm posed by the product could have been reduced or avoided by the adoption of a reasonable alternative design by the seller or other distributor, or a predecessor in the commercial chain of distribution, and the omission of the alternative design renders the product not reasonably safe;
c. is defective because of inadequate instructions or warnings when the foreseeable risks of harm posed by the product could have been reduced or avoided by the provision of reasonable instructions or warnings by the seller or other distributor, or a predecessor in the commercial chain of distribution, and the omission of the instructions or warnings renders the product not reasonably safe. ■

Liability Without Fault

Business Brief
Strict liability law imposes liability without fault on manufacturers, sellers, and lessors who make and distribute defective products that cause injury to users and others.

Unlike negligence, strict liability does not require the injured person to prove that the defendant breached a duty of care. *Strict liability is imposed irrespective of fault.* A seller can be found strictly liable even though he or she has exercised all possible care in the preparation and sale of his or her product.

The doctrine of strict liability applies to sellers and lessors of products who are engaged in the business of selling and leasing products. Casual sales and transactions by nonmerchants are not covered. Thus, a person who sells a defective product to a neighbor in a casual sale is not strictly liable if the product causes injury.

Web Site
Products Liability Law Page This Web page has all kinds of links to product-liability information, including information about asbestos, silicone breast implants, tobacco, medical malpractice, and more. Visit at **www.productslaw.com**.

Strict liability applies only to products, not services. In hybrid transactions involving both services and products, the dominant element of the transaction dictates whether strict liability applies. For example, in a medical operation that requires a blood transfusion, the operation would be the dominant element, and strict liability would not apply.[4] Strict liability may not be disclaimed.

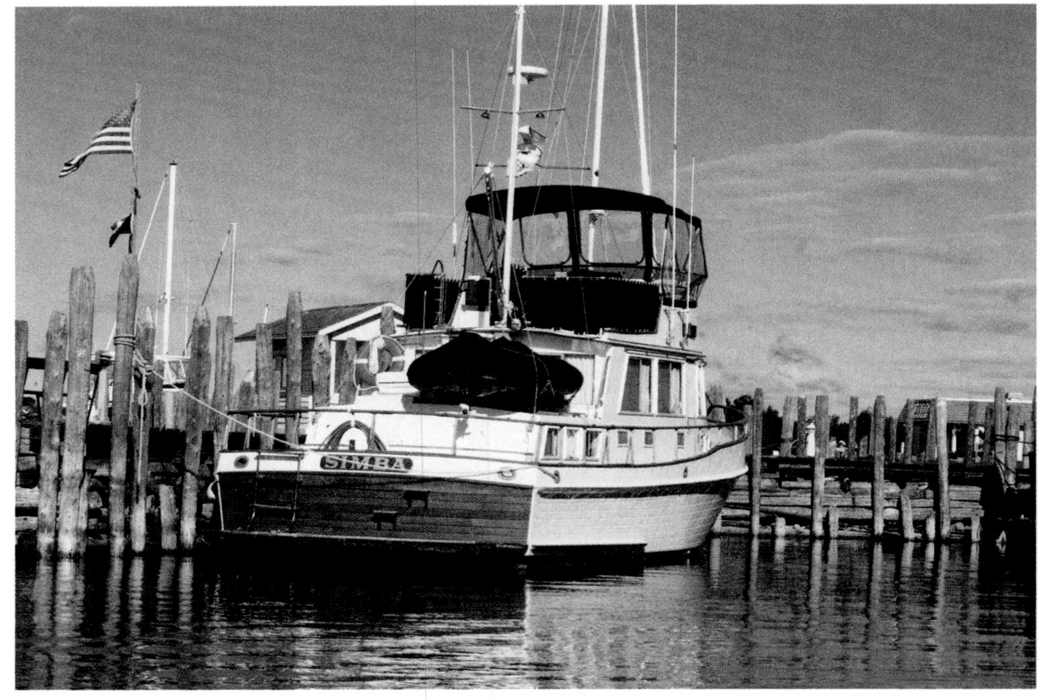

St. Ignace Bay, Michigan. The sale and lease of goods, such as this boat, are subject to product liability laws. *Strict liability* is a modern tort concept that only applies to transactions in goods and not to service contracts or contracts for the sale of real estate.

All in the Chain of Distribution Are Liable

All parties in the **chain of distribution** of a defective product are **strictly liable** for the injuries caused by that product. Thus, all manufacturers, distributors, wholesalers, retailers, lessors, and subcomponent manufacturers may be sued under this doctrine. This view is based on public policy. Lawmakers presume that sellers and lessors will insure against the risk of a strict liability lawsuit and spread the cost to their consumers by raising the price of products.

chain of distribution
All manufacturers, distributors, wholesalers, retailers, lessors, and subcomponent manufacturers involved in a transaction.

Consider This Example Suppose a subcomponent manufacturer produces a defective tire and sells it to a truck manufacturer. The truck manufacturer places the defective tire on one of its new-model trucks. The truck is distributed by a distributor to a retail dealer. Ultimately, the retail dealer sells the truck to a buyer. The defective tire causes an accident in which the buyer is injured. All of the parties in the tire's chain of distribution can be sued by the injured party; in this case, the liable parties are the subcomponent manufacturer, the truck manufacturer, the distributor, and the retailer.

A defendant who has not been negligent but who is made to pay a strict liability judgment can bring a separate action against the negligent party in the chain of distribution to recover its losses. In the preceding example, for instance, the retailer could sue the manufacturer to recover the strict liability judgment assessed against it. Exhibit 6.1 compares the doctrines of negligence and strict liability.

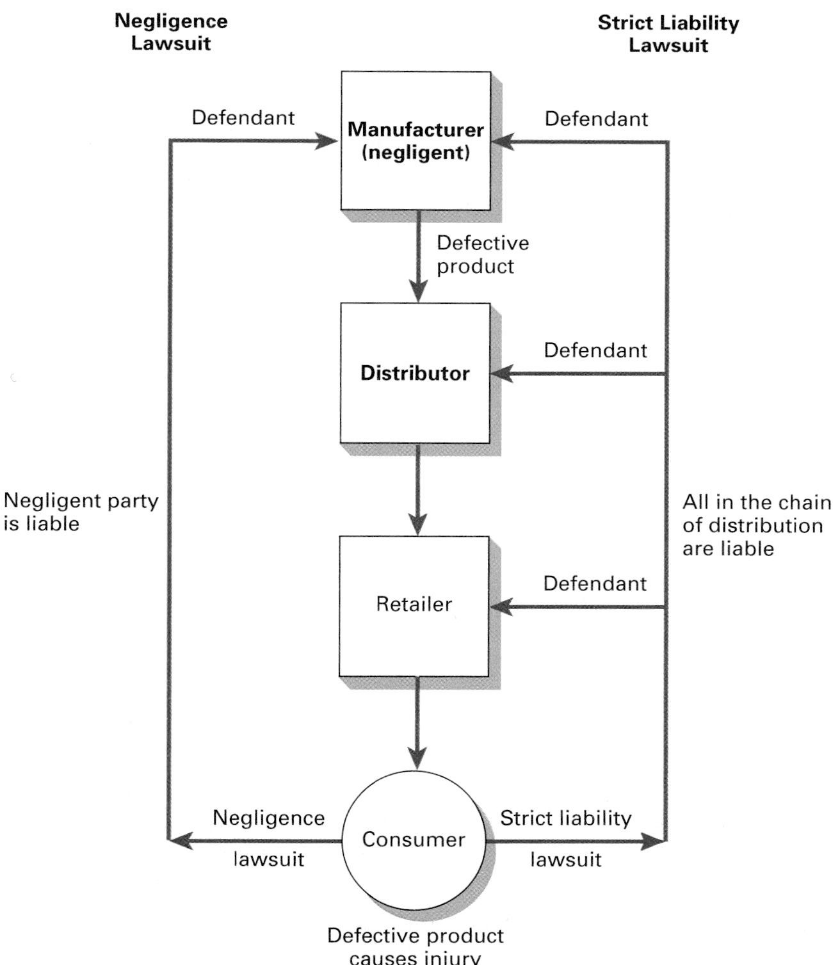

Exhibit 6.1
Doctrines of Negligence and Strict Liability Compared

Parties Who Can Recover for Strict Liability

Business Brief

Privity of contract is not required for a plaintiff to sue for strict liability.

Business Brief

Strict liability law imposes liability without fault on manufacturers, sellers, and lessors who make and distribute defective products that cause injury to users and others.

Business Brief

Punitive damages are often awarded in strict liability lawsuits if the plaintiff proves that the defendant either intentionally injured him or her or acted with reckless disregard for his or her safety.

Because strict liability is a tort doctrine, privity of contract between the plaintiff and the defendant is not required. In other words, the doctrine applies even if the injured party had no contractual relations with the defendant. Under strict liability, sellers and lessors are liable to the ultimate user or consumer. Users include the purchaser or lessee, family members, guests, employees, customers, and persons who passively enjoy the benefits of the product (e.g., passengers in automobiles).

Most jurisdictions have judicially or statutorily extended the protection of strict liability to bystanders. The courts have stated that bystanders should be entitled to even greater protection than a consumer or user. This is because consumers and users have the chance to inspect for defects and to limit their purchases to articles manufactured by reputable manufacturers and sold by reputable retailers, whereas bystanders do not have the same opportunity.

Damages Recoverable for Strict Liability

The damages recoverable in a strict liability action vary by jurisdiction. Damages for personal injuries are recoverable in all jurisdictions that have adopted the doctrine of strict liability, although some jurisdictions limit the dollar amount of the award. Property damage is recoverable in most jurisdictions, but economic loss (e.g., lost income) is recoverable in only a few jurisdictions. *Punitive damages* are generally allowed if the plaintiff can prove that the defendant either intentionally injured him or her or acted with reckless disregard for his or her safety.

Bhuton. Most other countries of the world have not adopted the doctrine of strict liability as it applies to products in the United States.

Entrepreneur and the Law

Entrepreneur Liable for Strict Liability

Entrepreneurs often own small and medium-sized retail stores as well as many wholesale and distributor businesses. In this capacity, they distribute and sell products made by manufacturers. Many of these products are sold in their original boxes or are otherwise sold without individual inspection by the retailer, wholesaler, or distributor. But what happens if the product has been produced defectively by the manufacturer, and the purchaser or user is injured by the product? Who is liable?

In the past, when negligence was the major legal theory asserted by the injured victim to recover damages, the negligent manufacturer paid, but the retailer, wholesaler, and distributor did not pay because they did nothing wrong. Gone are those days, however. With the advent of the legal theory of **strict liability**, all in the chain of distribution of a defective product are liable for any injury caused by the product, even though some of the parties are not at fault. Today, entrepreneurs and others who sell and distribute products made by others have to worry about being named in a products liability lawsuit and paying for injuries caused by the product.

To protect against such liability, retailers, wholesalers, and distributors should purchase products liability insurance. If the seller is embroiled in a products liability lawsuit, the insurance company will pay the costs of the defenses (e.g., attorneys' fees, court costs) as well as any settlement amount or judgment, up to the policy limits. The insured business is liable for any amount beyond the policy limit. Paying for products liability insurance raises the cost of doing business. ■

The Concept of Defect

To recover for strict liability, the injured party must first show that the product that caused the injury was somehow **defective**. (Remember that the injured party does not have to prove who caused the product to become defective.) Plaintiffs can allege multiple product defects in one lawsuit. A product can be found to be defective in many ways. The most common types of defects are *defects in manufacture*, *defects in design*, and *defects in packaging* and *failure to warn*. These defects are discussed in the following paragraphs.

defect
Something wrong, inadequate, or improper in manufacture, design, packaging, warning, or safety measures of a product.

Defect in Manufacture

A **defect in manufacture** occurs when the manufacturer fails to (1) properly assemble a product (2) properly test a product, or (3) adequately check the quality of the product. The following two cases are classic examples involving defect in manufacture.

defect in manufacture
A defect that occurs when the manufacturer fails to (1) properly assemble a product, (2) properly test a product, or (3) adequately check the quality of the product.

Shoshone Coca-Cola Bottling Co. v. Dolinski

420 P.2d 855, 1966 Nev. Lexis 260 (1967)
Supreme Court of Nevada

Case 6.4
Defect in Manufacture

Background and Facts

Leo Dolinski purchased a bottle of Squirt, a soft drink, from a vending machine at a Sea and Ski plant, his place of employment. Dolinski opened the bottle and consumed part of its contents. He immediately became ill. Upon examination, it was found that the bottle contained the decomposed body of a mouse, mouse hair, and mouse feces. Dolinski visited a doctor and was given medicine to counteract nausea. Dolinski suffered physical and mental distress from consuming the decomposed mouse and possessed an aversion to soft drinks. The Shoshone Coca-Cola Bottling Company (Shoshone) manufactured and distributed the Squirt bottle. Dolinski sued Shoshone, basing his lawsuit on the doctrine of strict liability. The state of Nevada had not previously recognized the doctrine of strict liability. However, the trial court adopted the doctrine of strict liability, and the jury returned a verdict in favor of the plaintiff. Shoshone appealed.

Issue

Should the state of Nevada judicially adopt the doctrine of strict liability? If so, was there a defect in the manufacture of the Squirt bottle that caused the plaintiff's injuries?

In The Language of The Court

Thompson, Justice We affirm the verdict and judgment since, in our views, public policy demands that one who places upon the market a bottled beverage in a condition dangerous for use must be held strictly liable to the ultimate user for injuries resulting from such use, although the seller has exercised all reasonable care. Though appellant Shoshone suggests that only the legislature may declare the policy of Nevada on this subject, the weight of the case authority is contra. As indicated, most states approving the doctrine of strict liability have done so by court declaration.

In the case at hand, Shoshone contends that insufficient proof was offered to establish that the mouse was in the bottle of Squirt when it left Shoshone's possession. The plaintiff offered the expert testimony of a toxicologist who examined the bottle and contents on the day the plaintiff drank from it. It was his opinion that the mouse "had been dead for a long time" and that the dark stains (mouse feces) that he found on the bottom of the bottle must have been there before the liquid was added. The jury apparently preferred the latter evidence that traced cause to the defendant.

Decision and Remedy

The Supreme Court of Nevada adopted the doctrine of strict liability and held that the evidence supported the trial court's finding that there was a defect in manufacture. Affirmed.

Case Questions

Critical Legal Thinking Should the courts adopt the theory of strict liability? Why or why not?

Ethics Was it ethical for Shoshone to argue that it was not liable to Dolinski?

Contemporary Business Should all in the chain of distribution of a defective product—even those parties who are not responsible for the defect—be held liable under the doctrine of strict liability? Or should liability be based only on fault?

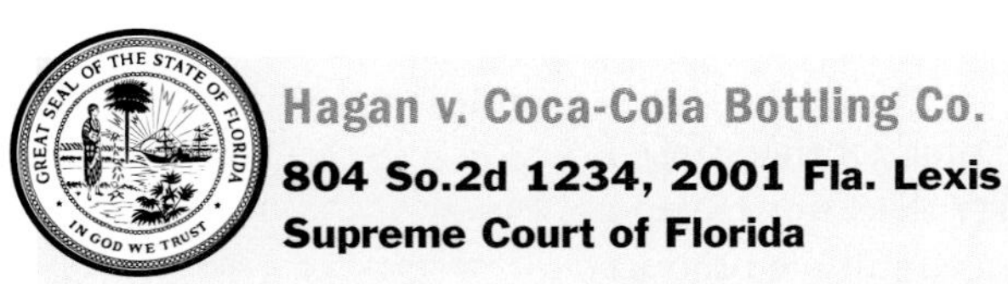

Case 6.5 Defect in Manufacture

Hagan v. Coca-Cola Bottling Co.
804 So.2d 1234, 2001 Fla. Lexis 2292 (2001)
Supreme Court of Florida

Background and Facts

In September 1992, Linda Hagan and her sister Barbara Parks drank from a bottle of Coke that they agreed tasted flat. Hagan then held the bottle up to a light and observed what appeared to be a condom. Both women were distressed, and Hagan immediately became nauseated. The next day they went to a health care facility and were given shots. Six months later both women were tested for HIV and the results were negative. Hagan and Parks sued Coca-Cola Bottling Co. for damages for emotional distress. Coca-Cola tested the contents of the bottle and testified at trial that the object in the bottle was a mold. The jury returned a verdict in favor of the plaintiffs and awarded $75,000 cash to Hagan and Parks. On appeal, the district court of appeals reversed this decision. Plaintiffs Hagan and Parks appealed to the Florida supreme court.

Issue

Can a plaintiff who has consumed a foreign substance in a food product recover damages for emotional distress without any accompanying physical injuries?

In The Language of The Court

Anstead, Justice The public has become accustomed to believing in and relying on the fact that packaged foods are fit for consumption. A producer or retailer of food should foresee that a person may well become physically or mentally ill after consuming part of a food product and then discovering a deleterious foreign object, such as an insect or rodent, in presumably wholesome food or drink. The manufacturer or retailer must expect to bear the costs of the resulting injuries. The mere observance of unwholesome food cannot be equated to consuming a portion of the same. We should not impose virtually unlimited liability in such cases. When a claim is based on an inert foreign object in a food product, we continue to require ingestion of a portion of the food before liability arises.

In *Way v. Tampa Coca-Cola Bottling Co.*, 260 So.2d 288 (Fla. 2d DCA 1972), the plaintiff drank from a bottle of soda and then, upon discovering a rat in the bottle, became nauseous and vomited. Plaintiff sued Coca-Cola. The court reasoned that recovery should be permitted because the evidence showed that the foreign substance in the bottle was loathsome, that it was reasonably foreseeable that its presence would cause nausea and mental distress, and the mental distress was evidence by the vomiting.

Decision and Remedy

The Florida supreme court held that a plaintiff need not prove the existence of a physical injury in order to recover damages for emotional distress caused by the consumption of a contaminated food or beverage. The court reversed the case for further proceedings, consistent with its opinion.

Case Questions

Critical Legal Thinking Should physical injuries have been required in this case, or is emotional distress sufficient to award damages? Explain.

Business Ethics Did Coca-Cola act ethically in fighting this case? Should it have settled the case earlier?

Contemporary Business Is there much room for fraudulent claims in product liability cases like the one in this case? Does the "indigestion rule" prevent most fraudulent claims?

Defect in Design

A **defect in design** can support a strict liability action. Design defects that have supported strict liability awards include toys that are designed with removable parts that could be swallowed by children, machines and appliances designed without proper safeguards, and trucks and other vehicles designed without warning device to let people know that the vehicle is backing up.

In evaluating the adequacy of a product's design, the courts apply a risk–utility analysis and consider the gravity of the danger posed by the design, the likelihood that injury will occur, the availability and cost of producing a safer alternative design, the social utility of the product, and other factors. The design defect case in the following case demonstrates the application of the risk–utility analysis.

defect in design
A defect that occurs when a product is improperly designed.

Web Site
Tobacco Control Archives The Tobacco Control Archives is a project sponsored by the University of California–San Francisco Library and Center for Knowledge Management. It collects materials relating to nonsmoking legislative initiatives and local ordinances. Visit at **galen.library.ucsf.edu/tobacco**.

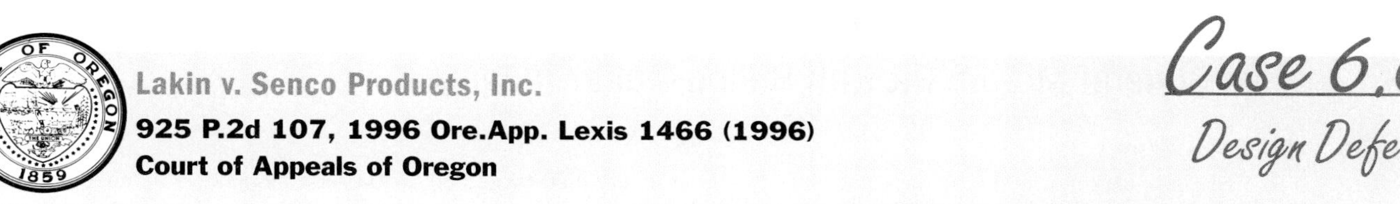

Lakin v. Senco Products, Inc.
925 P.2d 107, 1996 Ore.App. Lexis 1466 (1996)
Court of Appeals of Oregon

Case 6.6
Design Defect

Background and Facts

Senco Products, Inc. (Senco), manufactures and markets a variety of pneumatic nail guns, including the SN325 nail gun, which discharges 3.25 inch nails. The SN325 uses special nails designed and sold by Senco. The SN325 will discharge a nail only if two trigger mechanisms are activated; that is, the user must both squeeze the nail gun's finger trigger and press the nail gun's muzzle against a surface, activating the bottom trigger for safety. The SN325 can fire up to nine nails per second if the trigger is continuously depressed and the gun is bounced along the work surface, constantly reactivating the muzzle safety/trigger.

On December 1, 1990, John Lakin was using a Senco SN325 nail gun to help build a new home. When attempting to nail two-by-fours under the eaves of the garage, Lakin stood on tiptoe and raised a two-by-four over his head. As he held the board in position with his left hand and the nail gun in his right hand, he pressed the nose of the SN325 up against the board, depressed the safety, and pulled the finger trigger to fire the nail into the board. The gun fired the first nail and then, in a phenomenon known as "double firing," immediately discharged an unintended second nail that struck the first nail. The gun recoiled violently backward toward Lakin and, with Lakin's finger still on the trigger, came into contact with his cheek. That contact activated the safety/trigger, causing the nail gun to fire a third nail. This third nail went through Lakin's cheekbone and into his brain.

The nail penetrated the frontal lobe of the right hemisphere of Lakin's brain, blocked a major artery, and caused extensive tissue damage. Lakin was unconscious for several days and ultimately underwent multiple surgeries. He suffers permanent brain damage and is unable to perceive information from the left hemisphere of the brain. He also suffers partial paralysis of the left side of his body. Lakin has undergone a radical personality change and is prone to violent outbursts. He is unable to obtain employment. Lakin's previously warm and loving relationship with his wife and four children has been permanently altered. He can no longer live with his family and instead resides in a supervised group home for brain-injured persons. Lakin and his wife sued Senco for strict liability based on design defect. The trial court found Senco liable and awarded $3.6 million to Lakin, $457,000 to his wife, and $4 million in punitive damages against Senco. Senco appealed.

Issue

Is Senco liable to Lakin for strict liability based on a design defect in the SN325 that allowed it to double fire?

In The Language of The Court

Haselton, Judge The evidence disclosed that the SN325 double-fired once in every 15 firings. Defendant rushed the SN325's production in order to maintain its position in the market, modifying an existing nail gun model so that it could shoot longer nails, without engaging in additional testing to determine whether the use of loner nails in that model would increase the prevalence of double fire. A reasonable juror could plausibly infer that conscious profit/market share motives underlay the failure to engage in adequate product research, development, and testing.

After reviewing the entire record, we conclude that the amount of damages awarded was within the range that a rational juror would be entitled to award. Before John Lakin's injury, defendant knew from numerous complaints that it was highly probable that the SN325 would "double fire." Thus, it was foreseeable—indeed, highly likely given the SN325's recoil and "bump fire" potential—that serious injury could occur to someone when the nail gun double fired.

Decision and Remedy

The court of appeals applied the risk–utility analysis and held that the SN325 was defectively designed. The court affirmed the award of damages to Lakin and his wife.

Case Questions

Critical Legal Thinking Do you think the utility served by the nine-nail-per-second SN325 outweighed its risk of personal injury?

Business Ethics Did Senco act in a conscious disregard of safety factors when it designed, manufactured, and sold the SN325 nail gun?

Contemporary Business Do you think the award of punitive damages was warranted in this case?

Crashworthiness Doctrine

crashworthiness doctrine

A doctrine that says that automobile manufacturers are under a duty to design automobiles so they take into account the possibility of harm from a person's body striking something inside the automobile in the case of a car accident.

Often, when an automobile is involved in an accident, the driver or passengers are not injured by the blow itself. Instead, they are inured when their bodies strike something inside their own automobile (e.g., the dashboard or the steering wheel). This is commonly referred to as the "second collision." The courts have held that automobile manufacturers are under a duty to design automobiles to take into account the possibility of this second collision. This is called the **crashworthiness doctrine**. Failure to design an automobile to protect occupants from foreseeable dangers caused by a second collision subjects the manufacturer and dealer to strict liability.

Contemporary Business Environment

General Motors Hit with Billion-Dollar Judgment

On Christmas Eve, Patricia Anderson was driving her Chevrolet Malibu automobile, which was manufactured by the General Motors Corporation (GM), home from church. Her four young children, ages one through nine, and a neighbor, were also in the car. The Chevy Malibu was stopped at a stoplight at 89th Place and Figueroa Street in Los Angeles when a drunken driver plowed his car into the back of the Malibu at 50 to 70 mph. The Malibu burst into flames as its gas tank ruptured and ignited. Although no one died in the crash, the occupants of the Malibu were severely burned. Many required substantial and multiple skin grafts.

The two injured women and four injured children sued GM for product liability. They alleged that the fuel tank of the Chevy Malibu was defectively designed and placed too close to the rear bumper. GM countered that the tragic accident was the fault of the driver who struck the Malibu. The accident victims produced evidence that showed that GM knew that the car's fuel-tank design was unsafe but had not changed the design because of cost. The Chevy Malibu was one of GM's A-Class cars, which also included the Pontiac Grand Am, the Oldsmobile Cutlass, and the Chevrolet Monte Carlo, all of which have similar fuel-tank designs. The plaintiffs produced GM memos that said it would cost GM $8.59 per vehicle to produce and install a safer fuel tank design but that it would only cost the company an estimated $2.40 per car to not fix the cars and pay damages to injured victims.

After a 10-week trial, the jurors returned a verdict of $107 million in compensatory damages to the plaintiffs for injuries, disfigurement, and pain and suffering caused to them by the accident. The jury then tacked on $4.9 billion as punitive damages to punish GM. This was the largest amount ever awarded in a personal-injury lawsuit. GM, the world's largest automobile company, reported annual earnings of $3 billion in 1998, the year of the verdict. After the trial, one juror stated: "We're just like numbers. Statistics. That's something that is wrong."

GM asked the trial judge to throw out the trial. GM claimed that it was not given a fair trial because the trial court judge refused to allow the jury to hear evidence (1) that the driver of the other car was drunk and went to jail and (2) about crash-test data that showed the safety history of the vehicle. GM also claimed that the jury was prejudiced by repetitive personal attacks on GM as a "soulless company" and its lawyers as "hired guns" who consumed "cappuccinos and designer muffins." GM did not convince the judge that such animosity influenced the jury. GM also alleged that the jury was allowed to hear evidence that it should not have heard, namely, that GM had lobbied Congress in the 1970s to not adopt tougher standards for protecting fuel tanks in crashes.

In its posttrial motions, GM argued that the award of damages, specifically the $4.9 billion of punitive damages, was the result of bias and prejudice of the jury and asked the trial court judge to reduce the award of damages. This the trial court judge did do: He let the compensatory damage award stand but reduced the award of punitive damages to $1 billion. The revised award is equivalent to 2 percent of GM's net worth and 10 times the compensatory damages. GM faced more than 30 other lawsuits involving fuel tank explosions in it's A-Class cars. ■

Defect in Packaging

defect in packaging

A defect that occurs when a product has been placed in packaging that is insufficiently tamperproof.

Manufacturers owe a duty to design and provide safe packages for their products. This duty requires manufacturers to provide packages and containers that are tamperproof or that clearly indicate if they have been tampered with. Certain manufacturers, such as drug manufacturers, owe a duty to place their products in containers that cannot be opened by children. A manufacturer's failure to meet this duty subjects the manufacturer and others in the chain of distribution of the product to strict liability. In the following case, the court had to decide whether there was a **defect in packaging**.

Elsroth v. Johnson & Johnson

700 F.Supp. 151, 1988 U.S. Dist. Lexis 13167 (1988)
United States District Court, S.D. New York

Case 6.7
Defect in Packaging

Background and Facts

On February 4, 1986, Harriet Notarnicola purchased a box of Extra-Strength Tylenol capsules from a Bronxville, New York, grocery store owned by The Great Atlantic & Pacific Tea Co. (A&P). The Tylenol was manufactured by McNeil Consumer Products Co., a division of McNeilab, Inc. (McNeil), under the name Johnson & Johnson. Diane Elsroth was visiting her boyfriend, Michael Notarnicola, for a week, at the home of Michael's parents. Late on the night of February 7, Diane complained of a headache. Michael went to the kitchen, opened the box and plastic container of Extra-Strength Tylenol purchased by his mother at the A&P store, and returned with two capsules and a glass of water for Diane. A short time after ingesting the capsules, Diane retired. Her dead body was found the next day. The medical examiner concluded that the Tylenol capsules ingested by Diane were contaminated by a lethal dose of potassium cyanide. The murder remains unsolved, but evidence shows that the Tylenol bottle had been tampered with after the product left the manufacturer's control. An unknown third party purchased the Tylenol, breached the packaging, substituted cyanide for some of the medicine contained in several of the gelatin capsules, somehow resealed the container and box in such a way that the tampering was not readily detectable, and placed the contaminated box on the shelf of the A&P store. John Elsroth, administrator of Diane's estate, brought this strict liability action against McNeil and A&P, seeking $1 million in compensatory damages and $92 million in punitive damages.

Issue

Was there a defect in packaging that would support an action for strict liability?

In The Language of The Court

Goettel, District Judge Following issuance of the rule, the makers of Tylenol have marketed the product in tamper-resistant packaging with the following features: (1) a foil seal glued to the mouth of the container or bottle, (2) a "shrink seal" around the neck and cap of the container, and (3) a sealed box (the end flaps of which are glued shut) in which the product and container are placed.

McNeil, through its research, knew that this package could be violated by a determined tamperer using sophisticated means and that no evidence of this kind of sophisticated tampering would be visible to the average consumer. As one McNeil official put it, tampering by "the Rembrandt kind of criminals" could not be prevented by this type of packaging. McNeil was also operating under the constraint, however, as recognized by the Food and Drug Administration (FDA), that no packaging could prevent this kind of "exotic" tampering—tamperproof packaging is not possible.

The packaging alternative designed by McNeil employed not one, not two, but three of the tamper-resistant features listed as alternatives in the 1982 FDA regulations. When all of these factors are thrown into the mix, we find, as a matter of law, that under a utility/risk analysis this packaging was in a condition reasonably contemplated by the ultimate consumer and was not unreasonably dangerous for its intended use. Moreover, plaintiff has presented no evidence of what other steps might feasibly have been taken to ensure a higher degree of safety. If there are better tamper-resistant features available that would be feasible for use here, plaintiff has not described them. We return, however, to the fundamental premise: no packaging can boast of being tamperproof.

Decision and Remedy

The court held that there was not a defect in packaging. The defendants are not therefore strictly liable for Ms. Elsroth's death.

Case Questions

Critical Legal Thinking Should manufacturers be forced to make tamper-proof packaging for their products? Is this possible? What would be the expense?

Business Ethics Did any of the parties in the case act unethically?

Contemporary Business Do you think the plaintiff's seeking $92 million in punitive damages was warranted?

Failure to Warn

Certain products are inherently dangerous and cannot be made any safer and still accomplish the task for which they are designed. For example, certain useful drugs cause side effects, allergies, and other injuries to some users. Many machines and appliances include dangerous moving parts which, if removed, would defeat the purpose of the machine or appliance. Manufacturers and sellers of such products are under a *duty to warn* users about the product's dangerous propensities. A proper and conspicuous warning placed on the product insulates the manufacturer and others in the chain of distribution from strict liability. **Failure to warn** of these dangerous propensities is a defect that will support a strict liability action.

failure to warn
A defect that occurs when a manufacturer does not place a warning on the packaging of products that could cause injury if the danger is unknown.

The court found an inadequate warning in the following case.

Nowak v. Faberge USA, Inc.

32 F.3d 755, 1994 U.S. App. Lexis 16580 (1994)
United States Court of Appeals, Third Circuit

Case 6.8
Failure to Warn

Background and Facts

Faberge USA, Inc. (Faberge), manufactures Aqua Net, a hair spray that is sold in an aerosol can. In addition to the hair-holding spray, Aqua Net contains a mixture of butane or propane as the aerosol propellant and alcohol as a solvent. Alcohol, butane, and propane all are extremely flammable. Aerosol cans of Aqua Net carry a warning on the back stating, "Do not puncture" and "Do not use near fire or flame."

Alison Nowak, a 14-year old girl, tried to spray her hair with a newly purchased can of Aqua Net. The spray valve would not work properly, so she cut open the can with a can opener. She thought she could then pour the contents into an empty aerosol bottle and use it. Nowak was standing in the kitchen near a gas stove when she punctured the can. A cloud of hair spray gushed from the can, and the stove's pilot light ignited the spray into a ball of flame. Nowak suffered severe, permanently disfiguring burns over 20 percent of her body. Nowak sued Faberge for damages under strict liability, alleging that Faberge failed to warn her of the dangers of the flammability of Aqua Net. The jury held against Faberge and awarded Nowak $1.5 million. Faberge appealed.

Issue

Did Faberge adequately warn the plaintiff of the flammability of Aqua Net?

In The Language of The Court

Roth, Circuit Judge Under Pennsylvania strict liability law, a defect may be in the warnings given for the use of the product as well as in the design of that product. A product can be held to be defective if it is distributed without sufficient warning to notify the ultimate user of the dangers inherent in the product. We find that the district court made the threshold risk–utility determination that Faberge's product was defective under the facts by sending this case to the jury.

Decision and Remedy

The court of appeals affirmed the district court's judgment that Faberge had failed to warn the plaintiff of the dangers of flammability of its product and was therefore strictly liable.

Case Questions

Critical Legal Thinking Should the law recognize a failure to warn as a basis for imposing strict liability on manufacturers and sellers of products? Why or why not?

Business Ethics Did Faberge violate its duty of social responsibility in this case? Explain.

Contemporary Business Do you think this case was decided properly? What else could Faberge have done to avoid liability?

Los Angeles International Airport (LAX). Airline companies purchase product liability insurance to insure against product liability lawsuits.

Other Product Defects

Other product defects can prove the basis for a strict liability action. **Failure to provide adequate instructions** for either the safe assembly or safe use of a product is a defect that subjects the manufacturer and others in the chain of distribution to strict liability.

Other defects include inadequate testing of products, inadequate selection of component parts of materials, and improper certification of the safety of a product. The concept of "defect" is an expanding area of the law.

failure to provide adequate instructions
A defect that occurs when a manufacturer does not provide detailed directions for safe assembly and use of a product.

Defenses to Product Liability

Defendants in strict liability or negligence actions may raise several defenses to the imposition of liability. These defenses are discussed in the paragraphs that follow.

Supervening Event

For a seller to be held strictly liable, the product it sells must reach the consumer or user "without substantial change" in its condition.[5] Under the doctrine of **supervening**, or **intervening, event**, the original seller is not liable if the product is materially altered or modified after it leaves the seller's possession and the alteration or modification causes an injury. A supervening event absolves all prior sellers in the chain of distribution from strict liability.

supervening event
An alteration or a modification of a product by a party in the chain of distribution that absolves all prior sellers from strict liability.

Consider This Example A manufacturer produces a safe piece of equipment. It sells the equipment to a distributor, who removes a safety guard from the equipment. The distributor sells the equipment to a retailer, who sells it to a buyer. The buyer is injured because of the removal of the safety guard. The manufacturer can raise the defense of supervening event against the imposition of liability. However, the distributor and retailer are strictly liable for the buyer's injuries.

Generally Known Dangers

Certain products are inherently dangerous and are known to the general population to be so. Sellers are not strictly liable for failing to warn of **generally known dangers**. For example, it is a known fact that guns shoot bullets. Manufacturers of guns do not have to place a notice on the barrel of a gun warning of this generally known danger. However, the manufacturer would be under a duty to place a safety lock on the gun.

generally known dangers
A defense that acknowledges that certain products are inherently dangerous and are known to the general population to be so.

Government Contractor Defense

Many defense and other contractors manufacture products (e.g., rockets, airplanes) to government specifications. Most jurisdictions recognize a **government contractor defense** to product liability actions. To establish this defense, a government contractor must prove that (1) the precise specifications for the product were provided by the government, (2) the product conformed to those specifications, and (3) the contractor warned the government of any known defects or dangers of the product.

government contractor defense
A defense that says that a contractor who was provided specifications by the government is not liable for any defect in the product that occurs as a result of those specifications.

Contemporary Business Environment

Correction of a Product Defect

A manufacturer that produces a defective product and later discovers said defect must (1) notify purchasers and users of the defect and (2) correct the defect. Most manufacturers faced with this situation recall the defective product and either repair the defect or replace the product.

The seller must make reasonable efforts to notify purchasers and users of the defect and the procedure to correct it. Reasonable efforts normally consist of sending letters to known purchasers and users and placing notices in newspapers and magazines of general circulation. If a user ignores the notice and fails to have the defect corrected, the seller may raise this as a defense against further liability with respect to the defect. Many courts have held that reasonable notice is effective even against users who did not see the notice. ■

Assumption of the Risk

assumption of the risk
A defense in which the defendant must prove that (1) the plaintiff knew and appreciated the risk and (2) the plaintiff voluntarily assumed the risk.

Theoretically, the traditional doctrine of **assumption of the risk** is a defense to a product liability action. For this defense to apply, the defendant must prove that (1) the plaintiff knew and appreciated the risk and (2) the plaintiff voluntarily assumed the risk. In practice, the defense assumption of the risk is narrowly applied by the courts.

Misuse of a Product

misuse
A defense that relieves a seller of product liability if the user *abnormally* misused the product. Products must be designed to protect against *foreseeable* misuse.

Sometimes users are injured when they misuse a product. If they bring a product liability action, the defendant–seller may be able to assert the **misuse** as a defense. Whether the defense is effective depends on whether the misuse was foreseeable. The seller is relieved of product liability if the plaintiff has **abnormally misused** the product—that is, if there has been an *unforeseeable misuse* of the product. However, the seller is liable if there has been a *foreseeable misuse* of the product. This reasoning is intended to provide an incentive for manufacturers to design and manufacture safer products.

Statute of Limitations and Statute of Repose

statute of limitations
A statute that requires an injured person to bring an action within a certain number of years from the time that he or she was injured by the defective product.

statute of repose
A statute that limits the seller's liability to a certain number of years from the date when the product was first sold.

Most states have **statutes of limitations** that require an injured person to bring an action within a certain number of years from the time that he or she was injured by the defective product. This limitation period varies from state to state. Failure to bring an action within the appropriate time relieves the defendant of liability.

In most jurisdictions, the statute of limitations does not begin to run until the plaintiff suffers an injury. This subjects sellers and lessors to exposure for an unspecified period of time because a defective product may not cause an injury for years, or even decades, after it was sold. Because this may be unfair to the seller, some states have enacted **statutes of repose**. Statutes of repose limit the seller's liability to a certain number of years from the date when the product was first sold. The period of repose varies from state to state.

Concept Summary *Comparison of Statutes of Limitations and Statutes of Repose*

Statute	Begins to Run
Statute of limitations	When the plaintiff suffers injury
Statute of repose	When the product is first sold

Contributory and Comparative Negligence

Sometimes a person who is injured by a defective product is negligent and contributes to his or her own injuries. The defense of **contributory negligence** bars an injured plaintiff from recovering from the defendant in a negligence action. However, this doctrine generally does not bar recovery in strict liability actions.

Many states have held that the doctrine of **comparative negligence** (or **comparative fault**) applies to strict liability actions. Under this doctrine, a plaintiff who is contributorily negligent for his or her injuries is responsible for a *proportional share* of the damages. In other words, the damages are apportioned between the plaintiff and the defendant.

contributory negligence
A defense that says that a person who is injured by a defective product but has been negligent and has contributed to his or her own injuries cannot recover from the defendant.

comparative negligence
A doctrine that applies to strict liability actions and says that a plaintiff who is contributorily negligent for his or her injuries is responsible for a proportional share of the damages.

Consider This Example Suppose an automobile manufacturer produces a car with a hidden defect, and a consumer purchases the car from an automobile dealer. Assume that the consumer is injured in an automobile accident in which the defect is found to be 75 percent responsible for the accident and the consumer's own reckless driving is found to be 25 percent responsible. If the plaintiff suffers $1 million worth of injuries, the plaintiff may recover $750,000 from the defendant manufacturer and car dealer.

International Law

Product Liability Law in Japan

Japanese manufacturers sell many of the same products in Japan and the United States. In the United States, the products are subject to the same product liability laws as American companies. In Japan, they enjoy near immunity from product liability claims. For example, in almost 50 years, consumers have won only 150 product liability cases in Japan and recovered meager damages. In the same period, companies in the United States have lost tens of thousands of such suits and have paid out hundreds of millions of dollars in damages.

Product liability claims are rare in Japan for several reasons:

1. The plaintiff has the difficult burden of proving that the company was negligent. Japan has not adopted the U.S. doctrine of strict liability.
2. Japanese courts do not allow discovery. It is often impossible to prove that a product was defective if the plaintiff cannot obtain access to the defendant's files.
3. Win or lose, claimants must pay a percentage of any damages requested (not won) as court fees. This keeps damage requests low.
4. Awards that are granted by courts are small (at least by U.S. standards), and punitive damages are not available.

Consider the case of Japanese chemical maker Showa Denko. The company faces more than 1,000 lawsuits in the United States. The suits allege that the company's food supplement L-typtophan causes injuries. In one of those cases, Showa settled out of court with Randy Simmons, a 43-year-old Wichita, Kansas, resident who alleged that the food supplement caused him to become a quadriplegic. The same company has few Japan-based cases pending against it, alleging similar claims. There, the company currently offers only to reimburse Japanese customers the purchase price of the supplement.

Product liability laws of Japan differ from those in the United States.

International Law (continued)

The docile attitude of Japanese consumers is changing, and more injured consumers are suing to recover damages for their injuries. There is even a move by the Japanese government to adopt new consumer protection laws. However, the Diet, which has shown a probusiness sentiment in the past, is unlikely to expand the laws to anything near those in the United States.

Critics argue that the Japanese system leaves injured consumers unrecompensed for injuries caused by defective products. Some argue that the near immunity from product liability claims at home gives Japanese manufacturers an edge in selling goods in international markets. Proponents of the Japanese system argue that it promotes the development and sale of products free from the oppressive liability costs that manufacturers face in the United States. They point to the fact that liability insurance costs are sometimes 20 times higher in the United States than in Japan. ■

Warranties of Quality, p. 150

Express Warranty

Affirmation by a seller or lessor that the goods he or she is selling or leasing meet certain standards of quality, description, performance, or condition.

Implied Warranty of Merchantability

1. ***Implied warranty of merchantability.*** A warranty implied by law in sales and lease transactions that requires that the goods:
   a. Be fit for the ordinary purposes for which they are used
   b. Be adequately contained, packaged, and labeled
   c. Be of an even kind, quality, and quantity within each unit
   d. Conform to any promise or affirmation of fact made on the container or label
   e. Pass without objection in the trade
   f. Meet a fair or middle range of quality if the goods are fungible
2. ***Implied warranty of fitness for human consumption.*** A warranty implied by law that food products are fit for human consumption. States apply one of the two following tests:
   a. *Foreign substance test.* A food is unmerchantable if a foreign object in the food caused the plaintiff's injury.
   b. *Consumer expectation test.* A food is unmerchantable if an object in the food that a consumer would not expect to be there caused the plaintiff's injury.
   The UCC incorporates this warranty within the implied warranty of merchantability.

Implied Warranty of Fitness for a Particular Purpose

Implied warranty of fitness for a particular purpose. A warranty by a seller or lessor that the goods will meet the buyer's or lessee's expressed needs.

Magnuson-Moss Warranty Act

A federal statute that covers written warranties that apply to *consumer* products.

1. ***Full and Limited Warranties.*** If a good costs more than $10 and the warrantor makes an express warranty, the warranty must be labeled "full" or "limited."
   a. *Full warranty.* Guarantees free repair or replacement of a defective product. A time limit may be placed on the warranty.
   b. *Limited warranty.* Limits the scope of a full warranty in some way (e.g., return of the purchase price).

2. ***Limitation on Disclaiming Implied Warranties.*** If a seller or lessor makes an express warranty, he or she cannot disclaim or modify the implied warranties of merchantability and fitness for a particular purpose. A time limit may be placed on implied warranties but must correspond to the duration of the express warranty.

Product Liability Based on Fault, p. 156

Negligence

A seller or lessor reaches his or her duty of due care by producing a defective product that causes injury to the plaintiff. Privity of contract between the seller or lessor and the plaintiff is not required.

Misrepresentation

A seller or lessor fraudulently misrepresents the quality of a product, and the plaintiff relies on the misrepresentation and is injured thereby.

The Doctrine of Strict Liability, p. 157

Strict Liability in Tort

A manufacturer or seller who sells a defective product is liable to the ultimate user who is injured thereby. All in the chain of distribution are liable, irrespective of fault. Sometimes called *vertical liability.*

The Concept of Defect, p. 161

The Concept of Defect

To recover for strict liability, the injured party must show that the product that caused the injury was defective. The most common types of defects are:

1. Defect in manufacture
2. Defect in design
3. Defect in packaging
4. Failure to warn
5. Failure to provide adequate instructions for assembly of a product
6. Other defects

Defenses to Product Liability, p. 167

Defenses to Product Liability

A manufacturer or seller is not liable for damages caused by a product it manufactures or sells if one of the following defenses applies:

1. ***Supervening event.*** The product was materially altered or modified after it left the seller's possession and the alteration or modification caused an injury. Also called intervening event.
2. ***Generally known dangers.*** A seller is not liable for failing to warn about inherent dangers in products that are known to the general population.
3. ***Government contractor defense.*** A manufacturer produces a product to government specifications and warns the government of any known defects in the specified design.
4. ***Correction of a defect.*** A manufacturer or seller who learns about a defect in a product it has sold notifies purchasers and users of the defect and corrects the defect.
5. ***Assumption of the risk.*** The plaintiff knew and appreciated the risk and voluntarily assumed the risk.
6. ***Misuse of the product.***
    a. *Abnormal misuse.* The seller is not liable for injuries caused by the abnormal misuse of a product by the plaintiff. Also called unforeseeable misuse.
    b. *Foreseeable misuse.* The seller is liable for injuries caused by the foreseeable misuse of a product. The manufacturer must design products to be safe for foreseeable misuses.

Statutes of Limitation and Repose

1. ***Statute of limitations.*** Requires an injured person to bring a product liability lawsuit within a specified period of time after being injured by a defective product.
2. ***Statute of repose.*** Requires a person to bring a product liability lawsuit within a specified period of time after a defective product was first purchased or leased.

Contributory and Comparative Negligence

1. ***Contributory negligence.*** A person who is partially responsible for causing his or her own injuries may not recover anything from the manufacturer or seller of a defective product that caused the remainder of the person's injuries.
2. ***Comparative negligence.*** A person who is partially responsible for causing his or her own injuries is responsible for a proportional share of the damages. The manufacturer or seller of the defective product is responsible for the remainder of the plaintiff's damages. Also called *comparative fault.*

Internet Exercises and Case Questions

Working the Web Internet Exercises

Activities

1. Find statistics on the most frequent type of product liability cases filed in your jurisdiction. Start with Consumer Product Safety Data at **www.cpsc.gov/library/data.html**.
2. What is the statute of limitations on product liability in your jurisdiction? Does it matter if your case is filed under UCC Article 2 warranties, negligence, or strict liability under Section 402A of the *Restatement (Second) of Torts*? See *Restatement of Torts*, Section 402A, at **www.ali.org/ali/Tortpl.htm**. See also **www.law.cornell.edu/topics/products_liability.html**, which contains an overview of products-liability law, with links to key primary and secondary sources.
3. Does your state have a statute of repose for product liability cases?

Critical Legal Thinking Cases

6.1 Express Warranty The House of Zog manufactures and sells the "Golfing Gizmo," a training device designed to help golfers improve their swing. The device consists of a golf ball attached to one end of a cotton string, the other end of the string being tied to the middle of an elastic cord. The elastic cord is then stretched between two stakes placed in the ground, forming a "T" configuration. This allows the ball to return automatically after it has been struck. The "Golfing Gizmo" is sold in a package that states "COMPLETELY SAFE—BALL WILL NOT HIT PLAYER." In 1966, Louise Hauter gave a Golfing Gizmo to her 13-year-old son, Fred, for Christmas. One afternoon, Fred decided to use the device, which had been set up in his front yard. Having used the Gizmo before, Fred felt no apprehension as he took his normal swing at the ball. The last thing he remembered was pain and dizziness. Fred had been hit in the head by the ball and had suffered serious injuries. Fred Hauter sued the House of Zog. Who wins? [*Hauter v. Zogarts*, 14 Cal.3d 104, 120 Cal.Rptr. 681, 1975 Cal. Lexis 280 (Cal. 1975)]

6.2 Statement of Fact or Opinion? Jack Crothers went to Norm's Auto World to buy a used car. Maurice Boyd, a salesman at Norm's, showed Crothers a 1970 Dodge. While running the car's engine, Boyd told Crothers that the Dodge "had a rebuilt carburetor" and "was a good runner." After listening to the sales pitch, Crothers bought the car. As Crothers was driving the Dodge the next day, the car suddenly went out of control and crashed into a tree. Crothers was seriously injured. The cause of the crash was an obvious defect in the Dodge's accelerator linkage. Crothers sued Norm's Auto World. Who wins? [*Crothers v. Cohen*, 384 N.W.2d 562, 1986 Minn.App. Lexis 4202 (Minn.App. 1986)]

6.3 Implied Warranty of Merchantability Geraldine Maybank took a trip to New York City to visit her son and her two-year-old grandson. She borrowed her daughter's camera for the trip. Two days before leaving for New York, Maybank purchased a package of G.T.E. Sylvania Blue Dot flash cubes at a Kmart store. Kmart is owned by the S. S. Kresge Company. On the carton of the package were words to the effect that each bulb was safety coated. Upon arriving in New York, Maybank decided to take a picture of her grandson. She opened the carton of flash cubes and put one on the camera. When Maybank pushed down the lever to take a picture, the flash cube exploded. The explosion knocked her glasses off and caused cuts to her left eye. Maybank was hospitalized for eight days. Maybank sued S. S. Kresge Company. Who wins? [*Maybank v. S. S. Kresge Company*, 266 S.E.2d 409, 1980 N.C.App. Lexis 2927 (N.C.App. 1980)]

6.4 Implied Warranty of Merchantability Gladys Flippo went to a ladies' clothing store in Batesville, Arkansas, known as Mode O'Day Frock Shops of Hollywood. Flippo tried on two pairs of pants that were shown to her by a saleswoman. The first pair proved to be too small. When Flippo put on the second pair, she suddenly felt a burning sensation on her thigh. Flippo immediately removed the pants, shook them, and a spider fell to the ground. An examination of her thigh revealed a reddened area, which grew progressively worse. Flippo was subsequently hospitalized for 30 days. According to her physician, the injury was caused by the bite of a brown recluse spider. Flippo sued Mode O'Day Frock Shops. Is Mode O'Day Frock Shops liable? [*Flippo v. Mode O'Day Frock Shops of Hollywood*, 449 S.W.2d 692, 1970 Ark. Lexis 1165 (Ark. 1970)]

6.5 Implied Warranty of Fitness for Human Consumption Tina Koperwas went to a Publix Supermarket in Florida and bought a can of Doxsee Brand Clam Chowder. Keperwes opened the can of soup and prepared it at home. While eating the chowder, she bit down on a clam shell and injured one of her molars. Koperwas filed suit against Publix and Doxsee for breach of an implied warranty. In the lawsuit, Keperwes alleged that the clam chowder "was not fit for use as food, but was defective, unwholesome, and unfit for human consumption" and "was in such condition as to be dangerous to life and health." At the trial, Doxsee's general manager testified as to the state-of-the-art methods Doxsee uses in preparing its chowder. Are Publix Supermarkets and Doxsee liable for the injury to Keperwes's tooth? [*Koperwas v. Public Supermarkets, Inc.*, 534 S.2d 872, 1988 Fla.App. Lexis 5306 (Fla.App. 1988)]

6.6 Implied Warranty of Fitness for a Particular Purpose Dennis Walker is the owner of several pizza parlors in Nebraska. The stores operate under the name El Fredo Pizza Restaurants, Inc. Walker planned to open a new restaurant in 1973. A business associate suggested that Walker purchase an oven from the Roto-Flex Oven Co. Walker contacted an agent of Roto-Flex and negotiated to buy a new oven. Walker told the agent the particular purpose for which he was buying the oven—to cook pizza—and that he was relying on the agent's skill and judgment in selecting a suitable oven. Based on the agent's suggestions, Walker entered into a contract to purchase a custom-built Roto-Flex "Pizza Oven Special." The oven was installed in the new restaurant, and problems immediately ensued. The oven failed to bake pizzas properly because of uneven heating. Constant monitoring of the oven was required, and delays occurred in serving customers. Roto-Flex was notified of the problem and attempted to fix the oven. The oven, however, continued to bake pizzas improperly. El Fredo Pizza, Inc., sued Roto-Flex Oven Co. Was a warranty of fitness for a particular purpose created in this case? [*El Fredo Pizza, Inc. v. Roto-Flex Oven Co.*, 261 N.W.2d 358, 1978 Neb. Lexis 625 (Neb. 1978)]

6.7 Disclaimer of Warranties Cole Energy Company wanted to lease a gas compressor for use in its business of pumping and selling natural gas. Cole Energy began negotiating with the Ingersoll-Rand Company. On December 5, 1983, the two parties entered into a lease agreement for a KOA gas compressor. The lease agreement contained a section labeled "WARRANTIES." Part of the section read "THERE ARE NO IMPLIED WARRANTIES OF MERCHANTABILITY OR FITNESS FOR A PARTICULAR PURPOSE CONTAINED HEREIN." The gas compressor that was installed failed to function properly. As a result, Cole Energy lost business. Cole Energy sued Ingersoll-Rand for the breach of an implied warranty of merchantability. Is Ingersoll-Rand liable? [*Cole Energy Development Company v. Ingersoll-Rand Company*, 678 F.Supp. 208, 1988 U.S. Dist. Lexis 923 (C.D.III. 1988)]

6.8 Strict Liability Jeppesen and Company produces charts that graphically display approach procedures for airplanes landing at airports. These charts are drafted from tabular data supplied by the Federal Aviation Administration (FAA), a federal agency of the U.S. government. By law, Jeppesen cannot construct charts that include information different from that supplied by the FAA. On September 8, 1973, the pilot of an airplane owned by World Airways was on descent to land at the Cold Bay, Alaska, airport. The pilot was using an instrument approach procedure chart published by Jeppesen. The airplane crashed into a mountain near Cold Bay, killing all six crew members and destroying the aircraft. Evidence showed that the FAA data did not include the mountain. The heirs of the deceased crew members and World Airways brought a strict liability action against Jeppesen. Does the doctrine of strict liability apply to this case? Is Jeppesen liable? [*Brocklesby v. Jeppesen and Company*, 767 F.2d 1288, 1985 U.S. App. Lexis 21290 (9th Cir. 1985)]

6.9 Defect The Emerson Electric Co. manufactures and sells a product called the Weed Eater Model XR-90. The Weed Eater is a multipurpose weed-trimming and brush-cutting device. It consists of a handheld gasoline-powered engine connected to a long drive shaft, at the end of which can be attached various tools for cutting weeds and brush. One such attachment is a 10-inch circular sawblade capable of cutting through growth up to 2 inches in diameter. When this sawblade is attached to the Weed Eater, approximately 270 degrees of blade edge are exposed when in use. The owner's manual contained the following warning: "Keep children away. All people and pets should be kept at a safe distance from the work area, at least 30 feet, especially when using the blade." Donald Pearce, a 13-year-old boy, was helping his uncle clear an overgrown yard. The uncle was operating a Weed Eater XR-90 with the circular sawblade attachment. When Pearce stooped to pick something up off the ground about 6 to 10 feet behind and slightly to the left of where his uncle was operating the Weed Eater, the sawblade on the Weed Eater struck something near the ground. The Weed Eater kicked back to the left and cut off Pearce's right arm to the elbow. Pearce, through his mother, Charlotte Karns, sued Emerson to recover damages under strict liability. Is Emerson liable? [*Karns v. Emerson Electric Co.*, 817 F.2d 1452, 1987 U.S. App. Lexis 5608 (1987)]

6.10 Crashworthiness Doctrine At 11 P.M. on April 10, 1968, Verne Prior, driving on U.S. 101 under the influence of alcohol and drugs at a speed of 65 to 85 miles per hour, crashed his 1963 Chrysler into the left rear of a 1962 Chevrolet station wagon stopped on the shoulder of the freeway because of a flat tire. Christine Smith was sitting in the passenger seat of the parked car when the accident occurred. In the crash, the Chevrolet station wagon was knocked into a gully, where its fuel tank ruptured. The vehicle caught fire, and Smith suffered severe burn injuries. The Chevrolet station wagon was manufactured by General Motors Corporation. Evidence showed that the fuel tank was located in a vulnerable position in the back of the station wagon, outside the crossbars of the frame. Evidence further showed that if the fuel tank had been located underneath the body of the station wagon, between the crossbars of the frame, it would have been well protected in the collision. Smith sued General Motors for strict liability. Was the Chevrolet station wagon a defective product? [*Self v. General Motors Corporation*, 42 C.A.3d 1, 116 Cal.Rptr. 575, 1974 Cal.App. Lexis 1199 (Cal.App. 1974)]

6.11 Defect Virginia Burke purchased a bottle of "Le Domaine" champagne that was manufactured by Almaden Vineyards, Inc. At home, she removed the wine seal from the top of the bottle but did not remove the plastic cork. She set the bottle on the counter, intending to serve it in a few minutes. Shortly thereafter, the plastic cork spontaneously ejected from the bottle, ricocheted off the wall, and struck Burke in the left lens of her eyeglasses, shattering the lens and driving pieces of glass into her eye. The champagne bottle did not contain any warning of this danger. Evidence showed that Almaden had previously been notified of the spontaneous ejection of the cork from its champagne bottles. Burke sued Almaden to recover damages for strict liability. Is Almaden liable? [*Burke v. Almaden Vineyards, Inc.*, 86 C.A.3d 768, 150 Cal.Rptr. 419, 1978 Cal.App. Lexis 2123 (Cal.App. 1978)]

6.12 Assumption of Risk Lillian Horn was driving her Chevrolet station wagon, which was designed and manufactured by General Motors Corporation, down Laurel Canyon Boulevard in Los Angeles, California. Horn swerved to avoid a collision when a car coming toward her crossed the center line and was coming at her. In doing so, her hand knocked the horn cap off of the steering wheel, which exposed the area underneath the horn cap, including three sharp prongs that had held the horn cap to the steering wheel. A few seconds later, when her car hit an embankment, Horn's face was impaled on the three sharp exposed prongs, causing her severe facial injuries. Horn sued General Motors for strict liability. General Motors asserted the defense of assumption of the risk against Horn. Who wins? [*Horn v. General Motors Corporation*, 17 C.3d 359, 131 Cal.Rptr. 78, 1976 Cal. Lexis 283 (Cal. 1976)

6.13 Misuse On the morning of February 25, 1980, Elizabeth Horton (name changed to Ellsworth) wore a lady's flannelette nightgown inside out. As a result, two pockets on the sides of the nightgown were protruding from the sides of the nightgown. Ellsworth turned on the left front burner on the electric stove to "high" and placed a tea kettle of water on the burner. The kettle only partially covered the burner. As Horton reached above the stove to obtain coffee filters from one of the cupboards, the nightgown came in contact with the exposed portion of the burner and ignited. Ellsworth was severely burned and suffered permanent injuries. Ellsworth sued Sherme Lingerie, the seller of the nightgown, and Cone Mills Corporation, the manufacturer of the textile from which the nightgown was made, for strict liability. Was there a misuse of the product that would relieve the defendants of liability? [*Ellsworth v. Sherme Lingerie and Cone Mills Corporation*, 495 A.2d 348, 1985 Md. Lexis 920 (Md.App. 1985)]

6.14 Misuse The Wilcox-Crittendon Company manufactured harnesses, saddles, bridles, leads, and other items commonly used for horses, cattle, and other ranch and farm animals. One such item was a stallion or cattle tie, a five-inch-long iron hook with a one-inch ring at one end. The tongue on the ring opened outward to allow the hook to be attached to a rope or another object. In 1964, a purchasing agent for United Airlines, who was familiar with this type of hook because of earlier experiences on a farm, purchased one of these hooks from Keystone Brothers, a harness and saddlery wares outlet located in San Francisco, California. Four years later, on March 28, 1968, Edward Dosier, an employee of United Airlines, was working to install a new grinding machine at a United Airlines maintenance plant. As part of the installation process, Dosier attached the hook to a 1,700-pound counterweight and raised the counterweight into the air. While the counterweight was suspended in the air, Dosier reached under the counterweight to retrieve a missing bolt. The hook broke, and the counterweight fell and crushed Dosier's arm. Dosier sued Wilcox-Crittendon for strict liability. Who wins? [*Dosier v. Wilcox-Crittendon Company*, 45 Cal.App.3d. 74, 119 Cal.Rptr. 135, 1975 Cal.App. Lexis 1665 (Cal.App. 1975)]

Business Ethics Cases

6.15 Business Ethics During October 1978, Brian Keith, an actor, attended a boat show in Long Beach, California. At the boat show Keith obtained sales literature on a sailboat called the "Island Trader 42" from a sales representative of James Buchanan, a seller of sailboats. One sales brochure described the vessel as "a picture of sure-footed seaworthiness." Another brochure called the sailboat "a carefully well-equipped and very seaworthy live-aboard vessel." In November 1978, Keith purchased an Island Trader 41 sailboat from Buchanan for a total purchase price of $75,610. After delivery of the sailboat, a dispute arose in regard to the seaworthiness of the vessel. Keith sued Buchanan for breach of warranty. Buchanan defended, arguing that no warranty had been made. Was it ethical for Buchanan to try to avoid being held accountable for statements of quality about its product that were made in the sales brochures given Keith? Should sales "puffing" be considered to create an express warranty? Why or why not? Who wins this case? [*Keith v. Buchanan*, 173 Cal.App.3d 13, 220 Cal.Rptr. 392, 1985 Cal.App. Lexis 2603 (Cal.App. 1985)]

6.16 Business Ethics The Delano Growers' Cooperative Winery, a California winery, produces wine in bulk. Supreme Wine Co. Inc., operated a wine bottling plant in Boston. Since 1968, Supreme had purchased finished wine in bulk from Delano and other wine producers, which it then bottled and sold to retailers under the "Supreme" label. Supreme purchased all its sweet wine from Delano, and it was delivered to Supreme's bottling plant in tank cars. Supreme then pumped the wine into redwood vats in its building.

In 1973, Supreme began receiving widespread returns of sweet wine from its customers. All of the returned wine was produced by Delano. The wine was producing sediment, was cloudy, and contained a cottony or hairy substance. Supreme complained to Delano, which promised to correct the situation. Delano made other shipments of sweet wine to Supreme, but customers continued to return defective wine to Supreme. Evidence showed that the wine contained *lactobacillus trichodes*, also called "Fresno mold." More than 8,000 cases of wine were spoiled by the Fresno mold. When Supreme refused to pay an invoice of $25,825 for shipment of wine, Delano sued to collect this amount. Supreme filed a counterclaim to recover damages. Was it ethical for the seller to disavow liability in this case? Who wins? [*Delano Growers' Cooperative Winery v. Supreme Wine Co. Inc.*, 473 N.E.2d 1066, 1985 Mass. Lexis 1211 (Mass. 1985)]

6.17 Business Ethics Celestino Luque lived with his cousins Harry and Laura Dunn in Millbrae, California. The Dunns purchased a rotary lawn mower from Rhoads Hardware. The lawn mower was manufactured by Air Capital Manufacturing Company and was distributed by Garehime Corporation. On December 4, 1965, neighbors asked Luque to mow their lawn. While Luque was cutting the lawn, he noticed a small carton in the path of the lawn mower. Luque left the lawn mower in a stationary position with its motor running and walked around the side of the lawn mower to remove the carton. As he did so, he suddenly slipped on the wet grass and fell backward. Luque's left hand entered the unguarded hole of the lawn mower and was caught in its revolving blade, which turns at 175 miles per hour and 100 revolutions per second. Luque's hand was severely mangled and lacerated. The word *Caution* was printed above the unguarded hole on the lawn mower. Luque sued Rhoads Hardware, Air Capital, and Garehime Corporation for strict liability. The defendants argued that strict liability does not apply to *patent* (obvious) defects. Was it ethical for the defendants to argue that they were not liable for patent defects? Would patent defects ever be corrected if the defendants' contention was accepted by the court? Who wins? [*Luque v. McLean, Trustee*, 8 Cal.3d 136, 104 Cal.Rptr. 443, 1972 Cal. Lexis 245 (Cal. 1972)]

Briefing the Case Writing Assignment

Read Case A.6 in the Case Appendix [*Johnson v. Chicago Pneumatic Tool Company*]. Review and brief this case. In your brief, be sure to answer the following questions.

1. Who was the plaintiff? Who was the defendant?
2. What law did the plaintiff assert was violated by the defendant?
3. What was the defendant's defense? Explain.
4. Was this defense effective in this case?

Answers to Management Decision Questions

1. You should contact an attorney about commencing a product liability lawsuit for the harm suffered by your daughter. The various warranty and tort principles that permit injured parties to recover damages caused by defective products include breach of express and implied warranties and tort actions based on negligence and strict liability. In the landmark case *Henningsen v. Bloomfield Motors, Inc.*, 161 A.2d 69, 32 N.J. 358, 1960 N.J. Lexis 213 (1960) the court held that lack of privity did not prevent a third-party plaintiff from suing for breach of the implied warranty of merchantability. The UCC continued this evolutionary trend by limiting the doctrine of privity, saying that disclaimers and limitations of liability are ineffective against third parties.

   A person injured by a defective product may bring an action for negligence against the negligent party. In the landmark case *MacPherson v. Buick Motor Co.*, 111 N.E. 1050, 217 N.Y. 382, 1916 N.Y. Lexis 1324 (1916), the court held that an injured consumer could recover damages from the manufacturer of a product even though the consumer was only in privity with the retailer from whom he had purchased the product.

   In the landmark case *Greenmun v. Yuba Power Products, Inc.*, 377 P.2d 897, 59 Cal.2d 57, 1963 Cal. Lexis 140 (1963) the California supreme court adopted the doctrine of strict liability in tort as a basis for product liability actions. Most states have now adopted this doctrine as a basis for product liability actions.

   Because of several court rulings and as a matter of public policy, all parties in the chain of distribution of a defective product may be sued for the injuries caused by that product. Thus, the manufacturer, distributor, wholesaler, retailer, and subcomponent manufacturer of the paint may be sued.
2. Several defenses may come into play that may be asserted in a product liability case. The defenses that may be applicable in this situation include generally known dangers, assumption of risk, misuse of the product, and contributory and comparative negligence.

Endnotes

1. *Restatement (Second) of Torts*, § 395.
2. 111 N.E. 1050, 217 N.Y. 382, 1916 N.Y. Lexis 1324 (N.Y.App. 1916).
3. 59 Cal.2d 57, 27 Cal.Rptr. 697, 377 P.2d 897, 1963 Cal. Lexis 140 (1963).
4. Some states have enacted statutes that provide that the doctrine of strict liability does not apply to transactions involving the sale of blood or blood products.
5. *Restatement (Second) of Torts*, § 402A(1)(b).

7

Business Crimes and Criminal Law

"It is better that ten guilty persons escape, than that one innocent suffer."

—Sir William Blackstone
Commentaries on the Laws of England (1809)

Chapter Objectives

After studying this chapter, you should be able to:

1. Define and list the essential elements of a crime.
2. Describe criminal procedure, including arrest, indictment, arraignment, and the criminal trial.
3. Define major white-collar crimes, such as embezzlement, bribery, and criminal fraud.
4. Explain the constitutional safeguards provided by the Fourth, Fifth, Sixth, and Eighth Amendments to the U.S. Constitution.
5. List and describe laws involving computer and Internet crimes.

Chapter Contents

Management Decision Business Crimes and Criminal Law

You are the owner of an upscale nightclub. Over the years, John Smith, a local entrepreneur, has approached you several times about becoming a partner in your business. In the past you have ignored his request because you have heard rumors that he is involved in the illegal trafficking and selling of drugs in your community. Presently, you are having difficulty securing funds to expand your business. You are considering taking Mr. Smith up on his offer. After all, he has not been convicted of any illegal activity. You would remain the general manager of the nightclub, and Mr. Smith has indicated that he has no intention of actively participating in the management of the nightclub.

1. Is there potential criminal wrongdoing associated with making Mr. Smith a partner in your business?
2. Is it ethical for you to make Mr. Smith a business associate?

For members of society to peacefully coexist and commerce to flourish, people and their property must be protected from injury by other members of society. Federal, state, and local governments' **criminal laws** are intended to accomplish this by providing an incentive for persons to act reasonably in society and imposing penalties on persons who violate them.

The United States has one of the most advanced and humane criminal law systems in the world. It differs from any other criminal law systems in several respects. A person charged with a crime in the United States is *presumed innocent until proven guilty*. The *burden of proof* is on the government to prove that the accused is guilty of the crime charged. Further, the accused must be found guilty "beyond a reasonable doubt." Conviction requires unanimous jury vote. Under many other legal systems, a person accused of a crime is presumed guilty unless the person can prove he or she is not. A person charged with a crime in the United States is also provided with substantial constitutional safeguards during the criminal justice process.

Business Brief

In the United States, a person accused of a crime is *presumed innocent until proven guilty*. The government has the burden of proving that the accused is guilty of the crime charged.

London, England. Most industrialized countries and many other countries have well-developed criminal laws and legal systems to enforce these laws.

This chapter discusses crime, criminal procedure, crimes affecting business, white-collar crime, computer crime, inchoate crime, criminal penalties, and constitutional safeguards afforded criminal defendants.

Definition of a Crime

> Fraud includes the pretense of knowledge when knowledge there is none.
>
> C. J. Cardozo
> *Ultramares Corp. v. Touche (1931)*

crime
A violation of a statute for which the government imposes a punishment.

A **crime** is defined as any act done by an individual in violation of those duties that he or she owes to society and for the breach of which the law provides that the wrongdoer shall make amends to the public. Many activities have been considered crimes through the ages, whereas other crimes are of recent origin.

Penal Codes and Regulatory Statutes

penal codes
A collection of criminal statutes.

Statutes are the primary source of criminal law. Most states have adopted comprehensive **penal codes** that define in detail the activities considered to be crimes within their jurisdiction and the penalties that will be imposed for their commission. A comprehensive federal criminal code defines federal crimes.[1] In addition, state and federal regulatory statutes often provide for criminal violations and penalties. The state and federal legislatures are continually adding to the list of crimes.

> No! No! Sentence first—verdict afterward.
>
> Lewis Carroll
> *Alice in Wonderland, Ch. 12*

The penalty for committing a crime may consist of the imposition of a fine, imprisonment, both, or some other form of punishment (e.g., probation). Generally, imprisonment is imposed to (1) incapacitate the criminal so he or she will not harm others in society, (2) provide a means to rehabilitate the criminal, (3) deter others from similar conduct, and (4) inhibit personal retribution by the victim.

Parties to a Criminal Action

Business Brief
The plaintiff in a criminal trial is the government.

In a criminal lawsuit, the government (not a private party) is the **plaintiff**. The government is represented by a lawyer called the *prosecutor*. The accused is the **defendant**. The accused is represented by a *defense attorney*. If the accused cannot afford a defense lawyer, the government will provide one free of charge.

Classification of Crimes

All crimes can be classified in one of the following categories.

felony
The most serious type of crime; inherently evil crime. Most crimes against persons and some business-related crimes are felonies.

Felonies **Felonies** are the most serious kinds of crimes. Felonies include crimes that are *mala in se*, that is, inherently evil. Most crimes against persons (e.g., murder, rape, and the like) and certain business-related crimes (e.g., embezzlement and bribery) are felonies in most jurisdictions. Felonies are usually punishable by imprisonment. In some jurisdictions, certain felonies (e.g., first-degree murder) are punishable by death. Federal law[2] and some state laws require mandatory sentencing for specified crimes. Many statutes define different degrees of crimes (e.g., first-, second-, and third-degree murder). Each degree earns different penalties.

misdemeanor
A less serious crime than a felony; not inherently evil but prohibited by society. Many crimes against property are misdemeanors.

Misdemeanors **Misdemeanors** are less serious than felonies. They are crimes *mala prohibita*; that is, they are not inherently evil but are prohibited by society. Many crimes against property, such as robbery, burglary, and violations of regulatory statutes, are included in this category. Misdemeanors carry lesser penalties than felonies. They are usually punishable by fine and/or imprisonment for one year or less.

violation
A crime that is neither a felony nor a misdemeanor and that is usually punishable by a fine.

Violations Crimes such as traffic violations, jaywalking, and such are neither felonies nor misdemeanors. These crimes, which are called **violations**, are generally punishable by fines. Occasionally, a few days of imprisonment are imposed.

"Sweetie, show the Hazlitts the watercolors you made in jail."

Essential Elements of a Crime

The following two elements must be proven for a person to be found guilty of most crimes:

1. ***Criminal Act*** The defendant must have actually performed the prohibited act. The actual performance of the criminal act is called the **actus reus** (guilty act). Killing someone without legal jurisdiction is an example of *actus reus*. Sometimes, the omission of an act constitutes the requisite *actus reus*. For example, a crime has been committed if a taxpayer who is under a legal duty to file a tax return fails to do so. However, merely thinking about committing a crime is not a crime because no action has been taken.
2. ***Criminal Intent*** To be found guilty of a crime, the accused must be found to have possessed the requisite state of mind (i.e., specific or general intent) when the act was performed. This is called the **mens rea** (evil intent). *Specific intent* is found where the accused purposefully, intentionally, or with knowledge commits a prohibited act. *General intent* is found where there is a showing of recklessness or a lesser degree of mental culpability. The individual criminal statutes state whether the crime requires a showing of specific or general intent. Juries may infer an accused's intent from the facts and circumstances of the case. There is no crime if the requisite *mens rea* cannot be proven. Thus, no crime is committed if one person accidentally injures another person.

Some statutes impose criminal liability based on **strict**, or **absolute**, **liability**. That is, a finding of *mens rea* is not required. Criminal liability is imposed if the prohibited act is committed. Absolute liability is often imposed by regulatory statutes, such as environmental laws.

Web Site

U.S. Department of Justice The U.S. Department of Justice of the federal government prosecutes federal crimes. You can locate all sorts of Department of Justice information from its home page. Visit at **www.usdoj.gov**.

actus reus

"Guilty act"—the actual performance of a criminal act.

mens rea

"Evil intent"—the possession of the requisite state of mind to commit a prohibited act.

strict, or absolute, liability

A standard for imposing criminal liability without a finding of *mens rea* (intent).

Tibet. Religious beliefs are often reflected in the criminal laws of a country.

Criminal Acts as the Basis for Tort Actions

Business Brief
The same act may be the basis for both a criminal lawsuit and a civil lawsuit.

An injured party may bring a *civil tort action* against a wrongdoer who has caused the party injury during the commission of a criminal act. Civil lawsuits are separate from the government's criminal action against the wrongdoer. In many cases, a person injured by a criminal act will not sue the criminal to recover civil damages. This is because the criminal is often *judgment proof*—that is, the criminal does not have the money to pay a civil judgment.

Concept Summary Civil and Criminal Law Compared

Issue	Civil Law	Criminal Law
Party who brings the action	The plaintiff	The government
Trial by jury	Yes, except actions for equity	Yes
Burden of proof	Preponderance of the evidence	Beyond a reasonable doubt
Jury vote	Judgment for plaintiff requires specific jury vote (e.g., 9 of 12 jurors)	Conviction requires unanimous jury vote
Sanctions and penalties	Monetary damages and equitable remedies (e.g., injunction, specific performance)	Imprisonment, capital punishment, fine, and probation

The magnitude of a crime is proportionate to the magnitude of the injustice which prompts it. Hence, the smallest crimes may be actually the greatest.

Aristotle
The Rhetoric, BK. 1, Ch. XIV

Criminal Procedure

The court procedure for initiating and maintaining a criminal action is quite detailed. It includes both pretrial procedures and the actual trial.

Pretrial Criminal Procedure

Pretrial criminal procedure consists of several distinct stages, including *arrest*, *indictment* or *information*, *arraignment*, and *plea bargaining*.

Arrest Before the police can arrest a person for the commission of a crime, they usually must obtain an **arrest warrant** based on a showing of probable cause. *Probable cause* is defined as the substantial likelihood that the person either committed or is about to commit a crime. If there is no time for the police to obtain a warrant (e.g., if the police arrive during the commission of a crime, when a person is fleeing from the scene of a crime, or when it is likely that evidence will be destroyed), the policy may still arrest the suspect. *Warrantless arrests* are also judged by the probable cause standard.

arrest warrant
A document for a person's detainment, based on a showing of probable cause that the person committed the crime.

After a person is arrested, he or she is taken to the police station to be booked. *Booking* is the administrative procedure for recording the arrest, fingerprinting, and so on.

Indictment or Information Accused persons must be formally charged with a crime before they can be brought to trial. This is usually done by the issuance of a *grand jury indictment* or a *magistrate's information statement*.

Evidence of serious crimes, such as murder, is usually presented to a *grand jury*. Most grand juries comprise between 6 and 24 citizens who are charged with evaluating the evidence presented by the government. Grand jurors sit for a fixed period of time, such as one year. If the grand jury determines that there is sufficient evidence to hold the accused for trial, it issues an **indictment**. Note that the grand jury does not determine guilt. If an indictment is issued, the accused will be held for later trial.

indictment
The charge of having committed a crime (usually a felony), based on the judgment of a grand jury.

For lesser crimes (e.g., burglary, shoplifting, and such), the accused will be brought before a *magistrate* (judge). A magistrate who finds that there is enough evidence to hold the accused for trial will issue an **information**.

information
The charge of having committed a crime (usually a misdemeanor), based on the judgment of a judge (magistrate).

The case against the accused is dismissed if neither an indictment nor an information is issued.

Arraignment If an indictment or information is issued, the accused is brought before a court for an **arraignment** proceeding, during which the accused is (1) informed of the charges against him or her and (2) asked to enter a **plea**. The accused may plead *guilty*, *not guilty*, or *nolo contendere*. A plea of *nolo contendere* means that the accused agrees to the imposition of a penalty but does not admit guilt. A *nolo contendere* plea cannot be used as evidence of liability against the accused at a subsequent civil trial. Corporate defendants often enter this plea. The government has the option of accepting a *nolo contendere* plea or requiring the defendant to plead guilty or not guilty.

arraignment
A hearing during which the accused is brought before a court and is (1) informed of the charges against him or her and (2) asked to enter a plea.

In the following case, the U.S. Supreme Court held that a police officer may make a warrantless arrest pursuant to a minor criminal offense.

Case 7.1
Arrest

U.S. SUPREME COURT CASE
Atwater v. Lago Vista, Texas
532 U.S. 318, 121 S.Ct. 1536, 2001 U.S. Lexis 3366 (2001)
Supreme Court of the United States

Background and Facts

Texas law requires that front-seat drivers and passengers wear seat belts and that a driver secure any small child riding in front. In March 1997, Gail Atwater was driving her pickup truck in Lago Vista, Texas, with her three-year-old son and five-year-old daughter in the front seat. None of them were wearing seat belts. Bart Turek, a Lago Vista police officer, observed the seat-belt violation and pulled Atwater over. A friend of Atwater's

Atwater v. Lago Vista, Texas

532 U.S. 318, 121 S.Ct. 1536, 2001 U.S. Lexis 3366 (2001)
Supreme Court of the United States
(continued)

arrived at the scene and took charge of the children. Turek handcuffed Atwater, placed her in his squad car, and drove her to the police station. Atwater was booked, her "mug shot" was taken, and she was placed in a jail cell for about one hour until she was released on $310 bond. Atwater ultimately pleaded no contest to the misdemeanor seat-belt offenses and paid a $50 fine. Atwater sued the City of Lago Vista and the police officer for compensatory and punitive damages for allegedly violating her Fourth Amendment right to be free from unreasonable seizure. The district court ruled against Atwater, and the court of appeals affirmed. The U.S. Supreme Court granted certiorari to hear the appeal.

Supreme Court Issue

Does the Fourth Amendment permit police to make a warrantless arrest pursuant to a minor criminal offense?

In The Language of The U.S. Supreme Court

Souter, Justice There is no support for Atwater's position in this Court's cases. Both the legislative tradition of granting warrantless misdemeanor arrest authority and the judicial tradition of sustaining such statutes against constitutional attack are buttressed by legal commentary that, for more than a century now, has almost uniformly recognized the constitutionality of extending warrantless arrest power to misdemeanors without limitation to breaches of the peace. If an officer has probable cause to believe that an individual has committed even a very minor criminal offense in his presence, he may, without violating the Fourth Amendment, arrest the offender.

Decision and Remedy

The U.S. Supreme Court held that the Fourth Amendment permits police officers to make a warrantless arrest pursuant to a minor criminal offense. The judgment of the court of appeals was affirmed.

Case Questions

Critical Legal Thinking Do you agree with the U.S. Supreme Court's decision in this case? Why or why not?

Business Ethics Did the police officer act ethically in this case? Should he have used more discretion?

Contemporary Business What would be the consequences if the Supreme Court had held in favor of Atwater?

plea bargain
A situation in which the accused admits to a lesser crime than charged. In return, the government agrees to impose a lesser sentence than might have been obtained had the case gone to trial.

Plea Bargaining Sometimes the accused and the government enter into a **plea bargaining agreement**. The government engages in plea bargaining to save costs, avoid the risks of a trial, and prevent further overcrowding of the prisons. This type of arrangement allows the accused to admit to a lesser crime than charged. In return, the government agrees to impose a lesser penalty or sentence than might have been obtained had the case gone to trial.

The Criminal Trial

At a criminal trial, all jurors must *unanimously* agree before the accused is found *guilty* of the crime charged. If even one juror disagrees (i.e., has reasonable doubt) about the guilt of the accused, the accused is *not guilty* of the crime charged. If all of the jurors agree that the accused did not commit the crime, the accused is *innocent* of the crime charged. After trial, the following rules apply:

hung jury
A jury that cannot come to a unanimous decision about the defendant's guilt. The government may choose to retry the case.

- If the defendant is found guilty, he or she may appeal.
- If the defendant is found innocent, the government cannot appeal.
- If the jury cannot come to a unanimous decision about the defendant's guilt, the jury is considered a **hung jury**. The government may choose to retry the case before a new judge and jury.

Contemporary Business Environment

Money Laundering

The term *money laundering* is used to refer to the process by which criminals convert tainted proceeds into apparently legitimate funds or property. It applies equally to an international wire transfer of hundreds of millions of dollars in drug proceeds and the purchase of an automobile with funds robbed from a bank.

Money laundering is a federal crime. The following activities are among those that were criminalized by the Money Laundering Control Act:

- Knowingly engaging in a *financial transaction* involving the proceeds of some form of specified unlawful activity. Transactions covered include the sale of real property, personal property, intangible assets, and anything of value [18 U.S.C. § 1956].
- Knowingly engaging in a *monetary transaction* by, through, or to a financial institution involving property of a value greater than $10,000, which is derived from specified unlawful activity. Money transaction is defined as a deposit, withdrawal, or transfer between accounts and use of a monetary instrument [18 U.S.C. § 1957].

"Specified unlawful activity" includes narcotics activities and virtually any white-collar crime.

Money laundering statutes have been used to go after entities and persons involved in illegal check-cashing schemes, bribery, insurance fraud, Medicaid fraud, bankruptcy fraud, bank fraud, fraudulent transfer of property, criminal conspiracy, environmental crime, and other types of illegal activities.

Conviction for money laundering carries stiff penalties. Persons can be fined up to $500,000 or twice the value of the property involved, whichever is greater, and sentenced to up to 20 years in federal prison. In addition, violation subjects the defendant to provisions that mandate forfeiture to the government of any property involved in or traceable to the offense [18 U.S.C. §§ 981–982]. Any financial institution convicted of money laundering can have its charter revoked or its insurance of deposit accounts terminated.

To avoid running afoul of these increasingly complex statutes, banks and businesses must develop and implement policies and procedures to detect criminal activity and report money laundering by customers to the federal government. ■

Crimes Affecting Business

Many crimes are committed against business property. These crimes often involve the theft, misappropriation, or fraudulent taking of property. Many of the most important crimes against business property are discussed in the following paragraphs.

Robbery

In common law, **robbery** is defined as the taking of personal property from another person by the use of fear or force. For example, if a robber threatens to physically harm a storekeeper unless that victim surrenders the contents of the cash register, it is robbery. If a criminal pickpockets somebody's wallet, it is not robbery because there has been no use of force or fear. Robbery with a deadly weapon is generally considered aggravated robbery (or armed robbery) and carries a harsher penalty.

robbery
The taking of personal property from another person by use of fear or force.

Burglary

In common law, **burglary** is defined as "breaking and entering a dwelling at night" with the intent to commit a felony. Modern penal codes have broadened this definition to include daytime thefts from offices and commercial and other buildings. In addition, the "breaking-in" element has been abandoned by most modern definitions of burglary. Thus, unauthorized entering of a building through an unlocked door is sufficient. Aggravated burglary (or armed burglary) carries stiffer penalties.

burglary
The taking of personal property from another's home, office, commercial or other type of building.

Larceny

larceny
The taking of another's personal property other than from his or her person or building.

In common law, **larceny** is defined as the wrongful and fraudulent taking of another person's personal property. Most personal property—including tangible property, trade secrets, computer programs, and other business property—is subject to larceny. The stealing of automobiles and car stereos, pickpocketing, and such are larceny. Neither the use of force nor the entry of a building is required. Some states distinguish between grand larceny and petit larceny. This distinction depends on the value of the property taken.

Theft

Law cannot persuade, where it cannot punish.

Thomas Fuller
Gnomologia (1732)

Some states have dropped the distinction among the crimes of robbery, burglary, and larceny. Instead, these states group these crimes under the general crime of **theft**. Most of these states distinguish between grand theft and petit theft. The distinction depends on the value of the property taken.

Receiving Stolen Property

receiving stolen property
(1) Knowingly receiving stolen property and (2) intending to deprive the rightful owner of that property.

It is a crime for a person to (1) knowingly **receive stolen property** and (2) intend to deprive the rightful owner of that property. Knowledge and intent can be inferred from the circumstances. The stolen property can be any tangible property (e.g., personal property, money, negotiable instruments, stock certificates, and such).

Arson

arson
The willful or malicious burning of another's building.

In common law, **arson** is defined as the malicious or willful burning of the dwelling of another person. Modern penal codes expanded this definition to include the burning of all types of private, commercial, and public buildings. Thus, in most states, an owner who burns his or her own building to collect insurance proceeds can be found liable for arson. If arson is found, the insurance company does not have to pay proceeds of any insurance policy on the burned property.

Forgery

forgery
The fraudulent making or altering of a written document that affects the legal liability of another person.

The crime of **forgery** occurs if a written document is fraudulently made or altered and that change affects the legal liability of another person. Counterfeiting, falsifying public records, and materially altering legal documents are examples of forgery. One of the most common forms of forgery is the signing of another person's signature to a check or changing the amount of a check. Note that signing another person's signature without intent to defraud is not forgery. For example, forgery has not been committed if one spouse signs the other spouse's payroll check for deposit in a joint checking or savings account at the bank.

Extortion

extortion
A threat to expose something about another person unless that other person gives money or property. Often referred to as *blackmail*.

The crime of **extortion** means the obtaining of property from another, with his or her consent, induced by wrongful use of actual or threatened force, violence, or fear. For example, extortion occurs when a person threatens to expose something about another person unless that other person gives money or property. The truth or falsity of the information is immaterial. Extortion of private persons is commonly referred to as **blackmail**. Extortion of public official is called **extortion "under color of official right."**

Credit-Card Crimes

A substantial number of purchases in this country are made with credit cards. This poses a problem if someone steals and uses another person's credit cards. Many states have enacted statutes that make the misappropriation and use of credit cards a separate crime. In other states, credit-card crimes are prosecuted under the forgery statute.

At the present time in this country there is more danger that criminals will escape justice than that they will be subjected to tyranny.

J. Holmes Dissenting
Kepner v. United States (1904)

Bad Check Legislation

Many states have enacted *bad check legislation* that makes it a crime for a person to make, draw, or deliver a check at a time when that person knows that there are insufficient funds in the account to cover the amount of the check. Some states require proof that the accused intended to defraud the payee of the check.

Business Ethics

Whistle-Blowers Sing for Millions

The federal government is the largest purchaser of goods and services in the country. As such, it is also the target of substantial fraud by the firms it deals with. If caught, a government contractor that defrauds the government is subject to criminal prosecution. In addition, the federal government relies on a revamped law that elicits employees of government contractors and others to become modern-day bounty hunters and report anyone who defrauds the government. The law is the **Civil False Claims Act**, commonly known as the **whistle-blower statute**. This act was originally enacted in 1863 to protect the federal government from corrupt government contractors after the Civil War. It was strengthened in 1986 to provide a penalty of *treble damages* plus up to $10,000 per false claim against the defendant and allows the court to award between 15 and 30 percent of the recovery to the whistle-blower, who is now politely called a "relator." These lawsuits are called **qui tam** cases (from the Latin phrase "he who sues as much for the king as for himself").

The procedure for bringing a *qui tam* lawsuit is simple: The relator files the lawsuit, notifies the federal government, and then waits to see if the federal government chooses to intervene in the lawsuit. If the federal government intervenes, it pursues the lawsuit; if not, the relator must pursue the lawsuit alone, which is very costly. The federal government intervenes in only 20 percent of the *qui tam* cases filed, and 95 percent of the recoveries are from these cases. Many cases in which the federal government does not intervene are dropped. There is a strong incentive for a defendant to settle *qui tam* cases that are pursued by the federal government, however. If the defendant loses, it faces the possibility of treble damages, plus a penalty of up to $10,000 per false claim and a ban on ever doing business with the federal government again.

The greatest number of whistle-blower cases have involved hospitals and other medical facilities that have been caught overbilling the federal government under Medicare and other government aid programs. The second greatest number of cases have involved oil and gas companies that have cheated the federal government out of royalty and lease payments due on contracts for drilling on federal land. Other cases have been brought against government contractors that overbill the federal government for other products and services, file false claims to receive government subsidies, and overcharge the government for building and construction contracts. Sometimes a potential relator does not even know he or she has a whistle-blower claim. For example, Evelyn Knoob walked into a lawyer's office to file a worker's compensation claim worth $400 per week when she was placed on leave by her employer, Illinois Blue Cross/Blue Shield. After talking to her attorney, she filed a *qui tam* case against the Illinois Blues, alleging overbilling of the federal government. Several years later the defendants settled with the federal government for $150 million. Ms. Knoob's share was $29 million.

Proponents of the modern Civil False Claims Act cite that the federal government has recovered over $3 billion from fraudulent government contractors. They also allege that the act deters fraud and saves the federal government over $10 billion per year by making government contractors more honest. Detractors argue that the whistle-blower statute generates frivolous lawsuits by disgruntled employees who are taking a shot at the lottery. Currently, more than 600 new *qui tam* cases are filed each year.

1. Do you think there is much fraud in government contracting? Does the Civil False Claims Act make government contractors more honest?
2. Do employees face an ethical dilemma when filing a *qui tam* action against their employer? If so, how do you think most employees solve this dilemma? ■

White-Collar Crimes

white-collar crimes
Crimes usually involving cunning and deceit rather than physical force.

Certain types of crime are prone to being committed by businesspersons. These crimes are often referred to as **white-collar crimes**. These crimes usually involve cunning and deceit rather than physical force. Many of the most important white-collar crimes are discussed in the paragraphs that follow.

Embezzlement

embezzlement
The fraudulent conversion of property by a person to whom that property was entrusted.

Unknown in common law, the crime of **embezzlement** is not a statutory crime. Embezzlement is the fraudulent conversion of property by a person to whom that property was entrusted. Typically, embezzlement is committed by an employer's employees, agents, or representatives (e.g., accountants, lawyers, trust officers, treasurers). Embezzlers often try to cover their tracks by preparing false books, records, or entries.

The key element here is that the stolen property was *entrusted* to the embezzler. This differs from robbery, burglary, and larceny, where property is taken by someone not entrusted with the property. For example, embezzlement has been committed if a bank teller absconds with money that was deposited by depositors. The employer (the bank) entrusted the teller to take deposits from its customers.

In our complex society the accountant's certificate and the lawyer's opinion can be instruments for inflicting pecuniary loss more potent than the chisel or the crowbar.

Justice Blackmun
Dissenting Opinion,
Ernest & Ernst v. Hochfelder, 425 U.S. 185 (1976)

Criminal Fraud

criminal fraud
The act of obtaining title to property through deception or trickery. Also known as false pretenses or deceit.

Obtaining title to property through deception or trickery constitutes the crime of **false pretenses**. This crime is commonly referred to as **criminal fraud** or **deceit**.

Consider This Example Bob Anderson, a stockbroker, promises Mary Greenberg, a prospective investor, that he will use any money she invests to purchase interests in oil wells. Based on this promise, Ms. Greenberg decides to make the investment. Mr. Anderson never intended to invest the money. Instead, he used the money for his personal needs. This is criminal fraud.

mail fraud
The use of mail to defraud another person.

wire fraud
The use of telephone or telegraph to defraud another person.

Mail and Wire Fraud Federal law prohibits the use of mails or wires (e.g., telegraphs, telephone and Internet) to defraud another person. These crimes are called **mail fraud**[3] and **wire fraud**,[4] respectively. The government often prosecutes a suspect under these statutes if there is insufficient evidence to prove the real crime that the criminal was attempting to commit or did commit. The maximum penalty for mail, wire, and Internet fraud is 20 years in prison.

E-Commerce & Information Technology

Federal Law Helps Victims of Identity Fraud

For centuries, some people—for various purposes, mostly financial in nature—have attempted to take the identities of other persons. Today, taking on the identity of another can be extremely lucrative, earning the spoils of another's credit cards, bank accounts, Social Security benefits, and such. The use of new technology—computers and the Internet—have made such "identity fraud" even easier. But the victim of such fraud is left with funds stolen, a dismantled credit history, and thousands of dollars in costs trying to straighten out the mess. Identity fraud is the fastest-growing financial fraud in America. Credit-reporting firms say identity fraud cases have increased from 10,000 in 1990 to more than 500,000 cases per year today.

Consider the case of Mari Frank. She learned about her misfortune late one night in 1996 when she got a telephone call from the Bank of New York, asking why she had not made the monthly payment on her credit card. There was one hitch: Frank did not have a credit card with the bank. But Frank's double—who looked nothing like her but had taken Frank's name, background, Social Security number, credit history, and even her business cards—did. The imposter had bought $50,000 in clothing and luxury items and a Mustang convertible and had charged them to Frank's credit. The imposter had used Frank's identity for a year before the fraud was detected. It then took Frank over 500 hours and thousands of dollars in costs to clean up the situation and clear her credit history of the imposter's spending spree. Luckily, Frank was not responsible for more than $50 on her credit-card debts or for any other debt taken out in her name by the imposter. Several banks, however, had to write off the debts incurred by the imposter in Frank's name as bad debts. Identity fraud costs businesses over $1 billion per year.

To combat such fraud, Congress passed the **Identity Theft and Assumption Deterrence Act of 1998**. This act criminalizes identity fraud, making it a federal felony punishable with prison sentences ranging from 3 to 25 years. The act also appoints a federal administrative agency, the Federal Trade Commission (FTC), to help victims restore their credit and erase the impact of the imposter. Law enforcement officials suggest the following steps to protect against identity fraud: Never put your Social Security number on any document unless it is legally required, obtain and review copies of your credit report at least twice each year, and use safe passwords (e.g., other than maiden names and birthdays) on bank accounts and other accounts that require personal identification numbers (PINs). ■

Bribery

Bribery is one of the most prevalent forms of white-collar crime. A bribe can be money, property, favors, or anything else of value. The crime of commercial bribery prohibits the payment of bribes to private persons and businesses. This type of bribe is often referred to as a **kickback** or **payoff**. Intent is a necessary element of this crime. The offeror of a bribe commits the crime of bribery when the bribe is tendered. The offeree is guilty of the crime of bribery when he or she accepts the bribe. The offeror can be found liable for the crime of bribery even if the person to whom the bribe is offered rejects the bribe.

bribery
The act of one person giving another person money, property, favors, or anything else of value for a favor in return. Often referred to as a payoff or kickback.

Consider This Example Harriet Landers is the purchasing agent for the ABC Corporation and is in charge of purchasing equipment to be used by the corporation. Neal Brown, the sales representative of a company that make equipment that can be used by the ABC Corporation, offers to pay her a 10 percent kickback if she buys equipment from him. She accepts the bribe and orders the equipment. Both parties are guilty of bribery.

In common law, the crime of bribery is defined as the giving or receiving of anything of value in corrupt payment for an "official act" by a public official. Public officials include legislators, judges, jurors, witnesses at trial, administrative agency personnel, and other government officials. Modern penal codes also make it a crime to bribe public officials. For example, a developer who is constructing an apartment building cannot pay the building inspector to overlook a building code violation.

The following case involved the federal antibribery statute.

There can be no equal justice where the kind of trial a man gets depends on the amount of money he has.

J. Black
Griffin v. Illinois (1956)

Business Brief
Bribery is probably the most prevalent form of business crime.

Case 7.2 Bribery

U.S. SUPREME COURT CASE

United States v. Sun-Diamond Growers of California

526 U.S. 398, 119 S.Ct. 1402, 1999 U.S. Lexis 3001 (1999)
Supreme Court of the United States

Background and Facts

The Sun-Diamond Growers of California is a trade association that engages in marketing and lobbying activities on behalf of its 5,000 member-growers of raisins, figs, walnuts, prunes, and hazelnuts. Sun-Diamond gave Michael Epsy, U.S. secretary of agriculture, tickets to sporting events (worth $2,295), luggage ($2,427), meals ($665), and a crystal bowl ($524) while several matters in which Sun-Diamond members had an interest were pending before the secretary. The two matters were decided in Sun-Diamond's favor. The United States sued Sun-Diamond for making illegal gifts to a

United States v. Sun-Diamond Growers of California

526 U.S. 398, 119 S.Ct. 1402, 1999 U.S. Lexis 3001 (1999)

Supreme Court of the United States

(continued)

public official in violation of the federal antibribery and gratuity statute 18 U.S.C. Section 201(b) and 201(c). The jury convicted Sun-Diamond, and the district court ordered it to pay a fine of $400,000. The court of appeals reversed. The U.S. Supreme Court granted certiorari to hear the appeal.

Supreme Court Issue

Does a conviction under the federal antibribery and gratuity statute require a showing of a direct nexus between the value conferred on the public official and the official act performed by the public official in favor of the giver?

In The Language of The U.S. Supreme Court

Scalia, Justice The solicitor general of the United States contends that the statute requires only a showing that a gift was motivated, at least in part, by the recipient's capacity to exercise governmental power or influence in the donor's favor without necessarily showing that it was connected to a particular official act. We are inclined to believe this meaning incorrect because of the peculiar results that the government's reading would produce. It would criminalize, for example, token gifts to the president based on his official position and not linked to any identifiable act—such as the replica jerseys given by championship sports teams each year during ceremonial White House visits. Similarly, it would criminalize a high school principal's gift of a school baseball cap to the secretary of education, by reason of his office, on the occasion of the latter's visit to the school.

Decision and Remedy

The U.S. Supreme Court held that there must be proof of a direct nexus between the gratuity given and the public official's act before the federal antibribery and gratuity statute is violated. Because no such direct nexus was proven in this case, there is no violation of the federal antibribery and gratuity statute. The judgment of the court of appeals was affirmed.

Case Questions

Critical Legal Thinking Do you think the Supreme Court should have read the statute so narrowly? Why or why not?

Business Ethics Is it ethical for a government official to accept gifts and gratuities from parties who have actions or matters pending before the official? Do you think such gifts and gratuities are given with any return favor in mind?

Contemporary Business What is lobbying? Who are the winners and losers of lobbying?

White lily on pond, Japan. Different countries and cultures have different criminal laws. Some acts that are considered criminal in one country may not be thought so in other countries.

International Law

The Foreign Corrupt Practices Act

During the 1970s, several scandals were uncovered where American companies were found to have bribed foreign government officials to obtain lucrative contracts. Congressional investigations discovered that the making of such payments—or bribes—was pervasive in conducting international business. To prevent American companies from engaging in this type of conduct, the U.S. Congress enacted the **Foreign Corrupt Practices Act of 1977 (FCPA)** [15 U.S.C. § 78m]. Congress amended the FCPA as part of the Omnibus Trade and Competitiveness Act of 1988.

The FCPA attacks the problem in two ways. First, it requires firms to keep accurate books and records of all foreign transactions and to install internal accounting controls to ensure that transactions and payments are authorized. Inadvertent or technical errors in maintaining books and records do not violate the FCPA.

Second, the FCPA makes it illegal for American companies, or their officers, directors, agents, or employees, to bribe a foreign official, a foreign political party official, or a candidate for foreign political office. A bribe is illegal only where it is meant to influence the awarding of new business or the retention of a continuing business activity. Payments to secure ministerial, clerical, or routine government action (such as scheduling inspections, signing customs documents, unloading and loading of cargo, and the like) do not violate the FCPA.

The FCPA imposes criminal liability only in circumstances in which a person knowingly fails to maintain the proper system of accounting, pays the illegal bribe himself or herself, or supplies a payment to a third party or an agent, knowing that it will be used as a bribe. A firm can be fined up to $2 million, and an individual can be fined up to $100,000 and imprisoned for up to five years for violations of the FCPA.

The 1988 amendments created two defenses. One excuses a firm or person charged with bribery under the FCPA if the firm or person can show that the payment was lawful under the written laws of that country. The other allows a defendant to show that a payment was a reasonable and bona fide expenditure related to the furtherance or execution of a contract.

Some people argue that the FCPA is too soft and permits American firms to engage in the payment of bribes internally that would otherwise be illegal in this country. Others argue that the FCPA is difficult to interpret and apply and that American companies are placed at a disadvantage in international markets where commercial bribery is commonplace and firms from other countries are not hindered by laws similar to the FCPA. ■

Landmark Law

Racketeer Influenced and Corrupt Organizations Act (RICO)

Organized crime has a pervasive influence on many parts of the American economy. In 1980, Congress enacted the Organized Crime Control Act. The **Racketeer Influenced and Corrupt Organizations Act (RICO)** is part of this act [18 U.S.C. §§ 1961–1968]. Originally, RICO was intended to apply only to organized crime. However, the broad language of the RICO statute has been used against non-organized crime defendants as well. RICO, which provides for both criminal and civil penalties, is one of the most important laws affecting business today.

RICO makes it a federal crime to acquire or maintain an interest in, use income from, or conduct or participate in the affairs of an "enterprise" through a "pattern" of "racketeering activity." An *enterprise* is defined as a corporation, a partnership, a sole proprietorship, another business or organization, or the government. *Racketeering activity* consists of a number of specifically enumerated federal and state crimes, including such activities as gambling, arson, robbery, counterfeiting, and dealing in narcotics. Business-related crimes, such as bribery, embezzlement, mail fraud, and wire fraud, are also considered racketeering.

To prove a *pattern of racketeering*, at least two predicate acts must be committed by the defendant within a 10-year period. For example, committing two different frauds would be considered a pattern. Individual defendants found criminally liable for RICO violations can be fined up to $25,000 per violation, imprisoned for up to 20 years, or both. In addition, RICO provides for the *forfeiture* of any property or business interests (even interests in a legitimate business) that were gained because of RICO violations. This provision allows the government to recover investments made with monies derived from racketeering activities. The government may also seek civil penalties for RICO violations. These include injunctions, orders of dissolution, reorganization of business, and the divestiture of the defendant's interest in an enterprise.

Persons injured by a RICO violation can bring a private *civil* action against the violator to recover injury to business or property. A successful plaintiff may recover *treble damages* (three times actual loss), plus attorneys' fees. The following case involves the RICO statute. ■

U.S. SUPREME COURT CASE

Cedric Kushner Promotions, Ltd. v. Don King

533 U.S. 158, 121 S.Ct. 2087, 2001 U.S. Lexis 4311 (2001)

Supreme Court of the United States

Case 7.3

Racketeering

Background and Facts

Don King is the president and sole shareholder of Don King Productions, a corporation that promotes boxing matches. Cedric Kushner Promotions, Ltd., a corporation that also promotes boxing matches, sued Don King, claiming that King had conducted the boxing-related affairs of Don King Productions through a RICO pattern of illegal fraud and other crimes. The district court dismissed the complaint, holding that Don King was not a separate "person" from Don King Productions, and therefore the civil RICO provisions did not apply. The court of appeals affirmed. The U.S. Supreme Court granted certiorari.

Supreme Court Issue

In this case, are there two separate entities—a "person" and an "enterprise"—as required for the application of RICO's civil provisions?

In The Language of The U.S. Supreme Court

Breyer, Justice The corporate owner/employee, a natural person, is distinct from the corporation itself, a legally different entity with different rights and responsibilities due to its different legal status. And we can find nothing in the statute that requires more "separateness" than that.

Decision and Remedy

The U.S. Supreme Court held that Don King is a "person" separate from the corporate "enterprise" Don King Productions. The Supreme Court reversed the judgment of the court of appeals and remanded the case for trial.

Case Questions

Critical Legal Thinking What do the civil law provisions of RICO provide? What penalties are available for civil RICO violations?

Business Ethics Do you think there is much fraud in the promotion and staging of professional boxing matches?

Contemporary Business Do you think civil RICO is used more against mob or non-mob-related defendants? Why?

Inchoate Crimes

In addition to the substantive crimes previously discussed, a person can be held criminally liable for committing an *inchoate crime*. Inchoate crimes include incomplete crimes and crimes committed by nonparticipants. The most important inchoate crimes are discussed in the following paragraphs.

Criminal Conspiracy

criminal conspiracy

A situation in which two or more persons enter into an agreement to commit a crime and an overt act is taken to further the crime.

Business Brief

The use of computers to commit business crimes is increasing. Businesses must implement safeguards to prevent computer crimes.

A **criminal conspiracy** occurs when two or more persons enter into an *agreement* to commit a crime. To be liable for a criminal conspiracy, an *overt act* must be taken to further the crime. The crime itself does not have to be committed, however.

Consider This Example Two securities brokers agree over the telephone to commit a securities fraud. They also obtain a list of potential victims and prepare false financial statements necessary for the fraud. Because they entered into an agreement to commit a crime and took overt action, the brokers are guilty of the crime of criminal conspiracy even if they never carry out the securities fraud. The government usually brings criminal conspiracy charges if (1) the defendants have been thwarted in their efforts to commit the substantive crime or (2) there is insufficient evidence to prove the substantive crime.

Attempt to Commit a Crime

attempt to commit a crime

A situation in which a crime is attempted but not completed.

The **attempt to commit a crime** is itself a crime. For example, suppose a person wants to kill his or her neighbor. The person shoots at the neighbor but misses. The perpetrator is not liable for the crime of murder but is liable for the crime of attempted murder.

Aiding and Abetting the Commission of a Crime

Sometimes persons assist others in the commission of a crime. The act of **aiding and abetting the commission of a crime** is a crime. This concept, which is very broad, includes rendering support, assistance, or encouragement to the commission of a crime. Harboring a criminal after he or she has committed a crime is considered aiding and abetting.

aiding and abetting the commission of a crime
Rendering support, assistance, or encouragement to the commission of a crime; harboring a criminal after he or she has committed a crime.

The court addressed the issue of aiding and abetting in the following case.

Case 7.4 Aiding and Abetting

United States v. Cloud
872 F.2d 846, 1989 U.S. App. Lexis 4534 (1989)
United States Court of Appeals, Ninth Circuit

Background and Facts

In 1980, Ronald V. Cloud purchased the Cal-Neva Lodge, a hotel and casino complex located in the Lake Tahoe area near the California–Nevada border, for $10 million. Cloud was a sophisticated 68-year-old entrepreneur who is experienced in buying and selling real estate and has real estate holdings valued at more than $65 million. He also has experience in banking and finance, having been the founder and chairman of Continental National Bank of Fresno. After two years of mounting operation losses, Cloud closed the Cal-Neva Lodge and actively began seeking a new buyer. In December 1984, Cloud met with Jon Perroton and orally agreed to transfer the lodge to Perroton for approximately $17 million. On January 2, 1985, Perroton met with an executive of Hibernia Bank (Hibernia) to discuss a possible loan to finance the purchase of the lodge. Perroton made multiple false representations and presented false documents to obtain a $20 million loan from Hibernia. In particular, Perroton misrepresented the sale price for the lodge ($27.5 million) and stated that $7.5 million had already been paid to Cloud. An escrow was opened with Transamerica Title Company (Transamerica).

On January 15, 1985, Cloud and his attorney and Perroton met at Transamerica to sign mutual escrow instructions. Cloud reviewed the instructions and noticed that the sale price and down payment figures were incorrectly stated at $27.5 million and $7.5 million, respectively, and that the Hibernia loan was for $20 million, almost $3 million above what he knew to be the true sale price. Cloud signed the escrow instructions. Later, Cloud signed a settlement statement containing the same false figures and signed a grant deed to the property. The sale closed on January 23, 1985, with Hibernia making the $20 million loan to Perroton. Subsequently, when the loan went into default, Continental Insurance Company (Continental) paid Hibernia its loss of $7.5 million on the bank's blanket bond insurance policy. The United States sued Cloud for aiding and abetting a bank fraud in violation of federal law (18 U.S.C. §§ 2 and 1344). The jury convicted Cloud of the crime and ordered him to make restitution of $7.5 million to Continental. Cloud appealed.

Issue

Is Cloud guilty of aiding and abetting a bank fraud?

In The Language of The Court

Hall, Circuit Judge Aiding and abetting means to assist the perpetrator of a crime. An abettor's criminal intent may be inferred from the attendant facts and circumstances and need not be established by direct evidence.

The evidence in this case established that sometime in December 1984 or early January 1985, Jon Perroton launched a fraudulent scheme to obtain money from Hibernia Bank by means of false representations. The issue before this court is whether a rational trier of fact could conclude on the basis of all the evidence that Cloud at some point knowingly came aboard and participated in Perroton's bank fraud scheme. We conclude that a reasonable jury could have found that Cloud came aboard on January 15, 1985, at the meeting to sign the escrow instructions.

There was no question Cloud knew that the sale price was not $27.5 million, that he had not received $7.5 million outside of escrow, and that on their face the escrow instructions and settlement statement reflected these false figures. There is likewise no doubt that Cloud, who was a sophisticated businessman with extensive experience both in real estate transactions and in banking, knew that the escrow would not have closed and that the Hibernia funds would not have been disbursed if he had not signed the escrow instructions.

Decision

The court of appeals held that Cloud was guilty of the crime of aiding and abetting a bank fraud in violation of federal law. Affirmed.

Case Questions

Critical Legal Thinking Should the law recognize the crime of aiding and abetting? Why or why not?

Business Ethics Did Cloud act ethically in this case?

Contemporary Business What is the moral of this case? Do you think bank fraud of the type described in this case happens very frequently?

Corporate Criminal Liability

Business Brief

Corporations may be held criminally liable for actions of their officers, employees, or agents.

Business Brief

Corporate directors, officers, and employees are personally liable for the crimes they commit while acting on behalf of the corporation.

A corporation is a fictitious legal person that is granted legal existence by the state only after certain requirements are met. A corporation cannot act on its own behalf. Instead, it must act through *agents* such as managers, representatives, and employees.

The question of whether a corporation can be held criminally liable has intrigued legal scholars for some time. Originally, under the common law, it was generally held that corporations lacked the criminal mind (*mens rea*) to be held criminally liable. Modern courts, however, are more pragmatic. These courts have held that corporations are criminally liable for the acts of their managers, agents, and employees. In any event, because corporations cannot be put in prison, they are usually sanctioned with fines, loss of a license or franchise, and the like.

Corporate directors, officers, and employees are individually liable for crimes that they personally commit, whether for personal benefit or on behalf of the corporation. In addition, under certain circumstances a corporate manager can be held criminally liable for the criminal activities of his or her subordinates. To be held criminally liable, the manager must have failed to supervise the subordinate appropriately. This is an evolving area of the law.

Business Ethics

Hughes Aircraft Downed as a Criminal Conspirator

Hughes Aircraft Co., Inc. (Hughes), an aircraft manufacturer, contracted with the U.S. government to manufacture microelectronic circuits, known as "hybrids," which are used as components in weapons defense systems. The contract required Hughes to perform tests on each hybrid. A Hughes employee, Donald LaRue, was the supervisor responsible for ensuring the accuracy of the hybrid testing process. LaRue falsely reported that all tests had been performed and that each hybrid had passed the test. When LaRue's subordinates called his actions to the attention of LaRue's supervisors, the supervisors did nothing about it. Instead they responded that LaRue's decisions were his own and were not to be questioned. The United States sued Hughes and LaRue, charging criminal conspiracy to defraud the government. At trial, LaRue was acquitted, but Hughes was convicted of criminal conspiracy and fined $3.5 million. Hughes appealed it conviction, asserting that it should not be convicted of criminal conspiracy if its alleged co-conspirator, LaRue, was acquitted.

Should Hughes be acquitted as a matter of law because the same jury that convicted Hughes acquitted its alleged co-conspirator of the charge of criminal conspiracy? No. The court of appeals held that Hughes may be found guilty of criminal conspiracy even though its co-conspirator had been acquitted of the same crime, and affirmed Hughes's conviction.

The court of appeals, as a matter of law, held that the inconsistency of the jury verdicts of two defendants charged with criminal conspiracy does not mean that the convicted defendant should also be acquitted. The court noted that the jury may have been more lenient with defendant LaRue, an individual, than it was with Hughes, the corporate defendant. Moreover, the court stated that the jury could have found Hughes guilty of the required act of conspiracy based on evidence provided at trial by the other Hughes employees who were called as witnesses [*United States v. Hughes Aircraft Company, Inc.*, 20 F.3d 974, 1994 U.S. App. Lexis 5603 (9th Cir. 1994)]

1. Did LaRue act ethically in this case?
2. Did LaRue's supervisors act ethically in this case? ■

Constitutional Safeguards

The criminal is to go free because the constable has blundered.

C. J. Cardozo
People v. Defore (1926)

When our forefathers drafted the U.S. Constitution, they included provisions that protect persons from unreasonable government intrusion and provide safeguards for those accused of crimes. Although these safeguards originally applied only to federal cases, the

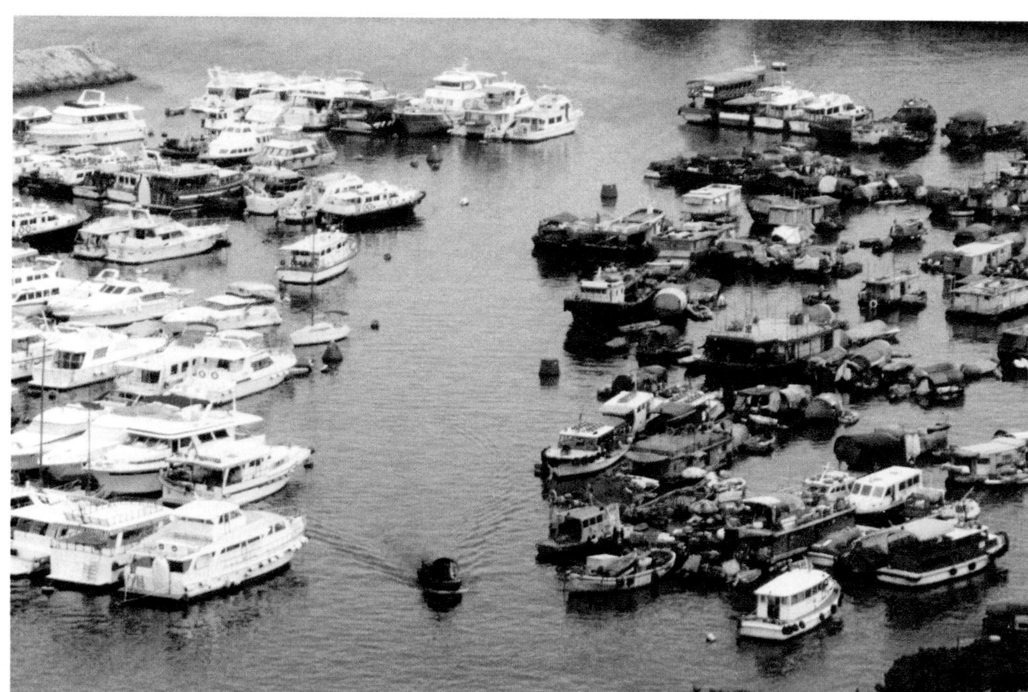

Hong Kong. Multinational corporations have to obey the criminal laws of all the countries in which they conduct business.

Fourteenth Amendment's Due Process Clause made them applicable to state criminal law cases as well. The most important of these constitutional safeguards are discussed in the following paragraphs.

Fourth Amendment Protection Against Unreasonable Search and Seizure

The *Fourth Amendment* to the U.S. Constitution protects persons and corporations from overzealous investigative activities by the government. It protects the rights of the people from **unreasonable search and seizure** by the government. It permits people to be secure in their persons, houses, papers, and effects.

"Reasonable" search and seizure by the government is lawful. **Search warrants** based on probable cause are necessary in most cases. Such a warrant specifically states the place and scope of the authorized search. General searches beyond the specified area are forbidden. *Warrantless searches* are permitted only (1) incident to arrest, (2) where evidence is in "plain view," or (3) where it is likely that evidence will be destroyed. Warrantless searches are also judged by the probable cause standard.

Evidence obtained from an unreasonable search and seizure is considered tainted evidence ("fruit of a tainted tree"). Under the **exclusionary rule**, such evidence generally can be prohibited from introduction at a trial or administrative proceeding against the person searched. However, this evidence is freely admissible against other persons. The U.S. Supreme Court created a *good faith exception* to the exclusionary rule.[5] This exception allows evidence otherwise obtained illegally to be introduced as evidence against the accused if the police officers who conducted the unreasonable search reasonably believed that they were acting pursuant to a lawful search warrant.

The following three U.S. Supreme Court cases examine the reach of the Fourth Amendment's protection against unreasonable search and seizure.

unreasonable search and seizure
Any search and seizure by the government that violates the Fourth Amendment.

search warrant
A warrant issued by a court that authorizes the police to search a designated place for specified contraband, articles, items, or documents. The search warrant must be based on probable cause.

exclusionary rule
A rule that says that evidence obtained from an unreasonable search and seizure can generally be prohibited from introduction at a trial or administrative proceeding against the person searched.

Case 7.5

Search

U.S. SUPREME COURT CASE

Kyllo v. United States

533 U.S. 27, 121 S.Ct. 2038, 2001 U.S. Lexis 4487 (2001)

Supreme Court of the United States

Background and Facts

In 1992, government agents suspected that marijuana was being grown in the home of Danny Kyllo, which was part of a triplex building in Florence, Oregon. Indoor marijuana growth typically requires high-intensity lamps. In order to determine whether an amount of heat was emanating from Kyllo's home consistent with the use of such lamps, federal agents used a thermal imager to scan the triplex. Thermal imagers detect infrared radiation and produce images of the radiation. The scan of Kyllo's home, which was performed from an automobile on the street, showed that the roof over the garage and a side wall of Kyllo's home were "hot." The federal agents concluded that Kyllo was using halide lights to grow marijuana in his house. The agents used this scanning evidence to obtain a search warrant authorizing a search of Kyllo's home. During the search, the agents found an indoor growing operation involving more than 100 marijuana plants.

Kyllo was indicted for manufacturing marijuana, a violation of federal criminal law. Kyllo moved to suppress the imaging evidence and the evidence it led to, arguing that it was an unreasonable search that violated the Fourth Amendment to the U.S. Constitution. The trial court disagreed with Kyllo and let the evidence be introduced and considered at trial. Kyllo then entered a conditional guilty plea and appealed the trial court's failure to suppress the challenged evidence. The court of appeals affirmed. The U.S. Supreme Court granted certiorari to hear the appeal.

Supreme Court Issue

Is the use of a thermal-imaging device aimed at a private home from a public street to detect relative amounts of heat within the home a "search" within the meaning of the Fourth Amendment?

In The Language of The U.S. Supreme Court

Scalia, Justice At the very core of the Fourth Amendment stands the right of a man to retreat into his own home and there be free from unreasonable government intrusion. With few exceptions, the question whether a warrantless search of a home is reasonable and hence constitutional must be answered no. On the other hand, the lawfulness of warrantless visual surveillance of a home has still been preserved. In fact we have held that visual observation is no "search" at all. We have applied the test on different occasions in holding that aerial surveillance of private homes and surrounding areas does not constitute a search.

The present case involves officers on a public street engaged in more than naked-eye surveillance of a home. The question we confront today is what limits there are upon this power of technology to shrink the realm of guaranteed privacy. We think that obtaining by sense-enhancing technology any information regarding the interior of the home that could not otherwise have been obtained without physical intrusion into a constitutionally protected area constitutes a search. This assures preservation of that degree of privacy against government that existed when the Fourth Amendment was adopted. On the basis of this criterion, the information obtained by the thermal imager in this case was the product of a search.

Decision and Remedy

The U.S. Supreme Court held that the use of a thermal-imaging device aimed at a private home from a public street to detect relative amounts of heat within the home is a "search" within the meaning of the Fourth Amendment. The Supreme Court reversed and remanded the case for further proceedings.

Case Questions

Critical Legal Thinking Is the Fourth Amendment's prohibition against unreasonable search and seizure an easy standard to apply? Explain.

Business Ethics Did the police act ethically in obtaining the evidence in this case? Did Kyllo act ethically in trying to suppress the evidence?

Contemporary Business How can the government catch entrepreneurs such as Kyllo? Explain.

Case 7.6

Search and Seizure

U.S. SUPREME COURT CASE

Maryland v. Dyson

527 U.S. 465, 119 S.Ct. 2013, 1999 U.S. Lexis 4200 (2001)

Supreme Court of the United States

Background and Facts

At 11 A.M. on July 2, 1996, a reliable informant gave a tip to a Maryland county sheriff that Kevin Darnell Dyson had gone to New York to buy drugs and would be returning to Maryland in a rented red Toyota automobile, license number DDY 787, with a large quantity of cocaine. When Dyson returned to Maryland in the rented car at 1 A.M. on July 3, the sheriff's deputies stopped and searched the vehicle, finding 23 grams of crack cocaine in a duffel bag in the trunk. Dyson was arrested, tried, and convicted of conspiracy to possess cocaine with intent to distribute. Dyson appealed, arguing that the cocaine evidence should have been suppressed because the sheriff had not obtained a search warrant before searching the car. The appellate court held for Dyson. The U.S. Supreme Court granted certiorari to hear the case.

Supreme Court Issue

If there is probable cause, must the police first obtain a search warrant before searching an automobile?

In The Language of The U.S. Supreme Court

The Fourth Amendment generally requires police to secure a warrant before conducting a search. There is an exception to this requirement for searches of vehicles. If a car is readily mobile and probable cause exists to believe it contains contraband, the Fourth Amendment permits police to search the vehicle without more. In this case, there was abundant probable cause that the car contained contraband.

Decision and Remedy

The U.S. Supreme Court held that under the "automobile exception" to the Fourth Amendment, an automobile can be searched by the police without a search warrant as long as there exists probable cause to conduct the search.

Case Questions

Critical Legal Thinking How would the Supreme Court have decided this case had there been no probable cause to search the vehicle?

Business Ethics Do defendants act ethically when they petition the court to suppress incriminating evidence?

Contemporary Business Are businesses subject to warrantless searches based on an informant's tip? Explain.

Case 7.7
Search and Seizure

U.S. SUPREME COURT CASE

City of Indianapolis v. Edmond

531 U.S. 32, 121 S.Ct. 447, 2000 U.S. Lexis 8084 (2000)

Supreme Court of the United States

Background and Facts

In August 1998, the police of the city of Indianapolis, Indiana, began to operate vehicle roadblock checkpoints on Indianapolis roads in an effort to interdict unlawful drugs. Once a car had been stopped, police questioned the driver and passengers and conducted an open-view examination of the vehicle from the outside. A narcotics-detection dog walked around outside each stopped vehicle. The police conducted a search and seizure of the occupants and vehicle only if particular suspicion developed from the initial investigation. The overall "hit rate" of the program was approximately 9 percent.

James Edmond and Joel Palmer, each attorneys who had been stopped at one of Indianapolis's checkpoints, filed a lawsuit on behalf of themselves and the class of all motorists who had been stopped or were subject to being stopped at such checkpoints. They claimed that the roadblocks violated the Fourth Amendment of the Constitution. The district court found for Indianapolis, but the court of appeals reversed. The U.S. Supreme Court granted certiorari to hear the appeal.

Supreme Court Issue

Do Indianapolis's highway checkpoint programs, whereby police, without individualized suspicion, stop vehicles for the primary purpose of discovering and interdicting illegal narcotics, violate the Fourth Amendment of the U.S. Constitution?

In The Language of The U.S. Supreme Court

O'Connor, Justice The Fourth Amendment requires that searches and seizures be reasonable. A search or seizure is ordinarily unreasonable in the absence of individualized suspicion of wrongdoing. We have recognized only limited circumstances in which the usual rule does not apply. We have upheld brief, suspicionless seizures of motorists at a fixed border patrol checkpoint designed to intercept illegal aliens, *United States v. Martinez-Fuerte*, 428 U.S. 543, 96 S.Ct. 3074 (1976), and at a sobriety checkpoint aimed at removing drunk drivers form the road, *Michigan Dept. of State Police v. Sitz*, 496 U.S. 444, 110 S.Ct. 2481 (1990). In none of these cases, however, did we indicate approval of a checkpoint program whose primary purpose was to detect evidence of ordinary criminal wrongdoing.

We have never approved a checkpoint program whose primary purpose was to detect evidence of ordinary criminal wrongdoing. Because the primary purpose of the Indianapolis narcotics checkpoint program is to uncover evidence of ordinary criminal wrongdoing, the program contravenes the Fourth Amendment. Of course, there are circumstances that may justify a law enforcement checkpoint where the primary purpose would otherwise, but for some emergency, relate to ordinary crime control. For example, the Fourth Amendment would almost certainly permit an appropriately tailored roadblock set up to thwart an imminent terrorist attack or to catch a dangerous criminal who is likely to flee by way of a particular route. The exigencies created

City of Indianapolis v. Edmond

531 U.S. 32, 121 S.Ct. 447, 2000 U.S. Lexis 8084 (2000)

Supreme Court of the United States

(continued)

by these scenarios are far removed from the circumstances under which authorities might simply stop cars as a matter of course to see if there just happens to be a felon leaving the jurisdiction.

Decision and Remedy

The U.S. Supreme Court held that Indianapolis's general highway checkpoints, whereby police, without individualized suspicion, stopped vehicles for the primary purpose of discovering and interdicting narcotics, was an unreasonable search and seizure in violation of the Fourth Amendment.

Case Questions

Critical Legal Thinking How did the Supreme Court reconcile its decision in this case with its prior decisions in *Martinez-Fuerte* and *Sitz*? Explain.

Business Ethics Should the 9 percent of criminals who were caught by the roadblock get off because of the Fourth Amendment?

Contemporary Business How big of a business is illegal narcotics sales in this country? Should this industry be legalized and taxed? Why or why not?

Searches of Business Premises

Generally, the government does not have the right to search business premises without a search warrant.[6] Certain hazardous and regulated industries—such as sellers of firearms and liquor, coal mines, and the like—are subject to warrantless searches if proper statutory procedures are met.

Fifth Amendment Privilege Against Self-Incrimination

The *Fifth Amendment* to the U.S. Constitution provides that no person "shall be compelled in any criminal case to be a witness against himself." Thus, a person cannot be compelled to give testimony against him- or herself, although nontestimonial evidence (e.g., fingerprints, body fluids, and the like) may be required. A person who asserts this right is described as having "taken the Fifth." This protection applies to federal cases and is extended to state and local criminal cases through the Due Process Clause of the Fourteenth Amendment.

The protection against **self-incrimination** applies only to natural persons who are accused of crimes. Therefore, artificial persons (such as corporations and partnerships) cannot raise this protection against incriminating testimony.[7] Thus, business records of corporations and partnerships are not generally protected from disclosure, even if they incriminate individuals who work for the business. However, certain "private papers" of businesspersons (such as personal diaries) are protected from disclosure.

self-incrimination

The giving of testimony that will likely subject a person to criminal prosecution. The Fifth Amendment states that no person shall be compelled in any criminal case to be a witness against him- or herself.

Business Brief

It is improper for a jury to infer guilt from the defendant's exercise of his or her constitutional right to remain silent.

Contemporary Business Environment

Miranda 2000

Most people have not read and memorized the provisions of the U.S. Constitution. The U.S. Supreme Court recognized this fact when it decided the landmark case *Miranda v. Arizona* in 1966 [384 U.S. 436, 86 S.Ct. 1602, 1996 U.S. Lexis 2817 (1966)]. In that case, the Supreme Court held that the Fifth Amendment privilege against self-incrimination is not useful unless a criminal suspect has knowledge of this right. Therefore, the Supreme Court required that the following warning—colloquially called the

"*Miranda* rights"—be read to a criminal suspect before he or she is interrogated by the police or other government officials:

- You have the right to remain silent.
- Anything you say can and will be used against you.
- You have the right to consult a lawyer, and to have a lawyer present with you during interrogation.
- If you cannot afford a lawyer, a lawyer will be appointed free of charge to represent you.

Any statements or confessions obtained from a suspect prior to being read his *Miranda* rights can be excluded from evidence at trial. *Miranda* has been criticized for letting guilty defendants go free. To combat this problem, the U.S. Congress enacted a statute, 18 U.S.C. Section 3501, which provided that a statement or confession by a suspect was admissible into evidence if it is "voluntarily" given, even if the suspect had not been read his or her *Miranda* rights. Many courts admitted confessions and other statements by defendants into evidence under this federal statute.

In 2000, the U.S. Supreme Court decided to revisit *Miranda* in *Dickerson v. United States* [530 U.S. 428, 120 S.Ct. 2326, 2000 U.S. Lexis 4305 (2000)] to test the lawfulness of Section 3501. In that case, the criminal defendant Dickerson was indicted for bank robbery. Before trial, Dickerson moved to suppress an incriminating statement he had made to the Federal Bureau of Investigation (FBI) prior to being read his *Miranda* rights. The court of appeals applied Section 3501 and admitted the statement at trial. Dickerson appealed to the U.S. Supreme Court to keep the statement out of trial. In a closely watched case, the Supreme Court upheld the *Miranda* ruling, finding that the *Miranda* decision was constitutionally based, and that Congress's attempt to lessen it by enacting Section 3501 was unconstitutional. In reaching its decision, the Supreme Court stated:

> We do not think there is justification for overruling *Miranda. Miranda* has become embedded in routine police practice to the point where the warnings have become part of our national culture. Whether or not we would agree with *Miranda*'s reasoning and its resulting rule, were we addressing the issue in the first instance, the principles of stare decisis weight heavily against overruling it now. We conclude that *Miranda* announced a constitutional rule that Congress may not supercede legislatively. Following the rule of stare decisis, we decline to overrule *Miranda* ourselves.

Thus, rather than being overturned or chipped away at, *Miranda* has been resurrected in its strict liability format: Police and government officials must read criminal suspects their *Miranda* rights; otherwise, the suspect's statements and confessions are inadmissible at trial. ■

Immunity from Prosecution On occasion, the government may want to obtain information from a suspect who has asserted his or her Fifth Amendment privilege against self-incrimination. The government can often achieve this by offering the suspect **immunity from prosecution**. Immunity from prosecution means that the government agrees not to use any evidence given by a person granted immunity against that person. Once immunity is granted, the suspect loses the right to assert his or her Fifth Amendment privilege. Grants of immunity are often given when the government wants the suspect to give information that will lead to the prosecution of other more important criminal suspects. Partial grants of immunity are also available. For example, a suspect may be granted immunity from prosecution for a serious crime, but not a lesser crime, in exchange for information. The suspect must agree to a partial grant of immunity.

immunity from prosecution
A situation in which the government agrees not to use any evidence given by a person granted immunity against that person.

Business Brief
Some persons who are granted immunity are placed in witness protection programs. Such a person is usually given a new identity, relocated, and found a job.

The Attorney–Client Privilege and Other Privileges To obtain a proper defense, the accused person must be able to tell his or her attorney facts about the case without fear that the attorney will be called as a witness against the accused. The **attorney–client privilege** is protected by the Fifth Amendment. Either the client or the attorney can raise this privilege. For the privilege to apply, the information must be told to the attorney in his or her capacity as an attorney, and not as a friend or neighbor or such.

The following privileges have also been recognized under the Fifth Amendment: (1) *psychiatrist/psychologist–patient privilege*, (2) *priest/minister/rabbi–penitent privilege*, (3) *spouse–spouse privilege*, and (4) *parent–child privilege*. There are some exceptions. For example, a spouse or child who is beaten by a spouse or parent may testify against the accused.

attorney–client privilege
A rule that says a client can tell his or her lawyer anything about the case without fear that the attorney will be called as a witness against the client.

Business Brief
There is no accountant–client privilege under federal law. Some states have enacted statutes that create an accountant–client privilege for state law criminal matters.

Contemporary Business Environment

Accountant–Client Privilege?

The common law has long recognized an attorney–client privilege that protects communications between a client and his or her lawyer from discovery in a lawsuit. In other words, lawyers cannot testify against their own clients. The rationale for this rule is that if any attorney could be called to testify against a client, the client might choose to withhold information from the attorney. This might prevent the attorney from preparing the best defense.

Although a similar situation occurs when accountants are supplied with information and documents by their clients, the U.S. Supreme Court has found that there is no corresponding accountant–client privilege under federal law. [*Couch v. U.S.*, 409 U.S. 322, 93 S.Ct. 611, 1973 U.S. Lexis 23 (1973)]. Thus, an accountant could be called as a witness in cases involving federal securities laws, federal mail or wire fraud, or federal RICO. Nevertheless, approximately 20 states have enacted special statutes that create an **accountant–client privilege**. An accountant cannot be called as a witness against a client in a court action in a state where these statutes are in effect. Federal courts do not recognize these laws, however. ■

Fifth Amendment Protection Against Double Jeopardy

Double Jeopardy Clause
A clause of the Fifth Amendment that protects persons from being tried twice for the same crime.

The **double jeopardy clause** of the *Fifth Amendment* protects persons from being tried twice for the same crime. For example, if the state tries a suspect for the crime of murder, and the suspect is found innocent, the state cannot bring another trial against the accused for the same crime. However, if the same criminal act involves several different crimes, the accused may be tried for each of the crimes without violating the Double Jeopardy Clause. Suppose the accused kills two people during a robbery. The accused may be tried for two murders and the robbery.

If the same act violates the laws of two or more jurisdictions, each jurisdiction may try the accused. For example, if an accused kidnaps a person in one state and brings the victim across a state border into another state, the act violates the laws of two states and the federal government. Thus, three jurisdictions can prosecute the accused without violating the Double Jeopardy Clause.

Moral Theory. Should the death penalty be permitted?

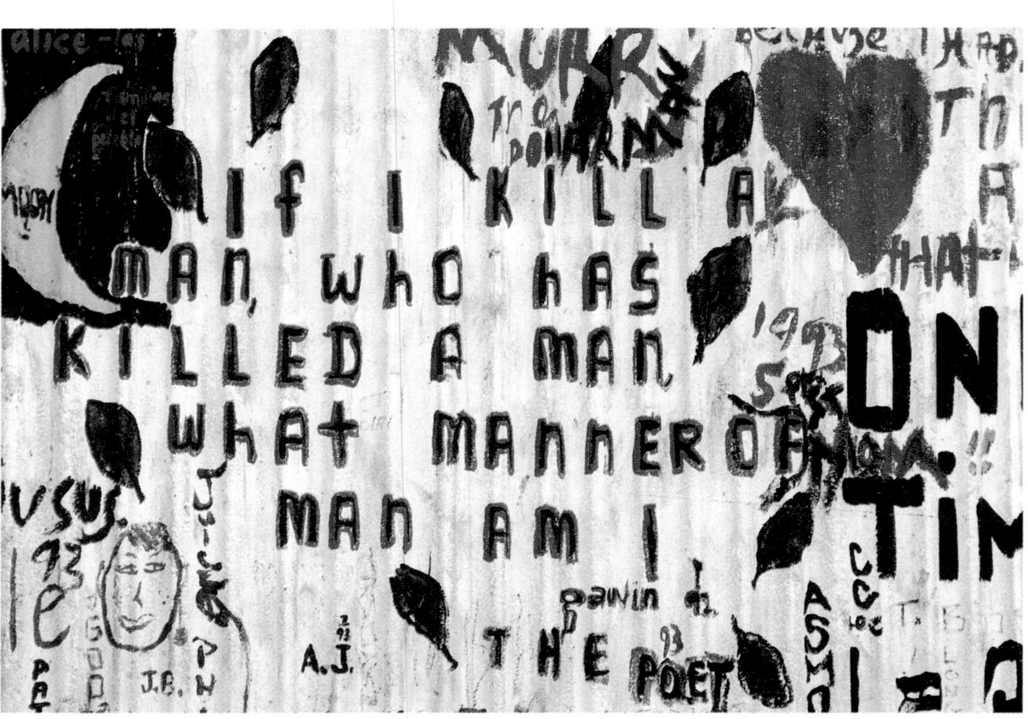

Sixth Amendment Right to a Public Jury Trial

The *Sixth Amendment* guarantees certain rights to criminal defendants. These rights are (1) to be tried by an impartial jury of the state or district in which the alleged crime was committed, (2) to confront (cross-examine) the witnesses against the accused, (3) to have the assistance of a lawyer, and (4) to have a speedy trial.[8]

Eighth Amendment Protection Against Cruel and Unusual Punishment

The *Eighth Amendment* protects criminal defendants from **cruel and unusual punishment**. For example, it prohibits the torture of criminals. However, this clause does not prohibit capital punishment.[9]

cruel and unusual punishment
A provision of the Eighth Amendment that protects criminal defendants from torture or other abusive punishment.

International Law

Hiding Money in Offshore Banks

Little did Christopher Columbus know in 1503 when he sailed past the Cayman Islands in the Caribbean that these tiny islands would become a bastion of international finance in the late twentieth and early twenty-first century. These tiny islands of 35,000 people host about 600 banks with over $500 million in deposits. Why is so much money being hoarded there? The answer is bank secrecy laws.

Every nation has banking laws, but all banking laws are not equal. What the Cayman Islands banking laws provide is confidentiality. In most instances, no party other than the depositor has the right to know the identity of the depositor, account number, or amount in the account. In fact, most accounts are held in the names of trusts instead of the depositors' actual names. This bank secrecy law has attracted many persons—and in some instances crooks—to park their ill-gotten gains in a Cayman Islands bank. Often the bank is no more than a lawyer's office.

Switzerland was once the primary location for depositing money that people did not want to be found. After some pressure from the United States and other countries, however, Switzerland entered into memorandums of understanding agreeing to cooperate with criminal investigations by these countries and to help uncover money deposited in Switzerland made through securities frauds and other crimes. Therefore, Switzerland has lost some of its luster as an international money hideout.

So Switzerland has been replaced by other places offering even more secret bank secrecy laws. The Cayman Islands is now the "Switzerland of the Caribbean." There are several other bank secrecy hideouts around the world, including The Bahamas in the Caribbean, the country of Lichtenstein in Europe, the Isle of Jersey off Great Britain, and the micro-island of Niue in the South Pacific. These tiny countries and islands follow the adage "Write a good law, and they will come." ■

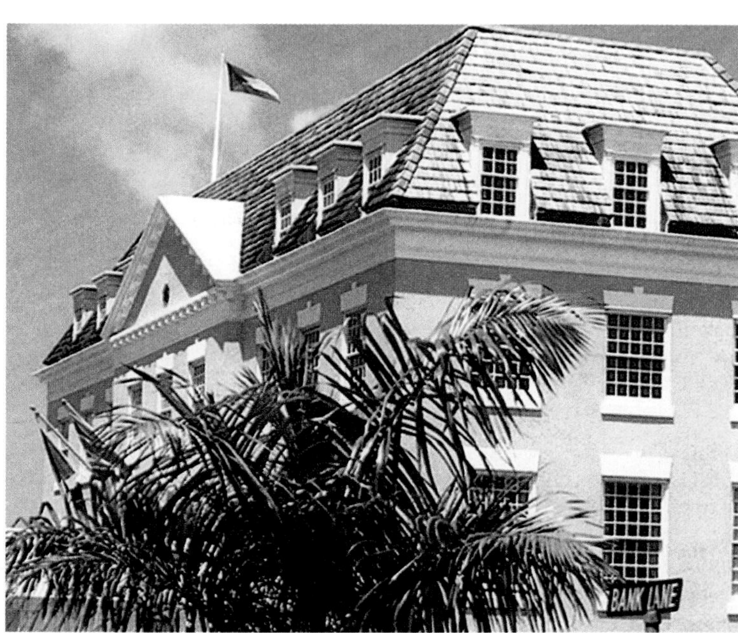

The Bahamas. Certain countries provide bank secrecy laws that protect the identity of depositors from disclosure. The Bahamas has such a law, and many of its chartered "banks" are no more than lawyers' offices in office buildings. Who do you think uses these bank accounts?

International Law

Federal Antiterrorism Act of 2001

The devastating terrorist attacks on the World Trade Center in New York and the Pentagon in Washington, DC, on September 11, 2001, shocked the nation. The attacks were organized and orchestrated by terrorists who crossed nations' borders easily, secretly planned and prepared for the attacks undetected, and financed the attacks using money located in banks in the United States, Great Britain, and other countries.

In response, Congress held hearings to investigate how to counter such terrorist activities. Congress enacted a new federal Antiterrorism Act that assists the government in detecting and preventing terrorist activities and investigating and prosecuting terrorists. The bill was signed into law by President Bush on October 26, 2001. The act contains the following main features:

- ***Special Intelligence Court*** The act authorizes a Special Intelligence Court to issue expanded wiretap orders and subpoenas to obtain evidence of suspected terrorism.
- ***Nationwide Search Warrant*** The act creates a nationwide search warrant to obtain evidence of terrorist activities. Previously, search warrants were limited to specific geographical locations.
- ***Roving Wiretaps*** The act permits "roving wiretaps" on a person suspected of involvement in terrorism so that any telephone or electronic device used by the person may be monitored. Previously, officials needed to obtain separate wiretap orders for each phone used by a suspect, which was ineffective against terrorists who used multiple telephones, including cellular phones.
- ***Sharing of Information*** The act permits evidence obtained during grand jury proceedings and evidence obtained by government law enforcement and intelligence agencies such as the FBI, Central Intelligence Agency (CIA), National Security Administration (NSA), Immigration and Naturalization Service (INS), U.S. Treasury Department, and other government agencies to be shared among the agencies. Previously, sharing of such information was restricted.
- ***Detention of Noncitizens*** The act gives the federal government authority to detain a nonresident in the United States for up to seven days without filing charges against that person if he or she is certified by the U.S. attorney general as being under suspicion of involvement in terrorist activities. Nonresidents who are certified by a court as a threat to national security may be held for up to six months without a trial. Aliens who raise funds for terrorist organizations may be deported.
- ***Bioterrorism Provision*** The act makes it illegal for people or groups to possess substances that can be used as biological or chemical weapons for any purpose besides a "peaceful" one.
- ***Anti-Money Laundering Provisions*** The act includes several provisions to discover, trace, and impound bank accounts used to fund terrorist activities. The act requires U.S. banks to determine sources of large overseas private bank accounts. Banks that refuse to disclose information about such accounts to U.S. investigators are subject to sanctions, including loss of license to conduct banking operations. The U.S. Treasury Department may cut off all dealings in the United States of foreign banking institutions located in nations with bank secrecy laws that refuse to disclose information about bank accounts to U.S. investigators. American banks are barred from doing business with offshore shell banks that have no connection to any regulated banking industry.

Proponents of the federal Antiterrorism Act argue that the new investigative and other powers granted by the act are necessary to give law enforcement and intelligence agencies tools necessary to detect and prevent terrorist activities and to investigate and prosecute terrorists. Critics of the act argue that civil liberties and many constitutional freedoms are trampled on by the provisions of the act. ■

International Law

International Criminal Court

In 1998, member nations of the United Nations negotiated a treaty to create a new **International Criminal Court**. The court hears and decides cases of "crimes against humanity." These include war crimes, genocide, and other crimes that violate humanitarian rights. It took more than four years for a sufficient number of member nations to ratify the treaty.

The International Criminal Court can only prosecute nationals of countries that have ratified the treaty. The United States, which had first signed the treaty, nullified its signature, refused to ratify the treaty, and withdrew from it. U.S. officials felt there were insufficient safeguards to protect U.S. soldiers serving on UN peacekeeping missions from being prosecuted in the court. Israel and China also voiced opposition to ratification.

The new court is located in The Hague. Its judges are appointed by member nations and began hearing cases in 2003. The court will be operated as other courts, with defendants being able to employ lawyers to represent them, to question witnesses, and to introduce evidence. If a defendant is found guilty of the crime charged, he or she will be held in the new court's own jail in The Hague. The treaty is not retroactive, so the court can only prosecute new alleged rights violations. ■

Chapter Summary

Definition of a Crime, p. 178

Specifics of a Criminal Trial

1. The accused is *presumed innocent until proven guilty.*
2. The plaintiff (the government) bears the *burden of proof.*
3. The government must prove *beyond a reasonable doubt* that the accused is guilty of the crime charged.
4. The accused does not have to testify against him- or herself.

Definition of a Crime

1. ***Crime.*** Any act done by a person in violation of those duties that he or she owes to society and for the breach of which the law provides a penalty.
2. ***Penal codes.*** State and federal statutes that define many crimes. Criminal conduct is also defined in many *regulatory statutes.*
3. Parties to a criminal lawsuit:
   a. *Plaintiff.* The government, which is represented by the *prosecuting attorney* (or *prosecutor*).
   b. *Defendant.* The person or business accused of the crime, who is represented by a *defense attorney.*

Classification of Crimes

1. ***Felonies.*** The most serious kinds of crimes. *Mala in se* (inherently evil). Usually punishable by imprisonment.
2. ***Misdemeanors.*** Less serious crimes than felonies. *Mala prohibita* (prohibited by society). Usually punishable by fine and/or imprisonment for less than one year.
3. ***Violations.*** Crimes that are neither felonies nor misdemeanors. Generally punishable by a fine.

Elements of a Crime

Most crimes require that the following two elements be proven:

1. ***Actus reus.*** Guilty act.
2. ***Mens rea.*** Evil intent.

Criminal Procedure, p. 180

Pretrial Criminal Procedure

1. ***Arrest.*** Make pursuant to an *arrest warrant* based upon showing of "probable cause," or, where permitted, by a *warrantless* arrest.
2. ***Indictment or information.*** Grand juries issue *indictments*; magistrates (judges) issue *informations.* These formally charge the accused with specific crimes.
3. ***Arraignment.*** The accused is informed of the charges against him or her and enters a *plea* in court. The plea may be *not guilty*, *guilty*, or *nolo contendere.*
4. ***Plea bargaining.*** The government and the accused may negotiate a settlement agreement wherein the accused agrees to admit to a lesser crime than charged.

Criminal Trial and Appeal

1. Criminal trial
   a. *Conviction.* Requires unanimous vote of the jury.
   b. *Innocent.* Requires unanimous vote of the jury.
   c. *Hung jury.* Nonunanimous vote of the jury. The government may prosecute the case again.
2. Appeal
   a. *Defendant.* May appeal his or her conviction.
   b. *Plaintiff (government).* May not appeal a verdict of innocent.

Crimes Affecting Business, p. 183

Crimes Affecting Business

1. ***Robbery.*** The taking of personal property from another by fear or force.
2. ***Burglary.*** The unauthorized entering of a building to commit a felony.
3. ***Larceny.*** The wrongful taking of another's property other than from his or her person or building.
4. ***Theft.*** The wrongful taking of another's property, whether by robbery, burglary, or larceny.
5. ***Receiving stolen property.*** A person knowingly receiving stolen property with the intent to deprive the rightful owner of that property.
6. ***Arson.*** The malicious and willful burning of another's building.
7. ***Forgery.*** Fraudulently making or altering a written document that affects the legal liability of another person.
8. ***Extortion.*** A threat to expose something about another person unless that person gives up money or property.
9. ***Credit-card crimes.*** The misappropriation or use of another person's credit card.
10. ***Bad check legislation.*** The making, drawing, or delivery of a check by a person when that person knows that there are insufficient funds in the account to cover the check.

White-Collar Crimes, p. 186

White-Collar Crimes

White-collar crimes. Crimes that are prone to be committed by businesspersons and that involve cunning and trickery rather than physical force.

1. ***Embezzlement.*** The fraudulent conversion of property by a person to whom the property was *entrusted.*
2. ***Criminal fraud.*** The act of obtaining title to another's property through deception or trickery. Also called *false pretenses* or *deceit.*
3. ***Mail fraud.*** The use of mail to defraud another person.
4. ***Wire fraud.*** The use of wire (telephone or telegraph) to defraud another person.
5. ***Bribery.*** The offer of payment of money or property or something else of value in return for an unwarranted favor. The payer of a bribe is also guilty of the crime of bribery.
   - *a.* *Commercial bribery* is the offer of a payment of a bribe to private persons and business. This is often referred to as a *kickback* or *payoff*
   - *b.* Bribery of public officials for an "official act" is a crime.
6. ***Racketeer Influenced and Corrupt Organizations Act (RICO).*** An act that makes it a federal crime to acquire or maintain an interest in, use income from, or conduct or participate in the affairs of an "enterprise" through a "pattern" of "racketeering activity." Criminal penalties include the *forfeiture* of any property or business interests gained through a RICO violation.

Inchoate Crimes, p. 190

Inchoate Crimes

Inchoate crimes. Crimes that are incomplete or that are committed by nonparticipants.

1. ***Criminal conspiracy.*** A crime in which two or more persons enter into an *agreement* to commit a crime and take some *overt act* to further the crime.
2. ***Attempt to commit a crime.*** The attempt to commit a crime is a crime even if the commission of the intended crime is unsuccessful.
3. ***Aiding and abetting the commission of a crime.*** Rendering support, assistance, or encouragement to the commission of a crime, or knowingly harboring a criminal after he or she has committed a crime.

Corporate Criminal Liability, p. 192

Corporate Criminal Liability

1. Corporate directors, officers, and employees are criminally liable for crimes they commit for personal benefit or on behalf of the corporation.

2. A corporation is criminally liable for crimes committed by directors, officers, and employees while acting on behalf of the corporation.

Constitutional Safeguards, p. 192

Fourth Amendment Protection Against Unreasonable Search and Seizure

This protection protects persons and corporations from *unreasonable searches and seizures.*

1. *Reasonable searches and seizures* based on *probable cause* are lawful:
   a. *Search warrant.* Stipulates the place and scope of the search.
   b. *Warrantless search.* Permitted only:
      i. Incident to an arrest.
      ii. Where evidence is in plain view.
      iii. Where it is likely that evidence will be destroyed.

2. ***Exclusionary rule.*** Evidence obtained from an unreasonable search and seizure is *tainted evidence* that may not be introduced at a government proceeding against the person searched.

3. ***Business premises.*** Protected by the Fourth Amendment, except that certain *regulated industries* may be subject to warrantless searches authorized by statute.

Fifth Amendment Privilege Against Self-Incrimination

Privilege against self-incrimination. Provides that no person "shall be compelled in any criminal case to be a witness against himself." A person asserting this privilege is said to have taken the Fifth.

1. ***Nontestimonial evidence.*** This evidence (e.g., fingerprints, body fluids, etc.) is not protected.

2. ***Businesses.*** The privilege applies only to natural persons; businesses cannot assert the privilege.

3. ***Miranda rights.*** A criminal suspect must be informed of his or her Fifth Amendment rights before the suspect can be interrogated by the police or government officials.

4. ***Immunity from prosecution.*** Granted by the government to obtain otherwise privileged evidence. The government agrees not to use the evidence given against the person who gave it.

5. ***Attorney–client privilege.*** An accused's lawyer cannot be called as a witness against the accused.

6. ***Other privileges.*** The following privileges have been recognized, with some limitations:
   a. Psychiatrist/psychologist–patient
   b. Priest/minister/rabbi–penitent
   c. Spouse–spouse
   d. Parent–child

7. ***Accountant–client privilege.*** Not recognized at the federal level. Some states recognize this privilege in state law actions.

Fifth Amendment Protection Against Double Jeopardy

Protects persons from being tried twice by the same jurisdiction for the same crime. If the act violates the laws of two or more jurisdictions, each jurisdiction may try the accused.

Sixth Amendment Right to a Public Jury Trial

Guarantees criminal defendants the following rights:

1. To be tried by an impartial jury

2. To confront the witness

3. To have the assistance of a lawyer

4. To have a speedy trial

Eighth Amendment Protection Against Cruel and Unusual Punishment

Protects criminal defendants from cruel and unusual punishment. Capital punishment is permitted.

Internet Exercises and Case Questions

Working the Web Internet Exercises

Activities

1. Check on the U.S. Department of Justice Web site for information about computer-related crimes: **www.usdoj.gov/criminal**.
2. See **www.hg.org/crime.html** for a comprehensive list of criminal law resources. Find the listing for your jurisdiction and research state laws relating to white-collar crime.

Critical Legal Thinking Cases

7.1 Criminal Liability of Corporations Representatives of hotels, restaurants, hotel and restaurant supply companies, and other businesses located in Portland, Oregon, organized an association to attract conventions to their city. Members were asked to make contributions equal to 1 percent of their sales to finance the association. To aid collections, hotel members, including Hilton Hotels Corporation, agreed to give preferential treatment to suppliers who paid their assessments and to curtail purchases from those who did not. This agreement violated federal antitrust laws. The United States sued the members of the association, including Hilton Hotels, for the crime of violating federal antitrust laws. Can a corporation be held criminally liable for the acts of its representatives? If so, what criminal penalties can be assessed against the corporation? [*United States v. Hilton Hotels Corp.*, 467 F.2d 1000, 1972 U.S. App. Lexis 7414 (9th Cir. 1973)]

7.2 Criminal Liability for Acts of Subordinates Acme Markets, Inc., is a national retail food chain with approximately 36,000 employees working in 874 retail stores and 16 warehouses. Mr. Park is the president and chief executive officer of the corporation. In April 1970, the FDA inspected Acme's Philadelphia warehouse and found unsanitary conditions, including rodent infestation. The FDA advised Mr. Park by letter of these conditions and demanded that they be corrected. In 1971, the FDA found that similar conditions existed at the warehouse. It again notified Park to correct the situation. An FDA inspection in March 1972 still showed unsanitary conditions and rodent infestation at the warehouse. Evidence showed that corporate employees did not take appropriate actions to correct this situation. The federal Food, Drug, and Cosmetic Act makes individuals, as well as corporations, criminally liable for violations of the act. The United States brought a criminal action against Mr. Park for the violations. Can a corporate officer such as Mr. Park be held criminally liable for actions of his subordinates? [*United States v. Park*, 421 U.S. 658, 95 S.Ct. 1903, 1975 U.S. Lexis 69 (1974)]

7.3 Receiving Stolen Property In December 1982, Whitehead bought a stereo from his friend, Walter Gibbs, for between $10 and $40. When Whitehead first saw the stereo, it was one of three in Gibbs's home. Whitehead knew that the stereo was new and was worth between $169 and $189. The stereo system, identified as one stolen in late 1982 from the J.C. Penney Warehouse, was found by police officers in Whitehead's bedroom on January 27, 1983. The serial number on the stereo had been scratched out. Is Whitehead guilty of any crime? Explain. [*Whitehead v. State of Georgia*, 313 S.E.2d 775, 1984 Ga.App. Lexis 1618 (Ga. App. 1984)]

7.4 Forgery Evidence showed that there was a burglary in which a checkbook belonging to Mary J. Harris, doing business as The Report Department, and a check encoder machine were stolen. Two of the checks from that checkbook were cashed at the Citizens & Southern National Bank branch office in Riverdale, Georgia, by Joseph Leon Foster, who was accompanied by a woman identified as Angela Foxworth. The bank teller who cashed the checks testified that the same man and woman cashed the checks on two different occasions at her drive-up window at the bank and that on both occasions they were in the same car. Each time the teller wrote the license tag number of the car on the back of the check. The teller testified that both times the checks and the driver's license used to identify the woman were passed to her by the man driving and that the man received the money from her. What crime has been committed? [*Foster v. State of Georgia*, 387 S.E.2d 637, 1989 Ga.App. Lexis 1456 (Ga. App. 1989)]

7.5 Extortion On February 3, 1987, the victim (Mr. X) went to the premises at 42 Taylor Terrace in New Milford, Connecticut, where his daughter and her husband lived. Lisa Percoco, who was Gregory Erhardt's girlfriend, was at the residence. Mr. X and Percoco were in the bedroom, partially dressed, engaging in sexual activity, when Erhardt entered the room and photographed them. He then informed Mr. X that unless he procured $5,000 and placed it in a mailbox at a designated address by 8 P.M. that night, Erhardt would show the photographs to Mr. X's wife. Mr. X proceeded to make telephone arrangements for the procurement and placement of the money according to Erhardt's instructions. If the money were paid, what crime would have been committed? [*State of Connecticut v. Erhardt*, 553 A.2d 188, 1989 Conn.App. Lexis 21 (Conn. App. 1989)]

7.6 Credit-Card Fraud Remi Olu Abod, a Nigerian national, obtained a Visa credit card that bore the name "Norman Skinner from a supplier." Abod purchased a counterfeit international driving permit bearing the name Norman Skinner at a passport photo shop in California. On June 27, 1984, Abod traveled from Los Angeles, California, to Corpus Christi, Texas. He first used the credit card to obtain $2,400 cash from each of two banks. He next appeared at a jewelry counter at Dillard's Department Store and tried to purchase $2,335 of jewelry with the credit card. When the store employee telephoned the Visa credit authorization center for approval, he was informed that the card was counterfeit. Corpus Christi police were summoned to the store, where they arrested Abod. What crime did Abod commit? [*United States v. Abod*, 770 F.2d 1293, 1985 U.S. App. Lexis 23107 (5th Cir. 1985)]

7.7 Criminal Fraud In 1978, Miriam Marlowe's husband purchased a life insurance policy on his own life, naming his wife as the beneficiary. After Marlowe's husband died in a swimming accident in July 1981, she received payment on the policy. Marlowe later met John Walton, a friend of a friend. He convinced her and her representative that he had a friend who worked for the State Department and had access to gold in Brazil, and that the gold could be purchased in Brazil for $100 an ounce and sold in the United States for $300 an ounce. Walton convinced Miriam to invest $25,000. Instead of investing the money in gold in Brazil, Walton opened an account at Tracy Collins Bank in the name of Jeffrey McIntyre Roberts and deposited Miriam's money in the account. He later withdrew the money in cash. What crime is Walton guilty of? [*State of Utah v. Roberts*, 711 P.2d 235, 1985 Utah Lexis 872 (Utah 1985)]

7.8 Embezzlement Marty W. Orr was employed as a deputy treasurer and bookkeeper in the treasurer's office of Washington County, Virginia. She was responsible for computing each day's revenue and depositing funds received on a daily basis. During the course of her work, she took cash totaling several thousand dollars. What crime has she committed? [*Orr v. Commonwealth of Virginia*, 344 S.E.2d 627, 1986 Va.App. Lexis 282 (Va. App. 1986)]

7.9 Bribery In 1979, the city of Peoria, Illinois, received federal funds from the Department of Housing and Urban Development (HUD) to be used for housing rehabilitation assistance. The city of Peoria designated United Neighborhoods, Inc. (UNI), a corporation, to administer the funds. Arthur Dixon was UNI's executive director, and James Lee Hinton was its housing rehabilitation coordinator. In these capacities, they were responsible for contracting with suppliers and tradespeople to provide the necessary goods and services to rehabilitate the houses. Evidence showed that Dixon and Hinton used their positions to extract 10 percent payments back on all contracts they awarded. What crime have they committed? [*Dixon and Hinton v. United States*, 465 U.S. 482, 104 S.Ct. 1172, 1984 U.S. Lexis 35 (1984)]

7.10 Attempt to Commit a Crime Mary G. Smith's MasterCard credit card was in her purse when it was stolen in June 1985. On June 28, 1985, Beulah Houston entered a Venture store located in Griffith, Indiana, and indicated to the manager of the jewelry department that she wished to purchase a man's watch. After making a selection, Houston handed the manager a MasterCard bearing the name Mary G. Smith. Upon contacting the bank for authorization, the manager was told to hold the card. Houston then left the store and was later arrested. Can Houston be convicted of attempt to commit credit-card fraud? [*Houston v. State of Indiana*, 528 N.E.2d 818, 1988 Ind.App. Lexis 716 (Ind. App. 1988)]

7.11 Administrative Search Lee Stuart Paulson owned the liquor license for My House, a bar in San Francisco. The California Department of Alcoholic Beverage Control is the administrative agency that regulates bars in that state. The California Business and Professions Code, which the department administers, prohibits "any kind of illegal activity on licensed premises." On February 11, 1988, an anonymous informer tipped the department that narcotic sales were occurring on the premises of My House and that the narcotics were kept in a safe behind the bar on the premises. A special department investigator entered the bar during its hours of operation, identified himself, and informed Paulson that he was conducting an inspection. The investigator, who did not have a search warrant, opened the safe without seeking Paulson's consent. Twenty-two bundles of cocaine, totaling 5.5 grams, were found in the safe. Paulson was arrested. At his criminal trial, Paulson challenged the lawfulness of the search. Was the warrantless search of the safe a lawful search? [*People v. Paulson*, 216 Cal.App.3d 1480, 265 Cal.Rptr. 579, 1990 Cal.App. Lexis 10 (Cal. App. 1990)]

7.12 Search Warrant The Center Art Galleries–Hawaii sells artwork. Approximately 20 percent of its business involves art by Salvador Dali. The federal government, which suspected the center of fraudulently selling forged Dali artwork, obtained identical search warrants for six locations controlled by the center. The warrants commanded the executing officer to seize items which were "evidence of violations of federal criminal law." The warrants did not describe the specific crimes suspected and did not stipulate that only items pertaining to the sale of Dali's work could be seized. There was no evidence of any criminal activity unrelated to that artist. Is the search warrant valid? [*Center Art Galleries–Hawaii, Inc. v. United States*, 875 F.2d 747, 1989 U.S. App. Lexis 6983 (9th Cir. 1989)]

7.13 Fifth Amendment's Privilege Against Self-Incrimination John Doe is the owner of several sole-proprietorship businesses. In 1980, during the course of an investigation of corruption in awarding county and municipal contracts, a federal grand jury served several subpoenas on John Doe, demanding the production of certain business records. The subpoenas demanded the production of the following record: (1) general ledgers and journals, (2) invoices, (3) bank statements and canceled checks, (4) financial statements, (5) telephone-company records, (6) safe-deposit box records, and (7) copies of tax returns. John Doe filed a motion in federal court, seeking to quash the subpoenas, alleging that producing these business records would violate his Fifth Amendment privilege of not testifying against himself. Do the records have to be disclosed? [*United States v. John Doe*, 465 U.S. 605, 104 S.Ct. 1237, 1984 U.S. Lexis 169 (1984)]

Business Ethics Cases

7.14 Business Ethics R. Foster Winans was a reporter for *The Wall Street Journal* from 1981 through 1984, during which time he wrote a column called "Heard on the Street." In the column, Winans would discuss the future prospects of companies and their securities. Evidence showed that positive comments would make a company's stock increase in value; negative comments would have the opposite result. Winans systematically leaked the contents of his future "Heard" columns prior to publication to Peter Brant, a stockbroker, in exchange for a share of the profits made by Brant. Upon discovery, Winans was convicted of wire and mail fraud, which are federal crimes. The crimes were committed within the state of New York. In September 1985, Winans entered into a book publishing contract with St. Martin's Press, and in 1988, St. Martin's published Winans's book *Trading Secrets*. The book details Winans's own actions that resulted in his federal conviction for insider trading. New York had previously adopted a "Son of Sam" law. The New York State Crimes Victims Board moved for an order directing St. Martin's to turn over the royalties due Winans, which would be deposited in an escrow account and held for the benefit of and payable to any victims of Winan's crimes. Who is legally entitled to the royalties? Is it ethical for a convicted criminal to make money by selling the media rights to the story about the crime? [*St. Martin's Press v. Zweibel*, *N.Y. Law Journal*, 2/26/90 (N.Y. Sup. 1990)].

7.15 Business Ethics In 1979, Leo Shaw, an attorney, entered into a partnership agreement with three other persons to build and operate an office building. From the outset, it was agreed that Shaw's role was to manage the operation of the building. Management of the property was Shaw's contribution to the partnership; the other three partners contributed the necessary capital. In January 1989, the other partners discovered that the loan on the building was in default and that foreclosure proceedings were imminent. Upon investigation, they discovered that Shaw had taken approximately $80,000 from the partnership's checking account. After heated discussions, Shaw repaid $13,000. In May 1989, when no further payment was forthcoming, a partner filed a civil suit against Shaw and notified the police. The state filed a criminal complaint against Shaw on March 15, 1990. On April 3, 1990, Shaw repaid the remaining funds as part of a civil settlement. At his criminal trial in November 1990, Shaw argued that the repayment of the money was a defense to the crime of embezzlement. Did Shaw act ethically in this case? Would your answer be different if he had really only "borrowed" the money and had intended to return it? [*People v. Shaw*, 10 Cal. App.4th 969, 12 Cal.Rptr.2d 665, 1992 Cal.App. Lexis 1256 (Cal. App. 1992)]

Briefing the Case Writing Assignment

Read Case A.7 in the Case Appendix [*Schalk v. Texas*]. This case is excerpted from the appellate court opinion. Review and brief the case. In your brief, be sure to answer the following questions.

1. What activities had the defendants engaged in?
2. What crime were the defendants accused of?
3. What was the decision of the appellate court?

Answers to Management Decision Questions

1. It is likely that Mr. Smith's offer to pour money into your business is a money-laundering scheme. The term *money laundering* is used to refer to the process by which criminals convert tainted proceeds into apparently legitimate funds or property. Money laundering is a federal crime. The Money Laundering Control Act makes it a crime to launder proceeds of certain criminal offenses called "specified unlawful activities." The activities are defined in various federal and state criminal statutes, including the Racketeer Influenced and Corrupt Organizations Act (RICO). "Specified unlawful activity" includes narcotic activities and virtually any white-collar crime. It is illegal to assist a person you know or suspect is participating in illegal activity.
2. *Ethics* may be defined as a set of moral principles or values that governs the conduct of an individual or a group. Most individuals consider illegal activity to be not only criminal but also ethically wrong. The fact that you have ignored Mr. Smith's request to become a business partner in the past because of your suspicions of his involvement in illegal activity and are now considering it because your company needs the funds he can supply would cause any arrangement you make with Mr. Smith to be morally reprehensible.

Endnotes

1. Title 18 of the U.S. Code contains the federal criminal code.
2. Sentencing Reform Act of 1984, 18 U.S.C. § 3551 et. seq. The sentencing guidelines for federal crimes, which were promulgated by the U.S. Sentencing Commission, became effective on November 1, 1987.
3. 18 U.S.C. § 1341.
4. 18 U.S.C. § 1343.
5. *United States v. Leon*, 468 U.S. 897, 104 S.Ct. 3405, 82 1984 U.S. Lexis 153 (1984).
6. *Marshall v. Barlow's Inc.*, 436 U.S. 307, 98 S.Ct. 1816, 1978 U.S. Lexis 26 (1978).
7. *Bellis v. United States*, 417 U.S. 85, 94 S.Ct. 2179, 1974 U.S. Lexis 58 (1974).
8. The Speedy Trial Act requires that a criminal defendant be brought to trial within 70 days after indictment [18 U.S.C. § 316(c)(1)]. Continuances may be granted by the court to serve the "ends of justice."
9. *Baldwin v. Alabama*, 472 U.S. 372, 105 S.Ct. 2727, 1985 U.S. Lexis 106 (1985).

8

Intellectual Property and Information Technology

"The Congress shall have the power . . . to promote the Progress of Science and useful Arts, by securing for limited Times to Authors and Inventors the exclusive Right to their respective Writings and Discoveries.

—Article I, Section 8, clause 8 of the U.S. Constitution

Chapter Objectives

After studying this chapter, you should be able to:

1. Describe the business tort of misappropriating a trade secret.
2. Describe how an invention can be patented under federal patent laws and the penalties for patent infringement.
3. List the writings that can be copyrighted and describe the penalties of copyright infringement.
4. Define trademarks and service marks, and describe the penalties for trademark infringement.
5. Describe international protection of intellectual property rights.

Chapter Contents

Management Decision Intellectual Property and Information Technology

You are the vice president of marketing for Burke Sporting Goods and Equipment, Inc. (Burke), the leading producer of sport balls. For over 20 years, your number-one seller has been the Kick It Ball, which is used in soccer games. As a matter of fact, other soccer balls are often referred to as Kick It Balls. Kick it Ball is a registered trademark. Recently, your competitors have used the term Kick It Ball in advertisements for their soccer balls. You are worried that sales of your product will decline because of confusion between your product and the soccer balls of your competitors.

1. What should Burke do to alleviate your concerns about this marketing dilemma?
2. If legal action is initiated against your competitors, what possible defenses may be asserted?

The U.S. economy is based on the freedom of ownership of property. In addition to real estate and personal property, **intellectual property rights** have value to both businesses and individuals. This is particularly the case in the modern era of the Information Age, computers, and the Internet.

intellectual property rights
The right to patents, copyrights, trademarks, trade secrets, trade names, domain names and other items of intellectual property that are very valuable business assets. Federal and state laws protect intellectual property rights from misappropriation and infringement.

Trade secrets form the basis of many successful businesses, which are protected from misappropriation. Federal law provides protections for intellectual property rights, such as patents, copyrights, and trademarks. In addition, businesses and individuals may register domain names to use on the Internet. Anyone who infringes on these rights may be stopped from doing so and is liable for damages.

This chapter discusses trade secrets, patents, copyrights, and trademarks.

Trade Secrets

Many businesses are successful because their **trade secrets** set them apart from their competitors. Trade secrets may be product formulas, patterns, designs, compilations of data, customer lists, or other business secrets. Many trade secrets either do not qualify to be—or simply are not—patented, copyrighted, or trademarked. Many states have adopted the **Uniform Trade Secrets Act** to give statutory protection to trade secrets.

trade secret
A product formula, pattern, design, compilation of data, customer list, or other business secret.

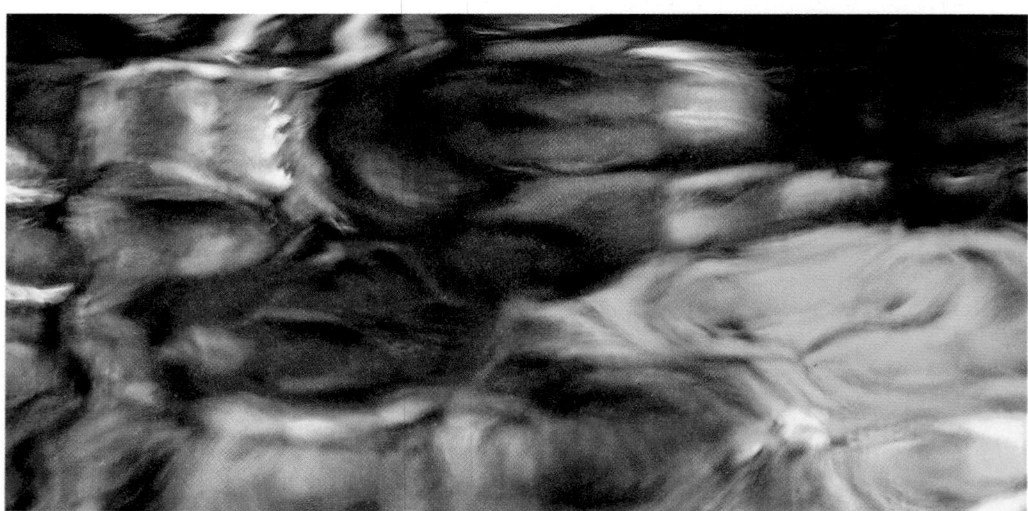

Reflecting Pool, Los Angeles County Museum of Art. Photographs, such as this one titled Colorful Dream, no longer need the © to be placed on it to be copyrighted.

State unfair competition laws allow the owner of a trade secret to bring a lawsuit for *misappropriation* against anyone who steals a trade secret. For the lawsuit to be actionable, the defendant (often an employee of the owner or a competitor) must have obtained the trade secret through unlawful means such as theft, bribery, or industrial espionage. No tort has occurred if there is no misappropriation. For example, a competitor can lawfully discover a trade secret by performing reverse engineering (i.e., taking apart and examining a rival's product).

The owner of a trade secret is obliged to take all reasonable precautions to prevent those secrets from being discovered by others. Such precautions include fencing in buildings, placing locks on doors, hiring security guards, and the like. If the owner fails to take such actions, the secret is no longer subject to protection under state unfair competition laws.

Ethics Brief

Businesses should take all necessary precautions to protect their trade secrets from unwanted discovery.

Generally, a successful plaintiff in a trade secret action can (1) recover the profits made by the offender from the use of the trade secret, (2) recover for damages, and (3) obtain an injunction prohibiting the offender from divulging or using the trade secret.

E-Commerce & Information Technology

The Economic Espionage Act

Although the stealing of trade secrets exposed the offender to a civil lawsuit by the injured party to recover economic damages, the offender seldom faced criminal charges except under a few state laws. All that changed with the enactment by Congress of the federal **Economic Espionage Act of 1996** [18 U.S.C. § § 1831–1839]. This act makes it a federal crime to steal another's trade secrets. Previously, no federal statute directly addressed economic espionage and the stealing of trade secrets.

Under the Espionage Act, it is a federal crime for any person to convert a trade secret to his or her benefit or for the benefit of others, knowing or intending that the act would cause injury to the owner of the trade secret. The definition of *trade secret* under the Espionage Act is very broad and parallels the definition used under the civil laws of misappropriating a trade secret. Under the Espionage Act, a trade secret includes any economic, business, financial, technical, scientific, or engineering information, including processes, software programs, and codes.

One of the major reasons for the passage of the Espionage Act was to address the ease of stealing trade secrets through computer espionage and using the Internet. For example, hundreds of pages of confidential information can be downloaded onto a small computer disk, placed in a pocket, and taken from the legal owner. In addition, computer hackers can crack into a company's computers and steal customer lists, databases, formulas, and other trade secrets. The Espionage Act is a very important weapon in addressing and penalizing computer and Internet espionage.

The Espionage Act provides for severe criminal penalties. An organization can be fined up to $5 million per criminal act and $10 million if the criminal act was committed to benefit a foreign government. The act imposes prison terms on individuals of up to 15 years per criminal violation, which can be increased to 25 years per violation if the criminal act was done with the intent to benefit a foreign government. By adding criminal penalties, the Espionage Act adds another weapon to safeguard trade secrets and intellectual property in this country. ■

Patents

When drafting the Constitution of the United States of America, the founders of the United States provided for protection of the works of inventors and writers. Article I, Section 8 of the Constitution provides, "The Congress shall have Power . . . To promote the Progress of Science and useful Arts, by securing for limited Times to Authors and Inventors the exclusive Right to their respective Writings and Discoveries." Pursuant to this power, Congress has enacted patent statutes to protect inventors' rights in their inventions.

"'How I Spent My Summer Vacation,' by Lilia Anya, all rights reserved, which includes the right to reproduce this essay or portions thereof in any form whatsoever, including, but not limited to, novel, screenplay, musical, television miniseries, home video, and interactive CD-ROM."

Medina, Fez, Morocco. One of the most important markets for the expansion of valuable intellectual property rights by U.S. companies is international markets.

Landmark Law

Federal Patent Statute

Pursuant to the express authority granted in the U.S. Constitution, Congress enacted the **Federal Patent Statute of 1952** [15 U.S.C § 1125(a)]. This law is intended to provide an incentive for inventors to invent and make their inventions public and to protect patented inventions from infringement. Federal patent law is exclusive; there are no state patent laws. The U.S. Court of Appeals for the Federal Circuit in Washington, DC, was created in 1982 to hear patent appeals. The court was established to promote uniformity in patent law.

Patent applications must contain a written description of the invention and be filed with the **U.S. Patent and Trademark Office** in Washington, DC. If a patent is granted, the invention is assigned a patent number. Patent holders usually affix the word *Patent* or *Pat.* and the patent number to the patented article. If a patent application is filed but a patent has not yet been issued, the applicant usually places the words *patent pending* on the article. Any party can challenge either the issuance of a patent or the validity of an existing patent. ■

Patenting an Invention

To be patented, an invention must be *novel*, *useful*, and *nonobvious*. In addition, only certain subject matters can be patented. Patentable subject matters include (1) machines; (2) processes; (3) compositions of matter; (4) improvements to existing machines, processes, or compositions of matter; (5) designs for an article of manufacture; (6) asexually reproduced plants; and (7) living material invented by a person. Abstractions and scientific principles cannot be patented unless they are part of the tangible environment. For example, Einstein's Theory of Relativity ($E = MC^2$) cannot be patented.

In the following case, the U.S. Supreme Court had to decide whether the subject matter was patentable.

Federal Patent Statute of 1952
A federal statute that establishes the requirements for obtaining a patent and protects patented inventions from infringement.

The patent system added the fuel of interest to the fire of genius.

Abraham Lincoln
Lectures on Discoveries, Inventions, and Improvements (1859)

Case 8.1
Patent

U.S. SUPREME COURT CASE

J.E.M. Ag Supply, Inc., dba Farm Advantage, Inc. v. Pioneer Hi-Bred International, Inc.

534 U.S. 124, 122 S.Ct. 593, 2001 U.S. Lexis 10949 (2001)
Supreme Court of the United States

Background and Facts

Pioneer Hi-Bred International, Inc. (Pioneer) has obtained 17 patents that cover the company's inbred and hybrid corn and corn seed products. A hybrid plant patent protects the plant, its seeds, variants, mutants, and modifications of the hybrid. Pioneer sells its patented hybrid seeds under a limited label license that provides: "License is granted solely to produce grain and/or forage." The license states that it "does not extend to the use of seed from such crop or the progeny thereof for propagation or seed multiplication." The license strictly prohibits "the use of such seed or progeny thereof for propagation or seed multiplication or for production or development of a hybrid or different variety of seed."

J.E.M. Ag Supply, Inc., doing business as Farm Advantage, Inc., purchased patented hybrid seeds from Pioneer in bags bearing this license agreement. Pioneer sued Farm Advantage, alleging that Farm Advantage infringed its patent and violated the license by creating seed from the hybrid corn products it grew from Pioneer's patented hybrid seed. Farm Advantage filed a counterclaim of patent invalidity, arguing that Pioneer hybrid plant seed patents are not patentable subject matter. The district court granted summary judgment to Pioneer, and the court of appeals affirmed. The U.S. Supreme Court agreed to hear the appeal.

Supreme Court Issue

Are sexually reproducing hybrid plants patentable subject matter?

In The Language of The U.S. Supreme Court

Thomas, Justice The text of 35 U.S.C. §101 provides; "Whoever invents or discovers any new and useful process, machine, manufacture, or composition of matter, or any new and useful improvement thereof, may obtain a patent therefor, subject to the conditions and requirements of this title." As this Court recognized over 20 years ago in *Diamond v. Chakrabarty*, 447 U.S. at 308 (1980), the language of §101 is extremely broad. "In choosing such expansive terms as 'manufacture' and 'composition of matter,' modified by the comprehensive 'any,' Congress plainly

J.E.M. Ag Supply, Inc., dba Farm Advantage, Inc. v. Pioneer Hi-Bred International, Inc.

534 U.S. 124, 122 S.Ct. 593, 2001 U.S. Lexis 10949 (2001)
Supreme Court of the United States
(continued)

contemplated that the patent laws would be given wide scope." This Court thus concluded in *Chakrabarty*, that living things were patentable under §101, and held that a manmade micro-organism fell within the scope of the statute.

Several years after *Chakrabarty*, The Patent and Trademark Office (PTO) Board of Patent Appeals and Interferences held that plants were within the understood meaning of "manufacture" or "composition of matter" and therefore were within the subject matter of §101. [*In re Hibberd*, 227 U.S.P.Q. (BNA) 443, 444 (1985).] It has been the unbroken practice of the PTO since that time to confer utility patents for plants. To obtain utility patent protection, a plant breeder must show that the plant he has developed is new, useful, and non-obvious. In addition, the plant must meet the specifications of §112, which require a written description of the plant and a deposit of seed that is publicly accessible.

Petitioner Farm Advantage essentially asks us to deny utility patent protection for sexually reproduced plants because it was unforeseen in 1930 that such plants could receive protection under §101. Denying patent protection under §101 simply because such coverage was thought technologically infeasible in 1930, however, would be inconsistent with the forward-looking perspective of the utility patent statute. As we noted in *Chakrabarty*, "Congress employed broad general language in drafting §101 precisely because new types of inventions are often unforeseeable."

Decision and Remedy

The U.S. Supreme Court held that sexually reproducing hybrid plants are patentable subject matter. The Supreme Court affirmed the judgment of the court of appeals.

Case Questions

Critical Legal Thinking Do you think sexually reproducing hybrid plants should be patentable subject matter? Why or why not?

Business Ethics Did Farm Advantage act ethically in this case? Explain.

Contemporary Business What are the economic implications of the U.S. Supreme Court's decision in this case?

International Law

Changes in Patent Law Mandated by GATT

In 1994, the **General Agreement on Tariffs and Trade (GATT)** established the **World Trade Organization (WTO)**, and international trade organization of which the United States is a member. GATT's intellectual property provisions, and implementing legislation passed by Congress, made the following important changes in U.S. patent law:

1. Patents are valid for *20 years*, instead of the previous term of 17 years.
2. The patent term begins to run from the date the patent application is *filed* instead of when the patent is issued, as was previously the case.

These changes, which became effective June 8, 1995, brought the U.S. patent system in harmony with the systems of the majority of other developed nations. The United States still follows the first-to-invent rule rather than the first-to-file rule followed by some other countries. In the following case, the U.S. Supreme Court held that an expired patent was in the public domain. ■

Case 8.2 Patent

U.S. SUPREME COURT CASE

TrafFix Devices, Inc. v. Marketing Displays, Inc.

532 U.S. 23, 121 S.Ct. 1255, 2001 U.S. Lexis 2457 (2001)
Supreme Court of the United States

Background and Facts

Temporary road signs with warnings such as "Road Work Ahead" and "Left Shoulder Closed" must withstand strong gusts of wind. An inventor named Robert Sarkisian obtained two utility patents for a mechanism built on two springs (the dual-spring design) to keep outdoor signs upright, despite adverse wind conditions. The patents were assigned to Marketing Displays, Inc. (MDI), which established a successful business manufacturing and selling sign stands incorporating the patented dual-spring feature. When the patents expired, a competitor, TrafFix Devices, Inc., sold sign stands using the patent-expired dual-spring design. MDI sued TrafFix, alleging that the visible dual-spring on its signs had gained trade dress protection under federal trademark laws. TrafFix argued that the expired patents were functional and had not gained trade dress protection. The district court agreed with TrafFix and held that MDI's previous patents were functional, that the patents had expired and entered the public domain, and that TrafFix could copy and sell its own version of the dual-spring design traffic signs. The court of appeals reversed the decision. TrafFix appealed to the U.S. Supreme Court.

Supreme Court Issue

Was the previously patented dual-spring design for traffic signs a functional invention that had entered the public domain upon the expiration of the patents and not subject to trade dress protection?

In The Language of The U.S. Supreme Court

Kennedy, Justice Trade dress protection must subsist with the recognition that in many instances there is no prohibition against copying goods and products. In general, unless an intellectual property right such as a patent or copyright protects an item, it will be subject to copying. As the Court has explained, copying is not always discouraged or disfavored by the laws which preserve our competitive economy. Allowing competitors to copy will have salutary effects in many instances. Reverse engineering of chemical and mechanical articles in the public domain often leads to significant advances in technology.

The principal question in this case is the effect of an expired patent on a claim of trade dress infringement. A prior patent, we conclude, has vital significance in resolving the trade dress claim. A utility patent is strong evidence that the features therein claimed are functional. If trade dress protection is sought for those features, the strong evidence of functionality based on the previous patent adds great weight to the statutory presumption that features are deemed functional until proved otherwise by the party seeking trade dress protection. Where the expired patent claimed the features in question, one who seeks to establish trade dress protection must carry the heavy burden of showing that the feature is not functional, for instance by showing that it is merely an ornamental, incidental, or arbitrary aspect of the device.

In the case before us, the central advance claimed in the expired utility patents is the dual-spring design; and the dual-spring design is the essential feature of the trade dress MDI now seeks to establish and to protect. The rule we have explained bars the trade dress claim, for MDI did not, and cannot, carry the burden of overcoming the strong evidentiary inference of functionality based on the disclosure of the dual-spring design in the claims of the expired patents.

Decision and Remedy

The U.S. Supreme Court held that the expired dual-spring design patents were functional, had not gained trade dress protection, and had therefore entered the public domain and were subject to copying by competitors of the prior patent holder. The Supreme Court reversed the decision of the court of appeals.

Case Questions

Critical Legal Thinking How long is a patent term? Do you think that the exclusive monopoly that the patent holder is given during this term is sufficient to spur invention?

Business Ethics Was it legal for TrafFix to copy MDI's expired patent design? Was it ethical for TrafFix to copy MDI's expired patent design?

Contemporary Business What do you think MDI was trying to accomplish by bringing this lawsuit? Explain.

Patent Infringement

Patent holders own exclusive rights to use and exploit their patents. **Patent infringement** occurs when someone makes unauthorized use of another's patent. In a suit for patent infringement, a successful plaintiff can recover (1) money damages equal to a reasonable royalty rate on the sale of the infringed articles, (2) other damages caused by the infringement (such as loss of customers), (3) an order requiring the destruction of the infringing article, an (4) an injunction preventing the infringer from such action in the future. The court has the discretion to award up to treble damages if the infringement was intentional.

patent infringement
Unauthorized use of another's patent. A patent holder may recover damages and other remedies against a patent infringer.

Entrepreneur and the Law

Inventor Wipes Ford's and Chrysler's Windshields Clean

In 1967, Robert Kearns, a professor at Wayne State University in Detroit, Michigan, patented his design for the electronic intermittent windshield wiper for automobiles and other vehicles. He peddled his invention around to many automobile manufacturers but never reached a licensing deal with any of them. In 1969, automobile manufacturers began producing cars with Kearns's invention. Virtually all cars sold in the United States today now have these wipers as standard equipment.

Entrepreneur and the Law

(continued)

Kearns filed patent infringement lawsuits against Ford in 1978 and Chrysler in 1982. He later filed patent infringement cases against virtually all automobile manufacturers. The Ford case went to trial first. Kearns sought $325 million in damages from Ford; Ford alleged that Kearns's patents were not valid because of obviousness and prior art. The jury disagreed with Ford and decided that Kearns's patents were valid. The jury ordered Ford to pay $5.2 million, plus interest. In 1990, Ford settled by paying Kearns $10.2 million and agreeing to drop all appeals. This represented 50¢ per Ford vehicle that used the wiper system.

Kearns sought $468 million in damages from Chrysler. In that case, Kearns fired his layers and represented himself. This was at least the fourth law firm hired and fired in the course of Kearns's patent infringement lawsuits. Kearns won a second victory: In 1991, the jury found that Chrysler had infringed Kearns's patents and awarded him $11.3 million. The court denied Kearns injunctive relief because his 17-year patents had expired years ago. The court of appeals affirmed the judgment, and the U.S. Supreme Court refused to hear Kearns's appeal. Kearns received over $21 million from Chrysler, which amounted to 90¢ for every vehicle sold by Chrysler with the wiper system.

In 1993 and 1994, courts dismissed Kearns's lawsuits against 23 automobile manufacturers, including General Motors, Porsche, Nissan, Toyota, Honda, and Rolls Royce, because Kearns failed to comply with court orders to disclose documents relevant to the cases. The district court then ordered Kearns to pay his fired lawyers $6.4 million in contingency fees. Thus ended Kearns's over-30-year saga and legal battle with the automobile industry. In an interview Kearns stated, "The patent system is a fraud pure and simple." ■

Entrepreneur and the Law

Protecting a Patent Is Expensive Business

Inventors spend years dreaming up new products and inventions, then file applications with the Patent and Trademark Office and wait to see if their patents are granted. The day the patent is issued is a cause for celebration—or is it? Ask Donald BonAsia. The young entrepreneur invented "fork-chops"—two eating utensils with chopsticks on one end and a knife and fork on the other end. He spent two years and $7,500 to receive a patent on his invention.

But his worst fear happened. Other manufacturers began copying his invention and selling them without seeking BonAsia's permission or paying him a royalty fee. BonAsia contacted a patent lawyer and found out the following: The normal cost to pursue a patent infringement case through trial is $1.5 million, and $1 million if it settles near trial. Attorneys typically want over $100,000 in retainer fees before filing a patent infringement case. BonAsia discovered that he had a patent but not enough money to protect it.

BonAsia'a plight is typical for small-time inventors who are under the misconception that a patent gives the holder an exclusive right to make the item. Wrong: What a patent gives the holder is the right to defend the patent and to try to stop others from making the patented article. BonAsia learned a valuable lesson: Patent law is usually the playing field of big corporations that have deep pockets to protect their patents. It may be that small entrepreneurs have the same legal rights; it is just that, as in many areas of the law, justice can only be obtained at a price. ■

One-Year "On Sale" Doctrine

Web Site

U.S. Patent and Trademark Office

The U.S. PTO has a Web site where you can download forms, order copies, link to legal materials, and find information about patents. Visit at **www.uspto.gov**.

Under the **one-year "on sale" doctrine**, also called the **public use doctrine**, a patent may not be granted if the invention was used by the public for more than one year prior to the filing of the patent application. This doctrine forces inventors to file their patent applications at the proper time.

Consider This Example Suppose Cindy Parsons invents a new invention on January 1. She allows the public to use this invention and does not file a patent application until February of the following year. The inventor has lost the right to patent her invention. The following U.S. Supreme Court case applied the one-year on-sale doctrine.

U.S. SUPREME COURT CASE

Case 8.3

Patent

Pfaff v. Wells Electronics Inc.

525 U.S. 55, 119 S.Ct. 304 1999 U.S. Lexis 18 (1998)
Supreme Court of the United States

Background and Facts

Wayne K. Pfaff commenced work on designing a computer chip socket in November 1980. Pfaff prepared detailed engineering drawings that described the design, dimensions, and materials to be used in making the socket. Prior to March 17, 1981, Pfaff showed a sketch of his design to representatives of Texas Instruments, a large company. On April 8, 1981, Texas Instruments and Pfaff signed a written contract confirming a previously placed verbal purchase order for 30,100 of his new sockets, for a total price of $91,000. Pfaff did not make a prototype of the new socket device before offering it for sale to Texas Instruments.

Pfaff filled the order in July 1981. The socket achieved substantial commercial success, as other companies placed orders. On April 19, 1982, Pfaff filed an application for a patent on his computer chip socket, and a patent was issued. When a competitor made a similar socket, Pfaff sued for patent infringement. The competitor countered that Pfaff did not have a valid patent because the one-year "on sale" doctrine of Section 102(b) of the federal patent statute had been violated. The district court held for Pfaff, but the court of appeals reversed the decision. The U.S. Supreme Court granted certiorari to hear the appeal.

Supreme Court Issue

Was the one-year "on sale" doctrine violated, thus invalidating Pfaff's patent on the computer chip socket?

In The Language of The U.S. Supreme Court

Stevens, Justice The primary meaning of the word *invention* in the Patent Act unquestionably refers to the inventor's conception rather than to a physical embodiment of that idea. The statute does not contain any express requirement that an invention must be reduced to practice before it can be patented.

It is well settled that an invention may be patented before it is reduced to practice. In 1888, this Court upheld a patent issued to Alexander Graham Bell even though he had filed his application before constructing a working telephone. *The Telephone Cases* [126 U.S. 1, 8 S.Ct. 778 (1888)]. When we apply the reasoning of *The Telephone Cases* to the facts of the case before us today, it is evident that Pfaff could have obtained a patent on his novel socket when he accepted the purchase order from Texas Instruments for 30,100 units.

Decision and Remedy

The U.S. Supreme Court held that the one-year "on sale" rule started to run on or before April 8, 1981, the date when Pfaff contracted in writing to sell sockets to Texas Instruments. Since the filing of his patent application on April 19, 1982, was more than one year later, his patent was invalidated pursuant to the one-year "on sale" doctrine. The judgment of the court of appeals was affirmed.

Case Questions

Critical Legal Thinking What does the one-year "on sale" doctrine provide? What is the public policy behind this rule?

Business Ethics Was it ethical for the competitor to copy and produce Pfaff's computer chip socket?

Contemporary Business How valuable is a patent? What were the economic consequences to Pfaff of the Supreme Court's decision? to others?

E-Commerce & Information Technology

Cyber Business Plans Are Patentable

Federal patent law recognizes four categories of innovation: (1) machines, (2) articles of manufacture, (3) compositions, and (4) processes. For centuries most patents involved tangible inventions, such as the telephone and the light bulb. But the computer and the Internet have changed the traditional view of what can be patented. Consider the case of *State Street Bank & Trust Co. v. Signature Financial Group, Inc.*, 149 F3d 1368, 1998 U.S.App. Lexis 16869 (Fed. Cir. 1998).

Signature Financial Group, Inc. (Signature), filed for and was granted a patent for a computerized accounting system that determines share prices through a series of mathematical calculations and is then used to manage mutual funds [U.S. Patent No. 5,193,056]. State Street Bank, another financial institution that wanted to offer a similar mutual fund investment program to clients, sued to have Signature's patent declared invalid. Signature defended, arguing that its intangible financial business model was a "process" that was protected under federal patent law. The U.S. Court of Appeals, Federal Circuit, upheld the patent as a "practical application of a mathematical, algorithm, formula, or calculation, because it produces a useful, concrete and tangible result."

Taking the lead from the *State Street* case, many persons and businesses have filed for and received patents for business and a financial models that are used over the Internet. Critics contend that Congress did not intend to grant patents for intangible processes when it enacted federal-patent law. Business plan patent holders counter that the trend reflects a necessary evolution in patent law and claim that business plan patterns are to the Internet Age what machine patents were to the Industrial Age. These proponents argue that critics had the same complaints when chemicals, polymers, and biotech patents were first granted. One thing is certain: The exponential growth in computer and Internet business plan patents will lead to an avalanche of patent litigation. ■

E-Commerce & Information Technology

Amazon.com Loses Its 1-Click Patent

Our forefathers believed that innovation was so important that they provided in the U.S. Constitution, as ratified by the states in 1788, for the protection of inventions. Since then, the U.S. Congress has enacted several patent statutes. The most recent major overhaul of the patent laws was completed in 1952, during the Industrial Age of the mechanical devices. But what happens when old laws meet the new technology of the Digital Age? Consider the following case.

Amazon.com, Inc., enables customers to find and purchase books, music, videos, consumer electronics, games, toys, gifts, and other items over the Internet by using its Web site, **www.amazon.com**. As an early entrant into this market, Amazon.com became a leader in electronic commerce. Other e-commerce retailers began offering goods and services for sale over the Web.

One problem that most of these e-commerce retailers faced was that over 50 percent of potential customers who went shopping online and selected items for purchase abandoned their transactions before checkout. To address this problem, Amazon.com devised a method that enabled online customers to purchase selected items with a single click of a computer mouse button. Only customers who had previously registered their name, address, and credit card number with Amazon.com could complete purchases by clicking an instant "buy" button. This ordering system was implemented by Amazon.com in September 1997. On September 21, 1997, Amazon.com applied for a patent for its one-click ordering system, and on September 28, 1998, the U.S. PTO granted patent No. 5,960,411 (411 patent) to Amazon.com. This was designated the 1-clik® ordering system by Amazon.com.

While Amazon.com's patent application was pending, other online retailers began offering similar one-click ordering systems. One was Barnesandnoble.com, which operates a Web site that sells books, software, music, videos, and other items. Barnesandnoble.com called its one-click ordering system "Express Lane." On October 21, 1999, Amazon.com sued Barnesandnoble.com, alleging patent infringement, and sought an injunction against Barnesandnoble.com from using its 1-click ordering system. Barnesandnoble.com defended, asserting that a one-click ordering system was clearly obvious and, therefore, did not meet the required "nonobvious" test of federal patent law for an invention to qualify for a patent.

The court was faced with several novel issues. The first was whether this business model—the one-click ordering system—qualified as patentable subject matter. Following the lead of the U.S. Court of Appeals in *State Street Bank & Trust Co. v. Signature Financial Group, Inc.*, 149 F.3d 1368 (Fed. Cir. 1998), the court acknowledged that business models qualify as a new breed of patentable subject matter. The second issue was whether the one-click ordering system was "nonobvious." After examining the evidence, the court decided that Amazon.com's 1-click system was nonobvious when it was invented in 1997.

Barnesandnoble.com appealed to the federal court of appeals, arguing that Amazon.com's 1-click ordering system was not novel or nonobvious as required by patent law. Barnesandnoble.com cited the following evidence that one-click ordering systems existed in the *prior art* before Amazon.com filed for its patent: (1) Since the 1990s the CompuServe Trend System provided for single-click ordering of stock charts over the Internet; (2) another Internet vendor's "WebBasket" allowed one-click ordering; (3) the "Oliver's Market" ordering system of another online vendor permitted one-click ordering; and (4) the book *Creating the Virtual Store*, published before Amazon.com filed for its '411 patent, suggested modifying software to provide for one-click ordering online. The federal court of appeals relied on these prior art references and reversed the trial court's grant of an injunction in favor of Amazon.com. The court of appeals allowed Barnesandnoble.com to use its Express Lane one-click ordering system. [*Amazon.com, Inc., v. Barnesandnoble.com, Inc.*, 239 F.3d 1343, 2001 U.S.App. Lexis 2163 (Fed. Cir. 2001)]. ■

Contemporary Business Environment

The American Inventors Protection Act

In 1999, Congress enacted the **American Inventors Protection Act**. This statute made significant changes in federal patent law. The act reorganized the U.S. PTO and granted the PTO new regulatory powers. The act does the following:

- Permits an inventor to file a provisional application with the PTO, pending the preparation and filing of a final and complete patent application. This part of the law grants "provisional rights" to an inventor for three months, pending the filing of a final application.
- Requires the PTO to issue a patent within three years after the filing of a patent application unless the applicant engages in dilatory activities.
- Provides that non–patent holders may challenge a patent as overly broad by requesting a contested reexamination of the patent application by the PTO. This provides that the reexamination will be within the confines of the PTO; the decision of the PTO can be appealed to the U.S. Court of Appeals for the Federal Circuit in Washington, DC.

The new act also upgrades the PTO commissioner to an assistant secretary of commerce with authority to advise the U.S. government on intellectual policy. ■

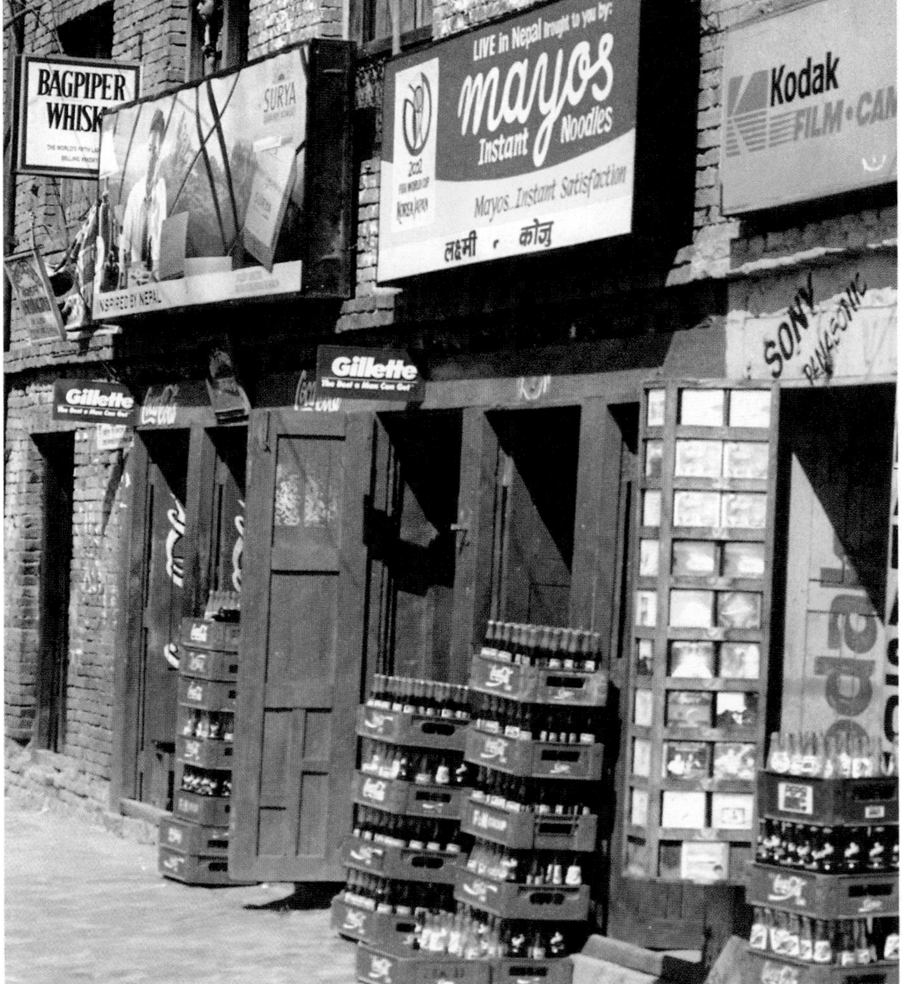

Nepal. Certain U.S. companies' brand names have worldwide name recognition.

Copyright

Article I, Section 8 of the Constitution of the United States of America authorizes Congress to enact statutes to protect the works of writers for limited times. Pursuant to this authority, Congress has enacted copyright statutes to protect writers' rights in their work.

Landmark Law

Federal Copyright Revision Act

Congress enacted a federal copyright law pursuant to an express grant of authority in the U.S. Constitution [17 U.S.C. §§ 101 et seq.]. This law protects the work of authors and other creative persons from the unauthorized use of their copyrighted materials and provides a financial incentive for authors to write, thereby increasing the number of creative works available in society. The **Copyright Revision Act of 1976** governs copyright law. Effective March 1, 1989, the United States became a member of the **Berne Convention**, an international copyright treaty. Federal copyright law is exclusive; there are no state copyright laws.

To be protected under federal copyright law, the work must be the original work of the author. Published and unpublished works may be copyrighted and registered with the **United States Copyright Office** in Washington, DC. Registration is permissive and voluntary and can be effected at any time during the term of the copyright. ■

Registration of Copyrights

Copyright Revision Act

A federal statute that (1) establishes the requirements for obtaining a copyright and (2) protects copyrighted works from infringement.

Business Brief

The expression of an idea is copyrightable. The idea itself is not.

Only *tangible writings*—writings that can be physically seen—are subject to copyright registration and protection. The term *writing* has been broadly defined to include books, periodicals, and newspapers; lectures, sermons, and addresses; musical compositions; plays, motion pictures, radio and television productions; maps; works of art, including paintings, drawings, sculpture, jewelry, glassware, tapestry, and lithographs; architectural drawings and models; photographs, including prints, slides, and filmstrips; greeting cards and picture postcards; photoplays, including feature films, cartoons, newsreels, travelogues, and training films; and sound recordings published in the form of tapes, cassettes, compact discs, and phonograph albums.

In the following case, the U.S. Supreme Court upheld Congress's extension of the copyright term.

Case 8.4

Copyright

U.S. SUPREME COURT CASE

Elred v. Ashcroft, Attorney General

537 U.S. 186, 123 S.Ct. 769, 2003 U.S. Lexis 751 (2003)

Supreme Court of the United States

Background and Facts

Article I, Section 8, Clause 8 of the U.S. Constitution provides that "Congress shall have Power . . . to promote the Progress of Science . . . by securing [to authors] for limited Times . . . the exclusive Right to their . . . Writings." The Nation's first copyright statute, enacted by Congress in 1790, provided for a copyright term of 14 years from publication, renewable for an additional 14 years. In 1831, Congress amended the original copyright term to 28 years from publication, renewable for an additional 14 years. In 1909 Congress kept the original term of 28 years but amended the extension to 28 years. In 1976, Congress amended the copyright term to be the author's life plus 50 years, and for a work for hire (commonly owned by businesses) to be the shorter of 75 years from publication or 100 years from creation. Each of the amendments of the copyright term by Congress applied to both new and existing works. A copyright that expires enters the public domain and may be copied by anyone without permission of the original copyright holder and without charge.

With several of the copyrights for its cartoon icons approaching the end of their copyright terms, in the mid-1990s the Walt Disney Company began lobbying Congress to add an additional 20 years to copyright terms. Other copyright holders joined in the lobbying. This extension would bring U.S. law in line with the European Union's longer copyright terms. In 1998, Congress enacted the Copyright Term Extension Act (CTEA), which lengthened the copyright terms by 20 years. The new copyright term was the author's life plus 70 years, and for a work for hire it was the shorter or 95 years from publication or 120 year from creation. The extensions applied to both new and existing works. Several parties (petitioners) who wanted to copy copyrighted works when they entered the public domain sued, arguing that the CTEA copyright extensions for existing works violated the Copyright Clause and the Freedom of Speech Clause of the U.S. Constitution. The district court and court of appeals held against the petitioners. The petitioners appealed to the U.S. Supreme Court.

Supreme Court Issue

Does the extended period of 20 years added to existing works by the CTEA violate either the Copyright Clause or Freedom of Speech Clause of the U.S. Constitution?

In The Language of The U.S. Supreme Court

Ginsburg, Justice In accord with the District Court and the Court of Appeals, we reject petitioners' challenges to the CTEA. In that 1998 legislation, as in all previous copyright term extensions, Congress placed existing and future copyrights in parity. In prescribing that alignment, we hold, Congress acted within its authority and did not transgress constitutional limitations. Petitioners' suit challenges the CTEA's constitutionality under both the Copyright Clause and the First Amendment. The District Court entered judgment for the Attorney General (respondent here). The court held that the CTEA does not violate the "limited times" restriction of the Copyright Clause because the CTEA's terms, though longer than the 1976 Act's terms, are still limited, not perpetual, and therefore fit within Congress' discretion. The court also held that "there are no First Amendment rights to use the copyrighted works of others."

The CTEA reflects judgments of a kind Congress typically makes, judgments we cannot dismiss as outside the Legislature's domain. As respondent Ashcroft describes, a key factor in the CTEA's passage was a 1993 European Union (EU) directive instructing EU members to establish a copyright term of life plus 70 years. By extending the baseline United States copyright term to life plus 70 years, Congress sought to ensure that American authors would receive the same copyright protection in Europe as their European counterparts.

In addition to spurring the creation and publication of new expression, copyright law contains built-in First Amendment accommodations. First, it distinguishes between ideas and expression and makes only the latter eligible for copyright protection. Specifically, 17 U.S.C. § 102(b) provides: "In no case does copyright protection for an original work of authorship extend to any idea, procedure, process, system, method of operation, concept, principle, or discovery, regardless of the form in which it is described, explained, illustrated, or embodied in such work." This idea/expression dichotomy strikes a definitional balance between the First Amendment and the Copyright Act by permitting free communication of facts while still protecting an author's expression.

Decision and Remedy

The U.S. Supreme Court held that the 20-year extensions to copyright terms granted by the 1998 CTEA did not violate the Copyright Clause or the Freedom of Speech Clause of the U.S. Constitution. The Supreme Court affirmed the decision of the court of appeals.

Case Questions

Critical Legal Thinking What is the purpose of the Copyright Clause of the U.S. Constitution? Do you think that the current copyright terms obey or violate the "limited times" provision of that clause?

Business Ethics Was it ethical for the Walt Disney Company to lobby for the copyright extension for existing works? What was the company's motive?

Contemporary Business What were the economic consequences of the U.S. Supreme Court's decision? Who were the winners? Who were the losers?

Contemporary Business Environment

Poems Qualify for Copyright Protection

Tangible writings, such as this poem, qualify for copyright protection:

Like oceans, we have spent
this time together before.
In galley slave pits you fed me
water and removed my slivers.
Riding Ch'u dynasty chariots
we perished on Mongol swords.
We toiled rocks in chains
and built Stonehenge,
drank with King Arthur
and danced with Black Elk.
We fled, hand-in-hand, dodging
Hitlers bullets, and
I carried you over the border
to have our baby in freedom.
During past full moons, the sun set
the seas in orbit
and as driftwood we tumbled
onto the shores of Los Angeles.
Another life together, my love?

Henry Cheeseman ■

Contemporary Business Environment

Martin Luther King, Jr.'s "I Have a Dream" Speech Copyrighted

Martin Luther King, Jr., was a leader of the Civil Rights movement in this country until he was shot outside a Memphis motel in 1968. King left behind a valuable legacy of intellectual property—speeches, sermons, letters, books, and unpublished manuscripts. The ownership rights to this intellectual property were left to his family—his widow, Coretta Scott King, and their children.

Since King's death, there has been an ongoing conflict between his heirs and some of the media. King's heirs have taken the position that copyright law protects King's intellectual property left to them, whereas some of the media and others argue that because King was such an influential figure in history, his works belong in the public domain.

Under the Copyright Act of 1976, as authorized by Article I, Section 8 of the U.S. Constitution, the right to King's works belongs to his heirs. The Kings license—for a fee—these intellectual property rights. The Kings also protect these intellectual property rights from copyright infringement. For example, the family sued *USA Today* for publishing the entire text of King's most famous speech—"I have a Dream"—without permission.

Copyright law does not restrict the media from publishing works about King and his life, however. Writers can write articles and books about King's life, editors can publish photographs of him, professors can teach courses about him, and producers can make films about King. What they cannot do is use his words without the permission of the King family.

Although some members of the media and the public will continue to criticize the King family for their stand on this issue, copyright law gives King's heirs rights to his intellectual property for 75 years after his death. ■

International Law

Berne Convention Eliminates Need for Copyright Notice

In 1989, the United States signed the Berne Convention. This international convention provides the copyright law that is now followed by most countries of the world. The convention made a major change in U.S. copyright law. Prior to 1989, to protect a copyright in a published work in the United States, the copyright holder had to place a copyright notice on the work that contained the following information: (1) the copyright holder's name, (2) a "(c)" or "©" or "Copyright" or "copr.," and (3) the year the material was copyrighted. Under the Berne Convention, however, notice is not required on works entering the public domain on or after March 1, 1989. Although notice is now permissive, it is recommended that notice be placed on copyrighted works to defeat a defendant's claim of innocent infringement. ■

Copyright Infringement

copyright infringement
An act in which a party copies a substantial and material part of the plaintiff's copyrighted work without permission. A copyright holder may recover damages and other remedies against the infringer.

Copyright infringement occurs when a party copies a substantial and material part of the plaintiff's copyrighted work without permission. The copying does not have to be either word for word or the entire work. A successful plaintiff can recover (1) the profit made by the infringer from the copyright infringement, (2) damages suffered by the plaintiff, (3) an order requiring the impoundment and destruction of the infringing works, and (4) an injunction preventing the infringer from doing so in the future. The court, in its discretion, can award statutory damages ranging from $200 for innocent infringements up to $100,000 for willful infringement in lieu of actual damages.

The court had to decide whether copyright infringement occurred in the following cases.

Ty, Inc. v. GMA Accessories, Inc.

132 F.3d 1167, 1997 U.S.App. Lexis 35974
United States Court of Appeals, Seventh Circuit

Case 8.5
Copyright

Background and Facts

In 1993, Ty, Inc., began selling the "Beanie Babies" line of small stuffed animals and introduced a new stuffed design each month. Beanie Babies became an immensely popular line of toys. Children, teenagers, and even adults collect some or all of the line of stuffed animals. Beanie Babies are copyrighted as "soft sculpture" under federal copyright law. Ty limits the production of individual Beanie Babies, thus, creating a secondary market in them. Some Beanie Babies that originally sold for $5 now have a price as high as $2,000. One Beanie Baby produced by Ty was Squealer the pig. Subsequently, GMA Accessories, Inc. (GMA), a competing toy manufacturer, brought out a line of its own small stuffed animals. One of GMA's animals was Preston the pig. GMA's Preston the pig was identical to Ty's Squealer. Ty sued GMA for copyright infringement. The district court granted a preliminary injunction against GMA prohibiting the company from producing Preston. GMA appealed.

Issue

Did GMA engage in copyright infringement?

In The Language of The Court

Posner, Chief Judge The two pigs are so nearly identical that if the second is a copy of the first, the second clearly infringes Ty's copyright. But identity is not infringement. The Copyright Act forbids only copying; if independent creation results in an identical work, the creator of that work is free to sell it. The practical basis for this rule is that unlike the case of patents and trademarks, the creator of an expressive work—an author or sculptor or composer—cannot canvass the entire universe of copyrighted works to discover whether his poem or song or, as in this case, "soft sculpture" is identical to some work in which copyright subsists, especially since unpublished, unregistered works are copyrightable. But identity can be powerful evidence of copying. The more a work is both like an already copyrighted work and—for this is equally important—unlike anything that is in the public domain, the less likely it is to be an independent creation.

The issue of copying can be broken down into two subissues. The first is whether the alleged copier had access to the work that he is claimed to have copied; the second is whether, if so, he used his access to copy. Here it is both. GMA's pig is strikingly similar to Ty's pig but not to anything in the public domain—a real pig, for example. The parties' bean-bag pigs bear little resemblance to real pigs. Real pigs are not the only pigs in the public domain. But GMA has not pointed to any fictional pig in the public domain that Preston resembles. Preston resembles only Squealer, and resembles him so closely as to warrant an inference that GMA copied Squealer.

Decision and Remedy

The court of appeals held that GMA engaged in copyright infringement and affirmed the district court's grant of the preliminary injunction against GMA.

Case Questions

Critical Legal Thinking Do copyright laws serve any useful purpose? What would be the consequences if copyright laws did not exist?

Business Ethics Did GMA act unethically in this case? Why do you think GMA fought this case all the way to the court of appeals?

Contemporary Business Did Ty have much to lose if it had not won this case? Explain.

U.S. SUPREME COURT CASE

New York Times Company, Inc. v. Tasini

533 U.S. 483, 121 S.Ct. 2381, 2001 U.S. Lexis 4667 (2001)
Supreme Court of the United States

Case 8.6
Copyright

Background and Facts

Between 1990 and 1993 Jonathan Tasini and other authors wrote articles that were printed in the *New York Times*, *Sports Illustrated*, and various other newspapers and magazines. The publishers hired the authors as independent contractors (freelancers) under contracts that did not secure consent from the authors to place their articles in electronic databases. At a later date, the publishers placed these articles in computerized databases and made them available to the public through subscription services from electronic publishers such as LexisNexis. The publishers did not pay the authors royalties on monies derived from electronic database sales. Tasini and other authors sued the publishers for copyright infringement. The district court granted the publishers summary judgment, but the court of appeals reversed the decision. The U.S. Supreme Court granted certiorari to hear the appeal.

New York Times Company, Inc. v. Tasini

533 U.S. 483, 121 S.Ct. 2381, 2001 U.S. Lexis 4667 (2001)
Supreme Court of the United States
(continued)

Supreme Court Issue

Did the publishers engage in copyright infringement when they placed and sold the authors' articles through electronic databases?

In The Language of The U.S. Supreme Court

Ginsburg, Justice In the instant case, the Authors wrote several Articles and gave the Print Publishers permission to publish the Articles in certain newspapers and magazines. It is undisputed that the Authors hold copyrights and, therefore, exclusive rights in the Articles. The crucial fact is that the Databases, like the hypothetical library, store and retrieve articles separately within a vast domain of diverse texts. Such a storage and retrieval system effectively overrides the Authors' exclusive right to control the individual reproduction and distribution of each Article. We conclude that the Electronic Publishers infringed the Authors' copyrights by reproducing and distributing the Articles in a manner not authorized by the Authors. We further conclude that the Print Publishers infringed the Authors' copyrights by authorizing the Electronic Publishers to place the Articles in the Databases and by aiding the Electronic Publishers in that endeavor.

Decision and Remedy

The U.S. Supreme Court held that the publishers infringed the authors' copyrights by publishing and selling the authors' articles through electronic databases without the permission of the authors to do so. The judgment of the court of appeals is affirmed.

Case Questions

Critical Legal Thinking When the original publisher–author contracts were written, was the placement of articles in electronic databases common?

Business Ethics Did the publishers act ethically in this case? What should they have done?

Contemporary Business Now that this case has been decided, what contract provision will new publisher agreements with freelancers contain? Explain.

E-Commerce & Information Technology

Napster Unplugged by the Court

In May 1999, 18-year-old Shawn Fanning cofounded Napster, Inc., and instantly created an Internet phenomenon. Using Napster software, Internet users could access digitally compressed MP3-format music files stored on other users' computers that were connected to the Internet. Although Napster did not actually provide a library of songs itself, it kept a directory available to its users that listed the names and computer locations of songs on its users' computers. The Napster program made possible free peer-to-peer swapping of music files, including those that were copyrighted.

There was one major problem. If copyrighted music was being copied for free, the songwriters, artists, and record companies that wrote, sang, and produced the songs were being cut out by the copiers and not paid anything. In December 1999, most of the world's biggest record labels, such as A&M Records, Sony Music, Universal Music, MCA Records, Warner Music, and EMI Group, sued Napster for contributory copyright infringement. The heavy metal band Metallica and rapper Dr. Dre joined the lawsuit against Napster.

Napster defended, arguing that it did nothing illegal. For 1½ years Napster continued to operate while the legal maneuverings wound their way through the federal courts. However, in February 2001 (Napster had more than 50 million users who were sharing more than 3 billion songs each month), the federal court of appeals issued an almost total victory for the record companies. Although the court did not hold that Napster was an actual copyright infringer (the individual computer users who used Napster to copy copyrighted songs were), the court did find Napster liable for *contributory copyright infringement* in violation of federal copyright law. The court stated that Napster "knowingly encourages and assists in the infringement of copyrights" by others. When Napster tried to argue that it did not know of its users' infringing conduct, the court cited a document written by Napster cofounder Sean Parker that mentioned "the need to remain ignorant of users' real names and IP addresses since they are exchanging pirated music." The court of appeals ordered the lower court to fashion an injunction that required Napster to block its users from swapping copyrighted songs when music the companies notify Napster that the songs are copyrighted and should be blocked. Eventually, Napster went bankrupt. Its brand name and Web site were sold to another company, which used it for lawful purposes, paying royalties to copyright holders for use of their songs.

Although winning a victory over Napster, the real victor was the new music-swapping technology. Faced with even more potent free music-swapping programs such as the Gnutella system, record companies began negotiating with record-sharing program owners to provide fee-based subscription services whereby users pay a monthly fee to swap copyrighted music, and the fees are then split with the record companies, songwriters, and artists. But even now record companies face new free music-swapping technologies and those originating in other countries where U.S. copyright laws do not reach. [*A&M Records v. Napster, Inc.*, 239 F.3d 1004, 2001 U.S. App. Lexis 1941 (9th Cir. 2001)] ■

The Fair Use Doctrine

The copyright holder's rights in the work are not absolute. The law permits certain limited unauthorized use of copyrighted materials under the **fair use doctrine**. The following uses are protected under this doctrine: (1) quotation of the copyrighted work for review or criticism or in a scholarly or technical work, (2) use in a parody or satire, (3) brief quotation in a news report, (4) reproduction by teacher or student of a small part of the work to illustrate a lesson, (5) incidental reproduction of a work in a newsreel or broadcast of an event being reported, and (6) reproduction of a work in a legislative or judicial proceeding. The copyright holder cannot recover for copyright infringement where fair use is found. The U.S. Supreme Court decided a fair use issue in the following case.

fair use doctrine
A doctrine that permits certain limited use of a copyright by someone other than the copyright holder without the permission of the copyright holder.

Web Site
U.S. Copyright Office Information about copyright basics, copyright law, copyright forms, copyright records, and other copyright materials can be found at this Web site. Visit at **www.loc.gov/copyright**.

Case 8.7
Fair Use

U.S. SUPREME COURT CASE
Campbell v. Acuff-Rose Music, Inc.
510 U.S. 569, 114 S.Ct. 1164, 1994 U.S. Lexis 2052 (1994)
Supreme Court of the United States

Background and Facts

In 1964, Roy Orbison collaborated with another songwriter and wrote a rock ballad called "Oh, Pretty Woman." The song was copyrighted under federal copyright law. Roy Orbison recorded the song, which became a memorable classic from the 1960s. The writers assigned their rights in the song to Acuff-Rose Music, Inc. (Acuff-Rose).

2 Live Crew is a popular rap music group led by Luther R. Campbell. In 1989, Campbell wrote a song called "Pretty Woman" that was a parody of Roy Orbison's original recording. The lyrics of Campbell's version differed from Roy Orbison's version, except for the first line, which was verbatim from the original. 2 Live Crew wrote Acuff-Rose and asked permission to record their rap version of the song and stated that they were willing to pay a fee for the right to do so. When Acuff-Rose refused the permission, 2 Live Crew recorded the song anyway and put it on their rap album "As Clean as They Wanna Be," which sold over 250,000 copies.

The rap version of "Pretty Woman" used the same rhythm as the original, although the rap version included additional sounds such as scraper noises, overlays of different keys, and altered drum beats. The lyrics of the two versions of the song follow.

Acuff-Rose sued 2 Live Crew and their record company, Luke Skywalker Records, for copyright infringement. The defendants asserted the affirmative defense of fair use based on parody. The district court found fair use, but the court of appeals reversed the decision. The U.S. Supreme Court agreed to hear the case.

Supreme Court Issue

Can commercial parody be fair use?

In The Language of The U.S. Supreme Court

Souter, Justice It is uncontested here that 2 Live Crew's song would be an infringement of Acuff-Rose's rights on "Oh, Pretty Woman," under the Copyright Act of 1976, but for a finding of fair use through parody. Modern dictionaries describe a parody as a "literary or artistic work that imitates the characteristic style of an author or a work for comic effect or ridicule." [*American Heritage Dictionary*, p. 1317 (3d ed. 1992)].

It is true, of course, that 2 Live Crew copied the characteristic opening bass riff (or musical phrase) of the original, and true that the words of the first line copy the Orbison lyrics. The words of 2 Live Crew's song then quickly degenerates into a play on words, substituting predictable lyrics with shocking ones that derisively demonstrate how bland and banal the Orbison song seems to them. 2 Live Crew juxtaposes the romantic musings of a man whose fantasy comes true, with degrading taunts, a bawdy demand for sex, and a sigh of relief from paternal responsibility. The later words can be taken as a comment on the naivete of the original of an earlier day, as a rejection of its sentiment that ignores the ugliness of street life and the debasement that it signifies. Parody needs to mimic an original to make its point. Suffice it to say here that, as to the lyrics, we think that no more was taken than necessary.

Campbell v. Acuff-Rose Music, Inc.

510 U.S. 569, 114 S.Ct. 1164, 1994 U.S. Lexis 2052 (1994)
Supreme Court of the United States
(continued)

Roy Orbison's Version of "Oh, Pretty Woman"
Pretty Woman, walking down the street,
Pretty Woman, the kind I like to meet,
Pretty Woman, I don't believe you, you're not the truth,
No one could look as good as you
Mercy
Pretty Woman, won't you pardon me,
Pretty Woman, I couldn't help but see,
Are you lonely just like me?
Pretty Woman, stop a while,
Pretty Woman, talk a while,
Pretty Woman give your smile to me
Pretty Woman, yeah, yeah, yeah
Pretty Woman, look my way,
Pretty Woman, say you'll stay with me
'Cause I need you, I'll treat you right
Come to me baby, Be mine tonight
Pretty Woman, don't walk on by,
Pretty Woman, don't make me cry,
Pretty Woman, don't walk away
Hey, O.K.
If that's the way it must be, O.K.
I guess I'll go on home, it's late
There'll be tomorrow night, but wait!
What do I see
Is she walking back to me?
Yeah, she's walking back to me!
Oh, Pretty Woman.

2 Live Crew's Version of "Pretty Woman"
Pretty Woman walkin' down the street
Pretty Woman girl you look so sweet
Pretty Woman you bring me down to that knee
Pretty Woman you make me wanna beg please
Oh, pretty woman
Big hairy woman you need to shave that stuff
Big hairy woman you know I bet it's tough
Big hairy woman all that hair it ain't legit'
Cause you look like "Cousin It"
Big hairy woman
Bald headed woman girl your hair won't grow
Bald headed woman you got a teeny weeny afro
Bald headed woman you know your hair could look nice
Bald headed woman first you got to roll it with rice
Bald headed woman here, let me get this hunk of biz for ya
Ya know what I'm saying you look better than rice a roni
Oh bald headed woman
Big hairy woman come on in
And don't forget your bald headed friend
Hey pretty woman let the boys
Jump in
Two timin' woman girl you know you ain't right
Two timin' woman you's out with my boy last night
Two timin' woman that takes a load off my mind
Two timin' woman now I know the baby ain't mine
Oh, two timin' woman
Oh pretty woman

Decision and Remedy

The U.S. Supreme Court held that commercial parody can qualify as fair use of another's copyrighted work. The Court reversed the judgment of the court of appeals and remanded the case for further proceedings.

Case Questions

Critical Legal Thinking Should there be a fair use exception to copyright infringement? What purpose is served by the fair use doctrine?

Business Ethics Did 2 Live Crew act ethically in using the "Oh, Pretty Woman" song even though the copyright holder denied them permission to do so?

Contemporary Business Do you think 2 Live Crew's parody version caused any economic loss to the original copyright holder?

E-Commerce & Information Technology

The Digital Millennium Copyright Act

The Internet makes it easier than ever before for people to illegally copy and distribute copyrighted works. To combat this, software and entertainment companies developed "wrappers" and encryption technology to protect their copyrighted works from unauthorized access. Not to be outdone, software pirates and other Internet users devised ways to crack these wrappers and protection devices. Seeing that they were losing the battle, software companies and the entertainment industry lobbied Congress to enact legislation that made the cracking of their wrappers and selling of technology to do so illegal. In1998, Congress responded by enacting the **Digital Millennium Copyright Act (DMCA)** [17 U.S.C. 1201], which does the following:

- Prohibits unauthorized *access* to copyrighted digital works by circumventing the wrapper or encryption technology that protects the intellectual property. This "black box" protection prohibits simply accessing the protected information and does not require that the accessed information be misused.
- Prohibits the manufacture and distribution of technologies, products, or services primarily designed for the purpose of circumventing wrappers or encryption protection. Multipurpose devices that can be used in ways other than cracking wrappers or encryption technology can be manufactured and sold without violating the DMCA.

The DMCA changes the traditional fair use doctrine of copyright law. Historically, it has never been a crime to access or make a copy of a copyrighted work; what has been a crime is the misuse of that information. This rule remains valid for the nondigital world of copyrighted works. The DMCA changes this rule for digital protected works, making it illegal to merely access the copyrighted material by breaking through the digital wrapper or encryption technology that protects the work. Thus, a professor who can access and quote a nondigital copyrighted work in a paper he or she is writing pursuant to the fair use doctrine would violate the DMCA by merely accessing a digital work protected by the act.

Congress granted exceptions to DMCA liability to

- Software developers to achieve compatibility of their software with the protected work.
- Federal, state, and local law enforcement agencies conducting criminal investigations.
- Parents who are protecting children from pornography or other harmful materials available on the Internet.
- Internet users who are identifying and disabling cookies and other identification devices that invade their personal privacy rights.
- Nonprofit libraries, educational institutions, and archives that access a protected work to determine whether to acquire the work.

The DMCA imposes civil and criminal penalties. A successful plaintiff in a civil action can recover actual damages from first-time offenders and treble damages from repeat offenders, costs and attorneys' fees, an order for the destruction of illegal products and devices, and an injunction against future violations by the offender. As an alternative to actual damages, a plaintiff can recover statutory damages of not less than $2,500 and up to $25,000 per act of circumvention. The following criminal penalties can be accessed for willful violations committed for "commercial advantage" or "private financial gain": First-time violators can be fined up to $500,000 and imprisoned for up to 5 years; subsequent violators can be fined up to $1 million and imprisoned for up to 10 years.

The passage of the DMCA marks a significant victory for the software and entertainment industries, who allege that the new law will allow a huge growth in electronic commerce. Opponents, such as academics, scientists, libraries, and consumers argue that the act restricts access to information that would have previously been available under the fair use doctrine. They also note that the act paves the way for the software and entertainment industries to impose a per-use fee for their works. In the end, the DMCA has elevated the protection of digital copyrighted works above the protection of nondigital copyrighted works. ■

E-Commerce & Information Technology

The NET Act: Criminal Copyright Infringement

A copyright holder owns a valuable right and may sue an infringer in a civil lawsuit to recover damages, injunctions, and other remedies for copyright infringement. In 1997, Congress enacted the **No Electronic Theft Act (NET Act)**, which criminalizes certain copyright infringement as well. The impetus for the passage of this act was the failure of the U.S. government to obtain criminal convictions against copyright infringers under existing, non-Internet-specific criminal statutes.

In one notable case, David LaMacchia, a 21-year-old student at the Massachusetts Institute of Technology (MIT), encouraged Internet users to upload computer games and software to a bulletin board. LaMacchia then made this software available free to Internet users without compensating the copyright holders. The worldwide traffic generated by the availability of free software attracted the notice of university and federal authorities. The U.S. government sued LaMacchia, asserting a violation of the federal wire fraud statute, but the federal court judge dismissed the case, holding that this statute's language did not prohibit LaMacchia's conduct because he did not recognize financial gain. [*United States v. LaMacchia*, 871 F.Supp. 535 (D. Mass. 1994)]

So Congress passed the NET Act to directly criminalize such copyright infringement. The NET Act prohibits any person from willfully infringing a copyright for the purpose of either commercial advantage or financial gain, or by reproduction or distribution even without commercial advantage or financial gain, including by electronic means, where the retail value of the copyrighted work exceeds $1,000. Criminal penalties for violating the act include imprisonment for up to one year and fines of up to $100,000.

The NET Act has closed the "LaMacchia loophole." For example, Jeffrey Gerald Levy, a 22-year-old University of Oregon senior, pleaded guilty to criminal copyright infringement in violation of the NET Act because he was caught maintaining a Web site on the university's server where the public could make copies of thousands of software programs, movies, and musical recordings. [*United States v. Levy* (D. Or. 1999)] The NET Act adds a new law for the federal government to criminally attack copyright infringement and curb digital piracy. ■

E-Commerce & Information Technology

Copyrighting Software

The advent of new technology challenges the ability of laws to protect it. For example, the invention of computers and the writing of software programs caused problems for existing copyright laws. These laws had to be changed to afford protection to software.

In 1980, Congress enacted the **Computer Software Copyright Act**, which amended the Copyright Act of 1976. The 1980 amendments included computer programs in the list of tangible items protected by copyright law. The amendments define *computer program* broadly as "a set of statements or instructions to be used directly or indirectly in a computer in order to bring about a certain result" [17 U.S.C. § 101].

A computer program is written first in programming language, which is called *source code*. It is then translated into another language, called *object code*, which is understood by the computer. In an important decision, *Apple Computer; Inc. v. Franklin Computer Corp.*, 714 F.2d 1240 (3d Cir. 1983), the court held that object code could be copyrighted.

As with other works, the creator of a copyrightable software program obtains automatic copyright protection. The **Judicial Improvement Act of 1990** authorizes the Register of Copyright to accept and record any document pertaining to computer software, and to issue a **certificate of recordation** to the recorder [P.L. 101–650]. Congress passed the **Semiconductor Chip Protection Act of 1984** to provide greater protection of the hardware components of a computer. This law protects masks that are used to create computer chips. A *mask* is an original layout of software programs that is used to create a semiconductor chip. This act is sometimes referred to as the "Mask Work Act." Notice on the work is optional, but when used must contain (1) the words *Mask Work* or the symbol *M* or (M) and (2) the name of the owner. [17 U.S.C. §§ 901–914] ■

Beijing, China. Now that China has joined the World Trade Organization (WTO), the country is expected to increase the enforcement of intellectual property rights.

Trademarks

Businesses often develop company names, as well as advertising slogans and commercial logos, to promote the sale of their goods and services. Companies, such as Nike, Microsoft, Louis Vuitton, and McDonald's, spend millions of dollars annually to gain market recognition from consumers. Congress enacted trademark acts to provide legal protection for these names, slogans, and logos.

Landmark Law

Federal Lanham Trademark Act

Trademark law is intended to (a) protect the owner's investment and goodwill in a **mark** and (2) prevent consumers from being confused as to the origin of goods and services. In 1946, Congress enacted the **Lanham Trademark Act** to provide federal protection to trademarks, service marks, and other marks [15 U.S.C. §§ 1114 et seq.]. Congress passed the **Trademark Law Revision Act of 1988**, which amended trademark law in several respects. The amendments made it easier to register a trademark but harder to maintain it. States may also enact trademark laws.

Trademarks are registered with the **U.S. PTO** in Washington, DC. The original registration of a mark is valid for 10 years and can be renewed for an unlimited number of 10-year periods. The registration of a trademark, which is given nationwide effect, serves as constructive notice that the mark is the registrant's personal property. The registrant is entitled to use the registered trademark symbol ® in connection with a registered trademark or service mark. Use of the symbol is not mandatory. Note that the frequently used notations "TM" and "SM" have no legal significance.

An applicant can register a mark six months prior to its proposed use in commerce. If the mark is not used within this period, the applicant loses the mark. ■

Marks That Can Be Trademarked

The following types of **marks** can be trademarked:

- ***Trademarks*** A **trademark** is a distinctive mark, symbol, name, word, motto, or device that identifies the *goods* of a particular business. For example, the words *Xerox, Coca-Cola*, and *IBM* are trademarks.
- ***Service marks*** A **service mark** is used to distinguish the *services* of the holder from those of its competitors. The trade names *United Airlines, Marriott Hotels*, and *Weight Watchers* are examples of service marks.
- ***Certification marks*** A **certification mark** is a mark that is used to certify that goods and services are of a certain quality or originate from particular geographical areas (for example, wines from the *Napa Valley* of California or *Florida* oranges). The owner of the mark is usually a nonprofit corporation that licenses producers that meet certain standards or conditions to use the mark.
- ***Collective marks*** A **collective mark** is a mark used by cooperatives, associations, and fraternal organizations. *Boy Scouts of America* is an example of a collective mark.

Certain marks cannot be registered. They include (1) the flag or coat of arms of the United States, any state, municipality, or foreign nation, (2) marks that are immoral or scandalous, (3) geographical names standing alone (e.g., "South"), (4) surnames standing alone (note that a surname can be registered if it is accompanied by a picture or fanciful name, such as *Smith Brothers' Cough Drops*, and (5) any mark that resembles a mark already registered with the federal PTO.

mark
The collective name for trademarks, service marks, certification marks, and collective marks that all can be trademarked.

trademark
A distinctive mark, symbol, name, word, motto, or device that identifies the goods of a particular business.

service mark
A mark that distinguishes the services of the holder from those of its competitors.

The law in respect to literature ought to remain upon the same footing as that which regards the profits of mechanical inventions and chemical discoveries.

William Wordsworth
Letter (1838)

Napa Valley, California. This certification mark designates California cheese manufacturers.

Registration of Trademarks

Lanham Trademark Act (as amended)
A federal statute that (1) establishes the requirements for obtaining a federal mark and (2) protects marks from infringement.

An applicant can register a mark if (1) it was in use in commerce (e.g., actually used in the sale of goods or services) or (2) the applicant verifies a bona fide intention to use the mark in commerce and actually does so within six months of its registration. Failure to do so during this period causes loss of the mark to the registrant. A party other than the registrant can submit an opposition to a proposed registration of a mark or the cancellation of a previously registered mark.

Distinctiveness of a Mark

distinctive
A brand name that is unique and fabricated.

secondary meaning
A brand name that has evolved from an ordinary term.

To qualify for federal protection, a mark must be **distinctive** or have acquired a "**secondary meaning**." For example, marks such as *Xerox* and *Acura* are *distinctive*. A term such as *English Leather*, which literally means leather processed in England, has taken on a secondary meaning as a trademark for an aftershave lotion. For example, Nike has trademarked its name *Nike*, its "*swoosh*" symbol, and its "*Just Do It*" slogan. Words that are *descriptive* but have no secondary meaning cannot be trademarked. For example, the word *cola* alone could not be trademarked.

In the following case, the U.S. Supreme Court held that color associated with a product could be trademarked.

Case 8.8

Trademark

U.S. SUPREME COURT CASE

Qualitex Company v. Jacobson Products Company, Inc.

514 U.S. 159, 115 S.Ct. 1300, 1995 U.S. Lexis 2408 (1995)
Supreme Court of the United States

Background and Facts

Since the 1950s, Qualitex Company has manufactured and sold dry cleaning pads with a special shade of green-gold color. The pads are used on cleaning presses at dry cleaning firms. Qualitex registered the special green-gold color of its pads with the PTO as a trademark. In 1989, Jacobson Products, a Qualitex rival, began to sell its own press pads to dry cleaning firms, and it colored these pads a similar green-gold. Qualitex sued Jacobson for trademark infringement. Qualitex won the lawsuit in the district court, but the court of appeals reversed the decision. Qualitex appealed to the U.S. Supreme Court.

Supreme Court Issue

Can color alone, when associated with a company's product, be trademarked under the Lanham Trademark Act?

In The Language of The U.S. Supreme Court

Breyer, Justice The Lanham Act gives a seller or producer the exclusive right to "register" a trademark and to prevent his or her competitors from using that trademark. Both the language of the Act and the basic underlying principles of trademark law would seem to include color within the universe of things that can qualify as a trademark. The language of the Lanham Act describes that universe in the broadest of terms. It says that trademarks "include any word, name, symbol, or device, or any combination thereof." Since human beings might use as a "symbol" or "device" almost anything at all that is capable of carrying meaning, this language, read literally, is not restrictive. The courts and the Patent and Trademark Office have authorized for use as a mark a particular shape (of a Coca-Cola bottle), a particular sound (of NBC's three chimes), and even a particular scent (of plumeria blossoms on sewing thread). If a shape, a sound, and a fragrance can act as symbols why, one might ask, can a color not do the same?

True, a product's color is unlike "fanciful," "arbitrary," or "suggestive" words or designs, which almost *automatically* tell a customer that they refer to a brand. The imaginary word "Suntost," or the words "Suntost Marmalade," on a jar of orange jam immediately would signal a brand or a product source; the jam's orange color does not do so. But, over time, customers may come to treat a particular color on a product or its packaging (say, a color that in context seems unusual, such as pink on a firm's insulating material or red on the head of a large industrial bolt) as signifying a brand. And, if so, that color would have come to identify and distinguish the goods. We cannot find in the basic objectives of trademark law any obvious theoretical objection to the use of color alone as a trademark, where that color has attained "secondary meaning" and therefore identifies and distinguishes a particular brand and thus indicates its "source."

It would seem, then, that color alone, at least sometimes, can meet the basic legal requirements for use as a trademark. It can act as a symbol that distinguishes a firm's goods and identifies their source, without serving any other significant function.

Indeed, the District Court, in this case, entered findings that show Qualitex's green-gold press pad color has met these requirements. The green-gold color acts as a symbol. Having developed secondary meaning (for customers identified the green-gold color as Qualitex's), it identifies the press pads' source. And, the green-gold color serves no other function. Although it is important to use *some* color on press pads to avoid noticeable stains, the court found no competitive need in the press pad industry for the green-gold color, since other colors are equally usable. Accordingly, trademark law would protect Qualitex's use of the green-gold color on its press pads.

Decision and Remedy

The U.S. Supreme Court held that color alone, when associated with a company's product, may be trademarked under the Lanham Trademark Act. The Supreme Court reversed the decision of the court of appeals.

Case Questions

Critical Legal Thinking Do you think Congress, when it enacted the federal Lanham Act, expected the courts to expand trademark protection to shapes, sounds, scents, and colors?

Business Ethics Was it ethical for Jacobson Products Company, Inc., to copy Qualitex Company's green-gold color on its competing press pads? What do you think was Jacobson Products Company's motive?

Contemporary Business Will the decision of the U.S. Supreme Court help or hurt business? Will the decision help or hurt consumers?

Trademark Infringement

The owner of a mark can sue a third party for the unauthorized use of a mark. To succeed in a **trademark infringement** case, the owner must prove that (1) the defendant infringed the plaintiff's mark by using it in an unauthorized manner and (2) such use is likely to cause confusion, mistake, or deception of the public as to the origin of the goods or services. A successful plaintiff can recover (1) the profits made by the infringer by the unauthorized use of the mark, (2) damages caused to the plaintiff's business and reputation, (3) an order requiring the defendant to destroy all goods containing the unauthorized mark, and (4) an injunction preventing the defendant from such infringement in the future. The court has discretion to award up to *treble* damages where intentional infringement is found.

trademark infringement

Unauthorized use of another's mark. The holder may recover damages and other remedies from the infringer.

Web Site

U.S. Patent and Trademark Office

The U.S. PTO has a Web site where you can download forms, order copies, link to legal materials, and find information about trademarks. Visit at **www.uspto.gov**.

Trade Dress

trade dress

Federal protection of the look and feel of a product, a product's packaging, or a service establishment.

Section 43(a) of the Lanham Act protects certain forms of **trade dress.** This consists of the "look and feel" of a product, a product's packaging or a service establishment. The area of trade dress protection is an evolving area of the law. In the following two cases, the U.S. Supreme Court attempted to define the limits of trade dress protection.

Case 8.9 Trade Dress

U.S. SUPREME COURT CASE

Two Pesos, Inc. v. Taco Cabana, Inc.

505 U.S. 763, 112 S.Ct. 2753, 1992 U.S. Lexis 4533 (1992)

Supreme Court of the United States

Background and Facts

Since 1975, Taco Cabana, Inc. (Taco Cabana), has operated a chain of fast-food Mexican restaurants in Texas. Its restaurants provide a festive eating atmosphere of interior dining and patio areas decorated with artifacts, bright colors, paintings, and murals. The exterior of its buildings has a vivid color scheme using top border paint and neon stripes. Bright awnings and umbrellas continue the theme.

Beginning in 1985, Two Pesos, Inc. (Two Pesos), opened a chain of competing Mexican fast-food restaurants in Texas. When Two Pesos adopted a motif similar to Taco Cabana's, Taco Cabana sued Two Pesos, alleging trade dress infringement in violation of Section 43(a) of the Lanham Trademark Act. Two Pesos argued that Taco Cabana's trade dress should not be protected because it had not yet acquired a secondary meaning. The court found that although Taco Cabana's trade dress had not yet acquired a secondary meaning, it was nonetheless distinctive and therefore protected. The court of appeals affirmed. Two Pesos appealed to the U.S. Supreme Court.

Supreme Court Issue

Must a restaurant's design have acquired a secondary meaning before it is protected as trade dress under Section 43(a) of the Lanham Trademark Act?

In The Language of The U.S. Supreme Court

White, Justice Trade dress is the total image of the business. Taco Cabana's trade dress may include the shape and general appearance of the exterior restaurant, the identifying sign, the interior kitchen floor plan, the decor, the menu, the equipment used to serve food, the servers' uniforms and other features reflecting on the total image of the restaurant. The trade dress of a product is essentially its total image and overall appearance.

Taco Cabana's trade dress was protected if it either was inherently distinctive or had acquired a secondary meaning. Trademark law requires a demonstration of secondary meaning only when the claimed trademark is not sufficiently distinctive of itself to identify the producer. The legal recognition of an inherently distinctive trademark or trade dress acknowledges the owner's legitimate proprietary interest in its unique and valuable informational device, regardless of whether substantial consumer association yet bestows the additional empirical protection of secondary meaning. The user of such a trade dress should be able to maintain what competitive position it has and continue to seek wider identification among potential customers.

We see no basis for requiring secondary meaning for inherently distinctive trade dress protection. Adding a secondary meaning requirement could have anticompetitive effects, creating particular burdens on the start-up of small companies. It would present special difficulties for a business, such as Taco Cabana, that seeks to start a new product in a limited area and then expand into new markets. Denying protection for inherently distinctive trade dress until after secondary meaning has been established would allow a competitor, which has not adopted a distinctive trade dress of its own, to appropriate the originator's dress in other markets and to deter the originator from expanding into and competing in these areas.

Decision and Remedy

The U.S. Supreme Court held that a restaurant's design does not have to have acquired a secondary meaning in the public's eye before it is protected as trade dress under Section 43(a) of the Lanham Trademark Act. The Supreme Court affirmed the decision of the court of appeals.

Case Questions

Critical Legal Thinking Should a business's trade dress be protected from copying by competitors? Why or why not?

Business Ethics Was it ethical for Two Pesos, Inc., to copy Taco Cabana, Inc.'s restaurant design? What do you think was the motive of Two Pesos?

Contemporary Business What were the economic consequences of the U.S. Supreme Court's decision? Who are the winners? Who are the losers?

U.S. SUPREME COURT CASE

Wal-Mart Stores, Inc. v. Samara Brothers, Inc.

529 U.S. 205, 120 S.Ct. 1339, 2000 U.S. Lexis 2197 (2000)
Supreme Court of the United States

Case 8.10
Trade Dress

Background and Facts

Samara Brothers, Inc. (Samara), is a designer and manufacturer of children's clothing. The core of Samara's business is its annual new line of spring and summer children's garments. Samara sold its clothing to retailers, who in turn sold the clothes to consumers. Wal-Mart Stores, Inc. (Wal-Mart), operates a large chain of budget warehouse stores that sell thousands of items at very low prices. In 1995, Wal-Mart contacted one of its suppliers, Judy-Philippine, Inc. (JPI), about the possibility of making a line of children's clothes just like Samara's successful line. Wal-Mart sent photographs of Samara's children's clothes to JPI (the name "Samara" was readily discernible on the labels of the garments) and directed JPI to produce children's clothes exactly like those in the photographs. JPI produced a line of children's clothes for Wal-Mart that copied the designs, colors, flower patterns, and so on of Samara's clothing. Wal-Mart then sold this line of children's clothing in its stores, making a gross profit of over $1.15 million on these clothes sales during the 1996 selling season.

Samara discovered that Wal-Mart was selling the knockoff clothes at a price that was lower than Samara's retailers were paying Samara for its clothes. After sending unsuccessful cease and desist letters to Wal-Mart, Samara sued Wal-Mart, alleging product trade dress infringement in violation of Section 43(a) of the Lanham Trademark Act. Although not finding that Samara's clothes had acquired a secondary meaning in the minds of the public, the district court held in favor of Samara and awarded damages. The court of appeals affirmed. Wal-Mart appealed to the U.S. Supreme Court.

Supreme Court Issue

Must a product's design have acquired a secondary meaning before it is protected as trade dress under Section 43(a) of the Lanham Trademark Act?

In The Language of The U.S. Supreme Court

Scalia, Justice In addition to protecting registered marks, the Lanham Act, in Section 43(a), gives a producer a cause of action for the use by any person of "any word, term, name, symbol, or device, or any combination thereof . . . which . . . is likely to cause confusion . . . as to the origin, sponsorship, or approval of his or her goods. . . . " It is this provision that is at issue in this case. The text of Section 43(a) provides little guidance as to the circumstances under which unregistered trade dress may be protected. It does require that a producer show that the allegedly infringing feature is not "functional," and is likely to cause confusion with the product for which protection is sought. We hold that, in an action for infringement of unregistered trade dress under Section 43(a) of the Lanham Act, a product's design is protectible only upon a showing of secondary meaning.

In *Two Pesos, Inc. v. Taco Cabana, Inc.*, 505 U.S. 763, 112 S.Ct. 2753, 1992 U.S. Lexis 4533 (1992), we held that the trade dress of a chain of Mexican restaurants, which the plaintiff described as a festive eating atmosphere having interior dining and patio areas decorated with artifacts, bright colors, paintings and murals, could be protected under Section 43(a) without a showing of secondary meaning. *Two Pesos* unquestionably establishes the legal principle that trade dress can be inherently distinctive, but it does not establish that *product-design* trade dress can be. *Two Pesos* is inapposite to our holding here because the trade dress at issue, the decor of a restaurant, seems to us not to constitute product *design*. It was either product packaging—which, as we have discussed, normally *is* taken by the consumer to indicate origin—or else some *tertium quid* that is akin to product packaging and has no bearing on the present case.

Decision and Remedy

The U.S. Supreme Court held that a product's design has to have acquired a secondary meaning in the public's eye before it is protected as trade dress under Section 43(a) of the Lanham Trademark Act. The Supreme Court reversed the decision of the court of appeals.

Case Questions

Critical Legal Thinking What is trade dress? What is secondary meaning? Can this case be reconciled with the previous case, Two Pesos, Inc. v. Taco Cabana, Inc., which held that no secondary meaning had to be shown to protect trade dress in product packaging?

Business Ethics Was it ethical for Wal-Mart to copy Samara Brothers' design for children's clothing? What was Wal-Mart's motive?

Contemporary Business What were the economic consequences of the U.S. Supreme Court's decision? Who are the winners? Who are the losers?

Generic Names

Most companies promote their trademarks and service marks to increase the public's awareness of the availability and quality of their products and services. At some point in time, however, the public may begin to treat the mark as a common name to denote the

generic name
A term for a mark that has become a common term for a product line or type of service and therefore has lost its trademark protection.

type of product or service being sold, rather than as the trademark or trade name of an individual seller. A trademark that becomes a common term for a product line or type of service is called a **generic name**. Once that happens, the term loses its protection under federal trademark law because it has become *descriptive* rather than *distinctive* (see Exhibit 8.1).

Exhibit 8.1

Reprinted with permission of Xerox Corporation

XEROX

Once a trademark, not always a trademark.

They were once proud trademarks, now they're just names. They failed to take precautions that would have helped them have a long and prosperous life.

We need your help to stay out of there. Whenever you use our name, please use it as a proper adjective in conjunction with our products and services: e.g., Xerox copiers or Xerox financial services. And never as a verb: "to Xerox" in place of "to copy," or as a noun: "Xeroxes" in place of "copies."

With your help and a precaution or two on our part, it's "Once the Xerox trademark, always the Xerox trademark."

Team Xerox. We document the world.

Business Brief
Nestlé Company, Inc., lost its trademark on the term "Toll House" for its chocolate chip cookies when a court ruled that the term had become generic because the public had come to associate the name Toll House with chocolate chip cookies in general, not only those sold by Nestlé [*Nestlé Company, Inc. v. Chester's Market, Inc.*, 571 F.Supp. 763 (D.Conn. 1983)].

E-commerce & Information Technology

AOL's You've Got Mail *a Generic Name*

America Online, Inc. (AOL), operates one of the world's largest interaction online services. More than 20 million people subscribe to, and are members of, AOL online service. For a basic monthly fee, AOL enables its members to receive computer information, access the Internet, and receive and send e-mail. For nearly a decade, AOL used the terms *You Have Mail* and *You've Got Mail* in connection with its automatic e-mail notification service. When an AOL member starts online and has e-mail, the cheerfully spoken words *You've Got Mail* are immediately heard. At the same time this voice sounds, a red signal flag is pictured prominently on the member's computer screen, above the phrase *You Have Mail*. AOL applied for service mark protection for the two phrases *You've Got Mail* and *You Have Mail*.

AT&T Corp. (AT&T), a telecommunications company, began offering Internet access, including e-mail services, to subscribers for a monthly fee. In December 1998, AT&T added a *You Have Mail!* notification to its e-mail service. AOL sent a letter to AT&T to cease and desist from using *You Have Mail!* When AT&T refused, AOL sued AT&T in federal district court for unauthorized appropriation and infringement of AOL's common-law service marks. AT&T argued that these terms were generic and that AOL had no protectable interest in them.

The district court held as a matter of law that the two phrases were generic and thus were not protected marks. The court stated that a mark is generic when it "identifies a class of product or service, regardless of source." The court found that *You Have Mail* and *You've Got Mail* are common words and phrases that are used for their ordinary meaning. The court stated that the phrases indicate to the public at large what the service is, not where it came from. The court cited evidence that many of AOL's competitors used the terms *mail* and *e-mail* when delivering e-mail to their subscribers. The court held that a generic term cannot receive service mark protection. The court granted summary judgment to AT&T and allowed it to use the term *You Have Mail!* when delivering e-mail to its subscribers. The court of appeals affirmed the judgment. [*America Online, Incorporated v. AT&T Corporation*, 243 F.3d 812, 2001 U.S.App. Lexis 2866 (4th Cir. 2001)] ■

State Antidilution Statutes

States recognize common law trademarks. In addition, many states have enacted their own trademark statutes. These state laws, which allow persons and companies to register trademarks and service marks, are often called **antidilution statutes**.They prevent others from infringing on and diluting a registrant's mark. Companies that only do business locally sometimes register under these laws.

antidilution statutes
State laws that allow persons and companies to register trademarks and service marks.

Contemporary Business Environment

Bootlegging of Live Music Outlawed

In 1995, the United States joined more than 130 other countries and became a member of the WTO. The WTO member nations adopted the international **Agreement on Trade-Related Aspects of Intellectual Property Rights (TRIPs)**, which outlawed unauthorized taping of sounds or images of live musical performances. To enforce this agreement in the United States, the U.S. Congress enacted the following federal antibootlegging statutes:

- ***18 U.S.C. 2319A*** This statute imposes criminal liability for the unauthorized taping of the sounds and images of live musical performances "knowingly and for purposes of commercial advantage or private financial gain." A first offense carries a prison term of up to 5 years; subsequent offenses carry prison terms of up to 10 years. The court can order unauthorized recordings to be destroyed.
- ***17 U.S.C. 1101*** This statute imposes civil liability for similar conduct but without the commercial advantage or private financial gain requirement. A successful plaintiff can recover actual damages and any profits made by the defendant, destruction of any unauthorized recordings, and an injunction against any future violations by the defendant.

Contemporary Business Environment
(continued)

It is important to note that both recording the sound of the concert and taking photographs of the performance are conduct that is outlawed by these statutes. The lawfulness of the anti-bootlegging statute has been upheld as a valid exercise of Congress's power under the Commerce Clause of the U.S. Constitution. [*United States v. Moghadam*, 175 F.3d 1269, 1999 U.S. App. Lexis 9510. (11th Cir. 1999)] ■

Concept Summary Types of Intellectual Property Protected by Federal Law

Type	Subject Matter	Term
Patent	Inventions (e.g., machines; processes; compositions of matter; designs for articles of manufacture; and improvements to existing machines, processes). Invention must be 1. Novel 2. Useful 3. Nonobvious *Public use doctrine:* Patent will no be granted if the invention was used in public for more than one year prior to the filing of the patent application.	Patents on articles of manufacture and processes: 20 years; design patents: 14 years.
Copyright	Tangible writing (e.g., books, magazines, newspapers, lectures, operas, plays, screenplays, musical compositions, maps, works of art, lithographs, photographs, postcards, greeting cards, motion pictures, newsreels, sound recordings, computer programs, and mask works fixed to semiconductor chips). Writing must be the original work of the author. *Fair use doctrine:* It permits use of copyrighted material without consent for limited uses (e.g., scholarly work, parody or satire, and brief quotation in news reports).	Author (individual registrant): life of author plus 70 years. Work for hire (business registrant) for the shorter of either (1) 120 years from the date of creation or (2) 95 years from the date of first publication.
Trademark	Marks (e.g., name, symbol, word, logo, or device). Marks include trademarks, service marks, certification marks, and collective marks. Mark must be distinctive or have acquired a secondary meaning. *Generic name:* A mark that becomes a common term for a product line or type of service loses its protection under federal trademark law.	Original registration: 10 years. Renewal registration: unlimited number of renewals for 10-year terms.

International Law

International Protection of Intellectual Property Rights

For centuries, national patent, copyright, and trademark laws defined the rights of inventors, authors, and businesses. These laws offered protection within a country's borders, but not in other countries. Beginning in the late 1800s, countries began entering into treaties and conventions with other countries that provided international protection of intellectual property rights.

The major convention that provides international protection to patents is the **1883 Convention of the Union of Paris (Paris Convention)**. The convention's major purpose is to allow the nationals of each member country to file for patents in all other member nations. The convention does not, however, eliminate the need to file separate patent applications in each member nation in which the applicant desires protection. The convention gives an applicant who has filed for a patent in one member country 12 months to submit applications in other member countries.

The Paris Convention also allows nationals of each member nation to file for trademarks and service marks in all other member nations on an individual, nondiscriminatory basis, even if the applicant does not own the mark in the country of origin. The applicant has six months after his or her original registration to submit application to other member countries.

The major copyright treaty is the **Berne Convention of 1886**, as revised. This convention provides for the recognition of a copyright in all member nations. The convention establishes a minimum copyright term of the life of the author plus 70 years and eliminates the requirement to put a © on copyrighted works.

In 1997, the World Intellectual Property Organization (WIPO), an agency of the United Nations, promulgated two new "Internet treaties." These treaties recognized the importance of new digital technologies and the Internet. The first treaty, the **WIPO Copyright Treaty**, extends copyright protection to computer programs and data compilations and grants copyright holders the exclusive right to make their works available on the Internet as well as by any other wire or wireless means. The second treaty, the **WIPO Phonogram Treaty**, gives performers and producers the exclusive right to broadcast, reproduce, and distribute copies of their performances by any means, including video recording, digital sound, or encryption signal. ■

Japan. International agreements, such as the Paris Convention, Berne Convention, Phonogram Treaty, and other treaties provide international protection of patents, copyrights, trademarks, domain names, and other intellectual property rights.

Web Site

International Trademark Association The International Trademark Association is an association of trademark owners and advisers worldwide. It is dedicated to the support and advancement of trademarks and related intellectual-property concepts as essential elements of effective national and international commerce. Visit at **www.inta.org**.

Chapter Summary

Trade Secrets, p. 208

Trade Secrets

1. ***Trade secret.*** A *trade secret* is a product, formula, pattern, design, compilation of data, customer list, or other business secret that makes a business successful. The owner of a trade secret must take reasonable precautions to prevent its trade secret from being discovered by others.
2. ***Misappropriation of a trade secret.*** The act of obtaining another's trade secret through unlawful means such as theft, bribery, or espionage. A successful plaintiff can recover profits, damages, and an injunction against the offender.
3. ***The Economic Espionage Act.*** A federal statute that makes it a crime for any person to convert a trade secret for his or another's benefit, knowing or intending to cause injury to the owners of the trade secret.

Patents, p. 209

Patents

Patent law is exclusively federal law; there are no state patent laws.

1. ***Patent.*** Patentable subject matter includes inventions such as machines; processes; compositions of matter; improvements to existing machines, processes, or compositions of matter; designs for articles of manufacture; asexually reproduced plants; and living matter invented by humans.
   a. Novel
   b. Useful
   c. Nonobvious
2. ***Business plans.*** In *State Street Bank & Trust Co. v. Signature Financial Group, Inc.*, the U.S. Court of Appeals held that business plans are patentable.
3. ***Patent application.*** An application containing a written description of the invention must be filed with the *United States Patent and Trademark Office (PTO)* in Washington, DC.
4. ***Term.*** Patents are valid for 20 years.
5. ***Public use doctrine.*** A patent may not be granted if the invention was used by the public for more than one year prior to the filing of the patent application.
6. ***Patent infringement.*** The unauthorized use of another's patent. The patent holder may recover damages and other remedies against the infringer.
7. ***The American Inventors Protection Act.*** This federal statute does the following:
   a. Permits an inventor to file a *provisional application* with the U.S. PTO three months pending the filing of a final patent application.
   b. Requires the PTO to issue a patent within three years after the filing of a patent application.
8. ***Patent appeals.*** Are heard by the *United States Court of Appeals for the Federal Circuit* in Washington, DC.

Copyrights, p. 218

Copyrights

Copyright law is exclusively federal law; there are no state copyright laws.

1. ***Copyright.*** Only tangible writings can be copyrighted. These include books, newspapers, addresses, musical compositions, motion pictures, works of art, architectural plans, greeting

cards, photographs, sound recordings, computer programs, and mask works fixed in semiconductor chips.

2. ***Requirements for copyright.*** The writing must be the original work of the author.
3. ***Copyright registration.*** Copyright registration is permissive and voluntary. Published and unpublished works may be registered with the *United States Copyright Office* in Washington, DC. Registration itself does not create the copyright.
4. ***Term.*** Copyrights are for the following terms:
   a. Individual holder. Life of the author plus 70 years.
   b. Business holder. Either (1) 120 years from the date of creation or (2) 95 years from the date of publication, whichever is shorter.
5. ***Copyright infringement.*** The copying of a substantial and material part of a copyrighted work without the holder's permission. The copyright holder may recover damages and other remedies against the infringer.
6. ***Fair use doctrine.*** Permits use of copyrighted material without the consent of the copyright holder for limited uses (e.g., scholarly work, parody or satire, and brief quotation in news reports).
7. ***Digital Millennium Copyright Act (DMCA).*** A federal statute enacted in 1998 that provides civil and criminal penalties that
   a. Prohibits the manufacture and distribution of technologies, products, or services primarily designed for the purpose of circumventing wrappers or encryption protection.
   b. Prohibits unauthorized *access* to copyrighted digital works by circumventing the wrapper or encryption technology that protects the intellectual property.
8. ***Visual Artists Rights Act.*** A federal statute that gives artists *moral rights* in their creation after the sale of the artwork.
9. ***No Electronic Theft Act (NET Act).*** A federal statute that makes it a crime for a person to willfully infringe a copyright work exceeding $1,000 in retail value.

Trademarks, p. 227

Trademarks and Service Marks

1. ***Mark.*** A trade name, symbol, word, logo, design, or device that distinguishes the owner's goods or services. Marks are often referred to collectively as *trademarks*. Types of marks are:
   a. Trademark. Identifies goods of a particular business.
   b. Service mark. Identifies services of a particular business.
   c. Certification mark. Certifies that goods or services are of a certain quality or origin.
   d. Collective mark. Used by cooperatives, associations, and fraternal organizations.
2. ***Requirements for a trademark.*** The mark must either (a) be *distinctive* or (b) have acquired a *secondary meaning*. The mark must have been used in commerce or the holder intends to use the mark in commerce and actually does so within six months after registering the mark.
3. ***Trademark registration.*** Marks are registered with the *United States PTO* in Washington, DC.
4. ***Term.*** The original registration of a mark is valid for 10 years and can be renewed for an unlimited number of 10-year periods.
5. ***Trademark infringement.*** The unauthorized use of another's registered mark. The mark holder may recover damages and other remedies from the infringer.
6. ***Generic name.*** A mark that becomes a common term for a product line or type of service loses its protection under federal trademark law.
7. ***Federal Trademark Dilution Act of 1995.*** A federal statute that protects famous marks from dilution. A violation of the act requires that the mark be famous, the use by the other party was commercial, and the use caused dilution of the distinctive quality of the mark.

Internet Exercises and Case Questions

Working the Web Internet Exercises

Activities

1. Research the Web to determine if your state has adopted the Uniform Trade Secrets Act. Visit the Trade Secrets home page, at **www.execpc.com/~mhallign/**.
2. The site **www.uspto.gov** contains information about the federal copyright registration system. Does the most recent copyright law require authors to use the copyright notice on printed material in order to protect it from infringement?
3. What is the current duration of a U.S. patent? What was the duration of a U.S. patent under previous law, and why was it changed? See **www.uspto.gov**.
4. Visit **www.wipo.int** and outline the process for international registration of a patent.

Critical Legal Thinking Cases

8.1 Trade Secret CRA-MAR Video Center, Inc., sells electronic equipment and videocassettes, as does its competitor, Koach's Sales Corporation. Both CRA-MAR and Koach's purchased computers from Radio Shack. CRA-MAR used the computer to store customer lists, movie lists, personnel files, and financial records. Because the computer was new to CRA-MAR, Randall Youts, Radio Shack's salesman and programmer, agreed to modify CRA-MAR's programs when needed, including the customer list program. At one point, CRA-MAR decided to send a mailing to everyone on its customer list. The computer was unable to perform the function, so Youts took the disks containing the customer lists to the Radio Shack store to work on the program. Somehow Koach's came into possession of CRA-MAR's customer lists and did advertising mailings to the parties on the lists. When CRA-MAR discovered this fact, it sued Koach's, seeking an injunction against any further use of its customer lists. Is a customer list a trade secret that can be protected from misappropriation? [*Koachs Sales Corp. v. CRA-MAR Video Center, Inc.*, 478 N.E.2d 110, 1985 Ind.App. Lexis 2432 (Ind. App. 1985)]

8.2 Trade Secret Acuson Corporation, a Delaware corporation, and Aloka Co., Ltd., a Japanese company, are competitors that both manufacture ultrasonic imaging equipment, a widely used medical diagnostic tool. The device uses sound waves to produce moving images of the inside of a patient's body, which a computer processes into an image that is displayed on a video monitor. Acuson's unit provides finer resolution than Aloka's unit. Both companies have sold many units to hospitals and medical centers. In November 1985, Aloka decided to purchase an Acuson unit. Aloka had another company make the actual purchase because it was concerned that Acuson would not sell the unit to a competitor. After the unit was shipped to Tokyo, Aloka's engineers partially dismantled the Acuson unit. They recorded their observations in notebooks. When Acuson discovered that Aloka had purchased one of its units, it sued Aloka, seeking an injunction and return of the unit. Is Aloka liable for misappropriation of a trade secret? [*Acuson Corp. v. Aloka Co., Ltd.*, 209 Cal.App.3d 425, 257 Cal.Rptr. 368, 1989 Cal.App. Lexis 317 (Cal. App. 1989)]

8.3 Patent In 1968, patent no. 3,397,928 (928) was issued to Edward M. Galle, an executive of Hughes Tool Company. Galle assigned the patent, and other related patents, to Hughes. The patent was for an O-ring rubber seal that was used to seal bearings in the cone of a rock bit that rotated to drill holes in rocks. Rock bits were used to drill oil wells. Hughes did not license its 928 patent, which was a substantial commercial success. Smith International, Inc., was Hughes's major competitor in this industry. Between 1971 and 1984, Smith made more than 460,000 rock bits (reaping sales of about $1.3 billion) that contained rubber seals that infringed on Hughes's patents. Hughes sued Smith for patent infringement and requested $1.2 billion in lost royalties and interest. Smith offered $20 million to $60 million in settlement. The case went to trial, and the court found Smith liable for patent infringement. How much should Hughes be awarded in damages? [*Smith Internat'l, Inc. v. Hughes Tool Co.*, 229 U.S.P.Q. 81, 1986 U.S. Dist. Lexis 28247 (Fed. Cir. 1986)]

8.4 Copyright When Spiro Agnew resigned as vice president of the United States, President Richard M. Nixon appointed Gerald R. Ford as vice president. In 1974, amid growing controversy surrounding the Watergate scandal, President Nixon resigned, and Vice President Ford acceded to the presidency. As president, Ford pardoned Nixon for any wrongdoing regarding the Watergate affair and related matters. Ford served as president until he was defeated by Jimmy Carter in the 1976 presidential election. In 1973, Ford entered into a contract with Harper & Row, Publishers, Inc., to publish his memoirs in book form. The memoirs were to contain significant unpublished materials concerning the Watergate affair and Ford's personal reflections on that time in history. The publisher instituted security measures to protect the confidentiality of the manuscript. Several weeks before the book was to be released, an unidentified person secretly brought a copy of the manuscript to Victor Navasky, editor of *The Nation*, a weekly political commentary magazine. Navasky, knowing that his possession of the purloined manuscript was not authorized, produced a 2,250-word piece titled "The Ford Memoirs" and published it in the April 3, 1979, issue of *The Nation*. Verbatim quotes of between 300 and 400 words from Ford's manuscript, including some of the most important parts, appeared in the article. Harper & Row sued the publishers of *The Nation* for copyright infringement. Who wins? [*Harper & Row, Publishers, Inc. v. Nation Enterprises*, 471 U.S. 539, 105 S.Ct. 2218, 1985 U.S. Lexis 17 (1985)]

8.5 Copyright The Sony Corporation of America manufactures videocassette recorders (VCRs) that can be used to videotape programs and films that are shown on television and cable stations. VCRs are used by consumers and others to videotape both copyrighted and uncopyrighted works. The primary use for

VCRs is by consumers for "time-shifting"—that is, taping a television program for viewing at a more convenient time. Universal City Studios, Inc, and Walt Disney Productions hold copyrights on a substantial number of motion-picture and audiovisual works that are shown on television and cable stations, which pay them a fee to do so. Some of Universal's and Disney's copyrighted works have been copied by consumers using Sony's VCRs. Universal and Disney sued Sony, seeking an injunction against the sale of VCRs by Sony. Is Sony liable for contributory copyright infringement? [*Sony Corp. of America v. Universal City Studios, Inc.*, 464 U.S. 417, 104 S.Ct. 774, 1984 U.S. Lexis 19 (1984)]

8.6 Fair Use Doctrine In the dark days of 1977, when the City of New York teetered on the brink of bankruptcy, on the television screens of America there appeared an image of a top-hatted Broadway showgirl, backed by an advancing phalanx of dancers, chanting: "I-I-I-I-I-I Love New Yo-o-o-o-o-o-o-rk." As an ad campaign for an ailing city, it was an unparalleled success. Crucial to the campaign was a brief but exhilarating musical theme written by Steve Karmin called "I Love New York." Elsmere Music, Inc., owned the copyright to the music. The success of the campaign did not go unnoticed. On May 20, 1978, the popular weekly variety program *Saturday Night Live* (*SNL*) performed a comedy sketch over National Broadcasting Company's network (NBC). In the sketch the cast of *SNL* portraying the mayor and members of the chamber of commerce of the biblical city of Sodom, were seen discussing Sodom's poor public image with out-of-towners and its effect on the tourist trade. In an attempt to recast Sodom's image in a more positive light, a new advertising campaign was revealed, with the highlight of the campaign being a song "I Love Sodom" sung a cappella by a chorus line of *SNL* regulars to the tune of "I Love New York." Elsmere Music did not see the humor of the sketch and sued NBC for copyright infringement. Who wins? [*Elsmere Music, Inc. v. National Broadcasting Co., Inc.*, 623 F.2d 252, 1980 U.S. App. Lexis 16820 (2d Cir. 1980)]

8.7 Copyright Professional Real Estate Investors, Inc., and Kenneth Irwin owned and operated La Mancha, a resort hotel in Palm Springs, California. Guests at La Mancha could rent movie videodiscs from the lobby gift shop for a $5 daily fee per disc, which could be charged on the hotel bill. Each guest room was equipped with a large-screen projection television and videodisc player. Guests viewed videodisc movies projected on the television screen in their rooms. After learning of these activities, Columbia Pictures Inc., and six other motion-picture studios (Columbia) that owned copyrights on films rented on videodisc at La Macha filed suit to prevent La Mancha from renting videodiscs to its guests, alleging copyright infringement. Is La Mancha liable for copyright infringement? [*Columbia Pictures Industries, Inc. v. Professional Real Estate Investors, Inc.*, 866 F.2d 278, 1989 U.S. App. Lexis 337 (9th Cir.1989)]

8.8 Trademark Clairol Incorporated manufactures and distributes hair tinting, dyeing, and coloring preparations. In 1956, Clairol embarked on an extensive advertising campaign to promote the sale of its "Miss Clairol" hair-color preparations that included advertisements in national magazines, on outdoor billboards, on radio and television, in mailing pieces, and on point-of-sale display materials to be used by retailers and beauty salons. The advertisements prominently displayed the slogans "Hair Color So Natural Only Her Hairdresser Knows for Sure" and "Does She or Doesn't She?" Clairol registered these slogans as trademarks. During the next decade Clairol spent more than $22 million for advertising materials, resulting in more than a billion separate audio and visual impressions using the slogans. Roux Laboratories, Inc., a manufacturer of hair-coloring products and a competitor of Clairol's, filed an opposition to Clairol's registration of the slogans as trademarks. Do the slogans qualify for trademark protection? [*Roux Laboratories, Inc. v. Clairol Inc.*, 427 F.2d 823, 1970 CCPA Lexis 344 (Cust.Pat.App. 1979)]

8.9 Trademark Since 1972, Mead Data Central, Inc., has provided computer-assisted legal research services to lawyers and others under the trademark "Lexis." Lexis is based on *lex*, the Latin word for law, and *IS*, for information systems. Through extensive sales and advertising, Mead has made Lexis a strong mark in the computerized legal research field, particularly among lawyers. However, Lexis is recognized by only 1 percent of the general population, with almost half of this 1 percent being attorneys. Toyota Motor Corporation has for many years manufactured automobiles, which it markets in the United States through its subsidiary Toyota Motor Sales, U.S.A., Inc. On August 24, 1987, Toyota announced a new line of luxury automobiles to be called Lexus. Toyota planned on spending almost $20 million for marketing and advertising Lexus during the first nine months of 1989. Mead filed suit against Toyota, alleging that Toyota's use of the name Lexus violated New York's antidilution statute and would cause injury to the business reputation of Mead and a dilution of the distinctive quality of the Lexis mark. Who wins? [*Mead Data Central, Inc. v. Toyota Motor Sales, U.S.A., Inc.*, 875 F.2d 1026, 1989 U.S. App. Lexis 6644 (2d Cir. 1989)]

8.10 Generic Name The Miller-Brewing Company, a national brewer, produces a reduced-calorie beer called "Miller Lite." Miller began selling beer under this name in the 1970s and has spent millions of dollars promoting the Miller Lite brand name on television, in print, and via other forms of advertising. Since July 11, 1980, Falstaff Brewing Corporation has been brewing and distributing a reduced-calorie beer called "Falstaff Lite." Miller brought suit under the Lanham Trademark Act, seeking an injunction to prevent Falstaff from using the term *Lite*. Is the term *Lite* a generic name that does not qualify for trademark protection? [*Miller Brewing Co. v. Falstaff Brewing Corp.*, 655 F.2d 5, 1981 U.S. App. Lexis 11345 (1st Cir. 1981)]

Business Ethics Cases

8.11 Business Ethics Integrated Cash Management Services, Inc. (ICM), designs and develops computer software programs and systems for banks and corporate financial departments. ICM's computer programs and systems are not copyrighted, but they are secret. After Alfred Sims Newlin and Behrouz Vafa completed graduate school, they were employed by ICM as computer programmers. They worked at ICM for several years, writing computer programs. In March 1987, they left ICM to work for Digital Transactions, Inc. (DTI). Before leaving ICM, however, they copied certain ICM files onto personal disks.

Within two weeks of starting to work at DTI, they created prototype computer programs that operated in substantially the same manner as comparable ICM programs and were designed to compete directly with ICM's programs. ICM sued Newlin, Vafa, and DTI for misappropriation of trade secrets. Are the defendants liable? Did the defendants act ethically in this case? [*Integrated Cash Management Services, Inc. v. Digital Transactions, Inc.* 920 F.2d 171, 1990 U.S. App. Lexis 20985 (2nd Cir. 1990)]

8.12 Business Ethics John W. Carson was the host and star of *The Tonight Show*, a well-known nightly television talk show broadcast by the National Broadcasting Company (NBC) until he retired in 1992. Carson also appeared as an entertainer in theaters and night clubs around the country. From the time that he began hosting *The Tonight Show* in 1962, he had been introduced on the show each night with the phrase "Here's Johnny." The phrase "Here's Johnny" was generally associated with Carson by a substantial segment of the television viewing public. Carson had licensed the use of the phrase to a chain of restaurants, a line of toiletries, and other business ventures. Johnny Carson Apparel, Inc., founded in 1970, manufactures and markets men's clothing to retail stores. Carson, president of Apparel and owner of 20 percent of its stock, had licensed Apparel to use the phrase "Here's Johnny" on labels for clothing and in advertising campaigns. The phrase had never been registered by Carson or Apparel as a trademark or service mark.

Earl Broxton was the owner and president of Here's Johnny Portable Toilets, Inc., a Michigan corporation that engages in the business of renting and selling "Here's Johnny" portable toilets. Broxton was aware when he formed the corporation that the phrase "Here's Johnny" was the introductory slogan for Carson on *The Tonight Show*. Broxton indicated that he coupled the phrase "Here's Johnny" with a second one, "The World's Foremost Commodian," to make a good play on the phrase. Shortly after Toilets went into business in 1976, Carson and Apparel sued Toilets, seeking an injunction prohibiting the further use of the phrase "Here's Johnny" as a corporate name for or in connection with the sale or rental of its portable toilets. Who wins? Did Broxton act ethically by appropriating the phrase "Here's Johnny" to promote the sale and rental of portable toilets? [*Carson v. Here's Johnny Portable Toilets, Inc.*, 698 F.2d 831, 1983 U.S. App. Lexis 30866 (6th Cir. 1983)]

8.13 Business Ethics Master Distributors, Inc. (MDI), manufactures and sells "Blue Max," a blue leader splicing tape that is used to attach undeveloped film to a leader cord for photo processing through a minilab machine that develops the film and prints the photographs. Leader tape can be created in any color, and MDI dyed its Blue Max tape aquamarine blue. Blue Max is well known and enjoys a reputation as the industry standard. Both distributors and customers often order Blue Max by asking for "the blue tape" or simply for "blue." When MDI learned that Pakor, Inc., was manufacturing and selling a brand of aquamarine blue leader splicing tape, "Pakor Blue," it brought suit for trademark infringement. Did Pakor act morally in copying MDI's color for its splicing tape? Why do you think Pakor did this? Was there trademark infringement? [*Master Distributors, Inc. v. Pakor Inc.*, 986 F.2d 219, 1993 U.S. App. Lexis 2312 (8th Cir. 1993)]

Briefing the Case Writing Assignment

Read Case A.8 in the Case Appendix [*Feist Publications, Inc. v. Rural Telephone Service Company, Inc.*]. This case is excerpted from the U.S. Supreme Court opinion. Review and brief the case. In your brief, be sure to answer the following questions.

1. Who was the plaintiff? Who was the defendant?

2. What had the defendant done that caused the plaintiff to sue?

3. What is the issue in this case?

4. What was the decision of the U.S. Supreme Court?

Answers to Management Decision Question

1. Burke can sue its competitors for the unauthorized use of a mark. In the United States, federal trademark law protects goods sold in interstate commerce. States also have trademark laws that protect products sold intrastate. To succeed in a trademark infringement case, the owner must prove that (1) the defendant infringed the plaintiff's mark by using it in an unauthorized manner and (2) such use is likely to cause confusion, mistake, or deception of the public as to the origin of the goods or services. One of the remedies available to a plaintiff in a trademark infringement suit is for the court to issue an injunction preventing the defendant from such infringement in the future.

2. Because the term Kick It Ball is used by the public to refer to different manufacturers' soccer balls, defendants in a trademark infringement case can raise the defense of generic name. *Generic name* is a term that has become a common term for a product line or type of service and therefore has lost its trademark protection. Several generic names, such as thermos, escalator, aspirin, cellophane, trampoline, lanolin, and kerosene, started out as trademarks for specific products but gradually became so common that they became generic names. Once a trademark is determined to be a generic name instead of a brand name, it can lose its trademark protection.

9

International and Comparative Law

"International law, or the law that governs between nations, has at times, been like the common law within states, a twilight existence during which it is hardly distinguishable from morality or justice, till at length the imprimatur of a court attests its jural quality."

—Justice Cardozo

New Jersey v. Delaware, 291 U.S. 361, 54 S.Ct. 407, 78 L.Ed. 847 (1934)

Chapter Objectives

After studying this chapter, you should be able to:

1. Describe the federal government's power under the Foreign Commerce and Treaty Clauses of the U.S. Constitution.
2. List and describe the sources of international law.
3. Describe the functions and governance of the United Nations.
4. Describe the North American Free Trade Agreement (NAFTA) and other regional economic organizations.
5. Describe the World Trade Organization (WTO) and explain how its dispute resolution procedure works.

Chapter Contents

- The United States and Foreign Affairs
- Sources of International Law
- The United Nations
- International Regional Organizations
- The World Trade Organization (WTO)
- Jurisdiction of National Courts to Decide International Disputes
- International Arbitration
- Criminal Prosecutions in the International Arena

Management Decision International and Comparative Law

As a result of the French government's opposition to the United States led war with Iraq in 2003 there have been organized efforts to boycott French products and services. You are the executive director of the Wisconsin Cheese Producers Association and have just learned that the French government, in retaliation, is spearheading a general boycott by its citizens of Wisconsin cheese products. This action by the French is likely to have a detrimental affect on the Wisconsin economy as well as the financial stability of the Wisconsin cheese industry. An emergency meeting of the association board has been scheduled, in which you are to present proposals for action by the association to end the strike. You are in the process of formulating a proposed course of action.

1. What legal options can your association pursue in the United States?
2. What recourse do you have on an international level?

international law
Law that governs affairs between nations and that regulates transactions between individuals and businesses of different countries.

International Law, important to both nations and businesses, has many unique features. First, there is no single legislative source of international law. All countries of the world and numerous international organizations are responsible for enacting international law. Second, there is no single world court that is responsible for interpreting international law. There are, however, several courts or tribunals that hear and decide international legal disputes of parties that agree to appear before them. Third, there is no world executive branch that can enforce international law. Thus, nations do not have to obey international law enacted by other countries or international organizations. Because of these uncertainties, some commentators question whether international law is really "law."

International Brief
International trade is increasing in importance for the United States and other countries of the world.

As technology and transportation bring nations closer together and American and foreign firms increase their global activities, international law will become even more

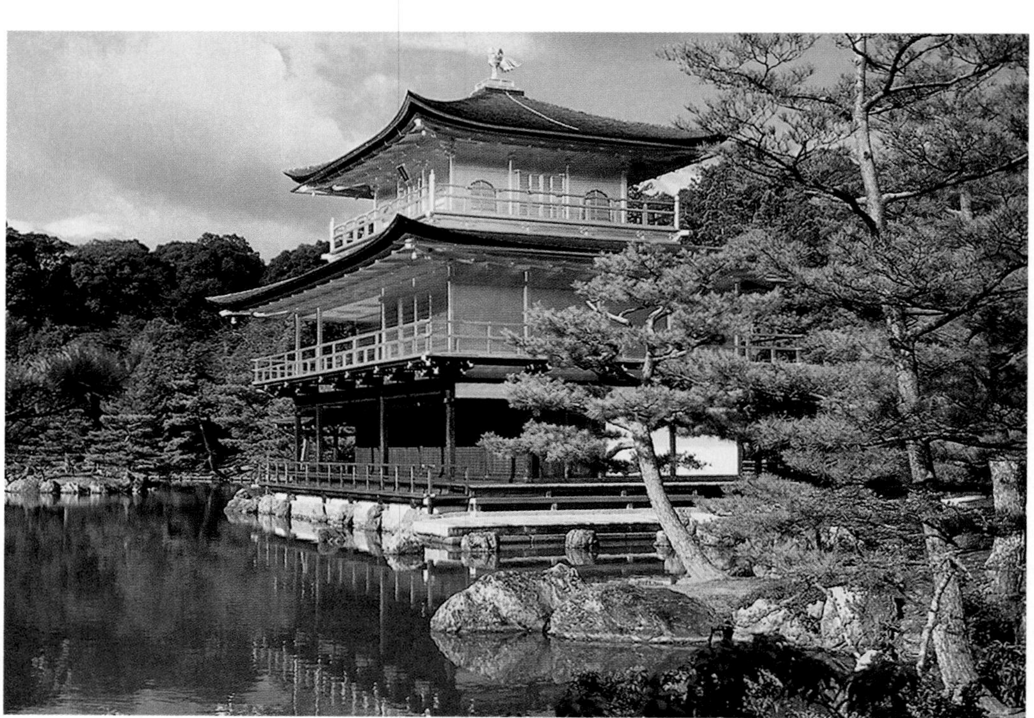

Kyoto, Japan. International law is important to both nations and businesses.

important to governments and businesses. This chapter introduces the main concepts of international law and discusses the sources of international law and the organizations responsible for its administration.

The United States and Foreign Affairs

The U.S. Constitution divides the power to regulate the internal affairs of this country between the federal and state governments. On the international level, however, the Constitution gives most of the power to the federal government. Two constitutional provisions establish this authority:

- ***Foreign Commerce Clause*** Article I, Section 8, clause 3 vests Congress with the power "to regulate commerce with foreign nations."
- ***Treaty Clause*** Article II, Section 2, clause 2 states that the president "shall have power, by and with the advice and consent of the Senate, to make treaties, provided two-thirds of the senators present concur."

The Constitution does not vest exclusive power over foreign affairs in the federal government, but any state or local law that unduly burdens foreign commerce is unconstitutional under the Foreign Commerce Clause. Under the Treaty Clause, only the federal government may enter into treaties with foreign nations. Under the Supremacy Clause of the Constitution, treaties become part of the "law of the land," and conflicting state or local law is void. The president is the agent of the United States in dealing with foreign countries.

In the following case, the U.S. Supreme Court struck down a state law as violating the Constitution.

Web Site

U.S. State Department The U.S. State Department has a Web site at which you can get situation updates, testimony, and briefings. Visit at **www.state.gov**.

Foreign Commerce Clause

A clause of the U.S. Constitution that vests Congress with the power "to regulate commerce with foreign nations."

Treaty Clause

A clause of the U.S. Constitution that states the president "shall have the power . . . to make treaties, provided two-thirds of the senators present concur."

U.S. SUPREME COURT CASE

Case 9.1

Foreign Affairs

Crosby, Secretary of Administration and Finance of Massachusetts v. National Foreign Trade Council

530 U.S. 363, 120 S.Ct. 2288, 2000 U.S. Lexis 4153 (2000)
Supreme Court of the United States

Background and Facts

The military regime of the country of Myanmar (called Burma prior to 1989) has been accused of major civil rights violations, including using forced and child labor, imprisoning and torturing political opponents, and harshly repressing ethnic minorities. These inhumane actions have been condemned by human rights organizations around the world.

The state legislators in the state of Massachusetts were so appalled at these actions that in June 1996 they enacted a state statute banning the state government from purchasing goods and services from any company that did business with Myanmar. In the meantime, Congress enacted its own federal statute that delegated power to the president to regulate the United States's dealings with Myanmar. The federal statute (1) banned all aid to the government of Myanmar except for humanitarian assistance, (2) authorized the president to impose economic sanctions against Myanmar, and (3) authorized the president to develop a comprehensive multilateral strategy to bring democracy to Myanmar. The National Foreign Trade Council (Council)—a powerful Washington, DC–based trade association with more than 500 member companies—filed a lawsuit against Massachusetts to have the state law declared unconstitutional. The Council argued that the Massachusetts "anti-Myanmar" statute was preempted by the Supremacy Clause of the U.S. Constitution, which makes federal law the "supreme law of the land" and gives the federal government the power to regulate foreign affairs. The district court and court of appeals ruled in favor of the Council. The U.S. Supreme Court agreed to hear the appeal from Massachusetts.

Supreme Court Issue

Does the Massachusetts anti-Myanmar state statute violate the Supremacy Clause of the U.S. Constitution?

In The Language of The U.S. Supreme Court

Within the sphere defined by Congress, then, the federal statute has placed the president in a position with as much discretion to exercise economic leverage against Burma, with an eye toward national security, as our law will admit. And it is just this plenitude

Crosby, Secretary of Administration and Finance of Massachusetts v. National Foreign Trade Council

530 U.S. 363, 120 S.Ct. 2288, 2000 U.S. Lexis 4153 (2000)
Supreme Court of the United States
(continued)

of executive authority that we think controls the issue of preemption here. The president has been given this authority not merely to make a political statement but to achieve a political result, and the fullness of his authority shows the importance in the congressional mind of reaching that result. It is simply implausible that Congress would have gone to such lengths to empower the president if it had been willing to compromise his effectiveness by deference to every provision of state statute or local ordinance that might, if enforced, blunt the consequences of discretionary presidential action.

We find it unlikely that Congress intended both to enable the president to protect national security by giving him the flexibility to suspend or terminate federal sanctions and simultaneously to allow Massachusetts to act at odds with the president's judgment of what national security requires. And that is just what the Massachusetts Burma law would do in imposing a different, state system of economic pressure against the Burmese political regime. This unyielding application undermines the president's intended statutory authority by making it impossible for him to restrain fully the coercive power of the national economy when he may choose to take the discretionary action open to him, whether he believes that the national interest requires sanctions to be lifted, or believes that the promise of lifting sanctions would move the Burmese regime in the democratic direction. Quite simply, if the Massachusetts law is enforceable the president has less to offer and less economic and diplomatic leverage as a consequence.

Decision and Remedy

The U.S. Supreme Court affirmed the court of appeals, finding that the Massachusetts and anti-Myanmar law conflicted with and was therefore preempted by the Supremacy Clause of the Constitution.

Case Questions

Critical Legal Thinking Should the federal government have sole power to regulate the foreign affairs of the United States? Or should the states share in this power?

Business Ethics Do you think companies that have goods manufactured in Myanmar violate any ethical principles? Explain.

Contemporary Business Did the Massachusetts anti-Myanmar law have any economic implications for business? What would have been the consequences if the U.S. Supreme Court had held that the Massachusetts anti-Myanmar statute was lawful?

Mandalay, Myanmar. Many companies in the United States and other countries do not do business in, or with companies from, Myanmar. This is because of alleged human rights violations by the military government of Myanmar. Does this policy help or hurt the people of Myanmar?

Sources of International Law

The **sources of international law** are those things that international tribunals rely on in deciding international disputes. **Article 38(1) of the Statute of the International Court of Justice** lists the following four sources of international law: *treaties and conventions, custom, general principles of law*, and *judicial decisions and teachings*. Most courts rely on the hierarchy suggested by this list; that is, treaties and conventions are turned to before custom, and so on. Each of these sources of law is discussed in the following paragraphs.

sources of international law
Those things that international tribunals rely on in settling international disputes.

Treaties and Conventions

Treaties and conventions are the equivalents of legislation at the international level. A **treaty** is an agreement or a contract between two or more nations that is formally signed by an authorized representative and ratified by the supreme power of each nation. *Bilateral treaties* are between two nations; *multilateral treaties* involve more than two nations. **Conventions** are treaties that are sponsored by international organizations, such as the United Nations. Conventions normally have many signatories.

Treaties and conventions address such matters as human rights, foreign aid, navigation, commerce, and the settlement of disputes. Most treaties are registered with and published by the United Nations.

treaty
The first source of international law, consisting of an agreement or a contract between two or more nations that are formally signed by an authorized representative and ratified by the supreme power of each nation.

convention
A treaty that is sponsored by an international organization.

E-Commerce & Information Technology

World Intellectual Property Organization (WIPO) Internet Treaties

In 1967, the United Nations (UN) created the **World Intellectual Property Organization (WIPO)**. WIPO is a special agency of the UN that administers international intellectual property conventions and treaties. More than 160 nations are members of WIPO. WIPO administers more than 20 major conventions and treaties affecting intellectual property, including the Paris Convention of 1883, which provides international patent and trademark protection, and the Berne Convention of 1886, which provides international copyright protection. The United States is a signatory to both of these conventions. In addition to administering existing conventions and treaties, WIPO develops and adopts new conventions and treaties.

WIPO convened its members in 1996 to address the impact that the new digital technologies and the Internet were having on intellectual property rights. The goal of the delegation was to conclude new conventions that would cover and expand copyright and intellectual property protection in the digital environment. After much negotiation, WIPO issued two new conventions collectively called the **Internet treaties**:

- ***Copyright Treaty*** This treaty grants copyright protection to computer programs and data compilations, protects the rights of copyright holders to make their works available on the Internet or by any other wire or wireless means, and extends copyright protection to rentals and means of distribution in addition to sale transactions.
- ***Phonogram Treaty*** This treaty provides protection to performers and producers by giving them exclusive rights to broadcast, reproduce, distribute, and rent copies of their performances, using any type of media, including video recordings, satellite transmissions, digital sound, and encrypted signals.

These two WIPO treaties go far to create new intellectual property rights and to grant protection to copyright holders over the Internet and in the digital marketplace. The United States signed the final act of the convention. ■

Custom

Custom between nations is an independent source of international law. Custom describes a practice followed by two or more nations when dealing with each other. It may be found in official government statements, diplomatic correspondence, policy statements, press

custom
The second source of international law, created through consistent, recurring practices between two or more nations over a period of time that have become recognized as binding.

releases, speeches, and the like. Two elements must be established to show that a practice has become a custom:

1. Consistent and recurring action by two or more nations over a considerable period of time.
2. Recognition that the custom is binding—that is, followed because of legal obligation rather than courtesy.

International Brief

Even customs that have not been elevated to the level of international law are still vitally important to the conduct of transnational business.

International customs evolve as mores, technology, forms of government, political parties, and other factors change throughout the world. Customs that have been recognized for some period of time are often codified in treaties.

General Principles of Law

general principles of law

The third source of international law, consisting of principles of law recognized by civilized nations. These are principles of law that are common to the national law of the parties to the dispute.

Courts and tribunals that decide international disputes frequently rely on **general principles of law** that are recognized by civilized nations. These are principles of law that are common to the *national* law of the parties to the dispute. They may be derived from constitutions, statutes, regulations, common law, or other sources of national law. In some cases, however, the countries' laws may differ concerning the matter in dispute.

Judicial Decisions and Teachings

judicial decisions and teachings

The fourth source of international law, consisting of judicial decisions and writings of the most qualified legal scholars of the various nations involved in the dispute.

A fourth source of law to which international tribunals can refer is **judicial decisions and teachings** of the most qualified scholars of the various nations involved in the dispute. Although international courts are not bound by the doctrine of *stare decisis* and may decide each case on its own merits, the courts often refer to their own past decisions for guidance. Court decisions of national courts do not create precedent for international courts.

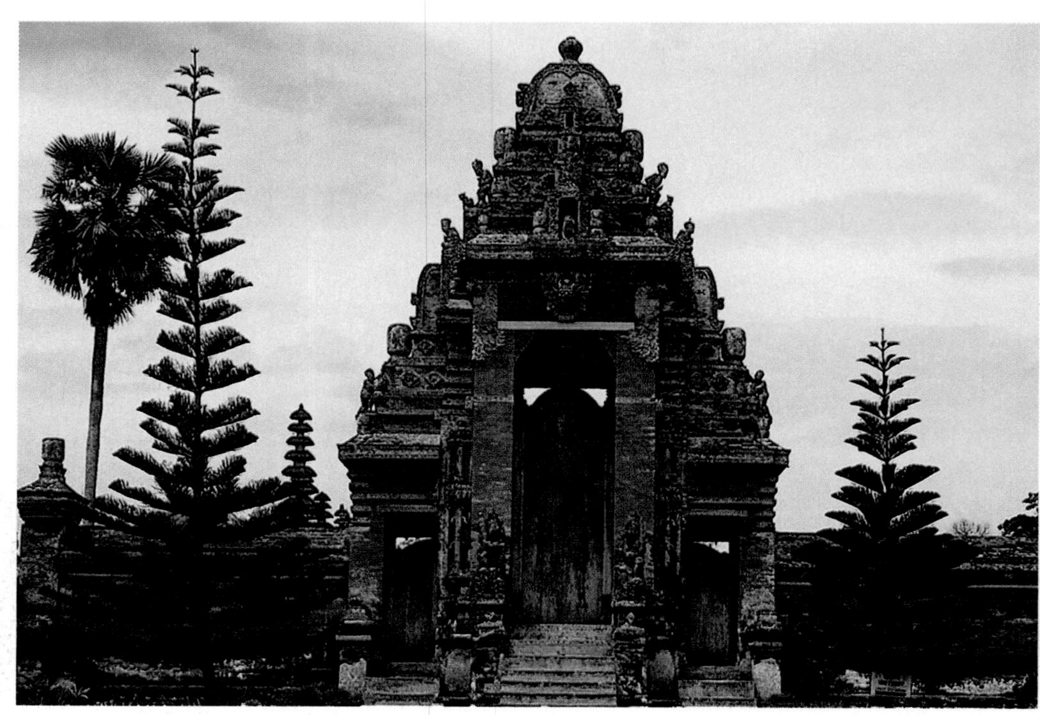

Indonesia. The federal government of the United States has exclusive power to regulate commerce with foreign nations.

The United Nations

One of the most important international organizations is the **United Nations (UN)**, which was created by a multilateral treaty on October 24, 1945.[1] Most countries of the world are members of the UN. The goals of the UN, which is headquartered in New York City, are to maintain peace and security in the world, promote economic and social cooperation, and protect human rights (see Exhibit 9.1).

Governance of the UN

The UN is governed by:

- **The General Assembly**, composed of all member nations. As the legislative body of the UN, it adopts resolutions concerning human rights, trade, finance and economics, and other matters within the scope of the UN Charter. Although resolutions have limited force, they are usually enforced through persuasion and the use of economic and other sanctions.
- **The Security Council**, composed of 15 member nations, 5 of which are permanent members (China, France, Russia, the United Kingdom, and the United States), and 10 other countries chosen by the members of the General Assembly to serve two-year terms. The council is primarily responsible for maintaining international peace and security and has authority to use armed forces.
- **The Secretariat**, which administers the day-to-day operations of the UN. It is headed by the *secretary-general*, who is elected by the General Assembly. The secretary-general may refer matters that threaten international peace and security to the Security Council and use his office to help solve international disputes.

Only when the world is civilized enough to keep promises will we get any kind of international law.

Julius Henry Cohen
(1946)

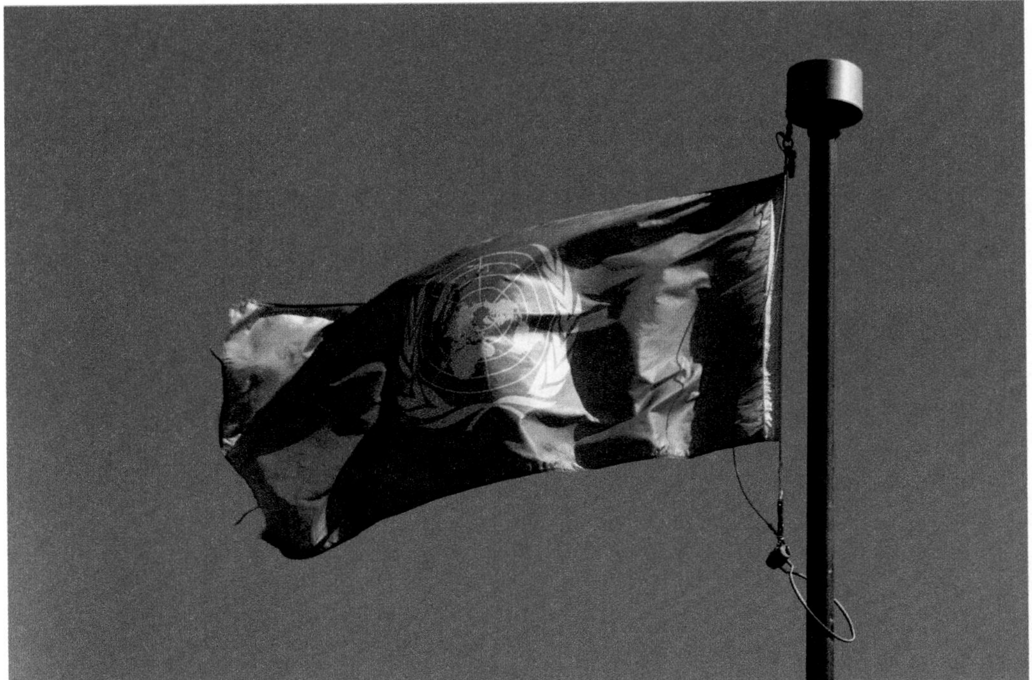

United Nations. The United Nations is an international organization created in 1945 to promote social and economic cooperation among nations and to protect human rights.

Exhibit 9.1

Selected Provisions from the Charter of the United Nations

Our respective Governments, through representatives assembled in the city of San Francisco, who have exhibited their full powers found to be in good and due form, have agreed to the present Charter of the United Nations and do hereby establish an international organization to be known as the United Nations.

Chapter 1. Purposes and Principles

Article 1 The Purposes of the United Nations are:

(1) To maintain international peace and security, and to that end: to take effective collective measures for the prevention and removal of threats to the peace, and for the suppression of acts of aggression or other breaches of the peace, and to bring about by peaceful means, and in conformity with the principles of justice and international law, adjustment or settlement of international disputes or situations which might lead to a breach of the peace;

(2) To develop friendly relations among nations based on respect for the principle of equal rights and self-determination of peoples, and to take other appropriate measures to strengthen universal peace;

(3) To achieve international co-operation in solving international problems of an economic, social, cultural, or humanitarian character, and in promoting and encouraging respect for human rights and for fundamental freedoms for all without distinction as to race, sex, language, or religion; and

(4) To be a centre for harmonizing the actions of nations in the attainment of these common ends.

Article 2 The Organization and its Members, in pursuit of the Purposes stated in Article 1, shall act in accordance with the following Principles.

(1) The Organization is based on the principle of the sovereign equality of all its Members.

(2) All Members, in order to ensure to all of them the rights and benefits resulting from membership, shall fulfill in good faith the obligations assumed by them in accordance with the present Charter.

(3) All Members shall settle their international disputes by peaceful means in such a manner that international peace and security, and justice, are not endangered.

(4) All Members shall refrain in their international relations from the threat or use of force against the territorial integrity or political independence of any state, or in any other manner inconsistent with the Purposes of the United Nations.

(5) All Members shall give the United Nations every assistance in any action it takes in accordance with the present Charter, and shall refrain from giving assistance to any state against which the United Nations is taking preventive or enforcement action.

(6) The Organization shall ensure that states which are not Members of the United Nations act in accordance with these Principles so far as may be necessary for the maintenance of international peace and security.

Web Site

ASIL Guide to Electronic Resources for International Law

This guide is a development project of the American Society of International Law. It has links to materials on all aspects of international law. Visit at **www.asil.org/resource/home.htm**.

The UN is also composed of various autonomous agencies that deal with a wide range of economic and social problems. These include UNESCO (United Nations Educational, Scientific, and Cultural Organization), UNICEF (United Nations International Children's Emergency Fund), the IMF (International Monetary Fund), the World Bank, and IFAD (International Fund for Agricultural Development).

International Court of Justice

International Court of Justice

The judicial branch of the United Nations that is located in The Hague, the Netherlands. Also called the *World Court*.

The **International Court of Justice (ICJ)**, also called the **World Court**, is located in The Hague, the Netherlands. It is the judicial branch of the UN. Only nations, not individuals or businesses, may have cases decided by this court. The ICJ may hear cases that nations refer to it as well as cases involving treaties and the UN Charter. A nation may seek redress on behalf of an individual or a business that has a claim against another country. The ICJ is composed of 15 judges who serve nine-year terms; not more than 2 judges may be from the same nation. A nation that is a party to a dispute before the ICJ may appoint 1 judge on an ad hoc basis for that case.

Regional Courts

Various treaties have created regional courts to handle disputes among member nations. For example, most regional economic organizations have established courts to enforce provisions of their respective treaties and to solve disputes among member nations. Regional courts, however, usually do not have mechanisms to enforce their judgments.

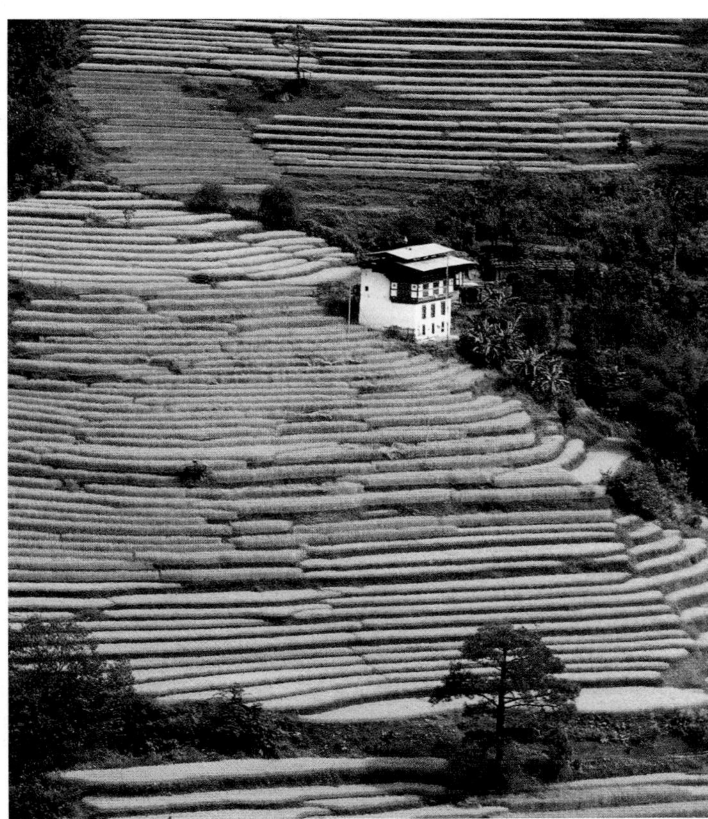

Bhutan. Even many of the smallest countries of the world are represented at the United Nations.

International Law

Holocaust Victims' Asset Litigation Settled

During World War II, the German Nazi regime engaged in years of persecution of Jews, including genocide, slave labor, and a wholesale and systematic looting of personal and business property of the Jewish victims. World War II ended in 1945 when the Allies defeated Germany and its Axis collaborators. During World War II, the European country of Switzerland remained neutral.

Switzerland has been a financial center to Europe for centuries. It is famous for its bank secrecy laws; that is, Swiss law protects the names of depositors and other information. Before and during the war, many Swiss banks held money and other property of Jews throughout Europe. And during the war, the Swiss banks obtained new clients—the Nazis—who stole their Jewish victims' property and placed it with the Swiss banks for safekeeping.

Over 50 years later, beginning in 1996, a series of class action lawsuits were filed in U.S. district courts by the survivors of the Holocaust and their heirs against Union Bank of Switzerland and many other Swiss banks. The plaintiffs alleged that during World War II the Swiss banks knowingly retained, concealed, and laundered the money and assets of Holocaust victims stolen by the Nazis. The lawsuits also alleged that Swiss banks did not pay money back to the Jewish survivors or to the heirs of the deceased victims that was on deposit at the banks once World War II was over.

After substantial negotiations, the plaintiffs reached a settlement with the defendant Swiss banks. The defendants dropped their defense that the claims were time-barred and agreed to pay $1.25 billion into a settlement fund. In exchange, the plaintiffs agreed to release all further claims against the banks. The district court judge approved the settlement agreement. Ernest Lobet, a survivor of the Holocaust, commented about the settlement:

> I have no quarrel with the settlement. I do not say it is fair, because fairness is a relative term. No amount of money can possibly be fair under those circumstances, but I'm quite sure it is the very best that could be done by the groups that negotiated for the settlement. The world is not perfect and the people that negotiated I'm sure tried their very best, and I think they deserve our cooperation and that they be supported and the settlement be approved.

A procedure was established for the plaintiffs to make claims against the settlement fund. [*In re Holocaust Victim Asset Litigation*, 105 F.Supp.2d 139, 2000 U.S. Dist. Lexis 10721 (E.D.N.Y. 2000)] ■

International Regional Organizations

There are several significant regional organizations whose members have agreed to work together to promote peace and security as well as economic, social, and cultural development. The most important of these organizations are discussed in the following paragraphs.

The European Union

European Union (Common Market)
An international region that comprises many countries of Western Europe. It was created to promote peace and security as well as economic, social, and cultural development.

One of the most important international regional organizations is the **European Union (EU)**, formerly called the **European Community**, or **Common Market**. The EU was created in 1957. The EU is composed of many countries of Western and Eastern Europe, including Austria, Belgium, Cyprus (Greek part), Denmark, Estonia, Finland, France, Germany, Greece, Hungary, Ireland, Italy, Latvia, Lithuania, Luxembourg, Malta, Netherlands, Poland, Portugal, Slovakia, Slovenia, Spain, Sweden, The Czech Republic, United Kingdom of Great Britain and Northern Ireland. The EU represents more than 400 million people and a gross community product that exceeds that of the United States, Canada, and Mexico combined.

When Kansas and Colorado have a quarrel over the water in the Arkansas River they don't call out the National Guard in each state and go to war over it. They bring a suit in the Supreme Court of the United States and abide by the decision. There isn't a reason in the world why we cannot do that internationally.

Harry S. Truman Speech *(1945)*

The EU's **Council of Ministers** is composed of representatives from each member country who meet periodically to coordinate efforts to fulfill the objectives of the treaty. The council votes on significant issues and changes to the treaty. Some matters require unanimity, whereas others require only a majority vote. The member nations have surrendered substantial sovereignty to the EU. The EU **commission**, which is independent of member nations, acts in the best interests of the union. The member nations have delegated substantial powers to the commission, including authority to enact legislation and to take enforcement actions to ensure member compliance with the treaty.

The EU treaty creates open borders for trade by providing for the free flow of capital, labor, goods, and services among member nations. Under the EU, customs duties have

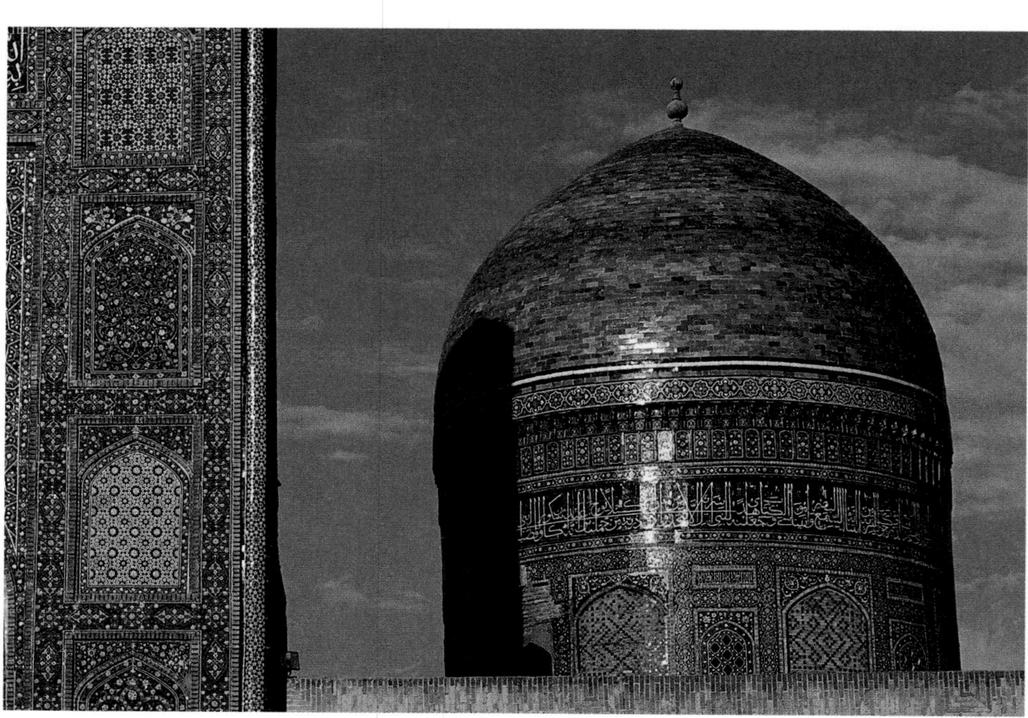

Islamic Mosque, Uzbekistan. Religious beliefs are often reflected in a nation's laws. For example, the Jewish, Hindu, and Islamic religions provide the basis for many nations' laws, such as those of Israel, India, and Egypt, respectively.

been eliminated among member nations. Common customs tariffs have been established for EU trade with the rest of the world. A single monetary unit, the euro, and a common monetary policy have been introduced. An EU central bank, equivalent to the U.S. Federal Reserve Board, has been established.

A unanimous vote of existing EU members is needed to admit a new member. Other Western European and some Eastern European countries are expected to apply for and be admitted as members of the EU.

European Court of Justice The **European Court of Justice**, located in Luxembourg, has jurisdiction to enforce EU law. Each EU member country appoints one judge to the court for a six-year term. The court decides disputes concerning member nations' compliance with EU law. The court follows civil law (rather than common law) traditions. Thus, the court may call witnesses, order documents to be produced, and hire experts.

European Court of Justice
The judicial branch of the European Union, located in Luxembourg. It has jurisdiction to enforce European Union law.

Member nations, EU institutions, and interested persons and businesses may bring actions before the court. Although national courts may interpret and enforce EU law, the European Court of Justice is the final arbiter of EU law. National courts are responsible for enforcing judgments of the European Court of Justice. Although the court's decisions are given great respect, the court has no means of enforcing its decisions against member nations.

An amendment to the Treaty of Rome created the **European Court of First Instance** (CFI), which is attached to the European Court of Justice. It has jurisdiction to hear actions brought by individuals and businesses. The purpose of the court is to relieve some of the European Court's caseload. The CFI started to hear cases in 1989.

Web Site
Eye on International Business Law
This is a site for links to all sorts of materials on international trade law and commercial arbitration. Visit at **www.uni-muenster.de/Jura.iwr/english/berger/linkse/linkse.html**.

Landmark Law

The North American Free Trade Agreement (NAFTA)

Mexico is a poor country with a population of about 90 million people. In the past, Mexico was dominated by government-run industries and protectionist laws. In the late 1980s, however, Mexico began a program to privatize its government-owned industries and to embrace capitalism.

In 1990, Mexican President Carlos Salinas de Gortari asked President George Bush to set up a two-country trade pact. Negotiations between the two countries began. Canada joined the negotiations eight months later, largely to make sure the United States did not undercut the earlier U.S.–Canada trade pact.

On August 12, 1992, after 14 months of arduous negotiations, the **North American Free Trade Agreement (NAFTA)** was signed by the leaders of the three countries. The treaty creates a free-trade zone stretching from the Yukon to the Yucatan, bringing together 360 million consumers in a $6.5 trillion market.

NAFTA eliminates or reduces most of the duties, tariffs, quotas, and other trade barriers between Mexico, the United States, and Canada. Agriculture, automobiles, computers, electronics, energy and petrochemicals, financial services, insurance telecommunications, and many other industries are affected. The treaty contains a safety valve: A country can reimpose tariffs if an import surge from one of the other nations hurts its economy or workers.

Some of the major features of the treaty are:

- Mexican tariffs on vehicles and light trucks were cut in half immediately. Mexican Trade barriers and restrictions on autos and auto parts were to be phased out over 10 years.
- All North American trade restrictions on textiles and apparel were to be eliminated within 10 years.
- Banks and securities firms are allowed to establish wholly owned subsidiaries in all three countries.
- Mexican import licenses, which cover about 25 percent of U.S. exports, were dropped immediately, and remaining Mexican tariffs were to be phased out over 15 years.
- Tariffs on import-sensitive American industries were to be phased out over 15 years.
- Intellectual property rights, such as patents, trademarks, and copyrights, receive increased protection.

Like other regional trading agreements, NAFTA allows the bloc to discriminate against outsiders and to cut deals among themselves. For example, only automobiles that consist of 62.5 percent North American content benefit from the treaty's tariff cuts.

Landmark Law

(continued)

NAFTA also includes special protection for favored industries with a lot of lobby muscle. For example, Mexico's oil industry, far and away its most lucrative, may keep out U.S. companies except on the most minimal basis. The U.S. sugar industry is protected by a quota system. Thus, many economists assert that NAFTA is not a "free trade" pact, but a *managed trade* agreement.

Proponents allege that NAFTA forms a supernational trading region that can more effectively compete with Japan and the European Community. Consumers in all three countries can expect lower prices on a wide variety of goods and services as trade barriers fall and competition increases.

Critics contend that NAFTA will shift American jobs—particularly blue-collar jobs—south of the border, where Mexican wage rates are about one-tenth of those in the United States. Environmentalists criticize the pact for not doing enough to prevent and clean up pollution in Mexico. ■

The parties to NAFTA are the United States, Canada, and Mexico.

International Law

Free Trade Area of the Americas (FTAA)

In April 2001, the leaders of 34 Western Hemisphere nations met at the Summit of the Americas in Quebec City, Canada, to discuss future trade opportunities in the hemisphere. The leaders agreed to a *Plan of Action* to create a regional Free Trade Area of the Americas (FTAA). The FTAA would be an extension of NAFTA, which currently exists between Canada, Mexico, and the United States. The proposed FTAA would include all of the countries of North, Central, and South America and would extend from Alaska in the north to Argentina in the south.

The FTAA would eliminate or reduce trade barriers among its member nations and create a trading zone of over 800 million people where trade of over $12 trillion could flourish between seamless economic borders. The plan is to create the FTAA by the year 2005. Negotiations of the details of the FTAA will be conducted for several years, with the United States and Brazil co-chairing the process.

The FTAA is supported by the United States and most large U.S. corporations. The FTAA is not without its critics, however. Labor unions fear loss of jobs, and environmentalists envision more loss of rain forests and further destruction of the environment caused by economic advancement. Brazil and several other nations have also voiced reservations. ■

Asian Economic Communities

My nationalism is intense internationalism. I am sick of the strife between nations or religions.

Gandhi

In 1967, the **Association of South East Asian Nations (ASEAN)** was created. The countries that belong to ASEAN are Brunei Darussalam, Cambodia, Indonesia, Laos, Malaysia, Myanmar, Philippines, Singapore, Thailand, and Vietnam. This is a cooperative association of diverse nations.

Two of the world's largest countries, Japan and China, do not belong to any significant economic community. Although not a member of ASEAN, Japan has been instrumental in providing financing for the countries that make up that organization. China also works closely with the countries of ASEAN and is a potential member of ASEAN.

Latin, Central, and South American Economic Communities

Countries of Latin America and the Caribbean have established several regional organizations to promote economic development and cooperation. These include (1) the **Central American Common Market**, composed of Costa Rica, El Salvador, Guatemala, Honduras, Nicaragua, and Panama; (2) the **MERCOSUR Common Market**, created by Argentina, Brazil, Paraguay, and Uruguay; (3) the **Caribbean Community**, whose member countries are Barbados, Belize, Dominica, Grenada, Jamaica, St. Kitts-Nevis-Anguilla, St. Lucia, St. Vincent, and Trinidad-Tobago; and (4) the **Andean Common Market (ANCOM)**, whose current members are Bolivia, Colombia, Ecuador, and Venezuela.

International Brief

The importance of regional organizations and their mutual agreements is increasing.

Mexico, the largest industrial country in Latin America and the Caribbean, has entered into a free trade agreement with all the countries of Central America as well as Chile, Colombia, and Venezuela.

African Economic Communities

Several regional economic communities have been formed in Africa. They include (1) the **Economic Community of West African States (ECOWAS)**, created by Dahomey, Gambia, Ghana, Guinea-Bissau, Ivory Coast, Liberia, Mali, Mauritania, Niger, Nigeria, Senegal, Sierra Leone, Togo, and Upper Volta; (2) the **Economic and Customs Union of Central Africa**, composed of Cameroon, Central African Republic, Chad, Congo, and Gabon; and (3) the **East African Community (EAC)**, created by Kenya, Tanzania, and Uganda. In 1991, 51 African countries of the **Organization of African Unity** signed a **Treaty Establishing the African Economic Community**. This wide-ranging treaty with its large organization of countries is expected to wield more power than the smaller African regional organizations.

International Brief

The development of a uniform body of law and the creation of tribunals to peacefully settle disputes between nations and commercial enterprises are necessary for the further development of international trade.

Middle Eastern Economic Communities

One of the most well-known economic organizations is **OPEC**, the **Organization of Petroleum Exporting Countries**. OPEC consists of eleven oil-producing and exporting countries from Africa, Asia, the Middle East, and South America. The member nations are Algeria, Indonesia, Iran, Iraq, Kuwait, Libya, Nigeria, Qatar, Saudi Arabia, United Arab Emirates, and Venezuela. OPEC sets quotas on the output of oil production by member nations. The **Gulf Cooperation Council** was established by Bahrain, Kuwait, Oman, Qatar, Saudi Arabia, and the United Arab Emirates to establish an economic trade area.

International Brief

By raising prices and restricting output, the OPEC cartel caused the "oil crisis" of the early 1970s in the United States and other countries.

International Law

Mexico Becomes an International Business Juggernaut

For decades the economy of Mexico was stagnant compared to that of the United States. But in 1992, Mexico joined the United States and Canada to create NAFTA, effective January 1, 1994. By reducing tariffs and eliminating most protectionism, the Mexican economy improved steadily under the new NAFTA rules.

There was one major problem: As of 1999, 85 percent of Mexico's imports went to the United States. Once Mexico saw that the regional trade pacts were good for its economy, it started seeking out new trading partners to balance its exports and reduce its reliance on the United States. Mexico also feared the consequences of China increasing its exports to the United States under the new China–U.S. trade pact. To boost its export trade, Mexico entered into individual trade treaties with more than a dozen Central and South American countries, including Chile and Colombia.

But Mexico decided to exploit its unique position and sought an even bigger deal. After much negotiation, in November 1999, Mexico signed an international trade agreement with the 15-member European Union (EU). This international trade agreement gave Mexico access to the markets of the United Kingdom, Germany, France, Spain, Greece, and the other European nations that represent more than 300 million people. The pact called for Europe to grant duty-free entry to most Mexican products, beginning in

International Law

(continued)

2000, and for Mexico to gradually open its markets to EU goods and services by 2007. The pact reduced tariffs and duties from an average of 12 percent to 2 percent or lower, depending on the types of goods and services.

With the creation of this new trade pact, Mexico became the only country other than Israel to have international trade agreements with the United States, Canada, and the European nations of the EU. This new position encourages European firms to establish factories in Mexico so that they can sell goods more cheaply in the United States and for U.S. firms to establish factories in Mexico as well so they can directly export goods more cheaply to the EU. The new trade pact with the EU assures that Mexico, already the world's eighth-largest trading country, will continue the growth in its industrial-export economy. ■

The World Trade Organization (WTO)

World Trade Organization (WTO)
An international organization of more than 130 member nations created to promote and enforce trade agreements among member nations.

In 1995, the **World Trade Organization (WTO)** was created as part of the Uruguay Round of trade negotiations on the *General Agreement on Tariffs and Trade (GATT)*. GATT is a multilateral treaty that establishes trade agreements and limits tariffs and trade restrictions among its more than 130 member nations.

The WTO is an international organization whose headquarters is located in Geneva, Switzerland. WTO members have entered into many trade agreements among themselves, including international agreements on investments, sale of goods, provision of services, intellectual property, licensing, tariffs, subsidies, and the removal of trade barriers.

International Law

China Joins the WTO

For the past 50 years, China and the United States have pursued divergent paths. China became the world's largest communist country and the United States the leading democracy. China maintained its agricultural base, while the United States pursued industrialization. China's businesses were state owned, while those in the United States were privately owned under a capitalist system. So what do these countries have in common? A new landmark trade pact. For over a decade, these two countries engaged in on-again, off-again trade negotiations. Then in November 1999 they formed a landmark trade pact.

In exchange for being granted the right to import most goods and services into the United States, China, which had substantially restricted imports into its country, agreed to open its markets to foreign goods and services in the following ways:

- ***Telecommunications*** Foreign telephone companies may own up to 50 percent of Chinese telephone companies.
- ***Entertainment*** China will double the number of U.S. films that can be imported into the country to 20 annually; the content of these films must be approved by the Chinese government.
- ***Banking and Financial Services*** Foreign banks may offer financial services to Chinese customers. China will allow foreign companies to own up to 49 percent of banks, insurance companies, and other financial-service companies.
- ***Distribution*** Foreigners may establish their own product distribution systems and sell directly to Chinese customers.
- ***Services*** Foreigners may establish their own repair and maintenance service businesses in China.
- ***Vehicle Sales*** China will permit foreign automobile manufacturers to sell and finance sales to Chinese customers.
- ***Farm Products*** China will eliminate subsidies of Chinese exports.
- ***Internet*** Foreign investors may own up to 50 percent of Chinese Internet businesses.

The China–U.S. trade agreement was a prelude to China's application to join the WTO. In 2002, China became a member of the WTO. China's entry into the WTO makes it a full partner in the world's trading system. The landmark China–U.S. trade pact is only one of many agreements that underscore the importance that trade and commerce now play in international politics.

The China–U.S. trade agreement is not without its critics. In the United States, labor unions criticize the agreement for its potential to ship U.S. manufacturing jobs to China, while environmentalists complain that little is being done to protect the environment from an industrialized economy the size of China. In China, workers at state-owned enterprises might lose their jobs to foreign capitalist companies that can produce goods and services more efficiently, and China's already impoverished farmers may be harmed by cheap farm products imported from other countries. But leaders from both countries thought the entry of China as a full member of the international trading community was worth these risks. ■

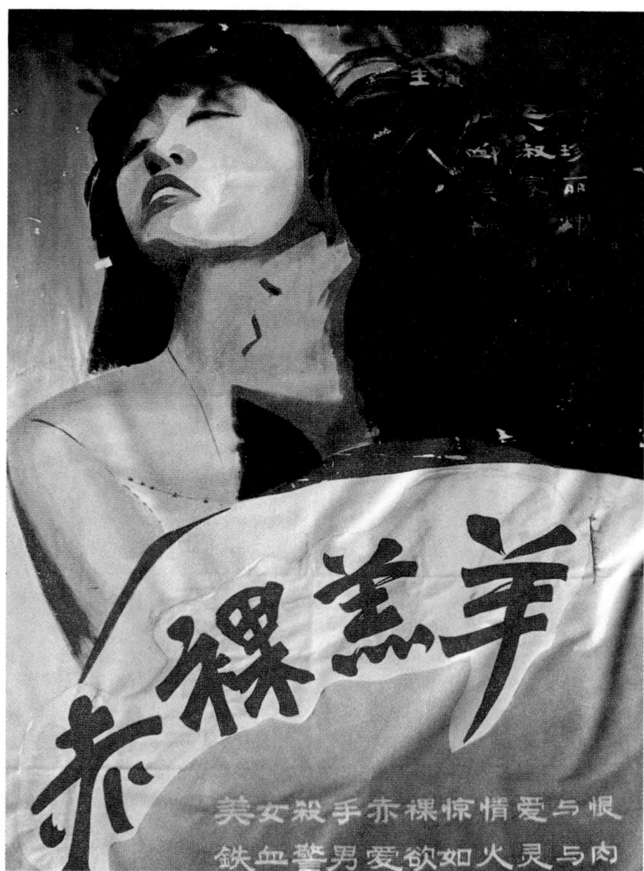

Advertisement, China. In 2002, China became a member of the WTO. By doing so, China opened its markets and became a full member of the international economic community.

WTO Dispute Resolution

One of the primary functions of the WTO is to hear and decide trade disputes between member nations. Before the creation of the WTO, GATT governed trade disputes between signatory nations. This system was inadequate because any member nation that was found to have violated any GATT trade agreement could itself veto any sanctions imposed by GATT's governing body. The WTO solved this problem by adopting a "judicial" mode of dispute resolution to replace GATT's more politically based one.

International Brief

One of the primary functions of the WTO is to hear and decide trade disputes between member nations.

A member nation that believes that another member nation has breached one of these agreements can initiate a proceeding to have the WTO hear and decide the dispute.

The dispute is first heard by a three-member **panel** of the WTO, which issues a "panel report." The members of the panel are professional judges from member nations. The report is the decision of the panel and contains its findings of fact and law and orders a remedy if a violation has been found. The report is then referred to the **dispute settlement body** of the WTO. This body is required to adopt the panel report unless the body, by consensus, agrees not to adopt it. Because each member nation has a representative on this settlement body, it can be presumed that panel reports will automatically be adopted because the winning nation to the dispute will almost assuredly vote to adopt it. This is a radical change from the former GATT settlement procedure. Under GATT, unanimity was required to enforce a panel report, and the losing party usually voted to "block" the implementation of a panel's findings against it. One of the most important features of the WTO is the elimination of this blocking power of member nations.

panel
A group of three WTO judges that hears trade disputes between member nations and issues a "panel report."

dispute settlement body
A board comprised of one representative from each WTO member nation that reviews panel reports.

The WTO creates an **appellate body** to which a party can appeal a decision of the dispute settlement body. This appeals court is composed of seven professional justices

appellate body
A panel of seven judges selected from WTO member nations that hears and decides appeals from decisions by the dispute settlement body.

Web Site

Legal Research on International Law Issues Using the Internet, by Lyonette Louis-Jacques This is an Internet site for finding links to all aspects of international law. Prof. Louis-Jacques has included major Web sites, international organizations, government agencies, publishers and vendors, databases, library catalogs, discussion groups, news sources, research guides, and more. Many of the links are annotated. Visit at **www.lob.uchicago.edu/~llou/forintlaw.html**.

selected from member nations. Appeals are heard by panels composed of three members of the appellate body. Appeals are limited to issues of law, not fact. The entire dispute proceeding is completed within 9 months when a panel report is not appealed and within 12 months when there is an appeal. A shortened period is available if the parties agree or if there is an urgent matter that must be decided quickly.

If a violation of a trade agreement is found, the general report and appellate decision can order the offending nation to cease from engaging in the violating practice and to pay damages to the other party. If the offending nation refuses to abide by the order, the WTO can order retaliatory trade sanctions (e.g., tariffs) by other member nations against the noncomplying nation.

International Law

WTO Takes a Bite Out of Japanese Apples

Japan produces and sells over $1.6 billion of apples annually, the majority of which are consumed there. The United States, which produces more than 100 varieties of apples, would like to export apples to Japan and compete for a share of this market. There's a problem, however. Although Japan has removed tariffs on U.S. apples, in accordance with WTO rules, the Japanese government has frustrated foreign apple growers with time-consuming apple-testing regulations that have in effect prevented the sale of most varieties of U.S. apples in Japan. Japan insists that these regulations are necessary to ensure the safety of apples imported into the country. U.S. apple growers argue that Japan's complex inspection, fumigation, quarantine, and handling regulations are calculated to accomplish what old tariffs used to do: block another country's goods from entering the market.

After attempts at negotiations failed to resolve the issue, U.S. apple growers took their case to court, the court of the WTO. There, the U.S. growers presented evidence that the Japanese rules lacked scientific merit and were blatant protectionist measures designed to shield local farmers from global competition. The Japanese government argued that its rules were required to protect against pests that could travel on the apples.

After hearing presentations by both sides, the Geneva-based WTO concluded that the Japanese apple-testing regulations lacked scientific merit and improperly impeded entry of foreign-grown apples into Japan. The WTO ordered that the apple-testing regulations be disbanded to allow the importation of foreign-grown apples into Japan. ■

The Future of the WTO

International Brief

By enforcing trade agreements among its more than 130 member nations, the WTO has become the world's most important trade organization.

The WTO, which has been referred to as the "Supreme Court of Trade," has become the world's most important trade organization. The WTO has jurisdiction to enforce the most important and comprehensive trade agreements in the world among its more than 130 member nations. Some critics argue that the WTO has been granted powers too great and will impinge upon the sovereignty of individual nations. Others herald the WTO as a much-needed world court that can peaceably solve trade disputes among nations.

International Law

WTO Audits U.S. Tax Laws

The number-one plaintiff in cases brought before the WTO has been the United States. It has initiated and won cases against Japan, Brazil, and the EU to knock down subsidies and other measures instituted by these countries to protect their industries from open trade. But in a recent and important case, the tables were turned on the United States, which lost an important case brought against it in the WTO by the EU.

This was the situation. The U.S. Tax Code provided that if U.S. companies ran the paperwork concerning the export of goods to Europe through the tax-haven countries in the Caribbean, then the goods would not be subject to U.S. export tax. The goods could be shipped directly from the United States to their destination in Europe, however, and still qualify for this tax saving, as long as paperwork (which is basically digital) was routed through the

Caribbean countries. The EU brought an action before the WTO against the United States, alleging that this tax break was an illegal export subsidy that violated WTO free-trade rules. After a hearing, the WTO ruled that the United States had engaged in a subtle and lucrative export subsidy that violated WTO trade laws. The WTO ordered the United States to dismantle this favorable tax subsidy. This ruling by the WTO is its most significant to date, repealing hundreds of millions of dollars of tax breaks sneakily given by the U.S. government to Microsoft Corporation, Boeing Company, and other large U.S. exporters. [World Trade Organization, 2001] ■

International Law

Old Enemies Become Economic Partners

During the late 1960s and early 1970s, the United States engaged in a military action to aid South Vietnam in its struggle against Communist North Vietnam. The might of the United States was unable to defeat the guerilla warfare of the Communists, and in 1972 the United States abandoned Vietnam. The Communists unified North and South Vietnam into one country. The war left visible scars—millions of Vietnamese soldiers and civilians on both sides died or were wounded, 50,000 U.S. soldiers died, and hundreds of thousands were wounded.

Vietnam and the United States remained enemies for the rest of the century. It was not until 1999 that the two countries opened diplomatic relations. In July 2000, Vietnam and the United States took a historical step and signed a trade pact that opened up each other's borders. The new deal took years to negotiate and had been abandoned several times by the Vietnamese Communist rulers who feared loss of power over Vietnam's economy. But after witnessing the trade deal struck by China and the United States, and fearing the loss of what little trade it did have with the United States to China, the Vietnamese leaders negotiated a final deal with the United States. The deal contains the following features:

- The United States reduces tariffs on Vietnamese imports from the current average of 40 percent to 3 percent.
- Vietnam eliminates the 50 percent surcharge it applies to the importation of American products.
- Vietnam adopts WTO standards for the protection of intellectual property rights (e.g., trademarks, copyrights, and patents).
- Over a five-year period Vietnam is to phase in entry of U.S. service industries such as distribution, legal, accounting, and engineering services.

The trade pact still allows many restrictions on U.S. companies doing business in Vietnam. For example, U.S. retailers will only be allowed one store in Vietnam. Also, U.S. companies desiring to do business in Vietnam are required to enter into joint ventures with Vietnamese partners, and U.S. ownership of cellular phone, satellite, and telecommunications companies is limited to 49 percent.

The new trade pact gives Vietnam much easier access to the rich U.S. consumer marketplace and gives U.S. companies entry into the Vietnamese marketplace, for both the manufacture and sale of goods. The United States has accomplished by an economic trade pact what it could not do through military action: convert a socialist redoubt into the world's newest capitalist recruit. Although Vietnam is not a member of the WTO, the trade pact will move Vietnam to adopt many of the world's global trading standards. ■

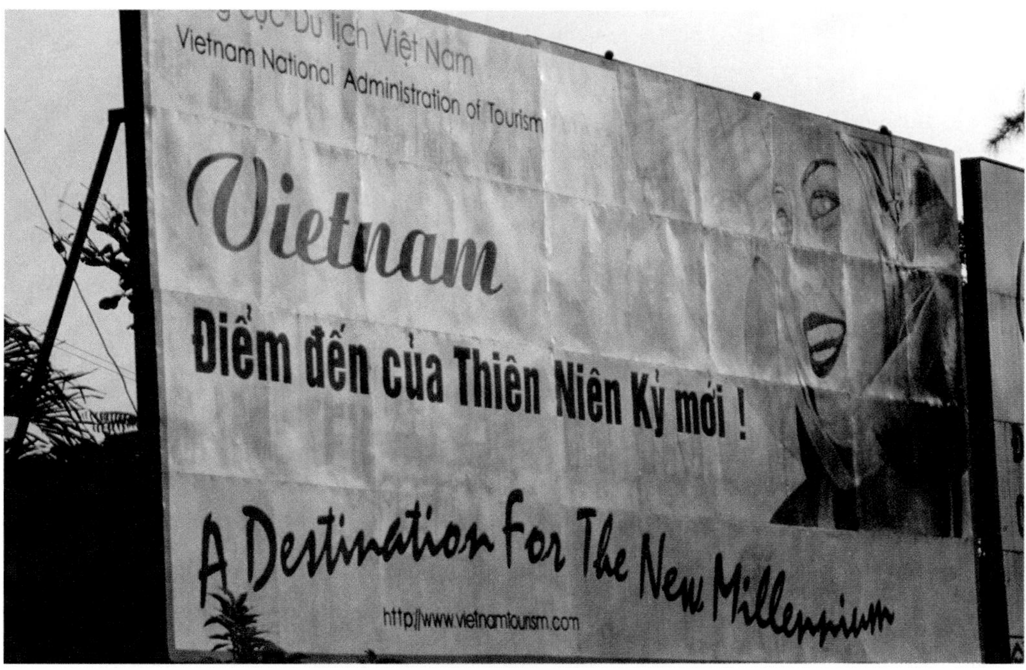

Vietnam. The United Sates and Vietnam have reestablished diplomatic relations and entered into an economic trade agreement.

Jurisdiction of National Courts to Decide International Disputes

national courts
The courts of individual nations.

International Brief
The majority of commercial litigation involving international business transactions is heard by national courts.

The majority of cases involving international law disputes are heard by **national courts** of individual nations. This is primarily the case for commercial disputes between private litigants that do not qualify to be heard by an international court. Some countries have specialized courts that hear international commercial disputes. Other countries permit such disputes to proceed through their regular court systems. In the United States, commercial disputes between U.S. companies and foreign governments or parties may be brought in federal district court.

Judicial Procedure

choice of forum clause
A clause in an international contract that designates which nation's court has jurisdiction to hear a case arising out of the contract. Also known as a *forum-selection clause.*

choice of law clause
A clause in an international contract that designates which nation's laws will be applied in deciding a dispute arising out of the contract.

A party seeking judicial resolution of an international dispute faces several problems, including which nation's courts will hear the case and what law should be applied to the case. Jurisdiction is often a highly contested issue. Absent an agreement providing otherwise, a case involving an international dispute will be brought in the national court of the plaintiff's home country.

Many international contracts contain a **choice of forum (or forum-selection) clause** that designates which nation's court has jurisdiction to hear a case arising out of contract. In addition, many contracts also include a **choice of law clause** that designates which nation's laws will be applied in deciding the case. Absent these two clauses, and without the parties agreeing to these matters, an international dispute may never be resolved.

Concept Summary *International Contract Clauses Affecting Jurisdiction and Choice of Law*

Clause	Description
Forum-selection	Designates the judicial or arbitral forum that will hear and decide the case.
Choice of law	Designates the law to be applied by the court or arbitrator in deciding the case.

The Act of State Doctrine

act of state doctrine
A doctrine that states that judges of one country cannot question the validity of an act committed by another country within that other country's borders. It is based on the principle that a country has absolute authority over what transpires within its own territory.

A general principle of international law is that a country has absolute authority over what transpires *within* its own territory. In furtherance of this principle, the **act of state doctrine** states that judges of one country cannot question the validity of an act committed by another country within that other country's own borders. In *United States v. Belmont,*[2] the U.S. Supreme Court declared, "Every sovereign state must recognize the independence of every other sovereign state; and the courts of one will not sit in judgment upon the acts of the government of another, done within its own territory." This restraint on the judiciary is justified under the doctrine of separation of powers and permits the executive branch of the federal government to arrange affairs with foreign governments.

U.S. SUPREME COURT CASE

W. S. Kirkpatrick & Co., Inc. v. Environmental Tectonics Corporation, International

493 U.S. 400, 110 S.Ct. 701, 1990 U.S. Lexis 486 (1990)
Supreme Court of the United States

Case 9.2
Act of State Doctrine

Background and Facts

In 1981, Harry Carpenter, a U.S. citizen and chairman of the board and chief executive officer of W. S. Kirkpatrick & Co., Inc. (Kirkpatrick), learned that the Republic of Nigeria was interested in contracting for the construction of an aeromedical center at Kaduna Air Force Base in Nigeria. He made arrangements with Benson "Tunde" Akindale, a Nigerian citizen, whereby Akindale would help secure the contract for Kirkpatrick by paying bribes to Nigerian officials. In accordance with the plan, the contract was awarded to a wholly owned subsidiary of Kirkpatrick; Kirkpatrick paid the agreed-upon funds to Akindale, which were dispersed as bribes to Nigerian officials. Environmental Tectonics Corporation, International (Environmental), an unsuccessful bidder for the Kaduna contract, learned of the bribes and informed the U.S. embassy in Lagos, Nigeria. In a criminal action, Carpenter and Kirkpatrick pleaded guilty to violating the U.S. Foreign Corrupt Practices Act. Environmental then brought this civil action against Carpenter, Kirkpatrick, and Akindale, seeking damages under federal and state racketeering and antitrust laws. The district court held that the action was barred by the act of state doctrine and dismissed the complaint. The court of appeals reversed. The defendants appealed to the U.S. Supreme Court.

Supreme Court Issue

Does the act of state doctrine bar the plaintiff's civil suit against the defendants?

In The Language of The U.S. Supreme Court

Scalia, Justice In every case in which we have held the act of state doctrine applicable, the relief sought or the defense interposed would have required a court in the United States to declare invalid the official act of a foreign sovereign performed within its own territory. In the present case, by contrast, neither the claim nor any asserted defense requires a determination that Nigeria's contract with Kirkpatrick was, or was not, effective. Act of state issues arise only when a court must decide—that is, when that outcome of the case turns upon—the effect of official action by a foreign sovereign. When that question is not in the case, neither is the act of state doctrine. That is the situation here.

The short of the matter is this: Courts in the United States have the power, and ordinarily the obligation, to decide cases and controversies properly presented to them. The act of state doctrine does not establish an exception for cases and controversies that may embarrass foreign governments, but merely requires that, in the process of deciding, the acts of foreign sovereigns taken within their own jurisdictions shall be deemed valid. That doctrine has no application to the present case because the validity of no foreign sovereign act is at issue.

Decision and Remedy

The Supreme Court held that the act of state doctrine did not apply to the case and therefore did not bar plaintiff Environmental's civil lawsuit against the defendants.

Case Questions

Critical Legal Thinking Should the act of state doctrine be followed by the United States?

Business Ethics Did Carpenter act ethically in obtaining the contract with the Nigerian government?

Contemporary Business What implications does the act of state doctrine have for business? Explain.

The Doctrine of Sovereign Immunity

One of the oldest principles of international law is the **doctrine of sovereign immunity**. Under this doctrine, *countries* are granted immunity from suits in courts in other countries. For example, if a U.S. citizen wanted to sue the government of China in a U.S. court, he or she could not (subject to the exceptions discussed below).

doctrine of sovereign immunity
A doctrine that states that countries are granted immunity from suits in courts of other countries.

Originally, the United States granted absolute immunity to foreign governments from suits in U.S. courts. In 1952, the United States switched to the principle of *qualified*, or *restricted*, *immunity*, which was eventually codified in the **Foreign Sovereign Immunities Act of 1976 (FSIA)**.[3] This act now exclusively governs suits against foreign nations in the United States, whether in federal or state court. Most Western nations have adopted the principle of restricted immunity. Other countries still follow the doctrine of absolute immunity.

Foreign Sovereign Immunities Act
An act that exclusively governs suits against foreign nations that are brought in federal or state courts in the United States. It codifies the principle of qualified, or restricted, immunity.

International Brief

A foreign nation may be sued in a court in the United States if that nation has engaged in a *commercial activity* that either (1) is carried on in the United States or (2) is carried on outside the United States but causes a direct effect in the United States.

Exceptions The FSIA provides that a foreign country is not immune from lawsuits in U.S. courts in the following two situations:

1. The foreign country has waived its immunity, either explicitly or by implication.
2. The action is based on a commercial activity carried on in the United States by the foreign country or carried on outside the United States but causing a direct effect in the United States.

What constitutes "commercial activity" is the most litigated aspect of the FSIA. If it is commercial activity, the foreign sovereign is subject to suit in the United States; if it is not, the foreign sovereign is immune from suit in this country. In the following case, the U.S. Supreme Court examined the commercial activity exception.

Case 9.3 Doctrine of Sovereign Immunity

U.S. SUPREME COURT CASE

Republic of Argentina v. Weltover, Inc.

504 U.S. 607, 112 S.Ct. 2160, 1992 U.S. Lexis 3542 (1992)

Supreme Court of the United States

Background and Facts

In an attempt to stabilize its currency, Argentina and its central bank, Banco Central (collectively Argentina), issued bonds called "Bonods." The bonds, which were sold to investors worldwide, provided for repayment in U.S. dollars through transfers on the London, Frankfurt, Zurich, and New York markets, at the bondholder's election. Argentina lacked sufficient foreign exchange to retire the bonds when they matured. Argentina unilaterally extended the time for payment and offered bondholders substitute instruments as a means of rescheduling the debts. Two Panamanian corporations and a Swiss bank refused the rescheduling and insisted that full payment be made in New York. When Argentina did not pay, they brought a breach of contract action against Argentina in U.S. district court in New York. Argentina moved to dismiss, alleging that it was not subject to suit in U.S. courts under the federal FSIA. The plaintiffs asserted that the "commercial activity" exception to the act applied, subjecting Argentina to suit in U.S. court. The district court denied Argentina's motion for dismissal, and the court of appeals affirmed. Argentina appealed to the U.S. Supreme Court.

Supreme Court Issue

Does the doctrine of sovereign immunity prevent the plaintiffs from suing Argentina in a U.S. court?

In The Language of The U.S. Supreme Court

Scalia, Justice When a foreign government acts, not as regulator of a market, but in the manner of a private player within it, the foreign sovereign's actions are "commercial" within the meaning of the FSIA. Thus, a foreign government's issuance of regulations limiting foreign currency exchange is a sovereign activity, because such authoritative control of commerce cannot be exercised by a private party; whereas a contract to buy army boots or even bullets is a "commercial" activity, because private companies can similarly use sales contracts to acquire goods.

The commercial character of the Bonods is confirmed by the fact that they are in almost all respects garden-variety debt instruments: They may be held by private parties; they are negotiable and may be traded on the international market; and they promise a future stream of cash income. We conclude that Argentina's issuance of the Bonods was a "commercial activity" under the FSIA. We have little difficulty concluding that Argentina's unilateral rescheduling of the maturity dates on the Bonods had a "direct effect" in the United States.

Decision and Remedy

The Supreme Court held that Argentina's issuance of the bonds was a commercial activity that had a direct effect in the United States. Therefore, the commercial activity exception to the FSIA applied, which allowed the plaintiffs to sue Argentina in a U.S. court.

Case Questions

Critical Legal Thinking Should the United States recognize the doctrine of absolute sovereign immunity or qualified immunity? Explain.

Business Ethics Did the government of Argentina act ethically in not paying the bonds when due and unilaterally rescheduling the debt?

Contemporary Business Is there more risk for investors who invest in obligations of foreign countries than in obligations of the U.S. government?

Concept Summary Act of State Doctrine and Sovereign Immunity Compared

Doctrine	Description
Act of state	An act of a government in its *own country* is not subject to suit in a foreign country's courts.
Sovereign immunity	An act of a government in a *foreign country* is not subject to suit in the foreign country. Some countries provide absolute immunity, whereas other countries (such as the United States) provide limited immunity.

International Law

Nationalization of Privately Owned Property by Foreign Nations

When a company invests capital in a foreign country in plants, equipment, bank accounts, and such, it runs the risk that that country may **nationalize** (seize) its assets. International law recognizes the right of nations to nationalize private property owned by foreigners if done for public purposes. Nationalization of assets occurs more often in underdeveloped or developing countries than in developed countries. Nationalization can be classified as

- ***Expropriation*** The owner of the property is paid just compensation by the government that seized the property.
- ***Confiscation*** The owner receives no payment or inadequate payment from the government that seized the property.

When a foreign government confiscates property of U.S. firms, there are few legal remedies available to the owners. The U.S. government may try to recover payment for the firms through diplomatic means, but this is often not successful.

The United States has created the **Overseas Private Investment Corporation (OPIC)**, a government agency that insures U.S. citizens and businesses against losses incurred as a result of the confiscation of their assets by foreign governments. This is often called **political risk insurance**. Low-cost premiums are charged for the insurance. Those insured that receive a payment under this insurance program must assign their claim against the foreign government to OPIC. The **United States Export-Import Bank (Eximbank)** also offers insurance protection against confiscation to U.S. firms engaged in exporting. Political risk insurance is also available through several private insurance companies. ■

International Arbitration

As an alternative to litigation, the parties to an international contract may agree that any dispute that arises between them regarding the transaction will be decided by mandatory arbitration. **Arbitration** is a nonjudicial method of dispute resolution whereby a neutral third party decides the case. The parties agree to be bound by the arbitrator's decision. Generally, arbitration is faster, less expensive, less formal, and more private than litigation.

arbitration
A nonjudicial method of dispute resolution whereby a neutral third party decides the case.

An **arbitration clause** should specify the arbitrator or the means of selecting the arbitrator. Several organizations conduct international arbitrations, including the American Arbitration Association, the International Chamber of Commerce, the International Center for the Settlement of Investment Disputes, and the United Nations Commission on International Trade Law. International arbitrators are usually businesspeople or lawyers experienced in worldwide commercial transactions. An arbitration clause should also specify the law to be applied by the arbitrator. Arbitration clauses are appearing in an increasing number of international contracts.

arbitration clause
A clause contained in many international contracts that stipulates that any dispute between the parties concerning the performance of the contract will be submitted to an arbitrator or arbitration panel for resolution.

Web Site

Research Guide to International Law on the Internet—International Environmental Law At this site, you can find treaties, documents, and Web sites. The list of Web sites is annotated. Visit at **www.spfo.unibo.it/spolfo/ENVLAW.htm**.

An arbitrator issues an *award*, not a judgment. An arbitrator does not have the power to enforce the award it renders. Therefore, if the losing party refuses to pay the award, the winning party must petition a court to enforce the award. More than 50 countries that conduct the bulk of worldwide commercial transactions are signatories to the **United Nations Convention on the Recognition and Enforcement of Foreign Arbitral Awards (Convention).**[4] The United States adopted the convention in 1970 and amended the Federal Arbitration Act to reflect this international law.[5] The recipient of an arbitral award subject to the convention can attach property of the loser that is located in any country that is a signatory to the convention.

International Law

Arbitration of International Business Disputes

Arbitration clauses often appear in international commercial agreements signed by U.S. companies that designate that a foreign country's arbitration system will hear and decide the dispute. Consider the following case.

Mitsubishi Motors Corporation (Mitsubishi) is a Japanese corporation that manufactures automobiles and has its principal place of business in Tokyo, Japan. Soler Chrysler-Plymouth, Inc. (Soler), is a Puerto Rican corporation with its principal place of business in Puerto Rico. On October 31, 1979, Soler entered into a sales and distributor agreement that gave Soler the right to sell Mitsubishi-manufactured automobiles within a designated area, including metropolitan San Juan. The agreement included an arbitration clause that stipulated, "All disputes, controversies, or differences which may arise between the parties out of this Agreement or for the breach thereof, shall be finally settled by arbitration in Japan in accordance with the rules and regulations of the Japan Commercial Arbitration Association." Initially, Soler did a brisk business in Mitsubishi-manufactured vehicles. In early 1981, the new-car market slackened, and Soler ran into serious difficulties in meeting the agreed-upon minimum sales volume. Soler repudiated its agreement with Mitsubishi. Mitsubishi requested arbitration before the Japan Commercial Arbitration Association and brought an action in U.S. district court in Puerto Rico for an order compelling arbitration. Soler filed a cross-complaint, alleging that Mitsubishi violated U.S. antitrust laws. The district court held that all claims were subject to arbitration. The court of appeals reversed as to the **antitrust claims**. Mitsubishi appealed to the U.S. Supreme Court, arguing that issues involving U.S. antitrust laws are subject to arbitration by an arbitration panel located in a foreign country.

The U.S. Supreme Court agreed with Mitsubishi and held that issues involving U.S. antitrust laws may be arbitrated by a foreign arbitration panel, it ordered the arbitration agreement between Soler and Mitsubishi enforced. The Supreme Court noted that by agreeing to arbitrate a statutory claim, a party does not forgo the substantive rights afforded by the statute; it only submits to their resolution in an arbitral, rather than a judicial, forum. It trades the procedures and opportunity for review of the courtroom for the simplicity, informality, and expedition of arbitration. In upholding international arbitration of the antitrust claims, the Supreme Court noted,

> The expansion of American business and industry will hardly be encouraged if, notwithstanding solemn contracts, we insist on a parochial concept that all disputes must be resolved under our laws and in our courts. We cannot have trade and commerce in world markets and international waters exclusively on our terms, governed by our laws, and resolved in our courts. We conclude that concerns of international comity, respect for the capacities of foreign and transnational tribunals, and sensitivity to the need of the international commercial system for predictability in the resolution of disputes require that we enforce the parties' arbitration agreement. [*Mitsubishi Motors Corporation v. Soler Chrysler-Plymouth, Inc., 473 U.S. 614, 105 S.Ct. 3346 (1985)*] ■

Criminal Prosecutions in the International Arena

extradition

The act of sending a person back to a country for criminal prosecution.

A nation has authority to criminally prosecute individuals or businesses that commit crimes within its territory or that violate that nation's laws, as well as its citizens (including businesses) that commit crimes elsewhere. One of the main problems of criminal prosecution, however, is that the perpetrator may be taking refuge in another country. In such cases, the person may be extradited (sent back) to the country seeking to criminally try him or her. The United States has entered into **extradition treaties** with many countries. If the perpetrator is not extradited, the crime may go unpunished.

International Law

Jewish Law and the Torah

Jewish law, which has existed for centuries, is a complex legal system based on ideology and theology of the Torah. The Torah prescribes comprehensive and integrated rules of religious, political, and legal life that together form Jewish thought. Jewish law is decided by rabbis who are scholars of the Torah and other Jewish scriptures. Rabbinic jurisprudence, known as **Halakhah**, is administered by rabbi-judges sitting as the **Beis Din**, Hebrew for the "house of judgment." As a court, the *Beis Din* has roots that go back 3,000 years.

Today, Jews are citizens of countries worldwide. As such, they are subject to the criminal and civil laws of their host countries. But Jews, no matter where they live, abide by the principles of the Torah in many legal matters, such as marriage, divorce, inheritance, and other family matters. Thus, the legal principles embedded in the Torah coexist with the secular laws of Jews' home countries.

The rabbinical judges tend to be actively involved in cases. True to its roots, the *Beis Din* is more a search for the truth than it is an adversarial process. ■

The legal principles in the Torah coexist with the secular laws of many countries.

International Law

Islamic Law and the Koran

Approximately 20 percent of the world's population is Muslim. Islam is the principal religion of Afghanistan, Algeria, Bangladesh, Egypt, Indonesia, Iran, Iraq, Jordan, Kuwait, Libya, Malaysia, Mali, Mauritania, Morocco, Niger, North Yemen, Oman, Pakistan, Qatar, Saudi Arabia, Somalia, South Yemen, Sudan, Syria, Tunisia, Turkey, and the United Arab Emirates. *Islamic law* (or *Shari'a*) is the only law in Saudi Arabia. In other Islamic countries, the *Shari'a* forms the basis of family law but coexists with other laws.

The Islamic law system is derived from the Koran, the Sunnah (decisions and sayings of the prophet Muhammad), and reasonings by Islamic scholars. By the tenth century A.D., Islamic scholars decided that no further improvement of the divine law could be made, closed the door of *ijtihad* (independent reasoning), and froze the evolution of Islamic law at that point. Islamic law prohibits *riba*, or the making of unearned or unjustified profit. Making a profit from the sale of goods or the provision of services is permitted. The most notable consequence of *riba* is that the payment of interest on loans is forbidden. To circumvent this result, the party with the money is permitted to purchase the item and resell it to the other party at a profit or to advance the money and become a trading partner who shares in the profits of the enterprise.

Today, Islamic law is primarily used in the areas of marriage, divorce, and inheritance and to a limited degree in criminal law. To resolve the tension between *Shari'a* and the practice of modern commercial law, the *Shari'a* is often ignored in commercial transactions. ■

International Law

Hindu Law—*Dharmasastra*

Over 20 percent of the world's population is Hindu. Most Hindus live in India, where they make up 80 percent of the population. Others live in Burma, Kenya, Malaysia, Pakistan, Singapore, Tanzania, and Uganda. *Hindu law* is a religious law. As such, individual Hindus apply this law to themselves, regardless of their nationality or place of domicile.

Classical Hindu law rests neither on civil codes nor on court decisions, but on the works of private scholars that were passed along for centuries by oral tradition and eventually were recorded in the *smitris* (law books). Hindu law—called *dharmasastra* in Sanskrit, that is, the doctrine of proper behavior—is linked to the divine revelation of Veda (the holy collection of Indian religious

International Law

(continued)

songs, prayers, hymns, and sayings written between 2000 and 1000 B.C.). Most Hindu law is concerned with family matters and the law of succession.

After India became a British colony, British judges applied a combination of Hindu law and common law in solving cases. This Anglo–Hindu law, as it was called, was ousted once India gained its independence. In the mid-1950s, India codified Hindu law by enacting the Hindu Marriage Act, the Hindu Minority and Guardianship Act, the Hindu Succession Act, and the Hindu Adoptions and Maintenance Act. Outside India, Anglo–Hindu law applies in most other countries populated by Hindus. ■

International Law

The Socialistic Law System

The youngest of the major legal systems in the world is the **Sino–Soviet socialist law system**, which applies to more than 30 percent of the people of the world. The Sino–Soviet theory of law is based on the philosophy of Karl Marx, which advocated the eradication of capitalism and the elimination of the private ownership of property. After the creation of the Soviet state following the Russian Revolution of 1917, Lenin replaced the old court system with a system of law meted out by workers, peasants, and the military. This legal nihilism (or absence of law) did not last long, and a formal legal system was restored pursuant to new criminal and civil law codes that promoted the socialist ideal. With its emphasis on codes, the Sino–Soviet legal system is a variant of the civil law.

Because private property in most respects is not permitted under Sino–Soviet law, the legal system comprises mostly public law. Therefore, property law, contract law, and business organization law (e.g., corporation and partnership law) that are prevalent in common law and civil law countries are not as important in Sino–Soviet law. Sino–Soviet public law preserves the authority of the state over property and the means of production.

As the republics of the now-dismantled Soviet Union and Eastern Bloc countries adopt free-market economies, Sino–Soviet public law is being replaced by laws establishing and protecting private property rights. Today, socialist law forms the basis of the legal systems of Angola, Cambodia, China, Cuba, Ethiopia, Guinea, Guyana, Laos, Libya, Mozambique, North Korea, Somalia, and Vietnam. But even Communist China is promoting capitalism and permitting individual ownership of property. This will require the development of business and property laws and the establishment of a court system to decide commercial and property-related disputes. ■

E-Commerce & Information Technology

Germany Becomes the World's E-Commerce Police

E-commerce—selling of products and services over the Internet—is exploding! American marketers, who are already used to compiling, maintaining, and selling lists of detailed information about customers and potential customers, welcome the ability not only to sell over the Internet but also to collect more detailed information about customer profiles. Now they can target sales pitches more accurately. Today, soon after a person subscribes to a magazine, he or she is inundated with advertising from myriad companies, often related to the subject of the new magazine. What has happened? The magazine has sold the new subscriber's name to companies, without the subscriber's permission. Compiling and selling customer lists is a very lucrative side business for many retailers. Companies also use "cross-marketing" to reach potential customers. For example, airlines commonly try to sell customers everything from car rentals to hotel services, to luxury goods.

In the United States, the compilation and selling of customer databases is all very legal. In the EU, however, as of October 25, 1998, the compilation and selling of consumer databases became highly regulated. Led by Germany, the EU, the world's largest economy, made up of many nations of Europe and surrounding areas, adopted the **European Union Directive on Data Protection**. This directive, which is law, establishes the following rules:

1. If a company wants personal information about an individual, it must get that person's permission after explaining what the information will be used for. For example, an airline would have to explain why it wants birth dates to distinguish one John Smith from another. A person can refuse to give the data.
2. Companies have to show customers their complete data profiles on demand, correct a profile if it is wrong, and delete it if it is objectionable.

3. Web site owners are not able to use "cookies," the data tags that hook into a login name, track the Web sites the user has explored, and send back consumer profiles.
4. Companies cannot engage in cross-marketing without customer permission.
5. A company cannot transmit personal data about EU citizens to users in other countries whose privacy laws do not meet EU standards.

Any company wanting to do business in any EU country has to abide by the law. Police from EU countries investigate companies to ensure that they abide by the directive, and companies and individuals may be prosecuted criminally for violating it. Citicorp, which issues credit cards in Europe, permits the Datenschutz—the German data police—to pay regular visits to its giant data-processing center in Sioux City, South Dakota, to ensure compliance with the new law. Other companies that wish to do business in the EU must do the same or be denied access to do business there.

This concerted directive from the EU attempts to dictate a norm for protecting privacy and e-commerce on the Internet to the rest of the world. The Germans argue that a global system requires global regulation to protect privacy rights, and they believe that the new directive accomplishes this goal. Regardless of whether the directive establishes a world standard, companies that want to do business in the EU must abide by its requirements. ■

The United States and Foreign Affairs, p. 243

The United States and Foreign Affairs

The following two provisions in the U.S. Constitution establish the federal government's authority to regulate international affairs:

1. ***Commerce Clause.*** Vests Congress with the power "to regulate commerce with foreign nations."
2. ***Treaty Clause.*** Gives the president the authority to enter into treaties with foreign nations, subject to a two-thirds vote of the Senate.

Sources of International Law, p. 245

Sources of International Law

1. ***Treaties and conventions.*** Agreements between nations that are formally ratified by the supreme power of each signatory nation. Conventions are treaties that are sponsored by international organizations (e.g., the United Nations).
2. ***Custom.*** Practices followed by two or more nations over a period of time when dealing with each other.
3. ***General principles of law.*** Principles of law that are common to the nations of the parties involved in a dispute.
4. ***Judicial decisions and teachings.*** Judicial decisions of national courts and teachings of the most qualified legal scholars of the nations of the parties involved in a dispute.

Principle of Comity

Courtesies granted by a nation to other nations that are not obligations of law but are based on respect, goodwill, and civility.

The United Nations, p. 247

The United Nations

Governance of the United Nations. An international organization located in New York City. Most countries of the world are members. Its goals are to maintain peace and security in the world, promote economic and social cooperation, and protect human rights.

International Regional Organizations, p. 250

Regional Economic Organizations

1. European Union (EU; formerly the Common Market)
2. Central American Common Market
3. MERCOSUR Common Market
4. Caribbean Community
5. Andean Common Market (ANCOM)
6. Economic Community of West African States (ECOWAS)
7. Economic and Customs Union of Central Africa
8. East African Community (EAC)
9. African Economic Community
10. Organization of Petroleum Exporting Countries (OPEC)
11. Gulf Cooperation Council
12. Association of South East Asian Nations (ASEAN)
13. North American Free Trade Agreement

The World Trade Organization (WTO), p. 254

World Trade Organization

World Trade Organization. An international organization headquartered in Geneva, Switzerland. Many countries of the world are members. Its goals are to limit tariff and trade restrictions and provide a mechanism for resolving trade disputes among its member nations.

Jurisdiction of National Courts to Decide International Disputes, p. 258

Principles of Judicial Restraint

National courts are limited by the following two principles of judicial restraint:

1. ***Act of state doctrine.*** States that judges of one country cannot question the validity of an act committed by another country *within* that other country's borders.
2. ***Doctrine of sovereign immunity.*** States that countries are granted immunity from suits in courts in other countries. Some countries provide for *absolute immunity*, and other countries (such as the United States) provide *qualified* or *restricted immunity. Exceptions*: The United States provides that a foreign country is not immune from lawsuits in U.S. courts if:
   a. The foreign country has *waived* its immunity.
   b. The foreign country has engaged in *commercial activity* in the United States or outside the United States that causes a direct effect in the United States.

International Arbitration, p. 261

International Arbitration

1. ***Arbitration.*** A nonjudicial method of dispute resolution whereby a neutral third party decides the case.
2. ***Arbitration clauses.*** Clauses included in many international contracts that require arbitration of disputes arising from the contract.

Criminal Prosecutions in the International Arena, p. 262

Criminal Prosecutions in the International Arena

Extradition treaty. A treaty between nations that provides a procedure for sending a person located in one country back to another country that seeks to criminally prosecute that person.

Internet Exercises and Case Questions

Working the Web Internet Exercises

Activities

1. Go to Hieros Gamos at **www.hg.org**. It is a huge international law site that contains laws from 230 countries in more than 50 languages. Look at the list of countries and review the legal structure of Afghanistan.
2. Go to **travel.state.gov/judicial_assistance.html**. Check on the procedures for enforcement of judgments in foreign countries. Why are there no treaties or conventions that make enforcement of U.S. judgments easier?
3. Survey the alternative dispute resolution (ADR) material at **search.info.usaid.gov**. What are some of the particular advantages to using ADR in other countries?
4. For an outstanding online lecture on many international law topics, visit **www.august1.com/pubs**. It contains outlines and online lectures from Professor Ray August.

Critical Legal Thinking Cases

9.1 Act of State Doctrine Prior to 1918, the Petrograd Metal Works, a Russian corporation, deposited a large sum of money with August Belmont, a private banker doing business in New York City under the name August Belmont & Co. (Belmont). In 1918, the Soviet government nationalized the corporation and appropriated all its property and assets wherever situated, including the deposit account with Belmont. As a result, the deposit became the property of the Soviet government. In 1933, the Soviet government and the United States entered into an agreement to settle claims and counterclaims between them. As part of the settlement, it was agreed that the Soviet government would take no steps to enforce claims against American nationals (including Belmont) and assigned all such claims to the United States. The United States brought this action against the executors of Belmont's estate to recover the money originally deposited with Belmont by Petrograd Metal Works. Who owns the money? [*United States v. Belmont*, 301 U.S. 324, 57 S.Ct. 758, 1937 U.S. Lexis 293 (1937)]

9.2 Act of State Doctrine Banco Nacional de Costa Rica is a bank wholly owned by the government of Costa Rica. It is subject to the rules and regulations adopted by the minister of finance and the central bank of Costa Rica. In December 1980, the bank borrowed $40 million from a consortium of private banks located in the United Kingdom and the United States. The bank signed promissory notes agreeing to repay the principal plus interest on the loan in four equal installments due on July 30, August 30, September 30, and October 30, 1981. The money was to be used to provide export financing of sugar and sugar products from Costa Rica. The loan agreements and promissory notes were signed in New York City, and the loan proceeds were tendered to the bank there.

On July 30, 1981, the bank paid the first installment on the loan. The bank did not, however, make the other three installment payments and defaulted on the loan. The lending banks sued the bank in U.S. district court in New York to recover the unpaid principal and interest. The bank alleged in defense that on August 27, 1981, the minister of finance and the central bank of Costa Rica issued a decree forbidding the repayment of loans by the bank to private lenders, including the lending banks in this case. The action was taken because Costa Rica was having trouble servicing debts to foreign creditors. The bank alleged that the act of state doctrine prevented the plaintiffs from recovering on their loans to the bank. Who wins? [*Libra Bank Limited v. Banco Nacional de Costa Rica*, 570 F.Supp. 870, 1983 U.S. Dist. Lexis 14677 (S.D.N.Y. 1983)]

9.3 Forum-Selection Clause Zapata Off-Shore Company is a Houston, Texas–based American corporation that engages in drilling oil wells throughout the world. Unterweser Reederei, GMBH, is a German corporation that provides ocean shipping and towing services. In November 1967, Zapata requested bids from companies to tow its self-elevating drilling rig "Chaparral" from Louisiana to a point off Ravenna, Italy, in the Adriatic Sea, where Zapata had agreed to drill certain wells. Unterweser submitted the lowest bid and was requested to submit a proposed contract to Zapata, which it did. The contract submitted by Unterweser contained the following provision: "Any dispute arising must be treated before the London Court of Justice." Zapata executed the contract without deleting or modifying this provision.

On January 5, 1968, Unterweser's deep sea tug *Bremen* departed Venice, Louisiana, with the Chaparral in tow, bound for Italy. On January 9, while the flotilla was in international waters in the middle of the Gulf of Mexico, a severe storm arose. The sharp roll of the Chaparral in Gulf waters caused portions of it to break off and fall into the sea, seriously damaging the Chaparral. Zapata instructed the *Bremen* to tow the Chaparral to Tampa, Florida, the nearest port of refuge, which it did. On January 12, Zapata filed suit against Unterweser and the *Bremen* in U.S. district court in Florida, alleging negligent towing and breach of contract. The defendants assert that suit can be brought only in the London Court of Justice. Who is correct? [*M/S Bremen and Unterweser Reederei, GMBH v. Zapata Off-Shore Company*, 407 U.S. 1, 92 S.Ct. 1907, 1972 U.S. Lexis 114 (1972)]

9.4 International Arbitration Alberto-Culver Company is an American company that is incorporated in Delaware and has its principal office in Illinois. It manufactures and distributes toiletries and hair care products in the United States and other countries. Fritz Scherk owned three interrelated businesses organized under the laws of Germany and Liechtenstein that were engaged in the manufacture of toiletries. After substantial negotiations, in February 1969, Alberto-Culver entered into a contract with Scherk to purchase his three companies, along with all rights held by these companies to trademarks in cosmetic goods. The contract contained a number of express warranties whereby Scherk guaranteed the sole and unencumbered ownership of these trademarks. The contract also contained a clause that provided that "any controversy or claim that shall arise out of this agreement or breach thereof" was to be referred to arbitration before the International Chamber of Commerce in Paris, France. The transaction closed in June 1969 in Geneva, Switzerland.

Nearly one year later, Alberto-Culver allegedly discovered that the trademark rights purchased under the contract were subject to substantial encumbrances that threatened to give other parties superior rights to the trademarks and to restrict or preclude Alberto-Culver's use of them. Alberto-Culver sued Scherk in U.S. district court in Illinois, alleging fraudulent misrepresentation in violation of Section 10(b) of the federal Securities Exchange Act of 1934. Scherk asserts in defense that the case is subject to mandatory arbitration in Paris. Who is correct? [*Scherk v. Alberto-Culver Co.*, 417 U.S. 506, 94 S.Ct. 2249, 1974 U.S. Lexis 73 (1974)]

Business Ethics Cases

9.5 Business Ethics Bank of Jamaica is wholly owned by the government of Jamaica. Chisholm & Co. is a Florida corporation that is owned by James Henry Chisholm, a Florida resident. The United States Export-Import Bank (Eximbank) provides financial services and credit insurance to export and import companies. In January 1982, the Bank of Jamaica and Chisholm & Co. agreed that Chisholm & Co. would arrange lines of credit from various banks and procure $50 million of credit insurance from Eximbank to be available to aid Jamaican importers. Chisholm & Co. was to be paid commissions for its services.

Chisholm & Co. negotiated and arranged for $50 million of credit insurance from Eximbank and lines of credit from Florida National Bank, Bankers Trust Company, and Irving Trust Company. Chisholm also arranged meetings between the Bank of Jamaica and the American banks. Unbeknownst to Chisholm & Co., the Bank of Jamaica went directly to Eximbank to exclude Chisholm & Co. from the Jamaica program and requested that the credit insurance be issued solely in the name of the Bank of Jamaica. As a result, Chisholm & Co.'s Eximbank insurance application was not considered. The Bank of Jamaica also obtained lines of credit from other companies and paid them commissions. Chisholm & Co. sued the Bank of Jamaica in the U.S. district court in Miami, Florida, alleging breach of contract and seeking damages. The Bank of Jamaica filed a motion to dismiss the complaint, alleging that its actions were protected by sovereign immunity. Who wins? Did the Bank of Jamaica act ethically in trying to avoid its contract obligations? [*Chisholm & Co. v. Bank of Jamaica*, 643 F.Supp. 1393, 1986 U.S. Dist. Lexis 20789 (S.D.Fla. 1986)]

9.6 Business Ethics Nigeria, an African nation, while in the midst of a boom period due to oil exports, entered into $1 billion of contracts with various countries to purchase huge quantities of Portland cement. Nigeria was going to use the cement to build and improve the country's infrastructure. Several of the contracts were with American companies, including Texas Trading & Milling Corporation (Texas Trading). Nigeria substantially overbought cement, and the country's docks and harbors became clogged with ships waiting to unload. Unable to accept delivery of the cement it had bought, Nigeria repudiated many of its contracts, including the one with Texas Trading. When Texas Trading sued Nigeria in a U.S. district court to recover damages for breach of contract, Nigeria asserted in defense that the doctrine of sovereign immunity protected it from liability. Who wins? [*Texas Trading & Milling Corp. v. Federal Republic of Nigeria*, 647 F.2d 300, 1981 U.S. App. Lexis 14231 (2nd Cir. 1981)]

Briefing the Case Writing Assignment

Read Case A.9 in the Case Appendix [*OHG v. Kolodny*]. This case is excerpted from the court's opinion. Review and brief the case. In your brief, be sure to answer the following questions.

1. In the German action, who was the plaintiff? Who was the defendant?
2. Who was the plaintiff in the New York action? Who was the defendant?
3. What was the decision of the German court? Would the decision under New York law have been different? Explain.
4. What was the plaintiff's argument to the New York court? Explain.
5. Did the enforcement of the German judgment violate New York's public policy?

Answers to Management Decision Questions

1. The association can encourage the government to prosecute U.S.-owned companies that violate U.S. anti-boycotting legislation. Congress has passed legislation, including the Export Administration Act of 1979 (EAA), that prohibits companies from complying with certain boycott-related requests. The EAA makes it unlawful to participate in another country's boycott of a country that in its own right is not subject to a U.S.-sponsored boycott. This law applies to "all U.S. persons." If American companies doing business in the U.S. or subsidiaries of American companies doing business in France comply with the boycott, they can be prosecuted in U.S. federal courts. "Primary boycotts" are allowed. It is "secondary boycotts that are illegal." This law would not apply to French-owned companies. Any attempt to file a complaint in the French courts would probably be futile.

2. The United States and the United Nations have supported sanctions and boycotts against Cuba and Iraq for many years. France can use these two situations to support the boycott. Furthermore, a country generally is free to decide whether to trade with another country. To be effective, any action by the association on the international level to end the French boycott should be coordinated through the U.S. government. Countries often grant courtesies to other countries that are not obligations of law but are based on respect, goodwill, and civility. The extension of such courtesies is referred to as the *principle of comity*. Your association can lobby its Congressional delegation to encourage the U.S. government to negotiate with the French based on the principle of comity in order to get the French to abandon its boycott of Wisconsin cheese. The United States can also address this issue through its ambassador to the United Nations.

France is a member of the European Union (EU). The United States entered into bilateral agreements of cooperation with the EU in 1991 and 1998, calling for positive comity between the countries. Thus, the United States can also solicit action on the part of the EU to either declare the French boycott illegal or to pressure France to abandon its boycott.

One of the primary functions of the World Trade Organization (WTO) is to hear and decide trade disputes between member nations. France and the United States are members of the WTO. A member nation that believes that another member nation has breached one of its agreements with a member nation can initiate proceedings to have the WTO hear and decide the case. If the offending nation refuses to abide by the order, the WTO can order retaliatory trade sanctions (e.g., tariffs) by other member nations against the noncomplying nation.

Endnotes

1. The Charter of the United Nations was entered into force on October 24, 1945; it was adopted by the United States on October 24, 1945 [59 Stat. 1031, T.S. 993, 3 Bevans 1153, 1976 Y.B.U.N. 1043].
2. 301 U.S. 324, 57 S.Ct. 758, 1937 U.S. Lexis 293 (1937).
3. 28 U.S.C. §§ 1602–1611.
4. 21 U.S.T. 2517, T.I.A.S. 6997.
5. 9 U.S.C. §§ 201–208.

10

Formation of Traditional and Online Contracts

"The movement of the progressive societies has hitherto been a movement from status to contract."

—Sir Henry Maine
Ancient Law, Ch. 5

Chapter Objectives

After studying this chapter, you should be able to:

1. List the elements necessary to form a valid contract.
2. Describe and distinguish among valid, void, voidable, and unenforceable contracts.
3. Define offer and acceptance.
4. Define consideration and analyze whether contracts are lacking in consideration.
5. Identify illegal contracts that are contrary to statutes and that violate public policy.

Chapter Contents

Management Decision Formation of Traditional and Online Contracts

You are a graduate student majoring in computer programming. After years of trial and error, you have authored a program that will allow an individual to download music to your computer instead of having to buy the more expensive CD-ROMs. You are considering asking several of your classmates to test the program for flaws. However, you are concerned about possible misuse and piracy of your software. The potential for purchase of this program by a major software distributor is assured. Before meeting with your classmates, you are considering contacting an attorney.

1. What can you do to protect your rights in this software?
2. What should you do once the program is ready for marketing?

Contracts are the basis of many of our daily activities. They provide the means for individuals and businesses to sell and otherwise transfer property, services, and other rights. The purchase of goods, such as books and automobiles, is based on sales contracts; the hiring of employees is based on service contracts; and the lease of an apartment is based on a rental contract. The list is almost endless. Without enforceable contracts, commerce would collapse.

Contracts are voluntarily entered into by parties. The terms of the contract become **private law** between the parties. One court has stated that "The contract between parties is the law between them and the courts are obliged to give legal effect to such contracts according to the true interests of the parties."[1]

This chapter introduces you to the study of contract law. Such topics as the definition of *contract* and the requirements for forming a contract are discussed.

The law has outgrown its primitive stage of formalism when the precise word was the sovereign talisman, and every slip was fatal. It takes a broader view today. A promise may be lacking, and yet the whole writing may be "instinct with an obligation," imperfectly expressed.

Justice Cardozo
Wood v. Duff-Gordon, 222 N.Y. 88, 91 (1917)

Marrakech, Morocco. Entering into contracts supports business and commerce worldwide.

Definition of Contract

A contract is an agreement that is enforceable by a court of law or equity. A simple and widely recognized definition of a contract is provided by the *Restatement (Second) of Contracts*: "A contract is a promise or a set of promises for the breach of which the law gives a remedy or the performance of which the law in some way recognizes a duty."[2]

Parties to a Contract

offeror
The party who makes an offer to enter into a contract.

offeree
The party to whom an offer to enter into a contract is made.

Every contract involves at least two parties. The **offeror** is the party who makes an offer to enter into a contract. The **offeree** is the party to whom the offer is made (see Exhibit 10.1). In making an offer, the offeror promises to do—or to refrain from doing—something. The offeree then has the power to create a contract by accepting the offeror's offer. A contract is created if the offer is accepted. No contract is created if the offer is not accepted.

Contemporary Business Environment

The Evolution of Modern Law of Contracts

The use of contracts originally developed in ancient times. The common law of contracts developed in England around the fifteenth century. American contract law evolved from the English common law.

At first, the United States adopted a *laissez-faire* approach to the law of contracts. The central theme of this theory was *freedom of contract*. The parties (such as consumers, shopkeepers, farmers, and traders) generally dealt with one another face-to-face, had equal knowledge and bargaining power, and had the opportunity to inspect the goods prior to sale. Contract terms were openly negotiated. There was little, if any, government regulation of the right to contract. This "pure" or **classical law of contracts** produced objective rules, which, in turn, produced certainty and predictability in the enforcement of contracts. It made sense until the Industrial Revolution.

The Industrial Revolution changed many of the underlying assumptions of pure contract law. For example, as large corporations developed and gained control of crucial resources, the traditional balance of parties' bargaining power shifted: Large corporations now had the most power. The chain of distribution for goods also changed because (1) buyers did not have to deal face-to-face with sellers and (2) there was not always an opportunity to inspect the goods prior to sale.

Eventually, sellers began using *form contracts* that offered their goods to buyers on a take-it-or-leave-it basis. The majority of contracts in this country today are form contracts. Automobile contracts, mortgage contracts, sales contracts for consumer goods, and such are examples of form contracts.

Both federal and state governments enacted statutes intended to protect consumers, creditors, and others from unfair contracts. In addition, the courts began to develop certain common law legal theories that allowed some oppressive or otherwise unjust contracts to be avoided. Today, under this **modern law of contracts**, there is substantial government regulation of the right to contract. ■

Exhibit 10.1
Parties to a Contract

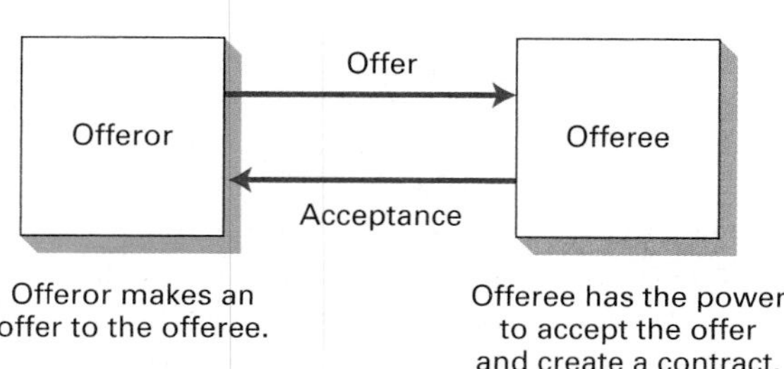
Offer
Offeror
Offeree
Acceptance
Offeror makes an offer to the offeree.
Offeree has the power to accept the offer and create a contract.

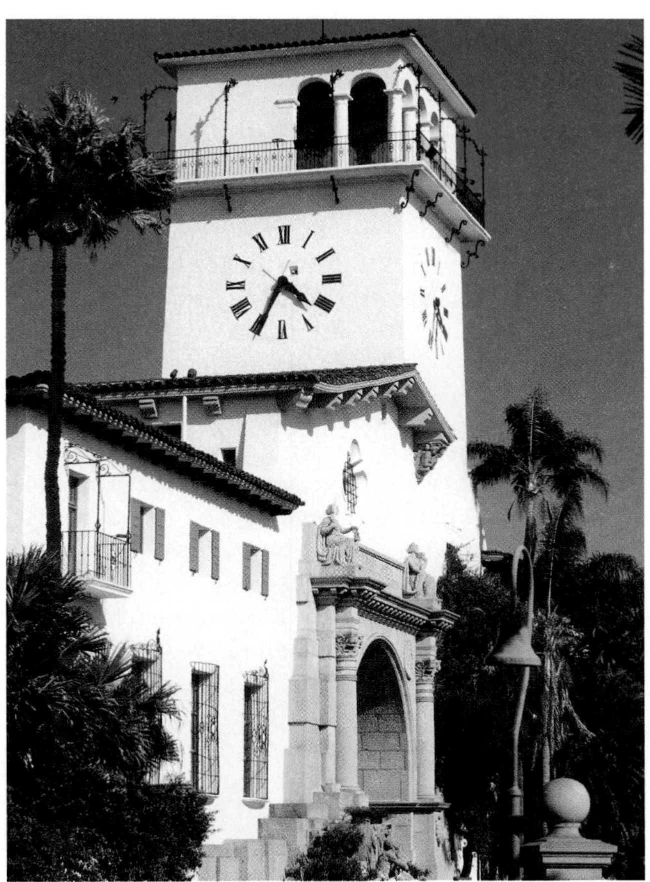

Courthouse, Santa Barbara, California. Courts are often called upon to enforce contracts between contracting parties.

Classifications of Contracts

There are several types of contracts, and they differ somewhat in formation, enforcement, performance, and discharge. The different types of contracts are discussed in the following paragraphs.

Bilateral and Unilateral Contracts

Contracts are either *bilateral* or *unilateral*, depending on what the offeree must do to accept the offeror's offer. The contract is **bilateral** if the offeror's promise is answered with the offeree's promise of acceptance. In other words, a bilateral contract is a "promise for a promise." This exchange of promises creates an enforceable contract. No act of performance is necessary to create a bilateral contract.

bilateral contract

A contract entered into by way of exchange of promises of the parties, a "promise for a promise."

A contract is **unilateral** if the offeror's offer can be accepted only by the performance of an act by the offeree. There is no contract until the offeree performs the requested act. An offer to create a unilateral contract cannot be accepted by a promise to perform. It is a "promise for an act."

unilateral contract

A contract in which the offeror's offer can be accepted only by the performance of an act by the offeree, a "promise for an act."

Consider These Examples Suppose Mary Douglas, the owner of the Chic Dress Shop, says to Peter Jones, a painter, "If you promise to paint my store by July 1, I will pay you $2,000." Peter promises to do so. A bilateral contract was created at the moment Peter promised to paint the dress shop (a promise for a promise). If Peter fails to paint the store, he can be sued for whatever damages result from his breach of contract. Similarly, Peter can sue Mary if she refuses to pay him after he has performed as promised.

Business Brief

Bilateral and unilateral contracts are distinguished according to the number of promises involved. Bilateral is "promise for promise." Unilateral is "promise for act."

Law cannot stand aside from the social changes around it.
William J. Brennan, Jr.

However, if Mary had said, "If you paint my shop by July 1, I will pay you $2,000," the offer would have created a unilateral contract. The offer can be accepted only by the painter's performance of the requested act. If Peter does not paint the shop by July 1, there has been no acceptance and the painter cannot be sued for damages.

Problems can arise if the offeror of a unilateral contract attempts to revoke an offer after the offeree has begun performance. Generally, an offer to create a unilateral contract can be revoked by the offeror anytime prior to the offeree's performance of the requested act. However, the offer cannot be revoked if the offeree has begun or substantially completed performance. For example, suppose Alan Matthews tells Sherry Levine that he will pay her $5,000 if she finishes the Boston Marathon. Alan cannot revoke the offer once Sherry starts running the marathon.

objective theory of contracts
A theory that says that the intent to contract is judged by the reasonable person standard and not by the subjective intent of the parties.

Objective Theory of Contracts The **objective theory of contracts** holds that the intent to enter into an express or implied-in-fact contract is judged by the **reasonable person standard**. Would a hypothetical reasonable person conclude that the parties intended to create a contract after considering (1) the words and conduct of the parties and (2) the surrounding circumstances? For example, no valid contract results from offers that are made in jest, anger, or undue excitement.

Under the objective theory of contracts, the subjective intent of a party to enter into a contract is irrelevant. The following case illustrates the application of the objective theory of contracts.

Case 10.1 Objective Theory of Contracts

City of Everett, Washington v. Mitchell
631 P.2d 366, 1981 Wash. Lexis 1139 (1981)
Supreme Court of Washington

Background and Facts

Al and Rosemary Mitchell owned a small secondhand store. On August 12, 1978, the Mitchells attended Alexander's Auction, where they frequently shopped to obtain merchandise for their business. While at the auction, they purchased a used safe for $50. They were told by the auctioneer that the inside compartment of the safe was locked and that no key could be found to unlock it. The safe was part of the Sumstad Estate. Several days after the auction, the Mitchells took the safe to a locksmith to have the locked compartment opened. When the locksmith opened the compartment, he found $32,207 in cash. The locksmith called the City of Everett Police, who impounded the money. The City of Everett commenced an interpleader action against the Sumstad Estate and the Mitchells. The trial court entered summary judgment in favor of Sumstad Estate. The court of appeals affirmed. The Mitchells appealed.

Issue

Was a contract formed between the seller and the buyer of the safe?

In The Language of The Court

Dolliver, Justice The objective manifestation theory of contracts lays stress on the outward manifestation of assent made by each party to the other. The subjective intention of the parties is irrelevant. A contract is an obligation attached by the mere force of law to certain acts of the parties, usually words, which ordinarily accompany and represent a known intent. If, however, it were proved by twenty bishops that either party, when he used the words intended something else than the usual meaning which the law imposes upon them, he would still be held.

The Mitchells were aware of the rule of the auction that all sales were final. Furthermore, the auctioneer made no statement reserving rights to any contents of the safe to the Estate. Under these circumstances, we hold reasonable persons would conclude that the auctioneer manifested an objective intent to sell the safe and its contents and that the parties mutually assented to enter into that sale of the safe and the contents of the locked compartment.

Decision and Remedy

The state supreme court held that under the objective theory of contracts, a contract was formed between the seller and the buyer of the safe. The court reversed the court of appeals' grant of summary judgment to the Sumstad Estate and remanded the case to the trial court for entry of judgment in favor of the Mitchells.

Case Questions

Critical Legal Thinking Does the objective theory of contracts work? Is it easy to define a *reasonable person*?

Business Ethics Did the seller of the safe act ethically in alleging that no contract had been made with the Mitchells?

Contemporary Business What do you think the economic consequences to business would be if the courts recognized a subjective theory of contracts?

Express and Implied Contracts

An **actual contract** (as distinguished from a quasi-contract, which is discussed later in this chapter) may be either *express* or *implied-in-fact*:

- **Express contracts** are stated in oral or written words. Examples of such contracts include an oral agreement to purchase a neighbor's bicycle and a written agreement to buy an automobile from a dealership.
- **Implied-in-fact contracts** are implied from the conduct of the parties. Implied-in-fact contracts leave more room for questions than express contracts.

express contract
An agreement that is expressed in written or oral words.

implied-in-fact contract
A contract in which agreement between parties has been inferred from their conduct.

Requirements for an Implied-in-Fact Contract The following elements must be established to create an implied-in-fact contract:

1. The plaintiff provided property or services to the defendant.
2. The plaintiff expected to be paid by the defendant for the property or services and did not provide the property or services gratuitously.
3. The defendant was given an opportunity to reject the property or services provided by the plaintiff but failed to do so.

Web Site
FindLaw FindLaw is a search engine that will help you find lots of legal information, including information on contracts. Visit at **www.findlaw.com**.

Entrepreneur and the Law

Owner of Scrabble Spelled "L-O-S-E-R"

Implied-in-fact contracts are implied from the conduct of the parties. Consider the following case.

Selchow & Richter (S&R) owns the trademark to the famous board game *Scrabble*. Mark Landsberg wrote a book on strategy for winning at *Scrabble* and contacted S&R to request permission to use the Scrabble trademark. In response, S&R requested a copy of Landsberg's manuscript, which he provided. After prolonged negotiations between the parties regarding the possibility of S&R's publication of the manuscript broke off, S&R brought out its own *Scrabble* strategy book. No express contract was ever entered into between Landsberg and S&R. Landsberg sued S&R and its subsidiary, Scrabble Crossword Game Players, Inc., for damages for breach of an implied contract.

Was there an implied-in-fact contract between the parties?

The district court and appellate court held that an implied-in-fact contract had been formed between the parties and that the contract was breached by the defendants. The court noted that the law allows for recovery for the breach of an implied-in-fact contract when the recipient of a valuable idea accepts and uses the information without paying for it, even though he knows that compensation is expected. Here, the court found that (1) Landsberg's disclosure of his manuscript was confidential and for the limited purpose of obtaining approval for the use of the *Scrabble* mark, and (2) given Landsberg's express intention to exploit his manuscript commercially, the defendant's use of any portion of it was conditioned on payment. Landsberg was awarded $440,300 in damages. ■

Quasi-Contracts (Implied-in-Law Contracts)

The equitable doctrine of **quasi-contract**, also called **implied-in-law contract**, provides that the court may award monetary damages to a plaintiff for providing work or services to a defendant even though no actual contract existed between the parties. This doctrine, which is intended to prevent *unjust enrichment* and *unjust detriment*, does not apply where there is an enforceable contract between the parties. In addition, recovery is generally based on the reasonable value of the services received by the defendant.

A quasi-contract is imposed where (1) one person confers a benefit on another, who retains the benefit, and (2) it would be unjust not to require that person to pay for the benefit received.

quasi-contract
An equitable doctrine whereby a court may award monetary damages to a plaintiff for providing work or services to a defendant even though no actual contract existed.

Ethics Brief
The doctrine of quasi-contract is intended to prevent unjust enrichment and unjust detriment.

Executed and Executory Contracts

executed contract

A contract that has been fully performed on both sides; a completed contract.

executory contract

A contract that has not been fully performed by either or both sides.

A completed contract—that is, one that has been fully performed on both sides—is called an **executed contract**. A contract that has not been performed by both sides is called an **executory contract**. Contracts that have been fully performed by one side but not by the other are classified as executory contracts.

Consider These Examples (1) Suppose Elizabeth Andrews signs a contract to purchase a new Jaguar automobile from Ace Motors. She has not yet paid for the car, and Ace Motors has not yet delivered it. This is an executory contract. (2) Assume that the car was paid for but Ace Motors has not yet delivered the car. Here, the contract is executed by Elizabeth but is executory as to Ace Motors. This is an executory contract. (3) Assume that Ace Motors now delivers the car to Elizabeth. The contract has been fully performed by both parties. It is an executed contract.

Contemporary Business Environment

Owner of *Mighty Morphin Power Rangers* Battles Logo Designer

Mighty Morphin Power Rangers was a phenomenal success as a television series. The Power Rangers battled to save the universe from all sorts of diabolical plots and bad guys. They were also featured in a profitable line of toys and garments bearing the Power Rangers' logo. The Power Rangers' name and logo are known to millions of children and their parents worldwide. The claim of ownership of the logo for the Power Rangers ended up in a battle itself, this time in a courtroom.

David Dees is a designer who works as d/b/a David Dees Illustration. Saban Entertainment, Inc. (Saban), which owns the copyright and trademark to Power Ranger figures and the name "Power Ranger," hired Dees as an independent contractor to design a logo for the Power Rangers. The contract signed by the parties was titled "Work-for-Hire/Independent Contractor Agreement." The contract was drafted by Saban with the help of its attorneys; Dees signed the agreement without the representation of legal counsel.

Dees designed the logo currently used for the Power Rangers and was paid $250 to transfer his copyright ownership in the logo. Subsequently, Dees sued Saban to recover damages for copyright and trademark infringement. Saban defended, arguing that a contract is a contract is a contract, and Dees was bound by the agreement he had signed.

The trial court agreed with Saban, finding that the "Work-for-Hire/Independent Contractor Agreement" was an enforceable contract between the parties and that Dees had transferred his ownership interests in the logo to Saban. Dees appealed. The court of appeals affirmed the judgment for Saban, stating, "The disputed agreement transferred plaintiff's copyright in the Mighty Morphin Power Rangers' logo with as much specificity as the law requires." The court found that a contract is a contract is a contract, at least in this case. Dees's appeal to the U.S. Supreme Court was denied. [*Dees, d/b/a David Dees Illustration v. Saban Entertainment, Inc.*, 131 F.3d 146, 1997 U.S. App. Lexis 39173 (1997)] ■

Valid, Void, Voidable, and Unenforceable Contracts

valid contract

A contract that meets all the essential elements to establish a contract; a contract that is enforceable by at least one of the parties.

void contract

A contract that has no legal effect; a nullity.

voidable contract

A contract in which one or both parties have the option to void their contractual obligations.

A **valid contract** is one that meets all of the essential elements to establish a contract. In other words, it must (1) consist of an agreement between the parties, (2) be supported by legally sufficient consideration, (3) be between parties with contractual capacity, and (4) accomplish a lawful object. Valid contracts are enforceable by at least one of the parties.

A **void contract** is one that has no legal effect. It is as if no contract had ever been created. For example, a contract to commit a crime is void. If a contract is void, neither party is obligated to perform, and neither party can enforce the contract.

A **voidable contract** is one where at least one party has the *option* to void his or her contractual obligations. If the contract is voided, both parties are released from their obligations under the contract. If the party with the option chooses to ratify the contract, both parties must fully perform their obligations. With certain exceptions, contracts may be voided by minors, insane persons, intoxicated persons, persons acting under duress, undue influence, or fraud, and cases involving mutual mistake.

An **unenforceable contract** is one where there is some legal defense to the enforcement of the contract. For example, if a contract is required to be in writing under the Statute of Frauds but is not, the contract is unenforceable. The parties may voluntarily perform a contract that is unenforceable.

unenforceable contract
A contract in which the essential elements to create a valid contract are met but there is some legal defense to the enforcement of the contract.

Concept Summary Classifications of Contracts

Formation	1. **Bilateral contract** A promise for a promise. 2. **Unilateral contract** A promise for an act. 3. **Express contract** A contract expressed in oral or written words. 4. **Implied-in-fact contract** A contract inferred from the conduct of the parties. 5. **Formal contract** A contract that requires a special form or method of creation. 6. **Informal contract** A contract that requires no special form or method of creation. 7. **Quasi-contract** A contract implied by law to prevent unjust enrichment.
Enforceability	1. **Valid contract** A contract that meets all of the essential elements to establish a contract. 2. **Void contract** No contract exists. 3. **Voidable contract** A contract in which a party has the option of voiding or enforcing the contract. 4. **Unenforceable contract** A contract that cannot be enforced because of a legal defense.
Performance	1. **Executed contract** A contract that is fully performed on both sides. 2. **Executory contract** A contract that is not fully performed by one or both parties.

E-Commerce & Information Technology

Ready for Love? Not Before You've Been NDA'd

You're out on a date and your partner whispers sweet nothings in your ear. What's a guy or girl to do? Quick, whip out a **nondisclosure agreement**—or NDA, as they are called—and have the other side sign it before responding. That is what many entrepreneurs and techies are doing, having their boyfriends, girlfriends, family members, friends, and others sign NDAs before revealing anything about what they are doing.

NDAs have been around for a long time, and traditionally they have been used among lawyers, investment bankers, and others involved in secret takeovers and other large corporate deals. NDAs swear the signatory to secrecy about confidential ideas, trade secrets, and other nonpublic information revealed by the party proffering the NDA. But today many entrepreneurs, particularly those in high-tech industries, are handing out NDAs as fast as business cards. An NDA serves a purpose in that it protects a person who has a great idea (or so he thinks) and wants to share it with a potential partner, investor, lawyer, or investment banker, but wants an assurance that the recipient of the information will not steal or reveal the information to anyone else.

NDAs are enforceable contracts, so if someone violates one, the disclosing party can sue the breaching party for damages. Bill Gates of Microsoft has plumbers and other persons who work on his house sign NDAs. Sabeer Bhatia, the founder of Hotmail, collected more than 400 NDAs in two years before selling his company to Microsoft for $400 million.

Although it may not be hard to get some people to sign NDAs, others balk. Some friends and relatives refuse to sign NDAs thrust on them because they present an aura of distrust. And it is particularly insulting to sign an NDA and then to hear a harebrained idea from the disclosing party. Industry bigwigs—venture capitalists, securities analysts, and successful technology companies—routinely refuse to sign NDAs because they see too many similar ideas and do not want their tongues tied by any single one. NDAs will continue to increase in use, however. So the next time you are at a party and you ask someone what they do, don't be surprised if you are NDA'd! ■

Requirements of a Contract

Contracts must not be the sports of an idle hour, mere matters of pleasantry and badinage, never intended by the parties to have any serious effect whatever.

Lord Stowell
Dalrymple v. Dalrymple (1811)

To be an enforceable contract, the following four basic requirements must be met:

1. ***Agreement*** To have an enforceable contract, there must be an agreement between the parties.
2. ***Consideration*** The promise must be supported by a bargained-for consideration that is legally sufficient.
3. ***Contractual Capacity*** The parties to a contract must have contractual capacity.
4. ***Lawful Object*** The object of the contract must be lawful.

The following text discusses these requirements in greater detail.

Contemporary Business Environment

The Uniform Commercial Code (UCC)

One of the major frustrations of businesspersons conducting interstate business is that they are subject to the laws of each of the states in which they operate. To address this problem, in 1949 the National Conference of Commissioners on Uniform State Laws promulgated the **Uniform Commercial Code** (UCC). The UCC is a **model act** that contains uniform rules that govern commercial transactions. To create this uniformity, individual states needed to enact the UCC as their commercial law statute. In fact, they did, and every state (except Louisiana, which has adopted only parts of the UCC) enacted the UCC as a commercial statute.

The UCC is divided into articles, with each article establishing uniform rules for a particular facet of commerce in this country. The articles of the UCC are

Article 1	General provisions
Article 2	Sales
Article 2A Revised	Leases
Article 3	Negotiable instruments
Article 4	Bank deposits and collections
Article 4A	Wire transfers
Article 5	Letters of credit
Article 6	Bulk transfers
Article 7	Documents of title
Article 8	Investment securities
Article 9	Secured transactions

The UCC is continually being revised to reflect changes in modern commercial practices and technology. For example, Article 2A was drafted to govern leases of personal property, and Article 4A was added to regulate the use of wire transfers in the banking system. Articles 3 and 4, which cover the creation and transfer of negotiable instruments and the clearing of checks through the banking system, were substantially amended in 1990. Article 2, which covers the sale of goods, currently is in the initial stages of revision. ■

Agreement

agreement
The manifestation by two or more persons of the substance of a contract.

offer
"The manifestation of willingness to enter into a bargain, so made as to justify another person in understanding that his assent to that bargain is invited and will conclude it." [*Restatement (Second) of Contracts* § 24]

Agreement is the manifestation by two or more persons of the substance of a contract. It requires an *offer* and *acceptance*. The process of reaching an agreement usually proceeds as follows: Prior to entering into a contract, the parties may engage in preliminary negotiations about price, time of performance, and such. At some point during these negotiations, one party makes an **offer**. The person who makes the offer is called the **offeror**, and the person to whom the offer is made is called the **offeree**. The offer sets forth the terms under which the offeror is willing to enter into the contract. The offeree has the power to create an agreement by accepting the offer.

Requirements of the Offer

Section 24 of the *Restatement (Second) of Contracts* defines an **offer** as "The manifestation of willingness to enter into a bargain, so made as to justify another person in understanding that his assent to that bargain is invited and will conclude it." These three elements are required for an offer to be effective:

1. The offeror must *objectively intend* to be bound by the offer.
2. The terms of the offer must be definite or reasonably *certain.*
3. The offer must be *communicated* to the offeree.

Intention The intent to enter into a contract is determined by asking whether a reasonable person viewing the circumstances would conclude that the parties intended to be legally bound. Therefore, no valid contract results from preliminary negotiations. For example, a question such as "Are you interested in selling your building for $2 million?" is not an offer. It is an invitation to make an offer or an invitation to negotiate. However, the statement, "I will buy your building for $2 million" is a valid offer because it indicates the offeror's present intent to contract.

A contract is a mutual promise.

William Paley
The Principles of Moral and Political Philosophy (1784)

Definiteness The terms of an offer must be clear enough for the offeree to be able to decide whether to accept or reject the terms of the offer. If the terms are indefinite, the courts cannot enforce the contract or determine an appropriate remedy for its breach.

Generally, an offer (and contract) must contain the following terms: (1) identification of the parties, (2) identification of the subject matter and quantity, (3) consideration to be paid, and (4) time of performance. Complex contracts usually state additional terms.

Business Brief
It is always best to expressly state all the essential terms in a contract. This practice will prevent many lawsuits.

Communication An offer cannot be accepted if it is not communicated to the offeree by the offeror or a representative or an agent of the offeror. For example, suppose Mr. Jones, the CEO of Ace Corporation, decides to sell a manufacturing division to Baker Corporation and puts the offer in writing. Assume that the offer is on Mr. Jones's desk. Suppose Mr. Griswald, the CFO of Baker Corporation, sees the offer when he visits Mr. Jones. Griswald tells his CEO about the offer. The offer is not acceptable because Mr. Jones never communicated it to the CEO of Baker Corporation.

Freedom of contracts begins where equality of bargaining power begins.

Oliver Wendell Holmes, Jr.
(1928)

"Your offer's a crumpled little ball in the middle of my desk."

Termination of the Offer

A valid offer gives the offeree the power to accept the offer and thereby create a contract. This power, however, does not continue indefinitely. An offer can be determined by the *action of the parties* or by *operation of law.*

Termination by Action of the Parties Under the common law, an *offeror* may revoke (i.e., withdraw) an offer any time prior to its acceptance by the offeree. Generally, this is so even if the offeror promised to keep the offer open for a longer period of time. The **revocation** may be (1) communicated to the offeree either by the offeror or a third party and (2) made by the offeror's express statement (e.g., "I hereby withdraw my offer") or by an act of the offeror that is inconsistent with the offer (e.g., selling the goods to another party). Most states provide that the revocation is not effective until it is actually received by the offeree or the offeree's agent.

revocation
Withdrawal of an offer by the offeror that terminates an offer.

An offer is terminated if the *offeree* rejects it. Any subsequent attempt by the offeree to accept the offer is ineffective and is construed as a new offer that the original offeror (now the offeree) is free to accept or reject. A **rejection** may be evidenced by the offeree's express words (oral or written) or conduct. Generally, a rejection is not effective until it is actually received by the offeror.

rejection
Express words or conduct by the offeree that rejects an offer. Rejection terminates the offer.

Consider This Example Harriet Jackson, sales manager of XYZ Corporation, offers to sell 1,000 computers to Ted Green, purchasing manager of General Corporation, for $250,000. The offer is made on August 1. Mr. Green telephones Ms. Jackson to say that he is not interested. This rejection terminates the offer. If Mr. Green later decides that he wants to purchase the computers, an entirely new contract must be formed.

A **counteroffer** by the *offeree* simultaneously terminates the offeror's offer and creates a new offer. For example, suppose in the prior example Mr. Green responds, "I think $250,000 is too high for the computers. I will pay you $200,000." He has made a counteroffer. Ms. Jackson's original offer is terminated, and the counteroffer is a new offer by Mr. Green that Ms. Jackson is free to accept or reject.

counteroffer
A response by an offeree that contains terms and conditions different from or in addition to those of the offer. A counteroffer terminates an offer.

Termination by Operation of the Law Offers can be terminated by operation of law through a **lapse of time**, destruction of the subject matter, death or incompetence of the offeror or offeree, or a supervening illegality.

lapse of time
A stated time period after which an offer expires. If no time is stated, an offer terminates after a reasonable time.

Business Brief
Destruction of the subject matter terminates an offer, but it does not terminate the contract if the offer has already been accepted, however.

The offer may state that it is effective only until a certain date. Unless otherwise stated, the time period begins to run when the offer is actually received by the offeree and terminates when the stated time period expires. Statements such as "This offer is good for 10 days" and "This offer must be accepted by January 1, 2004," are examples of such notices. If no time is stated in the offer, the offer terminates after a "reasonable time" dictated by the circumstances. A reasonable time to accept an offer to purchase stock traded on a national stock exchange may be a few moments, but a reasonable time to accept an offer to purchase a house may be a few days. Unless otherwise stated, an offer made face-to-face or during a telephone call usually expires after the conversation.

The offer terminates if the subject matter of the offer is destroyed through no fault of either party to its acceptance. For example, if a fire destroys an office building that has been listed for sale, the offer automatically terminates.

The death or incompetency of either the offeror or the offeree terminates the offer. Notice of the other party's death or incompetence is not a requirement.

If prior to the acceptance of an offer the object of the offer is made illegal, the offer terminates. This usually occurs when a statute is enacted or a court case is announced that makes the object of the offer illegal. This is called a **supervening illegality**. For example, suppose City Bank offers to loan ABC Corporation $5 million at an 18 percent interest

supervening illegality
The enactment of a statute or regulation or court decision that makes the object of an offer illegal. This terminates the offer.

rate. Prior to ABC's acceptance of the offer, the state **legislature** enacts a statute that sets a usury interest rate of 12 percent. City Bank's offer to ABC Corporation automatically terminates when the usury statute becomes effective.

Entrepreneur and the Law

Option Contracts

An offeree can prevent the offeror from revoking his or her offer by paying the offeror compensation to keep the offer open for an agreed-upon period of time. This payment is called an **option contract**. In other words, the offeror agrees not to sell the property to anyone but the offeree during the option period. The death of incompetency of either party does not terminate an option contract unless it is for the performance of a personal service.

Consider This Example Anne Mason offers to sell a piece of real estate to Harold Greenberg for $1 million. Greenberg wants time to make a decision, so he pays Mason $20,000 to keep her offer open to him for six months. At any time during the option period, Greenberg may exercise his option and pay Mason the $1 million purchase price. If he lets the option expire, however, Mason may keep the $20,000 and sell the property to someone else. ■

Acceptance

Acceptance is a manifestation of assent by the offeree to the terms of the offer in a manner invited or required by the offer, as measured by the objective theory of contracts. Recall that generally (1) unilateral contracts can be accepted only by the offeree's performance of the required act and (2) a bilateral contract can be accepted by an offeree who promises to perform (or, where permitted, by performance of) the requested act.

acceptance
A manifestation of assent by the offeree to the terms of the offer in a manner invited or required by the offer, as measured by the objective theory of contracts [*Restatement (Second) of Contracts* § 50]

Only the offeree has the legal power to accept an offer and create a contract. Third persons do not usually have the power to accept an offer. If an offer is made individually to two or more persons, each has the power to accept the offer. Once an offeree accepts the offer, though, it terminates as to the other offerees. An offer that is made to two or more persons jointly must be accepted jointly.

Trees Reflected in Water, Idaho. The common law of contracts follows the mirror image rule of contracting: A contract is made if the offeree accepts the terms offered by the offeror.

mirror image rule
A rule that states that in order for there to be an acceptance, the offeree must accept the terms as stated in the offer.

Unequivocal Acceptance The offeree's acceptance must be **unequivocal**. The **mirror image rule** requires the offeree to accept the offeror's terms. Generally, a "grumbling acceptance" is a legal acceptance. For example, a response such as "Okay, I'll take the car, but I sure wish you would make me a better deal" creates an enforceable contract. An acceptance is equivocal if certain conditions are added to the acceptance. For example, suppose the offeree had responded, "I accept, but only if you repaint the car red." There is no acceptance in this case.

Concept Summary *Offer and Acceptance*

Communication by Offeror	Effective When
Offer	Received by offeree
Revocation of offer	Received by offeree
Communication by Offeree	**Effective When**
Rejection of offer	Received by offeror
Counteroffer	Received by offeror
Acceptance of offer	Sent by offeree
Acceptance after previous rejection of offer	Received by offeror

mailbox rule
A rule that states that an acceptance is effective when it is dispatched, even if it is lost in transmission.

Mailbox Rule Under the common law of contracts, acceptance of a bilateral contract occurs at the time the offeree *dispatches* the acceptance by an authorized means of communication. This is called the **acceptance-upon-dispatch rule** or, more commonly, the **mailbox rule**. Under this rule, the acceptance is effective when it is dispatched, even if it is lost in transmission. If an offeree first dispatches a rejection and then sends an acceptance, the mailbox rule does not apply to the acceptance.[3]

The problem of lost acceptances can be minimized by expressly altering the mailbox rule. The offeror can do this by stating in the offer that acceptance is effective only upon actual receipt of the acceptance.

E-Commerce & Information Technology

Online Auctions

Auctions have been used traditionally to sell horses, antiques, paintings, and other such one-of-a-kind items. A bidder usually has to be physically present at a traditional auction to bid, although some auctions allow telephone bids from prequalified callers. Because of these restrictions, auctions used to occupy a small portion of the U.S. economy. But no more, thanks to the advent of the Internet.

Led by the giant online auction house eBay, online auctions have exploded on the Internet. eBay started as a small online auction house that made a market in such consumer collectibles as Pez dispensers and Beanie Babies. After seeing how successful this mode of business was for these items, eBay expanded into a full-service online auctioneer. By the year 2000, eBay was offering several million items each day for sale over the Internet. The millions of eBay's cybershoppers are loyal, spending an average of 130 minutes per month at the eBay auction site.

eBay does not own the items it sells. Instead, sellers list the items they want to auction on the eBay site, and buyers bid for the items. The purchase contract is between the cyberseller and the cyberbuyer. Payment is usually made by using PayPal. eBay takes a commission on items sold by its online auction house. In the beginning of online auctions, most of the goods sold were goods that were customarily sold at flea markets, antique stores, and classified advertisements. Today, many businesses have started using eBay auctions to sell their excess inventory or to sell mainstream consumer and business goods. Business sales through online auctions now exceed nonbusiness sales.

eBay is now receiving stiff competition from many other online auctioneers. The giant e-commerce leader Amazon.com conducts online auctions, and many small online auction houses specialize in selling jewelry, baseball cards, horses, and other items. eBay itself began offering localized auctions in individual cities for such large items as cars and furniture. Even traditional auction houses such as Sotheby's, which auctions pricey items such as paintings, jewelry, and antiques, have begun selling through online auctions. As proven by the success of eBay and other online auctioneers, consumers and businesses have embraced the dynamic pricing and fluid give-and-take of Internet auctions. Auctions, which have been around for most of history, are again giving fixed-priced selling, which has only been around for about 100 years, a run for its money. ■

Consideration

Consideration is a necessary element for the existence of a contract. Consideration is defined as the thing of value given in exchange for a promise. Consideration can come in many forms. The most common types consist of either a tangible payment (e.g., money or property) or the performance of an act (e.g., providing legal services). Less-usual forms of consideration include the forbearance of a legal right (e.g., accepting an out-of-court settlement in exchange for dropping a lawsuit) and noneconomic forms of consideration (e.g., refraining from "drinking, using tobacco, swearing, or playing cards or billiards for money" for a specified time period).[4]

consideration
Something of legal value given in exchange for a promise.

Written contracts are presumed to be supported by consideration. This is a rebuttable presumption that may be overcome by sufficient evidence. A few states provide that contracts made under seal cannot be challenged for lack of consideration.

Consideration consists of two elements: (1) Something of *legal value* must be given (e.g., either a legal benefit must be received or legal detriment suffered) and (2) there must be a *bargained-for exchange*. Each of these is discussed in the paragraphs that follow.

The law relating to public policy cannot remain immutable, it must change with the passage of time. The wind of change blows on it.

L. J. Danckwerts
Nagle v. Feilden (1966)

Legal Value

In a consideration, something of **legal value** must be given. Under the modern law of contracts, a contract is considered supported by legal value if (1) the promise suffers a *legal detriment* or (2) the promisor receives a *legal benefit*.

Business Brief
The more formal approach to finding consideration has been replaced by a modern definition that considers a contract supported by consideration if either (1) the promise suffers a legal detriment or (2) the promisor receives a legal benefit.

Consider This Example Suppose the Dallas Cowboys contract with a tailor to have the tailor make uniforms for the team. The tailor completes the uniforms, but the team manager thinks the color is wrong and refuses to allow the team to wear them. Here, there has

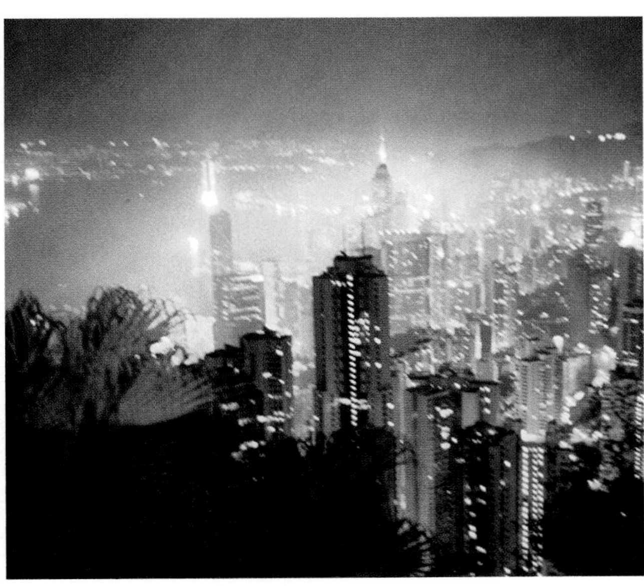

Hong Kong. Consideration must support a commercial or private contract.

been no benefit to either the manager or the players. However, the tailor has suffered a legal detriment (time spent making the uniforms). Under the modern rule of contracts, there is sufficiency of consideration and the contract is enforceable.

Bargained-for Exchange

bargained-for exchange
An exchange that parties engage in that leads to an enforceable contract.

gift promise
A promise that is unenforceable because it lacks consideration.

To be enforceable, a contract must arise from a **bargained-for exchange**. In most business contracts, the parties engage in such exchanges. The commercial setting in which business contracts are formed leads to this conclusion.

Gift promises, also called **gratuitous promises**, are unenforceable because they lack consideration. To change a gift promise into an enforceable promise, the promise must offer to do something in exchange—that is, consideration—for the promise. For instance, suppose Mrs. Colby promised to give her son $10,000 and then rescinded the promise. The son would have no recourse because it was a gift promise that lacked consideration. However, if Mrs. Colby promised her son $10,000 for getting an "A" in his business law course and the son performed as required, the contract would be enforceable. A completed gift promise cannot be rescinded for lack of consideration.

In the following case, the court had to determine whether a contract was supported by consideration.

Case 10.2
Consideration

Alden v. Presley
637 S.W.2d 862, 1982 Tenn. Lexis 340 (1982)
Supreme Court of Tennessee

Background and Facts

Elvis Presley, a singer of great renown and a man of substantial wealth, became engaged to Ginger Alden. He was generous with the Alden family, paying for landscaping the lawn, installing a swimming pool, and making other gifts. When his fiancé's mother, Jo Laverne Alden, sought to divorce her husband, Presley promised to pay off the remaining mortgage indebtedness on the Alden home, which Mrs. Alden was to receive in the divorce settlement. On August 16, 1977, Presley died suddenly, leaving the mortgage unpaid. When the legal representative of Presley's estate refused to pay the $39,587 mortgage, Mrs. Alden brought an action to enforce Presley's promise. The trial court denied recovery. Mrs. Alden appealed.

Issue

Was Presley's promise to pay the mortgage enforceable?

In The Language of The Court

Fones, Justice In the instant case, the trial held decedent did make a promise unsupported by consideration to plaintiff, that no gift was consummated for failure of delivery, that plaintiff suffered no detriment as she "wound up much better after her association with Elvis A. Presley than if he had never made any promise to Jo Laverne Alden." The court of appeals concurred in the finding that there was no gift for failure to deliver, holding that delivery is not complete unless complete dominion and control of the gift is surrendered by the donor and acquired by the donee.

Decision and Remedy

The state supreme court held that Presley's promise was a gratuitous executory promise that was not supported by consideration. As such, it was unenforceable against Presley's estate. The court dismissed the case and assessed costs against the plaintiff.

Case Questions

Critical Legal Thinking Should gratuitous promises be enforced?

Business Ethics Was it unethical for the representative of Presley's estate to refuse to complete the gift? Did he have any other choice?

Business Application Does it make a difference if a gift promise is executed or executory? Explain.

Contracts Lacking Consideration

illegal consideration
A promise to refrain from doing an illegal act. Such a promise will not support a contract.

Some contracts seem as if they are supported by consideration even though they are not. The following types of contracts fall into this category:

- ***Illegal Consideration*** A contract cannot be supported by a promise to refrain from doing an illegal act because that is **illegal consideration**. Contracts based on illegal consideration are void. For example, statements such as "I will burn your house down unless you agree to pay me $10,000" cannot become enforceable contracts. Even if the threatened party agrees to make the payment, the contract is unenforceable and void because it is supported by illegal consideration (arson is unlawful).

- ***Illusory Promises*** If the parties enter into a contract but one or both of the parties can choose not to perform their contractual obligations, the contract lacks consideration. Such promises, which are known as **illusory promises** (or **illusory contracts**), are unenforceable. For example, a contract that provides that one of the parties has to perform only if he or she chooses to do so is an illusory contract.

illusory promise
A contract into which parties enter but one or both of the parties can choose not to perform their contractual obligations. Such a contract lacks consideration.

- ***Moral Obligations*** Promises made out of a sense of **moral obligation** or honor are generally not enforceable on the ground that they lack consideration. In other words, moral consideration is not treated as legal consideration. Contracts based on love and affection and deathbed promises are examples of such promises. A minority of states hold that moral obligations are enforceable.
- ***Past Consideration*** A promise that is based on a party's **past consideration** (i.e., prior act or performance) lacks consideration. Such contracts are unenforceable unless some new consideration is given to support the contract.

  Consider This Example Felipe Chavez, who has worked for the Acme Corporation for 30 years, is retiring. The president of Acme says, "Because you were such a loyal employee, Acme will pay you a bonus of $25,000." The Corporation refuses to pay the $25,000. Unfortunately for Mr. Chavez, the contract is unenforceable because it is based on past consideration.

past consideration
A prior act or performance. Past consideration (e.g., prior acts) will not support a new contract. New consideration must be given.

- ***Preexisting Duty*** A promise lacks consideration if a person promises to perform an act or do something he or she is already under an obligation to do. This is called a **preexisting duty**. The promise is unenforceable because no new consideration has been given. For example, many states have adopted statutes that prohibit police officers from accepting rewards for apprehending criminals.

  In the private sector, the preexisting duty rule often arises when one of the parties to an existing contract seeks to change the terms of the contract during the course of its performance. Such midstream changes are unenforceable: The parties have a preexisting duty to perform according to the original terms of the contract.

preexisting duty
Something a person is already under an obligation to do. A promise lacks consideration in the case of preexisting duty.

Concept Summary *Contracts Lacking Consideration*

Type of Consideration	Description of Promise
Illegal consideration	Promise to refrain from doing an illegal act.
Illusory promise	Promise in which one or both parties can choose not to perform their obligation.
Moral obligation	Promise made out of a sense of moral obligation or honor or love or affection. Some states enforce these types of contracts.
Past consideration	Promise based on the past performance of the promisee.
Preexisting duty	Promise based on the preexisting duty of the promisee to perform. The promise is enforceable if (1) the parties rescind the contract and enter into a new contract or (2) there are unforeseen difficulties.

Contemporary Business Environment

Article 2 (Sales) of the UCC

Article 2 (Sales) of the UCC applies to *transactions in goods*—that is, the sale of goods [UCC 2-102]. All states except Louisiana have adopted some version of Article 2 of the UCC. A **sale** consists of the passing of title from a seller to a buyer for a price [UCC 2-106(1)]. For example, the purchase of the book is a sale subject to Article 2. This is so whether the book was paid for by cash, check, credit card, or another form of consideration.

Article 2 establishes a uniform law covering the formation, performance, and default of sales contracts.

Goods are defined as tangible things that are movable at the time of their identification to the contract [UCC 2-105(1)]. Specially manufactured goods and the unborn young of animals are examples of goods.

Money and intangible items, such as stocks, bonds, and patents, are not tangible goods. Therefore, they are not subject to Article 2.

Real estate is not subject to Article 2, either, because it is not movable [UCC 2-105(1)]. Minerals, structures, growing crops, and other things that are severable from real estate may be classified as goods subject to Article 2, however. For example, the sale and removal of a chandelier in a house is a sale of goods subject to Article 2 because its removal would not materially harm the realty. However, the sale and removal of the furnace would be a sale of real property because its removal would cause material harm [UCC 2-107(2)].

Contracts for the provision of services—including legal services, medical services, dental services, and such—are not covered by Article 2. Sometimes, however, a sale involves both the provision of a service and a good in the same transaction. This is referred to as a *mixed sale*. Article 2 applies only to mixed sales if the goods are the predominant part of the transaction. The UCC provides no guidance for deciding cases based on mixed sales. Therefore, the courts decide these issues on a case-by-case basis. ■

Capacity to Contract

Generally, the law presumes that the parties to a contract have the requisite **contractual capacity** to enter into the contract. However, certain persons do not have this capacity. They include minors, mentally incompetent persons, and intoxicated persons. Both the common law of contracts and many state statutes protect persons who lack contractual capacity from having contracts enforced against them. The party asserting incapacity, or his or her guardian, conservator, or other legal representative bears the burden of proof.

Minors

Minors do not always have the maturity, experience, or sophistication needed to enter into contracts with adults. States have enacted statutes that specify the *age of majority*. The most prevalent age of majority is 18 years for both males and females. Any age below the statutory age of majority is called the *period of minority*.

> The right of a minor to disaffirm his contract is based upon sound public policy to protect the minor from his own improvidence and the overreaching of adults.
>
> Justice Sullivan
> *Star Chevrolet v. Green (1985)*

infancy doctrine
A doctrine that allows minors to disaffirm (cancel) most contracts they have entered into with adults.

disaffirmance
The act of a minor to rescind a contract under the infancy doctrine. Disaffirmance may be done orally, in writing, or by the minor's conduct.

Infancy Doctrine To protect minors, the law recognizes the **infancy doctrine**, which allows minors to **disaffirm** (or **cancel**) most contracts they have entered into with adults. A minor's right to disaffirm a contract is based on public policy. The reasoning is that minors should be protected from unscrupulous behavior of adults.

Under the infancy doctrine, a minor has the option of choosing whether to enforce the contract (i.e., the contract is **voidable** by a minor). The adult party is bound to the minor's decision. If both parties to the contract are minors, both parties have the right to disaffirm the contract.

A minor can expressly disaffirm a contract orally, in writing, or by his or her conduct. No special formalities are required. The contract may be disaffirmed at any time prior to reaching the age of majority plus a "reasonable time." The designation of a reasonable time is determined on a case-by-case basis.

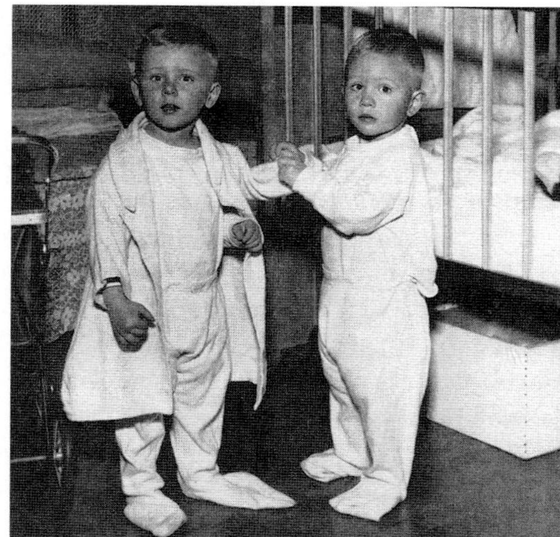

Twins. The infancy doctrine protects minors by permitting them to disavow (void) certain contracts. These contracts are voidable because only the minor, and not the adult on the other side of the contract, may disavow the contract.

Duties of Restoration and Restitution If the minor's contract is executory and neither party has performed, the minor can simply disaffirm the contract: There is nothing to recover because neither party has given the other party anything of value. However, if the parties have exchanged consideration and partially or fully performed the contract at the time the minor disaffirms the contract, the issue becomes one of what consideration or restitution must be made. The following rules apply:

- ***Competent Party's Duty of Restitution*** If the minor has transferred consideration—money, property, or other valuables—to the competent party before disaffirming the contract, that party must place the minor in status quo. That is, the minor must be restored to the same position he or she was in before the minor entered into the contract. This is usually done by returning the consideration to the minor. If the consideration has been sold or has depreciated in value, the competent party must pay the minor the cash equivalent. This is called the **competent party's duty of restitution**.
- ***Minor's Duty of Restoration or Restitution*** Generally, a minor is obligated only to return the goods or property he or she has received from the adult in the condition they are in at the time of disaffirmance (subject to several exceptions discussed later in this chapter). This is so even if an item has been consumed, lost, destroyed, or depreciated in value at the time of disaffirmance. This is called the **minor's duty of restoration**. This rule is based on the rationale that if a minor had to place the adult in status quo upon disaffirmance of a contract, there would be no incentive for an adult not to deal with a minor.

competent party's duty of restitution

A duty in which if a minor has transferred money, property, or other valuables to the competent party before disaffirming the contract, that party must place the minor back into status quo.

minor's duty of restoration

A minor's obligation to return goods or property at the time of disaffirmance. As a general rule, a minor is obligated only to return the goods or property he or she has received from the adult in the condition they are in at the time of disaffirmance.

Most states provide that the minor must put the adult in status quo upon disaffirmance of the contract if (1) the minor's intentional or grossly negligent conduct caused the loss of value to the adult's property or (2) the minor misrepresented his or her age when entering into the contract. A few states have enacted statutes that require the minor to make restitution of the reasonable value of the item when disaffirming any contract. This is called the minor's duty of restitution.

Ratification If a minor does not disaffirm a contract either during the period of minority or within a reasonable time after reaching the age of majority, the contract is considered ratified (accepted). This means that the minor (who is now an adult) is bound by the contract; the right to disaffirm the contract has been lost. Note that any attempt by a minor to ratify a contract while still a minor can be disaffirmed, just as the original contract can be disaffirmed.

ratification
The act of a minor after the minor has reached the age of majority by which he or she accepts a contract entered into when he or she was a minor.

The **ratification**, which relates back to the inception of the contract, can be by express oral or written words or implied from the minor's conduct (e.g., after reaching the age of majority the minor remains silent regarding the contract).

necessaries of life
The reasonable value of food, clothing, shelter, medical care, and other items considered necessary to the maintenance of life for which a minor must pay after he or she contracts for them.

Necessaries of Life Minors are obligated to pay for the **necessaries of life** that they contract for. Otherwise, many adults would refuse to sell these items to them. There is no standard definition of what is a *necessary of life*, but items such as food, clothing, shelter, medical services, and the like are generally understood to fit this category. Goods and services such as automobiles, tools of trade, education, and vocational training have also been found to be necessaries of life in some situations. The minor's age, lifestyle, and status in life influence what is considered necessary. For example, necessaries for a married minor are greater than those for an unmarried minor.

The seller's recovery is based on the equitable doctrine of **quasi-contract** rather than on the contract itself. Under this theory, the minor is obligated only to pay the reasonable value of the goods or services received. Reasonable value is determined on a case-by-case basis.

Contemporary Business Environment

Statutes That Make Minors Liable for Special Types of Contracts

The infancy doctrine of the common law of contracts allows minors to disaffirm many contracts they have entered into with adults. Based on public policy, many states have enacted statutes that make certain specified contracts enforceable against minors—that is, minors cannot assert the infancy doctrine against enforcement for these contracts. These usually include contracts for

- Medical, surgical, and pregnancy care
- Psychological counseling
- Health insurance
- Life insurance
- The performance of duties relating to stock and bond transfers, bank accounts, and the like
- Educational loan agreements
- Contracts to support children
- Contracts to enlist in the military
- Artistic, sports, and entertainment contracts that have been entered into with the approval of the court (many of these statutes require that a certain portion of the wages and fees earned by the minor be put in trust until the minor reaches the age of majority) ■

Mentally Incompetent Persons

Insanity vitiates all acts.
Sir John Nicholl
Countess of Portsmouth v. Earl of Portsmouth (1828)

Mental incapacity may arise because of mental illness, brain damage, mental retardation, senility, and the like. The law protects people suffering from substantial mental incapacity from enforcement of contracts against them because such persons may not understand the consequences of their actions in entering into a contract.

The law has developed the following two standards concerning contracts of mentally incompetent persons:

adjudged insane
A person who has been determined to be insane by a proper court or administrative agency. A contract entered into by such a person is void.

1. ***Adjudged Insane*** In certain cases, a relative, a loved one, or another interested party may institute a legal action to have someone declared legally (i.e., adjudged) insane. If, after hearing the evidence at a formal judicial or administrative hearing, the person is **adjudged insane**, the court will make that person a ward of the court and appoint a guardian to act on that person's behalf. If a person has been adjudged insane, any contract entered into by that person is *void*. That is, no contract exists. The court-appointed guardian is the only one who has the legal authority to enter into contracts on behalf of the person.

2. ***Insane, but Not Adjudged Insane*** If no formal ruling has been made, any contracts entered into by a person who suffers from a mental impairment that makes him legally insane are voidable by the insane person. Unless the other party does not have contractual capacity, he does not have the option to void the contract.

A person who has dealt with an insane person must place that insane person in status quo if the contract is either void or voided by the insane person. Most states hold that a party who did not know he or she was dealing with an insane person must be placed in status quo upon voidance of the contract. Insane persons are liable in quasi-contract to pay the reasonable value for necessaries of life they receive.

insane, but not adjudged insane
A person who is insane but has not been adjudged insane by a court or an administrative agency. A contract entered into by such person is generally voidable. Some states hold that such a contract is void.

Concept Summary *Disaffirmance of Contracts Based on Legal Insanity*

Type of Legal Insanity	Disaffirmance Rule
Adjudged insane	Contract is void. Neither party can enforce the contract.
Insane, but not adjudged insane	Contract is voidable by the insane person; the competent party cannot void the contract.

Intoxicated Persons

Most states provide that a contract entered into by an **intoxicated person** are voidable by that person. The intoxication may occur because of alcohol or drugs. The contract is not voidable by the other party if that party had contractual capacity.

Under the majority rule, the contract is voidable only if the person was so intoxicated when the contract was entered into that he or she was incapable of understanding or comprehending the nature of the transaction. In most states, this rule holds even if the intoxication was self-induced. The amount of alcohol or drugs that is necessary to be consumed by a person to be considered legally intoxicated to disaffirm contracts varies from case to case. The factors that are considered include the user's physical characteristics and his or her ability to "hold" intoxicants.

A person who disaffirms a contract based on intoxication generally must be returned to the status quo. In turn, the intoxicated person generally must return the consideration received under the contract to the other party and make restitution that returns the other party to status quo. After becoming sober, an intoxicated person can ratify the contracts he or she entered into while intoxicated. Intoxicated persons are liable in quasi-contract to pay the reasonable value for necessaries they receive.

intoxicated person
A person who is under contractual incapacity because of ingestion of alcohol or drugs to the point of incompetence.

"If there's no meaning in it," said the King, "that saves a world of trouble, you know, we needn't try to find any."

Lewis Carroll
Alice in Wonderland, Ch. 12

Contemporary Business Environment

Article 2A (Leases) of the UCC

Personal property leases are a billion-dollar industry. Consumer rentals of automobiles or equipment and commercial leases of such items as aircraft and industrial machinery fall into this category.

Article 2A of the UCC was promulgated in 1987. This article, cited as the **Uniform Commercial Code—Leases**, directly addresses personal property leases [UCC 2A-101]. It establishes a comprehensive, uniform law covering the formation, performance, and default of leases in goods [UCC 2A-102, 2A-103(h)].

Article 2A is similar to Article 2. In fact, many Article 2 provisions were changed to reflect leasing terminology and practices and carried over to Article 2A. Many states have adopted Article 2A, and many more are expected to do so in the future.

Contemporary Business Environment (continued)

A **lease** is a transfer of the right to the possession and use of the named goods for a set term in return for certain consideration [UCC 2A-103(1)(i)(x)]. The leased goods can be anything from a hand tool leased to an individual for a few hours to a complex line of industrial equipment leased to a multinational corporation for a number of years.

In an ordinary lease, the **lessor** is the person who transfers the right of possession and use of goods under the lease [UCC 2A-103(1)(p)]. The **lessee** is the person who acquires the right to possession and use of goods under a lease [UCC 2A-103(1)(n)]

A **consumer lease** is one with a value of $25,000 or less between a lessor regularly engaged in the business of leasing or selling and a lessee who leases the goods primarily for a personal, family, or household purpose [UCC 2A-103(1)(e)].

A **finance lease** is a three-party transaction consisting of the lessor, the lessee, and the **supplier** (or vendor) [UCC 2A-103(1)(g)]

Consider This Example The Row Chemical Company decides to use robotics to manufacture most of its products. It persuades Zand Corp. to design the robotic equipment that will meet its needs. To finance the purchase of the equipment, Row Chemical goes to City Bank, which purchases the robotics equipment from Zand Corp. and leases it to Row Chemical. City Bank is the lessor, Row Chemical is the lessee, and Zand Corp. is the supplier. ■

Legality

illegal contract
A contract to perform an illegal act. Cannot be enforced by either party to the contract.

An essential element for the formation of a contract is that the object of the contract be *lawful*. A contract to perform an illegal act is called an **illegal contract**. Illegal contracts are void. That is, they cannot be enforced by either party to the contract. Because illegal contracts are void, the parties cannot sue for nonperformance. Further, if an illegal contract is executed, the court will generally leave the parties where it finds them. Most contracts are presumed to be lawful. The burden of proving that a contract is unlawful rests on the party who asserts its illegality.

Illegality—Contracts Contrary to Statutes

A man must come into a court of equity with clean hands.
C. B. Eyre Dering v. Earl of Winchelsea (1787)

Both federal and state legislatures have enacted statutes that prohibit certain types of conduct. Contracts to perform an activity that is prohibited by statute are illegal contracts. Such contracts include gambling contracts, contracts that provide for usurious rates of interest, and contracts that violate Sabbath laws and licensing statutes.

gambling statutes
Statutes that make certain forms of gambling illegal.

Gambling Statutes All states either prohibit or regulate gambling, wagering, lotteries, and games of chance. States provide various criminal and civil penalties for illegal gambling. There are many exceptions to wagering laws. For example, many states have enacted **gambling statutes** that permit games of chance under a certain dollar amount, bingo games, lotteries conducted by religious and charitable organizations, and the like. Many states also permit and regulate horse racing, harness racing, dog racing, and state-operated lotteries.

In the following case, the court found an illegal contract and left the parties where it found them.

Case 10.3 Illegal Contract

Ryno v. Tyra
752 S.W.2d 148, 1988 Tex.App. Lexis 1646 (1988)
Court of Appeals of Texas

Background and Facts

R. D. Ryno, Jr., owned Bavarian Motors, an automobile dealership in Fort Worth, Texas. On March 5, 1981, Lee Tyra discussed purchasing a 1980 BMW M-1 from Ryno for $125,000. Ryno then suggested a double-or-nothing coin flip, to which Tyra agreed. When Tyra won the coin flip, Ryno said, "It's yours," and handed Tyra the keys and German title to the car. Tyra drove away in the car. This suit ensued as to the ownership of the car. The trial court held in favor of Tyra. Ryno appealed.

Issue

Was there an illegal contract? If so, who owns the car?

In The Language of The Court

Farris, Justice Ryno complains that the trial court erred in granting Tyra judgment because the judgment enforces a gambling contract. We find there was sufficient evidence to sustain the jury finding that Ryno intended to transfer to Tyra his ownership interest in the BMW at the time he delivered the documents, keys, and possession of the automobile to Tyra. We agree with appellant Ryno that his wager with Tyra was unenforceable. The trial court could not have compelled Ryno to honor his wager by delivering the BMW to Tyra. However, Ryno did deliver the BMW to Tyra and the facts incident to that delivery are sufficient to establish a transfer by gift of the BMW from Ryno to Tyra.

Decision and Remedy

Tyra, the patron at the car dealership who won the coin toss, owns the car. The appellate court found that there was an illegal contract and left the parties where it found them—that is, with Tyra in possession of the car. Affirmed.

Case Questions

Critical Legal Thinking Should the court have lent its resources to help Ryno recover the car?

Ethics Did Ryno act ethically in this case?

Contemporary Business What is the moral of this story if you ever win anything in an illegal gambling contract?

Usury Laws State **usury laws** set an upper limit on the annual interest rate that can be charged on certain types of loans. The limits vary from state to state. Lenders who charge a higher rate than the state limit are guilty of usury. The primary purpose of these laws is to protect unsophisticated borrowers from loan sharks and others who charge exorbitant rates of interest.

usury law
A law that sets an upper limit on the interest rate that can be charged on certain types of loans.

Sabbath Laws Certain states have enacted laws—called **Sabbath laws**, **Sunday laws**, or **blue laws**—that prohibit or limit the carrying on of certain secular activities on Sundays. Except for contracts for the necessaries of life, charitable donations, and such, these laws generally prohibit or invalidate executory contracts that are entered into on Sunday. Many states do not actively enforce these laws. In some states, they have even been found to be unconstitutional.

Sabbath law
A law that prohibits or limits the carrying on of certain secular activities on Sundays.

Licensing Statutes All states have **licensing statutes** that require members of certain professions and occupations to be licensed by the state in which they practice. Lawyers, doctors, real estate agents, insurance agents, certified public accountants, teachers, contractors, hairdressers, and such are among them. In most instances, a **license** is granted to a person who demonstrates that he or she has the proper schooling, experience, and moral character required by the relevant statute. Sometimes, a written examination is also required. Generally, unlicensed persons cannot recover payment for services that a regulatory statute requires a licensed person to provide.

licensing statute
A statute that requires a person or business to obtain a license from the government prior to engaging in a specified occupation or activity.

Consider This Example State law provides that legal services can be provided only by lawyers who have graduated from law school and passed the appropriate bar exam. Nevertheless, Jackie Yu, a first-year law student, agrees to draft a will for Randy McCabe for a $150 fee. Because Ms. Yu is not licensed to provide legal services, she has violated a regulatory statute. She cannot enforce the contract and recover payment from Mr. McCabe.

Illegality—Contracts Contrary to Public Policy

Certain contracts are illegal because they are **contrary to public policy**. Although *public policy* eludes a precise definition, the courts have held contracts to be contrary to public policy if they have a negative impact on society or interfere with the public's safety and welfare. Such contracts include immoral contracts, contracts in restraint of trade, certain covenants not to compete, and some exculpatory clauses.

contract contrary to public policy
A contract that has a negative impact on society or interferes with the public's safety and welfare.

contract in restraint of trade
A contract that unreasonably restrains trade.

Contracts in Restraint of Trade The general economic policy of this country favors competition. In common law, **contracts in restraint of trade**—that is, contracts that unreasonably restrain trade—were held to be unlawful. For example, it would be an illegal restraint of trade if all the bakers in a neighborhood agreed to fix the prices of the bread they sold. The bakers' contract would be void.

noncompete clause
An agreement whereby a person agrees not to engage in a specified business or occupation within a designated geographical area for a specified period of time following the sale.

Business Brief
Noncompete clauses are often used in the sale of business contracts to preserve the "goodwill" of the business for the new owner. Without a noncompete clause, the seller could open next to the buyer and serve previous customers.

Covenants Not to Compete Employment contracts often contain noncompete clauses that prohibit an employee from competing with his or her employer for a certain time period after leaving the employment. This agreement is called a covenant not to compete clause, or a **noncompete clause**.

A covenant not to compete that is ancillary to an employment contract is lawful if it is reasonable in three aspects: (1) the line of business protected, (2) the geographical area protected, and (3) the duration of the restriction. A covenant that is found to be unreasonable is not enforceable as written. The reasonableness of covenants not to compete is examined on a case-by-case basis. If a covenant not to compete is unreasonable, the courts may either refuse to enforce it or change it so that it is reasonable. Usually, the courts choose the first option.

Consider This Example Suppose Karen Ma is the Chief Financial Officer (CFO) of Aszic Software in San Diego, California. In her employment contract with Aszic, Karen agrees that when her employment with Aszic ends she will not accept a job as CFO of another software company in the state of California for a 10-year period. This covenant not to compete is reasonable in the line of business protected but is unreasonable in geographical scope and duration. It will not be enforced by the courts as written. The covenant not to compete would be reasonable and enforceable if it prohibited Ms. Ma only from accepting a job as CFO of a software company in the city of San Diego for 5 years.

A covenant not to compete that is not *ancillary* to a legitimate employment contract is void as against public policy because the noncompete clause is not protecting a legitimate business interest.

Entrepreneur and the Law

Using a Covenant Not to Compete with a Sale of a Business

Entrepreneurs and others often buy and sell businesses. The sale of a business includes its "goodwill" or reputation. To protect this goodwill after the sale, the seller often enters into an agreement with the buyer to not engage in a similar business or occupation within a specified geographical area for a specified period of time following the sale. This agreement is called a **covenant not to compete**, or a **noncompete clause**.

Covenants not to compete that are *ancillary* to a legitimate sale of a business or employment contract are lawful if they are reasonable in three aspects: (1) the line of business protected, (2) the geographical area protected, and (3) the duration of the restriction. If a covenant not to compete is unreasonable, the courts may either refuse to enforce it or change it so that it is reasonable.

Consider This Example Suppose Stacy Rogers is a certified public accountant (CPA) with her own lucrative accounting practice in Buffalo, New York. Her business includes a substantial amount of goodwill. When she sells her practice, she agrees not to open another accounting practice in the state of New York for a 10-year period. This covenant not to compete is reasonable in the line of business protected but is unreasonable in geographical scope and duration. It will not be enforced by the courts as written. The covenant not to compete would be reasonable and enforceable if it prohibited Ms. Rogers only from practicing as a CPA in the city of Buffalo for 5 years.

A covenant not to compete that is not *ancillary* to a legitimate business transaction is void as against public policy because the noncompete clause is not protecting a legitimate business interest. For example, a contract in which one accountant paid another accountant not to open an office nearby would be void as against public policy because it is not ancillary to a legitimate business transaction. ■

Exculpatory Clauses An **exculpatory clause** is a contractual provision that relieves one (or both) parties to the contract from tort liability. Exculpatory clauses can relieve a party of liability for ordinary negligence. They cannot be used in situations involving willful conduct, intentional torts, fraud, recklessness, or gross negligence. Exculpatory clauses are often found in leases, sales contracts, ticket stubs to sporting events, parking lot tickets, services contracts, and the like. Such clauses do not have to be reciprocal (i.e., one party may be relieved of tort liability while the other party is not).

exculpatory clause
A contractual provision that relieves one (or both) parties to the contract from tort liability for ordinary negligence.

Generally, the courts do not favor exculpatory clauses unless both parties have equal bargaining power. The courts are willing to permit competent parties of equal bargaining power to establish which of them bears the risk.

Consider This Example Trent Anderson voluntarily enrolled in a parachute jump course and signed a contract containing an exculpatory clause that relieved the parachute center of liability. After receiving proper instruction, he jumped from an airplane. Unfortunately, Trent was injured when he could not steer his parachute toward the target area. He sued the parachute center for damages, but the court enforced the exculpatory clause, reasoning that parachute jumping did not involve an essential service and that there was no decisive advantage in bargaining power between the parties.

Exculpatory clauses that either affect the *public interest* or result from superior bargaining power are usually found to be void as against public policy. Although the outcome varies with the circumstances of the case, the greater the degree that the party serves the general public, the greater the chance that the exculpatory clause will be struck down as illegal. The courts will consider such factors as the type of activity involved and the relative bargaining power, knowledge, experience, and sophistication of the parties, as well as other relevant factors. For example, exculpatory clauses used by many doctors and hospitals have been struck down as against public policy.

Immoral Contracts **Immoral contracts**—that is, contracts whose objective is the commission of an act that is considered immoral by society—may be found to be against public policy. For example, a contract that is based on sexual favors has been held to be an immoral contract and void as against public policy. Judges are not free to define morality based on their individual views. Instead, they must look to the practices and beliefs of society when defining immoral conduct.

immoral contract
A contract whose objective is the commission of an act that is considered immoral by society.

The following case raises the issue of whether a contract violates public policy and is therefore illegal.

Case 10.4 Illegal Contract

Flood v. Fidelity & Guaranty Life Insurance Co.
394 So.2d 1311, 1981 La.App. Lexis 3538 (1981)
Court of Appeals of Louisiana

Background and Facts

Ellen and Richard Flood, who were married in 1965, lived in a house trailer in Louisiana. Richard worked as a maintenance man, and Ellen was employed at an insurance agency. Evidence at trial showed that Ellen was unhappy with her marriage. Ellen took out a life insurance policy on her husband and named herself as beneficiary. The policy was issued by Fidelity & Guaranty Life Insurance Company (Fidelity). In June 1972, Richard became unexpectedly ill. He was taken to the hospital, where his condition improved. After a visit at the hospital from his wife, however, Richard died. Ellen was criminally charged with the murder of her husband by poisoning. Evidence showed that six medicine bottles at the couple's home, including Tylenol and paregoric bottles, contained arsenic. The court found that Ellen had fed Richard ice cubes laced with arsenic at the hospital. Ellen was tried and convicted of the murder of her husband. Ellen, as beneficiary of Richard's life insurance policy, requested Fidelity to pay her the benefits. Fidelity refused to pay the benefits and returned all premiums paid on the policy. This suit followed. The district court held in favor of Ellen Flood and awarded her the benefits of the life insurance policy. Fidelity appealed.

Issue

Was the life insurance policy an illegal contract that is void?

In The Language of The Court

Lear, Judge Louisiana follows the majority rule that holds, as a matter of public policy, that a beneficiary named in a life insurance

Flood v. Fidelity & Guaranty Life Insurance Co.
394 So.2d 1311, 1981 La.App. Lexis 3538 (1981)
Court of Appeals of Louisiana
(continued)

policy is not entitled to the proceeds of the insurance if the beneficiary feloniously kills the insured.

The genesis of this litigation is the escalating criminal action of Ellen Flood, bent on taking the life of her lawful husband. Our courts have previously adjudicated (1) the issue of the cause of death of Richard Flood, (2) the culprit in that death, and (3) the motives for the death. Under the peculiar circumstances of the case, it was unreasonable of the trial court not to consider and to assign great weight to the mountain of evidence tending to prove Mrs. Flood's scheme to defraud both the insurer, Fidelity, and the insured, Mr. Flood. It is clear to us that the entirety of the transaction here reviewed is tainted with the intendment of Ellen Flood to contravene the prohibitory law.

Life insurance policies are procured because life is, indeed, precarious and uncertain. Our law does not and cannot sanction any scheme that has as its purpose the certain infliction of death for, *inter alia*, financial gain through receipt of the proceeds of life insurance. To sanction this policy in any way would surely shackle the spirit, letter, and life of our laws.

Decision and Remedy

The appellate court held that the life insurance policy that Ellen Flood had taken out on the life of her husband was void based on public policy. Reversed.

Case Questions

Critical Legal Thinking Should Ellen Flood have been allowed to retain the insurance proceeds in this case?

Business Ethics Did Ellen Flood act unethically in this case? Did she act illegally?

Contemporary Business What would be the economic consequences if persons could recover insurance proceeds for losses caused by their illegal activities (e.g., murder, arson)?

Contemporary Business Environment

Unconscionable Contracts

The general rule of freedom of contract holds that if (1) the object of a contract is lawful and (2) the other elements for the formation of a contract are met, the courts will enforce a contract according to its terms. Although it is generally presumed that parties are capable of protecting their own interests when contracting, it is a fact of life that dominant parties sometimes take advantage of weaker parties. As a result, some lawful contracts are so oppressive or manifestly unfair that they are unjust. To prevent the enforcement of such contracts, the courts developed the equitable **doctrine of unconscionability**, which is based on public policy. A contract found to be unconscionable under this doctrine is called an **unconscionable contract**, or a **contract of adhesion**.

The courts are given substantial discretion in determining whether a contract or contract clause is unconscionable. There is no single definition of *unconscionability*. The doctrine may not be used merely to save a contracting party from a bad bargain.

The following elements must be shown to prove that a contract or clause in a contract is unconscionable:

1. The parties possessed severely unequal bargaining power.
2. The dominant party unreasonably used its unequal bargaining power to obtain oppressive or manifestly unfair contract terms.
3. The adhering party had no reasonable alternative.

In other words, the dominant party must *misuse* its greater power to obtain oppressive contract terms from the adhering party, and the adhering party must prove that it could not reasonably refuse to accept those terms. This situation is often proven by showing that the oppressive terms are contained in standard contracts used industry-wide.

If the court finds that a contract or contract clause is unconscionable, it may (1) refuse to enforce the contract, (2) refuse to enforce the unconscionable clause but enforce the remainder of the contract, or (3) limit the applicability of any unconscionable clause so as to avoid any unconscionable result. The appropriate remedy depends on the facts and circumstances of each case. Note that because unconscionability is a matter of law, the judge may opt to decide the case without a jury trial. ■

Third-Party Rights

With two exceptions, third parties do not acquire any rights under other people's contracts. These exceptions are (1) **assignees** to whom rights subsequently are transferred and (2) **intended third-party beneficiaries** to whom the contracting parties intended to give rights under the contract at the time of contracting.

Assignment

In many cases, the parties to a contract can transfer their rights under the contract to other parties. The transfer of contractual rights is called an **assignment of rights** or just an **assignment**. The party who owes the duty of performance is called the *obligor*. The party owed a right under the contract is called the *obligee*. An obligee who transfers the right to receive performance is called an **assignor**. The party to whom the right has been transferred is called the **assignee**. The assignee can assign the right to yet another person (called a **subsequent assignee**, or **subassignee**). Exhibit 10.2 illustrates these relationships.

assignment
The transfer of contractual rights by an obligee to another party.

assignor
An obligee who transfers a right.

assignee
A party to whom a right has been transferred.

Business Brief
Businesses often sell (assign) their accounts receivable to another party, called a "factor," for collection. Accounts receivable are usually sold at a discount to reflect risk of non-collection of some accounts.

Consider This Example Suppose the owner of a clothing store purchases $5,000 worth of goods on credit from a manufacturer. Payment is due in 120 days. Assume that the manufacturer needs cash before that period expires, so he sells his right to collect the money to a factor for $4,000. If the store owner is given proper notice of the assignment, he must pay $5,000 to the factor. The manufacturer is the assignor, and the factor is the assignee.

Generally, no formalities are required for a valid assignment of rights. Although the assignor often uses the word *assign*, other words or terms, such as *sell*, *transfer*, *convey*, *give*, and the like, are sufficient to indicate an intent to transfer a contract right.

Intended Beneficiaries

When the parties enter into a contract, they can agree that one of the party's performances should be rendered to or directly benefit a third party. Under such circumstances, the third party is called an **intended third-party beneficiary**. An intended third-party beneficiary can enforce the contract against the party who promised to render performance.[5]

intended beneficiary
A third party who is not in privity of contract but who has rights under the contract and can enforce the contract against the obligor.

Consider This Example Fred Richards hires a lawyer to draft his will. He directs the lawyer to leave all of his property to his best friend, Shari Silverman. Assume that (1) Mr. Richards dies and (2) the lawyer's negligence in drafting the will causes it to be invalid. Consequently, Mr. Richards's distant relatives receive the property under the state's inheritance statute. Ms. Silverman can sue the lawyer for damages because she was the intended beneficiary of the will.

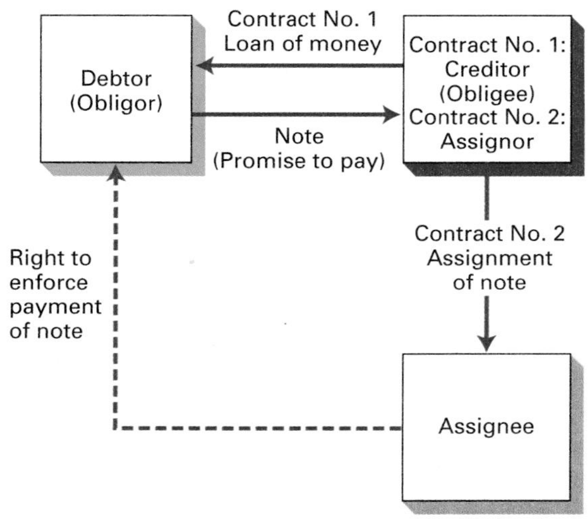

Exhibit 10.2
Assignment of a Right

Basketball hoop, University of Southern California campus. Many professional athletes' contracts contain clauses that permit the contracts to be assigned.

incidental beneficiary
A party who is unintentionally benefited by other people's contract.

In many instances, the parties to a contract unintentionally benefit a third party—called an **incidental beneficiary**—when the contract is performed. An incidental beneficiary has no rights to enforce or sue under other people's contracts. The courts are often asked to decide whether a third party is an intended or an incidental beneficiary.

International Law

The United Nations Convention on Contracts for the International Sale of Goods

The **United Nations Convention on Contracts for the International Sale of Goods (CISG)** came into effect on January 1, 1988, climaxing more than 50 years of negotiations. The CISG supersedes two earlier conventions, the Convention Relative to a Uniform Law on the International Sale of Goods (ULIS) and the Convention Relating to a Uniform Law on the Formation of Contracts for the International Sale of Goods (ULF).

Neither the ULIS nor the ULF was widely adopted because both were drafted without the participation of developing nations. The CISG, on the other hand, is the work of more than 60 countries and several international organizations. Many of its provisions are remarkably similar to those of the American UCC, for example. It incorporates rules from all the major legal systems. It has, accordingly, received widespread support from developed, developing, and Communist countries. Countries that have adopted it include Argentina, Austria, China, Egypt, Finland, France, Hungary, Italy, Mexico, Sweden, Syria, and the United States. Because the United States has ratified the CISG, Americans engaged in sales overseas need to be aware of the CISG.

The CISG applies to contracts for the international sale of goods. That is, the buyer and seller must have their places of business in different countries. In addition, either (1) both of the nations must be parties to the convention or (2) the contract specifies that the CISG has control. The contracting parties may agree to exclude (i.e., opt out of) or modify its application. In the United States, such a provision would be honored. ■

Singapore. The United Nations CISG provides rules for the enforcement of contracts for the international sale of goods if (1) the nations of the contracting parties recognize the CISG and (2) the international contract specifies that the CISG has control.

Definition of Contract, p. 272

Definition of Contract

"A promise or set of promises for the breach of which the law gives a remedy or the performance of which the law in some way recognizes a duty."

Parties to a Contract

1. *Offeror.* A party who makes an offer to enter into a contract.
2. *Offeree.* A party to whom an offer is made.

Classifications of Contracts, p. 273

Formation

1. ***Bilateral contract.*** A promise for a promise.
2. ***Unilateral contract.*** A promise for an act.
3. ***Express contract.*** A contract expressed in oral or written words.
4. ***Implied-in-fact contract.*** A contract implied from the conduct of the parties.
5. ***Quasi-contract.*** A contract implied by law to prevent unjust enrichment and unjust detriment.

Performance

1. ***Executed contract.*** A contract that is fully performed on both sides.
2. ***Executory contract.*** A contract that is not fully performed by one or both parties.

Enforceability

1. ***Valid contract.*** Meets all of the essential elements to establish a contract.
2. ***Void contract.*** No contract exists.
3. ***Voidable contract.*** One or both parties have the option of voiding or enforcing the contract.
4. ***Unenforceable contract.*** A contract that cannot be enforced because of a legal defense.

Requirements of a Contract, p. 278

Elements of a Contract

1. Agreement
2. Consideration
3. Contractual capacity
4. Lawful object

Agreement, p. 278

Offer

1. ***Offer.*** Manifestation by one party of a willingness to enter into a contract.
2. ***Offeror.*** A party who makes an offer.
3. ***Offeree.*** A party to whom an offer is made. This party has the power to create an agreement by accepting the terms of the offer.

Requirements of an Offer

1. ***Objection intent.*** The intent to enter into a contract is determined by the *objective theory of contracts*—that is, whether a reasonable person viewing the circumstances would conclude that the parties intended to be legally bound.
2. ***Definite terms.*** The terms of an offer must be definite so that the agreement between the parties can be determined. Reasonable terms (e.g., price, time for performance) may be *implied.*
3. ***Communication.*** The offer must be communicated to the offeree by the offeror.

Termination of an Offer by Action of the Parties

1. ***Revocation.*** The offeror may *revoke* (withdraw) an offer any time prior to its acceptance by the offeree.
2. ***Rejection.*** An offer is terminated if the offeree rejects the offer by his or her words or conduct.
3. ***Counteroffer.*** A counteroffer by the offeree terminates the offeror's offer (and creates a new offer).

Termination of an Offer by Operation of Law

1. ***Lapse of time.*** An offer terminates upon the expiration of a stated time in the offer. If no time is stated, the offer terminates after a "reasonable time."
2. ***Destruction of the subject matter.*** An offer terminates if the subject matter of the offer is destroyed prior to acceptance through no fault of either party.
3. ***Death or incompetency.*** The death or incompetency of either the offeror or the offeree prior to acceptance terminates the offer.
4. ***Supervening illegality.*** If, prior to the acceptance of an offer, the object of the offer is made illegal by statute, regulation, court decision, or other law, the offer terminates.

Acceptance

Acceptance. Manifestation of assent by the offeree to the terms of the offer. Acceptance of the offer by the offeree creates a contract.

1. ***Mirror image rule.*** Under the common law of contracts, the offeror must accept the terms offered by the offeror to create a contract. Any change in terms by the offeree constitutes a counteroffer, not an acceptance.

2. ***Acceptance-upon-dispatch rule.*** Unless otherwise provided in the offer, acceptance is effective when it is dispatched by the offeree. This is often called the *mailbox rule.*
3. ***Proper dispatch rule.*** An acceptance must be properly addressed, packaged, and have prepaid postage or delivery charges to be effective when dispatched. Generally, improperly dispatched acceptances are not effective until actually received by the offeror.

Consideration, p. 283

Consideration

A thing of value given in exchange for a promise. May be tangible or intangible property, performance of a service, forbearance of a legal right, or another thing of value.

Requirements of Consideration

1. ***Legal value.*** Something of legal value must be given. Either (a) the promise suffers a *legal detriment* or (b) the promisor receives a *legal benefit.*
2. ***Bargained-for exchange.*** A contract must arise from a bargained-for exchange. *Gift promises* (or gratuitous promises) are unenforceable because they lack consideration.

Adequacy of Consideration

Courts usually do not inquire into the adequacy of consideration. Thus, *nominal consideration* (e.g., $1) is usually sufficient.

Unenforceable Contracts

The following contracts are unenforceable because they lack consideration:

1. ***Illusory promise.*** If one or both parties to a contract can chose not to perform their contractual duties.
2. ***Moral obligation.*** Promise made out of a sense of moral obligation, honor, or love and affection.
3. ***Part consideration.*** Promise that is based on a party's past consideration.
4. ***Preexisting duty.*** Promise to perform an act or do something that a person is already under an obligation to do.

Capacity to Contract, p. 286

Minors

1. ***Infancy doctrine.*** Minors under the age of majority may *disaffirm* (cancel) most contracts they have entered into with adults. Such a contract is *voidable* by the minor but not by the adult.
2. ***Disaffirmance.*** Must occur before or within a reasonable time after the minor reaches the age of majority.
3. ***Competent party's duty of restitution.*** If a minor disaffirms a contract, the adult must place the minor in status quo by returning the value of the consideration that the minor paid.
4. ***Minor's duty upon disaffirmance:***
   a. *Minor's duty of restoration.* Generally, upon disaffirmance of a contract, a minor owes a duty to return the consideration to the adult in whatever condition it is at the time of disaffirmance.
   b. *Minor's duty of restitution.* A minor's duty to place the adult in status quo by returning the value of the consideration paid by the adult at the time of contracting if the minor (1) misrepresented his or her age or (2) intentionally or with gross negligence caused the loss to the adult's property.
5. ***Ratification.*** If a minor does not disaffirm a contract during the period of minority or within a reasonable time after reaching the age of majority, the contract is *ratified* (accepted).
6. ***Necessaries of life.*** Minors are obligated to pay the reasonable value for necessaries of life (e.g., food, clothing, shelter).
7. ***Special contracts.*** Many states have enacted statutes that make minors liable on certain types of contracts, such as for medical care, health and life insurance, educational loan agreements, and the like.

Mentally Incompetent Persons

1. ***Adjudged insane.*** Contracts by persons who have been adjudged insane are *void*. That is, the contract cannot be enforced by either the sane or insane party.
2. ***Insane, but not adjudged insane.*** Contracts by persons who are insane but have not been adjudged insane are *voidable* by the insane person but not by the competent party to the contract.
3. ***Duty of restitution.*** A person who has dealt with an insane person must place the insane person in status quo by returning the value of the consideration paid by the insane person at the time of contracting. Most states place the same duty on insane persons when they void a contract.
4. ***Necessaries of life.*** Insane persons are obligated to pay the reasonable value for necessaries of life.

Intoxicated Persons

1. ***Intoxicated persons.*** Contracts by intoxicated persons are *voidable* by the intoxicated person but not by the competent party to the contract.
2. ***Duty of restitution.*** Both parties owe a duty to place the other party in status quo by returning the value of the consideration paid by the other party at the time of contracting.
3. ***Necessaries of life.*** Intoxicated persons are obliged to pay the reasonable value for necessaries of life.

Legality, p. 290

Effect of Illegality

General rule. An illegal contract is *void*. Therefore, the parties cannot sue for nonperformance. If the contract has been executed, the court will *leave the parties where it finds them*.

Illegality—Contracts Contrary to Statutes

Contracts that violate statutes are illegal, void, and unenforceable.

1. ***Gambling statutes.*** Make certain types of gambling illegal.
2. ***Usury laws.*** Set the upper limit on the annual interest rate that can be charged on certain types of loans by certain lenders.
3. ***Sabbath laws.*** Prohibit or limit the carrying on of certain secular activities on Sundays. Also called *Sunday laws* or *blue laws*.
4. ***Licensing statutes.*** Licensing statutes enacted to protect the public. Unlicensed persons cannot recover payment for providing services that a licensed person is required to provide.

Illegality—Contracts Contrary to Public Policy

Contracts that violate public policy are illegal, void, and unenforceable.

1. ***Contracts in restraint of trade.*** Contracts that unreasonably restrain trade are illegal contracts.
2. ***Covenants not to compete.*** Contracts that provide that a seller of a business or an employee will not engage in a similar business or occupation within a specified geographical area for a specified time following the sale of the business or termination of employment. Also called *noncompete clauses*. They are illegal if they are *unreasonable* in scope, area, or time. Reasonable noncompete clauses are legal and enforceable.
3. ***Exculpatory clauses.*** Contract clauses that relieve one or both of the parties to the contract from tort liability for ordinary negligence. Exculpatory clauses that affect public interests, result from superior bargaining power, or that attempt to relieve one of the liability for intentional torts, fraud, recklessness, or gross negligence are illegal. Reasonable exculpatory clauses between parties of equal bargaining power are legal.
4. ***Immoral contracts.*** Contracts whose objective is the commission of an act that is considered immoral by society are illegal.

Third-Party Rights, p. 294

Assignment

1. *Assignment.* Transfer of contractual rights by a party to a contract to a third person.
2. *Assignor.* Contract party who assigns the contractual rights.
3. *Assignee.* Third person to whom contract rights are assigned.

The assignee "stands in the shoes of the assignor" and is entitled to performance of the contract by the obligor.

Intended Beneficiaries

A third person who is owed performance under other parties' contract. A person who is to be rendered performance gratuitously under a contract, for example, a beneficiary of a life insurance policy, may sue the promisor for nonperformance.

Internet Exercises and Case Questions

Working the Web Internet Exercises

Activities

1. Go to **www.findlaw.com** and review the extensive material on contracts. Determine the statute of limitations on written contracts in your jurisdiction.
2. Visit **cori.missouri.edu**. Use this site to aid in drafting specific types of contracts and/or clauses. Test your ability by visiting the site and searching for employment agreements with noncompetition clauses.
3. To review the basic elements of a contract, visit **www.freeadvice.com/law/518us.htm**.
4. For some tips on entering into contracts, see **www.itslegal.com/infonet/consumer/contracts.html**.
5. An extensive overview of contract law can be found at the Contracts home page (Craig Smith, Santa Barbara College of Law) **www.west.net/~smith/contracts.htm**. Review the Policing the Bargain page.
6. For international sales contracts, compare the CISG and the UCC by visiting the Web site **www.cisg.law.pace.edu**. It contains the entire text of the CISG and related information.

Critical Legal Thinking Cases

10.1 Objective Theory On July 24, 1973, Warren Treece appeared before the Washington State Gambling Commission to testify on an application for a license to distribute punchboards. During his testimony, Treece made the following statement: "I'll put a hundred thousand dollars to anyone to find a crooked board. If they find it, I'll pay it." The next day, Vernon Barnes watched a television news report of the proceeding and heard Treece's statement. He also read a newspaper report of the hearings that quoted Treece's statement. A number of years earlier, while employed as a bartender, Barnes had obtained two fraudulent punchboards. When Barnes presented the two crooked punchboards to Treece and demanded payment of the $100,000, Treece refused to pay. Did Treece's statement form the basis for an enforceable contract? [*Barnes v. Treece*, 549 P.2d 1152, 1976 Wash.App. Lexis 1418 (Wash.App. 1976)]

10.2 Essential Terms Ben Hunt and others operated a farm under the name S. B. H. Farms. Hunt went to McIlroy Bank and Trust and requested a loan to build hog houses, buy livestock, and expand farming operations. The bank agreed to loan S. B. H. Farms $175,000, for which short-term promissory notes were signed by Hunt and the other owners of S. B. H. Farms. At that time, oral discussions were held with the bank officer regarding long-term financing of S. B. H.'s farming operations. No dollar amount, interest rate, or repayment terms were discussed. When the owners of S. B. H. Farms defaulted on the promissory notes, the bank filed for foreclosure on the farm and other collateral. S. B. H. Farms counterclaimed for $750,000 damages, alleging that the bank breached its oral contract to provide long-term financing. Was there an oral contract for long-term financing? [*Hunt v. McIlroy Bank and Trust*, 616 S.W.2d 759, 1981 Ark.App. Lexis 716 (Ark.App. 1981)]

10.3 Counteroffer Glende Motor Company, an automobile dealer that sold new cars, leased premises from certain landlords. In October 1979, fire destroyed part of the leased premises, and Glende restored the leasehold premises. The landlords received payment of insurance proceeds for the fire. Glende sued the landlords to recover the insurance proceeds. On May 7, 1982, 10 days before the trial was to begin, the defendants jointly served on Glende a document titled "Offer to Compromise Before Trial," which was a settlement offer of $190,000. On May 16, Glende agreed to the amount of the settlement but made it contingent upon the execution of a new lease. On May 17, the defendants notified Glende that they were revoking the settlement offer. Glende thereafter tried to accept the original settlement offer. Has there been a settlement of the lawsuit? [*Glende Motor Company v. Superior Court*, 159 Cal.App.3d 389, 205 Cal.Rptr. 682 1984 Cal.App. Lexis 2435 (Cal.App. 1984)]

10.4 The Mailbox Rule William Jenkins and Nathalie Monk owned a building in Sacramento, California. In 1979, they leased the building to Tuneup Masters for five years. The lease provided that Tuneup Masters could extend the lease for an additional five years if it gave written notice of its intention to do so by certified or registered mail at least six months prior to the expiration of the term of the lease, which was August 1, 1983.

On July 29, 1983, Larry Selditz, vice president of Tuneup Masters, prepared a letter exercising the option, prepared and sealed an envelope with the letter in it, prepared U.S. Postal Service Form 3800 and affixed the certified mail sticker on the envelope, and had his secretary deliver the envelope to the Postal Service annex located on the ground floor of the office building. Postal personnel occupied the annex only between the hours of 9 A.M. and 10 A.M. At the end of each day, between 5 P.M. and 5:15 P.M., a postal employee picked up outgoing mail. The letter to the landlords was lost in the mail. The landlords thereafter refused to renew the lease and brought an unlawful detainer action against Tuneup Masters. Was the notice renewing the option effective? [*Jenkins v. Tuneup Masters*, 190 Cal.App.3d 1, 235 Cal.Rptr. 214, 1987 Cal.App. Lexis 1475 (Cal.App. 1987)]

10.5 Consideration When John W. Frasier died, he left a will that devised certain of his community and separate property to his wife, Lena, and their three children. These devises were more valuable to Lena than just her interest in the community property that she would otherwise have received without the will. The devise to her, however, was conditioned upon the filing of a waiver by Lena of her interest in the community property, and if she failed to file the waiver, she would then receive only her interest in the community property and nothing more. Lena hired her brother, D. L. Carter, an attorney, to represent her. Carter failed to file the waiver on Lena's behalf, thus preventing her from receiving her inheritance under the will. Instead, she received her interest in the community property, which was $19,358 less than she would have received under the will. Carter sent Lena the following letter:

> *This is to advise and confirm our agreement—that in the event the J. W. Frasier estate case now on appeal is not terminated so that you will receive settlement equal to your share of the estate as you would have done if your waiver had been filed in the estate in proper time, I will make up any balance to you in payments as suits my convenience and will pay interest on your loss at 6%.*

The appeal was decided against Lena. When she tried to enforce the contract against Carter, he alleged that the contract was not enforceable because it was not supported by valid consideration. Who wins? [*Frasier v. Carter*, 437 P.2d 32, 1968 Ida. Lexis 249 (Idaho 1968)]

10.6 Past Consideration A. J. Whitmire and R. Lee Whitmire were brothers. From 1923 to 1929, A. J. lived with his brother and his brother's wife, Lillie Mae. During this period, A. J. performed various services for his brother and sister-in-law. In 1925, R. Lee and Lillie Mae purchased some land. In 1944, in the presence of Lillie Mae, R. Lee told A. J., "When we're gone, this land is yours." A. J. had not done any work for R. Lee or Lillie Mae since 1929, and none was expected or provided in the future. On May 26, 1977, after both R. Lee and Lillie Mae had died, A. J. filed a claim with the estate of Lillie Mae, seeking specific performance of the 1944 promise. Does A. J. get the property? [*Whitmire v. Watkins*, 267 S.E.2d 6, 1980 Ga. Lexis 908 (Ga. 1980)]

10.7 Preexisting Duty Robert Chuckrow Construction Company was employed as the general contractor to build a Kenney Shoe Store. Chuckrow employed Ralph Gough to perform the carpentry work on the store. The contract with Gough stipulated that he was to provide all labor, materials, tools, equipment, scaffolding, and other items necessary to complete the carpentry work. On May 15, 1965, Gough's employees erected 38 trusses at the job site. The next day, 32 of the trusses fell off the building. The reason for the trusses' falling was unexplained, and evidence showed that it was not due to Chuckrow's fault or a deficiency in the building plans. Chuckrow told Gough that he would pay him to erect the trusses and continue work. When the job was complete, Chuckrow paid Gough the original contract price but refused to pay him for the additional cost of reerecting the trusses. Gough sued Chuckrow for this expense. Can Gough recover? [*Robert Chuckrow Construction Company v. Gough*, 159 S.E.2d 469, 1968 Ga.App. Lexis 1007 (Ga.App. 1968)]

10.8 Infancy Doctrine Charles Edwards Smith, a minor, purchased an automobile from Bobby Floars Toyota on August 15, 1973. Smith executed a security agreement to finance part of the balance due on the purchase price, agreeing to pay off the balance in 30 monthly installments. On September 25, 1973, Smith turned 18, which was the age of majority. Smith made 10 monthly payments after turning 18. He then decided to disaffirm the contract and stopped making the payments. Smith claims that he may disaffirm the contract entered into when he was a minor. Toyota argues that Smith had ratified the contract since attaining the age of majority. Who is correct? [*Bobby Floars Toyota, Inc. v. Smith*, 269 S.E.2d 320, 1980 N.C.App. Lexis 3263 (N.C.App. 1980)]

10.9 Necessities of Life Bobby L. Rogers, a 19-year-old emancipated minor, had to quit engineering school and go to work in order to support his wife and expected baby. Rogers contracted with Gastonia Personnel Corporation, an employment agency, agreeing to pay Gastonia a $295 fee if it found him employment. Soon thereafter, Rogers was employed by a company referred to him by Gastonia. Rogers sought to disaffirm the contract to pay Gastonia the $295 fee. Gastonia sues for the fee, claiming that the contract was for necessaries. Who wins? [*Gastonia Personnel Corporation v. Rogers*, 172 S.E.2d 19, 1970 N.C. Lexis 673 (N.C. 1970)]

10.10 Illegal Contract In 1972, Jordanos', Inc., suspected and accused one of its employees, Arthur T. Allen, of theft. The union to which Allen belonged negotiated an oral contract with Jordanos' whereby Allen agreed to accent a permanent layoff if Jordanos' would not report the suspected theft to the state's unemployment agency, so that Allen could collect unemployment benefits. Jordanos' agreed. It is a crime for an employer and employee to withhold relevant information from the state's unemployment agency. Jordanos' subsequently reported the suspected theft to the state's unemployment agency, and Allen was denied unemployment benefits. Allen sued Jordanos' for damages for breach of contract. Can Allen recover against Jordanos'? [*Allen v. Jordanos', Inc.*, 52 Cal.App. 3d 160, 125 Cal.Rptr. 31, 1975 Cal.App. Lexis 1442 (Cal.App. 1975)]

10.11 Covenant Not to Compete Gerry Morris owned a silk screening and lettering shop in Tucson, Arizona. On April 11, 1974, Morris entered into a contract to sell the business to Alfred and Connie Gann. The contract contained the following covenant not to compete: "Seller agrees not to enter into silk screening or lettering shop business within Tucson and a 100-mile radius of Tucson, for a period of ten (10) years from the date of this Agreement and will not compete in any manner whatsoever with buyers, and seller further agrees that he will refer all business contacts to buyers." Morris opened a silk screening and lettering business in competition with the Ganns and in violation of the noncompetition clause. The Ganns brought this action against Morris for breach of contract and to enforce the covenant not to compete. Is the covenant not to compete valid and enforceable in this case? [*Gann v. Morris*, 596 P.2d 43, 1979 Ariz.App. Lexis 487 (Ariz.App. 1979)]

10.12 Exculpatory Clause Grady Perkins owned the Raleigh Institute of Cosmetology, and Ray Monk and Rovetta Allen were employed as instructors at the institute. The school trains students to do hair styling and coloring, cosmetology, and other beauty services. The students receive practical training by providing services to members of the public under the supervision of the instructors. On March 28, 1985, Francis I. Alston went to the institute to have her hair colored and styled by a student who was under the supervision of Monk and Allen. Before receiving any services, Alston signed a written release form that released the institute and its employees from liability for their negligence. While coloring Alston's hair, the student negligently used a chemical that caused Alston's hair to fall out. Alston sued the institute, Perkins, Monk, and Allen for damages. The defendants asserted that the release form signed by Alston barred her suit. Is the exculpatory clause valid? [*Alston v. Monk*, 373 S.E.2d 463, 1988 N.C.App. Lexis 987 (N.C.App. 1988)]

10.13 Unconscionable Contract Bill Graham, an experienced promoter and producer of musical concerts, entered into a contract with Leon Russell, a rock singer who did business under the corporate name Scissor-Tail., Inc., whereby Graham would promote several concerts for Russell. Russell belonged to the American Federation of Musicians (AFM), a union that represented most big-name musicians. The contract between Graham and Russell was on a standard, preprinted form required to be used by all AFM members. The contract contained an arbitration clause that required any disputes regarding the contract to be heard and decided by the executive board of the AFM. When a monetary dispute arose between Graham and Russell regarding the division of proceeds from the concerts, Graham sued Russell in court. Russell filed a motion to compel arbitration. Graham asserted that the arbitration clause in the AFM contract is unconscionable. Is it? [*Graham v. Scissor-Tail, Inc.*, 28 Cal.App. 3d 807, 171 Cal.Reptr. 604, 1981 Cal. Lexis 115 (Cal.App. 1981)]

10.14 Assignment William John Cunningham, a professional basketball player, entered into a contract with Southern Sports Corporation, which owned the Carolina Cougars, a professional basketball team. The contract provided that Cunningham was to play basketball for the Cougars for a three-year period, commencing on October 2, 1971. The contract contained a provision that it could not be assigned to any other professional basketball franchise without Cunningham's approval. Subsequently, Southern Sports Corporation sold its assets, including its franchise and Cunningham's contract, to the Munchak Corporation. There was no change in the Cougars's location after the purchase. When Cunningham refused to play for the new owners, Munchak sued to enforce Cunningham's contract. Was Cunningham's contract assignable to the new owner? [*Munchak Corporation v. Cunningham*, 457 F.2d 721, 1972 U.S. App. Lexis 10272 (4th Cir. 1972)]

Business Ethics Cases

10.15 Business Ethics On Sunday, October 6, 1974, the Lewiston Lodge of Elks sponsored a golf tournament at the Fairlawn Country Club in Poland, Maine. For promotional purposes, Marcel Motors, an automobile dealership, agreed to give any golfer who shot a hole-in-one a new 1974 Dodge Colt. Fliers advertising the tournament were posted in the Elks Club and sent to potential participants. On the day of the tournament, the 1974 Dodge Colt was parked near the clubhouse, with one of the posters conspicuously displayed on the vehicle. Alphee Chenard, Jr., who had seen the promotional literature regarding the hole-in-one offer, registered for the tournament and paid the requisite entrance fee. While playing the thirteenth hole of the golf course, and in the presence of the other members of his foursome, Chenard shot a hole-in-one. When Marcel Motors refused to tender the automobile, Chenard sued for breach of contract. Was the contract a bilateral or a unilateral contract? Does Chenard win? Was it ethical for Marcel Motors to refuse to give the automobile to Chenard? [*Chenard v. Marcel Motors*, 387 A.2d 596, 1978 Me. Lexis 911 (Maine 1978)]

10.16 Business Ethics Ocean Dunes of Hutchinson Island Development Corporation was a developer of condominium units. Prior to the construction, Albert and Helen Colangelo entered into a purchase agreement to buy one of the units and paid a deposit to Ocean Dunes. A provision in the purchase agreement provided that

> *If Developer shall default in the performance of its obligations pursuant to this agreement, Purchaser's only remedy shall be to terminate this agreement, whereupon the Deposit shall be refunded to Purchaser and all rights and obligations thereunder shall thereupon become null and void.*

The purchase agreement provided that if the buyer defaulted, the developer could retain the buyer's deposit or sue the buyer for damages and any other legal or equitable remedy. When Ocean Dunes refused to sell the unit to the Colangelos, they sued seeking a decree of specific performance to require Ocean Dunes to sell them the unit. Ocean Dunes alleged that the above-quoted provision prevented the plaintiffs from seeking any legal or equitable remedy. Was the defendant's duty under the contract illusory? Was it ethical for Ocean Dunes to place the provision at issue in the contract? [*Ocean Dunes of Hutchinson Island Development Corporation v. Colangelo*, 463 So.2d 437, 1985 Fla.App. Lexis 12298 (Fla.App. 1985)]

10.17 Business Ethics Richard Zientara was friends with Chester and Bernice Kaszuba. All three were residents of Indiana. Bernice, who was employed in an Illinois tavern where Illinois state lottery tickets were sold, had previously obtained lottery tickets for Zientara because Indiana did not have a state lottery. In early April 1984, Zientara requested that Kaszuba purchase an Illinois lottery ticket for him. He gave Kaszuba the money for the ticket and the numbers 6-15-16-23-24-37. Kaszuba purchased the ticket, but when it turned out to be the winning combination worth $1,698,800, she refused to give the ticket to Zientara and unsuccessfully tried to collect the money. Zientara filed suit against Kaszuba in Indiana, claiming the ticket and proceeds thereof. Was the contract legal? Did the Kaszubas act ethically in this case? [*Kaszuba v. Zientara*, 506 N.E.2d 1, 1987 Ind. Lexis 874 (Ind. 1987)]

10.18 Business Ethics On August 31, 1965, Clifton and Cora Jones, who were welfare recipients, received a visit from a salesman representing You Shop at Home Service, Inc. After a sales representation, Jones signed a retail installment contract to purchase a home freezer unit for the sale price of $900.00. With the addition of time credit charges, credit life insurance, and credit property insurance, the contract price totaled $1,234.80. The freezer had a maximum retail value of $300.00. Evidence showed that the Joneses were unsophisticated and uneducated concerning contracts.

After paying $619.88, the Joneses brought an action to rescind the contract. Star Credit Corporation, which had come into possession of the credit contract, counterclaimed for $819.81, the amount remaining on the contract plus charges for missed payments. Is the contract unconscionable in the legal sense? If so, what remedy should be awarded? Was it ethical for the sales representatives to prey upon ignorant and unsophisticated consumers? Was it ethical for the Joneses to attempt to get out of the contract they signed? [*Jones v. Star Credit Corp.*, 298 N.Y.S.2d 264, 1969 N.Y.Misc. Lexis 1696 (N.Y.Sup. 1969)]

Briefing the Case Writing Assignment

Read Case A.10 in the Case Appendix [*Carnival Leisure Industries, Ltd. v. Aubin*]. This case is excerpted from the court of appeals opinion. Review and brief the case. In your brief, be sure to answer the following questions.

1. What were the plaintiff's contentions on appeal?
2. What law was applied by the court in this case—Bahamian law or Texas law? Why was that law applied?
3. What is the consequence of finding an illegal contract? Apply this rule to the facts of this case.
4. Did Aubin act ethically in avoiding an obligation that he knowingly made? Do you think he would have given back the money if he had won at gambling?

Answers to Management Decision Questions

1. You should have your classmates and others who may become aware of your project sign a nondisclosure agreement (NDA). NDAs are enforceable contracts that protect the confidentiality of secret information and swear the signatory to secrecy about confidential ideas, trade secrets, and other nonpublic information revealed by the party proffering the NDA. States have enacted legislation concerning the enforceability and validity of NDAs and other confidential agreements. Many entrepreneurs and technology innovators are having their boyfriends, girlfriends, family members, friends, and others sign NDAs before revealing anything about what they are doing. If your classmates violate the NDA, you can request a court to order the individuals to cease and desist from such action and sue for damages.
2. When the program is ready to be marketed, you should have the software program copyrighted. Copyright law protects the work of authors and other creative persons from the unauthorized use of their copyrighted materials. Software falls under the protection of the Copyright Revision Act of 1976. The unauthorized copying of this software would be prohibited under this statute.

Endnotes

1. *Rebstock v. Birthright Oil & Gas Co.*, 406 So.2d 636, 1981 La.App. Lexis 5242 (La.App. 1981).
2. *Restatement (Second) of Contracts*, § 1.
3. *Restatement (Second) of Contracts*, § 40.
4. *Hamer v. Sidway*, 124 N.Y. 538, 27 N.E. 256, 1891 N.Y. Lexis 1396 (N.Y. 1891).
5. *Restatement (Second) of Contracts*, § 302.

11

Performance of Contracts and Remedies for Breach

"When I use a word," Humpty Dumpty said, in rather a scornful tone, "it means just what I choose it to mean—neither more nor less."

"The question is," said Alice, "whether you can make words mean so many different things."

"The question is," said Humpty Dumpty, "which is to be master—that's all."

—Lewis Carroll
Alice's Adventures in Wonderland (1865)

Chapter Objectives

After studying this chapter, you should be able to:

1. Explain the genuineness of assent.
2. List and describe the contracts that must be in writing under the Statute of Frauds.
3. Describe the performance of a contract.
4. Describe compensatory, consequential, and liquidated damages.
5. Define the equitable remedies of specific performance, quasi-contract, and injunction.

Chapter Contents

- Genuineness of Assent
- Statute of Frauds—Writing Requirement
- Promises of Performance
- Discharge of Performance
- Performance and Breach
- Remedies

Management Decision Performance of Contracts and Remedies for Breach

You are a concert pianist who recently completed a year-long concert tour of Europe and the United States. The concert received rave revues, and you performed before sold-out audiences. Six months into the tour, you were offered a lucrative contract for a two-year engagement at a major Las Vegas casino. You informed the booking agency of the offer and threatened to leave the tour and accept the offer from the casino unless the booking agency agreed to double your performance fee. It agreed, and you completed the tour. The agency then refused to pay the extra compensation. You sued the agency for breach of contract.

1. Is the agency in breach of contract?
2. Was it ethical for the casino to approach you with the offer?

A verbal contract isn't worth the paper it's written on.

Samuel Goldwyn

As noted in Chapter 10, contracts are an important part of the daily lives of businesses and individuals. This chapter covers such topics as genuineness of assent, the requirements for contract performance, and the consequences for failure to perform. The role of contracts in international trade is also discussed.

Genuineness of Assent

A contract may not be enforced even if all of the required elements of a legal contract are met. This happens when the party against whom enforcement is sought raises certain defenses against its enforcement.

genuineness of assent
The requirement that a party's assent to a contract be genuine. Genuineness of assent is an issue in the areas of mistake, misrepresentation, duress, and undue influence.

One of the primary defenses to the enforcement of a contract is that the assent of one or both of the parties to the contract was not genuine or real. **Genuine assent** may be missing because a party entered into a contract based on *mistake*, *fraudulent misrepresentation*, *duress*, or *undue influence*. These defenses are discussed in the following paragraphs.

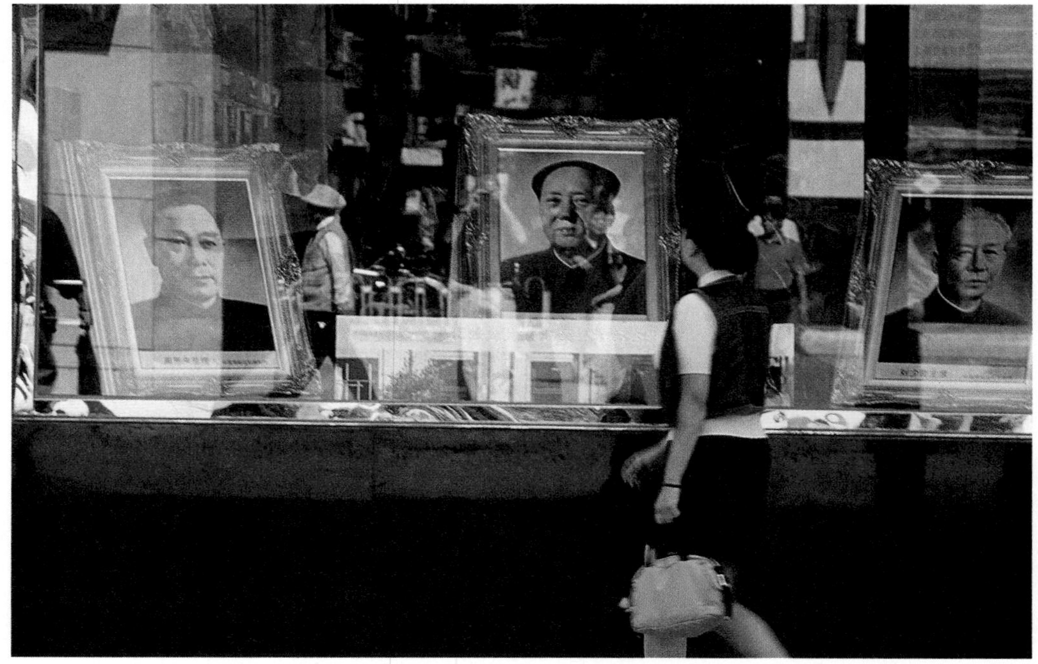

Beijing, China. Styles of contracting vary around the world. In many countries substantial time is necessary to build a relationship of trust before contract negotiations ensue.

Unilateral Mistakes

Unilateral mistakes occur when only one party is mistaken about a material fact regarding the subject matter of the contract. There are three types of situations in which the contract may not be enforced due to such a mistake:

unilateral mistake
A situation in which only one party is mistaken about a material fact regarding the subject matter of a contract.

1. One party makes a unilateral mistake of fact, and the other party knows (or should know) that a mistake has been made.
2. A unilateral mistake occurs because of a clerical or mathematical error that is not the result of gross negligence.
3. The mistake is so serious that enforcing the contract would be unconscionable.[1]

In most cases, however, the mistaken party will not be permitted to rescind the contract. The contract will be enforced on its terms.

Words are chameleons, which reflect the color of their environment.

L. Hand, J.
Commissioner v. National Carbide Co. (1948)

Consider This Example Suppose Trent Anderson wants to purchase a car from the showroom floor. He looks at several models. Although he decides to purchase a car with a sunroof, he does not tell the salesman about this preference. The model named in the contract he signs does not have this feature, although he believes it does. Mr. Anderson's unilateral mistake will not relieve him of his contractual obligation to purchase the car.

In the following case, the court had to decide whether to allow a party out of a contract because of its unilateral mistake.

Case 11.1 Unilateral Mistake

Wells Fargo Credit Corp. v. Martin
605 So.2d 531, 1992 Fla.App. Lexis 9927 (1992)
District Court of Appeals of Florida

Background and Facts
Wells Fargo Credit Corporation (Wells Fargo) obtained a judgment of foreclosure on a house owned by Mr. and Mrs. Clevenger. The total indebtedness stated in the judgment was $207,141. The foreclosure sale was scheduled for 11:00 A.M. on July 12, 1991, at the west front door of the Hillsborough County Courthouse. Wells Fargo was represented by a paralegal, who had attended more than 1,000 similar sales. Wells Fargo's handwritten instruction sheet informed the paralegal to make one bid at $115,000, the tax-appraised value of the property. Because the first "1" in the number was close to the "$," the paralegal misread the bid instruction as $15,000 and opened the bidding at that amount. Harley Martin, who was attending his first judicial sale, bid $20,000. The county clerk gave ample time for another bid and then announced "$20,000 going once, $20,000 going twice, sold to Harley. . . ." The paralegal screamed, "Stop, I'm sorry, I made a mistake!" The certificate of sale was issued to Martin. Wells Fargo filed suit to set aside the judicial sale based on its unilateral mistake. The trial court held for Martin. Wells Fargo appealed.

Issue
Does Wells Fargo's unilateral mistake constitute grounds for setting aside the judicial sale?

In The Language of The Court
Altenbernd, Judge We accept the trial court's conclusion that the amount of the sale was grossly inadequate. This inadequacy, however, occurred due to an avoidable, unilateral mistake by an agent of Wells Fargo. As between Wells Fargo and a good faith purchaser at the judicial sale, the trial court had the discretion to place the risk of this mistake upon Wells Fargo.

Thus, we affirm the trial court's orders denying relief to Wells Fargo.

We are certain that this result seems harsh to Wells Fargo. Nevertheless, Mr. Martin's bid was accepted when the clerk announced "sold." Without ruling that a unilateral mistake by the complaining party could never justify relief, we hold that the trial court had the discretion under these facts to make Wells Fargo suffer the loss.

Decision and Remedy
The appellate court held that Wells Fargo's unilateral mistake did not entitle it to relief from the judicial sale.

Case Questions
Critical Legal Thinking Should contracts be allowed to be rescinded because of unilateral mistakes? Why or why not?

Business Ethics Did Wells Fargo act ethically in trying to set aside the judicial sale?

Business Application Do you think mistakes such as that made by Wells Fargo happen very often in business?

Mutual Mistakes

mutual mistake of fact
A mistake made by both parties concerning a material fact that is important to the subject matter of the contract.

Either party may rescind a contract if there has been a **mutual mistake of a past or existing material fact.**[2] A material fact is one that is important to the subject matter of the contract. An ambiguity in a contract may constitute a mutual mistake of a material fact. An ambiguity occurs where a word or term in the contract is susceptible to more than one logical interpretation. If there has been a mutual mistake, the contract may be rescinded on the ground that no contract has been formed because there has been no "meeting of the minds" between the parties.

Most of the disputes in the world arise from words.
Lord Mansfield, C. J.
Morgan v. Jones (1773)

In the celebrated case of *Raffles v. Wichelhaus*,[3] which has become better known as the case of the good ship *Peerless*, the parties agreed on a sale of cotton that was to be delivered from Bombay by the ship. However, there were two ships named *Peerless*, and each party, in agreeing to the sale, was referring to a different ship. Because the sailing time of the two ships was materially different, neither party was willing to agree to shipment by the other *Peerless*. The court ruled that there was no binding contract because each party had a different ship in mind when the contract was entered into.

mutual mistake of value
A mistake that occurs if both parties know the object of the contract but are mistaken as to its value.

The courts must distinguish between *mutual mistakes of fact* and *mutual mistakes of value*. A **mutual mistake of value** exists if both parties know the object of the contract but are mistaken as to its value. Here, the contract remains enforceable by either party because the identity of the subject matter of the contract is not at issue. If the rule were different, almost all contracts could later be rescinded by the party who got the "worst" of the deal.

An honest man's word is as good as his bond.
Don Quixote

Consider This Example Suppose Eileen Spencer cleans her attic and finds a painting of tomato soup cans. She has no use for it, so she offers to sell it to Fred Lee for $100. Fred, who likes the painting, accepts the offer and pays Eileen $100. It is later discovered that the painting is worth $200,000 because it was painted by Andy Warhol. Neither party knew this at the time of contracting. It is a mistake of value. Eileen cannot recover the painting.

Fraudulent Misrepresentation

intentional misrepresentation
A misrepresentation that occurs when one person consciously decides to induce another person to rely and act on a misrepresentation. Also called *fraud*.

A **misrepresentation** occurs when an assertion is made that is not in accord with the facts.[4] An **intentional misrepresentation** occurs when one person consciously decides to induce another person to rely and act on a misrepresentation. Intentional misrepresentation is commonly referred to as **fraudulent misrepresentation**, or **fraud**. When a fraudulent misrepresentation is used to induce another to enter into a contract, the innocent party's assent to the contract is not genuine, and the contract is voidable by the innocent party.[5] The innocent party can either rescind the contract and obtain restitution or enforce the contract and sue for contract damages.

There are various types of fraud. Fraud can be categorized as follows:

fraud in the inception
Fraud that occurs if a person is deceived as to the nature of his or her act and does not know what he or she is signing.

- ***Fraud in the Inception*** **Fraud in the inception**, or **fraud in the factum**, occurs if a person is deceived as to the nature of his or her act and does not know what he or she is signing. Such contracts are void rather than just voidable. For example, suppose Heather brings her professor a grade card to sign. The professor signs the front of the grade card. On the back, however, are contract terms that transfer all of the professor's property to Heather. Here there is fraud in the inception. The contract is void.

fraud in the inducement
Fraud that occurs when the party knows what he or she is signing but has been fraudulently induced to enter into the contract.

- ***Fraud in the Inducement*** A great many fraud cases concern **fraud in the inducement**. Here, the innocent party knows what he or she is signing but has been fraudulently induced to enter into the contract. Such contracts are voidable by the innocent party.

  For example, suppose Lyle Green tells Candice Young he is forming a partnership to invest in drilling for oil and invites her to invest in this venture. In reality, though, Lyle Green intends to use whatever money he receives for his personal expenses, and he absconds with Ms. Young's $30,000 investment. Here there has been fraud in the inducement. Ms. Young can rescind the contract and recover the money from Lyle Greem—if he can be found.

- ***Fraud by Concealment*** **Fraud by concealment** occurs when one party takes specific action to conceal a material fact from another party. For example, suppose that ABC Blouses, Inc., contracts to buy a used sewing machine from Wear-Well Shirts, Inc. Wear-Well has not shown ABC the repair invoices from the sewing machine even though ABC asked to see them. Relying on the fact that the machine was not repaired, ABC bought the machine. If ABC discovers that a significant repair record has been concealed, it can sue Wear-Well for fraud.

fraud by concealment
Fraud that occurs when one party takes specific action to conceal a material fact from another party.

In the following case, the court allowed a contract to be rescinded.

Case 11.2
Fraud

Wilson v. Western National Life Insurance Co.
235 Cal.App.3d 981, 1 Cal.Rptr.2d 157, 1991 Cal.App. Lexis 1249 (1991)
California Court of Appeals

Background and Facts

Daniel and Doris Wilson were husband and wife. On August 13, 1985, Daniel fainted from a narcotics overdose and was rushed to the hospital unconscious. Doris accompanied him. Daniel responded to medication used to counteract a narcotics overdose and recovered. The emergency room physician noted that Daniel had probably suffered from a heroin overdose and had multiple puncture sites on his arms.

On October 8, 1985, Gil Cantrell, an gent for Western National Life Insurance Company (Western), met with the Wilsons in their home for the purpose of taking their application for life insurance. Cantrell asked questions and recorded the Wilsons' responses on a written application form. Daniel answered the following questions:

	Yes	No
13. In the past 10 years, have you been treated or joined an organization for alcoholism or drug addiction? If "Yes," explain on the reverse side.		X
17. In the past 5 years, have you consulted or been treated or examined by any physician or practitioner?		X

Both of the Wilsons signed the application form and paid the agent the first month's premium. Under insurance law and the application form, the life insurance policy took effect immediately. Daniel Wilson died from a drug overdose two days later. Western rescinded the policy and rejected Doris Wilson's claim to recover the policy's $50,000 death benefit for Daniel's death, alleging failure to disclose the August 13, 1985, incident. Doris sued to recover the death benefits. The trial court granted summary judgment for Western. Doris appealed.

Issue

Was there a concealment of a material fact that justified Western's rescission of the life insurance policy?

In The Language of The Court

Stone, Presiding Judge Plaintiff asserts the court erroneously granted summary judgment because Western failed to prove she or decedent made a misrepresentation in the application. We disagree.

In her deposition, plaintiff testified neither she nor decedent told Cantrell about decedent's fainting spell or his hospital treatment two months earlier. Thus, there is no question but that they omitted medical information. Knowledge of the true facts by plaintiff and decedent is beyond dispute.

Plaintiff further argues the misrepresentation, if one occurred, was not material. Plaintiff's argument must fail. The trial court properly found the omissions to be material and the evidence supporting its materiality uncontradicted. The trial court had before it evidence from Western that the application would not have been accepted, and decedent would not have been found to be insurable, had he disclosed on the application the episode in August when he became unconscious from a narcotics overdose.

A material misrepresentation or concealment entitles the injured party to rescission. Concealment, whether intentional or unintentional, entitles the injured party to rescind insurance. Western properly rescinded the insurance contract and its obligation to provide coverage terminated as of the date of application.

Decision and Remedy

The appellate court held that there was a concealment by the Wilsons that warranted rescission of the life insurance policy by Western.

Case Questions

Critical Legal Thinking Should a contract be allowed to be rescinded because of an *innocent* misrepresentation? Why or why not?

Business Ethics Do you think the concealment was intentional or innocent?

Business Application Do you think there is very much insurance fraud in this country? Explain.

Entrepreneur and the Law

Don't Be Taken by Fraud

Entrepreneurs and other business persons must be on guard in their commercial dealings not to be taken by fraud. Basically, if it sounds "too good to be true," it is a signal that the situation might be fraudulent. Other frauds are difficult to detect. To prove fraud, the following elements must be shown:

1. The wrongdoer made a false representation of material fact.
2. The wrongdoer intended to deceive the innocent party.
3. The innocent party justifiably relied on the misrepresentation.
4. The innocent party was injured.

Each of these elements is discussed in the following paragraphs.

1. ***Material Misrepresentation of Fact*** A misrepresentation may occur by words (oral or written) or by the conduct of the party. To be actionable as fraud, the misrepresentation must be of a past or existing *material fact*. This means that the misrepresentation must have been a significant factor in inducing the innocent party to enter into the contract. It does not have to be the sole factor. Statements of opinion or predictions about the future generally do not form the basis for fraud.
2. ***Intent to Deceive*** To prove fraud, the person making the misrepresentation must have either had knowledge that the representation was false or made it without sufficient knowledge of the truth. This is called **scienter** ("guilty mind"). The misrepresentation must have been made with the intent to deceive the innocent party. Intent can be inferred from the circumstances.
3. ***Reliance on the Misrepresentation*** A misrepresentation is not actionable unless the innocent party to whom the misrepresentation was directed acted upon it. Further, an innocent party who acts in reliance on the misrepresentation must justify his or her reliance. Justifiable reliance generally is found unless the innocent party knew that the misrepresentation was false or was so extravagant as to be obviously false. For example, reliance on a statement such as "This diamond ring is worth $10,000, but I'll sell it to you for $100" would not be justified.
4. ***Injury to the Innocent Party*** To recover damages, the innocent party must prove that the fraud caused economic injury. The measure of damages is the difference between the value of the property as represented and the actual value of the property. This measure of damages gives the innocent party the "benefit of the bargain." In the alternative, the buyer can rescind the contract and recover the purchase price. ■

Duress

duress
Situation that occurs when one party threatens to do a wrongful act unless the other party enters into a contract.

Duress occurs where one party threatens to do some wrongful act unless the other party enters into a contract. If a party to a contract has been forced into making the contract, the assent is not voluntary. Such contracts are not enforceable against the innocent party.

The threat to commit physical harm or extortion unless someone enters into a contract constitutes duress; so does a threat to bring (or not drop) a criminal lawsuit. This is so even if the criminal lawsuit is well founded.[6] However, a threat to bring (or not drop) a civil lawsuit does not constitute duress unless such a suit is frivolous or brought in bad faith.

> Every unjust decision is a reproach to the law or the judge who administers it. If the law should be in danger of doing injustice, then equity should be called in to remedy it. Equity was introduced to mitigate the rigour of the law.
>
> Lord Denning, M. R.
> *Re Vandervell's Trusts (1974)*

The courts have recognized another type of duress—*economic duress*. Economic duress usually occurs when one party to a contract refuses to perform his or her contractual duties unless the other party pays an increased price, enters into a second contract with the threatening party, or the like. The duressed party must prove that he or she had no choice but to give in to the threat.

Undue Influence

undue influence
One person's taking advantage of another person's mental, emotional, or physical weakness and unduly persuading that person to enter into a contract; the persuasion by the wrongdoer must overcome the free will of the innocent party.

The courts may permit the rescission of a contract based on the equitable doctrine of **undue influence**. Undue influence occurs when one person (the dominant party) takes advantage of another person's mental, emotional, or physical weakness and unduly persuades that person (the servient party) to enter into a contract. The persuasion by the wrongdoer must overcome the free will of the innocent party. A contract that is entered into because of undue influence is voidable by the innocent party.[7] Wills often are challenged as being made under undue influence.

The following elements must be shown to prove undue influence:

1. A fiduciary or confidential relationship must have existed between the parties.
2. The dominant party must have unduly used his or her influence to persuade the servient party to enter into a contract.

> Necessitous men are not, truly speaking, free men, but, to answer a present exigency, will submit to any terms that the crafty may impose upon them.
>
> Lord Thomas Henley
> *Vernon v. Bethell (1762)*

If there is a confidential relationship between persons—such as lawyer and client, doctor and patient, psychiatrist and patient—any contract made by the servient party that benefits the dominant party is presumed to be entered into under undue influence. This is a rebuttable presumption that can be overcome by proper evidence.

Statute of Frauds—Writing Requirement

Today, every state has enacted a **statute of frauds** that requires certain types of contracts to be in *writing*. This statute is intended to ensure that the terms of important contracts are not forgotten, misunderstood, or fabricated.

statute of frauds
A state statute that requires certain types of contracts to be in writing.

Generally, an *executory contract* that is not in writing even though the statute of frauds requires it to be is unenforceable by either party. (If the contract is valid in all other respects, however, it may be voluntarily performed by the parties.) The statute of frauds is usually raised by one party as a defense to the enforcement of the contract by the other party. If an oral contract that should have been in writing under the statute of frauds is already executed, neither party can seek to rescind the contract on the ground of noncompliance with the statute of frauds, however.

Contracts that are required to be in writing under the statute of frauds are discussed in the following paragraphs.

Bukhara, Uzbekistan. Oral contracts are used more in many foreign countries than they are in the United States.

Contracts Involving Interests in Land

Business Brief

Although only certain contracts must be in writing under the Statute of Frauds, it is good practice to place other contracts in writing so there is no dispute as to the terms of the contract at a later date.

To be enforceable, any contract that transfers an ownership interest in **real property** must be in writing under the statute of frauds. Real property includes the land itself, buildings, trees, soil, minerals, timber, plants, crops, fixtures, and things permanently affixed to the land or buildings. Certain personal property that is permanently affixed to the real property—for example, built-in cabinets in a house—are *fixtures* that are considered part of the real property.

Other contracts that transfer an ownership interest in land must be in writing under the statute of frauds. These interests include the following:

- ***Mortgages*** Borrowers often give a lender an interest in real property as security for the repayment of a loan. This must be done through the use of a written **mortgage** or **deed of trust**.
- ***Leases*** A **lease** is the transfer of the right to use real property for a specified period of time. Most statutes of frauds require leases for a term of more than one year to be in writing.
- ***Life Estates*** On some occasions, a person is given a **life estate** in real property. This means that the person has an interest in the land for the person's lifetime, and the interest will be transferred to another party on that person's death. A life estate is an ownership interest that must be in writing under the statute of frauds.
- ***Easements*** An **easement** is a given or required right to use another person's land without owning or leasing it. Easements may be either express or implied. Express easements must be in writing to be enforceable, whereas implied easements need not be written.

Statute of frauds: That unfortunate statute, the misguided application of which has been the cause of so many frauds.

Bacon, V. C.
Morgan v. Worthington (1878)

One-Year Rule

one-year rule
A rule that states that an executory contract that cannot be performed by its own terms within one year of its formation must be in writing.

According to the statute of frauds, an executory contract that cannot be performed by its own terms within one year of its formation must be in writing.[8] This **one-year rule** is intended to prevent disputes about contract terms that may otherwise occur toward the

Lake Huron. Contracts that transfer an ownership interest in real property such as this beachfront must be in writing under the statute of frauds.

end of a long-term contract. If the performance of the contract is possible within the one-year period, the contract may be oral.

The extension of an oral contract might cause the contract to violate the statute of frauds. For example, suppose the owner of a Burger King franchise hires Eugene Daly as a manager for 6 months. This contract may be oral. Assume that after 3 months, the owner and manager agree to extend the contract for an additional 11 months. At the time of the extension, the contract would be for 14 months (the 3 left on the contract plus 11 added by the extension). The modification would have to be in writing because it exceeds the one-year rule in the statute of frauds.

Business Brief
Employment contracts are often for periods longer than one year. These contracts should be in writing to be enforceable.

Collateral Promises

A **collateral** or **guaranty contract** occurs when one person agrees to answer for the debts or duties of another person. Collateral promises are required to be in writing under the statute of frauds.[9]

collateral contract
A promise in which one person agrees to answer for the debts or duties of another person.

In a guaranty situation, there are at least three parties and two contracts. (See Exhibit 11.1.) The *first contract*, which is known as the **original** or **primary contract**, is between the debtor and the creditor. It does not have to be in writing (unless another provision of the statute of frauds requires it to be). The *second contract*, called the **guaranty contract**, is between the person who agrees to pay the debt if the primary debtor does not (i.e., the **guarantor**) and the original creditor. The guarantor's liability is secondary because it does not arise unless the party primarily liable fails to perform.

guarantor
The person who agrees to pay the debt if the primary debtor does not.

Consider This Example Jay Hoberman, recent college graduate, offers to purchase a new automobile on credit from a General Motors dealership. Because the purchaser does not have a credit history, the dealer will agree to sell the car only if there is a guarantor. Jay's mother signs the guaranty contract. She becomes responsible for any payments her son fails to make.

To break an oral agreement which is not legally binding is morally wrong.
Talmud, Bava Metzi'a

Contracts for the Sale of Goods

Section 201 of the Uniform Commercial Code (UCC) is the basic statute of frauds provision for sales contracts. It requires that contracts for the sale of goods costing *$500 or more* be in writing to be enforceable.[10] If the contract price of an original sales contract is below $500 and does not have to be in writing under the **UCC Statute of Frauds**, but if a modification of the contract increases in sales price to $500 or more, the modification has to be in writing to be enforceable.[11]

UCC Statute of Frauds
A provision for contracts that says that the sale of *goods* costing $500 or more must be in writing.

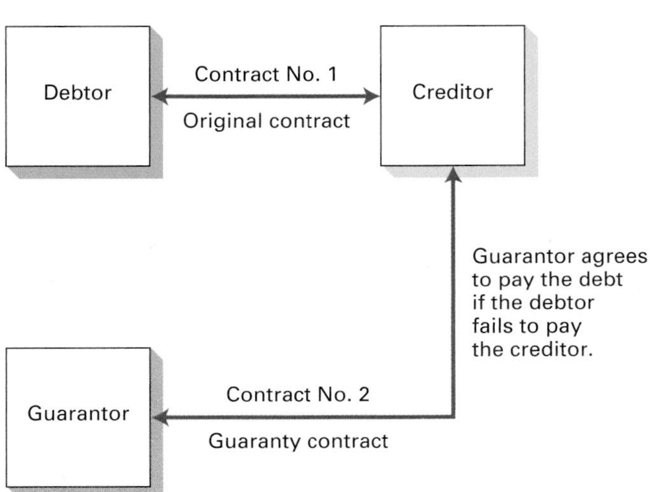

Exhibit 11.1
Original and Guaranty Contracts

Mackinac Island, Michigan. The UCC requires contracts for the sale of goods costing $500 or more, such as these horses, to be in writing.

Agents' Contracts

Many state statutes of frauds require that *agents' contracts* to sell property covered by the statute of frauds be in writing to be enforceable. This requirement is often referred to as the **equal dignity rule**.

equal dignity rule
A rule that says that agents' contracts to sell property covered by the statute of frauds must be in writing to be enforceable.

Consider This Example Suppose Barney Berkowitz hires Cynthia Lamont, a licensed Century 21 real estate agent, to sell his house. Because a contract to sell real estate must be in writing pursuant to the statute of frauds, the equal dignity rule requires the agent's contract to be in writing as well. Some state statutes of frauds expressly list the agent's contracts that must be in writing.

Entrepreneur and the Law

An Oral Contract Isn't Worth the Paper It's Written On

The statute of frauds, which requires certain contracts to be in writing in order to be enforceable, is designed to prevent fraud. Entrepreneurs and other business persons should know the requirements of the state's statute of frauds; otherwise, they may find themselves with an unenforceable oral contract. Consider the following case.

Whitman Heffernan Rhein & Co., Inc. (Whitman) is a company that provides financial advice to firms planning acquisitions and mergers. The Griffin Company (Griffin), which is owned primarily by Merv Griffin, was negotiating to purchase Resorts International, Inc., from Donald Trump. Whitman alleged that it entered into an oral contract to provide Griffin with financial and investment advice in connection with the negotiation of the purchase of Resorts International. Once Griffin completed the acquisition of Resorts International from Trump, Whitman requested payment for its services from Griffin. When Griffin did not pay, Whitman sued Griffin to recover payment. Griffin asserted the New York Statute of Frauds in defense, arguing that Whitman's alleged contract to provide services in negotiating the purchase of a business had to be in writing to be enforceable, and because Whitman's complaint alleged that it was an oral contract, it was not enforceable.

The New York court agreed with Griffin and held that the alleged contract was oral and therefore barred by the statute of frauds. The court stated:

> New York General Obligations Law § 5-701(a)(10) provides that an agreement is void, unless evidenced by a writing signed by the party to be charged, if the agreement is a contract to pay compensation for services rendered in negotiating the purchase of a business. The term "negotiating" includes assisting in the consummation of the transaction.

The moral of the story for entrepreneurs and other business persons is to get it in writing! [*Whitman Heffernan Rhein & Co., Inc. v. The Griffin Co.*, 557 N.Y.S.2d 342, 1990 N.Y.App.Div. Lexis 8334 (NY 1990)] ■

E-Commerce & Information Technology

Electronic Contracts Meet Writing Requirement of the Statute of Frauds

In 2000, the federal government enacted the **Electronic Signature in Global and National Commerce Act**. This act is a federal statute enacted by Congress and signed by the president that therefore has national reach. The act is designed to place the world of electronic commerce on a par with the world of paper contracts in the United States.

One of the main features of the act is that it recognizes electronic contracts as meeting the writing requirement of the statute of frauds for most contracts. Statutes of frauds are state laws that require certain types of contracts to be in writing. The 2000 federal act provides that electronically signed contracts cannot be denied effect because they are in electronic form or delivered electronically. The act also provides that record retention requirements are satisfied if the records are stored electronically.

The federal law was passed with several provisions to protect consumers. First, consumers must consent to receiving electronic records and contracts. Second, to receive electronic records, consumers must be able to demonstrate that they have access to the electronic records. Third, businesses must tell consumers that they have the right to receive hard-copy documents of transactions. ■

Promissory Estoppel

The doctrine of **promissory estoppel**, or **equitable estoppel**, is another equitable exception to the strict application of the statute of frauds. The *Restatement (Second) of Contracts* version of promissory estoppel provides that if parties enter into an oral contract that should be in writing under the statute of frauds, the oral promise is enforceable against the promisor if these three conditions are met: (1) The promise induces action or forbearance of action by another; (2) the reliance on the oral promise was foreseeable; and (3) injustice can be avoided only by enforcing the oral promise.[12] Where this doctrine applies, the promisor is **estopped** (prevented) from raising the statute of frauds as a defense to the enforcement of the oral contract.

promissory estoppel
An equitable doctrine that permits enforcement of oral contracts that should have been in writing. It is applied to avoid injustice.

As the following case illustrates, the court can refuse to enforce the statute of frauds if enforcement would cause an inequitable result.

Case 11.3

Equity

Sutton v. Warner

12 Cal.App.4th 415, 15 Cal.Rptr.2d 632, 1993 Cal.App. Lexis 22 (1993)
California Court of Appeals

Background and Facts

In 1983, Arlene and Donald Warner inherited a one-third interest in a home at 101 Molimo Street in San Francisco. The Warners bought out the other heirs and obtained a $170,000 loan on the property. Donald Warner and Kenneth Sutton were friends. In January 1984, Donald Warner proposed that Sutton and his wife purchase the residence. His proposal included a $15,000 down payment toward the purchase price of $185,000. The Suttons were to pay all mortgage payments and real estate taxes on the property for five years, and at any time during the five-year period

Sutton v. Warner

12 Cal.App.4th 415, 15 Cal.Rptr.2d 632, 1993 Cal.App. Lexis 22 (1993)
California Court of Appeals
(continued)

they could purchase the house. All this was agreed to orally. The Suttons paid the down payment and cash payments equal to the monthly mortgage ($1,881) to the Warners. They paid the annual property taxes on the house. The Suttons also made improvements to the property. In July 1988, the Warners reneged on the sales/option agreement. At that time the house had risen in value to between $250,000 and $320,000. The Suttons sued for specific performance of the sales agreement. The Warners defended, alleging that the oral promise to sell real estate had to be in writing under the Statute of Frauds and was therefore unenforceable. The trial court applied the equitable doctrine of part performance and ordered specific performance. The Warners appealed.

Issue

Does the equitable doctrine of part performance take this oral contract for the sale of real property out of the Statute of Frauds?

In The Language of The Court

Kline, Presiding Judge The doctrine of part performance by the purchaser is a well-recognized exception to the Statute of Frauds as applied to contracts for the sale of real property. The question here, then, is whether the continued possession of the property by the Suttons and their other actions are sufficiently related to the option contract to constitute part performance. The trial court responded in the affirmative. After entering the oral agreement, the Suttons made a $15,000 down payment and increased their monthly payments to the Warners from the original monthly rental payment to payments in the precise amount of the variable mortgage payments due under the $170,000 loan. They reimbursed the Warners for property taxes in the sum of $800 every six months.

Although it was disputed whether the dollar value of improvements made by the Suttons in reliance upon the oral agreement constituted "substantial" improvements, it is undisputed that many of the improvements—such as painting the interior of the house and the installation of a toilet and entry lamp—were done by the Suttons' own labor. The trial court found that these actions were unequivocally related to the purchase agreement.

The actions taken by the Suttons in reliance upon the oral agreement, when considered together with the Warners' admission that there was an oral agreement of some duration, satisfy both elements of the part performance doctrine.

The record supports the trial court's determination that part performance by the Suttons sufficed to remove the bar of the statute.

Decision and Remedy

The appellate court held that the doctrine of part performance applied and that the Statute of Frauds did not prevent the enforcement of the oral contract to sell real estate.

Case Questions

Critical Legal Thinking What purposes are served by the Statute of Frauds? Explain.

Business Ethics Did the Warners act ethically in this case? Did the Statute of Frauds give them a justifiable reason not to go through with the deal?

Business Application Should important business contracts be written? Why or why not?

Formality of the Writing

Counsel Randle Jackson: "In the book of nature, my lords, it is written."

Ellenborough: "Will you have the goodness to mention the page, Sir, if you please."

Lord Campbell
Lives of the Chief Justices (1857)

Many written commercial contracts are long, detailed documents that have been negotiated by the parties and drafted and reviewed by their lawyers. Other written contracts are preprinted forms that are prepared in advance to be used in recurring situations.

However, a written contract does not have to be either drafted by a lawyer or formally typed to be legally binding. Generally, the law only requires a writing containing the essential terms of the parties' agreement. Any writing—including letters, telegrams, invoices, sales receipts, handwritten agreements written on scraps of paper, and such—can be an enforceable contract under this rule.

Required Signature

Business Brief
Only the signature of the party against whom enforcement is sought needs to be on the written contract.

The statute of frauds and the UCC require a written contract, whatever its form, to be signed *by the party against whom enforcement is sought*. The signature of the person who is enforcing the contract is not necessary. Thus, a written contract may be enforceable against one party but not the other party.

Consider This Example Suppose Travis McQuire and Holly Berger, who are not merchants, enter into an oral contract whereby Ms. Berger agrees to sell her motor home to Mr. McQuire for $35,000. She sends him a signed letter setting forth the terms of their agreement. The contract can be enforced against Ms. Berger because she signed a written memorandum (i.e., the letter) containing the essential terms of the contract. However, the contract cannot be enforced against Mr. McQuire because he can raise the statute of frauds as a defense.

Generally, the signature may appear anywhere on the writing. In addition, it does not have to be a person's full legal name. The person's last name, first name, nickname, initials, seal, stamp, engraving, or other symbol or mark (e.g., an X) that indicates the person's intent can be binding. The signature may be affixed by an authorized agent.

Convenience is the basis of mercantile law.

Lord Mansfield
Medcalf v. Hall (1782)

International Law

Japanese *Hankos* and Chinese *Chops* as Signatures

Americans, Europeans, and many others in the world use their personal hand-applied signatures on legal documents. In Japan, China, and other countries of Asia, however, individuals often do not use their hand-applied signatures to sign legal documents. Instead, they follow the age-old tradition of using a stamp as their signature. The stamp is a character or set of characters carved onto the end of a cylinder-shaped piece held in a person's hand. The characters are carved onto one end of the cylinder. The owner places this end in ink and then applies this end to the document to be signed, leaving an imprint that serves as the owner's signature. In Japan this is called a *hanko*; in China it is called a *chop*. *Hankos* and *chops* are registered with the government. *Hankos* and *chops* can be made of ivory, jade, agate, gold, animal's horn, wood, or even plastic.

In societies that use personal signatures, if a signature is suspected of being forged, the victim can hire handwriting experts and use modern technology to prove it is not his or her signature. In Japan, China, and other countries where *hankos* and *chops* are used, it is much more difficult to prove forgery because anyone in possession of another's *hanko* or *chop* can apply it. Some people predict the demise of the *hanko* and *chop* because of the possible problem of fraud and the increased use of hand-applied signatures by younger persons in countries used to using the *hanko* and *chop*. Others predict that the rich tradition of using a *hanko* or *chop* will continue. ■

Angkor Wat, Cambodia. In many parts of the world, the parties usually engage in negotiations that involve substantial posturing prior to agreeing on a final price.

Promises of Performance

He who derives the advantage ought to sustain the burden.

Legal Maxim

In contracts, parties make certain promises to each other. These promises may be classified as *covenants* or *conditions*. The differences between these are discussed in the following paragraphs.

Covenants

covenant

An unconditional promise to perform.

Business Brief

Nonperformance of a covenant is a breach of contract that gives the other party the right to sue.

A **covenant** is an unconditional promise to perform. Nonperformance of a covenant is a breach of contract that gives the other party the right to sue. For example, if Medcliff Corporation borrows $100,000 from a bank and signs a promissory note to repay this amount plus 10 percent interest in one year, this promise is a covenant. That is, it is an unconditional promise to perform.

Conditions of Performance

condition

A qualification of a promise that becomes a covenant if it is met.

A conditional promise (or qualified promise) is not as definite as a covenant. The promisor's duty to perform (or not perform) arises only if the **condition** does (or does not) occur.[13] However, it becomes a covenant if the condition is met.

Generally, contractual language such as *if*, *on condition that*, *provided that*, *when*, *after*, *as soon as*, and the like indicates a condition. A single contract may contain numerous conditions that trigger or excuse performance. There are two types of conditions: *conditions precedent* and *conditions subsequent*.

condition precedent

A condition that requires the occurrence of an event before a party is obligated to perform a duty under a contract.

Conditions Precedent If a contract requires the occurrence (or nonoccurrence) of an event before a party is obligated to perform a contractual duty, there is a **condition precedent**. The happening (or nonhappening) of the event triggers the contract or duty of performance. If the event does not occur, no duty to perform arises because there is a failure of condition.

Statue, China. International contracts contain covenants and conditions of performance as specified or implied by law.

For example, suppose E. I. duPont offers Joan Andrews a job as an industrial engineer upon her graduation from college. If Ms. Andrews graduates, the condition has been met. If the employer refuses to hire Ms. Andrews at that time, she can sue the employer for breach of contract. However, if Ms. Andrews does not graduate, duPont is not obligated to hire her because there has been a failure of condition.

Conditions Subsequent A **condition subsequent** exists when a contract provides that the occurrence or nonoccurrence of a specific event automatically excuses the performance of an existing duty to perform. For example, many employment contracts include a clause that permits the employer to terminate the contract if the employee fails a drug test.

condition subsequent
A condition, if it occurs, that automatically excuses the performance of an existing contractual duty to perform.

Concept Summary Types of Conditions

Type of Condition	Description
Condition precedent	A specified event must occur (or not occur) before a party is obligated to perform contractual duties.
Condition subsequent	The occurrence (or nonoccurrence) of a specified event excuses the performance of an existing contractual duty to perform.

Discharge of Performance

A party's duty to perform under a contract may be discharged by *mutual agreement* of the parties or by *impossibility of performance*. These methods of discharge are discussed in the paragraphs that follow.

> The foundation of Justice is good faith.
>
> Cicero
> *(106–43 B.C.) De Officiis, Bk. 1, Ch. VII*

Discharge by Agreement

In many situations, the parties to a contract mutually decide to discharge their contractual duties. The different types of mutual agreements are discussed below.

Business Brief
The parties to a contract may mutually agree to discharge (end) their contractual duties.

> The meaning of words varies according to the circumstances of and concerning which they are used.
>
> Blackburn, J.
> *Allgood v. Blake (1873)*

- *Mutual Rescission* If a contract is wholly or partially executory on both sides, the parties can agree to rescind (i.e., cancel) the contract. **Mutual rescission** requires the parties to enter into a second agreement that expressly terminates the first one. Unilateral rescission of the contract by one of the parties without the other party's consent is not effective. Unilateral rescission of a contract constitutes a breach of that contract.
- *Novation* A **novation agreement** (commonly called **novation**) substitutes a third party for one of the original contracting parties. The new substituted party is obligated to perform the contract. All three parties must agree to the substitution. In a novation, the exiting party is relieved of liability on the contract.
- *Accord and Satisfaction* The parties to a contract may agree to settle a contract dispute by an **accord and a satisfaction**. The agreement whereby the parties agree to accept something different in satisfaction of the original contract is called an **accord**. The performance of an accord is called a **satisfaction**. An accord does not discharge the original contract. It only suspends it until the accord is performed. Satisfaction of the accord discharges both the original contract and the accord. If an accord is not satisfied when it is due, the aggrieved party may enforce either (1) the accord or (2) the original contract.

novation
An agreement that substitutes a new party for one of the original contracting parties and relieves the exiting party of liability on the contract.

accord and satisfaction
The settlement of a contract dispute.

Discharge by Impossibility

Under certain circumstances, the nonperformance of contractual duties is excused—discharged—because of *impossibility of performance.*

impossibility of performance
Nonperformance that is excused if the contract becomes impossible to perform; it must be objective impossibility, not subjective.

Impossibility of performance (or **objective impossibility**) occurs if a contract becomes impossible to perform.[14] The impossibility must be objective impossibility ("it cannot be done") rather than subjective impossibility ("I cannot do it"). The following types of objective impossibility excuse nonperformance:

> If a man will improvidently bind himself up by a voluntary deed, and not reserve a liberty to himself by a power of revocation, this court will not loose the fetters he hath put upon himself, but he must lie down under his own folly.
>
> Lord Nottingham, L. C.
> *Villers v. Beaumont (1682)*

1. The death or incapacity of the promisor prior to the performance of a personal service contract. For example, if a professional athlete dies prior to or during a contract period, her contract with the team is discharged.
2. The destruction of the subject matter of a contract prior to performance. For instance, if a building is destroyed by fire, the lessees are discharged from further performance unless otherwise provided in the lease.
3. A supervening illegality makes performance of the contract illegal. For example, suppose an art dealer contracts to purchase native art found in a foreign country. The contract is discharged if the foreign country enacts a law forbidding native art from being exported from the country before the contract is performed.

In the following case, the court had to decide whether there was impossibility of performance.

Case 11.4 Impossibility of Performance

Parker v. Arthur Murray, Inc.
295 N.E.2d 487, 1973 Ill.App. Lexis 2760 (1973)
Appellate Court of Illinois

Background and Facts

In November 1959, Ryland S. Parker, a 37-year-old college-educated bachelor, went to the Arthur Murray Studios (Arthur Murray) in Oak Park, Illinois, to redeem a certificate entitling him to three free dancing lessons. At that time he lived alone in a one-room attic apartment. During the free lessons the instructor told Parker that he had "exceptional potential to be a fine and accomplished dancer." Parker thereupon signed a contract for more lessons. Parker attended lessons regularly and was praised and encouraged by his instructors despite his lack of progress. Contract extensions and new contracts for additional instructional hours were executed, which Parker prepaid. Each written contract contained the bold-type words, "NONCANCELLABLE CONTRACT." On September 24, 1961, Parker was severely injured in an automobile accident, rendering him incapable of continuing his dancing lessons. At that time he had contracted for a total of 2,734 hours of dance lessons, for which he had prepaid $24,812. When Arthur Murray refused to refund any of the money, Parker sued to rescind the outstanding contracts. The trial courts held in favor of Parker and ordered Arthur Murray to return the prepaid contract payments. Arthur Murray appealed.

Issue

Does the doctrine of impossibility excuse Parker's performance of the personal service contracts?

In The Language of The Court

Stamos, Presiding Justice Plaintiff was granted rescission on the ground of impossibility of performance. Defendants do not deny that the doctrine of impossibility of performance is generally applicable to the case at bar. Rather they assert that certain contract provisions bring the case within the *Restatement's* limitation that the doctrine is inapplicable if "the contract indicates a contrary intention." It is contended that such bold-type phrases as "NONCANCELLABLE CONTRACT," "NONCANCELLABLE NEGOTIABLE CONTRACT," and "I UNDERSTAND THAT NO REFUNDS WILL BE MADE UNDER THE TERMS OF THIS CONTRACT" manifested the parties' mutual intent to waive their respective rights to invoke the doctrine of impossibility.

This is a construction that we find unacceptable. Courts engage in the construction and interpretation of contracts with the sole aim of determining the intention of the parties. We need rely on no construction aids to conclude that plaintiff never contemplated that by signing a contract with such terms as "NONCANCELLABLE" and "NO REFUNDS," he was waiving a remedy expressly recognized by Illinois courts. Although neither party to a contract should be relieved from performance on the ground that good business judgment was lacking, a court will not place upon language a ridiculous construction. We conclude that plaintiff did not waive his right to assert the doctrine of impossibility.

Suffice it to say that overwhelming evidence supported plaintiff's contention that he was incapable of continuing his lessons.

Decision and Remedy

The appellate court held that the doctrine of impossibility of performance excused Parker's performance of the personal service contracts. Affirmed.

Case Questions

Critical Legal Thinking Should the doctrine of impossibility excuse parties from performance of their contracts? Why or why not?

Business Ethics Did Arthur Murray act ethically in not returning Parker's money?

Contemporary Business Why do you think Arthur Murray fought this case?

Commercial Impracticability

Many states recognize the doctrine of **commercial impracticability** as an excuse of nonperformance of contracts. Commercial impracticability excuses performance if an unforeseeable event makes it impractical for the promisor to perform. This doctrine has not yet been fully developed by the courts. It is examined on a case-by-case basis.

commercial impracticability
Nonperformance that is excused if an extreme or unexpected development or expense makes it impractical for the promisor to perform.

Consider This Example A utility company enters into a contract to purchase uranium for its nuclear-powered generator from a uranium supplier at a fixed price of $1 million per year for five years. Suppose a new uranium cartel is formed worldwide and the supplier must pay $3 million for uranium to supply the utility with each year's supply. In this case, the court would likely allow the supplier to rescind its contract with the utility based on commercial impracticability. Note that it is not impossible for the supplier to supply the uranium.

Entrepreneur and the Law

Force Majeure Clauses

Parties may agree in a contract that certain events will excuse nonperformance of the contract. These clauses are called **force majeure clauses.**

Usually, force majeure clauses excuse nonperformance caused by natural disasters such as floods, tornadoes, earthquakes, and such. Modern clauses often excuse nonperformance due to labor strikes, shortages of raw materials, and the like. ■

Performance and Breach

If a contractual duty has not been discharged (i.e., terminated) or excused (i.e., relieved of legal liability), the contracting party owes an absolute duty (i.e., covenant) to perform the duty. There are three types of performance of a contract: (1) *complete performance*, (2) *substantial performance* (or minor breach), and (3) *inferior performance* (or material breach). These concepts are discussed in the following paragraphs.

No cause of action arises from a bare promise.

Legal Maxim

Complete Performance

Most contracts are discharged by the **complete**, or **strict**, **performance** of the contracting parties. Complete performance occurs when a party to a contract renders performance exactly as required by the contract. A fully performed contract is called an **executed contract**.

complete performance
A type of performance that occurs when a party to a contract renders performance exactly as required by the contract; it discharges that party's obligations under the contract.

Vietnam. As capitalism increases around the world, the performance and judicial enforcement of contracts will become more important.

Note that **tender of performance** also discharges a party's contractual obligations. *Tender* is an unconditional and absolute offer by a contracting party to perform his or her obligations under the contract.

Consider This Example Suppose Ashley's Dress Shops, Inc., contracts to purchase dresses from a dress manufacturer for $25,000. Ashley's has performed its obligation under the contract once it tenders the $25,000 to the manufacturer. If the manufacturer fails to deliver the dresses, Ashley's can sue it for breach of contract.

Substantial Performance: Minor Breach

substantial performance
Performance by a contracting party that deviates only slightly from complete performance.

Substantial performance occurs when there has been a **minor breach** of contract. In other words, it occurs when a party to a contract renders performance that deviates only slightly from complete performance. The nonbreaching party may either (1) convince the breaching party to elevate his or her performance to complete performance, (2) deduct the cost to repair the defect from the contract price and remit the balance to the breaching party, or (3) sue the breaching party to recover the cost to repair the defect if the breaching party has already been paid.

There is grim irony in speaking of freedom of contract of those who, because of their economic necessities, give their service for less than is needful to keep body and soul together.

Harian Fiske Stone
Morchead v. N.Y. ex rel. Tipaldo (1936)

Consider This Example Suppose Donald Trump contracts with Big Apple Construction Co. to have Big Apple construct an office building for $50 million. The architectural plans call for installation of three-ply windows in the building. Big Apple constructs the building exactly to plan except that it installs two-ply windows. There has been substantial performance. It would cost $300,000 to install the correct windows. If Big Apple agrees to replace the windows, its performance is elevated to complete performance, and Trump must remit the entire contract price. However, if Trump has to hire someone else to replace the windows, he may deduct this cost of repair from the contract price and remit the difference to Big Apple.

Inferior Performance: Material Breach

A **material breach** of a contract occurs when a party fails to perform certain express or implied obligations that impair or destroy the essence of the contract. When a material breach occurs, it is called **inferior performance**. Because there is no clear line between a minor breach and a material breach, determination is made on a case-by-case basis.

material breach
A breach that occurs when a party renders inferior performance of his or her contractual duties.

inferior performance
Performance that occurs when a party fails to perform express or implied contractual obligations that impair or destroy the essence of the contract.

Where there has been a material breach of a contract, the nonbreaching party has two choices:

1. The nonbreaching party may *rescind* the contract, seek restitution of any compensation paid under the contract to the breaching party, and be discharged from any further performance under the contract.
2. The nonbreaching party may treat the contract as being in effect and sue the breaching party to recover *damages*.

Consider This Example Suppose a university contracts with a general contractor to build a new three-story building with classroom space for 1,000 students. However, the completed building can support the weight of only 500 students because the contractor used inferior materials. The defect cannot be repaired without rebuilding the entire structure. Because this is a material breach, the university may rescind the contract and require removal of the building. The university is discharged of any obligations under the contract and is free to employ another contractor to rebuild the building. Alternatively, the university could accept the building and deduct damages caused by the defect from the contract price.

Men keep their agreements when it is an advantage to both parties not to break them.

Solon
(c. 600 B.C.)

Concept Summary Types of Performance

Type of Performance	Legal Consequence
Complete performance	The contract is discharged.
Substantial performance (minor breach)	The nonbreaching party may recover damages caused by the breach.
Inferior performance (material breach)	The nonbreaching party may either (1) rescind the contract and recover restitution or (2) affirm the contract and recover damages.

E-Commerce & Information Technology

Breach of an Internet Contract

A contract is a contract is a contract, even if it is over the Internet. Consider the following case. The Hotmail Corporation (Hotmail) is a Silicon Valley company that provides free e-mail on the Internet. Hotmail's online services allow its millions of registered subscribers to exchange e-mail messages on the Internet. The company registered the name "Hotmail" as a federal trademark and obtained the Internet domain name "hotmail.com." Every e-mail sent by a Hotmail subscriber automatically displays Hotmail's domain name and mark. To become a Hotmail subscriber, one must agree to abide by a service agreement by clicking an "accept" prompt on the computer screen. This click-wrap contract expressly prohibits subscribers from using Hotmail's services to send unsolicited commercial bulk e-mail, or "spam," or to send obscene or pornographic messages. The transmission of spam is a practice widely condemned by the Internet community.

In the fall of 1997, Hotmail discovered that defendants Van$ Money Pie Inc., ALS Enterprises, Inc., LCGM, Inc., and the Genesis Network, Inc., created Hotmail accounts that were facilitating their sending spam e-mail to Hotmail subscribers. The spam messages advertised pornography and "get-rich-quick" schemes, among other things. Hotmail was inundated with complaints from its subscribers who had received the spam, and it faced the loss of customers as well as an overloading of its services from the spam e-mail.

E-Commerce & Information Technology (continued)

Hotmail sued the defendants in district court for breach of contract and sought a preliminary injunction to enjoin the defendants from sending spam e-mail using Hotmail accounts, and the Hotmail domain name and mark. This district court agreed with Hotmail on its breach of contract claim, stating

> The evidence supports a finding that plaintiff Hotmail will likely prevail on its breach of contract claim and that there are at least serious questions going to the merits of this claim in that plaintiff has presented evidence of the following: that defendants obtained a number of Hotmail mailboxes and access to Hotmail's services; that in so doing defendants agreed to abide by Hotmail's Terms of Service which prohibit using a Hotmail account for purposes of sending spam and/or pornography; that defendants breached their contract with Hotmail by using Hotmail's services to facilitate sending spam and/or pornography; that Hotmail complied with the conditions of the contract except those from which its performance was excused; and that if defendants are not enjoined they will continue to create such accounts in violation of the Terms of Service.

The district court enforced the click-wrap contract and held the defendants in breach of Hotmail's Internet contract. The court issued a preliminary injunction prohibiting the defendants from using Hotmail accounts or Hotmail's domain name or mark to send spam. [*Hotmail Corporation v. Van$ Money Pie, Inc.*, 47 U.S.P.Q.2d, 1998 U.S. Dist. Lexis 10729 1020 (N.D.Cal. 1998)] ■

Anticipatory Breach

anticipatory breach
A breach that occurs when one contracting party informs the other that he or she will not perform his or her contractual duties when due.

Anticipatory breach (or **anticipatory repudiation**) of a contract occurs when one contracting party informs the other in advance that he or she will not perform his or her contractual duties when due. This type of material breach can be expressly stated or implied from the conduct of the repudiator. Where there is an anticipatory repudiation, the nonbreaching party's obligations under the contract are discharged immediately. The nonbreaching party also has the right to sue the repudiating party when the anticipatory breach occurs; there is no need to wait until performance is due.[15]

Remedies

> It is a vain thing to imagine a right without a remedy; for want of right and want of remedy are reciprocal.
>
> C. J. Holt
> *Ashby v. White (1703)*

The most common remedy for a breach of contract is an award of *monetary damages*. This is often called the "law remedy." However, if a monetary award does not provide adequate relief, the court may order any one of several *equitable remedies*, including specific performance, reformation, quasi-contract, and injunction. Equitable remedies are based on the concept of fairness.

Monetary Damages

monetary damages
Financial damages that a nonbreaching party may recover from a breaching party whether the breach was minor or material.

A nonbreaching party may recover **monetary damages** from a breaching party. Monetary damages are available whether the breach was minor or material. Several types of monetary damages may be awarded, including *compensatory*, *consequential*, *nominal*, and *liquidated damages*.

Compensatory Damages

compensatory damages
A remedy intended to compensate a nonbreaching party for the loss of a bargain; they place the nonbreaching party in the same position as if the contract had been fully performed by restoring the "benefits of the bargain."

Compensatory damages are intended to compensate a nonbreaching party for the loss of a bargain. In other words, they place the nonbreaching party in the same position as if the contract had been fully performed by restoring the "benefit of the bargain."

Consider This Example Suppose Lederle Laboratories enters into a written contract to employ a manager for three years at a salary of $6,000 per month. Before work is to start, the manager is informed that he will not be needed. This is a material breach of contract.

Assume that the manager finds another job, but it pays only $5,000 a month. The manager may recover $1,000 per month for 36 months ($36,000 total) from Lederle Laboratories as compensatory damages. These damages place the manager in the same situation as if the contract with Lederle had been performed.

Consequential Damages

In addition to compensatory damages, a nonbreaching party can sometimes recover **special** or **consequential damages** from the breaching party. Consequential damages are *foreseeable* damages that arise from circumstances outside the contract. To be liable for consequential damages, the breaching party must know or have reason to know that the breach will cause special damages to the other party.

consequential damages
Foreseeable damages that arise from circumstances outside the contract. In order to be liable for these damages, the breaching party must know or have reason to know that the breach will cause special damages to the other party.

The very definition of a good award is that it gives dissatisfaction to both parties.

M. R. Plumer
Goodman v. Sayers (1820)

Consider This Example Suppose Soan-Allen Co., a wholesaler, enters into a contract to purchase 1,000 men's suits for $150 each from the Fabric Manufacturing Co., a manufacturer. Prior to contracting, the wholesaler tells the manufacturer that the suits will be resold to retailers for $225. The manufacturer breaches the contract by failing to manufacture the suits. The wholesaler cannot get the suits manufactured by anyone else in time to meet his contracts. He can recover $75,000 of lost profits on the resale contracts (1,000 suits × $75 profit) as consequential damages from the manufacturer because the manufacturer knew of this special damage to Soan-Allen Co. if it breached the contract.

Liquidated Damages

Under certain circumstances, the parties to a contract may agree in advance to the amount of damage payable upon a breach of contract. These are called **liquidated damages**. To be lawful, the actual damages must be difficult or impracticable to determine, and the liquidated amount must be reasonable in the circumstances.[16] An enforceable liquidated damage clause is an exclusive remedy even if actual damages are later determined to be different.

Business Brief
Many businesses include liquidated damage clauses in their commercial contracts. This helps to provide certainty, avoid lawsuits, and provide an incentive to enter into contracts.

A liquidated damage clause is considered a **penalty** if actual damages are clearly determinable in advance or the liquidated damages are excessive or unconscionable. If a liquidated damage clause is found to be a penalty, it is unenforceable. The nonbreaching party may then recover actual damages.

Concept Summary Types of Monetary Damages

Type of Damage	Description
Compensatory	Damages that compensate a nonbreaching party for the loss of a bargain. It places the nonbreaching party in the same position as if the contract had been fully performed.
Consequential	Damages that compensate a nonbreaching party for foreseeable special damages. The breaching party must have known or should have known that these damages would result from the breach.
Liquidated	An agreement by the parties in advance that sets the amount of damages recoverable in case of breach. These damages are lawful if they do not cause a penalty.

Punitive Damages

punitive damages
Damages that are awarded to punish the defendant, to deter the defendant from similar conduct in the future, and to set an example for others.

Generally, **punitive damages** are not recoverable for breach of contract. They are recoverable, however, for certain *tortious* conduct that may be associated with the nonperformance of a contract. This includes fraud, intentional conduct, or other egregious conduct. Punitive damages are in addition to actual damages and may be kept by the plaintiff. Punitive damages are awarded to punish the defendant, to deter the defendant from similar conduct in the future, and to set an example for others.

Mitigation of Damages

mitigation
A situation in which a nonbreaching party is under a legal duty to avoid or reduce damages caused by a breach of contract.

If a contract has been breached, the law places a duty on the innocent nonbreaching party to take reasonable efforts to mitigate (i.e., avoid and reduce) the resulting damages. The extent of **mitigation** required depends on the type of contract involved. For example, if an employer breaches an employment contract, the employee owes a duty to mitigate damages by trying to find substitute employment. The employee is only required to accept comparable employment. The courts consider such factors as compensation, rank, status, job description, and geographical location in determining the comparability of jobs.

In the following case, the court had to decide whether a job was comparable.

Case 11.5 Duty to Mitigate Damages

Parker v. Twentieth Century-Fox Film Corp.
3 Cal.3d 176, 89 Cal.Rptr. 737, 1970 Cal. Lexis 199 (1970)
California Supreme Court

Background and Facts

On August 6, 1965, Twentieth Century-Fox Film Corporation (Fox), a major film production studio, entered into an employment contract with Shirley MacLaine Parker (Parker), an actress. Under the contract, Parker was to play the leading female role in a musical production called *Bloomer Girl*, to be filmed in Los Angeles. In the movie, Parker would be able to use her talents as a dancer and as an actress. The contract provided that Parker was to be paid guaranteed compensation of $53,571.42 per week for 14 weeks commencing on May 23, 1966, for a total of $750,000. On April 4, 1966, Fox sent Parker a letter notifying her that it was not going to film *Bloomer Girl*. The letter, however, offered Parker the leading female role in a film tentatively entitled *Big Country*, which was to be a dramatic western to be filmed in Australia. The compensation Fox offered Parker was identical to that offered for *Bloomer Girl*. Fox gave Parker one week to accept. She did not, and the offer expired. Parker sued Fox to recover the guaranteed compensation provided in the *Bloomer Girl* contract. The trial court granted summary judgment to Parker. Fox appealed.

Issue

Was the job that Fox offered Parker in *Big Country* comparable employment that Parker was obligated to accept to mitigate damages?

In The Language of The Court

Burke, Justice The general rule is that the measure of recovery by a wrongfully discharged employee is the amount of salary agreed upon for the period of service, less the amount that the employer affirmatively proves the employee has earned or with reasonable effort might have earned from other employment. However, before projected earnings from other employment opportunities not sought or accepted by the discharged employee can be applied, in mitigation, the employer must show that the other employment was comparable, or substantially similar, to that of which the employee has been deprived; the employee's rejection of or failure to seek other available employment of a different or inferior kind may not be resorted to in order to mitigate damages.

Applying the foregoing rules to the record in the present case, with all intendments in favor of the party opposing the summary judgment motion—here, defendant Fox—it is clear that the trial court correctly ruled that plaintiff's failure to accept defendant's tendered substitute employment could not be applied in mitigation of damages because the offer of the *Big Country* lead was of employment both different and inferior, and that no factual dispute was presented on that issue. The mere circumstances that *Bloomer Girl* was to be a musical review, calling upon plaintiff's talents as a dancer as well as an actress, and was to be produced in the City of Los Angeles, whereas *Big Country* was a straight dramatic role in a Western-type story taking place in an opal mine in Australia, demonstrates the difference in kind between the two employments: The female lead as a dramatic actress in a Western-style motion picture can by no stretch of imagination be considered the equivalent of or substantially similar to the lead in a song-and-dance production.

Decision and Remedy

The state supreme court held that the job that Fox offered to Parker in *Big Country* was not comparable employment to the role Fox had contracted Parker to play in *Bloomer Girl*. Therefore, Parker did not fail to mitigate damages by refusing to accept such employment. The supreme court affirmed the trial court's summary judgment.

Case Questions

Critical Legal Thinking Should nonbreaching parties be under a duty to mitigate damages caused by the breaching party? Why or why not?

Business Ethics Did Fox act ethically in this case? Did Parker?

Business Application Who is more likely to be able to mitigate damages when there is a breach of an employment contract: (1) the president of a large corporation, (2) a middle manager, or (3) a bank teller?

Rescission and Restitution

Rescission is an action to *undo* a contract. It is available where there has been a material breach of contract, fraud, duress, undue influence, or mistake. Generally, in order to rescind a contract, the parties must make **restitution** of the consideration they received under the contract.[17] Restitution consists of returning the goods, property, money, or other consideration received from the other party. If possible, the actual goods or property must be returned. If the goods or property has been consumed or is otherwise unavailable, restitution must be made by conveying a cash equivalent. The rescinding party must give adequate notice of the rescission to the breaching party. *Rescission* and *restitution* restore the parties to the position they occupied prior to the contract.

rescission
An action to rescind (undo) a contract. Rescission is available if there has been a material breach of contract, fraud, duress, undue influence, or mistake.

restitution
Returning of goods or property received from the other party in order to rescind a contract; if the actual goods or property is not available, a cash equivalent must be made.

Consider This Example Suppose Filene's Department Store contracts to purchase $100,000 of goods from a sweater manufacturer. The store pays $10,000 as a down payment, and the first $20,000 of goods are delivered. The goods are materially defective, and the defect cannot be cured. This is a material breach. Filene's can rescind the contract. The store is entitled to receive its down payment back from the manufacturer, and the manufacturer is entitled to receive the goods back from the store.

Unconscionable Contracts

The general rule of freedom of contract holds that if (1) the object of a contract is lawful and (2) the other elements for the formation of a contract are met, the courts will enforce a contract according to its terms. Although it is generally presumed that parties are capable of protecting their own interests when contracting, it is a fact of life that dominant parties sometimes take advantage of weaker parties. As a result, some lawful contracts are so oppressive or manifestly unfair that they are unjust. To prevent the enforcement of such contracts, the courts developed the equitable doctrine of **unconscionability**, which is based on public policy. A contract found to be unconscionable under this doctrine is called an **unconscionable contract**, or a **contract of adhesion**.

unconscionability
A doctrine under which courts may deny enforcement of unfair or oppressive contracts.

The courts are given substantial discretion in determining whether a contract or contract clause is unconscionable. There is no single definition of *unconscionability*. The doctrine may not be used merely to save a contracting party from a bad bargain.

The following elements must be shown to prove that a contract or clause in a contract is unconscionable:

1. The parties possessed severely unequal bargaining power.
2. The dominant party unreasonably used its unequal bargaining power to obtain oppressive or manifestly unfair contract terms.
3. The adhering party had no reasonable alternative.

An unconscionable contract is one which no man in his senses and not under delusion would make on the one hand, and as no honest and fair man would accept on the other.

Chief Justice Fuller
Hume v. United States, 132 U.S. 406, 10 S.Ct. 134, 33 L.Ed. 393 (1889)

If the court finds that a contract or contract clause is unconscionable, it may (1) refuse to enforce the contract, (2) refuse to enforce the unconscionable clause but enforce the remainder of the contract, or (3) limit the applicability of any unconscionable clause so as to avoid any unconscionable result. The appropriate remedy depends on the facts and circumstances of each case. Note that because unconscionability is a matter of law, the judge may opt to decide an unconscionability case without a jury trial.

Ethics Brief
Unconscionability is extremely subjective. Just because the result seems unfair does not mean that it is unconscionable.

Equitable Remedies

equitable remedies
Remedies that may be awarded by a judge where there has been a breach of contract and either (1) the legal remedy is not adequate or (2) the judge wants to prevent unjust enrichment.

Equitable remedies are available if there has been a breach of contract that cannot be adequately compensated by a legal remedy. They are also available to prevent unjust enrichment. The most common equitable remedies are *specific performance*, *reformation*, *quasi-contract*, and *injunction*.

Specific Performance

specific performance
A remedy that orders the breaching party to perform the acts promised in the contract. Specific performance is usually awarded in cases in which the subject matter is unique, such as in contracts involving land, heirlooms, paintings, and the like.

An award of **specific performance** orders the breaching party to *perform* the acts promised in the contract. The courts have the discretion to award this remedy if the subject matter of the contract is unique.[18] This remedy is available to enforce land contracts because every piece of real property is considered to be unique. Works of art, antiques, items of sentimental value, rare coins, stamps, heirlooms, and such also fit the requirement for uniqueness. Most other personal property does not. Specific performance of personal service contracts is not granted because the courts would find it difficult or impracticable to supervise or monitor performance of the contract.

Entrepreneur and the Law

Hard Dealing for the Hard Rock Cafe

In the 1970s, Peter Morton operated a popular restaurant and tourist attraction in England known as the "Hard Rock Cafe." At that time, Milton Okun of the United States inquired about investing in the business. Morton declined Okun's offer but indicated that if he contemplated expanding the business to the United States, he would contact Okun. In December 1981, Morton located a site suitable for a Hard Rock Cafe in Los Angeles, California. Morton contacted Okun and offered him stock in the general partnership. An agreement was executed on March 2, 1982, whereby Okun contributed $100,000 in exchange for a 20 percent interest in the general partnership. Paragraph 9 of the agreement gave Okun the option to participate in future Hard Rock Cafes with the same 20 percent interest.

After Morton raised funds from limited partners, the Hard Rock Cafe opened in the Beverly Center in Los Angeles and was a commercial success. As a result, Morton decided to exploit the San Francisco market. Per their agreement, Morton offered Okun a 20 percent interest, which Okun accepted.

In 1984, while Morton was finalizing plans for operating a Hard Rock Cafe in Chicago, Illinois, Morton and Okun had a disagreement. Morton advised Okun that he planned to exclude Okun from participating in the venture. Okun offered to participate on the terms of their 1982 agreement. Morton rejected that offer and proceeded with the development of restaurants in Houston, Honolulu, and Chicago, without offering Okun a general partnership interest in these ventures. Okun sued Morton for breach of contract, seeking an order of specific performance of their 1982 agreement. The trial court held in favor of Okun and ordered specific performance of the contract. Morton appealed.

Can the 1982 agreement between Morton and Okun be specifically performed?

The court of appeals noted that as a whole, the terms of the agreement were sufficient to establish from the outset the ways in which future ventures were to be financed, owned, and operated by the parties. The fundamental structure of all such undertakings was to be based on the 20/80 ratio established for the creation of the L.A. Hard Rock Cafe. The court stated that although the agreement admittedly does not deal in specifics, neither law nor equity requires that every term and condition be set forth in the contract. In light of the fact that neither defendant nor plaintiff could predict with any degree of certainty the success of the Los Angeles operation, it is not surprising that Paragraph 9 was drafted broadly enough to accommodate changing circumstances and unforeseen developments.

The defendant asserted, however, that specific performance should not have been granted because enforcement of the contract will require continuous and protracted judicial supervision. The courts of this state have generally followed this "archaic" rule. This case merely involves the offering of an opportunity to participate in a business venture and the concomitant payment of capital and expenses for that participation.

The court stated, "We are not here concerned with the day-to-day management of any particular Hard Rock Cafe or related enterprises that would require the close and ongoing cooperation of the parties or the court." The defendant retains the discretion under the terms of the judgment to structure each venture as he pleases so long as he maintains the 20/80 ratio and does nothing to interfere with or burden plaintiff's right to participate in the deal. Under these circumstances, the court concluded that the decree of specific performance is not unduly burdensome nor requires inordinate supervision by the trial court.

The appellate court held that the subject matter of the agreement between Morton and Okun was unique and therefore that the agreement can be specifically enforced. [*Okun v. Morton*, 203 Cal.App.3d 805, 250 Cal.Rptr. 220, 1988 Cal.App. Lexis 732 (Cal.App. 1988)] ■

Reformation

Reformation is an equitable doctrine that permits the court to *rewrite* a contract to express the parties' true intentions. For example, suppose a clerical error is made during the typing of the contract and both parties sign the contract without discovering the error. If a dispute later arises, the court can reform the contract to correct the clerical error to read as the parties originally intended.

reformation
An equitable doctrine that permits the court to rewrite a contract to express the parties' true intentions.

Quasi-contract

A **quasi-contract** (also called **quantum meruit** or an **implied-in-law contract**) is an equitable doctrine that permits the recovery of compensation even though no enforceable contract exists between the parties because of lack of consideration, because the Statute of Frauds has run out, or the like. Such contracts are imposed by law to prevent unjust enrichment. Under quasi-contract, a party can recover the reasonable value of the services or materials provided. For example, a physician who stops to render aid to an unconscious victim of an automobile accident may recover the reasonable value of his services from that person.

quasi-contract
An equitable doctrine that permits the recovery of compensation even though no enforceable contract exists between the parties.

Injunction

An **injunction** is a court order that "prohibits" a person from doing a certain act. To obtain an injunction, the requesting party must show that he or she will suffer irreparable injury unless the injunction is issued.

injunction
A court order that prohibits a person from doing a certain act.

Consider This Example Suppose a professional football team enters into a five-year employment contract with a "superstar" quarterback. The quarterback breaches the contract and enters into a contract to play for a competing team. Here, the first team can seek an injunction to prevent the quarterback from playing for the other team.

That what is agreed to be done, must be considered as done.

Lord Hardwicke, L. C.
Guidot v. Guidot (1745)

Concept Summary Types of Equitable Remedies

Type of Equitable Remedy	Description
Specific performance	Court order that the breaching party must perform the acts promised in the contract. The subject matter of the contract must be unique.
Reformation	Court rewriting of a contract to express the parties' true intentions. Usually used to correct clerical errors.
Quasi-contract	Doctrine that permits the recovery of damages for breach of an implied-in-law contract where no actual contract exists between the parties. Only the reasonable value of the services or materials may be recovered.
Injunction	Court order that prohibits a party from doing a certain act. Available in contract actions only in limited circumstances.

International Law

Use of Letters of Credit in International Trade

The major risks in any business transaction involving the sale of goods are (1) that the seller will not be paid after delivering the goods and (2) that the buyer will not receive the goods after paying for them. These risks are even more acute in international transactions where the buyer and seller may not know each other, the parties are dealing at long distance, and the judicial systems of the parties' countries may not have jurisdiction to decide a dispute if one should arise. The irrevocable **letter of credit** has been developed to manage these risks in international sales. The function of a letter of credit is to substitute the credit of a recognized international bank for that of the buyer.

An irrevocable letter of credit works this way. Suppose a buyer in one country and a seller in another country enter into a contract for the sale of goods. The buyer goes to his or her bank and pays the bank a fee to issue a letter of credit in which the bank agrees to pay the amount of the letter (which is the amount of the purchase price of the goods) to the seller's bank if certain conditions are met. These conditions are usually the delivery of documents indicating that the seller has placed the goods in the hands of a shipper. The buyer is called the **account party**, the bank that issues the letter of credit is called the **issuing bank**, and the seller is called the **beneficiary** of the letter of credit.

The issuing bank then forwards the letter of credit to a bank that the seller has designated in his or her country. This bank, which is called the **correspondent** or **confirming bank**, relays the letter of credit to the seller. Now that the seller sees that he or she is guaranteed payment, he or she makes arrangements to ship the goods and receives a **bill of lading** from the carrier proving so. The seller then delivers these documents to the confirming bank. The confirming bank examines the documents and, if it finds them in order, pays the seller and forwards the documents to the issuing bank. By this time, the buyer has usually paid the amount of the purchase price to the issuing bank (unless an extension of credit has been arranged), and the issuing bank then charges the buyer's account. The issuing bank forwards the bill of lading and other necessary documents to the buyer, who then picks up the goods from the shipper when they arrive.

If the documents (e.g., the bill of lading, proof of insurance) conform to the conditions specified in the letter of credit, the issuing bank must pay the letter of credit. If the account party does not pay the issuing bank, the bank's only recourse is to sue the account party to recover damages.

Article 5 (Letters of Credit) of the UCC governs letters of credit unless otherwise agreed by the parties. The International Chamber of Commerce has promulgated the **Uniform Customs and Practices for Documentary Credits (UCP)**, which contains rules governing the formation and performance of letters of credit. Although the UCP is neither a treaty nor a legislative enactment, most banks incorporate the terms of the UCP in letters of credit they issue. ■

Chapter Summary

Genuineness of Assent, p. 306

Unilateral Mistakes

Unilateral mistake. Occurs when only one party is mistaken about a material fact regarding the subject matter of the contract. The legal consequences are:

1. ***General rule.*** The mistaken party is not permitted to rescind the contract.
2. ***Exceptions.*** The mistaken party can rescind the contract if:
   a. The other party knew or should have known of the mistake and took advantage of it.
   b. The mistake occurred because of a clerical or mathematical error that was not the result of gross negligence.
   c. The mistake is so serious that enforcing the contract would be unconscionable.

Mutual Mistakes

1. ***Mutual mistake of fact.*** Both parties are mistaken about the essence or object of the contract. Either party may rescind the contract.
2. ***Mutual mistake of value.*** Both parties know the object of the contract but are mistaken as to its value. Neither party may rescind the contract.

Elements of Fraud

Fraudulent misrepresentation. Fraud in which a person intentionally makes an assertion that is not in accord with the facts. Also called *fraud.*

1. ***Elements of fraud:***
   a. The wrongdoer made a false representation of material fact.
   b. The wrongdoer intended to deceive the innocent party.
   c. The innocent party justifiably relied on the misrepresentation.
   d. The innocent party was injured.
2. ***Legal consequences if fraudulent misrepresentation is found.*** The innocent party may:
   a. Rescind the contract and obtain restitution, or
   b. Enforce the contract and sue for damages

Types of Fraud

Common types of fraud:

1. ***Fraud in the inception.*** An innocent person is deceived as to the nature of his or her act. Also called *fraud in the factum.*
2. ***Fraud in the inducement.*** The wrongdoer fraudulently induces another party to enter into a contract.
3. ***Fraud by concealment.*** The wrongdoer takes specific action to conceal a material fact from the other party.

Duress

One party threatens to do some wrongful act unless the other party enters into a contract. A contract entered into under duress cannot be enforced.

Types of duress:

1. Physical duress
2. Extortion
3. Economic duress

Undue Influence

One person takes advantage of another person's mental, emotional, or physical weakness and unduly persuades that person to enter into a contract. A contract entered into under undue influence cannot be enforced.

1. ***Elements of undue influence:***
   a. A fiduciary or confidential relationship existed between the dominant and servient parties.
   b. The dominant party unduly used his or her influence to persuade the servient party to enter into a contract.
2. ***Presumption.*** If there is a confidential relationship between persons, any contract by the servient party that benefits the dominant party is presumed to be entered into under undue influence. This is a *rebuttable presumption.*

Statute of Frauds—Writing Requirement, p. 311

Writing Requirement

Statute of Frauds. A state statute that requires the following contracts to be in writing:

1. ***Contracts involving the transfer of interests in real property.*** Includes contracts for the sale of land, buildings, and items attached to land, mortgages, leases for a term of more than one year, and express easements.
   a. Part performance exception. Permits the specific enforcement of oral contracts for the sale of land when they have been partially performed to avoid injustice.
2. Contracts that cannot be performed within one year of their formation.

3. ***Collateral contracts.*** Occur where one person promises to answer for the debts of another person. Also called *guaranty contracts.*
   a. *Main purpose exception.* Permits enforcement of oral collateral promise if main or leading purpose of collateral promise is to benefit the guarantor.
4. Contracts for the sale of goods costing $500 or more. [UCC § 201]
5. Agents' contracts to sell real estate.
6. Promises made in consideration of marriage, such as prenuptial agreements.

Promissory Estoppel

Equitable doctrine that prevents the application of the Statute of Frauds. It permits the enforcement of oral contracts that should otherwise be in writing under the Statute of Frauds to prevent injustice or unjust enrichment.

Sufficiency of the Writing

1. ***Formality of the writing.*** A written contract does not have to be formal or drafted by a lawyer to be enforceable. Informal contracts, such as handwritten notes, letters, invoices, and the like, are enforceable contracts.
2. ***Required signature.*** The party against whom enforcement of the contract is sought must have signed the contract. The signature may be the person's full legal name, last name, first name, nickname, initials, or other symbol or mark.

Promises of Performance, p. 318

Covenants

Unconditional promises to perform. Nonperformance of a covenant is a breach of contract that gives the other party the right to sue.

Conditions of Performance

Condition. Promisor's duty to perform or not perform arises only if the *condition* does or does not occur. Also called a *qualified promise.* There are two types:

1. ***Condition precedent.*** Requires the occurrence or nonoccurrence of an event before a party is obligated to perform.
2. ***Condition subsequent.*** Provides that the occurrence or nonoccurrence of a specific event automatically excuses performance under a contract.

Discharge of Performance, p. 319

Discharge by Agreement

1. ***Mutual rescission.*** The parties mutually agree to rescind an executory contract.
2. ***Novation.*** The parties agree to the substitution of a third party for one of the original parties. The exiting party is relieved of liability, and the entering party is obligated to perform the contract.
3. ***Accord and satisfaction.*** The parties agree to settle a contract dispute. The *satisfaction* of the *accord* discharges the original contract.
4. ***Force majeure clause.*** The parties stipulate in the contract what events will excuse performance.

Discharge by Impossibility

1. ***Impossibility of performance.*** The contract is objectively impossible to perform because of an event.
2. ***Commercial impracticability.*** The contract is impractical for the promisor to perform because of an event.

Performance and Breach, p. 321

Levels of Performance

1. ***Complete performance.*** A party renders performance exactly as required by the contract. That party's contractual duties are discharged.
2. ***Substantial performance.*** A party renders performance that deviates only slightly from complete performance. There is a *minor breach*. The nonbreaching party may recover damages caused by the breach.
3. ***Inferior performance.*** A party fails to perform express or implied contractual duties that impair or destroy the essence of the contract. There is a *material breach*. The nonbreaching party may either (1) rescind the contract and recover restitution or (2) affirm the contract and recover damages.

Anticipatory Breach

One contracting party informs the other party—by express words or by contract—that he or she will not perform his or her contractual duties when due. Gives an immediate cause of action to the nonbreaching party to sue for breach of contract. Also called *anticipatory repudiation*.

Remedies, p. 324

Monetary Damages

1. ***Compensatory damages.*** Damages that compensate a nonbreaching party for the loss of the contract. Restore the "benefit of the bargain" to the nonbreaching party as if the contract had been fully performed.
2. ***Consequential damages.*** Foreseeable damages that arise from circumstances outside the contract and of which the breaching party either knew or had reason to know. Also called *special damages*.
3. ***Liquidated damages.*** Damages payable upon breach of contract that are agreed on in advance by the contracting parties. Liquidated damages substitute for actual damages. For a liquidated damage clause to be lawful, the following two conditions must be met:
   a. The actual damages must be extremely difficult or impracticable to determine.
   b. The liquidated amount must be a reasonable estimate of the harm that would result from the breach.

A liquidated damage clause is considered a *penalty* if actual damages are clearly determinable in advance or the liquidated damages are excessive or unconscionable. A penalty is unenforceable, and the nonbreaching party may recover actual damages.

Mitigation of Damages

The duty the law places on a nonbreaching party to take reasonable efforts to avoid or reduce the resulting damages from a breach of contract. To mitigate a breach of an employment contract, the nonbreaching party must only accept "comparable" employment.

Rescission and Restitution

Rescission is an action by a nonbreaching party to undo a contract. Available upon the material breach of a contract. The parties must make *restitution* of the consideration they have received from the other party. *Rescission* and *restitution* restore the parties to the positions they occupied prior to the contract.

Unconscionable Contracts

Unconscionable contracts. Contracts that are oppressively unfair or unjust. Also called *contracts of adhesion*.

1. ***Elements of unconscionable contracts:***
   a. The parties possessed severely unequal bargaining power.
   b. The dominant party unreasonably used its power to obtain oppressive or manifestly unfair contract terms.
   c. The adhering party had no reasonable alternative.

2. ***Remedies for unconscionability.*** Where a contract or contract clause is found to be unconscionable, the court may do one of the following:
   a. Refuse to enforce the contract
   b. Refuse to enforce the unconscionable clause but enforce the remainder of the contract.
   c. Limit the applicability of any unconscionable clause so as to avoid any unconscionable result.

Equitable Remedies

Equitable remedies are available if the nonbreaching party cannot be adequately compensated by a legal remedy or to prevent unjust enrichment.

1. ***Specific performance.*** Court order that requires the breaching party to perform his or her contractual duties. Only available if the subject matter of the contract is *unique.*
2. ***Reformation.*** Permits the court to rewrite a contract to express the parties' true intention. Available to correct clerical and mathematical errors.
3. ***Quasi-contract.*** Permits the court to order recovery of compensation even though no enforceable contract exists between the parties. Used to prevent unjust enrichment. Also called an *implied-in-law contract* or *quantum meruit.*
4. ***Injunction.*** Court order that prohibits a person from doing a certain act. The requesting party must show that he or she will suffer irreparable injury if the injunction is not granted.

Judgment

The court issues a judgment to the successful plaintiff in a breach of contract action. The judgment specifies the remedy that the nonbreaching party has against the breaching party.

Internet Exercises and Case Questions

Working the Web Internet Exercises

Activities

1. For an interesting case involving genuineness of assent go to **www.legalwa.org** and type in *Barnes v. Treece, 15 Wn. App. 437.*
2. While common law contract principles have general application, many contracts are regulated on an industry-wide basis, by state statutes. See **www.law.cornell.edu/topics/topic2.html#particular** for examples.
3. For an overview of defenses to contract claims, see **www.west.net/~smith/contracts.htm**.
4. A good case can be lost because of a statute of limitations. These statutes vary by state and by type of claim. See **www.nolo.com/encyclopedia/articles/cm/timely.html** for a summary of the statutes; find your state law at the site.
5. Review the basic principles of remedies at **consumer.pub.findlaw.com/newcontent/consumerlaw/chp15_b.html**. Compare with **www.lectlaw.com/files/bul08.htm**.
6. The newest developments relating to online contracts are reviewed at **www.wiz.com/issue14/f02.html**. See also **profs.1p.findlaw.com/signatures/index.html**.

Critical Legal Thinking Cases

11.1 Unilateral Mistake Mrs. Chaney died in 1985, leaving a house in Annapolis, Maryland. The representative of her estate listed the property for sale with a real estate broker, stating that the property was approximately 15,650 square feet. Drs. Steele and Faust made an offer of $300,000 for the property, which was accepted by the estate. A contract for the sale of the property was signed by all of the parties on July 3, 1985. When a subsequent survey done before the deed was transferred showed that the property had an area of 22,047 square feet, the estate requested the buyers to pay more money for the property. When the estate refused to transfer the property to the buyers, they sued for specific performance. Can the estate rescind the contract? [*Steele v. Goettee*, 542 A.2d 847, 1988 Md. Lexis 91 (Md.App. 1988)]

11.2 Mutual Mistake Ron Boskett, a part-time coin dealer, purchased a dime purportedly minted in 1916 at the Denver mint for nearly $450. The fact that the D on the coin signified Denver mintage made the coin rare and valuable. Boskett sold the coin to Beachcomber Coins, Inc., a retail coin dealer, for $500. A principal of Beachcomber examined the coin for 15 or 45 minutes prior to its purchase. Soon thereafter, Beachcomber received an offer of $700 for the coin, subject to certification of its genuineness by the American Numismatic Society. When this organization labeled the coin counterfeit, Beachcomber sued Boskett to rescind the purchase of the coin. Can Beachcomber rescind the contract? [*Beachcomber Coins, Inc. v. Boskett*, 400 A.2d 78, 1979 N.J.Super. Lexis 659 (NJ 1979)]

11.3 Fraud Robert McClure owned a vehicle salvage and rebuilding business. He listed the business for sale and had a brochure printed that described the business and stated that during 1981 the business grossed $581,117 and netted

$142,727. Fred H. Campbell saw the brochure and inquired about buying the business. Campbell hired a CPA to review McClure's business records and tax returns, but the CPA could not reconcile these with the income claimed for the business in the brochure. When Campbell asked McClure about the discrepancy, McClure stated that the business records and tax returns did not accurately reflect the cash flow or profits of the business because it was such a high-cash operation that much of the cash was not being reported to the Internal Revenue Service on tax returns. McClure signed a warranty that stated that the true income of the business was as represented in the brochure. Campbell bought the business based on these representations. However, the business, although operated in substantially the same manner as when owned by McClure, failed to yield a net income similar to that warranted by McClure. Evidence showed that McClure's representations were substantially overstated. Campbell sued McClure for damages for fraud. Who wins? [*Campbell v. McClure*, 182 Cal.App.3d 806, 227 Cal.Rptr. 450, 1986 Cal.App. Lexis 1751 (Cal.App. 1986)]

11.4 Undue Influence Conrad Schaneman, Sr., had eight sons and five daughters. He owned four 80-acre farms in the Scottsbluff area of Nebraska. Conrad was born in Russia and could not read or write English. Prior to 1974, all of his children had frequent contact with Conrad and helped with his needs. In 1974, his eldest son, Lawrence, advised the other children that he would henceforth manage his father's business affairs. On March 18, 1975, after much urging by Lawrence, Conrad deeded the farm to Lawrence for $23,500. Evidence showed that at the time of the sale the reasonable fair market value of the farm was between $145,000 and $160,000. At the time of the conveyance, Conrad was more than 80 years old; had deteriorated in health; suffered from heart problems, diabetes, high and uncontrollable blood sugar levels; weighed almost 300 pounds; had difficulty breathing; could not walk more than 15 feet; and had to have a jack hoist lift him into and out of the bathtub. He was for all purposes an invalid, relying on Lawrence for most of his personal needs, transportation, banking, and other business mattes. After Conrad died, the conservators of the estate brought an action to cancel the deed transferring the farm to Lawrence. Can the conservators cancel the deed? [*Schaneman v. Schaneman*, 291 N.W.2d 412, 1980 Neb. Lexis 823 (NE 1980)]

11.5 Statute of Frauds In 1955, Robert Briggs and his wife purchased a home located at 167 Lower Orchard Drive, Levittown, Pennsylvania. They made a $100 down payment and borrowed the balance of $11,600 on a 30-year mortgage. In late 1961, when the Briggs family was behind on mortgage payments, it entered into an oral contract to sell the house to Winfield and Emma Sackett if the Sacketts would pay the three months' arrearages on the loan and agree to make the future payments on the mortgage. Mrs. Briggs and Mrs. Sackett were sisters. The Sacketts paid the arrearages, moved into the house, and had lived there continuously. In 1976, Robert Briggs filed an action to void the oral contract as in violation of the Statute of Frauds and evict the Sacketts from the house. Who wins? [*Briggs v. Sackett*, 418 A.2d 586, 1980 Pa.Super. Lexis 2034 (Pa.App. 1980)]

11.6 Guaranty Contract On May 17, 1979, David Brown met with Stan Steele, a loan officer with the Bank of Idaho (now First Interstate Bank), to discuss borrowing $5,000 from the bank to start a new business. After learning that he did not qualify for the loan on the basis of his own financial strength, Brown told Steele that his former employers, James and Donna West of California, might be willing to guarantee the payment of the loan. On May 18, 1979, Steele talked to Mr. West, who orally stated on the telephone that he would personally guarantee the loan to Brown. Based on this guarantee, the bank loaned Brown $5,000. The bank sent a written guarantee to Mr. and Mrs. West for their signature, but it was never returned to the bank. When Brown defaulted on the loan, the bank filed suit against the Wests to recover on their guarantee contract. Are the Wests liable? [*First Interstate Bank of Idaho, N.A. v. West*, 693 P.2d 1053, 1984 Ida. Lexis 600 (ID 1984)]

11.7 Condition Shumann Investments, Inc., hired Pace Construction Corporation, a general contractor, to build "Outlet World of Pasco County." In turn, pace hired OBS Company, Inc., a subcontractor, to perform the framing, drywall, insulation, and stucco work on the project. The contract between Pace and OBS stipulated: "Final payment shall not become due unless and until the following conditions precedent to final payment have been satisfied . . . (c) receipt of final payment for subcontractor's work by contractor from owner." When Shumann refused to pay Pace, Pace refused to pay OBS. OBS sued Pace to recover payment. Who wins? [*Pace Construction Corporation v. OBS Company, Inc.*, 531 So.2d 737, 1988 Fla.App. Lexis 4020 (Fla.App. 1988)]

11.8 Anticipatory Repudiation In September 1976, Muhammad Ali successfully defended his heavyweight boxing championship of the world by defeating Ken Norton. Shortly after the fight, Ali held a press conference and, as he had done on several occasions before, announced his retirement from boxing. At that time Ali had beaten every challenger except Duane Bobick, whom he had not yet fought. In November 1976, Madison Square Garden Boxing, Inc. (MSGB), a fight promoter, offered Ali $2.5 million if he would fight Bobick. Ali agreed, stating, "We are back in business again." MSGB and Ali signed a Fighters' Agreement, and MSGB paid Ali $125,000 advance payment. The fight was to take place in Madison Square Garden on a date in February 1977. On November 30, 1976, Ali told MSGB that he was retiring from boxing and would not fight Bobick in February. Must MSGB wait until the date performance is due to sue Ali for breach of contract? [*Madison Square Garden Boxing, Inc. v. Muhammad Ali*, 430 F.Supp. 679, 1977 U.S. Dist. Lexis 16101 (N.D.Ill. 1977)]

11.9 Damages Raquel Welch was a movie actress who appeared in about 30 films between 1965 and 1980. She was considered a sex symbol, and her only serious dramatic role was as a roller derby queen in *Kansas City Bomber*. About 1980, Michael Phillips and David Ward developed a film package based on the John Steinbeck novella *Cannery Row*. In early 1981, Metro-Goldwyn-Mayer Film Co. (MGM) accepted to produce the project and entered into a contract with Welch to play the leading female character, a prostitute named Suzy. At 40 years old, Welch relished the chance to direct her career toward more serious roles. Welch was to receive $250,000 from MGM, with payment being divided into weekly increments during filming. Filming began on December 1, 1980. On December 22, 1980, MGM fired Welch and replaced her with another actress, Debra Winger. Welch sued MGM to recover the balance of $194,444 that remained unpaid under the contract. Who wins? [*Welch v. Metro-Goldwyn-Mayer Film Co.*, 207 Cal.App.3d 164, 254 Cal.Rptr. 645, 1988 Cal.App. Lexis 1202 (Cal.App. 1989)]

11.10 Damages On August 28, 1979, Ptarmigan Investment Company, a partnership, entered into a contract with Gundersons, Inc., a South Dakota corporation in the business of golf course construction. The contract provided that Gundersons would construct a golf course for Ptarmigan for a contract price of $1,294,129. Gundersons immediately started work and completed about one-third of the work by late November 1979, when bad weather forced cessation of most work. Ptarmigan paid Gundersons for the work to that date. In the spring of 1980, Ptarmigan ran out of funds and was unable to pay for the completion of the golf course. Gundersons sued Ptarmigan and its individual partners to recover the lost profits that it would have made on the remaining two-thirds of the contract. Can Gundersons recover these lost profits as damages? [*Gundersons, Inc. v. Ptarmigan Investment Company*, 678 P.2d 1061, 1983 Colo.App. Lexis 1133 (Colo.App. 1983)]

11.11 Liquidated Damages In December 1974, H. S. Perlin Company, Inc. (Perlin), and Morse Signal Devices of San Diego entered into a contract whereby Morse agreed to provide burglar and fire alarm service to Perlin's coin and stamp store. Perlin paid $50 per month for this service. The contract contained a liquidated damages clause by Perlin based on Morse's failure of service. During the evening of August 25, 1980, a burglary occurred at Perlin's store. Before entering the store, the burglars cut a telephone line that ran from the burglar system in Perlin's store to Morse's central location. When the line was cut, a signal indicated the interruption of service at Morse's central station. Inexplicably, Morse took no further steps to investigate the interruption of service at Perlin's store. The burglars stole stamps and coins with a wholesale value of $958,000, and Perlin did not have insurance against this loss. Perlin sued Morse to recover damages. Is the liquidated damages clause enforceable? [*H. S. Perlin Company, Inc. v. Morse Signal Devices of San Diego*, 209 Cal.App.3d 1289, 258 Cal.Rptr. 1, 1989 Cal.App. Lexis 400 (Cal.App. 1989)]

11.12 Specific Performance Liz Claiborne, Inc., is a large maker of women's better sportswear in the United States and a well-known name in fashion, with sales of more than $1 billion a year. Claiborne distributes its products through 9,000 retail outlets in the United States. Avon Products, Inc., is a major producer of fragrances, toiletries, and cosmetics, with sales of more than $3 billion a year. Claiborne, which desired to promote its well-known name on perfumes and cosmetics, entered into a joint venture with Avon whereby Claiborne would make available its name, trademarks, and marketing experience, and Avon would engage in the procurement and manufacture of the fragrances, toiletries, and cosmetics. The parties would equally share the financial requirements of the joint venture. In 1986, its first year of operation, the joint venture had sales of more than $16 million. In the second year, sales increased to $26 million, making it one of the fastest-growing fragrance and cosmetic lines in the country. In 1987, Avon sought to "uncouple" the joint venture. Avon thereafter refused to procure and manufacture the line of fragrances and cosmetics for the joint venture. When Claiborne could not obtain the necessary fragrances and cosmetics from any other source for the fall/Christmas season, Claiborne sued Avon for breach of contract, seeking specific performance of the contract by Avon. Is specific performance an appropriate remedy in this case? [*Liz Claiborne, Inc. v. Avon Products, Inc.*, 530 N.Y.S.2d 425, 141 A.D.2d 329, 1988 N.Y.App.Div. Lexis 6423 (N.Y.Sup.App. 1988)]

11.13 Quasi-Contract Wood Dimension, Inc., manufactured stereo speakers for resale to other companies. Fisher Corporation, a major customer, accounted for 30 percent to 50 percent of Wood's business. In early 1982, Fisher stopped buying from Wood. In order to regain Fisher's business, the president of Wood solicited the help of L. Dale Watson, who had known the vice president of Fisher for many years. Wood agreed to pay Watson 5 percent of all Fisher's orders if he succeeded in persuading Fisher to buy at Wood again. They shook hands to seal the agreement. Due to Watson's efforts, Fisher again became a customer of Wood's. In May 1984, Wood terminated Watson. Between that time and July 1985, Fisher placed orders of almost $10 million with Wood. Although the oral contract between Wood and Watson was terminable at will, Watson sued Wood to recover commissions on Fisher's orders that were placed under the theory of quasi-contract. Can Watson recover these damages under the theory of quasi-contract? [*Watson v. Wood Dimension, Inc.*, 209 Cal.App.3d 1359, 257 Cal.Rptr. 816, 1989 Cal.App. Lexis 399 (Cal.App. 1989)]

11.14 Injunction In 1982, Anita Baker, a then-unknown singer, signed a multiyear recording contract with Beverly Glen Music, Inc. Baker recorded a record album for Beverly Glen that was moderately successful. After having some difficulties with Beverly Glen, Baker was offered a considerably more lucrative contract by Warner Communications, Inc. Baker accepted the Warner offer and informed Beverly Glen that she would not complete her contract because she had entered into an agreement with Warner. Beverly Glen sued Baker, and Warner and sought an injunction to prevent Baker from performing as a singer for Warner. Is an injunction an appropriate remedy in this case? [*Beverly Glen Music, Inc. v. Warner Communications, Inc.*, 178 Cal.App.3d 1142, 224 Cal.Rptr. 260, 1986 Cal.App. Lexis 2729 (Cal.App. 1986)]

Business Ethics Cases

11.15 Business Ethics The First Baptist Church of Moultrie, Georgia, invited bids for the construction of a music, education, and recreation building. The bids, which were to be opened on May 15, 1986, were to be accompanied by a bid bond of 5 percent of the bid amount. Barber Contracting Company submitted a bid in the amount of $1,860,000. A bid bond in the amount of 5 percent of the bid—$93,000—was issued by The American Insurance Company. The bids were opened by the church on May 15, 1986, as planned, and Barber's was the lowest bid.

On May 16, 1986, Albert W. Barber, the president of Barber Contracting Company, informed the church that its bid was in error and should have been $143,120 higher. The error was caused in totaling the material costs on Barber's estimate worksheets. The church had not been provided these worksheets. On May 20, 1986, Barber sent a letter to the church, stating that it was withdrawing its bid. The next day the church sent a construction contract to Barber containing the original bid amount. When Barber refused to sign the contract and refused to do the work for the original contract price, the church signed a contract with the second-lowest bidder, H & H Construction and Supply Company, Inc., to complete the work for $1,919,272. The church sued Barber Contracting Company and The

American Insurance Company, seeking to recover the amount of the bid bond. Who wins? Did Barber act ethically in trying to get out of the contract? Did the church act ethically in trying to enforce Barber's bid? [*First Baptist Church of Moultrie v. Barber Contracting Co.*, 377 S.E.2d 717, 1989 Ga.App. Lexis 25 (Ga.App. 1989)]

11.16 Business Ethics Adolfo Mozzetti, who owned a construction company, orally promised his son, Remo, that if Remo would manage the family business for their mutual benefit and would take care of him for the rest of his life, he would leave the family home to Remo. Section 2714 of the Delaware Code requires contracts for the transfer of land to be in writing. Section 2715 of the Delaware Code requires testamentary transfers of real property to be in writing. Remo performed as requested—he managed the family business and took care of his father until the father died. When the father died, his will devised the family home to his daughter, Lucia M. Shepard. Remo brought this action to enforce his father's oral promise that the home belonged to him. The daughter argued that the will should be upheld. Who wins? Did the daughter act ethically in trying to defeat the father's promise to leave the property to the son? Did the son act ethically in trying to defeat his father's will? [*Shepard v. Mozzetti*, 545 A.2d 621, 1988 Del. Lexis 217 (DE 1988)]

11.17 Business Ethics Walgreen Company has operated a pharmacy in the Southgate Mall in Milwaukee since 1951, when the mall opened. Its current lease, signed in 1971 and carrying a 30-year-term, contains an exclusivity clause in which the landlord, Sara Creek Property Company, promises not to lease space in the mall to anyone else who wants to operate a pharmacy or a store containing a pharmacy. In 1990, after its anchor tenant went broke, Sara Creek informed Walgreen that it intended to lease the anchor tenant space to Phar-Mor Corporation. Phar-Mor, a "deep discount" chain, would occupy 100,000 square feet, of which 12,000 square feet would be occupied by a pharmacy the same size as Walgreen's. The entrances to the two stores would be within a few hundred feet of each other. Walgreen sued Sara Creek for breach of contract and sought a permanent injunction against Sara Creek's leasing the anchor premises to Phar-Mor. Do the facts of this case justify the issuance of a permanent injunction? Did Sara Creek act ethically in not living up to the contract? [*Walgreen Co. v. Sara Creek Property Co.*, 966 F.2d 273, 1992 U.S. App. Lexis 14847 (7th Cir. 1992)]

Briefing the Case Writing Assignment

Read Case A.11 in the Case Appendix [*E. B. Harvey & Company, Inc. v. Protective Systems, Inc.*]. This case is excerpted from the appellate court opinion. Review and brief the case. In your brief, be sure to answer the following questions.

1. What were Protective Systems's duties under the contract?
2. What amount of damages was Protective Systems liable for under the express terms of the contract?
3. Was Protective Systems negligent in this case?
4. What policy considerations did the court cite in upholding the liquidated damages clause?

Answers to Management Decision Question

1. No, the agency is not in breach of contract. A contract is an agreement between two or more competent parties to do or not do some legal thing for consideration and is enforceable in a court of law. If a contract duty has not been discharged or excused, a contracting party owes an absolute duty to perform the duty. (Cheeseman) In other words, you had a preexisting duty to finish the tour according to the original terms. The agreement to pay the additional compensation fails as a contract because of lack of consideration. A promise lacks consideration if a person promised to perform an act or do something he or she is already under an obligation to do.
2. Yes, under present ethical assumptions, one should be free from predatory interference in contractual dealings with others. Today, corporations are considered to owe some degree of social responsibility for their actions. (Cheeseman) In addition, if you had breached your contract with the agency through your failure to perform, you could be sued for breach of contract, and an injunction could be issued, preventing you from working for the casino during the remaining term of the contract with the agency. The casino could be sued under tort theory for wrongful interference with a contractual relationship.

Endnotes

1. *Restatement (Second) of Contracts*, § 153.
2. *Restatement (Second) of Contracts*, § 152.
3. 159 Eng.Rep. 375 (1864).
4. *Restatement (Second) of Contracts*, § 159.
5. *Restatement (Second) of Contracts*, §§ 163 and 164.
6. *Restatement (Second) of Contracts*, § 176.
7. *Restatement (Second) of Contracts*, § 177.
8. *Restatement (Second) of Contracts*, § 130.
9. *Restatement (Second) of Contracts*, § 112.
10. UCC § 2-201(1).
11. UCC § 2-209(3).
12. *Restatement (Second) of Contracts*, § 139.
13. *Restatement (Second) of Contracts*, § 224, defines a *condition* as "an event, not certain to occur, which must occur, unless its nonperformance is excused, before performance under a contract is due."
14. *Restatement (Second) of Contracts*, § 261.
15. *Restatement (Second) of Contracts*, § 253; UCC § 2-610.
16. *Restatement (Second) of Contracts*, § 356(1).
17. *Restatement (Second) of Contracts*, § 370.
18. *Restatement (Second) of Contracts*, § 359.

12

Internet Law and Electronic Commerce

"Through the use of chat rooms, any person with a phone line can become a town crier with a voice that resonates farther than it could from any soapbox. Through the use of Web pages, mail exploders, and newsgroups, the same individual can become a pamphleteer."

—Justice Stevens
Reno v. American Civil Liberties Union, 521 U.S. 844 (1997)

Chapter Objectives

After studying this chapter, you should be able to:

1. Describe the free-speech protection granted to the Internet by the U.S. Supreme Court.
2. Describe the process for obtaining Internet domain names and the procedure for arbitrating Internet domain name disputes.
3. Define license and the parties to a licensing agreement.
4. Describe the provisions of the Federal Electronics Signatures Act for e-commerce.
5. Describe the Uniform Electronic Transactions Act (UETA) and the Uniform Computer Information Transactions Act (UCITA).

Chapter Contents

- The Internet
- Internet Domain Names
- Licensing of Information Rights

Management Decision Internet Law and Electronic Commerce

As a young entrepreneur, you are contemplating entering into an e-commerce business with your friend, Thomas Jefferson Smith. Your company will allow individuals to trade college textbooks on your site for a modest fee. You are in the process of establishing an Internet Web site. You have suggested that the domain name of the Web site should be ThomasJefferson.com because of the public's familiarity with that name. Your friend is concerned about the legality of using the name Thomas Jefferson as a domain name. He is also concerned about lawsuits being filed by heirs of President Jefferson.

1. Should you be concerned about the legal implications associated with establishing a Web site?
2. What is the law concerning the use of the name of a famous persons as an Internet domain name?

In the late 1990s and early 2000s the use of the Internet and the World Wide Web, and the sale of goods and services through **e-commerce**, exploded. Large and small businesses began selling goods and services over the Internet through Web sites and registered domain names. Consumers and businesses can purchase almost any good or service they want over the Internet, using such sites as Amazon.com, eBay, and others. In addition, software and information may be licensed either by physically purchasing the software or information and installing it on a computer or by merely downloading the software or information directly into a computer.

Many legal scholars and lawyers argued that traditional rules of contract law do not adequately meet the needs of Internet transactions and software and information licensing.

e-commerce
The sale of goods and services by computer over the Internet.

Business Brief
The use of the Internet and the sale of goods and services through e-commerce has exploded in the United States and worldwide.

E-Commerce. The development of electronic commerce has required courts to apply existing laws to new businesses and spurred the federal Congress and state legislatures to enact new laws to govern modern means of communications and the conduct of electronic business.

These concerns led to an effort to create a new contract law for electronic transactions. After much debate, the National Conference of Commissioners on Uniform Sate Laws developed the **Uniform Electronic Transactions Act (UETA)** and the **Uniform Computer Information Transactions Act (UCITA)**. These model acts provide uniform and comprehensive rules for contracts involving computer information transactions and software and information licenses.

Uniform Computer Information Transactions Act (UCITA)
A model act that provides uniform and comprehensive rules for contracts involving computer information transactions and software and information licenses.

This chapter covers the registration of domain names and the operation of Web businesses and explains how the UETA and UCITA and other laws regulate the creation, transfer, and enforcement of e-commerce and informational rights licensing contracts.

The Internet

Internet
A collection of millions of computers that provide a network of electronic connections between computers.

The **Internet**, or **Net**, is a collection of millions of computers that provide a network of electronic connections between the computers. The Internet began in 1969, when the U.S. Department of Defense wanted to create communications for military and national defense purposes. Building on this start, in the 1980s the National Science Foundation, the federal government's main scientific and technical agency, established the Net to facilitate high-speed communications among research centers at academic and research institutions around the world.

Our legal system faces no theoretical dilemma but a single continuous problem: how to apply to ever changing conditions the never changing principles of freedom.
Earl Warren (1995)

Eventually, individuals and businesses began using the Internet for communication of information and data. In 1980 there were fewer than 250 computers hooked to the Internet. Growth was rapid in the late 1990s and into the early 2000s, and today there are several hundred million computers connected to the Internet. The Internet's evolution helped usher in the Information Age of today.

In the following case, the U.S. Supreme Court reviewed an important issue concerning free speech over the Internet.

U.S. SUPREME COURT CASE

Reno, Attorney General of the United States v. American Civil Liberties Union

521 U.S. 844, 117 S.Ct. 2329, 1997 U.S. Lexis 4037 (1997)
Supreme Court of the United States

Case 12.1 Free Speech and the Internet

Background and Facts

Congress enacted the Telecommunications Act of 1996. Title V of the act, known as the Communications Decency Act of 1996 (CDA), contained two important statutory provisions challenged in this case. The first provision, the "indecent transmission" provision, prohibits the knowing transmission of obscene or indecent messages over the Internet to a recipient under 18 years of age. The second provision, the "patently offensive display" provision, prohibits the knowing sending or displaying of patently offensive messages over the Internet in a manner that is available to a person under 18 years of age. Both provisions provide for criminal penalties, including sentencing to jail. Immediately after the statute was signed into law, 47 plaintiffs, consisting of Internet companies and users, sued the United States, alleging that these provisions violated the Freedom of Speech Clause of the First Amendment to the U.S. Constitution. The district court entered a preliminary injunction against enforcement of the challenged provisions. The U.S. Supreme Court agreed to hear the appeal.

Supreme Court Issue

Do the indecent transmission and the patently offensive display provisions of the CDA violate the Freedom of Speech Clause of the First Amendment of the U.S. Constitution?

In The Language of The U.S. Supreme Court

Stevens, Justice Each medium of expression may present its own problems. Thus, some of our cases have recognized special justifications for regulation of the broadcast media that are not applicable to other speakers. In these cases, the Court relied on the history of extensive government regulation of the broadcast medium, the scarcity of available frequencies at its inception, and its "invasive" nature. Those factors are not present in cyberspace. Neither before nor after the enactment of the CDA have the vast democratic fora of the Internet been subject to the type of government supervision and regulation that has attended the broadcast industry. Moreover, the Internet is not as "invasive" as radio or television. The District Court specifically found that "communications over the Internet do not invade an individual's home or appear on one's computer screen unbidden. Users seldom encounter content by accident." It also found that "almost all sexually explicit images are preceded by warnings as to the content," and cited testimony that "odds are slim that a user would come across a sexually explicit site by accident."

Unlike the conditions that prevailed when Congress first authorized regulation of the broadcast spectrum, the Internet can hardly be considered a "scarce" expressive commodity. It provides relatively unlimited, low-cost capacity for communication of all kinds. This dynamic, multifaceted category of communication includes not only traditional print and news services, but also audio, video, and still images, as well as interactive, realtime dialogue. Through the use of chat rooms, any person with a phone line can become a town crier with a voice that resonates farther than it could from any soapbox. Through the use of Web pages, mail exploders, and newsgroups, the same individual can become a pamphleteer. As the District Court found, "the content on the Internet is as diverse as human thought."

The vagueness of the CDA is a matter of special concern for two reasons. First, the CDA is a content-based regulation of speech. The vagueness of such a regulation raises special First Amendment concerns because of its obvious chilling effect on free speech. Second, the CDA is a criminal statute. In addition to the opprobrium and stigma of a criminal conviction, the CDA threatens violators with penalties including up to two years in prison for each act of violation. The severity of criminal sanctions may well cause speakers to remain silent rather than communicate even arguably unlawful words, ideas, and images. Given the vague contours of the coverage of the statute, it unquestionably silences some speakers whose messages would be entitled to constitutional protection.

Systems have been developed to help parents control the material that may be available on a home computer with Internet access. A system may either limit a computer's access to an approved list of sources that have been identified as containing no adult material, it may block designated inappropriate sites, or it may attempt to block messages containing identifiable objectionable features. Although parental control software currently can screen for certain suggestive words or for known sexually explicit sites, it cannot now screen for sexually explicit images. Nevertheless, the evidence indicates that a reasonably effective method by which parents can prevent their children from accessing sexually explicit and other material which parents may believe is inappropriate for their children will soon be available.

We are persuaded that the CDA lacks the precision that the First Amendment requires when a statute regulates the content of speech. In order to deny minors access to potentially harmful speech, the CDA effectively suppresses a large amount of speech that adults have a constitutional right to receive and to address to one another. In evaluating the free speech rights of adults, we have made it perfectly clear that sexual expression which is indecent but not obscene is protected by the First Amendment.

Decision and Remedy

The U.S. Supreme Court held that the indecent transmission and the patently offensive display provisions of the CDA violated the free speech rights of the plaintiffs. The Supreme Court affirmed the decision of the district court.

Case Questions

Critical Legal Thinking Should the Internet be treated differently from other types of media, such as radio, cable, and television, when it comes to First Amendment free speech issues? Explain.

Business Ethics What goals was Congress trying to accomplish by enacting the challenged provisions in this case? Are these laudable goals? Are there any goals of others that are opposed to these goals? Explain.

Contemporary Business Does the Supreme Court's decision have any important economic consequences? If so, to whom?

Electronic Mail

Electronic mail, or **e-mail**, is one of the most widely used applications for communication over the Internet. Using e-mail, individuals can instantaneously communicate in electronic writing with others around the world. Each person can have an e-mail address that identifies him or her by a unique address. E-mail will continue to grow in use in the future as it replaces some telephone and paper correspondence and increases new communication between persons.

electronic mail (e-mail)
Electronic written communication between individuals using computers connected to the Internet.

E-Commerce & Information Technology

E-Mail Contracts

E-mail has exploded as a means of personal and business communication. In the business environment, e-mail is sometimes the method used to negotiate and agree on contract terms and to send and agree to the final contract. The question presented is whether an e-mail contract is enforceable. Assuming that all of the elements to establish a contract are present, an e-mail contract is valid and enforceable. The main problem in a lawsuit seeking to enforce an e-mail contract is evidence, but this problem, which exists in almost all lawsuits, can be overcome by printing out the e-mail contract and its prior e-mail negotiations, if necessary.

A further issue arises if the contract is required to be in writing by the state statute of frauds. Because the parties to an e-mail contract can print a paper version of the electronic contract, this would meet the writing requirement of the statute of frauds. The analogy would be that a contract that is printed from the e-mail message is not different from a contract that is printed on the same printer from a word-processing program. Thus, e-mail contracts meet the writing requirements for enforceable contracts. ■

E-Commerce & Information Technology

Electronic Communications Privacy Act

E-mail, computer data, and other electronic communications are sent daily by millions of people using computers and the Internet. Recognizing how the use of computer and electronic communications raise special issues of privacy, the federal government enacted the **Electronic Communications Privacy Act (ECPA)**. The ECPA makes it a crime to intercept an "electronic communication" at the point of transmission, while in transit, when stored by a router or server, or after receipt by the intended recipient. An electronic communication includes any transfer of signals, writings, images, sounds, data, or intelligence of any nature. The ECPA makes it illegal to access stored e-mail as well as e-mail in transmission.

The ECPA provides that stored electronic communications may be accessed without violating the law by the following:

1. The party or entity providing the electronic communication service. The primary example would be an employer who can access stored e-mail communications of employees using the employer's service.
2. Government and law enforcement entities that are investigating suspected illegal activity. Disclosure would be required only pursuant to a validly issued warrant.

The ECPA provides for criminal penalties. In addition, the ECPA provides that an injured party may sue for civil damages for violations of the act. ■

The World Wide Web

World Wide Web
An electronic connection of millions of computers that support a standard set of rules for the exchange of information.

The **World Wide Web** consists of millions of computers that support a standard set of rules for the exchange of information called Hypertext Transfer Protocol (HTTP). Web-based documents are formatted using common coding languages such as Hypertext Markup Language (HTML) and Java. Businesses and individuals can hook up to the Web by registering with a service such as America Online (AOL).

Web Site
Legal Research Using the Internet, by Lyonette Louis-Jacques This guide, written by a law librarian at the University of Chicago, explains why the Internet is useful for legal research. Visit at **www.lib.uchicago.edu/~~llou/mpoctalk.html**.

Individuals and businesses can have their own Web sites. A Web site is composed of electronic documents known as Web pages. The Web sites and pages are stored on servers throughout the world. They are viewed by using Web browser software such as Microsoft Internet Explorer and Netscape Navigator. Each Web site has a unique online address. Web pages can contain a full range of multimedia content, including text, images, video, sound, and animation. Web pages can include references, called *hyperlinks*, or *links*, to other Web pages or sites.

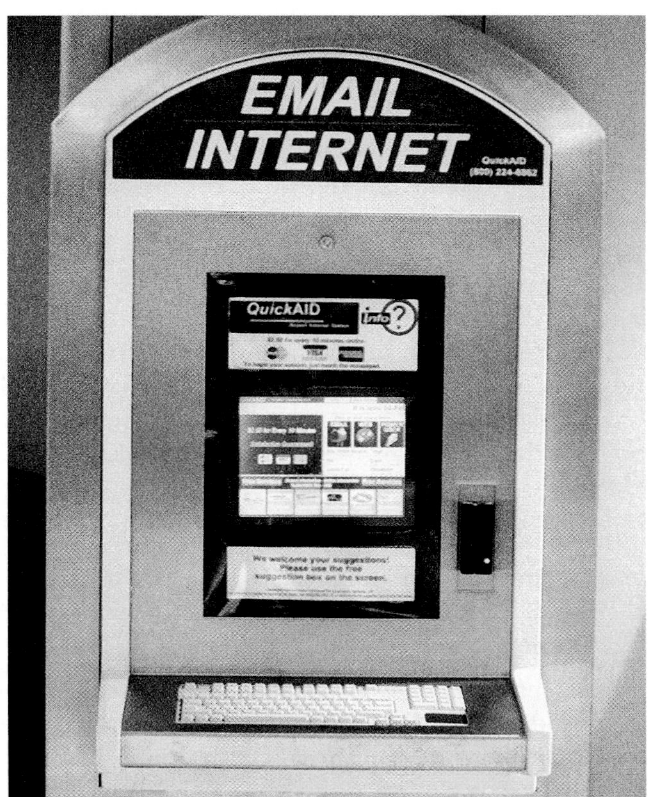

Kiosk for Internet Services. The evolution of the World Wide Web and the Internet has changed how business is conducted.

The Web has made it extremely attractive to conduct commercial activities online. Companies such as Amazon.com and eBay are e-commerce powerhouses that sell all sorts of goods and services. Existing companies, such as Wal-Mart, Merrill Lynch, and Dell Computers, sell their goods and services online as well. E-commerce over the Web will continue to grow dramatically each year.

International Law

China Opens the Internet

In November 1999, China and the United Sates entered into a historic trade pact that reduced tariffs and other barriers to entry for selling goods and services between the two countries. Prior to this trade pact, China had announced that it would not allow investment by foreign firms in China's Internet markets. In exchange for the United States opening its borders to more Chinese-made goods, China agreed to allow U.S. firms to invest in China's Internet business.

Although it agreed to open its Internet markets, China has placed restrictions on foreign investment in Internet businesses. These restrictions include the following:

- Foreign companies cannot own more than 50 percent of any Internet business in China.
- Foreign companies must obtain a special license from the Chinese government for such investments.
- China will regulate the content of Internet Web sites, including advertisements placed on the Web.

Critics of the pact argue that China could use the licensing procedures and content-approval rules to erect bureaucratic nontariff barriers to entry. Proponents argue that China has an incentive not to enforce the restrictions too harshly because strict enforcement would cause China to lose much-needed foreign investment and technological knowledge and to risk retaliatory actions by the United Sates. Others argue that there are always ways around such restrictions, such as the traditional method of paying the appropriate government officials to get things done. In the borderless world of the Internet, some foreign companies may set up business in countries and areas near China and offer Internet services to China from these locations.

With over 1.2 billion people, China offers a great potential for the growth of the use of the Internet and e-commerce. If foreign companies are allowed up to a 50 percent investment in Internet companies and businesses in China, this is still far better than being shut out of the market altogether. ■

Internet Domain Names

domain name
A unique name that identifies an individual's or a company's Web site.

Each Web site is identified by a unique Internet **domain name**. For example, the domain name for the publisher of this book is **www.prenhall.com**. Some of the top-level suffixes for domain names are *com* for commercial use, *net* for networks, *org* for organizations, and *edu* for educational institutions.

Business Brief
Domain names may be registered by filing the appropriate form with a domain name registration service and paying the appropriate fee.

Domain names can be registered. The first step in registering a domain name is determining whether any other party already owns the name. For this purpose, InterNIC maintains a "Whois" database that contains the domain names that have been registered. The InterNIC Web site is located online at **internic.net**. Domain names can also be registered at Network Solutions, Inc.'s, Web site, which is located at **www.networksolutions.com**, as well as at other sites. An applicant must complete a registration form, which can be done online. It costs less than $50 to register a domain for one year, and the fee may be paid by credit card online.

The most commonly used top-level extensions for domain names are:

- ***.com*** This extension represents the word *commercial* and is the most widely used extension in the world. Most businesses prefer a .com domain name because it is a highly recognized business symbol.
- ***.net*** This extension represents the word *network*, and is most commonly used by Internet service providers, Web-hosting companies, and other businesses that are directly involved in the infrastructure of the Internet. Some businesses also choose domain names with a .net extension.
- ***.org*** This extension represents the word *organization* and is primarily used by non-profit groups and trade associations.
- ***.info*** This extension signifies a "resource" Web site. It is an unrestricted global name that may be used by businesses, individuals, and organizations.
- ***.biz*** This extension is used for small-business Web sites.
- ***.us*** This extension is for U.S. Web sites. Many businesses choose this extension, which is a relatively new extension.
- ***.cc*** This extension was originally the country code for Coco Keeling Islands, but it is now unrestricted and may be registered by anyone from any country. It is often registered by businesses.
- ***.bz*** This extension was originally the country code for Belize, but it is now unrestricted and may be registered by anyone from any country. It is commonly used by small businesses.
- ***.name*** This new extension is for individuals, who can use it to register personalized domain names.
- ***.museum*** This extension enables museums, museum associations, and museum professionals to register their own Web sites.
- ***.coop*** This extension represents the word *co-operative* and may be used by cooperative associations around the world.
- ***.aero*** This extension is exclusively reserved for the aviation community. It enables organizations and individuals to reserve Web sites.
- ***.pro*** This extension is available to professionals, such as doctors, lawyers, consultants, and other professionals.
- ***.edu*** This extension is for educational institutions.

Entrepreneur and the Law

Web Domain Names Sold for Millions

What is a name worth? Plenty! It used to be that a person could make money by trademarking a name before a large company wanted to use the name for a product or service or as a new company name. Once in possession of the trademark, the owner could sell it at a profit if some company wanted it desperately enough. But trying to guess what names would be wanted took some work. In addition, trademark law required the name to be used in commerce. Although trademarking and selling trademark names is still a way to make money, the hottest area for name-selling is registering and selling Internet domain names.

Take the case of the domain name *business.com*. This name, which was originally registered as a domain name for $70, was sold to entrepreneur Marc Ostrofsky for $150,000 in 1996. Many people at the time thought this was an outrageous sum to pay for a domain name—that is, until Mr. Ostrofsky turned around and resold the name to ECompanies in 1999 for $7.5 million. That was the most ever paid for an Internet domain name. ECompanies thought it was a bargain and plans to use the domain name for its new Web site, where it will offer a form of Internet Yellow Pages.

Other domain names have been sold at high prices, too. *Altavista.com* was purchased by Compaq Computer for its Internet search engine. Other domain names sold for high prices include *wine.com* for $3 million, *bingo.com* for $1.1 million, *wallstreet.com* for $1 million, and *drugs.com* for $800,000. As commerce over the Internet increases and as unregistered memorable names become harder to find, transactions in the sale of domain names are expected to accelerate, with multimillion-dollar prices being paid for the most desirable names—which were originally registered for $70 or less. ■

E-Commerce & Information Technology

Anticybersquatting Act Passed by Congress

When the famous actress Julia Roberts tried to register her name as the Internet domain name juliaroberts.com, she discovered that someone else had already registered this domain name. So what's a famous person to do? Rely on Congress to pass a law that helps him or her. And that is exactly what the U.S. Congress did.

In November 1999, the U.S. Congress enacted, and the president signed, the **Anticybersquatting Consumer Protection Act (ACPA)** [15 U.S.C. § 1125(d)]. The act was specifically aimed at cybersquatters who register Internet domain names of famous companies and people and hold them hostage by demanding ransom payments from the famous company or person. In the past, trademark law was of little help, either because the famous person's name was not trademarked or because, even if the name was trademarked, trademark law required distribution of goods or services to find infringement, and most cybersquatters did not distribute goods or services but merely sat on the Internet domain name. The act has two fundamental requirements: (1) The name must be famous and (2) the domain name must have been registered in bad faith. Thus, the law prohibits the act of cybersquatting itself if it is done in *bad faith*.

The first issue in applying the statute is whether the domain name is the famous name of someone else. Trademarked names qualify; nontrademarked names—such as those of famous actors, actresses, singers, sports exhibitures, political exhibitures, and such—also are protected. In determining bad faith, the law provides that courts may consider the extent to which the domain name resembles the holder's name or the famous person's name, whether goods or services are sold under the name, the holder's offer to sell or transfer the name, and whether the holder has acquired multiple Internet domain names of famous companies and persons.

The act provides for the issuance of cease-and-desist orders and injunctions by the court. In addition, the law adds monetary penalties: A plaintiff has the option of seeking statutory damages of between $1,000 and $300,000 in lieu of proving damages. The ACPA gives owners of trademarks and persons with famous names a new weapon to attack the kidnapping of Internet domain names by cyberpirates. Julia Roberts immediately sued the holder of juliaroberts.com for violating the act and won the right to her own domain name. The singer Sting was not so lucky, however, when he found that sting.com was already taken. The court ruled that because the word *sting* is generic and can be found in the dictionary, Sting had no claim under the ACPA to the domain name. ■

The following cases show the application of the Anticybersquatting Consumer Protection Act.

E. & J. Gallo Winery v. Spider Webs Ltd.

286 F.3d 270, 2002 U.S. App. Lexis 5928 (2002)
United States Court of Appeals, Fifth Circuit

Case 12.2

Anticybersquatting Consumer Protection Act

Background and Facts

Ernest and Julio Gallo Winery (Gallo) is a famous maker of wines that is located in California. The company registered the trademark "Ernest & Julio Gallo" in 1964 with the United States Patent and Trademark Office. The company has spent over $500 million promoting its brand name and has sold more than four billion bottles of wine. Its name has taken on a secondary meaning as a famous trademark name. In 1999, Steve, Pierce, and Fred Thumann created Spider Webs Ltd., a limited partnership, to register Internet domain names. Spider Webs registered more than 2,000 Internet domain names, including ernestandjuliogallo.com. Spider Webs is in the business of selling some of its domain names. Gallo filed suit against Spider Webs Ltd. and the Thumanns, alleging violation of the federal ACPA. The district court held in favor of Gallo and ordered Spider Webs to transfer the domain name ernestandjuliogallo.com to Gallo. Spider Webs Ltd. appealed.

Issue

Did Spider Webs Ltd. and the Thumanns act in bad faith in registering the Internet domain name ernestandjuliogallo.com?

In The Language of The Court

Jolly, Judge Spider Webs does not appeal the holdings that Gallo had a valid registration in its mark, that the mark is famous and distinctive, and that the domain name registered by Spider Webs is identical or confusingly similar to Gallo's mark. However, Spider Webs argues that they did not act with a "bad faith intent to profit," as required by the ACPA.

We turn now to consider the listed bad-faith factors as they apply to this case. Spider Webs has no intellectual property rights or trademark in the name "ernestandjuliogallo," aside from its registered domain name. The domain name does not contain the name of Spider Webs or any of the other defendants. Spider Webs had no "prior use" (or any current use) of the domain name in connection with the bona fide offering of goods or services. Spider Webs's use is commercial, and there is no indication that it is a fair use. Steve Thumann admitted that the domain name was valuable and that they hoped Gallo would contact them so that they could "assist" Gallo in some way. Additionally, there is uncontradicted evidence that Spider Webs was engaged in commerce in the selling of domain names and that they hoped to sell this domain name some day. The ACPA was passed to address situations just like this one.

Finally, there was evidence presented that Gallo's mark is distinctive and famous. Gallo registered the mark, which is a family name, thirty-eight years ago, and "Gallo" has clearly become associated with wine in the United States such that its evolution to "secondary meaning" status may not be seriously questioned. The circumstances of this case all indicate that Spider Webs knew Gallo had a famous mark in which Gallo had built up goodwill, and that they hoped to profit from this by registering "ernestandjuliogallo.com" and waiting for Gallo to contact them so they could "assist" Gallo.

Decision and Remedy

The court of appeals held that the name Ernest and Julio Gallo was a famous trademark name and that Spider Webs Ltd. and the Thumanns acted in bad faith when they registered the Internet domain name ernestandjulio.com. The court of appeals upheld the district court's decision, ordering the defendants to transfer the domain name to plaintiff E. & J. Gallo Winery.

Case Questions

Critical Legal Thinking Should Congress have enacted the ACPA? Is it really consumers who are being protected? Explain.

Business Ethics Did the defendants act ethically in registering so many Internet domain names? What was the defendant's motive?

Contemporary Business How valuable is a company's trademark name? Does the ACPA protect that value? Explain.

People for the Ethical Treatment of Animals v. Daughney

263 F.3d 359, 2001 U.S. App. Lexis 19028 (2001)
United States Court of Appeals, Fourth Circuit

Case 12.3

Anticybersquatting Consumer Protection Act

Background and Facts

People for the Ethical Treatment of Animals (PETA) is a nonprofit organization. PETA is an animal rights organization with more than 600,000 members worldwide who are dedicated to promoting and heightening public awareness of animal protection issues, and it opposes the exploitation of animals for food, clothing, and entertainment. The organization has trademarked the term PETA. In 1995, Michael E. Doughney registered the Internet domain name peta.org. When this Web site was accessed, the words "People Eating Tasty Animals" appeared in large, bold print. Under the title, the viewer would see a statement that the Web site was a resource for those who enjoy eating meat, wearing fur and leather, hunting, and animal research. The Web site contained links to various meat, fur, leather, hunting, and animal research organizations. Doughney stated that he would sell the domain name peta.org to PETA. PETA sued Doughney, alleging a violation of the federal ACPA. The district court held in favor of PETA and ordered Doughney to transfer the Internet domain name peta.org to PETA. Doughney appealed.

Issue

Did Doughney act in bad faith in violation of the federal ACPA in registering the Internet domain name peta.org?

In The Language of The Court

Gregory, Judge To establish an ACPA violation, PETA was required to (1) prove that Doughney had a bad faith intent to profit from using the peta.org domain name, and (2) that the peta.org domain name is identical or confusingly similar to, or dilutive of, the distinctive and famous PETA Mark.

The district court properly concluded that Doughney (I) had no intellectual property right in peta.org; (II) peta.org is not Doughney's name or a name otherwise used to identify Doughney; (III) Doughney had no prior use of peta.org in connection with the bona fide offering of any goods or services; (IV) Doughney used the PETA Mark in a commercial manner; (V) Doughney "clearly intended to confuse, mislead and divert Internet users into accessing his Web site which contained information antithetical and therefore harmful to the goodwill represented by the PETA Mark"; (VI) Doughney made statements on his web site and in the press recommending that PETA attempt to "settle" with him and "make him an offer"; (VII) Doughney made false statements when registering the domain name; and (VIII) Doughney registered other domain names that are identical or similar to the marks or names of other famous people and organizations.

Decision and Remedy

The court of appeals held that the name PETA was a famous trademark name and that Doughney had acted in bad faith when he registered the Internet domain name peta.org. The court of appeals affirmed the district court's decision ordering Doughney to transfer the domain name peta.org to plaintiff PETA.

Case Questions

Critical Legal Thinking If it were not for the federal ACPA, would PETA have had any recourse in this case?

Business Ethics Did Doughney act ethically in this case? Explain.

Contemporary Business What would be the consequences if the ACPA did not protect businesses and organizations from attacks like the one in this case? Explain.

Case 12.4

Anticybersquatting Consumer Protection Act

Virtual Works, Inc. v. Volkswagen of America, Inc. and Volkswagen Aktiengesellschaft

238 F.3d 264, 2001 U.S. App. Lexis 831 (2001)
United States Court of Appeals, Fourth Circuit

Background and Facts

Volkswagen Aktiengesellschaft and Volkswagen of America, Inc. (Volkswagen) are companies that produce and sell automobiles under the famous "Volkswagen" trademark in the United States. Virtual Works, Inc., is a small service provider located in the United States. In 1996, Virtual Works, Inc., registered the Internet domain name vw.net with the domain registry Network Solutions, Inc. At the time of registration, the owners of Virtual Works, Christopher Grimes and James Anderson, were aware that some Internet users might think that vw.net was affiliated with Volkswagen. They talked about Volkswagen and the possibility that Volkswagen might purchase the domain name vw.net. Two years later, Anderson called Volkswagen and stated that Volkswagen had 24 hours to purchase the vw.net domain name, or the name would be sold to the highest bidder. Volkswagen sued Virtual Works to recover the name under the federal ACPA. The district court held in favor of Volkswagen and ordered Virtual Works to relinquish its rights to the domain name vw.net to Volkswagen. Virtual Works appealed.

Issue

Did Virtual Works, Inc., act in bad faith in violation of the federal ACPA in registering the Internet domain name vw.net?

In The Language of The Court

Wilkinson, Chief Judge The ACPA was enacted in 1999 in response to concerns over the proliferation of cybersquatting—the Internet version of a land grab. According to the Senate Report accompanying the Act: "Trademark owners are facing a new form of piracy on the Internet caused by acts of 'cybersquatting,' which refers to the deliberate, bad-faith, and abusive registration of Internet domain names in violation of the rights of trademark owners." Cybersquatting is the practice of registering well-known brand names as Internet domain names in order to force the rightful owners of the marks to pay for the right to engage in electronic commerce under their own brand name.

The district court held that Virtual Works had no right to or interest in the VW mark and that Virtual Works had never been referred to or done business under the name VW. The district court found that the famousness of the VW mark also favored Volkswagen. Unfortunately for Virtual Works, however, there is both circumstantial and direct evidence establishing bad faith. The following uncontested facts all provide circumstantial evidence of Virtual Works' bad faith with respect to the VW mark: 1) the famousness of the VW mark; 2) the similarly of vw.net to the VW mark; 3) the admission that Virtual Works never once did business as VW nor identified itself as such; and 4) the

Virtual Works, Inc. v. Volkswagen of America, Inc. and Volkswagen Aktiengesellschaft

238 F.3d 264, 2001 U.S. App. Lexis 831 (2001)
United States Court of Appeals, Fourth Circuit
(continued)

availability of vwi.org and vwi.net as the time Virtual Works registered vw.net. Notably, either of these domain names would have satisfied Virtual Works' own stated criterion of registering a domain name that used only two or three letters and would have eliminated any risk of confusion with respect to the VW mark.

Volkswagen, however, points to direct evidence regarding Virtual Works' intent—the statements made at registration. Grimes' deposition reveals that when registering vw.net, he and Anderson specifically acknowledged that vw.net might be confused with Volkswagen by some Internet users. They nevertheless decided to register the address for their own use, but left open the possibility of one day selling the site to Volkswagen "for a lot of money." Moreover, the facts affirmatively support the claim that Virtual Works had a bad faith intent to profit when it attempted to sell vw.net to Volkswagen. Viewed in its totality, the evidence establishes that at the time Virtual Works proposed to sell vw.net to Volkswagen, it was motivated by a bad faith intent to profit from the famousness of the VW mark. This is the sort of misconduct that Congress sought to discourage.

Decision and Remedy

The court of appeals held that Virtual Works had attempted to profit in bad faith from Volkswagen's famous trademark when Virtual Works registered the Internet domain name vw.net. The court of appeals affirmed the district court's decision, ordering Virtual Works to transfer the domain name vw.net to plaintiff Volkswagen.

Case Questions

Critical Legal Thinking What public purpose does the federal ACPA serve? Whose interests are served by enforcement of the act?

Business Ethics Did the owners of Virtual Works act ethically in this case? Explain.

Contemporary Business What are the economic consequences of the court's decision in this case? Explain.

E-Commerce & Information Technology

Domain Name Disputes Set for Arbitration

Under a contract with the United States government, the **Internet Corporation for Assigned Names and Numbers (ICANN)** is responsible for regulating the issuance of domain names on the Internet. ICANN contracted with Network Solutions, a private company, to register domain names. Until June 1999, Network Solutions was the exclusive registrar for all domain names bearing .com, .net, and .org. Since then, other registrars of domain names have been approved by ICANN.

Domain names are sometimes challenged for infringing on trademarks or service marks owned by businesses and individuals. In addition, the passage of the federal ACPA of 1999 allows owners of famous names to challenge similar domain names that have been registered in bad faith. Civil lawsuits alleging violations of trademark law or the anticybersquatting law may take years to go to trial and cost a fortune to pursue.

In October 1999, ICANN approved an arbitration procedure for challenging cybersquatting. This procedure, called the **Uniform Dispute Resolution Policy (UDRP)**, requires all ICANN-approved registrars of domain names to agree to use this dispute resolution policy as part of their accreditation. The UDRP requires arbitration of domain name disputes. The dispute is heard by an arbitration panel approved by ICANN. ICANN has approved the World Intellectual Property Organization (WIPO), an agency of the United Nations, as an arbitrator of domain name disputes. ICANN has also approved several private companies, including the National Arbitration Forum and the Disputes.org/eResolution.ca Consortium, to be dispute resolution arbitrators. In a UDRP arbitration hearing, a panel of trademark and intellectual property experts, who usually are scholars, retired judges, or other professionals, hear and decide the dispute. The decision of the arbitration panel can be appealed to the U.S. courts.

In its first ruling under the UDRP, the WIPO held that Michael Bosman, a resident of Redlands, California, had registered the domain name **www.worldwrestlingfederation.com** in bad faith. The World Wrestling Federation (WWF), a promoter of professional wrestling, had long owned the trademark to its name. Bosman, after registering the domain name, contacted the WWF and offered to sell it to the trademark holder. Instead of buying the name, WWF filed a case with the WIPO. The WIPO arbitrator found that Bosman registered the domain name in bad faith in violation of the law. The arbitrator noted that the domain name was not Bosman's nickname or a name of any family member and that he had not made any use of the name. The arbitrator concluded that the domain name was identical to the WWF's trademark and that Bosman had no legal rights to the domain name. The arbitrator ordered the domain name transferred to the WWF. ■

Cambodia. Internet access is available in many countries of the world.

E-Commerce & Information Technology

Armani Outmaneuvered for Domain Name

G. A. Modefine S. A. is the owner of the famous "Armani" trademark under which it produces and sells upscale and high-priced apparel. The Armani label is recognized worldwide. But Modefine was surprised when it tried to register for the domain name armani.com and found that it had already been taken. Modefine brought an arbitration action in the WIPO's Arbitration and Mediation Center against the domain name owner to recover the armani.com domain name under the UDRP. To win, Modefine had to prove that the domain name was identical or confusingly similar to its trademark, the owner who registered the name did not have a legitimate interest in the name, and the owner registered the name in bad faith.

The person who owned the domain name, Anand Ramnath Mani, appeared at the proceeding and defended his ownership rights. The arbitrator found that Modefine's trademark and Mr. Mani's domain name were identical but held that Mr. Mani had a legitimate claim to the domain name. The arbitrator wrote that it is "common practice for people to register domain names which are based upon initials and a name, acronyms or otherwise variants of their full names." The court rejected Modefine's claim that Mr. Mani's offer to sell the name for $1,935 constituted bad faith. The arbitrator ruled against Modefine and permitted Mr. Mani to own the domain name armani.com. [*G. A. Modefine S. A. v. A. R. Mani*, WIPO, No. D2001-0537 (2001)] ■

International Law

Gold Rush for Country Domain Names

When the domain name system was created, only a handful of high-level generic suffixes were provided for individuals and businesses, such as *.com* and *.net*. The cyber rush for names bearing these suffixes was on, and many of the names were quickly claimed. Once all the good names were taken, unsuccessful .com and .net applicants tried to figure out what "dot" names to register. They discovered that in addition to the .com and .net generic suffixes, every country was assigned its own two-letter country code suffix to administer as it wished. Many countries decided that they were sitting on new gold that they could mine.

International Law

(continued)

One example of a country that has capitalized on its country domain name is Tuvalu, which consists of a small group of islands with just over 10,000 inhabitants, located in the South Pacific. Tuvalu was assigned the country code .tv. Because its country code is so commonly used as a shorthand version for the word *television*, it is easily recognizable. So Tuvalu joined forces with a new entrepreneurial Internet company called Dot-TV and began marketing domain names with the suffix .tv—at a price. Sales have been brisk as individuals and businesses have rushed to register domain names bearing the suffix .tv. Thus, countries can market their country code suffixes as part of domain names as an alternative to .com, .net, and .biz names that have already been taken. ■

Licensing of Information Rights

Uniform Computer Information Transactions Act (UCITA)
A model state law that creates contract law for the licensing of information technology rights.

Much of the new cyberspace economy is based on electronic contracts and the licensing of computer information. E-commerce created problems for forming contracts over the Internet, enforcing e-commerce contracts, and providing consumer protection. To address these problems, the National Conference of Commissioners on Uniform State Laws (a group of lawyers, judges, and legal scholars) drafted the **UCITA**.

E-Commerce & Information Technology

The Uniform Computer Information Transactions Act (UCITA)

In July 1999, after years of study and debate, the National Conference of Commissioners on Uniform State Laws (a group of lawyers, judges, and legal scholars) issued the **UCITA**. This is a model act that establishes a uniform and comprehensive set of rules that governs the creation, performance, and enforcement of computer information transactions. A computer information transaction is an agreement to create, transfer, or license computer information or information rights [UCITA § 102(a)(11)].

The UCITA does not become law until a state's legislature enacts it as a state statute. States have adopted the UCITA or laws similar to the UCITA as their law for computer transactions and the licensing of informational rights.

Any provision of the UCITA that are preempted by federal law are unenforceable to the extent of the preemption [UCITA § 105(a)]. Unless displaced by the UCITA, state law and equity principles, including principal and agent law, fraud, duress, mistake, trade secret law, and other state laws, supplement the UCITA [UCITA § 114]. ■

Licensing

Business Brief
Intellectual property and information rights are valuable assets of individuals and businesses.

Intellectual property and information rights are an extremely important asset of many individuals and companies. Patent, trademark, copyright, trade secret, and other laws protect intellectual property from misappropriation and infringement (see Chapter 8).

license
A contract that transfers limited rights in intellectual property and informational rights.

The owners of intellectual property and information rights often wish to transfer limited rights in the property or information to parties for specified purposes and limited duration. The agreement that is used to transfer such limited rights is called a **license**, which is defined as follows [UCITA § 102(a)(40)]:

> License means a contract that authorizes access to, or use, distribution, performance, modification, or reproduction of, information or informational rights, but expressly limits the access or uses authorized or expressly grants fewer than all rights in the information, whether or not the transferee has title to a licensed copy. The term includes an access contract, a lease of a computer program, and a consignment of a copy.

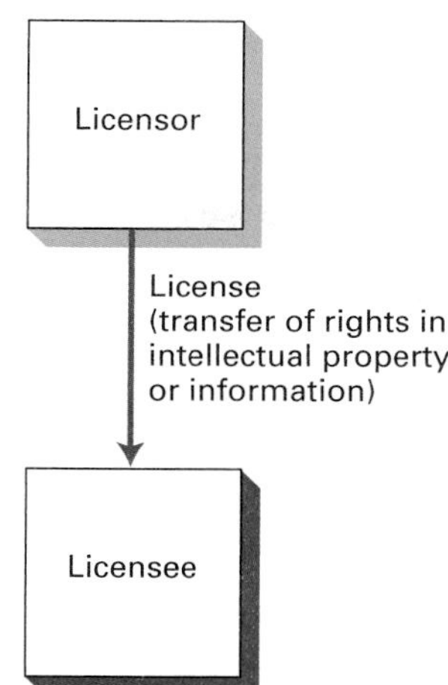

Exhibit 12.1
Licensing Arrangement

The parties to a license are the licensor and the licensee. The **licensor** is the party who owns the intellectual property or information rights and obligates him- or herself to transfer rights in the property or information to the licensee. The **licensee** is the party who is granted limited rights in or access to the intellectual property of information rights [UCITA § 102(a)(41), (42)]. A licensing arrangement is illustrated in Exhibit 12.1.

A license grants the contractual rights expressly described in the license and the right to use any information rights within the licensor's control that are necessary to exercise the expressly described rights [UCITA § 307(a)].

licensor
The owner of intellectual property or information rights, who transfers rights in the property or information to the licensee.

licensee
The party who is granted limited rights in or access to intellectual property or information rights owned by the licensor.

Exclusive License

A license can grant the licensee the exclusive rights to use information. An **exclusive license** means that for the specified duration of the license, the licensor will not grant to any other person rights to the same information [UCITA § 307(f)(2)].

exclusive license
A license that grants the licensee exclusive rights to use information rights for a specified duration.

China. The Chinese and English written languages are the most used languages on the Internet.

Licensing Agreement

licensing agreement
A detailed and comprehensive written agreement between the licensor and licensee that sets forth the express terms of their agreement.

The licensor and licensee usually enter into a written **licensing agreement** that expressly states the terms of their agreement. Licensing agreements tend to be very detailed and comprehensive contracts. This is primarily because of the nature of the subject matter and the limited uses granted in the intellectual property or information rights.

E-Commerce & Information Technology

Software and Information Access Contracts

Sometimes instead of transferring a copy of information to a licensee, a software license grants the licensee the right to access information in the possession of the licensor. This type of license is called an **access contract**. Access contracts provide for access by the licensee to the information for an agreed-upon time or number of uses. The licensee's access to the information must be available at times and in a manner that complies with the express terms of the license. If such terms are not stated in the agreement, access by the licensee shall be at times and in a manner that is reasonable for the particular type of contract in light of ordinary standards of the business, trade, or industry.

The licensee's right of access is to information as periodically modified and updated by the licensor. A change in the content of the information is not a breach of contract unless the change conflicts with express terms in the license. An occasional failure to have access available is not a breach of contract if it is either (1) normal in the business, trade, or industry or (2) caused by scheduling downtime; reasonable periods of failure of equipment, communications, or computer programs; or reasonable needs for maintenance [UCITA § 611]. ■

E-Commerce & Information Technology

Counteroffers Ineffectual Against Electronic Agents

In today's e-commerce, many sellers use electronic agents to sell goods and services. An *electronic agent* is any telephonic or computer system that has been established by a seller to accept orders. Voice mail and Web page order systems are examples of electronic agents.

In the past, when humans dealt with each other face-to-face, by telephone, or in writing, their negotiations might have consisted of an exchange of several offers and counteroffers until agreed-upon terms were reached and a contract was formed. Each new counteroffer extinguished the previous offer and became a new viable offer. Most electronic agents do not have the ability to evaluate and accept counteroffers or to make counteroffers. The UCITA recognizes this limitation of e-commerce and provides that a contract is formed if an individual takes action that causes the electronic agent to cause performance or promise benefits to the individual. Thus, counteroffers are not effective against electronic agents [UCITA § 206(a)].

Consider This Example "Birdie" is an electronic ordering system for placing orders for electronic information sold by the Green Company, a producer of computer software and electronic information. Freddie Calloway dials the Green Company's toll-free telephone number and orders new software for $1,000 using the Birdie voice mail electronic ordering system. Freddie enters the product code and description, his mailing address and credit card information, and other data needed to complete the transaction, but at the end of the order states "I will accept this software if, after two weeks of use, I am satisfied with the software." Because Freddie has placed the order with an electronic agent, Freddie has ordered the software, and his counteroffer is ineffectual. ■

E-Commerce & Information Technology

The Federal Electronic Signature Act

In the world of pen-and-paper, it used to be "Sign on the dotted line," "Put your John Hancock right here," or "Sign by the X." No more. In the e-commerce world it is now "What is your mother's maiden name?" "Slide your smart card in the sensor" or "Look into the iris scanner." But are electronic signatures sufficient to form an enforceable contract? The courts and state legislatures of the 50 states have wrestled with this question, often reaching inconsistent decisions on whether electronic contracts meet the writing and signature requirements of the state Statutes of Frauds.

In 2000, the federal government stepped into the breach and enacted the **Electronic Signature in Global and National Commerce Act (E-Sign Act)**. This act is a federal statute enacted by Congress and signed by the president; it therefore has national reach. The act is designed to place the world of electronic commerce on a par with the world of paper contracts in the United States.

Electronic Signature

One of the main features of the federal law is that it recognizes an *electronic signature*, or *e-signature*. The act gives an e-signature the same force and effect as a pen-inscribed signature on paper. The act is technology neutral, however, in that the law does not define or decide which technologies should be used to create a legally binding signature in cyberspace. Loosely defined, a *digital signature* is some electronic method that identifies an individual. The challenge is to make sure that someone who uses a digital signature is the person he or she claims to be. The act provides that a digital signature can basically be verified in one of three ways:

1. By something the signatory knows, such as a secret password, a pet's name, and so forth.
2. By something a person has, such as smart card, which looks like a credit card and stores personal information.
3. By biometrics, which uses a device that digitally recognizes fingerprints or the retina or iris of the eye.

The verification of electronic signatures has created a need for the use of scanners and methods for verifying personal information. ■

E-Commerce & Information Technology

Consumers Saved from Electronic Errors

Under the common law of contracts, many parties who make unilateral mistakes while contracting are not relieved of the consequences of their error. The UCITA, which governs licenses of informational rights, is more lenient. The UCITA provides that consumers are not bound by their unilateral electronic errors if the consumer

1. Promptly upon learning of the error notifies the other party of the error.
2. Does not use or receive any benefit from the information, or make the information or benefit available to a third party.
3. Delivers all copies of the information to the third party or destroys all copies of the information, pursuant to reasonable instructions from the other party.
4. Pays all shipping, reshipping, and processing costs of the other party. [UCITA § 217]

Section 217 of the UCITA applies only to consumers who make electronic errors in contracting. Electronic errors by nonconsumers are handled under the common law of contracts or the Uniform Commercial Code (UCC), whichever applies. The UCITA does not relieve a consumer of his or her electronic error if the other party provides a reasonable method to detect and correct or avoid the error.

Thus, many sellers establish methods whereby the buyer must verify the information and purchase order a second time before an electronic order is processed. This procedure strips the consumer of the defense of UCITA Section 217.

Consider This Example Kai, a consumer, intends to order 10 copies of a video game over the Internet from Cybertendo, a video game producer. In fact, Kai makes an error and orders 110 games. The electronic agent maintaining Cybertendo's Web site's ordering process electronically disburses 110 games. The next morning Kai discovers his mistake and immediately e-mails Cybertendo, describing the mistake and offering to return or destroy the copies at his expense. When Kai receives the games, he returns the 110 copies unused. Under the UCITA, Kai has no contract obligation for 110 copies but bears the cost of returning them to Cybertendo or destroying them if Cybertendo instructs him to do so. If Cybertendo's Web site's electronic ordering system had asked Kai to confirm his order of 110 copies of the purchase order, and Kai had confirmed the original order of 110 copies, Kai would have had to pay for the 110 copies, even if his confirmation had been in error. ■

E-Commerce & Information Technology

Electronic Self-Help

When a licensor licenses its software to a licensee, it expects that the licensee will abide by the terms of the license. This includes protecting the licensor's trade secrets, using the software or information pursuant to the terms of the license, and paying the agreed-upon license fee. Just like normal contracts, however, electronic licenses can be breached by licensees. If such a breach occurs, the licensor can resort to remedies provided in the UCITA. Sections 815 and 816 of the UCITA provide that a licensor can resort to electronic self-help if a breach occurs—for example, if the licensee fails to pay the license fee. Such electronic self-help can consist of activating disabling bugs and time bombs that have been embedded in the software or information that will prevent the licensee from further using the software or information.

Section 816 provides that a licensor is entitled to use electronic self-help only if the following requirements are met:

1. The licensee specifically agrees to the inclusion in the license of self-help as a remedy. General assent to the license is not sufficient; there must be a specific self-help option to which the licensee assents.
2. The licensor must give the licensee at least 15 days' notice prior to the disabling action. The notice must contain the name and location of the person to whom the licensee can communicate regarding the issue. The notice period allows the licensee to make lawful adjustments to minimize the effects of the licensor's self-help or to seek a judicial remedy to combat the use of the self-help.
3. The licensor may not use self-help if it would cause a breach of the peace, risk personal injury, cause significant damage or injury to information other than the licensee's information, result in injury to the public health or safety, or cause grave harm to national security.

A licensor who violates these provisions and uses self-help improperly is liable for damages. This liability cannot be disclaimed. The UCITA gives licensees the right to obtain an expedited hearing in court if any of the self-help restrictions are violated. Licensors will continue to install and use such self-help devices, subject to the requirements and restrictions of the UCITA. ■

Breach of License Agreements

It will be of little avail to the people, that the laws are made by men of their own choice, if the laws be so voluminous that they cannot be read, or so incoherent that they cannot be understood.

Alexander Hamilton
The Federalist Papers (1788)

The parties to a contract for the licensing of information owe a duty to perform the obligations stated in the contract. If a party fails to perform as required, there is a breach of the contract. Breach of contract by one party to a licensing agreement gives the nonbreaching party certain rights, including recovering damages or other remedies [UCITA § 701].

Licensee's Refusal of Defective Tender If the licensor tenders a copy that is a material breach of the contract, the nonbreaching party to whom tender is made may either (1) refuse the tender, (2) accept the tender, or (3) accept any commercially reasonable units and refuse the rest [UCITA § 704].

Licensee's Revocation of Acceptance If a licensee has accepted tender of a copy where the nonconformity is a material breach, the licensee may later revoke his or her acceptance if (1) acceptance was made because discovery was difficult at the time of tender but was then later discovered or (2) the nonconformity was discovered at the time of tender but the licensor agreed to cure the defect, and the defect has not been reasonably cured [UCITA §707].

Web Site

CataLaw CataLaw is a catalog of catalogs of law on the Internet. It speeds research by arranging all legal and government indexes on the Internet into a single, simple, intuitive meta-index. Visit at **www.catalaw.com**.

Adequate Assurance of Performance Each party to a license agreement expects to receive due performance from the other party. If any reasonable grounds arise prior to the performance date that make one party think that the other party might not deliver performance when due, the aggrieved party may demand adequate assurance of due performance from the other party. Until such assurance is received, the aggrieved party may, if commercially reasonable, suspend performance until assurance is received. Failure to provide assurance within 30 days permits the aggrieved party to repudiate the contract [UCITA § 708].

Remedies

The UCITA provides certain *remedies* to an aggrieved party upon the breach of a licensing agreement. A party may not recover more than once for the same loss, and his or her remedy (other than liquidated damages) may not exceed the loss caused by the breach [UCITA § 801]. The UCITA provides that a cause of action must be commenced within one year after the breach was or should have been discovered, but not more than five years after the breach actually occurred [UCITA § 805]. Remedies are discussed in the following paragraphs.

Business Brief
The UCITA provides various remedies that injured parties can obtain against breaching parties.

Cancellation If there has been a material breach of a contract that has not been cured or waived, the aggrieved party may cancel the contract. **Cancellation** is effective when the canceling party notifies the breaching party of the cancellation. Upon cancellation, the breaching party in possession or control of copies, information, documentation, or other materials that are the property of the other party must use commercially reasonable efforts to return them or hold them for disposal on instructions from the other party. All obligations that are executory on both sides at the time of cancellation are discharged [UCITA § 802(a), (b)].

Upon cancellation of a license, the licensor has the right to have all copies of the licensed information returned by the licensee and to prevent the licensee from continued use of the licensed information.

cancellation
The termination of a contract by a contracting party upon the material breach of the contract by the other party.

Licensor's Damages If a licensee breaches a contract, the licensor may sue the licensee and recover monetary damages, called **licensor's damages**, caused by the breach, plus any consequential and incidental damages [UCITA § 808]. A licensor can recover *lost profits* caused by the licensee's failure to accept or complete performance of the contract. Lost profits is a proper measure of damages in this case because the licensor has effectively unlimited capability to make access available to others so there will be no license to substitute to reduce damages owed by the breaching licensee.

licensor's damages
If a licensee breaches a contract, the licensor may sue the licensee and recover monetary damages caused by the breach.

Consider This Example iSuperSoftware.com licenses a master disk of its software program to Distributors, Inc., to make and distribute 10,000 copies of the software. This is a nonexclusive license, and the license fee is $1 million. It costs iSuperSoftware.com $15 to produce the disk. If Distributors, Inc., refuses the disk and breaches the contract, iSuperSoftware.com can recover $1 million less $15 as damages for the profits lost on the transaction.

Business Brief
If the contract is a *nonexclusive license*, the licensor can recover lost profits caused by the licensee's failure to accept or complete performance of the contract.

Licensor's Right to Cure Unlike the common law of contracts, the UCITA provides that a licensor has a **right to cure** a breach of a license in certain circumstances. A breach of contract may be cured if (1) the time of performance of the contract has not expired and the licensor makes conforming performance within the time of performance, (2) the time of performance has expired but the licensor had reasonable grounds to believe the performance would be acceptable and then the licensor has a reasonable time to make conforming performance, or (3) the licensor makes a conforming performance before the licensee cancels the contract. In all three situations, the licensor must reasonably notify the licensee of its intent to cure [UCITA § 703(a)].

right to cure
A right of a licensor to repair a contract under certain conditions.

Business Brief
When a licensor breaches a contract, the licensee may sue and recover monetary damages from the licensor.

Licensee's Damages When a licensor breaches a contract, the licensee may sue and recover monetary damages from the licensor. The amount of the damages depends on the facts of the situation. Upon the licensor's breach, the licensee may either (1) cover by purchasing other electronic information from another source and recover the difference between the value of the promised performance from the licensor and the cost of cover or (2) not cover and recover the value of the performance from the licensor. **Cover** is a licensee's right to engage in a commercially reasonable substitute transaction. The licensee may obtain an award of consequential and incidental damages in either case. A licensee cannot obtain excessive or double recovery [UCITA § 809].

cover
A right of a licensee's to engage in a commercially reasonable substitute transaction after the licensor has breached the contract.

Web Site

The Law Engine The Law Engine links to many online law sources from a well-organized, single-page format. Visit at **www.fastsearch.com/law**.

Consider This Example Auction.com is an Internet company that operates an online auction service. Auction.com enters into a contract with MicroHard, Inc., a software producer, for a site license to use MicroHard, Inc.'s software. Auction.com agrees to pay $500,000 as an initial license fee and $10,000 per month for the license duration of three years. Before Auction.com pays any money under the license, MicroHard, Inc., breaches the contract and does not deliver the software. Auction.com covers by licensing commercially similar software from another software company for the payment of a $600,000 initial licensing fee and $11,000 per month for the license duration of three years. Under the facts of this case, Auction.com can recover $100,000 for the increased initial fee and $36,000 for the increased monthly costs from MicroHard, Inc., for breach of contract.

specific performance

A judgment of a court ordering a licensor to specifically perform a license by making the contracted-for unique information available to the licensee.

Licensee Can Obtain Specific Performance The UCITA provides the remedy of **specific performance** if the parties have agreed to this remedy in their contract or if the agreed-upon performance is unique. The test of uniqueness requires the court to examine the total situation that characterizes the contract [UCITA § 811].

Web Site

Internet Legal Resource Guide The Internet Legal Resource Guide is a categorized index of 3,100 selected Web sites in 238 nations, islands, and territories. Visit at **www.ilrg.com**.

Consider This Example Nedra enters into a licensing agreement to obtain access to certain informational rights from Info, Inc., for a specified monthly license fee. The data are proprietary to Info, Inc., and are not available from any other vendor. If Info, Inc., breaches the license and refuses to give Nedra access to the information, Nedra can sue and obtain an order of specific performance whereby the court orders Info, Inc., to make the contracted-for information available to Nedra for the duration of the license.

Limitations of Remedies

The UCITA provides that the parties to an agreement may limit the remedies available for breach of a contract. This is done by including provisions in the contract. Remedies may be restricted to return of copies and repayment of the licensing fee or limiting the remedy to the repair or replacement of the nonconforming copies. Limitation of remedies in licenses subject to the UCITA is enforceable unless the remedies are unconscionable [UCITA § 803].

In the following case, the court upheld a limitation-on-remedies clause in a software license.

Case 12.5
Software License

M.A. Mortenson Company, Inc. v. Timberline Software Corporation

970 P. 2d 803 1999 Wash. App. Lexis 185 (1999)

Court of Appeals of Washington

Background and Facts

The Timberline Software Corporation (Timberline) produces software programs that are used by contractors to prepare bids to do work on construction projects. The M.A. Mortenson Company (Mortenson), a contractor, had been using Timberline software for some time without any problem. In 1993, Timberline introduced an advanced version of its bidding software program called *Precision*. Mortenson, as the licensee, entered into a license agreement with Timberline, the licensor, to license the use of the Precision software. Timberline delivered the software to Mortenson, and a Timberline representative installed the software on Mortenson's computer. The software license agreement contained the following terms, which were printed on the outside of the envelope in which the software disks were packaged and on the inside cover of the user's manual, and they also appear on the introductory computer screen each time the software program is executed:

> Carefully read the following terms and conditions before using the programs. Use of the programs indicates your acknowledgement that you have read this license, understand it, and agree to be bound by its terms and conditions. If you do not agree to these terms and conditions, promptly return the programs and user manuals to the place of purchase and your purchase price will be refunded. You agree that your use of the program acknowledges that you have read this license, understand it, and agree to be bound by its terms and conditions.
>
> Limitation of remedies and liability: Neither Timberline nor anyone else who has been involved in the creation, production or delivery of the programs or user manuals shall be liable to you for any damages of any type, including but not limited to, any lost profits, lost savings, loss of anticipated benefits, or other incidental or consequential damages arising out of the use or inability to use such programs, whether arising out of contract, negligence, strict tort, or under any warranty, or otherwise, even if Timberline has been advised of the possibility of such damages or for any other claim by any other party. Timberline's liability for damages in no event shall exceed the license fee paid for the right to use the programs.

On December 2, 1993, Mortenson used the Precision software and prepared a bid to do contracting work for the Harborview Hospital project. While preparing the bid, the program aborted at least five times before Mortenson's employees finished the bid. Subsequently, Mortenson claimed that its bid was $2 million under what it should have been had the Precision software program worked correctly. Mortenson sued Timberline to recover consequential damages, arguing that the Precision software calculated an inaccurate bid. Timberline defended, alleging that the limitation-of-remedies clause in the software license prevented Mortenson's lawsuit. Mortenson countered that the limitation-of-remedies clause was unconscionable and therefore unenforceable. The trial court granted summary judgment to Timberline and dismissed the lawsuit. Mortenson appealed.

Issue

Was the limitation of remedies clause in the Timberline software license unconscionable?

In The Language of The Court

Webster, Judge Mortenson makes much of the fact that Timberline never mentioned the license agreement or any of its terms during the negotiations. But the negotiations between the parties involved only the number of copies and the price. Timberline's failure to bring up the license terms during price-quantity discussions is hardly surprising. We hold that the terms of the present license agreement are part of the contract as formed between the parties. We find that Mortenson's installation and use of the software manifested its assent to the terms of the license and that it is bound by all terms of that license that are not found to be illegal or unconscionable.

Whether a limitation on consequential damages is unconscionable is a question of law. Considering all the circumstances surrounding the transaction in this case, the limitations clause is not unconscionable. Although Mortenson and Timberline did not specifically negotiate the limitations of remedies clause, this one factor is not conclusive. The introductory screen warned that use of the program was subject to a license. This warning placed Mortenson on notice that use of the software was governed by a license. Mortenson had reasonable opportunity to learn and understand the terms of the agreement. The limitations provision was not hidden in a maze of fine print but appeared in all capital letters. Finally, such limitations provisions are widely used in the computer software industry.

Limitations of consequential damages in commercial transactions are prima facie conscionable. Such clauses are standard in the software industry and do not shock the conscience. Indeed, they are useful in making software affordable. If software developers were prohibited from limiting consequential damages, the significant costs to the industry would be passed on to the consumer. We conclude that the limitations of remedies provision is not unconscionable. Thus, the limitations of remedies clause bars Mortenson's claim for consequential damage.

Decision and Remedy

The court of appeals held that the limitation-of-remedies clause in the software license was conspicuous and not unconscionable and that it therefore prohibited Mortenson's lawsuit to recover consequential damages from Timberline. The court of appeals affirmed the trial court's grant of summary judgments to Timberline and dismissed the case.

Case Questions

Critical Legal Thinking What does the doctrine of unconscionability provide? Does the doctrine serve any useful purpose?

Business Ethics Did Timberline act ethically when it included a limitation-of-remedies clause in its software license?

Contemporary Business What would the business consequences be if limitation-of-remedies clauses in software licenses were all held to be *per se* illegal?

Liquidation of Damages The parties to a license may provide that damages for breach of contract may be liquidated. **Liquidated damages** are damages that are specified in the contract rather than determined by the court. The amount of liquidated damages must be reasonable in light of the loss anticipated at the time of contracting or the anticipated difficulties of proving loss in the event of breach. The fixing of unreasonably large liquidated damages is void [UCITA § 804].

liquidated damages

Damages that are specified in a contract rather than determined by a court.

Bagan, Myanmar. Some countries are behind in developing or permitting Internet access.

Chapter Summary

The Internet, p. 340

The Internet and World Wide Web

1. ***Internet.*** A collection of millions of computers that provide a network of electronic connections between computers.
2. ***World Wide Web.*** An electronic connection of computers that support a standard set of rules for the exchange of information called Hypertext Transfer Protocol (HTTP).
3. ***Electronic mail (e-mail).*** Electronic written communication between individuals using computers connected to the Internet.
4. ***E-mail contracts.*** Contracts that are formed electronically over the Internet using e-mail.

Electronic Privacy

Electronic Communications Privacy Act. A federal statute that makes it a crime to intercept an electronic communication at the point of transmission, while in transit, when stored by a router or server, or after receipt by the intended recipient.

Internet Domain Names, p. 344

Domain Name

1. ***Domain name.*** A unique name that identifies an individual's or a company's Web site.
2. ***Internet Corporation for Assigned Names and Numbers (ICANN).*** ICANN is responsible for regulating the issuance of domain names on the Internet. ICANN approves registrars of domain names.
3. ***Domain name registration.*** Domain names are registered by filing the appropriate form with a domain name registration service and paying the appropriate fee.

Anticybersquatting Act

1. ***Anticybersquatting Consumer Protection Act (ACPA).*** A federal statute that permits a court to issue cease-and-desist orders and injunctions and to aware monetary damages against anyone who has registered a domain name (1) of a famous name and (2) in bad faith.
2. ***Uniform Dispute Resolution Policy (UDRP).*** A policy that requires all ICANN-approved registrars of domain names to agree to use an arbitration procedure for challenging cybersquatting as part of their accreditation.

Licensing of Information Rights, p. 350

License

1. ***License.*** A contract that transfers limited rights in intellectual property and informational rights.
2. ***Licensor.*** The owner of intellectual property or information rights who transfers rights in the property or information to the licensee.
3. ***Licensee.*** The party who is granted limited rights or access to intellectual property or information rights owned by the licensor.
4. ***Licensing agreement.*** Detailed and comprehensive written agreement between the licensor and licensee that sets forth the express terms of their agreement.
5. ***Access contract.*** A type of license that grants the licensee access to the licensed information for an agreed-upon time or number of uses.

The Uniform Computer Information Transactions Act (UCITA)

The Uniform Computer Information Transactions Act (UCITA). A model act issued by the National Conference of Commissioners on Uniform State Laws that establishes a uniform and comprehensive set of rules that governs the creation, performance, and enforcement of computer information transactions.

1. ***Adoption of UCITA by states.*** The UCITA does not become law until a state's legislature enacts it as a state statute.

Special Provisions of the UCITA

1. ***Counteroffer rule.*** Counteroffers are not effective against electronic agents. This is because most electronic agents do not have the ability to evaluate and accept counteroffers or make counteroffers.
2. ***Electronic errors.*** The UCITA provides that *consumers* are not bound by their unilateral electronic errors if the consumer
   a. Promptly upon learning of the error notifies the other party of the error.
   b. Does not use or receive any benefit from the information, or make the information or benefit available to a third party.
   c. Delivers all copies of the information to the third party or destroys all copies of the information pursuant to reasonable instructions from the other party.
   d. Pays all shipping, reshipping, and processing costs of the other party.
3. ***Electronic self-help.*** If an electronic license has been breached by a licensee, the licensor can resort to electronic self-help such as activating disabling bugs and time bombs that have been embedded in the software or information that will prevent the licensee from further using the software or information. A licensor is entitled to use electronic self-help only if the following requirements are met:
   a. The licensee specifically agrees to the inclusion in the license of self-help as a remedy.
   b. The licensor must give the licensee at least 15 days' notice prior to the disabling action.
   c. The licensor may not use self-help if it would cause a breach of the peace, risk personal injury, cause significant damage or injury to information other than the licensee's information, result in injury to the public health or safety, or cause grave harm to national security.

Electronic Signatures

The Electronic Signature in Global and National Commerce Act (E-Sign Act). A federal statute that recognizes and gives electronic signatures—e-signatures—the same force and effect as a pen-inscribed signature on paper. The act is technology neutral in that the law does not define or decide which technologies should be used to create a legally binding signature in cyberspace.

1. ***Exemption.*** Any state that has enacted the Uniform Electronic Transactions Act (UETA) is exempt from the E-Sign Act.

Internet Exercises and Case Questions

Working the Web Internet Exercises

Activities

1. Research the Web to determine if your state has adopted the Uniform Electronic Transactions Act (UETA) or the Uniform Computer Information Transactions Act (UCITA). Start with **www.hg.org/cgi-bin/redir.cgi?url=www.law.cornell.edu/uniform/vol7.html**.
2. For a discussion of the Federal Dilution Act, featuring Barbie, Elvis, and Coca-Cola, see **cyber.law.harvard.edu/property/respect/antibarbie.html**.
3. For an overview of the Federal Electronic Signatures Act, explore the law review article "Are Online Business Transactions Executed by Electronic Signatures Legally Binding?" at **www.law.duke.edu/journals/dltr/Articles/2001dltr0005.html**.
4. Domain name dispute resolution procedures are presented in great detail at **lweb.law.harvard.edu/udrp/library.html**. Check this site for everything from an overview to sample pleading forms.

Critical Legal Thinking Cases

12.1 Domain Name Francis Net, a freshman in college and computer expert, browses Web sites for hours each day. One day she thinks to herself, "I can make money registering domain names and selling them for a fortune." She has recently seen an advertisement for Classic Coke, a cola drink produced and marketed by the Coca Cola Company. The Coca Cola Company has a famous trademark on the term *Classic Coke* and has spent millions of dollars advertising this brand and making the term famous throughout the United States and the world. Francis goes to the Web site www.networksolutions.com, an Internet domain name registration service, to see if the Internet domain name classiccoke.com has been taken. She discovers that it is available, so she immediately registers the Internet domain name classiccoke.com for herself and pays the $70 registration fee with her credit card. Coca Cola Company decides to register the Internet domain name classiccoke.com, but when it checks at Network Solutions, Inc.'s, Web site, it discovers that Francis Net has already registered the Internet domain name. Coca Cola Company contacts Francis, who demands $500,000 for the name. Coca Cola Company sues Francis to prevent Francis from using the Internet domain name classiccoke.com and to recover it from her under the federal ACPA. Who wins?

12.2 Domain Name Francis Net, a freshman in college and computer expert, browses Internet Web sites for hours each day. One day she thinks to herself, "I can make money registering domain names and selling them for a fortune." She has recently seen advertisements for Classic Coke, a cola drink produced and marketed by the Coca Cola Company, and for Pepsi, a cola drink produced and marketed by Pepsi, Inc. The Coca Cola Company has a famous trademark on the term Classic Coke, and Pepsi, Inc., has a famous trademark on Pepsi; both companies have spent millions of dollars advertising their brands and making the terms famous throughout the United States and the world. Francis, realizing that she cannot trade off the famous names Classic Coke or Pepsi, thinks about what terms soda manufacturers might want to use as their domain name. Francis, who has traveled throughout the country, realizes that in some parts of the United States people call soda by the name pop. Francis goes to the Web site www.networksolutions.com, an Internet domain name registration service, to see if the Internet domain name pop.com has been taken. She discovers that it is available, so she immediately registers the Internet domain name pop.com for herself and pays the $70 registration fee with her credit card. Coca Cola Company decides to register the Internet domain name pop.com, but when it checks at Network Solutions, Inc.'s, Web site, it discovers that Francis Net has already registered the Internet domain name pop.com. Coca Cola Company contracts Francis, who demands $200,000 for the name. Coca Cola Company sues Francis to prevent Francis from using the Internet domain name pop.com and to recover it from her under the federal ACPA. Who wins?

12.3 E-Mail Contract The Litle Steel Company is a small steel fabricator that makes steel parts for various metal machine shop clients. When Litle Steel Company receives an order from a client, it must locate and purchase 10 tons of a certain grade of steel to complete the order. The Litle Steel Company sends an e-mail message to West Coast Steel Company, a large steel company, inquiring about the availability of 10 tons of the described grade of steel. The West Coast Steel Company replies by e-mail that it has available the required 10 tons of steel and quotes $450 per ton. The Litle Steel Company's purchasing agent replies by e-mail that the Litle Steel Company will purchase the 10 tons of described steel at the quoted price of $450 per ton. The e-mails are signed electronically by the Litle Steel Company's purchasing agent and the selling agent of the West Coast Steel Company. When the steel arrives at the Litle Steel Company's plant, the Litle Steel Company rejects the shipment, claiming the defense of the statute of frauds. The West Coast Steel Company sues the Litle Steel Company for damages. Who wins?

12.4 Electronic Contract The Minute Steel Company is a small steel fabricator that makes steel parts for various metal machine shop clients. When Minute Steel Company receives an order from a client, it must locate and purchase 10 tons of a certain grade of steel to complete the order. The Minute Steel Company's purchasing agent opens the Internet and goes to a Web site called steelauction.com. This is a Web site where sellers and buyers of steel can locate one another and make deals. On this Web site, the purchasing agent for Minute Steel Company finds that the East Coast Steel Company, a large steel company, has available the required 10 tons of the described steel at $450 per ton. The Minute Steel Company's agent agrees online to purchase the 10 tons of described steel at the quoted price of $450 per ton from East Coast Steel Company. The record and the signatures of both sides agreeing to the transaction are electronic. When the steel arrives at the Minute Steel Company's plant, the Minute Steel Company rejects the shipment, claiming the defense of the statute of frauds and invalid signatures. The UETA applies to the transaction. The East Coast Steel Company sues the Minute Steel Company for damages. Who wins?

12.5 Contract Einstein Financial Analysts, Inc. (EFA), has developed an electronic database that has recorded the number of plastic pails manufactured and sold in the United States since plastic was first invented. Using this data, and a complicated patented software mathematical formula developed by EFA, a user can predict with 100 percent accuracy (historically) how the stock of each of the companies of the Dow Jones Industrial Average will perform on any given day of the year. William Buffet, an astute billionaire investor, wants to increase his wealth, so he enters into an agreement with EFA whereby he is granted the sole right to use the EFA data (updated daily) and its financial model for the next five years. Buffet pays EFA $100 million for the right to the data and mathematical formula. After using the data and software formula for one week, Buffet discovers that EFA has also transferred the right to use the EFA plastic pail database and software formula to his competitor. Buffet sues EFA. What type of arrangement has EFA and Buffet entered into? Who wins?

12.6 Encryption Technology The Silicon Encryption Company, Inc. (SEC), has developed a very powerful encryption technology that permits a user to establish an encryption code that no person or computer program can figure out. Therefore, the encryption code developed by SEC is impenetrable when it is wrapped around electronic data. Imports, Inc., a U.S. company organized in the state of Florida, contacts SEC about acquiring the encryption technology. SEC conducts a reasonable investigation and due diligence review of Imports, Inc., and finds that the company is an importer of goods from around the world; SEC discovers no adverse information about Imports, Inc. SEC decides to deal with Imports, Inc., and Imports, Inc., pays SEC $10 million for the right to use SEC's encryption technology for five years. After one year, the U.S. government believes that Imports, Inc., is engaged in smuggling illegal drugs into the United States and has used SEC's encryption technology to protect any data implicating Import, Inc., in the illegal activity. The U.S. Department of Justice prosecutes Imports, Inc., for the crime of illegal drug smuggling, but the government loses the case because it cannot produce the necessary evidence that is protected by SEC's encryption technology. The U.S. Department of Justice therefore sues SEC for selling its powerful encryption technology to Imports, Inc. Is SEC guilty?

12.7 License An Internet firm called Info.com, Inc., licenses computer software and electronic information over the Internet. Info.com has a Web site, info.com, where users can license Info.com software and electronic information. The Web site is operated by an electronic agent; a potential user enters Info.com's Web site and looks at available software and electronic information that is available from Info.com. Mildred Hayward pulls up the Info.com Web site on her computer screen and decides to order a certain type of Info.com software. Hayward enters the appropriate product code and description; her name, mailing address, and credit card information; and other data needed to complete the order for a three-year license at $300 per month; the electronic agent has Hayward verify all the information a second time. When Hayward has completed verifying the information, she types at the end of her order, "I accept this electronic software only if after I have used it for two months do I still personally like it." Info.com's electronic agent delivers a copy of the software to Hayward, who downloads the copy of the software onto her computer. Two weeks later Hayward sends the copy of the software back to Info.com stating, "Read our contract: I personally don't like this software; cancel my license." Info.com sues Hayward to recover the license payments for three years. Who wins?

12.8 Electronic Signature David Abacus uses the Internet to place an order to license software for his computer from Inet.License, Inc. (Inet), through Inet's electronic Web site ordering system. Inet's Web page order form asks David to type in his name, mailing address, telephone number, e-mail address, credit card information, computer location information, and personal identification number. Inet's electronic agent requests that David verify the information a second time before it accepts the order, which David does. The license duration is two years, at a license fee of $300 per month. Only after receiving the verification of information does Inet's electronic agent place the order and send an electronic copy of the software to David's computer, where he installs the new software program. David later refuses to pay the license fee due Inet because he claims his electronic signature and information were not authentic. Inet sues David to recover the license fee. Is David's electronic signature enforceable against him?

12.9 License Tiffany Pan, a consumer, intends to order three copies of a financial software program from iSoftware, Inc. Tiffany, using her computer, enters iSoftware's Web site isoftware.com and places an order with the electronic agent taking orders for the Web site. The license provides for a duration of three years at $300 per month for each copy of the software program. Tiffany enters the necessary product code and description; her name, mailing address, and credit card information; and other data necessary to place the order. When the electronic order form prompts Tiffany to enter the number of copies of the software program she is ordering, Tiffany mistakenly types in "30." Isoftware's electronic agent places the order and ships 30 copies of the software program to Tiffany. When Tiffany receives the 30 copies of the software program, she ships them back to iSoftware with a note stating, "Sorry, there has been a mistake. I only meant to order 3 copies of the software, not 30." When iSoftware bills Tiffany for the license fees for the 30 copies, Tiffany refuses to pay. Isoftware sues Tiffany to recover the license fees for 30 copies. Who wins?

12.10 License Silvia Miofsky licenses a software program from Accura.com, Inc., to sort information from a database to be used in Silvia's financial planning business. The license is for three years, and the license fee is $500 per month. The new software program from Accura.com will be used to run in conjunction with other software programs and databases used by Silvia in her business. The licensing agreement between Accura.com and Silvia and the label on the software package state that the copy of the licensed software program has been tested by Accura.com and will run without error. Silvia installs the copy of Accura.com's software, but every fifth or sixth time the program is run, it fails to operate properly and shuts down Silvia's computer and other programs. Silvia sends the software, marked *defective*, back to Accura.com. When Accura.com bills Silvia for the unpaid license fees for the three years of the license, Silvia refuses to pay. Accura.com sues Silvia to recover the license fees under the three-year license. Who wins?

12.11 License Harold Harrington operates a large personal financial planning business. He contacts Hardware/Software, Inc., a seller of software programs and electronic information, about licensing a software program from Hardware/Software. Harold tells the Hardware/Software sales representative about the scope and volume of his business and his business needs and informs the Hardware/Software representative that he is relying on her to select the software that will meet his business needs. The Hardware/Software sales representative selects the software program called PerFinPlan III for Harold's business. The license is $500 per month for three years. Harold installs the PerFinPlan III software. The software, however, is inadequate to handle the financial planning requirements of Harold's clients. After one month, Harold notifies the sales representative for Hardware/Software that the PerFinPlan III software does not meet his described business needs. Harold returns the copy of the software to Hardware/Software and demands the return of his one month's license fee. Hardware/Software sues Harold to recover the unpaid license fees for the duration of the license. Who wins?

12.12 License Metatag, Inc., is a developer and distributor of software and electronic information rights over the Internet. Metatag produces a software program called Virtual 4-D Links; a user of the program merely types in the name of a city and address anywhere in the world, and the computer transports the user there and creates a four-dimensional space and a sixth-sense unknown to the world before. The software license is nonexclusive, and Metatag licenses its Virtual 4-D Link to millions of users worldwide. Nolan Bates, who has lived alone with his mother too long, licenses the Virtual 4-D Link program for five years for a $350 per month license fee. Bates uses the program for two months before his mother discovers why he has had a smile on his face lately. Bates, upon his mother's urging, returns the Virtual 4-D Link software program to Metatag, stating that he is canceling the license. Metatag sues Bates to recover the unpaid license fees. Who wins?

Business Ethics Cases

12.13 Business Ethics BluePeace.org is a new environmentalist group that has decided that expounding its environmental causes over the Internet is the best and most efficient way to spend its time and money to advance its environmental causes. To draw attention to its Web sites, BluePeace.org comes up with catchy Internet domain names. One is macyswearus.org, another is exxonvaldezesseals.org, and another is generalmotorscrashesdummies.org. The macyswearus.org Web site first shows beautiful women dressed in mink fur coats sold by Macy's Department Stores and then goes into graphic photos of minks being slaughtered and skinned and made into the coats. The exxonvaldezesseals.org Web site first shows a beautiful pristine bay in Alaska with the Exxon Valdez oil tanker quietly sailing through the waters and then shows photos of the ship breaking open and spewing forth oil and then seals who are gooed with oil, suffocating and dying on the shoreline. The Web site generalmotorscrashesdummies.org shows a General Motors automobile involved in normal crash tests with dummies followed by photographs of automobile accident scenes where people and children lay bleeding and dying after an accident involving General Motors automobiles. Macy's Department Stores, the Exxon Oil Company, and the General Motors Corporation sue BluePeace.org for violating the federal ACPA. Who wins? Has BluePeace.org acted unethically in this case?

12.14 Business Ethics Apricot.com is a major software developer that licenses software to be used over the Internet. One of its programs, called Match, is a search engine that searches personal ads on the Internet and provides a match for users for potential dates and possible marriage partners. Nolan Bates subscribes to the Match software program from Apricot.com. The license duration is five years, at $200 per month license fee. For each subscriber, Apricot.com produces a separate Web page that shows photos of the subscriber and personal data. Bates places a photo of himself with his mother, with the caption, "Male, 30 years old, lives with mother, likes quiet nights at home." Bates licenses the Apricot.com Match software and uses it 12 hours each day, searching for his Internet match. Bates does not pay Apricot.com the required monthly licensing fee for any of the three months he uses the software. After using the Match software but refusing to pay Apricot.com its licensing fee, Apricot.com activates the disabling bug in the software and disables the Match software on Bates's computer. Apricot.com did this with no warning to Bates. It then sends a letter to Bates stating, "Loser, the license is canceled!" Bates sues Apricot.com for disabling the Match software program. Who wins? Did Bates act ethically? Did Apricot.com act ethically?

Briefing the Case Writing Assignment

Read Case A. 12 in the Case Appendix [*Toys "R" Us, Inc. v. Abir*]. This case is excerpted from the district court opinion. Review and brief the case. In your brief, be sure to answer the following questions.

1. What law did Toys "R" Us assert had been violated?
2. What elements must be shown to prove that this law has been violated?
3. Did the court find that the law had been violated?
4. Was defendant Abir's conduct ethical?

Answers to Management Decision Questions

1. Individuals and businesses can have their own Web sites. The Web has made it extremely attractive to conduct commercial activities online. E-commerce over the Web will continue to grow in the future. Each Web site is identified by a unique Internet domain name. A domain name will become part of a uniform resource locator (URL) that is an address of a document or Web site on the Internet. Under present trademark protection law, the "right of privacy provision" prohibits federal registration of any trademark that "consists of or comprises a name, portrait or signature identifying a particular living individual except by his written consent, or the name, signature or portrait of a deceased President of the United States during the life of his widow, if any, except by the written consent of the widow." Except as noted, the law does not apply to deceased persons' names. Therefore, you need not be overly concerned about your legal rights to establish this Web site or use the suggested domain name.
2. Domain names can be registered and must meet the same requirements as other applications for federal trademark registration. An issue that arises in the examination of trademark applications is the use of a famous person's name as a trademark by another person. In November 1999, the U.S. Congress passed the Anticybersquatting Consumer Protection Act. This act was specifically aimed at cybersquatters who register Internet domain names of famous companies and people and hold them hostage by demanding ransom payments from the famous company or person. The act has two fundamental requirements: (1) The name must be famous and (2) the domain name must have been registered in bad faith. According to the language of the act, "Any person who registers a domain name that consists of the name of another living person, or a name substantially and confusingly similar thereto, without that person's consent, with the specific intent to profit from such name by selling the domain name for financial gain to that person or any third party, shall be liable in a civil action by such person."

   A famous person may initiate arbitration proceedings through the Internet Corporation for Assigned Names and Numbers (ICANN) and win the name back.

13

Agency Law

"Let every eye negotiate for itself, and trust no agent."

—William Shakespeare
Much Ado About Nothing (1598)

Chapter Objectives

After studying this chapter, you should be able to:

1. Define agency.
2. Identify and define a principal–independent contractor relationship.
3. List and describe the agent's duties to the principal and the principal's duties to the agent.
4. Describe the principal's and agent's liability on third-party contracts.
5. Identify and describe the principal's liability for the tortious conduct of an agent.

Chapter Contents

Management Decision Agency Law

You work for Uptown Realty, a company that provides comprehensive brokerage and appraisal services to buyers and sellers of residential and commercial property located in and around Boston, Massachusetts. Its agents assist in both negotiating sales agreements and securing mortgages. Uptown recently hired the Walker Painting Company (Walker) to paint the inside and outside of its headquarters. Walker was given complete freedom to determine its working hours and used its own painters. At the completion of the job, Walker was to be paid $5,000. You work as a painter for Walker. You fell from a defective ladder while painting the outside of Uptown Realty and were severely injured.

1. What is your employment relationship with Uptown Realty? What is your employment relationship with Walker?
2. In a negligence lawsuit, should Uptown Realty be sued?
3. What is the employment relationship between Uptown Realty and its real estate clients?

If businesspeople had to personally conduct all of their business, the scope of their activities would be severely curtailed. Partnerships would not be able to operate; corporations could not act through managers and employees; and sole proprietorships would not be able to hire employees. The use of agents (or agency), which allows one person to act on behalf of another, solves this problem.

There are many examples of agency relationships. They include a salesperson who sells goods for a store, an executive who works for a corporation, a partner who acts on behalf of a partnership, an attorney who is hired to represent a client, a real estate broker who is employed to sell a house, and so on. Agency is governed by a large body of common law, known as **agency law**. This law, which is a mixture of contract law and tort law, is discussed in this chapter.

agency law
The large body of common law that governs agency: a mixture of contract law and tort law.

Independent Contractor. Prentice Hall Publishing's contract with the author of this book creates an independent contractor status between the two parties.

The Nature of Agency

Agency relationships are formed by the mutual consent of a principal and an agent. Section 1(1) of the *Restatement (Second) of Agency* defines *agency* as a *fiduciary relationship* "which results from the manifestation of consent by one person to another that the other shall act in his behalf and subject to his control, and consent by the other so to act." The *Restatement (Second) of Agency* is the reference source of the rules of agency. A party who employs another person to act on his or her behalf is called a **principal**. A party who agrees to act on behalf of another is called an **agent**. The principal–agent relationship is commonly referred to as an **agency**. This relationships is depicted in Exhibit 13.1.

principal
A party who employs another person to act on his or her behalf.

agent
A party who agrees to act on behalf of another.

agency
The principal–agent relationship: the fiduciary relationship "which results from the manifestation of consent by one person to another that the other shall act in his behalf and subject to his control, and consent by the other so to act."

Web Site

Restatement of the Law of Agency
The *Restatement of the Law of Agency* deals with the relations between principal and agent, principal and third person, and agent and third person. It was developed by the American Law Institute. Visit at **www.ali.org/ali/agency.htm**.

Business Brief

Some agency relationships are prohibited by law.

Persons Who Can Initiate an Agency Relationship

Any person who has the capacity to contract can appoint an agent to act on his or her behalf. Generally, persons who lack **contractual capacity**, such as insane persons and minors, cannot appoint agents. However, the court can appoint a legal guardian or another representative to handle the affairs of insane persons, minors, and others who lack capacity to contract. With court approval, these representatives can enter into enforceable contracts on behalf of the persons they represent.

An agency can be created only to accomplish a lawful purpose. Agency contracts that are created for illegal purposes or are against public policy are void and unenforceable. For example, a principal cannot hire an agent to kill another person. Some agency relationships are prohibited by law. For example, unlicensed agents cannot be hired to perform the duties of certain licensed professionals (e.g., doctors and lawyers).

Kinds of Employment Relationships

Businesses usually have three kinds of **employment relationships**: (1) employer–employee relationships; (2) principal–agent relationships; and (3) principal–independent contractor relationships. These relationships are discussed in the following paragraphs.

employment relationships
Business relationships, including (1) employer–employee, (2) principal–agent, and (3) principal–independent contractor.

Exhibit 13.1
The Principal–Agent Relationship

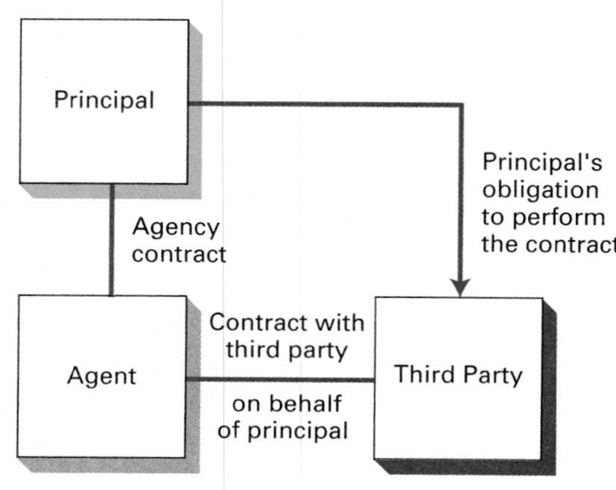

Employer—Employee Relationship

An **employer–employee relationship** exists when an employer hires an employee to perform some form of service. For example, a welder on General Motors Corporation's assembly line is employed in an employer–employee relationship because he performs a physical task.

employer-employee relationship A relationship that results when an employer hires an employee to perform some form of service.

An employee is not an agent unless he or she is specifically empowered to enter into contracts on the principal employer's behalf. Employees may only enter into contracts that are within the scope of their employment. The welder in the previous example is not an agent because he cannot enter into contracts on behalf of General Motors Company. If the company empowered him to enter into contracts, he would become an agent.

Principal—Agent Relationship

A **principal–agent relationship** is formed when an employer hires an employee and gives that employee authority to act and enter into contracts on his or her behalf. The extent of this authority is governed by an express agreement between the parties and implied from the circumstances of the agency. For example, the president of a corporation usually has the authority to enter into major contracts on the corporation's behalf, but a supervisor on the corporation's assembly line may have the authority only to purchase the supplies necessary to keep the line running.

principal-agent relationship A relationship in which an employer hires an employee and gives that employee authority to act and enter into contracts on his or her behalf.

Principal—Independent Contractor Relationship

Principals often employ outsiders—that is, persons and businesses who are not employees—to perform certain tasks on their behalf. These persons and businesses are called **independent contractors**. Doctors, dentists, consultants, stockbrokers, architects, certified public accountants, real estate brokers, and plumbers are examples of those in professions and trades that commonly act as independent contractors. An independent contractor who is a professional, such as a lawyer, is called a *professional agent*.

independent contractor A person or business who is not an employee who is employed by a principal to perform a certain task on his or her behalf.

Boat Dock, Mackinac Island, Michigan. Often, persons and businesses employ independent contractors to perform work and services for them.

A principal can authorize an independent contractor to enter into contracts. Principals are bound by the authorized contracts of their independent contractors. For example, if a client authorizes an attorney to settle a case within a certain dollar amount, and the attorney does so, the settlement agreement is binding.

Concept Summary *Kinds of Employment Relationships*

Type of Relationship	Description
Employer–employee	The employer has the right to control the physical conduct of the employee.
Principal–agent	The agent has authority to act on behalf of the principal, as authorized by the principal and implied from the agency. An employee is often the agent of his or her employer.
Principal–independent contractor	The principal has no control over the details of the independent contractor's conduct. An independent contractor is usually not an agent of the principal.

Contemporary Business Environment

Employment at Will

Employees who are offered express employment contracts for a definite term cannot be discharged in violation of the contract. Most employees, however, do not have employment contracts. They are considered **at-will employees**.

Under common law, an at-will employee could be discharged by an employer at any time for any reason. This laissez-faire doctrine gave the employer great flexibility in responding to its changing needs. It also caused unfair results for some employees. Today, there are many statutory, contract, public policy, and tort exceptions to the at-will doctrine. These exceptions are:

- ***Statutory Exception*** Federal and state statutes that restrict the employment at-will doctrine include federal labor laws that prohibit employers from discharging employee members of labor unions in violation of labor laws or collective bargaining agreements. Title VII and other federal and state antidiscrimination laws that prohibit employers from engaging in race, sex, religious, age, disability, or other forms of discrimination are other examples of such laws.
- ***Contract Exception*** The courts have held that an **implied-in-fact contract** can be created between an employer and an employee. Implied-in-fact contracts develop from the conduct of the parties. For example, a company bulletin, handbook, or personnel policy might mention that employees who do their jobs properly will not be discharged. This can be construed as an implied promise that an employee can be discharged only for good cause. Thus, the employer's ability to discharge an employee at will is removed. An employee who is discharged in violation of an implied-in-fact contract can sue the employer for breach of contract.
- ***Public Policy Exception*** The most used common law exception to the employment at-will doctrine is the **public policy exception**. This rule states that an employee cannot be discharged if such discharge violates the public policy of the jurisdiction. For example, discharging an employee for serving as a juror, refusing to do an act in violation of the law (e.g., refusing to engage in dumping of toxic wastes in violation of environmental protection laws), refusing to engage in illegal research (e.g., research that violates patent laws or animal protection laws), refusing to distribute defective products, and the like have been held to violate public policy.

An employee who has been *wrongfully discharged* can sue his or her employer for damages and other remedies (reinstatement, back pay, and such). Punitive damages may be recovered if the employer has engaged in fraud or other intentional conduct. ■

Formation of an Agency Relationship

An agency and the resulting authority of an agent can arise in any of these four ways: (1) express agency, (2) implied agency, (3) apparent agency, and (4) agency by ratification. Each of these types of agencies is discussed in the paragraphs that follow.

Express Agency

Express agency is the most common form of agency. In an express agency, the agent has the authority to contract or otherwise act on the principal's behalf as expressly stated in the agency agreement. In addition, the agent may also possess certain implied or apparent authority to act on the principal's behalf (as discussed later in this chapter).

express agency
An agency that occurs when a principal and an agent expressly agree to enter into an agency agreement with each other.

Express agency occurs when a principal and an agent expressly agree to enter into an agency agreement with each other. Express agency contracts can be either oral or written, unless the statute of frauds stipulates that they must be written. For example, in most states, a real estate broker's contract to sell real estate must be in writing.

If the principal and agent enter into an **exclusive agency contract**, the principal cannot employ any agent other than the exclusive agent. If the principal does so, the exclusive agent can recover damages from the principal. If an agency is not an exclusive agency, the principal can employ more than one agent to try to accomplish a stated purpose. When multiple agents are employed, the agencies with all of the agents terminate when any one of the agents accomplishes the stated purpose.

exclusive agency contract
A contract that a principal and an agent enter into that says the principal cannot employ any agent other than the exclusive agent.

Power of Attorney A **power of attorney** is one of the most formal types of express agency agreements. It is often used to give an agent the power to sign legal documents, such as deeds to real estate, on behalf of the principal. There are two kinds of powers of attorney: **general**, which confers broad powers on the agent to act in any matters on the principal's behalf, and **special**, which limits the agent to those acts specifically enumerated in an agreement. The agent is called an **attorney-in-fact** even though he or she does not have to be a lawyer. Powers of attorney must be written. Usually, they must be notarized. A general power of attorney is shown in Exhibit 13.2.

power of attorney
An express agency agreement that is often used to give an agent the power to sign legal documents on behalf of the principal.

Implied Agency

In many situations, a principal and an agent do not expressly create an agency. Instead, the agency is implied from the conduct of the parties. This type of agency is referred to as **implied agency**. The extent of the agent's authority is determined from the particular facts and circumstances of the particular situation. Implied agency can be conferred by either industry custom, prior dealing between the parties, the agent's position, the acts deemed necessary to carry out the agent's duties, and other factors the court deems relevant. Implied agency cannot conflict with express agency or with stated limitations on express agency.

implied agency
An agency that occurs when a principal and an agent do not expressly create an agency, but it is inferred from the conduct of the parties.

Incidental Authority Often, even an express agency agreement does not provide enough detail to cover all contingencies that may arise in the future regarding the performance of the agency. In this case, the agent possesses certain implied authority to act. This implied authority is sometimes referred to as incidental authority.

Emergency Powers Certain emergency situations may arise in the course of an agency. If the agent cannot contact the principal for instructions, the agent has implied emergency powers to take all actions reasonably necessary to protect the principal's property and rights.

Exhibit 13.2

A Sample General Power of Attorney

Power of Attorney

Know All Men by These Presents: That ____

____

the undersigned (jointly and severally, if more than one) hereby make, constitute and appoint ______________

____

My true and lawful Attorney for me and in my name, place and stead and for my use and benefit:

(a) To ask, demand, sue for, recover, collect and receive each and every sum of money, debt, account, legacy, bequest, interest, dividend, annuity and demand (which now is or hereafter shall become due, owing or payable) belonging to or claimed by me, and to use and take any lawful means for the recovery thereof by legal process or otherwise, and to execute and deliver a satisfaction or release therefor, together with the right and power to compromise or compound any claim or demand;

(b) To exercise any or all of the following powers as to real property, any interest therein and/or any building thereon: To contract for, purchase, receive and take possession thereof and of evidence of title thereto; to lease the same for any term or purpose, including leases for business, residence, and oil and/or mineral development; to sell, exchange, grant or convey the same with or without warranty; and to mortgage, transfer in trust, or otherwise encumber or hypothecate the same to secure payment of a negotiable or non-negotiable note or performance of any obligation or agreement;

(c) To exercise any or all of the following powers as to all kinds of personal property and goods, wares and merchandise, chosen in action and other property in possession or in action: To contract for, buy, sell, exchange, transfer and in any legal manner deal in and with the same and to mortgage, transfer in trust, or otherwise encumber or hypothecate the same to secure payment of a negotiable or non-negotiable note or performance of any obligation or agreement;

(d) To borrow money and to execute and deliver negotiable or non-negotiable notes therefor with or without security, and to loan money and receive negotiable or non-negotiable notes therefor with such security as said Attorney shall deem proper;

(e) To create, amend, supplement and terminate any trust and to instruct and advise the trustee of any trust wherein I am or may be trustor or beneficiary; to represent and vote stock, exercise stock rights, accept and deal with any dividend, distribution or bonus, join in any corporate financing reorganization, merger, liquidation, consolidation or other action and the extension, compromise, conversion, adjustment, enforcement or foreclosure, singly or in conjunction with others of any corporate stock, bond, note, debenture or other security; to compound, compromise, adjust, settle and satisfy any obligation, secured or unsecured, owing by or to me and to give or accept any property and/or money whether or not equal to or less in value than the amount owning in payment, settlement or satisfaction thereof;

(f) To transact business of any kind or class and as my act and deed to sign, execute, acknowledge and deliver any deed, lease, assignment of lease covenant, indenture, indemnity, agreement, mortgage, deed of trust, assignment of mortgage or of the beneficial interest under deed of trust, extension or renewal of any obligation, subordination or waiver or priority, hypothecation, bottomry, charter-party, bill of lading, bill of sale, bill, bond, note, whether negotiable or non-negotiable, receipt, evidence of debt, full or partial release or satisfaction of mortgage, judgment and other debt, request for partial or full reconveyance of deed of trust and such other instruments in writing of any kind or class as may be necessary or proper in the premises.

Giving and Granting unto my said Attorney full power and authority to do and perform all and every act and thing whatsoever, requisite, necessary or appropriate to be done in and about the premises as fully to all intents, and purposes as I might or could do if personally present, hereby ratifying all that my said Attorney shall lawfully do or cause to be done by virtue of these presents. The powers and authority hereby conferred upon my said Attorney shall be applicable to all real and personal property or interests therein now owned or hereafter required by me and whenever situate.

My said Attorney is empowered hereby to determine in said Attorney's sole discretion the time when, purpose for and manner in which any power herein conferred upon said Attorney shall be exercised, and the conditions, provisions and covenants of any instrument or document which may be executed by said Attorney pursuant hereto and in the acquisition or disposition of real or personal property, my said Attorney shall haveexclusive power to fix the terms thereof for cash, credit and/or property, and if on credit with or without security.

The undersigned, if a married person, hereby further authorizes and empowers my said Attorney, as my duly authorized agent, to join in my behalf, in the execution of any instrument by which any community real property or any interest therein, now owned or hereafter acquired by my spouse and myself, or either of us, is sold, leased, encumbered, or conveyed.

When the context to requires, the masculine gender includes the feminine and/or neuter, and the singular number includes the plural.

Witness my hand this ______________ **day of** ______________________________, **20**____.

STATE OF CALIFORNIA
COUNTY OF } SS

On ____________________ before me, the undersigned, a Notary Public in and for said State personally appeared ____________

____

____

____

____________________ personally known to me (or proved to me on the basis of satisfactory evidence) to be the person ____________ whose name ____________ subscribed to the within instrument and acknowledge that ________ ____________ executed the same.

WITNESS my hand and official seal.

Signature ______________________________

____

Name (Typed or Printed)

(This area for official seal)

Apparent Agency

apparent agency

Agency that arises when a principal creates the appearance of an agency that in actuality does not exist.

Apparent agency (or **agency by estoppel**) arises when a principal creates the appearance of an agency that in actuality does not exist. Where an apparent agency is established, the principal is estopped from denying the agency relationship and is bound to contracts entered into by the apparent agent while acting within the scope of the apparent agency. Note that it is the principal's actions—not the agent's—that create an apparent agency.

Consider This Example Suppose Georgia Pacific, Inc., interviews Albert Iorio for a sales representative position. Mr. Iorio, accompanied by Jane Franklin, the national sales manager, visits retail stores located in the open sales territory. While visiting one store, Jane tells the store manager, "I wish I had more sales reps like Albert." Nevertheless, Albert is not hired. If Albert later enters into contracts with the store on behalf of Georgia Pacific and Jane has not controverted the impression of Albert she left with the store manager, the company will be bound to the contract.

Ethics Brief

Where an apparent agency is established, the principal is *estopped* from denying the agency relationship.

Contemporary Business Environment

Apparent Agency in Franchising

Franchising has become a major form of conducting business in the United States. In a franchise agreement, one company (called the franchisor) licenses another company (called the franchisee) to use its trade name, trademarks and service marks, and trade secrets. Many fast-food restaurants, gasoline stations, motels and hotels, and other businesses operate in this fashion.

The franchisor and franchisee are independently owned businesses. A principal–agent relationship usually is not created by the franchise. If no express or implied agency is created, the franchisor would not normally be civilly liable for the tortious conduct (e.g., negligence) of the franchisee. Liability could be imposed on the franchisor, however, if an apparent agency is shown. Consider the following case.

The Howard Johnson Company (HJ) operates a chain of hotels, motels, and restaurants across the United States. Approximately 75 percent of the HJ motor lodges are owned and operated by franchisees that are licensed by HJ to do business under the "Howard Johnson" trade name and trademarks. The rest are company owned.

Orlando Executive Park, Inc. (OEP), is a corporate franchisee that owns and operates an HJ motor lodge franchise in Orlando, Florida. The motor lodge is part of a large complex known as "Howard Johnson's Plaza," located off Interstate 4. The motor lodge contains approximately 300 guest rooms in six separate buildings.

P.D.R. (name withheld by the court), a 35-year-old married woman and mother of a small child, worked as a supervisor for a restaurant chain. Her work occasionally required her to travel and stay overnight in Orlando. On October 22, 1975, P.D.R. stopped at the HJ motor lodge in Orlando. At approximately 9:30 P.M., P.D.R. registered for her previously reserved room at the lodge. The registration form did not inform her that the hotel was an HJ franchisee. P.D.R. parked her car in the motor lodge parking lot and proceeded with her suitcase to her ground-floor room in Building A, which was located directly behind the registration office. P.D.R. then went back to her car to get some papers. After obtaining the papers from her car, P.D.R. returned to Building A. As she proceeded down an interior hallway of the building toward her room, she was accosted by a man she had previously seen standing behind the registration office. The man struck her in the throat and neck and choked her until she became semiconscious. When P.D.R. fell to the floor, her assailant sat on top of her and stripped her of her jewelry. He then dragged her down the hallway and beneath a secluded stairway, where he brutally beat her. The assailant then disappeared into the night and has never been identified.

P.D.R. suffered serious physical and psychological injury, including memory loss, mental confusion, and an inability to tolerate and communicate with people. She lost her job within one year of the assault. P.D.R. suffers permanent injury that requires expensive, long-term medical and psychiatric treatment. P.D.R. brought a tort action against OEP and HJ and sought actual and punitive damages against both of them.

The jury had little trouble finding that OEP had breached its duty of care and was liable. Evidence showed that other criminal activity had occurred previously on the premises but that OEP failed to warn guests, including P.D.R., of the danger. In fact, OEP management actively discouraged criminal investigations by the sheriff's deputies, thus minimizing any deterrent effect they may have had. Further evidence showed that the dark and secluded stairwell area where P.D.R. was dragged was a security hazard that should have been boarded up or better lit.

The jury also found HJ liable to P.D.R. under the doctrine of apparent agency. The appellate court stated:

> While OEP might not be HJ's agent for all purposes, the signs, national advertising, uniformity of building design and color schemes allow the public to assume that this and other similar motor lodges are under the same ownership. An HJ official testified that it was the HJ marketing strategy to appear as a "chain that sells a product across the nation."

The court continued.

> There was sufficient evidence for the jury to reasonably conclude that HJ represented to the traveling public that it could expect a particular level of service at a Howard Johnson Motor Lodge. The uniformity of signs, design and color schemes easily leads the public to believe that each motor lodge is under common ownership or conforms to common standards, and the jury could find they are intended to do so.

The appellate court upheld an award of $750,000 compensatory damages against OEP and HJ jointly. [*Orlando Executive Park, Inc. v. P.D.R.*, 402 So.2d 442, 1981 Fla.App. Lexis 20565 (Fla. App. 1981)] ■

Agency by Ratification

agency by ratification
An agency that occurs when (1) a person misrepresents him- or herself as another's agent when in fact he or she is not and (2) the purported principal ratifies the unauthorized act.

Agency by ratification occurs when (1) a person misrepresents himself or herself as another's agent when in fact he or she is not and (2) the purported principal ratifies (accepts) the unauthorized act. In such cases, the principal is bound to perform, and the agent is relieved of any liability for misrepresentation.

Consider This Example Bill Levine sees a house for sale and thinks his friend Sherry Maxwell would want it. Bill Levine enters into a contract to purchase the house from the seller and signs the contract "Bill Levine, agent for Sherry Maxwell." Because Bill is not Sherry Maxwell's agent, she is not bound to the contract. However, if Sherry agrees to purchase the house, there is an agency by ratification. The ratification "relates back" to the moment Bill Levine entered into the contract. Upon ratification of the contract, Sherry Maxwell is obligated to purchase the house.

Concept Summary *Formation of Agency Relationships*

Type of Agency	Definition	Enforcement of the Contract
Express	Authority is expressly given to the agent by the principal.	Principal and third party are bound to the contract.
Implied	Authority is implied from the conduct of the parties, custom and usage of trade, or act incidental to carrying out the agent's duties.	Principal and third party acts are bound to the contract.
Apparent	Authority created when the principal leads a third party into believing that the agent has authority.	Principal and third party are bound to the contract.
By ratification	Acts of the agent committed outside the scope of his or her authority.	Principal and third party are not bound to the contract unless the principal ratifies the contract.

An Agent's Duties

An agent owes certain duties to a principal. These duties may be either set forth in the agency agreement or implied by law. Generally, agents owe the principal the duties of (1) performance, (2) notification, (3) loyalty, and (4) accountability. Each of these duties is discussed in the paragraphs that follow.

Duty of Performance

duty of performance
An agent's duty to a principal that includes (1) performing the lawful duties expressed in the contract and (2) meeting the standards of reasonable care, skill, and diligence implicit in all contracts.

An agent who enters into a contract with a principal has two distinct obligations: (1) performing the lawful duties expressed in the contract and (2) meeting the standards of reasonable care, skill, and diligence implicit in all contracts. Collectively, these duties are referred to as the agent's **duty of performance**.

Normally, an agent is required to render the same standard of care, skill, and diligence that a fictitious reasonable agent in the same occupation would render in the same locality and under the same circumstances. For instance, a general medical practitioner in a rural area would be held to the standard of a reasonable general practitioner in rural areas. That standard might be different for a general medical practitioner in a big city. In some professions, such as accounting, a national standard of performance (called "generally accepted accounting standards") is imposed. If an agent holds himself or herself as possessing higher-than-customary skills, the agent will be held to this higher standard of performance. For example, a lawyer who claims to be a specialist in securities law will be held to a reasonable specialist-in-securities-law standard.

An agent who does not perform his or her express duties or fails to use the standard degree of care, skill, or diligence is liable to the principal for breach of contract. An agent who has negligently (or intentionally) failed to perform property is also liable in tort.

Duty of Notification

In the course of an agency, the agent usually learns information that is important to the principal. This information may come from third parties or other sources. The agent's duty to notify the principal of such information is called the **duty of notification**. The agent is liable to the principal for any injuries resulting from a breach of this duty.

duty of notification
An agent's duty to notify the principal of information he or she learns from a third party or another source that is important to the principal.

Imputed Knowledge Most information learned by an agent in the course of the agency is **imputed** to the principal. This means that the principal is assumed to know what the agent knows. This is so even if the agent does not tell the principal certain relevant information.

imputed knowledge
Information that is learned by the agent that is attributed to the principal.

Business Ethics

Agent's Duty of Loyalty

Because the agency relationship is based on trust and confidence, an agent owes the principal a **duty of loyalty** in all agency-related matters. Thus, an agent owes a fiduciary duty not to act adversely to the interests of the principal. If this duty is breached, the agent is liable to the principal. The most common types of breaches of loyalty by an agent are discussed below:

- ***Self-dealing*** Agents generally are prohibited from undisclosed self-dealing with the principal. For example, a real estate agent who is employed to purchase real estate for a principal cannot secretly sell his own property in the transaction. However, the deal is lawful if the principal agrees to buy the property after the agent discloses his or her ownership.
- ***Usurping an Opportunity*** An agent cannot usurp an opportunity that belongs to the principal. For example, a third-party offer to an agent must be conveyed to the principal. The agent cannot appropriate the opportunity for himself or herself unless the principal rejects it after due consideration. Opportunities to purchase real estate, businesses, products, ideas, and other property are subject to this rule.
- ***Competing with the Principal*** Agents are prohibited from competing with the principal during the course of an agency unless the principal agrees to the competition. The reason for this rule is that an agent cannot meet his or her duty of loyalty when his or her personal interests conflict with the principal's interests. If the parties have not entered into an enforceable covenant-not-to-compete, an agent is free to compete with the principal once the agency has ended.
- ***Misuse of Confidential Information*** In the course of an agency, the agent often acquires confidential information about the principal's affairs (e.g., business plans, technological innovations, customer lists, trade secrets). The agent is under a legal duty not to disclose or misuse such information either during or after the course of the agency. There is no prohibition against using general information, knowledge, or experience acquired during the course of the agency.
- ***Dual Agency*** An agent cannot meet a duty of loyalty to two parties who have conflicting interests. Dual agency occurs when an agent acts for two or more different principals in the same transaction. This practice generally is prohibited unless all of the parties involved in the transaction agree to it. If an agent acts as an undisclosed dual agent, he or she must forfeit all compensation received in the transaction. Some agents, such as middlemen and finders, are not considered dual agents. This is because they only bring interested parties together; they do not take part in any negotiations.

1. Describe an agent's fiduciary duty of loyalty.
2. What remedies should be imposed against an agent who breaches his or her loyalty to the principal? ■

Duty of Accountability

duty of accountability
A duty that an agent owes to maintain an accurate accounting of all transactions undertaken on the principal's behalf.

Unless otherwise agreed, an agent owes a duty to maintain an accurate accounting of all transactions undertaken on the principal's behalf. This **duty of accountability** includes keeping records of all property and money received and expended during the course of the agency. A principal has a right to demand an accounting from the agent at any time, and the agent owes a legal duty to make the accounting. This duty also requires the agent to (1) maintain a separate account for the principal and (2) use the principal's property in an authorized manner.

Ethics Brief
A constructive trust is created by law, rather than agreement, to impose a duty to transfer property to another.

Any property, money, or other benefit received by the agent in the course of an agency belongs to the principal. For example, all secret profits received by the agent are the property of the principal. If an agent breaches the agency contract, the principal can sue the agent to recover damages caused by breach. The court can impose a *constructive trust* on any secret profits on property purchased with secret profits for the benefit of the principal.

A Principal's Duties

A principal owes certain duties to an agent. These duties, which can be expressed in the agency contract or implied by law, include (1) the duty of compensation, (2) the duties of reimbursement and indemnification, and (3) the duty of cooperation.

Duty of Compensation

duty of compensation
A duty that a principal owes to pay an agreed-upon amount to the agent either upon the completion of the agency or at some other mutually agreeable time.

A principal owes a **duty of compensation** to an agent for services provided. Usually, the agency contract (whether written or oral) specifies the compensation to be paid. The principal must pay this amount either upon the completion of the agency or at some other mutually agreeable time.

Backyard Basketball Hoop. Basketball players and other professional sports figures usually hire sports agents to represent them in negotiations with owners of the professional teams they are interested in playing for. Professional sports stars also use sports agents to negotiate endorsement contracts with sporting goods companies and other advertisers.

If there is no agreement as to the amount of compensation, the law implies a promise that the principal will pay the agent the customary fee paid in the industry. If the compensation cannot be established by custom, the principal owes a duty to pay the reasonable value of the agent's services.

There is no duty to compensate a gratuitous agent. However, gratuitous agents who agree to provide their services free of charge may be paid voluntarily.

Certain types of agents traditionally perform their services on a *contingency fee* basis. Under this type of arrangement, the principal owes a duty to pay the agent the agreed-upon contingency fee only if the agency is completed. Real estate brokers, finders, lawyers, and salespersons often work on this basis.

Business Brief

Many plaintiffs' lawyers agree to take cases on a contingency-fee basis.

Duties of Reimbursement and Indemnification

In carrying out the agency, an agent may spend his or her own money on the principal's behalf. Unless otherwise agreed, the principal owes a **duty of reimbursement** to the agent for all such expenses if they were (1) authorized by the principal, (2) within the scope of the agency, and (3) necessary to discharge the agent's duties in carrying out the agency. For example, a principal must reimburse an agent for authorized business trips taken on the principal's behalf.

duty of reimbursement

A duty that a principal owes to repay money to the agent if the agent spent his or her own money during the agency on the principal's behalf.

A principal also owes a **duty of indemnification** to the agent for any losses the agent suffers because of the principal. This duty usually arises where an agent is held liable for the principal's misconduct. For example, suppose an agent enters into an authorized contract with a third party on the principal's behalf, the principal fails to perform on the contract, and the third party recovers a judgment against the agent. The agent can recover indemnification of this amount from the principal.

duty of indemnification

A duty that a principal owes to protect the agent for losses the agent suffered during the agency because of the principal's misconduct.

Duty of Cooperation

Unless otherwise agreed, the principal owes a **duty of cooperation** to cooperate and assist the agent in the performance of the agent's duties and the accomplishment of the agency. For example, unless otherwise agreed, a principal who employs a real estate agent to sell his or her house owes a duty to allow the agent to show the house to prospective purchasers during reasonable hours.

duty of cooperation

A duty that a principal owes to cooperate with and assist the agent in the performance of the agent's duties and the accomplishment of the agency.

International Law

International Licensing

A company that owns a valuable property right or expertise—such as a patent or another form of technology—may wish to distribute it or products that contain it in foreign countries without selling it. A method for doing so is the **license**. In licensing, one party (the *licensor*) sells the right to use its patent or other technology in another country to another company (the *licensee*). The licensor and licensee are independent entities. The licensee is usually granted an exclusive right to sell the technology or product in a specified territory (e.g., a countrywide license). The licensee usually pays royalties or other fees to the licensor.

Consider This Example The Walt Disney Company, which is a U.S. company, often grants licenses to businesses in other countries to put Mickey Mouse, Mulan, and its other trademarked characters on clothing, toys, and other items sold in other countries. The Walt Disney Company is the licensor, and the foreign company is the licensee.

Many Internet companies license software and other intellectual property in conducting international e-commerce.

If licensing is used, the exporter (1) does not have to sell its valuable property right, (2) is not subject to the tort or contract liability of the licensee, (3) often avoids any restrictions against foreign entry into a country, (4) does not have to make a substantial investment in foreign country operations, and (5) can control the use of its property right through specific contract provisions (e.g., grant only a limited-time license, impose quality control standards). ■

Contract Liability to Third Parties

A principal who authorizes an agent to enter into a contract with a third party is liable on the contract. Thus, the third party can enforce the contract and recover damages if the principal fails to perform it.

The agent can also be held liable on the contract in certain circumstances. Imposition of such liability depends on whether the agency is classified as (1) *fully disclosed*, (2) *partially disclosed*, or (3) *undisclosed*.

Fully Disclosed Agency

Business Brief

In a fully disclosed agency, the principal is liable to the third party on the contract; the agent is not liable.

A **fully disclosed agency** results if the third party entering into the contract knows (1) that the agent is acting as an agent for a principal and (2) the actual identity of the principal.[1] The third party has the requisite knowledge if the principal's identity is disclosed to the third party by either the agent or some other source.

In a fully disclosed agency, the contract is between the principal and the third party. Thus, the principal, who is called a *fully disclosed principal*, is liable on the contract. The agent, however, is not liable on the contract because the third party relied on the principal's credit and reputation when the contract was made. An agent is liable on the contract if he or she guarantees that the principal will perform the contract.

Partially Disclosed Agency

Business Brief

In a partially disclosed agency, both the principal and the agent are liable to the third party if the principal fails to perform the contract.

A **partially disclosed agency** occurs if the agent discloses his or her agency status but does not reveal the principal's identity, and the third party does not know the principal's identity from another source. The nondisclosure may be because (1) the principal instructs the agent not to disclose his or her identity to the third party or (2) the agent forgets to tell the third party the principal's identity. In this kind of agency, the principal is called a *partially disclosed principal*.

In a partially disclosed agency, both the principal and the agent are liable on third-party contracts.[2] This is because the third party must rely on the agent's reputation, integrity, and credit because the principal is unidentified. If the agent is made to pay the contract, the agent can sue the principal for indemnification. The third party and the agent can agree to relieve the agent's liability.

Undisclosed Agency

Business Brief

In an undisclosed agency, both the principal and the agent are liable to the third party if the principal fails to perform the contract.

An **undisclosed agency** occurs when the third party is unaware of either the existence of an agency or the principal's identity. The principal is called an *undisclosed principal*. Undisclosed agencies are lawful. They are often used when the principal feels that the terms of the contract would be changed if his or her identity were known. For example, a wealthy person may use an undisclosed agency to purchase property if he or she thinks that the seller would raise the price of the property if his or her identity were revealed.

In an undisclosed agency, both the principal and the agent are liable on the contract with the third party. This is because the agent, by not divulging that he or she is acting as an agent, becomes a principal to the contract. The third party relies on the reputation and credit of the agent in entering into the contract. If the principal fails to perform the contract, the third party can recover against the principal or the agent. If the agent is made to pay the contract, he or she can recover indemnification from the principal.

In the following case, the court was presented with the issue of whether an agent was liable on a contract.

Case 13.1
Undisclosed Agency

You'll See Seafoods, Inc. v. Gravois
520 So.2d 461, 1988 La.App. Lexis 186 (1988)
Court of Appeals of Louisiana

Background and Facts

In 1978, James Gravois purchased a restaurant and named it "The Captain's Raft." The restaurant was actually owned by Computer Tax Services of LA, Inc., a corporation owned by Gravois. Gravois did not inform the managers, employees, or suppliers that the restaurant was owned by a corporation. Further, the menus were printed with the name "The Captain's Raft," with no indication it was a corporate entity. Supplies purchased by the restaurant were paid for with checks signed by Gravois with no indication of his agency capacity.

You'll See Seafoods, Inc. (You'll See), supplied fresh seafood to the restaurant and was paid for the merchandise with checks signed by Gravois. On February 28, 1984, You'll See filed suit against Gravois d.b.a. The Captain's Raft to recover unpaid invoices. Gravois responded by saying that he was merely acting as an agent for a corporate principal. The corporation was in bankruptcy.

Issue

Was Gravois liable on the debt owed You'll See Seafoods, Inc.?

In The Language of The Court

Kliebert, Judge Under Louisiana law, an agent is liable to those with whom he contracts on behalf of his principal when he has bound himself personally by entering into an agreement without disclosing the identity of his principal, and the agent has the burden of proving he disclosed his capacity and the identity of his principal if he wishes to escape personal liability. Express notice of the agent's status and the principal's identity is not required if the facts and circumstances indicate that a third party should have known or was put on notice of the principal–agent relationship.

Pretermitting the questions of whether Gravois established corporate ownership of the restaurant, after review of the record before us we discern no clear error in the trial court's factual finding that You'll See was unaware an agency relationship existed between Gravois and the corporation. Although Gravois contends he was under no obligation to disclose his corporate capacity because he neither placed the orders nor accepted from You'll See, he does not deny that he spoke on occasion with the president/representative of You'll See and signed all checks issued against the You'll See account without indicating he was acting in a corporate capacity. As Gravois failed to disclose the alleged agency relationship, he is individually liable for all debts incurred.

Decision and Remedy

The appellate court held that Gravois was an agent for an undisclosed corporate principal and, therefore, was liable for the debts owed to You'll See Seafoods, Inc.

Case Questions

Critical Legal Thinking Should agents for undisclosed principals be held personally liable on contracts? Why or why not?

Business Ethics Did Gravois act ethically in arguing that the debts owed to You'll See belonged to the corporation and not to himself individually?

Contemporary Business Why do you think Gravois wanted the debts to be placed in the corporation? Why do you think You'll See did not want the debts placed in the corporation?

Agent Exceeding the Scope of Authority

An agent who enters into a contract on behalf of another party impliedly warrants that he or she has the authority to do so. This is called the agent's **implied warranty of authority**. If the agent exceeds the scope of his or her authority, the principal is not liable on the contract unless the principal **ratifies** it. The agent, however, is liable to the third party for breaching the implied warranty of authority. To recover, the third party must show (1) reliance on the agent's representation and (2) ignorance of the agent's lack of status.

implied warranty of authority
A case in which an agent who enters into a contract on behalf of another party impliedly warrants that he or she has the authority to do so.

ratification
A principal's acceptance of an agent's unauthorized contract.

Consider This Example Suppose Sam, Sara, Satchel, Samantha, and Simone form a rock band called SSSSex. SSSSex is a voluntary association without any legal status. Sam enters into a contract with Rocky's Musical Instruments to purchase instruments and equipment for the band on credit and signs the contract, "Sam, for SSSSex." When SSSSex fails to pay the debt, Rocky's can sue Sam and recover. Sam must pay the debt because he breached his implied warranty of authority when he acted as an agent for a *nonexistent principal*; that is, the purported principal was not a legal entity upon which liability could be imposed.

Concept Summary Contract Liability of Principals and Agents to Third Parties

Type of Agency	Principal Liable	Agent Liable
Fully disclosed	Yes	No, unless the agent (1) acts as a principal or (2) guarantees the performance of the contract.
Partially disclosed	Yes	Yes, unless the third party relieves the agent's liability.
Undisclosed	Yes	Yes.
Nonexistent	No, unless the principal ratifies the contract	Yes, the agent is liable for breaching the implied warranty of authority.

Entrepreneur and the Law

Signing Properly as an Agent

The agent's signature on a contract entered into on the principal's behalf is important. It can establish the agent's status and, therefore, his or her liability. For instance, in a fully disclosed agency, the agent's signature must clearly indicate that he or she is acting as an agent for a specifically identified principal. Examples of proper signatures include "Allison Adams, agent for Peter Perceival," "Peter Perceival, by Allison Adams, agent," and "Peter Perceival, by Allison Adams."

An agent who is authorized to sign a contract for a fully disclosed principal but fails to properly do so can be held personally liable on the contract. For example, in the prior example, a partially disclosed agency would be created if the contract was signed "Allison Adams, agent." If Adams merely signed the contract "Allison Adams," the agency would be an undisclosed agency. In both these instances the agent is liable on the contract. ■

Tort Liability to Third Parties

Business Brief

The use of agents creates tort liability exposure for principals. A principal is only liable for the tortious conduct of agents committed within their *scope of employment*, however.

The principal and the agent are each personally liable for their own tortious conduct. The principal is liable for the tortious conduct of an agent who is acting within the scope of his or her authority. The agent, however, is liable for the tortious conduct of the principal only if he or she directly or indirectly participates in or aids and abets the principal's conduct.

The courts have applied a broad and flexible standard in interpreting scope of authority in the context of employment. Although other factors may also be considered, the courts rely on the following factors to determine whether an agent's conduct occurred within the scope of his or her employment:

- Was the act specifically requested or authorized by the principal?
- Was it the kind of act that the agent was employed to perform?
- Did the act occur substantially within the time period of employment authorized by the principal?
- Did the act occur substantially within the location of employment authorized by the employer?
- Was the agent advancing the principal's purpose when the act occurred?

Where liability is found, tort remedies are available to the injured party. These remedies include recovery for medical expenses, lost wages, pain and suffering, emotional distress and, in some cases, punitive damages. As discussed in the following paragraphs, the three main sources of tort liability for principals and agents are misrepresentation, negligence, and intentional torts.

An agent's scope of employment was at issue in the following case.

Case 13.2 Agent's Scope of Employment

Edgewater Motels, Inc. v. Gatzke and Walgreen Co.

277 N.W.2d 11, 1979 Minn. Lexis 1381 (1979)
Supreme Court of Minnesota

Background and Facts

Arlen Gatzke (Gatzke) was a district manager for the Walgreen Company (Walgreen). In August 1979, Gatzke was sent to Duluth, Minnesota, to supervise the opening of a new Walgreen store. In Duluth, Gatzke stayed at the Edgewater Motel (Edgewater). While in Duluth, Gatzke was "on call" 24 hours a day to other Walgreen stores located in his territory. About midnight on the evening of August 23, 1979, Gatzke, after working 17 hours that day, went with several other Walgreen employees to a restaurant and bar to drink. Within one hour's time, Gatzke had consumed three doubles and one single brandy Manhattan. About 1:30 A.M., he went back to the Edgewater Motel and filled out his expense report. Soon thereafter a fire broke out in Gatzke's motel room. Gatzke escaped, but the fire spread and caused extensive damage to the motel. Evidence showed that Gatzke smoked two packs of cigarettes a day. An expert fire reconstruction witness testified that the fire started from a lit cigarette in or next to the wastepaper basket in Gatzke's room. Edgewater Motels, Inc., sued Gatzke and Walgreen. The parties stipulated that the damage to the Edgewater Motel was $330,360. The jury returned a verdict against defendants Gatzke and Walgreen. The court granted Walgreen's posttrial motion for judgment notwithstanding the verdict. Plaintiff Edgewater and defendant Gatzke appealed.

Issue

Was Gatzke's act of smoking within his "scope of employment," making his principal, the Walgreen Company, vicariously liable for his negligence?

In The Language of The Court

Scott, Justice The question of whether smoking can be within an employee's scope of employment is a close one, but after careful consideration of the issue we are persuaded by the reasoning of the courts that hold that smoking can be an act within an employee's scope of employment. It seems only logical to conclude that an employee does not abandon his employment as a matter of law while temporarily acting for his personal comfort when such activities involve only slight deviations from work that are reasonable under the circumstances. We hold that an employer can be held vicariously liable for his employee's negligent smoking of a cigarette if he was otherwise acting in the scope of his employment at the time of the negligent act.

The record contains a reasonable basis from which a jury could find that Gatzke was involved in serving his employer's interests at the time he was at the bar. Gatzke testified that, while at the Bellows, he discussed the operation of the newly opened Walgreen's store with other Walgreen employees. But more important, even assuming that Gatzke was outside the scope of his employment while he was at the bar, there is evidence from which a jury could reasonably find that Gatzke resumed his employment activities after he returned to his motel room and filled out his expense account.

Additionally, the record indicates that Gatzke was an executive type of employee who had no set working hours. He considered himself a 24-hour-a-day man; his room at the Edgewater Motel was his "office away from home." It was therefore also reasonable for the jury to determine that the filling out of his expense account was done within authorized time and space limits of his employment. In light of the above, we hold it was reasonable for the jury to find that Gatzke was acting within the scope of his employment when he completed his expense account.

Decision and Remedy

The state supreme court held that Gatzke's negligent act of smoking was within the scope of his employment while acting as an employee of the Walgreen Company. The supreme court reinstated the jury's verdict, awarding damages to plaintiff Edgewater Motels, Inc.

Case Questions

Critical Legal Thinking Should smoking cigarettes be held to be within an employee's "scope of employment"? Why or why not?

Business Ethics Do employers owe a duty to police the personal habits of their employees?

Contemporary Business Because of the dangers of smoking, would employers be justified in hiring only nonsmokers as employees?

Misrepresentation

intentional misrepresentation Misrepresentation that occurs when an agent makes an untrue statement that he or she knows is not true.

innocent misrepresentation Misrepresentation that occurs when an agent makes an untrue statement that he or she honestly and reasonably believes to be true.

Intentional misrepresentations are also known as **fraud** or **deceit**. They occur when an agent makes statements that he or she knows are not true. An **innocent misrepresentation** occurs when an agent negligently makes a misrepresentation to a third party.

A principal is liable for the intentional and innocent misrepresentations made by an agent acting within the scope of employment. The third party can either (1) rescind the contract with the principal and recover any consideration paid or (2) affirm the contract and recover damages.

Consider This Example Assume that (1) a car salesman is employed to sell the principal's car and (2) the principal tells the agent that the car was repaired after it was involved in a major accident. If the agent intentionally tells the buyer that the car was never involved in an accident, the agent has made an intentional misrepresentation. Both the principal and the agent are liable for this misrepresentation.

Negligence

respondeat superior A rule that says an employer is liable for the tortious conduct of its employees or agents while they are acting within the scope of its authority.

Principals are liable for the negligent conduct of agents acting within the scope of their employment. This liability is based on the common law doctrine of **respondeat superior** ("let the master answer"), which, in turn, is based on the legal theory of *vicarious liability* (liability without fault). In other words, the principal is liable because of his or her employment contract with the negligent agent, not because the principal was personally at fault.

This doctrine rests on the principle that if someone (i.e., the principal) expects to derive certain benefits from acting through others (i.e., an agent), that person should also bear the liability for injuries caused to third parties by the negligent conduct of an agent who is acting within the scope of his or her employment.

frolic and detour A situation in which an agent does something during the course of his employment to further his own interests rather than the principal's.

Frolic and Detour Agents sometimes do things during the course of their employment to further their own interests rather than the principal's. For example, an agent might take a detour to run a personal errand while on assignment for the principal. This is commonly referred to as a **frolic and detour**. Negligence actions stemming from frolic and detour are examined on a case-by-case basis. Agents are always personally liable for their tortious conduct in such situations. Principals generally are relieved of liability if the agent's frolic and detour is substantial. However, if the deviation is minor, the principal is liable for the injuries caused by the agent's tortious conduct.

Consider These Examples A salesperson stops home for lunch while on an assignment for his principal. While leaving his home, the agent hits and injures a pedestrian with his automobile. The principal is liable if the agent's home was not too far out of the way from the agent's assignment. However, the principal would not be liable if an agent who is supposed to be on assignment to Los Angeles flies to San Francisco to meet a friend and is involved in an accident. The facts and circumstances of each case determine its outcome.

"coming and going" rule A rule that says a principal is generally not liable for injuries caused by its agents and employees while they are on their way to and from work.

The "Coming and Going" Rule Under the common law, a principal generally is not liable for injuries caused by its agents and employees while they are on their way to or from work. This **"coming and going" rule** applies even if the principal supplies the agent's automobile or other transportation or pays for gasoline, repairs, and other automobile operating expenses. This rule is quite logical. Because principals do not control where their agents and employees live, they should not be held liable for tortious conduct of agents on their way to and from work.

Dual-Purpose Mission Sometimes, principals request that agents run errands or conduct other acts on their behalf while the agent or employee is on personal business. In this case, the agent is on a **dual-purpose mission**. That is, he or she is acting partly for himself or herself and partly for the principal. Most jurisdictions hold both the principal and the agent liable if the agent injures someone while on such a mission.

dual-purpose mission
An errand or another act that a principal requests of an agent while the agent is on his or her own personal business.

Consider This Example Suppose a principal asks an employee to drop a package off at a client's office on the employee's way home. If the employee negligently injures a pedestrian while on this dual-purpose mission, the principal is liable to the pedestrian.

Intentional Torts

Intentional torts include such acts as assault, battery, false imprisonment, and other intentional conduct that cause injury to another person. A principal is not liable for the intentional torts of agents and employees that are committed outside the principal's scope of business. For example, if an employee attends a sporting event after working hours and gets into a fight with another spectator at the event, the employer is not liable.

intentional tort
A tort that occurs when a person has intentionally committed a wrong against (1) another person or his or her character or (2) another person's property.

However, a principal is liable under the doctrine of vicarious liability for intentional torts of agents and employees committed within the agent's scope of employment. The courts generally apply one of the tests discussed below in determining whether an agent's intentional torts were committed within the agent's scope of employment.

The Motivation Test Under the **motivation test**, if the agent's motivation in committing an intentional tort was to promote the principal's business, the principal is liable for any injury caused by the tort. However, if the agent's motivation in committing the intentional tort was personal, the principal is not liable, even if the tort took place during business hours or on business premises. For example, a principal is not liable if his agent was motivated by jealousy to beat up someone on the job who dated her boyfriend.

motivation test
A test to determine the liability of the principal; if the agent's motivation in committing the intentional tort is to promote the principal's business, then the principal is liable for any injury caused by the tort.

The Work-Related Test Some jurisdictions have rejected the motivation test as too narrow. These jurisdictions apply the **work-related test** instead. Under this test, if an agent commits an intentional tort within a work-related time or space—for example, during working hours or on the principal's premises—the principal is liable for any injuries caused by the agent's intentional torts. Under this test, the agent's motivation is immaterial.

work-related test
A test to determine the liability of a principal; if an agent commits an intentional tort within a work-related time or space, the principal is liable for any injury caused by the agent's intentional tort.

In the following case, the court applied the work-related test in determining whether an employer was liable for an agent's intentional tort.

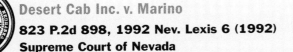

Case 13.3 Work-Related Test

Desert Cab Inc. v. Marino
823 P.2d 898, 1992 Nev. Lexis 6 (1992)
Supreme Court of Nevada

Background and Facts

On October 6, 1986, Maria Marino, a cab driver with Yellow-Checkered Cab Company (Yellow Cab), and James Edwards, a cab driver with Desert Cab Inc. (Desert Cab), parked their cabs at the taxicab stand at the Sundance Hotel and Casino in Las Vegas to await fares. Marino's cab occupied the first position in the line, and Edwards's cab occupied the third. As Marino stood alongside her cab conversing with the driver of another taxi, Edwards began verbally harassing her from inside his cab. When Marino approached Edwards to inquire as to the reason for the harassment, a verbal argument ensued. Edwards jumped from his cab, grabbed Marino by her neck and shoulders, began choking her, and threw her in front of his taxicab. A bystander pulled Edwards off Marino and escorted her back to her cab. Marino sustained injuries that rendered her unable to work for a time. Edwards was convicted of misdemeanor assault and battery. Marino brought a personal injury action against Desert Cab. The jury found Desert Cab liable and awarded Marino $65,000. Desert Cab appealed.

Issue

Is Desert Cab liable for the intentional tort of its employee?

Desert Cab Inc. v. Marino

823 P.2d 898, 1992 Nev. Lexis 6 (1992)
Supreme Court of Nevada
(continued)

In The Language of The Court

Per Curiam The district court admitted into evidence the judgment of Edwards' misdemeanor assault and battery conviction. The court found this evidence to conclusively prove Edwards' civil liability to Marino. Edwards' judgment of conviction provides conclusive evidence of his civil liability to Marino.

A finding that Edwards committed a wrongful act by attacking Marino is a prerequisite to imposing liability upon Desert Cab. In order to find Desert Cab liable, Marino still had to establish that Desert Cab was "responsible" for Edwards' conduct. Desert Cab could be found "responsible" only if Marino proved that the attack arose out of the course and scope of Edwards' employment with Desert Cab. We affirm the judgment of the district court.

Decision and Remedy

The appellate court held that Desert Cab was liable for the intentional tort committed by its employee.

Case Questions

Critical Legal Thinking Should employers be held liable for the intentional torts of their employees?

Business Ethics Did Desert Cab act ethically in denying liability?

Contemporary Business Should employers give prospective employees psychological examinations to determine if they have any dangerous propensities?

Concept Summary Tort Liability of Principals and Agents to Third Parties

Agent's Conduct	Agent Liable	Principal Liable
Misrepresentation	Yes	The principal is liable for the intentional and innocent misrepresentations made by an agent acting within the scope of his or her authority.
Negligence	Yes	The principal is liable under the doctrine of *respondeat superior* if the agent's negligent act was committed within his or her scope of employment.
Intentional tort	Yes	Motivation test: The principal is liable if the agent's motivation in committing the intentional tort was to promote the principal's business.
	Yes	Work-related test: The principal is liable if the agent committed the intentional tort within work-related time and space.

Independent Contractors

independent contractor
"A person who contracts with another to do something for him who is not controlled by the other nor subject to the other's right to control with respect to his physical conduct in the performance of the undertaking" [*Restatement (Second) of Agency*].

Section 2 of the *Restatement (Second) of Agency* defines an **independent contractor** as "A person who contracts with another to do something for him who is not controlled by the other nor subject to the other's right to control with respect to his physical conduct in the performance of the undertaking."

Independent contractors usually work for a number of clients, have their own offices, hire employees, and control the performance of their work. Merely labeling someone an "independent contractor" is not enough. The crucial factor in determining whether someone is an employee or an independent contractor is the *degree of control* that the employer has over the agent. Critical factors in determining independent contractor status include:

- Whether the worker is engaged in a distinct occupation or an independently established business

- The length of time the agent has been employed by the principal
- The amount of time that the agent works for the principal
- Whether the principal supplies the tools and equipment used in the work
- The method of payment, whether by time or by the job
- The degree of skill necessary to complete the task
- Whether the worker hires employees to assist him or her
- Whether the employer has the right to control the manner and means of accomplishing the desired result

If an examination of these factors shows that the principal asserts little control, the person is an independent contractor. Substantial control indicates an employer–employee relationship.

Business Brief
The crucial factor in determining whether a person is an employee or an independent contractor is the *degree of control* that the principal has over that person.

Contemporary Business Environment

Liability for Independent Contractor's Torts

Generally, a principal is not liable for the torts of its independent contractors. Independent contractors are personally liable for their own torts. The rationale behind this rule is that principals do not control the means by which the results are accomplished. Nevertheless, there are several exceptions to this rule:

- ***Nondelegable Duties*** Certain duties may not be delegated. For example, railroads owe a duty to maintain safe railroad crossings. They cannot escape this liability by assigning the task to an independent contractor.
- ***Special Risks*** Principals cannot avoid strict liability for dangerous activities assigned to independent contractors. For example, the use of explosives, clearing land by fire, crop dusting, and such involve special risks that are shared by the principal.
- ***Negligence in the Selection of an Independent Contractor*** A principal who hires an unqualified or knowingly dangerous person as an independent contractor is liable if that person injures someone while on the job. ■

Lighthouse, Straits of Mackinac. Common carriers, such as freighters and other ships that carry goods for others, are independent contractors. Risk of loss of goods depends on the shipping terms used in the shipping contract.

Business Ethics

Principal Liable for Repo Man's Tort

Yvonne Sanchez borrowed money from MBank El Paso (MBank) to purchase an automobile. She gave MBank a security interest in the vehicle to secure the loan. When Sanchez defaulted on the loan, MBank hired El Paso Recovery Service, an independent contractor, to repossess the automobile. The two men who were dispatched to Sanchez's house found the car parked in the driveway and hooked it to a tow truck. Sanchez demanded that they cease their efforts and leave the premises, but the men nonetheless continued with the repossession. Before the men could tow the automobile into the street, Sanchez jumped into the car, locked the doors, and refused to leave. The men towed the car at a high rate of speed to the repossession yard. They parked the car in the fenced repossession yard, with Sanchez inside, and padlocked the gate. Sanchez was left in the repossession lot with a Doberman Pinscher guard dog loose in the yard. Later, she was rescued by the police. The law prohibits the repossession of a vehicle if a breach of peace would occur. Sanchez filed suit against MBank, alleging that it was liable for the tortious conduct of El Paso Recovery Service. The trial court granted summary judgment to MBank, but the court of appeals reversed. MBank appealed.

The supreme court of Texas held that MBank, the principal, was liable for the tortious conduct of El Paso Recovery Service, an independent contractor. The court held that the act of repossessing an automobile from a defaulting debtor is an inherently dangerous activity and a nondelegable duty. The court concluded that El Paso Recovery Service had breached the peace in repossessing the car from Sanchez and caused her physical and emotional harm. The court held that MBank, the principal, could not escape liability by hiring an independent contractor to do this task. The court found MBank liable to Sanchez. [*MBank El Paso, N.A. v. Sanchez*, 836 S.W.2d 151, 1992 Tex. Lexis 97 (1992)]

1. Did the independent contractor act responsibly in this case?
2. Should the principal bank have been held liable in this case? Why or why not? ■

Termination of an Agency

An agency contract is similar to other contracts in that it can be terminated either by an act of the parties or by operation of law. These different methods of termination are discussed next. Note that once an agency relationship is terminated, the agent can no longer represent the principal or bind the principal to contracts.

Termination by Acts of the Parties

termination by acts of the parties
Termination of an agency that can occur by the following acts of the parties: (1) mutual agreement, (2) lapse of time, (3) purpose achieved, and (4) occurrence of a specified event.

The parties to an agency contract can terminate an agency contract by agreement or by their actions. The four methods of **termination** of an agency relationship **by acts of the parties** are:

1. ***Mutual Agreement*** As with any contract, the parties to an agency contract can mutually agree to terminate their agreement. By doing so, the parties relieve each other of any further rights, duties, obligations, or powers provided for in the agency contract. Either party can propose the termination of an agency contract.
2. ***Lapse of Time*** Agency contracts are often written for a specific period of time. The agency terminates when the specified time period elapses. Suppose, for example, that the principal and agent enter into an agency contract "beginning January 1, 2003, and ending December 31, 2006." The agency automatically terminates on December 31, 2006. If the agency contract does not set forth a specific termination date, the agency terminates after a reasonable time has elapsed. The courts often look to the custom of an industry in determining the reasonable time for the termination of the agency.
3. ***Purpose Achieved*** A principal can employ an agent for the time it takes to accomplish a certain task, purpose, or result. Such agencies automatically terminate when they are completed. For example, suppose a principal employs a licensed real estate broker to sell his house. The agency terminates when the house is sold and the principal pays the broker the agreed-upon compensation.

4. ***Occurrence of a Specified Event*** An agency contract can specify that the agency exists until a specified event occurs. The agency terminates when the specified event happens. For example, if a principal employs an agent to take care of her dog until she returns from a trip, the agency terminates when the principal returns from the trip.

Entrepreneur and the Law

Notification Required at the Termination of an Agency

If an agency is terminated by agreement between the parties, the principal is under a duty to give certain third parties notification of the termination. Unless otherwise required, the notice can be from the principal or some other source (e.g., the agent). If an agency terminates by operation of law, there is no duty to notify third parties about the termination, however.

The termination of an agency extinguishes an agent's actual authority to act on the principal's behalf. However, if the principal fails to give the proper notice of termination to a third party, the agent still has apparent authority to bind the principal to contracts with these third parties. If this happens, the contract is enforceable against the principal. The principal's only recourse is against the agent, to recover damages caused by these unauthorized contracts.

The following notification requirements must be met:

- ***Parties Who Dealt with the Agent*** Direct notice of termination must be given to all persons with whom the agent dealt. Although the notice may be either written or oral, it is better practice to give written notice.
- ***Parties Who Have Knowledge of the Agency*** The principal must give direct or constructive notice to any third party who has knowledge of the agency but with whom the agent has not dealt. Direct notice often is in the form of a letter. Constructive notice usually consists of placing a notice of the termination of the agency in a newspaper serving the relevant community. This notice is effective even against persons who do not see it.
- ***Parties Who Have No Knowledge of the Agency*** Generally, a principal is not obligated to give notice of termination to strangers who have no knowledge of the agency. However, a principal who has given the agent written authority to act but fails to recover the writing upon termination of the agency may be liable to strangers who later rely on this writing and deal with the agent. The laws of most states provide that this liability can be avoided by giving constructive notice (e.g., newspaper announcement) of the termination of the agency. ■

Termination by Operation of Law

Agency contracts can be terminated by **operation of law** as well as by agreement. The six methods of terminating an agency relationship by operation of law are:

termination by operation of law
An agency's termination by operation of law, including (1) death of the principal or agent, (2) insanity of the principal or agent, (3) bankruptcy of the principal, (4) impossibility of performance, (5) changed circumstances, and (6) war between the principal's and agent's countries.

1. ***Death*** The death of either the principal or the agent terminates the agency relationship. This rule is based on the old legal principle that because a dead person cannot act, no one can act for him or her. Note that the agency terminates even if one party is unaware of the other party's death. An agent's actions that take place after the principal's death do not bind the principal's estate.
2. ***Insanity*** The insanity of either the principal or the agent generally terminates the agency relationship. A few states have modified this rule to provide that a contract entered into by an agent on behalf of an insane principal is enforceable if (1) the insane person has not been adjudged insane, (2) the third party does not have knowledge of the principal's insanity at the time of contracting, and (3) the enforcement of the contract will prevent injustice.
3. ***Bankruptcy*** The agency relationship is terminated if the principal is declared bankrupt. Bankruptcy requires the filing of a petition for bankruptcy under federal bankruptcy law. With few exceptions, neither the appointment of a state court receiver nor the principal's financial difficulties or insolvency terminates the agency relationship. The agent's bankruptcy usually does not terminate an agency unless the agent's credit standing is important to the agency relationship.

4. ***Impossibility*** The agency relationship terminates if a situation arises that makes its fulfillment impossible. The following circumstances can lead to termination on this ground:
   - ***The loss or destruction of the subject matter of the agency.*** For example, assume that a principal employs an agent to sell his horse, but the horse dies before it is sold. The agency relationship terminates at the moment the horse dies.
   - ***The loss of a required qualification.*** For example, suppose a principal employs a licensed real estate agent to sell her house, and the real estate agent's license is revoked. The agency terminates at the moment the license is revoked.
   - ***A change in the law.*** For example, suppose that a principal employs an agent to trap alligators. If a law is passed that makes trapping alligators illegal, the agency contract terminates when the law becomes effective.
5. ***Changed Circumstances*** An agency terminates when there is an unusual change in circumstances that would lead the agent to believe that the principal's original instructions should no longer be valid. For example, a principal employs a licensed real estate agent to sell a farm for $100,000. The agent thereafter learns that oil has been discovered on the property that makes it worth $1 million. The agency terminates because of this change in circumstances.
6. ***War*** The outbreak of a war between the principal's country and the agent's country terminates the agency relationship between the parties. Such an occurrence usually makes the performance of the agency contract impossible.

Contemporary Business Environment

Irrevocable Agency

An **agency coupled with an interest** is a special type of agency relationship that is created for the agent's benefit. This type of agency is irrevocable by the principal (e.g., the principal cannot terminate it). An agency coupled with an interest is commonly used in security agreements to secure loans. An agency coupled with an interest is not terminated by the death or incapacity of either the principal or the agent. It terminates only when the agent's obligations are performed. However, the parties can expressly agree that an agency coupled with an interest is terminated.

Consider This Example Heidi Norville owns a piece of real estate. She goes to Wells Fargo Bank to obtain a loan on the property. The bank makes the loan but requires her to sign a security agreement (e.g., a mortgage) pledging the property as collateral for the loan. The security agreement contains a clause that appoints that bank as Ms. Norville's agent and permits the bank to sell the property and recover the amount of the loan from the sale proceeds if she defaults on her payments. This agency is irrevocable by Ms. Norville, the principal. ■

Wrongful Termination of an Agency or Employment Contract

Generally, agency and employment contracts that do not specify a definite time for their termination can be terminated at will by either the principal or the agent without liability to the other party. When a principal terminates an agency contract, it is called a **revocation of authority**. When an agent terminates an agency, it is called a **renunciation of authority**.

Unless an agency is irrevocable, both the principal and the agent have an individual power to unilaterally terminate any agency contract. Note that having the power to terminate an agency agreement is not the same as having the right to terminate it. The unilateral termination of an agency contract may be wrongful. If the principal's or agent's termination of an agency contract breaches the contract, the other party can sue for damages for **wrongful termination**.

wrongful termination
The termination of an agency contract in violation of the terms of the agency contract. The nonbreaching party may recover damages from the breaching party.

Consider This Example A principal employs a licensed real estate agent to sell his house. The agency contract gives the agent an exclusive listing for three months. After one month, the principal unilaterally terminates the agency. The principal has the power to do so, and the agent can no longer act on behalf of the principal. However, because the principal did not have the right to terminate the contract, the agent can sue him and recover damages (i.e., lost commission) for wrongful termination.

Business Brief
The distinction between the *power* and the *right* to terminate an agency is critical. Be certain it is clear.

International Law

Strategic Alliances in Foreign Countries

A **strategic alliance** is an agreement between two or more businesses from different countries to accomplish a specific purpose or function. For example, an agreement between an American automobile company and a Japanese automobile company to jointly produce an automobile to be sold in the United States is a joint venture. A joint venture may also be between a corporation and a foreign government.

Joint ventures are often entered into if it is (1) commercially efficient to do so (e.g., neither party has sufficient capital or expertise to accomplish the objective alone) or (2) required by law (e.g., some countries prohibit a foreign company from owning more than 49 percent of a business that operates in the country). ■

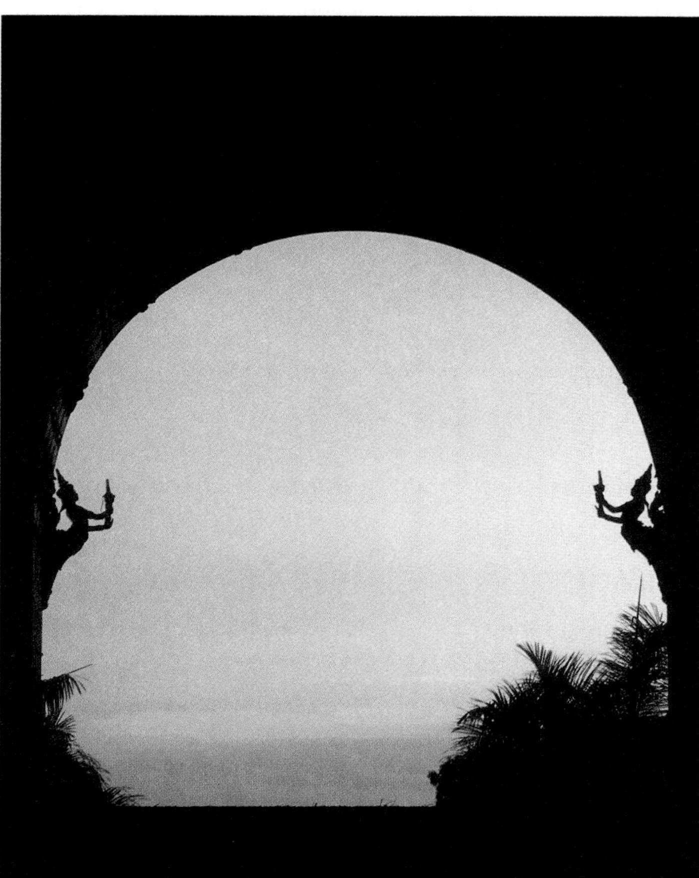

Laos. Multinational companies often use agents to represent them to conduct business in foreign countries.

Chapter Summary

The Nature of Agency, p. 366

The Nature of Agency

1. ***Agency.*** A fiduciary relationship that results from the manifestation of consent by one person to act on behalf of another person with that person's consent.
2. ***Parties:***
   a. *Principal.* Party who employs another person to act on his or her behalf.
   b. *Agent.* Party who agrees to act on behalf of another person.

Kinds of Employment Relationships, p. 366

Employer–Employee Relationship

An employer hires an employee to perform some form of physical service. An employee is not an agent unless the principal authorizes him or her to enter into contracts on the principal's behalf.

Principal–Agent Relationship

An employer hires an employee and authorizes the employee to enter into contracts on the employer's behalf.

Principal–Independent Contractor Relationship

The principal employs a person who is not an employee of the principal. The independent contractor has authority only to enter into contracts authorized by the principal.

Formation of an Agency Relationship, p. 369

Express Agency

Principal and agent expressly agree in words to enter into an agency agreement. The agency contract may be oral or written unless the statute of frauds requires it to be in writing.

Implied Agency

An agency is implied (inferred) from the conduct of the parties.

Apparent Agency

Arises when a principal creates an appearance of an agency that in actuality does not exist. Also called *agency by estoppel* or *ostensible agency.*

Agency by Ratification

Occurs when a person misrepresents him- or herself as another's agent when he or she is not and the purported principal ratifies (accepts) the unauthorized act.

An Agent's Duties, p. 372

Duty of Performance

Performance of the lawful duties expressed in the agency contract with reasonable care, skill and diligence.

Duty of Notification

An agent owes a duty to notify the principal of any information he learns that is important to the agency. Information learned by the agent in the course of the agency is *imputed* to the principal.

Duty of Loyalty

An agent's duty not to act adversely to the interests of the principal. The most common breaches of loyalty are:

1. ***Self-dealing.*** Agent cannot deal with the principal unless his or her position is disclosed and the principal agrees to deal with the agent.
2. ***Usurping an opportunity.*** Agent cannot usurp (take) an opportunity belonging to the principal as his or her own.
3. ***Competing with the principal.*** Agent is prohibited from competing with the principal during the course of an agency unless the principal agrees to the competition.
4. ***Misuse of confidential information.*** Agent is under a legal duty not to disclose or misuse confidential information learned within the course of an agency.
5. ***Dual agency.*** Agent cannot act on behalf of two different principals in same transaction unless the principals agree.

Duty of Accountability

Agent must maintain an accurate accounting of all transactions undertaken on the principal's behalf. A principal may demand an accounting from the agent at any time.

A Principal's Duties, p. 374

Duty of Compensation

Principal must pay the agent agreed-upon compensation. If there is no agreement, the principal must pay what is customary in the industry, or, if there is no custom, then the reasonable value of the services.

Duties of Reimbursement and Indemnification

Principal must *reimburse* an agent for all expenses paid that were authorized by the principal, within the scope of the agency, and necessary to discharge the agent's duties. The principal must *indemnify* the agent for any losses suffered because of the principal's misconduct.

Duty of Cooperation

The principal must cooperate with and assist the agent in the performance of the agent's duties and the accomplishment of the agency.

Contract Liability to Third Parties, p. 376

Fully Disclosed Agency

The third party entering into the contract knows that the agent is acting for a principal and knows the identity of the principal. The principal is liable on the contract; the agent is not liable on the contract.

Partially Disclosed Agency

The third party knows that the agent is acting for a principal but does not know the identity of the principal. Both the principal and the agent are liable on the contract.

Undisclosed Agency

The third party does not know that the agent is acting for a principal. Both the principal and the agent are liable on the contract.

Tort Liability to Third Parties, p. 378

Tort Liability

Principals are liable for the *tortious conduct* of an agent who is acting within the *scope of his or her authority*. Liability is imposed for misrepresentation, negligence, and intentional torts.

Misrepresentation

Principals are liable for intentional and innocent misrepresentations made by an agent acting within the scope of his or her employment.

Negligence

Principals are liable for the negligent conduct of agents acting within the scope of their employment. Special negligence doctrines include:

1. ***Frolic and detour.*** Principals are generally relieved of liability if the agent's negligent act occurred on a substantial frolic and detour from the scope of employment.
2. ***"Coming and going" rule.*** Principals are not liable if the agent's tortious conduct occurred while on the way to or from work.
3. ***Dual-purpose mission.*** If the agent is acting on his or her own behalf and on behalf of the principal, the principal is generally liable for the agent's tortious conduct.

Intentional Torts

States apply one of the following rules:

1. ***Motivation test.*** The principal is liable if the agent's intentional tort was committed to promote the principal's business.
2. ***Work-related test.*** The principal is liable if the agent's intentional tort was committed within a work-related time or space.

Agents are personally liable for their own tortious conduct.

Independent Contractors, p. 382

Liability for Independent Contractor's Torts

Generally, principals are not liable for the tortious conduct of independent contractors. Exceptions to the rule are for:

1. ***Nondelegable duties***
2. ***Special risks***
3. ***Negligence in selecting an independent contractor***

Independent contractors are personally liable for their own torts.

Termination of an Agency, p. 384

Termination by Acts of the Parties

The following *acts of the parties* terminate agency contracts:

1. ***Mutual agreement.*** Parties mutually agree to terminate an agency contract.
2. ***Lapse of time.*** The stipulated time period of the agency expires.
3. ***Purpose achieved.*** The stipulated purpose of the agency is achieved.
4. ***Occurrence of a specified event.*** The occurrence of a stipulated event happens.

Notification of Termination

If an agency is terminated by agreement between the parties, the principal must notify third parties as follows:

1. ***Parties who dealt with the agent.*** Direct notice must be given to these parties.
2. ***Parties who have knowledge of the agency.*** Direct or constructive (e.g., public notice in newspapers) notice must be given to these parties.
3. ***Parties who have no knowledge of the agency.*** No notice needs to be given to these parties.

If the proper notice of the termination of the agency is not given, the agent has *apparent authority* to bind the principal to contracts.

The principal and agent both have the *power* to terminate an agency at any time. After termination, the agent can no longer act on behalf of the principal. The terminating party may not, however, have had the *right* to terminate the agency and may be held liable for damages caused by *wrongful termination* of the agency.

Termination of Operation of Law

Agency contracts can be terminated by *operation of law*. This includes the following methods:

1. ***Death.*** Death of either the principal or the agent.
2. ***Insanity.*** Insanity of either the principal or the agent.
3. ***Bankruptcy.*** Bankruptcy of the principal.
4. ***Impossibility.*** A situation arises that makes the performance of the agency contract impossible.
5. ***Changed circumstances.*** An unusual circumstance would lead the agent to believe that the principal's original instructions are no longer valid.
6. ***War.*** Outbreak of war between the principal's country and the agent's country.

Irrevocable Agency

An *agency coupled with an interest* is a special type of agency that is irrevocable by the principal. Commonly used in security interests to secure loans.

Wrongful Termination of an Agency Contract

If an agency is for an agreed-upon term or purpose, the *unilateral termination* of the agency contract by either the principal or the agent constitutes the *wrongful termination* of the agency. The breaching party is liable to the other party for damages caused by the breach.

Internet Exercises and Case Questions

Working the Web Internet Exercises

Activities

1. Visit Nolo Press at **www.nolo.com/category/ic_home.html** to find general information regarding the classification of independent contractor versus employee.
2. A quick overview of the topic of agency from a practical business perspective can be found at **consumer.pub.findlaw.com/newcontent/consumerlaw/chp2_h.html**. See also Law About . . . Agency at **www.law.cornell.edu/topics/agency.html**.
3. One way to create an agency is to execute a power of attorney. See **smallbiz.biz.findlaw.com/bookshelf/sblg/sblgchp13_f.html** for information and **consumer.pub.findlaw.com/nllg/forms/128.html** for a form.
4. Agency law is very important and widely used in international business ventures. For an example of how the law is applied in another country, Iran, see **www.nourlaw.com/guide_to_iranian_market/Agency.html**.

Critical Legal Thinking Cases

13.1 Creation of an Agency Renaldo, Inc., d/b/a Baker Street, owns and operates a nightclub in Georgia. On the evening in question, plaintiff Ginn became "silly drunk" at the nightclub and was asked by several patrons and the manager to leave the premises. The police were called, and Ginn left the premises. When Ginn realized that his jacket was still in the nightclub, he attempted to reenter the premises. He was met at the door by the manager, who refused him admittance. When Ginn persisted, an unidentified patron, without the approval of the manager, pushed Ginn, who lost his balance and fell backward. To break his fall, Ginn put his hand against the door jamb. The unidentified patron slammed the door on Ginn's hand and held it shut for several minutes. Ginn, who suffered severe injuries to his right hand, sued the nightclub for damages. Was the unidentified patron an agent of the nightclub? [*Ginn v. Renaldo, Inc.*, 359 S.E.2d 390, 1987 Ga.App. Lexis 2023 (Ga. App. 1987)]

13.2 Independent Contractor The Butler Telephone Company, Inc. (Butler), contracted with the Sandidge Construction Company to lay 18 miles of telephone cable in a rural area. In the contract, Butler reserved the right to inspect the work for compliance with the terms of the contract. Butler did not control how Sandidge performed the work. Johnnie Carl Pugh, an employee of Sandidge, was killed on the job when the sides to an excavation in which he was working caved in on top of him. Evidence disclosed that the excavation was not properly shored or sloped and that it violated general safety standards. Pugh's parents and estate brought a wrongful death action against Butler. Is Butler liable? [*Pugh v. Butler Telephone Company, Inc.*, 512 So.2d 1317, 1987 Ala. Lexis 4468 (AL 1987)]

13.3 Independent Contractor Mercedes Connolly and her husband purchased airline tickets and a tour package for a tour to South Africa from Judy Samuelson, a travel agent doing business as International Tours of Manhattan. Samuelson sold tickets for a variety of airline companies and tour operators, including African Adventurers, which was the tour operator for Connolly's tour. Connolly injured her left ankle and foot on September 27, 1984, while the tour group was on a walking tour to see hippopotami in a river at the Sabi Sabi Game Reserve. Mercedes fell while trying to cross a six-inch-deep stream. She sued Samuelson for damages. Is Samuelson liable? [*Connolly v. Samuelson*, 671 F.Supp. 1312, 1987 U.S. Dist. Lexis 8308 (D.Kan. 1987)]

13.4 Implied Agency Tom and Judith Sullivan owned real property on which they obtained a loan from the Federal Land Bank of Omaha (FLB). The property secured the loan. The Sullivans defaulted on the loan, and the FLB brought an action to foreclose on the mortgage. The FLB hired an independent lawyer to handle the case. The lawyer wrote a letter to the Sullivans, outlining a settlement offer. A copy of the letter was sent to the FLB's regional office in Yankton, South Dakota. The regional office did not notify the attorney that he did not have authority to offer the settlement without the FLB's permission. When the Sullivans accepted the settlement offer, the FLB regional office refused to approve the deal. The Sullivans sued to enforce it. Did the attorney for the FLB have authority to settle the case? [*Federal Land Bank of Omaha v. Sullivan*, 430 N.W.2d 700, 1988 S.D. Lexis 150 (SD 1988)]

13.5 Apparent Agency Gene Mohr and James Loyd each own 50 percent of Tri-County Farm Equipment Company. Tri-County has its depository bank account at First National Bank of Olathe, Kansas. Loyd also personally owns an oil business known as Earthworm Energy, which has its bank account at the State Bank of Stanley. Neither Mohr nor Tri-County has any ownership interest in Earthworm. Mohr did not indicate to the State Bank of Stanley that Loyd had any authority to personally sign checks on behalf of Tri-County. In 1982, Loyd took eight checks that were payable to Tri-County and endorsed and deposited them into Earthworm's account at the State Bank of Stanley. Mohr brought an action for conversion against the State Bank of Stanley to recover the amount of the checks. The bank argued in defense that Loyd had apparent authority to deposit the checks in his personal business account. Did Loyd possess apparent authority? [*Mohr v. State Bank of Stanley*, 734 P.2d 1071, 1987 Kan. Lexis 297 (KA 1987)]

13.6 Ratification After Francis Pusateri retired, he met with Gilbert J. Johnson, a stockbroker with E. F. Hutton & Co., Inc., and informed Johnson that he wished to invest in tax-free bonds and money market accounts. Pusateri opened an investment account with E. F. Hutton and checked the box stating his objective was "tax-free income and moderate growth." During the course of a year, Johnson churned Pusateri's account to make commissions and invested Pusateri's funds in volatile securities and options. Johnson kept telling Pusateri that his account was making money, and the monthly statement from E. F. Hutton did not indicate otherwise. The manager at E. F. Hutton was aware of Johnson's activities but did nothing to prevent them. When Johnson left E. F. Hutton, Pusateri's account—which had been called the "laughingstock" of the office—had shrunk from $196,000 to $96,880, Pusateri sued E. F. Hutton for damages. Is E. F. Hutton liable? [*Pusateri v. E. F. Hutton & Co., Inc.*, 180 Cal.App.3d 247, 225 Cal.Rptr. 526, 1986 Cal.App. Lexis 1502 (Cal. App. 1986)]

13.7 Reasonable Care and Skill Norman R. Barton and his wife decided to vacation in Florida in November 1984. In March 1984, they contacted Wonderful World of Travel, Inc., a travel agency licensed by the state of Ohio, to make the arrangements. They requested a room with a view of the ocean, a kitchenette so they would be saved the expense of dining out, free parking, and a free spa. In August, with the Bartons' approval, the travel agency made reservations at the Beau Rivage motel in Bal Harbour, Florida. The travel agency did not confirm the reservations prior to the Bartons' departure in November. When the Bartons arrived at the motel, they found it closed, chained, and guarded. The only other hotel or motel in the area was a Sheraton, which was almost triple the room cost of the Beau Rivage. The Sheraton overlooked the ocean, but it did not have a kitchenette, free parking, or free spa privileges. The Bartons stayed at the Sheraton. They sued the travel agent upon their return. Is the travel agent liable for the increased costs incurred by the Bartons? [*Barton v. Wonderful World of Travel, Inc.*, 502 N.E.2d 715, 1986 Ohio Misc. Lexis 57 (Ohio Mun. 1986)]

13.8 Imputed Knowledge On March 31, 1981, Iota Management Corporation entered into a contract to purchase the Bel Air West Motor Hotel in the City of St. Louis from Boulevard Investment Company. The agreement contained the following warranty: "Seller has no actual notice of any substantial defect in the structure of the Hotel or in any of its plumbing, heating, air-conditioning, electrical, or utility systems."

When the buyer inspected the premises, no leaks in the pipes were visible. Iota purchased the hotel for $2 million. When Iota removed some of the walls and ceilings during remodeling, it found evidence of prior repairs to leaking pipes and ducts, as well as devices for catching water (e.g., milk cartons, cookie sheets, and buckets). The estimate to repair these leaks was $500,000. Evidence at trial showed that Cecil Lillibridge, who was Boulevard's maintenance supervisor from 1975 until the sale of the hotel in 1981, had actual knowledge of these problems and had repaired some of the pipes. Iota sued Boulevard to rescind the contract. Is Boulevard liable? [*Iota Management Corporation v. Boulevard Investment Company*, 731 S.W.2d 399, 1987 Mo.App. Lexis 4027 (Mo. App. 1987)]

13.9 Dual Agency Chemical Bank is the primary bank for Washington Steel Corporation. As an agent for Washington Steel, Chemical Bank expressly and impliedly promised that it would advance the best interests and welfare of Washington Steel. During the course of the agency, Washington Steel provided the bank with comprehensive and confidential financial information, other data, and future business plans.

At some point during the agency, TW Corporation and others approached Chemical Bank to request a loan of $7 million to make a hostile tender offer for the stock of Washington Steel. Chemical Bank agreed and became an agent for TW. Management at Chemical Bank did not disclose its adverse relationship with TW to Washington Steel, did not request Washington Steel's permission to act as an agent for TW, and directed employees of the bank to conceal the bank's involvement with TW from Washington Steel. After TW commenced its public tender offer, Washington Steel filed suit, seeking to obtain an injunction against Chemical Bank and TW. Who wins? [*Washington Steel Corporation v. TW Corporation*, 465 F.Supp. 1100, 1979 U.S. Dist Lexis 14391 (W.D.Pa. 1979)]

13.10 Duty of Loyalty Peter Shields was the president and a member of the board of directors of Production Finishing Corporation from 1974 through August 1981. The company provided steel polishing services. It did most, if not all, of the polishing work in the Detroit area, except for that of the Ford Motor Company. (Ford did its own polishing.) Shields discussed this matter with Ford on behalf of Production Finishing on a number of occasions. When Shields learned that Ford was discontinuing its polishing operation, he incorporated Flat Rock Metal and submitted a confidential proposal to Ford that provided that he would buy Ford's equipment and provide polishing services to Ford. It was not until he resigned from Production Finishing that he informed the board of directors that he was pursuing the Ford business himself. Production Finishing sued Shields. Did Shields breach his fiduciary duty of loyalty to Production Finishing? [*Production Finishing Corporation v. Shields*, 405 N.W.2d 171, 1987 Mich.App. Lexis 2379 (Mich. App. 1987)]

13.11 Personal Guaranty In May 1978, Sebastian International, Inc., entered into a five-year lease for a building in Chadsworth, California. In September 1980, with the consent of the master lessors, Sebastian sublet the building to West Valley Grinding, Inc. In conjunction with the execution of the sublease, the corporate officers of West Valley, including Kenneth E. Peck, each signed a guaranty of lease, personally ensuring the payment of West Valley's rental obligations. The guaranty contract referred to Peck in his individual capacity; however, on the signature line he was identified as "Kenneth Peck, Vice President." In May 1981, West Valley went out of business, leaving 24 months remaining on the sublease. After unsuccessful attempts to secure another sublessee, Sebastian surrendered the leasehold back to the master lessors and brought suit against Peck to recover the unpaid rent. Peck argues he is not personally liable because his signature was that of an agent for a disclosed principal and not that of a principal himself. Who wins? [*Sebastian International, Inc. v. Peck*, 195 Cal.App.3d 803, 240 Cal.Rptr. 911, 1987 Cal.App. Lexis 2237 (Cal. App. 1987)]

13.12 Contract Liability G. Elvin Grinder of Marbury, Maryland, was a building contractor who, prior to May 1, 1973, did business as an individual and traded as "Grinder Construction." Grinder maintained an open account, on his individual credit, with Bryans Road Building & Supply Co., Inc. Grinder would purchase materials and supplies from Bryans on credit and later pay the invoices. On May 1, 1973, G. Elvin Grinder Construction, Inc., a Maryland corporation, was formed, with Grinder personally owning 52 percent of the stock of the corporation. Grinder did not inform Bryans that he had incorporated and continued to purchase supplies on credit from Bryans under the name "Grinder Construction." In May 1978, after certain invoices were not paid by Grinder, Bryans sued Grinder personally to recover. Grinder asserted that the debts were owed by the corporation. Bryans amended its complaint to include the corporation as a defendant. Who is liable to Bryans? [*Grinder v. Bryans Road Building & Supply Co., Inc.*, 432 A.2d 453, 1981 Md. Lexis 246 (Md. App. 1981)]

13.13 Contract Liability In the spring of 1974, certain residents of Harrisville, Utah, organized Golden Spike Little League for the youngsters of the town. This was an unincorporated association. David Anderson and several other organizers contracted with Smith & Edwards, a sporting goods store, which agreed to give them favorable prices on merchandise. During the course of the summer, parents went into Smith & Edwards and picked up uniforms and equipment for their children and other Little Leaguers. At the end of the summer, Smith & Edwards sent them a bill for $3,900. Fund-raising activities produced only $149, and the organizers refused to pay the difference. Smith & Edwards sued Anderson and the other organizers for the unpaid balance. Are the organizers personally liable for the debt? [*Smith & Edwards v. Anderson*, 577 P.2d 132, 1978 Utah Lexis 1269 (UT 1978)]

13.14 Tort Liability Intrastate Radiotelephone, Inc., is a public utility that supplies radiotelephone utility service to the general public for radiotelephones, pocket pagers, and beepers. Robert Kranhold, an employee of Intrastate, was authorized to use his personal vehicle on company business. On the morning of March 9, 1976, when Kranhold was driving his vehicle to Intrastate's main office, he negligently struck a motorcycle being driven by Michael S. Largey, causing severe and permanent injuries to Largey. The accident occurred at the intersection where Intrastate's main office is located. Evidence showed that Kranhold acted as a consultant to Intrastate, worked both in and out of Intrastate's offices, had no set hours of work, often attended meetings at Intrastate's offices, and went to Intrastate's offices to pick things up or drop things off. Largey sued Intrastate for damages. Is Intrastate liable? [*Largey v. Radiotelephone, Inc.*, 136 Cal.App.3d 660, 186 Cal.Rptr. 520, 1982 Cal.App. Lexis 2049 (Cal. App. 1982)]

Business Ethics Cases

13.15 Business Ethics The Hagues, husband and wife, owned a 160-acre tract that they decided to sell. On March 19, 1976, they entered into a listing agreement with Harvey C. Hilgendorf, a licensed real estate broker, which gave Hilgendorf the exclusive right to sell the property for a period of 12 months. Hague agreed to pay Hilgendorf a commission of 6 percent of the accepted sale price if a bona fide buyer was found during the listing period.

By letter on August 13, 1976, Hague terminated the listing agreement with Hilgendorf. Hilgendorf did not acquiesce to Hague's termination, however. On September 30, 1976, Hilgendorf presented an offer to the Hagues from a buyer willing to purchase the property at the full listing price. The Hagues ignored the offer and sold the property to another buyer. Hilgendorf sued the Hagues for breach of the agency agreement. Did the Hagues act ethically in this case? Who wins the lawsuit? [*Hilgendorf v. Hague*, 293 N.W.2d 272, 1980 Iowa Sup. Lexis 882 (IA 1980)]

13.16 Business Ethics The National Biscuit Company (Nabisco) is a corporation that produces and distributes cookies and other food products to grocery stores and other outlets across the nation. In October 1968, Nabisco hired Ronnell Lynch as a cookie salesman-trainee. On March 1, 1969, Lynch was assigned his own sales territory. Lynch's duties involved making sales calls, taking orders, and making sure that shelves of stores in his territory were stocked with Nabisco products. During the period March 1 to May 1, 1969, Nabisco received numerous complaints from store owners in Lynch's territory that Lynch was overly aggressive and was taking shelf space for Nabisco products that was reserved for competing brands.

On May 1, 1969, Lynch visited a grocery store that was managed by Jerome Lange. Lynch was there to place previously delivered merchandise on the store's shelves. An argument developed between Lynch and Lange. Lynch became very angry and started swearing. Lange, the store manager, told Lynch to stop swearing or leave the store because children were present. Lynch became uncontrollably angry and went behind the counter and dared Lange to a fight. When Lange refused to fight, Lynch proceeded to viciously assault and batter Lange, causing severe injuries. Lange sued Nabisco. Was it ethical for Nabisco to deny liability in this case? Do you think the prior complaints against Lynch had any effect on the decision reached in this case? Is Nabisco liable for the intentional tort (assault and battery) of its employee, Lynch? [*Lange v. National Biscuit Company*, 211 N.W.2d 783, 1973 Minn. Lexis 1106 (MN 1983)]

Briefing the Case Writing Assignment

Read Case A.13 in the Case Appendix [*District of Columbia v. Howell*]. This case is excerpted from the court of appeals opinion. Review and brief the case. In your brief, be sure to answer the following questions.

1. Was A. Louis Jagoe hired by the District of Columbia as an employee or as an independent contractor?
2. Describe the accident that occurred. Who was injured?
3. Normally, an employer is not liable for the tortious conduct of an independent contractor it has hired. Describe the "special risks" exception to this rule.
4. What damages were awarded to the plaintiff?

Answers to Management Decision Questions

1. Businesses usually have three kinds of employment relationships: (1) employer–employee relationships, (2) principal–agent relationships, and (3) principal–independent contractor relationships. The employer–employee relationship results when an employer hires an employee to perform some form of physical service. In the principal–agent relationship, an employer hires an employee and gives that employee authority to act and enter into contracts on his or her behalf. In a principal–independent contractor relationship, a principal employs an outsider—that is, persons and businesses who are not employees—to perform tasks on their behalf. You have no employment relationship with Uptown Realty. You are in an employer–employee relationship with Walker.
2. Uptown Realty should not be included as a defendant in a negligence lawsuit. Generally, a principal is not liable for the torts of its independent contractors. Independent contractors are personally liable for their own torts. Falling from a defective ladder supplied by an independent contractor and not by a principal does not qualify as an exception under this rule. The exceptions to the rule include nondelegable duties, special risks, and negligence in the selection of an independent contractor.

Endnotes

1. *Restatement (Second) of Agency*, § 4.
2. *Restatement (Second) of Agency*, § 321.

14

Entrepreneurships, Sole Proprietorships, and Franchising

"Commerce never really flourishes so much, as when it is delivered from the guardianship of legislators and ministers."

—William Godwin
Enquiry Concerning Political Justice (1798)

Chapter Objectives

After studying this chapter, you should be able to:

1. Describe the role of entrepreneurs in starting and operating businesses.
2. Define sole proprietorship and the liability of a sole proprietor.
3. Describe how a business files for a d.b.a.—a fictitious business name.
4. Define franchise and identify the parties to a franchise arrangement.
5. Identify the contract liability and tort liability of franchisors and franchisees.

Chapter Contents

- Entrepreneurial Forms of Conducting Business
- Sole Proprietorship
- Franchises
- The Franchise Agreement
- Contract and Tort Liability of Franchisors and Franchisees
- Termination of Franchises

Management Decision — Entrepreneurship, Sole Proprietorships, and Franchising

As president of Coney Island Hot Dog, Inc., a fast-food franchisor, you are looking for ways to expand the market for your hot dogs. In particular, you researched the pros and cons of licensing franchisees to operate in eastern Canada. Further licensing in the United States offers little potential for expansion, and the familiarity of the Canadians with Coney Island and its famous hot dogs makes the potential for expansion into this market an acceptable risk and a likely lucrative investment. The chairman of the board has asked you to present a report to the board concerning this matter and to make recommendations.

1. What different types of franchise agreements currently exist? What franchise agreement should you suggest for the Canadian market?
2. What common terms should you include in the franchise agreement?

entrepreneur
A person who forms and operates a new business either by him- or herself or with others.

An **entrepreneur** is a person who forms and operates a new business. An entrepreneur may start the business by him- or herself or cofound the business with others. Most businesses started by entrepreneurs are small, although some grow into substantial organizations. For example, Bill Gates started Microsoft Corporation, which grew into the giant software and Internet company. Michael Dell started Dell Computers as a mail-order business; it has become a leader in computer sales. Entrepreneurs in this country and around the world create new businesses daily that hire employees, provide new products and services, and make economies of countries grow.

It has been uniformly laid down in this Court, as far back as we can remember, that good faith is the basis of all mercantile transactions.

Buller, J.
Salomons v. Nissen (1788)

Franchising is an important method for distributing goods and services to the public. Originally pioneered by the automobile and soft drink industries, franchising today is used in many forms of business. The 700,000-plus franchise outlets in the United

Restaurant, Sault Ste. Marie, Michigan. Entrepreneurs have many choices of legal forms for conducting their businesses, such as this restaurant.

States account for over 25 percent of retail sales and about 15 percent of the gross national product (GNP).

This chapter discusses law related to entrepreneurships, sole proprietorships, and franchising.

Entrepreneurial Forms of Conducting Business

Entrepreneurs contemplating starting a business have many options when choosing the legal form in which to conduct the business. Each of these forms of business has advantages and disadvantages for the entrepreneur. The major forms for conducting businesses and professions are:

1. Sole proprietorship
2. General partnership
3. Limited partnership
4. Limited liability partnership
5. Limited liability company
6. Corporation

These forms of business are discussed in this chapter and the following chapters.

It is the privilege of a trader in a free country, in all matters not contrary to law, to regulate his own mode of carrying it on according to his own discretion and choice.

B. Alderson
Hilton v. Eckersly (1855)

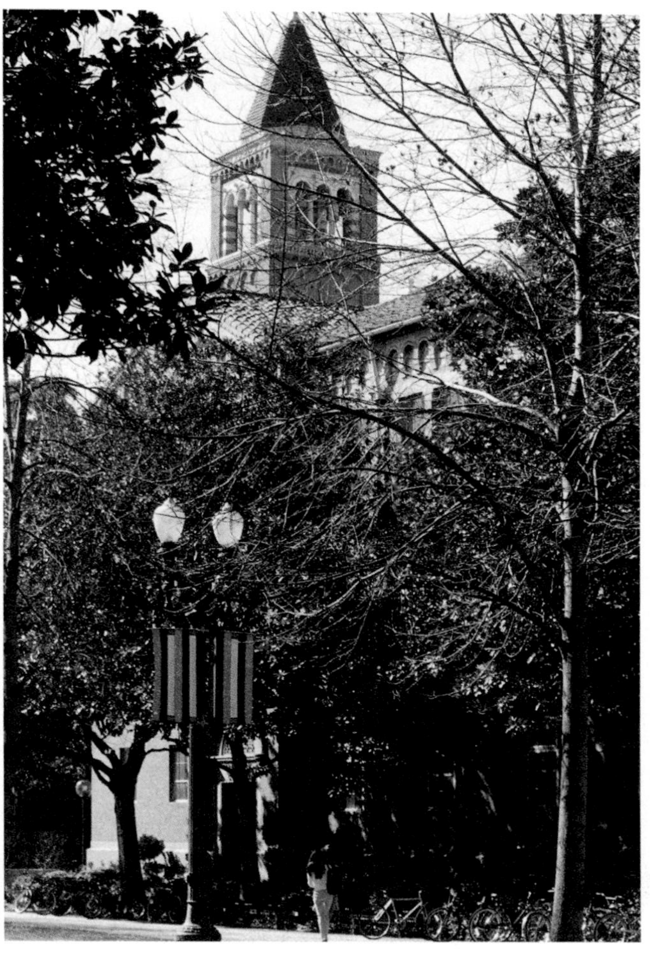

University Campus. Many of today's students will become tomorrow's entrepreneurs.

Entrepreneur and the Law

The Entrepreneurial Spirit: The Creation of Amazon.com

In 1994, Jeff Bezos, the son of a Cuban immigrant to the United States, had made it big. After graduating from Princeton University, he had gone to Wall Street, where he worked for a hedge fund. But Bezos saw an even greater opportunity: online commerce. So he quit his job, jumped in the car with his wife, MacKenzie, and headed west. While she drove, he typed on his laptop computer. Bezos drew up a list of 20 products that he figured he could sell online, but then narrowed it to 2—books and music. Bezos settled on books for two reasons. First, there are more to sell (about 1.3 million books in print versus 300,000 music titles). Second, the Goliaths of publishing seemed less imposing than the six record companies that dominated music; there were thousands of bookstores, the largest of which was Barnes & Noble, with 12 percent of the industry's $25 billion annual sales.

After checking out Colorado and Oregon, Bezos and his wife settled in Seattle, Washington. They rented a house, hired four employees, and started Amazon.com out of their garage. Bezos and his family incorporated the business, sold some stock to friends and other investors, and kept the rest of the stock themselves. Bezos took a traditional business—bookselling—online. He reasoned that books were fungible—everyone sold the same product—and that a portion of a traditional bookseller's cost represented the real estate on which the store sat. So Bezos lined up a distribution center in Oregon and began taking orders in cyberspace. Amazon.com sold its first book in July 1995.

Amazon.com became a success, at least at selling books. However, it was not a success at making a profit, and it lost money for years. But Bezo's business plan called for building a client base and making "Amazon.com" a readily recognized e-commerce name. He accomplished these goals, attracting a client base of over 10 million loyal book-buying customers and getting the Amazon.com brand name to be recognized by more than one-quarter of Americans. Like most startups, Amazon.com needed more seed money.

Undeterred by the company's unprofitableness, the venture capitalist firm Kleiner Perkins Caufield & Byer put up $10 million for preferred stock, which represented a 15 percent stake in Amazon.com.

Following on the heels of its book-selling success, Amazon.com began selling other products over the Internet, including CDs, videos, gifts, greeting cards, and thousands of other items. Amazon.com entered the world of online auctions; linked with other companies selling pet supplies, drugstore goods, and more; and agreed to pay fees of 4 to 8 percent to other Web site owners that linked a purchaser to Amazon.com. Purchasers pay Amazon.com by credit card, submitted over the telephone or the Web, and the transaction is guarded by encryption. Amazon.com offers one-click ordering, which lets buyers store credit card information and addresses after their first purchase.

After several years of operation and quick growth, Amazon.com needed more money to reach its goals. In May 1997, it went public, raising over $40 million by selling stock for $18 per share. The price of Amazon.com doubled on the first day of trading and reached $200 per share over the next year, before retreating. Bezos became a billionaire before the age of 34. Bezos and his family own about 40 percent of Amazon.com. In the span of less than five years, Bezos had taken his business plan and created the largest, most recognized e-commerce company in the world. This entrepreneur's dream became reality. But when asked if he feared Barnes & Noble's entry into online bookselling, Bezos replied that he feared "two guys or girls in a garage" more because they represented the most dangerous of competitors—entrepreneurs. ■

Sole Proprietorship

sole proprietorship
A form of business in which the owner is actually the business; the business is not a separate legal entity.

It is the spirit and not the form of law that keeps justice alive.
Earl Warren
The Law and the Future (1955)

Sole proprietorships are the simplest form of business organization. The owner is the business. There is no separate legal entity. Sole proprietorships are the most common form of business organization in the United States. Many small businesses—and a few large ones—operate in this way.

There are several major advantages to operating a business as a sole proprietorship. They include the following:

1. They are easy to form and have low costs.
2. The owner has the right to make all management decisions concerning the business, including those involving hiring and firing employees.

3. The sole proprietor owns all of the business and has the right to receive all of the business's profits.
4. A sole proprietorship can be easily transferred or sold if and when the owner desires to do so; no other approval (such as from partners or shareholders) is necessary.

There are important disadvantages to this business form, too. For example, (1) the sole proprietor's access to the capital is limited to personal funds plus any loans he or she can obtain, and (2) the sole proprietor is legally responsible for the business's contracts and the torts he or she or any of his or her employees commit in the course of employment.

Web Site

Small Business Administration (SBA) The SBA guarantees loans to small businesses and provides other resources. Visit at **www.sba.gov**.

Business Brief

Sole proprietorships are the most common form of business organization in the United States.

Creation of a Sole Proprietorship

It is easy to create a sole proprietorship. There are no formalities, and no federal or state government approval is required. Some local governments require all businesses, including sole proprietorships, to obtain licenses to do business within the city. If no other form of business organization is chosen, the business is by default a sole proprietorship.

Business Brief

A sole proprietorship is easy to form and requires no formal filing with state or federal government authorities.

Entrepreneur and the Law

d.b.a.—"Doing Business As"

A sole proprietorship can operate under the name of the sole proprietor or under a *trade name*. For example, the author of this book can operate a sole proprietorship under the name "Henry R. Cheeseman" or under a trade name such as "The Big Cheese." Operating under a trade name is commonly designated as a **d.b.a. (doing business as)** (e.g., Henry R. Cheeseman, d.b.a. The Big Cheese).

Most states require all businesses that operate under a trade name to file a **fictitious business name statement** (or **certificate of trade name**) with the appropriate government agency. The statement must contain the name and address of the applicant, the trade name, and the address of the business. Most states also require notice of the trade name to be published in a newspaper of general circulation serving the area in which the applicant does business.

These requirements are intended to disclose the real owner's name to the public. Noncompliance can result in a fine. Some states prohibit violators from maintaining lawsuits in the state's courts. A sample fictitious business name statement is shown in Exhibit 14.1. ■

Personal Liability of Sole Proprietors

The sole proprietor bears the risk of loss of the business; that is, the owner will lose his or her entire capital contribution if the business fails. In addition, the sole proprietor has *unlimited personal liability* (see Exhibit 14.2). Therefore, creditors may recover claims against the business from the sole proprietor's personal assets (e.g., home, automobile, and bank accounts).

Business Brief

A major detriment of operating a business as a sole proprietorship is that the owner is personally liable for the debts of the business.

Consider This Example Suppose Ken Smith opens a clothing store called "The Rap Shop" and operates it as a sole proprietorship. Smith files the proper statement and publishes the necessary notice of the use of the trade name. He contributes $25,000 of his personal funds to the business and borrows $100,000 in the name of the business from a bank. Assume that after several months Smith closes the business because it was unsuccessful. At the time it is closed, the business has no assets, owes the bank $100,000, and owes rent, trade credit, and other debts of $25,000. Here, Smith is personally liable to pay the bank and all of the debts from his personal assets.

There shall be one law for the native and for the stranger who sojourns among you.

Moses
Exodus 12:49

Exhibit 14.1

Sample Fictitious Business Name Statement

Return To:

Name: Kerry Fields, Esq.
Address: 115 S. Chaparral Court
City: Anaheim, CA 92808
Telephone # (714) 283-0140
Cust. Ref. # 53247

☒ First Filing ☐ Renewal Filing
Current Registration No.

PUBLISH IN:

COUNTY CLERK'S FILING STAMP

FICTITIOUS BUSINESS NAME STATEMENT

THE FOLLOWING PERSON(S) IS (ARE) DOING BUSINESS AS:

1 Fictitious Business Name(s)
The Big Cheese

2 Street address & Principal place of Business in California — Zip Code
1000 Exposition Boulevard — Los Angeles — California — 90089

3

Full name of Registrant		(if corporation - incorporated in what state)	
Henry R. Cheeseman			
Residence Address	City	State	Zip Code
575 Barrington Ave.	Los Angeles	California	90049
Full Name of Registrant		(if corporation - incorporated in what state)	
Residence Address	City	State	Zip Code
Full name of Registrant		(if corporation - incorporated in what state)	
Residence Address	City	State	Zip Code
Full name of Registrant		(if corporation - incorporated in what state)	
Residence Address	City	State	Zip Code

4 This Business is conducted by: (check one only)
(X) an Individual ( ) co-partners ( ) a general partnership ( ) husband and wife ( ) joint venture ( ) a corporation ( ) a business trust ( ) a limited partnership ( ) an unincorporated association other than a partnership ( ) other—(*please specify*) ________

5 The registrant commenced to transact business under the fictitious business name or names listed above on ________

6

a. Signed:

Henry R. Cheeseman (signature) — SIGNATURE
Henry R. Cheeseman — TYPE OR PRINT NAME

SIGNATURE — TYPE OR PRINT NAME

SIGNATURE — TYPE OR PRINT NAME

b. If Registrant a corporation sign below:

CORPORATION NAME

SIGNATURE & TITLE

TYPE OR PRINT NAME

This statement was filed with the County Clerk of Los Angeles County on date indicated by file stamp above.

NOTICE THIS FICTITIOUS NAME STATEMENT EXPIRES FIVE YEARS FROM THE DATE IT WAS FILED IN THE OFFICE OF THE COUNTY CLERK. A NEW FICTITIOUS BUSINESS NAME STATEMENT MUST BE FILED BEFORE THAT TIME. THE FILING OF THIS STATEMENT DOES NOT OF ITSELF AUTHORIZE THE USE IN THIS STATE OF A FICTITIOUS BUSINESS NAME IN VIOLATION OF THE RIGHTS OF ANOTHER UNDER FEDERAL, STATE, OR COMMON LAW (SEE SECTION 14400 ET SEQ., BUSINESS AND PROFESSIONS CODE).

I HEREBY CERTIFY THAT THIS COPY IS A CORRECT COPY OF THE ORIGINAL STATEMENT ON FILE IN MY OFFICE.

Helen Pitts
COUNTY CLERK

BY Deborah Cantrell DEPUTY

FILE NO. 081646

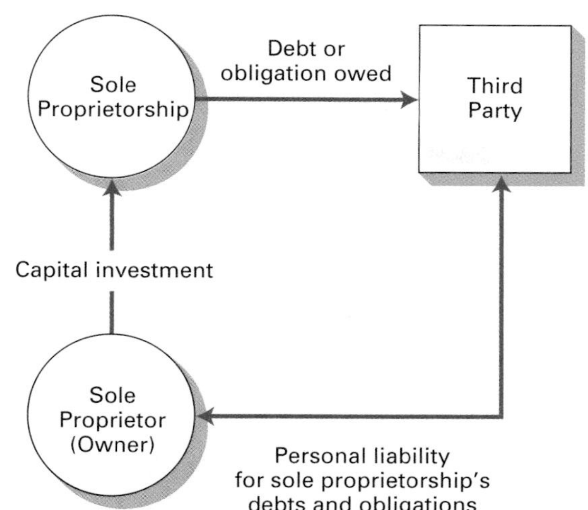

Exhibit 14.2
Sole Proprietorship

Entrepreneur and the Law

Sole Proprietorship and Sole Proprietor Are One and the Same

The law holds that a sole proprietorship is not a distinct legal entity. Instead, the sole proprietorship and the sole proprietor are one and the same. The following case demonstrates this principle.

James Schuster was a sole proprietor d.b.a. Diversity Heating and Plumbing. Diversity Heating was in the business of selling, installing, and servicing heating and plumbing systems. George Vernon and others (Vernon) owned a building that needed a new boiler. In November 1989, Vernon hired Diversity Heating to install a new boiler in the building. Diversity Heating installed the boiler and gave a warranty that the boiler would not crack for 10 years. On October 20, 1993, James Schuster died. On that date, James's son, Jerry Schuster, inherited his father's business and thereafter ran the business as a sole proprietorship as d.b.a. Diversity Heating and Plumbing. In February 1994, the boiler installed in Vernon's building broke and could not be repaired. Vernon demanded that Jerry Schuster honor the warranty and replace the boiler. When Jerry Schuster refused to do so, Vernon had the boiler replaced at a cost of $8,203 and sued Jerry Schuster to recover this amount for breach of warranty. The trial court dismissed Vernon's complaint, but the appellate court reinstated the case. Jerry Schuster appealed to the supreme court of Illinois. The issue presented to the supreme court was Is Jerry Schuster liable for the warranty made by his father?

The supreme court held that Jerry Schuster was not liable for the warranty made by his father. The court stated

> Common identity of ownership is lacking when one sole proprietorship succeeds another. It is well settled that a sole proprietorship has no legal identity separate from that of the individual who owns it. The sole proprietor may do business under a fictitious name if he or she chooses. However, doing business under another name does not create an entity distinct from the person operating the business. The individual who does business as a sole proprietor under one or several names remains one person, personally liable for all his or her obligations. There is generally no continuity of existence because on the death of the sole proprietor, the sole proprietorship obviously ends.
>
> In this case, therefore, it must be remembered that "Diversity Heating" has no legal existence. Diversity Heating was only a pseudonym for James Schuster. Once he died, Diversity Heating ceased to exist. Now, Diversity Heating is only a pseudonym for the defendant, Jerry Schuster. Once sole proprietor James Schuster died, he could not be the same sole proprietor as defendant Jerry Schuster who became a sole proprietor after his father's death. James Schuster and Jerry Schuster, one succeeding the other, cannot be the same entity. Even though defendant Jerry Schuster inherited Diversity Heating from his father, defendant would not have continued his father's sole proprietorship, but rather would have started a new sole proprietorship.

This case demonstrates the legal principle that a sole proprietorship has no legal status separate from its owner. The sole proprietorship and sole proprietor are one and the same. In this case, Vernon should have made a claim against the estate of James Schuster, the sole proprietor who made the warranty, and not against Jerry Schuster. [*Vernon v. Schuster, d/b/a/ Diversity Heating and Plumbing*, 688 N.E.2d 1172, 1997 Ill. Lexis 482 (IL 1997)] ■

Myanmar. Around the world many businesses are conducted as sole proprietorships.

International Law

Conducting International Business Using Agents, Representatives, and Distributors

A corporation organized in one country may wish to conduct business in other countries. To do so, it has a variety of choices available to it, depending on the extent of involvement and market penetration desired, the amount of capital to be invested, the legal and cultural restrictions of the foreign country, and so on. Several major forms of conducting business in a foreign country are by direct selling or by using sales agents, representatives, or distributors.

Direct Export and Import Sales

The simplest form of conducting international business is to engage in *direct export* or *import* sale. For example, if Ladera Corporation wishes to sell equipment overseas, it can merely enter into a contract with a company in a foreign country that wishes to buy the equipment. Ladera Corporation is the *exporter*, and the firm in the foreign country is the *importer*. If a U.S. company buys goods from a firm in a foreign country, the roles are reversed. The main benefits of conducting international business this way are that (1) it is inexpensive and (2) it usually involves just entering into contracts.

Sales Agents, Representatives, and Distributorships

Companies wishing to do business in a foreign country often appoint a local agent or representative to represent them in that country. A *sales representative* may solicit and take orders for his or her foreign employer but does not have the authority to bind the company contractually. A *sales agent*, on the other hand, may enter into contracts on his or her foreign employer's behalf. The scope of a sales agent's or representative's authority should be explicitly stated in the employment agreement. Sales agents and representatives do not take title to the goods. They are usually paid commissions for business that they generate.

Another commonly used form for engaging in international sales is through a *foreign distributor*. Often, the distributor is a local firm that is separate and independent from the exporter. A distributor is usually given an exclusive territory (e.g., a country or portion of a country). A distributor takes title to the goods and makes a profit on the resale of the goods in the foreign country. A foreign distributor generally is used when a company wants a greater presence in a foreign market than is possible through a sales agent or representative. ■

franchise

An arrangement that is established when one party licenses another party to use the franchisor's trade name, trademarks, commercial symbols, patents, copyrights, and other property in the distribution and selling of goods and services.

Franchises

A **franchise** is established when one party (the **franchisor** or **licensor**) licenses another party (the *franchisee* or *licensee*) to use the franchisor's trade name, trademarks, commercial symbols, patents, copyrights, and other property in the distribution and selling of goods

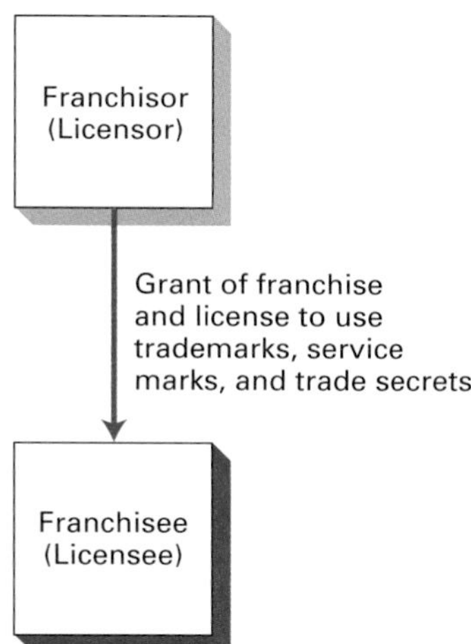

Exhibit 14.3

Parties to a Typical Franchise Arrangement

and services. Generally, the franchisor and the franchisee are established as separate corporations. The term *franchise* refers to both the agreement between the parties and the franchise outlet.

There are several advantages to franchising, including (1) the franchisor can reach lucrative new markets, (2) the franchisee has access to the franchisor's knowledge and resources while running an independent business, and (3) consumers are assured of uniform product quality.

A typical franchise arrangement is illustrated in Exhibit 14.3.

Types of Franchises

There are three basic forms of franchises. They are discussed in the paragraphs that follow.

Distributorship Franchises In a **distributorship franchise**, the franchisor manufactures a product and licenses a retail dealer to distribute the product to the public. For example, the Ford Motor Company manufactures automobiles and franchises independently owned automobile dealers (franchisees) to sell them to the public.

distributorship franchise
A franchise in which the franchisor manufactures a product and licenses a retail franchisee to distribute the product to the public.

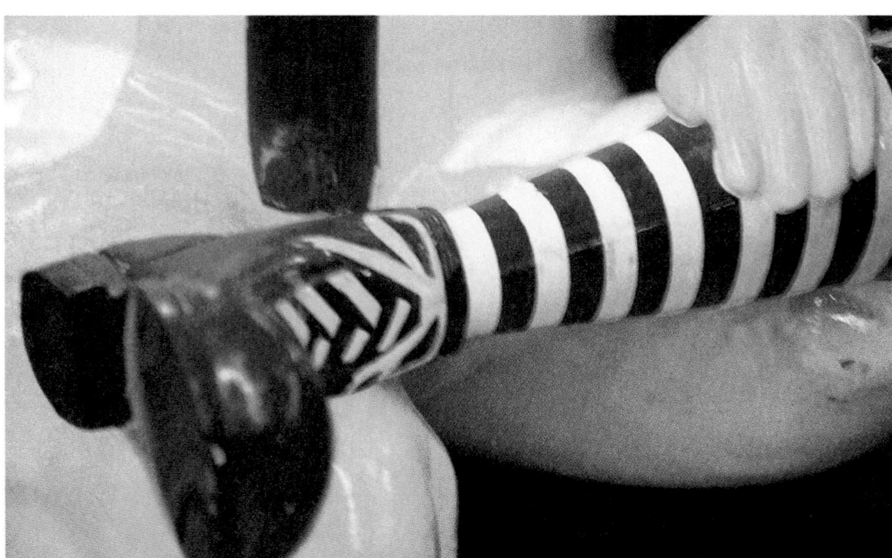

Franchise Outlet. Franchising is a major form of business in the United States.

processing plant franchise
A franchise in which the franchisor provides a secret formula or process to the franchisee, and the franchisee manufactures the product and distributes it to retail dealers.

Processing Plant Franchise In a **processing plant franchise**, the franchisor provides a secret formula or the like to the franchisee. The franchisee then manufactures the product at its own location and distributes it to retail dealers. For example, the Coca-Cola Corporation, which owns the secret formulas for making Coca-Cola and other soft drinks, licenses regional bottling companies to manufacture and distribute soft drinks under the name "Coca-Cola" and other brand names.

chain-style franchise
A franchise in which the franchisor licenses the franchisee to make and sell its products or distribute services to the public from a retail outlet serving an exclusive territory.

Chain-Style Franchises In a **chain-style franchise**, the franchisor licenses the franchisee to make and sell its products or services to the public from a retail outlet serving an exclusive geographical territory. Most fast-food franchises use this form. For example, the Pizza Hut Corporation franchises independently owned restaurant franchises to make and sell pizzas to the public under the "Pizza Hut" name.

International Law

Starbucks Invades the World

Starbucks Coffee has been a tremendous success in the United States. Beginning with a single outlet in Seattle, Washington, the company has expanded Starbucks Coffee shops across the country. Now even some of the smaller cities in America have Starbucks Coffee shops. The company expanded in the United States through company-owned stores; that is, Starbucks had not granted franchises in the United States.

When Starbucks wanted to enter overseas markets, however, it realized it could not expand solely through company-owned outlets. This was because (1) government restrictions in some countries prohibit 100 percent ownership of a business by a foreign investor and (2) the company lacked the business expertise and cultural knowledge necessary to enter many foreign markets. To enter foreign markets, Starbucks turned to franchising.

After substantial research and investigation, Starbucks decided it would grant **area franchises** to local foreign companies to develop Starbucks outlets in these countries. In an area franchise, the franchisor grants the franchisee a franchise for an agreed-upon geographical area. The local foreign company then determines where to locate Starbucks outlets in its assigned territory. The foreign company pays Starbucks for the area franchise.

An area franchise is usually granted the authority to negotiate and sell franchises in the designated area on behalf of the franchisor. In this arrangement, the franchisee is also called the *subfranchisor* (see Exhibit 14.4).

Franchising and the use of area franchises allow major U.S. companies, and companies around the world, to enter foreign markets more easily, efficiently, and economically than would expanding to many foreign countries through company-owned outlets. ■

Exhibit 14.4
Example of an Area Franchise

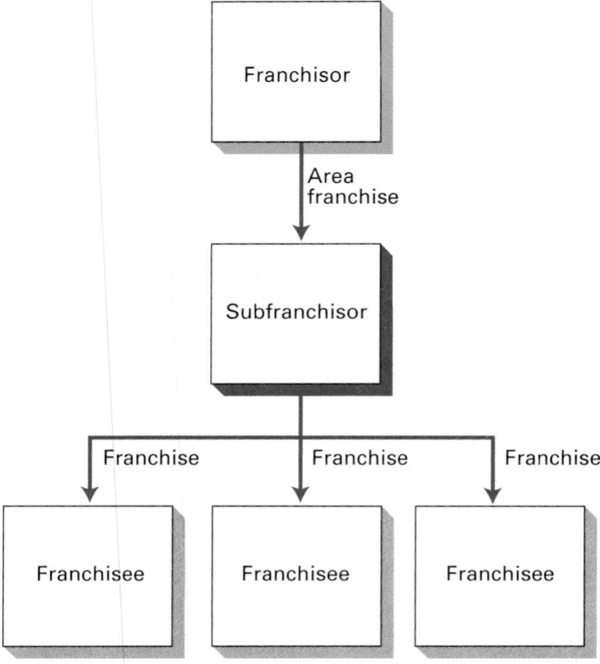

Disclosure Protection

In the past, certain franchisors made material misrepresentations and omissions of facts to potential franchisees concerning the financial future of their franchises. Since then, the **Federal Trade Commission (FTC)** and many states have enacted laws that promote full disclosure to prospective franchisees.

Federal Trade Commission (FTC)
A federal government agency empowered to enforce federal franchising rules.

State Disclosure Laws Prior to the 1970s, franchising was not highly regulated by either state or federal governments. In 1971, California enacted its *Franchise Investment Law*,[1] which requires franchisors to register and deliver disclosure documents to prospective franchisees. Since then, many other states have enacted franchise disclosure statutes. For a while, franchisors struggled to comply with the various state statutes. Finally, in the mid-1970s, state franchise administrators developed a uniform disclosure document called the **Uniform Franchise Offering Circular (UFOC)**.

The UFOC and state laws require the franchisor to make specific presale disclosures to prospective franchisees. Information that must be disclosed includes a description of the franchisor's business, balance sheets and income statements of the franchisor for the preceding three years, material terms of the franchise agreement, any restrictions on the franchisee's territory, grounds for termination of the franchise, and other relevant information.

Uniform Franchise Offering Circular (UFOC)
A uniform disclosure document that requires the franchisor to make specific presale disclosures to prospective franchisees.

FTC's Franchise Rule In 1979, the **FTC franchise rule** became law. The FTC rule requires franchisors to make full presale disclosure nationwide to prospective franchisees.[2] The FTC does not require the registration of the disclosure document prior to its use. The UFOC satisfies both state regulations and the FTC. If a franchisor violates FTC disclosure rules, the wrongdoer is subject to an injunction against further franchise sales, civil fines of up to $10,000 per violation, and an FTC civil action on behalf of injured franchisees to recover damages from the franchisor that were caused by the violation.

FTC franchise rule
A rule set out by the FTC that requires franchisors to make full presale disclosures to prospective franchisees.

Entrepreneur and the Law

Required Disclosures by Franchisors to Prospective Franchisees

Many potential franchisees are entrepreneurs who want to own and operate their own business. Franchisors, on the other hand, are looking for potential franchisees to whom to sell their franchises. In the past, there has been some fraud by franchisors and failure to disclose important information to prospective franchisees. To remedy this situation, the FTC has adopted the following rules.

First, if a franchisor makes sales or earnings projections for a potential franchise location that is based on the actual sales, income, or profit figures of an existing franchise, the franchisor must disclose the following:

- The number and percentage of its actual franchises that have obtained such results; and
- A cautionary statement in at least 12-point boldface type that reads **"Caution: Some outlets have sold (or earned) this amount. There is no assurance you'll do as well. If you rely upon our figures, you must accept the risk of not doing so well."**

Second, if a franchisor makes sales or earnings projections based on hypothetical examples, the franchisor must disclose the following:

- The assumptions underlying the estimates;
- The number and percentage of actual franchises that have obtained such results; and
- A cautionary statement in at least 12-point boldface print that reads **"Caution: These figures are only estimates of what we think you may earn. There is no assurance you'll do as well. If you rely upon our figures, you must accept the risk of not doing so well."**

Third, the FTC requires that the following statement appear in at least 12-point boldface type on the cover of a franchisor's required disclosure statement to prospective franchisees:

> To protect you, we've required your franchisor to give you this information.

Entrepreneur and the Law (continued)

We haven't checked it, and don't know if it's correct. It should help you make up your mind. Study it carefully. While it includes some information about your contract, don't rely on it alone to understand your contract. Read all of your contract carefully. Buying a franchise is a complicated investment. Take your time to decide. If possible, show your contract and this information to an adviser, like a lawyer or an accountant. If you find anything you think may be wrong or anything important that's been left out, you should let us know about it. It may be against the law. There may also be laws on franchising in your state. Ask your state agencies about them.

The FTC hopes that the required disclosures by franchisors will protect prospective entrepreneur-franchisees from fraud and from acting on insufficient information. ■

The Franchise Agreement

franchise agreement
An agreement that a franchisor and a franchisee enter into that sets forth the terms and conditions of the franchise.

A prospective franchisee must apply to the franchisor for a franchise. The application often includes detailed information about the applicant's previous employment, financial and educational history, credit status, and so on. If an applicant is approved, the parties enter into a **franchise agreement** that sets forth the terms and conditions of the franchise. Although some states permit oral franchise agreements, most have enacted a Statute of Frauds that requires franchise agreements to be in writing. To prevent unjust enrichment, the courts will occasionally enforce oral franchise agreements that violate the Statute of Frauds.

Common Terms of a Franchise Agreement

Business Brief
The public expects each franchisee of a franchisor to sell products or services of a similar quality. If one franchisee sells products or services of a lesser quality, it reflects on the entire franchise. Therefore, a franchisor should set exacting quality control standards in the franchise agreement.

Web Site
The Franchise Handbook Online
This Web site contains articles on franchising, lists of worldwide franchise associations, and a directory of business opportunities. Visit at **www.franchise1.com**.

Franchise agreements do not usually have much room for negotiation. Generally, the agreement is a standard form contract prepared by the franchisor. Franchise agreements cover the following topics:

1. ***Quality Control Standards*** The franchisor's most important assets are its name and reputation. The quality control standards set out in the franchise agreement—such as the franchisor's right to make periodic inspections of the franchisee's premises and operations—are intended to protect these assets. Failure to meet the proper standards can result in loss of the franchise.
2. ***Training Requirements*** Franchisees and their personnel usually are required to attend training programs either on-site or at the franchisor's training facilities.
3. ***Covenant Not to Compete*** Covenants not to compete prohibit franchisees from competing with the franchisor during a specific time and in a specified area after the termination of the franchise. Unreasonable (overextensive) covenants not to compete are void.
4. ***Arbitration Clause*** Most franchise agreements contain an arbitration clause that provides that any claim or controversy arising from the franchise agreement or an alleged breach thereof is subject to arbitration. The U.S. Supreme Court has held such clauses to be enforceable.[3]
5. ***Other Terms and Conditions*** Capital requirements, including the following, are included in the agreement: restrictions on the use of the franchisor's trade name, trademarks, and logo; standards of operation; duration of the franchise; recordkeeping requirements; sign requirements; hours of operation; prohibition as to the sale or assignment of the franchise; conditions for the termination of the franchise; and other specific terms pertinent to the operation of the franchise and the protection of the parties' rights.

Japan. The major growth in franchising opportunities for U.S. franchisors, such as McDonald's, is in international markets.

Franchise Fees

Franchise fees payable by the franchisee are usually stipulated in the franchise agreement. The franchisor may require the franchisee to pay any or all of the following fees:

1. ***Initial License Fee*** A lump-sum payment for the privilege of being granted a franchise.
2. ***Royalty Fee*** A fee for the continued use of the franchisor's trade name, property, and assistance that is often computed as a percentage of the franchisee's gross sales.
3. ***Assessment Fee*** A fee for such things as advertising and promotional campaigns and administrative costs, billed either as a flat monthly fee or an annual fee or as a percentage of gross sales.
4. ***Lease Fees*** Payment for any land or equipment leased from the franchisor, billed either as a flat monthly fee or an annual fee or as a percentage of gross sales or other agreed-upon amount.
5. ***Cost of Supplies*** Payment for supplies purchased from the franchisor.

Sample provisions from a franchise agreement are set forth in Exhibit 14.5.

Business Brief

A franchisee should be careful to understand the fees he or she is responsible for paying to the franchisor pursuant to the franchise agreement.

Web Site

International Franchise Association At the International Franchise Association site, you can search by company name, category, investment range, and location. This site serves as a resource center for current and prospective franchisees and franchisors. Visit at **www.franchise.org**.

Exhibit 14.5

Sample Provisions from a Franchise Agreement

FRANCHISE AGREEMENT

Agreement, this 2nd day of January, 2004, between ALASKA PANCAKE HOUSE, INC., an Alaska corporation located in Anchorage, Alaska (hereinafter called the Company) and PANCAKE SYRUP COMPANY, INC., a Michigan corporation located in Detroit, Michigan (hereinafter called the Franchisee), for one KLONDIKE PANCAKE HOUSE restaurant to be located in the City of Mackinac Island, Michigan.

RECITALS

A. The Company is the owner of proprietary and other rights and interests in various service marks, trademarks, and trade names used in its business including the trade name and service mark "KLONDIKE PANCAKE HOUSE."

B. The Company operates and enfranchises others to operate restaurants under the trade name and service mark "KLONDIKE PANCAKE HOUSE" using certain recipes, formulas, food preparation procedures, business methods, business forms, and business policies it has developed. The Company has also developed a body of knowledge pertaining to the establishment and operation of restaurants. The Franchisee acknowledges that he does not presently know these recipes, formulas, food preparation procedures, business methods, or business policies, nor does the Franchisee have these business forms or access to the Company's body of knowledge.

C. The Franchisee intends to enter the restaurant business and desires access to the Company's recipes, formulas, food preparation procedures, business methods, business forms, business policies, and body of knowledge pertaining to the operation of a restaurant. In addition, the Franchisee desires access to information pertaining to new developments and techniques in the Company's restaurant business.

D. The Franchisee desires to participate in the use of the Company's rights in its service marks and trademarks in connection with the operation of one restaurant to be located at a site approved by the Company and the Franchisee.

E. The Franchisee understands that information received from the Company or from any of its officers, employees, agents, or franchisees is confidential and has been developed with a great deal of effort and expense. The Franchisee acknowledges that the information is being made available to him so that he may more effectively establish and operate a restaurant.

F. The Company has granted, and will continue to grant others, access to its recipes, formulas, food preparation procedures, business methods, business forms, business policies, and body of knowledge pertaining to the operation of restaurants and information pertaining to new developments and techniques in its business.

G. The Company has and will continue to license others to use its service marks and trademarks in connection with the operation of restaurants at Company-approved locations.

H. The Franchise Fee and Royalty constitute the sole consideration to the Company for the use by the Franchisee of its body of knowledge, systems, and trademark rights.

I. The Franchisee acknowledges that he received the Company's franchise offering prospectus at or prior to the first personal meeting with a Company representative and at least ten (10) business days prior to the signing of this Agreement and that he has been given the opportunity to clarify provisions he did not understand and to consult with an attorney or other professional advisor. Franchisee represents he understands and agrees to be bound by the terms, conditions, and obligations of this Agreement.

J. The Franchisee acknowledges that he understands that the success of the business to be operated by him under this Agreement depends primarily upon his efforts and that neither the Company nor any of its agents or representatives have made any oral, written, or visual representations or projections of actual or potential sales, earnings, or net or gross profits. Franchisee understands that the restaurant operated under this Agreement may lose money or fail.

AGREEMENT

Acknowledging the above recitals, the parties hereto agree as follows:

1. Upon execution of this Agreement, the Franchisee shall pay to the Company a Franchise Fee of $30,000 that shall not be refunded in any event.
2. The Franchisee shall also pay to the Company, weekly, a Royalty equal to eight (8%) percent of the gross sales from each restaurant that he operates throughout the term of this Agreement. "Gross sales" means all sales or revenues derived from the Franchisee's location exclusive of sales taxes.
3. The Company hereby grants to the Franchisee:
   a. Access to the Company's recipes, formulas, food preparation procedures, business methods, business forms, business policies, and body of knowledge pertaining to the operation of a restaurant.
   b. Access to information pertaining to new developments and techniques in the Company's restaurant business.
   c. License to use of the Company's rights in and to its service marks and trademarks in connection with the operation of one restaurant to be located at a site approved by the Company and the Franchisee.
4. The Company agrees to:
   a. Provide a training program for the operator of restaurants using the Company's recipes, formulas, food preparation procedures, business methods, business forms, and business policies. The Franchisee shall pay all transportation, lodging, and other expenses incurred in attending the program. The Franchisee must attend the training program before opening his restaurant.
   b. Provide a Company Representative that the Franchisee may call upon for consultation concerning the operation of his business.
   c. Provide the Franchise with a program of assistance that shall include periodic consultations with a Company Representative, publish a periodical advising of new developments and techniques in the Company's restaurant business, and grant access to Company personnel for consultations concerning the operation of his business.
5. The Franchisee agrees to:
   a. Begin operation of a restaurant within 365 days. The restaurant will be at a location found by the Franchisee and approved by the Company. The Company or one of its designees will lease the premises and sublet them to the Franchisee at cost. The Franchisee will then construct and equip his unit in accordance with Company specifications contained in the Operating Manual. Upon written request from the Franchisee, the Company will grant a 180-day extension that is effective immediately upon receipt of the request. Under certain circumstances, and at the sole discretion of the Company, the Company may grant additional time in which to open the business. In all instances, the location of each unit must be approved by the Company and the Franchisee. If the restaurant is not operating within 365 days, or within any approved extensions, this Agreement will automatically expire.
   b. Operate his business in compliance with applicable laws and governmental regulations. The Franchisee will obtain at his expense, and keep in force, any permits, licenses, or other consents required for the leasing, construction, or operation of his business. In addition, the Franchisee shall operate his restaurant in accordance with the Company's Operation Manual, which may be amended from time to time as a result of experience, changes in the law, or changes in the marketplace. The Franchisee shall refrain from conducting any business or selling any products other than those approved by the Company at the approved location.
   c. Be responsible for all costs of operating his unit, including but not limited to, advertising, taxes, insurance, food products, labor, and utilities. Insurance shall include, but not be limited to, comprehensive liability insurance including products liability coverage in the minimum amount of $1,000,000. The Franchisee shall keep these policies in force for the mutual benefit of the parties. In addition, the Franchisee shall save the Company harm from any claim of any type that arises in connection with the operation of his business.

Breach of the Franchise Agreement

A lawful franchise agreement is an enforceable contract. Each party owes a duty to adhere to and perform under the terms of the franchise agreement. If the agreement is breached, the aggrieved party can sue the breaching party for rescission of the agreement, restitution, and damages.

Business Brief

If a franchise agreement is breached, the aggrieved party can sue the breaching party for rescission of the agreement, restitution, and damages.

Business Ethics

Häagen-Dazs Ice Cream Franchise Melts

Franchise agreements are detailed documents that are carefully drafted to spell out the rights and duties of the parties. A franchisee must be careful to read and understand the terms of the agreement, as the following case demonstrates.

In the late 1950s, Reuben Mattus developed a "super premium" ice cream and named it "Häagen-Dazs" to give the product a Scandinavian flair. Mattus began selling Häagen-Dazs ice cream in prepackaged pints to small stores and delicatessens in the New York metropolitan area. During the 1970s, sales of the product were expanded into some grocery stores and other retail outlets.

In 1976, Mattus's daughter, Doris Mattus-Hurley, opened the first "Häagen-Dazs Shoppe" in Brooklyn Heights, New York. After this shop prospered, Mattus-Hurley began franchising other shops to independent franchisees throughout the country. Häagen-Dazs ice cream is manufactured, distributed, and franchised through a variety of corporate entities (collectively referred to as Häagen-Dazs). The franchise agreement, which has been the same since 1978, grants a limited license to the franchisee to operate a single shop under the Häagen-Dazs trademark at a specific location for a specified term, ranging from 5 to 12 years. The franchisee agrees to purchase all its ice cream from the franchisor at prices set by Häagen-Dazs.

In 1983, the Pillsbury Company (Pillsbury), a diversified international food and restaurant company headquartered in Minneapolis, Minnesota, purchased the Häagen-Dazs Company, including its franchise operations. The franchise agreements were assigned to Pillsbury as part of the sale. Pillsbury decided that it could maximize sales of Häagen-Dazs ice cream by expanding sales through methods of distribution that did not involve franchises. Pillsbury substantially increased sales of Häagen-Dazs products to national grocery store chains, convenience stores such as 7-Eleven, and other retail outlets.

This change severely harmed sales at existing franchises. Franchisees located in many states sued Pillsbury, alleging breach of the franchise agreement. Plaintiffs claimed that the defendant breached the franchise agreement by distributing Häagen-Dazs ice cream through nonfranchised outlets that were not "upscale" and by mass distribution of prepackaged pints that competed with franchise outlet sales.

The district court held that the express terms of the franchise agreement had not been violated. The franchise agreement expressly reserved the right of the franchisor to distribute Häagen-Dazs products "through not only Häagen-Dazs Shoppes, but through any other distribution method, which may from time to time be established." The court held that this language gave Pillsbury the right to aggressively distribute prepackaged pints of Häagen-Dazs ice cream through nonfranchise outlets, even though that distribution adversely affected retail sales by franchisees. The district court granted Pillsbury's motion for summary judgment. [*Carlock v. Pillsbury Company*, 719 F.Supp. 791, 1989 U.S. Dist. Lexis 9370 (D. Minn. 1989)]

1. Even though the express terms of the franchise agreement allowed Pillsbury to distribute Häagen-Dazs ice cream through nonfranchise outlets, do you think Pillsbury acted ethically in doing so?
2. Should a covenant of good faith and fair dealing be implied in franchise agreements? Why or why not?

Trademark Law, Trade Secrets, and Franchising

A franchisor's ability to maintain the public's perception of the quality of the goods and services associated with its trade name, **trademarks**, and **service marks** is the essence of its success. The sizes of the advertising budgets of many franchisors supports this view.

trademarks and service marks

Distinctive marks, symbols, names, words, mottoes, or devices that identify the goods or services of a particular franchisor.

Trademarks The **Lanham Trademark Act**, which was enacted in 1946, provides for the registration of trademarks and service marks with the federal **Patent and Trademark Office** in Washington, D.C. Most franchisors license the use of their trade names, trademarks, and service marks and prohibit their franchisees from misusing these marks.

Anyone who uses a mark without authorization may be sued for *trademark infringement*. The trademark holder can sue to recover damages and obtain an injunction prohibiting further unauthorized use of the mark.

trade secrets
Ideas that make a franchise successful but that do not qualify for trademark, patent, or copyright protection.

Misappropriation of Trade Secrets **Trade secrets** are ideas that make a franchise successful but that do not qualify for trademark, patent, or copyright protection. Most state laws protect trade secrets.

The misappropriation of a trade secret is called *unfair competition*. The holder of the trade secret can sue the offending party for damages and obtain an injunction to prohibit further unauthorized use of the trade secret.

Business Ethics

Franchisee's Fraudulent Scoop Caught

Baskin-Robbins Ice Cream Company (Baskin-Robbins) is a franchisor that has established a system of more than 2,700 franchise ice cream retail stores nationwide. The franchisees agree to purchase ice cream in bulk only from Baskin-Robbins or an authorized Baskin-Robbins source, to sell only Baskin-Robbins ice cream under the "Baskin-Robbins" marks, and to keep specific business hours. Franchisees agree to pay ice cream invoices to Baskin-Robbins when due. If ice cream invoices are not paid within seven days of delivery of the ice cream, payment by certified check is required. If such check is not received, prepayment in cash is then required. If Baskin-Robbins must institute a lawsuit for a breach of franchise agreement, the franchisee is required to pay all costs incurred by Baskin-Robbins if it is successful in lawsuit.

In 1978, Baskin-Robbins entered into a standard Franchise Agreement with D&L Ice Cream Company, Inc., (D&L), granting it a franchise to operate a retail ice cream store in Brooklyn, New York. During the course of the franchise, D&L consistently failed to maintain proper business hours and failed to satisfy ice cream invoices when due. Baskin-Robbins properly invoked its right to require payment by certified check. When such payment was not received, Baskin-Robbins required prepayment for ice cream deliveries. D&L then purchased bulk ice cream from other manufacturers and sold it in its store, bearing the Baskin-Robbins trademarks. Upon discovering this fact, Baskin-Robbins sent a notice of termination to D&L. D&L ignored the notice and continued to operate the Baskin-Robbins store and sell other brands of ice cream in cups and containers bearing the Baskin-Robbins trademarks. Baskin-Robbins sued D&L for trademark infringement.

The court stated that the sale by a franchised licensee of unauthorized products—that is, products outside the scope of the license—is likely to confuse the public into believing that such products are in fact manufactured or authorized by the trademark owner, when in fact they are not. The court concluded that D&L had engaged in trademark infringement. The court held that Baskin-Robbins was entitled to a permanent injunction, to recover outstanding monies owed by D&L, to all profits made by D&L as a result of the trademark infringement, and to full costs and attorneys' fees incurred in connection with this litigation. [*Baskin-Robbins Ice Cream Co. v. D&L Ice Cream Co., Inc.,* 576 F.Supp. 1055, 1983 U.S. Dist. Lexis 11057 (E.D. N.Y. 1983)]

1. Did D&L act ethically in this case?
2. Do you think there was trademark infringement in this case? ■

Contract and Tort Liability of Franchisors and Franchisees

Business Brief
Franchisors and franchisees are liable for their own contracts and torts.

Franchisors and franchisees are liable for their own *contracts*. The same is true of *tort liability*. For example, if a person is injured by a franchisee's negligence, the franchisee is liable.

In the following case, the court held that a franchisor was directly liable to the plaintiffs.

Case 14.1 Franchisor's Tort Liability

Martin v. McDonald's Corporation
572 N.E.2d 1073, 1991 Ill.App. Lexis 715 (1991)
Appellate Court of Illinois

Background and Facts

McDonald's Corporation (McDonald's) is a franchisor that licenses franchisees to operate fast-food restaurants and to use McDonald's trademarks and service marks. One such franchise, which was located in Oak Forest, Illinois, was owned and operated by McDonald's Restaurants of Illinois, the franchisee.

Recognizing the threat of armed robbery at its franchises, especially in the time period immediately after closing, McDonald's established an entire corporate division to deal with security problems at franchises. McDonald's prepared a manual for restaurant security operations and required its franchisees to adhere to these procedures.

Jim Carlson was the McDonald's regional security manager for the area in which the Oak Forest franchise was located. Carlson visited the Oak Forest franchise on October 31, 1979, to inform the manager of security procedures. He specifically mentioned these rules: (1) No one should throw garbage out the back door after dark and (2) trash and grease were to be taken out the side glass door at least one hour prior to closing. During his inspection, Carlson noted that the locks had to be changed at the restaurant, and an alarm system needed to be installed for the back door. Carlson never followed up to determine whether these security measures had been taken.

On the evening of November 29, 1979, a six-woman crew, all teenagers, was working to clean up and close the Oak Forest restaurant. Laura Martin, Therese Dudek, and Maureen Kincaid were members of that crew. A person later identified as Peter Logan appeared at the back of the restaurant with a gun. He ordered the crew to open the safe and get him the money and then ordered them into the refrigerator. In the course of moving the crew into the refrigerator, Logan shot and killed Martin and assaulted Dudek and Kincaid. Dudek and Kincaid suffered severe emotional distress from the assault.

Evidence showed that Logan had entered the restaurant through the back door. Trial testimony proved that the work crew used the back door exclusively, both before and after dark, and emptied garbage and grease through the back door all day and all night. In addition, there was evidence that the latch on the back door did not work properly. Evidence also showed that the crew had not been instructed about the use of the back door after dark and had never received copies of the McDonald's security manual, and that the required warning about not using the back door after dark had not been posted at the restaurant.

Martin's parents, Dudek, and Kincaid sued McDonald's to recover damages for negligence. The trial court awarded damages of $1,003,445 to the Martins for the wrongful death of their daughter, and it awarded $125,000 each to Dudek and Kincaid. McDonald's appealed.

Issue

Is McDonald's liable for negligence?

In The Language of The Court

McNulty, Judge The trial court correctly determined that McDonald's Corporation had a duty to protect plaintiffs Laura Martin, Maureen Kincaid, and Therese Dudek from harm. Although it did not specifically state that such duty was "assumed," there is ample support in case law and the facts of this case to support a determination that McDonald's Corporation voluntarily assumed a duty to provide security to plaintiffs and protect them from harm.

Once McDonald's Corporation assumed the duty to provide security and protection to plaintiffs, it had the obligation to perform this duty with due care and competence, and any failure to do so would lead to a finding of breach of duty. Accordingly, there was ample evidence for the jury to determine that McDonald's had breached its assumed duty to plaintiffs.

Decision and Remedy

The appellate court held that McDonald's was negligent for not following up and making sure that the security deficiencies it had found at the Oak Forest franchise had been corrected. Affirmed.

Case Questions

Critical Legal Thinking Should businesses be held liable for criminal actions of others? Why or why not?

Business Ethics Should McDonald's have denied liability in this case?

Contemporary Business What is the benefit to a franchisor to establish and require its franchisees to adhere to security rules? Is there any potential detriment? Explain.

Independent Contractor Status

If properly organized and operated, the franchisor and franchisee are separate legal entities. Therefore, the franchisor deals with the franchisee as an *independent contractor*. Because there is no agency relationship, neither party is liable for the contracts or torts of the other.

In the following case, the court applied the independent contractor rule and held that the franchisor was not liable for the tortious conduct of a franchisee.

Business Brief

If properly organized and operated as a separate business, a franchisee is not the agent of the franchisor, and the franchisor is not liable for the franchisee's contracts or torts.

Case 14.2

Franchisee as an Independent Contractor

Cislaw v. Southland Corp.
4 Cal.App.4th 1284, 6 Cal.Rptr.2d 386, 1992 Cal.App. Lexis 375 (1992)
Court of Appeals of California

Background and Facts

The Southland Corporation (Southland) owns the "7-Eleven" trademark and licenses franchisees to operate convenience stores using this trademark. Each franchise is independently owned and operated. The franchise agreement stipulates that the franchisee is an independent contractor who is authorized to make all inventory, employment, and operational decisions for the franchise.

Timothy Cislaw, 17 years old, died of respiratory failure on May 10, 1984. His parents filed a wrongful death action against the franchise and Southland, alleging that Timothy's death resulted from his consumption of Djarum Specials (clove cigarettes) sold at a Costa Mesa, California, 7-Eleven franchise store. The Costa Mesa 7-Eleven was franchised to Charles Trujillo and Patricia Colwell-Trujillo. After answering the complaint, Southland moved for summary judgment, arguing that it was not liable for the alleged tortious conduct of its franchisee because the franchisee was an independent contractor. The plaintiffs alleged that the franchisee was Southland's agent, and therefore Southland was liable for its agent's alleged negligence of selling the clove cigarettes to their son. The trial court granted Southland's motion. The Cislaws appealed.

Issue

Was the Costa Mesa franchisee an agent of Southland?

In The Language of The Court

Sonenshine, Associate Justice In this field of franchise agreements, the question of whether the franchisee is an independent contractor or an agent is ordinarily one of fact, depending on whether the franchisor exercises complete or substantial control over the franchisee.

Colwell-Trujillo said that, as provided under the franchise agreement, she exercised "full and complete control over" the store's employees and "any and all labor relations," including "hiring, firing, disciplining, compensation and work schedules." She attested, "I could purchase whatever inventory I chose and from whomever I wanted and I did so." She decided how much of any particular item to order, how frequently to order it, and what to charge for it. Colwell-Trujillo stated, "Southland had no control over my decision to sell or not sell clove cigarettes at the store. It was my sole decision to sell clove cigarettes. I alone set the prices. In no way did Southland ever advertise, promote or merchandise the clove cigarettes sold in my store."

The agreement recites that the franchisees are independent contractors, and two provisions give the Trujillos the right to make all inventory, employment and operational decisions. The Cislaws were not entitled to proceed to trial.

Decision and Remedy

The court of appeals held that the Costa Mesa 7-Eleven franchise was not an agent of Southland but was an independent contractor. Affirmed.

Case Questions

Critical Legal Thinking Should franchisors be automatically held liable for the tortious conduct of their franchisees? Why or why not?

Business Ethics Did the Cislaws act ethically in suing Southland?

Contemporary Business How careful must a franchisor be to retain enough control to protect the quality of the goods and services sold by its franchisees but not to retain too much control so as to become liable for the actions of its franchisees?

Agency Status

If the franchisee is the *actual* or *apparent agent* of the franchisor, the franchisor is responsible for the torts and contracts the franchise committed or entered into within the scope of the agency. **Apparent agency** is created when a frachisor leads a third party into believing that the franchisee is its agent. For example, a franchisor and franchisee who use the same trade name and trademarks and make no effort to inform the public of their separate legal status may find themselves in such a situation. However, mere use of the same name does not automatically make the franchisor liable for the franchisee's actions.

apparent agency
Agency that arises when a franchisor creates the appearance that a franchisee is its agent when in fact an actual agency does not exist.

In the following case, the court found that a franchisee was the apparent agent of the franchisor, thereby making the franchisor liable for the tortious conduct of the franchisee.

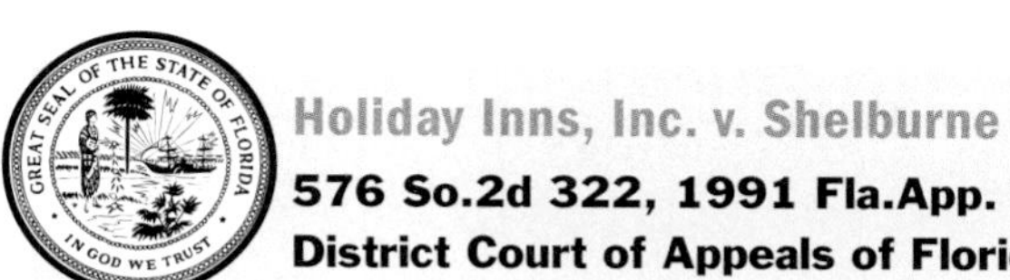

Case 14.3 Franchisor as an Apparent Agent

Holiday Inns, Inc. v. Shelburne
576 So.2d 322, 1991 Fla.App. Lexis 585 (1991)
District Court of Appeals of Florida

Background and Facts

Holiday Inns, Inc. (Holiday Inns), is a franchisor that licenses franchisees to operate hotels using its trademarks and service marks. Holiday Inns licensed Hospitality Venture to operate a franchised hotel in Fort Pierce, Florida. The Rodeo Bar, which had a reputation as the "hottest bar in town," was located in the hotel.

The Fort Pierce Holiday Inn and Rodeo Bar did not have sufficient parking, so security guards posted in the Holiday Inn parking lot required Rodeo Bar patrons to park in vacant lots that surrounded the hotel but that were not owned by the hotel. The main duty of the guards was to keep the parking lot open for hotel guests. Two unarmed security guards were on duty on the night in question. One guard was drinking on the job, and the other was an untrained temporary fill-in.

The record disclosed that although the Rodeo bar had a capacity of 240 people, the bar regularly admitted 270 to 300 people, with 50 to 75 people waiting outside. Fights occurred all the time in the bar and the parking lots, and often there were three or four fights a night. Police reports involving 58 offenses, including several weapons charges and battery and assault charges, had been filed during the previous 18 months.

On the night in question, the two groups involved in the altercation did not leave the Rodeo Bar until closing time. According to the record, these individuals exchanged remarks as they moved toward their respective vehicles in the vacant parking lots adjacent to the Holiday Inn. Ultimately, a fight erupted. The evidence shows that during the course of physical combat, Mr. Carter shot David Rice, Scott Turner, and Robert Shelburne. Rice died from his injuries.

Rice's heirs, Turner, and Shelburne sued the franchisee, Hospitality Venture, and the franchisor, Holiday Inns, for damages. The trial court found Hospitality Ventures negligent for not providing sufficient security to prevent the foreseeable incident that took the life of Rice and injured Turner and Shelburne. The court also found that Hospitality Venture was the apparent agent of Holiday Inns, and therefore Holiday Inns was vicariously liable for its franchisee's tortious conduct. Turner was awarded $3,825,000 for his injuries, Shelburne received $1 million, and Rice's interests were awarded $1 million. Hospitality Venture and Holiday Inns appealed.

Issue

Are the franchisee and the franchisor liable?

In The Language of The Court

Hersey, Chief Judge There was testimony that Holiday Inns, Inc. gave Hospitality Venture, the franchisee, use of the Holiday Inns, Inc. logo and made the franchisee part of the corporation's reservation system. In fact, Holiday Inns, Inc.'s standard sign was displayed in front of the Fort Pierce Holiday Inn in order to draw customers through name recognition. Clearly, this evidence shows that Holiday Inns, Inc. represented to the public that this particular hotel was a part of the national chain of Holiday Inns and that it could find a certain level of service and safety at its hotel and bar.

Clearly, on the question of reliance, the jury had a right to conclude that appellees believed exactly what Holiday Inns, Inc. wanted them to believe—that the Fort Pierce Holiday Inn and its Rodeo Bar were part of the Holiday Inns' system. For these reasons, the evidence supported the jury's finding that Hospitality Venture was the apparent agent of Holiday Inns, Inc. and was acting within the scope of its apparent authority.

Decision and Remedy

The court of appeals held that the franchisee was negligent and that the franchisee was the apparent agent of the franchisor. Affirmed.

Case Questions

Critical Legal Thinking What does the doctrine of apparent agency provide? How does it differ from actual agency?

Business Ethics Did Hospitality Venture act ethically in denying liability? Did Holiday Inns act ethically in denying liability?

Contemporary Business Why do you think the plaintiffs included Holiday Inns as a defendant in their lawsuit? Do you think the damages that were awarded were warranted?

Entrepreneur and the Law

Licensing: Pokémon Invades the United States

In the 1990s, the Japanese company Nintendo's animated Pokémon creatures were a huge hit in Japan. In this role-playing game, children manipulate Pokémon characters with different stated strengths and weaknesses in a variant of the rock, paper, scissors game. The several hundred cute, gender-neutral characters, with such names as Pikachu, Piyo Piyo, Dalki, and Dragon Ball, show up in TV cartoons and Nintendo video games and on playing cards, book bags, and thousands of other items. Japanese children are crazy about acquiring the next Pokémon character. When one new character was introduced at the Nintendo Science World Fair in Japan, more than 100,000 kids lined up to get it.

Entrepreneur and the Law

(continued)

But would American children buy into oddly animated creatures and their interactive games? Nintendo had doubts and did not want to take the exporting risk directly. Up stepped Alfred Kahn and Thomas Kenney, both prior toy company executives, who formed 4Kids Entertainment, Inc., a U.S. company. They approached Nintendo about bringing the Pokémon games and characters to the United States through the concept of licensing. In 1997, after much negotiation, Nintendo agreed to allow 4Kids to be its licensing agent in the United States.

4Kids went looking for its first television deal, but the major TV networks turned it down. Not to be deterred, 4Kids syndicated the TV series on its own, dubbed episodes in English, and gave them free to TV stations in exchange for a percentage of advertising revenue.

Within four months, Pokémon was the top-rated syndicated kids' program in the United States. After this TV success, Nintendo released the first Pokémon video games in the United States, followed by trading cards, comic books, home videos, and compact discs. 4Kids has signed more than 100 licensing deals for Pokémon, including those with Hasbro toy company as its master toy licensee and Time Warner for the Pokémon TV series. The first Pokémon movie, *Mewtwo Strikes Back*, was released in 1999 in the United States and was a huge hit. The Pokémon craze reached a fever pitch in the United States as it had in Japan.

The Pokémon invasion of the United States has reaped a plethora of royalties for Nintendo and its local entrepreneurs. Neither Nintendo nor 4Kids will disclose their licensing arrangement or royalty fees. But retailers usually pay a licensing fee of 5 to 15 percent of their retail sales, and licensing agents such as 4Kids typically earn commissions of 20 to 50 percent of that royalty. With Pokémon sales exceeding $1 billion in the United States, 4Kids may have earned up to $75 million, making its owners multimillionaires. Nintendo claims that it needs licensing agents such as 4Kids to enter a foreign market because of the expertise they bring in finding hot companies in the foreign country to produce and market t-shirts, school supplies, athletic shoes, and the thousands of other items its Pokémon characters now appear on in the United States. Licensing agents, such as 4Kids, take the ball and run with it, sometimes very successfully. ■

Termination of Franchises

A franchise agreement usually contains provisions that permit the franchisor to terminate the franchise if certain events occur. The franchisor's right to terminate a franchise has been the source of litigation.

Termination "For Cause"

Business Brief

A franchisor can terminate a franchise agreement for "just cause" (e.g., nonpayment of franchise fees by the franchisee, continued failure to meet quality control standards).

Most franchise agreements permit franchisors to terminate a franchise "for cause." For example, the continued failure of a franchisee to meet legitimate quality control standards would be deemed just cause.

Unreasonably strict application of a just-cause termination clause constitutes wrongful termination. A single failure to meet a quality control standard, for example, is not cause for termination.

In the following case, the court held that a franchisor had properly terminated a franchisee.

Case 14.4

Franchise Termination

Dunkin'Donuts of America, Inc. v. Middletown Donut Corp.

495 A.2d 66, 1985 N.J. Lexis 2369 (1985)

Supreme Court of New Jersey

Background and Facts

Dunkin' Donuts of America, Inc. (Dunkin' Donuts), is a franchisor that has licensed hundreds of franchised doughnut shops throughout the country. Gerald Smothergill, through two corporations, entered into franchise and lease agreements with Dunkin' Donuts to operate Dunkin' Donuts franchise stores in Middletown and West Long Branch, New Jersey. Smothergill paid about $115,000 for the two franchises. Under each franchise agreement, Smothergill was required to keep accurate sales records, pay a basic franchise fee of 4.9 percent of gross sales, and pay an advertising fee of 2 percent of gross sales. The lease agreements were conditioned on Smothergill's remaining a franchisee in good standing under the franchise agreements.

In August 1978, Dunkin' Donuts notified Smothergill that his franchise agreements were being terminated due to his intentional underreporting of gross sales. The termination notice provided an opportunity for Smothergill to cure the breach by making prompt payment of the amounts due. Smothergill made no attempt to cure and refused to abandon his Dunkin' Donuts stores. Dunkin' Donuts sued to enforce its claimed right of termination and to collect damages. The trial court permitted Dunkin' Donuts to terminate the franchise agreements. The appellate court affirmed. Smothergill appealed.

Issue

Was the franchise agreement properly terminated "for cause" by Dunkin' Donuts?

In The language of The Court

Clifford, Justice At the conclusion of the trial, the trial court found as fact that Smothergill had been guilty of substantial, intentional, and long-continued underreporting of gross sales at both of his Dunkin' Donuts stores. The court determined that Smothergill had failed to keep the financial records that were required under the franchise agreements and that the failure to keep records was not the result of carelessness or incompetence. Rather, Smothergill's delinquency in recordkeeping was part of a deliberate effort to underreport sales, which in turn would result in the underpayment of franchise fees, underpayment of advertising fund fees, underpayment of rental override charges, and evasion of federal and state taxes. In short, the trial court found as fact that Smothergill was "guilty of unconscionable cheating."

Here the franchise deserves to have the full weight of the legal remedies fall upon him. He has been found guilty of unconscionable cheating. Dunkin' Donuts, as franchisor of a sizable network of New Jersey franchises, has a real and legitimate interest in maintaining the integrity of its system. Other Dunkin' Donuts franchisees also have an interest in promoting honest reporting because a percentage of their reported gross sales are pooled in a common advertising fund that benefits all. To the extent that a franchisee such as Smothergill underreports gross sales, he cheats not only the franchisor but all other franchisees as well. Upon signing the Dunkin' Donuts franchise agreement, both franchisor and franchisee were aware of the rules of the game. Those rules seem fair. A franchisee who gets caught with his hand in the proverbial cookie jar (or doughnut box, as the case may be) must suffer the known consequences.

Decision and Remedy

The state supreme court held that Smothergill intentionally breached the franchise agreements and that Dunkin' Donuts had properly terminated Smothergill as a franchisee.

Case Questions

Critical Legal Thinking Should franchisors be permitted to terminate franchisees "at will"? Or is the rule that they can only terminate franchisees "for cause" a better rule? Explain.

Business Ethics Did Smothergill act ethically in this case?

Contemporary Business Do you think many franchisees "cheat" when franchise royalty fees are based on sales?

Wrongful Termination

Termination-at-will clauses in franchise agreements are generally held to be void on the grounds that they are unconscionable. The rationale for this position is that the franchisee has spent time, money, and effort developing the franchise.

If a franchise is terminated without just cause, the franchisee can sue the franchisor for **wrongful termination**. The franchisee can then recover damages caused by the unlawful termination and recover the franchise.

wrongful termination
Termination of a franchise without just cause.

International Law

International Franchising

Franchising as a form of business is well established in the United States. Sometimes it seems that certain types of franchises (e.g., gasoline stations) have saturated the market. The international market presently offers the greatest opportunity for U.S. franchisors to expand their businesses. Many U.S. franchisors view international expansion as their number-one priority. However, in addition to providing lucrative new markets, international franchising also poses difficulties and risks.

The expansion into other countries through franchising means that U.S. franchisors can expand internationally without the huge capital investments that would be required if they tried to penetrate these markets with company-owned stores or branches. In

International Law (continued)

addition, a foreign franchisee will know things about the cultural and business traditions of the foreign country that the franchisor will not. Consequently, the franchisee will be better able to serve the consumers and customers in the particular market.

Utilizing this foreign expertise probably means that U.S. franchisors will grant area franchises in many foreign countries. The U.S. franchisor will rely on the area franchisee to locate, investigate, and approve individual franchisees.

Foreign franchising is not without difficulties, however. For example, the host country's laws may differ from U.S. laws. This will have to be taken into consideration in drafting the franchise agreement and operating the franchise. Foreign cultures may also require different advertising, marketing, and promotional approaches. In addition, the franchisor may be subjecting itself to government regulation in the host country. A regional group such as the European Community (EC) may possibly become involved. Finally, different dispute settlement procedures may be in place that will have to be used if there is a dispute between the U.S. franchisor and the foreign franchisee.

To aid the development of U.S. franchising abroad, the *U.S. Agency for International Development (USAID)* guarantees loans to U.S. franchisors' area licensees and franchisees in developing countries. The foreign franchisee seeks financing from its own bank, and USAID backs 50 percent of the loan through a guarantee. Franchisors must apply and be approved to participate in the program.

In addition to U.S. franchisors' expanding to other countries, foreign franchisors also view the United States as a potential market. This provides an opportunity for U.S. entrepreneurs to become franchisees for foreign franchisors. As a result, in the future, U.S. consumers are able to purchase foreign goods and services from franchises located in this country. ■

Chapter Summary

Entrepreneurial Forms of Conducting Business, p. 397

Forms of Conducting Business

Entrepreneurs may choose to conduct business using any of the following forms:

1. Sole proprietorship.
2. General partnership.
3. Limited partnership.
4. Limited liability partnership (LLP).
5. Limited liability company (LLC).
6. Corporation.

Sole Proprietorship, p. 398

Sole Proprietorship

A form of business in which the owner and the business are one. The business is not a separate legal entity.

Business Name

A sole proprietorship can operate under the name of the sole proprietor or a *trade name*. Operating under a trade name is commonly designated as *d.b.a. (doing business as)*. If a trade name is used, a *fictitious business name statement* must be filed with the appropriate state government office.

Personal Liability of Sole Proprietors

The sole proprietor is personally liable for the debts and obligations of the sole proprietorship.

Franchises, p. 402

Franchises

A franchise is established when one party licenses another party to use the franchisor's trade name, trademarks, commercial symbols, patents, copyrights, and other property in the distribution and selling of goods and services.

1. ***Franchisor.*** The party who does the licensing in a franchise arrangement. Also called the *licensor*.
2. ***Franchisee.*** The party who is licensed by the franchisor in a franchise arrangement. Also called the licensee.

Types of Franchises

1. ***Distributorship franchise.*** The franchisor manufactures a product and licenses a retail franchisee to distribute the product to the public.
2. ***Processing plant franchise.*** The franchisor provides a secret formula or process to the franchisee, and the franchisee manufactures the product and distributes it to retail dealers.
3. ***Chain-style franchise.*** The franchisor licenses the franchisee to make and sell its products or distribute its services to the public from a retail outlet serving an exclusive territory.
4. ***Area franchise.*** The franchisor authorizes the franchisee to negotiate and sell franchises on behalf of the franchisor in designated areas. The area franchisee is called a *subfranchisor*.

State Disclosure Laws

Many states have enacted statutes that require franchisors to make specific presale disclosures to prospective franchisees. Some states use a uniform disclosure document called the *Uniform Franchise Offering Circular (UFOC)*.

FTC's Franchise Rule

The *FTC* requires franchisors to make presale disclosures to prospective franchisees. If the franchisor uses actual or hypothetical sales or income data in its sales materials, the franchisor must disclose assumptions underlying any estimates and how many franchises have obtained such results, and it must provide a mandated precautionary statement.

The Franchise Agreement, p. 406

The Franchise Agreement

An agreement that the franchisor and the franchisee enter into that sets forth the terms and conditions of the franchise (e.g., quality control standards, covenant-not-to-compete).

Franchise Fees

Franchise fees. A franchisee may be required to pay any or all of the following fees to the franchisor:

1. ***Initial license fee.*** A lump-sum payment for the privilege of being granted a franchise.
2. ***Royalty fee.*** A fee for the continued use of the franchisor's trade name, property, and assistance that is often computed as a percentage of the franchisee's gross sales.
3. ***Assessment fee.*** A fee for such things as advertising and promotional campaigns, administrative costs, and the like, billed either as a flat monthly fee or an annual fee or as a percentage of gross sales.
4. ***Lease fee.*** A fee for any land or equipment leased from the franchisor, billed either as a flat monthly fee or an annual fee or as a percentage of gross sales or other agreed-upon amount.
5. ***Cost of supplies.*** Payment for supplies purchased from the franchisor.

Trademarks

1. ***Trademarks and service marks.*** Distinctive marks, symbols, names, words, mottoes, or devices that identify the goods or services of a particular franchisor.
2. ***Licensing of marks.*** A franchisor *licenses* the use of its trademarks and service marks to its franchisees in the franchise agreement.
3. ***Trademark infringement.*** Anyone who uses a mark without authorization from the franchisor may be sued for *trademark infringement*. The franchisor can recover damages and obtain an injunction prohibiting further unauthorized use of the mark.

Misappropriation of Trade Secrets

1. ***Trade secrets.*** Ideas, formulas, and methods of doing business that make a franchise successful but do not qualify for trademark, patent, or copyright protection.
2. ***Misappropriation of trade secrets.*** Anyone who steals and uses a franchisor's trade secret is liable for misappropriation of a trade secret. The franchisor can recover damages and obtain an injunction prohibiting further unauthorized use of the trade secret.

Contract and Tort Liability of Franchisors and Franchisees, p. 410

Contract and Tort Liability

1. Franchisors and franchisees are liable for their own contracts and torts.
2. ***Independent contractor.*** A separately organized and operated business that is not the agent of another party with whom it does business. This is the typical franchisor–franchisee arrangement. There is no agency relationship, so neither party is liable for the other's contracts or torts.
3. ***Actual agency.*** An arrangement in which a franchisor expressly or implicitly by its conduct makes a franchisee its agent. The franchisor is liable for the contracts entered into and torts committed by the franchisee while acting within the scope of the agency.
4. ***Apparent agency.*** Agency that arises when a franchisor creates the appearance that a franchisee is its agent when in fact an actual agency does not exist. The franchisor is liable for the contracts entered into and torts committed by the franchisee acting as an apparent agent.

Termination of Franchises, p. 414

Termination of Franchises

Termination "for cause." Most franchise agreements, and state and federal laws, permit a franchisor to terminate a franchise "for cause" (e.g., nonpayment of franchise fees by the franchisee, continued failure of the franchisee to meet quality control standards).

Wrongful Termination

1. ***Termination at will.*** Most state and federal laws regulating franchising prohibit franchisors from terminating franchises at will. This is to prevent a franchisor from taking advantage of the good will developed at the franchise location by the franchisee.
2. ***Wrongful termination.*** If a franchisor terminates a franchise agreement without just cause, the franchisee can sue the franchisor for *wrongful termination*. The franchisee can recover damages caused by the wrongful termination and recover the franchise.

Internet Exercises and Case Questions

Working the Web Internet Exercises

Activities

1. Review the recent FTC cases of alleged abusive practices of franchisors at **www.ftc.gov/bcp/franchise/1999-2000cases.htm**. How would you advise a franchisee client to protect against such practices? For information on federal law regarding franchising, see **www.ftc.gov/bcp/franchise/netfran.htm**.
2. Franchising makes extensive use of licensing of intellectual property, especially trademarks and trade secrets. Use the Web sites listed below to find examples of licensing agreements and the disputes that they can sometimes produce:
   - The Trade Secrets home page, at **www.execpc.com/mhallign**
   - All About Trademarks, at **www.ggmark.com**

- Intellectual Property Digital Library, at **ipdl.wipo.int**
- Intellectual Property Mall, at **www.fplc.edu/ipmall/pointbox/pb_copy.htm**
- JurisNotes.Com—A source for all aspects of intellectual property law, at **www.jurisnotes.com**
- Marksonline—For free trademark search and domain name search, at **www.marksonline.com**
- The Intellectual Property Law Server, at **www.cybercommercelaw.com**

Critical Legal Thinking Cases

14.1 Franchise Agreement H&R Block, Inc. (Block), is a franchisor that licenses franchisees to provide tax preparation services to customers under the "H&R Block" service mark. In 1975, June McCart was granted a Block franchise at 900 Main Street, Rochester, New York. From 1972 to 1979, her husband, Robert, was involved in the operation of a Block franchise in Rensselaer, New York. After that, he assisted June in the operation of her Block franchise. All the McCarts' income during the time in question came from the Block franchises.

The Block franchise agreement that June signed contained a provision whereby she agreed not to compete (1) in the business of tax preparation (2) within 250 miles of the franchise (3) for a period of two years after the termination of the franchise. Robert did not sign the Rochester franchise agreement. On December 31, 1981, June wrote a letter to Block, giving notice that she was terminating the franchise. Shortly thereafter, the McCarts sent a letter to people who had been clients of the Rochester Block office, informing them that June was leaving Block and that Robert was opening a tax preparation service in which June would assist him. Block granted a new franchise in Rochester to another franchisee. It sued the McCarts to enforce the covenant not to compete against them. Who wins? [*McCart v. H&R Block, Inc.*, 470 n.E.2d 756, 1984 Ind.App. Lexis 3039 (Ind. App. 1984)]

14.2 Franchise Agreement Libby-Broadway Drive-In, Inc. (Libby), is a corporation licensed to operate a McDonald's fast-food franchise restaurant by the McDonald's System, Inc. (McDonald's). Libby was granted a license to operate a McDonald's in Cleveland, Ohio, and was granted an exclusive territory in which McDonald's could not grant another franchise. The area was described as "bound on the north by the south side of Miles Avenue, on the west and south side by Turney Road, on the east by Warrensville Center Road." In December 1976, McDonald's granted a franchise to another franchisee to operate a McDonald's restaurant on the west side of Turney Road. Libby sued McDonald's, alleging a breach of the franchise agreement. Is McDonald's liable? [*Libby-Broadway Drive-In, Inc. v. McDonald's System, Inc.*, 391 N.E.2d 1, 1979 Ill.App. Lexis 2698 (Ill. App. 1979)]

14.3 Disclosure My Pie International, Inc. (My Pie), an Illinois corporation, is a franchisor that licenses franchisees to open pie shops under its trademark name. My Pie licensed 13 restaurants throughout the country, including one owned by Dowmont, Inc. (Dowmont), In Glen Ellyn, Illinois. The Illinois Franchise Disclosure Act requires a franchisor that desires to issue franchises in the state to register with the state or qualify for an exemption from registration and to make certain disclosures to prospective franchisees. My Pie granted the license to Dowmont without registering with the state of Illinois or qualifying for an exemption from registration and without making the required disclosures to Dowmont. Dowmont operated its restaurant as a "My Pie" franchise between July 1976 and May 1980, and since then it has operated it under the name "Arnold's." Dowmont paid franchise royalty fees to My Pie prior to May 1980. My Pie sued Dowmont for breach of the franchise agreement to recover royalties it claimed were due from Dowmont. Dowmont filed a counter-claim seeking to rescind the franchise agreement and recover the royalties it paid to My Pie. Who wins? [*My Pie International, Inc. v. Dowmont, Inc.*, 687 F.2d 919, 1982 U.S. App. Lexis 16537 (7th Cir. 1982)]

14.4 Tort Liability Georgia Girl Fashions, Inc. (Georgia Girl), is a franchisor that licenses franchisees to operate women's retail clothing stores under the "Georgia Girl" trademark. Georgia Girl granted a franchise to a franchisee to operate a store on South Cobb Drive in Smyrna, Georgia. Georgia Girl did not supervise or control the day-to-day operations of the franchisee. Melanie McMullan entered the store to exchange a blouse that she had previously purchased at the store. When she found nothing that she wished to exchange the blouse for, she began to leave the store. At that time, she was physically restrained and accused of shoplifting the blouse. McMullan was taken to the local jail, where she was held until her claim of prior purchase could be verified. The store then dropped the charges against her, and she was released from jail. McMullan filed an action against the store owner and Georgia Girl to recover damages for false imprisonment. Is Georgia Girl liable? [*McMullan v. Georgia Girl Fashions, Inc.*, 348 S.E.2d 748, 1986 Ga.App. Lexis 2093 (Ga. App. 1988)]

14.5 Tort Liability The Seven-Up Company (Seven-Up) is a franchisor that licenses local bottling companies to manufacture, bottle, and distribute soft drinks using the "7-Up" trademark. The Brooks Bottling Company (Brooks) is a Seven-Up franchisee that bottles and sells 7-Up soft drinks to stores in Michigan. Under the franchise agreement, the franchisee is required to purchase the 7-Up syrup from Seven-Up, but it can purchase its bottles, cartons, and other supplies from independent suppliers if Seven-Up approves the design of these articles.

Brooks used cartons designed and manufactured by Olinkraft, Inc., using a design that Seven-Up had approved. Sharon Proos Kosters, a customer at Meijers Thrifty Acre Store in Holland, Michigan, removed a cardboard carton containing six bottles of 7-Up from a grocery store shelf, put it under her arm, and walked toward the checkout counter. As she did so, a bottle slipped out of the carton, fell on the floor, and exploded, causing a piece of glass to strike Kosters in her eye as she looked down; she was blinded in that eye. Evidence showed that the 7-Up carton was designed to be held from the top and was made without a strip on the side of the carton that would prevent a bottle from slipping out if held underneath. Kosters sued Seven-Up to recover damages for her injuries. Is Seven-Up liable? [*Kosters v. Seven-Up Company*, 595 F.2d 347, 1979 U.S. App. Lexis 15945 (6th Cir. 1979)]

14.6 Trademark The Kentucky fried Chicken Corporation (KFC) is the franchisor of Kentucky Fried Chicken restaurants. Franchisees must purchase equipment and supplies from manufacturers approved in writing by KFC. Equipment includes cookers, fryers, ovens, and the like; supplies include carry-out boxes, napkins, towelettes, and plastic eating utensils known as "sporks." These products are not trade secrets. KFC may not "unreasonably withhold" approval of any suppliers who apply and whose goods are tested and found to meet KFC's quality control standards. The 10 manufacturers who went through KFC's approval process were approved. KFC also sells supplies to franchisees in competition with these independent suppliers. All supplies, whether produced by KFC or the independent suppliers, must contain "Kentucky Fried Chicken" trademarks.

Upon formation in 1972, Diversified Container Corporation (Diversified) began manufacturing and selling supplies to KFC franchisees without applying for or receiving KFC's approval. All the items sold by Diversified contained KFC trademarks. Diversified represented to franchisees that its products met "all standards" of KFC and that it sold "approved supplies." Diversified even affixed KFC trademarks to the shipping boxes in which it delivered supplies to franchisees. Evidence showed that Diversified's products did not meet the quality control standards set by KFC. KFC sued Diversified for trademark infringement. Who wins? [*Kentucky Fried Chicken Corporation v. Diversified Container Corporation*, 549 F.2d 368, 1977 U.S. App. Lexis 14128 (5th Cir. 1977)]

14.7 Trademarks Ramada Inns, Inc. (Ramada Inns), is a franchisor that licenses franchisees to operate motor hotels using the "Ramada Inns" trademarks and service marks. In August 1977, the Gadsden Motor Company (Gadsden), a partnership, purchased a motel in Attalla, Alabama, and entered into a franchise agreement with Ramada Inns to operate it as a Ramada Inns motor hotel. In 1982, the motel began receiving poor ratings from Ramada Inns inspectors, and Gadsden fell behind on its monthly franchise fee payments. Despite proddings from Ramada Inns, the motel never met Ramada Inns's operational standards again. On November 17, 1983, Ramada Inns properly terminated the franchise agreement, citing quality deficiencies and Gadsden's failure to pay past-due franchise fees. The termination notice directed Gadsden to remove any materials or signs identifying the motel as a Ramada Inns. Gadsden continued using Ramada Inns's signage, trademarks, and service marks inside and outside the motel. In September 1984, Ramada Inns sued Gadsden for trademark infringement. Who wins? [*Ramada Inns, Inc. v. Gadsden Motel Company*, 804 F.2d 1562, 1986 U.S. App. Lexis 34279 (11th Cir.)]

14.8 Termination of a Franchise In 1976, Amoco Oil Company (Amoco) purchased the land in question and constructed a two-bay gasoline station at a total cost of $125,000. The property was then leased to Robert F. Burns, who operated an Amoco franchise gasoline station. The franchise was maintained through a series of written one-year leases. The leases provided for automatic renewal unless either party gave written notice of cancellation prior to the end of the current term. On June 8, 1977, Amoco gave Burns written notice of nonrenewal and directed Burns to vacate the premises effective September 10, 1977. Evidence showed that the gasoline station had been suffering a steadily decreasing sales volume and that the station was an unprofitable location for Amoco. Evidence further showed that no reasonable steps could be taken to increase the sales volume at the site to make it profitable. Amoco planned on discontinuing the sale of gasoline at the site and selling the property. Burns sued Amoco for wrongful termination. Who wins? [*Amoco Oil Company v. Burns*, 437 A.2d 381, 1981 Pa. Lexis 906 (Pa. 1981)]

14.9 Termination of a Franchise Kawasaki Motors Corporation (Kawasaki), a Japanese corporation, manufactures motorcycles that its distributes in the United States through its subsidiary, Kawasaki Motors Corporation, U.S.A. (Kawasaki USA). Kawasaki USA is a franchisor that grants franchises to dealerships to sell Kawasaki motorcycles. In 1971, Kawasaki USA granted the Kawasaki Shop of Aurora, Inc. (Dealer), a franchise to sell Kawasaki motorcycles in Aurora, Illinois. The franchise changed locations twice. Both moves were within the five-mile exclusive territory granted Dealer in the franchise agreement.

Dealer did not obtain Kawasaki USA's written approval for either move, as required by the franchise agreement. Kawasaki USA acquiesed to the first move but not the second. At the second new location, Dealer also operated Honda and Suzuki motorcycle franchises and was negotiating to operate a Yamaha franchise. The Kawasaki franchise agreement expressly permitted multiline dealerships. Kawasaki USA objected to the second move, asserting that the dealer had not received written approval for the move, as required by the franchise agreement. Evidence showed, however, that the real reason Kawasaki objected to the move was because it did not want its motorcycles to be sold at the same location as other manufacturers' motorcycles. Kawasaki terminated the dealer's franchise. Dealer sued Kawasaki USA for wrongful termination. Who wins? [*Kawasaki Shop of Aurora, Inc. v. Kawasaki Motors Corporation, U.S.A.*, 544 N.E.2d 457, 1989 Ill. App. Lexis 1442 (Ill. App. 1989)]

Business Ethics Cases

14.10 Business Ethics Southland Corporation (Southland) owned the "7-Eleven" trademark and licenses franchisees throughout the country to operate 7-Eleven stores. The franchise agreement provides for fees to be paid to Southland by each franchisee based on a percentage of gross profits. In return, franchisees receive a lease of premises, a license to use the 7-Eleven trademark and trade secrets, advertising merchandise, and bookkeeping assistance. Vallerie Campbell purchased an existing 7-Eleven store in Fontana, California, and became a Southland franchisee. The franchise was designated #13974 by Southland. As part of the purchase, she applied to the state of California for transfer of the beer and wine license from the prior owner. Southland also executed the application. California approved the transfer and issued the license to "Campbell Vallerie Southland #13974."

On September 9, 1978, an employee of Campbell's store sold beer to Jesse Lewis Cope, a minor who was allegedly intoxicated at the time. After drinking the beer, Cope drove his vehicle and struck another vehicle. Two occupants of the other vehicle, Denise Wickham and Tyrone Crosby, were severely injured, and a third occupant, Cedrick Johnson, was killed. Johnson (through his parents), Wickham, and Crosby sued Southland—but not

Campbell—to recover damages. Is Southland legally liable for the tortious acts of its franchisee? Is it morally responsible? [*Wickham v. The Southland Corporation*, 168 Cal.App.3d 49, 213 Cal.Rptr. 825, 1985 Cal.App. Lexis 2070 (Cal.App. 1985)]

14.11 Business Ethics The Kentucky Fried Chicken Corporation (KFC), with its principal place of business in Louisville, Kentucky, is the franchisor of Kentucky Fried Chicken restaurants. KFC's registered trademarks and service marks include "Kentucky Fried Chicken," "It's Finger Lickin' Good," and the portrait of Colonel Harlan Sanders. KFC grants a license to its franchisees to use these marks in connection with the preparation and sale of "Original Recipe Kentucky Fried Chicken." Original Recipe Kentucky Fried Chicken, which is sold only by KFC franchisees, is prepared by a special cooking process featuring the use of a secret recipe seasoning known as "KFC Seasonings." This blend of seasoning was developed by KFC's founder, Colonel Harlan Sanders. As a condition of each franchise agreement, KFC requires that its franchisees use only KFC Seasoning in connection with the preparation and sale of Kentucky Fried Chicken.

KFC Seasoning is a trade secret. To make the seasoning, KFC has entered into contracts with two spice blenders, the John W. Sexton Company, Inc. (Sexton), and Strange Company (Strange). Each of these companies blends approximately one-half the spices of KFC Seasoning; neither has knowledge of the complete formulation of KFC Seasoning, and both entered into secrecy agreements to maintain the confidentiality of their formulation. After the seasoning is blended by Sexton and Strange, it is mixed together and sold directly to all KFC franchisees. KFC does not receive a royalty or other economic benefit from the sale of KFC Seasoning. KFC's relationship with Sexton and Strange has existed for more than 25 years; no other companies are licensed to blend KFC Seasoning.

Marion-Kay Company, Inc. (Marion-Kay), is a spice blender engaged in the manufacture of chicken seasoning known as "Marion-Kay Seasoning." In 1973, Marion-Kay requested permission from KFC to sell its seasoning products to KFC franchisees. KFC refused the request. In 1977, KFC learned that Marion-Kay was supplying some KFC franchisees with Marion-Kay seasoning and demanded it cease this practice. When Marion-Kay refused, KFC sued it for interference with contractual relations. Marion-Kay filed a counterclaim, alleging violation of antitrust law. Who wins? Was KFC justified in preventing Marion-Kay from blending its seasonings? Did Marion-Kay act morally in selling seasoning to KFC franchisees? [*KFC Corporation v. Marion-Kay Company, Inc.*, 620 F.Supp. 1160, 1985 U.S. Dist. Lexis 14766 (S.D.Ind. 1985)]

Briefing the Case Writing Assignment

Read Case A.14 in the Case Appendix [*Little v. Howard Johnson Company*]. This case is excerpted from the court of appeals opinion. Review and brief the case. In your brief, be sure to answer the following questions.

1. Describe how the plaintiff was injured. Whom did she sue?
2. Was Howard Johnson Company directly liable for the plaintiff's injuries? Explain.
3. Was the franchisee an actual agent of Howard Johnson Company?
4. Did Howard Johnson's actions create an apparent agency between it and the franchisee?

Answers to Management Decision Questions

1. After consulting with Coney Island attorneys, you determined that the types of franchise arrangements currently in existence include:
   a. Distributorship franchises, through which the franchisor manufactures a product and licenses a retail dealer to distribute the product to the public.
   b. Processing plant franchises, in which the franchisor provides a secret formula or the like to the franchisee. The franchisee then manufactures the product at its own location and distributes it to retail dealers.
   c. Chain-style franchises, through which the franchisor licenses the franchisee to make and sell its products or services to the public from a retail outlet serving an exclusive geographical territory.
   d. Area franchises by which the franchisor grants to the franchisee a franchise for an agreed-upon geographical area.

   Currently, Coney Island franchisees in the United States operate under chain-style franchise agreements. This practice should be continued in Canada. In addition, your research indicated that the International Franchise Association (IFA), an association for U.S. franchisors, maintains close ties with national franchise associations in other countries, including Canada. You should recommend to the board that Coney Island join this association.
2. Your current franchise agreements include quality control standards, training requirements, covenants not to compete, and arbitration agreements. In addition, your Canadian franchise agreements should include a forum-selection clause that designates a certain court to hear any dispute concerning nonperformance that cannot be settled through arbitration procedures.

Endnotes

1. Cal.Corp. Code §§ 31000–31019.
2. 16 CFR Part 436.
3. *Southland Corporation v. Keating*, 465 U.S. 1, 104 S.Ct. 852, 1984 U.S. Lexis 2 (1985).

15

Partnerships and Limited Liability Companies

"There are a great many of us who will adhere to that ancient principle that we prefer to be governed by the power of laws, and not by the power of men."

—Woodrow Wilson
Speech, September 25, 1912

Chapter Objectives

After studying this chapter, you should be able to:

1. Define general partnership and explain the contract and tort liability of partners.
2. Define limited partnership and describe the liability of general and limited partners.
3. Define limited liability partnership (LLP) and describe the limited liability of partners of an LLP.
4. Define limited liability company (LLC) and describe the limited liability shield provided by an LLC.
5. Compare a member-managed LLC to a manager-managed LLC.

Chapter Contents

- General Partnerships
- Limited Partnerships
- Limited Liability Partnerships (LLPs)
- Limited Liability Companies (LLCs)

Management Decision Partnerships and Limited Liability Companies

Cheryl Barber, President of Barber Construction Company, a family-owned business located in Raleigh, North Carolina, recently approached you concerning entering into a business arrangement to develop an upscale residential subdivision in Wake County on 1,000 acres of undeveloped property that you own. Because of the continued development of Research Triangle Park, the population growth in Wake County is predicted to rise sharply over the next several years. However, you are concerned about the personal liability associated with such a venture. A friend has suggested that you form a limited liability company (LLC).

1. Can an LLC be formed in the state of North Carolina?
2. Is the LLC form of business organization suitable for this type of a business venture? Why or why not?

A person who wants to start a business must decide whether the business should operate as one of the major forms of business organization—*sole proprietorship, general partnership, limited partnership, limited liability partnership (LLP), limited liability company (LLC),* or *corporation*—or under some other available legal business form. The selection depends on many factors, including the ease and cost of formation, the capital requirements of the business, the flexibility of management decisions, government restrictions, the extent of personal liability, tax considerations, and the like.

This chapter discusses noncorporate forms of business, including general partnerships, limited partnerships, LLPs, and LLCs. Corporations are discussed in Chapter 16.

It has been uniformly laid down in this Court, as far back as we can remember, that good faith is the basis of all mercantile transactions.

Buller, J.
Salomons v. Nissen (1788)

General Partnerships

General, or *ordinary, partnerships* have been recognized since ancient times. The English common law of partnerships governed early U.S. partnerships. The individual states expanded the body of partnership law.

Palm Desert, California. Many businesses, such as the one that owns these windmills near Palm Springs, California, are operated as limited partnerships.

Exhibit 15.1
General Partnership

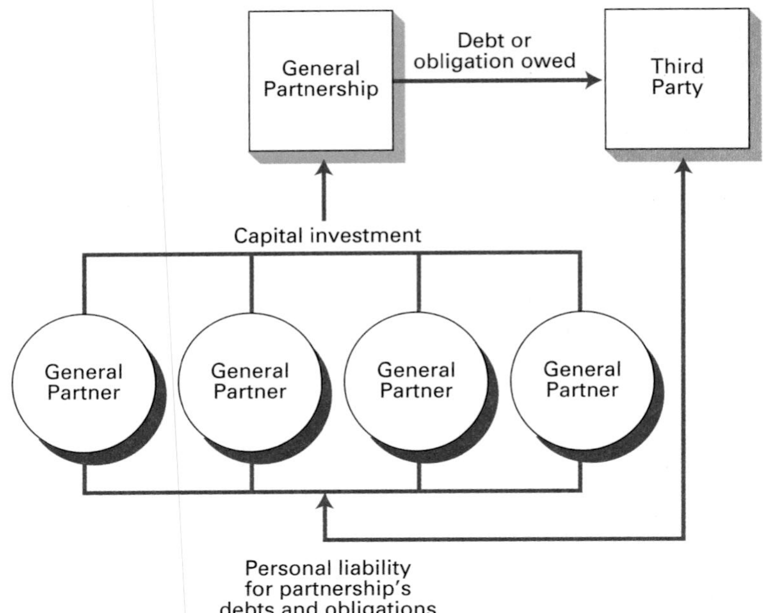

general partnership
A voluntary association of two or more persons for carrying on a business as co-owners for profit. Also called a *partnership*.

A **general partnership**, or partnership, is a voluntary association of two or more persons for carrying on a business as co-owners for profit. The formation of a partnership creates certain rights and duties among partners and with third parties. These rights and duties are established in the partnership agreement and by law. **General partners**, or **partners**, are personally liable for the debts and obligations of the partnership (see Exhibit 15.1).

Uniform Partnership Act

Uniform Partnership Act (UPA)
A model act that codifies partnership law. Most states have adopted the UPA in whole or in part.

In 1914, the National Conference of Commissioners on Uniform State Laws (a group of lawyers, judges, and legal scholars) promulgated the **Uniform Partnership Act (UPA)**. The UPA codifies partnership law. Its goal was to establish consistent partnership law that was uniform throughout the United States. The UPA has been adopted in whole or in part by 48 states,[1] the District of Columbia, Guam, and the Virgin Islands. Because it is so important, the UPA forms the basis of the study of general partnerships in this chapter.

One of the most fruitful sources of ruin to men of the world is the recklessness or want of principle of partners, and it is one of the perils to which every man exposes himself who enters into partnership with another.

Malins, V.C.
Mackay v. Douglas, 14 Eq. 106 at 118 (1872)

The UPA covers most problems that arise in the formation, operation, and dissolution of ordinary partnerships. Other rules of law or equity govern if there is no applicable provision of the UPA [UPA § 5].

The UPA adopted the **entity theory** of partnership, which considers partnerships as separate legal entities. As such, partnerships can hold title to personal and real property, transact business in the partnership name, and the like.

Partnership Name

Business Brief
Partnerships often operate under fictitious business names. A business that does so must file a fictitious business name statement with the appropriate government agency.

An ordinary partnership can operate under the names of any one or more of the partners or under a fictitious business name. If the partnership operates under a fictitious name, it must file a *fictitious name statement* with the appropriate government agency and publish a notice of the name in a newspaper of general circulation where the partnership does business. The name selected by a partnership cannot indicate that it is a corporation (e.g., it cannot contain the term *Inc.*) and cannot be similar to the name used by any existing business entity.

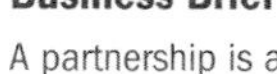

Formation of a Partnership

A b[illegible]st meet four criteria to qualify as a partnership under the UPA [UPA § 6(1)]. It [illegible]ciation of two or more persons (2) carrying on a business (3) as co-[illegible]hips are voluntary associations of two or more persons. All [illegible]n of each co-partner. A person cannot be forced to be [illegible] a partner. The UPA definition of *person* includes [illegible] limited partnerships), corporations, and other asso-[illegible]n, or profession—must be carried on. The organiza-[illegible]tive in order to qualify as a partnership, even though [illegible] make a profit.

Business Brief
A partnership is a *voluntary* association. A person cannot be forced to be a partner or to accept another person as a partner.

[illegible] formed with little or no formality. Co-ownership of a [illegible]tnership. The most important factor in determining co-[illegible]hare the business's profits and management responsibility. [illegible]ss profits is prima facie evidence of a partnership because [illegible]en the right to share in the business's profits. No inference [illegible]ip is drawn if profits are received in payment of (1) a debt [illegible]ents or otherwise, (2) wages owed to an employee, (3) rent [illegible] annuity owed to a widow, widower, or representative of a [illegible] owed on a loan, or (6) consideration for the sale of goodwill [illegible] agreement to share losses of a business is strong evidence of a [illegible]

The partner of my partner is not my partner.

Legal Maxim

[illegible] in the management of a business is important evidence for [illegible]f a partnership, but it is not conclusive evidence because the [illegible]gement is sometimes given to employees, creditors, and others. [illegible] the existence of a partnership if a person is given the right to [illegible] management of a business.

Business Brief
It is compelling evidence of the existence of a partnership if persons are given the right to share in profits, losses, and management of a business.

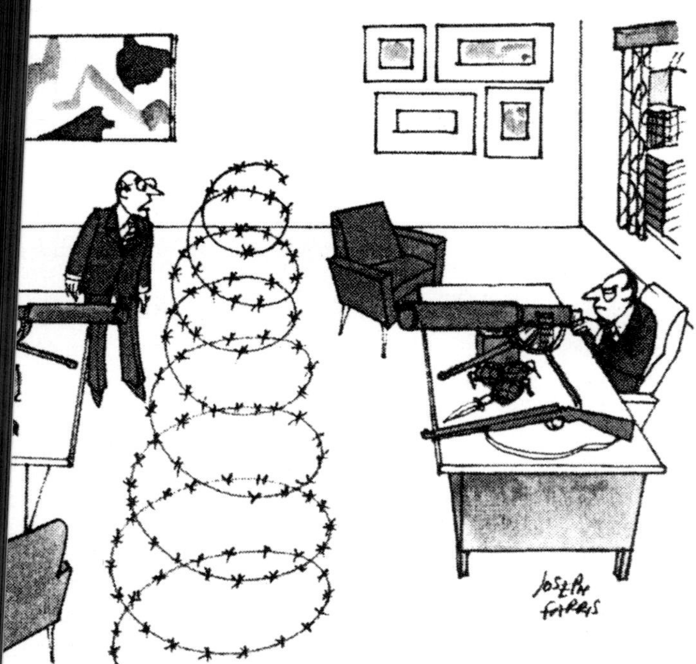

"*What happened to our working partnership?*"

The Partnership Agreement

> It is the privilege of a trader in a free country, in all matters not contrary to law, to regulate his own mode of carrying it on according to his own discretion and choice.
>
> B. Alderson
> *Hilton v. Eckersley (1855)*

Web Site

Legal Information for U.S. Business Organizations At this site, you will find numerous links relating to all forms of business in the United States. These links include information pertaining to structure, taxation, legal requirements for formation, and many other pertinent topics. Visit at **www.maprip.org/library/legal/legal/htm**.

The agreement to form a partnership may be oral, written, or implied from the conduct of the parties. It may even be created inadvertently. No formalities are necessary, although a few states require general partnerships to file certificates of partnership with an appropriate government agency. Partnerships that exist for more than one year or are authorized to deal in real estate must be in writing under the statute of frauds.

It is good practice for partners to put their partnership agreement in writing. A written document is important evidence of the terms of the agreement, particularly if a dispute arises among the partners.

A written partnership agreement is called a **partnership agreement** or **articles of partnership**. The partners can agree to almost any terms in their partnership agreement, except terms that are illegal. The articles of partnership can be short and simple or long and complex. If the agreement fails to provide for an essential term or contingency, the provisions of the UPA control. Thus, the UPA acts as a gap-filling device to the partners' agreement.

In the following case, the court had to decide whether a partnership had been created.

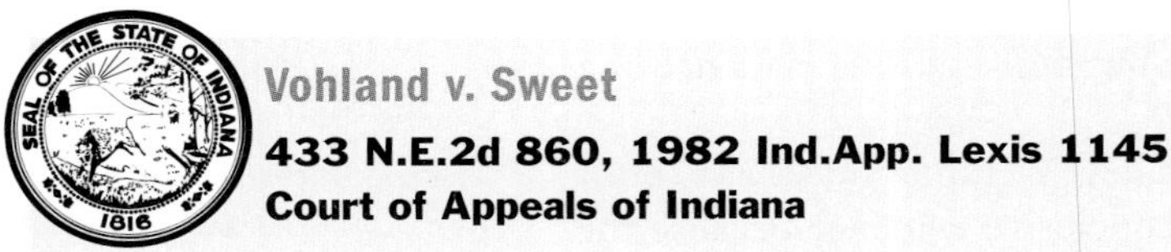

Vohland v. Sweet
433 N.E.2d 860, 1982 Ind.App. Lexis 1145
Court of Appeals of Indiana

Case 15.1 General Partnership

Background and Facts

Norman E. Sweet began working for Charles Vohland as an hourly employee at a garden nursery owned by Vohland in 1956, when he was a youngster. Upon completion of military service (from 1958 to 1960), Sweet resumed his former employment. In 1963, Charles Vohland retired, and his son Paul Vohland (Vohland) commenced what became known as Vohland's Nursery, the business of which was landscape gardening. Vohland purchased the interests of his brothers and sisters in the nursery. At the time, Sweet's status changed: He was to receive a 20 percent share of the net profit of the business after all expenses were paid, including labor, supplies, plants, and other expenses. Sweet contributed no capital to the enterprise. The compensation was paid on an irregular basis—every several weeks, Vohland and Sweet would sit down, compute the income received and expenses paid, and Sweet would be issued a check for 20 percent of the balance. No Social Security or income taxes were withheld from Sweet's checks.

Vohland and Sweet did not enter into a written agreement. No partnership income tax returns were filed by the business. Sweet's tax returns declared that he was a self-employed salesman. He paid self-employment Social Security taxes. Vohland handled all of the finances and books of the nursery and borrowed money from the bank solely on his own name for business purposes. Vohland made most of the sales for the business. Sweet managed the physical aspects of the nursery, supervised the care of the nursery stock, and oversaw the performance of the contracts for customers. Sweet testified that in the early 1970s, Vohland told him that

> He was going to take me in and that I wouldn't have to punch a time clock anymore, that I would be on a commission basis and that I would be—have more of an interest in the business if I had an interest in the business. He referred to it as a "piece of the action."

Vohland denied making this statement. Sweet brought this action for dissolution of the alleged partnership and for an accounting. He sought payment for 20 percent of the business's inventory. The trial court held in favor of Sweet and awarded him $58,733. Vohland appealed.

Issue

Did Vohland and Sweet enter into a partnership?

In The Language of The Court

Neal, Judge We note that both parties referred to the 20% as "commissions". To us the term "commission," unless defined, does not mean the same thing as a share of the net profits. However, this term, when used by landscape gardeners and not lawyers, should not be restricted to its technical definition. "Commission" was used to refer to Sweet's share of the profits, and the receipt of a share of the profits is prima facie evidence of a partnership.

Though evidence is conflicting, there is evidence that the payments were not wages, but a share of the profit of a partnership. It can readily be inferred from the evidence most favorable to support the judgment that the parties intended a community of interest in any increment in the value of the capital and in the profit.

is not controlling, and contribu- There is evidence from which it intended to do the things that tnership, regardless of how they nship.

a partnership had been created irmed.

Case Questions

Critical Legal Thinking Do you think a partnership was formed in this case? Should all partnership agreements be required to be in writing?

Business Ethics Do you think either party acted unethically in this case?

Contemporary Business What are the economic consequences of founding a partnership?

Management

ent to the contrary, all partners have equal rights in the man- rtnership business. In other words, each partner has one vote, al size of his or her capital contribution or share in the part- UPA, a simple majority decides most ordinary partnership e vote is tied, the action being voted on is considered to be agree to modify the majority rule by delegating management ee of partners or to a managing partner.

Business Brief

Unless otherwise agreed, each partner has a right to participate in the management of a partnership and has an equal vote on partnership matters.

g

to sue the partnership or other partners at law. Instead, they are g an **action for an accounting** against other partners. An dicial proceeding in which the court is authorized to (1) review artners' transactions and (2) award each partner his or her share [UPA § 24]. It results in a money judgment for or against part- ance struck.

action for an accounting

A formal judicial proceeding in which the court is authorized to (1) review the partnership and the partners' transactions and (2) award each partner his or her share of the partnership assets.

trepreneur and the Law

tners' Rights to Share in Profits

he UPA mandates that a partner has in the partnership's profits and ership agreements often provide that e allocated in proportion to the part- . The right to share in the profits of the to be the right to share in the earnings pital.

LeAnn Pearson and Mark Butler form contributes $75,000 capital and 00 capital. They do not have an ofits or losses are to be shared. makes $100,000 in profits. Under the UPA, Pearson and Butler share in the profits equally—$50,000 each.

Where a partnership agreement provides for the sharing of profits but is silent as to how losses are to be shared, losses are shared in the same proportion as profits. The reverse is not true, however. If a partnership agreement provides for the sharing of losses but is silent as to how profits are to be shared, profits are shared equally.

Expressly providing how profits and losses are to be shared by partners can increase the benefits to partners. For example, partners with high incomes from other sources can benefit most from the losses generated by a partnership. ■

ty

artnership must act through its agents, that is, its partners. Contracts ppliers, customers, lenders, or others on the partnership's behalf are nership.

joint liability
Partners are *jointly liable* for contracts and debts of the partnership. This means that a plaintiff must name the partnership and all of the partners as defendants. If successful, the plaintiff can recover the entire amount of the judgment from any or all of the partners.

Under the UPA, partners are **jointly liable** for the contracts and debts of the partnership [UPA § 15(b)]. This means that a third party who sues to recover on a partnership contract or debt must name all of the partners in the lawsuit. If such a lawsuit is successful, the plaintiff can collect the entire amount of the judgment against any or all of the partners. If the third party's suit does not name all of the partners, the judgment cannot be collected against any of the partners or the partnership assets. Similarly, releasing any partner from the lawsuit releases them all.

A partner who is made to pay more than his or her proportionate share of contract liability may seek **indemnification** from the partnership and from those partners who have not paid their share of the loss.

In the following case, the court found partners jointly liable on a partnership contract.

Case 15.2 Joint Liability of General Partners

Edward A. Kemmler Memorial Foundation v. Mitchell
584 N.E.2d 695, 1992 Ohio Lexis 205 (1992)
Supreme Court of Ohio

Background and Facts

Clifford W. Davis and Dr. William D. Mitchell formed a general partnership to purchase and operate rental properties for investment purposes. The partnership purchased a parcel of real property from the Edward A. Kemmler Memorial Foundation (Foundation) on credit. Davis signed a $150,000 promissory note to the Foundation as "Cliff W. Davis, Partner." Prior to executing the note, Davis and Mitchell entered into an agreement that provided that only Davis, and not Mitchell, would be personally liable on the note to the Foundation. They did not inform the Foundation of this side agreement, however. When the partnership defaulted on the note, the Foundation sued the partnership and both partners to recover on the note. Mitchell asserted in defense that the side agreement with Davis relieved him of personal liability. The trial court found Davis and Mitchell jointly liable. The appellate court reversed, excusing Mitchell from liability. The Foundation appealed.

Issue

Are both partners, Davis and Mitchell, jointly liable on the note?

In The Language of The Court

Brown, Justice Every partner is an agent of the partnership for the purpose of its business, and the act of every partner, including the execution in the partnership name of any instrument, for apparently carrying on in the usual way the business of the partnership of which he is a member binds the partnership, unless the partner so acting has in fact no authority to act for the partnership in the particular matter, and the person with whom he is dealing has knowledge of the fact that he has no such authority.

Thus, if a promissory note is executed in the name of the partnership, the partnership is bound, unless a contradictory agreement between the partners is known to the parties with whom they are dealing. The trial court found that the Foundation had no knowledge of the agreement between Davis and Mitchell regarding Mitchell's liability for the note.

Decision and Remedy

The Ohio supreme court held that both partners were jointly liable on the note. Reversed.

Case Questions

Critical Legal Thinking What is joint liability? Should one general partner be liable to pay a judgment against the partnership?

Business Ethics Should Davis and Mitchell have notified the Foundation of their side agreement?

Contemporary Business Is it financially dangerous to be a partner in a general partnership? Explain.

Tort Liability

joint and several liability
Tort liability of a partnership in which the partners are liable together and separately. This means that the plaintiff can sue one or more of the partners separately. If successful, the plaintiff can recover the entire amount of the judgment from any or all of the defendant-partners.

While acting on partnership business, a partner or an employee of the partnership may commit a tort that causes injury to a third person. This tort could be caused by a negligent act, a breach of trust (such as embezzlement from a customer's account), a breach of fiduciary duty, defamation, fraud, or other intentional tort. The partnership is liable if the act is committed while the person is acting within the ordinary course of partnership business or with the authority of his or her co-partners.

Under the UPA, partners are **jointly and severally liable** for torts and breaches of trust [UPA § 15(a)]. This is so even if a partner did not participate in the commission of

rmits a third party to sue one or more of the partners sep-
ted only against the partners who are sued. The partnership
pay tort liability may seek indemnification from the partner
act. A release of one partner does not discharge the liability

pose Nicole, Jim, and Maureen form a partnership. Assume
business, causes an automobile accident that injures Kurt, a
,000 in injuries. Kurt, at his option, can sue Nicole, Jim, or
wo of them, or all of them.

A new partner who is admitted to a partnership is liable for
tions (**antecedent debts**) of the partnership only to the extent
ution. The new partner is personally liable for debts and obli-
tnership after becoming a partner.

It is when merchants dispute about their own rules that they invoke the law.

J. Brett
Robinsone v. Mollett (1875)

ntemporary Business Environment

and Several Liability of General Partners

e of joint and several liability in the
a and Joseph Antenucci were both
artners in a medical practice. Both
erman during her pregnancy. Her son,
with severe physical problems.
and natural guardian, brought this
gainst both doctors. The jury found
dical malpractice but that Antenucci
e verdict totaled $4 million. The trial
gainst Pena but not against Antenucci.
a posttrial motion for judgment against

d severally liable for the medical mal-
ena? The court said yes.

The court noted that a partnership is liable for the tortious act of a partner, and a partner is jointly and severally liable for tortious acts chargeable to the partnership.

When a tort is committed by the partnership, the wrong is imputable to all of the partners jointly and severally, and an action may be brought against all of any of them in their individual capacities or against the partnership as an entity. Therefore, even though the jury found that defendant Antenucci was not guilty of malpractice in his treatment of the patient, but that defendant Pena, his partner, *was* guilty of malpractice in his treatment of the patient, they were both jointly and severally liable for the malpractice committed by defendant Pena by operation of law. [*Zuckerman v. Antenucci*, 478 N.Y.S.2d 578, 1984 N.Y.Misc. Lexis 3283 (N.Y. 1984)] ■

mary Personal Liability of General Partners

oint Liability	Joint and Several Liability
Contract action.	Tort action.
Plaintiff must name all partners as defendants.	Plaintiff can sue partners individually.
If successful, the plaintiff can recover the judgment against all or any of the defendants.	If successful, the plaintiff can recover the judgment against all or any of the named defendants.
Partner who pays judgment can recover contribution from other partners for their share of the judgment.	Partner who pays judgment can recover contribution from other partners for their share of the judgment.

Dissolution of Partnerships

The duration of a partnership can be for a fixed term (e.g., five years) or until a particular undertaking is accomplished (e.g., until a real estate development is completed) or it can be for an unspecified term. A partnership with a fixed duration is called a **partnership for a term**. A partnership with no fixed duration is called a **partnership at will**.

partnership for a term
A partnership with a fixed duration.

partnership at will
A partnership with no fixed duration.

A partner has the *power* to withdraw and dissolve the partnership at any time, but he or she may not have the *right* to do so. For example, a partner who withdraws from a partnership before the expiration of the term stated in the partnership agreement does not have the right to do so. The partner's action causes a **wrongful dissolution** of the partnership. The partner is liable for damages caused by the wrongful dissolution of the partnership.

wrongful dissolution
A partner's withdrawal from a partnership when he or she does not have the right to do so.

Notice of Dissolution The dissolution of a partnership terminates the partners' actual authority to enter into contracts or otherwise act on behalf of the partnership. Notice of dissolution must be given to certain third parties. The degree of notice depends on the relationship of the third party with the partnership [UPA § 35]:

Business Brief
If a partnership is dissolved, notice of the dissolution must be given to certain third parties. Partners may be liable for debts and obligations incurred on behalf of the partnership after the dissolution if the required notice is not given.

1. Third parties who have actually dealt with the partnership must be given **actual notice** (verbal or written) of dissolution or have acquired knowledge of the dissolution from another source.
2. Third parties who have not dealt with the partnership but have knowledge of it must be given either actual or **constructive notice** of dissolution. Constructive notice consists of publishing a notice of dissolution in a newspaper of general circulation serving the area where the business of the partnership was regularly conducted.
3. Third parties who have not dealt with the partnership and do not have knowledge of it do not have to be given notice.

constructive notice
Usually, written notice to a third party that is put into general circulation, such as in a newspaper.

If proper notice is not given to a required third party after the dissolution of a partnership and a partner enters into a contract with the third party, liability may arise on the grounds of *apparent authority*.

Entrepreneur and the Law

Continuation of a Partnership After Dissolution

The surviving or remaining partners are given the right to continue a partnership after dissolution. It is good practice for the partners of a partnership to enter into a *continuation agreement* that expressly sets forth the events that allow for continuation of the partnership, the amount to be paid outgoing partners, and other details.

When a partnership is continued, the old partnership is dissolved, and a new partnership is created. The new partnership is composed of the remaining partners and any new partners admitted to the partnership. The creditors of the old partnership become creditors of the new partnership and have equal status with the creditors of the new partnership [UPA § 41].

The dissolution of a partnership does not of itself discharge the liability of outgoing partners for existing partnership debts and obligations. An outgoing partner can be relieved of liability if the outgoing partner, the continuing partners, and the creditor enter into a **novation agreement** that expressly relieves the outgoing partner of liability [UPA § 36]. ■

emporary Business Environment

f Survivorship

her partners of the specific
partnership [UPA § 25(1)].
exists only in a partnership.
eceased partner's right in spe-
the remaining partner or part-
er heirs or next of kin. This is
pon the death of the last surviv-
artnership property vest in the
tative [UPA § 25(2)C]. The *value*
t in the partnership passes to
pon his or her death, however.

Consider This Example Jamie, Harold, Shou-Ju, and Jesus form a general partnership to operate a new restaurant. After their first restaurant is successful, they expand until the partnership owns 100 restaurants. At that time Jaime dies. None of the partnership assets transfer to Jaime's heirs; for example, they do not get 25 of the restaurants. Instead, under the right of survivorship, they inherit Jamie's ownership interest, and his heirs now have the right to receive Jamie's one-quarter of the partnership's profits each year. ■

rnational Law

erships Outside the United States

organizations are essentially the
tates. Partnership law, in particu-
n both countries (and in countries
partnership is an association of
n a business with the intent to

cluding France and Germany, every
, including a partnership, is a "com-
llschaft in German). A French part-
any, is considered as having sepa-
ity independent from its partners
sue or be sued in its own name. At
t can also opt to be treated as a
xes as if it were a corporation. In
artnership does not have a separate
, even though a German partnership
rs who own the property, and the
d.
categorized as companies in both
main associations of persons who
r the actions of their company.
ssociations, they must have two or

ed to generate profits for the part-
he partnership agreement may
uch clauses can exclude a particular
er the profits or losses of the com-
ause is void.

A specialized form of partnership, the limited partnership, is recognized in the civil law countries. At least one partner must be a general partner (with personal unlimited liability) and one must be a limited partner. Limited partners have limited liability of the kind that investors in stock companies have. They may invest only cash or property in France, but in Germany services may be fixed and recognized as a contribution. In both countries persons can be either general or limited partners, but they cannot be both. In France, limited partners can participate in the internal administration of the partnership. In Germany, they can participate in internal administration and be given broad powers to deal with third parties on behalf of the partnership.

Germany recognizes another type of partnership, known as the silent partnership. This is a secret relationship between the partners that is unknown to third parties. The active partner conducts the business in his or her name alone, never mentioning the silent partner. So long as the silent partner's participation is not disclosed, the silent partner's risk is limited to the amount he or she invested. Silent partnerships are useful business forms for investment in Germany because the interest paid to the silent partner is treated as interest on a loan and is therefore tax deductible as a business expense from the earnings of the active partner. In France, where partnerships are regarded as separate legal entities, a silent partnership is not recognized as a separate entity and, therefore, is not governed by partnership law. ■

Cambodia. Partnerships have been used as a form of business for centuries.

Limited Partnerships

Limited partnerships are statutory creations that have been used since the Middle Ages. They include both general (manager) and limited (investor) partners. Today, all states have enacted statutes that provide for the creation of limited partnerships. In most states these partnerships are called **limited partnerships** or **special partnerships**. Limited partnerships are used for such business ventures as investing in real estate, drilling oil and gas wells, investing in movie productions, and the like.

limited partnership
A special form of partnership that is formed only if certain formalities are followed. A limited partnership has both general and limited partners.

Revised Uniform Limited Partnership Act (RULPA)
A 1976 revision of the ULPA that provides a more modern, comprehensive law for the formation, operation, and dissolution of limited partnerships.

The great can protect themselves, but the poor and humble require the arm and shield of the law.

Andrew Jackson
(1767–1845)

The Revised Uniform Limited Partnership Act

In 1916 the National Conference of Commissioners on Uniform State Laws, a group composed of lawyers, judges, and legal scholars, promulgated the **Uniform Limited Partnership Act (ULPA)**. The ULPA contains a uniform set of provisions for the formation, operation, and dissolution of limited partnerships. Most states originally enacted this law.

In 1976, the National Conference on Uniform State Laws promulgated the **Revised Uniform Limited Partnership Act (RULPA)**, which provides a more modern, comprehensive law for the formation, operation, and dissolution of limited partnerships. This law supersedes the ULPA in the states that have adopted it. The RULPA provides the basic foundation for the discussion of limited partnership law in the following pages.

general partners
Partners in a limited partnership who invest capital, manage the business, and are personally liable for partnership debts.

limited partners
Partners in a limited partnership who invest capital but do not participate in management and are not personally liable for partnership debts beyond their capital contribution.

General and Limited Partners

Limited partnerships have two types of partners: (1) **general partners**, who invest capital, manage the business, and are personally liable for partnership debts, and (2) **limited partners**, who invest capital but do not participate in management and are not personally liable for partnership debts beyond their capital contribution (see Exhibit 15.2).

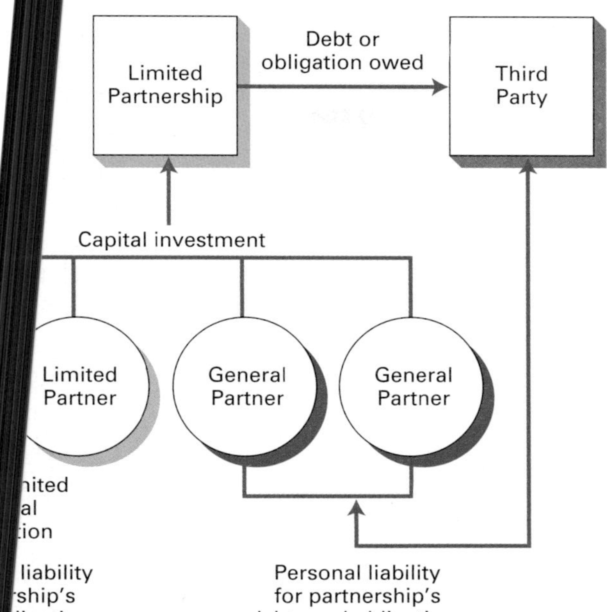

Exhibit 15.2
Limited Partnership

ited
al
ion
liability
ship's
ligations

p must have one or more general partners and one or more lim- 101(7)]. There are no restrictions on the number of general or in a limited partnership. Any person may be a general or limited atural persons, partnerships, limited partnerships, trusts, estates, ations. A person may be both a general and a limited partner in rship.

its a corporation to be the sole general partner of a limited part- permissible, it affects the liability of the limited partnership. ited partners are liable only to the extent of their capital contri- ration acting as general partner is liable only to the extent of its

A judge should not stand in judgment over a person whom he likes or dislikes.

Talmud
(A.D. 1st–6th cent.)

ted Partnerships

mited partnership is formal and requires public disclosure. The with the statutory requirements of the RULPA or other state

PA, two or more persons must execute and sign a **certificate of limited** PA §§ 201 and 206]. The certificate must contain the following

certificate of limited partnership
A document that two or more persons must execute and sign that makes the limited partnership legal and binding.

e limited partnership
aracter of the business
the principal place of business, and the name and address of the agent ce of legal process
business address of each general and limited partner
e on which the limited partnership is to dissolve
of cash, property, or services (and description of property or services) y each partner, and any contributions of cash, property, or services e made in the future
atters that the general partners determine to include

Business Brief
It is good practice to have a written partnership agreement that sets forth in detail the rights and duties of the partners. This will reduce later disputes and lawsuits.

The certificate of limited partnership must be filed with the secretary of state of the appropriate state and, if required by state law, with the country recorder in the county or counties in which the limited partnership carries on business. The limited partnership is formed when the certificate of limited partnership is filed.

Limited Partnership Agreement

limited partnership agreement A document that sets forth the rights and duties of the general and limited partners, the terms and conditions regarding the operation, termination, and dissolution of the partnership, and so on.

Although not required by law, the partners of a limited partnership often draft and execute a **limited partnership agreement** (also called the **articles of limited partnership**) that sets forth the rights and duties of the general and limited partner, the terms and conditions regarding the operation, termination, and dissolution of the partnership, and so on. Where there is no such agreement, the certificate of limited partnership serves as the articles of limited partnership.

The limited partnership agreement may specify how profits and losses from the limited partnership are to be allocated among the general and limited partners. If there is no such agreement, the RULPA provides that profits and losses from a limited partnership are shared on the basis of the value of the partner's capital contribution [RULPA § 503]. A limited partner is not liable for losses beyond his or her capital contribution.

Morality cannot be legislated, but behavior can be regulated. Judicial decrees may not change the heart, but they can restrain the heartless.

Martin Luther King, Jr.
Strength to Love (1963)

In addition, it is good practice to establish voting rights in the limited partnership agreement or certificate of limited partnership. The limited partnership agreement can provide which transactions must be approved by which partners (i.e., general, limited, or both). General and limited partners may be given unequal voting rights.

Business Brief
A limited partner may be held liable as a general partner if the limited partnership is defectively formed.

Defective Formation Defective formation occurs when (1) a certificate of limited partnership is not properly filed, (2) there are defects in a certificate that is filed, or (3) some other statutory requirement for the creation of a limited partnership is not met. If there is a substantial defect in the creation of a limited partnership, persons who thought they were limited partners can find themselves liable as general partners. Such persons who erroneously but in good faith believe they have become limited partners can escape liability as general partners by either (1) causing the appropriate certificate of limited partnership (or certificate of amendment) to be filed or (2) withdrawing from any future equity participation in the enterprise and causing a certificate showing this withdrawal to be filed. Nevertheless, the limited partner remains liable to any third party who transacts business with the enterprise before either certificate is filed if the third person believed in good faith that the partner was a general partner at the time of the transaction [RULPA § 304].

Laws too gentle are seldom obeyed; too severe, seldom executed.

Benjamin Franklin
Poor Richard's Almanack (1756)

Liability of General and Limited Partners

Business Brief
General partners of a limited partnership have unlimited liability for debts and obligations of the partnership. Limited partners are liable only up to their capital contribution.

Business Brief
If a limited partner participates in management, he or she can become liable as a general partner.

The **general partners** of a limited partnership have unlimited liability for the debts and obligations of the limited partnership. This liability extends to debts that cannot be satisfied with the existing capital of the limited partnership. Generally, **limited partners** are liable only for the debts and obligations of the limited partnership up to their capital contributions.

As a trade-off for limited liability, limited partners give up their right to participate in the control and management of the limited partnership. This means, in part, that limited partners have no right to bind the partnership to contracts or other obligations. Under the RULPA, a limited partner is liable as a general partner if his or her participation in the control of the business is substantially the same as that of a general partner, but the limited partner is liable only to persons who reasonably believed him or her to be a general partner [RULPA § 303(a)].

Entrepreneur and the Law

Limited Partner Liable on Personal Guarantee

Many small businesses, including limited partnerships, attempt to borrow money from banks or obtain extensions of credit from suppliers. Often these lenders require owners of small businesses to personally guarantee the loan to the business; otherwise, the extensions of credit will not be made. Consider the following case.

Linnane Magnavox Home Entertainment Center (Linnane Magnavox) was a limited partnership that was organized under the laws of Kansas. Paul T. Linnane was the sole general partner, and Richard Gale Stover was the limited partner. Stover was the silent partner who provided the capital for the partnership. Stover took no part in the day-to-day management or control of the partnership, employment or discharge of employees, the purchase or sale of inventory, or any other incident of partnership business. In November 1977, Linnane Magnavox entered into a contract with General Electric Credit Corporation (GE Credit) whereby GE Credit would provide financing to the partnership. GE Credit refused to grant credit to the undercapitalized partnership unless Stover signed as the guarantor of the credit. It was not until Stover furnished his personal financial statements to GE Credit and personally signed the credit agreement as a guarantor that it extended credit to the partnership. When Linnane Magnavox defaulted on the debt and Paul Linnane was adjudicated bankrupt, GE Credit sued Stover to recover on the debt. The trial court held in favor of GE Credit. Stover appealed. Is Stover, the limited partner, personally liable for Linnane Magnavox's debt to GE Credit?

The court of appeals held that defendant Stover was liable to pay the debts of Linnane Magnavox to GE Credit. The court stated:

> The question for decision was whether, for the purpose of the extension of credit to Linnane Magnavox, Stover put his personal assets at stake and GE Credit was therefore induced to extend its credit to the partnership. The evidence before the trial court was that GE Credit would not have extended credit to Linnane Magnavox had not Stover signed the credit agreement. It was a stipulated fact that prior to the execution of the credit agreement, GE Credit requested, and Stover furnished, his personal financial statement. In terms of partnership principle, the question is that of holding out: whether the Stover signature induced GE Credit to extend credit on reliance that Stover would be personally bound on those obligations. Stover had every reason to know that his unqualified signature on the documents would bind his personal credit as that of the general partner.

The court held the limited partner Stover to his word. [*General Electric Credit Corporation v. Stover*, 708 S.W.2d 355, 1986 Mo.App. Lexis 3931 (MO 1986)] ■

Concept Summary Liability of Limited Partners

General rule	Limited partners are not individually liable for the obligations or conduct of the partnership beyond the amount of their capital contribution.
Exceptions to the general rule	Limited partners are individually liable for the debts, obligations, and tortious acts of the partnership in three situations: 1. **Defective Formation** There has not been substantial compliance in good faith with the statutory requirements to create a limited partnership. Exception: Persons who erroneously believed themselves to be limited partners either (1) caused the appropriate certificate of limited partnership or amendment thereto to be filed or (2) withdrew from any future equity participation in the profits of the partnership and caused a certificate of withdrawal to be filed. 2. **Participation in Management** The limited partner participated in the management and control of the partnership. Exception: The limited partner was properly employed by the partnership as a manager or executive. 3. **Personal Guarantee** The limited partner signed an enforceable personal guarantee that guarantees the performance of the limited partnership.

Contemporary Business Environment

Master Limited Partnerships

One of the major drawbacks for investors who are limited partners in a limited partnership is that their investment usually is not liquid because there is no readily available market for buying and selling limited partnership interests. The introduction of **master limited partnerships (MLPs)** is changing this situation.

An MLP is a limited partnership whose limited partnership interests are traded on organized securities exchanges such as the New York Stock Exchange. Often, MLPs are created by corporations that transfer certain corporate assets (such as real

estate) to an MLP and then sell limi sts to
the public. The corporation usually r l partner. Some MLPs are formed to make .
There are tax benefits to owning interest
in an MLP rather than corporate stoc ne
tax—partnership income and losses individual partner's income tax return. Profi ns of
MLPs also avoid the double taxation s.
The use of MLPs is expected to in ■

Limited Liability Partnerships (LLPs)

limited liability partnership (LLP)
A form of partnership in which all partners are limited partners and there are no general partners.

Many states have enacted legislation to permit the creation of **lin ner-**
ships (LLPs). In an LLP, there does not have to be a general par nally
liable for the debts and obligations of the partnership. Instead, *a* ited
partners who stand to lose only their capital contribution shoul fail.
None of the partners is personally liable for the debts and obligati ship
beyond his or her capital contribution (see Exhibit 15.3).

LLPs enjoy the "flow-through" tax benefit of other types of part ere
is no tax paid at the partnership level, and all profits and losses are di-
vidual partners' income tax returns.

Articles of Partnership

articles of partnership
A public document that must be filed with the secretary of state to form a limited liability partnership.

LLPs must be created formally by filing **articles of partnership** w of
state of the state in which the LLP is organized. This is a public d P
is a **domestic LLP** in the state in which it is organized. The LLP la -

Exhibit 15.3
Limited Liability Partnership (LLP)

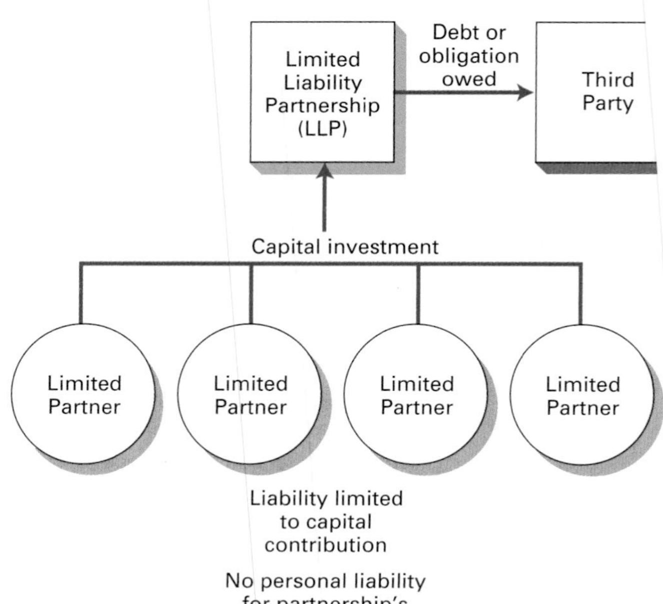

erns the operation of the LLP. An LLP may do business in other states, however. To do so, the LLP must register as a **foreign LLP** in any state in which it wants to conduct business.

Liability Insurance Required

In most states LLP law restricts the use of LLPs to certain types of professionals, such as accountants and lawyers. Many state laws require LLPs to carry a minimum of $1 million of liability insurance that covers negligence, wrongful acts, and misconduct by partners or employees of the LLP. This requirement guarantees that injured third parties will have compensation to recover for their injuries and is a quid pro quo for permitting partners of LLPs to have limited liability.

Justice is the end of government. It is the end of civil society. It ever has been, and ever will be pursued, until it be obtained, or until liberty be lost in the pursuit.

James Madison
The Federalist No. 51 (1788)

Contemporary Business Environment

Accounting Firms Operate as LLPs

Prior to the advent of the LLP form of doing business, accounting firms operated as general partnerships. As such, the general partners were personally liable for the debts and obligations of the general partnership. In large accounting firms, this personal liability was rarely imposed. This was because the general partnership usually carried sufficient liability insurance to cover most awards to third-party plaintiffs in negligence tort actions. Creditors usually extended credit to the large accounting firms based on the reputation of the firms and the fact that these large accounting firms had sufficient capital in the partnership to meet most loan obligations.

Beginning in the early 1980s, large accounting firms were hit with many large court judgments. These cases were brought in conjunction with the failure of large savings banks and commercial banks and the failure of other large firms that accountants had audited. Many of these firms failed because of fraud by their major owners and officers. The shareholders and creditors of these failed companies sued the auditors, alleging that the auditors had been negligent in not catching the fraud. Many juries agreed and awarded large sums against the accounting firms. Sometimes the accounting firm's liability insurance was not enough to cover the judgment, thus imposing personal liability on partners. General partners in accounting firms became worried that the inability of the profession to shield itself from such liability jeopardized the profession.

In response, in the 1990s, state legislatures created a new form of business, the LLP. This entity was particularly created for accountants, lawyers, and other professionals to offer their services under an umbrella of limited liability. The partners of an LLP have limited liability up to their capital contribution; the partners do not have personal liability for the debts and liabilities of the LLP, however.

Once LLPs were permitted by law, all of the Big Five accounting firms changed their status from general partnerships to LLPs. The signs and letterheads of each of the Big Five accounting firms prominently announce that the accounting firm is an "LLP." Many accounting firms other than the Big Five have also changed over to LLP status, as have many law firms. The LLP form of business has changed how accountants, lawyers, and other professionals offer their services. ■

Limited Liability Companies (LLCs)

In recent years, a majority of states have approved a new form of business entity called a **limited liability company (LLC)**. An LLC is an unincorporated business entity that combines the most favorable attributes of general partnerships, limited partnerships, and corporations. An LLC may elect to be taxed as a partnership, the owners can manage the business, and the owners have limited liability. Many entrepreneurs who begin new businesses choose the LLC as their legal form for conducting business. The formation and operation of LLCs are discussed in the following pages.

limited liability company (LLC)
An unincorporated business entity that combines the most favorable attributes of general partnerships, limited partnerships, and corporations.

LLCs are creatures of state law, not federal law. LLCs can only be created pursuant to the laws of the state in which the LLC is being organized. These statutes, commonly referred to as **limited liability company codes**, regulate the formation, operation, and

limited liability company codes
State statutes that regulate the formation, operation, and dissolution of LLCs.

dissolution of LLCs. The state legislature may amend its LL… ne. The courts interpret state LLC statutes to decide LLC and membe…

legal entity
A separate legal entity—an *artificial person*—distinct from its members that can own property, sue and be sued, enter into and enforce contracts, and such.

An LLC is a separate **legal entity** (or legal person) di… embers [ULLCA § 201]. LLCs are treated as artificial persons that can… ter into and enforce contracts, hold title to and transfer property, and b… l crimi-nally liable for violations of law.

Members' Limited Liability

member
An owner of an LLC.

limited liability
Liability in which members are liable for the LLC's debts, obligations, and liabilities only to the extent of their capital contributions.

The owners of LLCs are usually called **members**. The general rul… are not personally liable to third parties for the debts, obligations, an… LLC beyond their capital contributions. Members are said to have **limi**… xhibit 15.4). The debts, obligations, and liabilities of an LLC, whether… tracts, torts, or otherwise, are solely those of the LLC [ULLCA § 303(a)…

Consider This Example Jasmin, Shan-Yi, and Vanessa form ar… con-tributes $25,000 in capital. The LLC operates for a period of tim… bor-rows money from banks and purchases goods on credit from supp… time, the LLC experiences financial difficulty and goes out of business. … with $500,000 in debts, each of the members will lose her capital contri… but will not be personally liable for the rest of the unpaid debts of LLC…

The Uniform Limited Liability Company Act

Uniform Limited Liability Company Act (ULLCA)
A model act that provides comprehensive and uniform laws for the formation, operation, and dissolution of LLCs.

In 1995, the National Conference of Commissioners of Uniform St… of lawyers, judges, and legal scholars) issued the **Uniform Limited Lia… Act (ULLCA)**. The ULLCA codifies LLC law. Its goal is to establish … LC law that is uniform throughout the United States. The ULLCA co… ms that arise in the formation, operation, and termination of LLCs. The… aw unless a state adopts it as its LLC statute. Many states have adopte… he

Exhibit 15.4
Limited Liability Company (LLC)

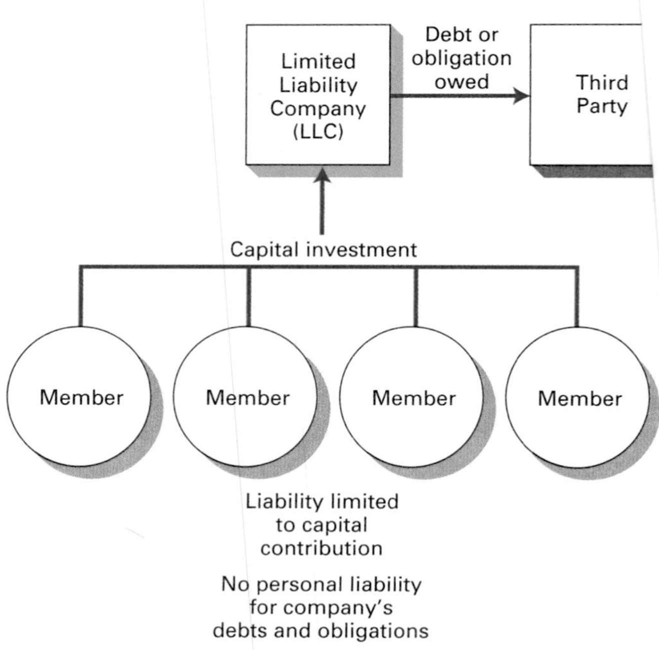

ULLCA as their limited liability company law. Because it is so important, the ULLCA forms the basis of the study of LLCs in this chapter.

In the following case, the court addressed the issue of the limited liability of a member of an LLC.

Business Brief

An LLC combines the tax benefits of a partnership with the limited personal liability attributes of a corporation.

Case 15.3 Limited Liability Company

Page v. Roscoe, LLC

497 S.E.2nd 422, 1998 N.C.App. Lexis 169

Court of Appeals of North Carolina

Background and Facts

Dale C. Bone was a member of Roscoe, LLC, an LLC organized under the laws of North Carolina. In August 1994, Roscoe, LLC, purchased two acres of land near the town of Apex, North Carolina. In January 1995, Apex approved Roscoe, LLC's, plan to construct and operate a propane gas bulk storage and distribution facility on the land. This use was permitted under Apex's zoning ordinance. In April 1995, Daylene Page and other homeowners in the area sued Roscoe, LLC, and Dale C. Bone, alleging that the gas storage facility, if constructed, would constitute a nuisance. In December 1995, after the trial court denied the plaintiffs' motion to obtain a preliminary injunction against construction of the facility, the plaintiffs dismissed the lawsuit. Subsequently, Bone sued the plaintiffs for sanctions to recover attorneys' fees he had spent in defending against the plaintiffs' lawsuit. The trial court ordered the plaintiffs to pay Bone's attorneys' fees. The plaintiffs appealed.

Issue

Were the sanctions warranted against the plaintiffs for naming an individual member of an LLC in the lawsuit they brought against the LLC?

In The Language of The Court

Walker, Judge We do find that the allegations against Bone individually are not well-grounded in law. N.C.Gen.Stat. § 57C-3-30 (1993) provides in pertinent part:

(a) A person who is a member or manager, or both, of a limited liability company is not liable for the obligations of a limited liability company solely by reason of being a member or manager or both, and does not become so by participating, in whatever capacity, in the management or control of the business.

(b) A member of a limited liability company is not a proper party to proceedings by or against a limited liability company.

The record sustains the trial court's conclusion that no acts by Bone, individually, were properly alleged. Therefore, under the above statute, it was improper to name an individual member of a limited liability company as a party defendant without any evidence to support it. As such, the naming of Bone as an individual defendant was not well-grounded in law.

Decision and Remedy

The court of appeals held that Bone, as a member of Roscoe, LLC, was not liable as a matter of law for the acts of the LLC and was therefore improperly named as a defendant in the lawsuit filed by the plaintiffs. The plaintiffs were held liable for sanctions and were required to pay Bone's attorneys' fees the he expended in defending against the plaintiffs' lawsuit.

Case Questions

Critical Legal Thinking Should members of an LLC be released from personal liability for the debts and obligations incurred by the LLC?

Business Ethics Did the plaintiff homeowners act ethically in naming Bone as a defendant? Why do you think they named Bone as a defendant?

Contemporary Business Is this case good precedent for business persons wishing to conduct business as LLCs?

Personal Guarantees A member is personally liable for the debts of an LLC only if he or she agrees to be in either the articles of organization or other writing, or if he or she personally guarantees the repayment of the LLC's debts [ULLCA § 303(c)].

Web Site

LLC-USA This site is a good resource for people interested in LLCs. Visit at **www.llc-usa.com**.

Consider This Example Patricia, Arnold, and Emory form a new LLC. When they go to a bank to have the LLC borrow money from the bank, the bank refuses to make the loan to such a new LLC unless the members personally guarantee the loan. To obtain the loan, Patricia, Arnold, and Emory sign personal guarantees with the bank, agreeing to repay the loan if the LLC does not. In this case, if the LLC fails to repay the loan, the bank may enforce the personal guarantees and recover the amount of the loan from the members.

Business Brief

A member is personally liable if he or she personally guarantees repayment of the debts of the LLC.

Contemporary Business Environment

DreamWorks SKG, LLC: Script for a Movie Company

In 1995, Steven Spielberg, Jeffrey Katzenberg, and David Geffen formed **DreamWorks SKG**, which is a major movie and recording production company. Spielberg's fame and money came from directing such films as *E. T.*, Katzenberg was a leading executive at Disney, and Geffen built and sold Geffen Records. These multimillionaire, multimedia giants combined their talents to form a formidable entertainment company.

Interestingly, DreamWorks was hatched as a Delaware LLC. The organizers chose to form an LLC because it is taxed as a partnership, and the profits (or losses) flow directly to the owners, but as with a corporation, the owners are protected from personal liability beyond their capital contributions.

DreamWorks issued several classes of stock, or interests. The three principals put up $100 million ($33.3 million each) for **"SKG" stock**, which grants the principals 100 percent voting control and 67 percent of the firm's profits. In addition, each principal has a seven-year employment contract that pays him $1 million annually, plus other fringe benefits and perquisites on terms that are customary for similarly situ ... he entertainment industry.

DreamWorks raised the other $9 ... billion capital from other investors, who re ... ture profits. The other investors were iss ... asses of stock:

Class	Investment
A	Outside investors. Cla ... to big investors with over $2 ... Microsoft's cofounder, ... ed $500 million of Class A stoc ... got seats on the board of ...
S	Outside investors. Clas ... ed for smallish, "strategic" in ... r companies for cross-market ...
E	Employees. Employees ... ht to participate in an emp ... e plan. ■

Formation of an LLC

articles of organization

The formal document that must be filed with the secretary of state to form an LLC.

Forming an LLC is very similar to organizing a corporation. T ... sons (which include individuals, partnerships, corporations, and associ ... an LLC for any lawful purpose. To form an LLC, **articles of organi**... filed with the appropriate state office, usually the Secretary of State's ... ibit 15.5). The articles of organization must state the LLC's name, ... her information required by statute or that the organizers deem impor... The name of an LLC must contain the words *Limited Liability Company* ... ion *L.L.C.* or *L.C.*

Entrepreneur and the Law

Why Operate a Business as an LLC?

Why should LLC be used instead of an S Corporation or a partnership? S Corporations and partnerships are subject to many restrictions and adverse consequences that do not exist with an LLC. Some differences are:

- S Corporations cannot have shareholders other than estates, certain trusts, and individuals (who cannot be nonresident aliens). S Corporations can have no more than 75 shareholders and one class of stock and may not own more than 80 percent of another corporation. LLCs have no such restrictions.
- In a general partnership, the partners a... for the obligations of the partnership. M... have limited liability.
- Limited partnerships must have at least ... who is personally liable for the obligation... ship (although this partner can be a corp... partners are precluded from participating ... ment of the business. An LLC provides li... members, even though they participate in ... the business. ■

Exhibit 15.5

Sample Articles of Organization

ARTICLES OF ORGANIZATION
FOR FLORIDA LIMITED LIABILITY COMPANY

ARTICLE I - NAME

The name of the Limited Liability Company is
iCitrusSystems.com

ARTICLE II - ADDRESS

The mailing address and street address of the principal office of the Limited Liability Company is

3000 Dade Boulevard
Suite 200
Miami Beach, Florida 33139

ARTICLE III - DURATION

The period of duration for the Limited Liability Company shall be
50 years

ARTICLE IV - MANAGEMENT

The Limited Liability Company is to be managed by a manager and the name and address of such manager is

Susan Escobar
1000 Collins Avenue
Miami Beach, Florida 33141

____
Thomas Blandford

____
Pam Rosales

Conversion of an Existing Business to an LLC Many LLCs are formed by entrepreneurs to start new businesses. In addition, many existing businesses may want to convert to LLCs to obtain its tax benefits and limited liability shield. General partnerships, limited partnerships, and corporations may be converted to LLCs. The conversion takes effect when the articles of organization are filed with the secretary of state.

Business Brief

Some existing businesses, such as general partnerships, limited partnerships, and corporations, may want to convert to LLCs. The law permits such conversions.

Operating Agreement

Members of an LLC may enter into an **operating agreement** that regulates the affairs of the company and the conduct of its business and governs relations among the members, managers, and the company [ULLCA § 103(a)]. The operating agreement may be amended by the approval of all members, unless otherwise provided in the agreement. The operating agreement and amendments may be oral but are usually written.

operating agreement

An agreement entered into by members that governs the affairs and business of the LLC and the relations among members, managers, and the LLC.

Contemporary Business Environment

"Check-the-Box" Regulations for Partnership Taxation of LLCs

An LLC is an unincorporated business entity formed under state law. Because an LLC is neither a partnership nor a corporation, a question arises as to how it should be taxed for federal income tax purposes. Under the Internal Revenue Code, a partnership is not taxed at the entity level, but its income or losses "flow through" to the partners' individual income tax returns. This avoids double taxation. On the other hand, corporations are generally taxed once at the entity level and then again if they pay dividends to shareholders, who must pay tax on these dividends when they file their personal

Contemporary Business Environment
(continued)

income tax returns. Thus, there is double taxation with a corporation.

In most cases, an LLC would prefer to be taxed as a partnership rather than as a corporation. When the first LLC was formed under Wyoming law, the Internal Revenue Service (IRS) issued a Revenue Ruling that classified the LLC as a partnership for federal income tax purposes. After this initial ruling, the IRS issued regulations that provided that an LLC could be taxed as a partnership if it gave up two of the following corporate attributes: (1) associates, (2) objective to carry on the business for a profit, (3) centralized management, (4) limited liability, (5) continuity of life, and (6) free transferability of interests. To obtain partnership taxation, in most instances LLCs gave up continuity of life by stating a term for the LLC (e.g., 50 years) and free transferability of interests by agreeing to buy-and-sell agreements and other restrictions on the sale or transfer of their ownership interests.

This method of obtaining partnership taxation was used by LLCs until 1997. Effective January 1, 1997, the IRS adopted **"Check-the-Box" Regulations** that made it easier for LLCs to be taxed as partnerships. These regulations provide that a business entity falls into one of the following categories:

1. ***Per se Corporations*** These are d ... ns incorporated under the state law ar ... orations for federal income tax purpose
2. ***Eligible Entities*** These are define ... than *per se* corporations. Eligible entitie ... rated businesses with two or more ov ... s, LLPs, limited partnerships, and gener ... eligible entity is taxed as a partnership ... be taxed as a corporation.
3. ***Single-Owner Entity*** A single-owne ... a sole proprietorship unless the owner ... as a corporation.

The Check-the-Box Regulations hav ... t provide that eligible entities, such as an LLC, ... nerships with flow-through taxation unless an e ... be taxed as a corporation. This election is mad ... 32 with the IRS; this form must be signed by a ... ager who is given authority to sign such an ... -the-Box Regulations make it easier for LLC ... ship taxation status for federal income tax p ... tes automatically apply the federal classific ... e income tax purposes, although a few d

Member-Managed and Manager-Managed LLCs

member-managed LLC

An LLC that has not designated that it is a manager-managed LLC in its articles of organization.

manager-managed LLC

An LLC that has designated in its articles of organization that it is a manager-managed LLC.

An LLC can be either a **member-managed LLC** or a **manager-ma** ... LLC is a member-managed LLC unless it is designated as a member-ma ... articles of organization [ULLCA § 203(a)(6)].

The designation of an LLC as a member-managed LLC or ma ... LLC is important in determining who has authority to bind the LLC to ... member-managed LLC, all members have agency authority to bind the L ... On the other hand, in a manager-managed LLC, only the designated m ... hority to bind the LLC to contracts; nonmanager members do not hav ... An LLC is only bound to contracts that are in the ordinary course of busi ... LC has authorized [ULLCA § 301].

Entrepreneur and the Law
Management of a Limited Liability Company

In a member-managed LLC, each member has equal rights in the management of the business of the LLC, irrespective of the size of his or her capital contribution. Any matter relating to the business of the LLC is decided by a majority vote of the members [ULLCA § 404(a)].

Consider This Example Allison, Jaeson, Stacy, Lan-Wei, and Ivy form NorthWest.com, LLC. Allison contributes $100,000 capital, and each of the other four members contrib ... tal. When deciding whether to add another l ... the business, Stacy, Lan-Wei, and Ivy vote to ... Allison and Jaeson vote against it. The line ... added to the LLC's business because three ... while two members voted no. It does not ma ... members who voted no contributed $125,00 tively versus $75,000 in capital contributed by the three members who voted yes.

In a manager-managed LLC, the members and nonmembers who are designated managers control the management of the LLC. The members who are not managers have no rights to manage the LLC unless otherwise provided in the operating agreement. A manager must be appointed by a vote of a majority of the members; managers may also be removed by a vote of the majority of the members [ULLCA § 404(b)(3)]. In a manager-managed LLC, each manager has equal rights in the management and conduct of the company's business. Any matter relating to the business of the LLC may be exclusively decided by the managers by a majority vote of the managers [ULLCA § 403(b)].

Certain actions cannot be delegated to managers but must be voted on by all members of the LLC. These include (1) amending the articles of organization, (2) amending the operating agreement, (3) admitting new members, (4) consenting to dissolve the LLC, (5) consenting to merge the LLC with another entity, and (6) selling, leasing, or disposing of all or substantially all of the LLC's property [ULLCA § 404(c)].

A member or manager may appoint a proxy to vote or otherwise act for him or her by signing an appropriate proxy card [ULLCA § 404(e)]. ■

Duty of Loyalty Owed to LLC

A member of a member-managed LLC and a manager of a manager-managed LLC owe a **duty of loyalty** to the LLC. This means that these parties must act honestly in their dealings with the LLC. The duty of loyalty includes the duty not to usurp the LLC's opportunities, make secret profits, secretly deal with the LLC, secretly compete with the LLC, or represent any interest adverse to that of the LLC [ULLCA § 409(b)]. For example, making secret kickbacks on the purchase of goods by the LLC and transacting business with the LLC without first disclosing this position and obtaining approval from the LLC to do so are breaches of duty of loyalty.

duty of loyalty
A duty owed by a member of a member-managed LLC and a manager of a manager-managed LLC to be honest in his or her dealings with the LLC and to not act adversely to the interests of the LLC.

In the following case, the court found a member-manager of an LLC to have breached his fiduciary duty of loyalty.

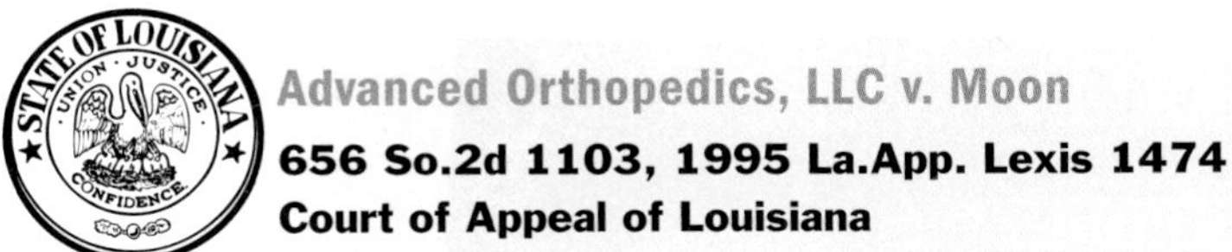

Case 15.4 Liability of a Member

Advanced Orthopedics, LLC v. Moon
656 So.2d 1103, 1995 La.App. Lexis 1474
Court of Appeal of Louisiana

Background and Facts

In November 1992, Bryon Heath and John Moon organized an LLC called "Advanced Orthopedics, L.L.C." (Advanced) under the Louisiana law. The articles of organization were filed with the Louisiana secretary of state's office, which issued a certificate of organization establishing the LLC. Advanced, under the management of Heath and Moon, provided prosthetic and orthotic services to the community. By June 1993, Moon and Heath were having difficulties managing Advanced together. While at Advanced, Moon took steps to set up a competing business. By November 1993, Moon opened his own prosthetic and orthotic services business. He thereafter resigned from Advanced.

Advanced filed a petition for permanent injunction and damages against Moon, alleging that Moon violated his fiduciary duty of loyalty to Advanced by setting up his competing business while still a member-manager of Advanced. The trial court granted a preliminary injunction in favor of Advanced, enjoining Moon from soliciting any of Advanced's patients or using any of Advanced's records. The court rejected Moon's defense that Advanced was not a legally formed LLC because he allegedly did not have the subjective intent to form an LLC. Moon appealed.

Issue

Was an LLC formed by Heath and Moon, thereby justifying the trial court's finding that Moon had violated his fiduciary duty of loyalty to Advanced?

In The Language of The Court

Gothard, Judge In Moon's first assignment of error, he argues that he did not have the subjective intent to form an L.L.C. with Heath. During the year that Moon participated in the management of Advanced, he never questioned its viability as an L.L.C. He testified in his deposition that he reviewed informational materials regarding LLC's prior to Advanced's inception and that he knew that he and Heath were operating their business as an L.L.C. Advanced clearly provided enough evidence to the trial court to support its argument that an L.L.C. was formed and operating.

On appeal, Moon argues that he did not adequately understand the concept of an L.L.C. Attaining a certain level of understanding regarding LLCs is not a prerequisite to the formation of and participation in one. After a thorough review of the record, we cannot find any support for Moon's assertion that somehow he did not have the subjective intent to form an L.L.C. with Heath.

Advanced Orthopedics, LLC v. Moon

656 So.2d 1103, 1995 La.App. Lexis 1474
Court of Appeal of Louisiana
(continued)

Decision and Remedy

The court of appeal held that Heath and Moon had formed an LLC and upheld the trial court's finding that Moon had violated his fiduciary duty of loyalty to the LLC. The court of appeals affirmed the decision of the trial court.

Case Questions

Critical Legal Thinking Should the law impose fiduciary duties of loyalty and care on member-managers and managers of LLCs? Why or why not?

Business Ethics Do you think Moon a nying that an LLC had been formed?

Contemporary Business What are the tions if a member-manager or manager comp ner LLC? Should this practice be illegal?

Continuation of an LLC

This trial is a travesty: it's a travesty of a mockery of a sham of a mockery of a travesty of two mockeries of a sham. I move for a mistrial.

Woody Allen
Bananas (1971)

At the expiration of the term of a term LLC, some of its member ontinue the LLC. At the expiration of its term, a term LLC can be conti uations. First, the members of the LLC may vote prior to the expiration da ie LLC for an additional specified term. This requires the unanimous vot embers and the filing of an amendment to the articles of organization wit f state, stating this fact. Second, absent the unanimous vote to continue th e LLC may be continued as an at-will LLC by a simple majority vote of th e LLC [ULLCA § 411(b)].

International Law

LLCs in Foreign Countries

The use of the LLC as a form of conducting business in the United States is a recent occurrence. In 1977, Wyoming was the first state in the United States to enact legislation creating an LLC as a legal form for conducting business. This new form of business received little attention until the early 1990s when several more states enacted legislation to allow the creation of LLCs. The evolution of LLCs then grew at blinding speed, with all states having enacted LLC statutes by 1998. Most LLC laws are quite similar, although some differences do exist between the state statutes.

The United States did not invent the LLC as a form of business, however. An LLC form of business has been used in different countries of the world for a long time. The **limitada**, a form of business used in Latin America, has many similarities to the LLC. *Limitadas* have been used in Argentina, Brazil, Mexico, and other Latin American countries for a century. These entities share the features of limited liability of owners and centralized management with the LLC. In creating its LLC law, the State of Florida noted that its LLC law was necessary to provide a form of business similar to Latin *limitadas*, with which Central and South American investors were familiar.

On the European continent, an equival ss to the LLC has existed for centuries. In Spai **sociedad de responsibilidades limitada**. LLCs provide for limited liability of owners an- agement. Germany was one of the last Eu add the LLC as a form of business—one c England, an antecedent to the LLC called t was developed around 1555. These comp cally partnerships, had limited liability of owners y of ownership interests, and centralized mana hat of modern LLCs.

In the United States, the LLC has rapidl ness of choice for non-publicly traded busin use of LLCs by entrepreneurs and other busines received much attention in this country, it m that the LLC is not a U.S. invention but is ar of business that has been in use in other co for centuries. ■

General Partnerships, p. 423

G

UPA). A model act that codifies partnership law. Most states have UPA.

ips. A theory that holds that partnerships are *separate legal entities* onal and real property, transact business in the partnership name, and

Partnerships do not pay federal income taxes. The income and losses ndividual partners' federal income tax returns.

nerships

association of two or more persons to carry on as co-owners of a busi-

2. ***Partners***... general partnership can operate under the names of any one or more of the partners or under a fictitious business name.

The Partnership Agreement

Agreement establishing a general partnership. It sets forth terms of the partnership. It is good practice to have a written partnership agreement that the partners sign.

1. ***Certificate of partnership.*** A document that general partnerships must file with the appropriate state government agency in some states.

Contract Liability

1. ***Partners' contract authority.*** A contract entered into by a partner with a third party on behalf of a partnership is binding on the partnership.
2. ***Ratification.*** The partners can decide to *ratify* an unauthorized contract. The ratification binds the partnership to the contract from the time of execution.
3. ***Partnership liability.*** A partnership is liable for the contracts entered into on its behalf by partners acting with express, implied, or apparent authority, or where unauthorized contracts have been ratified by the partners.

Tort Liability

1. ***Tort.*** Occurs when a partner causes injury to a third party by his or her negligent act, breach of trust, breach of fiduciary duty, or intentional tort.
2. ***Partnership liability.*** The partnership is liable to third persons who are injured by torts committed by a partner while he or she is acting within the ordinary course of partnership business.
3. ***Joint and several liability of partners.*** Partners are *personally liable* for torts committed by partners acting on partnership business. This liability is *joint and several.* This means that the plaintiff can sue *one or more* of the partners separately. If successful, the plaintiff can recover the entire amount of the judgment from any or all of the defendant-partners.

Liability of Incoming Partners

A new partner who is admitted to the partnership is liable for the existing debts and obligations (*antecedent debts*) of the partnership only to the extent of his or her capital contribution. The new partner is personally liable for debts and obligations incurred by the partnership after becoming a partner.

Dissolution of Partnerships

The change in the relation of the partners caused by any partner ceasing to be associated in the carrying on of the business.

Wrongful Dissolution

Occurs when a partner withdraws from a partnership without having the *right* to do so at the time. The partner is liable for damages caused by the wrongful dissolution of the partnership.

Notice of Dissolution

1. ***Notice of dissolution of partners.*** Notice of dissolution must be given to all partners. If a partner who has not received notice of dissolution enters into a contract on behalf of the partnership in the course of partnership business, the contract is binding on all of the partners.
2. ***Notice of dissolution to third parties.*** The following notice must be given to third parties when a partnership has been dissolved other than by operation of law:
   a. *Actual notice.* Must be given to third parties who have actually dealt with the partnership.
   b. *Constructive notice.* Must be given to third parties who have not dealt with the partnership but have knowledge of it. Constructive notice is given by publishing a notice of dissolution in a newspaper of general circulation serving the area where the business of the partnership is conducted.
   c. *No notice.* Parties who have not dealt with the partnership and do not have knowledge of it do not have to be given notice.

Continuation of the Partnership after Dissolution

The surviving or remaining partners are given the right to continue the partnership after dissolution. When a partnership is continued, the old partnership is dissolved and a new partnership is created.

1. ***Continuation agreement.*** A document that expressly sets forth the events that allow for continuation of the partnership, the amount to be paid to outgoing partners, and other details.
2. ***Creditors' status.*** The creditors of the old partnership become creditors of the new partnership and have equal status with the creditors of the new partnership.
3. ***Liability of outgoing partners.*** An outgoing partner is liable for existing partnership debts unless the creditor, other partners, and the outgoing partner enter into a *novation agreement* that expressly relieves the outgoing partner of liability to the creditor.

Limited Partnerships, p. 432

Uniform Limited Partnership Act

1. ***Uniform Limited Partnership Act (ULPA).*** A 1916 model act that contains a uniform set of provisions for the formation, operation, and dissolution of limited partnerships.
2. ***Revised Uniform Limited Partnership Act (RULPA).*** A 1976 revision of the ULPA that provides a more modern comprehensive law for the formation, operation, and dissolution of limited partnerships.

Limited Partnerships

1. ***Limited partnerships.*** A special form of partnership that has both limited and general partners.
   a. *General partners.* Partners in a limited partnership who invest capital, manage the business, and are personally liable for partnership debts.
   b. *Limited partners.* Partners in a limited partnership who invest capital but do not participate in management and are not personally liable for partnership debts beyond their capital contributions.
2. ***Corporation as sole general partner.*** A corporation may be the sole general partner of a limited partnership. Shareholders of corporations are liable only up to their capital contributions.

Formation of Limited Partnerships

1. ***Certificate of limited partnership.*** A document that two or more persons must execute and sign that establishes a limited partnership. The certificate of limited partnership must be filed with the secretary of state of the appropriate state.
2. ***Limited partnership agreement.*** A document that sets forth the rights and duties of general and limited partners, the terms and conditions regarding the operation, termination, and dissolution of the partnership, and so on.
3. ***Offering circular.*** Document that is provided to investors of limited partnership interests that describes the issuer, its business, the terms of the partnership agreement, and other relevant information.
4. ***Defective formation.*** Occurs when (a) a certificate of limited partnership is not properly filed, (b) there are defects in a certificate that is filed, or (c) some other statutory requirement for the creation of a limited partnership is not met. A limited partner may be held liable as a general partner if the limited partnership is defectively formed.

Share of Profits and Losses

Share of profits and losses. Unless otherwise agreed, profits and losses from a limited partnership are shared on the basis of the value of the partner's capital contributions. A limited partner is not liable for losses beyond his or her capital contribution. The limited partnership agreement may specify how profits and losses are to be allocated among the general and limited partners.

Liability of General and Limited Partners

1. ***General partners.*** General partners of a limited partnership have *unlimited personal liability* for the debts and obligations of the limited partnership.
2. ***Limited partners.*** Limited partners of a limited partnership are liable only for the debts and obligations of the limited partnership up to their capital contributions.
3. ***Limited partner and management.*** Limited partners have no right to participate in the management of the partnership. A limited partner is *liable as a general partner* if his or her participation in the control of the business is substantially the same as that of a general partner, but the limited partner is liable only to persons who reasonably believed him or her to be a general partner.

Limited Liability Partnerships (LLPs), p. 436

Limited Liability Partnership

1. ***Limited liability partnership (LLP).*** A form of business in which there does not have to be a general partner who is personally liable for debts and obligations of the partnership. All partners are limited partners and stand to lose only their capital contribution should the partnership fail. LLPs are formed by accountants and other professionals as allowed by LLP law.
2. ***Partners.*** Owners of an LLP.
3. ***Articles of partnership.*** A document that the partners of an LLP must execute, sign, and file with the secretary of state of the appropriate state to form an LLP.
4. ***Taxation.*** An LLP does not pay federal income taxes unless it elects to do so. If an LLP is taxed as a partnership, the income and losses of the LLP flow onto individual partners' federal income tax returns.

Limited Liability Companies (LLCs), p. 437

Limited Liability Company

1. ***Limited liability company (LLC).*** A special form of unincorporated business entity that combines the tax benefits of a partnership with the limited personal liability attribute of a corporation.
2. ***Members.*** Owners of an LLC.
3. ***Articles of organization.*** A document that owners of an LLC must execute, sign, and file with the secretary of state of the appropriate state to form an LLC.

4. ***Operating agreement.*** An agreement entered into among members that governs the affairs and business of the LLC and the relations among partners, managers, and the LLC.
5. ***Taxation.*** An LLC does not pay federal income taxes unless it elects to do so. In an LLC is taxed as a partnership, the income and losses of the LLP flow onto individual members' federal income tax returns.
6. ***Member-managed and manager-managed LLC.*** An LLC can be either a *member-managed LLC* or a *manager-managed LLC*. An LLC is a member-managed LLC unless it is designated as a manager-managed LLC.
   a. *Member-managed LLC.* All members of the LLC have agency authority to bind the LLC to contracts.
   b. *Manager-managed LLC.* Only the designated managers have authority to bind the LLC to contracts.

Internet Exercises and Case Questions

Working the Web Internet Exercises

Activities

1. Review the materials at **smallbiz.biz.findlaw.com/planning/index.html?planning/wa**. Compare with the text discussion of partnerships. Can you see why lawyers generally advise business clients *not* to do business in a partnership form?
2. A checklist of questions about partnership can be found at **www.nolo.com/lawcenter/faqs/detail.cfm/objectID/D2C7200B-28A8-49FB-9EA5E2B7E7F15CB5**. Use it as a self-test.
3. Study the provisions of the ULPA at **www.law.upenn.edu/bll/ulc/ulpa/final2001.htm**.
4. Check your state statute on LLPs. Are they permitted in your jurisdiction? Are there any limitations on the type of businesses allowed to operate as an LLP? See LII: Law About . . . Partnership at **www.law.cornell.edu/topics/partnership.html**.
5. Check your state statute on LLCs. How many persons are required to form an LLC? Try **www.4inc.com/llcfaq.htm**.

Critical Legal Thinking Cases

15.1 General Partnership In early 1986, Thomas Smithson, a house builder and small-scale property developer, decided that a certain tract of undeveloped land in Franklin, Tennessee, would be extremely attractive for development into a subdivision. Smithson contacted the owner of the property, Monsanto Chemical Company, and was told that the company would sell the property at the "right price."

Smithson did not have the funds with which to embark unassisted in the endeavor, so he contacted Frank White, a coowner of the Andrews Realty Company, and two agents of the firm, Dennis Devrow and Temple Ennis. Smithson showed them a sketch map with the proposed layout of the lots, roads, and so forth. Smithson testified that they all orally agreed to develop the property together, and in lieu of making a financial investment, Smithson would oversee the engineering of the property. Subsequently, H. R. Morgan was brought into the deal to provide additional financing.

Smithson later discovered that White had contacted Monsanto directly. When challenged about this, White assured Smithson that he was still "part of the deal" but refused to put the agreement in writing. White, Devrow, Ennis, and Morgan purchased the property from Monsanto. They then sold it to H.A.H. Associates, a corporation, for a $184,000 profit. When they refused to pay Smithson, he sued to recover an equal share of the profits. Was a partnership formed between Smithson and the defendants? [*Smithson v. White*, 1988 Tenn.App. Lexis 221 (Tenn.App. 1988)]

15.2 General Partnership Richard Filip owned Trans Texas Properties. Tracy Peoples was an employee of the company. In order to obtain credit to advertise in the *Austin American-Statesman* newspaper, which was owned by Cox Enterprises, Inc., Peoples completed a credit application that listed Jack Elliot as a partner in Trans Texas. Evidence showed that Elliot did not own interest in Trans Texas and did not consent to or authorize Peoples to make this representation to Cox. Cox made no effort to verify the accuracy of the representation and extended credit to Trans Texas. When Trans Texas defaulted on payments owed Cox, Cox sued both Filip and Elliot to recover the debt. Is Elliot liable? [*Cox Enterprises, Inc. v. Filip and Elliot*, 538 S.W.2d 836, 1976 Tex.App. Lexis 2947 (Tex.App. 1976)]

15.3 Tort Liability In January 1977, Charles Fial and Roger J. Steeby entered into a partnership called "Audit Consultants" to perform auditing services. Pursuant to the agreement, they shared equally the equity, income, and profits of the partnership. Originally, they performed the auditing services themselves, but as business increased, they engaged independent contractors to do some of the audit work. Fial's activities generated approximately 80 percent of the partnership's revenues. Unhappy with their agreement to divide the profits equally, Fial wrote a letter to Steeby on July 11, 1984, dissolving the partnership.

Fial asserted that the clients should be assigned based on who brought them into the business. Fial formed a new business called "Audit Consultants of Colorado, Inc." He then terminated the partnership's contracts with many clients and put them under contract under his new firm. Fial also terminated the partnership's contracts with the independent-contractor auditors and signed many of these auditors with his new firm. The partnership terminated on May 24, 1985. Steeby brought an action against Fial, alleging breach of fiduciary duty and seeking a final accounting. Who wins? [*Steeby v. Fial*, 765 P.2d 1081, 1988 Colo.App. Lexis 409 (Colo.App. 1988)]

15.4 Fiduciary Duty Edgar and Selwyn Husted, attorneys, formed Husted and Husted, a law partnership. Herman McCloud, who was the executor of his mother's estate, hired them as attorneys for the estate. When taxes were due on the estate, Edgar told McCloud to make a check for $18,000 payable to the Husted and Husted Trust Account and that he would pay the IRS from this account. There was no Husted and Husted trust account. Instead, Edgar deposited the check into his own personal account and converted the funds to his own personal use. When Edgar's misconduct was uncovered, McCloud sued the law firm for conversion of estate funds. Is the partnership liable for Edgar's actions? [*Husted v. McCloud*, 436 N.E.2d 341, 1982 Ind.App. Lexis 1244 (Ind.App. 1982)]

15.5 Tort Liability Thomas McGrath was a partner in the law firm of Torbenson, Thatcher, McGrath, Treadwell & Schoonmaker. At approximately 4:30 P.M. on February 11, 1980, McGrath went to a restaurant-cocktail establishment in Kirkland, Washington. From that time until about 11:00 P.M. he imbibed considerable alcohol while socializing and discussing personal and firm-related business. After 11 o'clock, McGrath did not discuss firm business but continued to socialize and drink until approximately 1:45 A.M., when he and Frederick Hayes, another bar patron, exchanged words. Shortly thereafter, the two encountered each other outside, and after another exchange, McGrath shot Hayes. Hayes sued McGrath and the law firm for damages. Who is liable? [*Hayes v. Torbenson, Thatcher, McGrath, Treadwell & Schoonmaker*, 749 P.2d 178, 1988 Wash.App. Lexis 27 (Wash.App. 1988)]

15.6 Notice of Dissolution In 1976, Leonard Sumter, Sr., entered into a partnership agreement with his son, Michael T. Sumter, to conduct a plumbing business in Shreveport, Louisiana, under the name "Sumter Plumbing Company." On June 10, 1976, the father, on behalf of the partnership, executed a credit application with Thermal Supply of Louisiana, Inc., (Thermal) for an open account to purchase supplies on credit. From that date until the spring of 1980, the Sumters purchased plumbing supplies from Thermal on credit and paid their bills without fail. Both partners and one employee signed for supplies at Thermal. In May 1980, the partnership was dissolved, and all outstanding debts to Thermal were paid in full. The Sumters did not, however, notify Thermal that the partnership had been dissolved.

A year later, the son decided to reenter the plumbing business. He used the name previously used by the former partnership, listed the same post office address for billing purposes, and hired the employee of the former partnership who signed for supplies at Thermal. The father decided not to become involved in this venture. The son began purchasing supplies on credit from Thermal on the open credit account of the former partnership. Thermal was not informed that he was operating a new business. When the son defaulted on payments to Thermal, it sued the original partnership to recover the debt. Is the father liable for these debts? [*Thermal Supply of Louisiana, Inc. v. Sumter*, 452 So.2d 312, 1984 La.App. Lexis 8975 (La.App. 1984)]

15.7 Liability of General Partners Pat McGowan, Val Somers, and Brent Robertson were general partners of Vermont Place, a limited partnership formed on January 20, 1984, for the purpose of constructing duplexes on an undeveloped tract of land in Fort Smith, Arkansas. The general partners appointed McGowan and his company, Advance Development Corporation, to develop the project, including contracting with material men, mechanics, and other suppliers. None of the limited partners took part in the management or control of the partnership.

On September 3, 1984, Somers and Robertson discovered that McGowan had not been paying the suppliers. They removed McGowan from the partnership and took over the project. The suppliers sued the partnership to recover the money owed them. The partnership assets were not sufficient to pay all of their claims. Who is liable to the suppliers? [*National Lumber Company v. Advance Development Corporation*, 732 S.W.2d 840, 1987 Ark. Lexis 2225 (Ark. 1987)]

15.8 Liability of Limited Partners Union Station Associates of New London (USANL) is a limited partnership formed under the laws of Connecticut. Allen M. Schultz, Anderson Notter Associates, and the Lepton Trust were limited partners. The limited partners did not take part in the management of the partnership. The National Railroad Passenger Association (NRPA) entered into an agreement to lease part of a railroad facility from USANL. The NRPA sued the USANL for allegedly breaching the lease and also named the limited partnership as defendants. Are the limited partners liable? [*National Railroad Passenger Association v. Union Station Associates of New London*, 643 Supp. 192, 1986 U.S. Dist. Lexis 22190 (D.D.C. 1986)]

15.9 Formation of a Limited Partnership Robert K. Powers and Lee M. Solomon were among other limited partners of the Cosmopolitan Chinook Hotel, a limited partnership. On October 25, 1972, Cosmopolitan entered into a contract to lease and purchase neon signs from Dwinell's Central Neon. The contract identified Cosmopolitan as a "partnership" and was signed on behalf of the partnership, "R. Powers, President." At the time the contract was entered into, Cosmopolitan had taken no steps to file its certificate of limited partnership with the state, as required by limited partnership law. The certificate was not filed with the state until several months after the contract was signed. When Cosmopolitan defaulted on payments due under the contract, Dwinell's sued Cosmopolitan and its general and limited partners. Are the limited partners liable? [*Dwinell's Central Neon v. Cosmopolitan Chinook Hotel*, 587 P.2d 191, 1978 Wash.App. Lexis 2735 (Wash.App. 1978)]

15.10 Limited Liability Company Harold, Jasmine, Caesar, and Yuan form "Microhard.com, LLC," an LLC, to sell computer hardware and software over the Internet. Microhard.com, LLC, hires Heather, a recent graduate of the University of Chicago and a brilliant software designer, as an employee. Heather's job is to design and develop software that will execute a computer command when the computer user thinks of the next command he or she wants to execute on the computer.

Using Heather's research, Microhard.com, LLC, develops the "Third Eye" software program that does this. Microhard.com, LLC, sends Heather to the annual Comdex computer show in Las Vegas, Nevada, to unveil this revolutionary software. Heather goes to Las Vegas and while there rents an automobile to get from the hotel to the computer show and to meet interested buyers at different locations in Las Vegas. While Heather is driving from her hotel to the site of the Comdex computer show, she negligently causes an accident in which she runs over Harold Singer, a pedestrian. Singer, who suffers severe personal injuries, sues Microhard.com, LLC; Heather; Harold; Jasmine; Caesar; and Yuan to recover monetary damages for his injuries. Who is liable?

15.11 Limited Liability Company Juan, Min-Yi, and Chelsea form "Unlimited, LLC, an LLC that operates a chain of women's retail clothing stores that sell eclectic women's clothing. The company is a manager-managed LLC, and Min-Yi has been designated in the articles of organization filed with the secretary of state as the manager of Unlimited, LLC. Min-Yi sees a store location on Rodeo Drive in Beverly Hills, California, that she thinks would be an excellent location for an Unlimited store. Min-Yi enters into a five-year lease on behalf of Unlimited, LLC, with Landlord, Inc., the owner of the store building, to lease the store at $100,000 rent per year. While visiting Chicago, Chelsea sees a store location on North Michigan Avenue in Chicago that she thinks is a perfect location for an Unlimited store. Chelsea enters into a five-year lease on behalf of Unlimited, LLC, with Real Estate, Inc., the owner of the store building, to lease the store location at $100,000 rent per year. Is Unlimited, LLC, bound to either of these leases?

15.12 Limited Liability Company Donna, Arnold, Jose, and Won-Suk form an LLC called "Millennium Foods, LLC," to operate an organic foods grocery store in Portland, Oregon. Donna and Arnold each contribute $25,000 capital, Jose contributes $50,000, and Won-Suk contributes $100,000. The LLC's articles of organization are silent as to how profits and losses of the LLC are to be divided. The organic foods grocery store is an immediate success and Millennium Foods, LLC makes $200,000 profit the first year. Jose and Won-Suk want the profits distributed based on the amount of the members' capital contribution. Arnold and Donna think the profits should be distributed equally. Who is correct?

Business Ethics Cases

15.13 Business Ethics Harriet Hankin, Samuel Hankin, Moe Henry Hankin, Perch P. Hankin, and Pauline Hankin, and their spouses, for many years operated a family partnership composed of vast real estate holdings. Some of the properties included restaurants, industrial buildings, shopping centers, golf courses, a motel chain, and hundreds of acres of developable ground, estimated to be worth $72 million in 1977. In that year, because of family disagreement and discontent, the Hankin family agreed to dissolve the partnership. When they could not agree on how to liquidate the partnership assets, in August 1977, Harriet and Samuel (collectively called Harriet) initiated this equity action.

Based on assurances from Moe and Perch that they would sell the partnership assets as quickly as possible and at the highest possible price, the court appointed them as liquidators of the partnership during the winding-up period. Based on similar assurances, the court again appointed them liquidators for the partnership in 1979. But by 1981, only enough property had been sold to retire the debt of the partnership. Evidence showed that Moe and Perch had not aggressively marketed the remaining properties and that Moe wished to purchase some of the properties for himself at a substantial discount from their estimated value. Six years and three appeals to the superior court later, Harriet brought this action seeking the appointment of a receiver to liquidate the remaining partnership assets.

Did the winding-up partners breach their fiduciary duties? Should the court appoint a receiver to liquidate the remaining partnership assets? Did Moe Henry Hankin act ethically in this case? [*Hankin v. Hankin*, 493 A.2d 675, 1985 Pa. Lexis 337 (Pa. 1985)]

15.14 Business Ethics Angela, Yoko, Cherise, and Serena want to start a new business that designs and manufactures toys for children. At a meeting where the owners want to decide what type of legal form to use to operate the business, Cherise states

> *We should use a limited liability company to operate our business because this form of business provides us, the owners, with a limited liability shield, which means that if the business gets sued and loses, we the owners are not personally liable to the injured party except up to our capital contribution in the business.*

The others agree and form an LLC called Fuzzy Toys, LLC, to conduct the member-managed business. Each of the four owners contributes $50,000 as her capital contribution to the LLC. Fuzzy Toys, LLC, purchases $800,000 of liability insurance from Allied Insurance Company and starts business. Fuzzy Toys, LLC, designs and produces "Heidi," a new toy doll and female action figure. The new toy doll is an instant success, and Fuzzy Toys, LLC, produces and sells millions of these female action figures. After a few months, however, the LLC starts getting complaints that one of the parts of the female action figure is breaking off quite regularly and some children are swallowing the part. The concerned member-managers of Fuzzy Toys, LLC, issue an immediate recall of the female action figure, but before all of the dolls are returned for a refund, Catherine, a seven-year-old child, swallows the toy's part and is severely injured. Catherine, through her mother, sues Fuzzy Toys, LLC, Allied Insurance Company, Angela, Yoko, Cherise, and Serena to recover damages for product liability. At the time of suit, Fuzzy Toys, LLC, has $200,000 of assets. The jury awards Catherine $10 million for her injuries. Who is liable to Catherine and for how much? How much does Catherine recover? Did Angela, Yoko, Cherise, and Serena act ethically in using an LLC as a form of conducting their toy business? Explain.

Briefing the Case Writing Assignment

Read Case A.15 in the Case Appendix [*Catalina Mortgage Company, Inc. v. Monier*]. This case is excerpted from the supreme court of Arizona's opinion. Review and brief the case. In your brief, be sure to answer the following questions.

1. Who was the plaintiff? Who were the defendants?
2. What business arrangement were the defendants engaged in? How did this lead to the lawsuit?
3. What is joint and several liability?
4. Did the court impose joint and several liability in this case?

Answers to Management Decision Questions

1. Yes, the company can be created pursuant to the laws of the state of North Carolina because that is the state in which the LLC would operate. Chapter 57C of the General Statutes of North Carolina authorizes the formation of LLCs in the State of North Carolina: "Each limited liability company has the same powers as an individual to do all things necessary or convenient to carry out its business and affairs.
2. Yes, an LLC would be ideal for entering into a business venture with Barber Construction. When forming a business organization, there are several types of organizational structures to choose from. An LLC is an unincorporated business that combines the most favorable attributes of general partnerships, limited partnerships, and corporations. An LLC can sue or be sued, enter into and enforce contracts, hold title to and transfer property, and be found civilly and criminally liable for violation of law. The characteristic of this organizational structure that makes it most beneficial for investment purposes is the fact that members have limited liability and tax advantages. The debts, obligations, and liabilities of an LLC, whether arising from contracts, torts, or otherwise, are solely those of the LLC unless a member agrees otherwise. An LLC does not pay federal income taxes unless it elects to do so. If an LLC is taxed as a partnership, the income and losses of the LLC flow onto individual members' federal income tax returns. An LLC will expire according to the agreement of the parties.

Endnote

1. Georgia and Louisiana have not adopted the UPA. These states have enacted their own partnership statutes.

16

Domestic and Multinational Corporations

"The biggest corporation, like the humblest private citizen, must be held to strict compliance with the will of the people."

—Theodore Roosevelt
Speech, 1902

Chapter Objectives

After studying this chapter, you should be able to:

1. Define corporation and list the major characteristics of a corporation.
2. Describe the process of forming a corporation.
3. Describe the function of shareholders, directors, and officers in managing the affairs of a corporation.
4. Describe a director's and an officer's duty of care and the business judgment rule.
5. Describe multinational corporations and their role in international trade.

Chapter Contents

Management Decision Domestic and Multinational Corporations

You are the plant manager of Roanoke Sporting Authority, Inc. (Roanoke), a manufacturer of sporting clothing products. Roanoke is experiencing financial difficulty. Records indicate that employee theft is on the rise and that employees have been observed leaving the premises during work hours and returning before their shift is over. Local health and safety standards require all doors in manufacturing plants to be unlocked at all times. Mr. Green, the president and a member of the board of directors, has demanded that the situation be corrected and has suggested that the doors of the plant be locked during second- and third-shift operations.

1. What are the general duties that you and the president owe the employees and shareholders of Roanoke?
2. Should you do as your boss suggested? Why or why not?

Corporations are the most dominant form of business organization in the United States. They generate more than 85 percent of the country's gross business receipts. Corporations range in size from one owner to thousands of owners. Owners of corporations are called **shareholders**.

corporation
A fictitious legal entity that is created according to statutory requirements.

shareholders
The owners of corporations, whose ownership interests are evidenced by stock certificates.

Corporations were first formed in medieval Europe. Great Britain granted charters to certain trading companies from the 1500s to the 1700s. The English law of corporations applied in most of the colonies until 1776. After the Revolutionary War, the states of the United States developed their own corporation law.

Originally, corporate charters were individually granted by state legislatures. In the late 1700s, however, the states began enacting **general corporation statutes** (**corporation codes**) that permitted corporations to be formed without the separate approval of the legislature. Today, most corporations are formed pursuant to general corporation laws of the states.

corporation codes
State statutes that regulate the formation, operation, and dissolution of corporations.

The nature, formation, operation, and financing of corporations are discussed in this chapter.

London. Multinational corporations conduct business throughout the world. They are subject to the laws of each country in which they conduct business.

Web Site

Many large corporations have well-developed Web sites. Here are some good examples:

Information corporation: Microsoft. Visit at **www.microsoft.com**.

Service corporation: Federal Express. Visit at **www.fedex.com**.

International corporation: Mercedes-Benz. Visit at **www.mercedes-benz.com**.

Publishing corporation: Prentice Hall (business law site). Visit at **www.prenhall.com/phblaw**.

The Nature of the Corporation

A corporation is a separate **legal entity** (or **legal person**) for most purposes. Corporations are treated, in effect, as artificial persons created by the state who can sue or be sued in their own names, enter into and enforce contracts, hold title to and transfer property, and be found civilly and criminally liable for violations of law. Corporations cannot be put in prison, so the normal criminal penalty is the assessment of a fine, loss of a license, or other sanction.

Contemporary Business Environment

Characteristics of Corporations

Corporations have the following unique characteristics:

1. ***Limited Liability of Shareholders*** As separate legal entities, corporations are liable for their own contracts and debts. Generally, the shareholders have only **limited liability**. That is, they are liable only to the extent of their capital contribution.
2. ***Free Transferability of Shares*** Corporate shares are freely transferable by the shareholder by sale, assignment, pledge, or gift unless they are issued pursuant to certain exemptions from securities registration. Shareholders may agree among themselves on restrictions on the transfer of shares. National securities markets, such as the New York Stock Exchange, the American Stock Exchange, and NASDAQ, have been developed for the organized sale of securities.
3. ***Perpetual Existence*** Corporations exist in perpetuity unless a specific duration is stated in the corporation's articles of incorporation. The existence of a corporation can be voluntarily terminated by the shareholders. Corporations may be involuntarily terminated by the corporation's creditors if an involuntary petition for bankruptcy against the corporation is granted. The death, insanity, or bankruptcy of a shareholder, a director, or an officer of the corporation does not affect its existence.
4. ***Centralized Management*** The *board of directors* makes policy decisions concerning the operation of the corporation. The members of the board of directors are elected by the shareholders. The directors, in turn, appoint corporate *officers* to run the corporation's day-to-day operations. Together, the directors and the officers form the corporate "management." ■

Revised Model Business Corporation Act (RMBCA)

A 1984 revision of the MBCA that arranged the provisions of the original act more logically, revised the language to be more consistent, and made substantial changes in the provisions.

Business Brief

A corporation is a separate legal entity—an *artificial person*—that can own property, sue and be sued, enter into contracts, and such.

domestic corporation

A corporation in the state in which it was formed.

foreign corporation

A corporation in any state or jurisdiction other than the one in which it was formed.

The Revised Model Business Corporation Act

The Committee on Corporate Laws of the American Bar Association drafted the **Model Business Corporation Act (MBCA)** in 1950. The model act was intended to provide a uniform law regulating the formation, operation, and termination of corporations.

In 1984, the committee completely revised the MBCA and issued the **Revised Model Business Corporation Act (RMBCA)**. Certain provisions of the RMBCA have been amended since 1984. The RMBCA arranged the provisions of the original act more logically, revised the language of the act to be more consistent, and made substantial changes in the provisions of the model act. Many states have adopted all or part of the RMBCA as their **corporation codes**. The RMBCA serves as the basis for the discussion of corporations law in this book.

Classification of Corporations

A private, for-profit corporation is a **domestic corporation** in the state in which it is incorporated. It is a **foreign corporation** in all other states and jurisdictions. For example, suppose a corporation is incorporated in Texas and does business in Montana. The corpo-

Japan. Multinational corporations have grown to immense size and power in recent years. For example, the Mitsubishi Group of Japan operates subsidiary corporations in many nations of the world.

ration is a domestic corporation in Texas and a foreign corporation in Montana. An **alien corporation** is a corporation that is incorporated in another country.

alien corporation
A corporation that is incorporated in another country.

Nonprofit corporations are formed for charitable, educational, religious, or scientific purposes.

Government-owned (or **public**) **corporations** are formed to meet a specific governmental or political purpose. For example, most cities and towns are formed as corporations, as are most water, school, sewage, and park districts. Local government corporations are often called **municipal corporations**.

Concept Summary Types of Corporations

Type of Corporation	Description
Domestic	A corporation is a domestic corporation in the state in which it is incorporated.
Foreign	A corporation is a foreign corporation in states other than the one in which it is incorporated.
Alien	A corporation is an alien corporation in the United States if it is incorporated in another country.

Incorporation Procedures

Corporations are creatures of statute. Thus, the organizers of the corporation must comply with the state's incorporating statute to form a corporation. Although relatively similar, the procedure for **incorporating** a corporation varies somewhat from state to state. The procedure for incorporating a corporation is discussed in the following paragraphs.

limited liability
A situation in which shareholders are liable for the corporation's debts and obligations only to the extent of their capital contributions.

Business Brief

Corporations are creatures of statute: They can be formed only if certain statutory formalities are followed.

Business Brief

More than half of the corporations listed on the New York Stock Exchange are incorporated in Delaware because of its laws that favor management.

Selecting a State for Incorporation

A corporation can be incorporated in only one state, even though it can do business in all other states in which it qualifies to do business. In choosing a state for incorporation, the incorporators, directors, and/or shareholders must consider the corporations law of the states under consideration.

For the sake of convenience, most corporations (particularly small ones) choose the state in which the corporation will be doing most of its business as the state for incorporation. Large corporations generally opt to incorporate in the state with the laws that are most favorable to the corporation's internal operations (e.g., Delaware).

Entrepreneur and the Law

Selecting a Corporate Name

When starting a new corporation, the organizers must choose a name for the entity. To ensure that the name selected is not already being used by another business, the organizers should take the following steps [RMBCA § 4.01]:

- Choose a name (and alternative names) for the corporation. The name must contain the words *corporation*, *company*, *incorporated*, or *limited*, or an abbreviation of one of these words (i.e., *Corp.*, *Co.*, *Inc.*, *Ltd.*).
- Make sure that the name chosen does not contain any word or phrase that indicates or implies that the corporation is organized for any purpose other than those stated in the articles of incorporation. For example, a corporate name cannot contain the word *bank* if it is not authorized to conduct the business of banking.
- Determine whether the name selected is federally trademarked by another company and is therefore unavailable for use. Trademark lawyers and specialized firms will conduct trademark searches for a fee.
- Determine whether the chosen name is similar to other nontrademarked names and therefore unavailable for use. Lawyers and specialized firms will conduct such searches for a fee.
- Determine whether the name selected is available as a domain name on the Internet. If the domain name is already owned by another person or business, the new corporation cannot use this domain name to conduct e-commerce over the Internet. Therefore, it is advisable to select another corporate name. ■

Articles of Incorporation

articles of incorporation

The basic governing document of the corporation. This document must be filed with the secretary of state of the state of incorporation.

Business Brief

Failure to file articles of incorporation exposes purported shareholders to personal liability for the business's debts and obligations.

The **articles of incorporation** (or **corporate charter**) is the basic governing document of the corporation. It must be drafted and filed with, and approved by, the state before the corporation can be officially incorporated. Under the RMBCA, the articles of incorporation must include [RMBCA § 2.02(a)]

1. The name of the corporation
2. The number of shares the corporation is authorized to issue
3. The address of the corporation's initial registered office and the name of the initial registered agent
4. The name and address of each incorporator

The articles of incorporation may also include provisions concerning (1) the period of duration, which may be perpetual, (2) the purpose or purposes for which the corporation is organized, (3) limitation or regulation of the powers of the corporation, (4) regulation of the affairs of the corporation, and (5) any provision that would otherwise be contained in the corporation's bylaws.

The RMBCA provides that corporate existence begins when the articles of incorporation are filed. The secretary of state's filing of the articles of incorporation is *conclusive proof* that the incorporators satisfied all conditions to incorporations. The corollary to this rule is that failure to file articles of incorporation is conclusive proof of the nonexistence of the corporation.

Exhibit 16.1

Sample Articles of Incorporation

**ARTICLES OF INCORPORATION
OF
THE BIG CHEESE CORPORATION**

ONE: The name of this corporation is:

THE BIG CHEESE CORPORATION

TWO: The purpose of this corporation is to engage in any lawful act or activity for which a corporation may be organized under the General Corporation Law of California other than the banking business, the trust company business, or the practice of a profession permitted to be incorporated by the California Corporations Code.

THREE: The name and address in this state of the corporation's initial agent for service of process is:

Nikki Nguyen, Esq.
1000 Main Street
Suite 800
Los Angeles, California 90010

FOUR: This corporation is authorized to issue only one class of shares which shall be designated common stock. The total number of shares it is authorized to issue is 1,000,000 shares.

FIVE: The names and addresses of the persons who are appointed to act as the initial directors of this corporation are:

Shou-Yi Kang	100 Maple Street Los Angeles, California 90005
Frederick Richards	200 Spruce Road Los Angeles, California 90006
Jessie Qian	300 Palm Drive Los Angeles, California 90007
Richard Eastin	400 Willow Lane Los Angeles, California 90008

SIX: The liability of the directors of the corporation from monetary damages shall be eliminated to the fullest extent possible under California law.

SEVEN: The corporation is authorized to provide indemnification of agents (as defined in Section 317 of the Corporations Code) for breach of duty to the corporation and its stockholders through bylaw provisions or through agreements with the agents, or both, in excess of the indemnification otherwise permitted by Section 317 of the Corporations Code, subject to the limits on such excess indemnification set forth in Section 204 of the Corporations Code.

IN WITNESS WHEREOF, the undersigned, being all the persons named above as the initial directors, have executed these Articles of Incorporation.

Dated: January 1, 2003

The articles of incorporation can be amended to contain any provision that could have been lawfully included in the original document. After the amendment is approved by the shareholders, the corporation must file **articles of amendment** with the secretary of state [RMBCA § 10.06].

Exhibit 16.1 illustrates a sample articles of incorporation.

articles of amendment

A document that must be filed with the secretary of state when the amendment to the articles of incorporation is approved by the shareholders.

Corporate Bylaws

In addition to the articles of incorporation, corporations are governed by their **bylaws**. Either the incorporators or initial directors can adopt the bylaws of the corporation. The bylaws are much more detailed than are the articles of incorporation. Bylaws may contain any provision for managing the business and affairs of the corporation that are not inconsistent with law or the articles of incorporation [RMBCA § 2.06]. They do not have to be filed with any government official. The bylaws are binding on the directors, officers, and shareholders of the corporation.

bylaws

A detailed set of rules that are adopted by the board of directors after the corporation is incorporated that contains provisions for managing the business and the affairs of the corporation.

Business Brief

The bylaws, which are much more detailed than the articles of incorporation, regulate the internal management structure of the corporation.

The bylaws govern the internal management structure of the corporation. Typically, they specify the time and place of the annual shareholders' meeting, how special meetings of shareholders are called, the time and place of annual and monthly board of directors' meetings, how special meetings of the board of directors are called, the notice required for meetings, the quorum necessary to hold a shareholders' or board of directors' meeting, the required vote necessary to enact a corporate matter, the corporate officers and their duties, the committees of the board of directors and their duties, where the records of the corporation are to be kept, directors' and shareholders' inspection rights of corporate records, the procedure for transferring shares of the corporation, and such.

The board of directors has the authority to amend the bylaws unless the articles of incorporation reserve that right for the shareholders. The shareholders of the corporation have the absolute right to amend the bylaws even though the bylaws may also be amended by the board of directors. Sample provisions of corporate bylaws are set forth in Exhibit 16.2.

Exhibit 16.2

Sample Provisions from Corporate Bylaws

BYLAWS
of
THE BIG CHEESE CORPORATION

ARTICLE I Offices

Section 1. Principal Executive Office. The corporation's principal executive office shall be fixed and located at such place as the Board of Directors (herein called the "Board") shall determine. The Board is granted full power and authority to change said principal executive office from one location to another.

Section 2. Other Offices. Branch or subordinate offices may be established at any time by the Board at any place or places.

ARTICLE II Shareholders

Section 1. Annual Meetings. The annual meetings of shareholders shall be held on such date and at such time as may be fixed by the Board. At such meetings, directors shall be elected and any other proper business may be transacted.

Section 2. Special Meetings. Special meetings of the shareholders may be called at any time by the Board, the Chairman of the Board, the President, or by the holders of shares entitled to cast not less than ten percent of the votes at such meeting. Upon request in writing to the Chairman of the Board, the President, any Vice President or the Secretary by any person (other than the Board) entitled to call a special meeting of shareholders, the officer forthwith shall cause notice to be given to the shareholders entitled to vote that a meeting will be held at a time requested by the person or persons calling the meeting, not less than thirty-five nor more than sixty days after the receipt of the request. If the notice is not given within twenty days after receipt of the request, the persons entitled to call the meeting may give the notice.

Section 3. Quorum. A majority of the shares entitled to vote, represented in person or by proxy, shall constitute a quorum at any meeting of shareholders. If a quorum is present, the affirmative vote of a majority of the shares represented and voting at the meeting (which shares voting affirmatively also constitute at least a majority of the required quorum) shall be the act of the shareholders, unless the vote of a greater number or voting by classes is required by law or by the Articles, except as provided in the following sentence. The shareholders present at a duly called or held meeting at which a quorum is present may continue to do business until adjournment, notwithstanding the withdrawal of enough shareholders to leave less than a quorum, if any action taken (other than adjournment) is approved by at least a majority of the shares required to constitute a quorum.

ARTICLE III Directors

Section 1. Election and term of office. The directors shall be elected at each annual meeting of the shareholders, but if any such annual meeting is not held or the directors are not elected thereat, the directors may be elected at any special meeting of shareholders held for that purpose. Each director shall hold office until the next annual meeting and until a successor has been elected and qualified.

Section 2. Quorum. A majority of the authorized number of directors constitutes a quorum of the Board for the transaction of business. Every act or decision done or made by a majority of the directors present at a meeting duly held at which a quorum is present shall be regarded as the act of the Board, unless a greater number be required by law or by the Articles. A meeting at which a quorum is initially present may continue to transact business notwithstanding the withdrawal of directors, if any action taken is approved by at least a majority of the required quorum for such meeting.

Section 3. Participation in Meetings by Conference Telephone. Members of the Board may participate in a meeting through use of conference telephone or similar communications equipment, so long as all members participating in such meeting can hear one another.

Section 4. Action Without Meeting. Any action required or permitted to be taken by the Board may be taken without a meeting if all members of the board shall individually or collectively consent in writing to such action. Such consent or consents shall have the same effect as a unanimous vote of the Board and shall be filed with the minutes of the proceedings of the Board.

Organizational Meeting

An **organizational meeting** of the initial directors of the corporation must be held after the articles of incorporation are filed. At this meeting, the directors must adopt the bylaws, elect corporate officers, and transact such other business as may come before the meeting [RMBCA § 2.05]. The latter category includes such matters as accepting share subscriptions, approving the form of the stock certificate, authorizing the issuance of the shares, ratifying or adopting promoters' contracts, selecting a bank, choosing an auditor, forming committees of the board of directors, fixing the salaries of officers, hiring employees, authorizing the filing of applications for government licenses to transact the business of the corporation, and empowering corporate officers to enter into contacts on behalf of the corporation.

organizational meeting
A meeting that must be held by the initial directors of the corporation after the articles of incorporation are filed.

Entrepreneur and the Law

S Corporations

Corporations are separate legal entities. As such, they generally must pay corporate income taxes to federal and state governments. If a corporation distributes its profits to shareholders in the form of dividends, shareholders must pay personal income tax on the dividends. This *double taxation* of corporation is one of the major disadvantages of doing business in the corporate form. Some corporations and their shareholders can avoid double taxation by electing to be an S Corporation.

In 1982, Congress enacted the **Subchapter S Revision Act**. The act divided all corporations into two groups: **S Corporations**, which are those that elect to be taxed under Subchapter S, and **C Corporations**, which are all other corporations [26 U.S.C. §§ 6242 et seq.].

If a corporation elects to be taxed as an S Corporation, it pays no federal income tax at the corporate level. As in a partnership, the corporation's income or loss flows to the shareholders' individual income tax returns. Thus, this election is particularly advantageous if (1) the corporation is expected to have losses that can be offset against other income of the shareholders or (2) the corporation is expected to make profits and the shareholders' income tax brackets are lower than the corporation's. Profits are taxed to the shareholders even if the income is not distributed. The shares retain other attributes of the corporate form, including limited liability.

Corporations that meet the following criteria can elect to be taxed as S Corporations:

1. The corporation must be a domestic corporation.
2. The corporation cannot be a member of an affiliated group.
3. The corporation can have no more than 75 shareholders.
4. Shareholders must be individuals, estates, or certain trusts. Corporations and partnerships cannot be shareholders.
5. Shareholders must be citizens or residents of the United States. Nonresident aliens cannot be shareholders.
6. The corporation cannot have more than one class of stock. Shareholders do not have to have equal voting rights.
7. No more than 20 percent of the corporation's income can be from passive investment income.

An S Corporation election is made by filing a Form 2553 with the Internal Revenue Service (IRS). The election can be rescinded by shareholders who collectively own at least a majority of the shares of the corporation. However, if the election is rescinded, another S Corporation election cannot be made for five years. ■

Authorized, Issued, and Outstanding Shares

The number of shares provided for in a corporation's articles of incorporation are called **authorized shares** [RMBCA § 6.01]. The shareholders may vote to amend the articles of incorporation to increase this amount. Authorized shares that have been sold by the corporation are called **issued shares**. Not all authorized shares have to be issued at the same time. Authorized shares that have not been issued are called **unissued shares**. The board of directors can vote to issue unissued shares at any time without shareholder approval.

authorized shares
The number of shares provided for in a corporation's articles of incorporation.

issued shares
Shares that have been sold by the corporation.

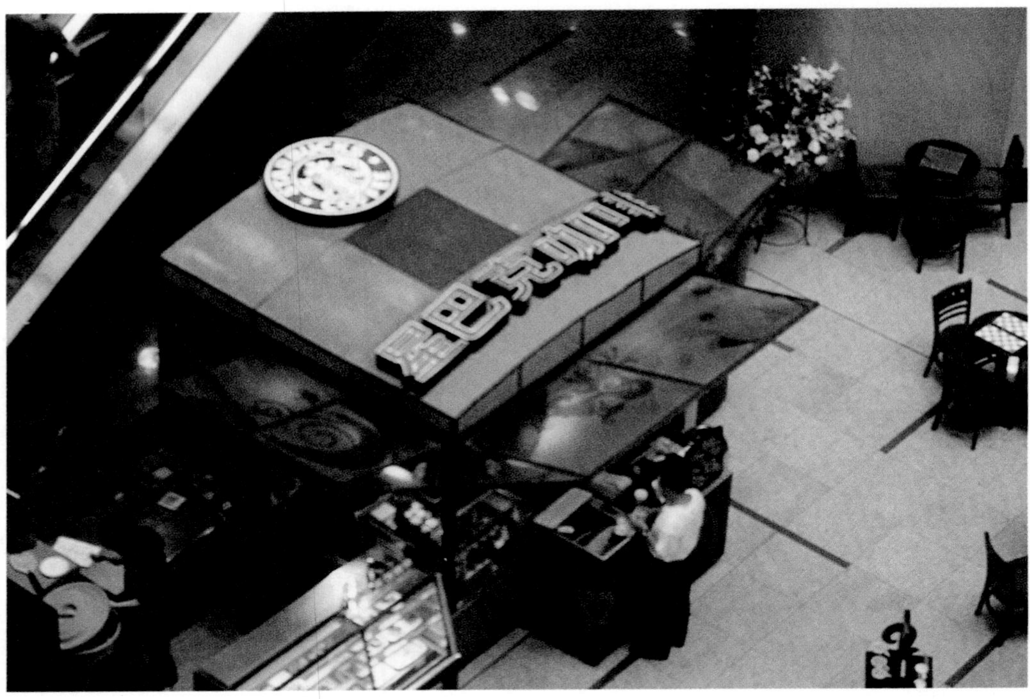

Beijing, China. Commercial opportunities for multinational corporations will increase as new markets open up around the world.

treasury shares
Shares of stock repurchased by the company itself.

outstanding shares
Shares of stock that are in shareholder hands.

A corporation is permitted to repurchase its own shares. Repurchased shares are commonly called **treasury shares**. Treasury shares cannot be voted by the corporation, and dividends are not paid on these shares. Treasury shares can be reissued by the corporation. The shares that are in shareholder hands, whether originally issued or reissued treasury shares, are called **outstanding shares**. Only outstanding shares have the right to vote.

Concept Summary Types of Shares

Type of Share	Description
Authorized	Shares authorized in the corporation's articles of incorporation.
Issued	Shares sold by the corporation.
Treasury	Shares repurchased by the corporation. They do not have the right to vote.
Outstanding	Issued shares minus treasury shares. These shares have the right to vote.

Financing the Corporation

Business Brief
Equity securities represent ownership rights in the corporation. They are also called *stocks*.

A corporation needs to finance the operation of its business. The most common way to do this is by selling equity securities and debt securities. *Equity securities* (or *stocks*) represent ownership rights in the corporation. *Debt securities* do not. Instead, they represent debts owed to creditors of the corporation. Funds may also be obtained by borrowing money from banks, receiving an extension of credit from suppliers, or selling commercial paper to investors.

Common Stock

Common stock is an equity security that represents the residual value of the corporation. Common stock has no preferences. That is, creditors and preferred shareholders must receive their required interest and dividend payments before common shareholders receive anything. Common stock does not have a fixed maturity date. If the corporation is liquidated, the creditors and preferred shareholders are paid the value of their interests first, and the common shareholders are paid the value of their interest (if any) last. Corporations may issue different classes of common stock [RMBCA §§ 6.01 (a) and (b)].

common stock
A type of equity security that represents the *residual* value of the corporation.

Persons who own common stock are called **common stockholders**. A common stockholder's investment in the corporation is represented by a **common stock certificate**. Common stockholders have the right to elect directors and to vote on mergers and other important matters. In return for their investment, common shareholders receive **dividends** declared by the board of directors.

common stockholder
A person who owns common stock.

common stock certificate
A document that represents the common shareholder's investment in a corporation.

Common shares are sometimes categorized as either par or no par. **Par value** is a value assigned to common shares by the corporation, usually in the articles of incorporation, that sets the lowest price at which the shares may be issued by the corporation. It does not affect the market value of the shares. Most shares that are issued by corporations are *no par shares*. No par shares are not assigned a par value. The RMBCA eliminates the concept of par value.

par value
A value assigned to common shares by the corporation that sets the lowest price at which the shares may be issued by the corporation.

Preferred Stock

Preferred stock is an equity security that is given certain *preferences and rights over common stock* [RMBCA § 6.01 (c)]. The owners of preferred stock are called **preferred stockholders**. Preferred stockholders are issued *preferred stock certificates* to evidence their ownership interest in the corporation.

preferred stock
A type of equity security that is given certain preferences and rights over common stock.

preferred stockholder
A person who owns preferred stock.

Preferred stock can be issued in classes or series. One class of preferred stock can be given preferences over another class of preferred stock. Like common stockholders, preferred shareholders have limited liability. Preferred shareholders generally are not given the right to vote for the election of directors or such. However, they are often given the right to vote if there is a merger or if the corporation has not made the required dividend payments for a certain period of time (e.g., three years).

Contemporary Business Environment

Preferences of Preferred Stock

Preferences of preferred stock must be set forth in the articles of incorporation. Preferred stock may have any or all of the following preferences or rights:

- ***Dividend Preference*** A **dividend preference** is the right to receive a *fixed dividend* at set periods during the year (e.g., quarterly). The dividend rate is usually a set percentage of the initial offering price. For example, suppose a stockholder purchases $10,000 of a preferred stock that pays an 8 percent dividend annually. The stockholder has the right to receive $800 each year as a dividend on the preferred stock.
- ***Liquidation Preference*** The right to be paid before common stockholders if the corporation is dissolved and liquidation is called a **liquidation preference**. A liquidation preference is normally a stated dollar amount. For example, a corporation issues a preferred stock that has a liquidation preference of $200. This means that if the corporation is dissolved and liquidated, the holder of each preferred share will receive at least $200 before the common shareholders receive anything. Note that because the corporation must pay its creditors first, there may be insufficient funds to pay this preference.

Contemporary Business Environment
(continued)

- ***Cumulative Dividend Right*** Corporations must pay a preferred dividend if they have the earnings to do so. **Cumulative preferred stock** provides that any missed dividend payments must be paid in the future to preferred shareholders before the common shareholders can receive any dividends. The amount of unpaid cumulative dividends is called dividend *arrearages*. Usually, arrearages can be accumulated for only a limited period of time (such as three years). If the preferred stock is **noncumulative**, there is no right of accumulation. In other words, the corporation does not have to pay any missed dividends.
- ***Right to Participate in Profits*** **Participating preferred stock** allows the stockholders to participate in the profits of the corporation along with the common stockholders. Participation is in addition to the fixed dividend paid on preferred stock. The terms of participation vary widely. Usually, the common stockholders must be paid a certain amount of dividends before participation is allowed. **Nonparticipating preferred stock** does not have a right to participate in the profits of the corporation beyond its fixed dividend rate. Most preferred stock falls into this category.
- ***Conversion Right*** **Convertible preferred stock** permits the stockholders to convert their shares into common stock. The terms and exchange rate of the conversion are established when the shares are issued. The holders of the convertible preferred stock usually exercise this option if the corporation's common stock increases significantly in value. Preferred stock without a conversion feature is called **nonconvertible preferred stock**. Nonconvertible stock is more common than convertible preferred stock.

The preceding list of preferences and rights is not exhaustive [RMBCA § 6.01(d)]. Corporations may establish other preferences and rights for preferred stock. ■

redeemable preferred stock
Stock that permits the corporation to buy back the preferred stock at some future date.

Redeemable Stock **Redeemable preferred stock** (or **callable preferred stock**) permits the corporation to redeem (i.e., buy back) the preferred stock at some future date. The terms of the redemption are established when the shares are issued. Corporations usually redeem the shares when the current interest rate falls below the dividend rate of the preferred shares. Preferred stock that is not redeemable is called **nonredeemable preferred stock**. Nonredeemable stock is more common than redeemable preferred stock.

Debt Securities

debt securities
Securities that establish a debtor–creditor relationship in which the corporation borrows money from the investor to whom the debt security is issued.

A corporation often raises funds by issuing debt securities [RMBCA § 3.02(7)]. **Debt securities** (also called **fixed income securities**) establish a debtor–creditor relationship in which the corporation borrows money from the investor to whom the debt security is issued. The corporation promises to pay interest on the amount borrowed and to repay the principal at some stated maturity date in the future. The corporation is the *debtor*, and the holder is the *creditor*. There are three classifications of debt securities: debentures, bonds, and notes.

debenture
A long-term, unsecured debt instrument that is based on the corporation's general credit standing.

A **debenture** is a long-term (often 30 years or more), unsecured debt instrument that is based on the corporation's general credit standing. If the corporation encounters financial difficulty, unsecured debenture holders are treated as general creditors of the corporation (i.e., they are paid only after the secured creditors' claims are met).

bond
A long-term debt security that is secured by some form of collateral.

A **bond** is a long-term debt security that is secured by some form of *collateral* (e.g., real estate, personal property). Thus, bonds are the same as debentures except that they are secured. Secured bondholders can foreclose on the collateral in the event of nonpayment of interest, principal, or other specified events.

note
A debt security with a maturity of five years or less.

A **note** is a debt security with a maturity of five years or less. Notes can be either unsecured or secured. They usually do not contain a conversion feature. They are sometimes made redeemable.

International Law

Organization and Operation of the Multinational Corporation

In the past, the size, power, and range of activities of corporations were limited. This changed at the beginning of the twentieth century, when corporations won the right to own the stock in each other. National corporate networks soon followed. Eventually, parent corporations, mostly American, expanded these networks overseas by setting up subsidiary corporations under the laws of other countries. These international networks (or multinational enterprises) are made up of companies of different nationalities that constitute a single economic unit connected by shareholding, managerial control, or contractual agreement. The simplest international operating structure is one that subcontracts with independent firms in the host country to carry out sales or purchases. "National multinational" firms that establish wholly owned branches and subsidiaries overseas are somewhat more complex. "International multinational" firms are even more complicated. They are made up of two or more parents from different countries that co-own operating businesses in two or more countries.

The Ford Motor Company is an example of a national multinational firm. Organized in the United States at the beginning of the twentieth century, Ford has always viewed the entire world as its market. The company's policy is for the American parent to own and control all of its overseas subsidiaries. Ford's 10 European subsidiaries are all owned entirely by the American parent. The Mitsubishi Group is another example of this organizational format. It is actually made up of several Japanese companies that use joint directors' meetings to coordinate their activities in Japan and overseas.

The Royal Dutch/Shell Group is an example of an international multinational corporation. In 1907, the Dutch and British parents each formed a wholly owned holding company in their respective countries. Each then transferred the ownership of the operating subsidiary to the holding company and exchanged shares in the holding companies. The Dutch parent held 60 percent of each holding company, and the British parent held 40 percent. In addition, the management and operation of the two companies were organized to function as a single economic unit. Unilever, Dunlop, Pirelli, and VFW/Fokker also operate under an international multinational umbrella.

There is a special type of international multinational: a publicly owned transnational enterprise. One example is Air Afrique, which was created by several West African countries through the use of a treaty granting each government a voice in the company's operation. ■

Shareholders

A corporation's shareholders *own* the corporation. Nevertheless, they are not agents of the corporation (i.e., they cannot bind the corporation to any contracts), and the only management duties they have are the right to vote on matters such as the election of directors and the approval of fundamental changes in the corporation.

Business Brief
Shareholders are not agents of a corporation. They cannot bind the corporation to contracts.

Shareholder Meetings

Annual shareholders' meetings are held to elect directors, choose an independent auditor, or take other actions. The meetings must be held at the time fixed in the bylaws. If the meeting is not held within either 15 months of the last annual meeting or 6 months after the end of the corporation's fiscal year, whichever is earlier, a shareholder may petition the court to order the meeting held.

annual shareholders' meeting
A meeting of the shareholders of a corporation that must be held annually by the corporation to elect directors and to vote on other matters.

Special shareholders' meetings may be called by the board of directors, the holders of at least 10 percent of the voting shares of the corporation, or any other person authorized to do so by the articles of incorporation or bylaws (e.g., the president) [RMBCA § 7.02]. Special meetings may be held to consider important or emergency issues, such as a merger or consolidation of the corporation with one or more other corporations, the removal of directors, amendment of the articles of incorporation, or dissolution of the corporation.

special shareholders' meeting
Meetings of shareholders that may be called to consider and vote on important or emergency issues, such as a proposed merger, amending the articles of incorporation, and such.

Any act that can be taken at a shareholders' meeting can be taken without a meeting if all of the corporate shareholders sign a written consent form approving the action.

Proxies Shareholders do not have to attend the shareholders' meeting to vote. Shareholders may vote by *proxy*; that is, they can appoint another person (the proxy) as their agent to vote at the shareholders' meeting. The proxy may be directed exactly how to vote the shares or may be authorized to vote the shares at his or her discretion. Proxies must be in writing. The written document itself is called the **proxy** (or **proxy card**).

proxy
The written document that a shareholder signs, authorizing another person to vote his or her shares at the shareholders' meetings in the event of the shareholder's absence.

quorum
The required number of shares that must be represented in person or by proxy to hold a shareholder's meeting.

Quorum and Vote Required Unless otherwise provided in the articles of incorporation, if a majority of shares entitled to vote are represented at the meeting in person or by proxy, there is a **quorum** to hold the meeting.

The affirmative vote of the majority of the voting shares represented at a shareholders' meeting constitutes an act of the shareholders for actions other than for the election of directors [RMBCA § 7.25(c)].

Consider This Example Suppose there are 20,000 shares of a corporation outstanding. Assume that a shareholders' meeting is duly called to amend the articles of incorporation and that 10,001 shares are represented at the meeting. A quorum is present because a majority of the shares entitled to vote are represented at the meeting. Suppose that 5,001 shares are voted in favor of the amendment. The amendment passes. In this example, just over 25 percent of the shares of the corporation bound the other shareholders to the action taken at the shareholders' meeting.

The articles of incorporation or the bylaws of a corporation can require a greater than majority of shares to constitute quorum or the vote of the shareholders [RMBCA § 7.27]. This is called a **supramajority** (or **supermajority**) **voting requirement**. Such votes are often required to approve mergers, consolidations, the sale of substantially all of the assets of the corporation, and such.

supramajority voting requirement
A requirement that a greater than majority of shares constitutes quorum or the vote of the shareholders.

Contemporary Business Environment

Election of Directors by Straight and Cumulative Voting

The election of directors by shareholders may be by one of the following two methods.

Straight (Noncumulative) Voting

Unless otherwise stated in the corporation's articles of incorporation, voting for the election of directors is by the **straight voting** method. This voting method is quite simple: Each shareholder votes the number of shares he or she owns on candidates for each of the positions open for election. Thus, a majority shareholder can elect the entire board of directors.

Consider This Example Assume that a corporation has 10,000 outstanding shares. Erin Caldwell owns 5,100 shares (or 51 percent) and Michael Rhodes owns 4,900 shares (49 percent). Suppose that three directors of the corporation are to be elected. Caldwell casts 5,100 votes each for her chosen candidates. Rhodes votes 4,900 shares for each of his chosen candidates, who are different from those favored by Caldwell. Each of the three candidates whom Caldwell voted for wins, with 5,100 votes.

Cumulative Voting

The articles of incorporation may provide for **cumulative voting** for the election of directors. Under this method, a shareholder can accumulate all of his or her votes and vote them all for one candidate or split them among several candidates. This means that each shareholder is entitled to multiply the number of shares he or she owns by the number of directors to be elected and cast the product for a single candidate or distribute the product among two or more candidates [RMBCA § 7.28]. Cumulative voting gives a minority shareholder a better opportunity to elect someone to the board of directors.

Consider This Example Suppose Lisa Monroe owns 1,000 shares. Assume that four directors are to be elected to the board. Under cumulative voting, Monroe can multiply the number of shares she owns by the number of directors to be elected. She can take the resulting number of votes (4,000) and cast them all for one candidate or split them. Examples of cumulative voting are set forth in Exhibit 16.3. ■

Exhibit 16.3

Examples of Cumulative Voting

Formula for Cumulative Voting. A shareholder can use the following formula to determine whether or not he or she owns a sufficient number of shares to elect a director to the board of directors using cumulative voting:

$$\frac{S \times T}{D + 1} + 1 = X$$

where X is the number of shares needed by a shareholder to elect a director to the board, S is the number of shares that actually vote at the shareholders' meeting, T is the number of directors the shareholder wants to elect, and D is the number of directors to be elected at the shareholders' meeting.

Example 1 Suppose there are 9,000 outstanding shares of a corporation. Shareholder 1 owns 1,000 shares, Shareholder 2 owns 4,000 shares, and Shareholder 3 owns 4,000 shares. Assume nine directors are to be elected to the board of directors. All the shares are voted. Under cumulative voting, does Shareholder 1 have enough votes to elect a director to the board? The answer is yes:

$$\frac{9{,}000 \times 1}{9 + 1} + 1 = 901$$

Example 2 If a board of directors is divided into classes and elected by staggered elections, the ability of a minority shareholder to elect a director to the board is diminished. Suppose in Example 1 that the corporation staggered the election of the board of directors so that three directors are elected each year to serve three-year terms. How many shares would a shareholder have to own to elect a director to the board?

$$\frac{9{,}000 \times 1}{3 + 1} + 1 = 2{,}251$$

Because of the staggered election of the board of directors, Shareholder 1 (who owns 1,000 shares) would not be able to elect a director to the board without the assistance of another shareholder.

Preemptive Rights

The articles of incorporation can grant shareholders preemptive rights. **Preemptive rights** give existing shareholders the option of subscribing to new shares being issued by the corporation in proportion to their current ownership interest in the corporation [RMBCA § 6.30]. Such a purchase can prevent a shareholder's interest in the corporation from being *diluted.* Shareholders are given a reasonable period of time (such as 30 days) to exercise their preemptive rights. If the shareholders do not exercise their preemptive rights during this time, the shares can then be sold to anyone.

preemptive rights
Rights that give existing shareholders the option of subscribing to new shares being issued in proportion to their current ownership interest.

Consider This Example Suppose that the ABC Corporation has 10,000 outstanding shares and that Lina Norton owns 1,000 shares (10 percent). Assume that the corporation plans to raise more capital by issuing another 10,000 shares of stock. With preemptive rights, Ms. Norton must be offered the option to purchase 1,000 of the 10,000 new shares before they are offered to the public. If she does not purchase them, her ownership in the corporation will be diluted from 10 percent to 5 percent.

It appears to me that the atmosphere of the temple of Justice is polluted by the presence of such things as companies.

James, L. J
Wilson v. Church (1879)

Business Ethics

Shareholder Resolutions: Do They Promote Social Responsibility of Business?

Shareholders have become more active in corporate governance, as witnessed by the hundreds of shareholder resolutions that are filed each year for vote at annual shareholder meetings.

During the 1980s, apartheid in South Africa was the primary issue of shareholder issues. Prompted by such proposals and the publicity they generated, many U.S. companies left South Africa. The world pressure worked, and South Africa ended apartheid. Free elections were held, and new leaders were elected. The U.S. corporations and other corporations from around the world have returned to doing business in South Africa.

In the 1990s, the fastest growth was in shareholder resolutions urging more corporate sensitivity to the environment. The bigger corporate target in this area was Exxon Corporation, whose March 1989 *Valdez* oil spill fouled the Alaska coastline. Other environmental issues that appeared as shareholder resolutions addressed global warming and the ozone layer, overcutting of the rain forests in Brazil, and the saving of the spotted owl in the Northwest. Shareholder resolutions promoting environmental concerns are expected to continue to increase in the future.

Several new themes have emerged as well. Ever since the Securities and Exchange Commission (SEC), which oversees what resolutions can be included in proxy statements, reversed an earlier position and has now held that cigarette smoking is an area in which shareholders are entitled to vote, resolutions opposing tobacco products are appearing in proxy statements. These resolutions urge cigarette manufacturers, such as Philip Morris Company and American Brands, to quit producing cigarettes and media companies to quit advertising them. Such resolutions are expected to increase in the future.

Other recent shareholder resolutions deal with proposals to prohibit animal testing by companies, place a moratorium on nuclear weapons and a ban on the use of nuclear power, and dismantle antitakeover devices.

Most shareholder resolutions have a slim chance of being enacted because large-scale investors usually support management. They can, however, cause a corporation to change the way it does business. For example, to avoid the adverse publicity such issues can create, some corporations voluntarily adopt the changes contained in shareholder proposals. Others negotiate settlements with the sponsors of resolutions to get the measures off the agenda before the annual shareholders' meetings.

Furthermore, shareholder resolutions are no longer just the bailiwick of individual or eccentric shareholders. Many state, municipal, and private pension funds now advocate socially responsible investing. These funds, which own billions of dollars of stock in American companies, are flexing their muscles and sponsoring shareholder resolutions to protect the environment, promote ethics, and curtail the greed of corporate managers.

1. Do you think shareholder proposals cause companies to act in a more socially responsible way? Explain.
2. Should investors be socially conscious when making investments? Why or why not? ■

Cambodia. Shareholder resolutions often challenge corporate policies. For example, is it socially responsible for U.S. businesses to have goods made in countries that do not have substantial worker protection laws?

Dividends

For-profit corporations operate to make a profit. The objective of the shareholders is to share in those profits, either through capital appreciation, the receipt of dividends, or both. **Dividends** are paid at the discretion of the board of directors [RMBCA § 6.40]. The directors are responsible for determining when, where, how, and how much will be paid in dividends. They may opt to retain the profits in the corporation to be used for corporate purposes instead of as dividends. This authority cannot be delegated to a committee of the board of directors or to officers of the corporation.

Business Brief

Dividends are not automatically paid to shareholders; they are paid at the discretion of the board of directors.

When a corporation declares a dividend, it sets a date, usually a few weeks prior to the actual payment, that is called the **record date**. Persons who are shareholders on that date are entitled to receive the dividend even if they sell their shares before the payment date, Once declared, a cash or property dividend cannot be revoked. Shareholders can sue to recover declared but unpaid dividends.

record date

A date that determines whether a shareholder receives payment of a declared dividend.

Derivative Lawsuits

If a corporation is harmed by someone, the directors of the corporation have the authority to bring an action on behalf of the corporation against the offending party to recover damages or other relief. If the corporation fails to bring the lawsuit, shareholders have the right to bring the lawsuit on behalf of the corporation. This is called a **derivative action** or **derivative lawsuit** [RMBCA § 7.40].

derivative lawsuit

A lawsuit a shareholder brings against an offending party on behalf of the corporation when the corporation fails to bring the lawsuit.

A shareholder can bring a derivative action if he or she (1) was a shareholder of the corporation at the time of the act complained of; (2) fairly and adequately represents the interests of the corporation; and (3) made a written demand upon the corporation to take suitable actions, and either the corporation rejected the demand or 90 days have expired from the date of the demand.

A derivative lawsuit will be dismissed by the court if either a majority of independent directors or a panel of independent persons appointed by the court determines that the lawsuit is not in the best interests of the corporation. This decision must be reached in good faith and only after conducting a reasonable inquiry.

If a shareholder derivative action is successful, any award goes into the corporate treasury. The plaintiff-shareholder is entitled to recover payment for reasonable expenses, including attorneys' fees, incurred in bringing and maintaining the derivative action. Any settlement of a derivative action requires court approval. The following case concerns a derivative lawsuit.

U.S. SUPREME COURT CASE

Kamen v. Kemper Financial Services, Inc.

500 U.S. 90, 111 S.Ct. 1711, 1991 U.S. Lexis 2782 (1991)

Supreme Court of the United States

Case 16.1

Derivative Lawsuit

Background and Facts

Jill S. Kamen is a shareholder of Cash Equivalent Fund, Inc. (Fund), a mutual fund that employs Kemper Financial Services, Inc. (Kemper), as its investment advisor. Kamen brought a derivative lawsuit on behalf of Fund against Kemper, alleging that Kemper violated fiduciary duties owed to Fund, as imposed by the Investment Company Act of 1940 (Act), a federal statute. Kamen did not make a demand on Fund's board of directors to sue Kemper any earlier. She alleged that it would have been futile to do so because the directors were acting in a conspiracy with

Kamen v. Kemper Financial Services, Inc.

500 U.S. 90, 111 S.Ct. 1711, 1991 U.S. Lexis 2782 (1991)
Supreme Court of the United States
(continued)

Kemper. The Act was silent as to the rule concerning derivative actions under the Act. The trial court granted Kemper's motion to dismiss the lawsuit. The court of appeals adopted a "universal demand rule" as part of the federal common law and affirmed. This rule requires a shareholder always to make a demand on the directors of a corporation before bringing a derivative lawsuit. Kamen appealed to the U.S. Supreme Court.

Supreme Court Issue

Should federal law adopt the universal demand rule for bringing derivative actions?

In The Language of The U.S. Supreme Court

Marshall, Justice The presumption that state laws should be incorporated into federal common law is particularly strong in areas in which private parties have entered legal relationship with the expectation that their rights and obligations would be governed by state law standards. Corporation law is one such area. Corporations are creatures of state law, state law which is the font of corporate directors' powers. Consequently, we conclude that gaps in federal statutes bearing on the allocation of governing power within the corporation should be filled with state law.

The purpose of requiring a precomplaint demand is to protect the directors' prerogative to take over the litigation or to oppose it. Thus, the demand requirement implements the basic principle of corporate governance that the decisions of a corporation—including the decision to initiate litigation—should be made by the board of directors or the majority of shareholders. To the extent that a jurisdiction recognizes the futility exception to demand, the jurisdiction places a limit upon the directors' usual power to control the initiation of corporate litigation. Demand typically is deemed to be futile when a majority of the directors have participated in or approved the alleged wrongdoing. Superimposing a rule of universal demand over the corporate doctrine of these States would clearly upset the balance that they have struck between the power of the individual shareholder and the power of the directors to control corporate litigation.

Decision and Remedy

The U.S. Supreme Court refused to adopt the universal demand rule as federal common law but instead held that federal law should follow the appropriate state law concerning demands in derivative lawsuits if a federal statute is silent as to this issue. Reversed.

Case Questions

Critical Legal Thinking Which do you think is the better rule: (1) the universal demand rule or (2) the futility exception rule? Why?

Business Ethics Should Kamen have given the directors of fund the opportunity to have sued Kemper before she did?

Contemporary Business Do derivative lawsuits serve any legitimate purposes? Explain.

Disregard of the Corporate Entity

limited liability
Liability that shareholders of a corporation have, only to the extent of their capital contribution. Shareholders are generally not personally liable for debts and obligations of the corporation.

piercing the corporate veil
A doctrine that says that if a shareholder dominates a corporation and misuses it for improper purposes, a court of equity can disregard the corporate entity and hold the shareholder personally liable for the corporation's debts and obligations.

Shareholders of a corporation generally have **limited liability** (i.e., they are liable for the debts and obligations of the corporation only to the extent of their capital contribution). However, if a shareholder or shareholders dominate a corporation and misuse it for improper purposes, a court of equity can *disregard the corporate entity* and hold the shareholders of a corporation personally liable for the corporation's debts and obligations. This doctrine is commonly referred to as **piercing the corporate veil**. It is often resorted to by unpaid creditors who are trying to collect from shareholders a debt owed by the corporation. The piercing the corporate veil doctrine is also called the *alter ego doctrine* because the corporation has become the *alter ego* of the shareholder.

Courts will pierce the corporate veil if (1) the corporation has been formed without sufficient capital (i.e., *thin capitalization*) or (2) separateness has not been maintained between the corporation and its shareholders (e.g., commingling of personal and corporate assets, failure to hold required shareholders' meetings, failure to maintain corporate records and books). The courts examine this doctrine on a case-by-case basis.

The piercing the corporate veil doctrine was raised in the following case.

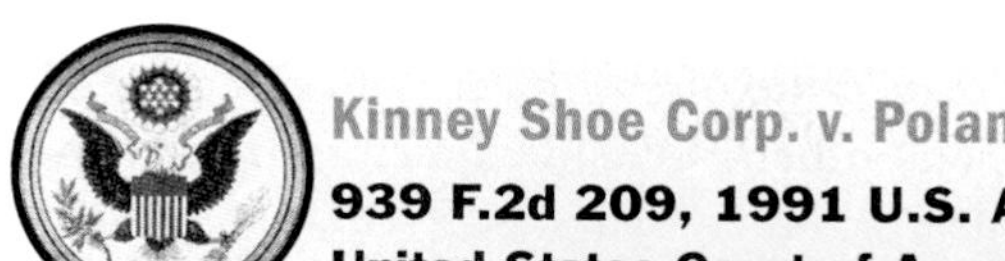

Kinney Shoe Corp. v. Polan
939 F.2d 209, 1991 U.S. App. Lexis 15304 (1991)
United States Court of Appeals, Fourth Circuit

Case 16.2
Piercing the Corporate Veil

Background and Facts

In 1984, Lincoln M. Polan formed Industrial Realty Company (Industrial), a West Virginia corporation. Polan was the sole shareholder of Industrial. Although a certificate of incorporation was issued, no organizational meeting was held, and no officers were elected. Industrial issued no stock certificates because nothing was ever paid in to the corporation. Other corporate formalities were not observed. Polan, on behalf of Industrial, signed a lease to sublease commercial space in a building controlled by Kinney Shoe Corporation (Kinney). The first rental payment to Kinney was made out of Polan's personal funds, and no further payments were made on the lease. Kinney filed suit against Industrial and obtained a judgment of $66,400 for unpaid rent. When the amount was unpaid by Industrial, Kinney sued Polan individually and sought to pierce the corporate veil to collect from Polan. The district court held for Polan. Kinney appealed.

Issue

Is Polan personally liable for Industrial's debts?

In The Language of The Court

Chapman, Senior Circuit Judge Kinney seeks to pierce the corporate veil of Industrial so as to hold Polan personally liable on the sublease debt. The Supreme Court of Appeals of West Virginia has set forth a two prong test to be used in determining whether to pierce a corporate veil in a breach of contract case. This test raises two issues: first, is the unity of interest and ownership such that the separate personalities of the corporation and the individual shareholder no longer exist; and second, would an equitable result occur if the acts are treated as those of the corporation alone.

The district court found that the two prong test had been satisfied. The court concluded that Polan's failure to carry out the corporate formalities with respect to Industrial, coupled with Industrial's gross undercapitalization, resulted in damage to Kinney. We agree. It is undisputed that Industrial was not adequately capitalized. Actually, it had no paid in capital. Polan had put nothing into this corporation, and it did not observe any corporate formalities. Polan was obviously trying to limit his liability by setting up a paper curtain constructed of nothing more than Industrial's certificate of incorporation. These facts present the classic scenario for an action to pierce the corporate veil so as to reach the responsible party and produce an equitable result.

Decision and Remedy

The court of appeals pierced the corporate veil and held Polan personally liable on Industrial's debt to Kinney. Reversed.

Case Questions

Critical Legal Thinking Is the doctrine of piercing the corporate veil needed? Should parties such as Kinney bear the risk of dealing with corporations such as Industrial?

Business Ethics Is it ethical for persons to form corporations to avoid personal liability? Should this be allowed?

Contemporary Business What is the risk if corporate formalities are not observed? Explain.

Directors and Officers

Directors and officers have different rights in managing the corporation. The directors are responsible for making policy decisions and employing officers. The officers are responsible for the corporation's day-to-day operations. The rights, duties, and liability of corporate directors and officers are discussed in the following paragraphs.

Business Brief
The directors of a corporation are responsible for formulating the *policy* decisions affecting the corporation.

Board of Directors

Typically, **boards of directors** are composed of inside directors and outside directors. An **inside director** is a person who is also an officer of the corporation. For example, the president of a corporation often sits as a director of the corporation.

board of directors
A panel of decision makers, the members of which are elected by a corporation's shareholders.

inside director
A member of the board of directors who is also an officer of the corporation.

outside director
A member of the board of directors who is not an officer of the corporation.

An **outside director** is a person who sits on the board of directors of a corporation but is not an officer of that corporation. Outside directors are often officers and directors of other corporations, bankers, lawyers, professors, and others. Outside directors are usually selected for their business knowledge and expertise.

The board of directors of a corporation is responsible for formulating the policy decisions affecting the management, supervision, and control of the operation of the corporation [RMBCA § 8.01]. Such policy decisions include deciding the business or businesses in which the corporation should be engaged, selecting and removing the top officers of the corporation, determining the capital structure of the corporation, declaring dividends, and the like.

resolution
A decision by the board of directors that approves a transaction.

The board may initiate certain actions that require shareholders' approval. These actions are initiated when the board of directors adopts a **resolution** that approves a transaction and recommends that it be submitted to the shareholders for a vote. Examples of such transactions include mergers, sales of substantially all of the corporation's assets outside the course of ordinary business operations, amendment of the articles of incorporation, and the voluntary dissolution of the corporation.

Business Brief
The terms of office of directors may be *staggered* so that only a portion of the board of directors is up for election each year.

Director's Term of Office The term of a director's office expires at the next annual shareholders' meeting following his or her election, unless terms are staggered. The RMBCA allows boards of directors that consist of nine or more members to be divided into two or three classes (each class to be as nearly equal in number as possible) that are elected to serve *staggered terms* of two or three years [RMBCA § 8.06]. The specifics of such an arrangement must be outlined in the articles of incorporation.

The law does not permit the stockholders to create a sterilized board of directors.
Collins, J.
Manson v. Curtis (1918)

Consider This Example Suppose a board of directors consists of nine directors. The board can be divided into three classes each, each class to be elected to serve a three-year term. Only three directors of the nine-member board would come up for election each year. This nine-member board could also be divided into two classes of five and four directors, each class to be elected to two-year terms.

Meetings of the Board of Directors

The directors can act only as a board. They cannot act individually on the corporation's behalf. Every director has the right to participate in any meeting of the board of directors. Each director has one vote. Directors cannot vote by proxy.

regular meeting
A meeting held by the board of directors at the time and place established in the bylaws.

special meeting
A meeting convened by the board of directors to discuss new shares, merger proposals, hostile takeover attempts, and so forth.

Regular meetings of the board of directors are held at the times and places established in the bylaws. Such meetings can be held without notice. The board can call **special meetings** as provided in the bylaws [RMBCA § 8.20(a)]. They are usually convened for such reasons as issuing new shares, considering proposals to merge with other corporations, adopting maneuvers to defend against hostile takeover attempts, and the like.

The board of directors may act without a meeting if all of the directors sign written consent forms that set forth the actions taken. Such consent has the effect of a unanimous vote. The RMBCA permits meetings of the board to be held via conference calls.

The director is really a watchdog, and the watchdog has no right, without the knowledge of his master, to take a sop from a possible wolf.
L. J. Bowen
Re The North Australian Territory Co. Ltd. (1891)

Quorum and Voting A simple majority of the number of directors established in the articles of incorporation or bylaws usually constitutes a *quorum* for transacting business. However, the articles of incorporation and bylaws may increase this number. If a quorum is present, the approval and disapproval of a majority of the quorum binds the entire board. The articles of incorporation or bylaws can require a greater than majority of directors to constitute a quorum or the vote of the board.

Contemporary Business Environment

Committees of the Board of Directors

In the current complex business world, the demands on directors have increased. To help handle this increased workload, boards of directors have turned to creating committees of their members to handle specific duties. Board members with special expertise or interests are appointed to the various committees.

Unless the articles of incorporation or bylaws provide otherwise, the board of directors may create committees of the board and delegate certain powers to those committees [RMBCA § 8.25]. All members of these committees must be directors. An act of a committee pursuant to delegated authority is the act of the board of directors.

Committees commonly appointed by the board of directors include the following:

- ***Executive Committee*** Has authority to (1) act on certain matters on behalf of the board during the interim period between board meetings and (2) conduct preliminary investigations of proposals on behalf of the full board. Most members of the committee are inside directors because it is easier for them to meet to address corporate matters.
- ***Audit Committee*** Appoints the independent public accountants and supervises the audit of the financial records of the corporation by the accountants.
- ***Nominating Committee*** Nominates the management slate of directors to be submitted for shareholder vote.
- ***Compensation Committee*** Approves management compensation, including salaries, bonuses, stock option plans, fringe benefits, and such.
- ***Investment Committee*** Is responsible for investing and reinvesting the funds of the corporation.
- ***Litigation Committee*** Reviews and decides whether to pursue requests by shareholders for the corporation to sue persons who have allegedly harmed the corporation.

The following powers cannot be delegated to committees but must be exercised by the board itself: (1) declaring dividends, (2) initiating actions that require shareholders' approval, (3) appointing members to fill vacancies on the board, (4) amending the bylaws, (5) approving a plan of merger that does not require shareholder approval (short-form merger), and (6) authorizing the issuance of shares. ■

E-Commerce & Information Technology

Delaware Amends Corporation Code to Recognize Electronic Communications

The state of Delaware leads the nation as the preferred site for incorporation of the largest corporations in the United States. This is the result of the Delaware Corporation Code itself, as well as the expertise of the Delaware courts in resolving corporate disputes. In order to keep this leadership position, in 2000 the state legislature amended the Delaware General Corporation law to recognize evolving electronic technology. The major changes to the law are:

- Delivery of notices to stockholders may be made electronically if the stockholder consents to the delivery of notice in this form.
- Proxy solicitation for shareholder votes may be made by electronic transmission.
- The shareholder list of a corporation that must be made available during the 10 days prior to a stockholder meeting may be made available either at the principal place of business of the corporation or by posting the list on an electronic network.
- Stockholders who are not physically present at meetings may be deemed present, participate in, and vote at the meeting by electronic communication; a meeting may be held solely by electronic communication without a physical location.
- The election of directors of the corporation may be held by electronic transmission.
- Directors' actions by unanimous consent may be taken by electronic transmission.

The use of electronic transmission, electronic networks, and communications by e-mail make the operation and administration of corporate affairs more efficient in Delaware. Other states have amended their corporation codes to recognize the importance of electronic communications. ■

Corporate Officers

officers
Employees of a corporation who are appointed by the board of directors to manage the day-to-day operations of the corporation.

The board of directors has the authority to appoint the **officers** of the corporation. The officers are elected by the board of directors at such time and by such manner as prescribed in the corporation's bylaws. The directors can delegate certain management authority to the officers of the corporation.

At minimum, most corporations have the following officers: (1) a president, (2) one or more vice presidents, (3) a secretary, and (4) a treasurer. The bylaws or the board of directors can authorize duly appointed officers the power to appoint assistant officers. One individual may simultaneously hold more than one office in the corporation [RMBCA § 8.40]. The duties of each officer are specified in the bylaws of the corporation.

Officers of the corporation have such authority as may be provided in the bylaws of the corporation or as determined by resolution of the board of directors.

Concept Summary Management of a Corporation

Management Group	Function
Shareholders	Own the corporation. They vote on the directors and other major actions to be taken by the corporation.
Board of directors	Responsible for making policy decisions and employing the major officers for the corporation. They also make recommendations regarding actions to be taken by the shareholders.
Officers	Responsible for the day-to-day operation of the corporation, including acting as agents for the corporation, hiring other officers and employees, and the like.

Duty of Loyalty

duty of loyalty
A duty that directors and officers have not to act adversely to the interests of the corporation and to subordinate their personal interests to those of the corporation and its shareholders.

The **duty of loyalty** requires directors and officers to subordinate their personal interests to those of the corporation and its shareholders. Justice Benjamin Cardozo defined this duty of loyalty as follows:

> [A corporate director or officer] owes loyalty and allegiance to the corporation—a loyalty that is undivided and an allegiance that is influenced by no consideration other than the welfare of the corporation. Any adverse interest of a director [or officer] will be subjected to a scrutiny rigid and uncompromising. He may not profit at the expense of his corporation and in conflict with its rights; he may not for personal gain divert unto himself the opportunities that in equity and fairness belong to the corporation.
>
> Many forms of conduct permissible in a workaday world for those acting at arm's length are forbidden to those bound by fiduciary ties. Not honesty alone, but the punctilio of an honor the most sensitive, is then the standard of behavior. As to this there has developed a tradition that is unbending and inveterate.[1]

If a director or an officer breaches his or her duty of loyalty and makes a secret profit on a transaction, the corporation can sue the director or officer to recover the secret profit.

Contemporary Business Environment

The Sarbanes-Oxley Act of 2002

During the late 1990s and early 2000s, the U.S. economy was wracked by a number of business and accounting scandals. Companies such as Enron, Tyco, and Worldcom engaged in fraudulent conduct, leading to the conviction of many corporate officers of financial crimes. Many of these companies went bankrupt, causing huge losses to their shareholders, employees, and creditors. Accounting firms were caught conspiring to conceal this fraudulent conduct, and one of them, the prior Big 5 accounting firm Arthur Andersen, went under. Boards of directors were also complacent, not keeping a watchful eye over the conduct of their officers and employees.

In response, Congress enacted the federal **Sarbanes-Oxley Act of 2002**. This act established far-reaching new rules regarding corporate governance, established independence between public accounting firms and the public companies they audit, and created new government oversight over public corporations and their officers and the public accountants that audit public companies. The act also created new criminal penalties for violations of its provisions and other federal criminal laws. The provisions of the act apply to public companies.

The goals of the Sarbanes-Oxley Act are to improve corporate governance rules, eliminate conflicts of interest, and instill confidence in investors and the public that management will run public companies in the best interests of all constituents. Although the Sarbanes-Oxley Act applies only to public companies, private companies and nonprofit organizations will be influenced by the act's accounting and corporate governance rules.

A summary of important provisions of the Sarbanes-Oxley Act follows.

Establishment of the Public Company Accounting Oversight Board

The act creates the Public Company Accounting Oversight Board (Board). The Board consists of five financially literate members who are appointed by the Securities and Exchange Commission (SEC) for five-year terms. Two of the members must be certified public accountants (CPAs), and three must not be CPAs. The SEC has oversight and enforcement authority over the Board. The Board has the authority to adopt rules concerning auditing, accounting quality control, independence, and ethics of public companies and public accountants.

Public Accounting Firms Must Register with the Board

In order to audit a public company, a public accounting firm must register with the Board. Registered accounting firms that audit more than 100 public companies annually are subject to inspection and review by the Board once a year; all other public accounting firms must be audited by the Board every three years. The Board may discipline public accountants and accounting firms and order sanctions for intentional or reckless conduct, including suspension or revocation of registration with the Board, placing temporary limitations on activities, and assessing civil money penalties.

Separation of Audit and Nonaudit Services

The act makes it unlawful for a registered public accounting firm to simultaneously provide audit and certain nonaudit services to a public company. If a public accounting firm audits a public company, the accounting firm may not provide the following nonaudit services to the client: (1) bookkeeping services; (2) financial information systems; (3) appraisal or valuation services; (4) internal audit services; (5) management functions; (6) human resources; (7) broker, dealer, or investment services; (8) investment banking services; (9) legal services; (10) or any other services the Board determines. A certified public accounting firm may provide tax services to audit clients if such tax services are preapproved by the audit committee of the client.

Audit Reports Sign-Offs

Each audit by a certified public accounting firm is assigned an audit partner of the firm to supervise the audit and approve the audit report. The act requires that a second partner of the accounting firm review and approve audit reports prepared by the firm. All audit papers must be retained for at least seven years. The lead audit partner and reviewing partner must rotate off an audit every five years.

Prohibited Employment

Any person who is employed by a public accounting firm that audits a client cannot be employed by that client as the chief executive officer (CEO), chief financial officer (CFO), controller, chief accounting officer, or equivalent position for a period of one year following the audit.

Audit Committee

A public company must have an audit committee. Members of the audit committee must be members of the board of directors and must be independent—that is, not employed or receiving compensation from the company or any of its subsidiaries for services other than as a board member and member of the audit committee. At least one member of the audit committee must be a financial expert, based on either education or prior experience, so as to understand generally accepted accounting principles, preparation of financial statements, and audit committee functions.

The audit committee is responsible for the appointment, payment of compensation, and oversight of public accounting firms employed to audit the company. The audit committee must preapprove all audit and permissible nonaudit services to be performed by a public accounting firm. The audit committee has authority to employ independent legal counsel and other advisors.

Internal Control Procedures of Public Companies

The act requires public companies to establish and maintain adequate internal controls and procedures for financial reporting. The act required public companies to prepare an assessment of the effectiveness of its internal quality controls at the end of each fiscal year.

Contemporary Business Environment
(continued)

Off-Balance-Sheet Items
Annual and quarterly reports of public companies must disclose material off-balance-sheet transactions and relationships with other entities that may have a material effect on the financial condition of the public company.

CEO and CFO Certification
The CEO and CFO of a public company must file a statement accompanying each annual and quarterly report, certifying that the signing officer has reviewed the report, based on the officer's knowledge the report does not contain any untrue statement of a material fact or omit to state a material fact that would make the statement misleading and that the financial statement and disclosures fairly present, in all material aspects, the operation and financial condition of the company. A knowing and willful violation is punishable for up to 20 years in prison and a fine of not more than $5 million.

Reimbursement of Bonuses and Incentive Pay
If a public company is required to restate its financial statements because of material noncompliance with financial reporting requirements, the CEO and CFO must reimburse the company for any bonuses, incentive pay, or securities trading profits made because of the noncompliance.

Prohibition on Personal Loans
The act prohibits public companies from making personal loans to its directors or executive officers.

Tampering with Evidence
The act makes it a crime for any person to knowingly alter, destroy, mutilate, conceal, or create any document to impair , impede, influence, or obstruct any federal investigation. A violation is punishable for up to 20 years in prison and a monetary fine.

Bar from Acting as an Officer or a Director
The SEC may issue an order prohibiting any person who has committed securities fraud from acting as an officer or a director of a public company. ■

Duty of Care

duty of care
A duty that corporate directors and officers have to use care and diligence when acting on behalf of the corporation.

negligence
Failure of a corporate director or officer to exercise the duty of care while conducting the corporation's business.

The **duty of care** requires corporate directors and officers to use *care and diligence* when acting on behalf of the corporation. To meet this duty, the directors and officers must discharge their duties (1) in good faith, (2) with the care that an *ordinary prudent person* in a like position would use under similar circumstances, and (3) in a manner he or she reasonably believes to be in the best interests of the corporation [RMBCA §§ 8.30(a) and 8.42(a)].

A director or an officer who breaches this duty of care is personally liable to the corporation and its shareholders for any damages caused by the breach. Such breaches, which are normally caused by **negligence**, often involve a director's or an officer's failure to (1) make a reasonable investigation of a corporate matter, (2) attend board meetings on a regular basis, (3) properly supervise a subordinate who causes a loss to the corporation through embezzlement and such, or (4) keep adequately informed about corporate affairs. Breaches are examined by the courts on a case-by-case basis.

Contemporary Business Environment
The Business Judgment Rule

The determination of whether a corporate director or officer has met his or her duty of care is measured as of the time the decision is made; the benefit of hindsight is not a factor. Therefore, the directors and officers are not liable to the corporation or its shareholders for honest mistakes of judgment. This is called the **business judgment rule**.

Consider This Example Suppose after conducting considerable research and investigation, the directors of a major automobile company decide to produce a large and expensive automobile. When the car is introduced to the public for sale, few of the automobiles are sold because of the public's interest in buying smaller, less expensive automobiles. Because this was an honest mistake of judgment on the part of corporate management, their judgment is shielded by the business judgment rule.

Were it not for the protection afforded by the business judgment rule, many high-risk but socially desirable endeavors might not be undertaken. The court had to decide whether directors were protected by the business judgment rule in the following case. ■

Smith v. Van Gorkom

488 A.2d 858, 1985 Del. Lexis 421 (1985)
Supreme Court of Delaware

Case 16.3

Business Judgment Rule

Background and Facts

Trans Union Corporation (Trans Union) was a publicly traded, diversified holding company that was incorporated in Delaware. Its principal earnings were generated by its railcar leasing business. Jerome W. Van Gorkom was a Trans Union officer for more than 24 years, its chief executive officer for more than 17 years, and the chairman of the board of directors for 2 years. Van Gorkom, a lawyer and certified public accountant, owned 75,000 shares of Trans Union. He was approaching 65 years of age and mandatory retirement. Trans Union's board of directors was composed of 10 members—5 inside and 5 outside directors.

In September 1980, Van Gorkom decided to meet with Jay A. Pritzker, a well-known corporate takeover specialist and a social acquaintance of Van Gorkom's, to discuss the possible sale of Trans Union to Pritzker. Van Gorkom met Pritzker at Pritzker's home on Saturday, September 13, 1980. He did so without consulting Trans Union's board of directors. At this meeting, Van Gorkom proposed a sale of Trans Union to Pritzker at a price of $55 per share. The stock was trading at about $38 in the market. On Monday, September 15, Pritzker notified Van Gorkom that he was interested in the $55 cash-out merger proposal. Van Gorkom, along with two inside directors, privately met with Pritzker on September 16 and 17. After meeting with Van Gorkom on Thursday, September 18, Pritzker notified his attorney to begin drafting the merger documents.

On Friday, September 19, Van Gorkom called a special meeting of Trans Union's board of directors for the following day. The board members were not told the purpose of the meeting. At the meeting, Van Gorkom disclosed the Pritzker offer and described its terms in a 20-minute presentation. Neither the merger agreement nor a written summary of the terms of agreement was furnished to the directors. No valuation study as to the value of Trans Union was prepared for the meeting. After two hours, the board voted in favor of the cash-out merger with Pritzker's company at $55 per share for trans Union's stock. The board also voted not to solicit other offers. The merger agreement was executed by Van Gorkom during the evening of September 20, at a formal social event he hosted for the opening of the Chicago Lyric Opera's season. Neither he nor any other director read the agreement prior to its signing and delivery to Pritzker.

Trans Union's board of directors recommended that the merger be approved by its shareholders and distributed proxy materials to the shareholders stating that the $55 per share price for their stock was fair. In the meantime, Trans Union's board of directors took steps to dissuade two other possible suitors who showed an interest in purchasing Trans Union. On February 10, 1981, 69.9 percent of the shares of Trans Union stock was voted in favor of the merger. The merger was consummated. Alden Smith and other Trans Union shareholders sued Van Gorkom and the other directors for damages. The plaintiffs alleged that the defendants were negligent in their conduct in selling Trans Union to Pritzker. The Delaware Court of Chancery held in favor of the defendants. The plaintiffs appealed.

Issue

Did Trans Union's directors breach their duty of care?

In The Language of The Court

Horsey, Justice In the specific context of a proposed merger of domestic corporations, a director has a duty, along with his fellow directors, to act in an informed and deliberate manner in determining whether to approve an agreement of merger before submitting the proposal to the stockholders. Certainly in the merger context, a director may not abdicate that duty by leaving to the shareholders alone the decision to approve or disapprove the agreement. Only an agreement of merger satisfying these requirements may be submitted to the shareholders. It is against these standards that the conduct of the directors of Trans Union must be tested, as a matter of law and as a matter of fact, regarding their exercise of an informed business judgment in voting to approve the Pritzker merger approval.

The issue of whether the directors reached an informed decision to sell the company on September 20, 1980 must be determined only upon the basis of the information then reasonably available to the directors and relevant to their decision to accept the Pritzker merger proposal. On the record before us, we must conclude that the board of directors did not reach an informed business judgment on September 20, 1980 in voting to sell the company for $55 per share pursuant to the Pritzker cash-out merger proposals. Our reasons, in summary, are as follows:

The directors (1) did not adequately inform themselves as to Van Gorkom's role in forcing the sale of the company and in establishing the per share purchase price; (2) they were uninformed as to the intrinsic value of the company; and (3) given these circumstances, at a minimum, they were grossly negligent in approving the sale of the company upon two hours' consideration, without prior notice, and without the exigency of a crisis or emergency.

Without any documents before them concerning the proposed transaction, the members of the board were required to rely entirely upon Van Gorkom's 20-minute oral presentation of the proposal. No written summary of the terms of the merger was presented; the directors were given no documentation to support the adequacy of $55 price per share for sale of the company; and the board had before it nothing more than Van Gorkom's statement of his understanding of the substance of an agreement that he admittedly had never read, or that any member of the board had ever seen. Thus, the record compels the conclusion that on September 20 the board lacked valuation information to reach an informed business judgment as to the fairness of $55 per share for sale of the company. We conclude that Trans Union's board was grossly negligent in that it failed to act with informed reasonable deliberation in agreeing to the Pritzker merger proposal on September 20, 1980.

Smith v. Van Gorkom
488 A.2d 858, 1985 Del. Lexis 421 (1985)
Supreme Court of Delaware
(continued)

Decision and Remedy

The supreme court of Delaware held that the defendant directors had breached their duty of care. The supreme court remanded the case to the court of chancery to conduct an evidentiary hearing to determine the fair value of the shares represented by the plaintiffs' class. If that value was higher than $55 per share, the difference was to be awarded to the plaintiffs as damages. Reversed and remanded.

Case Questions

Critical Legal Thinking What does the business judgment rule provide? Is this a good rule? Explain.

Business Ethics Do you think van Gorkum and the other directors had the shareholders' best interests in mind? Were the plaintiff-shareholders being greedy?

Contemporary Business Is there any liability exposure for sitting on a board of directors?

Concept Summary Fiduciary Duties of Corporation Directors and Officers

Duty	Description	Violation
Duty of obedience	Duty to act within the authority conferred by law and the corporation.	Acts outside the corporate officer's or director's authority.
Duty of care	Duty to use care and diligence when acting on behalf of the corporation. This duty is discharged if an officer or director acts: 1. In good faith. 2. With the care that an ordinary prudent person in a like position would use under similar circumstances. 3. In a manner he or she reasonably believes to be in the best interests of the corporation.	Acts of negligence and mismanagement. Such acts include failure to: 1. Make a reasonable investigation of a corporate matter. 2. Attend board meetings on a regular basis. 3. Properly supervise a subordinate who causes a loss to the corporation. 4. Keep adequately informed about corporate matters. 5. Take other actions necessary to discharge duties.
Duty of loyalty	Duty to subordinate personal interests to those of the corporation and its shareholders.	Acts of disloyalty. Such acts include unauthorized: 1. Self-dealing with the corporation. 2. Usurping of a corporate opportunity. 3. Competing with the corporation. 4. Making a secret profit that belongs to the corporation.

International Law

Conducting International Business Through a Branch Office or a Subsidiary Corporation

A corporation that wants to conduct business in a foreign country has the choice of conducting the business through a branch office or a subsidiary corporation. There are different costs, efficiencies, rules, and liability exposure associated with each of these forms of conducting international business.

Branch Office

A company can enter a foreign market by establishing a **branch** in the foreign country. Branches are often used where a corporation wants to enter a foreign market in a substantial way but wants to retain exclusive control over the operation. For example, an American manufacturing company can establish a presence in a foreign country by building a plant there. A branch is not a separate corporation or legal entity (see Exhibit 16.4). It is merely an extension of the corporate owner and is wholly owned by the home corporation.

There are detriments to this form of operation. For instance, it is expensive (because the owner must build or lease plant or office premises), and it exposes the owner to tort and contract liability in the foreign country and to foreign laws.

Subsidiary Corporation

A business can enter a foreign market by establishing a separate corporation to conduct business in a foreign country. Such a corporation, which is called a **subsidiary**, must be formed pursuant to the laws of the country in which it is to be located. The **parent corporation** usually owns all or a majority of the subsidiary corporation. The parent corporation and the subsidiary corporation are separate legal entities that are individually capitalized (see Exhibit 16.5).

A foreign subsidiary is usually used where the parent corporation wants to establish a substantial presence in a foreign country. The benefit of using a subsidiary corporation over a branch is that it isolates the parent corporation from the tort and contract liability of the subsidiary corporation (and vice versa), unless the foreign country's laws provide otherwise. On the other hand, establishing and operating a subsidiary corporation in a foreign country is often expensive and complicated. Also, it exposes the subsidiary corporation to the laws of the foreign country.

Exhibit 16.4

Conducting International Business Using a Branch Office

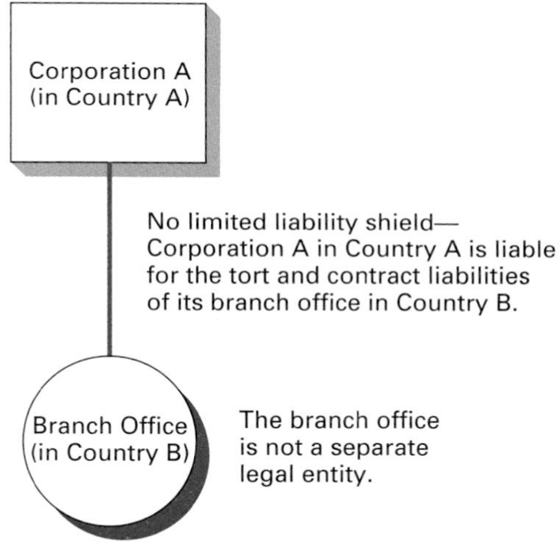

Exhibit 16.5

Conducting International Business Using a Subsidiary Corporation

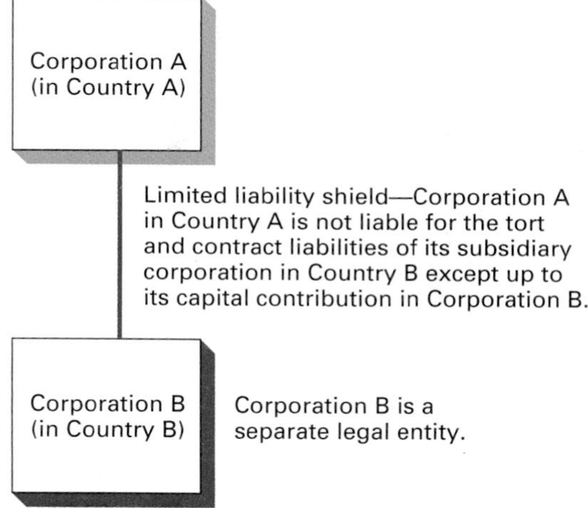

Consider These Examples Ford Motor Company, Inc., a U.S. corporation organized in the State of Delaware, opens a branch office in India to sell its automobiles there. If an employee at the branch office in India negligently injures an Indian citizen while on a test drive, Ford Motor Company, Inc., in the United States is wholly liable for the injured person's damages. Suppose instead that Ford Motor Company, Inc., forms a subsidiary corporation called Ford.India Corporation in India, pursuant to Indian law. Ford Motor Company, Inc., is the parent corporation and shareholder of Ford.India Corporation; Ford.India Corporation is the subsidiary corporation. If an employee of Ford.India Corporation negligently injures an Indian citizen while on a test drive, only Ford.India Corporation is liable; Ford Motor Company, Inc., in the United States is not liable other than it may lose its capital contribution in Ford.India Corporation if the judgment is large. ■

Mergers and Acquisitions

Corporations may agree to friendly acquisitions or combinations of one another. This may be by merger or consolidation. These types of combinations are discussed in the following paragraphs.

Business Brief

Mergers, consolidations, share exchanges, and sales of assets are *friendly* in nature. That is, both corporations have agreed to the combination of corporations or acquisitions of assets.

Mergers

A **merger** occurs when one corporation is absorbed into another corporation and ceases to exist. The corporation that continues to exist is called the *surviving corporation*. The other is called the *merged corporation* [RMBCA § 11.01]. The surviving corporation gains all the rights, privileges, powers, duties, obligations, and liabilities of the merged corporation.

merger

A situation in which one corporation is absorbed into another corporation and ceases to exist.

Exhibit 16.6
Example of a Merger

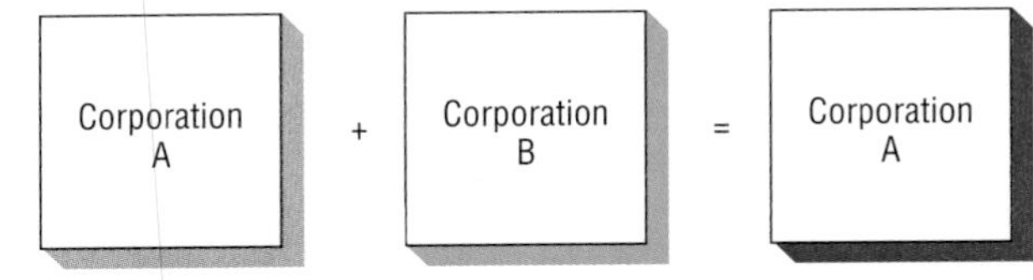

Title to property owned by the merged corporation transfers to the surviving corporation without formality or deeds. The shareholders of the merged corporation receive stock or securities of the surviving corporation or other consideration as provided in the plan of merger.

Suppose, for example, that Corporation A and Corporation B merge and it is agreed that Corporation A will absorb Corporation B. Corporation A is the surviving corporation. Corporation B is the merged corporation. A symbolic representation of this merger is A + B = A (see Exhibit 16.6).

Corporation: An ingenious device for obtaining individual profit without individual responsibility.
Ambrose Bierce
The Devil's Dictionary (1911)

Required Approvals

An ordinary merger requires (1) the recommendation of the board of directors of each corporation and (2) an affirmative vote of the majority of shares of each corporation that are entitled to vote [RMBCA § 11.03]. The articles of incorporation or corporate bylaws can require the approval of a *supramajority*, such as 80 percent of the voting shares.

The approval of the surviving corporation's shareholders is not required if the merger increases the number of voting shares of the surviving corporation by 20 percent or less.

The approved **articles of merger** must be filed with the secretary of state. The state normally issues a **certificate of merger** to the surviving corporation after all the formalities are met and the requisite fees are paid.

To supervise wisely the great corporations is well: but to look backward to the days when business was polite pillage and regard our great business concerns as piratical institutions carrying letters of marque and reprisal is a grave error born in the minds of little men. When these little men legislate they set the brakes going uphill.
Elbert Hubbard
(1856–1915) Notebook

short-form merger
A merger between a parent corporation and a subsidiary corporation that does not require the vote of the shareholders of either corporation or the board of directors of the subsidiary corporation.

Short-Form Mergers If one corporation (called the **parent corporation**) owns 90 percent or more of the outstanding stock of another corporation (known as the **subsidiary corporation**), a **short-form merger** procedure may be followed to merge the two corporations. The short-form merger procedure is simpler than an ordinary merger because neither the approval of the shareholders of either corporation nor of the board of directors of the subsidiary corporation is needed. All that is required is the approval of the board of directors of the parent corporation [RMBCA § 11.04].

Dissenting Shareholder Appraisal Rights

dissenting shareholder appraisal rights
Rights of shareholders who object to a proposed merger, share exchange, or sale or lease of all or substantially all of the property of a corporation to have their shares valued by the court and receive cash payment of this values from the corporation.

Specific shareholders sometimes object to a proposed ordinary or short-form merger, even though the transaction received the required approvals. Objecting shareholders are provided a statutory right to dissent and obtain payment of the fair value of their shares [RMBCA § 13.02]. This is referred to as a **dissenting shareholder appraisal right** (or **appraisal right**). Shareholders have no recourse unless the transaction is unlawful or fraudulent.

The corporation must notify shareholders of the existence of their appraisal rights before the transaction can be voted on. To obtain appraisal rights, a dissenting shareholder must (1) deliver written notice of his or her intent to demand payment of his or her shares to the corporation before the vote is taken and (2) not vote his or her shares in favor of the proposed action. The shareholder must deposit his or her share certificates with the corporation. Shareholders who fail to comply with these statutory procedures lose their appraisal rights.

As soon as the proposed action is taken, the corporation must pay each dissenting shareholder the amount the corporation estimates to be the fair value of his or her shares, plus accrued interest. If the dissenter is dissatisfied, the corporation must petition the court to determine the fair value of the shares.

Business Brief

The court must determine the "fair value" of the shares of dissenting shareholders. Courts usually use appraisers to assist in determining this value.

After a hearing, the court will issue an order declaring the fair value of the shares. Appraisers may be appointed to help in determining this value. Court costs and appraisal fees are usually paid by the corporation. However, the court can assess these costs against the dissenters if they acted arbitrarily, vexatiously, or not in good faith.

E-Commerce & Information Technology

Internet Alliances in China

By the year 2005, China will have the largest number of Internet users in the world. Leading Internet companies in the United States have eyed this market for its tremendous growth potential. But China prohibits complete ownership of Internet companies in China by foreigners. In addition, the legendary Chinese "connections" method of conducting business places another hurdle in the way of foreign companies wishing to do business there. So what is the main way to tap into this Internet market? Strategic alliances.

A major strategic alliance by U.S. companies in China was their tie-in and investment in China.com. China.com is a Chinese-language Web portal backed by investments by U.S. companies America Online (AOL), Sun Microsystems, and Nortel. China.com became China's largest Internet company when it raised over \$84 million in an initial public offering in July 1999. Intel Corp., another major U.S. company, has aligned itself with Sohu.com, a Chinese Internet company located in Beijing. CMGI Inc., a U.S. Internet holding company, has joined with Pacific Century CyberWorks (PCCW), a Hong Kong company, to sell Web content and e-commerce services to the exploding Chinese Internet market from its base in Hong Kong.

Although the Chinese government has permitted these strategic alliances, it has stated that it will not allow foreign companies to own Internet service providers (ISPs) in China. Some U.S. companies have set up ISPs in countries and areas near China, which will be able to serve the Chinese market. The information industries minister of China has announced that China will control the content of materials delivered via the Internet in China.

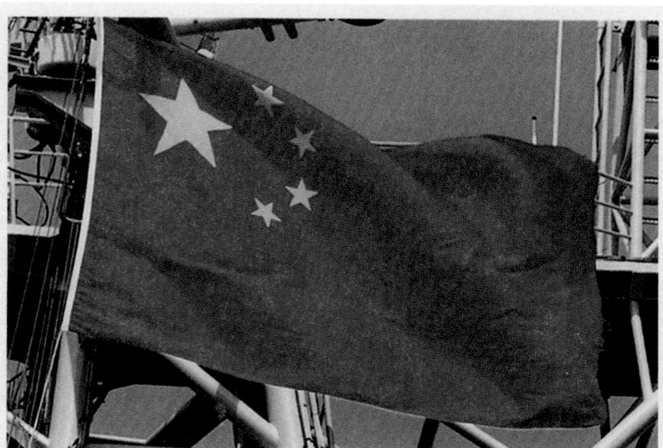

China's recent entry into the World Trade Organization (WTO) will increase trade between China and other countries.

Analysts predict that this will be hard to do given the global nature of the Internet.

Based on the Communist government's rules in China and a culture that favors business connections, U.S. Internet companies will continue to enter the Chinese Internet market through strategic alliances with Chinese Internet firms. These strategic alliances bring together the expertise of all parties, bring China fully into the information age, and provide Internet users in China the most affordable options. ■

Tender Offers

Recall that a merger, a consolidation, a share exchange, and a sale of assets all require the approval of the board of directors of the corporation whose assets or shares are to be acquired. If the board of directors of the target corporation does not agree to the merger or

Exhibit 16.7

Illustration of a Tender Offer

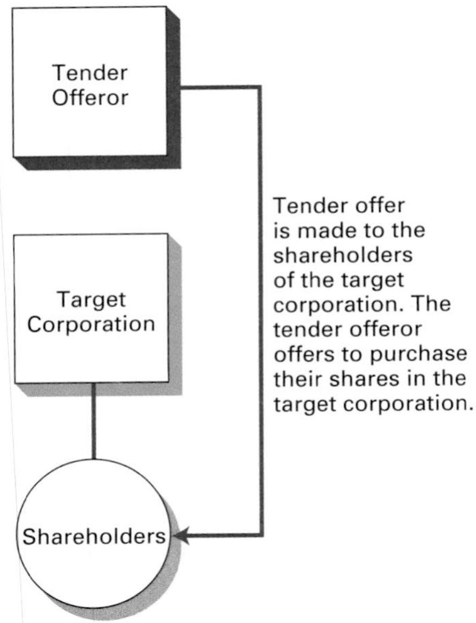

tender offer
An offer that an acquirer makes directly to a target corporation's shareholders in an effort to acquire the target corporation.

target corporation
The corporation that is proposed to be acquired in a tender offer situation.

tender offeror
The party that makes a tender offer.

acquisition, the acquiring corporation can make a **tender offer** for the shares directly to the shareholders of the **target corporation**. The shareholders make individual decisions about whether to sell their shares to the **tender offeror** (see Exhibit 16.7). Such offers are often referred to as **hostile tender offers**.

The tender offeror's board of directors must approve the offer, although the shareholders do not have to approve. The offer can be made for all or a portion of the shares of the target corporation.

In a tender offer, the tendering corporation and the target corporation retain their separate legal status. A successful tender offer is sometimes, however, followed by a merger of the two corporations.

The Williams Act

Prior to 1968, tender offers were not federally regulated. However, securities that were issued in conjunction with such offers had to be registered with the SEC or qualify for an exemption from registration. Tender offers made with cash were not subject to any federal disclosure requirements.

Williams Act
A 1968 amendment to the Securities Exchange Act of 1934 that specifically regulates all tender offers.

In 1968, Congress enacted the **Williams Act** as an amendment to the Securities Exchange Act of 1934.[2] This act specifically regulates all tender offers, whether they are made with securities, cash, or other considerations. The act establishes certain disclosure requirements and antifraud provisions.

The Williams Act does not require the tender offeror to notify either the management of the target company or the SEC until the offer is made. Detailed information regarding the terms, conditions, and other information concerning the tender offer must be disclosed at that time.

Section 14(e)
A provision of the Williams Act that prohibits fraudulent, deceptive, and manipulative practices in connection with a tender offer.

Section 14(e) of the Williams Act prohibits fraudulent, deceptive, and manipulative practices in connection with a tender offer.[3] Violations of this section may result in *civil* charges brought by the SEC or *criminal* charges brought by the Justice Department. The courts have implied a private civil cause of action under Section 14(e).

Therefore, a shareholder who has been injured by a violation of Section 14(e) can sue the wrongdoer for damages.

Fighting a Tender Offer

The incumbent managers of many targets of hostile tender offers do not want the corporation taken over by the tender offeror. Therefore, they engage in varied activities to impede and defeat the tender offer. Some of the strategies and tactics used by incumbent managers in defending against hostile tender offers are described as follows:

Business Brief

Target corporations initiate and implement a variety of defensive maneuvers and tactics to defend against unwanted hostile tender offers.

1. ***Persuasion of Shareholders*** Media campaigns are organized to convince shareholders that the tender offer is not in their best interests.
2. ***Delaying Lawsuits*** Lawsuits are filed, alleging that the tender offer violates securities laws, antitrust laws, or other laws. The time gained by this tactic gives management the opportunity to erect or implement other defensive maneuvers.
3. ***Selling a Crown Jewel*** Such assets as profitable divisions or real estate that are particularly attractive to outside interests—called **crown jewels**—are sold. This tactic makes the target corporation less attractive to the tender offer.
4. ***Adopting a Poison Pill*** Poison pills are defensive strategies that are built into the target corporation's articles of incorporation, corporate bylaws, or contracts and leases. For example, contracts and leases may provide that they will expire if the ownership of the corporation changes hands. These tactics make the target corporation more expensive to the tender offeror.
5. ***White Knight Merger*** White knight mergers are mergers with friendly parties, that is, parties that promise to leave the target corporation and/or its management intact.
6. ***Pac-Man (or Reverse) Tender Offer*** The target corporation makes a tender offer on the tender offeror. This is called a **pac-man tender offer**. Thus, the target corporation tries to purchase the tender offeror.
7. ***Issuing Additional Stock*** Placing additional stock on the market increases the number of outstanding shares that the tender offeror must purchase in order to gain control of the target corporation.
8. ***Creating an Employee Stock Ownership (ESOP)*** A company creates an ESOP and places a certain percentage of the corporation's securities (e.g., 15 percent) in it. The ESOP is then expected to vote the shares it owns against the potential acquirer in a proxy contest or tender offer because the beneficiaries (i.e., the employees) have a vested interest in keeping the company intact.
9. ***Flip-Over and Flip-In Rights Plans*** These plans provide that existing shareholders of the target corporation may convert their shares for a greater amount (e.g., twice the value) of shares of the acquiring corporation (*flip-over rights plan*) or debt securities of the target company (*flip-in rights plan*). Rights plans are triggered if the acquiring firm acquires a certain percentage (e.g., 20 percent) of the shares of the target corporation. They make it more expensive for the acquiring firm to take over the target corporation.
10. ***Greenmail and Standstill Agreement*** Most tender offerors purchase a block of stock in the target corporation before making an offer. Occasionally, the tender offeror will agree to give up its tender offer and agree not to purchase any further shares if the target corporation agrees to buy back the stock at a premium over fair market value. This payment is called **greenmail**. The agreement of the tender offeror to abandon its tender offer and not purchase any additional stock is called a *standstill agreement*.

crown jewel

A valuable asset of the target corporation's that the tender offeror particularly wants to acquire in the tender offer.

pac-man tender offer

An offer in which a corporation that is the target of a tender offer makes a *reverse tender offer* for the stock of the tender offeror.

The usual trade and commerce is cheating all round by consent.

Thomas Fuller
Gnomologia (1732)

greenmail

The purchase by a target corporation of its stock from an actual or perceived tender offeror at a premium.

There are many other strategies and tactics that target companies initiate and implement in defending against a tender offer.

State Antitakeover Statutes

state antitakeover statutes
Statutes enacted by state legislatures that protect from hostile takeovers corporations incorporated in or doing business in the state.

Many states have enacted statutes that are aimed at protecting from hostile takeovers corporations that are either incorporated in or do business within the state. Many of these states statutes have been challenged as being unconstitutional because they violate the Williams Act and the Commerce and Supremacy Clauses of the U.S. Constitution.

The lawfulness of one such **state antitakeover statute** was at issue in the following case.

U.S. SUPREME COURT CASE

CTS Corp. v. Dynamics Corp.

481 U.S. 69, 107 S.Ct. 1637, 1987 U.S. Lexis 1811 (1987)

Supreme Court of the United States

Case 16.4

State Antitakeover Statute

Background and Facts

On March 4, 1986, Indiana enacted the Control Share Acquisitions Chapter act. The act covers corporations that (1) are incorporated in Indiana and have at least 100 shareholders, (2) have their primary place of business or substantial assets in Indiana, and (3) have either 10 percent of their shareholders in Indiana or 10 percent of their shares owned by Indiana residents. The act provides that if any entity acquires 20 percent or more of the voting shares of a covered corporation, the acquirer loses voting rights to these shares unless a majority of the disinterested shareholders of the acquired corporation vote to restore such voting rights. The acquirer can request that such vote be held within 50 days after its acquisition. If the shareholders do not restore the voting rights, the target corporation may redeem the shares from the acquirer at fair market value, but it is not required to do so.

On March 10, 1986, Dynamics Corporation of America (Dynamics), a Delaware corporation, announced a tender offer for 1 million shares of CTS Corporation (CTS), an Indiana corporation covered by the act. The purchase of these shares would have brought the voting interest of Dynamics in CTS to 27.5 percent. Dynamics sued in federal court, alleging that Indiana's Control Share Acquisitions Chapter was unconstitutional. The federal district court held for Dynamics. The court of appeals affirmed. CTS appealed.

Supreme Court Issue

Does the Indiana Control Share Acquisitions Chapter conflict with the Williams Act or violate the Commerce Clause of the U.S. Constitution by unduly burdening interstate commerce?

In The Language of The U.S. Supreme Court

Powell, Justice The first question in this case is whether the Williams Act preempts the Indiana Act. As we have stated frequently, absent an explicit indication by Congress of an intent to preempt state laws, a state statute is preempted only where compliance with both federal and state regulations is a physical impossibility or where the state law stands as an obstacle to the accomplishment and execution of the full purposes and objectives of Congress. Because it is entirely possible for entities to comply with both the Williams and the Indiana acts, the state statute can be preempted only if it frustrates the purposes of the federal law.

The statute now before the court protects the independent shareholder against both of the contending parties. Thus, the act furthers a basic purpose of the Williams Act, placing investors on an equal footing with the takeover bidder. The Indiana Act operates on the assumption, implicit in the Williams Act, that independent shareholders faced with tender offers often are at a disadvantage. By allowing such shareholders to vote as a group, the act protects them from the coercive aspects of some tender offers. If, for example, shareholders believe that a successful tender offer will be followed by a purchase of nontendering shares at a depressed price [in a second tier merger], individual shareholders may tender their shares—even if they doubt the tender offer is in the corporation's best interest—to protect themselves from being forced to sell their shares at a depressed price. In such a situation under the Indiana Act, the shareholders as a group, acting in the corporation's best interest, could reject the offer although individual shareholders might be inclined to accept it. The desire of the Indiana legislature to protect shareholders of Indiana corporations from this type of coercive offer does not conflict with the Williams Act. Rather, it furthers the federal policy of investor protection.

Decision and Remedy

The U.S. Supreme Court held that the Indiana Control Share Acquisitions Chapter neither conflicted with the Williams Act nor violated the Commerce Clause of the U.S. Constitution. Reversed.

Case Questions

Critical Legal Thinking Should states be permitted to adopt antitakeover statutes? Why or why not? Whom do you think these statutes actually protect?

Business Ethics Is it ethical for a target corporation's management to assert a state antitakeover statute?

Contemporary Business What are the economic effects of a state antitakeover statute?

Kyrgyzstan. The opportunities for U.S.-based multinational companies will increase as other countries of the world open up their markets to free trade.

International Law

Maquiladoras in Mexico

In 1965, Mexico and the United States created a duty-free export assembly zone located right across the border from the United States. Many U.S. companies located assembly plants in this zone to take advantage of Mexico's plentiful and cheap labor and abundant factory space. These assembly plants are call *maquiladoras*. Equipment and parts can be imported from the United States to the duty-free zones in Mexico as long as the finished products assembled there are exported back to the United States. Multinational companies rushed to set up *maquiladoras* in these duty-free zones in Mexico. The *maquiladoras* helped Mexico to grow into the world's thirteenth-largest exporter. In recent years the *maquiladoras* have shipped nearly half of Mexico's merchandise exports.

Maquiladoras originally made low-end garments and small appliances, but they evolved into producing higher-end manufacturing products such as automobile parts. The *maquiladoras* are currently under competitive pressure as the manufacturing of goods has shifted to even cheaper-labor countries, such as China, Indonesia, Vietnam, and other Asian countries. Currently, there is a trend for *maquiladoras* to reinvent themselves with advanced technology and better-trained labor to produce high-technology products such as computers, electronic goods, and big-screen TVs. Although under competitive pressures and pressures to change their output, *maquiladoras* will remain a major source of employment and exports for Mexico. ■

The Nature of the Corporation, p. 454

Nature of the Corporation

1. ***Corporation.*** A legal entity created pursuant to the laws of the state of incorporation.
2. ***Corporation Codes.*** State statutes that govern the formation, operation, and dissolution of corporations.

The Corporation as a "Legal Person"

A corporation is a separate legal entity—an *artificial person*—that can own property, sue and be sued, enter into contracts, and such.

Characteristics of Corporations

1. ***Limited liability of shareholders.*** Shareholders are liable for the debts and obligations of the corporation only to the extent of their capital contributions.
2. ***Free transferability of shares.*** Shares of a corporation are freely transferable by shareholders unless they are expressly restricted.
3. ***Perpetual existence.*** Corporations exist in perpetuity unless a specific duration is stated in the corporation's articles of incorporation.
4. ***Centralized management.*** The *board of directors* of the corporation makes policy decisions of the corporation. Corporate *officers* appointed by the board of directors run the corporation's day-to-day operations. Together, the directors and officers form the corporation's "management."

The Revised Model Business Corporation Act

1. ***Model Business Corporation Act (MBCA).*** A model act drafted in 1950 that was intended to provide a uniform law for the regulation of corporations.
2. ***Revised Model Business Corporation Act (RMBCA).*** A revision of the MBCA promulgated in 1984 that arranged the provisions of the model act more logically, revised the language to be more consistent, and made substantial changes that modernized the provisions of the act.

Classifications of Corporations

1. ***Domestic corporation.*** A corporation in the state in which it is incorporated.
2. ***Foreign corporation.*** A corporation in any state other than the one in which it is incorporated. A domestic corportion often transacts business in states other than its state of incorporation; hence it is a foreign corporation in these other states. A foreign corporation must obtain a *certificate of authority* from these other states in order to transact intrastate business in those states.
3. ***Alien corporation.*** A corporation that is incorporated in another country. Alien corporations are treated as foreign corporations for most purposes.
4. ***Nonprofit corporation.*** A corporation that is formed to operate charitable institutions, colleges, universities, and other not-for-profit entities. *There are no shareholders of these corporations.*
5. ***Public corporation.*** A corporation formed to meet a specific governmental or political purpose. Also called a *government-owned corporation. Municipal corporations* (i.e., cities) are an example.

Incorporation Procedures, p. 455

Incorporation Procedures

1. ***Incorporation.*** The process of incorporating (forming) a new corporation.
2. ***Corporation Code.*** Corporations are creatures of statute; they can be formed only if certain statutory formalities contained in the state's corporation code are followed.

Selecting a State of Incorporation

A corporation can be incorporated in only one state, although it can conduct business in other states.

Corporate Name

A corporate name selected for a new corporation must be distinguishable from existing corporate names. A corporate name may be reserved for a limited period of time while the corporation is being formed.

Articles of Incorporation

The basic governing document of a corporation. This document must be filed with the secretary of state of the state of incorporation. It is a public document. It is also called the *corporate charter*.

1. ***Information to be set forth in the articles of incorporation.*** The corporation code of each state sets out the information that must be included in the articles of incorporation. Additional information may be included in the articles of incorporation as deemed necessary or desirable by the incorporators.

2. ***Amending the articles of incorporation.*** The articles of incorporation can be amended to contain any provision that could have been lawfully included in the original articles of incorporation. After an amendment is approved by the shareholders, the corporation must file *articles of amendment* with the secretary of state.

Corporate Bylaws

Bylaws. A detailed set of rules that are adopted by the board of directors after a corporation is formed that contain provisions for managing the business and affairs of the corporation. This document does not have to be filed with the secretary of state.

Organizational Meeting

A meeting that must be held by the initial directors of the corporation after the articles of incorporation are filed. At this meeting, the directors adopt the bylaws, elect corporate officers, ratify promoters' contracts, adopt a corporate seal, and transact such other business as may come before the meeting.

Authorized, Issued, and Outstanding Shares

1. ***Authorized shares.*** The number of shares provided for in the articles of incorporation. The shareholders may amend the articles of incorporation to increase this amount.
2. ***Issued shares.*** Authorized shares that have been sold by the corporation.
3. ***Unissued shares.*** Authorized shares that have not been sold by the corporation.
4. ***Treasury shares.*** Issued shares that have been repurchased by the corporation. They may be resold by the corporation.
5. ***Outstanding shares.*** Shares that are in shareholder hands, whether originally issued or reissued treasury shares. Only outstanding shares have the right to vote.

Financing the Corporation, p. 460

Financing the Corporation

Equity securities. Securities that represent the ownership rights to the corporation. They are called *stocks*. Equity securities consist of *common stock* and *preferred stock*.

Common Stock

A type of equity security that represents the *residual value* of the corporation. Common stock has no preferences, and its shareholders are paid dividends and assets upon liquidation only after creditors and preferred shareholders have been paid.

1. ***Common stockholder.*** A person who owns common stock.
2. ***Common stock certificate.*** A document that represents the common shareholders' investment in the corporation.
3. ***Par value.*** A value assigned by the corporation to common shares that sets the lowest price at which the shares may be issued by the corporation. *No par shares* are not assigned a par value. The RMBCA has eliminated the concept of par value.

Preferred Stock

A type of equity security that is given certain preferences and rights over common stock.

1. ***Preferred stockholder.*** A person who owns preferred stock.
2. ***Preferred stock certificate.*** A document that represents the preferred stockholders' investment in the corporation.
3. ***Preferences and rights.*** Preferred stock may have any or all of the following preferences or rights:
   a. *Dividend preference.* The right to receive a fixed dividend at stipulated periods during the year (e.g., quarterly).
   b. *Liquidation preference.* The right to be paid a stated dollar amount if the corporation is dissolved and liquidated. The corporation must pay its creditors first, however.

   c. Cumulative dividend right. Cumulative preferred stock is stock that provides that any missed dividend payments must be paid in the future to the preferred shareholders before the common shareholders can receive any dividends.

   d. Right to participate in profits. Participating preferred stock is preferred stock that allows the stockholder to participate in the profits of the corporation along with the common stockholders on an expressly stated basis.

   e. Conversion right. Convertible preferred stock is preferred stock that permits stockholders to convert their shares into common stock at a stipulated conversion price.

4. ***Redeemable preferred stock.*** Preferred stock that may be bought back by the corporation at a specified price at some future date. This is also called *callable preferred stock.*

Debt Securities

Securities that establish a *debtor–creditor* relationship in which the corporation borrows money from the investor to whom the debt security is issued.

1. ***Debenture.*** A *long-term unsecured debt* instrument that is based on the corporation's general credit rating.
2. ***Bond.*** A *long-term* debt security that is *secured* by some form of property. The property securing the bond is called *collateral.* In the event of nonpayment of interest, principal, or other specified events, bondholders can foreclose on and obtain the collateral.
3. ***Note.*** A *short-term* debt instrument with a maturity of five years or less. It can either be unsecured or secured.

Shareholders, p. 463

Rights of Shareholders

Ownership rights. Shareholders of a corporation own the corporation.

Shareholder Meetings

1. ***Annual shareholders' meeting.*** Meeting of the shareholders of a corporation that must be held annually by the corporation to elect directors and to vote on other matters.
2. ***Special shareholders' meeting.*** Meeting of shareholders that may be called to consider and vote on important or emergency matters, such as proposed merger, amending the articles of incorporation, and so forth.

Proxies

1. ***Proxy.*** Shareholders may appoint another person (the *proxy*) as their agent to vote their shares at shareholders' meetings.
2. ***Proxy card.*** Document that a shareholder signs that authorizes another person to vote his or her shares at a shareholders' meeting.

Voting Requirements

1. ***Record date.*** A date specified in the corporate bylaws that determines whether a shareholder may vote at a shareholders' meeting. Only persons that are shareholders on the record date are permitted to vote at the meeting.
2. ***Quorum.*** The required number of shares that must be represented in person or by proxy in order to hold a shareholders' meeting. The RMBCA establishes a majority of outstanding shares as a quorum.
3. ***Vote required for elections other than for directors.*** The affirmative vote of the *majority* of the voting shares represented at a shareholders' meeting constitutes an act of the shareholders for actions other than for the election of directors.
4. ***Supramajority voting requirement.*** The articles of incorporation or bylaws can require a greater than majority of shares to constitute quorum or the vote of the shareholders (e.g., 80 percent). Also called *supermajority voting requirement.*

5. ***Voting methods for electing directors:***
   a. *Straight (noncumulative) voting.* Unless otherwise stated, each shareholder votes the number of shares he or she owns on candidates for each of the positions open for election. The candidate or candidates with the most votes win the open position or positions.
   b. *Cumulative voting.* The articles of incorporation may provide for cumulative voting. Under this method, a shareholder is entitled to multiply the number of shares he or she owns by the number of directors to be elected and cast the product for a single candidate or distribute the product among two or more candidates.

Shareholder Proposals

Proposal submitted by a shareholder or group of shareholders to be considered and voted upon by the corporation's shareholders. Most shareholder proposals concern social issues (e.g., protection of the environment, discontinuation of the manufacture and sale of dangerous products).

1. ***Inclusion in proxy materials.*** If management does not oppose the proposal, it may be included in the proxy materials issued by the corporation. If management opposes the shareholder proposal, the SEC rules on whether the proposal must be submitted to the shareholders in the corporation's proxy materials.
2. ***Requirements.*** To be included in the corporation's proxy materials, the shareholder proposal must (a) not violate federal or state law, (b) relate to the corporation's business, (c) concern policy issues (and not the day-to-day operations of the corporation), and (d) not concern the payment of dividends.

Preemptive Rights

Rights that give existing shareholders the option of subscribing to new shares being issued by the corporation in proportion to their current ownership interest.

Dividends

1. ***Directors' authority to pay dividends.*** The board of directors has the *discretion* to pay *dividends* to shareholders or *retain earnings* for use by the corporation.
2. ***Record date.*** When a corporation declares a dividend, it sets a date usually a few weeks prior to the actual payment that establishes the *record date* for payment of the dividend. Shareholders as of that date will be paid the dividend.

Derivative Lawsuits

A lawsuit a shareholder brings on behalf of the corporation against an offending party who has injured the corporation when the directors of the corporation fail to bring the suit. The shareholders must make a written *demand* upon the corporation to bring the lawsuit, and the corporation either rejects it or 90 days expire without the corporation's bringing the requested lawsuit.

Liability of Shareholders

Limited liability. Shareholders of corporations generally have *limited liability*: That is, they are liable for the debts and obligations of the corporation only to the *extent of their capital contribution* to the corporation.

Disregard of the Corporate Entity

Shareholders may be found *personally liable* for the debts and obligations of the corporation under the following doctrine:

1. ***Piercing the corporate veil.*** Courts can *disregard the corporate entity* and hold shareholders personally liable for the debts and obligations of the corporations if (a) the corporation has been formed without sufficient capital (*thin capitalization*) or (b) separateness has not been maintained between the corporation and its shareholders (e.g., commingling of personal and corporate assets, failure to hold required shareholders' meetings). Also called the *alter ego doctrine*.

Directors and Officers, p. 469

Rights of Directors

1. ***Board of directors.*** A panel of decision makers for the corporation, the members of which are elected by the shareholders.
2. ***Policy decisions.*** The directors of a corporation are responsible for formulating the *policy* decisions affecting the corporation, such as deciding what businesses to engage in, determining the capital structure of the corporation, selecting and removing top officers of the corporation, and the like.
3. ***Resolution.*** The board of directors can adopt a resolution that approves a transaction that requires shareholder vote and recommends it to shareholders.

Selecting Directors

1. ***Inside director.*** A member of the board of directors who is also an officer of the corporation.
2. ***Outside director.*** A member of the board of directors who is not an officer of the corporation.

Term of Office

1. ***Annual term.*** The term of a director's office expires at the next annual shareholders' meeting following his or her election, unless terms are staggered.
2. ***Staggered terms.*** If a board of directors consists of nine or more members, it may be divided into two or three *classes* (each class to be as nearly equal in number as possible), and classes can be elected to serve *staggered terms* for two or three years.

Meetings of the Board of Directors

1. ***Regular meeting.*** A meeting of the board of directors held at the time and place scheduled in the bylaws.
2. ***Special meeting.*** A meeting of the board of directors convened to discuss an important or emergency matter, such as a proposed merger or a hostile takeover attempt.
3. ***Written consents.*** The board of directors may act without a meeting if all the directors sign written consents that set forth the action taken.
4. ***Conference call.*** The board of directors may meet via conference call if all the directors can hear and participate in the call.
5. ***Quorum.*** A simple *majority* of the number of directors established in the articles of incorporation or bylaws constitutes a quorum for transacting business.
6. ***Vote.*** The approval or disapproval of a *majority* of the quorum binds the entire board.
7. ***Supramajority.*** The articles of incorporation or bylaws may require a greater than majority of directors to constitute quorum or the vote of the board.

Committees of the Board of Directors

Committees of the board of directors. Unless the articles of incorporation or bylaws provide otherwise, the board of directors may create committees of its members and delegate certain powers to those committees. The most common committees are:

1. ***Executive committee.*** Has authority to (1) act on certain matters during the interim period between board meetings and (2) conduct preliminary investigations of proposals on behalf of the board.
2. ***Audit committee.*** Recommends independent public accountants and supervises the audit of the financial records of the corporation by the accountants.
3. ***Nominating committee.*** Nominates the management slate of directors to be submitted for shareholder vote.
4. ***Compensation committee.*** Approves management compensation, including salaries, bonuses, stock option plans, fringe benefits, and such.
5. ***Investment committee.*** Responsible for investing and reinvesting the funds of the corporation.
6. ***Litigation committee.*** Reviews and decides whether to pursue requests by shareholders for the corporation to sue persons who have allegedly harmed the corporation.

Officers

Officers. Employees of the corporation who are appointed by the board of directors to manage *day-to-day operations* of the corporation.

Duty of Loyalty

A duty that directors and officers have not to act adversely to the interests of the corporation and to subordinate their personal interests to those of the corporation and its shareholders.

Common examples of breaches of the duty of loyalty:

1. ***Self-dealing.*** The corporation may void any transaction with a director or an officer if it is *unfair to the corporation.* This usually involves undisclosed self-dealing by a director or an officer with the corporation.
2. ***Usurping a corporate opportunity.*** A director or an officer may not personally *usurp* (*steal*) an opportunity that belongs to the corporation. The corporation can acquire the opportunity from the director or officer and recover any profits made by the director or officer.
3. ***Competing with the corporation.*** Directors and officers may not compete with their corporation unless the competitive activity has been fully disclosed to the corporation and approved by a majority of disinterested directors or shareholders.

Duty of Care

A duty that corporate directors and officers have to use care and diligence when acting on behalf of the corporation. This duty is discharged if they perform their duties (a) in good faith, (b) with the care that an *ordinary prudent person* in a like position would use under similar circumstances, and (c) in a manner they reasonably believe to be in the best interests of the corporation.

1. ***Negligence.*** Failure of a corporate director or officer to exercise this duty of care when conducting the corporation's business.
2. ***Business judgment rule.*** A rule that says that directors and officers are not liable to the corporation or its shareholders for honest mistakes of judgment.

Mergers and Acquisitions, p. 477

Mergers and Acquisitions

Mergers, consolidations, and share exchanges are *friendly* combinations of corporations.

1. ***Merger.*** Occurs when one corporation is absorbed into another corporation and ceases to exist. The corporation that continues to exist after a merger is called the *surviving corporation.* The corporation that is absorbed in the merger and ceases to exist as a separate entity is called the *merged corporation.*

Required Approvals

1. ***Required approvals.*** An ordinary merger or share exchange requires (a) the recommendation of the board of directors of each corporation and (b) an affirmative vote of the majority of shares of each corporation that are entitled to vote (unless a greater vote is required).
2. ***No shareholders' vote required.*** The approval of the surviving corporation's shareholders in not required if the merger or share exchange increases the number of voting shares of the surviving corporation by 20 percent or less.
3. ***Articles of merger.*** A document that must be filed with the secretary of state once the merger is completed.

Short-Form Mergers

A merger between a *parent corporation* and a *subsidiary corporation* in which the parent corporation owns 90 percent or more of the subsidiary corporation.

1. ***Required approval.*** Only the approval of the board of directors of the parent corporation is required to effectuate a short-form merger. The votes of the shareholders of either corporation and the board of directors of the subsidiary corporation are not required.

Dissenting Shareholder Appraisal Rights

Statutory rights of shareholders who object to a proposed merger, share exchange, or sale or lease of all or substantially all of the property of the corporation to have their shares valued by the court and receive cash payment of this value from the corporation.

1. ***Procedures.*** The corporation must notify shareholders of their appraisal rights. To obtain appraisal rights, the shareholder must (a) deliver written notice to the corporation of his or her intent to demand payment of his or her shares before the vote is taken and (b) not vote his or her shares in favor of the proposed action.
2. ***Fair value.*** If the shareholder does not accept the value offered by the corporation, the court will determine the *fair value* of the shares. The court may hire appraisers to assist in making this determination. Costs of this proceeding are usually borne by the corporation.

Tender Offers, p. 479

Tender Offers

An offer that an acquirer makes directly to a *target corporation's shareholders* in an effort to acquire the target corporation or gain control of the target corporation.

1. ***Tender offeror.*** The party that makes a tender offer.
2. ***Target corporation.*** The corporation that is proposed to be acquired in a tender offer situation.

The Williams Act

Federal statute that regulates all tender offers. The SEC is empowered to administer the Williams Act.

Antifraud Provision

Section 14(e). A provision of the Williams Act that prohibits fraudulent, deceptive, and manipulative practices in connection with a tender offer.

Fighting a Tender Offer

The management of the target corporation often takes one or more of the following steps to try to defeat a hostile tender offer:

1. Persuade the shareholders not to tender their shares.
2. File delaying lawsuits (e.g., antitrust lawsuits).
3. Sell the *crown jewel* (e.g., a valuable asset that the tender offeror is particularly interested in acquiring).
4. Adopt *poison pills* (e.g., contract provisions that make contracts and leases expire).
5. Find a *white knight* to purchase the corporation in a friendly acquisition.
6. Conduct a *pac-man tender offer* (i.e., a reverse tender offer to acquire the tender offeror).
7. Issue additional stock to friendly parties.
8. Create an *Employee Stock Ownership Plan (ESOP)* and issue stock to the ESOP.
9. Adopt *flip-over* and *flip-in rights plans* that make it more expensive for the tender offeror to acquire shares.
10. Pay *greenmail* by purchasing the shares held by the tender offeror at a premium. Obtain a *standstill agreement* whereby the offeror agrees not to purchase shares of the target corporation for a stipulated period of time.
11. Engage in other strategies and tactics that make it more difficult for a tender offeror to complete its tender offer.

State Antitakeover Statutes

Statutes enacted by state legislatures that are aimed at protecting corporations that are either incorporated in or doing business within the state from hostile takeovers.

1. ***Lawfulness.*** State antitakeover statutes are lawful if they do not conflict with the federal *Williams Act* or unduly burden interstate commerce in violation of the *Commerce Clause* of the U.S. Constitution.

Internet Exercises and Case Questions

Working the Web Internet Exercises

Activities

1. Create a hypothetical corporation by preparing articles of incorporation, bylaws, and a shareholder agreement, using forms suitable for your state. For a list of state corporation statutes, see **www.law.cornell.edu/topics/state_statutes.html#corporations**.
2. Prepare minutes of the organizational meeting for your newly formed corporation. See Findlaw's Compilation of State Corporation and Business Forms, at **www.findlaw.com/11stategov/indexcorp.html**.
3. For more coverage of the background on directors' and officers' liability, see **www.griffincom.com/docont.htm**. For a lengthy list of topics, see **guide.lp.findlaw.com/01topics/08corp/index.html**. For a quick overview of corporate law, see **www.nolo.com/category/sb_home.html**.
4. For socially responsible investing information, see **www.socialinvest.org**.

Critical Legal Thinking Cases

16.1 Limited Liability of Shareholders Joseph M. Billy was an employee of the USM Corporation. USM is a publicly held corporation. On October 21, 1976, Billy was at work when a 4,600-pound ram from a vertical boring mill broke loose and crushed him to death. Billy's widow brought suit against USM, alleging that the accident was caused by certain defects in the manufacture and design of the vertical boring mill and in the two moving parts directly involved in the accident, a metal lifting arm and the 4,600-pound ram. If Mrs. Billy's suit is successful, can the shareholders of USM Corporation be held personally liable for any judgment against USM? [*Billy v. Consolidated Mach. Tool Corp.*, 412 N.E.2d 934, 51 N.Y.2d 152, 1980 N.Y. Lexis 2638 (N.Y. App. 1980)]

16.2 Preferred Stock On June 24, 1970, Commonwealth Edison, Co., Inc., through its underwriters, sold 1 million shares of preferred stock at an offering price of $100 per share. Commonwealth Edison wanted to issue the stock with a dividend rate of 9.26 percent, but its major underwriter, First Boston Corporation, advised that a rate of 9.44 percent should be paid. According to First Boston, a shortage of investment funds existed and a higher dividend rate was necessary for a successful stock with the high dividend rate being paid on this preferred stock. On April 2, 1971, Commonwealth Edison's vice chairman was quoted in the report of the annual meeting of the corporation as saying, "We were disappointed in the 9.44 percent dividend rate on the preferred stock we sold last August, but we expect to refinance it when market conditions make it feasible." On March 20, 1972, Commonwealth Edison, pursuant to the terms under which the stock was sold, bought back the 1 million shares of preferred stock at a price of $110 per share. What type of preferred stock is this? [*The Franklin Life Insurance Company v. Commonwealth Edison Company*, 451 F.Supp. 602, 1978 U.S. Dist. Lexis 17604 (S.D.Ill. 1978)]

16.3 Dividends Gay's SuperMarkets, Inc., was a corporation formed under the laws of the state of Maine. Hannaford Bros. Co. held 51 percent of the corporation's common stock. Lawrence F. Gay and his brother Carrol were both minority shareholders in Super Markets. Lawrence Gay was also the manager of the corporation's store at Machias, Maine. On July 5, 1971, he was dismissed from his job. At the January 1972 meeting of the Super Markets's board of directors, a decision was made not to declare a stock dividend for 1971. The directors cited expected losses from increased competition and the expense of opening a new store as reasons for not paying a dividend. Lawrence Gay claims that the reason for not paying a dividend was to force him to sell his shares in Super Markets. Lawrence sued to force the corporation to declare a dividend. Who wins? [*Gay v. Gay's Super Markets, Inc.*, 343 A.2d 577, 1975 Me. Lexis 391 (Maine 1975)]

16.4 Duty of Loyalty Edward Hellenbrand ran a comedy club known as the Comedy Cottage, In Rosemont, Illinois. The business was incorporated, with Hellenbrand and his wife as the corporation's sole shareholders. The corporation leased the premises in which the club was located. In 1978, Hellenbrand hired Jay Berk as general manager of the club. In 1980, Berk was made vice president of the corporation and given 10 percent of its stock. Hellenbrand experienced health problems and moved to Nevada, leaving Berk to manage the daily affairs of the business. In June 1984, the ownership of the building where Comedy Cottage was located changed hands. Shortly thereafter, the club's lease on the premises expired. Hellenbrand instructed Berk to negotiate a new lease. Berk arranged a month-to-month lease but had the lease agreement drawn up in his name instead of that of the corporation. When Hellenbrand learned of this, he fired Berk. Berk continued to lease the building in his own name, and he opened his own club there, known as the Comedy Company, Inc. Hellebrand sued Berk for an injunction to prevent Berk from leasing the building. Who wins? [*Comedy Cottage, Inc. v. Berk*, 495 N.E.2d 1006, 1986 Ill.App. Lexis 2486 (Ill. App. 1986)]

16.5 Duty of Loyalty Lawrence Gaffney was the president and general manager of Ideal Tape Co. Ideal, which was a subsidiary of Chelsea Industries, Inc., was engaged in the business of manufacturing pressure-sensitive tape. In 1975, Gaffney recruited three other Ideal executives to join him in starting a tape manufacturing business. The four men remained at Ideal for the two years it took them to plan the new enterprise. During this time, they used their positions at Ideal to travel around the country to gather business ideas, recruit potential customers, and purchase equipment for their business. At no time did they reveal to Chelsea their intention to open a competing business. In November 1977, the new business was incorporated as Action Manufacturing Co. When executives at Chelsea discovered the existence of the new venture, Gaffney and the others resigned from Chelsea. Chelsea sued them for damages. Who wins? [*Chelsea Industries, Inc. v. Gaffney*, 449 N.E.2d 320, 1983 Mass. Lexis 1413 (Mass. Sup. 1983)]

16.6 Derivative Lawsuit In 1948, four brothers—Monnie, Mechel, Merko, and Sam Dotlich—formed a partnership to run a heavy-equipment rental business. By 1957, the company had been incorporated as Dotlich Brothers, Inc. Each of the brothers owned 25 percent of the corporation's stock, and each served on the board of directors. In 1951, the business acquired a 56-acre tract of land in Speedway, Indiana. This land was held in the name of Monnie Dotlich. Each of the brothers was aware of this arrangement. By 1976, the corporation had purchased six other pieces of property, which were all held in Monnie's name. Sam Dotlich was not informed that Monnie was the record owner of these properties. In 1976, Sam discovered this irregularity and requested that the board of directors take action to remedy the situation. When the board refused to do so, Sam initiated a lawsuit on behalf of the corporation. Can Sam bring this lawsuit? [*Dotlich v. Dotlich*, 475 N.E.2d 331, 1985 Ind.App. Lexis 2233 (Ind. App. 1985)]

16.7 Piercing the Corporate Veil M. R. Watters was the majority shareholder of several closely held corporations, including Wildhorn Ranch, Inc. All these businesses were run out of Watters' home in Rocky Ford, Colorado. Wildhorn operated a resort called the Wildhorn Ranch Resort in Teller County, Colorado. Although Watters claimed that the ranch was owned by the corporation, the deed for the property listed Watters as the owner. Watters paid little attention to corporate formalities, holding corporate meetings at his house, never taking minutes of these meetings, and paying the debts of one corporation with the assets of another. During August 1986, two guests of Wildhorn Ranch Resort drowned while operating a paddleboat at the ranch. The family of the deceased guests sued for damages. Can Watters be held personally liable? [*Geringer v. Wildhorn Ranch, Inc.*, 706 F.Supp. 1442, 1988 U.S. Dist. Lexis 15701 (D.Colo.1988)]

16.8 Shareholder Proposal The National Medical Committee for Human Rights is a nonprofit corporation that is organized to advance concerns for human life. The committee received a gift of shares of Dow Chemical stock. Dow manufactured napalm, a chemical defoliant that was used during the Vietnam conflict. The committee objected to the sale of napalm by Dow primarily because of its concerns for human life. The committee owned sufficient shares for a long enough time to propose a shareholders' resolution as long as it met the other requirements to propose such a resolution. The committee proposed that the following resolution be included in the proxy materials circulated by management for the 1969 annual shareholders' meetings:

> *RESOLVED, that the shareholders of the Dow Chemical Company request that the Board of Directors, in accordance with the law, consider the advisability of adopting a resolution setting forth an amendment to the composite certificate of incorporation of the Dow Chemical Company that the company shall not make napalm.*

Dow's management refused to include the requested resolution in its proxy materials. The committee sued, alleging that its resolution met the requirements to be included in the proxy materials. Who wins? [*National Medical Committee for Human Rights v. Securities and Exchange Commission*, 432 F.2d 659, 1970 U.S. App. Lexis 8284 (D.C. Cir. 1970)]

16.9 Dissenting Shareholder Appraisal Rights Over a period of several years, the Curtiss-Wright Corporation purchased 65 percent of the stock of Dorr-Oliver Incorporated. In early 1979, Curtiss-Wright's board of directors decided that a merger with Dorr-Oliver would be beneficial to Curtiss-Wright. The board voted to approve a merger of the two companies and to pay $23 per share to the stockholders of Dorr-Oliver. The Dorr-Oliver board and 80 percent of Dorr-Oliver's shareholders approved the merger. The merger became effective on May 31, 1979. John Bershad, a minority shareholder of Dorr-Oliver, voted against the merger but thereafter tendered his 100 shares and received payment of $2,300. Bershad subsequently sued, alleging that the $23 per share paid to Dorr-Oliver shareholders was grossly inadequate. Can Bershad obtain minority shareholder appraisal rights? [*Bershad v. Curtiss-Wright Corporation*, 535 A.2d 840, 1987 Del. Lexis 1313 (DE 1987)]

16.10 Fighting a Tender Offer On October 30, 1981, Mobil Corporation made a tender offer to purchase up to 40 million outstanding common shares of stock in Marathon Oil Company for $85 per share in cash. It further stated its intentions to follow the purchase with a merger of the two companies. Mobil was primarily interested in acquiring Marathon's oil and mineral interests in certain properties, including the Yates Field. The Marathon directors immediately held a board meeting and determined to find a white knight. Negotiations developed between Marathon and U.S. Steel Corporation. On November 18, 1981, Marathon and U.S. Steel entered into an agreement whereby U.S. Steel would make a tender offer of 30 million common shares of Marathon stock at $125 per share, to be followed by a merger of the two companies.

The Marathon–U.S. Steel agreement was subject to the following two conditions: (1) U.S. Steel was given an irrevocable option to purchase 10 million authorized but unissued shares of Marathon common stock for $90 per share (or 17 percent of Marathon's outstanding shares) and (2) U.S. Steel was given an option to purchase Marathon's interest in oil and mineral rights in Yates Field for $2.8 billion. The latter option could be exercised only if U.S. Steel's offer did not succeed and if a third party gained control of Marathon. Evidence showed that Marathon's interest in the Yates Field was worth up to $3.6 billion. Marathon did not give Mobil either of these two options. Mobil sued, alleging that these two options violated Section 14(e) of the Williams Acts. Who wins? [*Mobil Corporation v. Marathon Oil Company*, 669 F.2d 366, 1981 U.S. App. Lexis 14958 (6th Cir. 1981)]

16.11 Fighting a Tender Offer The Fruehauf Corporation is engaged in the manufacture of large trucks and industrial vehicles. The Edelman group made a cash tender offer for the shares of Fruehauf for $48.50 per share. The stock had sold in the low $20-per-share range for a few months earlier. Fruehauf's management decided to make a competing management-led leveraged buyout (MBO) tender offer for the company in conjunction with Merrill Lynch. The MBO would be funded using $375 million borrowed from Merrill Lynch, $375 million borrowed from Manufacturers Hanover Bank, and $100 million contributed by Fruehauf Corporation. Total equity contributions to the new company under the MBO would be only $25 million: $10 million to $15 million from management and the rest from Merrill Lynch. In return for their equity contributions, management would receive between 40 percent and 60 percent of the new company.

Fruehauf's management agreed to pay $30 million to Merrill Lynch for brokerage fees that Merrill Lynch could keep even if the deal did not go through. Management also agreed to a "no shop" clause whereby they agreed not to seek a better deal with another bidder. Incumbent management received better information about the goings-on. They also gave themselves golden parachutes that would raise the money for management's equity position in the new company.

The Edelman group informed Fruehauf's management that it could top their bid, but Fruehauf's management did not give them the opportunity to present their offer. Management's offer was accepted. The Edelman group sued, seeking an injunction. Did Fruehauf's management violate the business judgment rule? [*Edelman v. Fruehauf Corporation*, 798 F.2d 882, 1986 U.S. App. Lexis 27911 (6th Cir. 1986)]

16.12 State Antitakeover Statute The state of Wisconsin enacted an antitakeover statute that protects corporations that are incorporated in Wisconsin and have their headquarters, substantial operations, or 10 percent of their shares or shareholders in the state. The statute prevents any party that acquires a 10 percent interest in a covered corporation from engaging in a business combination (e.g., merger) with the covered corporation for three years unless approval of the management is obtained in advance of the combination. Wisconsin firms cannot opt out of the law. This statute effectively eliminates hostile leveraged buyouts because buyers must rely on the assets and income of the target company to help pay off the debt incurred in effectuating the takeover.

The Universal Foods Corporation is a Wisconsin corporation covered by the statute. On December 1, 1988, Amanda Acquisition Corporation commenced a cash tender offer for up to 75 percent of the stock of Universal. Universal asserted the Wisconsin law. Is Wisconsin's antitakeover statute lawful? [*Amanda Acquisition Corporation v. Universal Foods*, 877 F.2d 496, 1989 U.S. App. Lexis 9024 (7th Cir. 1989), cert. denied 493 U.S. 955, 110 S.Ct. 367, 1989 U.S. Lexis 5238 (1989)]

Business Ethics Cases

16.13 Business Ethics Jon-T Chemicals, Inc., was an Oklahoma corporation engaged in the fertilizer and chemicals business. John H. Thomas was its majority shareholder and its president and board chairman. In April 1971, Chemicals incorporated Jon-T Farms, Inc., as a wholly owned subsidiary to engage in the farming and land-leasing business. Chemicals invested $10,000 to establish Farms. All the directors and officers of Farms were directors and officers of Chemicals, and Thomas was its president and board chairman. In addition, Farms used offices, computers, and accountants of Chemicals without paying a fee, and Chemicals paid the salary of Farms's only employee. Chemicals made regular informed advances to pay Farms's expenses. This reached $7.5 million by January 1975.

Thomas and Farms engaged in a scheme whereby they submitted fraudulent applications for agricultural subsidies from the federal government under the Uplands Cotton Program. As a result of these applications, the Commodity Credit Corporation, a government agency, paid more than $2.5 million in subsidies to Thomas and Farms. After discovering the fraud, the federal government obtained criminal convictions against Thomas and Farms. In a separate civil action, the federal government obtained a $4.7 million judgment against Thomas and Farms, finding them jointly and severally liable for the tort of fraud. Farms declared bankruptcy, and Thomas was unable to pay the judgment. Because Thomas and Farms were insolvent, the federal government sued Chemicals to recover the judgment. Was Farms the alter ego of Chemicals, permitting the United States to pierce the corporate veil and recover the judgment from Chemicals? Did Thomas act ethically in this case? [*United States of America v. Jon-T Chemicals, Inc.*, 768 F.2d 686, 1985 U.S. App. Lexis 21255 (5th Cir. 1985)]

16.14 Business Ethics MCA, Inc., a corporate holding company, owned 92 percent of the stock of Universal Pictures Company (Universal) and 100 percent of the stock of Universal City Studios, Inc. On March 25, 1996, these two subsidiaries merged pursuant to Delaware's short-form merger statute. The minority shareholders of Universal were offered $75 per share for their shares. Francis I. Du Pont & Company and other minority shareholders (plaintiffs) rejected the offer and then perfected their dissenting shareholder appraisal rights. On March 29, 1973, an appraiser filed a final report in which he found the value of the Universal stock to be $91.47 per share. Both parties filed exceptions to this report.

The parties' ultimate disagreement was, of course, over the value of the stock. Plaintiffs submitted that the true value was $131.89 per share; defendant $52.36. The computations were as follows:

Plaintiffs

Value Factor	Value	Weight	Result
Earnings	$129.12	70%	$ 90.38
Market	144.36	20	28.87
Assets	126.46	10	12.64
		Value per share	$131.89

Defendants

Value Factor	Value	Weight	Result
Earnings	$51.93	70%	$36.35
Market	41.66	20	8.33
Assets	76.77	10	7.68
		Value per share	$52.36

Appraiser

Value Factor	Value	Weight	Result
Earnings	$92.89	80%	$74.31
Assets	85.82	20	17.16
		Value per share	$91.47

Defendant took exception to the appraiser's failure to find that in the years prior to merger, the industry was declining and that Universal was ranked near its bottom. And it argued that Universal was in the business of producing and distributing feature motion pictures for theatrical exhibition. It contended that such business, generally, was in a severe decline at the time of merger and that Universal, in particular, was in a vulnerable position because it had failed to diversify, its feature films were of low commercial quality, and, unlike other motion picture companies, substantially all of its film library had already been committed to distributors for television exhibition. In short, defendant pictured Universal as a weak "wasting asset" corporation in a sick industry with poor prospects for revival.

The stockholders saw a different company. They said that Universal's business was indeed the production and distribution of feature films, but not merely for theatrical exhibition. They argued that there was a dramatic increase in the television market for such feature films at the time of the merger. This new market, they contended, gave greater new value to a fully amortized film library and significantly enhanced the value of Universal's current and future productions. They equated the television market to the acquisition of a new and highly profitable business whose earnings potential was just beginning to be realized at the time of the merger. Finally, say plaintiffs, the theatrical market itself was recovering in 1966. Thus, they painted the portrait of a well-situated corporation in a rejuvenated industry.

Did the parties act ethically in arriving at their proposed value of the company? What was the value of the minority shareholders' shares of Universal? [*Francis I. Du Pont & Company v. Universal City Studios, Inc.*, 312 A.2d 344, 1973 Del.Ch. Lexis 123 (Del.Ch. 1973)]

Briefing the Case Writing Assignment

Read Case A.16 in the Case Appendix [*United States v. WRW Corporation*]. This case is excerpted from the court of appeals opinion. Review and brief the case. In your brief, be sure to answer the following questions.

1. Who was the plaintiff? What was it suing for?
2. Who were the defendants?
3. Explain the doctrine of piercing the corporate veil.
4. Did the court find the defendants personally liable?

Answers to Management Decision Questions

1. A corporation's directors and officers owe the fiduciary duties of trust and confidence to the corporation and shareholders. More specifically, they owe the (a) duty of obedience, (b) duty of care, and (c) duty of loyalty. The duty of obedience dictates that they act within the authority conferred upon them by the state corporation statute, the articles of incorporation, the corporate bylaws, and the resolutions adopted by the board of directors. The duty of care requires officers to use care and diligence when acting on behalf of the corporation. The duty of loyalty requires directors and officers to subordinate their personal interest to those of the corporation and its shareholder. Employees who breach their fiduciary duties are personally liable for any resultant damages caused to the corporation or its shareholders.
2. Under no circumstances should you follow the suggestions of your boss. Generally speaking, the corporate form of business organization protects officers and boards of directors from personal liability from the torts and crimes of the corporations they serve. However, there are situations when the courts will pierce the corporate veil and allow third parties to sue corporate officers and directors for physical damage as well as monetary damages caused by their corporate activity. Also, as a U.S. citizen, you are subject to criminal persecution for your crimes, including those committed as a corporate officer or employee. To intentionally violate health and safety laws and to knowingly subject employees to a dangerous work environment is totally irresponsible and morally indefensible. The law does not require corporate employees to take actions that are illegal or tortious. You would not be protected from liability by a defense of "I was just following my employer's directions." The potential liability from a peril such as a plant fire could subject the corporation to millions of dollars in criminal fines and personal damage claims. Locking plant doors in violation of state law would constitute a breach of the fiduciary duty you and your boss owe the shareholders of Atlantic, and the **Business Judgment Rule** does not apply. This rule says that directors are not liable to the corporation or its shareholders for honest mistakes of judgment.

   Putting into effect better inventory controls and employee production quotas is a better solution. Also, the benefits of additional security personnel cannot be underestimated. The bottom line cannot always be the overriding factor when making business decisions. More and more, society is demanding increased social responsibility on the part of corporations and corporate officers and directors.

Endnotes

1. *Meinhard v. Salmon*, 164 N.E. 545, 546, 1928 N.Y. Lexis 830 (N.Y. App. 1928).
2. 15 U.S.C. Sections 78n(d) and (e).
3. 15 U.S.C. Section 78n(e).

17 Labor and Worker Protection Laws

"Strong responsible unions are essential to industrial fair play. Without them the labor bargain is wholly one-sided."

—Louis D. Brandeis
(1935)

Chapter Objectives

After studying this chapter, you should be able to:

1. Describe how a union is organized and the process of collective bargaining.
2. Describe employees' right to strike and picket.
3. Explain how state workers' compensation programs work and describe the benefits available.
4. Describe employers' duty to provide safe working conditions under the Occupational Safety and Health Act.
5. List the benefits provided by unemployment compensation and Social Security laws.

Chapter Contents

- Federal Labor Law
- Organizing a Union
- Collective Bargaining
- Strikes and Picketing
- Internal Union Affairs
- Workers' Compensation Acts
- Occupational Safety and Health Act
- Fair Labor Standards Act
- Employee Retirement Income Security Act (ERISA)
- Consolidated Omnibus Budget Reconciliation Act (COBRA)
- Immigration Reform and Control Act
- Unemployment Compensation
- Social Security

Management Decision Labor and Worker Protection Laws

Last year, you retired from your position as a full-time instructor in the Science Department at Tennessee Community College (Tennessee). Recently, you were hired to teach three sections of Chemistry I as an adjunct faculty member at Tennessee. On your way to class one afternoon, you slipped and fell as a result of water in the hallway of the Natural and Allied Science Building where the classes were held. There had been severe thunderstorms with accompanying rain in the area that afternoon. You are physically unable to teach the last two months of classes.

1. Are you eligible for workers' compensation benefits?
2. How are workers' compensation claims handled?

Ethics Brief

Prior to this century, the doctrine of *laissez-faire* governed the employment relationship. Since then, federal and state governments have enacted a multitude of statutes that regulate employment.

Management and union may be likened to that serpent of the fables who on one body had two heads that fighting with poisoned fangs, killed themselves.

Peter Drucker
The New Society (1951)

Before the Industrial Revolution, the doctrine of laissez-faire governed the employment relationship in this country. Generally, this meant that employment was subject to the common law of contracts and agency law. In most instances, employees and employers had somewhat equal bargaining power.

This changed dramatically when the country became industrialized in the late 1800s. For one thing, large corporate employers had much more bargaining power than their employees. For another, the issues of child labor, unsafe working conditions, long hours, and low pay caused concern. Both federal and state legislation sought to protect workers' rights, and labor unions were made lawful. Today, employment law is a mixture of contract law, agency law, and government regulation.

This chapter discusses employment laws, labor unions, worker safety, and security, and immigration laws.

Mackinac Bridge, Michigan. Workers on this bridge are covered by workers' compensation, occupational safety, and other labor and protection laws.

Federal Labor Law

In the 1880s, few laws protected workers against employment abuses. The workers reacted by organizing unions in an attempt to gain bargaining strength. Unlike unions in many European countries, unions in the United States did not form their own political party. By the early 1900s, employers used violent tactics against workers who were trying to organize into unions. The courts generally sided with employers in such disputes.

Business Brief

Unions in the United States have not formed their own political party as they have in many other countries.

History of American Labor Unions

The **American Federation of Labor (AFL)** was formed in 1886, under the leadership of Samuel Gompers. Only skilled craft workers such as silversmiths and artisans were allowed to belong. Semiskilled and unskilled workers could not become members. In 1935, after an unsuccessful attempt to take over the AFL, John L. Lewis formed the **Congress of Industrial Organizations (CIO)**. The CIO permitted semiskilled and unskilled workers to become members. In 1955, the AFL and CIO combined to form the **AFL-CIO**. Individual unions (such as the United Auto Workers and United Steel Workers) may choose to belong to the AFL-CIO, but not all unions opt to join.

Today, approximately 15 percent of private-sector wage and salary workers belong to labor unions. Many government employees also belong to unions.

AFL-CIO

The 1955 combination of the AFL and the CIO.

Web Site

AFL-CIO The mission of the AFL-CIO is to improve the lives of working families and to bring economic justice to the workplace. Find out about unions on this useful Web site. Visit at **www.aflcio.org**.

Landmark Law

Federal Labor Union Statutes

In the early 1900s, members of the labor movement lobbied Congress to pass laws to protect their rights to organize and bargain with management. During the Great Depression of the 1930s, several statutes that were enacted gave workers certain rights and protections. Other statutes have been added since then. The major federal statutes in this area are:

- ***Norris-LaGuardia Act*** Enacted in 1932 [29 U.S.C. §§ 101–110 and 113–115], this act stipulates that it is legal for employees to organize. Thus, it removes the federal courts' power to enjoin peaceful union activity. In response, the courts often ignored the act or found union "violence" to escape their provisions.
- ***National Labor Relations Act (NLRA)*** This act, also known as the Wagner Act, was enacted in 1935 [29 U.S.C. §§ 151 et seq.]. The NLRA establishes the right of employees to form, join, and assist labor organizations; to bargain collectively with employers; and to engage in concerted activity to promote these rights. The act places an affirmative duty on employers to bargain and deal in good faith with unions. This act is the heart of American labor law.
- ***Labor–Management Relations Act*** Industrywide strikes occurred in the rail, maritime, coal, lumber, oil, automobile, and textile industries between 1945 and 1947. As a result, public sympathy for unions waned. In 1947, Congress enacted the Labor–Management Relations Act (the Taft-Hartley Act) [29 U.S.C. §§ 141 et seq.], which amended the Wagner Act. This act (1) expands the activities that labor unions can engage in, (2) gives employers the right to engage in free-speech efforts against unions prior to a union election, and (3) gives the president the right to seek an injunction (for up to 80 days) against a strike that would create a national emergency.
- ***Labor–Management Reporting and Disclosure Act*** After discovering substantial corruption in labor unions, Congress enacted the Labor–Management Reporting and Disclosure Act of 1959 (the Landrum-Griffin Act) [29 U.S.C. §§ 153 and 158–164]. This act regulates internal union affairs and establishes the rights of union members. Specifics of this act include (1) a requirement for regularly scheduled elections for union officials by secret ballot, (2) a prohibition against ex-convicts and communists from holding union office, and (3) a rule that makes union officials accountable for union funds and property.
- ***Railway Labor Act*** The Railway Labor Act of 1926, as amended in 1934, covers employees of railroad and airline carriers [45 U.S.C. §§ 151–162 and 181–188]. This act permits self-organization of employees, prohibits interference with this right, and provides for the adjustment of grievances. ■

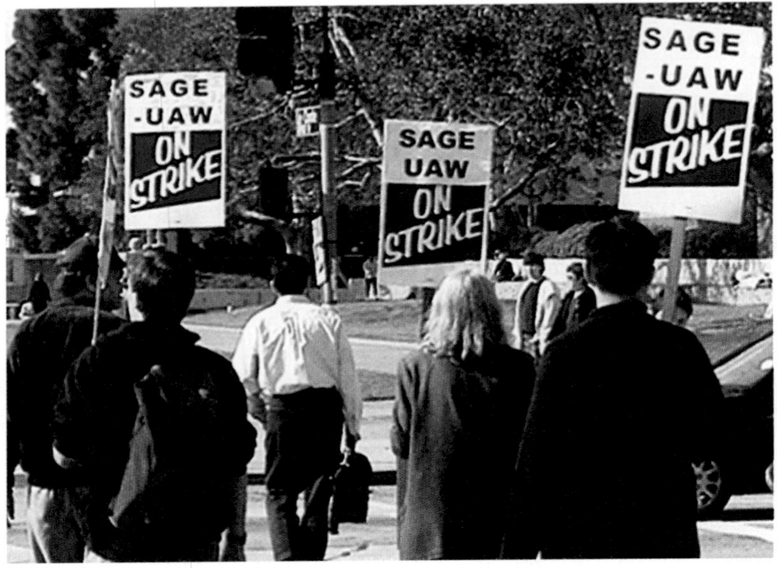

UCLA Campus, Los Angeles, California. In the United States, federal labor laws protect the rights of workers to form and join unions and to engage in peaceful strikes and picketing. Here, teaching assistants at the University of California picket to have the United Auto Workers recognized as their union.

National Labor Relations Board (NLRB)

National Labor Relations Board (NLRB)
A federal administrative agency that oversees union elections, prevents employers and unions from engaging in illegal and unfair labor practices, and enforces and interprets certain federal labor laws.

The National Labor Relations Act created the **National Labor Relations Board (NLRB)**. The NLRB is an administrative body comprised of five members appointed by the president and approved by the Senate. The NLRB oversees union elections, prevents employers and unions from engaging in illegal and unfair labor practices, and enforces and interprets certain federal labor laws. The decisions of the NLRB are enforceable in court.

Business Ethics

Work or Featherbedding?

Unions often oppose change that would cause members to lose their jobs. Union workers steadfastly defend their right to preserve their jobs. Others argue that unions sometimes use their economic muscle to preserve jobs that are no longer necessary, an action called *featherbedding*. Featherbedding impedes technological progress and raises the cost of goods and services to consumers. Consider these views in the following case.

Longshoremen are employed by steamship and stevedoring companies to load and unload cargo into and out of oceangoing vessels at the pier. Cargo arriving at the pier on trucks or railroad cars is transferred piece by piece from the truck or railroad car to the ship by the longshoremen. The longshoremen check the cargo, sort it, place it on pallets, move it by forklift to the side of the ship, and lift it by means of a sling or hook into the ship's hold. The process is reversed for cargo taken off ships. The longshoremen are represented by a union, the International Longshoremen's Association (ILA).

The introduction of "containerization" revolutionized the transportation of cargo. Containers are large metal boxes that are designed to fit onto trucks and railroad cars and can be removed and placed on ships without unloading and loading their contents. When a ship reaches its destination, the containers are loaded onto trucks or railroad cars for transport to their destination. Containerization eliminates most of the work traditionally performed by longshoremen.

After a prolonged strike, ILA and the steamship and stevedoring companies reached an agreement whereby 80 percent of the containers could pass over the pier intact and be loaded onto the ships. The remaining 20 percent of the containers must be unloaded and reloaded by longshoremen, even if this work is unnecessary. This agreement was called the Rules on Containers (Rules). Several transportation companies brought suit, challenging the legality of the Rules under federal labor law. The NLRB held the Rules to be unlawful. The court of appeals reversed. NLRB appealed to the U.S. Supreme Court.

The Supreme Court sided with ILA and upheld the Rules. The Court concluded that Congress, in enacting federal labor law, had no thought of prohibiting labor agreements directed to work preservation. In essence, that is the purpose of a union. The Supreme Court stated:

> The question is not whether the Rules represent the most rational or efficient response to innovation, but whether they are a legally permissible effort to preserve jobs. We

have often noted that a basic premises of the labor laws is that collective discussions backed by the parties' economic weapons will result in decisions that are better for both management and labor and for society as a whole. The Rules represent a negotiated compromise of a volatile problem bearing directly on the well-being of our national economy. [*National Labor Relations Board v. International Longshoremen's Association, AFL-CIO,* 473 U.S. 61, 105 S.Ct. 3045, 1985 U.S. Lexis 83 (1985)]

1. Is it ethical for members of a union to strike to preserve jobs that are no longer needed?
2. Should work preservation be considered a legitimate goal of federal labor policy? Why or why not?
3. Will the decision of the Supreme Court increase or decrease the cost of goods and services to consumers? Explain. ■

Organizing a Union

Section 7 of the NLRA gives employees the right to join together and form a union.[1] The group that the union is seeking to represent—which is called the **appropriate bargaining unit** or **bargaining unit**—must be defined before the union can petition for an election. This group can be the employees of a single company or plant, a group within a single company (e.g., maintenance workers at all of a company's plants), or an entire industry (e.g., nurses at all hospitals in the country). Managers and professional employees may not belong to unions formed by employees whom they manage.

Section 7 of the NLRA
A law that gives employees the right to join together and form a union.

appropriate bargaining unit
The group that a union seeks to represent.

Types of Union Elections

If it can be shown that at least 30 percent of the employees in the bargaining unit are interested in joining or forming a union, the NLRB can be petitioned to investigate and set an election date. Most union elections are contested by the employer. The NLRB is

Business Brief
If a majority of the employees of the appropriate bargaining unit vote to join a union, the union is certified as the bargaining agent of *all* the employees of that unit, even those who did not vote for the union.

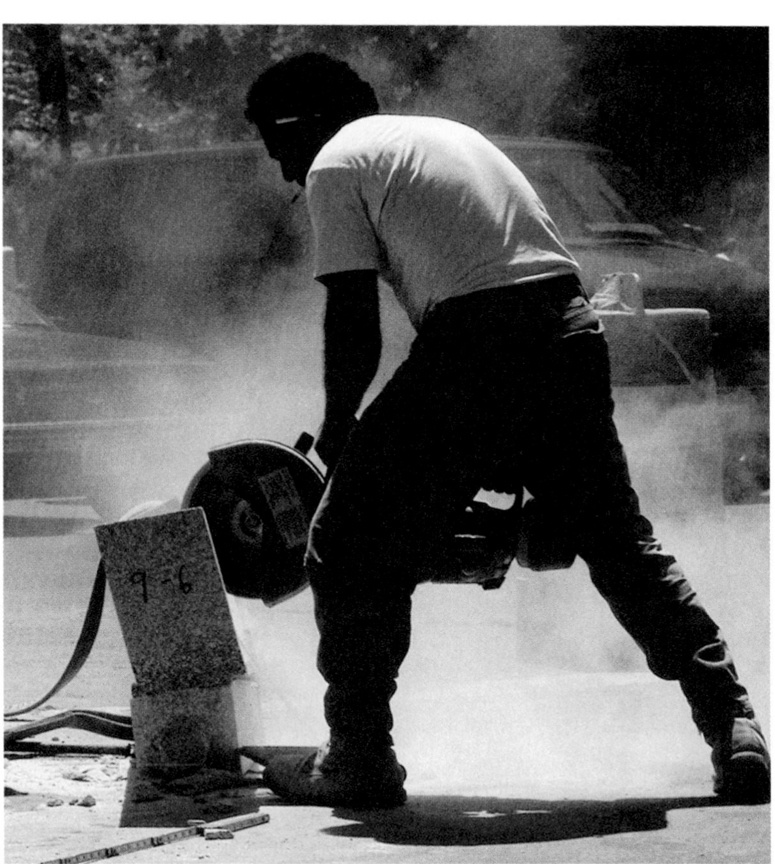

Washington D.C. Federal labor laws protect the rights of workers to form and join unions.

required to supervise all *contested elections*. A simple majority vote (over 50 percent) wins the election. For example, if 51 of 100 employees vote for the union, the union is certified as the bargaining agent for all 100 employees. If management does not contest the election, a *consent election* may be held without NLRB supervision.

If employees no longer want to be represented by a union, a *decertification election* will be held. Such elections must be supervised by the NLRB.

Union Solicitation on Company Property

Ethics Brief

An employer may restrict union solicitation activities by employees to nonworking areas during employees' free time (e.g., coffee breaks, lunch hours, and before and after work).

If union solicitation is being conducted by employees, an employer may restrict solicitation activities to the employees' free time (e.g., coffee breaks, lunch hours, and before and after work). The activities may also be limited to nonworking areas such as the cafeteria, rest room, or parking lot. Off-duty employees may be barred from union solicitation on company premises, and nonemployees (e.g., union management) may be prohibited from soliciting on behalf of the union anywhere on company property.

inaccessibility exception

A rule that permits employees and union officials to engage in union solicitation on company property if the employees are beyond reach of reasonable union efforts to communicate with them.

An exception to this rule applies if the location of the business and the living quarters of the employees place the employees beyond the reach of reasonable union efforts to communicate with them. This so-called **inaccessibility exception** applies to logging camps, mining towns, company towns, and the like. Employers may dismiss employees who violate these rules.

In the following case, the U.S. Supreme Court addressed the issue of whether an employer had to allow nonemployee union organizers on its property.

U.S. SUPREME COURT CASE

Lechmere, Inc. v. National Labor Relations Board

502 U.S. 527, 112 S.Ct. 841, 1992 U.S. Lexis 555 (1992)

Supreme Court of the United States

Case 17.1

Organizing a Union

Background and Facts

Lechmere, Inc. (Lechmere), owns and operates a retail store in the Lechmere Shopping Plaza in Newington, Connecticut. Thirteen smaller stores are located between Lechmere's store and the parking lot, which is owned by Lechmere. In June 1987, the United Food and Commercial Workers Union, AFL-CIO (Union), attempted to organize Lechmere's 200 employees, none of whom belonged to a union. After a full-page advertisement in a local newspaper drew little response, nonemployee Union organizers entered Lechmere's parking lot and began placing handbills on windshields of cars parked in the employee section of the parking lot. Lechmere's manager informed the organizers that Lechmere prohibited solicitation or handbill distribution of any kind on the property and asked them to leave. They did so, and Lechmere personnel removed the handbills. Union organizers renewed their handbill effort in the parking lot on several subsequent occasions, but each time, they were asked to leave, and the handbills were removed. Union filed a grievance with the NLRB. The NLRB ruled in favor of Union and ordered Lechmere to allow handbill distribution in the parking lot. The court of appeals affirmed. Lechmere appealed to the U.S. Supreme Court.

Supreme Court Issue

May a store owner prohibit nonemployee union organizers from distributing leaflets in a shopping mall parking lot owned by the store?

In The Language of The U.S. Supreme Court

Thomas, Justice In practice, nonemployee organizational trespassing had generally been prohibited except where "unique obstacles" prevented nontrespassory methods of communication with the employees. The inaccessibility exception is a narrow one. It does not apply wherever nontrespassory access to employees may be cumbersome or less-than-ideally effective, but only where the location of a plant and the living quarters of the employees place the employees beyond the reach of reasonable union efforts to communicate with them.

Although the employees live in a large metropolitan area (Greater Hartford), that fact does not in itself render them "inaccessible." Their accessibility is suggested by the union's success in contacting a substantial percentage of them directly, via mailing, phone calls, and home visits. Such direct contact, of course, is not a necessary element of "reasonably effective" communication; signs or advertising also may suffice. In this case, other alternative means of communication were readily available. Thus, signs (displayed, for example, from the public grassy strip adjoining Lechmere's parking lot) would have informed the employees about the union's organizational efforts. Access to employees, not success in winning them over, is the critical issue.

Decision and Remedy

The U.S. Supreme Court held that under the facts of this case, Lechmere could prohibit nonemployee Union organizers from distributing leaflets to employees in the store's parking lot. Reversed.

Case Questions

Critical Legal Thinking Should property rights take precedence over a union's right to organize employees?

Business Ethics Is it ethical for an employer to deny union organizers access to company property to conduct their organization efforts? Is it ethical for union organizers to demand this as a right?

Contemporary Business What implications does this case have for business? Is this a pro- or antibusiness decision?

Illegal Interference with an Election

Section 8(a) of the NLRA makes it an **unfair labor practice** for an employer to interfere with, coerce, or restrain employees from exercising their statutory right to form and join unions. Threats of loss of benefits for joining the union, statements such as "I'll close this plant if a union comes in here," and the like are unfair labor practices. An employer may not form a company union.

Section 8(a) of the NLRA
A law that makes it an *unfair labor practice* for an employer to interfere with, coerce, or restrain employees from exercising their statutory right to form and join unions.

Section 8(b) of the NLRA prohibits unions from engaging in unfair labor practices that interfere with a union election. Coercion, physical threats, and such are unfair labor practices. Where an unfair labor practice has been found, the NLRB (or the courts) may issue a cease-and-desist order or an injunction to restrain unfair labor practices and may set aside an election and order a new election.

Section 8(b) of the NLRA
A law that prohibits unions from engaging in unfair labor practices that interfere with a union election.

In the following case, the Supreme Court found that an employer had engaged in an unfair labor practice and ordered a new election.

Case 17.2 Unfair Labor Practice

U.S. SUPREME COURT CASE
National Labor Relations Board v. Exchange Parts Co.
375 U.S. 405, 84 S.Ct. 457, 1964 U.S. Lexis 2263 (1964)
Supreme Court of the United States

Background and Facts

Exchange Parts Co. (Exchange Parts) is engaged in the business of rebuilding automobile parts in Fort Worth, Texas. Prior to November 1959, its employees were not represented by a union. On November 9, 1959, the International Brotherhood of Boilermakers, Iron Shipbuilders, Blacksmiths, Forgers and Helpers, AFL-CIO (Union), advised Exchange Parts that it was going to conduct a campaign to organize the workers at the plant. After obtaining sufficient support from members of the appropriate bargaining unit, Union petitioned the NLRB to set an election date. After completing its investigation on February 19, 1960, the NLRB issued an order setting March 18, 1960, as the election date. On February 25, 1960, Exchange Parts held a dinner for its employees at which management announced a new company benefit allowing employees to have an extra holiday (their birthday). On March 4, Exchange Parts sent a letter to its employees that announced new increased wages for overtime pay and an extended vacation plan for employees. Union subsequently lost the election. Union filed a complaint with the NLRB, and the court held in favor of Union and ordered a new election. The court of appeals reversed. The NLRB appealed to the U.S. Supreme Court.

Supreme Court Issue

Is it an unfair practice for an employer to confer new economic benefits on its employees on the eve of a union election?

In The Language of The U.S. Supreme Court

Harlan, Justice The broad purpose of Section 8(a) is to establish the right of employees to organize for mutual aid without employer interference. We have no doubt that it prohibits not only intrusive threats but also conduct immediately favorable to employees that is undertaken with the express purpose of impinging upon their freedom of choice for or against unionization and is reasonably calculated to have that effect. The danger inherent in well-timed increases in benefits is the suggestion of a "fist inside a velvet glove." Employees are not likely to miss the inference that the

National Labor Relations Board v. Exchange Parts Co.

375 U.S. 405, 84 S.Ct. 457, 1964 U.S. Lexis 2263 (1964)
Supreme Court of the United States
(continued)

source of benefits now conferred is also the source from which future benefits must flow and which may dry up if it is not obliged.

We cannot agree with the court of appeals that enforcement of the NLRB's order will have the ironic result of discouraging benefits for labor. The beneficence of an employer is likely to be ephemeral if prompted by a threat of unionization that is subsequently removed. Insulating the right of collective organization from calculated goodwill of this sort deprives employees of little that has lasting value.

Decision and Remedy

The U.S. Supreme Court held that an employer's conferral of benefits on employees on the eve of a union election, which are designed to affect the outcome of that election, is an unfair labor practice. Reversed.

Case Questions

Critical Legal Thinking Should a company be prohibited from taking away (or giving) economic benefits in its fight with a union?

Business Ethics Was it ethical for the employer in this case to increase employee benefits on the eve of the union election?

Contemporary Business Do you think the employer's conduct in this case constituted a "fist in a velvet glove"? Were the benefits conferred in this case likely to be ephemeral?

Contemporary Business Environment

Plant Closing Act

Often, a company would choose to close a plant without giving its employees prior notice of the closing. To remedy this situation, on August 4, 1988, Congress enacted the **Worker Adjustment and Retraining Notification (WARN) Act**, also called the **Plant Closing Act** [P.L. 100–379, 102 Stat. 840]. The act, which covers employers with 100 or more employees, requires employers to give their employees 60 days' notice before engaging in certain plant closings or layoffs.

If the employees are represented by a union, the notice must be given to the union; if they are not, the notice must be given to the employees individually.

The actions covered by the act are

- ***Plant Closings*** A permanent or temporary shut-down of a single site that results in a loss of employment of 50 or more employees during any 30-day period.
- ***Mass Layoffs*** A reduction of 33 percent of the employees or at least 50 employees during any 30-day period.

An employer is exempted from having to give such notice if

1. The closing or layoff is caused by business circumstances that were not reasonably foreseeable as of the time that the notice would have been required.
2. The business was actively seeking capital or business that, if obtained, would have avoided or postponed the shutdown and the employer in good faith believed that giving notice would have precluded it from obtaining the needed capital or business. ■

Collective Bargaining

collective bargaining
The act of negotiating contract terms between an employer and the members of a union.

collective bargaining agreement
The resulting contract from a collective bargaining procedure.

Once a union has been elected, the employer and the union discuss the terms of employment of union members and try to negotiate a contract that embodies these terms. The act of negotiating is called **collective bargaining**, and the resulting contract is called a **collective bargaining agreement**. The employer and the union must negotiate with each other in good faith. Among other things, this prohibits making take-it-or-leave-it proposals.

Subjects of Collective Bargaining

Web Site
U.S. National Labor Relations Board
The NLRB is an independent federal agency created in 1935 to enforce the NLRA. Visit at **www.nlrb.gov**.

Wages, hours, and other terms and conditions of employment are *compulsory subjects* of collective bargaining. Fringe benefits, health benefits, retirement plans, work assignments, safety rules, and the like are included in this category. *Illegal* subjects (e.g., closed shops and discrimination) may not be negotiated.

Subjects that are not compulsory or illegal are *permissive* subjects of collective bargaining. These include such issues as the size and composition of the supervisory force, location of plants, corporate reorganizations, and the like. These subjects may be bargained for if the company and union agree to do so.

The following case presents the issue of whether an employer's decision to close a business unit is a compulsory subject of collective bargaining.

Ethics Brief

An employer may not sponsor or control a union.

Case 17.3 Subjects of Collective Bargaining

U.S. SUPREME COURT CASE

First National Maintenance Corp. v. National Labor Relations Board

452 U.S. 666, 101 S.Ct. 2573, 1981 U.S. Lexis 117 (1981)
Supreme Court of the United States

Background and Facts

The First National Maintenance Corp. (First Maintenance) is engaged in the business of providing cleaning, maintenance, and related services to commercial buildings in the New York City area. It contracts with and hires personnel separately for each customer, and it does not transfer employees between locations. On March 31, 1977, a majority of the employees of First Maintenance selected the National Union of Hospital and Health Care Employees, Retail, Wholesale and Department Store Union, AFL-CIO (Union), to represent them as their bargaining agent.

One of First Maintenance's customers was the Greenpark Care Center (Greenpark) in Brooklyn. First Maintenance became aware that it was losing money at Greenpark, but Greenpark would not agree to an increase in the fee charged for First Maintenance's services. On July 6, 1977, First Maintenance discontinued its contract with Greenpark and dismissed its employees who had been working there. Union filed an unfair labor practice charge with the NLRB. The NLRB ordered First Maintenance to bargain with Union about its decision to terminate the Greenpark contract. The court of appeals enforced the NLRB's order. First Maintenance appealed to the U.S. Supreme Court.

Supreme Court Issue

Is closing a part of a business operation a mandatory subject of collective bargaining?

In The Language of The U.S. Supreme Court

Blackmun, Justice Although parties are free to bargain about any legal subject, Congress has limited the mandate or duty to bargain on matters of "wages, hours, and other terms and conditions of employment." Congress deliberately left the words "wages, hours, and other terms and conditions of employment" without further definition, for it did not intend to deprive the NLRB of the power further to define those terms in light of specific industrial practices. Nonetheless, in establishing what issues must be submitted to the process of bargaining, Congress had no expectation that the elected union representative would become an equal partner in the running of the business enterprise in which the union's members are employed.

Some management decisions, such as the choice of advertising and promotion, product type and design, and financing arrangements, have only an indirect and attenuated impact on the employment relationship. Other management decisions, such as layoffs and recalls, production quotas, and work rules, are almost exclusively an aspect of the relationship between employer and employee. The present case concerns a third type of management decision, one that had a direct impact on employment, since jobs were inexorably eliminated by the termination, but had as its focus only the economic profitability of the contract with Greenpark, a concern under these facts wholly apart from the employment relationship. This decision, involving a change in the scope and direction of the enterprise, is akin to the decision whether to be in business at all.

There is an important difference between permitted bargaining and mandated bargaining. Labeling this type of decision mandatory could afford a union with a powerful tool for achieving delay, a power that might be used to thwart management's intentions in a manner unrelated to any feasible solution the union might propose. The decision to halt work at this specific location represented a significant change in First Maintenance's operations, a change not unlike opening a new line of business or going out of business entirely.

Decision and Remedy

The Supreme Court held that an employer's decision to close a business unit is not part of the terms and conditions over which Congress mandated bargaining. Reversed and remanded.

Case Questions

Critical Legal Thinking Do you think the closing of part of a company's operations should be a mandatory subject of collective bargaining? Why or why not?

Business Ethics Does a company owe a duty not to discontinue nonprofitable operations because it would cause employees to lose their jobs?

Contemporary Business What would have been the economic consequences if the Court had decided the case the other way?

Union Security Agreements

To obtain the greatest power possible, elected unions sometimes try to install a *union security agreement*. The two types of security agreements are

union shop
An establishment in which an employee must join the union within a certain number of days after being hired.

agency shop
An establishment in which an employee does not have to join the union but must pay a fee equal to the union dues.

- ***Union Shop*** Under a **union shop** agreement, an employee must join the union within a certain number of days (e.g., 30 days) after being hired. Employees who do not join must be discharged by the employer upon notice from the union. Union members pay union dues to the union. Union shops are lawful.
- ***Agency Shop*** Under an **agency shop** agreement, employees do not have to become union members, but they do have to pay an agency fee (an amount equal to union dues) to the union. Agency shops are lawful.

Upon proper notification by the union, union and agency shop employers are required to (1) deduct union dues and agency fees from employees' wages and (2) forward these dues to the union. This is called a *check-off provision*. The following case involves the legality of a union security clause.

Case 17.4 Union Security Clause

U.S. SUPREME COURT CASE
Marquez v. Screen Actors Guild, Inc.
525 U.S. 33, 119 S.Ct 292, 1998 U.S. Lexis 7110 (1998)
Supreme Court of the United States

Background and Facts

The Screen Actors Guild (SAG) is a labor union that represents performers in the entertainment industry. In 1994, Lakeside Productions, an entertainment production company, signed a collective bargaining agreement with SAG, making SAG the exclusive union for performers that Lakeside hired for its productions. The collective bargaining agreement contained a standard union security clause, providing that any performer who worked for Lakeside must be a member of SAG. Naomi Marquez, a part-time actress, auditioned for a one-line role in a TV episode to be filmed by Lakeside and won the part. When Marquez did not pay the $500 membership fee to SAG, Lakeside hired another actress for the part. Marquez sued SAG and Lakeside, alleging that the union security clause was unlawful. The district court held for the defendants, and the court of appeals affirmed. The U.S. Supreme Court granted certiorari to hear the appeal.

Supreme Court Issue

Does the union security clause negotiated between Lakeside Productions and SAG violate federal labor law?

In The Language of The U.S. Supreme Court

O'Connor, Justice Section 8(a)(3) of the National Labor Relations Act (NLRA), permits unions and employers to negotiate an agreement that requires union "membership" as a condition of employment for all employees.

The conclusion that Section 8(a)(3) permits union security clauses is not the end of the story. First, in *NLRB v. General Motors Corp.*, 373 U.S. 734, 742, 83 S.Ct. 1453, we held that although Section 8(a)(3) states that unions may negotiate a clause requiring "membership" in the union, an employee can satisfy the membership condition merely by paying to the union an amount equal to the union's initiation fees and dues. In other words, the membership that may be required as a condition of employment is whittled down to its financial core.

Second, in *Communications Workers v. Beck*, 487 U.S. 735, 108 S.Ct. 2641, we considered whether the employee's "financial core" obligation included a duty to pay for support of union activities beyond those activities undertaken by the union as the exclusive bargaining representative. We held that the language of Section 8(a)(3) does not permit unions to exact dues or fees from employees for activities that are not germane to collective bargaining, grievance adjustment, or contract administration.

As a result of these two conclusions, Section 8(a)(3) permits unions and employers to require only that employees pay the fees and dues necessary to support the union's activities as the employees' exclusive bargaining representative.

Decision and Remedy

The U.S. Supreme Court held that the union security clause negotiated between Lakeside Productions and SAG was lawful under federal labor law. The judgment of the court of appeals was affirmed.

Case Questions

Critical Legal Thinking What does an exclusive union security clause provide? Under this agreement, must a worker join a labor union? Explain.

Business Ethics Did SAG and Lakeside act ethically in this case?

Contemporary Business Do the decisions of the U.S. Supreme Court regarding union security agreements prevent the "free rider" problem? Explain.

Contemporary Business Environment

State Right-to-Work Laws

In 1947, Congress amended the Taft-Hartley Act by enacting Section 14(b), which provides: "Nothing in this Act shall be construed as authorizing the execution or application of agreements requiring membership in a labor organization as a condition of employment in any State or Territory in which such execution or application is prohibited by State or Territorial Law." In other words, states can enact **right-to-work laws**—either by constitutional amendment or statute—that outlaw union and agency shops.

If a sate enacts a right-to-work law, individual employees cannot be forced to join a union or pay union dues and fees even though a union has been elected by other employees. Right-to-work laws are often enacted by states to attract new businesses to a nonunion and low-wage environment. Unions vehemently oppose the enactment of right-to-work laws because they substantially erode union power.

Today, the following 22 states have enacted right-to-work laws:

Alabama	Nevada
Arizona	North Carolina
Arkansas	North Dakota
Florida	Oklahoma
Georgia	South Carolina
Idaho	South Dakota
Iowa	Tennessee
Kansas	Texas
Louisiana	Utah
Mississippi	Virginia
Nebraska	Wyoming

The remedies for violation of right-to-work laws vary from state to state but usually include damages to persons injured by the violation, injunctive relief, and often criminal penalties. ■

Strikes and Picketing

The NLRA gives union management the right to recommend that the union call a **strike** if a collective bargaining agreement cannot be reached. Before there can be a strike, though, a majority vote of the union's members must agree to the action.

strike

A cessation of work by union members in order to obtain economic benefits or correct an unfair labor practice.

Employer Lockout

If an employer reasonably anticipates a strike by some of its employees, it may prevent those employees from entering the plant or premises. This is called an **employer lockout**.

employer lockout

An act of an employer to prevent employees from entering the work premises when the employer reasonably anticipates a strike.

Ranch, Idaho. The State of Idaho has enacted a state right-to-work law.

Crossover and Replacement Workers

Individual members of a union do not have to honor a strike. They may (1) choose not to strike or (2) return to work after joining the strikers for a time. Employees who choose either of these options are known as **crossover workers**.

crossover worker
A person who does not honor a strike who either (1) chooses not to strike or (2) returns to work after joining the strikers for a time.

Once a strike begins, the employer may continue operations by using management personnel and hiring **replacement workers** to take the place of the striking employees. Replacement workers can be hired on either a temporary or permanent basis. If replacement workers are given permanent status, they do not have to be dismissed when the strike is over.

replacement worker
A worker who is hired to take the place of a striking worker. A replacement worker can be hired on either a temporary or permanent basis.

Illegal Strikes

Several types of strikes have been held to be illegal and are not protected by federal labor law. Illegal strikes are:

- ***Violent Strikes*** Striking employees cause substantial damage to property of the employer or a third party. Courts usually tolerate a certain amount of isolated violence before finding that the entire strike is illegal.
- ***Sit-Down Strikes*** Striking employees continue to occupy the employer's premises. Such strikes are illegal because they deny the employer's statutory right to continue its operations during the strike.
- ***Partial or Intermittent Strikes*** Employees strike part of the day or workweek and work the other part. This type of strike is illegal because it interferes with the employer's right to operate its facilities at full operation.
- ***Wildcat Strikes*** Individual union members go on strike without proper authorization from the union. The courts have recognized that a wildcat strike becomes lawful if it is quickly ratified by the union.
- ***Strikes During the 60-Day Cooling-Off Period*** Strikes begin during the mandatory 60-day **cooling-on period**. This time is designed to give the employer and the union time to negotiate a settlement of the union grievances and avoid a strike. Any strike without a proper 60-day notice is illegal.
- ***Strikes in Violation of a No-Strike Clause*** Strikes take place in violation of a negotiated no-strike clause, under which an employer gives economic benefits to the union and, in exchange, the union agrees that no strike will be called for a set time.

Illegal strikers may be discharged by the employer with no rights to reinstatement.

Web Site
Bureau of Labor Statistics
Keeping statistics is one of the things our government does best. Here you will find statistics on employment, unemployment, prices, living conditions, and more. Visit at **stats.bls.gov**.

cooling-off period
A period that is required so a union can give an employer at least 60 days' notice before a strike can commence.

Picketing

Striking union members often engage in **picketing** in support of their strike. Picketing usually takes the form of the striking employees and union representatives walking in front of the employer's premises carrying signs announcing their strike. It is used to put pressure on an employer to settle a strike. The right to picket is implied from the NLRA.

picketing
The action of strikers walking in front of the employer's premises, carrying signs announcing their strike.

Picketing is lawful unless it (1) is accompanied by violence, (2) obstructs customers from entering the employer's place of business, (3) prevents nonstriking employees from entering the employer's premises, or (4) prevents pickups and deliveries at the employer's place of business. An employer may seek an injunction against unlawful picketing.

Business Brief
The right of workers to form, join, and assist labor unions is a statutorily protected right in the United States.

Secondary Boycott Picketing Unions sometimes try to bring pressure against an employer by picketing the employer's suppliers or customers. Such **secondary boycott picketing** is lawful only if it is product picketing (i.e., if the picketing is against the primary employer's product). The picketing is illegal if it is directed against the neutral employer instead of the struck employer's product.

secondary boycott picketing
A type of picketing in which unions try to bring pressure against an employer by picketing his or her suppliers or customers.

Consider This Example Suppose the apple pickers' union in the state of Washington goes on strike against its primary employers, the apple growers. Picketing the apple orchards may do little to draw attention of the strike to the public. Therefore, members of the apple pickers' union may picket grocery stores in metropolitan areas that sell Washington apples. If the signs the picketers carry ask shoppers at the grocery stores not to buy Washington apples, the secondary boycott is lawful. However, it is unlawful if the signs ask customers not to shop at the grocery stores.

Web Site

Bureau of International Labor Affairs Find out all about international labor issues at this Web site. Visit at **www.dol.gov/ilab**.

Business Ethics

Labor Union Violence Punished

The primary purpose of a union is to organize employees so that they will have greater bargaining power in negotiating wages and other terms of employment with their employers. If an agreement with an employer is not reached, the union may call a strike of its members and set up picket lines at the employer's place of business to try to bring added pressure on the employer to settle. But when does pressure cross over the ethical line? Consider the following case.

Peter Vargas and Kenneth Henderson owned Chino Farms Market, a grocery store. The employees at the market belonged to the Retail Clerk's Union Local 1428. When the existing collective bargaining agreement expired, the parties began negotiations for a new contract. After several months, the negotiations reached an impasse, and the union workers went out on strike. Vargas, Henderson, and workers they hired tried to operate the store.

On the first night of the strike. Henderson voiced concern about the employees' welfare to the union's local agent who replied, "We don't care about the people. We're going to break you." The union hired professional picketers to join the striking workers on the picket line.

During the course of the picketing, which lasted approximately one year, the picketers

- Blocked the entrances to the store.
- Blocked the driveways leading to the store's parking lot.
- Swore at and threatened customers.
- Scattered nails and carpet tacks over the parking lot.
- Broke windows of delivery trucks trying to make deliveries to the store.
- Spray-painted delivery trucks.
- Painted graffiti on the exterior walls at the store.
- Pushed the store's shopping carts into the street.
- Threw eggs and other food at the store.
- Threw water balloons at customers.
- Placed horse manure in front of the store to offend customers.
- Physically attacked workers at the store and destroyed their vehicles.

The owners of the store obtained court injunctions against the picketers engaging in such conduct. When presented with the injunctions, the picketers tore them up. Customers who complained about the picketers' activities simply stopped shopping at the market. The market was driven out of business.

Vargas and Henderson sued the union for the tort of intentional interference with business relations. The jury found that the striking workers had engaged in illegal activities while picketing the market and that these activities had been condoned by the union. The jury awarded Chino Farms Market $2,602,765 in compensatory damages and $2,602,765 in punitive damages against the union. The court of appeals affirmed the judgment [*Vargas v. Retail Clerk's Union Local 1428*, 212 Cal.App. 3d 319, 260 Cal.Rptr. 650, 1989 Cal.App. Lexis 741 (Cal. App. 1989)]

1. Were the picketers' activities morally reprehensible?
2. Why did the picketers engage in violent and dangerous activities during their strike?
3. Was the award of damages, particularly punitive damages, warranted in this case? ■

Internal Union Affairs

Unions may adopt **internal union rules** to regulate the operation of the union, acquire and maintain union membership, and the like. The undemocratic manner in which many unions were formulating these rules prompted Congress to enact **Title I of the Landrum-Griffin Act**. Title I, which is often referred to as **labor's "bill of rights,"** gives each union member equal rights and privileges to nominate candidates for union office, vote in elections, and participate in membership meetings. It further guarantees union members the right of free speech and assembly, provides for due process (notice and hearing), and permits union members to initiate judicial or administrative action.

Title I of the Landrum-Griffin Act
An act that is referred to as labor's "bill of rights" that gives each union member equal rights and privileges to nominate candidates for union office, vote in elections, and participate in membership meetings.

Vietnam. Workers in many other countries are not accorded the same rights to form and join unions as provided by federal labor law in the United States.

No private business monopoly, producer organization or cartel wields the market (and physical) power or commands the discipline over its members which many unions have achieved.

Gottfried Haberler
Economic Growth and Stability (1974)

A union may discipline members for participating in certain activities, including (1) walking off the job in a nonsanctioned strike, (2) working for wages below union scale, (3) spying for an employer, and (4) any other unauthorized activity that has an adverse economic impact on the union. A union may not punish a union member for participating in a civic duty, such as testifying in court against the union.

Contemporary Business Environment

Drug Testing of Employees

Drug testing of employees or prospective employees by private and public employers has increased dramatically in the past decade. Employers see drug testing as a way to increase productivity and decrease liability exposure. Job applicants and employees often view drug testing as an invasion of privacy. Although the courts have not been totally consistent in deciding drug-testing cases, several trends have emerged.

Generally, preemployment drug screening has been upheld by the courts. Because job applicants have a lower expectation of privacy than incumbent employees, legal challenges are less likely. Drug testing of incumbent employees by private employers is usually upheld where the employer either has a reasonable suspicion that an employee is impaired or drug testing is required after an accident has occurred.

When the government is the employer, an additional challenge is usually raised against drug testing. Plaintiffs usually say that it constitutes an unreasonable search and seizure by the government in violation of the Fourth Amendment of the U.S. Constitution. This issue was raised in two case decided by the U.S. Supreme Court.

In *Skinner v. Railway Labor Executives' Association* [489 U.S. 602, 109 S.Ct. 1402, 1989 U.S. Lexis 1568 (1989)], the Supreme Court upheld the postaccident testing of railway workers even if the employer has no reason to suspect drug use. The Court upheld a Federal Railroad Administration (FRA) rule that regulations require blood and urine tests of every employee involved in a "major accident" and permit testing of any worker who violates certain safety rules. These rules were prompted by an investigation that revealed that alcohol and drug use by railroad employees contributed to a substantial number of train accidents.

After deciding *Skinner*, the Court moved on to consider the case of *National Treasury Employees Union v. Von Raab* [489 U.S. 656, 109 S.Ct. 1384, 1989 U.S. Lexis 6033 (1989)]. In *Von Raab*, the Supreme Court decided that the U.S. Customs Service, which is responsible for protecting the nation's borders and seizing illegal drugs, could require applicants for jobs that required them to interdict illegal drugs, carry a gun, or handle "classified material" to take a urine test for illegal drugs. The Court stated that even off-duty use of illicit substances can affect their effectiveness because of the risk of bribery and blackmail. ■

Workers' Compensation Acts

Many types of employment are dangerous, and each year many workers are injured on the job. Under common law, employees who were injured on the job could sue their employer for negligence. This time-consuming process placed the employee at odds with his or her employer. In addition, there was no guarantee that the employee would win the case. Ultimately, many injured workers—or the heirs of deceased workers—were left uncompensated.

Workers' compensation acts were enacted in response to the unfairness of that result. These acts create an administrative procedure for workers to receive compensation for injuries that occur on the job. First, the injured worker files a claim with the appropriate state government agency (often called the workers' compensation board or commission). Next, that entity determines the legitimacy of the claim. If the worker disagrees with the agency's findings, he or she may appeal the decision through the state court system.

workers' compensation acts
Acts that compensate workers and their families if workers are injured in connection with their jobs.

Business Brief
Depending on the state, employers are required either to pay for workers' compensation insurance or to self-insure by making payments into a contingency fund. This is a substantial expense for business.

Workers' compensation benefits are paid according to preset limits established by statute or regulation. The amounts that are recoverable vary from state to state.

Employment-Related Injury

For an injury to be compensable under workers' compensation, the claimant must prove that the injury arose out of and in the course of his or her employment. An accident that occurs while an employee is actively working is clearly within the scope of this rule. Accidents that occur at a company cafeteria or while on a business lunch for an employer are covered. Accidents that happen while the employee is at an off-premises restaurant during his or her personal lunch hour are not covered. Many workers' compensation acts include stress as a compensable work-related injury.

Business Brief
To recover under workers' compensation, the worker's injuries must have been employment related.

Exclusive Remedy

Workers' compensation is an exclusive remedy. Thus, workers cannot sue their employers in court for damages. There is no exception to this rule: If an employer intentionally injures a worker, the worker can collect workers' compensation benefits and sue the employer. Workers' compensation acts do not bar injured workers from suing responsible third parties to recover damages.

In the following case, the court had to decide whether an accident was work related.

Business Brief
Generally, workers' compensation is an *exclusive remedy* for an injured employee. It precludes the injured employee from suing the employer for other damages or remedies. An exception is when an employer intentionally injures an employee.

Soo Locks, Michigan. Employers are required to cover employees with workers' compensation insurance.

Case 17.5 Workers' Compensation

Smith v. Workers' Compensation Appeals Board

191 Cal.App.3d 127, 236 Cal.Rptr. 248, 1987 Cal.App. Lexis 1587 (1987)
Court of Appeals of California

Background and Facts

Ronald Wayne Smith was employed by Modesto High School as a temporary math instructor. In addition, he coached the girls' baseball and basketball teams. The contract under which he was employed stated that he "may be required to devote a reasonable amount of time to other duties" in addition to instructional duties. The teachers in the school system were evaluated once a year regarding both instructional duties and noninstructional duties, including "sponsorship or the supervision of out-of-classroom student activities."

The high school's math club holds an annual end-of-year outing. For the 1983–1984 school year, a picnic was scheduled for June 7, 1984, at the Modesto Reservoir. The students invited their math teachers, including Smith, to attend. The food was paid for by math club members' dues. Smith attended the picnic with his wife and three children. One of the students brought along a windsurfer. Smith watched the students as they used it before and after the picnic. When Smith tried it himself, he fell and was seriously injured. He died shortly thereafter. Mrs. Smith filed a claim for workers' compensation benefits, which was objected to by the employer. The workers' compensation judge denied benefits. The Workers' Compensation Appeals Board affirmed. Mrs. Smith appealed.

Issue

Was Smith engaged in employment-related activities when the accident occurred?

In The Language of The Court

Ballantyne, Associate Justice In the instant case, decedent was a temporary instructor at Modesto High. As such, he was more vulnerable to pressure or suggestion that he participate in extracurricular activities to better his chances of being rehired. The math club was an official school club. Notices of meetings to plan the picnic appeared in the school bulletin. The picnic was not an impromptu and informal gathering. Students were required to submit permission slips to the school. The food for the event was paid for out of the math club funds. The school was more than minimally involved in the picnic. Teachers were encouraged to involve themselves in extracurricular activities of the school, thus conferring the benefit of better teacher–student relationships. More importantly, teachers were evaluated on whether they shared equally in the sponsorship or the supervision of out-of-classroom student activities, and decedent had been commended for his participation in this area. We are persuaded to conclude that the employee's heir should be compensated.

Respondent argues that if this court finds that decedent's attendance at the picnic was required by his employment, then his activities in using the windsurfer were outside the course and scope of his employment. An injury is deemed to have arisen out of one's employment if there is an incidental or causal connection between the employment and the accident. Because attendance at the picnic was an implied requirement of decedent's employment, his accident that resulted from his engaging in the recreational activities that were part and parcel of the picnic's "entertainment" is causally connected to his employment.

Decision and Remedy

The court of appeals held that decedent's accident was causally connected to his employment for purposes of awarding workers' compensation benefits to his heirs. Reversed and remanded.

Case Questions

Critical Legal Thinking Should workers' compensation benefits be awarded only for accidents that occur at the job site? Why or why not?

Business Ethics Did the employer act ethically in objecting to the payment of benefits in this case?

Contemporary Business How costly is workers' compensation for business? Do you think that many fraudulent workers' compensation claims are filed?

Contemporary Business Environment

Employee Polygraph Protection Act

In the past, some employers used polygraph (lie detector) tests to screen job applicants and employees. To correct abuses in this practice and to protect workers' privacy, Congress enacted the **Employee Polygraph Protection Act of 1988** [29 U.S.C. §§ 2001–2009]. The act prohibits most private employers from using polygraph tests. Federal and state governments are not covered by the act. Polygraph tests may also be used by

- Employers in matters dealing with national defense (e.g., certain defense contractors).
- Security services that hire employees who protect the public health and safety (e.g., guards at electric power plants).
- Drug manufacturers and distributors that hire employees that will have access to the drugs.
- Employers that are investigating incidents of theft, embezzlement, espionage, and the like by current employees. The employer must have a reasonable suspicion that the employee was involved in the incident.

The act requires private employers that are permitted to use polygraph testing to follow certain procedures, including giving notice to the person to be tested, using licensed examiners, and prohibiting certain questions (e.g., those relating to the religion or sexual behavior of the subject).

The act is administered by the Department of Labor, which has the authority to adopt regulations to enforce the act. It can assess civil penalties up to $10,000 and can seek injunctive and legal relief against violators. Employees and job applicants are given a private right of action to sue under the act. ■

Occupational Safety and Health Act

In 1970, Congress enacted the **Occupational Safety and Health Act**[2] to promote safety in the workplace. Virtually all private employers are within the scope of the act, but federal, state, and local governments are exempt. Industries regulated by other federal safety legislation also are exempt.[3] The act also established the **Occupational Safety and Health Administration (OSHA)**, a federal administrative agency within the Department of Labor. The act imposes recordkeeping and reporting requirements on employers and requires them to post notices in the workplace, informing employees of their rights under the act.

Occupational Safety and Health Act
A federal act enacted in 1970 that promotes safety in the workplace.

Web Site
OSHA OSHA is a federal agency created to enforce occupational safety laws. Visit at **www.osha.gov**.

Specific and General Duty Standards

OSHA is empowered to administer the Occupational Safety and Health Act and adopt rules and regulations to interpret and enforce it. OSHA has adopted thousands of regulations to enforce the safety standards established by the act. These include the following:

- ***Specific Duty Standards*** Many of the OSHA standards address safety problems of a **specific duty** nature. For example, OSHA standards establish safety requirements for equipment (e.g., safety guards), set maximum exposure levels to hazardous chemicals, regulate the location of machinery, establish safety procedures for employees, and the like.
- ***General Duty Standards*** The act imposes a **general duty** on an employer to provide a work environment "free from recognized hazards that are causing or are likely to cause death or serious physical harm to his employees."[4] This is so even if no specific regulation applies to the situation.

specific duty
A duty of a specific nature (e.g., requirement for a safety guard on a particular type of equipment).

general duty
A duty that an employer has to provide a work environment "free from recognized hazards that are causing or are likely to cause death or serious physical harm to his employees."

OSHA is empowered to inspect places of employment for health hazards and safety violations. If a violation is found, OSHA can issue a *written citation* that requires the employer to abate or correct the situation. Contested citations are reviewed by the Occupational Safety and Health Review Commission. Its decision is appealable to the federal circuit court of appeals. Employers who violate the act, OSHA rules and regulations, or OSHA citations are subject to both civil and criminal penalties.

Restaurant. The federal Occupational Safety and Health Act establishes certain job safety standards that employers must comply with.

In the following case, the U.S. Supreme Court upheld a finding of a violation of the Occupational Safety and Health Act.

Case 17.6

Occupational Safety

U.S. SUPREME COURT CASE

Chao, Secretary of Labor v. Mallord Bay Drilling, Inc.

534 U.S. 253, 122 S.Ct. 738, 2002 U.S. Lexis 403 (2002)

Supreme Court of the United States

Background and Facts

Mallard Bay Drilling, Inc., operates a fleet of barges off the Louisiana coast that drill for oil and gas. On April 9, 1997, one of its barges, "Rig 52," was towed to a location in the territorial waters off Louisiana, where it drilled a well over two miles deep. On June 16, 1997, when the crew had nearly completed drilling, an explosion occurred, killing four members of the crew and injuring two others. The U.S. Coast Guard conducted an investigation and determined that natural gas had leaked from the well, spread throughout the barge, and was ignited by sparks in the pump room. Based on this information, OSHA cited Mallard Bay Drilling for three violations of the Occupational Safety and Health Act. The three violations were that Mallard Bay Drilling had (1) failed to train employees in emergency response, (2) failed to develop and implement an emergency response plan, and (3) failed to promptly evacuate employees from the drilling rig. The administrative law judge and the Occupational Safety and Health Review Commission held against respondent Mallard Bay Drilling. Respondent Mallard Bay Drilling appealed to the U.S. court of appeals, alleging that Rig 52 was not a "workplace" that was regulated by OSHA. The court of appeals held in favor of Mallard Bay Drilling. OSHA appealed the case to the U.S. Supreme Court.

Supreme Court Issue

Was Rig 52 a "workplace" that was subject to regulation by OSHA?

In The Language of The U.S. Supreme Court

Stevens, Justice The Occupational and Safety Health Act imposes on covered employers a duty to provide working conditions that "are free from recognized hazards that are causing or are likely to cause death or serious bodily harm" to their employees, as well as an obligation to comply with safety standards promulgated by the Secretary of Labor. We think it equally clear that Rig 52 was a "workplace" as that term is defined in Section 4(a) of the Act. The vessel was located within the geographic area described in the definition: "a State," namely Louisiana. Nothing in the text of Section 4(a) attaches any significance to the fact that the barge was anchored in navigable waters. Rather, the other geographic areas described in Section 4(a) support a reading of that provision that includes a State's navigable waters: for example, Section 4(a) covers the Outer Continental Shelf, and sensibly extends to drilling operations attached thereto.

Decision and Remedy

The U.S. Supreme Court held that Rig 52 was a "workplace" that was subject to regulation by OSHA. The Supreme Court reversed the decision of the court of appeals and upheld the Occupational Safety and Health Review Commission's citations against respondent Mallard Bay Drilling, Inc.

Case Questions

Critical Legal Thinking What is the public policy that underlies the occupational safety laws? Explain.

Business Ethics Was it ethical for Mallard Bay Drilling, Inc., to argue that Rig 52 was not a workplace subject to OSHA regulation?

Contemporary Business Does compliance with occupational safety and health laws cost businesses very much money? Is the cost worth the benefits?

Business Ethics

Roofing Company Nailed by OSHA

Corbesco, Inc. (Corbesco), an industrial roofing and siding installation company, was hired to put metal roofing and siding over the skeletal structure of five aircraft hangars at Chennault Air Base in Louisiana. In April 1987, Corbesco assigned three of its employees to work on the partially completed flat roof of Hangar B, a large single-story building measuring 60 feet high, 374 feet wide, and 574 feet long. On April 2, 1987, one of the workers, Roger Matthew, who was on his knees installing insulation of the roof, lost his balance and fell 60 feet to the concrete below. He was killed by the fall. The next day, an OSHA compliance officer cited Corbesco for failing to install a safety net under the work site. The officer cited a general industry standard that provides that safety nets should be provided when workers are more than 25 feet above the ground [25 C.F.R. § 1926.105(a)]. The

Department of Labor affirmed the citation against Corbesco. Corbesco appealed.

Did Corbesco violate the OSHA general industry regulation that required employers to install safety nets below employees working more than 25 feet above the ground?

The court of appeals noted the OSHA rule that stated if a workplace is more than 25 feet above the ground, an employer must furnish some form of fall protection. The language of Section 1926.105(a) gave Corbesco knowledge of this general duty. However, the essence of Corbesco's claim is that it believed that it was complying with the regulation. Corbesco was required to furnish its worker with a safety net only if none of the following safety devices was being used: "Ladders, scaffolds, catch platforms, temporary floors, safety lines, or safety belts." Corbesco agues that the flat roof on which the employees were working served as a "temporary floor" and that the language of the standard is not specific enough to notify it otherwise.

The court held that Corbesco had constructive notice that it was required to install safety nets under its crew while they were working on the edge of a flat roof some 60 feet above a concrete floor. The commission frequently had said that a flat roof cannot serve as a temporary floor if workers must operate along the perimeter of such a roof because it does not provide fall protection; either a safety net or one of the alternate safety devices listed in Section 1926.105(a) must be used. A reasonable construction company in Corbesco's position would have known about these interpretations of this standard.

The court of appeals held that Corbesco violated 25 C.F.R. Section 1926.105(a) by not providing a safety net below its employees who were working more than 60 feet above the ground. [*Corbesco, Inc. v. Dole, Secretary of Labor*, 926 F.2d 422, 1991 U.S. App. Lexis 3369 (5th Cir. 1991)]

1. Did Corbesco act ethically in arguing that the flat roof created a temporary floor that relieved it of the duty to install a safety net under it?
2. Why are occupational safety laws enacted? Would just letting employees sue their employers for injuries caused by unsafe working conditions accomplish the same result? Explain.

Fair Labor Standards Act (FLSA)

In 1938, Congress enacted the **Fair Labor Standards Act (FLSA)** to protect workers.[5] The FLSA applies to private employers and employees engaged in the production of goods for interstate commerce.

Fair Labor Standards Act (FLSA) A federal act enacted in 1938 to protect workers. It prohibits child labor and establishes minimum wage and overtime pay requirements.

Child Labor

The FLSA forbids the use of oppressive child labor and makes it unlawful to ship goods produced by businesses that use oppressive child labor. The Department of Labor has adopted the following regulations that define lawful child labor: (1) children under the age of 14 cannot work except as newspaper deliverers; (2) children ages 14 and 15 may work limited hours in nonhazardous jobs approved by the Department of Labor (e.g., restaurants and gasoline stations); and (3) children ages 16 and 17 may work unlimited hours in nonhazardous jobs. The Department of Labor determines which occupations are hazardous (e.g., mining, roofing, and working with explosives). Children who work in agricultural employment and child actors and performers are exempt from these restrictions. Persons age 18 and older may work at any job whether it is hazardous or not.

It is difficult to imagine any grounds, other than our own personal economic predilections, for saying that the contract of employment is any the less an appropriate subject of legislation than are scores of others, in dealing with which this Court has held that legislatures may curtail individual freedom in the public interest.

Justice Stone
Dissenting Opinion, Morehead v. New York (1936)

Entrepreneur and the Law

Minimum Wage and Overtime Pay Requirements

The FLSA establishes minimum wage and overtime pay requirements for workers. Managerial, administrative, and professional employees are exempt from the act's wage and hour provisions. As outlined below, the FLSA requires employers to pay covered workers at least the minimum wage for their regular work hours. Overtime pay is also mandated.

- ***Minimum Wage*** The minimum wage is set by Congress and can be changed. In 2003, it was set at $5.15 per hour. The Department of Labor permits employers to pay less than the minimum wage to students and apprentices. An employer may reduce minimum wages by an amount equal to the reasonable cost of food and lodging provided to employees.
- ***Overtime Pay*** Under the FLSA, an employer cannot require nonexempt employees to work more than 40 hours per week unless they are paid one-and-a-half times their regular pay for each hour worked in excess of 40 hours. Each week is treated separately. For example, if an employee works 50 hours one week and 30 hours the next, the employer owes the employee 10 hours of overtime pay for the first week.

E-Commerce & Information Technology

Microsoft Violates Employment Law

Microsoft Corporation is the world's largest provider of computer operating systems, software programs, and Internet browsers. The company has grown into a monopoly and made one of its founders, Bill Gates, the richest person in the world. But the company has been caught nickel-and-diming some of its workers out of their stock option benefits. It all started with an Internal Revenue Service (IRS) investigation. Here is the story.

Microsoft is headquartered in the state of Washington. In addition to having regular employees, Microsoft used the services of other workers who are classified as *independent contractors* (called *freelancers*) and temporary agency employees (called *temps*). Most of these special employees worked full time for Microsoft, doing jobs that were identical to jobs performed by Microsoft's regular employees. Microsoft paid the special employees by check as outside workers. In 1990, the IRS conducted an employment tax examination and determined that Microsoft had misclassified these special workers as independent contractors and that the workers in these positions should be reclassified as "employees" for federal tax purposes.

The IRS used the following factors to reach the conclusion that the special workers were Microsoft employees rather than independent contractors:

- The party that has the right to control the manner and means by which the service or product is produced.
- The skill required.
- The source of the instrumentalities and tools.
- The location of the work.
- The duration of the relationship between the parties.
- The extent of the hiring party's discretion over when and how long to work.
- The hiring party's role in hiring and paying assistants.
- Whether the work is part of the regular business of the hiring party.

The IRS applied these factors to both the freelancers and temps who worked at Microsoft and found both to be employees of Microsoft. But that was not the end of the story. Plaintiff Donna Vizcaino and other freelancers sued Microsoft in a class action lawsuit, alleging that they were denied employment benefits, especially employee stock options, that were paid to regular employees. Microsoft contributed 3 percent of an employee's salary to the stock option plan. The court of appeals agreed with the plaintiffs, citing the Internal Revenue Code that requires such stock option plans to be available to all employees. Thus, Microsoft's attempts to define certain full-time employees as freelancers and temps was rebuffed by the courts [*Vizcaino v. United States District Court for the Western District of Washington*, 173 F.3d 713, 1999 U.S. App. Lexis 9057 (9th Cir. 1999)]. ■

Employee Retirement Income Security Act (ERISA)

Employee Retirement Income Security Act (ERISA)
A federal act designed to prevent fraud and other abuses associated with private pension funds.

Employers are not required to establish pension plans for their employees. If they do, however, they are subject to the recordkeeping, disclosure, and other requirements of the **Employee Retirement Income Security Act (ERISA).**[6] ERISA is a complex act designed to prevent fraud and other abuses associated with private pension funds. Federal, state, and local government pension funds are exempt from its coverage. ERISA is administered by the Department of Labor and the IRS.

Among other things, ERISA requires pension plans to be in writing and to name a pension fund manager. The plan manager owes a fiduciary duty to act as a "prudent person" in managing the fund and investing its assets. No more tan 10 percent of a pension fund's assets can be invested in the securities of the sponsoring employer.

Vesting occurs when an employee has a nonforfeitable right to receive pension benefits. First, ERISA provides for immediate vesting of each employee's own contributions to the plan. Second, it requires employers' contributions to be either (1) completely forfeitable for a set period of up to five years and totally vested after that (*cliff vesting*) or (2) gradually vested over a seven-year period and completely vested after that time.

Consolidated Omnibus Budget Reconciliation Act (COBRA)

The **Consolidated Omnibus Budget Reconciliation Act of 1985 (COBRA)**[7] provides that an employee of a private employer or the employee's beneficiaries must be offered the opportunity to continue his or her group health insurance after the voluntary or involuntary termination of a worker's employment or the loss of coverage due to certain qualifying events defined in the law. The employer must notify covered employees and their beneficiaries of their rights under COBRA. To continue coverage, a person must pay the required group rate premium. Government employees are subject to parallel provisions found in the Public Health Service Act.

Consolidated Omnibus Budget Reconciliation Act (COBRA)
A federal law that permits employees and their beneficiaries to continue their group health insurance after an employee's employment has ended.

Landmark Law

Family and Medical Leave Act

In February 1993, Congress enacted the **Family and Medical Leave Act.** The act guarantees workers unpaid time off from work for medical emergencies. The act, which applies to companies with 50 or more workers as well as federal, state, and local governments, covers about half of the nation's workforce. To be covered by the act, an employee must have worked for the employer for at least one year and have performed more than 1,250 hours of service during the previous 12-month period.

Covered employers are required to provide up to 12 weeks of unpaid leave during any 12-month period due to the

1. Birth of, and care for, a child.
2. Placement of a child for adoption or in foster care.
3. Serious health condition that makes the employee unable to perform his or her duties.
4. Care for a spouse, child, or parent with a serious health problem.

Leave because of the birth of a child or the placement of a child for adoption or foster care cannot be taken intermittently unless the employer agrees. Other leaves may be taken on an intermittent basis. The employer may require medical proof of claimed serious health conditions.

An eligible employee who takes leave must, upon returning to work, be restored to either the same or an equivalent position with equivalent employment benefits and pay. The restored employee is not entitled to the accrual of seniority during the leave period, however. A covered employer may deny restoration to a salaried employee who is among the highest-paid 10 percent of that employer's employees if the denial is necessary to prevent "substantial and grievous economic injury" to the employer's operations. ■

Tibet. Workers in many other countries are not accorded the same worker protection laws as those provided by many state and federal laws in the United States.

Immigration Reform and Control Act (IRCA)

Immigration Reform and Control Act of 1986 (IRCA)

A federal statute that makes it unlawful for employers to hire illegal immigrants.

INS Form I-9

A form that must be filled out by all U.S. employers for each employee. It states that the employer has inspected the employee's legal qualifications to work.

The **Immigration Reform and Control Act of 1986 (IRCA)** is administered by the U.S. Immigration and Naturalization Service (INS).[8] The act makes it unlawful for employers to hire illegal immigrants. As of June 1, 1987, all U.S. employers must complete **INS Form I-9** for each employee. The form attests that the employer has inspected documents of the employee and has determined that he or she is either a U.S. citizen or otherwise qualified to work in the country (e.g., has a proper work visa). Employers must maintain records and post in the workplace notices of the contents of the law. Violators are subject to both civil and criminal penalties.

The following case involved the application of immigration law.

Case 17.7 Immigration Law

U.S. SUPREME COURT CASE
Hoffman Plastic Compounds, Inc. v. National Labor Relations Board

535 U.S. 137, 122 S.Ct. 1275, 2002 U.S. Lexis 2147 (2002)
Supreme Court of the United States

Background and Facts

Hoffman Plastic Compounds, Inc. (Hoffman), custom-formulates chemical compounds used by businesses. In May 1988, Hoffman hired Jose Castro as an employee to operate various vending machines. Unbeknownst to Hoffman, Castro was an illegal alien who showed Hoffman a birth certificate belonging to a friend who was born in Texas. Using this false birth certificate, Castro fraudulently obtained a California driver's license and a Social Security card, which were also shown to Hoffman. Hoffman relied on these documents and hired Castro.

In January 1992, Hoffman dismissed Castro and several other employees who had been supporting the formation of a union at Hoffman. Castro sued Hoffman, alleging that Hoffman had violated the NLRA, a federal statute that permits employees to organize a union, and alleging that he was due back pay for the time period for which he had been fired. The NLRB, a federal agency, found Hoffman had violated the NLRA and awarded $66,951 in back pay to Castro. Hoffman appealed, alleging that the federal immigration law prohibited the award of back pay to an illegal immigrant. The court of appeals affirmed the NLRB's order against Hoffman. Hoffman appealed to the U.S. Supreme Court.

Supreme Court Issue

Does federal immigration law prohibit the award of back pay to an illegal immigrant worker where the employer has violated national labor laws in dismissing the illegal immigrant worker?

In The Language of The Supreme Court

If an employer unknowingly hires an unauthorized alien, or if the alien becomes unauthorized while employed, the employer is compelled to discharge the worker upon discovery of the worker's undocumented status. Employers who violate the Immigration Reform and Control Act (IRCA) are punished by civil fines and may be subject to criminal prosecution. IRCA also makes it a crime for an unauthorized alien to subvert the employer verification system by tendering fraudulent documents. It thus prohibits aliens from using or attempting to use "any forged, counterfeit, altered, or falsely made document" or "any document lawfully issued to or with respect to a person other than the possessor" for purposes of obtaining employment in the United States. Aliens who use or attempt to use such documents are subject to fines and criminal prosecution. There is no dispute that Castro's use of false documents to obtain employment with Hoffman violated these provisions.

Under the IRCA regime, it is impossible for an undocumented alien to obtain employment in the United States without some party directly contravening explicit congressional policies. Either the undocumented alien tenders fraudulent identification, which subverts the cornerstone of IRCA's enforcement mechanism, or the employer knowingly hires the undocumented alien in direct contradiction of its IRCA obligations. The NLRB asks that we overlook this fact and allow it to award back pay to an illegal alien for years of work not performed, for wages that could not lawfully have been earned, and for a job obtained in the first instance by a criminal fraud. We find, however, that awarding back pay to illegal aliens runs counter to policies underlying IRCA, policies the NLRB has no authority to enforce or administer. Therefore, as we have consistently held in like circumstances, the award lies beyond the bounds of the NLRB's remedial discretion.

Indeed, awarding back pay in a case like this not only trivializes the immigration laws, it also condones and encourages future violations. We therefore conclude that allowing the Board to award back pay to illegal aliens would unduly trench upon explicit statutory prohibitions critical to federal immigration policy, as expressed in IRCA. It would encourage the successful evasion of apprehension by immigration authorities, condone prior violations of the immigration laws, and encourage future violations.

Decision and Remedy

The U.S. Supreme Court held that the NLRB's award of back pay to plaintiff Castro violated federal immigration law of the United States. The Supreme Court reversed the judgment of the court of appeals.

Case Questions

Critical Legal Thinking Do current immigration laws work to keep illegal immigrants from securing jobs in the United States? Explain.

Business Ethics Did Hoffman act ethically in denying it owed Castro back pay? Did Castro act ethically in using false documents to secure employment?

Contemporary Business Does America's policy of providing legal working visas to immigrants to temporarily work in this country help or hurt the country? Explain.

Unemployment Compensation

In 1935, Congress established an unemployment compensation program to assist workers who were temporarily unemployed. Under the **Federal Unemployment Tax Act (FUTA)**[9] and state laws enacted to implement the program, employers are required to pay unemployment contributions (taxes). The tax rate and unemployment wage level are subject to change. Employees do not pay unemployment taxes.

Federal Unemployment Tax Act (FUTA)
A federal act that requires employers to pay unemployment taxes; unemployment compensation is paid to workers who are temporarily unemployed.

State governments administer unemployment compensation programs under general guidelines set by the federal government. Each state establishes its own eligibility requirements and the amount and duration of the benefits. To collect benefits, applicants must be able and available for work and seeking employment. Workers who have been let go because of bad conduct (e.g., illegal activity, drug use on the job) or who voluntarily quit work without just cause are not eligible to receive benefits.

Social Security

In 1935, Congress established the federal **Social Security** system to provide limited retirement and death benefits to certain employees and their dependents. The Social Security system is administered by the Social Security Administration. The program has expanded greatly since it was first enacted. Today, it provides benefits to approximately 9 out of every 10 workers.[10]

Social Security
A federal system that provides limited retirement and death benefits to covered employees and their dependents.

Social Security benefits include (1) retirement benefits, (2) survivors' benefits to family members of deceased workers, (3) disability benefits, and (4) medical and hospitalization benefits (Medicare).

Under the **Federal Insurance Contributions Act (FICA)**,[11] employees and employers must make contributions (pay taxes) into the Social Security fund. The employer must pay a matching amount. Social Security does not operate like a savings account. Instead, current contributions are used to fund current claims. The employer is responsible for deducting employees' portions from their wages and remitting the entire payment to the IRS.

Federal Insurance Contributions Act (FICA)
A federal act that says employees and employers must make contributions into the Social Security fund.

Under the **Self-Employment Contributions Act**,[12] self-employed individuals must pay Social Security, too. The amount of taxes self-employed individuals must pay is equal to the combined employer–employee amount.

Self-Employment Contributions Act
A federal act that says self-employed persons must pay Social Security taxes equal to the combined employer–employee amount.

Failure to submit Social Security taxes subjects the violator to interest payments, penalties, and possible criminal liability. Social Security taxes may be changed by act of Congress.

International Law

Mexican Labor Laws

Labor and employment in Mexico are subject to the **Federal Labor Law of Mexico**, which is administered by the **Labor Board of Conciliation and Arbitration**. Because this law promotes unionized labor, labor unions are easy to form. Most collective bargaining agreements are unlimited in duration, although the terms of the agreements are usually revised biannually. Under Mexican law if there is a strike, the plant will shut down. This will force the parties to settle the strike.

The Mexican government publishes a biannual list of required salaries, by occupation. Manual laborers must be paid weekly, whereas other employees must be paid in pay periods not exceeding 15 days. Employees receive an overtime bonus of 25 percent of their wages for working on Sunday. Employees are also paid a bonus equivalent to at least 15 days' pay as a Christmas bonus. Under the law, employers must include workers in profit-sharing programs that distribute 8 percent of earnings, before taxes, to the workers.

Employees who pass a 30-day trial period may not be dismissed for lack of qualification for the job. After 1 year, employees can be dismissed only for statutory reasons. An employee who is unjustly dismissed is entitled to recover 3 months' severance pay plus 20 days' salary for each year of employment.

Another Mexican law establishes a social security system. Both the employer and employee must contribute to this system. Employers must pay fees for workers' compensation, disability, old age, unemployment, death, and maternity leave benefits. In addition, employers are required to contribute an amount equivalent to 5 percent of their employees' wages to the national housing fund, 1 percent to day-care facilities, 1 percent to public education, and 1 percent to payroll taxes.

Although the foregoing employment benefits may seem generous, in reality they are not. There are several reasons for this. First, the cost of a minimum-wage employee in Mexico, including wages, benefits, and taxes, is less than $1 per hour. Second, Mexican labor laws have not been stringently enforced by the government. Many U.S. companies have moved manufacturing plants to Mexico to take advantage of the low wage rates there. ■

Chapter Summary

Federal Labor Law, p. 497

Federal Labor Statutes

Federal labor statutes include:

1. ***Norris-LaGuardia Act.*** Made it legal for employees to organize.
2. ***National Labor Relations Act (NLRA).*** Established the right of employees to form, join, and assist labor unions. Also called the *Wagner Act*.
3. ***Labor–Management Relations Act.*** Expanded the activities labor unions could engage in, gave employers free speech rights to oppose unionization, and gave the president the right to seek injunctions against strikes that would create a national emergency. Also called the *Taft-Hartley Act*.
4. ***Labor–Management Reporting and Disclosure Act.*** Called labor's "bill of rights," this act gives union members the right to nominate candidates for union offices and vote in union elections. Also called the *Landrum-Griffin Act*.
5. ***Railway Labor Act.*** Governs union rights of railroad and airline employees.

National Labor Relations Board (NLRB)

Federal administrative agency empowered to administer federal labor law, oversee union elections, and decide labor disputes.

Organizing a Union, p. 499

Organizing a Union

1. ***Section 7 of the NLRA.*** Gives employees the right to join together and form a union.
2. ***Appropriate bargaining unit.*** Group of employees that a union is seeking to represent.

Types of Union Elections

1. ***Contested election.*** Management contests the union. The NLRB must supervise the election.
2. ***Consent election.*** Management does not contest the union election.
3. ***Decertification election.*** Election to determine if the employees want to reject a union as their representative. The NLRB must supervise the election.

Union Solicitation on Company Property

1. ***Employees.*** Employer may restrict solicitation activities to the employees' free time (e.g., breaks, lunch hours) and before and after work.
2. ***Nonemployee union representatives.*** Employer may prohibit solicitation on company property unless the employees cannot otherwise be contacted.

Illegal Interference with an Election

1. ***Section 8(a) of the NLRA.*** Makes it an *unfair labor practice* for an employer to interfere with, coerce, or restrain employees from exercising their right to form and join unions.
2. ***Section 8(b) of the NLRA.*** Makes it an unfair labor practice for a *union* to interfere with a union election.

Collective Bargaining, p. 502

Collective Bargaining

Process whereby the union and employer negotiate the terms and conditions of employment for the covered employee union members.

1. ***Collective bargaining agreement.*** Contract resulting from collective bargaining.

Subjects of Collective Bargaining

1. ***Compulsory subjects.*** Wages, hours, and other terms and conditions of employment (e.g., vacations, medical benefits, etc.)
2. ***Illegal subjects.*** Subjects that may not be negotiated (e.g., discrimination).
3. ***Permissive subjects.*** Subjects that are not compulsory or illegal (e.g., closing of plants).

Union Security Agreements

1. ***Union shop.*** An establishment in which an employee must join a union within a certain number of days after being hired.
2. ***Agency shop.*** An establishment in which employees do not have to join the union but must pay an *agency fee* equal to union dues.
3. ***Check-off provision.*** Requires employers to deduct union and agency dues from employees' wages and remit these payments to the union.

State Right-to-Work Laws

States may enact statutes that make union shops and agency shops illegal. Here, individual employees may choose not to join the union.

Strikes and Picketing, p. 505

Strikes

A *strike* is a cessation of work by union members in order to obtain economic benefits, to correct an unfair labor practice, or to preserve their work. The NLRA gives union employees the right to strike.

Employer Lockout

An employer may lock employees out of its premises if it reasonably anticipates a strike.

Crossover Workers and Replacement Workers

Crossover worker. An employee who does not honor a strike who either (1) chooses not to strike or (2) returns to work after joining strikers for a time.

Replacement worker. A person who is hired to take the place of a striking worker. The employer may offer such an employee a permanent position.

Illegal Strikes

1. ***Violent strike.*** Striking employees cause substantial damage to the employer's or a third party's property.
2. ***Sit-down strike.*** Employees occupy and refuse to leave the employer's premises.
3. ***Partial or intermittent strike.*** Employees strike for only parts of each day or week.
4. ***Wildcat strike.*** Strike not sanctioned by the union.
5. ***Strike during the 60-day cooling-off period.*** Strike where the union has not given the employer at least 60 days' prior notice of the strike.
6. ***Strike in violation of a no-strike clause.*** Strike that violates a no-strike clause in a collective bargaining agreement.

Picketing

Striking employees and union organizers walking around the employer's premises, usually carrying signs, notifying the public of their grievance against the employer.

1. ***Illegal picketing.*** Picketing is illegal if it is accompanied by violence or obstructs customers, nonstriking workers, or suppliers from entering the employer's premises.
2. ***Secondary boycott.*** Picketing conducted at a third party's premises. *Product picketing* against the products of the struck employer is lawful. Picketing is illegal if it is directed against the neutral employer.

Internal Union Affairs, p. 507

Internal Union Rules

Title I of the Landrum-Griffin Act. A federal law that gives each union member equal rights and privileges to nominate candidates for union office, vote in union elections, and participate in membership meetings. Commonly called *labor's "bill of rights."*

Workers' Compensation Acts, p. 509

Workers' Compensation Acts

State statutes that create an administrative procedure for workers to receive payments for job-related injuries.

1. ***Workers' compensation insurance.*** Most states require employers to carry private or government-sponsored workers' compensation insurance. Some states permit employers to self-insure.

Employment-Related Injury

To be compensable under workers' compensation, the claimant must prove that the injury arose out of and in the course of his or her employment.

Exclusive Remedy

Workers' compensation is an exclusive remedy. Thus, workers cannot sue their employers to recover damages for job-related injuries.

1. ***Exceptions to the exclusive-remedy rule.*** Workers may recover damages from their employers for job-related injuries if the employer:
   a. Does not provide workers' compensation.
   b. Intentionally causes the worker's injuries.

2. ***Lawsuits against third parties.*** Workers' compensation acts do not bar injured workers from suing responsible third parties to recover damages (e.g., manufacturer of a defective machine that caused the worker's injuries).

Occupational Safety and Health Act, p. 511

Occupational Safety and Health Act

Federal statute that requires employers to provide safe working conditions.

1. ***Occupational Safety and Health Administration (OSHA).*** Federal administrative agency that administers and enforces the Occupational Safety and Health Act.

Specific and General Duty Standards

1. ***Specific duty standards.*** Safety standards for specific equipment (e.g., lathe) or industry (e.g., mining).
2. ***General duty standards.*** Impose a general duty on employers to provide safe working conditions.

Fair Labor Standards Act (FLSA), p. 513

Fair Labor Standards Act (FLSA)

A federal statute that protects workers.

Child Labor

The FLSA forbids the use of illegal child labor. The U.S. Department of Labor defines illegal child labor.

Minimum Wage and Overtime Pay Requirements

1. ***Minimum wage.*** The minimum wage is set by Congress and can be changed. The minimum wage, as of 2003, is $5.15 per hour.
2. ***Overtime pay.*** An employer cannot require employees to work more than 40 hours per week unless they are paid 1.5 times their regular pay for each hour worked in excess of 40 hours.

Employee Retirement Income Security Act (ERISA), p. 514

Employee Retirement Income Security Act (ERISA)

A federal statute that governs the establishment and administration of private pension programs to prevent fraud and other abuses.

Consolidated Omnibus Budget Reconciliation Act (COBRA), p. 515

Consolidated Omnibus Budget Reconciliation Act (COBRA)

A federal statute that requires an employer to offer an employee or the employee's beneficiaries the opportunity to continue health benefits (upon payment of the premium) after termination of employment due to the voluntary or involuntary termination of the worker's employment.

Immigration Reform and Control Act (IRCA), p. 516

Immigration Reform and Control Act (IRCA)

A federal statute that prohibits employers from employing illegal immigrants. Employers must require workers to prove that they are U.S. citizens or have proper work visas to work in this country.

Unemployment Compensation, p. 517

Unemployment Compensation

A state and federal program that pays compensation to unemployed persons who meet certain qualifying standards. Employers are required to pay unemployment compensation payments to the government to fund the program. Authorized by the *Federal Unemployment Tax Act (FUTA)* and state laws.

Social Security, p. 517

Social Security

A federal government program that provides limited retirement, disability, and medical care and hospitalization to covered employees and their dependents. Employers and employees pay taxes to fund the program.

Internet Exercises and Case Questions

Working the Web Internet Exercises

Activities

1. For an overview of labor law, see Labor and Employment Law at **jurist.law.pitt.edu/sg_lab.htm**.

2. Visit the Web site of one of the largest labor unions at **www.aflcio.org**.

3. Check the current unemployment rate at the Department of Labor: **www.dol.gov**. Is it higher or lower than it was one year ago?

Critical Legal Thinking Cases

17.1 Unfair Labor Practice In July 1965, the Teamsters Union began a campaign to organize the employees at a Sinclair Company plant. When the president of Sinclair learned of the Teamsters' drive, he talked with all of his employees and emphasized the results of a long 1952 strike that he claimed "almost put out company out of business" and expressed worry that the employees were forgetting the "lessons of the past." He emphasized that the company was on "thin ice" financially, that the Teamsters' "only weapon is to strike," and that a strike "could lead to the closing of the plant" because the company had manufacturing facilities elsewhere. He also noted that because of the employees' ages and the limited usefulness of their skills, they might not be able to find reemployment if they lost their jobs. Finally, he sent literature to the employees, stating that "the Teamsters Union is a strike happy outfit" and that they were under "hoodlum control," and he included a cartoon showing the preparation of a grave for the Sinclair Company and other headstones containing the names of other plants allegedly victimized by unions. The Teamsters lost the election 7 to 6 and then filed an unfair labor practice charge with the NLRB. Did the company violate labor law? [*N.L.R.B. v. Gissel Packing Co.*, 395 U.S. 575, 89 S.Ct. 1918, 1969 U.S. Lexis 3172 (1969)]

17.2 Right-to-Work Law Mobil Oil Corporation had its headquarters office in Beaumont, Texas. It operated a fleet of eight oceangoing tankers that transport its petroleum products from Texas to ports on the East Coast. A typical trip on a tanker from Beaumont to New York took about five days. No more than 10 percent to 20 percent of the seamen's work time was spent in Texas. The 300 or so seamen who were employed to work on the tankers belonged to the Oil, Chemical & Atomic Workers International Union, AFL-CIO, which had an agency shop agreement with Mobil. The state of Texas enacted a right-to-work law. Mobil sued the union, claiming that the agency shop agreement was unenforceable because it violated the Texas right-to-work law. Who wins? [*Oil, Chemical & Atomic Workers International Union, AFL-CIO v. Mobil Oil Corp.*, 426 U.S. 407, 96 S.Ct. 2140, 1976 U.S. Lexis 106 (1976)]

17.3 Work Preservation The Frouge Corporation was the general contractor on a housing project in Philadelphia. The carpenter-employees of Frouge were represented by the Carpenters' International Union. Traditional jobs of carpenters included mortising blank wooden doors for doorknobs, routing them for hinges, and beveling them to fit between the door jambs. The union had entered into a collective bargaining agreement with Frouge that provided that no member of the union would handle any doors that had been fitted prior to being furnished to the job site. The housing project called for 3,600 doors. Frouge contracted for the purchase of premachined doors that were already mortised, routed, and beveled.

When the union ordered its members not to hang the prefabricated doors, the National Woodwork Manufacturers Association filed an unfair labor practice charge against the union with the NLRB. Was the union's refusal to hang prefabricated doors lawful? [*National Woodwork Manufacturers Association v. N.L.R.B.*, U.S. 612, 87 S.Ct. 1250, 1967 U.S. Lexis 2858 (1967)]

17.4 Featherbedding Most local musicians belong to the American Federation of Musicians (Union), which represents more than 200,000 members in the United Sates. Union was divided into separate local unions that represent the members from a certain geographical area. Gamble Enterprises, Inc., owns and operates the Palace Theater in Akron, Ohio, which stages the performances of local and traveling musicians. The union adopted the following rule: "Traveling members cannot, without the consent of a Local, play any presentation performance unless a local house orchestra is also employed." This meant that the theater owner might have to pay two bands or orchestras. Gamble's refusal to abide by this rule caused the union to block the appearances of traveling bands and orchestras. Gamble filed an unfair labor practice charge with the NLRB. Is the union rule lawful? [*N.L.R.B. v. Gamble Enterprises, Inc.*, 345 U.S. 117, 73 S.Ct. 560, 1953 U.S. Lexis 2620 (1953)]

17.5 Illegal Strike In September 1966, the employees of the Shop Rite Foods, Inc.'s, warehouse in Lubbock, Texas, elected the United Packinghouse, Food and Allied Workers (Union) as its bargaining agent. Negotiations for a collective bargaining agreement began in late November 1966. In February and March 1967, when an agreement had not yet been reached, the company found excess amounts of damage to merchandise in its warehouse and concluded that it was being intentionally caused by dissident employees as a pressure tactic to secure concessions from the company. The company notified the union representative that employees caught doing such acts would be terminated; the Union representative in turn notified the employees. On March 31, 1967, a Shop Rite manager observed an employee in the flour section—where he had no business to be—making quick motions with his hands. The manager found that several bags of flour had been cut. The employee was immediately fired. Another employee and fellow union member led about 30 other employees in an immediate walkout. The company discharged these employees and refused to rehire them. The employees filed a grievance with the NLRB. Can they get their jobs back? [*N.L.R.B. v. Shop Rite Foods, Inc.*, 430 F.2d 786, 1970 U.S. App. Lexis 7613 (5th Cir. 1970)]

17.6 Employer Lockout The American Shipbuilding Company operates a shipyard in Chicago, Illinois, where it repairs Great Lakes ships during the winter months, when freezing on the Great Lakes renders shipping impossible. The workers at the shipyard are represented by several unions. On May 1, 1961, the unions notified the company of their intention to seek modification of the current collective bargaining agreement when it expired on August 1, 1961. On five previous occasions, agreements had been preceded by strikes (including illegal strikes) that were called just after the ships had arrived in the shipyard for repairs so that the unions increased their leverage in negotiations with the company.

Based on this prior history, the company displayed anxiety about the unions' strike plans and possible work stoppage. On August 1, 1961, after extended negotiations, the company and the unions reached an impasse in their collective bargaining. In response, the company decided to lay off most of the workers at the shipyard. It sent them the following notice: "Because of the labor dispute which has been unresolved since August 1, 1961, you are laid off until further notice." The unions filed unfair labor practice charges with the NLRB. Were the company's actions legal? [*American Ship Building Company v. N.L.R.B.*, 380 U.S. 300, 85 S.Ct. 955, 1965 U.S. Lexis 2310 (1965)]

17.7 Secondary Boycott Safeco Title Insurance Company is a major insurance company that underwrites title insurance for real estate in the state of Washington. Five local title companies act as insurance brokers who exclusively sell Safeco insurance. In 1972, Local 1001 of the Retail Store Employees Union, AFL-CIO, was elected as the bargaining agent for certain Safeco employees. When negotiations between Safeco and the union reached an impasse, the employees went on strike. The union did not confine its picketing to Safeco's office in Seattle but also picketed each of the five local title companies. The picketers carried signs declaring that Safeco had no contract with the union and distributed handbills asking consumers to support the strike by canceling their Safeco insurance policies. The local title companies filed a complaint with the NLRB. Was the picketing of the neutral title insurance companies lawful? [*N.L.R.B. v. Retail Store Employees Union, Local 1001, Retail Clerks International Association, AFL-CIO*, 447 U.S. 607, 100 S.Ct. 2372, 1980 U.S. Lexis 133 (1980)]

17.8 Workers' Compensation John B. Wilson was employed by the City of Modesto, California, as a police officer. He was a member of the special emergency reaction team (SERT), a tactical unit of the city's police department that is trained and equipped to handle highly dangerous criminal situations. Membership in SERT is voluntary for police officers. No additional pay or benefits are involved. To be a member of SERT, each officer is required to pass physical tests four times a year. One such test requires members to run two miles in 17 minutes. Other tests call for a minimum number of pushups, pullups, and situps. Officers who do not belong to SERT are not required to undergo these physical tests. On June 27, 1984, Wilson completed his patrol shift, changed clothes, and drove to the Modesto Junior College track. While running there, he injured his left ankle. Wilson filed a claim for workers' compensation benefits, which was contested by his employer. Who wins? [*Wilson v. Workers' Compensation Appeals Board*, 196 Cal.App.3d 902, 239 Cal.Rptr. 719, 1987 Cal.App. Lexis 2382 (Cal. App. 1987)]

17.9 Workers' Compensation Joseph Albanese was employed as a working foreman by Atlantic Steel Company, Inc., for approximately 20 years prior to 1970. His duties included the supervision of plant employees. In 1967, the business was sold to a new owner. In 1969, after the employees voted to unionize, friction developed between Albanese and the workers. Part of the problem was caused by management's decision to eliminate overtime work, which required Albanese to go out into the shop and prod the workers to expedite the work. Additional problems resulted from the activities of Albanese's direct supervisor, the plant manager. On one occasion in 1968, the manager informed Albanese that the company practice of distributing Thanksgiving turkeys was to be discontinued. In 1969, the manager told Albanese that the company did not intend to give the workers a Christmas bonus. The plant manager also informed Albanese that he did not intend to pay overtime wages to a worker. On each occasion, after Albanese relayed the information to the workers, the plant manager reversed his own decision. After the last incident, Albanese became distressed and developed chest pains and nausea. When the chest pains became sharper, he went home to bed. Albanese has not worked since. He has experienced continuing pain, sweatiness, shortness of breath, headaches, and depression. Albanese filed a claim for workers' compensation based on stress. The employer contested the claim. Who wins? [*Albanese's Case*, 389 N.E.2d 83, 1979 Mass. Lexis 795 (MA 1979)]

17.10 Occupational Safety Getty Oil Company operates a separation facility where it gathers gas and oil from wells and transmits them to an outgoing pipeline under high pressure. Getty engineers designed and produced a pressure vessel, called a fluid booster, that was to be installed to increase pressure in the system. Robinson, a Getty engineer, was instructed to install the vessel. Robinson picked up the vessel from the welding shop without having it tested. After he completed the installation, the pressure valve was put into operation. When the pressure increased from 300 to 930 pounds per square inch, an explosion occurred. Robinson died from the explosion, and another Getty employee was seriously injured. The secretary of labor issued a citation against Getty for violating the general duty provision for worker safety contained in the Occupational Safety and Health Act. Getty challenged the citation. Who wins? [*Getty Oil Company v. Occupational Safety and Health Review Commission*, 530 F.2d 1143, 1976 U.S. App. Lexis 11640 (5th Cir. 1976)]

17.11 ERISA United Artists is a Maryland corporation doing business in the state of Texas. United Pension Fund (Plan) is a defined-contribution, employee pension-benefit plan sponsored by United Artists for its employees. Each employee has his or her own individual pension account, but Plan assets are pooled for investment purposes. The Plan is administered by a board of trustees. During the period 1977 through 1986, seven of the trustees caused the Plan to make a series of loans to themselves. The trustees did not (1) require the borrowers to submit written applications for the subject loans, (2) assess the prospective borrowers' ability to repay the loans, (3) specify a period in which the loans were to be repaid, or (4) call the loans when they remained unpaid. The trustees also charged less than fair-market-value interest rates for the loans. The secretary of labor sued the trustees, alleging that they breached their fiduciary duty in violation of ERISA. Who wins? [*McLaughlin v. Rowley*, 698 F.Supp. 1333, 1988 U.S. Dist. 12674 (N.D.Tex. 1988)]

17.12 Drug Testing Air traffic controllers are federal government employees who are responsible for directing commercial and private air traffic in this country. They are subject to regulation by the secretary of transportation. The secretary adopted a regulation that provides for postaccident urinalysis drug testing of air traffic controllers responsible for the airspace in which an airplane accident has occurred. The National Air Traffic Controllers Association, MEBA/NNU, AFL-CIO sued, alleging that such drug testing was an unreasonable search and seizure in violation of the Fourth Amendment to the U.S. Constitution. Who wins? [*National Air Traffic Controllers Assn., MEBA/NNU, AFL-CIO v. Burnley*, 700 F.Supp. 1043, 1988 U.S. Dist. Lexis 15884 (N.D.Cal. 1988)]

17.13 Unemployment Benefits Devon Overstreet worked as a bus driver for the Chicago Transit Authority (CTA) for more than six years. She took a sick leave from January 30 to March 15, 1985. Because she had been on sick leave for more than seven days, the CTA required her to take a medical examination. The blood and urine analysis indicated the presence of cocaine. A second test confirmed this finding. On March 20, 1985, the CTA suspended her and placed her in the Employee's Assistance Program for substance abuse for not less than 30 days, with a chance of reassignment to a nonoperating job if she successfully completed the program. The program is an alternative to discharge and is available at the election of the employee. Overstreet filed for unemployment compensation benefits. The CTA contested her claim. Who wins? [*Overstreet v. Illinois Department of Employment Security*, 522 N.E.2d 185, 1988 Ill.App. Lexis 269 (Ill. App. 1988)]

17.14 Plant Closing Act Arrow Automotive Industries, Inc. (Arrow), is engaged in the remanufacture and distribution of automobile and truck parts. All of its operating plants produce identical product lines. Arrow is planning to open a new facility in Santa Maria, California. The employees at the Arrow plant in Hudson, Massachusetts, are represented by the United Automobile, Aerospace, and Agricultural Implement Workers of America (Union). The Hudson plant has a history of unprofitable operations. The union called a strike when the existing collective bargaining agreement expired and a new agreement could not be reached. After several months, the board of directors of the company voted to close the striking plant. The closing gave Arrow a 24 percent increase in gross profits and freed capital and equipment for the new Santa Maria plant. In addition, the existing customers of the Hudson plant could be serviced by the Spartanburg plant, which was currently being underutilized. What would have to be done if the Plant Closing Act applied to this situation? [*Arrow Automotive Industries, Inc., v. N.L.R.B.*, 853 F.2d 223, 1988 U.S. App. Lexis 10091 (4th Cir. 1988)]

Business Ethics Cases

17.15 Business Ethics Whirlpool Corporation operates a manufacturing plant in Marion, Ohio, for the production of household appliances. Overhead conveyors transport appliance components throughout the plant. To protect employees from objects that occasionally fall from the conveyors, Whirlpool installed a horizontal wire-mesh guard screen approximately 20 feet above the plant floor. The mesh screen is welded to angle-iron frames suspended from the building's structural steel skeleton.

Maintenance employees spend several hours each week removing objects from the screen, replacing paper spread on the screen to catch grease drippings from the materials on the conveyors, and performing occasional maintenance work on the conveyors. To perform these duties, maintenance employees usually are able to stand on the iron frames, but sometimes they find it necessary to step onto the steel-mesh screen itself. Several employees have fallen partly through the screen. On June 28, 1974, a maintenance employee fell to his death through the guard screen.

On July 7, 1974, two maintenance employees, Virgil Deemer and Thomas Cornwell, met with the plant supervisor to voice their concern about the safety of the screen. Unsatisfied with the supervisor's response, on July 9 they met with the plant safety director and voiced similar concerns. When they asked him for the name, address, and telephone number of the local OSHA office, he told them they "had better stop and think about" what they were doing. The safety director then furnished them with the requested information, and later that day one of the men contacted the regional OSHA office and discussed the guard screen.

The next day, Deemer and Cornwell reported for the night shift at 10:45 P.M. Their foreman directed the two men to perform their usual maintenance duties on a section of the screen. Claiming that the screen was unsafe, they refused to carry out the directive. The foreman sent them to the personnel office, where they were ordered to punch out without working or being paid for the remaining six hours of the shift. The two men subsequently received written reprimands, which were placed in their employment files.

The secretary of labor filed suit, alleging that Whirlpool's actions constituted discrimination against the two men in violation of the Occupational Safety and Health Act. Did Whirlpool act ethically in this case? Can employees engage in self-help under certain circumstances under OSHA regulations? [*Whirlpool Corporation v. Marshall, Secretary of Labor*, 445 U.S. 1, 100 S.Ct. 883, 1980 U.S. Lexis 81 (1980)]

17.16 Business Ethics On April 23, 1971, the International Association of Machinists and Aerospace Workers, AFL-CIO (Union), began soliciting the employees of Whitcraft Houseboat Division to organize a union. On April 26, 27, and 28, Whitcraft management dispersed congregating groups of employees. During these three days, production was down almost 50 percent. On April 28, Whitcraft adopted the following no-solicitation rule and mailed a copy to each employee and posted it around the workplace:

> *As you well know working time is for work. No one will be allowed to solicit or distribute literature during our working time, that is, when he or she should be working. Anyone doing so and neglecting his work or interfering with the work of another employee will be subject to discharge.*

On April 30, a manager of Whitcraft found that two employees of the company were engaged in union solicitation during working hours in a working area. The company discharged them for violating the no-solicitation rule. Was their discharge lawful? Did the company act ethically in discharging the employees? [*Whitcraft Houseboat Division, North American Rockwell Corporation v. International Association of Machinists and Aerospace Workers, AFL-CIO*, 195 N.L.R.B. 1046 (1972)]

Briefing the Case Writing Assignment

Read Case A.17 in the Case Appendix [*Wiljef Transportation, Inc. v. National Labor Relations Board*]. This case is excerpted from the court of appeals opinion. Review and brief the case. In your brief, be sure to answer the following questions.

1. Who was the plaintiff? Who was the defendant?
2. What did the defendant do that caused the plaintiff to file this action?
3. What is an unfair labor practice?
4. Did the court find an unfair labor practice in this case?

Answers to Management Decision Questions

1. You may be eligible to receive workers' compensation benefits. Workers' compensation laws have been enacted in all states. According to the Workers' Compensation Division of the Tennessee Department of Labor and Workforce Development, any employer who has five full-time or part-time employees is required to have workers' compensation insurance. State employment compensation acts provide medical and disability benefits to employees who are injured as the result of an accident that occurs in the course of employment. As an adjunct faculty member, you would be covered under Tennessee law. Because you were in the building to teach a class, you should have little difficulty proving that the injury arose out of and in the course of your employment. Generally, workers' compensation is an exclusive remedy for an injured employee. It precludes the injured employee from suing the employer for other damages or remedies. An exception occurs when an employer intentionally injures an employee.
2. Workers' compensation acts create an administrative procedure for workers to receive compensation for injuries that occur on the job. First, the injured worker files a claim with the appropriate state government agency. Next, that entity determines the legitimacy of the claim. If the worker agrees with the agency's findings, he or she may appeal the decision through the state court system. Workers' compensation benefits are paid according to preset limits established by statute or regulation. The amounts that are recoverable vary from state to state.

Endnotes

1. Section 7 of the NLRA provides that employees shall have the right to self-organization; to form, join, or assist labor organizations; to bargain collectively through representatives of their own choosing; and to engage in other concerted activities for the purpose of collective bargaining or other mutual aid protection.
2. 29 U.S.C. § 651–678.
3. For example, the Railway Safety Act and the Coal Mine Safety Act regulate workplace safety of railway workers and coal miners, respectively.
4. 29 U.S.C. § 654(a)(1).
5. 29 U.S.C. §§ 201 et seq.
6. 29 U.S.C. §§ 1001 et seq.
7. Internal Revenue Code § 4980B(f), 26 U.S.C. § 1161(a).
8. 29 U.S.C. § 1802.
9. 26 U.S.C. §§ 3301–3311.
10. Some federal, state, and local government employees who are covered by comparable legislation are not subject to the Social Security Act.
11. 26 U.S.C. §§ 3101–3126.
12. 26 U.S.C. §§ 1401–1403.

18

Equal Opportunity in Employment

"What people have always sought is equality of rights before the law. For rights that were not open to all equally would not be rights."

—Cicero (106–43 B.C.)
De officiis, Bk. II, Ch. XII

Chapter Objectives

After studying this chapter, you should be able to:

1. Describe the scope of coverage of Title VII of the Civil Rights Act of 1964.
2. Identify race, color, and national origin discrimination that violates Title VII.
3. Identify sex discrimination—including sexual harassment—that violates Title VII.
4. Describe the scope of coverage of the Age Discrimination in Employment Act.
5. Describe the protections afforded by the Americans with Disabilities Act of 1990.

Chapter Contents

- Equal Employment Opportunity Commission (EEOC)
- Title VII of the Civil Rights Act of 1964
- Defenses to a Title VII Action
- Equal Pay Act of 1963
- Americans with Disabilities Act of 1990
- Affirmative Action
- State and Local Government Antidiscrimination Laws

Management Decision Equal Opportunity in Employment

You manage Tiny Tots, a family-owned daycare center that provides round-the-clock childcare services for children ages 3 through kindergarten age. The center is opened Monday through Friday and has 30 employees. Currently, there are no male employees, and the owners have indicated that they would like to keep it that way. The owners decided to expand the business and operate seven days a week. You advertised in the local newspaper for applicants for several positions, including teachers, teacher assistants, and cooks. Several qualified males have applied for these positions.

1. Does the hiring policy of Tiny Tots violate employment laws?
2. What are the legal rights of males who are not hired as a result of this policy?

Under common law, employers could terminate an employee at any time and for whatever reason. In this same vein, employers were free to hire and promote anyone they chose without violating the law. This often created unreasonable hardship on employees and erected employment barriers to certain minority classes.

Starting in the 1960s, Congress began enacting a comprehensive set of federal laws that eliminated major forms of employment discrimination. These laws, which were passed to guarantee **equal employment opportunity** to all employees and job applicants, have been broadly interpreted by the federal courts, particularly the U.S. Supreme Court. States have also enacted antidiscrimination laws.

equal opportunity in employment
The right of all employees and job applicants (1) to be treated without discrimination and (2) to be able to sue employers if they are discriminated against.

This chapter discusses federal and state equal opportunity in employment laws.

Equal Employment Opportunity Commission (EEOC)

Equal Employment Opportunity Commission (EEOC)
The federal administrative agency that is responsible for enforcing most federal antidiscrimination laws.

The **Equal Employment Opportunity Commission (EEOC)** is the federal agency responsible for enforcing most federal antidiscrimination laws. The members of the EEOC are appointed by the U.S. president. The EEOC is empowered to conduct investigations, interpret the statutes, encourage conciliation between employees and employers, and bring suit to enforce the law. The EEOC can also seek injunctive relief.

Handicap Parking Space. Title I of the Americans with Disabilities Act (ADA) requires employers to make reasonable accommodations for individuals with disabilities that do not cause undue hardship to the employer.

Landmark Law

Title VII of the Civil Rights Act of 1964

After substantial debate, Congress enacted the **Civil Rights Act of 1964**. **Title VII** of the Civil Rights Act of 1964 (titled the **Fair Employment Practices Act**) was intended to eliminate job discrimination based on the following *protected classes: (1) race, (2) color, (3) religion, (4) sex, and (5) national origin*. As amended by the **Equal Employment Opportunity Act of 1972**, Section 703(a)(2) of Title VII provides in pertinent part that

> It shall be an unlawful employment practice for an employer
>
> (1) to fail or refuse to hire or to discharge any individual, or otherwise to discriminate against any individual with respect to his compensation, terms, conditions, or privileges of employment, because of such individual's race, color, religion, sex, or national origin; or
>
> (2) to limit, segregate, or classify his employees or applicants for employment in any way which would deprive or tend to deprive any individual of employment opportunities or otherwise adversely affect his status as an employee, because of such individual's race, color, religion, sex, or national origin. ■

Title VII of the Civil Rights Act of 1964

Scope of Coverage of Title VII

Title VII of the Civil Rights Act of 1964, also called the **Fair Employment Practices Act**, applies to (1) employers with 15 or more employees, (2) all employment agencies, (3) labor unions with 15 or more members, (4) state and local governments and their agencies, and (5) most federal government employment. Indian tribes and tax-exempt private clubs are expressly excluded from coverage.[1]

Title VII of the Civil Rights Act of 1964 (Fair Employment Practices Act)
An act that is intended to eliminate job discrimination based on five protected classes: *race, color, religion, sex,* and *national origin*.

Title VII prohibits discrimination in hiring, decisions regarding promotion or demotion, payment of compensation and fringe benefits, availability of job training and apprenticeship opportunities, referral systems for employment, decisions regarding dismissal, work rules, and any other "*term, condition, or privilege*" of employment. Any employee of covered employers, including undocumented aliens,[2] may bring actions for employment discrimination under Title VII.

Forms of Title VII Actions

Business Brief
Title VII applies to any term, condition, or privilege of employment, including but not limited to hiring, firing, promotion, and payment of fringe benefits decisions.

Title VII prohibits the following forms of employment discrimination based on any of the five prohibited factors listed previously:

1. ***Disparate Treatment Discrimination*** **Disparate treatment discrimination** occurs when an employer treats a specific *individual* less favorably than others because of that person's race, color, national origin, sex, or religion. In such situations, the complainant must prove that (1) he or she belongs to a Title VII protected class, (2) he or she applied for and was qualified for the employment position, (3) he or she was rejected despite this, and (4) the employer kept the position open and sought applicants from persons with the complainant's qualifications.[3]

disparate treatment discrimination
An employer's discrimination against a specific *individual* because of his or her race, color, national origin, sex, or religion.

2. ***Disparate Impact Discrimination*** **Disparate impact discrimination** occurs when an employer discriminates against an entire protected *class*. Many disparate impact cases are brought as class action lawsuits. Often, this type of discrimination is proven through statistical data about the employer's employment practices. The plaintiff must demonstrate a *casual link* between the challenged practice and the statistical imbalance. Showing a statistical disparity between the percentage of protected class

disparate impact discrimination
An employer's discrimination against an entire protected *class*. An example would be where a facially neutral employment practice or rule causes an adverse impact on a protected class.

employees versus the percentage of the population that the protected class makes within the surrounding community is not enough, by itself, to prove discrimination. Disparate impact discrimination occurs when an employer adopts a work rule that is neutral on its face but is shown to cause an adverse impact on a protected class.

God . . . hath made of one blood all nations of men for to dwell on the face of the earth.

Bible, Acts 17:26

Procedure for Bringing a Title VII Action To bring an action under Title VII, a private complainant must first file a complaint with the EEOC.[4] The EEOC is given the opportunity to sue the employer on the complainant's behalf. If the EEOC chooses not to bring suit, it will issue a *right to sue letter* to the complainant. This gives the complainant the right to sue the employer.

Ethics Brief

As originally proposed, sex discrimination was not included in Title VII. The amendment (Equal Employment Opportunity Act), designed to kill the entire legislation, backfired when the Civil Rights Act of 1964 passed.

Remedies for Violations of Title VII A successful plaintiff in a Title VII action can recover up to two years' back pay and reasonable attorneys' fees. In cases involving malice or reckless indifference to federally protected rights, the aggrieved party can recover compensatory and punitive damages. The statute caps the amounts that are recoverable on the basis of the size of the employer: (1) 15 to 100 employees, $50,000; (2) 101 to 200 employees, $100,000; (3) 201 to 500 employees, $200,00; (4) more than 500 employees, $300,000.

The courts also have broad authority to grant equitable remedies. For instance, the courts can order reinstatement, grant fictional seniority, and issue injunctions to compel the hiring or promotion of protected minorities.

Race, Color, and National Origin Discrimination

Rights matter most when they are claimed by unpopular minorities.

Michael Kirby, J.
Sydney Morning Herald
November 30, 1985

Title VII of the Civil Rights Act of 1964 was primarily enacted to prohibit employment discrimination based on *race, color, and national origin. Race* refers to broad categories such as black, Caucasian, Asian, and Native American. *Color* refers to the color of a person's skin. *National origin* refers to the country of a person's ancestors or cultural characteristics. The following two cases demonstrate race and national origin discrimination, respectively.

Case 18.1 Race Discrimination

National Association for the Advancement of Colored People, Newark Branch v. Town of Harrison, New Jersey

907 F.2d 1408, 1990 U.S. App. Lexis 11793 (1990)

United States Court of Appeals, Third Circuit

Background and Facts

The town of Harrison, New Jersey (Harrison), had followed a policy of hiring only town residents as town employees for as long as any townspeople could remember. In 1978, New Jersey adopted the Act Concerning Residency Requirements for Municipal and County Employees, which permitted towns, cities, and countries in the state to require that their employees be bona fide residents of the local government unit. Pursuant to this statute, Harrison adopted Ordinance 747, which stipulated that "all officers and employees of the Town shall, as a condition of employment, be bona fide residents of the Town."

Although Harrison is a small industrial community located in Hudson County, New Jersey, it is clearly aligned with Essex County to the west and is considered an extension of the city of Newark, which it abuts. Adjacent counties are within an easy commute of Harrison. Only 0.2 percent of Harrison's population is black. None of the 51 police officers, 55 firefighters, or 80 nonuniformed employees of the town are black. Several blacks who were members of the National Association for the Advancement of Colored People, Newark Branch (NAACP) applied for employment with Harrison but were rejected because they did not meet the residency requirement. The NAACP sued Harrison for employment discrimination.

Issue

Does the residency requirement of the town of Harrison violate Title VII of the Civil Rights Act of 1964?

In The Language of The Court

Debevoise, District Judge The geographical area from which Harrison draws employees includes its own county of Hudson as well as Bergen, Essex, and Union counties. These four counties have a total civilian labor force of 1,353,555 of which 214,747 are black. By reason of the geographical location and the flow of transportation facilities, Harrison could reasonably be viewed as functionally a component of the city of Newark and a part of Essex County. Newark's population is approximately 60% black. Essex

County's civilian labor force totals 391,612 of which 130,397 (or 33.3%) are black. It would be hard to conclude that among the very substantial number of black workers in the four-county labor market there are not large numbers of persons qualified to serve as police officers, firefighters, clerk typists, and laborers.

I find that the evidence also compels the conclusion that the residency requirements are the cause of at least a substantial part of the disparity. For all practical purposes, Harrison has no black residents. Thus, to limit employment or applications for employment to residents effectively excludes black persons from employment by the municipality. There is strong evidence that, if the residency requirement were removed, qualified black persons would seek positions with Harrison's municipal government. Thus, Harrison's facially neutral residency requirements have been shown to have a disproportionate impact upon black persons.

Decision and Remedy

The district court held that the plaintiffs had established that the ordinance constituted disparate impact race discrimination in violation of Title VII of the Civil Rights Act of 1964. The court issued an injunction against enforcement of the ordinance.

Case Questions

Critical legal Thinking Would the same residency requirement rule cause disparate impact discrimination if it were adopted by New York City or Los Angeles?

Business Ethics Did the town of Harrison act ethically when it adopted the residency requirements?

Contemporary Business Could a private business impose a residency requirement on its employees?

Case 18.2 National Origin Discrimination

Rivera v. Baccarat, Inc.
10 F.Supp.2d 318, 1998 U.S. Dist. Lexis 9099 (1998)
United States District Court, S. D. New York

Background and Facts

Irma Rivera is a Hispanic woman who was born in Puerto Rico. In September 1984, she began working for Baccarat, Inc. (Baccarat), a distributor of fine crystal, as a sales representative in its retail store in Manhattan. Rivera was the top sales representative at the Baccarat store from 1992 through 1994. J. D. Watts, the store's manager, stated that Rivera was "one of the best salespeople I have encountered in my 15 years in quality tabletop and gift retailing."

In October 1994, Jean Luc Negre became the new president of Baccarat, with ultimate authority for personnel decisions. Sometime later, Negre angrily told Rivera that he did not like her attitude and that he did not want her to speak Spanish on the job. On July 14, 1995, Dennis Russell, the chief financial officer of Baccarat, notified Rivera that Negre had made a decision to terminate her. Rivera pressed Russell to tell her why she was being fired. According to Rivera, he replied, "Irma, he doesn't want Hispanics." Ivette Brigantty, another Hispanic sales representative, was also terminated by Negre. The non-Hispanic salesperson was retained by the store. Rivera sued Baccarat for national origin discrimination in violation of Title VII of the Civil Rights Act. The jury found Baccarat liable. Baccarat appealed.

Issue

Did Baccarat engage in unlawful national origin discrimination?

In The Language of The Court

Francis, United States Magistrate Under Equal Employment Opportunity Commission regulations, national origin discrimination includes the denial of employment opportunity because an individual has the linguistic characteristics of a national origin group. Accent and national origin are obviously inextricably intertwined in many cases. Thus, unless any employee's accent materially interferes with her job performance, it cannot legally be the basis for an adverse employment action.

In this case, Ms. Rivera testified that during her one face-to-face meeting with Mr. Negre, he specifically stated that he did not like her accent. While Baccarat characterizes this as a single stray remark insufficient to support a finding of discriminatory intent, its probative value, if credited, is substantial. It is a statement by the president of the company who himself made the decision to terminate Ms. Rivera. Mr. Negre's criticism of Ms. Rivera's accent, his statement that he did not want Hispanic sales employees, and the fact that two Hispanic sales representatives were discharged while the non-Hispanic salesperson was retained all buttress the jury's finding of liability.

Decision and Remedy

The district court held that Baccarat had engaged in national origin discrimination in violation of Title VII. The court awarded Ms. Rivera $104,373 in damages, attorneys' fees of $102,437, and prejudgment interest.

Case Questions

Critical Legal Thinking Why did Congress include national origin discrimination under Title VII? How does it differ from race discrimination?

Business Ethics Did the president of Baccarat act ethically in this case?

Contemporary Business Do you think national origin discrimination is very prevalent in business?

Sex Discrimination

sex discrimination
Discrimination against a person solely because of his or her sex.

Pregnancy Discrimination Act
An amendment to Title VII that forbids employment discrimination because of "pregnancy, childbirth, or related medical conditions."

Although the prohibition against **sex discrimination** applies equally to men and women, the overwhelming majority of Title VII sex discrimination cases are brought by women. The old airline practice of ignoring the marital status of male flight attendants but hiring only single female flight attendants is an example of such discrimination.

In 1978, the **Pregnancy Discrimination Act** was enacted as an amendment to Title VII.[5] This amendment forbids employment discrimination because of "pregnancy, childbirth, or related medical conditions." Thus, a work rule that prohibits the hiring of pregnant women violated Title VII.

In the following case, the court found sex discrimination in violation of Title VII.

Case 18.3
Sex Discrimination

Barbano v. Madison County
922 F.2d 139, 1990 U.S. App. Lexis 22494 (1990)
United States Court of Appeals, Second Circuit

Background and Facts

In February 1980, the position of director of the Madison County Veterans Service Agency became vacant. The Madison County Board of Supervisors (Board) appointed a committee of five men to hold interviews. Maureen E. Barbano applied for the position and was interviewed by the committee. Upon entering the interview, Barbano heard someone say, "Oh, another woman." When the interview began, Donald Greene, a committee member, said he would not consider "some woman" for the position. He then asked Barbano personal questions about her plans on having a family and whether her husband would object to her transporting male veterans. When Barbano said the questions were irrelevant and discriminatory, Greene replied that the questions were relevant because he did not want to hire a woman who would get pregnant and quit. Another committee member said the questions were relevant. No committee member said they were not relevant or asked Barbano any substantive questions.

The committee interviewed several other candidates and found them all (including Barbano) to be qualified for the position. Ultimately, the Board acted on the committee's recommendation and hired a male candidate. Barbano sued Madison County for sex discrimination in violation of Title VII. The district court held in favor of Barbano and awarded her $55,000 in back pay, prejudgment interest, and attorneys' fees. Madison County appealed.

Issue

Did the defendant engage in sex discrimination in violation of Title VII?

In The Language of The Court

Feinberg, Circuit Judge There is little doubt that Greene's statements during the interview were discriminatory. He said he would not consider "some woman" for the position. His questioning Barbano about whether she would get pregnant and quit was also discriminatory, since it was unrelated to a bona fide occupational qualification. Similarly, Greene's questions about whether Barbano's husband would mind if she had to "run around the country with men," and that he would not want his wife to do it, were discriminatory.

Given the discriminatory tenor of the interview, and the acquiescence of the other Committee members to Greene's line of questioning, it follows that the trial court judge could find that those present at the interview, and not merely Greene, discriminated against Barbano. The record before us supports the district court's finding that the Board discriminated in making the hiring decision.

Decision and Remedy

The court of appeals held that the defendant, Madison County, had engaged in sex discrimination in violation of Title VII. The court affirmed the award of damages to plaintiff Barbano.

Case Questions

Critical Legal Thinking Why are questions concerning family obligations made illegal by Title VII?

Business Ethics Was Greene's conduct morally reprehensible?

Contemporary Business What actions should employers take to make sure their interviewers and other personnel understand Title VII and other antidiscrimination laws?

Sexual Harassment

In the modern work environment, coworkers sometimes become sexually interested or involved with each other voluntarily. On other occasions, though, a coworker's sexual advances are not welcome.

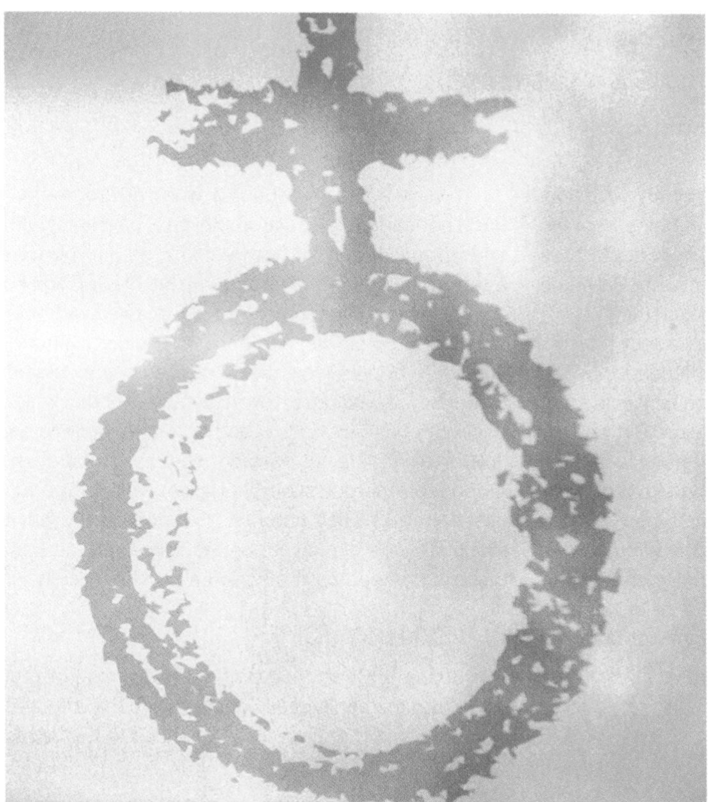

Sign in Window. Title VII prohibits sexual harassment that causes a hostile work environment.

Refusing to hire or promote someone unless he or she has sex with the manager or supervisor is sex discrimination that violates Title VII. Other forms of conduct, such as lewd remarks, touching, intimidation, posting of indecent materials and other verbal or physical conduct of a sexual nature, constitute **sexual harassment** and violate Title VII.[6]

sexual harassment
Lewd remarks, touching, intimidation, posting of indecent material, and other verbal or physical conduct of a sexual nature that occur on the job.

To determine what conduct creates a hostile work environment, the Supreme Court stated:

> We can say that whether an environment is "hostile" or "abusive" can be determined only by looking at all the circumstances. These may include the frequency of the discriminatory conduct; its severity; whether it is physically threatening or humiliating, or a mere offensive utterance; and whether it unreasonably interferes with an employee's work performance.[7]

In the following case, the Supreme Court decided that the challenged conduct created a hostile work environment.

Business Brief
To prevent future lawsuits, employers should be fully aware of federal and state equal employment opportunity (EEO) laws and implement policies and procedures to adhere to them.

Case 18.4
Sexual Harassment

U.S. SUPREME COURT CASE
Harris v. Forklift Systems, Inc.
510 U.S. 17, 114 S.Ct. 367, 1993 U.S. Lexis 7155 (1993)
Supreme Court of the United States

Background and Facts

Teresa Harris worked as a manager at Forklift Systems, Inc. (Forklift), an equipment rental company, from April 1985 until October 1987. Charles Hardy was Forklift's president. Throughout Harris's time at Forklift, Hardy often insulted her because of her sex and made her the target of unwanted sexual innuendos. Hardy told Harris on several occasions, in the presence of other employees, "You're a woman, what do you know" and "We need a man as the rental manager"; at least once, he told her she was "a dumb ass woman." Again in front of others, he suggested that the two of them

Harris v. Forklift Systems, Inc.

510 U.S. 17, 114 S.Ct. 367, 1993 U.S. Lexis 7155 (1993)
Supreme Court of the United States
(continued)

"go to the Holiday Inn to negotiate Harris's raise." Hardy occasionally asked Harris and other female employees to get coins from his front pants pocket. He threw objects on the ground in front of Harris and other women and asked them to pick the objects up. He made sexual innuendos about Harris's and other women's clothing.

In mid-August 1987, Harris complained to Hardy about his conduct. Hardy said he was surprised that Harris was offended, claimed he was only joking, and apologized. He also promised he would stop, and based on this assurance, Harris stayed on the job. But in early September, Hardy began anew: While Harris was arranging a deal with one of Forklift's customers, he asked her, again in front of other employees, "What did you do, promise the guy some sex Saturday night?" On October 1, Harris collected her paycheck and quit.

Harris then sued Forklift, claiming that Hardy's conduct had created an abusive work environment for her because of her gender. The district court held that because Harris had not suffered severe psychological injury, she could not recover. The court of appeals affirmed. Harris appealed to the U.S. Supreme Court.

Supreme Court Issue

Must conduct, to be actionable as abusive work environment harassment, seriously affect the victim's psychological well-being?

In The Language of The U.S. Supreme Court

O'Connor, Justice When the workplace is permeated with discriminatory intimidation, ridicule, and insult, that is sufficiently severe or pervasive to alter the conditions of the victim's employment and create an abusive working environment, Title VII is violated.

A discriminatorily abusive work environment, even one that does not seriously affect employees' psychological well-being, can and often will detract from employees' job performance, discourage employees from remaining on the job, or keep them from advancing in their careers. Moreover, even without regard to these tangible effects, the very fact that the discriminatory conduct was so severe or pervasive that it created a work environment abusive to employees because of their race, gender, religion, or national origin offends Title VII's broad rule of workplace equality.

Certainly Title VII bars conduct that would seriously affect a reasonable person's psychological well-being, but the statute is not limited to such conduct. So long as the environment would reasonably be perceived, and is perceived, as hostile or abusive, there is no need for it also to be psychologically injurious.

Decision and Remedy

The Supreme Court held that Title VII does not require a victim to prove that the challenged conduct seriously affected her psychological well-being. The case was remanded to the district court for trial.

Case Questions

Critical Legal Thinking Should an employer be held liable for sexual harassment committed by one of its employees?

Business Ethics What penalty should be assessed against Hardy for his conduct?

Contemporary Business How can businesses eliminate sexual harassment on the job?

Contemporary Business Environment

The Reasonable Woman Standard

In most cases, the courts use a "reasonable person" standard to determine whether certain conduct violates the norms of society. This traditional standard was used in sexual harassment cases until recently, when several courts held that it was inappropriate. A "reasonable woman" standard was adopted in its place. The following case illustrates how this new standard works.

Kerry Ellison worked as a revenue agent for the Internal Revenue Service. A male co-worker, whose desk was 20 feet from Ellison's, wrote her detailed love letters. When Ellison complained, the male employee was transferred to another location for six months, but then he was transferred back. He again wrote love letters to Ellison. The IRS did not take any further action to transfer the male employee elsewhere. Ellison filed a Title VII action against her employer, claiming sexual harassment. The district court granted the defendant's motion for summary judgment.

The court of appeals reversed and remanded the case. In doing so, the court articulated the **reasonable woman standard** for examining sexual harassment cases brought by females. The court stated:

> We believe that in evaluating the severity and pervasiveness of sexual harassment, we should focus on the perspective of the victim. If we only examined whether a reasonable person would engage in allegedly harassing conduct, we would run the risk of reinforcing the prevailing level of discrimination. We therefore prefer to analyze harassment from the victim's perspective. Conduct that many men consider unobjectionable may offend many women. We hold that a female plaintiff states a prima facie case of hostile environment sexual harassment when she alleges conduct which a reasonable woman would consider sufficiently severe or pervasive to alter the conditions of employment and create an abusive working environment. [*Ellison v. Brady, Secretary of Treasury*, 924 F.2d 872, 1991 U.S. App. Lexis 875 (9th Cir. 1991)] ■

E-Commerce & Information Technology

E-Mail's Role in Hostile Work Environment Lawsuits

The use of e-mail in business has dramatically increased efficiency and information sharing among employees. Managers and workers alike can communicate with each other, send documents, and keep each other apprised of business developments. In many organizations, e-mail has replaced the telephone as the most used method of communication and has eliminated the need for many meetings. This is a boon for business. But the downside is that e-mail has increased the exposure of businesses to sexual and racial harassment lawsuits. For example, the largest settlement regarding a sexual harassment case arose from e-mail. In 1995, Chevron Corporation paid $2.2 million to settle sexual harassment charges brought by female employees for offensive e-mail messages sent by male coworkers, including one about "25 Reasons Beer is Better Than Women." The employees had signed a complaint letter about the e-mail harassment, but the company had ignored the complaint.

E-mail often sets the social tone of an office and has been permitted to be slightly ribald. At some point, however, e-mail conduct becomes impermissible and crosses the line to actionable sexual or racial harassment. The standard of whether e-mail creates an illegal hostile work environment is the same as that for measuring harassment in any other context. The offensive conduct must be severe and cannot consist of isolated or trivial remarks and incidents. And, as in other harassment cases, an employer may raise the defense that requires two elements: (1) the employer exercised reasonable care to prevent and correct the behavior and (2) the plaintiff employee unreasonably failed to take advantage of any preventive or corrective opportunities provided by the employer or to avoid the harm.

E-mail differs from many other incidents of harassment because it is subtle and insidious. Unlike with paper pin-up calendars in plain view, an employer does not readily see e-mail messages. Obscenity pulled off the Internet or scanned into a computer can be sent as a clipping to an e-mail message. Because e-mail is hidden, to detect offensive messages, employers must take action to review e-mail messages on its network. Courts have generally held that an employee does not have an expectation of privacy of e-mail. Stored e-mail is the property of the employer, which may review it freely. Employers can also use software to scan and filter e-mail messages that contain any of a predefined list of objectionable words or phrases or certain "to" or "from" headers. Employers can also use software programs to scan graphics and block X-rated pictures.

E-mail has not only increased the possibility of there being sexual or racial harassment on the job, but it has also become the smoking gun that undermines a company's attempt to defend such cases. Therefore, employers must adopt policies pertaining to the use of e-mail by their employees and make their employees aware that certain e-mail messages constitute sexual or racial harassment and violate the law. Employers should make periodic inspections and audits of stored e-mail to ensure that employees are complying with the company's antiharassment policies. ■

Same-Sex Discrimination The U.S. Supreme Court has held that same-sex sexual harassment is actionable under Title VII.[8] State and local laws also prohibit this form of discrimination.

Business Brief
Title VII prohibits same-sex employment discrimination.

Contemporary Business Environment

Employers May Prove an Affirmative Defense in Some Sexual Harassment Cases

The law of sexual harassment has been evolving since the U.S. Supreme Court first recognized it as a violation of Title VII in *Meritor Savings Bank, FSB v. Vinson*, 477 U.S. 57, 106 S.Ct. 2399 (1986). During the 1997 term, the Supreme Court, in two parallel decisions, again established important rules for sexual harassment cases brought under Title VII.

In *Faragher v. City of Boca Raton* and *Burlington Industries, Inc. v. Ellerth*, female plaintiffs sued their employers, proving that their supervisors had engaged in unconsented physical touching and verbal sexual harassment. In both cases, the female employee quit her job and sued her employer for sexual harassment in violation of Title VII. In the first case, the employer had never disseminated a policy against sexual harassment to its employees. In the second case, the employer had disseminated its policy against sexual harassment to its employees and had put into place a complaint system that was not used by the female employee. After trials and appeals, the U.S. Supreme Court accepted these two cases for review to decide the following issue: Are employers strictly liable for the sexual harassment of their employees?

In *Faragher* and *Burlington Industries*, the Supreme Court issued opinions that reject automatic or strict liability. The Court

Contemporary Business Environment

(continued)

announced that an employer may raise an *affirmative defense* against liability or damages by proving the following two elements:

1. The employer exercised reasonable care to prevent and correct promptly any sexual-harassing behavior.
2. The plaintiff employee unreasonably failed to take advantage of any preventive or corrective opportunities provided by the employer or to otherwise avoid harm.

The defendant employer has the burden of proving this affirmative defense. Courts should consider the following factors in determining whether such defense has been proven: (1) did the employer have an antiharassing policy? (2) did the employer have a complaint mechanism in place? (3) were employees informed of the antiharassment policy and complaint procedure? and (4) other factors the court deems relevant. Since the U.S. Supreme Court has announced this rule, it is the job of lower federal courts to apply the affirmative defense to specific cases. [*Faragher v. City of Boca Raton*, 524 U.S. 775, 118 S.Ct. 2275, 1998 U.S. Lexis 4216 (1998); *Burlington Industries, Inc. v. Ellerth*, 524 U.S. 742, 118 S.Ct. 2257, 1998 U.S. Lexis 4217 (1998)] ■

Religious Discrimination

Title VII prohibits employment discrimination based on a person's religion. Religions include traditional religions, other religions that recognize a supreme being, and religions based on ethical or spiritual tenets. Many **religious discrimination** cases involve a conflict between an employer's work rule and an employee's religious beliefs (e.g., when an employee is required to work on his or her religious holiday).

religious discrimination
Discrimination against a person solely because of his or her religion or religious practices.

The right of an employee to practice his or her religion is not absolute. Under Title VII, an employer is under a duty to *reasonably accommodate* the religious observances, practices, or beliefs of its employees if it does not cause an *undue hardship* on the employer. The courts must apply these general standards to specific fact situations. In making their decisions, the courts must consider such factors as the size of the employer, the importance of the employee's position, and the availability of alternative workers.

Ethics Brief
Employers owe a duty to *reasonably accommodate* an employee's religious practices, observances, or beliefs if it does not cause *undue hardship* to the employer.

Title VII expressly permits religious organizations to give preference in employment to individuals of a particular religion. For example, if a person applies for a job with a religious organization but does not subscribe to its religious tenets, the organization may refuse to hire that person.

Business Brief
Employers can select and promote employees based on merit without violating Title VII.

Forbidden City, Beijing, China. Foreign nationals employed in foreign countries by U.S.-controlled companies are not covered by Title VII; U.S. citizens employed by U.S.-controlled companies in foreign countries are covered by Title VII, however.

Defenses to a Title VII Action

Title VII and case law recognize the following defenses to a charge of discrimination under Title VII.

Merit

Employers can select or promote employees based on *merit*. Merit decisions are often based on work, educational experience, and professionally developed ability tests. To be lawful under Title VII, the requirement must be job related. For example, requiring a person to pass a typing test to be hired as a typist would be lawful. Requiring a person to pass a college-level English composition test to be employed as a maintenance worker would violate Title VII.

Seniority

Many employers maintain *seniority* systems that reward long-term employees. Higher wages, fringe benefits, and other preferential treatment (e.g., choice of working hours and vacation schedule) are examples of such rewards. Seniority systems provide an incentive for employees to stay with the company. Such systems are lawful if they are not the result of intentional discrimination.

Ethics Brief

An employer may maintain a seniority system that rewards long-term employees. Such systems are lawful if they are not the result of intentional discrimination.

Web Site

U.S. Equal Employment Opportunity Commission The mission of the EEOC is to promote equal opportunity employment by enforcing the federal civil rights employment laws through administrative and judicial actions, education, and technical assistance. Visit at **www.eeoc.gov**.

Bona Fide Occupational Qualification (BFOQ)

Discrimination based on protected classes (other than race or color) is permitted if it is shown to be a **bona fide occupational qualification (BFOQ)**. To be legal, a BFOQ must be both *job related* and a *business necessity*. For example, allowing only women to be locker room attendants in a women's gym is a valid BFOQ, but prohibiting males from being managers or instructors at the same gym would not be a BFOQ. As the following case shows, BFOQ exceptions are narrowly interpreted by the courts.

bona fide occupational qualification (BFOQ)

Employment discrimination based on a protected class (other than race or color) that is lawful if it is *job related* and a *business necessity*. This exception is narrowly interpreted by the courts.

Case 18.5

Bona Fide Occupational Qualification

U.S. SUPREME COURT CASE

International Union, United Automobile, Aerospace and Agricultural Implement Workers of America, UAW v. Johnson Controls, Inc.

499 U.S. 187, 111 S.Ct. 1196, 1991 U.S. Lexis 1715 (1991)

Supreme Court of the United States

Background and Facts

Johnson Controls, Inc. (Johnson Controls), manufacturers batteries. Lead is the primary ingredient in the manufacturing process. Exposure to lead entails health risks, including risk of harm to any fetus carried by a female employee. To protect unborn children from such risk, Johnson Controls adopted an employment rule that prevented pregnant women and women of childbearing age from working at jobs involving lead exposure. Only women who were sterilized or could prove they could not have children were not affected by the rule. Consequently, most female employees were relegated to lower-paying clerical jobs at the company. Several female employees filed a class action suit challenging Johnson Controls's fetal-protection policy as sex discrimination in violation of Title VII. The district court held that the policy was justified as a BFOQ and granted summary judgment to Johnson Controls. The court of appeals affirmed. The plaintiffs appealed to the U.S. Supreme Court.

Supreme Court Issue

Is Johnson Controls's fetal-protection policy a BFOQ?

In The Language of The U.S. Supreme Court

Blackmun, Justice The bids in Johnson Controls' policy is obvious. Fertile men, but not fertile women, are given a choice as to whether they wish to risk their reproductive health for a particular job. Johnson Controls' fetal-protection policy explicitly discriminates against women on the basis of their sex. The policy excludes women with childbearing capacity from lead-exposed jobs and so creates a facial classification based on gender.

The bona fide occupational qualification's (BFOQ) defense is written narrowly, and this Court has read it narrowly. We have no difficulty concluding that Johnson Controls cannot establish a BFOQ. Fertile women, as far as appears in the record, participate in the manufacture of batteries as efficiently as anyone else.

International Union, United Automobile, Aerospace and Agricultural Implement Workers of America, UAW v. Johnson Controls, Inc.

499 U.S. 187, 111 S.Ct. 1196, 1991 U.S. Lexis 1715 (1991)

Supreme Court of the United States

(continued)

Johnson Controls' professed moral and ethical concerns about the welfare of the next generation do not suffice to establish a BFOQ of female sterility. Decisions about he welfare of future children must be left to the parents who conceive, bear, support, and raise them rather than to the employers who hire those parents.

Decision and Remedy

The U.S. Supreme Court held that Johnson Controls's fetal-protection policy was not a BFOQ. Instead, it was sex discrimination in violation of Title VII. Reversed and remanded.

Case Questions

Critical Legal Thinking Should any BFOQ exceptions to Title VII actions be permitted: Why or why not?

Business Ethics Should Johnson Controls's moral and ethical concerns about the welfare of the next generation justify its actions?

Contemporary Business Does Johnson Controls have any tort liability to children who are born injured by exposure to lead? How can Johnson Controls limit such liability?

Concept Summary Title VII of the Civil Rights Act of 1964

Covered Employers and Employment Decisions	1. **Employers** Employers with 15 or more employees for 20 weeks in the current or preceding year, all emploment agencies, labor unions with 15 or more members, state and local governments, and most federal agencies. 2. **Employment Decisions** Decisions regarding hiring; promotion; demotion; payment of salaries, wages, and fringe benefits; dismissal; job training and apprenticeships; work rules; or any other *term*, *condition*, or *privilege* of employment. Decision to admit a partner to a partnership is also covered.
Protected Classes	1. **Race** Broad class of individuals with common charactertistics (e.g., black, Caucasian, Asian, Native American). 2. **Color** Color of a person's skin (e.g., light-skinned person, dark-skinned person). 3. **National Origin** A person's country of origin or national heritage (e.g., Italian, Hispanic). 4. **Sex** A person's sex, whether male or female. Includes sexual harassment and discrimination against females who are pregnant. 5. **Religion** A person's religious beliefs. An employer has a duty to reasonably accommodate an employee's religious beliefs if it does not cause an undue hardship on the employer.
Types of Discrimination	1. **Disparate Treatment Discrimination** Discrimination against a specific individual because that person belongs to a protected class. 2. **Disparate Impact Discrimination** Discrimination that occurs where a neutral-looking employment rule causes discrimination against a protected class.
Defenses	1. **Merit** Job-related experience, education, or unbiased employment test. 2. **Seniority** Length of time an employee has been employed by the employer. Intentional discrimination based on seniority is unlawful. 3. **Bona Fide Occupational Qualification (BFOQ)** Discrimination based on sex or religion is permitted if it is a valid BFOQ for the position. Qualification based on race or color is not a permissible BFOQ.
Remedies	1. The court may order the payment of two years' back pay, issue an injunction awarding reinstatement, grant fictional seniority, or order some other equitable remedy. The court can also award compensatory and punitive damages in cases involving an employer's malice or reckless indifference to federally protected rights.

International Law

International Reach of U.S. Antidiscrimination Laws

Does Title VII extend beyond the territorial reach of the United States? The **Civil Rights Act of 1991** stipulates that it does. The 1991 act expressly protects *U.S. citizens*—but not foreign nationals—employed in a foreign country by U.S.-controlled employers. Foreign operations not controlled by U.S. employers are not covered.

An employer of a U.S. citizen abroad is subject to claims under Title VII in the following two situations:

1. An employer that is incorporated in the United States and operates a branch office in a foreign country is liable for Title VII violations against U.S. citizens that occur in its foreign operation.
2. If a U.S. parent corporation owns a foreign corporation that is incorporated in another country, the foreign-controlled subsidiary is subject to Title VII because the 1991 act expressly states that discriminatory practices of "controlled foreign corporations" are presumed to be acts engaged in by the parent corporation.

The 1991 act contains an express exception that protects employers from conflicting foreign laws. If required conduct under Title VII would cause the employer to violate the law of a foreign nation (e.g., foreign law does not permit the employment of female workers), compliance with Title VII is excused.

The 1991 act also extends its international reach to the Americans with Disabilities Act (ADA) and the Age Discrimination in Employment Act (ADEA). Both of these acts are discussed later in this chapter. ■

Equal Pay Act of 1963

Discrimination often takes the form of different pay scales for men and women performing the same job. The **Equal Pay Act of 1963** protects both sexes from pay discrimination based on sex.[9] This act covers all levels of private-sector employees and state and local government employees. Federal workers are not covered, however.

Equal Pay Act of 1963
An act that protects both sexes from pay discrimination based on sex; extends to jobs that require equal skill, equal effort, equal responsibility, and similar working conditions.

The act prohibits disparity in pay for jobs that require *equal skill* (i.e., equal experience), *equal effort* (i.e., mental and physical exertion), *equal responsibility* (i.e., equal supervision and accountability), or *similar working conditions* (e.g., dangers of injury, exposure to the elements). To make this determination, the courts examine the actual requirements of jobs to determine whether they are equal and similar. If two jobs are determined to be equal and similar, an employer cannot pay disparate wages to members of different sexes.

Employees can bring a private cause of action against an employer for violating the act. Back pay and liquidated damages are recoverable. In addition, the employer must increase the wages of the discriminated-against employee to eliminate the unlawful disparity of wages. The wages of other employees may not be lowered.

By what justice can an association of citizens be held together when there is no equality among the citizens?

Cicero
De Re Publica De Legibus J XXXII 49

Criteria That Justify a Differential in Wages

The Equal Pay Act expressly provides four criteria that justify a differential in wages. These defenses include payment systems that are based on

- **Seniority**
- **Merit** (as long as there is some identifiable measurement standard)
- **Quantity or quality of product** (commission, piecework, or quality-control–based payment systems are permitted)
- "**Any factor other than sex**" (including shift differentials, i.e., night versus day shifts)

Business Brief
The Equal Pay Act expressly provides four criteria that justify a differential in wages. The employer bears the burden of proving these defenses.

The employer bears the burden of proving these defenses. An employer asserted the "any factor other than sex" defense in the following case.

Case 18.6 Equal Pay Act

Glenn v. General Motors Corporation
841 F.2d 1567, 1988 U.S. App. Lexis 5005 (1988)
United States Court of Appeals, Eleventh Circuit

Background and Facts

Sheila Ann Glenn, Patricia Johns, and Robbie Nugent, three female employees of General Motors Corporation (GM), sued their employer for violation of the Equal Pay Act. The three females worked in the tools stores department of GM as "Follow Ups." A Follow Up basically ensures that adequate tools are on hand in GM plants to keep the plants running. From 1975 through 1985, the three women were paid less than all their male comparators in the same position, and the most highly paid of the three earned less than the lowest-paid man. When hired, all three women received lower starting salaries than men hired at the same time. The trial court held in favor of the three women and awarded damages against GM. GM appealed.

Issue

Did GM violate the Equal Pay Act?

In The Language of The U.S. Supreme Court

Johnson, Circuit Judge Once the appellees established a prima facie case, the burden shifted to GM to prove that the difference in pay was justified by one of the four exceptions in the Equal Pay Act: (1) a seniority system, (2) a merit system, (3) a system that measures earnings by quantity or quality of production, (4) a differential based on any factor other than sex.

GM seeks to justify the pay disparity on the fourth ground—a factor other than sex.

GM seeks to defend the pay disparity as a result of the market force theory. This court and the Supreme Court have long rejected the market force theory as a "factor other than sex." The argument that supply and demand dictates that women may be paid less is exactly the kind of evil that the Equal Pay Act was designed to eliminate and has been rejected. The market force theory that a woman will work for less than a man is not a valid consideration under the Equal Pay Act.

Decision and Remedy

The court of appeals held that GM had violated the Equal Pay Act and affirmed the award of damages to the plaintiffs.

Case Questions

Critical Legal Thinking Do you think the Equal Pay Act was necessary to eliminate pay disparities between men and women?

Business Ethics Was it ethical for GM to pay women less than men for the same job?

Contemporary Business What does the market force theory provide? Does it make economic sense?

Landmark Law
Age Discrimination in Employment Act of 1967

In the past, some employers discriminated against employees and prospective employees based on their age. For example, employers often refused to hire older workers. The **Age Discrimination in Employment Act (ADEA)**, which prohibits certain *age discrimination* practices, was enacted in 1967 [29 U.S.C. §§ 621–634].

The ADEA covers nonfederal employers with at least 20 employees, labor unions with at least 25 members, and all employment agencies. State and local government employees except those in policy-making positions are covered, as well as employees of certain sectors of the federal government.

The ADEA prohibits age discrimination in all employment decisions, including hiring, promotions, payment of compensation, and other terms and conditions of employment. The **Older Workers Benefit Protection Act (OWBPA)** amended the ADEA to prohibit age discrimination with regard to employee benefits. Employers cannot use employment advertisements that discriminate against applicants covered by ADEA. The same defenses that are available in a Title VII action are also available in an ADEA action.

Protected Age Categories

Originally, the ADEA prohibited employment discrimination against persons between the ages of 40 and 65. In 1978, its coverage was extended to persons up to the age of 70. Further amendments completely eliminated an age ceiling, so ADEA now applies to employees who are 40 and older. As a result, covered employers cannot establish mandatory retirement ages for their employees.

Because persons under 40 are not protected by the ADEA, an employer can maintain an employment policy of hiring only workers who are 40 years of age or older without violating the ADEA. However, the employer could not maintain an employment practice whereby it hired only persons 50 years of age and older because it would discriminate against persons aged 40 to 49.

The ADEA is administered by the EEOC. Private plaintiffs can also sue under the ADEA. A successful plaintiff in an ADEA action can recover back wages, attorneys' fees, and equitable relief, including hiring, reinstatement, and promotion. Where a violation of ADEA is found, the employer must raise the wages of the discriminated-against employee. It cannot lower the wages of other employees. The following case raises the issue of age discrimination. ■

U.S. SUPREME COURT CASE

Reeves v. Sanderson Plumbing Products, Inc.

530 U.S. 133, 120 S.Ct. 2097, 2000 U.S. Lexis 3966 (2000)
Supreme Court of the United States

Case 18.7
Age Discrimination

Background and Facts

In October 1995, Roger Reeves was 57 years old and had spent 40 years employed by Sanderson Plumbing Products, Inc., a manufacturer of toilet seats and covers. Reeves worked as a supervisor of a production line in a department known as the "Hinge Room." Reeves's responsibilities included recording the attendance and hours of the workers under his supervision. In the summer of 1995, the president of Sanderson Plumbing fired Reeves, asserting that Reeves had failed to maintain accurate attendance records. Sanderson Plumbing replaced Reeves with a worker in his 30s. Reeves sued Sanderson Plumbing for violating the ADEA, alleging that Sanderson's stated reason for discharging him was false and the real reason was to discriminate against him because of his age. The jury held in favor of Reeves, but the court of appeals reversed. The U.S. Supreme Court granted certiorari to hear the appeal.

Supreme Court Issue

Did plaintiff Reeves properly raise the issue to the jury of the falsity of Sanderson Plumbing's claim as to why he had been fired?

In The Language of The U.S. Supreme Court

Ginsburg, Justice First, the plaintiff must establish a prima facie case of discrimination. It is undisputed that petitioner Reeves satisfied this burden here: (i) at the time he was fired, he was a member of the class protected by the ADEA (individuals who are at least 40 years of age) (ii) he was otherwise qualified for the position of Hinge Room supervisor, (iii) he was discharged by respondent, and (iv) respondent successively hired three persons in their thirties to fill petitioner's position. The burden therefore shifted to respondent to produce evidence that the plaintiff was rejected, or someone else was preferred, for a legitimate, nondiscriminatory reason. Respondent met this burden by offering admissible evidence sufficient for the trier of fact to conclude that petitioner was fired because of his failure to maintain accurate attendance records.

Although intermediate evidentiary burdens shift back and forth under this framework, the ultimate burden of persuading the trier of fact that the defendant intentionally discriminated against the plaintiff remains at all times with the plaintiff. And in attempting to satisfy this burden, the plaintiff—once the employer produces sufficient evidence to support a nondiscriminatory explanation for its decision—must be afforded the opportunity to prove by a preponderance of the evidence that the legitimate reasons offered by the defendant were not its true reasons, but were a pretext for discrimination. That is, the plaintiff may attempt to establish that he was the victim of intentional discrimination by showing that the employer's proffered explanation is unworthy of credence. Petitioner offered evidence that he had properly maintained the attendance records. It is permissible for the trier of fact to infer the ultimate fact of discrimination from the falsity of the employer's explanation.

Decision and Remedy

The U.S. Supreme Court held that plaintiff Reeves had presented sufficient evidence to the jury that Sanderson Plumbing's asserted justification for dismissing him was false, and thus permitted the jury to conclude that Sanderson Plumbing had unlawfully discriminated against him.

Case Questions

Critical Legal Thinking Does the Supreme Court's back-and-forth burden-shifting approach in employment discrimination lawsuits work well? Do you think it leads to fair decisions in most cases?

Business Ethics Did Sanderson Plumbing act ethically in this case? Why do you think it used a false pretense to fire Reeves?

Contemporary Business Are there economic reasons for employers to prefer to discharge older employees? Explain.

Americans with Disabilities Act of 1990

Some individuals suffer from physical and mental disabilities. In many instances, these disabilities do not prohibit the disabled person from performing certain jobs. To protect disabled persons from being discriminated against in employment, Congress enacted the federal **Americans with Disabilities Act of 1990**.

Americans with Disabilities Act (ADA) of 1990
An act that imposes obligations on employers and providers of public transportation, telecommunications, and public accommodations to accommodate individuals with disabilities.

Landmark Law

Americans with Disabilities Act of 1990

The **Americans with Disabilities Act (ADA)**, which was signed into law on July 26, 1990, is the most comprehensive piece of civil rights legislation since the Civil Rights Act of 1964 [42 U.S.C. §§ 1201 et seq.]. The ADA imposes obligations on employers and providers of public transportation, telecommunications, and public accommodations to accommodate individuals with disabilities.

Title I of the ADA

Title I of the ADA prohibits employment discrimination against qualified individuals with disabilities in regard to job application procedures, hiring, compensation, training, promotion, and termination. Title I, which became effective July 26, 1992, covers employers with 25 or more employees for two years after the effective data and those with 15 or more employees thereafter. The United States, corporations wholly owned by the United States, and bona fide tax-exempt private membership clubs are exempt from Title I coverage.

Title I requires an employer to make reasonable accommodations to individuals with disabilities that do not cause undue hardship to the employer. *Reasonable accommodations* may include making facilities readily accessible to individuals with disabilities, providing part-time or modified work schedules, acquiring equipment or devices, modifying examination and training materials, and providing qualified readers or interpreters.

Employers are not obligated to provide accommodations that would impose an *undue burden*. This means actions that would require significant difficulty or expense. Factors such as the nature and cost of accommodation, the overall financial resources of the employer, and the employer's type of operation are considered by the EEOC and the courts. Obviously, what may be a significant difficulty or expense for a small employer may not be an undue hardship for a large employer. ■

Qualified Individual with a Disability

qualified individual with a disability

A person who (1) has a physical or mental impairment that substantially limits one or more of his or her major life activities, (2) has a record of such impairment, or (3) is regarded as having such impairment.

A **qualified individual with a disability** is a person who, with or without reasonable accommodation, can perform the essential functions of the job that person desires or holds. A disabled person is someone who (1) has a physical or mental impairment that substantially limits one or more of his or her major life activities, (2) has a record of such impairment, or (3) is regarded as having such impairment. Mental retardation, paraplegia, schizophrenia, cerebral palsy, epilepsy, diabetes, muscular dystrophy, multiple sclerosis, cancer, infection with HIV (human immunodeficiency virus), and visual, speech, and hearing impairments are covered under the ADA. A current user of illegal drugs or an alcoholic who uses alcohol or is under the influence of alcohol at the workplace is not covered. However, recovering alcoholics and former users of illegal drugs are protected.

Forbidden Conduct

Title I limits an employer's ability to inquire into or test for an applicant's disabilities. Title I forbids an employer from asking a job applicant about the existence, nature, and severity of a disability. An employer may, however, inquire about the applicant's ability to perform job-related functions. Preemployment medical examinations are forbidden before a job offer. Once a job offer has been made, an employer may require a medical examination and may condition the offer on the examination results, as long as all entering employees are subject to such an examination. The information must be kept confidential.

Procedure and Remedies

Web Site

ADA Document Center This site contains the statute itself, regulations, technical sheets, and other assistance documents. Visit at **janweb.icdi.wvu.edu/kinder.**

Title I, which is administered by the EEOC, borrows much of its procedural framework from Title VII of the Civil Rights Act of 1964. An aggrieved individual must first file a charge with the EEOC, which may take action against the employer or permit the individual to pursue a private cause of action.

Relief can take the form of an injunction, hiring or reinstatement (with back pay), payment of attorneys' fees, and recovery of compensatory and punitive damages (subject to the same caps as Title VII damages). In the following cases, the U.S. Supreme Court addressed the issue of what is a disability for purposes of the ADA.

Case 18.8

Americans with Disabilities Act

U.S. SUPREME COURT CASE

Sutton v. United Air Lines, Inc.

527 U.S. 471, 119 S.Ct. 2139, 1999 U.S. Lexis 4371 (1999)
Supreme Court of the United States

Background and Facts

In 1992, Karen Sutton and Kimberly Hinton (petitioners), twin sisters, applied to United Air Lines, Inc., for employment as commercial airline pilots. They met United's education and experience requirements and the Federal Aviation Administration (FAA) certification qualifications. Both of the petitioners have severe myopia, with uncorrected visual acuity of 20/200 or worse and 20/400 or worse. Each of the petitioners has vision that is 20/20 or better with the use of corrective lens. Without corrective lens, neither of the petitioners can see to conduct activities such a driving a vehicle, watching television, or shopping in public stores, but with corrective lens both function identically to persons without similar impairment. United rejected the petitioners' employment applications because they did not meet United's minimum visual requirement of uncorrected visual acuity of 20/100 or better. Petitioners filed a charge of disability discrimination against United for allegedly violating the ADA. The district court dismissed the petitioners' complaint and the circuit court of appeals affirmed. The petitioners appealed to the U.S. Supreme Court, which granted review.

Issue

Are the petitioners disabled within the meaning of the ADA?

In The Language of The U.S. Supreme Court

O'Connor, Justice With respect to the disability definition, our decision turns on whether disability is to be determined with or without reference to corrective measures. Petitioners maintain that whether an impairment is substantially limiting should be determined without regard to corrective measures. United, in turn, maintains that an impairment does not substantially limit a major life activity if it is corrected. We conclude that United is correct. Looking at ADA as a whole, it is apparent that if a person is taking measures to correct for, or mitigate, a physical or mental impairment, the effects of those measures—both positive and negative—must be taken into account when judging whether that person is "substantially limited" in a major life activity and thus "disabled" under the ADA.

The ADA defines a "disability" as "a physical or mental impairment that substantially limits one or more of the major life activities" of an individual. A person whose physical or mental impairment is corrected by medication or other measures does not have an impairment that presently substantially limits a major life activity. To be sure, a person whose physical or mental impairment is corrected by mitigating measures still has an impairment, but if the impairment is corrected it does not substantially limit a major life activity.

Decision and Remedy

The U.S. Supreme Court held that *disability* under the ADA does not include persons with corrected conditions, such as petitioners' corrected vision. The Supreme Court concluded that the petitioners' complaint was properly dismissed. Affirmed.

Case Questions

Critical Legal Thinking Does the ADA promote an important social policy? Do you think a federal law was needed to effectuate this policy?

Business Ethics Did United act ethically in this case? What reasons underlie its decision not to hire the petitioners?

Contemporary Business What is the business implication of the U.S. Supreme Court's decision? What would have been the economic implications for business if the Supreme Court would have held in the petitioners' favor?

Case 18.9

Americans with Disabilities Act

U.S. SUPREME COURT CASE

PGA Tour, Inc. v. Martin

532 U.S. 661, 121 S.Ct. 1879, 2001 U.S. Lexis 4115 (2001)
2001 U.S. Lexis 415, WL
Supreme Court of the United States

Background and Facts

The PGA Tour, Inc., is a nonprofit entity that sponsors professional golf tournaments. The PGA has adopted a set of rules that apply to its golf tour. One rule requires golfers to walk the golf course during PGA-sponsored tournaments. Casey Martin is a talented amateur golfer who won many Oregon junior events, and the state championship as a high school senior. He played on the Stanford University golf team and won

PGA Tour, Inc. v. Martin

532 U.S. 661, 121 S.Ct. 1879, 2001 U.S. Lexis 4115 (2001)
2001 U.S. Lexis 415, WL
Supreme Court of the United States
(continued)

the 1994 National Collegiate Athletic Association (NCAA) championship.

Martin has been afflicted with Klippel-Trenaunay-Weber Syndrome, a degenerative circulatory disorder that obstructs the flow of blood from his right leg to his heart. The disease is progressive and has atrophied his right leg. Walking causes him pain, fatigue, and anxiety, with significant risk of hemorrhaging. Martin is an individual with a disability as defined by the ADA. When Martin turned professional, he qualified for the PGA Tour. He made a request to use a golf cart while playing in PGA tournaments. When the PGA denied his request, Martin sued the PGA for violation of the ADA for not making reasonable accommodations for his disability. The district court sided with Martin and ordered the PGA to permit Martin to use a golf cart. The court of appeals affirmed. The U.S. Supreme Court agreed to hear the appeal.

Supreme Court Issue

Does the ADA require the PGA Tour, Inc., to accommodate Casey Martin, a disabled professional golfer, by permitting him to use a golf cart while playing in PGA-sponsored golf tournaments?

In The Language of The U.S. Supreme Court

Stevens, Justice In this case, the narrow dispute is whether allowing Martin to use a golf cart, despite the walking requirement that applies to the PGA Tour tournaments, is a modification that would "fundamentally alter the nature" of those events.

As an initial matter, we observe that the use of carts is not itself inconsistent with the fundamental character of the game of golf. From early on, the essence of the game has been shot-making—using clubs to cause a ball to progress from the teeing ground to a hole some distance away with as few strokes as possible. Golf carts started appearing with increasing regularity on American golf course in the 1950's. Today they are everywhere. And they are encouraged. For one thing, they often speed up play, and for another, they are great revenue producers.

The force of petitioner PGA Tour's argument is, first of all, mitigated by the fact that golf is a game in which it is impossible to guarantee that all competitors will play under exactly the same conditions or that an individual's ability will be the sole determinant of the outcome. For example, changes in the weather may produce harder greens and more head winds for the tournament leader than for his closest pursuers. A lucky bounce may save a shot or two. Whether such happenstance events are more or less probable than the likelihood that a golfer afflicted with Klippel-Trenaunay-Weber Syndrome would one day qualify for the PGA Tour, they at least demonstrate that pure chance may have a greater impact on the outcome of elite golf tournaments than the fatigue resulting from the enforcement of the walking rule. The District Court credited the testimony of a professor in physiology and expert on fatigue, who calculated the calories expended in walking a golf course (about five miles) to be approximately 500 calories—"nutritionally-less than a Big Mac."

Decision and Remedy

The U.S. Supreme Court held that the ADA requires that the PGA Tour, Inc., accommodate Casey Martin, a disabled professional golfer, by allowing him to use a golf cart while competing in PGA-sponsored professional golf tournaments. The judgment of the court of appeals was affirmed.

Case Questions

Critical Legal Thinking Do you agree with U.S. Supreme Court's decision? Will the decision open a floodgate of similar lawsuits?

Business Ethics Was Casey Martin just asking for "fairness," or was he asking for an advantage when competing in professional golf tournaments?

Contemporary Business Is the PGA Tour a lucrative business? Will the Supreme Court's ruling have any effect on the revenues generated by the PGA Tour?

Case 18.10 Americans with Disabilities Act

U.S. SUPREME COURT CASE

Toyota Motor Manufacturing, Kentucky, Inc. v. Williams

534 U.S. 184, 122 S.Ct. 681, 2002 U.S. Lexis 400 (2002)
Supreme Court of the United States

Background and Facts

In 1990, Ella Williams began working at an automobile plant in Georgetown, Kentucky, that was owned by Toyota Motor Manufacturing, Kentucky, Inc. (Toyota). Williams worked on an engine fabrication assembly line, where her duties included work with pneumatic tools. Use of these tools eventually caused pain in Williams's hands, wrists, and arms. Williams consulted her personal physician, who diagnosed that Williams had bilateral carpal tunnel syndrome. Her physician placed Williams on permanent work restrictions that precluded her from lifting more than 20 pounds or engaging in constant repetitive flexing or extension of her wrists or elbows. To accommodate these restrictions, Toyota placed Williams on a Quality Control Inspection team, where she visually inspected painted cars moving slowly down a conveyor. Williams was required to open and shut doors, trunks, and hoods of inspected vehicles. Williams requested that Toyota accommodate her medical condition by allowing her to only visually inspect automobiles, but Toyota refused. Toyota eventually terminated Williams, citing her poor attendance record.

Williams sued Toyota, alleging a violation of the ADA. The district court granted summary judgment to Toyota, finding that Williams was not disabled. The court of appeals reversed, finding that Williams was disabled because she could not perform the manual tasks at her job. Toyota appealed to the U.S. Supreme Court.

Supreme Court Issue

Did the court of appeals apply the proper standard in making a disability determination based solely on Williams' ability to perform specific manual tasks at the job?

In The Language of The U.S. Supreme Court

Even assuming that working is a major life activity, a claimant would be required to show an inability to work in a "broad range of jobs," rather than a specific job.

While the Court of Appeals in this case addressed the different major life activity of performing manual tasks, its analysis focused on respondent's inability to perform manual tasks associated only with her job. This was error. When addressing the major life activity of performing manual tasks, the central inquiry must be whether the claimant is unable to perform the variety of tasks central to most people's daily lives, not whether the claimant is unable to perform the tasks associated with her specific job.

There is also no support in the Act, our previous opinions, or the regulations for the Court of Appeals' idea that the question of whether an impairment constitutes a disability is to be answered only by analyzing the effect of the impairment in the workplace.

Even more critically, the manual tasks unique to any particular job are not necessarily important parts of most people's lives. As a result, occupation-specific tasks may have only limited relevance to the manual task inquiry. In this case, repetitive work with hands and arms extended at or above shoulder levels for extended periods of time, the manual task on which the Court of Appeals relied, is not an important part of most people's daily lives. The court, therefore, should not have considered respondent's inability to do such manual work in her specialized assembly line job as sufficient proof that she was substantially limited in performing manual tasks.

At the same time, the Court of Appeals appears to have discarded the very type of evidence that it should have focused upon. It treated as irrelevant the fact that respondent can . . . tend to her personal hygiene and carry out personal or household chores. Yet household chores, bathing, and brushing one's teeth are among the types of manual tasks of central importance to people's daily lives, and should have been part of the assessment of whether respondent was substantially limited in performing manual tasks. In addition, according to respondent's deposition testimony, even after her condition worsened, she could still brush her teeth, wash her face, bathe, tend her flower garden, fix breakfast, do laundry, and pick up around the house.

Decision and Remedy

The U.S. Supreme Court held that in addition to job-related tasks, the court of appeals should also have considered non-job-related tasks in making a disability determination. The Supreme Court reversed the court of appeals's grant of summary judgment for Williams and remanded the case for further proceedings, consistent with its opinion.

Case Questions

Critical Legal Thinking Do you agree with the Supreme Court's definition of *disability* in this case? Why or why not?

Business Ethics Do you think many disability claims are fraudulent? How can fraudulent claims be prevented?

Contemporary Business Does the Supreme Court's decision in this case favor businesses or employees? Explain.

U.S. SUPREME COURT CASE

Chevron U.S.A. Inc. v. Echazabal

536 U.S. 73, 122 S.Ct. 2045, 2002 U.S. Lexis 4202 (2002)

Supreme Court of the United States

Case 18.11

Americans with Disabilities Act

Background and Facts

Beginning in 1972, Mario Echazabal worked for independent contractors at an oil refinery owned by Chevron U.S.A. Inc. Echazabal twice applied for a job directly with Chevron, which offered to hire him if he could pass the company's physical examination. Each time, the exam showed liver abnormality or damage, the cause eventually being identified as hepatitis C, which Chevron's doctors said would be aggravated by continued exposure to toxins at Chevron's refinery. In each instance, Chevron withdrew the offer, and the second time Chevron asked the independent contractor who employed Echazabal at the refinery to either reassign him to a job without exposure to harmful chemicals or to remove him from the refinery altogether. The contractor laid off Echazabal in early 1996. Echazabal sued Chevron, alleging that Chevron violated the ADA by refusing to hire him and even refusing to let him continue working in the refinery because of a disability, his liver condition. Chevron defended, asserting a regulation of the EEOC that permitted a defense that a worker's disability on the job would pose a "direct threat" to his health. The district court entered judgment for Chevron, but the court of appeals reversed. Chevron appealed to the U.S. Supreme Court.

Chevron U.S.A. Inc. v. Echazabal

536 U.S. 73, 122 S.Ct. 2045, 2002 U.S. Lexis 4202 (2002)

Supreme Court of the United States

(continued)

Supreme Court Issue

Is the EEOC's "direct threat" to oneself rule lawful?

In The Language of The U.S. Supreme Court

Souter, Justice Section 102 of the Americans with Disabilities Act of 1990 creates an affirmative defense for action shown to be job-related for the position in question and consistent with business necessity. Such a standard may include a requirement that an individual shall not pose a direct threat to the health or safety of other individuals in the workplace if the individual cannot perform the job safely with reasonable accommodation. By regulation, the EEOC carries the defense one step further, in allowing an employer to screen out a potential worker with a disability not only for risks that he would pose to others in the workplace but for risks on the job to his own health or safety as well.

Decision and Remedy

The U.S. Supreme Court held that the direct threat to oneself defense was lawful to a charge of disability discrimination under the ADA. The Supreme Court reversed the decision of the court of appeals and remanded the case for proceedings, consistent with its opinion.

Case Questions

Critical Legal Thinking Do you think that the direct threat to oneself defense is a good law? Why or why not?

Business Ethics Did Chevron act ethically by not hiring Echazabal? Did Chevron act ethically in asking the independent contractor Echazabal worked for to either reassign him or remove him from jobs at the Chevron refinery?

Contemporary Business Why did Chevron refuse to hire Echazabal at its refinery? Explain.

Landmark Law

Civil Rights Act of 1866

The **Civil Rights Act of 1866** was enacted after the Civil War. *Section 1981* of this act states that all persons "have the same right . . . to make and enforce contracts . . . as is enjoyed by white persons" [42 U.S.C. § 1981]. Employment decisions are covered because the employment relationship is contractual. Most employers other than the federal government are subject to this act.

Section 1981 expressly prohibits racial discrimination; it has also been held to forbid discrimination based on national origin. Although most racial and national origin employment discrimination cases are brought under Title VII, there are two reasons that a complainant would bring the action under Section 1981: (1) A private plaintiff can bring an action without going through the procedural requirements of Title VII, and (2) there is no limitations period on the recovery of back pay and no cap on the recovery of compensatory or punitive damages. ■

Entrepreneur and the Law

Small Businesses Exempt from Federal Equal Opportunity in Employment Laws

In passing federal equal opportunity in employment laws, Congress exempted small businesses from the reach of many of these laws. In several of these statutes, Congress set a threshold number of employees that an employer must have to be covered by each act. Some of the threshold requirements are

- ***Title VII*** Employers with 15 or more employees.
- ***Age Discrimination in Employment Act*** Employers with 20 or more employees.
- ***Americans with Disabilities Act of 1990*** Employers with 15 or more employees.

The rationale behind these exemptions is that it may be too costly for small employers to comply with the laws and face lawsuits that could arise thereunder. These employers should make every effort to comply with these laws, however. ■

Myanmar. In some countries, females do not have equality of rights under the law, as provided in the United States and other countries.

Affirmative Action

Employers often adopt **affirmative action plans** that provide that certain job preferences will be given to minority or other protected-class applicants when an employer makes an employment decision. Such plans can be voluntarily adopted by employers, undertaken to settle a discrimination action, or ordered by the courts. Employee approval is not required.

affirmative action
A policy that provides that certain job preferences will be given to minority or other protected-class applicants when an employer makes an employment decision.

Affirmative action plans are often controversial. Proponents of such plans argue that the plans are necessary to address imbalances in the workforce and to remedy past discrimination against protected classes. Opponents argue that affirmative action plans actually cause **reverse discrimination**, cause work hardship on innocent employees, and lead to the employment of less qualified individuals.

reverse discrimination
Discrimination against a group that is usually thought of as a majority.

The Civil Rights Act of 1991 prohibits the practice of "race norming" and other practices that are used to alter or adjust test scores on the basis of race. It does not affect how an employer uses accurately reported test scores or require that test scores be used at all in making employment decisions, however.

Contemporary Business Environment

Affirmative Action Narrowed

Affirmative action was dealt a severe blow when, in April 1995, the U.S. Supreme Court refused to hear appeals in two cases that gave victories to white men in reverse discrimination lawsuits. These decisions show a willingness by the courts to apply the Equal Protection Clause of the U.S. Constitution and equal opportunity in employment laws to protect white employees as well as minorities from discrimination.

The first case involved an affirmative action plan implemented by the city of Birmingham, Alabama, to ensure the promotion of black firefighters. The case began over 30 years ago, when black firefighters sued the city for discrimination because it had only a few black firefighters and none in supervisory positions. After a heated lawsuit, in 1981 the city agreed to promote white and black firefighters to the rank of lieutenant on a 1-to-1 basis until the number of blacks equaled the 28 percent of the surrounding county's workforce that was black. The target was reached in 1989, but the city continued this quota system.

In 1989, several white firefighters challenged the city's affirmative action plan. The white firefighters lost in federal district court, but the court of appeals reversed, finding that the city's

Contemporary Business Environment

(continued)

affirmative action plan violated the Equal Protection Clause of the Constitution and Title VII. The court of appeals denounced the city's plan as outright racial balancing, stating, "We can imagine nothing less conducive to eliminating the vestiges of past discrimination than a government separating its employees into two categories, black and nonblack, and allocating a rigid, inflexible number of promotions to each group, year in and year out."

The second case was brought by Frederick Claus, a white engineer with a bachelor's degree in electrical engineering who had worked 29 years for his employer, Duquesne Light Co. Claus, along with four other whites and one black, sought promotion for an open managerial job. The black employee did not have a bachelor's degree or the required seven years' experience for the position. When the company applied its affirmative action plan and chose the black employee for the position, Claus sued under Title VII, claiming that he was a victim of racial discrimination. The jury agreed and awarded him $25,000 in compensatory damages and $400,000 in punitive damages. The court of appeals upheld the verdict.

Without comment, the U.S. Supreme Court turned down appeals in both cases [*Arrington v. Wilks*, 514 U.S. 1065, 115 S.Ct. 1695, 1995 U.S. Lexis 2648 (1995); *Duquesne Light Co. v. Claus*, 514 U.S. 1067, 115 S.Ct. 1700, 1995 U.S. Lexis 2678 (1995)].

What is left of affirmative action? For one thing, affirmative action was not held to be per se illegal in either case. Instead, the courts of appeals held that an affirmative action plan, to be legal, must be "narrowly tailored" to achieve some "compelling interest." In these two cases, the courts found that the affirmative action plans were not narrowly tailored but were blatant quotas that were unlawful. Government and private employers must now tailor their affirmative action programs narrowly or face reverse discrimination lawsuits by passed-over nonminority employees. ■

Racial discrimination in any form and in any degree has no justifiable part whatever in our democratic way of life. It is unattractive in any setting but it is utterly revolting among a free people who have embraced the principles set forth in the Constitution of the United States.

Murphy, J., dissenting opinion
Korematsu v. U.S. (1944)

State and Local Government Antidiscrimination Laws

Many state and local governments have adopted laws that prevent discrimination in employment. These laws usually include classes protected by federal equal opportunity laws, as well as classes of persons not protected by federal laws, such as homosexuals and other minority groups.

International Law

Japan Adopts an Equal Opportunity in Employment Law

Prior to April 1, 1999, job openings in Japan were restricted by sex; that is, jobs could be reserved for men only without violating the law. Classified advertisements in major Japanese newspapers typically listed "men only" jobs, which were executive positions and high-paying blue collar jobs. "Women only" listings tended to be for nursing, secretarial, food-service, and other low-paying jobs. Japanese women hold only 10 percent of professional positions, as compared to 45 percent in the United States. Only 8 out of every 1,000 factory workers in Japan are women, compared to 160 per 1,000 in the United States. In addition to gender-based discrimination, sexual harassment against females in the workplace was usually ignored.

All this changed with Japan's enactment of the **Equal Employment Opportunity and Labor Standard Law** in 1999. The new statute grants equal opportunity rights to females in being hired for jobs and promoted to higher positions. The law bans the use of gender-specific advertising, so the "men only" and "women only" job listings have disappeared. Women may not compete equally, under the law, for jobs and promotions. The new law also makes other gender-based discrimination illegal. For example, prior to the new law, women were banned from working after 10:00 P.M. or putting in more than six hours of overtime per week. Both of these restrictions have been removed, allowing females to earn higher wages from working night shifts and overtime. Women are still forbidden from holding positions involving heavy lifting and those involving certain chemicals.

The Equal Opportunity Law prohibits sexual harassment in the workplace. Prior to the passage of the new law, sexual harassment—known in Japan as *seku hara*—was difficult to sue for. Previously, companies could veto any sexual harassment complaint brought against them, which helped explain why fewer than a dozen cases were even ruled on during the 1990s. Under the new law, a woman can file a complaint with the Labor Ministry, a government administrative agency empowered to investigate such charges. So companies are now advising male managers to remove X-rated calendars from offices and to not pressure female employees to accompany them to karaoke, dancing, or other endeavors. ■

Equal Employment Opportunity Commission (EEOC), p. 528

Equal Employment Opportunity Commission (EEOC)

A federal administrative agency responsible for administering, interpreting, and enforcing most federal equal employment opportunity (antidiscrimination) laws.

Title VII of the Civil Rights Act of 1964, p. 529

Title VII of the Civil Rights Act of 1964

A federal statute that prohibits job discrimination based on the (1) race, (2) color, (3) religion, (4) sex, or (5) national origin of the job applicant.

Scope of Coverage of Title VII

1. ***Employment decisions subject to Title VII.*** Decisions regarding hiring; promotion; demotion; payment of salaries, wages, and fringe benefits; job training and apprenticeships; work rules; or any other "term, condition, or privilege of employment."

Forms of Title VII Actions

1. ***Disparate treatment discrimination.*** Occurs when an employer treats a specific *individual* less favorably than others because of that person's race, color, national origin, sex, or religion. To be successful, the complainant must prove:
   a. He or she belongs to a Title VII protected class.
   b. He or she applied for and was qualified for the employment position.
   c. He or she was rejected despite these qualifications.
   d. The employer kept the position open and sought applicants from persons with the complainant's qualifications.
2. ***Disparate impact discrimination.*** Occurs when an employer discriminates against an entire protected *class*. May be proven by statistical data that demonstrate a causal link between the challenged practice and the statistical imbalance. *Neutral employment rules* that have an adverse impact on a protected class constitute disparate impact discrimination.

Procedure for Bringing a Title VII Action

1. ***Complaint.*** A private complainant must file a complaint with the EEOC. The EEOC is given the opportunity to sue the employer on the complainant's behalf.
2. ***Right to sue letter.*** If the EEOC chooses not to bring suit, it will issue a *right to sue letter* that authorizes the complainant to sue the employer.

Remedies for Violations of Title VII

A successful plaintiff in a Title VII action can recover up to two years' back pay, compensatory and punitive damages (subject to certain caps based on the size of the defendant employer), reasonable attorneys' fees, and equitable remedies such as reinstatement, fictional seniority, and injunctions.

Protected Classes

Protected classes. Employment discrimination based on the following protected classes is forbidden by Title VII:

1. ***Race***
2. ***Color***
3. ***National origin***
4. ***Sex***
5. ***Religion***

Race, Color, and National Origin Discrimination

1. ***Race.*** Broad class of individuals with common physical characteristics (e.g., black, Caucasian, Asian Native American).
2. ***Color.*** Color of a person's skin (e.g., light-skinned person, dark-skinned person).
3. ***National origin.*** A person's country of origin or national heritage (e.g., Italian, Hispanic).

Sex Discrimination

1. ***Sex.*** A person's sex, whether male or female.
2. ***Pregnancy.*** The *Pregnancy Discrimination Act of 1978* amended Title VII to forbid employment discrimination because of "pregnancy, childbirth, or related medical conditions."
3. ***Sexual harassment.*** Lewd remarks, touching, intimidation, posting of indecent materials, and other verbal or physical conduct of a sexual nature that occurs on the job. Sexual harassment that creates a *hostile work environment* violates Title VII [*Meritor Savings Bank v. Vinson*, 477 U.S. 57 (1986)].
4. ***Sexual preference.*** Title VII does not apply to employment discrimination based on sexual preference.

Title VII: Religious Discrimination

Discrimination solely because of a person's religions beliefs or practices. An employer has a duty to *reasonably accommodate* an employee's religious beliefs if it does not cause an *undue hardship* on the employer.

Defenses to a Title VII Action, p. 537

Defenses to a Title VII Action

1. ***Merit.*** Job-related experience, education, or unbiased employment test.
2. ***Seniority.*** Length of time an employee has been employed by the employer. Intentional discrimination based on seniority is unlawful.
3. ***Bona fide occupational qualification (BFOQ).*** Employment discrimination based on the sex, religion, or national origin of an applicant is permitted if it is a valid *BFOQ* for the position. To be legal, a BFOQ must be *job related* and a *business necessity*. BFOQ exceptions are narrowly interpreted by the courts.

Equal Pay Act of 1963, p. 539

Equal Pay Act

A federal statute that forbids pay discrimination for the same job based on the sex of the employee performing the job. There cannot be pay disparity based on sex for jobs that require equal skill, equal effort, equal responsibility, and similar working conditions.

1. ***Criteria that justify a differential in wages.*** The Equal Pay Act stipulates that the following four criteria justify a differential in wages:
   a. *Seniority*
   b. *Merit*
   c. *Quantity or quality of work* (commission, piecework, or quality-control–based pay systems)
   d. *Any factor other than sex* (e.g., night versus day shifts)

Age Discrimination in Employment Act of 1967, p. 540

Age Discrimination in Employment Act (ADEA)

A federal statute that prohibits employment discrimination against applicants and employees who are 40 years of age and older.

1. ***Older Workers Benefit Protection Act (OWBPA).*** A federal statute that amended the ADEA to prohibit age discrimination with respect to employment benefits.

2. ***Defenses.*** The same defenses that are available in a Title VII action are also available in an ADEA action.
3. ***Remedies.*** A successful plaintiff can recover back wages, attorneys' fees, and equitable relief, including hiring, reinstatement, and promotion.

Americans with Disabilities Act of 1990, p. 541

Americans with Disabilities Act of 1990 (ADA)

A federal statute that imposes obligations on employers and providers of public transportation, telecommunications, and public accommodations to accommodate individuals with disabilities.

Title I of the ADA

A federal law that prohibits employment discrimination against qualified individuals with disabilities.

1. ***Reasonable accommodation.*** Title I requires employers to make *reasonable accommodations* to accommodate employees with disabilities that do not cause *undue hardship* to the employer.

Qualified Individual with a Disability

A person who (1) has a physical or mental impairment that substantially limits one or more of his or her major life functions, (2) has a record of such impairment, or (3) is regarded as having such impairment.

Procedure and Remedies

A successful plaintiff can recover back pay, compensatory and punitive damages (subject to certain caps based on the size of the defendant employer), reasonable attorneys' fees, and equitable remedies such as hiring, reinstatement, or promotion.

Civil Rights Act of 1866, p. 546

Civil Rights Act of 1866

1. ***Section 1981 of the Civil Rights Act of 1866.*** A federal statute enacted after the Civil War that states that all persons "have the same right . . . to make and enforce contracts . . . as is enjoyed by white persons."
2. ***Protected class.*** Section 1981 prohibits *race* and *national origin* discrimination concerning employment contracts.
3. ***Remedies.*** A successful plaintiff can recover back pay, compensatory and punitive damages, reasonable attorneys' fees, and equitable remedies. There is no limitations period on the recovery of back pay, and there is no cap on the recovery of compensatory or punitive damages.

Affirmative Action, p. 547

Affirmative Action and Reverse Discrimination

A policy that provides that certain job preferences will be given to minority or other protected-class applicants when an employer makes an employment decision.

1. ***Lawfulness of affirmative action plans.*** An employer may adopt a voluntary affirmative action plan that uses race or other protected-class status as a "*plus factor*" in making employment decisions. *Race norming*—the practice of altering or adjusting test scores on the basis of race—is unlawful.
2. ***Reverse discrimination.*** Discrimination against a person who is a member of a group that is usually thought of as a majority. Very few reverse discrimination lawsuits are successful.

State and Local Government Antidiscrimination Laws, p. 548

State and Local Government Antidiscrimination Laws

Many state and local governments have adopted laws that prevent discrimination in employment. These laws usually include classes protected by federal equal opportunity laws (e.g., race, color, national origin, sex, religion, age, disability, and such), as well as classes not protected by federal law (e.g., homosexuals).

Internet Exercises and Case Questions

Working the Web Internet Exercises

Activities

1. Review the case *Gupta v. Florida Bd. of Regents* (5/17/2000, No. 98-5392) via the Cornell Discrimination Web site at **www.law.cornell.edu/topics/employiment_discrimination.html**. According go the 11th circuit court of appeals, is it sexual harassment to make comments to coworkers such as "You are looking very beautiful"?
2. Review Congress's statement of purpose in the ADEA. Has this law served to accomplish that purpose? See the U.S. Equal Employment Opportunity Commission site at **www.eeoc.gov** and the Law About . . . Employment Discrimination site at **www.law.cornell.edu/topics/employment_discrimination.html**.
3. For a discussion of the courts' definition of *disability*, see "The Supreme Court's Definition of Disability Under the ADA: A Return to the Dark Ages" at **www.law.ua.edu/lawreview/tucker521.htm**.
4. Find the case *PGA Tour, Inc. v. Martin* involving the ADA and a professional golfer. Do you agree with the court's decision? Try the Cornell disability site.

Critical Legal Thinking Cases

18.1 Equal Pay Act For years, certain state laws prevented females from working at night. Therefore, Corning Glass Works employed male workers for night inspection jobs and female workers for day inspection jobs. Males working the night shift were paid higher wages than were females who worked the day shift. When the law changed and Corning began hiring females for night shift jobs, it instituted a "red circle" wage rate that permitted previously hired male night shift workers to continue to receive higher wages than newly hired night shift workers. Does this violate the Equal Pay Act? [*Corning Glass Works v. Brennan, Secretary of Labor*, 417 U.S. 188, 94 S.Ct. 2223, 1974 U.S. Lexis 62 (1974)]

18.2 Race Discrimination Winnie Teal is a black employee of the Department of Income Maintenance of the State of Connecticut. The first step to being promoted to a supervisor position is to attain a passing score on a written test. When the written test was administered, 54 percent of the black candidates passed and 68 percent of the white candidates passed. Teal, who failed the examination, filed a disparate impact Title VII action alleging that the test was biased against blacks. To reach a nondiscriminatory bottom-line result, the employer promoted 22.9 percent of the black candidates who passed the test but only 13.5 percent of the white candidates who passed. Teal was not promoted because she did not pass the test. Is this result a defense to Teal's Title VII action? [*Connecticut v. Teal*, 457 U.S. 440, 102 S.Ct. 2525, 1982 U.S. Lexis 131 (1982)]

18.3 Sex Discrimination The Los Angeles Department of Water and Power maintains a pension plan for its employees that is funded by both employer and employee contributions. The plan pays men and women retirees pensions with the same monthly benefits. However, because statistically women on average live several years longer than men, female employees are required to make monthly contributions to the pension fund that are 14.84 percent higher than the contributions required of male employees. Because employee contributions are withheld from paychecks, a female employee takes home less pay than a male employee earning the same salary. Does this practice violate Title VII? [*City of Los Angeles Department of Water and Power v. Manhart*, 435 U.S. 702, 98 S.Ct. 1370, 1978 U.S. Lexis 23 (1978)]

18.4 Hostile Work Environment Shirley Huddleston became the first female sales representative of Roger Dean Chevrolet, Inc. (RDC), in West Palm Beach, Florida. Shortly after she began working at RDC, Philip Geraci, a fellow sales representative, and other male employees began making derogatory comments to and about her, expelled gas in her presence, called her a bitch and a whore, and such. Many of these remarks were made in front of customers. The sales manager of RDC participated in the harassment. On several occasions, Huddleston complained about this conduct to RDC's general manager. Was Title VII violated? [*Huddleston v. Roger Dean Chevrolet, Inc.*, 845 F.2d 900, 1988 U.S. App. Lexis 6823 (11th Cir. 1988)]

18.5 Pregnancy Discrimination Act The Newport News Shipbuilding and Dry Dock Company provides hospitalization and medical–surgical coverage to its employees and dependents of employees. Under the plan, all covered males, including employees and spouses of female employees, were treated alike for purposes of hospitalization coverage. All covered females, including employees or spouses of male employees, were treated alike except for one major exception: Female employees were provided full hospital coverage for pregnancy, whereas female spouses of male employees were provided limited hospital coverage for pregnancy. Does this practice violate Title VII? [*Newport News Shipbuilding and Dry Dock Company v. EEOC*, 462 U.S. 669, 103 S.Ct. 2622, 1983 U.S. Lexis 73 (1983)]

18.6 National Origin Discrimination The Federal Bureau of Investigation (FBI) engaged in a pattern and practice of discrimination against Hispanic FBI agents. Job assignments and promotions were areas that were especially affected. Bernardo M. Perez, an Hispanic, brought this Title VII action against the FBI. Did the FBI violate Title VII? [*Perez v. Federal Bureau of Investigation*, 714 F.Supp. 1414, 1989 U.S. Dist. Lexis 8426 (W.D. Texas 1989)]

18.7 Color Discrimination Walker, a clerk typist with the IRS, is a light-skinned black. Her supervisor is a dark-skinned black. Walker filed an action alleging that she was terminated by her supervisor in violation of Title VII. Does she have a cause of action under Title VII? [*Walker v. Internal Revenue Service*, 713 F.Supp. 403, 1989 U.S. Dist. Lexis 5260 (N.D.Ga. 1989)]

18.8 Religious Discrimination Trans World Airlines (TWA), an airline, operates a large maintenance and overhaul base for its airplanes at Kansas City, Missouri. Because of its essential role, the stores department at the base must operate 24 hours per day, 365 days per year. The employees at the base are represented by the International Association of Machinists and

Aerospace Workers (Union). TWA and the Union entered into a collective bargaining agreement that includes a seniority system for the assignment of jobs and shifts.

Larry Hardison was hired by TWA to work as a clerk in the stores department. Soon after beginning work, Hardison joined the Worldwide Church of God, which does not allow its members to work from sunset on Friday until sunset on Saturday and on certain religious holidays. Hardison, who had the second lowest seniority within the stores department, did not have enough seniority to observe his Sabbath regularly. When Hardison asked for special consideration, TWA offered to allow him to take his Sabbath off if he could switch shifts with another employee-union member. None of the other employees would do so. TWA refused Hardison's request for a four-day workweek because it would have to either hire and train a part-time worker to work on Saturdays or incur the cost of paying overtime to an existing full-time worker on Saturdays. Hardison sued TWA for religious discrimination in violation of Title VII. Did TWA's actions violate Title VII? [*Trans World Airlines v. Hardison*, 432 U.S. 63, 97 S.Ct. 2264, 1977 U.S. Lexis 115 (1977)]

18.9 Bona Fide Occupational Qualification At the age of 60, Manuel Fragante emigrated from the Philippines to Hawaii. In response to a newspaper ad, Fragante applied for an entry-level civil service clerk job with the City of Honolulu's Division of Motor Vehicles and Licensing. The job required constant oral communication with the public, either at the information counter or on the telephone. Fragante scored the highest of 731 test takers on a written examination that tested word usage, grammar, and spelling. As part of the application process, two civil service employees who were familiar with the demands of the position interviewed Fragante. They testified that his accent made it difficult to understand him. Fragante was not hired for the position, which was filled by another applicant. Fragante sued, alleging national origin discrimination in violation of Title VII. Who wins? [*Fragante v. City and County of Honolulu*, 888 F.2d 591, 1989 U.S. App. Lexis 2636 (9th Cir. 1989)]

18.10 Age Discrimination Walker Boyd Fite was an employee of First Tennessee Production Credit Association for 19 years. He had attained the position of vice president–credit. During the course of his employment, he never received an unsatisfactory review. On December 26, 1983, at the age of 57, Fite was hospitalized with a kidney stone. On January 5, 1984, while Fite was recovering at home, an officer of First Tennessee called to inform him that he had been retired as of December 31, 1983. A few days later, Fite received a letter stating that he had been retired because of poor job performance. Fite sued First Tennessee for age discrimination. Who wins? [*Fite v. First Tennessee Production Credit Association*, 861 F.2d 884, 1988 U.S. App. Lexis 14759 (6th Cir. 1989)]

18.11 Disability Discrimination Woolworth Davis, Salvatore D'Elia, and Herbert Sims, Jr., applied for various jobs with the City of Philadelphia. The City of Philadelphia receives federal government assistance. When Davis reported for a medical examination, scars revealed that he had previously injected illegal drugs intravenously. D'Elia, a former narcotics addict, had been enrolled in a methadone program. Sims was a former user of morphine and heroin during his two-year tour of duty with the armed forces. Although the three applicants were rehabilitated and otherwise qualified for the position, the City of Philadelphia refused to hire them because of their past drug use. The three applicants sued the City of Philadelphia, alleging a violation of the Rehabilitation Act of 1973. Are the three applicants protected by the act? [*Davis v. Bucher*, 451 F.Supp. 791, 1978 U.S. Dist. Lexis 17470 (E.D.Pa. 1978)]

Business Ethics Cases

18.12 Business Ethics Dianne Rawlinson, 22 years old, was a college graduate whose major course of study was correctional psychology. After graduation, she applied for a position as a correctional counselor (prison guard) with the Alabama Board of Corrections. Her application was rejected because she failed to meet the minimum 120-pound weight requirement of an Alabama statute that also established a height minimum of 5 feet 2 inches. In addition, the Alabama Board of Corrections adopted Administrative Regulation 204, which established gender criteria for assigning correctional counselors to maximum-security prisons for "contact positions." These are correctional counselor positions that require continual close physical proximity to inmates. Under this rule, Rawlinson did not qualify for contact positions with male prisoners in Alabama maximum-security prisons. Rawlinson brought this class action lawsuit against Dothard, who was the director of the Department of Public Safety of Alabama. Does either the height–weight requirement or the contact position rule constitute a bona fide occupational qualification that justifies the sexual discrimination in this case? Does society owe a duty of social responsibility to protect women from dangerous job positions? Or is this "romantic paternalism"? [*Dothard, Director, Department of Public Safety of Alabama v. Rawlinson*, 433 U.S. 321, 97 S.Ct. 2720, 1977 U.S. Lexis 143 (1977)]

18.13 Business Ethics Rita Machakos, a white female, worked for the Civil Rights Division (CRD) of the Department of Justice. During her employment, she was denied promotion to certain paralegal positions. In each instance, the individual selected was a black female. Evidence showed that the CRD maintained an institutional and systematic discrimination policy that favored minority employees over white employees. Machakos sued the CRD for race discrimination under Title VII. Who wins? [*Machakos v. Attorney General of the United States*, 859 F.2d 1487, 1988 U.S. App. Lexis 14672 (D.C.Cir. 1988)]

Briefing the Case Writing Assignment

Read Case A.18 in the Case Appendix [*Robinson v. Jacksonville Shipyards, Inc.*]. This case is excerpted from the district court opinion. Review and brief the case. In your brief, be sure to answer the following questions.

1. Who is the plaintiff? Who is the defendant?
2. What is sexual harassment?
3. Did the court find sexual harassment in this case?
4. What remedy did the court order?

Answers to Management Decision Questions

1. As amended by the **Equal Employment Act of 1972,** Section 703(a)(2) of **Title VII of the Civil Rights Act of 1964** states that:

> It shall be an unlawful employment practice for an employer
> (1) to fail or refuse to hire or to discharge any individual, or otherwise to discriminate against any individual with respect to his compensation, terms, conditions, or privileges of employment, because of such individual's race, color, religion, sex, or national origin; or
> (2) to limit, segregate, or classify his employees or applicants for employment in any way which would deprive or tend to deprive any individual of employment opportunities or otherwise adversely affect his status as an employee, because of such individual's race, color, religion, sex, or national origin.

2. Male applicants who are adversely affected by the employment practices at Tiny Tots can bring an action for employment discrimination under **Title VII**. To bring an action under **Title VII**, a private complainant must first file a complaint with the EEOC. The EEOC is given the right to sue the employer on the complainant's behalf. If the EEOC chooses not to bring suit, it will issue a **right to sue letter** to the complainant. This gives the complainant the right to sue the employer. Monetary as well as equitable damages are available. In addition, reasonable attorneys' fees can be collected.

Endnotes

1. 42 U.S.C. §§ 2000e et seq. Other portions of the Civil Rights Act of 1964 prohibit discrimination in housing, education, and other facets of life.
2. *Equal Employment Opportunity Commission v. Tortilleria "La Mejor,"* 758 F.Supp. 585, 1991 U.S. Dist. Lexis 5754 (E.D.Cal. 1991).
3. *McDonnell Douglas v. Green*, 411 U.S. 792, 93 S.Ct. 1817, 1973 U.S. Lexis 154 (1973).
4. In some states, the complaint must be filed with the appropriate state agency rather than the EEOC.
5. 42 U.S.C. § 2000e(K).
6. *Meritor Savings Bank v. Vinson*, 477 U.S. 57, 106 S.Ct. 2399, 1986 U.S. Lexis 108 (1986).
7. *Harris v. Forklift Systems, Inc.*, 510 U.S. 17, 114 S.Ct. 367, 1993 U.S. Lexis 7155 (1993).
8. *Omcale v. Sundowner Offshore Services, Incorporated*, 523 U.S. 75, 118 S.Ct. 998, 1998 U.S. Lexis 1599 (1998).
9. 29 U.S.C. § 206(d).

19

Administrative Law and Consumer Protection

"I should regret to find that the law was powerless to enforce the most elementary principles of commercial morality."

—Lord Herschell
Reddaway v. Banham (1896), A.C. 199, at p. 209.

Chapter Objectives

After studying this chapter, you should be able to:

1. Describe government regulation and the functions of administrative agencies.
2. Describe the federal Food and Drug Administration's regulation of food, food additives, drugs, cosmetics, and medicinal devices.
3. Explain the coverage of consumer product safety acts.
4. Identify unfair and deceptive practices that violate Section 5 of the Federal Trade Commission Act.
5. Describe the coverage of consumer credit protection statutes.

Chapter Contents

- Government Regulation
- Administrative Agencies
- The FDA's Administration of the Federal Food, Drug, and Cosmetic Act (FOCA)
- Regulation of Product Safety
- Unfair and Deceptive Practices
- Federal Consumer-Debtor Protection Laws

Management Decision Administrative Law and Consumer Protection

You run a medium-size poultry farm and processing plant located along the banks of the Catawba River in York County, South Carolina. Your plant has been in operation for 10 years, and you sell your poultry products directly to retailers located in South Carolina, North Carolina, and Georgia. Your poultry farm and processing plant uses water from the river. Recently, fish in the river have been dying at an unusual rate. Upon examination by state and local environmental agencies, it was determined that contaminated by-products from other manufacturing plants located along the river have leaked from the ground and have contaminated the river. You are concerned about the legal ramifications surrounding the pollution of the river.

1. What are some of the federal laws that may have been broken, and which environmental agencies are responsible for carrying out the provisions of those acts?
2. What is the basis of federal administrative regulatory authority?

administrative agencies
Agencies that the legislative and executive branches of federal and state governments establish.

caveat emptor
"Let the buyer beware," the traditional guideline of sales transactions.

consumer protection laws
Federal and state statutes and regulations that promote product safety and prohibit abusive, unfair, and deceptive business practices.

Congress and the executive branch of government have created more than 100 federal **administrative agencies**. These agencies are intended to provide resources and expertise in dealing with complex commercial organizations and businesses. In addition, state governments have created many state administrative agencies. Thousands of *rules and regulations* regarding business operations have been adopted and enforced by federal and state administrative agencies. Since the 1960s, the number of administrative agencies, and the regulations they produce have increased substantially. Because of their importance administrative agencies are informally referred to as the *fourth branch of government*.

Originally, sales transactions in this country were guided by the principle of **caveat emptor** ("let the buyer beware"). To promote product safety and prohibit abusive, unfair, and deceptive selling practices, federal and state governments have enacted a variety of statutes that regulate the behavior of businesses that deal with consumers. These laws are collectively referred to as **consumer protection laws**.

This chapter discusses administrative agencies and consumer protection laws.

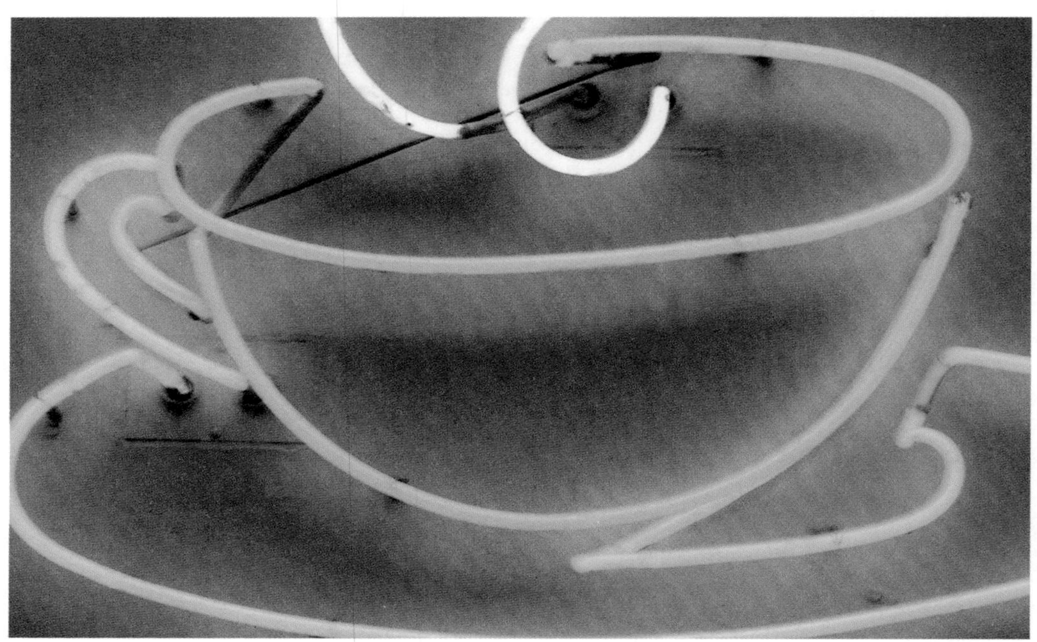

Sign on Restaurant. The shipment, distribution, and sale of adulterated food, and false labeling of food, are prohibited by the federal Food, Drug, and Cosmetic Act.

Government Regulation

The government's recordkeeping and reporting requirements form a large part of administrative law. Other government regulations concern proper business purpose and conduct, entry restrictions into an industry, government rate setting, and the like.

Proponents of government regulation argue that it is needed to protect consumers and others from unethical and deceptive business practices. Opponents say that the time and compliance and enforcement costs outweigh the benefits of regulation. The debate rages on, but one fact is certain: Government regulation will continue to affect business operations.

Business Brief

Businesses spend billions of dollars each year complying with government regulation.

General Government Regulation

Most government regulation applies to many businesses and industries collectively. For example, the National Labor Relations Board (NLRB) is empowered to regulate the formation and operation of labor unions in most industries, the Occupational Safety and Health Administration (OSHA) is authorized to formulate and enact safety and health standards for the workplace, the Consumer Product Safety Commission (CPSC) is empowered to establish mandatory safety standards for products sold in this country, and the Securities and Exchange Commission (SEC) is authorized to enforce federal securities laws that apply to issuers and persons who trade in securities.

Business Brief

Businesses are subject to *general government regulation* (e.g., antidiscrimination laws) that applies to many businesses and industries collectively.

Specific Government Regulation

Congress and the executive branch created some administrative agencies to monitor certain regulated industries. For example, the Federal Communications Commission (FCC) regulates the operation of television and radio stations, the Interstate Commerce Commission (ICC) regulates railroads, the Federal Aviation Administration (FAA) regulates commercial airlines, and the Office of the Comptroller of the Currency (OCC) regulates national banks. Although a detailed discussion of these agencies and the laws they administer is beyond the scope of this book, it is important to know that they exist.

Business Brief

Many industries are subject to specific regulation that regulates companies in each industry (e.g., banking television, railroads).

International Law

What Does "Made in America" Mean?

Many goods contain the label "Made in America." But what does this label really mean? In 1998, the Federal Trade Commission (FTC), the administrative agency charged with protecting consumers from deception, issued new standards that define "Made in America." The new standards try to balance domestic origin claims and the global marketplace.

The 1998 FTC guidelines require goods that are "substantially made" in the United States to bear the "Made in America" label. This new test rejects the "wholly domestic" 100 percent standard. Instead, the FTC states that a marketer may claim the "Made in America" label if either of the following "safe harbor" rules is met:

1. At least 75 percent of the total costs of manufacturing the product are U.S. manufacturing costs.
2. The final product was last "substantially transformed" in the United States. This rule requires that the manufacturing process results in a new and different article of commerce having a name, character, and use different than what existed prior to processing. For example, using foreign steel to make a new automobile qualifies, but adding a tail light to an already-made automobile would not.

The FTC guidelines also permit marketers to make qualified U.S. origin claims even where their products would not meet the unqualified "Made in America" label. For example, a product assembled in the United States but made primarily with foreign parts could be labeled "Made in USA of foreign parts."

The new labeling law is designed to protect consumers from false "Made in USA" claims. The FTC is empowered to seek sanctions against violators and to turn over fraudulent cases to the Department of Justice for criminal prosecution. ■

Administrative Agencies

Good government is an empire of laws.

John Adams
Thoughts on Government (1776)

Administrative agencies are generally established with the goal of creating a body of professionals who are experts in a particular field. These experts have delegated authority to regulate an individual industry or a specific area of commerce.

Administrative agencies are created by federal, state, and local governments. They range from large, complex federal agencies, such as the Department of Homeland Security, to local zoning boards. Many administrative agencies are given the authority to adopt **rules and regulations** that enforce and interpret statutory law. (The rule-making power of administrative agencies is discussed later in this chapter.)

rules and regulations
Laws that administrative agencies adopt to interpret the statutes that they are authorized to enforce.

Federal Administrative Agencies

The most pervasive government regulations have developed from the statutes enforced by and the rules and regulations adopted by **federal administrative agencies**. The majority of federal administrative agencies—including the Department of Justice, the Department of Housing and Urban Development, the Department of Labor, the Department of Transportation, and the Department of Commerce—are part of the executive branch of government.

federal administrative agencies
Administrative agencies that are part of the executive or legislative branch of government.

Congress has established many federal administrative agencies. These agencies are independent of the executive branch and have broad regulatory powers over key areas of the national economy. Many of these independent agencies are discussed elsewhere in this book.

State Administrative Agencies

All states have created administrative agencies to enforce and interpret state law. For example, most states have a corporations department to enforce state corporations law, a banking department to regulate the operation of banks, fish and game departments, and workers' compensation boards. **States administrative agencies** also have a profound effect on business. Local governments and municipalities create administrative agencies, such as zoning commissions, to administer local law.

state administrative agencies
Administrative agencies that states create to enforce and interpret state law.

In the following case, the U.S. Supreme Court had to determine the lawfulness of a government regulation.

Case 19.1
Administrative Law

U.S. SUPREME COURT CASE
National Cable & Telecommunications Association, Inc. v. Gulf Power Company
534 U.S. 327, 122 S.Ct. 782, 2002 U.S. Lexis 491 (2002)
Supreme Court of the United States

Background and Facts

Since the inception of cable television, cable companies have sought means to run wire into the home of each cable subscriber. They found it convenient to lease space on telephone and utility poles for their cable lines. Congress enacted the federal Pole Attachments Act, which requires the FCC to regulate this practice and to set reasonable rates, terms, and conditions of pole attachments.

Since the original act was passed, cable operators have developed broadband Internet service to provide over their cables. In addition, wireless telecommunications companies have sought to place attachments to poles to provide better wireless services. The FCC issued orders permitting both broadband Internet services over cable wires and wireless equipment attachments to poles. Certain pole-owning utilities challenged these orders as violating the FCC's statutory and regulatory authority. The FCC upheld the orders. The court of appeals reversed. The cable and wireless communications companies appealed to the U.S. Supreme Court.

Supreme Court Issue

Are the two attachments sought in this case—Internet services commingled with cable and wireless equipment attachments—covered by the Pole Attachments Act and therefore properly regulated by the FCC?

In The Language of The U.S. Supreme Court

Kennedy, Justice We turn first to the question whether the Act applies to attachments that provide high-speed Internet access at the same time as cable television, the commingled services at issue here.

No one disputes that a cable attached by a cable television company, which provides only cable television service, is an attachment "by a cable television system." If one day its cable provides high-speed Internet access, in addition to cable television service, the cable does not cease, at that instant, to be an attachment "by a cable television system." The addition of a service does not change the character of the attaching entity. And this is what matters under the statute.

This is our own, best reading of the statute, which we find unambiguous. If the statute were thought ambiguous, however, the FCC's reading must be accepted nonetheless, provided it is a reasonable interpretation.

The second question presented is whether and to what extent the equipment of wireless telecommunications providers is susceptible of FCC regulations under the Act. A provider of wireless telecommunications service is a provider of telecommunications service, so its attachment is a pole attachment. Attachments of wires by wireless providers of telecommunications service are covered by the Act. It follows, in our view, that wireless associated equipment which is indistinguishable from the associated equipment of wire-based telecommunications providers would also be covered. The proposed distinction—between prototypical wire-based associated equipment and the wireless associated equipment which allegedly falls outside of the rationale of the Act—finds no support in the text.

Decision and Remedy

The U.S. Supreme Court held that the attachments at issue—broadband Internet services offered over cable lines and wireless equipment—fall within the Pole Attachments Act. Therefore, the FCC's decision to assert jurisdiction over these pole attachments is reasonable. The judgment of the court of appeals was reversed, and the case was remanded for further proceedings, consistent with the Supreme Court's opinion.

Case Questions

Critical Legal Thinking Do you think the Supreme Court's interpretation of the Pole Attachments Act was reasonable? Why or why not?

Business Ethics Why did the owners of the poles bring this lawsuit? Explain.

Contemporary Business Is such government regulation as was at issue in this case—pole attachments—necessary? Do such regulations help or hinder business?

Entrepreneur and the Law

U.S. Department of Agriculture Administers Farming Laws

In May 1862, Congress created the **U.S. Department of Agriculture (USDA)** to administer the country's farm-oriented programs. The USDA, which is headed by the secretary of agriculture, a cabinet-level post, is composed of several administrative agencies and programs. Other federal administrative agencies (such as the Veterans Administration and the Environmental Protection Agency [EPA]) and state administrative agencies also have an impact on farming operations. The USDA may affect farmers through (1) rule making, (2) adjudication proceedings, and (3) reparation proceedings that decide disputes between private parties (discussed later).

The federal statutes administered by the USDA include the following:

- Agricultural Marketing Agreement Act
- Animal Quarantine Act
- Animal Welfare Act
- Archaeological Resources Protection Act
- Beef Research and Information Act
- Cotton Research and Promotion Act
- Egg Products Inspection Act
- Egg Research and Consumer Information Act
- Endangered Species Act
- Federal Land Policy and Management Act
- Federal Meat Inspection Act
- Federal Seed Act
- Horse Protection Act
- Meat Inspection Act
- Packers and Stockyards Act
- Perishable Agricultural Commodities Act
- Potato Research and Promotion Act
- Poultry Production Inspection Act
- Poultry Products Protection Act
- Swine Health Protection Act
- United States Cotton Standards Act
- United States Grain Standards Act
- United States Warehouse Act
- Virus-Serum-Toxin Act
- Wheat and Wheat Foods Research and Nutrition Education Act ■

Cattle. The USDA, a federal administrative agency, administers and enforces numerous federal statutes that regulate the safety of agricultural and food products.

Landmark Law

Administrative Procedure Act

In 1946, Congress enacted the **Administrative Procedure Act (APA)** [5 U.S.C. § § 551 et seq.]. This act establishes certain administrative procedures that federal administrative agencies must follow in conducting their affairs. For example, the APA establishes notice and hearing requirements, rules for conducting agency adjudicative actions, and procedures for rule making. Most states have enacted administrative procedural acts that govern state administrative agencies.

Administrative law judges (ALJs) preside over administrative proceedings. They decide questions of law and fact concerning the case. There is no jury. The ALJ is an employee of the administrative agency. Both the administrative agency and the respondent may be represented by counsel. Witnesses may be examined and cross-examined, evidence may be introduced, objections may be made, and such.

The ALJ's decision is issued in the form of an **order**. The order must state the reasons for the ALJ's decision.

The order becomes final if it is not appealed. An appeal consists of a review by the agency. The agency review can result in new findings of fact and law. Further appeal can be made to the appropriate federal court (in federal agency actions) or state court (in state agency actions). ■

Administrative Law

Business Brief

Administrative agencies are often criticized for creating too much "red tape" for businesses and individuals.

Administrative law is a combination of substantive and procedural law. Each federal administrative agency is empowered to administer a particular statute or statutes. For example, the SEC is authorized to enforce the Securities Act of 1933, the Securities Exchange Act of 1934, and other federal statutes dealing with securities markets. These statutes are the *substantive law* that is enforced by the agency.

Delegation of Powers

delegation doctrine

A doctrine that says that when an administrative agency is created, it is delegated certain powers; the agency can use only those legislative, judicial, and executive powers that are delegated to it.

Because the U.S. Constitution does not stipulate that administrative agencies are a separate branch of the government, they must be created by the legislative or executive branch. When an administrative agency is created, it is delegated certain powers. The agency has only the legislative, judicial, and executive powers that are delegated to it. This is called the **delegation doctrine**.

Thus, an agency can adopt a rule or regulation (a legislative function), prosecute a violation of the statute or rule (an executive function), and adjudicate the dispute (a judicial function). The courts have generally upheld this combined power of administrative agencies as being constitutional. If an administrative agency acts outside the scope of its delegated powers, it is an unconstitutional act.

Entrepreneur and the Law

Licensing Powers of Administrative Agencies

Statutes often require the issuance of a government *license* before a person can enter certain types of industries (e.g., the operation of banks, television, and radio stations, commercial airlines) or professions (e.g., doctors, lawyers, dentists, certified public accountants, contractors). Most administrative agencies have the power to determine whether to grant licenses to applicants.

Applicants must usually submit detailed applications to the appropriate administrative agency. In addition, the agency usually accepts written comments from interested parties and holds hearings on the matter. The administrative agency's decision is subject to judicial review. However, the courts generally defer to the expertise of administrative agencies in licensing matters. ■

Administrative Searches

Administrative agencies are usually granted powers, such as the investigation and prosecution of possible violations of statutes, administrative rules, and administrative orders. To perform these functions successfully, the agency must often obtain information from the persons and businesses under investigation as well as from other sources.

Sometimes a physical inspection of the business premises is crucial to an investigation. Most inspections by administrative agencies are considered "searches" that are subject to the Fourth Amendment of the U.S. Constitution. The Fourth Amendment protects persons (including businesses) from **unreasonable search and seizures.**

unreasonable search and seizure Any search and seizure by the government that violates the Fourth Amendment.

In the following cases, the U.S. Supreme Court had to decide whether searches of businesses by administrative agencies violated the Fourth Amendment.

U.S. SUPREME COURT CASE

Dow Chemical Company v. United States

476 U.S. 227, 106 S.Ct. 1819, 1986 U.S. Lexis 155 (1986)

Supreme Court of the United States

Case 19.2 Administrative Search

Background and Facts

Since the 1890s, Dow Chemical Company (Dow) has manufactured chemicals at a facility in Midland, Michigan. Its complex covers 2,000 acres and contains a number of chemical-processing plants. Many of these are "open-air" plants, with reactor equipment, loading and storage facilities, motors, transfer lines, and piping conduits located in the open areas between the buildings. Dow has undertaken elaborate precautions to secure the facility from unwelcome intrusion: An eight-foot-high chain-link fence completely surrounds the facility, security personnel guard the plant and monitor it by closed-circuit television, unauthorized entry into the facility triggers alarm systems, motion detectors indicate movement of persons within restricted areas, and the use of camera equipment by anyone other than authorized Dow personnel is prohibited. Dow considers its entire facility a trade secret.

The EPA is a federal administrative agency empowered to administer and enforce the federal Clean Air Act. In 1978, Dow denied an EPA request to conduct an on-site inspection of the Midland facility. The EPA did not seek an administrative search warrant. Instead, the EPA employed a commercial aerial photographer to take photographs of the facility from altitudes of 12,000, 3,000, and 1,200 feet. Using a standard floor-mounted, precision aerial-mapping camera, this firm took approximately 75 color photographs of various parts of the plant. When the photographs taken from 1,200 feet were enlarged, it was possible to discern equipment, pipes, and power lines as small as one-half inch in diameter.

Dow Chemical Company v. United States

476 U.S. 227, 106 S.Ct. 1819, 1986 U.S. Lexis 155 (1986)
Supreme Court of the United States
(continued)

Several weeks later, after Dow learned about the EPA-authorized flight from independent sources, it filed suit against the EPA. The district court held in favor of Dow and issued an injunction against the EPA's use of the photographs. The court of appeals reversed. Dow appealed.

Supreme Court Issue

Did the EPA's aerial photography of Dow's plant constitute an unreasonable search in violation of the Fourth Amendment to the U.S. Constitution?

In The Language of The U.S. Supreme Court

Burger, Chief Justice We turn to Dow's contention that taking aerial photographs constituted a search without warrant, thereby violating Dow's rights under the Fourth Amendment. Plainly a business establishment or an industrial or commercial facility enjoys certain protections under the Fourth Amendment. Dow plainly has a reasonable, legitimate, and objective expectation of privacy within the interior of its covered buildings, and it is equally clear that expectation is one society is prepared to observe. Dow's inner manufacturing areas are elaborately secured to ensure they are not open or exposed to the public from the ground. Any actual physical entry by EPA into any enclosed area would raise significantly different questions, because the businessman, like the occupant of a residence, has a constitutional right to go about his business free from unreasonable official entries upon his private commercial property.

The issue raised by Dow's claim of search and seizure, however, concerns aerial observation of a 2,000-acre outdoor manufacturing facility without physical entry. The intimate activities associated with family privacy and the home and its curtilage simply do not reach the outdoor areas or spaces between structures and buildings of a manufacturing plant. The government has greater latitude to conduct warrantless inspections of commercial property because the expectation of privacy that the owner enjoys in such property differs significantly from the sanctity accorded an individual's home. We emphasized that unlike a homeowner's interest in his dwelling, the interest of the owner of commercial property is not one in being free from any inspections. And with regard to regulatory inspections, we have held that what is observable by the public is observable without warrant, by the government inspector as well.

Here, EPA was not employing some unique sensory device that, for example, could penetrate the walls of buildings and record conversations in Dow's plants, offices, or laboratories, but rather a conventional, albeit precise, commercial camera commonly used in map making. It may well be, as the government concedes, that the surveillance of private property by using highly sophisticated surveillance equipment not generally available to the public, such as satellite technology, might be constitutionally proscribed absent warrant. But the photographs here are not so revealing of intimate details as to raise constitutional concerns. Although they undoubtedly give EPA more detailed information than naked-eye views, they remain limited to an outline of the facility's buildings and equipment. The mere fact that human vision is enhanced somewhat, at least to the degree here, does not give rise to constitutional problems.

Decision and Remedy

The Supreme Court held that the taking of photographs of an industrial plant complex from navigable airspace is not a search prohibited by the Fourth Amendment. Affirmed.

Case Questions

Critical Legal Thinking Should the government be given greater latitude to conduct warrantless searches of business property than personal homes? Why or why not?

Business Ethics Did the EPA act ethically in this case?

Contemporary Business Could Dow have in any way protected itself from the search conducted in this case?

Case 19.3 Administrative Search

U.S. SUPREME COURT CASE

New York v. Burger

482 U.S. 691, 107 S.Ct. 2636, 1987 U.S. Lexis 2725 (1987)
Supreme Court of the United States

Background and Facts

Joseph Burger is the owner of a junkyard in Brooklyn, New York. His business consists, in part, of dismantling automobiles and selling their parts. The State of New York enacted a statute that requires automobile junkyards to keep certain records. The statute authorizes warrantless searches of vehicle dismantlers and automobile junkyards without prior notice. At approximately noon on November 17, 1982, five plainclothes officers of the Auto Crimes Division of the New York City Police Department entered Burger's junkyard to conduct a surprise inspection. Burger did not have either a license to conduct the business or records of the automobiles and vehicle parts on his premises, as required by state law. After conducting an inspection of the premises, the officers determined that Burger was in possession of stolen vehicles and parts. He was arrested and charged with criminal possession of stolen property. Burger moved to suppress the evidence. The New York supreme court and appellate division held the search to be constitutional. The New York court of appeals reversed. New York appealed.

Supreme Court Issue

Does the warrantless search of an automobile junkyard pursuant to a state statute that authorizes such search constitute an unreasonable search and seizure in violation of the Fourth Amendment to the U.S. Constitution?

In The Language of The U.S. Supreme Court

Blackman, Justice The Court has long recognized that the Fourth Amendment's prohibition on unreasonable searches and seizures is applicable to commercial premises, as well as to private homes.

An expectation of privacy in commercial premises, however, is different from, and indeed less than, a similar expectation in an individual's home. This expectation is particularly attenuated in commercial property employed in "closely regulated" industries. Because the owner or operator of commercial premises in a closely regulated industry has a reduced expectation of privacy, the warrant and probable cause requirements—which fulfill the traditional Fourth Amendment standard of reasonableness for a government search—have a lessened application in this context. The nature of the regulatory statute reveals that the operation of a junkyard, part of which is devoted to vehicle dismantling, is a closely regulated business in the state of New York. A warrantless inspection of commercial premises may well be reasonable within the meaning of the Fourth Amendment.

The New York regulatory scheme satisfies the three criteria necessary to make reasonable warrantless inspections. First, the state has a substantial interest in regulating the vehicle dismantling and automobile junkyard industry because motor vehicle theft has increased in the state of New York and because the problem of theft is associated with this industry. Second, regulation of the vehicle dismantling industry reasonably serves the state's substantial interest in eradicating automobile theft. It is well established that the theft problem can be addressed effectively by controlling the receiver of, or market in, stolen property. Automobile junkyards and vehicle dismantlers provide the major market for stolen vehicles and vehicle parts. Third, the New York law provides a constitutionally adequate substitute for a warrant. The statute informs the operator of a vehicle dismantling business that inspections will be made on a regular basis.

Decision and Remedy

The U.S. Supreme Court held that the New York statute that authorizes warrantless searches of vehicle-dismantling businesses and automobile junkyards does not constitute an unreasonable search in violation of the Fourth Amendment to the U.S. Constitution. The Supreme Court reversed the judgment of the New York court of appeals and remanded the case for further proceedings, consistent with its decision.

Case Questions

Critical Legal Thinking Should the Fourth Amendment's protection against unreasonable searches and seizures apply to businesses? Why or why not?

Business Ethics Was it ethical for the defendant to assert the Fourth Amendment's prohibition against unreasonable search and seizure?

Contemporary Business Is auto theft a big business? Will the New York law that regulates vehicle-dismantling businesses and junkyards help to alleviate this crime?

The FDA's Administration of the Federal Food, Drug, and Cosmetic Act (FDCA)

The **Food and Drug Administration (FDA)**, a federal government agency, is empowered to regulate food, food additives, drugs, cosmetics, and medicinal devices.

Food and Drug Administration (FDA)
A federal administrative agency that administers and enforces the federal Food, Drug, and Cosmetic Act (FDCA) and other federal consumer protection laws.

Landmark Law

Federal Food, Drug, and Cosmetic Act

The first federal statute regulating the wholesomeness of food and drug products was enacted in 1906. A much more comprehensive act—the federal **Food, Drug, and Cosmetic Act (FDCA)**—was enacted in 1938 [21 U.S.C. § 301]. This act, as amended, provides the basis for the regulation of much of the testing, manufacture, distribution, and sale of foods, drugs, cosmetics, and medicinal products and devices in the United States. The act is administered by the **FDA**.

Before certain food additives, drugs, cosmetics, and medicinal devices can be sold to the public, they must receive FDA approval. An applicant must submit an application to the FDA that contains relevant information about the safety and uses of the product. The FDA, after considering the evidence, will either approve or deny the application.

The FDA can seek search warrants and conduct inspections; obtain orders for the seizure, recall, and condemnation of products; seek injunctions; and turn over suspected criminal violations to the U.S. Department of Justice for prosecution. ■

Regulation of Food

Food, Drug, and Cosmetic Act (FDCA)
A federal statute enacted in 1938 that provides the basis for the regulation of much of the testing, manufacture, distribution, and sale of foods, drugs, cosmetics, and medicinal products.

The **Food, Drug, and Cosmetic Act (FDCA)** prohibits the shipment, distribution, or sale of *adulterated food*. Food is deemed adulterated if it consists in whole or in part of any "filthy, putrid, or decomposed substance" or if it is otherwise "unfit for food." Note that food does not have to be entirely pure to be distributed or sold—it only has to be unadulterated.

The FDCA also prohibits *false and misleading labeling* of food products. In addition, it mandates affirmative disclosure of information on food labels, including the name of the food, the name and place of the manufacturer, and a statement of ingredients. A manufacturer may be held liable for deceptive labeling or packaging.

In 1995, the FDA issued new regulations that establish safety standards for seafood and shellfish. The FDA is authorized to conduct inspections of seafood processors to ensure compliance with these new regulations.

Contemporary Business Environment

A Hidden Source of Protein in Peanut Butter

So you take a big bite of a peanut butter sandwich and savor the taste. It has been processed by a food manufacturer and inspected by the federal government, so you think that it is pure peanut butter. Not necessarily. Under federal FDA guidelines, peanut butter may contain up to 30 insect fragments per 3 ounces and still be considered "safe" for human consumption.

The FDA has set ceilings, or "action levels," for certain contaminants, or "defects," as the FDA likes to call them, for various foods. Several of these action levels are

- Golden raisins—35 fly eggs per 8 ounces
- Popcorn—two rodent hairs per pound
- Shelled peanuts—20 insects per 100 pounds
- Canned mushrooms—20 maggots per 3 1/2 ounces
- Tomato juice—10 fly eggs per 3 1/2 ounces

The FDA can mount inspections and raids to enforce its action levels. If it finds that the federal tolerance system has been violated, it can seize the offending food and destroy it at the owner's expense. For example, in the Great Peanut Raid of 1991, the FDA seized 8.5 million pounds of peanuts shipped to the United States from foreign countries. The FDA found that these peanuts contained illegal levels of contamination and sent them back to their home countries.

The courts have upheld the presence of some contamination in food as lawful under the federal FDCA. For example, in one case the court found that 28 insect parts in 9 pounds of butter did not violate the act. The court stated, "Few foods contain no natural or unavoidable defects. Even with modern technology, all defects in foods cannot be eliminated." [*United States v. Capital City Foods, Inc.*, 345 F. Supp. 277, 1972 U.S. Dist. Lexis 12796 (ND 1972)] ■

Beverly Hills, California. Restaurants and other food providers are subject to stringent state and federal health and consumer protection laws.

Business Ethics

Less Baloney on the Shelves

For much of its existence, the federal FDA has been a paper tiger that was led by wine-and-dine-with-the-industry regulators. In April 1991, the FDA shocked the food industry by having U.S. marshals seize 24,000 half-gallon cartons of "Citrus Hill Fresh Choice" orange juice, which is made by mammoth food processor Proctor & Gamble (P&G). After trying for a year to get P&G to remove the word *fresh* from the carton—the product is made from concentrate and is pasteurized—the FDA finally got tough. P&G gave in after two days and agreed to remove the word *fresh* from its Citrus Hill products.

Next on the FDA's hit list were Best Foods, which markets Mazola Corn Oil; Great Foods of America, makers of HeartBeat Canola Oil; and again P&G, manufacturer of Crisco Corn Oil. These companies had prominently advertised their cooking oils as having "no cholesterol," and some even added cute little hearts to the label. Although the claim was literally true (these oils do not contain cholesterol), they are in fact 100% fat—which is not especially good for the heart. The FDA felt that these companies were hoodwinking the public and ordered the companies to take the "no cholesterol" labels off their vegetable oils.

In late 1990, Congress passed a sweeping truth-in-labeling law called the **Nutrition Labeling and Education Act**. The statute requires food manufacturers and processors to provide more nutritional information on virtually all foods and bars them from making scientifically unsubstantiated health claims.

This law requires the more than 20,000 food labels found on grocery store shelves to disclose the number of calories derived from fat and the amount of dietary fiber, saturated fat, cholesterol, and a variety of other substances. The law applies to packaged foods as well as fruits, vegetables, and raw seafood. Meat, poultry, and egg products, which are regulated by the Department of Agriculture, are exempt from the act.

In December 1992, the FDA announced final regulations to implement the act. The regulations require food processors to provide uniform information about serving sizes and nutrients on labels of the food products they sell and establish standard definitions for *light, low fat, natural*, and other terms routinely bandied about by food processors.

With the new law on the books and a tough new stand, the FDA is coming out of its corner with its gloves on. The American consumer can only come out a winner.

1. Did Proctor & Gamble act ethically when it used the word *fresh* on its orange juice cartons? Why do you think it did this?
2. Do you think labeling laws serve a useful purpose? Explain.

Regulation of Drugs

The FDCA gives the FDA the authority to regulate the testing, manufacture, distribution, and sale of drugs. The **Drug Amendment to the FDCA**,[1] enacted in 1962, gives the FDA broad powers to license new drugs in the United States. After a new drug application is filed, the FDA holds a hearing and investigates the merits of the application. This process can take many years. The FDA may withdraw approval of any previously licensed drug.

This law requires all users of prescription and nonprescription drugs to receive proper directions for use (including the method and duration of use) and adequate warnings about any related side effects. The manufacture, distribution, and sale of adulterated or misbranded drugs are prohibited.

In the following case, the U.S. Supreme Court held that the FDA, a federal administrative agency, could not regulate tobacco as a drug.

Web Site

U.S. Food and Drug Administration
The FDA's Web site links you to information about foods, human drugs, animal drugs, cosmetics, and many other subjects. Visit at **www.fda.gov.**

Case 19.4 Regulation of a "Drug"

U.S. SUPREME COURT CASE

Food and Drug Administration v. Brown & Williamson Tobacco Corporation

529 U.S. 120, 120 S.Ct. 1291, 2000 U.S. Lexis 2195, (2000)
Supreme Court of the United States

Background and Facts

The FDA is a federal administrative agency empowered to administer the FDCA. Pursuant to this act, the FDA can regulate "drugs" and medical "devices." Based on its perceived power under FDCA, the FDA enacted a rule regulating tobacco products. The rule:

Food and Drug Administration v. Brown & Williamson Tobacco Corporation

529 U.S. 120, 120 S.Ct. 1291, 2000 U.S. Lexis 2195, (2000)
Supreme Court of the United States
(continued)

1. Prohibits the sale of cigarettes and smokeless tobacco to persons younger than 18.
2. Requires retailers to verify through photo identification the age of all purchasers younger than 27.
3. Prohibits the sale of cigarettes in quantities smaller than 20.
4. Prohibits the distribution of free samples.
5. Prohibits sales through self-service displays and vending machines except in adult-only locations.
6. Requires print advertising to appear in black-and-white, text-only format.
7. Prohibits outdoor advertising within 1,000 feet of any public school or playground.
8. Prohibits the distribution of any promotional items, such as t-shirts or hats, bearing the manufacturer's brand.
9. Prohibits a manufacturer from sponsoring any athletic, musical, artistic, or other social or cultural event using its brand name.
10. Requires that the statement "A Nicotine-Delivery Device for Persons 18 or Older" appear on all tobacco products.

A group of tobacco manufacturers and advertisers filed a lawsuit in district court, asserting that the FDA did not have authority to regulate tobacco as a "drug" or "device" that delivered nicotine to the body. The district court certified the issue to the court of appeals, which held that the FDCA did not grant the FDA power to regulate tobacco products. The U.S. Supreme Court granted certiorari to hear the appeal.

Supreme Court Issue

Does the FDCA grant the FDA authority to regulate tobacco products as a "drug" or "device"?

In The Language of The U.S. Supreme Court

O'Connor, Justice Regardless of how serious the problem an administrative agency seeks to address, however, it may not exercise its authority in a manner that is inconsistent with the administrative structure that Congress enacted into law. Congress has foreclosed the removal of tobacco products from the market. A provision of the United States Code currently in force states that "the marketing of tobacco constitutes one of the greatest basic industries of the United States with ramifying activities which directly affect interstate and foreign commerce at every point, and stable conditions therein are necessary to the general welfare." More importantly, Congress has directly addressed the problem of tobacco and health through legislation on six occasions since 1965. See Federal Cigarette Labeling and Advertising Act (FCLAA), Public Health Cigarette Smoking Act of 1969, Alcohol and Drug Abuse Amendments of 1983, Comprehensive Smoking Education Act, Comprehensive Smokeless Tobacco Health Education Act of 1986, and Alcohol, Drug Abuse, and Mental Health Administration Reorganization Act. When Congress enacted these statutes, the adverse health consequences of tobacco use were well known, as were nicotine's pharmacological effects. Nonetheless, Congress stopped well short of ordering a ban. Instead, it has generally regulated the labeling and advertisement of tobacco products.

Considering the FDC Act as a whole, it is clear that Congress intended to exclude tobacco products from the FDA's jurisdiction. A fundamental precept of the FDC Act is that any product regulated by the FDA—but not banned—must b safe for its intended use. Consequently, if tobacco products were within the FDA's jurisdiction, the FDC Act would require the FDA to remove them from the market entirely. But a ban would contradict Congress' clear intent as expressed in its more recent, tobacco-specific legislation. The inescapable conclusion is that there is no room for tobacco products within the FDC Act's regulatory scheme.

By no means do we question the seriousness of the problem that the FDA has sought to address. The agency has amply demonstrated that tobacco use, particularly among children and adolescents, poses perhaps the single most significant threat to public health in the United States. Nonetheless, no matter how important, conspicuous, and controversial the issue, an administrative agency's power to regulate in the public interest must always be grounded in a valid grant of authority from Congress. And, in our anxiety to effectuate the congressional purpose of protecting the public, we must take care not to extend the scope of the statute beyond the point where Congress indicated it would stop. Reading the FDC Act as a whole, as well as in conjunction with Congress' subsequent tobacco-specific legislation, it is plain that Congress has not given the FDA the authority that it seeks to exercise here.

Decision and Remedy

The U.S Supreme Court held that the FDA does not have authority under the FDCA to regulate tobacco products as a "drug" or "device." The judgment of the court of the appeal was affirmed.

Case Questions

Critical Legal Thinking Did the FDA exceed its delegated authority under the FDCA by enacting its tobacco products rules?

Business Ethics Do you think that the cigarette companies have "bought off" Congress? Explain your answer.

Contemporary Business Do the state and federal governments have a stake in cigarette product sales? What economic effects would a ban on cigarette sales cause to state and federal governments?

Business Ethics

Sometimes Viagra Stirs the Heart too Quickly

The anti-impotency drug Viagra, introduced in 1997, was heralded as the most important drug to hit the market since the birth control pill. Viagra is prescribed by doctors to male patients who cannot have or have trouble getting erections, and it helps such men have intercourse. It became wildly successful and is now used by millions of men worldwide. In the United States, the FDA approved the drug for use by the general public. A black market for Viagra has developed in countries where the drug has not been given government approval. Pfizer, the manufacturer of the drug, is receiving a financial bounty from its now-famous drug.

It seems, however, that Viagra not only gets men's hearts stirring again, but it may also cause their hearts to explode, literally. After hundreds of deaths of men taking the drug were reported, the FDA investigated and found that men with certain health predispositions may be at risk of death if they take Viagra. Therefore, the FDA now requires Viagra labels to warn individuals with the following conditions to be careful when taking the drug:

- Men who have had a heart attack or an irregular heartbeat in the past six months.
- Men who have a history of cardiac failure or coronary artery disease that caused angina.
- Men who have significant high or low blood pressure.

Viagra causes visual disturbance—particularly the ability to distinguish between blue and green—in about 3 percent of the men who use it. And Viagra sometimes works too well, causing priapism, or painful erections that last up to four hours. Doctors and consumers must also be warned against these conditions.

Pfizer asserts that its explosively popular drug was not the culprit in the reported deaths, but that the drug was taken by men with health problems who should have not used it. By requiring the new warnings, the FDA wants men with the noted risk factors to first ask, "Is sex a good idea for me?" before taking Viagra.

1. Are there risks in taking many of the prescription drugs on the market today?
2. In applying a cost–benefit analysis to the development and marketing of a drug, when is the point reached where the cost (in injuries, side effects, and deaths) exceeds the benefits to society? Discuss.

Regulation of Cosmetics

The FDA's definition of cosmetics includes substances and preparations for cleansing, altering the appearance of, and promoting the attractiveness of a person. For example, eye shadow and other facial makeup are cosmetics subject to FDA regulation. Ordinary household soap is expressly exempted from this definition.

The FDA has issued regulations that require cosmetics to be labeled, to disclose ingredients, and to contain warnings if they are carcinogenic (cancer causing) or otherwise dangerous to a person's health. The manufacture, distribution, and sale of adulterated or misbranded cosmetics are prohibited. The FDA may remove from commerce cosmetics that contain unsubstantiated claims of preserving youth, increasing vitality, growing hair, and such.

Ethics Brief

The federal Public Health Cigarette Smoking Act of 1985 requires cigarette manufacturers to place certain warnings on cigarette packages. Do you think these warnings adequately warn consumers of the dangers of smoking?

Regulation of Medicinal Devices

In 1976, Congress enacted the **Medical Devices Amendments to the FDCA.**[2] This amendment gives the FDA authority to regulate medical devices, such as heart pacemakers, kidney dialysis machines, defibrillators, surgical equipment, and other diagnostic, therapeutic, and health devices. The mislabeling of such devices is prohibited. The FDA is empowered to remove "quack" devices from the market.

In the following case, the U.S. Supreme Court had to decide whether the FDCA preempted a state law lawsuit.

Medical Devices Amendments to the FDCA

Amendments enacted in 1976 that gives the FDA authority to regulate medical devices and equipment.

U.S. SUPREME COURT CASE

Buckman Company v. Plaintiffs' Legal Committee

531 U.S. 341, 121 S.Ct. 1012, 2001 U.S. Lexis 1701 (2001)

Supreme Court of the United States

Case 19.5

Federal Preemption

Background and Facts

The AcroMed Corporation developed orthopedic bone screws to be placed in the pedicles of patients' spines during surgical operations. With the help of Buckman Company, a consulting service, AcroMed filed applications with the FDA, a federal administrative agency, for approval to sell this medical device. The federal FDCA and the Medical Device Amendments of 1976 (MDA), federal statutes, required the FDA's approval before the device could be marketed. After reviewing the information submitted by AcroMed and Buckman, the FDA approved the device for sale. The bone screws have been used in thousands of surgical operations.

However, more than 2,000 lawsuits were filed by patients who had the bone screws installed, claiming that they have been injured by the screws. The plaintiffs based their lawsuits on state law tort claims that fraud had been committed on the FDA by AcroMed and Buckman in the information submitted in the applications filed with the FDA. The defendants brought a motion to have the cases dismissed, alleging that the plaintiffs were prohibited from suing for "fraud on the FDA" because the federal law—the FDCA and MDA—preempted any state law tort claim. The district court dismissed the plaintiffs' cases, but the court of appeals reversed, allowing the plaintiffs to sue. The U.S. Supreme Court granted review.

Supreme Court Issue

Is the plaintiffs' state law "fraud on the FDA" tort claim preempted by federal law?

In The Language of The U.S. Supreme Court

Policing fraud against federal agencies is hardly a field which the States have traditionally occupied. To the contrary, the relationship between a federal agency and the entity it regulates is inherently federal in character because the relationship originates from, is governed by, and terminates according to federal law. Given this analytical framework, we hold that the plaintiffs' state-law fraud-on-the-FDA claims conflict with, and are therefore impliedly preempted by federal law. The conflict stems from the fact that the federal statutory scheme amply empowers the FDA to punish and deter fraud against the Agency, and that this authority is used by the Agency to achieve a somewhat delicate balance of statutory objectives. The balance sought by the Agency can be skewed by allowing fraud-on-the FDA claims under state tort law.

Decision and Remedy

The U.S. Supreme Court held that the plaintiffs' state law "fraud on the FDA" tort claim was preempted by valid federal law. The cases against the defendants were dismissed.

Case Questions

Critical Legal Thinking What does the "fraud on the FDA" claim state? Why did the Supreme Court hold that the plaintiffs could not assert this theory?

Business Ethics Was it ethical for the defendants to try to avoid facing the merits of the lawsuit rather than hide behind the federal preemption doctrine?

Contemporary Business Do you think consumers are adequately protected by the federal FDA? Why or why not?

Other Acts Administered by the FDA

Business Brief

In many FDA actions, the proceeding is brought against the product.

In addition to the FDCA, the FDA administers the following statutes and amendments to the FDCA:

- ***Pesticide Amendment of 1954***[3] Authorizes the FDA to establish tolerances for pesticides used on agricultural products.
- ***Food Additives Amendment of 1958***[4] Requires FDA approval of new food ingredients or articles that come in contact with food, such as wrapping and packaging materials.
- ***Color Additives Amendment of 1960***[5] Requires FDA approval of color additives used in foods, drugs, and cosmetics.
- ***Animal Drug Amendment of 1968***[6] Requires FDA approval of any new animal drug or additive to animal food.
- ***Biologies Act of 1902***[7] Gives the FDA power to regulate biological products, including vaccines, blood, blood components and derivatives, and allergenic products.

Things are seldom what they seem.
Skim milk masquerades as cream.
Highlows pass as patent leathers.
Jackdaws strut in peacock's feathers.

William S. Gilbert
H.M.S. Pinafore, Act II

- ***Section 361 of the Public Health Service Act***[8] Gives the FDA power to regulate and set standards for sanitation at food service establishments (including colleges and universities) and on interstate carriers (e.g., airlines and railroads).
- ***Section 354 of the Public Health Service Act***[9] and the ***Radiation for Health and Safety Act of 1968***[10] Empower the FDA to regulate the manufacture, distribution, and use of x-ray machines, microwave ovens, ultrasound equipment, and other products that are capable of emitting radiation.

International Law

United Nations Biosafety Protocol for Genetically Altered Foods

Many food processors in the United States and around the world genetically modify some foods by adding genes from other organisms to help crops grow faster or ward off pests. In the past, food processors did not notify consumers that they were purchasing genetically modified agricultural products. Although the companies insist that genetically altered foods are safe, consumers and many countries began to demand that such foods be clearly labeled so that buyers could decide for themselves. When most large food processors balked at this idea, the consumers went to their lawmakers.

The most concerned countries in the world regarding this issue were in Europe. Led by Germany, many European countries wanted to require genetically engineered food products to be labeled as such and be transported separately from nonaltered agricultural products. Some European countries wanted genetically altered foods to be banned completely. The United States, a major exporter of agricultural products and the leader in the development of biotech foods, argued that these countries were using this issue to erect trade barriers to keep U.S.-produced food products out of their countries in violation of international trade treaties and conventions administered by the World Trade Organization (WTO), which had reduced or eliminated many international trade restrictions.

In January 2000, a compromise was reached when 138 countries, including the United States, agreed to the United Nations–sponsored **Biosafety Protocol**. After much negotiation, the countries agreed that all genetically engineered foods would be clearly labeled with the phrase "May contain living modified organisms." This allows consumers to decide on their own whether to purchase such altered food products. In addition, the containers in which such goods are shipped must also be clearly marked as containing genetically altered food products. This compromise ensures that new biosafety labeling rules will coexist with the free trade agreements of the WTO. ■

Morocco. Many other countries of the world have different means of distributing and regulating the production and sale of food products than the United States.

Regulation of Product Safety

To promote product safety, the federal government has enacted several statutes that directly regulate the manufacture and distribution of consumer products.[11] These acts are discussed in the paragraphs that follow.

Consumer Product Safety Act (CPSA)

Consumer Product Safety Act (CPSA)
A federal statute that created the Consumer Product Safety Commission regulates potentially dangerous consumer products.

Web Site
Consumer Product Safety Commission The mandate of the CPSC is "to protect the public against unreasonable risks of injuries and deaths associated with consumer products." You can find out about unsafe products and recalls from this site. Visit at **www.cpsc.gov.**.

In 1972, Congress enacted the **Consumer Product Safety Act (CPSA)**[12] that created the **Consumer Product Safety Commission (CPSC)**. The CPSC is an independent federal regulatory agency empowered to (1) adopt rules and regulations to interpret and enforce the CPSA, (2) conduct research on the safety of consumer products, and (3) collect data regarding injuries caused by consumer products. Certain consumer products, including motor vehicles, boats, aircraft, and firearms, are regulated by other government agencies.

Because the CPSC regulates potentially dangerous consumer products, it issues product safety standards for consumer products that pose an unreasonable risk of injury. If a consumer product is found to be imminently hazardous—that is, its use can cause an unreasonable risk of death or serious injury or illness—the manufacturer can be required to recall, repair, or replace the product or take other corrective action. Alternatively, the CPSC can seek injunctions, bring actions to seize hazardous consumer products, see civil penalties for knowing violations of the act or CPSC rules, and seek criminal penalties for knowing and willful violations of the act or of CPSC rules. A private party can sue for an injunction to prevent violations of the act or of CPSC rules and regulations.

Business Ethics

Should All-Terrain Vehicles Be Grounded?

All-terrain vehicles (ATVs) are three- and four-wheeled motorized vehicles generally characterized by large low-pressure tires, a relatively high center of gravity, a seat designed to be straddled by the operator, and handlebars for steering. They are sold by a variety of manufacturers.

ATVs are intended for off-road, recreational use over rough roads and various nonpaved terrain. The ATV industry's television and print advertising promotes ATVs as "family fun vehicles" that pose little danger to their operators. The truth is that ATVs are extremely dangerous, particularly when operated by inexperienced youthful riders. The danger of death or serious injury associated with the operation of ATVs has received wide public attention. Both the Senate and the House of Representatives have held hearings concerning the dangers of ATVs.

In December 1986, after receiving substantial public comment, the CPSC filed an emergency action in federal district court against the manufacturers of ATVs. The CPSC formally referred the matter to the U.S. Department of Justice to seek a judicial declaration that ATVs present an "imminent and unreasonable risk of death, serious illness, and severe personal injury."

The case never made it to trial, however. The CPSC and the defendant ATV and manufacturers entered into a settlement whereby the defendants signed a consent decree in which they agreed to discontinue the "family fun" advertising of ATVs, provide warnings of their danger, publish manuals for their safe operation, provide training to ATV buyers, and set age-limit restrictions for the sale and use of certain ATV models. The CPSC agreed to the settlement because it was designed to alert consumers and would help reduce the hazards of using ATVs.

Several consumer groups thought that the CPSC had sold out and sought to intervene in the action to compel it to get tougher. Some consumer groups wanted an outright ban on the sale of ATVs in this country. The court of appeals rejected the interveners' arguments and upheld the consent decree. The court held that the settlement reached between the CPSC and the ATV industry was "fair, adequate, reasonable, and in the general public interest." The court stated, "No decree designed to protect consumers has ever gone this far in meeting such a massive national consumer problem." [*United States v. American Honda Motor Co., Inc.*, 143 F.R.D. 1 (D.D.C. 1992)]

1. Do you think that the CPSC acted in the public's best interest by entering into the consent decree with the ATV industry?
2. Should the government just "butt out" and let consumers assume the risk of dangerous activities in which they want to participate?

Fair Packaging and Labeling Act

The **Fair Packaging and Labeling Act**[13] requires the labels on consumer goods to identify the product; the manufacturer, processor, or packager of the product and its address; the net quantity of the contents of the package; and the quantity of each serving if the number of servings is stated. The label must use simple and clear language that a consumer can understand. This act is administered by the FTC and Department of Health and Human Services.

Fair Packaging and Labeling Act A federal statute that requires the labels on consumer goods to identify the product; the manufacturer, processor, or packager of the product and its address; the net quantity of the contents of the package; and the quantity of each serving.

Poison Prevention Packaging Act

Many children suffer serious injury or death when they open household products and inhale, ingest, or otherwise mishandle dangerous products. The **Poison Prevention Packaging Act**[14] is intended to avoid this problem by requiring manufacturers to provide "childproof" containers and packages for all household products.

Business Ethics

Lemon Laws Protect Consumers from Sour Deals

In the past, consumers who purchased automobiles and other vehicles that developed nagging mechanical problems had to try to convince the dealer or manufacturer to correct the problem. If the problem was not corrected, the consumer's only recourse was to seek redress through costly and time-consuming litigation. Today, most states have enacted **lemon laws**, which give consumers a new weapon in this battle.

Lemon laws provide a procedure for consumers to follow to correct recurring problems in vehicles. Lemon laws establish an administrative procedure that is less formal than a court proceeding. Most of these laws require that an arbitrator decide the dispute between a consumer and car dealer. Lemon laws stipulate that if the dealer or manufacturer does not correct a recurring defect in a vehicle within a specified number of tries (e.g., four tries) within a specified period of time (e.g., two years), the purchaser can rescind the purchase and recover a full refund of the vehicle's purchase price.

To properly invoke a state's lemon law, a consumer should take the following steps:

- Notify the car dealer immediately of any mechanical or other problems that develop in the vehicle.
- Take the vehicle back to the dealer for the statutory number of times to give the dealer the opportunity to correct the defects.
- File a claim with the appropriate state agency, seeking arbitration of the claim if the defect is not corrected during the number of times and time period established by the state's lemon law.
- Attend the arbitration hearing and present evidence to substantiate the claim that the vehicle suffered from a defect that was not corrected by the dealer or manufacturer within the statutorily presented period.

1. In general, do you think automobile dealerships are very scrupulous?
2. Are lemon laws needed to protect consumers? ■

Unfair and Deceptive Practices

Sellers sometimes engage in unfair, deceptive, or abusive sales techniques. If these practices result in fraud, an injured consumer can bring a civil action to recover damages. Such actions are not always brought, though, because it is difficult, costly, and time-consuming to prove fraud. Therefore, the federal government has enacted statutes to regulate seller's behavior.

Section 5 of the Federal Trade Commission Act

The **Federal Trade Commission Act (FTC Act)** was enacted in 1914.[15] The **Federal Trade Commission (FTC)** was created the following year. The FTC is empowered to enforce the FTC Act as well as other federal consumer protection statutes.

Federal Trade Commission (FTC) A federal administrative agency empowered to enforce the Federal Trade Commission Act and other federal consumer protection statutes.

China. Consumer and environmental protection regulation is being developed by countries worldwide.

Section 5 of the FTC Act

A portion of the FTC Act that prohibits *unfair and deceptive* practices.

Like a gun that fires at the muzzle and kicks over at the breach, a cheating transaction hurts the cheater as much as the man cheated.

Henry Ward Beecher
Proverbs from Plymouth Pulpit (1887)

Web Site

FTC—Bureau of Consumer Protection This bureau's mandate is to protect consumers against unfair, deceptive, or fraudulent practices. It enforces a variety of consumer protection laws, as well as trade-regulation rules. Visit at **www.ftc.gov/bcp/bcp.htm**.

Section 5 of the FTC Act, as amended, prohibits *unfair and deceptive practices*. It has been used extensively to regulate business conduct. This section gives the FTC the authority to bring an administrative proceeding to attack a deceptive or unfair practice. If, after a public administrative hearing, the FTC finds a violation of Section 5, it may order a cease- and-desist order, an affirmative disclosure to consumers, corrective advertising, or the like. The FTC may sue in state or federal court to obtain compensation on behalf of consumers. The decision of the FTC may be appealed to federal court.

False and Deceptive Advertising

Advertising is false and deceptive under Section 5 if it (1) contains misinformation or omits important information that is likely to mislead a "reasonable consumer" or (2) makes an unsubstantiated claim (e.g., "This product is 33 percent better than our competitor's"). Proof of actual deception is not required. Statements of opinion and "sales talk" (e.g., "This is a great car") do not constitute deceptive advertising.

In the following case, the U.S. Supreme Court found false and deceptive advertising in violation of Section 5 of the FTC Act.

U.S. SUPREME COURT CASE

Federal Trade Commission v. Colgate-Palmolive Co.

380 U.S. 374, 85 S.Ct. 1035, 1965 U.S. Lexis 2300 (1965)

Supreme Court of the United States

Case 19.6

Consumer Protection

Background and Facts

The Colgate-Palmolive Co. (Colgate), manufactures and sells a shaving cream called "Rapid Shave." Colgate hired Ted Bates & Company (Bates), an advertising agency, to prepare television commercials designed to show that Rapid Shave could shave the toughest beards. With Colgate's consent, Bates prepared a television commercial that included the sandpaper test. The announcer informed the audience, "To prove Rapid Shave's super-moisturizing power, we put it right from this can onto this tough, dry sandpaper. And off in a stroke."

While the announcer was speaking, Rapid Shave was applied to a substance that appeared to be sandpaper, and immediately a razor was shown shaving the substance clean. Evidence showed that the substance resembling sandpaper was in fact a simulated prop or "mock-up" made of Plexiglas to which sand had been glued. The FTC issued a complaint against Colgate and Bates, alleging a violation of Section 5 of the FTC Act. The FTC held against the defendants. The court of appeals reversed. The FTC appealed to the U.S. Supreme Court.

Supreme Court Issue

Did the defendants engage in false and deceptive advertising in violation of Section 5 of the FTC Act?

In The Language of The U.S. Supreme Court

Warren, Chief Justice We agree with the FTC that the undisclosed use of Plexiglas in the present commercial was a material deceptive practice. Respondents claim that it will be impractical to inform the viewing public that it is not seeing an actual test, experiment or demonstration, but we think it inconceivable that the ingenious advertising world will be unable, if it so desires, to conform to the FTC's insistence that the public be not misinformed.

If, however, it becomes impossible or impractical to show simulated demonstrations on television in a truthful manner, this indicates that television is not a medium that lends itself to this type of commercial, not that the commercial must survive at all costs. Similarly unpersuasive is respondents' objection that the FTC's decision discriminates against sellers whose product claims cannot be verified on television without the use of stimulation. All methods of advertising do not equally favor every seller. If the inherent limitations of a method do not permit its use in the way a seller desires, the seller cannot by material misrepresentation compensate for those limitations.

The court of appeals could find no difference between the Rapid Shave commercial and a commercial which extolled the goodness of ice cream while giving viewers a picture of a scoop of mashed potatoes appearing to be ice cream. We do not understand this difficulty. In the ice cream case the mashed potatoes prop is not being used for additional proof of the product claim, while the purpose of the Rapid Shave commercial is to give the viewer objective proof of the claims made. If in the ice cream hypothetical the focus of the commercial becomes the undisclosed potato prop and the viewer is invited, explicitly or by implication, to see for himself the truth of the claims about the ice cream's rich texture and full color, and perhaps compared to a rival product, then the commercial has become similar to the one now before us. Clearly, however, a commercial which depicts happy actors delightedly eating ice cream that is in fact mashed potatoes or drinking a product appearing to be coffee but which is in fact some other substance is not covered by the present order.

Decision and Remedy

The U.S. Supreme Court held that Colgate and Bates had engaged in false and deceptive advertising. Reversed and remanded.

Case Questions

Critical Legal Thinking Does the government owe a duty to protect consumers from false and misleading business practices?

Business Ethics Did Colgate and Bates act ethically in this case? Do you think the viewing public believed the commercial?

Contemporary Business Do you think Colgate needed "some fencing in"?

Bait and Switch

Bait and switch is another type of deceptive advertising under Section 5. It occurs when a seller advertises the availability of a low-cost discounted item (the "bait") to attract customers to its store. Once the customers are in the store, however, the seller pressures them to purchase more expensive merchandise (the "switch").

It is often difficult to determine when a seller has engaged in this practice. The FTC states that a bait and switch occurs if the seller refuses to show consumers the advertised merchandise, discourages employees from selling the advertised merchandise, or fails to have adequate quantities of the merchandise available.

bait and switch
A type of deceptive advertising that occurs when a seller advertises the availability of a low-cost discounted item but then pressures the buyer into purchasing more expensive merchandise.

Door-to-Door Sales

Some salespersons sell merchandise and services door-to-door. In some situations, these salespersons use aggressive sales tactics to overcome a consumer's resistance to the sale. To protect consumers from ill-advised decisions, many states have enacted laws that give the consumer a certain number of days to rescind (cancel) a door-to-door sales contract. The usual period is three days. The consumer must send a required notice of cancellation to the seller. An FTC regulation requires the salesperson to permit cancellation of the contract within the stipulated time.

Business Brief
Many states have enacted statutes that permit consumers to rescind contracts made at home with door-to-door sales representatives within a three-day period after signing the contract.

Unsolicited Merchandise

Postal Reorganization Act An act that makes the mailing of unsolicited merchandise an unfair trade practice.

The **Postal Reorganization Act**[16] makes the mailing of unsolicited merchandise an unfair trade practice. The act permits persons who receive unsolicited merchandise through the mail to retain, use, discard, or otherwise dispose of the merchandise without incurring any obligation to pay for it or return it. Unsolicited mailings by charitable organizations and mailings made by mistake are excepted from this rule.

Business Ethics

Kraft No Longer the "Big Cheese"

Kraft, Inc. (Kraft), the king of cheese producers in the United States, makes and sells Singles American Pasteurized Process Cheese slices (Singles) that can be used on sandwiches and for other purposes. When Kraft's dominant position in this market began to be eroded by imitation cheese slices made from vegetable oil and other products, Kraft designed a new advertising campaign to tout the health benefits of its Singles. In its campaign, Kraft advertised that (1) a slice of its Singles contained the same amount of calcium as five ounces of milk and (2) its Singles contained more calcium than most imitation slices.

The FTC filed charges against Kraft, claiming that neither of these statements was true. The FTC found that although Kraft uses five ounces of milk in making each Kraft Single, about one-third of the calcium contained in the milk is lost during processing. The FTC also found that most imitation slices sold in the United States contain the same amount of calcium as Kraft Singles. The FTC held that Kraft's advertisements constituted unfair and deceptive advertising in violation of Section 5 of the FTC Act because they were likely to mislead consumers. The FTC ordered Kraft to cease and desist from making these misrepresentations. The court of appeals upheld the FTC's order. [*Kraft, Inc. v. Federal Trade Commission*, 970 F.2d 311, 1992 U.S. App. Lexis 17575 (7th Cir. 1992)]

1. Do you think Kraft made untrue statements?
2. Was the punishment sufficient in this case? Why or why not? ■

E-Commerce & Information Technology

Anti-Spam Statute Upheld

As most computer users have experienced, when they open their e-mail, they often find lots of spam—unsolicited commercial e-mail messages selling anything from everyday products and services to sexually explicit materials. But spamming can reach outrageous proportions as spammers can send hundreds of thousands, even millions, of messages with a touch of a button. Consider the following case.

The State of Washington enacted an anti-spam statute that prohibits false and misleading commercial e-mail messages. Jason Heckel, an Oregon resident doing business as Natural Instincts, sent 100,000 to 1 million unsolicited commercial e-mail messages per week, many to Washington residents, trying to sell his 46-page booklet "How to Profit from the Internet." The State of Washington sued Heckel for violating its anti-spam statute. Heckel allegedly did what many spammers do to get someone to read their messages; he disguised the message's point of origin and transmission path. The trial court dismissed the lawsuit, finding that Washington's anti-spam statute caused an undue burden on interstate commerce. The Washington supreme court upheld the statute, finding the law to be constitutional. The court stated:

> The Act limits the harm that deceptive commercial e-mail causes Washington businesses and citizens. The Act prohibits e-mail solicitors from using misleading information in the subject line or transmission path of any commercial e-mail message to Washington residents or from a computer located in Washington. We find that the local benefits of the Act outweigh any conceivable burdens the Act places on those sending commercial e-mail messages. Consequently, we hold that the Act does not violate the dormant Commerce Clause of the United States Constitution.

Many other states have enacted similar ant-spam statutes. [*State v. Heckel*, 24 P.3d 404, 2001 Wash. Lexis 388 (WA 2001)] ■

Outdoor Market, Kashgar. Most other countries do not have as extensive consumer protection laws as the United States.

Federal Consumer-Debtor Protection Laws

Creditors have been known to engage in various abusive, deceptive, and unfair practices when dealing with consumer-debtors. To protect consumer-debtors from such practices, the federal government has enacted a comprehensive scheme of laws concerning the extension and collection of credit. These laws are discussed in the following section.

Business Brief
The federal government protects *consumer-debtors* (borrowers) from abusive, deceptive, and unfair practices by *creditors* (lenders).

Landmark Law

Truth-in-Lending Act

In 1968, Congress enacted the **Truth-in-Lending Act (TILA)** as part of the Consumer Credit Protection Act (CCPA) [15 U.S.C. § § 1601 et seq.]. The TILA, as amended, requires creditors to make certain disclosures to debtors in consumer transactions that do not exceed $25,000 (e.g., retail installment sales, automobile loans) and real estate loans of any amount on the debtor's principal dwelling.

The TILA covers only creditors who regularly (1) extend credit for goods or services to consumers or (2) arrange such credit in the ordinary course of their business. Consumer credit is defined as credit extended to natural persons for personal, family, or household purposes.

Regulation Z

The TILA is administered by the Federal Reserve Board, which has the authority to adopt regulations to enforce and interpret the act. **Regulation Z**, which sets forth detailed rules for compliance with the TILA, was adopted under this authority [12 C.F. R. 226]. The uniform disclosures required by the TILA and Regulation Z are intended to help consumers shop for the best credit terms.

The TILA and Regulation Z require the following information to be disclosed by the creditor to the consumer-debtor:

- Cash price of the product or service
- Down payment and trade-in allowance
- Unpaid cash price
- Finance charge, including interest, points, and other fees paid for the extension of credit
- Annual percentage rate (APR) of the finance charges
- Charges not included in the finance charge (such as appraisal fees)
- Total dollar amount financed
- Date the finance charge begins to accrue
- Number, amounts, and due dates of payments
- A description of any security interest
- Penalties to be assessed for delinquent payments and late charges
- Prepayment penalties
- Comparative costs of credit (optional) ■

Consumer Leasing Act (CLA)

Consumer Leasing Act (CLA)
An amendment to the TILA that extends the TILA's coverage to lease terms in consumer leases.

Consumers often opt to lease consumer products such as automobiles and large appliances rather than purchase them. As originally enacted, the TILA applied only to certain forms of leases. The **Consumer Leasing Act (CLA)** extended the TILA's coverage to lease terms in consumer leases.[17] The CLA applies to lessors who engage in leasing or arranging leases for consumer goods in the ordinary course of their business. Casual leases (such as leases between consumers) and leases of real property (such as a lease on an apartment) are not subject to the CLA. Creditors who violate the CLA are subject to the same civil and criminal penalties as those provided in the TILA.

Fair Credit and Charge Card Disclosure Act of 1988

Fair Credit and Charge Card Disclosure Act of 1988
An amendment to the TILA that requires disclosure of credit terms on credit- and charge-card solicitations and applications.

Business Brief
Issuers of credit cards are subject to certain rules concerning (1) unsolicited credit cards, (2) faulty products purchased with credit cards, and (3) lost or stolen credit cards.

The **Fair Credit and Charge Card Disclosure Act of 1988**[18] amended the TILA to require disclosure of credit terms on credit- and charge-card solicitations and applications.

The regulations adopted under the act require that any direct written solicitation to a consumer display, in tabular form, the following information: (1) the APR, (2) any annual membership fee, (3) any minimum or fixed finance charge, (4) any transaction charge for use of the card for purchases, and (5) a statement that charges are due when the periodic statement is received by the debtor.

Contemporary Business Environment

Credit-Card Rules Protect Consumers

Many consumer purchases are made with *credit cards*. Cardholders are liable to pay for authorized purchases even if they exceed the established dollar limit of the credit card. The TILA regulates the issuance and use of credit cards in the following ways:

- ***Unsolicited Credit Cards*** Issuers (e.g., Visa, MasterCard) are not prohibited from sending an *unsolicited credit card*. However, the TILA stipulates that the addressee is not liable for any charges made on an unsolicited card that is lost or stolen prior to its acceptance by the addressee. Acceptance of the card makes the addressee liable for authorized charges made with it.
- ***Faulty Products*** A consumer who unknowingly purchases a faulty product with a credit card may withhold payments to the credit-card issuer until the dispute over the defect is resolved. The cardholder may notify the issuer about the defect immediately or wait until receipt of the billing statement. If the consumer and the seller cannot resolve the dispute (e.g., by replacing or repairing the defective product), the credit-card issuer is under a duty to intervene. If the dispute cannot be settled, a legal action may be necessary to resolve the dispute.
- ***Lost or Stolen Credit Cards*** Sometimes credit cards are lost or stolen from the cardholder. The TILA limits the cardholder's liability to $50 per card for unauthorized charges made on the card before the issuer is notified that the card is missing. There is no liability if the issuer is notified before the missing card is used.

Consider This Example Suppose Karen loses her Visa credit card. Before Karen realizes that she has lost the card, Michael finds it and charges $750 of goods. When Karen discovers the card is missing, she notifies Visa. Karen is liable for only $50 of the $750 of unauthorized charges. If Karen had notified Visa prior to the charges being made on her card, she would not have been liable for the $50. ■

Equal Credit Opportunity Act (ECOA)

Equal Credit Opportunity Act (ECOA)
A federal statute that prohibits discrimination in the extension of credit based on sex, marital status, race, color, national origin, religion, age, or receipt of income from public assistance programs.

The **Equal Credit Opportunity Act (ECOA)** was enacted in 1975.[19] The ECOA, as amended, prohibits discrimination in the extension of credit based on sex, marital status, race, color, national origin, religion, age, or receipt of income from public assistance programs. The ECOA applies to all creditors who extend or arrange credit in the ordinary course of their business, including banks, savings and loan associations, automobile dealers, real estate brokers, credit-card issuers, and the like.

The creditor must notify the applicant within 30 days regarding the action taken on a credit application. If the creditor takes an **adverse action** (i.e., denies, revokes, or changes the credit terms), the creditor must provide the applicant with a statement containing the specific reasons for the action. If a creditor violates the ECOA, the consumer may bring a civil action against the creditor and recover actual damages (including emotional distress and embarrassment).

adverse action
A denial or revocation of credit or a change in the credit terms offered.

Fair Credit Reporting Act (FCRA)

The 1970 Congress enacted the **Fair Credit Reporting Act (FCRA)** as Title VI of the TILA.[20] This act protects consumers who are subjects of a **credit report** by setting out guidelines for consumer reporting agencies—that is, credit bureaus that compile and sell credit reports for a fee.

Fair Credit Reporting Act (FCRA)
An amendment to the TILA that protects customers who are subjects of a credit report by setting out guidelines for credit bureaus.

credit report
Information about a person's credit history that can be secured from a credit bureau.

The consumer may request the following information at any time: (1) the nature and substance of all the information in the consumer's credit file (except medical information), (2) the sources of this information (except sources used solely for investigative reports), and (3) the names of recipients of a credit report within the past 6 months, or 10 months if it was used for employment purposes.

Consumer reporting agencies are required to maintain reasonable procedures to ensure the accuracy of their information. If a consumer challenges the accuracy of pertinent information contained in the credit file, the agency may be compelled to reinvestigate. If the agency cannot find an error, despite the consumer's complaint, the consumer may file a 100-word written statement of his or her version of the disputed information.

> He begs of them that borrowed of him.
>
> James Kelly
> *Scottish Proverbs (1721)*

If a consumer reporting agency or user violates the FCRA, the injured consumer may bring a civil action against the violator and recover actual damages. The FCRA also provides for criminal penalties.

Fair Debt Collection Practices Act (FDCPA)

In 1977, Congress enacted the **Fair Debt Collection Practices Act (FDCPA).**[21] This act protects consumer-debtors from abusive, deceptive, and unfair practices used by **debt collectors**. The FDCPA expressly prohibits debt collectors from using certain practices. They are (1) harassing, abusive, or intimidating tactics (e.g., threats of violence and obscene or abusive language), (2) false or misleading misrepresentations (e.g., posing as a police officer or attorney), and (3) unfair or unconscionable practices (e.g., threatening the debtor with imprisonment).

Fair Debt Collection Practices Act (FDCPA)
An act enacted in 1977 that protects consumer-debtors from abusive, deceptive, and unfair practices used by debt collectors.

debt collector
An agent who collects debts for other parties.

Business Brief
The Fair Debt Collection Practices Act prohibits certain contact by the creditor with third parties and the debtor.

In some circumstances, the debt collector may not contact the debtor. These situations include the following:

1. At any inconvenient time. The FDCPA provides that convenient hours are between 8:00 A.M. and 9:00 P.M. unless this time is otherwise inconvenient for the debtor (e.g., the debtor works a night shift and sleeps during the day).
2. At inconvenient places, such as at a place of worship or social events.
3. At the debtor's place of employment if the employer objects to such contact.
4. If the debtor is represented by an attorney.
5. If the debtor gives a written notice to the debt collector that he or she refuses to pay the debt or does not want the debt collector to contact him or her again.

> To contract new debts is not the way to pay old ones.
>
> George Washington
> *Letter to James Welch (1799)*

The FDCPA limits the contact that a debt collector may have with third persons other than the debtor's spouse or parents. Such contacts are strictly limited. Unless the court has given its approval, third parties can be consulted only for the purpose of locating the debtor. They can be contacted only once. The debt collector may not inform the third person that the consumer owes a debt that is in the process of collection. A debtor may bring a civil action against a debt collector for intentionally violating the FDCPA.

International Law

Consumer Protection Laws in Mexico

In the decades following World War II, Mexico developed both an industrial base that created jobs in manufacturing and in service industries and a large consumer base. The ever-growing consumer population gave rise to increased consumer complaints of faulty products, consumer fraud, false advertising, and unfair business practices.

Prior to 1975, the traditional civil remedies provided by mercantile codes in Mexico provided little protection for Mexican consumers because they favored merchants and service providers. In addition, legal cases brought in the civil court system were slow, procedurally complicated, and costly.

In 1975, the Mexican Federal Congress enacted the **Federal Consumer Protection Act (FCPA)** [D.O. Dec. 22, 1975 (Mex.)]. The FCPA was modeled after several U.S. consumer protection statutes. The fact that most consumer transactions are codified and regulated in Mexico in a single statute is a clear advantage for Mexican consumers. The provisions of the FCPA are granted the highest legal rank in Mexico, second only to constitutional precepts.

The FCPA contains the following legal rules designed to protect consumers:

- The legal relationship between the merchant and the consumer is based on the "principle of truthfulness." This includes advertising, labeling, instructions, and warnings.
- Consumer contracts must be drafted in precise and clear language.
- Warranties of any goods and services are legally enforceable.
- Public authorities have the power to establish maximum interest rates and total expenses associated with consumer credit. Total disclosure is required in consumer credit transactions.
- Consumers have the legal right to modify, through judicial means, clauses included in adhesion or unconscionable contracts.
- Federal authorities have the power to regulate offers, advertising, and conduct of sales by businesses selling goods or services to consumers.
- Consumer protection rules contained in the FCPA may not be legally renounced.

The FCPA also created agencies to enforce its rules. For example, it created the **Federal Attorney General for Consumer Affairs**, an independent agency of the Mexican government that is empowered to represent the interests of consumers in proceedings before federal administrative agencies and federal courts.

The **Consumer Affairs Office** is empowered to settle disputes between suppliers and consumers as a *compositeur amiable*. A consumer may file a complaint with this office, which then acts as a conciliator or arbitrator to try to settle the dispute. Most consumer disputes are settled using the conciliation and arbitration method of the Consumer Affairs Office, even though the parties have the option of using traditional judicial avenues.

The **National Consumer Institute** educates the Mexican population concerning their rights and obligations as consumers. The work of the Institute has established a "consumer protection consciousness" among Mexican consumers and merchants selling goods and services in Mexico. ■

Chapter Summary

Government Regulation, p. 557

Government Regulation of Business

1. ***General government regulation.*** Government regulation that applies to many industries (e.g., antidiscrimination laws).
2. ***Specific government regulation.*** Government regulation that applies to a specific industry (e.g., banking laws).

Administrative Agencies, p. 558

Administrative Agencies

1. ***Administrative agencies.*** Created by federal and state legislative and executive branches. Consist of professionals having an area of expertise in a certain area of commerce, who interpret and apply designated statutes.
2. ***Administrative rules and regulations.*** Administrative agencies are empowered to adopt rules and regulations that interpret and advance the laws they enforce.
3. ***Administrative Procedure Act.*** An act that establishes procedures (i.e., notice, hearing, and such) to be followed by federal agencies in conducting their affairs. States have enacted their own procedural acts to govern state agencies.

The FDA's Administration of the Federal Food, Drug, and Cosmetic Act (FDCA), p. 563

Federal Food, Drug, and Cosmetic Act (FDCA)

A federal statute that regulates the testing, manufacture, distribution, and sale of foods, food additives, drugs, cosmetics, and medical products.

Required FDA Approval

1. ***Federal Food and Drug Administration (FDA).*** A federal administrative agency empowered to interpret and enforce the federal FDCA and other federal consumer protection laws.
2. ***Powers of the FDA.*** The FDA has the power to approve or deny applications by private companies to distribute drugs, food additives, and medical devices to the public.

Regulation of Food, Drugs, and Cosmetics

Adulterated food. The FDA prohibits the shipment, distribution, or sale of *adulterated* or *misbranded* food, drugs, cosmetics, or medical devices.

Other Acts Administered by the FDA

The FDA also has authority to administer the following health-related federal statutes and amendments:

1. Pesticide Amendment of 1954
2. Food Additives Amendment of 1958
3. Color Additives Amendment of 1960
4. Animal Drug Amendment of 1968
5. Biologies Act of 1902
6. Public Health Service Act
7. Radiation for Health and Safety of 1968

Regulation of Product Safety, p. 570

Consumer Product Safety Act (CPSA)

A federal statute that regulates the safety of consumer products. It created the Consumer Product Safety Commission.

1. ***Consumer Product Safety Commission (CPSC).*** A federal administrative agency that is empowered to
   a. interpret and enforce the CPSA,
   b. conduct research on safety, and
   c. collect data regarding injuries.

Consumer Product Safety Statutes Administered by the CPSC

The CPSC also has authority to administer the following federal consumer product safety acts:

1. Consumer Product Safety Act (CPSA)
2. Fair Packaging and Labeling Act
3. Poison Prevention Packaging Act

Unfair and Deceptive Practices, p. 571

Section 5 of the Federal Trade Commission Act (FTC Act)

A federal statute that prohibits unfair and deceptive practices, including false and deceptive advertising, abusive sales tactics, consumer fraud, and other unfair business practices.

Federal Trade Commission (FTC). A federal administrative agency that is empowered to enforce the Federal Trade Commission Act and other federal consumer protection statutes.

Federal Consumer-Debtor Protection Laws, p. 575

Truth-in-Lending Act (TILA)

A federal statute that requires creditors to make certain disclosures to consumer-debtors in most consumer credit transactions. It mandates disclosure of a single-figure *annual percentage rate (APR).*

Regulation Z. Regulation adopted by the Federal Reserve Board to enforce and interpret the TILA.

Consumer Leasing Act

A federal statute that requires lessors to make disclosures to lessees in most consumer lease transactions.

Fair Credit and Charge Card Disclosure Act of 1988

A federal statute that requires disclosure of certain credit terms to credit card holders. The act provides the following protections:

1. ***Unsolicited credit cards.*** A consumer is not liable for any charges on an unsolicited credit card that is lost or stolen prior to its acceptance by the addressee.
2. ***Faulty products.*** A consumer who unknowingly purchases a faulty product with a credit card may withhold payment to the credit card issuer until the dispute over the defect is resolved.
3. ***Lost or stolen credit cards.*** A cardholder's liability for unauthorized charges on a lost or stolen credit card is limited to $50 per card before the issuer is notified that the card is missing. The cardholder has no liability if the issuer is notified before the missing card is used.

Equal Credit Opportunity Act (ECOA)

Federal statute that prohibits discrimination in the extension of credit based on the applicant's sex, marital status, race, color, national origin, religion, age, or receipt of income from public assistance programs.

1. ***Notification.*** The ECOA requires a creditor to notify a consumer-debtor of the reasons for an *adverse action* on a credit application.

Fair Credit Reporting Act (FCRA)

A federal statute that regulates credit reporting agencies and establishes a procedure for a consumer-debtor to have errors in credit reports corrected.

1. ***100-word statement.*** The act permits a consumer-debtor to place a 100-word written statement in his or her credit report file concerning any unresolved dispute. This information must be conveyed to anyone seeking a credit report on the debtor.
2. ***Obsolete information.*** The act requires a credit report to be kept up-to-date and to delete obsolete information from the credit report file.

Fair Debt Collection Practices Act (FDCPA)

Federal statute that protects consumer-debtors from abusive, deceptive, and unfair practices used by debt collectors.

1. ***Prohibited contact.*** The FDCPA prohibits or limits the creditor from making certain contact with third parties and the debtor concerning a debt it is trying to collect.

Internet Exercises and Case Questions

Working the Web Internet Exercises

Activities

1. How does administrative law work? What makes it administrative? An overview of administrative law and procedure is collected at **www.law.fsu.edu/library/admin**.
2. Cases and related materials can be found at **www.law.cornell.edu/topics/adminstrative.html**.
3. Check the CPSC site for information on window blinds and/or batteries for notebook computers. See **www.cpsc.gov**.
4. Find out what "Made in the U.S.A." means, according to the FTC Web site. See **www.ftc.gov**.
5. Review the FDA Enforcement Reports for a detailed list of recent violators. Are any of your favorite foods listed? See the FDA site **www.fda.gov**.
6. Go to the FTC site and find the "Top Ten Dot Cons" at **www.ftc.gov/bcp/menu-credit.htm**. See also **www.law.cornell.edu/topics/consumer_credit.html** for an overview of consumer credit law with links to key primary and secondary sources.

Critical Legal Thinking Cases

19.1 Adulterated Food Barry Engel owned and operated the Gel Spice Co., Inc., which specialized in the importation and packaging of various food spices for resale. All of the spices Gel Spice imported were unloaded at a pier in New York City and taken to a warehouse on McDonald Avenue. Storage and repacking of the spices took place in the warehouse. Between July 1976 and January 1979, the McDonald Avenue warehouse was inspected four times by investigators from the FDA. The investigators found live rats in bags of basil leaves, rodent droppings in boxes of chili peppers, and mammalian urine in bags of sesame seeds. The investigators produced additional evidence that showed that spices packaged and sold from the warehouse contained insects, rodent excreta pellets, rodent hair, and rodent urine. The FDA brought criminal charges against Engel and Gel Spice. Are they guilty? [*United States v. Gel Spice Co., Inc.*, 601 F.Supp. 1205, 1984 U.S. Dist. Lexis 21041 (E.D.N.Y. 1984)]

19.2 Food Additive Coco Rico, Inc., manufactures a coconut concentrate called "Coco Rico" for use as an ingredient in soft drinks. The concentrate that is sold to beverage bottlers in Puerto Rico contains potassium nitrate, which is added for the purpose of developing and fixing a desirable color and flavor. Puerto Rico is subject to U.S. federal laws, including those administered by the FDA. The FDA has not approved the use of potassium nitrate as a food additive in soft drinks. The FDA learned of the use of the Coco Rico concentrate in soft drinks and on March 10, 1982, obtained a warrant from a federal district court to search the premises of a Puerto Rican bottler. On March 24, 1982, government investigators discovered three lots of soft drinks containing Coco Rico on the premises of the bottler and seized them pursuant to the warrant. Coco Rico, Inc., sued to reclaim the soft drinks. Who wins? [*United States v. An Article of Food*, 752 F.2d 11, 1985 U.S. App. Lexis 27849 (1st Cir. 1985)]

19.3 Regulation of Drugs Dey Laboratories, Inc., is a drug manufacturer operating in the state of Texas. In 1983, Dey scientists created an inhalant known as ASI. The only active ingredient in ASI is atropine sulfate. The inhalant is sold to physicians, who then prescribe the medication for patients suffering from asthma, bronchitis, and other pulmonary diseases. In May 1983, Dey filed a new drug application with the FDA. By September 1983, Dey was advised that its application would not be approved. In spite of the lack of FDA approval, Dey began marketing ASI in November 1983. On August 25, 1985, the United States filed a complaint for forfeiture of all ASI manufactured by Dey. The inhalant was seized, and Dey sued to have the FDA's seizure declared illegal. Who wins? [*United States v. Atropine Sulfate 1.0 MG (Article of Drug)*, 843 F.2d 860, 1988 U.S. App. Lexis 5817 (5th Cir. 1988)]

19.4 Cosmetics FBNH Enterprizes, Inc., is a distributor of a product known as French Bronze Tablets. The purpose of the tablets is to allow a person to achieve an even tan without exposure to the sun. When ingested, the tablets impart color to the skin through the use of various ingredients, one of which is canthaxanthin, a coloring agent. Canthaxanthin has not been approved for use by the FDA as a coloring additive. The FDA became aware that FBNH was marketing the tablets and that each contains 30 milligrams of canthaxanthin. On June 16, 1988, the FDA files a lawsuit seeking the forfeiture and condemnation of eight cases of the tablets in the possession of FBNH. FBNH challenged the government's right to seize the tablets. Who wins? [*United States v. Eight Unlabeled Cases of an Article of Cosmetic*, 888 F.2d 945, 1989 U.S. App. Lexis 15589 (2nd Cir. 1989)]

19.5 Medical Device Amendments General Medical Company manufactures and markets a product known as the "drionic" antiperspirant device. The device is designed as a substitute for chemical antiperspirants or for the extensive medical treatment for those who suffer from greatly increased perspiration. The device consists of a housing for two wool felt pads and a battery. The pads are soaked in ordinary tap water and then placed against the treated area, typically the hands, feet, and underarms. An electrical current is passed through the pads and the area of skin between the pads for about 20 minutes. Ions (atoms carrying an electrical charge) are thereby transmitted across the skin. General Medical claims this process works in controlling perspiration in the treated area. The FDA seeks to regulate the device. Does it have the authority to do so? [*General Medical Company v. United States Food and Drug Administration*, 770 F.2d 214, 1985 U.S. App. Lexis 21251 (D.C. Cir. 1985)]

19.6 Poison Prevention Packaging Act In June 1980, Joseph Wahba had a prescription filled at Zuckerman's Pharmacy in Brooklyn, New York. The prescription was for Lomotil, a drug used to counteract stomach disorders. The pharmacy dispensed 30 tablets in a small, plastic container unequipped with a "child-proof" cap. Joseph took the medicine home, where it was discovered by Wahba's two-year-old son, Mark. Mark opened the container and ingested approximately 20 pills before Mark's mother saw him and stopped him. She rushed him to a hospital but, despite the efforts of the doctors, Mark lapsed into a coma and died. The Wahbas sued H&N Prescription Center, Inc., the company that owns Zuckerman's Pharmacy, for damages. Who wins? [*Wahba v. H&N Prescription Center, Inc.*, 539 F.Supp. 352, 1982 U.S. Dist. Lexis 12327 (E.D.N.Y. 1982)]

19.7 Truth-in-Lending In June 1979, Elizabeth Valentine purchased a home in Philadelphia, Pennsylvania. In October 1979, she applied for and received a $4,500 home loan from Salmon Building and Loan Association for the purpose of paneling the cellar walls and redecorating the house. Salmon took a security interest in the house as collateral for the loan. Although Valentine was given a disclosure document by Salmon, nowhere on the document were "finance charges" disclosed. The document did notify Valentine that Salmon had a security interest in the house. In May 1982, Valentine sued Salmon (which had since merged with Influential Savings and Loan Association) to rescind the loan. Who wins? [*Valentine v. Influential Savings and Loan Association*, 572 F.Supp. 36 (E.D.Pa. 1983)]

19.8 Consumer Leasing Act In April 1986, Joyce Givens entered into a rental agreement with Rent-A-Center, Inc., whereby she rented a bar and entertainment center. The agreement provided that she must pay in advance to keep the furniture for periods of one week or one month. Givens could terminate the agreement at any time by making arrangements for the furniture's return. Givens made payments between April and August of 1986. After that, she failed to make any further payments but continued to possess the property. When Rent-A-Center became aware that Givens had moved and taken the furniture with her, in violation of the rental agreement, it filed a criminal complaint against her. On January 9, 1988, Givens agreed to return the furniture, and Rent-A-Center dropped the charges. After Rent-A-Center recovered the furniture, Givens sued the company, claiming that the agreement she had signed violated the Consumer Leasing Act. Who wins? [*Givens v. Rent-A-Center, Inc.*, 720 F.Supp. 160, 1988 U.S. Dist. Lexis 16839 (S.D.Ala. 1988)]

19.9 Fair Credit Billing Oscar S. Gray had been an American Express cardholder since 1964. In 1980, Gray used his card to purchase airline tickets costing $9,312. American Express agreed that Gray could pay for the tickets in 12 equal monthly installments. In January and February of 1981, Gray made substantial prepayments of $3,500 and $1,156, respectively. When his March bill arrived, Gray was surprised because American Express had converted the deferred payment plan to a currently due charge, making the entire amount for the tickets due and payable. Gray paid the normal monthly charge under the deferred payment plan and informed American Express by letter dated April 22, 1981, of its error. In the letter, Gray identified himself, his card number, and the nature of the error. Gray did not learn of any adverse action by American Express until almost one year later, on the night of his and his wife's anniversary. When he offered his American Express card to pay for their anniversary dinner, the restaurant informed Gray that American Express had canceled his account and had instructed the restaurant to destroy the card. Gray sued American Express. Did American Express violate the Fair Credit Billing Act? [*Gray v. American Express Company*, 743 F.2d 10, 1984 US. App. Lexis 19033 (D.C. Cir. 1984)]

19.10 Fair Credit Reporting Act The San Antonio Retail Merchants Association (SARMA) is a business engaged in selling computerized credit reports. In November 1974, William Daniel Thompson, Jr., opened a credit account with Gordon's Jewelers in San Antonio, listing his Social Security number as 457-68-5778. Thompson subsequently ran up a delinquent account of $77.25 at Gordon's that was later charged off as a bad debt. Gordon's reported the bad debt to SARMA, which placed the information and a derogatory credit rating in Thompson's file No. 5867114.

In early 1978, William Douglas Thompson III applied for credit with Gulf Oil and Wards. He listed his Social Security number as 407-86-4065. On February 9, 1978, a worker in the credit department at Gulf accepted file No. 5867114 from SARMA as the credit history of William. Thereafter, SARMA combined the credit reports of the two men. William was denied credit by both Gulf and Wards on the basis of this erroneous information. It was not until June 1979 that William learned of the mistake. After straightening out the facts with Gordon's, William requested SARMA to correct the error. SARMA took no action on William's complaint for four months. William Douglas Thompson III sued SARMA for violating the Fair Credit Reporting Act. Who wins? [*Thompson v. San Antonio Retail Merchants Association*, 682 F.2d 509, 1982 U.S. App. Lexis 16612 (5th Cir. 1982)]

19.11 Fair Debt Collection Practices Act Stanley M. Juras was a student at Montana State University (MSU) from 1972 to 1976. During his years at MSU, Juras took out several student loans from the school under the National Direct Student Loan program. By the time Juras left MSA, he owed the school more than $5,000. Juras defaulted on these loans and MSU assigned the debt to Aman Collection Service, Inc., for purposes of collection. Aman obtained a judgment against Juras in a Montana state court for $5,015 on the debt and $1,920 in interest and attorney's fees. Juras, who now lived in California, still refused to pay these amounts. On May 5, 1982, a vice president of Aman, Mr. Gloss, telephoned Juras twice in California before 8:00 A.M. Pacific Standard Time. Mr. Gloss told Juras that if he did not pay the debt, he would not receive a college transcript. Juras sued Aman, claiming that the telephone calls violated the Fair Debt Collection Practices Act. Gloss testified at trial that he made the calls before 8:00 A.M. because he had forgotten the difference in time zones between California and Aman's offices in South Dakota. Who wins? [*Juras v. Aman Collection Services, Inc.*, 829 F.2d 739, 1987 U.S. App. Lexis 12888 (9th Cir. 1987)]

Business Ethics Cases

19.12 Business Ethics Charles of the Ritz Distributors Corporation is a New York corporation engaged in the sale and distribution of a product called Rejuvenescence Cream. The extensive advertising campaign that accompanied the sale of the cream placed emphasis upon the supposed rejuvenating powers of the product. The ads claimed that the cream would bring to the user's "skin quickly the clear radiance" and "the petal-like quality and texture of youth." Another advertisement claimed that the product would "restore natural moisture necessary for a live, healthy skin" with the result that "Your face need not know drought years." The FTC learned of the ads and asked several experts to investigate application of cosmetics to overcome skin conditions that result from psychological changes occurring with the passage of time. The FTC issued a cease-and-desist order in regard to the advertising. Ritz appealed the FTC's decision to a federal court. Did Ritz act ethically in making its advertising claims? Who wins? [*Charles of the Ritz Distributing Corp. v. FTC*, 143 F.2d 676, 144 U.S. App. Lexis 3172 (2nd Cir. 1944)]

19.13 Business Ethics Leon A. Tashof operated a store known as the New York Jewelry Company. The store was located in an area that serves low-income consumers, many of whom have low-paying jobs and have no bank or charge accounts. About 85 percent of the store's sales are made on credit. The store advertised eyeglasses "from $7.50 complete," including "lenses, frames, and case." Tashof advertised this sale extensively on radio and in newspapers. Evidence showed that of the 1,400 pairs of eyeglasses sold by the store, fewer than 10 were sold for $7.50; the rest were more-expensive glasses. The FTC sued Tashof for engaging in "bait and switch" marketing. Was Tashof's conduct ethical? Who wins? [*Tashof v. Federal Trade Commission*, 437 F.2d 707, 1970 U.S. App. Lexis 5809 (D.C. Cir. 1970)]

Briefing the Case Writing Assignment

Read Case A.19 in the Case Appendix [*X-Tra Art, Inc. v. Consumer Product Safety Commission*]. This case is excerpted from the district court opinion. Review and brief the case. In your brief, be sure to answer the following questions.

1. Who were the plaintiffs? Who was the defendant?
2. What product was being sold by the plaintiffs?
3. What act was alleged to have been violated by the plaintiffs?
4. In whose favor did the district court decide the case?

Answers to Management Decision Questions

1. There are several federal laws that may have been broken. The federal **Food, Drug, and Cosmetic Act of 1938**, as amended, provides the basis for the regulation of much of the testing, manufacture, distribution, and sale of foods, drugs, cosmetics, and medicinal products and devices in the United States. The FDA administers the act. The Department of Agriculture administers the **Agricultural Marketing Act of 1946**, the **Poultry Inspection Act of 1957**, and the **Poultry Inspection Act of 1957**. Its protection role also includes wildlife damage management, the welfare of animals, human health and safety, and ecosystems vulnerable to invasive pests and pathogens.
2. The **Commerce Clause** of the U.S. Constitution grants Congress the power "to regulate commerce with foreign nations, and among the several states, and with Indian tribes." Because the U.S. Constitution does not stipulate that administrative agencies are a separate branch of the government, they must be created by the legislative or executive branch. The agency has only the legislative, judicial, and executive powers that are delegated to it. The courts have generally upheld the combined powers of administrative agencies as being constitutional. An administrative agency acting outside the scope of its delegated powers is an unconstitutional act.

Endnotes

1. 21 U.S.C. § 321.
2. 21 U.S.C. § § 360(c) et seq.
3. 21 U.S.C. § 346(a).
4. 21 U.S.C. § 348.
5. 21 U.S.C. § 376(a).
6. 21 U.S.C. § 360(b).
7. 21 U.S.C. § 357.
8. 42 U.S.C. § 264.
9. 42 U.S.C. § 263(b).
10. 42 U.S.C. § 263.
11. A consumer who is injured by a defective product can bring a civil action to recover damages from his or her injuries.
12. 15 U.S.C. § 2051.
13. 15 U.S.C. § § 1451 et seq.
14. 15 U.S.C. § 1471.
15. 15 U.S.C. § § 41–51.
16. 39 U.S.C. § 3009.
17. 15 U.S.C. § § 1667 et seq.
18. 15 U.S.C. § 1637.
19. 15 U.S.C. § 1691.
20. 15 U.S.C. § § 1681 et seq.
21. 15 U.S.C. § 1692.

20

Environmental Protection

"All animals are equal but some animals are more equal than others."

—George Orwell
Animal Farm (1945)

Chapter Objectives

After studying this chapter, you should be able to:

1. Describe an environmental impact statement and identify when one is needed.
2. Describe the national ambient air quality standards required by the Clean Air Act.
3. Describe the effluent water standards required by the Clean Water Act.
4. Explain how environmental laws regulate the use of toxic substances.
5. Describe the government's authority to recover the cost of cleaning up hazardous waste sites pursuant to the Superfund law.

Chapter Contents

- Environmental Protection
- Air Pollution
- Water Pollution
- Toxic Substances
- Hazardous Waste
- Nuclear Waste
- Noise Pollution
- State Environmental Protection Laws

Management Decision Environmental Protection

Currently, you serve as the director of parks and recreation for Apex, Virginia, a small township located on the banks of the James River. To attract tourists, Apex is in the process of designing and building a public golf course on recently acquired land. In addition, a private company has agreed to develop a theme park close to the golf course. The chief contractor for the golf course has just discovered dwarf wedge mussels in a creek that flows through the property. He informed you that the dwarf wedge mussel is on the federal endangered species list for the southeastern United States.

1. How does a species acquire designation as an endangered species?
2. Will the discovery of the dwarf mussel in the creek affect the ongoing development of this property?

In producing and consuming products, businesses and consumers generate air pollution, water pollution, and hazardous and toxic wastes that cause harm to the environment and to human health. Although environmental protection has been a concern since medieval England enacted laws regulating the burning of soft coal, pollution has now reached alarming rates in this country and the world.

This chapter is concerned with how the federal and state governments are trying to contain the levels of pollution and to clean up hazardous waste sites in this country. It examines the scope and impact of the major environmental protection laws applicable to businesses and individuals.

Business Brief

Although pollution of many forms has been around for centuries, only in recent times have federal and state governments enacted laws prohibiting or limiting many forms of pollution and requiring their cleanup.

La Jolla, California. The federal and state governments have enacted many statutes to protect the environment from pollution.

Those who hike the Appalachian Trail into Sunfish Pond, New Jersey, and camp or sleep there, or run the Allagash in Maine, or climb the Guadalupes in West Texas, or who canoe and portage the Quentico Superior in Minnesota, certainly should have standing to defend those natural wonders before courts or agencies, though they live 3,000 miles away. Then there will be assurances that all of the forms of life will stand before the court—the pileated woodpecker as well as the coyote and bear, the lemmings as well as the trout in the streams. Those inarticulate members of the ecological group cannot speak. But those people who have so frequented the place as to know its values and wonders will be able to speak for the entire ecological community.

Justice Douglas
Dissenting Opinion Sierra Club v. Morton, Secretary of the Interior 31 L.Ed.2d 636 (1972)

Environmental Protection

Under common law, both individuals and the government could bring a civil suit against the offending party. Individuals could bring a private civil suit based on *private nuisance* to recover damages from the polluting party. The injured party could also sue for an injunction to prevent further pollution by the offending party. The government could bring a lawsuit against a polluter based on the common law theory of *public nuisance*. By the 1950s and 1960s, federal and state governments realized that this approach was not enough to contain the problems caused by pollution and began enacting legislation to protect the environment.

Web Site

Environmental Protection Agency (EPA) The mission of the U.S. EPA is to "protect human health and to safeguard the environment." At the EPA Web site, you can find out about projects and programs, researchers and scientists, children's health, and more. Visit at **www.epa.gov**.

In the 1970s, the federal government began enacting statutes to protect our nation's air and water from pollution. Federal legislation was also enacted to regulate hazardous wastes and to protect wildlife. In many instances, states enacted their own environmental laws that now coexist with federal law as long as they do not directly conflict with the federal law or unduly burden interstate commerce. These laws provide both civil and criminal penalties. The development of such a vast body of law in such a short period of time is unprecedented in U.S. history. Environmental protection is one of the most important, and costly, issues facing business and society today.

The Environmental Protection Agency (EPA)

Environmental Protection Agency (EPA)
An administrative agency created by Congress in 1970 to coordinate the implementation and enforcement of the federal environmental protection laws.

In 1970, Congress created the **Environmental Protection Agency (EPA)** to coordinate the implementation and enforcement of the federal environmental protection laws. The EPA has broad rule-making powers to adopt regulations to advance the laws that it is empowered to administer. The agency also has adjudicative powers to hold hearings, make decisions, and order remedies for violations of federal environmental laws. In addition, the EPA can initiate judicial proceedings in court against suspected violators of federal environmental laws.

Landmark Law

National Environmental Policy Act

The **National Environmental Policy Act (NEPA)**, which was enacted in 1969, became effective January 1, 1970 [42 U.S.C. §§ 4321 et seq.]. The **Council on Environmental Quality** was created under this act. The NEPA mandates that the federal government consider the "adverse impact" of proposed legislation, rule making, or other federal government action on the environment before the action is implemented.

Environmental Impact Statement

The NEPA and rules adopted thereunder require that an **environmental impact statement (EIS)** must be prepared for all proposed legislation or major federal action that significantly affects the quality of the human environment. The purpose of the EIS is to provide enough information about the environment to enable the federal government to determine the feasibility of the project. The EIS is also used as evidence in court whenever a federal action is challenged as violating the NEPA or other federal environmental protection laws. Examples of actions that require an EIS include proposals to build a new federally funded highway, to license nuclear plants, and the like.

The EIS must (1) describe the affected environment, (2) describe the impact of the proposed federal action on the environment, (3) identify and discuss alternatives to the proposed action, (4) list the resources that will be committed to the action, and (5) contain a cost–benefit analysis of the proposed action and alternative actions. Expert professionals, such as engineers, geologists, and accountants, may be consulted during the preparation of the EIS.

Once an EIS is prepared, it is subject to public review. The public has 30 days in which to submit comments to the EPA. After the comments have been received and reviewed, the EPA will issue an order that states whether the proposed federal action may proceed. Decisions of the EPA are appealable to the appropriate U.S. court of appeals.

The NEPA does not apply to action by state or local governments or private parties. Most states and many local governments have enacted laws that require an environmental impact statement to be prepared regarding proposed state and local government action as well as private development. ■

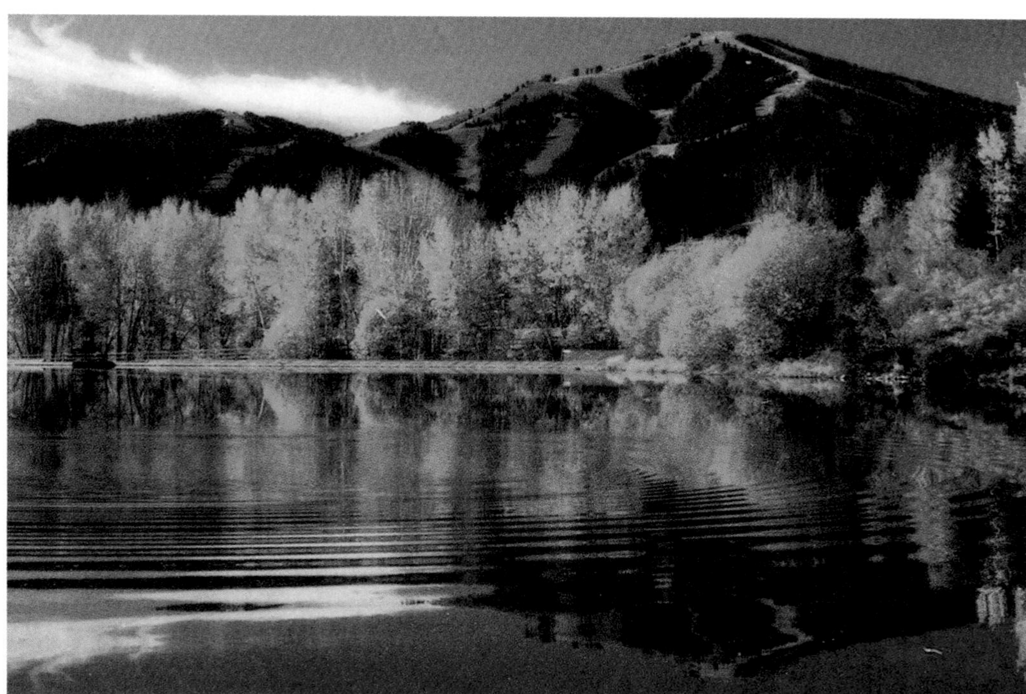

Baldy Mountain, Sun Valley, Idaho. An environmental impact statement (EIS) must be prepared to consider the adverse impact any federal government action will have on the environment.

Air Pollution

One of the major problems facing this country is **air pollution**. Prior to the advent of the internal combustion engine, most air pollution consisted of smoke from factories and homes. Today, most air pollution is invisible and odorless. The air pollution is caused by both mobile sources (such as automobiles) and stationary sources (such as public utilities, manufacturing facilities, and households).

air pollution
Pollution caused by factories, homes, vehicles, and the like that affects the air.

Landmark Law
The Clean Air Act

The federal government's first legislation concerning air pollution came in 1955, when it authorized funds for air pollution research. The **Clean Air Act** was enacted in 1963 to assist states in dealing with air pollution. The act was amended in 1970 and 1977 and, most recently, by the **Clean Air Act Amendments of 1990** [42 U.S.C. §§ 7401 et seq.]. The Clean Air Act, as amended, provides comprehensive regulation of air quality in this country.

National Ambient Air Quality Standards

The Clean Air Act directs the EPA to establish **national ambient air quality standards (NAAQS)** for certain pollutants. These standards are set at two different levels: primary (to protect human beings) and secondary (to protect vegetation, matter, climate, visibility, and economic values). Specific standards have been established for carbon monoxide, nitrogen oxide, sulfur oxide, ozone, lead, and particulate matter.

Although the EPA establishes air quality standards, the states are responsible for their enforcement. The federal government has the right to enforce these air pollution standards if the states fail to do so. Each state is required to prepare a *state implementation plan* (SIP) that sets out how the state plans to meet the federal standards. The EPA has divided each state into *air quality control regions (AQCRs)*. Each region is monitored to ensure compliance. The Clean Air Act was at issue in the following case. ■

U.S. SUPREME COURT CASE

Whitman, Administrator of Environmental Protection Agency v. American Trucking Association

531 U.S. 457, 121 S.Ct. 903, 2001 U.S. Lexis 1952 (2001)
Supreme Court of the United States

Background and Facts

Section 109 of the federal Clean Air Act requires the administrator of the EPA, a federal administrative agency, to set NAAQS for air pollutants. Section 109 instructs the EPA to set NAAQS at levels "to protect the public health" with "an adequate margin of safety." Pursuant to Section 109, the EPA issued new standards for ozone and particular matter emitted from the operation of trucks. The American Trucking Association sued the EPA, arguing that the EPA must consider the cost caused to trucking firms before issuing the NAAQS. The EPA argued that it did not have to do so under the statute. The district court held for the American Trucking Association, but the court of appeals held for the EPA on this issue. The U.S. Supreme Court granted review.

Supreme Court Issue

Under Section 109 of the federal Clean Air Act, must the EPA consider the cost imposed on trucking firms before setting NAAQS for ozone and particulate matter emissions from trucks?

In The Language of The U.S. Supreme Court

Scalia, Justice Section 109 instructs the EPA to set primary ambient air quality standards "the attainment and maintenance of which are requisite to protect the public health" with "an adequate margin of safety." Were it not for the hundreds of pages of briefing respondent American Trucking Association have submitted on the issue, one would have thought it fairly clear that this text does not permit the EPA to consider costs in setting the standards. The language, as one scholar has noted, "is absolute." The EPA, based on the information about health effects contained in the technical criteria documents is to identify the maximum airborne concentration of a pollutant that the public health can tolerate, decrease the concentration to provide an adequate margin of safety, and set the standard at that level. Nowhere are the costs of achieving such a standard made part of that initial calculation.

Respondent argues many more factors than air pollution affect public health. In particular, the economic cost of implementing a very stringent standard might produce health losses sufficient to offset the health gains achieved in cleaning the air—for example, by closing down whole industries and thereby impoverishing the workers and consumers dependent upon those industries. That is unquestionably true. Accordingly, to prevail in their present challenge, respondent must show a textual commitment of authority to the EPA to consider costs in setting NAAQS under Section 109. Congress does not alter the fundamental details of a regulatory scheme in vague terms or ancillary provisions—it does not, one might say, hide elephants in mouseholes. Respondent's textual arguments ultimately founder upon this principle.

Decision and Remedy

The U.S. Supreme Court held that the statutory language of Section 109 of the Clean Air Act does not require the EPA to consider the cost to trucking firms for implementing the NAAQS set by the EPA. The judgment of the court of appeals was affirmed as to this issue.

Case Questions

Critical Legal Thinking Do you think the statutory language of Section 109 was clear in this case?

Business Ethics Would the "public health" be compromised under the trucking firms' argument? Why did the trucking firms resist the NAAQS set by the EPA?

Contemporary Business What are the economic consequences of the Supreme Court's ruling? Explain.

Stationary Sources of Air Pollution

stationary sources
Sources of air pollution such as industrial plants, oil refineries, and public utilities.

Substantial amounts of air pollution are emitted by **stationary sources** (e.g., industrial plants, oil refineries, public utilities). The Clean Air Act requires states to identify major stationary sources and develop plans to reduce air pollution from these sources.

Mobile Sources of Air Pollution

mobile sources
Sources of air pollution such as automobiles, trucks, buses, motorcycles, and airplanes.

Automobile and other vehicle emissions are one of the major sources of air pollution in this country. In an effort to control emissions from these **mobile sources**, the Clean Air Act requires air pollution controls to be installed on motor vehicles. Emission standards have been set for automobiles, trucks, busses, motorcycles, and airplanes. (The Federal Aviation Administration is responsible for enforcing pollution standards for airplanes.)

The manufacture of automobiles is regulated to ensure compliance with EPA emission standards. The Clean Air Act requires new automobiles and light-duty trucks to meet air quality control standards. The EPA can require automobile manufacturers to recall and repair or replace pollution control equipment that does not meet these requirements. In addition, the Clean Air Act authorizes the EPA to regulate air pollution caused by fuel and fuel additives.

Nonattainment Areas

Regions that do not meet the air quality standards are designated **nonattainment areas**. Nonattainment areas are classified into one of five categories—(1) marginal, (2) moderate, (3) serious, (4) severe, and (5) extreme—based on the degree to which they exceed the ozone standard. Deadlines are established for areas to meet the attainment level. States must submit compliance plans that (1) identify major sources of air pollution and require them to install pollution control equipment, (2) institute permit systems for new stationary sources, and (3) implement inspection programs to monitor mobile sources. States that fail to develop or implement an approved plan are subject to the following sanctions: (1) loss of federal highway funds and (2) limitations on new sources of emissions (e.g., the EPA can prohibit the construction of a new pollution-causing industrial plant in the nonattainment area).

nonattainment areas
Regions that do not meet air quality standards.

Web Site

WWW Virtual Library—Environment
The Virtual Library site is a collection point for different subject-based "libraries" of Web links. It was developed to keep track of and to organize Web pages. Each virtual library is divided by subject. Visit at **earthsystems.org/Environment.shtml**.

Contemporary Business Environment

Smog Swapping

Businesses have long thought that the enforcement of environmental laws was too burdensome and cumbersome, whereas environmentalists argue that current laws have not brought about sufficient reductions in pollution. Today, the "command and control" environmental regulation—the amount of pollution a plant can produce—is giving way to a market-based trading scheme. It is hoped that the new scheme will reduce pollution without unduly burdening businesses.

The **Clean Air Act Amendments of 1990** include a new program that allows companies to trade sulfur dioxide emissions (which are responsible for acid rain). Under this plan, companies still face strict quotas for reducing such emissions, but they are free to satisfy their limits by buying pollution credits from other companies.

Consider This Example Company A uses all of its 2,000-pound limit, and it wants to add equipment that would increase the amount of emissions it produces. Company B also has a 2,000-pound limit, but it uses only 1,500 pounds. Company A can buy pollution credits from Company B. The credits are deducted in pounds of pollution allowed per day. For every 1.2 pounds of pollution eliminated by the selling company, the program allows the creation of only 1 pound of pollution by the buying company. This system is designed to reduce overall pollution. Trades cannot happen until the EPA certifies the pollution credits for sale.

The Southern California Air Quality Management District (AQMD), where the air pollution levels exceed federal health standards more than 180 days each year, has also adopted an extensive market-based trading program. The program covers the three pollutants most responsible for smog: sulfur oxide, nitrogen oxide, and reactive organic gas.

There is even a movement at the United Nations to create an international market for trading emission credits for carbon dioxide. Carbon dioxide is the main cause of global warming.

Markets are developing for the trading of pollution credits. For example, the Chicago Board of Trade will offer futures contracts on pollution credits. Manufacturers, refiners, utilities, and speculators would buy and sell pollution credits on these markets. Companies that buy credits can lock in pollution rights for the future.

Businesses argue that the market-based trading of pollution credits will work to reduce pollution in this country. They feel that trading is the best way to solve social and environmental problems at the least cost to society. Critics, most notably environmental groups, contend that the system will be hard to monitor. They also assert that it is immoral to allow companies to buy and sell the right to pollute the environment. ■

Toxic Air Pollutants

Section 112 of the Clean Air Act requires the EPA to identify **toxic air pollutants** that cause serious illness or death to humans.[1] So far, more than 200 chemicals have been listed as toxic, including asbestos, mercury, vinyl chloride, benzene, beryllium, and radionuclides.

toxic air pollutants
Air pollutants that cause serious illness or death to humans.

Web Site
Greenpeace International
Greenpeace International is an activist environmental organization. Visit at **www.greenpeace.org**.

The act requires the EPA to establish standards for these chemicals and requires stationary sources to install equipment and technology to control emissions of toxic substances. EPA standards for toxic substances are set without regard to economic or technological feasibility.

The EPA's setting of the level for a toxic pollutant was challenged in the following case.

Case 20.2
Clean Air Act

Natural Resources Defense Council, Inc. v. Environmental Protection Agency
824 F.2d 1146, 1987 U.S. App. Lexis 10013 (1987)
United States Court of Appeals, District of Columbia Circuit

Background and Facts

Vinyl chloride, a gaseous synthetic chemical used in the manufacture of plastics, is a strong carcinogen. The EPA issued a notice of proposed rule making to establish emission standards for vinyl chloride as a toxic pollutant under Section 112 of the Clean Air Act. Section 112 stipulates that the EPA must set minimum emission standards for toxic air pollutants at the level that in its judgment "provides an ample margin of safety to protect the public health." The EPA issued a final order that required emissions of vinyl chloride to be set at a level that would provide an ample margin of safety for human beings. The National Resources Defense Council, Inc. (NRDC), an environmental activist organization, sued the EPA, alleging that its final order violated Section 112. The NRDC argued that the EPA must set a zero level of emissions of vinyl chloride.

Issue

Must the EPA set a zero level of emissions of the toxic pollutant vinyl chloride?

In The Language of The Court

To accept the NRDC's zero level of emissions rule we would have to conclude that Congress mandated massive economic and social dislocations by shutting down entire industries. That is not a reasonable way to read the legislative history. The EPA has determined that zero-emissions standards for toxic pollutants would result in the elimination of such activities as the generation of electricity from either coal burning or nuclear energy; the manufacture of steel; the mining, smelting, or refining of virtually any mineral (e.g., copper, iron, lead, zinc, and limestone); the manufacture of synthetic organic chemicals; and the refining, storage, or dispensing of any petroleum product. It is simply not possible that Congress intended such havoc in the American economy, and not a single representative or senator mentioned the fact. Thus, we find no support for the NRDC's extreme position in the language or legislative history of the act.

Decision and Remedy

The court of appeals held that the EPA must reach a determination of what amount of vinyl chloride is "safe" and then set emission standards accordingly to provide for an "ample margin of safety."

Case Questions

Critical Legal Thinking Should emission levels of toxic pollutants be set at "risk-free" levels rather than just "safe" levels? Explain.

Business Ethics Do environmental activist groups and organizations serve an important public purpose? Explain.

Contemporary Business Can you think of instances in which environmental laws should be used to shut down whole industries? Explain.

Contemporary Business Environment
Indoor Air Pollution: A Frontier for Environmental Litigation

Most people who live or work in our country's urban centers have grown to accept air pollution as an unavoidable peril of modern life. What many of these people do not realize, however, is that they should not breathe a sigh of relief upon entering their offices or homes. According to officials of the EPA, the air inside some buildings may be 100 times more polluted than outside air.

Indoor air pollution, or **sick building syndrome**, has two primary causes. In an effort to reduce dependence on foreign oil, many recently constructed office buildings were overly insulated and built with sealed windows and no outside air ducts. As a result, absolutely no fresh air enters many workplaces. This absence of fresh air can cause headaches, fatigue, and dizziness among workers.

The other chief cause of sick building syndrome, which is believed to affect up to one-third of U.S. office buildings, is hazardous chemicals and construction materials. In the office, these include everything from asbestos to noxious fumes emitted from copy machines, carbonless paper, and cleaning fluids. In the home, radon, an odorless gas that is emitted from the natural breakdown of uranium in soil, poses a particularly widespread danger. Four million to 10 million homes in the United States have radon levels in excess of EPA guidelines. Radon gas damages and may destroy lung tissue. It is estimated that radon causes 20,000 deaths each year.

Indoor air pollution has placed businesses between a rock and a hard place. Employer inactivity in the face of this danger will surely result in higher health care bills for employee illnesses as doctors increasingly attribute a wide range of symptoms to sick building syndrome. Indoor air pollution also adversely affects worker productivity and morale and increases absenteeism. On the other hand, the costs of eliminating these conditions can be colossal.

Experts predict that sick building syndrome is likely to spawn a flood of litigation, and that a wide range of parties will be sued. Manufacturers, employers, home sellers, builders, engineers, and architects will increasingly be forced to defend themselves against tort and breach of contract actions filed by homeowners, employees, and others affected by indoor air pollution. Federal and state governments may also be dragged into court to pay for defects in their buildings and to defend their regulatory standards. Insurance companies will undoubtedly be drawn into costly lawsuits stemming from indoor air pollution.

Presently, the government has not adopted any regulations governing indoor air quality. ■

Water Pollution

Water pollution affects human health, recreation, agriculture, and business. Pollution of waterways by industry and humans has caused severe ecological and environmental problems, including water sources that are unsafe for drinking water, fish, birds, and animals.

water pollution
Pollution of lakes, rivers, oceans, and other bodies of water.

The federal government has enacted a comprehensive scheme of statutes and regulations to prevent and control water pollution. The first regulation dates back to the **River and Harbor Act**, which was enacted in 1886. This act, as codified in 1899, established a permit system for the discharge of refuse, wastes, and sewage into the nation's navigable waterways. This permit system was replaced in 1972 by the **National Pollutant Discharge Elimination System (NPDES)**, which requires any person who proposes to discharge pollution into the water to obtain a permit from the EPA. The EPA can deny or set restrictions on such permits.

River and Harbor Act
A federal statute enacted in 1886 that established a permit system for the discharge of refuse, wastes, and sewage into U.S. navigable waterways.

Landmark Law

Clean Water Act

In 1948, Congress enacted the **Federal Water Pollution Control Act (FWPCA)** to regulate water pollution. This act was amended several times before it was updated by the Clean Water Act of 1972, the Clean Water Act of 1977, and the Water Quality Act of 1987. The FWPCA, as amended, is simply referred to as the **Clean Water Act** [33 U.S.C. §§ 1251 et seq.]. This act is administered by the EPA.

Pursuant to the Clean Water Act, the EPA has established water quality standards that define which bodies of water can be used for public drinking water, recreation (such as swimming), propagation of fish and wildlife, and agricultural and industrial uses.

States are primarily responsible for enforcing the provisions of the Clean Water Act and EPA regulations adopted thereunder. If a state fails to do so, the federal government may enforce the act. ■

St. Ignace, Michigan. Federal environmental protection statutes control water pollution.

Point Sources of Water Pollution

point sources
Sources of water pollution such as paper mills, manufacturing plants, electric utility plants, and sewage plants.

The Clean Water Act authorizes the EPA to establish water pollution control standards for **point sources** of water pollution (i.e., mines, manufacturing plants, paper mills, electric utility plants, municipal sewage plants, and other stationary sources of water pollution). The EPA issues guidelines as to the best available technologies. Dischargers of pollutants are required to keep records, maintain monitoring equipment, and keep samples of discharges. The following case involves the application of the Clean Water Act.

U.S. SUPREME COURT CASE

Case 20.3
Clean Water Act

Friends of the Earth, Incorporated v. Laidlaw Environmental Services (TOC), Inc.

528 U.S. 167, 120 S.Ct. 693, 2000 U.S. Lexis 501 (2000)
Supreme Court of the United States

Background and Facts

Laidlaw Environmental Services (TOC), Inc., operated a hazardous waste incinerator facility in Roebuck, South Carolina, where it discharged wastes into the North Tyger River. Between 1987 and 1995, Laidlaw discharged into the river wastes that exceeded the mercury limits allowed at the site. Mercury is a dangerous pollutant. The South Carolina Department of Health and Environmental Control (DHEC) sued Laidlaw. Laidlaw, which had gained an economic benefit of over $1 million by making these illegal discharges, reached a settlement with the DHEC whereby it paid $100,000 in penalties.

The Friends of the Earth, Incorporated (FOE), and other environmental groups brought a lawsuit against Laidlaw, seeking to obtain civil penalties permitted in civil-citizen lawsuits under the federal Clean Water Act. Laidlaw argued that FOE could not sue because Laidlaw had already reached a settlement with the state of South Carolina. The district court held for FOE and ordered Laidlaw to pay $405,800 in civil penalties; the court also ordered a hearing to determine the amount of attorneys' fees to be awarded FOE. The court of appeals reversed. The U.S. Supreme Court granted review.

Supreme Court Issue

Does settlement with a state for environmental violations make moot a civil-citizen lawsuit under the federal Clean Water Act?

In The Language of The U.S. Supreme Court

Ginsburg, Justice It can scarcely be doubted that, for a plaintiff who is injured or faces the threat of future injury due to illegal conduct ongoing at the time of suit, a sanction that effectively abates that conduct and prevents its recurrence provides a form of redress. Civil penalties can fit that description. To the extent that they encourage defendants to discontinue current violations and deter them from committing future ones, they afford redress to citizen plaintiffs who are injured or threatened with injury as a consequence of ongoing unlawful conduct.

Decision and Remedy

The U.S. Supreme Court held that defendant Laidlaw was subject to FOE's civil-citizen lawsuit for damages under the Clean Water Act, even though Laidlaw had previously been sued and reached a settlement with the state of South Carolina. The Supreme Court remanded the case for a determination of the attorneys' fees to be awarded to FOE.

Case Questions

Critical Legal Thinking Should citizens be permitted to bring lawsuits to enforce environmental laws? Or should only the government have this power? Explain.

Business Ethics Did Laidlaw act ethically in this case?

Contemporary Business Did Laidlaw come out ahead financially in its settlement with the state of South Carolina?

Thermal Pollution

The Clean Water Act expressly forbids **thermal pollution** because the discharge of heated waters or materials into the nation's waterways may upset the ecological balance; decrease the oxygen content of water; and harm fish, birds, and other animals that use the waterways.[2] Sources of thermal pollution (such as electric utility companies and manufacturing plants) are subject to the provisions of the Clean Water Act and regulations adopted by the EPA.

thermal pollution
Pollution created by heated water or material being discharged into waterways. It upsets the ecological balance and decreases the oxygen content.

Wetlands

Wetlands are defined as areas that are inundated or saturated by surface water or ground water that support vegetation typically adapted for life in saturated soil conditions. Wetlands include swamps, marshes, bogs, and similar areas that support birds, animals, and vegetative life. The Clean Water Act forbids the filling or dredging of wetlands unless a permit has been obtained from the **Army Corps of Engineers (Corps)**. The Corps is empowered to adopt regulations and conduct administrative proceedings to enforce the act.

wetlands
Areas that are inundated or saturated by surface water or ground water that support vegetation typically adapted for life in such conditions.

Safe Drinking Water Act

The **Safe Drinking Water Act**,[3] which was enacted in 1974 and amended in 1986, authorizes the EPA to establish national primary drinking water standards (minimum quality of water for human consumption). The act also prohibits the dumping of wastes into wells used for drinking water. The states are primarily responsible for enforcing the act. If a state fails to do so, the federal government can enforce the act.

Safe Drinking Water Act
A federal statute enacted in 1974 and amended in 1986 that authorizes the EPA to establish national primary drinking water standards.

Ocean Dumping

The **Marine Protection, Research, and Sanctuaries Act**,[4] enacted in 1972, extends environmental protection to the oceans. It (1) requires a permit for dumping wastes and other foreign materials into ocean waters and (2) establishes marine sanctuaries in ocean waters as far seaward as the edge of the Continental Shelf and in the Great Lakes and their connecting waters.

Marine Protection, Research, and Sanctuaries Act
A federal statute enacted in 1972 that extends environmental protection to the oceans.

Oil Spills

The Clean Water Act authorizes the U.S. government to clean up oil spills and spills of other hazardous substances in ocean waters within 12 miles of the shore and on the Continental Shelf and to recover the cleanup costs from responsible parties.

The following case involved the definition of *navigable waters* under the Clean Water Act.

Ethics Brief
When the oil tanker *Exxon Valdez* ran aground off Alaska in 1989, the oil industry was not prepared to respond to the emergency.

Case 20.4 Clean Water Act

U.S. SUPREME COURT CASE

Solid Waste Agency of Northern Cook County, Illinois v. United States Army Corps of Engineers

531 U.S. 159, 121 S.Ct. 675, 2001 U.S. Lexis 640 (2001)

Supreme Court of the United States

Background and Facts

Section 404 of the federal Clean Water Act regulates the discharge of dredged or fill material into *navigable waters*. The U.S. Army Corps of Engineers (Corps) is authorized to enforce this statute and to issue permits for discharge of dredged or fill material into navigable waters in the United States. The Solid Waste Agency of Northern Cook County, Illinois (Agency), a consortium of 23 suburban Chicago cities and villages, located a 533-acre parcel of real property that was a closed sand and gravel pit mining operation as a proposed disposal site for baled nonhazardous solid waste. Long since abandoned, the old mining site had permanent and seasonal water ponds of varying size and depth that served several species of migrating birds. The ponds were not connected to any water tributary but were filled by rain water and melting snow. When the Corps refused to issue a permit, the Agency sued the Corps, arguing that the Corps had no jurisdiction over the site because it did not contain any *navigable waters*. The district court held for the Corps, and the court of appeals affirmed. The U.S. Supreme Court granted review.

Supreme Court Issue

Does the gravel and sand pit contain *navigable waters* that give the Corps jurisdiction over the site?

In The Language of The U.S. Supreme Court

Rehnquist, Chief Justice Congress passed the CWA for the stated purpose of restoring and maintaining the chemical, physical, and biological integrity of the Nation's waters. Relevant here, Section 404 authorizes respondents U.S. Army Corps of Engineers to regulate the discharge of fill material into "navigable waters," which the statute defines as "the waters of the United States, including the territorial seas." Respondents have interpreted these words to cover the abandoned gravel pit at issue here because it is used as habitat for migratory birds. We thus decline respondents' invitation to hold that isolated ponds, some only seasonal, wholly located within Illinois, fall under § 404's definition of "navigable waters" because they serve as habitat for migratory birds. As counsel for respondents conceded at oral argument, such a ruling would assume that the use of the word *navigable* in the statute does not have any independent significance.

Decision and Remedy

The U.S. Supreme Court held that the ponds located on the sand and gravel pit are not *navigable waters* as defined by Section 404 of the Clean Water Act. Therefore, the Corps does not have authority or jurisdiction over these ponds. The judgment of the court of appeals was reversed.

Case Questions

Critical Legal Thinking Do you think that the U.S. Supreme Court properly interpreted the term *navigable waters* as used in Section 404 of the Clean Water Act?

Business Ethics Did the petitioner Solid Waste Agency act ethically in placing a waste disposal site on an area where the habitat of several species of migrating birds could be destroyed?

Contemporary Business In the United States, has a proper balance been struck between the protection of the environment and the ability of businesses to operate without too much burden from these laws? Explain.

Contemporary Business Environment

The Oil Pollution Act

In March 1989, the *Exxon Valdez*, an oil supertanker, ran aground in Prince William Sound in Alaska, spilling millions of gallons of oil into the water. Exxon and the oil industry were not prepared to respond to this emergency. The first cleanup barge did not reach the site until 14 hours after the oil spill. The response was totally inadequate, and the oil eventually contaminated 1,100 miles of shoreline. Tens of thousands of dead animals and birds lay strewn on the shore, and there were unknown numbers of dead fish.

Two factors—the devastation caused by the *Exxon Valdez* catastrophe and the oil industry's ill-preparedness to address oil spills—caused Congress to enact the **Oil Pollution Act of 1990 (OPA)**. This act, which is administered by the U.S. Coast Guard, requires the oil industry to adopt procedures that can more readily respond to oil spills.

The OPA contains strict requirements for constructing oil tankers. It requires new ships to have double hulls and phases out single-hull tankers between 1995 and 2010. Barges must be double-hulled by 2015. The tanker industry is upset about the double-hull requirement and is seeking a less expensive means to ensure protection in case of a mishap.

The OPA also requires each tanker owner–operator to establish an oil pollution cleanup contingency plan. The Coast Guard has issued regulations for emergency response plans by tankers operating in U.S. waters. Under the OPA and Coast Guard regulations, tanker owner–operators must have enough personnel and equipment to handle a "worst case" spill of an entire cargo in "adverse" weather conditions. They also have to contract with an oil-spill response company. In response, 20 major oil companies funded the creation of the Marine Spill Response Corporation. Other response firms are also being set up by other oil companies.

The Coast guard must issue a certificate to a tanker owner–operator before oil may be brought to the United States. To obtain the certificate, the tanker owner–operator must prove that it is fully insured to cover any liability that may occur from an oil spill.

It is hoped that the emergency response procedures mandated by the OPA will not be needed. But at least next time the mechanism will be in place to respond more quickly and adequately to such a spill so that an environmental catastrophe the size of that caused by the *Exxon Valdez* will never occur again. ■

International Law

The Law of the Sea

For centuries, the oceans were considered "high seas" over which no nation had jurisdiction. In the middle of the nineteenth century, coastal nations began claiming exclusive rights to territorial waters and seabeds that bordered their nations. Nations claimed exclusive rights to seas extending anywhere from 12 to 200 miles from the shoreline. Most of these national laws were enacted to protect fishing rights.

In 1971, the United Nations Convention on the Law of the Sea (LOS Convention) established a 200-mile exclusive economic zone (EEZ) for coastal nations. This convention grants sovereign rights to coastal nations to explore, exploit, conserve, and manage living resources in their EEZs. It also grants these nations sovereign rights over nonliving resources of the seabed and subsoil in the EEZs.

The LOS Convention grants all nations the freedom of navigation and overflight over EEZs as well as the right to lay submarine cables and pipelines. In exercising these rights, nations must comply with the lawful and nondiscriminatory laws of the coastal nation. A coastal nation may permit other nations to fish and use the waters and seabeds of its EEZ, subject to conservation and other laws established by the coastal nation.

The LOS Convention gives coastal nations the right to board and inspect ships, arrest a ship and its crew, and institute legal proceedings against violators. Appeals may be made to the International Tribunal for the Law of the Sea. ■

Toxic Substances

The use of chemicals for agricultural, industrial, and mining uses has greatly increased productivity in this country. Unfortunately, many of these chemicals contain **toxic substances** that cause cancer, birth defects, and other health-related problems in human beings, as well as injury or death to birds, animals, fish, and vegetation. Because of these dangers, the federal government has enacted legislation to regulate the use of toxic substances. Two of these statutes are discussed in the following paragraphs.

toxic substances
Chemicals used for agricultural, industrial, and mining uses that cause injury to humans, birds, animals, fish, and vegetation.

Insecticide, Fungicide, and Rodenticide Act

Farmers and ranchers use chemical pesticides, herbicides, fungicides, and rodenticides to kill insects, pests, and weeds. Evidence shows that the use of some of these chemicals on foods, and their residual accumulation in soil, poses health hazards. In 1947, Congress enacted the **Insecticide, Fungicide, and Rodenticide Act**, which gave the federal government authority to regulate pesticides and related chemicals. This act, which was substantially amended in 1972,[5] is administered by the EPA.

Insecticide, Fungicide, and Rodenticide Act
A federal statute that requires pesticides, herbicides, fungicides, and rodenticides to be registered with the EPA; the EPA may deny, suspend, or cancel registration.

Under the act, pesticides must be registered with the EPA before they can be sold. The EPA may deny registration, certify either general or restricted use, or set limits on the amount of chemical residue permitted on crops sold for human or animal consumption. The EPA has authority to register and inspect pesticide manufacturing facilities.

The EPA may suspend the registration of a registered pesticide that it finds poses an imminent danger or emergency. If the EPA finds that the use of a registered pesticide poses environmental risks (but not imminent danger), it may initiate a proceeding to cancel the registration of the pesticide. After reviewing the evidence, the EPA may cancel a registration if it finds use of the pesticide would cause unreasonably adverse effects on the environment.

Botanical Gardens, Huntington Library, San Marino, California. The federal Clean Air Act, Clean Water Act, Toxic Substances Control Act, and other federal statutes protect plant life, animal life, and the environment from pollution.

Toxic Substances Control Act

Toxic Substances Control Act A federal statute enacted in 1976 that requires manufacturers and processors to test new chemicals to determine their effect on human health and the environment before the EPA will allow them to be marketed.

Many chemical compounds that are used in the manufacture of plastics and other products are toxic (e.g., PCBs, asbestos). Hundreds of new chemicals and chemical compounds that may be toxic are discovered each year. In 1976, Congress enacted the **Toxic Substances Control Act**[6] and gave the EPA authority to administer the act.

The act requires manufacturers and processors to test new chemicals to determine the effect on human health and the environment and to report the results to the EPA before they can be marketed. The EPA may limit or prohibit the manufacture and sale of toxic substances, or remove them from commerce, if it finds that they pose an imminent hazard or an unreasonable risk of injury to human health or the environment. The EPA also requires special labeling of toxic substances.

International Law

Kyoto Protocol Reduces Greenhouse Gases

For decades, scientists have been concerned that *greenhouse gases*—particularly from carbon dioxide created by burning coal, oil, and gas—were causing a global warming effect and creating a hole in the ozone layer around the earth. In 1997, after much debate, the countries of the world met in Kyoto, Japan, and proposed the **Kyoto Protocol**, an international treaty to reduce greenhouse gases. The deal almost fell apart; but in 2001, 178 countries agreed to abide by the rules of the Kyoto Protocol.

The Kyoto Protocol calls for the reduction of greenhouse gases worldwide to 5.2 percent below 1990 levels, with this goal to be reached by 2012. The protocol originally set targets for 39 industrialized countries; however, developing nations are not covered by the initial emission control standards. The protocol calls for member nations to create a $400 million fund to help developing nations adopt technology to reduce greenhouse gases. The United States was not a signatory to the Kyoto Protocol but instead chose to adopt its own laws to control greenhouse gas emissions. ■

Tibet. Many areas of the world must protect the environment from pollution.

Hazardous Waste

Wastes, which often contain hazardous substances that can harm the environment or pose a danger to human health, are generated by agriculture, mining, industry, other businesses, and households. Wastes consist of garbage, sewage, industrial discharges, old equipment, and such. The mishandling and disposal of **hazardous wastes** can cause air, water, and **land pollution**.

hazardous waste
Waste that may cause or significantly contribute to an increase in mortality or serious illness or pose a hazard to human health or the environment if improperly managed.

land pollution
Pollution of the land that is generally caused by hazardous waste being disposed of in an improper manner.

Prior to the mid-1970s, the disposal of solid waste was generally regarded as a problem for local governments. However, discovery of thousands of dump sites and landfills containing hazardous wastes caused concern at the federal level. To prevent future problems, and to assist in cleaning up past problems, Congress enacted the statutes discussed in the following paragraphs to deal with hazardous waste.

Resource Conservation and Recovery Act (RCRA)

In 1976, Congress enacted the **Resource Conservation and Recovery Act (RCRA)**,[7] which regulates the disposal of new hazardous wastes. This act, which has been amended several times, authorizes the EPA to regulate facilities that generate, treat, store, transport, and dispose of hazardous wastes. States have primary responsibility for implementing the standards established by the act and EPA regulations. If states fail to act, the EPA can enforce the act.

Resource Conservation and Recovery Act (RCRA)
A federal statute that authorizes the EPA to regulate facilities that generate, treat, store, transport, and dispose of hazardous wastes.

The act defines hazardous waste as a solid waste that may cause or significantly contribute to an increase in mortality or serious illness or pose a hazard to human health or the environment if improperly managed. The EPA has designated substances that are toxic, radioactive, or corrosive or that ignite as hazardous and can add to the list of hazardous wastes as needed.

Pursuant to its authority under the act, the EPA has implemented a "cradle to grave" tracking system and regulation of hazardous substances. Under the act, anyone who generates, treats, stores, or transports hazardous wastes must obtain a government permit to do so. The EPA establishes standards and procedures for the safe treatment, storage, disposal, and transportation of hazardous wastes. Under the act, the EPA is authorized to regulate underground storage facilities, such as underground gasoline tanks.

Business Ethics

Illegal Dumping of Pollutants Is a Crime

Environmental laws establish methods and procedures for treating and disposing of contaminated wastes. Persons and businesses sometimes intentionally violate environmental laws by secretly dumping polluted materials into the environment. Consider the following case.

Mark Irby was plant manager of a waste-water treatment plant. The record shows that Irby ordered employees of the plant to bypass the treatment system afterhours and to discharge approximately 500,000 gallons of raw untreated sewage and partially treated sludge sewage at least twice a week for two years into the Reedy River. The court found that these discharges caused environmental damage. Irby was charged with criminal violation of the Clean Water Act. The jury convicted him of six criminal violations of the act, and the district court sentenced him to the maximum allowable jail sentence (33 months). Irby challenged his sentence.

The court of appeals held that Irby exercised decision-making authority in directing the employees of the waste-water treatment plant to discharge the untreated sewage into the Reedy River. The court also held that the offense resulted in an ongoing, continuous, and repetitive discharge of pollutants into the environment, thus justifying the imposition of the 33 months of jail time. The court stated, "There was absolutely no acceptance of responsibility in this case. No remorse whatsoever was shown by Irby." [*United States v. Irby*, 944 F.2d 902, 1991 U.S. App. Lexis 27736 (4th Cir. 1991)]

1. Did Irby act ethically in this case?
2. What is the incentive for businesses and organizations to avoid obeying environmental laws? ■

Landmark Law

Comprehensive Environmental Response, Compensation, and Liability Act (Superfund)

In 1980, Congress enacted the **Comprehensive Environmental Response, Compensation, and Liability Act (CERCLA)**, which is commonly called "Superfund" [43 U.S.C. § 9601 et seq.]. The act, which was significantly amended in 1986, is administered by the EPA. The act gives the federal government a mandate to deal with hazardous wastes that have been spilled, stored, or abandoned.

Designated Hazardous Waste Sites

The Superfund requires the EPA to (1) identify sites in the United States where hazardous wastes have been disposed, stored, abandoned, or spilled and (2) rank these sites regarding the severity of the risk. More than 25,000 sites have been identified. The EPA considers such factors as the types of hazardous waste, the toxicity of the waste, the types of pollution (air, water, land, or other pollution) caused by the waste, the number of people potentially affected by the risk, and other factors when it ranks the sites. The hazardous waste sites with the highest ranking are put on the National Priority List. The sites on this list receive first consideration for cleanup. Before the cleanup can begin, though, engineering and scientific studies are conducted to determine the best method for cleaning up the waste site. The EPA has the authority to clean up hazardous priority or nonpriority sites quickly to prevent fire, explosion, contamination of drinking water, or other imminent danger.

The Superfund provides for the creation of a fund to finance the cleanup of hazardous waste sites (hence the name *Superfund*). The fund is financed through taxes on chemicals, feedstocks, motor fuels, and other products that contain hazardous substances.

Liability for Cleanup of Superfund Sites

The EPA can order a responsible party to clean up a hazardous waste site. If that party fails to do so, the EPA can clean up the site and recover the cost of the cleanup. The Superfund imposes strict liability—that is, liability without fault. The EPA can recover the cost of the cleanup from (1) the generator who deposited the waste, (2) the transporter of the waste to the site, (3) the owner of the site at the time of the disposal, and (4) the current owner and operator of the site. Liability is *joint and several*; that is, a person who is responsible for only a fraction of the hazardous waste may be liable for all the cleanup costs. The Superfund permits states and private parties who clean up hazardous waste sites to seek reimbursement from the fund.

The Superfund contains a **right to know provision** that requires businesses to (1) disclose the presence of certain listed chemicals to the community, (2) annually disclose emissions of chemical substances released into the environment, and (3) immediately notify the government of spills, accidents, and other emergencies involving hazardous substances. ■

Entrepreneur and the Law

Superfund Law Cleans Car Wash Owner

Jim Wilson nearly forgot that he had once owned a car wash in Sherman Oaks, California, 30 years before, until he received a bill in the mail from the EPA for $142,500. The bill was his share of the $600 million cost of cleaning up a toxic waste site in Monterey Park, some 20 miles from the site of his prior car wash. The EPA had designated the Monterey Park location, which had been a waste disposal site, as a Superfund site and was now sending bills to about 700 prior users to recover money to clean up the site. By designating a Superfund site, the EPA is responsible by law to clean up the site and seek compensation from "polluters" to pay for the cleanup costs.

What was Jim Wilson's sin? He had sent soapy nontoxic carwash water to the Monterey Park dump site in the 1960s. Wilson correctly argues that what he did was legal under existing laws when he did it. The Superfund law, however, was drafted to apply retroactively; that is, a party can be held liable for violating the law for actions it took before the Superfund law was enacted by Congress. Although the retroactive application of the law has been challenged, the federal courts have held that the Superfund law does not violate the Due Process Clause of the U.S. Constitution.

Superfund is a tort law that imposes *strict liability*, or liability without fault, and *joint and several liability*, which means that each individual defendant is legally liable for the entire cleanup cost, no matter how small that defendant's pollution was relative to all the pollution at the site. Thus, under these two legal principles, any defendant could be held liable for the entire cleanup cost of an EPA Superfund site without being found to be at fault. Superfund law also allows liable private parties to sue to recover from other polluters for their share of the cleanup costs. Thus, if a party should decide to ignore the EPA's bill, it can be sued by other polluters.

If a party settles with the EPA by paying the bill sent to it, it generally is not liable beyond this amount. If a party does not pay the bill, it risks lawsuits from the EPA and other polluters and could be assessed liability much greater than the billed amount. Persons who receive EPA Superfund bills claim that this law is unfair because the EPA has a hammer that forces them to pay. In addition, if a party decides to fight the bill, it could pay hundreds of thousands of dollars in legal fees, with little probability of winning. Wilson and others like him claim that they have been steamcleaned by the EPA. The EPA claims that Wilson owes a duty to clean the EPA Superfund site as well as he did cars. ■

Nuclear Waste

Nuclear-powered fuel plants create radioactive wastes that maintain a high level of *radioactivity*. Radioactivity can cause injury and death to humans and other life and can also cause severe damage to the environment. Accidents, human error, faulty construction, and such all can be causes of **radiation pollution**.

radiation pollution
Emissions from radioactive wastes that can cause injury and death to humans and other life and can cause severe damage to the environment.

Regulation of nuclear energy in this country is primarily placed with the following two federal agencies:

1. ***Nuclear Regulatory Commission*** The **Nuclear Regulatory Commission (NRC)**, which was created by Congress in 1977, licenses the construction and opening of commercial nuclear power plants. It continually monitors the operation of nuclear power plants and may close a plant if safety violations are found.
2. ***EPA*** The EPA is empowered to set standards for radioactivity in the environment and to regulate the disposal of radioactive waste. The EPA also regulates thermal pollution from nuclear power plants and emissions from uranium mines and mills.

Nuclear Regulatory Commission (NRC)
A federal agency that licenses the construction and opening of commercial nuclear power plants.

Nuclear Waste Policy Act of 1982
A federal statute that says the federal government must select and develop a permanent site for the disposal of nuclear waste.

Currently, nuclear wastes are stored on an interim basis at the power plants that generated the wastes or other temporary sites. **The Nuclear Waste Policy Act of 1982**[8] mandates that the federal government select and develop a permanent site for the disposal of nuclear wastes.

Business Ethics

Disclosing Environmental Liabilities to Shareholders

In the past, most corporations did not disclose environmental liabilities in the financial statements given to shareholders and others. As of 1992, the Securities and Exchange Commission (SEC) adopted rules requiring companies to report their environmental liabilities in their financial statements. The SEC and the EPA share information concerning corporations' compliance with environmental laws. Failure to disclose environmental liabilities under the new rules subjects violators to civil and criminal penalties.

In developing a program to access and report environmental liabilities, companies should take the following steps:

- Designate a senior officer to be responsible for the environmental disclosure process. This environmental officer should report directly to the president and the board of directors.
- Create a committee of the board of directors to oversee the environmental compliance and disclosure process of the company.
- Retain outside environmental consultants, if feasible, to assist in the data gathering, evaluation, and disclosure process. This will lead to a more objective assessment of environmental liabilities.
- Review the company's environmental exposure and make a list of the important environmental problems facing the company.
- Decide which environmental problems are "material" and must be disclosed under SEC rules. Also decide whether additional information should be disclosed.
- Document what the company is doing to rectify its environmental problems. Also document why the company thought it was doing the right thing in taking the action it took.
- Prepare the environmental disclosure report as required by the SEC and include the relevant information from this report in the financial statements of the company.
- Monitor new developments and reassess whether additional disclosures have to be periodically made to the SEC, EPA, shareholders, and others. ■

Landmark Law

The Endangered Species Act

Many species of animals are endangered or threatened with extinction. The reduction of certain species of wildlife may be caused by environmental pollution, real estate development, or hunting. The **Endangered Species Act** was enacted in 1973 [16 U.S.C. §§ 1531 et seq.]. The act, as amended, protects *endangered* and *threatened* species of animals and plants. The secretary of the interior is empowered to declare a form of wildlife *endangered* or *threatened*. The act requires the EPA and the Department of Commerce to designate *critical habitats* for each endangered and threatened species. Real estate and other development in these areas is prohibited or severely limited. The secretary of commerce is empowered to enforce the provisions of the act as to marine species.

In addition, the Endangered Species Act, which applies to both government and private persons, prohibits the *taking* of any endangered species. *Taking* is defined as an act intended to "harass, harm, pursue, hunt, shoot, wound, kill, trap, capture, or collect" an endangered animal or plant.

Other Federal Laws that Protect Wildlife

Numerous other federal laws protect wildlife. These include (1) the Migratory Bird Treaty Act, (2) the Bald Eagle Protection Act, (3) the Wild Free-Roaming Horses and Burros Act, (4) the Marine Mammal Protection Act, (5) the Migratory Bird Conservation Act, (6) the Fishery Conservation and Management Act, (7) the Fish and Wildlife Coordination Act, and (8) the National Wildlife Refuse System. Many states have enacted statutes that protect and preserve wildlife. The Endangered Species Act was applied in the following case. ■

U.S. SUPREME COURT CASE

Tennessee Valley Authority v. Hill, Secretary of the Interior

437 U.S. 153, 98 S.Ct. 2279, 1978 U.S. Lexis 33 (1978)
Supreme Court of the United States

Case 20.5

Endangered Species Act

Background and Facts

The Tennessee Valley Authority (TVA) is a wholly owned public corporation of the United State that operates a series of dams, reservoirs, and water projects that provide electric power, irrigation, and flood control to areas in several southern states. In 1967, with appropriations from Congress, the TVA began construction of the Tellico Dam on the Little Tennessee River. When completed, the dam would impound water covering 16,500 acres, thereby converting the river's shallow, fast-flowing waters into a deep reservoir over 30 miles in length. Construction of the dam continued until 1977, when it was completed.

In 1973, a University of Tennessee ichthyologist found a previously unknown species of perch called the Percina (Imostoma) Tansai—or "snail darter"—in the Little Tennessee River. After further investigation, it was determined that approximately 10,000 to 15,000 of these 3-inch, tannish-colored fish existed in the river's waters that would be flooded by the operation of the Tellico Dam. The snail darter was not found anywhere else in the world. It feeds exclusively on snails and requires substantial oxygen, both supplied by the fast-moving waters of the Little Tennessee River. The impounding of the water behind the Tellico Dam would destroy the snail darter's food and oxygen supplies, thus causing its extinction. Evidence was introduced showing that the TVA could not, at any time, successfully transplant the snail darter to any other habitat.

Also in 1973, Congress enacted the Endangered Species Act (Act). The act authorizes the secretary of the interior (Secretary) to declare species of animal life *endangered* and to identify the *critical habitat* of these creatures. When a species or its habitat is so listed, Section 7 of the act mandates that the secretary take such action as is necessary to ensure that actions of the federal government do not jeopardize the continued existence of such endangered species. The secretary declared the snail darter an endangered species and the area that would be affected by the dam its critical habitat.

Congress continued to appropriate funds for the construction of the dam, which was completed at a cost of over $100 million. In 1976, a regional association of biological scientists, a Tennessee conservation group, and several individuals filed an action seeking to enjoin the TVA from closing the gates of the dam and impounding the water in the reservoir on the grounds that those actions would violate Section 7 of the act by causing the extinction of the snail darter. The district court held in favor of the TVA. The court of appeals reversed and remanded, with instructions to the district court to issue a permanent injunction halting the operation of the Tellico Dam. The TVA appealed to the U.S. Supreme Court.

Supreme Court Issue

Would the TVA be in violation of the Endangered Species Act if it operated the Tellico Dam?

In The Language of The U.S. Supreme Court

Burger, Chief Justice It may seem curious to some that the survival of a relatively small number of 3-inch fish among all the countless millions of species would require the permanent halting of a virtually completed dam for which Congress has expended more than $100 million. We conclude, however, that the explicit provisions of the Endangered Species Act required precisely this result.

One would be hard pressed to find a statutory provision whose terms were any plainer than those in Section 7 of the Endangered Species Act. Its very words affirmatively command all federal agencies to ensure that actions authorized, funded, or carried out by them do not jeopardize the continued existence of an endangered species or result in the destruction or modification of habitat of such species. This language admits no exception. Nonetheless, petitioner TVA urges that the Act cannot reasonably be interpreted as applying to a federal project that was well under way when Congress passed the Endangered Species Act of 1973. To sustain that position, however, we would be forced to ignore the ordinary meaning of plain language.

Examination of the language, history, and structure of the legislation under review here indicates beyond doubt that Congress intended endangered species to be afforded the highest of priorities. As it was passed, the Endangered Species Act of 1973 represented the most comprehensive legislation for the preservation of endangered species ever enacted by any nation. Virtually all dealings with endangered species, including taking, possession, transportation, and sale, were prohibited. Section 7 of the Act, which of course is relied upon by respondents in this case, provides a particularly good gauge of congressional intent.

Decision and Remedy

The Supreme Court held that the Endangered Species Act prohibited the impoundment of the Little Tennessee River by the Tellico Dam. Affirmed.

Note

Eventually, after substantial research and investigation, it was determined that the snail darter could live in another habitat that was found for it. After the snail darter was removed, at government expense, to this new location, the TVA was permitted to close the gates of the Tellico Dam and begin its operation.

Case Questions

Critical Legal Thinking Should the law protect endangered species? Why or why not?

Business Ethics Did the TVA act ethically in this case by completing construction of the dam?

Contemporary Business Do you think the cost of constructing the Tellico Dam ($100 million) should have been considered by the Court in reaching its decision?

Monterey, California. Greenpeace International is an organization that engages in activism to protect animals, including fish and birds, and the environment. Greenpeace members often use physically combative tactics to block hunters from killing seals.

Noise Pollution

noise pollution
Unwanted sound from planes, manufacturing plants, motor vehicles, construction equipment, stereos, and the like.

Unwanted sound affects almost every member of society on a daily basis. The sources of **noise pollution** include airplanes, manufacturing plants, motor vehicles, construction equipment, lawn mowers, radios, toys, automobile alarms, and such. Noise pollution causes hearing loss, loss of sleep, depression, and other emotional and psychological symptoms and injuries.

Noise Control Act

Noise Control Act
A federal statute enacted in 1972 that authorizes the EPA to establish noise standards for products sold in the United States.

The **Noise Control Act**,[9] enacted in 1972, authorizes the EPA to establish noise standards for products sold in the United States. The EPA, jointly with the Federal Aviation Administration (FAA), establishes noise limitations on new aircraft. The EPA, jointly with the Department of Transportation, regulates noise emissions from trucks, railroads, and interstate carriers. Other federal agencies also regulate noise pollution. For example, the Occupational Safety and Health Administration (OSHA) regulates noise levels in the workplace.

The **Quiet Communities Act**[10] authorizes the federal government to provide financial and technical assistance to state and local governments in controlling noise pollution. The act, which was enacted in 1978, is administered by the EPA.

State Environmental Protection Laws

Business Brief
States are entitled to set pollution standards that are stricter than federal requirements.

Many state and local governments have enacted statutes and ordinances to protect the environment. For example, most states require that an EIS or a report be prepared for any proposed state action. In addition, under their police power to protect the "health, safety, and welfare" of their residents, many states require private industry to prepare EISs for proposed developments.

Some states have enacted special environmental statutes to protect unique areas within their boundaries. For example, Florida has enacted laws to protect the Everglades, and California has enacted laws to protect its Pacific Ocean coastline. Businesses must consult state environmental protection laws before engaging in major developments.

International Law

Transborder Pollution

Countries can adopt laws to govern, prevent, and clean up pollution occurring within their own borders. However, in some instances, another country is the source of the pollution. This is called **transborder pollution**.

Whether the affected country has any recourse against the polluting country depends on whether the two countries have entered into a treaty concerning such an occurrence and whether the polluting country wants to abide by the provisions of the treaty. For example, the United States has entered into several treaties with Canada and Mexico that coordinate their efforts to control transborder pollution. The countries have agreed to regulate transborder air pollution (particularly acid rain) and water pollution. These three countries have created the North American Commission on Environmental Cooperation (CEC), a regional international agency located in Montreal, Canada, to review and coordinate environmental issues affecting the North American continent.

One of the most important international environmental issues focuses on the rain forests in Brazil and other South American countries. The rain forests are being clear-cut at an alarming rate. Environmental activists are trying to save the rain forests, but to no avail. It is difficult for countries such as the United States and those of Western Europe, that have cut down over 90 percent of their own forests, to try to convince Brazil and its neighbors not to cut down the rain forests.

In June 1992, an **Earth Summit** was held in Rio de Janeiro, Brazil. Most countries sent representatives to this conference. The countries at the summit signed the Rio Declaration, which directs signatory nations to enact effective environmental legislation. In addition, two treaties emerged from the summit, the Climate Change Control Convention (CCCC) and the Convention on Biological Diversity (CBD).

The focus of the CCCC is the stabilization of the greenhouse gas concentration in the atmosphere that is causing a hole in the ozone layer. The CBD is directed at ensuring that patents and inventions do not harm the environment.

It is obvious that environmental problems are not confined to individual countries. International cooperation is necessary to protect the environment and prevent global pollution. ■

International Bridges. This bridge links the twin cities of Sault Ste. Marie Canada and United States. Countries are working together to reduce transborder pollution.

Chapter Summary

Environmental Protection, p. 586

Environmental Protection

Environmental protection laws. Federal and state governments have enacted environmental protection statutes to control pollution and to penalize those who violate these statutes.

The Environmental Protection Agency (EPA)

A federal administrative agency created in 1970 that is empowered to implement and enforce federal environmental protection statutes. The EPA can adopt regulations to interpret and enforce the laws it is authorized to administer.

National Environmental Policy Act (NEPA)

A federal statute that mandates that the federal government consider the *adverse impact* a federal government action would have on the environment before the action is implemented.

Environmental Impact Statement (EIS)

A document that must be prepared for all proposed legislation or major federal action that significantly affects the quality of the human environment. The EIS must (1) describe the affected environment, (2) describe the impact of the proposed federal action on the environment, (3) identify and discuss alternatives to the proposed action, (4) list the resources that will be committed to the action, and (5) contain a cost–benefit analysis of the proposed action and alternative actions.

Air Pollution, p. 587

Air Pollution

Pollution caused by factories, homes, vehicles, and the like that affects the air.

Clean Air Act

A federal statute enacted in 1963 and amended several times that regulates air pollution.

National Ambient Air Quality Standards (NAAQS)

Standards for certain pollutants set by the EPA that protect (1) human beings (*primary*) and (2) vegetation, matter, climate, visibility, and economic values (*secondary*).

1. ***Nonattainment areas.*** Regions that do not meet federal air quality standards. They are classified into one of five categories—(1) marginal, (2) moderate, (3) serious, (4) severe, and (5) extreme—based on the degree to which they exceed federal air quality standards. States that fail to develop or implement an approved plan to correct deficiencies are subject to sanctions.

Stationary Sources of Air Pollution

Sources of air pollution such as industrial plants, oil refineries, and public utilities.

1. ***Pollution control.*** Stationary sources are required to install pollution control equipment.

Mobile Sources of Air Pollution

Sources of air pollution such as automobiles, trucks, buses, motorcycles, and airplanes.

1. ***Pollution controls.*** The Clean Air Act requires air pollution controls to be installed on automobiles and other sources of mobile air pollution.

Toxic Air Pollutants

Pollutants that cause serious illness or death. The EPA has identified more than 180 toxic air pollutants.

Water Pollution, p. 591

Water Pollution

Pollution of lakes, rivers, oceans, and other bodies of water.

1. ***River and Harbor Act of 1886.*** A statute that established a permit system for the discharge of refuse, wastes, and sewage into U.S. navigable waters.

Clean Water Act

Federal Water Pollution Control Act (FWPCA) of 1948. A federal statute that regulates water pollution. As amended, called the *Clean Water Act.*

Point Sources of Water Pollution

Sources of water pollution such as paper mills, manufacturing plants, electric utility plants, and sewage plants.

1. ***Pollution controls.*** Point sources are required to install pollution control equipment.

Thermal Pollution

Heated water or material discharged into waterways that upsets the ecological balance and decreases the oxygen content. Thermal pollution is subject to the provisions of the Clean Water Act.

Wetlands

Areas that are inundated or saturated by surface or groundwater that support vegetation typically adapted for life in such conditions. The Clean Water Act forbids the filling or dredging of wetlands unless a permit has been obtained from the *Army Corps of Engineers.*

Safe Drinking Water

The *Safe Drinking Water Act of 1974* authorizes the EPA to establish national minimum quality of water standards for human consumption. States are primarily responsible for enforcing the act. If a state fails to do so, the federal government can enforce the act.

Ocean Dumping

Marine Protection, Research, and Sanctuaries Act of 1972. A federal statute that extends environmental protection to oceans. It requires a permit for dumping wastes and other foreign materials into ocean waters.

Oil Spills

The Clean Water Act authorizes the U.S. government to clean up oil spills and spills of other hazardous substances in ocean waters within 12 miles of the shore and on the Continental Shelf. The act authorizes the federal government to recover the cleanup costs from responsible parties.

Toxic Substances, p. 595

Toxic Substances

Chemicals used for agricultural, industrial, and mining uses that cause injury to humans, birds, animals, fish, and vegetation.

Federal Insecticide, Fungicide, and Rodenticide Act

A federal statute that requires pesticides, herbicides, fungicides, and rodenticides to be registered with the EPA. The EPA may deny, suspend, or cancel registration.

Toxic Substances Control Act

A federal statute that requires manufacturers and processors to test new chemicals to determine their effect on human health and the environment before the EPA will allow them to be marketed. The EPA requires special labeling of toxic substances.

Hazardous Waste, p. 597

Hazardous Waste

Solid waste that may cause or significantly contribute to an increase in mortality or serious illness or pose a hazard to human health or the environment if improperly managed.

1. ***Land pollution.*** Pollution of the land that is generally caused by hazardous waste being disposed of in an improper manner.

Resource Conservation and Recovery Act

A federal statute that authorizes the EPA to regulate facilities that generate, treat, store, transport, and dispose of hazardous wastes.

Comprehensive Environmental Response, Compensation, and Liability Act (Superfund)

A federal statute that gives the federal government a mandate to deal with hazardous wastes that have been spilled, stored, or abandoned. This act is commonly called Superfund.

1. ***Hazardous waste sites.*** This act requires the EPA to identify sites in the United States where hazardous wastes have been disposed, stored, spilled, or abandoned, and to rank these sites regarding the severity of the risk. The EPA has identified more than 25,000 hazardous waste sites.
2. ***Superfund.*** The act created a fund to finance the cleanup of hazardous waste sites (hence, the name Superfund). The fund is financed through taxes on chemicals, feedstocks, motor fuels, and other products that contain hazardous substances.
3. ***Liability for cleanup costs.*** The EPA can order a responsible party to clean up a hazardous waste site. If that party fails to do so, the EPA can clean up the site and recover the cost of the cleanup from the responsible party or parties. Superfund imposes *strict liability* (liability without fault). Liability is *joint and several* (i.e., a party who is only partially responsible may be liable for all the cleanup costs).
4. ***Right to know provision.*** A provision in Superfund that requires businesses to (1) disclose the presence of certain listed chemicals to the community, (2) annually disclose emissions of chemical substances released into the environment, and (3) immediately notify the government of spills, accidents, and other emergencies involving hazardous substances.

Nuclear Waste, p. 599

Nuclear Waste

Radioactive wastes generated by nuclear-powered fuel plants.

1. ***Radioactive pollution.*** Emissions from radioactive wastes that can cause injury and death to humans and other life and can cause severe damage to the environment.
2. ***Nuclear Regulatory Commission (NRC).*** A federal agency that licenses the construction and opening of commercial nuclear power plants. The NRC may deny or remove a license.
3. ***Nuclear Waste Policy Act of 1982.*** A federal statute that says the federal government must select and develop a permanent site for the disposal of nuclear wastes.

Preservation of Wildlife and Plants, p. 600

Endangered Species Act

A federal statute that protects endangered and threatened species of animals.

1. ***Critical habitat.*** The act requires the EPA to designate "critical habitats" for each endangered and threatened species.
2. ***Taking.*** The act prohibits the "taking" (e.g., hunting, trapping, harming) of any endangered species.

Other Federal Laws that Protect Wildlife

Other federal laws that protect wildlife include:

1. Migratory Bird Treaty Act
2. Bald Eagle Protection Act
3. Wild Free-Roaming Horses and Burros Act
4. Marine Mammal Protection Act
5. Migratory Bird Conservation Act
6. Fishery Conservation and Management Act
7. Fish and Wildlife Coordination Act
8. National Wildlife Refuse System

Noise Pollution, p. 602

Noise Pollution

Unwanted sound from planes, manufacturing plants, motor vehicles, construction equipment, stereos, and the like.

Noise Control Act

A federal statute that authorizes the EPA to establish noise standards for products sold in the United States.

1. ***Quiet Communities Act.*** A federal statute that authorizes the federal government to provide financial and technical assistance to state and local governments in controlling noise pollution.

State Environmental Protection Laws, p. 602

State Environmental Protection Laws

Many state and local governments have enacted statutes and ordinances to protect the environment. States and local governments are entitled to set pollution control standards that are stricter than federal requirements.

Internet Exercises and Case Questions

Working the Web Internet Exercises

Activities

1. Find the EPA Superfund toxic waste cleanup sites in your state. See the EPA Web site, at **www.epa.gov**.
2. Compare the position of Greenpeace International, the Sierra Club, and others on drilling in the Arctic National Wildlife Refuse:

   Greenpeace International
   www.greenpeace.org

   Sierra Club
   www.sierraclub.org

   National Audubon Society
   www.audubon.org

   Natural Resources Defense Council
   www.nrdc.org

   EarthWatch Institute
   www.earthwatch.org/index.html

   World Environmental Law
   www.hg.org/environ.html

3. Compare your state's environmental laws to the federal controls in the area of water and air pollution. For an overview of land-use law, with links to key primary and secondary sources, see Law About . . . Land Use, at **www.law.cornell.edu/topics/land_use.html**.
4. Is your state home to any of the animals protected by the Endangered Species Act? Which ones? See the Earth Justice Legal Defense Fund site at **www.earthjustice.org**, and the Environmental Defense Fund site, at **www.edf.org**.

Critical Legal Thinking Cases

20.1 Environmental Impact Statement The U.S. Forest Service is responsible for managing the country's national forests for recreational and other purposes. This includes issuing special use permits to private companies to operate ski areas on federal lands. Sandy Butte is a 6,000-foot mountain located in the Okanogan National Forest in Okanogan County, Washington. Sandy Butte, like the Methow Valley it overlooks, is a pristine, unspoiled, sparsely populated area located within the North Cascades National Park. Large populations of mule deer and other animals exist in the park.

In 1978, Methow Recreation, Inc. (MRI), applied to the Forest Service for a special use permit to develop and operate its proposed Early Winters Ski Resort on Sandy Butte and a 1,165-acre parcel of private land it had acquired adjacent to the national forest. The proposed development would make use of approximately 3,900 acres of Sandy Butte to provide up to 16 ski lifts capable of accommodating 10,500 skiers at one time. Is an environmental impact statement required? [*Robertson v. Methow Valley Citizens Council*, 490 U.S. 332, 109 S.Ct. 1835, 104 L.Ed.2d 351, 1989 U.S. Lexis 2160 (1989)]

20.2 Clean Air Act Pursuant to the Clean Air Act, the state of New Mexico divided its territory into eight air quality control regions, one of which consisted of the city of Albuquerque and parts of three counties (AQCR 2). AQCR 2 was a nonattainment area for purposes of carbon monoxide (CO). The act requires states to prepare and submit a state implementation plan showing how they will attain compliance and have the plan approved by the EPA. As part of the plan, the state must implement a vehicle emission control inspection and maintenance program (I/M program). New Mexico filed an SIP but failed to implement an enforceable I/M program. The EPA engaged in formal, public rule making, disapproved New Mexico's SIP, and imposed sanctions by cutting off certain federal funds that New Mexico would have otherwise received. New Mexico challenges the EPA's action. Who wins? [*New Mexico Environmental Improvement Division v. Thomas, Administrator, U.S. Environmental Protection Agency*, 789 F.2d 825, 1986 U.S. App. Lexis 24575 (10th Cir. 1986)]

20.3 Clean Air Act Pilot Petroleum Associates, Inc., and various affiliated companies distribute gasoline to retail gasoline stations in the State of New York. Pilot owns some of these stations and leases them out to individual operators who are under contract to purchase gasoline from Pilot. At various times during 1984, the EPS took samples of gasoline from five different service stations to which Pilot had sold unleaded gasoline. These samples showed that Pilot had delivered "unleaded gasoline that contained amounts of lead in excess of that permitted by the Clean Air Act and EPA regulations." The United States brought criminal charges against Pilot for violating the act and EPA regulations and sought fines from Pilot. Who wins? [*United States v. Pilot Petroleum Associates, Inc.*, 712 F.Supp. 1077, 1989 U.S. Dist. Lexis 6119 (E.D.N.Y. 1989)]

20.4 Clean Water Act Placer mining is a method used to mine for gold in streambeds of Alaska. The miner removes soil, mud, and clay from the streambed, places it in an on-site sluice box, and separates the gold from the other matter by forcing water through the paydirt. The water in the sluice box is discharged into the stream, causing aesthetic and water quality impacts on the water both in the immediate vicinity and downstream. Toxic metals, including arsenic, cadmium, lead, zinc, and copper are found in higher concentrations in streams where mining occurs than in nonmining streams.

In 1988, after public notice and comment, the EPA issued rules that require placer miners to use the best practical control technology (BPCT) to control discharges of nontoxic pollutants and the best available control technology (BACT) to control discharges of toxic pollutants. The BACT standard requires miners to construct settling ponds and recycle water through these ponds before discharging the water into the streambed. This method requires substantial expenditure. The Alaska Miners Association challenged the EPA's rule making. Who wins? [*Rybachek v. U.S. Environmental Protection Agency*, 904 F.2d 1276, 1990 U.S. App. Lexis 7833 (9th Cir. 1990)]

20.5 Wetlands Leslie Salt Company owns a 153-acre tract of undeveloped land south of San Francisco. The property abuts the San Francisco National Wildlife Refuse and lies approximately one-quarter mile from Newark Slough, a tidal arm of San Francisco Bay. Originally the property was pasture land. The first change occurred in the early 1900s, when Leslie's predecessors constructed facilities to manufacture salt on the property. They excavated pits and created large, shallow, watertight basins on the property. Salt production on the property was stopped in 1959. The construction of a sewer line and public roads on and around the property created ditches and culverts on the property. Newark Slough is connected to the property by these culverts, and tidewaters reach the property. Water accumulates in the ponds, ditches, and culverts, providing wetland vegetation to wildlife and migratory birds. Fish live in the ponds on the property. In 1985, Leslie started to dig a ditch to drain the property and began construction to block the culvert that connected the property to the Newark Slough. The Army Corps of Engineers issued a cease-and-desist order against Leslie. Leslie challenged the order. Who wins? [*Leslie Salt Co. v. United States*, 896 F.2d 354, 1990 U.S. App. Lexis 1524 (9th Cir.)]

20.6 Water Pollution The Reserve Mining Company (Reserve) owns and operates a mine in Minnesota that is located on the shores of Lake Superior and produces hazardous waste. In 1947, Reserve obtained a permit from the state of Minnesota to dump its wastes into Lake Superior. The permits prohibited discharges that would "result in any clouding or discoloration of the water outside the specific discharge zone" or "result in any material adverse affects on public water supplies." Reserve discharged its wastes into Lake Superior for years, until they reached 67,000 tons per day in the early 1970s. Evidence showed that the discharges caused discoloration of surface waters outside the zone of discharge and contained carcinogens that adversely affected public water supplies. The United States sued Reserve for engaging in unlawful water pollution. Who wins? [*United States v. Reserve Mining Co.*, 412 F.Supp. 705, 1976 U.S. Dist. Lexis 15262 (D.Minn. 1976)]

20.7 Pesticides DDT was a pesticide that was sprayed by farmers on cotton, soybean, peanut, and other crops to control insects and pests. Evidence showed that DDT was an uncontrollable, durable chemical that persisted in the aquatic and terrestrial environments. Given its insolubility in water and its propensity to be stored in tissue, it collected in the food chain and was passed up to higher forms of aquatic and terrestrial life. Evidence also showed that DDT could persist in soil for many years and that it moved along with eroding soil. DDT had been found in remote areas and in ocean species, such as whales, far from any known area of application. DDT killed and injured birds, fish, and animals and affected their reproductive capabilities. DDT also posed a threat to human life because it was carcinogenic. The EPA brought a proceeding to cancel all registrations of DDT products and uses. Thirty-one registrants challenged the proposed cancellation. Who wins? [*Consolidated DDT Hearings*, 37 Fed.Reg. 13.369 (EPA 1972)]

20.8 Toxic Substances During the U.S. involvement in the Vietnam conflict, the U.S. military used a herbicide called "Agent Orange." It was sprayed from airplanes to defoliate the jungles of Vietnam. People on the ground, including U.S. soldiers, were exposed to the spray. Agent Orange contains dioxin, a poison that causes cancer and other health problems. After returning home from Vietnam, often years later, veterans who had been exposed to Agent Orange began contracting cancer, suffering skin problems, and having children with birth defects. The veterans brought a class action lawsuit against Monsanto Company, Dow Chemical Company, and several other chemical companies that manufactured the Agent Orange used in Vietnam. This action, which would have been the largest, and probably the longest, private toxic injury action in history, was set to go to trial in May 1984, when the defendants offered to establish a $180 million trust fund for the plaintiffs. The settlement would provide each veteran who was exposed to Agent Orange with approximately $2,000 in damages. Should the veterans accept the settlement? [Agent Orange Settlement (E.D.N.Y. 1984)]

20.9 Hazardous Waste Douglas Hoflin was the director of the Public Works Department for Ocean Shores, Washington. From 1975 to 1982, the department purchased 3,500 gallons of paint for road maintenance. As painting jobs were finished, the 55-gallon drums that had contained the paint were returned to the department's yard. The paint used contained hazardous substances such as lead. When 14 of the drums were discovered to still contain unused paint, Hoflin instructed employees to haul the paint drums to the city's sewage treatment plant and bury them. The employees dug a hole on the grounds of the treatment plant and dumped the drums in. Some of the drums were rusted and leaking. The hole was not deep enough, so the employees crushed the drums with a front-end loader to make them fit. The refuse was then covered with sand. Almost two years later, one of the city's employees reported the incident to state authorities, who referred the matter to the EPA. Investigation showed that the paint had contaminated the soil. The United States brought criminal charges against Hoflin for aiding and abetting the illegal dumping of hazardous waste. Who wins? [*United States v. Hoflin*, 880 F.2d 1033, 1989 U.S. App. Lexis 10169 (9th Cir. 1989)]

20.10 Nuclear Power Metropolitan Edison Company owns and operates two nuclear-fueled power plants at Three Mile Island near Harrisburg, Pennsylvania. Both power plants were licensed by the NRC after extensive proceedings and investigations, including the preparation of the required environmental impact statements. On March 28, 1979, when one of the power plants was shut down for refueling, the other plant suffered a serious accident that damaged the reactor. The governor of Pennsylvania recommended an evacuation of all pregnant women and small children, and many area residents did leave their homes for several days. As it turned out, no dangerous radiation was released.

People Against Nuclear Energy (PANE), an association of area residents who opposed further operation of either nuclear power plant at Three Mile Island, sued to enjoin the plants from reopening. They argued that the reopening of the plants would cause severe psychological health damage to persons living in the vicinity and serious damage to the stability and cohesiveness of the community. Are these reasons sufficient to prevent the reopening of the nuclear power plants? [*Metropolitan Edison Co. v. People Against Nuclear Energy*, 460 U.S. 766, 103 S.Ct. 1556, 75 L.Ed.2d 534, 1983 U.S. Lexis 21 (1983)]

20.11 Endangered Species The red-cockaded woodpecker is a small bird that lives almost exclusively in old pine forests throughout the southern United States. Its survival depends upon a very specialized habitat of pine trees that are at least 30, if not 60, years old, in which they build their nests and forage for insects. The population of this bird decreased substantially between 1978 and 1987 as pine forests were destroyed by clear-cutting. The secretary of the interior has named the red-cockaded woodpecker as an endangered species.

The Forest Service, which is under the authority of the secretary of agriculture, manages federal forests and is charged with duties to provide recreation, protect wildlife, and provide timber. To accomplish the charge of providing timber, the Forest Service leases national forest lands to private companies for lumbering. When the Forest Service proposed to lease several national forests in Texas, where the red-cockaded woodpecker lives, to private companies for lumbering, the Sierra Club sued. The Sierra Club seeks to enjoin the Forest Service from leasing these national forests for lumbering. Who wins? [*Sierra Club v. Lyng, Secretary of Agriculture*, 694 F.Supp. 1260, 1988 U.S. Dist. Lexis 9203 (E.D.Tex. 1990)]

Business Ethics Cases

20.12 Ethical Perspective The state of Michigan owns approximately 57,000 acres of land that comprise the Pigeon River County State Forest in southwestern Michigan. On June 12, 1977, Shell Oil Company applied to the Michigan Department of Natural Resources (DNR) for a permit to drill 10 exploratory oil wells in the forest. Roads had to be constructed to reach the proposed drill sites. Evidence showed that the only sizable elk herd east of the Mississippi River annually used the forest as its habitat and returned to this range every year to breed. Experts testified that elk avoid roads, even when there is no traffic, and that the construction of the roads and wells would destroy the elk herd's habitat. Michigan law prohibits activities that adversely impact natural resources. The West Michigan Environmental Action Council sued the DNR, seeking to enjoin the DNR from granting the drilling permits to Shell. Who wins? [*West Michigan Environmental Action Council, Inc. v. Natural Resources Commission*, 275 N.W.2d 538, 1979 Mich. Lexis 347 (Mich. 1979)]

20.13 Ethical Perspective Riverside Bayview Homes, Inc. (Riverside), owns 80 acres of low-lying marshland (wetlands) near the shores of Lake St. Clair in Macomb County, Michigan. In 1976, Riverside began to place fill materials on its property as part of its preparations for construction of a housing development. Riverside did not obtain a permit from the Army Corps of Engineers. Upon discovery of Riverside's activities, the Corps sued, seeking to enjoin Riverside from discharging a pollutant (fill) onto wetlands. Is the subject property subject to the Corps of Engineers permit system? Did Riverside act ethically in this case? [*United States v. Riverside Bayview Homes, Inc.*, 474 U.S. 121, 106 S.Ct. 455, 88 L.Ed.2d 419, 1985 U.S. Lexis 145 (1985)]

Briefing the Case Writing Assignment

Read Case A.20 in the Case Appendix [*FMC Corp. v. United States Department of Commerce*]. This case is excerpted from the district court opinion. Review and brief the case. In your brief, be sure to answer the following questions:

1. Who was the plaintiff? Who was the defendant?

2. What statute was applied in this case? What does the statute provide?

3. Succinctly state the issue the court had to decide.

4. What was the district court decision?

Answers to Management Decision Questions

1. The **Endangered Species Act** was enacted in 1973. The act, as amended, protects endangered and threatened species of animals. The secretary of the interior is empowered to declare a form of wildlife "endangered" or "threatened." The act requires the EPA and the Department of Commerce to designate "critical" habitats for each endangered and threatened species.

2. Your development plans are ruined. You cannot ignore the implications of this discovery. Once you inform the appropriate authorities of the dwarf wedge mussels, the creek and surrounding land will be designated as a critical habitant. Real estate and other development in these areas will be prohibited or severely limited. The secretary of commerce is empowered to enforce the provisions of the act as to marine species. In addition, the Endangered Species Act, which applies to both government and private persons, prohibits the "taking" of any endangered species. Taking is defined as an act intended to "harass, harm, pursue, hunt, shoot, wound, kill, trap, capture, or collect" an endangered animal or plant.

Endnotes

1. 42 U.S.C. § 7412(b).
2. 33 U.S.C. § 1254(t).
3. 21 U.S.C. § 349; 42 U.S.C. §§ 201 and 300F et seq.
4. 16 U.S.C. §§ 1431 et seq.; 33 U.S.C. §§ 1407 et seq.
5. 7 U.S.C. §§ 135 et seq.
6. 15 U.S.C. §§ 2601 et seq.
7. 42 U.S.C. § 6901 et seq.
8. 42 U.S.C. §§ 10101 et seq.
9. 42 U.S.C. § 4901.
10. 42 U.S.C. § 4913.

21

Antitrust Law

"While competition cannot be created by statutory enactment, it can in large measure be revived by changing the laws and forbidding the practices that killed it, and by enacting laws that will give it heart and occasion again. We can arrest and prevent monopoly."

—Woodrow Wilson
Speech, August 7, 1912

Chapter Objectives

After studying this chapter, you should be able to:

1. Describe the enforcement of federal antitrust laws.
2. Describe the horizontal and vertical restraints of trade that violate Section 1 of the Sherman Act.
3. Identify acts of monopolization that violate Section 2 of the Sherman Act.
4. Explain how the lawfulness of mergers is examined under Section 7 of the Clayton Act.
5. Apply Section 5 of the Federal Trade Commission Act to antitrust cases.

Chapter Contents

- Federal Antitrust Laws
- Section 1 of the Sherman Act—Restraints of Trade
- Horizontal Restraints of Trade
- Vertical Restraints of Trade
- Defenses to Section 1 of the Sherman Act
- Section 2 of the Sherman Act—Monopolization
- Section 7 of the Clayton Act—Mergers
- Section 3 of the Clayton Act—Tying Arrangements
- Section 2 of the Clayton Act—Price Discrimination
- Section 5 of the FTC Act—Unfair Methods of Competition
- Exemptions from Antitrust Laws
- State Antitrust Laws

Management Decision Antitrust Law

While attending the annual conference of the Western Locksmiths Association, you meet several other locksmiths from your state. During the Charity Golf Tournament, you team with three other locksmiths from your hometown. The discussion on the golf course turns to the service charges that are being paid by your customers. You learn that on the average the other locksmiths were charging higher rates than you. Charlie, one of your foursome, suggests that the four of you all charge the same rate. The rate he suggests is lower than the industry average for your county.

1. Should you do as Charlie suggests? Why or why not?
2. If you go along with the plan and charge the same rates as the others do, can competitors who are injured as a result sue for damages?

The American economic system was built on the theory of freedom of competition. After the Civil War, however, the American economy changed from a rural and agricultural economy to an industrialized and urban one. Many large industrial trusts were formed during this period. These arrangements resulted in a series of monopolies in basic industries such as oil and gas, sugar, cotton, and whiskey.

Because the common law could not deal effectively with these monopolies, Congress enacted a comprehensive system of **antitrust laws** to limit anticompetitive behavior. Almost all industries, businesses, and professions operating in the United States were affected. Although many states have also enacted antitrust laws, most actions in this area are brought under federal law.

antitrust laws
Laws enacted to limit anticompetitive behavior in almost all industries, businesses, and professions operating in the United States.

This chapter discusses federal and state antitrust laws.

Oriole Park at Camden Yards, Baltimore, Maryland. In 1922, the U.S. Supreme Court held that professional baseball was exempt from federal antitrust law.

Federal Antitrust Laws

The **Sherman Act**, enacted in 1890, made certain restraints of trade and monopolistic acts illegal. Both the **Clayton Act** and the **Federal Trade Commission Act (FTC Act)** were enacted in 1914. The Clayton Act regulates mergers and prohibits certain exclusive dealing arrangements. The FTC Act prohibits unfair methods of competition. The **Robinson-Patman Act**, which prohibits price discrimination, was enacted in 1930.

The notion that a business is clothed with a public interest and has been devoted to the public use is little more than a fiction intended to beautify what is disagreeable to the sufferers.

Holmes, J.
Tyson & Bro-United Theatre Ticket Offices v. Banton (1927)

Antitrust Enforcement

The federal antitrust statutes are broadly drafted to reflect the government's enforcement policy and to allow it to respond to economic, business, and technological changes. Each administration that occupies the White House adopts an enforcement policy for antitrust laws. From the 1940s through the 1970s, antitrust enforcement was quite stringent. During the 1980s, government enforcement of antitrust laws was more relaxed. During the 1990s, antitrust enforcement increased.

Business Brief

Each administration that occupies the White House adopts an enforcement policy for antitrust laws.

Antitrust Penalties

Federal antitrust laws provide for both government and private lawsuits.

Government Actions The federal government is authorized to bring actions to enforce federal antitrust laws. Government enforcement of federal antitrust laws is divided between the Antitrust Division of the Department of Justice and the Bureau of Competition of the Federal Trade Commission (FTC).

The Sherman Act is the only major antitrust act with *criminal* sanctions. Intent is the prerequisite for criminal liability under this act. Penalties for individuals include fines of up to $350,000 per violation and up to three years in prison; corporations may be fined up to $10 million per violation.[1]

The government may seek *civil* damages, including treble damages, for violations of antitrust laws.[2] Broad remedial powers allow the courts to order a number of civil remedies, including orders for divestiture of assets, cancellation of contracts, liquidation of businesses, licensing of patents, and such. Private parties cannot intervene in public antitrust actions brought by the government.

Business Brief

The Sherman Act is the only major federal antitrust act that provides for *criminal* penalties.

Web Site

Federal Trade Commission The FTC works for consumer protection and a competitive marketplace. One of its missions is antitrust enforcement. Visit at **www.ftc.gov**.

Private Actions **Section 4** of the **Clayton Act** permits any person who suffers antitrust injury in his or her "business or property" to bring a *private civil action* against the offenders.[3] Consumers who have to pay higher prices because of an antitrust violation have recourse under this provision.[4] To recover damages, plaintiffs must prove that they suffered *antitrust injuries* caused by the prohibited act. The courts have required that consumers must have dealt *directly* with the alleged violators to have standing to sue; indirect injury resulting from higher prices being "passed on" is insufficient.

Successful plaintiffs may recover **treble damages** (i.e., triple the amount of the damages), plus reasonable costs and attorneys' fees. Damages may be calculated as lost profits, an increase in the cost of doing business, or a decrease in the value of tangible or intangible property caused by the antitrust violation. This rule applies to all violations of the Sherman Act, the Clayton Act, and the Robinson-Patman Act. Only actual damages—not treble damages—may be recovered for violations of the FTC Act.

A private plaintiff has four years from the date on which an antitrust injury occurred to bring a private civil treble damage action. Only damages incurred during this four-year period are recoverable. This statute is *tolled* (i.e., does not run) during a suit by the government.

Ethics Brief

Businesses or individuals who are found to violate federal antitrust laws may be assessed *treble* (triple) damages in private civil lawsuit by any person who suffers injury in his or her business or property because of the violation.

Web Site

American Bar Association, Section of Antitrust Law Members of this section stay up-to-date on pertinent antitrust developments, including those involving mergers and acquisitions, joint ventures, distribution and franchising arrangements, pricing practices, collaboration among competitors, class actions, and refusal to deal. Visit at **www.abanet.org/antitrust/home.html**.

Ethics Brief

Many defendants settle government-brought antitrust lawsuits by entering pleas of *nolo contendere* in criminal actions and *consent decree* in civil actions. These pleas cannot be used as evidence in a subsequent private civil action.

Effect of a Government Judgment A government judgment against a defendant for an antitrust violation may be used as prima facie evidence of liability in a private civil treble damage action. Antitrust defendants often opt to settle government-brought antitrust actions by entering a plea of *nolo contendere* in a criminal action or a *consent decree* in a government civil action. These pleas usually subject the defendant to penalty without an admission of guilt or liability.

Section 16 of the **Clayton Act** permits the government or a private plaintiff to obtain an injunction against anticompetitive behavior that violates antitrust laws.[5] Only the FTC may obtain an injunction under the FTC Act.

Section 1 of the Sherman Act—Restraints of Trade

Section 1 of the Sherman Act

An act that prohibits *contracts, combinations*, and *conspiracies* in restraint of trade.

In 1890 Congress enacted the **Sherman Antitrust Act**. The purpose of the act was to outlaw anticompetitive behavior. The Sherman Act has been called the "Magna Carta of free enterprise."[6] The two main provisions of the Sherman Act—Section 1 and Section 2—are discussed in the following materials.

Landmark Law

Sherman Act Section 1

Section 1 of the **Sherman Act** is intended to prohibit certain concerted anticompetitive activities. It provides that [15 U.S.C. § 1]

> Every contract, combination in the form of trust or otherwise, or conspiracy, in restraint of trade or commerce along the several states, or with foreign nations, is hereby declared to be illegal. Every person who shall make any contract or engage in any combination or conspiracy hereby declared to be illegal shall be deemed guilty of a felony.

In other words, Section 1 outlaws *contracts, combinations*, and *conspiracies* in restraint of trade. Thus, it applies to unlawful conduct by *two or more parties*. The agreement may be written, oral, or inferred from the conduct of the parties.

Section 1 outlaws certain *restraints of trade*. The two tests the U.S. Supreme Court has developed for determining the lawfulness of a restraint—of the *rule of reason* and the *per se rule*—are discussed in the paragraphs that follow. ■

Rule of Reason

Landmark Law

In *Standard Oil Company of New Jersey v. United States* (1911), the U.S. Supreme Court adopted the "rule of reason" standard for analyzing Sherman Act Section 1 cases.

rule of reason

A rule that holds that only unreasonable restraints of trade violate Section 1 of the Sherman Act. The court must examine the pro- and anticompetitive effects of the challenged restraint.

If Section 1 were read literally, it would prohibit almost all contracts. In the landmark case *Standard Oil Company of New Jersey v. United States*,[7] the Supreme Court adopted the **rule of reason** standard for analyzing Section 1 cases. This rule holds that only *unreasonable restraints of trade* violate Section 1 of the Sherman Act. Reasonable restraints are lawful. The courts examine the following factors in applying the rule of reason:

- The pro- and anticompetitive effects of the challenged restraint.
- The competitive structure of the industry.
- The firm's market share and power.
- The history and duration of the restraint.
- Other relevant factors.

Per Se Rule

per se rule

A rule that is applicable to those restraints of trade considered inherently anticompetitive. Once this determination is made, the court will not permit any defenses or justifications to save it.

The Supreme Court adopted a **per se rule** that is applicable to those restraints of trade considered inherently anticompetitive. No balancing of pro- and anticompetitive effects is necessary in such cases: The restraint is automatically in violation of Section 1 of the Sherman Act. Once a restraint is characterized as a *per se* violation, no defenses or justifications for the restraint will save it, and no further evidence need be considered. Restraints that are not characterized as *per se* violations are examined under the rule of reason.

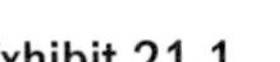

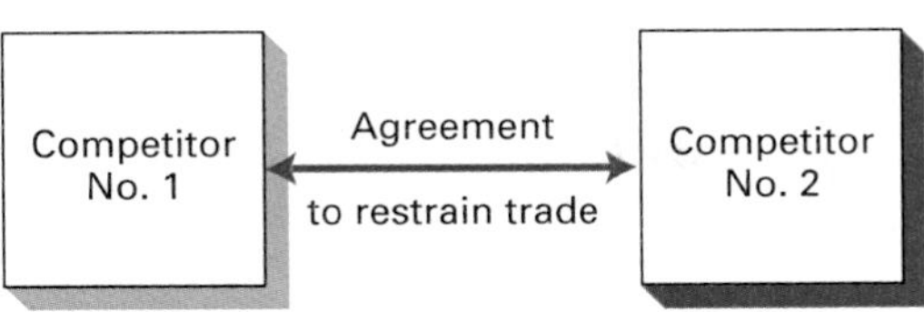

Exhibit 21.1
Horizontal Restraint of Trade

Horizontal Restraints of Trade

A **horizontal restraint of trade** occurs when two or more competitors at the *same level of distribution* enter into a contract, combination, or conspiracy to restrain trade (see Exhibit 21.1). Many horizontal restraints fall under the *per se* rule; others are examined under the rule of reason. The most common forms of horizontal restraint are discussed in the following paragraphs.

horizontal restraint of trade
A restraint of trade that occurs when two or more competitors at the same *level of distribution* enter into a contract, combination, or conspiracy to restrain trade.

Price-Fixing

Horizontal **price-fixing** occurs if the competitors in the same line of business agree to set the price of goods or services they sell. Price-fixing is defined as raising, depressing, fixing, pegging, or stabilizing the price of a commodity or service. Illegal price-fixing includes setting minimum or maximum prices or fixing the quantity of a product or service to be produced or provided. Although most price-fixing agreements occur between sellers, an agreement among buyers to set the price they will pay for goods or services is also price-fixing. The plaintiff bears the burden of proving a price-fixing agreement.

price-fixing
A situation in which competitors in the same line of business agree to set the price of the goods or services they sell; raising, depressing, fixing, pegging, or stabilizing the price of a commodity or service.

Price-fixing is a *per se violation* of Section 1 of the Sherman Act. No defenses or justifications of any kind—such as "the price-fixing helps consumers or protects competitors from ruinous competition"—can prevent the *per se* rule from applying.

The following case illustrates price-fixing.

Case 21.1
Price-Fixing

U.S. SUPREME COURT CASE
Federal Trade Commission v. Superior Court Trial Lawyers Association
493 U.S. 411, 110 S.Ct. 768, 1990 U.S. Lexis 638 (1990)
Supreme Court of the United States

Background and Facts

In the District of Columbia (District), lawyers in private practice are appointed to represent indigent defendants in less serious felony and misdemeanor cases. These private attorneys are paid pursuant to District's Criminal Justice Act (CJA), which in 1982 provided for fees of $30 per hour for court time and $20 per hour for out-of-court time. Most appointments went to approximately 100 lawyers called "CJA regulars," who handled more than 25,000 cases in 1982. These lawyers derived almost all of their income from representing indigents.

The CJA regulars belonged to the Superior Court Trial Lawyers Association (SCTLA), which was a professional organization and not a labor union. Beginning in 1982, SCTLA unsuccessfully tried to persuade District to increase CJA rates. In August 1983, about 100 CJA lawyers resolved not to accept any new cases after September 6, 1983, if legislation providing for an increase in fees was not passed by that date. When the legislation was not enacted, on September 6, most CJA regulars refused to accept new assignments. As anticipated, their action had a severe impact on District's criminal justice system, which within 10 days was on the brink of collapse.

The FTC filed a complaint against SCTLA, alleging that SCTLA's actions restrained trade in violation of federal antitrust law. FTC held against SCTLA. The court of appeals vacated the FTC order. The U.S. Supreme Court agreed to hear FTC's appeal.

Supreme Court Issue

Did the actions of SCTLA constitute price-fixing and a *per se* violation of Section 1 of the Sherman Act?

Federal Trade Commission v. Superior Court Trial Lawyers Association

493 U.S. 411, 110 S.Ct. 768, 1990 U.S. Lexis 638 (1990)
Supreme Court of the United States
(continued)

In The Language of The U.S. Supreme Court

Stevens, Justice Prior to the boycott CJA lawyers were in competition with one another, each deciding independently whether and how often to offer to provide services to the District at CJA rates. The agreement among the CJA lawyers was designed to obtain higher prices for their services and was implemented by a concerted refusal to serve the only customer in the market for the particular services that CJA regulars offered. This constriction of supply is the essence of price-fixing.

The horizontal arrangement among these competitors was unquestionably a "naked restraint" on price and output. The social justifications preferred for respondents' restraint of trade thus do not make it any less unlawful. The statutory policy underlying the Sherman Act precludes inquiry into the question whether competition is good or bad. No matter how altruistic the motives of respondents may have been, it is undisputed that their immediate objective was to increase the price that they would be paid for their services. The per se rules are, of course, the product of judicial interpretations of the Sherman Act, but the rules nevertheless have the same force and effect as any other statutory commands.

Decision and Remedy

The U.S. Supreme Court held that SCTLA lawyers' horizontal agreement to fix prices was a *per se* violation of Section 1 of the Sherman Act. Reversed and remanded.

Case Questions

Critical Legal Thinking Do you think that *per se* rules are necessary? Or should the courts be required to examine fully the pro- and anticompetitive effects of an activity to determine whether it violates Section 1 of the Sherman Act?

Business Ethics Do you think CJA lawyers were acting "altruistically"? Did District act ethically by keeping CJA rates low and refusing to increase them?

Contemporary Business Should professionals be subject to antitrust laws? Why or why not?

Division of Markets

division of markets
A situation in which competitors agree that each will serve only a designated portion of the market.

Competitors who agree that each will serve only a designated portion of the market are engaging in a **division of markets** (or **market sharing**), which is a *per se* violation of Section 1 of the Sherman Act. Each market segment is considered a small monopoly served only by its designated "owner." Horizontal market-sharing arrangements include division by geographical territory, customers, and products.

In the following case, the Supreme Court examined an agreement to see if it constituted a division of markets.

Case 21.2
Division of Markets

U.S. SUPREME COURT CASE

Palmer v. BRG of Georgia, Inc.

498 U.S. 46, 111 S.Ct. 401, 1990 U.S. Lexis 5901 (1990)
Supreme Court of the United States

Background and Facts

Harcourt Brace Jovanovich Legal and Professional Publications (HBJ) is the nation's largest provider of bar review materials and lecture services. In 1976, HBJ began offering a Georgia bar review course in direct competition with BRG of Georgia, Inc. (BRG), the only other main provider of bar review services in the state. In 1980, HBJ and BRG entered into an agreement whereby BRG was granted an exclusive license to market HBJ bar review materials in Georgia in exchange for paying HBJ $100 per student enrolled by BRG in the course. HBJ agreed not to compete with BRG in Georgia, and BRG agreed not to compete with HBJ outside of Georgia. Immediately after the 1980 agreement, the price of BRG's course was increased from $150 to $400. Jay Palmer and other law school graduates who took the BRG bar review course in preparation for the 1985 Georgia bar exam sued BRG and HBJ, alleging a violation of Section 1 of the Sherman Act. The district court held in favor of the defendants. The court of appeals affirmed. The Supreme Court agreed to hear the plaintiffs' appeal.

Supreme Court Issue

Did the BRG–HBJ agreement constitute a division of markets and a *per se* violation of Section 1 of the Sherman Act?

In The Language of The U.S. Supreme Court

Per Curiam The revenue-sharing formula in the 1980 agreement between BRG and HBJ, coupled with the price increase that took place immediately after the parties agreed to cease competing with each other, indicates that this agreement was formed for the purpose and with the effect of raising the price of the bar review course.

Here, HBJ and BRG had previously competed in the Georgia market; under their allocation agreement, BRG received that market, while HBJ received the remainder of the United States. Each agreed not to compete in the other's territories. Such agreements are anticompetitive. Thus, the agreement between HBJ and BRG was unlawful on its face.

Decision and Remedy

The U.S. Supreme Court held that the agreement between BRG and HBJ constituted a division of markets and as such was a *per se* violation of Section 1 of the Sherman Act. Reversed and remanded.

Case Questions

Critical Legal Thinking Should the division of markets be considered a *per se* violation of Section 1 of the Sherman Act? Or should the rule of reason apply?

Business Ethics Did BRG and HBJ act ethically in this case? Should the defendants, as bar review providers, have been aware of the antitrust law that prohibits division of markets?

Contemporary Business Why do you think BRG and HBJ entered into the 1980 agreement?

Group Boycotts

A **group boycott** (or **refusal to deal**) occurs when two or more competitors at one level of distribution agree not to deal with others at a different level of distribution. For example, a boycott would occur if a group of television manufacturers agreed not to sell their products to certain discount retailers (see Exhibit 21.2). A boycott would also occur if a group of rental car companies agreed not to purchase Chrysler automobiles for their fleets (see Exhibit 21.3).

Although in the past the U.S. Supreme Court has held that group boycotts were *per se* illegal, recent Supreme Court decisions have held that only certain group boycotts are *per se* illegal. Others are to be examined under the rule of reason. Nevertheless, most group boycotts are found to be illegal.

group boycott

A situation in which two or more competitors at one level of distribution agree not to deal with others at another level of distribution.

People of the same trade seldom meet together, even for merriment and diversion, but that the conversation ends in a conspiracy against the public, or in some contrivance to raise prices.

Adam Smith
The Wealth of Nations (1776)

Other Horizontal Agreements

Some agreements entered into by competitors at the same level of distribution—including trade association activities and rules, exchange of nonprice information, participation in joint ventures, and the like—are examined using the rule of reason. Reasonable restraints are lawful; unreasonable restraints violate Section 1 of the Sherman Act.

The rule of reason test was applied in the following case.

Business Brief

Note that for a Sherman Act Section 1 violation, it is *essential* to show *concerted activity*; one party, acting alone, cannot be liable.

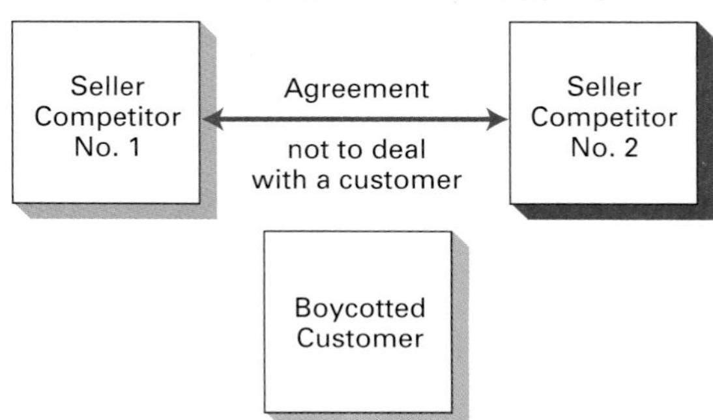

Exhibit 21.2

Group Boycott by Sellers

Exhibit 21.3

Group Boycott by Purchasers

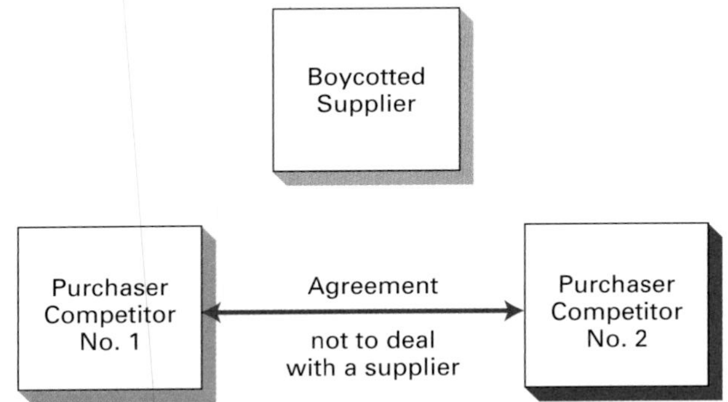

Case 21.3

Group Boycott

U.S. SUPREME COURT CASE

NYNEX Corporation v. Discon, Incorporated

525 U.S. 128, 119 S.Ct. 493, 1998 U.S. Lexis 8080 (1998)

Supreme Court of the United States

Background and Facts

The NYNEX Corporation owned New York Telephone, a provider of local telephone services on the east coast of the United States. NYNEX also owned the Material Enterprises Company (Material), an entity that purchases services for the removal of old switching equipment and other obsolete telephone equipment from New York Telephone's physical locations. For years, Material contracted with Discon Incorporated, an independent company, to provide this equipment removal service. After several years, Material did not renew Discon's contract, and instead contracted with AT&T to provide these removal services. Discon, which went out of business, sued NYNEX, Material, New York Telephone, and AT&T for engaging in a group boycott not to deal with Discon, an alleged *per se* violation of Sherman Act Section 1. The district court dismissed Discon's complaint. The court of appeals affirmed. The U.S. Supreme Court granted review.

Supreme Court Issue

Did the conduct of the defendants amount to a horizontal agreement necessary to constitute a *per se* group boycott violation of Section 1 of the Sherman Act?

In The Language of The U.S. Supreme Court

Breyer, Justice We conclude no boycott-related *per se* rule applies. Our conclusion rests in large part upon precedent, for precedent limits the *per se* rule in the boycott context to cases involving horizontal agreements among direct competitors.

Decision and Remedy

The U.S. Supreme Court held that a *per se* violation of Section 1 of the Sherman Act requires a horizontal agreement to not deal with another party. The Supreme Court held that the antitrust rule that group boycotts are illegal *per se* did not apply to a single buyer's (Material's) decision to purchase from one supplier rather than another supplier.

Case Questions

Critical Legal Thinking Describe a *per se* illegal group boycott. Why did the Supreme Court find that one did not exist in this case?

Business Ethics Was there anything unethical about Material's decision not to renew its contract with Discon? Would your answer be different if Material knew that such a decision would put Discon out of business?

Contemporary Business Should businesses be allowed to make exclusive decisions about whom to deal with without facing antitrust lawsuits?

Business Ethics

The Department of Justice Flunks the Ivy League Schools

Many college students think that tuition is too high and financial aid too low. After conducting an investigation, the U.S. Department of Justice thought so, too. It brought an action against the eight Ivy League schools (Brown, Columbia, Cornell, Dartmouth, Harvard, Princeton, the University of Pennsylvania, and Yale) and the Massachusetts Institute of Technology (M.I.T.). The Department of Justice alleged that these schools had conspired and engaged in horizontal restraint of trade in violation of Section 1 of the Sherman Act. The facts of the case are as follows.

For years, the administrators of the Ivy League schools met annually to trade information about applicants seeking scholarships. They then agreed to offer scholarships to the students they thought would attend their schools. Scholarships were not offered to those less likely to attend. The schools defended this practice as preventing "overlap"—that is, certain students getting scholarship offers from many schools and other applicants receiving no scholarship offers. The schools figured this would save administrative costs as well as best serve the interests of the students.

The Department of Justice did not think so. It felt that this trading of information and agreements to offer scholarships only to specified students constituted price-fixing by explicitly fixing the amount of scholarship money applicants were paid to attend school. The Department of Justice lawyers pointed to what they learned in Economics 101 and asserted that this collegiate cartel was no different from any other cartel—it denied customers (students) the right to "comparison shop" just as they would for other services.

After weathering bad publicity, the eight Ivy League schools agreed to settle the case with the Department of Justice. Under the terms of the consent decree, the schools agreed not to share financial aid information or discuss future tuition levels or faculty salaries with other schools. M.I.T. chose to fight the case in court and lost. The court found M.I.T. guilty of price-fixing and enjoined the challenged practices. [*United States v. Brown University*, 5 F.3d 658, 1993 U.S. App. Lexis 23895 (3d Cir. 1993)]

1. Do you think the schools acted ethically in this case?
2. Did their "overlap" argument justify their actions? ■

Vertical Restraints of Trade

A **vertical restraint of trade** occurs when two or more parties on *different levels of distribution* enter into a contact, combination, or conspiracy to restrain trade (see Exhibit 21.4). The Supreme Court has applied both the *per se* rule and the rule of reason in determining the legality of vertical restraints of trade under Section 1 of the Sherman Act. The most common forms of vertical restraint are discussed in the following paragraphs.

vertical restraint of trade
A restraint of trade that occurs when two or more parties on *different levels of distribution* enter into a contract, combination, or conspiracy to restrain trade.

Resale Price Maintenance

Resale pricing maintenance (or **vertical price-fixing**) is a *per se* violation of Section 1 of the Sherman Act. It occurs when a party at one level of distribution enters into an agreement with a party at another level to adhere to a price schedule that either sets or stabilizes prices. For example, a computer manufacturer that sells its computers only to retailers that agree to resell them at the minimum prices set by the manufacturer is engaged in this illegal practice.

resale price maintenance
A *per se* violation of Section 1 of the Sherman Act that occurs when a party at one level of distribution enters into an agreement with a party at another level to adhere to a price schedule that either sets or stabilizes prices.

In the following case, the Supreme Court had to decide whether the setting of a maximum resale price was a *per se* violation of Section 1 of the Sherman Act.

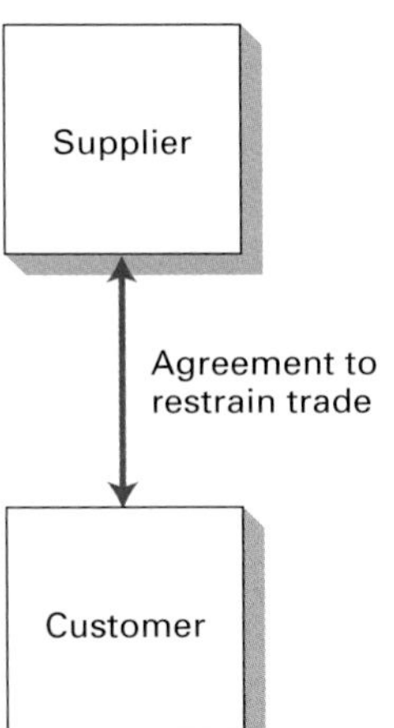

Exhibit 21.4
Vertical Restraint of Trade

Case 21.4 Resale Price Maintenance

U.S. SUPREME COURT CASE

State Oil Company v. Khan

522 U.S. 3, 118 S.Ct. 275, 1997 U.S. Lexis 6705 (1997)

Supreme Court of the United States

Background and Facts

Barkat U. Khan and his corporation entered into an agreement with State Oil Company to lease and operate a gas station and convenience store owned by State Oil. The agreement provided that Khan would obtain his station's gasoline supply from State Oil. The agreement also provided that Khan could charge any price for the gasoline he sold to the station's customers, but if the price charged was higher than State Oil's "suggested retail price," the excess was to be rebated to State Oil. Khan could also choose to sell gasoline for less than State Oil's suggested retail price. After operating the station under these terms for about one year, Khan lost the station back to State Oil for falling behind in lease payments. Khan sued State Oil, alleging that the maximum resale price required by State Oil was a *per se* violation of Section 1 of the Sherman Act. The district court entered summary judgment for State Oil. The court of appeals reversed and held that the maximum resale price set by State Oil was a *per se* violation of Section 1. The court of appeals cited a previous U.S. Supreme Court case—*Albrecht v. Herald Co.*, 390 U.S. 145 (1968)—that held that the setting of maximum resale prices also was a *per se* violation of Section 1. State Oil appealed to the U.S. Supreme Court.

Supreme Court Issue

Is the establishment of a maximum resale price by a supplier a *per se* violation of Section 1 of the Sherman Act?

In The Language of The U.S. Supreme Court

O'Connor, Justice Although the Sherman Act, by its terms, prohibits every agreement "in restraint of trade," this Court has long recognized that Congress intended to outlaw only unreasonable restraints. As a consequence, most antitrust claims are analyzed under a rule of reason, according to which the finder of fact must decide whether the questioned practice imposes an unreasonable restraint on competition, taking into account a variety of factors, including specific information about the relevant business, its condition before and after the restraint was imposed, and the restraint's history, nature, and effect. Some types of restraints, however, have such predictable and pernicious anticompetitive effect, and such limited potential for procompetitive benefit, that they are deemed unlawful *per se*.

We find it difficult to maintain that vertically-imposed maximum prices could harm consumers or competition to the extent necessary to justify their *per se* invalidation. Although we have acknowledged the possibility that maximum pricing might mask minimum pricing, we believe that such conduct can be appropriately recognized and punished under the rule of reason. Indeed, both courts and antitrusts scholars noted that *Albrecht's* rule may actually harm consumers and manufacturers. After reconsidering *Albrecht's* rationale and the substantial criticism the decision has received, we conclude that there is insufficient economic justification for *per se* invalidation of vertical maximum price fixing.

In overruling *Albrecht*, we of course do not hold that all vertical maximum price fixing is *per se* lawful. Instead, vertical maximum price fixing, like the majority of commercial arrangements subject to the antitrust laws, should be evaluated under the rule of reason. In our view, rule-of-reason analysis will effectively identify those situations in which vertical maximum price fixing amounts to anticompetitive conduct.

Decision and Remedy

The U.S. Supreme Court reversed *Albrecht*. The Supreme Court held that the setting of a maximum resale price is not a *per se* violation of Section 1 of the Sherman Act. The Court remanded the case for trial, using the rule of reason standard.

Case Questions

Critical Thinking How often do you think the U.S. Supreme Court reverses itself? Do you think it should have done so in this case?

Business Ethics Was the State Oil contract that set a maximum resale price in this case lawful under the rule of reason standard?

Contemporary Business How will this decision affect suppliers and the retailers they sell to? Explain.

Nonprice Vertical Restraints

nonprice vertical restraints
Restraints of trade that are unlawful under Section 1 of the Sherman Act if their anticompetitive effects outweigh their procompetitive effects.

The legality of **nonprice vertical restraints** of trade under Section 1 of the Sherman Act is examined using the rule of reason.[8] Nonprice restraints are unlawful under this analysis if their anticompetitive effects outweigh their procompetitive effects. Nonprice vertical restraints include situations where a manufacturer assigns exclusive territories to retail dealers or limits the number of dealers that may be located in a certain territory.

Entrepreneur and the Law

How Trade Association Members Can Avoid Antitrust Liability

Trade associations are organizations that are formed by industry members to promote the industry, provide education to members, formulate rules for self-regulation of the industry, and conduct lobbying and other activities.

Trade associations usually hold annual and other meetings that industry members attend. To avoid antitrust problems, attendees should avoid sharing and discussing certain information with each other. Here are some activities to avoid:

- Do not discuss or exchange price information about current or future sales to customers.
- Do not agree to share or split customers or geographical areas.
- Do not agree to operate only during agreed-upon hours. ■

Defenses to Section 1 of the Sherman Act

The courts have recognized several defenses to alleged violations of Section 1 of the Sherman Act. These defenses are discussed in the following paragraphs.

Unilateral Refusal to Deal

The U.S. Supreme Court has held that a firm can unilaterally choose not to deal with another party without being liable under Section 1 of the Sherman Act. A **unilateral refusal to deal** is not a violation of Section 1 because there is no concerted action with others. This rule was announced in *United States v. Colgate & Co.* and is therefore often referred to as the "**Colgate doctrine**."[9]

unilateral refusal to deal
A unilateral choice by one party not to deal with another party. This does not violate Section 1 of the Sherman Act because there is not concerted action.

Conscious Parallelism

If two or more firms act the same, but no concerted action is shown, there is no violation of Section 1 of the Sherman Act. This doctrine is often referred to as **conscious parallelism**. For example, if two competing manufacturers of a similar product both separately reach an independent decision not to deal with a retailer, there is no violation of Section 1 of the Sherman Act. The key is that each of the manufacturers acted on its own.

Ethics Brief
If two or more firms act the same, but no concerted action is shown, there is no violation of Section 1 of the Sherman Act under the doctrine of conscious parallelism.

Noerr Doctrine

The ***Noerr doctrine*** holds that two or more persons may petition the executive, legislative, or judicial branch of the government or administrative agencies to enact laws or to take other action without violating the antitrust laws. The rationale behind this doctrine is that the right to petition the government has precedence because it is guaranteed by the Bill of Rights.[10] For example, General Motors and Ford could collectively petition Congress to pass a law that would limit the import of foreign automobiles into this country.

There is an exception to this doctrine. Under, the *"sham" exception*, petitioners are not protected if their petition or lawsuit is baseless—that is, if a reasonable petitioner or litigant could not realistically expect to succeed on its merits. If the protection of the Noerr doctrine is lost, an antitrust action may be maintained against those parties who had asserted its protection.

Ethics Brief
Under the *Noerr doctrine*, two or more persons may petition the executive, legislative, or judicial branch of the government or administrative agencies to enact laws or take other action without violating the antitrust laws.

Section 2 of the Sherman Act—Monopolization

Section 2 of the Sherman Act
An act that prohibits the act of monopolization and attempts or conspiracies to monopolize trade.

By definition, monopolies have the ability to affect the price of goods and services. **Section 2 of the Sherman Act** was enacted in response to widespread concern about the power generated by this type of anticompetitive activity.

Landmark Law
Sherman Act Section 2

Section 2 of the Sherman Act prohibits the act of monopolization. It provides that [15 U.S.C. § 2]

> Every person who shall monopolize, or attempt to monopolize, or combine or conspire with any other person or persons, to monopolize any part of the trade or commerce among the several States, or with foreign nations, shall be deemed guilty of a felony.

Proving that a defendant is in violation of Section 2 means proving that the defendant (1) possesses monopoly power in the relative market and (2) is engaged in a willful act of monopolization to acquire or maintain the power. ■

Defining the Relevant Market

Identifying the **relevant market** for a Section 2 action requires defining the relevant product or service market and geographical market. The definition of the relevant market often determines whether the defendant has monopoly power. Consequently, this determination is often litigated.

relevant product or service market
A relevant market that includes substitute products or services that are reasonably interchangeable with the defendant's products or services.

relevant geographical market
A relevant market that is defined as the area in which the defendant and its competitors sell a product or service.

The **relevant product or service market** generally includes substitute products or services that are reasonably interchangeable with the defendant's products or services. Defendants often try to make their market share seem smaller by arguing for a broad definition of the product or service market. Plaintiffs, on the other hand, usually argue for a narrow definition.

The **relevant geographical market** is usually defined as the area in which the defendant and its competitors sell the product or service. This may be a national, regional, state, or local area, depending on the circumstances.

Monopoly Power

monopoly power
The power to control prices or exclude competition, measured by the market share the defendant possesses in the relevant market.

For an antitrust action to be sustained, the defendant must possess **monopoly power** in the relevant market. Monopoly power is defined by the courts to be the power to control prices or exclude competition. The courts generally apply the following guidelines: Market share above 70 percent is monopoly power; market share under 20 percent is not monopoly power. Otherwise, the courts generally prefer to examine the facts and circumstances of each case before making this determination.

Willful Act of Monopolizing

act of monopolizing
A required act for there to be a violation of Section 2 of the Sherman Act. Possession of monopoly power without such act does not violate Section 2.

Section 2 outlaws the **act of monopolizing**, not monopolies. Any act that otherwise violates any other antitrust law (such as illegal restraints of trade in violation of Section 1 of the Sherman Act) is an act of monopolization that violates Section 2. When coupled with monopoly power, certain otherwise lawful acts have been held to constitute an act of monopolization. For example, *predatory pricing*—that is, pricing below average or marginal cost—that is intended to drive out competition has been held to violate Section 2.[11]

Defenses to Monopolization

Only two narrow defenses to a charge of monopolizing have been recognized: (1) innocent acquisition (e.g., acquisition because of a *superior business acumen*, skill, foresight, or industry) and (2) *natural monopoly* (e.g., a small market that can support only one competitor, such as a small-town newspaper). If a monopoly that fits into one of these categories exercises its power in a predatory or exclusionary way, the defense is lost.

Business Brief
Note carefully that, in contrast to Section 1, which requires *concerted action*, Section 2 may apply to individual behavior.

Attempts and Conspiracies to Monopolize

Firms that *attempt* or *conspire* to monopolize a relevant market may be found liable under Section 2 of the Sherman Act. A single firm may be found liable for monopolizing or attempting to monopolize. Two or more firms may be found liable for conspiring to monopolize.

E-Commerce & Information Technology

United States v. Microsoft Corporation

Not since the days of John D. Rockefeller and the Standard Oil trust has the power of one man's company transfixed so many people as Bill Gates's Microsoft Corporation. In less than 25 years, Microsoft grew from a startup company into the world's largest software company, whose products touch the lives of virtually everyone who uses a personal computer. Microsoft dominates the software market with its Windows operating system, which is used on most of the world's personal computers.

One market that Microsoft did not dominate was the rapidly growing Internet Web browser market. Netscape developed its Navigator Internet Web browser, and by 1994 it controlled over 80 percent of the market. This posed a serious threat to Microsoft because not only was Navigator extremely popular, but it bypassed Microsoft's operating system altogether. Microsoft called a meeting with Netscape to offer a "special relationship" that meant that Navigator would be absorbed into Microsoft Windows. Netscape refused.

Microsoft began a campaign to defeat Netscape. Microsoft developed its own browser, called *Explorer*, and attached it to its Windows operating system for free. Microsoft warned Apple, a manufacturer of personal computers, that it would cancel Microsoft's all-important Office software unless Apple used Explorer; Apple capitulated and made Explorer its Web browser. Microsoft muscled AOL into offering Explorer in return for a small placement on the Windows desktop if it would not offer Netscape anywhere on its online service. AOL agreed. Microsoft gave Compaq, a maker of personal computers, a lower price for Windows in return for placing a Microsoft icon for the Explorer Web browser on Compaq's computers. And when Intel developed technology that would set its own software standards in competition with Microsoft's Windows, Microsoft threatened to cut support for Intel PCs. Intel promptly stopped work on its new technology.

After investigating, the U.S. government and 19 states sued Microsoft in a civil antitrust case. After a nine-month trial and four months of failed settlement negotiations, U.S. District Court Judge Thomas Penfield Jackson decided the case, finding that (1) Microsoft had used predatory and anticompetitive conduct to illegally maintain its monopoly in the Windows operating system in violation of Section 2 of the Sherman Act, (2) Microsoft had illegally attempted to monopolize the market for Internet browsing software in violation of Section 2 of the Sherman Act, and (3) Microsoft illegally bundled its Web browser Explorer with its successful Windows operating system, thus engaging in a tying arrangement in violation of Section 1 of the Sherman Act.

The district judge rendered a decision that prohibited Microsoft from engaging in such conduct in the future and ordered that Microsoft be split into two separate companies, one company that owns the operating systems such as Windows, and a second company that owns software, Internet browsers, and other computer applications. On appeal, the court of appeals upheld the finding that Microsoft had engaged in monopolization in violation of Section 2, but it reversed the ruling ordering the breakup of the company. The case was remanded for further proceedings.

Microsoft appealed the decision. In the meantime, Microsoft must defend more than 100 civil class action antitrust lawsuits brought against it by competitors and consumers. The case was eventually decided by the federal district court, ordering Microsoft Corporation to (1) refrain from engaging in coercive practices and (2) make some of the code for its operating systems available to other software companies under reasonable licensing arrangements so that they could design their software to be used in conjunction with Microsoft's operating system. [*United States v. Microsoft Corporation*, 2002 U.S. Dist. Lexis 22864 (District Court, D.C. 2002)] ■

Concept Summary The Sherman Act

Section	Description
1	Prohibits contracts, combinations, and conspiracies in restraint of trade. To violate Section 1, the restraint must be found to be unreasonable under either of two tests: 1. Rule of reason 2. *Per se* rule Requires the concerted action of two or more parties.
2	Prohibits the act of monopolizing and attempts or conspiracies to monopolize. Can be violated by the conduct of one firm.

Section 7 of the Clayton Act—Mergers

In the late 1800s and early 1900s, *mergers* led to increased concentration of wealth in the hands of a few wealthy individuals and large corporations. In response, in 1914 Congress enacted Section 7 of the Clayton Act that gave the federal government the power to check anticompetitive mergers.

Landmark Law

Clayton Act Section 7

Originally, **Section 7 of the Clayton Act** applied only to stock mergers. The **Celler Kefauver Act**, which was enacted in 1950, widened Section 7's scope to include asset acquisitions [15 U.S.C. § 18]. Today, Section 7 applies to all methods of external expansion, including technical mergers, consolidations, purchases of assets, subsidiary operations, joint ventures, and other combinations.

Section 7 of the Clayton Act provides that it is unlawful for a person or business to acquire stock or assets of another "where in any line of commerce or in any activity affecting commerce in any section of the country, the effect of such acquisition may be substantially to lessen competition, or to tend to create a monopoly." In determining whether a merger is lawful under Section 7 of the Clayton Act, the courts must examine the elements discussed in the following paragraphs. ■

Line of Commerce

line of commerce
Products or services that consumers use as substitutes. If an increase in the price of one product or service leads consumers to purchase another product or service, the two products are substitutes for each other.

Determining the **line of commerce** that will be affected by the merger involves defining the relevant *product or service market*. Traditionally, the courts have done this by applying the functional interchangeability test. Under this test, the relevant line of commerce includes products or services that consumers use as substitutes. If two products are substitutes for each other, they are considered as part of the same line of commerce. For example, suppose a price increase for regular coffee causes consumers to switch to Sanka (decaffeinated coffee). The two products are part of the same line of commerce because they are interchangeable.

Section of the Country

section of the country
A division of the United States that is based on the relevant geographical market; the geographical area that will feel the direct and immediate effects of a merger.

Defining the relevant **section of the country** consists of determining the relevant *geographical market*. The courts traditionally identify this market as the geographical area that will feel the direct and immediate effects of the merger. It may be a local, state, or regional market, the entire country, or some other geographical area. For example, Anheuser-Busch and the Miller Brewing Company sell beer nationally, whereas a local brewery, such as Anchor Steam, sells beer only in the western states. If Anheuser-Busch and the Miller Brewing Company plan to merge, the relevant section of the country is the nation; if Anheuser-Busch intends to acquire a local brewery that sells beer in the West, the relevant section of the country is the western states.

Probability of a Substantial Lessening of Competition

After the relevant product or service and geographical market have been defined, the court must determine whether a merger or an acquisition is **likely to substantially lessen competition or create a monopoly**. If the court feels that the merger is likely to do either, it may prevent the merger. Section 7 tries to prevent potentially anticompetitive mergers before they occur. It deals in probabilities; an actual showing of the lessening of competition is not required.

probability of a substantial lessening of competition
A probability that a merger will substantially lessen competition or create a monopoly that prompts the court to prevent the merger under Section 7 of the Clayton Act.

In applying Section 7, mergers are generally classified as one of the following: *horizontal merger*, *vertical merger*, *market extension merger*, or *conglomerate merger*. Each of these is discussed in the paragraphs that follow.

Horizontal Mergers

A **horizontal merger** is a merger between two or more companies that compete in the same business and geographical market. The merger of two grocery store chains that serve the same geographical market fits this definition. Such mergers are subjected to strict review under Section 7 because they clearly result in an increase in concentration in the relevant market. For example, if General Motors Corporation and Ford Motor Company tried to merge, this horizontal merger would clearly violate Section 7.

horizontal merger
A merger between two or more companies that compete in the same business and geographical market.

In the landmark case *United States v. Philadelphia National Bank*,[12] the U.S. Supreme Court adopted the *presumptive illegality test* for determining the lawfulness of horizontal mergers. This test finds horizontal mergers presumptively illegal under Section 7 if (1) the merged firm would have a 30 percent or more market share in the relevant market and (2) the merger would cause an increase in concentration of 33 percent or more in the relevant market. This presumption is rebuttable—that is, the defendants may overcome it by introducing evidence that shows that the merger does not violate Section 7.

This test is not the only criterion for evaluating the lawfulness of a merger. The court must also examine factors such as the trend toward concentration in the relevant market, the past history of the firms involved, the aggressiveness of the merged firms, the economic efficiency of the proposed merger, and consumer welfare.

E-Commerce & Information Technology

AOL Acquires Time Warner in Megamerger

In 1989, entrepreneur Steve Case introduced a nationwide service called America Online (AOL) that provided Internet access to subscribers. In 1990, this upstart company was in desperate need of cash and offered to sell 11 percent ownership to media giant Time Warner for $5 million. Time Warner rejected the offer. Ten years later AOL made a second offer to Time Warner, this time to buy Time Warner for $180 billion in AOL stock. Time Warner accepted the offer. Although the agreement is called a merger, there is no doubt as to who the buyer is: AOL, the new-kid-on-the-block and member of the high-tech community, is buying the venerable media company Time Warner. The name of the new company was changed to "AOL Time Warner" and the trading symbol for the new company was changed to "AOL." When announced in January 2000, the AOL–Time Warner merger was the largest merger in history.

E-Commerce & Information Technology (continued)

AOL had only become a public company seven years prior to the merger, when it sold stock to the public at $11 per share. Since that time, its stock had increased 35,000 percent in value. At the time of the merger announcement, AOL was worth more than 2.5 times more than Time Warner on the stock market. With no historical reference to valuing Internet companies, AOL and Time Warner negotiated a trade that valued AOL 1.5 times more than Time Warner. This gave a premium of 70 percent to each Time Warner stockholder over the then-current stock price per share. After the merger, the AOL stockholders would own 55 percent of the $350 billion merged company. The Time Warner part of the merger, with more than 82,000 employees, would provide 80 percent of the profits compared to AOL, with its 12,000 employees.

The merger married content with the Internet. Time Warner is a media conglomerate that owns Warner Bros. Studios, New Line Cinema, and Castle Rock film companies; Warner Bros; and HBO television companies, Time Warner Cable, TNT, TBS, and CNN cable companies; Warner and Elektra music labels; 33 magazines, including *Time*, *People*, and *Sports Illustrated*; and Time Warner and Little, Brown book publishers. AOL, on the other hand, is a high-tech Internet company that owns America Online Internet service, AOL sites, MapQuest, MovieFone, CompuServe, Netscape, and part of DIRECTV; and deals with regional bells for providing DSL service and strategic alliances with other Internet companies. The merger also combined customer databases. AOL had 25 million Internet subscribers, while Time Warner had 28 million magazine subscribers, 35 million HBO subscribers, and 75 million households that had the TBS and TNT television channels.

The federal government antitrust authorities examined the horizontal merger. The government decided not to challenge it after the parties agreed to divest certain assets. Three years after the merger, the performance of the AOL side of the company had done very poorly and the price of the merged company's stock had decreased considerably. The company's name was changed back to "Time Warner" and the trading symbol was changed to "TWX." This was just one example of a high-tech merger gone sour. ■

Vertical Mergers

vertical merger
A merger that integrates the operations of a supplier and a customer.

backward vertical merger
A vertical merger in which the customer acquires the supplier.

forward vertical merger
A vertical merger in which the supplier acquires the customer.

A **vertical merger** is a merger that integrates the operations of a supplier and a customer. For example, if Prentice Hall, Inc., a textbook publisher, acquired a paper mill, it would be a **backward vertical merger**. If a book publisher, such as Doubleday, acquired a retail bookstore chain, such as B. Dalton Bookstores, it would be a **forward vertical merger**. In examining the legality of vertical mergers, the courts usually consider such factors as the past history of the firms, the trend toward concentration in the industries involved, the barriers to entry, the economic efficiencies of the merger, and the elimination of potential competition caused by the merger.

Vertical mergers do not create an increase in market share because the merging firms serve different markets. They may, however, cause anticompetitive effects such as *foreclosing* competitors from either selling goods or services to or buying them from the merged firm.

Consider This Example Assume that a furniture manufacturer acquires a chain of retail furniture stores. The merger is unlawful if it is likely that the merged firm will not buy furniture from other manufacturers or sell furniture to other retailers.

Market Extension Mergers

market extension merger
A merger between two companies in similar fields whose sales do not overlap.

A **market extension merger** is a merger between two companies in similar fields whose sales do not overlap. The merger may expand the acquiring firm's geographical or product market. For example, a merger between two regional brewers that do not sell beer in the same geographical area is called a *geographical market extension merger*. A merger between sellers of similar products, such as a soft drink manufacturer and an orange juice producer, is called a *product market extension merger*. The legality of market extension mergers is examined under Section 7 of the Clayton Act. Market extension mergers are treated like conglomerate mergers.

Conglomerate Mergers

Conglomerate mergers are mergers that do not fit into any other category. That is, they are mergers between firms in totally unrelated businesses. For example, if an oil company such as Exxon merged with a clothing retailer such as Neiman-Marcus, the result would be a conglomerate merger. Section 7 examines the lawfulness of such mergers under the *unfair advantage theory*, the *potential competition theory*, and the *potential reciprocity theory*, which are discussed in the paragraphs that follow.

conglomerate merger
A merger that does not fit into any other category; a merger between firms in totally unrelated businesses.

Unfair Advantage Theory The **unfair advantage theory** holds that a merger may not give the acquiring firm an unfair advantage over its competitors in finance, marketing, or expertise. This rule is intended to prevent wealthy companies from overwhelming the competition in a given market.

unfair advantage theory
A theory that holds that a merger may not give the acquiring firm an unfair advantage over its competitors in finance, marketing, or expertise.

Potential Competition Theory The **potential competition** (or **waiting-in-the-wings**) **theory** reasons that the real or implied threat of increased competition keeps businesses more competitive. A merger that would eliminate this perception can be enjoined under Section 7. For example, if IBM were perceived as a potential entrant to the fax machine business de novo, it could not merge with a large manufacturer of such machines.

potential competition theory
A theory that reasons that the real or implied threat of increased competition keeps businesses more competitive. A merger that would eliminate this perception can be enjoined under Section 7.

Potential Reciprocity Theory A merger may be enjoined if **potential reciprocity** can be shown between the merged firms and other firms. For example, suppose the New York Times Company (Company) purchases paper supplies from Hammermill, a paper manufacturer. Hammermill, in turn, purchases the raw materials for its paper from Northwest Logging Company (Northwest). Assume that Company proposes to merge with Northwest. In this merger, the potential danger is that Company can threaten not to purchase its paper supplies from Hammermill unless Hammermill agrees to purchase all its logs from Northwest. The potential reciprocity theory is illustrated in Exhibit 21.5.

potential reciprocity theory
A theory that says that if Company A, which supplies materials to Company B, mergers with Company C (which in turn gets its supplies from Company B), the newly merged company can coerce Company B into dealing exclusively with it.

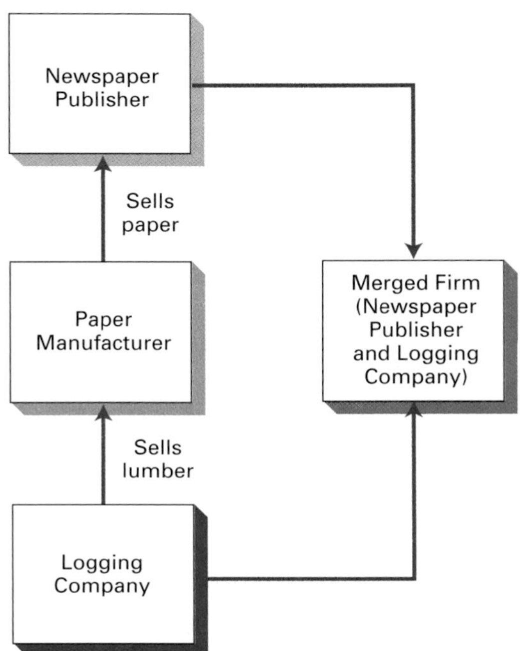

Exhibit 21.5
Potential Reciprocity Theory

Defenses to Section 7 Actions

The Supreme Court has recognized two defenses to Section 7 actions. These defenses can be raised even if the merger would otherwise violate Section 7. The defenses are

- ***The Failing Company Doctrine*** According to this defense, a competitor may merge with a failing company if (1) there is no other reasonable alternative for the failing company, (2) no other purchaser is available, and (3) the assets of the failing company would completely disappear from the market if the anticompetitive merger were not allowed to go through.
- ***The Small Company Doctrine*** The courts have permitted two or more small companies to merge without liability under Section 7 if the merger allows them to compete more effectively with a large company.

Premerger Notification

Hart-Scott-Rodino Antitrust Improvement Act

An act that requires certain firms to notify the FTC and the Department of Justice in advance of a proposed merger. Unless the government challenges the proposed merger within 30 days, the merger may proceed.

In 1976, premerger notification rules were enacted pursuant to the **Hart-Scott-Rodino Antitrust Improvement Act.**[13] These rules require certain firms to notify the FTC and the Department of Justice of any proposed merger. This gives those agencies time to investigate and challenge any mergers they deem anticompetitive. If the merger is reportable, the parties must file the notification form and wait 30 days. If within the waiting period the government sues, the suit is entitled to expedited treatment in the courts.

Section 3 of the Clayton Act—Tying Arrangements

Section 3 of the Clayton Act

An at that prohibits tying arrangements involving sales and leases of goods.

tying arrangement

A restraint of trade in which a seller refuses to sell one product to a customer unless the customer agrees to purchase a second product from the seller.

Section 1 of the Sherman Act

An act that prohibits tying arrangements involving goods, services, intangible property, and real property.

Section 3 of the Clayton Act prohibits tying arrangements involving sales and leases of goods (tangible personal property).[14] **Tying arrangements** are vertical trade restraints that involve the seller's refusal to sell a product (the *tying* item) to a customer unless the customer purchases a second product (the *tied* item). **Section 1 of the Sherman Act** (restraints of trade) forbids tying arrangements involving goods, services, intangible property, and real property.

The defendant must be shown to have had sufficient economic power in the tying product market to restrain competition in the tied product market. Suppose, for example, that a manufacturer makes one patented product and one unpatented product. A tie-in arrangement occurs if the manufacturer refuses to sell the patented product to a buyer unless the buyer also purchases the unpatented product.

A tying arrangement is lawful if there is some justifiable reason for it. For example, the protection of quality control coupled with a trade secret may save a tie-in arrangement.

Consider This Example Coca-Cola Company owns the right to the formula for the syrup to make Coca-Cola, which is a trade secret. Suppose Coca-Cola requires its distributors to purchase the syrup to make Coca-Cola from it. The tying product is the Coca-Cola franchise distributorship, and the tied product is the syrup. Here, the tying arrangement is lawful because a trade secret is involved and quality control must be preserved.

Contemporary Business Environment

Kodak's Copier Replacement Parts Jammed

Tying arrangements require that there be two products—the *tying* product and the *tied* product. A defendant who proves that the products are not separate cannot be held liable for a tying arrangement. Consider the following case.

Eastman Kodak Company (Kodak) manufacturers and sells complex high-volume photocopier machines and micrographics equipment, such as microfilmers, scanners, microfilm viewers, and data-processing peripherals. Kodak equipment is unique because its equipment and parts are not compatible with other manufacturers' equipment and parts, and vice versa.

Kodak provides replacement parts and services for its machines. After the initial warranty period, Kodak provides service either through annual service contracts (which include all necessary parts) or on a per-call basis. Kodak manufactures some of the parts itself; the rest are made to order for Kodak by independent original equipment manufacturers (OEMs). Beginning in the early 1980s, independent service organizations (ISOs) began repairing and servicing Kodak equipment at prices substantially lower than Kodak's. ISOs purchased parts from Kodak and OEMs. Kodak customers sometimes purchased parts from Kodak but hired ISOs to do the actual repairs. Some customers found that the ISO service was of higher quality than Kodak service.

In 1985 and 1986, Kodak implemented a policy to limit ISO access to Kodak parts. Kodak also implemented a policy of selling replacement parts only to owners of Kodak equipment who used Kodak to service and repair their machines. Through these policies, Kodak intended to make it difficult for ISOs to sell service for Kodak machines. It succeeded. Many ISOs were forced out of business, and others lost substantial revenue.

In 1987, many ISOs sued Kodak, alleging that Kodak had unlawfully tied the sale of service for Kodak machines to the sale of parts, in violation of Section 1 of the Sherman Act. Kodak moved for summary judgment, alleging that parts and service were only one item—repair. The district court granted Kodak's motion, but the court of appeals reversed. The U.S. Supreme Court granted certiorari.

The Supreme Court held that the sale of replacement parts and the provision of services to install these parts and repair Kodak machines could be found to be two separate and distinct markets that would support a charge of unlawful tying. The Court found that there was sufficient evidence of a tie between service and parts to deny Kodak's motion for summary judgment. The Court held that the ISOs were entitled to a trial on their claim against Kodak and remanded the case for this trial. [*Eastman Kodak Company v. Image Technical Services, Inc.*, 504 U.S. 451, 112 S.Ct. 2072, 1992 U.S. Lexis 3405 (1992)]. ■

Section 2 of the Clayton Act—Price Discrimination

Businesses in the American economy survive by selling their goods and services at prices that allow them to make a profit. Sellers often offer favorable terms to their preferred customers. **Price discrimination** occurs if the seller does this without just cause. The rules regarding this type of unlawful trade practice are found in **Section 2** of the **Clayton Act**, which is commonly referred to as the **Robinson-Patman Act**.

Landmark Law

The Robinson-Patman Act

Section 2(a) of the **Robinson-Patman Act** contains the following basic prohibition against price discrimination in the sale of goods [15 U.S.C. § 13(a)]:

> It shall be unlawful for any person engaged in commerce, either directly or indirectly, to discriminate in price between different purchases of commodities of like grade and quality, where either or any of the purchases involved in such discrimination are in commerce, where the effect of such discrimination may be substantially to lessen competition or tend to create a monopoly in any line of commerce, or to injure, destroy, or prevent competition with any person who either grants or knowingly receives the benefit of such discrimination, or with customers of either of them.

This section does not apply to the sale of services, real estate, intangible property, securities, leases, consignments, or gifts. Mixed sales (i.e., those involving both services and commodities) are controlled by the dominant nature of the transaction. ■

Direct Price Discrimination

Section 2(a) of the Robinson-Patman Act

An act that prohibits direct and indirect price discrimination by sellers of a commodity of a like grade and quality where the effect of such discrimination may be to substantially lessen competition or to tend to create a monopoly in any line of commerce.

To prove a violation of **Section 2(a) of the Robinson-Patman Act**, the following elements of price discrimination must be shown:

- ***Sales to Two or More Purchasers*** To violate Section 2(a), the price discrimination must involve sales to at least two different purchasers at approximately the same time. It is legal to make two or more sales of the same product to the same purchaser at different prices. The Robinson-Patman Act requires that the discrimination occur "in commerce."
- ***Commodities of Like Grade and Quality*** A Section 2(a) violation must involve goods of "like grade and quality." To avoid this rule, sellers sometimes try to differentiate identical or similar products by using brand names. Nevertheless, as one court stated, "Four Roses under any other name would still swill the same."[15]
- ***Injury*** To recover damages, the plaintiff must have suffered actual injury because of the price discrimination. The injured party may be the purchaser who did not receive the favored price (*primary line injury*), that party's customers to whom the lower price could not be passed along (*secondary line injury*), and so on down the line (*tertiary line injury*).

Business Brief

To prove a violation of Section 2(a), the following elements must be shown: (1) The defendant sold commodities of like grade and quality (2) to two or more purchasers at different prices at approximately the same time, and (3) the plaintiff suffered injury because of the price discrimination.

A plaintiff who has not suffered injury because of the price discrimination cannot recover. For example, assume that a wholesaler sells Michelin tires to General Motors more inexpensively than to Ford Motor Company. If Ford could have purchased comparable Michelin tires elsewhere at the lower price, it cannot recover.

Indirect Price Discrimination

indirect price discrimination

A form of price discrimination (e.g., favorable credit terms) that is less readily apparent than direct forms of price discrimination.

Because direct forms of price discrimination are readily apparent, sellers of goods have devised sophisticated ways to provide discriminatory prices to favored customers. Favorable credit terms, freight charges, and such are examples of **indirect price discrimination** that violate the Robinson-Patman Act.

Defenses to Section 2(a) Actions

The Robinson-Patman Act establishes three statutory defenses to Section 2(a) liability: (1) cost justification, (2) changing conditions, and (3) meeting the competition. These defenses are discussed in the following paragraphs.

cost justification defense

A defense in a Section 2(a) action that provides that a seller's price discrimination is not unlawful if the price differential is due to "differences in the cost of manufacture, sale, or delivery" of the product.

Cost Justification Section 2(a) provides that a seller's price discrimination is not unlawful if the price differential is due to "differences in the cost of manufacture, sale, or delivery" of the product. This is called the **cost justification defense**. For example, quantity or volume discounts are lawful to the extent they are supported by cost savings. Sellers may classify buyers into various broad groups and compute an average cost of selling to the group. The seller may then charge members of different groups different prices without being liable for price discrimination. The seller bears the burden of proving this defense.

Consider This Example If the Procter & Gamble Company can prove that bulk shipping rates make it less costly to deliver 10,000 boxes of Tide than lesser quantities, it may charge purchasers accordingly. However, Procter & Gamble may not simply lower its price per box because the buyer is a good customer.

Changing Conditions Price discrimination is not unlawful if it is in response to "changing conditions in the market for or the marketability of the goods." For example, the price of goods can be lowered to subsequent purchasers to reflect the deterioration of perishable goods (e.g., fish), obsolescence of seasonable goods (e.g., winter coats sold in the spring), a distress sale pursuant to court order, or discontinuance of a business. This is called the **changing conditions defense**.

changing conditions defense
A price discrimination defense that claims that prices were lowered in response to changing conditions in the market for or the marketability of the goods.

Meeting the Competition The **meeting the competition defense** to price discrimination is stipulated in **Section 2(b) of the Robinson-Patman Act.**[16] This defense holds that a seller may lawfully engage in price discrimination to meet a competitor's price. For example, assume Rockport sells its "ProWalker" shoe nationally at $100 per pair, while the Great Lakes Shoe Co. (Great Lakes), which produces and sells a comparable walking shoe, sells its product only in Michigan and Wisconsin. If Great Lakes sells its walking shoes at $75 per pair, Rockport can do the same in Michigan and Wisconsin. Rockport does not have to reduce the price of the shoe in the other 48 states. The seller can only meet, not beat, the competitor's price, however.

meeting the competition defense
A defense stipulated in Section 2(b) that says that a seller may lawfully engage in price discrimination to meet a competitor's price.

Section 5 of the FTC Act—Unfair Methods of Competition

In 1914, Congress enacted the **FTC Act** and created the **FTC**. **Section 5 of the FTC Act** prohibits *unfair methods of competition and unfair or deceptive acts or practices* in or affecting commerce [15 U.S.C. § 45].

Section 5 of the Federal Trade Commission Act
An act that prohibits unfair methods of competition and unfair and deceptive acts or practices.

Section 5, which is broader than the other antitrust laws, covers conduct that (1) violates any provision of the Sherman Act or the Clayton Act, (2) violates the "spirit" of those acts, (3) fills the gaps of those acts, and (4) offends public policy, or is immoral, oppressive, unscrupulous, or unethical, or causes substantial injury to competitors or consumers.

The FTC is exclusively empowered to enforce the FTC Act. It can issue interpretative rules, general statements of policy, trade regulation rules, and guidelines that define unfair or deceptive practices, and can conduct investigations of suspected antitrust violations. It can also issue cease-and-desist orders against violators. These orders are appealable to federal court. The FTC Act provides for a private civil cause of action for injured parties. Treble damages are not available.

Web Site
U.S. Department of Justice, Antitrust Division This site provides links to the latest information on antitrust cases. Visit at **www.uskoj.gov/atr**.

E-Commerce & Information Technology

Unfair and Deceptive Acts Prohibited over the Internet

Little did Congress know over 90 years ago when it passed the FTC that Section 5 of the act would be used to prosecute fraud over the Internet. Section 5 prohibits "unfair and deceptive" acts affecting commerce. The FTC has demonstrated recently that old laws can learn new tricks. Consider the following case.

Powerful search engines have been developed to allow surfers to browse the Internet and connect to Web sites in which they are interested. Certain scammers came up with a scheme in which they entice unwitting surfers to connect to their porn sites and not allow them to get out. The scheme worked as follows. The scammers made fake copies of more than 25 million popular Web sites, such as the *Harvard Business Review*, *Japanese Friendship Gardens*, and others. Search engines trolling the Web for new pages found these Web sites and added them to their listings. The scammers added to the faked Web pages an extra bit of coding so that as soon as surfers found the bogus Web page, it rerouted—"page-jacked"—them to the scammer's porn Web site. Once there, the user was "mouse-trapped" at the porn site, and efforts to escape led only to new porn pages appearing. The porn site operators made money by selling advertisements, and ad prices were often based on the number of "hits" on the site.

The FTC, a federal government agency, investigated and sued porn site operators in federal court for violating Section 5 of the FTC Act. The court found that the porn site operators had engaged in unfair and deceptive practices in violation of Section 5 and issued an injunction to shut down the porn sites and ordered the operators not to engage in such conduct in the future. ■

Exemptions from Antitrust Laws

Certain industries and businesses are exempt from federal antitrust laws. The three categories of exemptions—*statutory*, *implied*, and *state action*—are discussed in the paragraphs that follow.

Statutory Exemptions

statutory exemptions
Exemptions from antitrust laws that are expressly provided in statutes enacted by Congress.

Certain statutes expressly exempt some forms of business and other activities from the reach of antitrust laws. **Statutory exemptions** include labor unions,[17] agricultural cooperatives,[18] export activities of American companies,[19] and insurance business that is regulated by a state.[20] Other statutes exempt railroad, utility, shipping, and securities industries from most of the reach of antitrust laws.

Implied Exemptions

implied exemptions
Exemptions from antitrust laws that are implied by the federal courts.

The federal courts have implied several exemptions from antitrust laws. Examples of **implied exemptions** include professional baseball (but not other professional sports) and airlines.[21] The airline exemption was granted on the ground that railroads and other forms of transportation were expressly exempt. The Supreme Court has held that professionals such as lawyers do not qualify for an implied exemption from antitrust laws.[22] The Supreme Court strictly construes implied exemptions from antitrust laws.

State Action Exemptions

state action exemptions
Exemptions in which business activities that are mandated by state law are exempt from federal antitrust laws.

The U.S. Supreme Court has held that economic regulations mandated by state law are exempt from federal antitrust laws. The **state action exemption** extends to businesses that must comply with these regulations.

Consider This Example States may set the rates that public utilities (e.g., gas, electric, and cable television companies) may charge their customers. The states that set these rates and the companies that must abide by them are not liable for price-fixing in violation of federal antitrust law.

State Antitrust Laws

Most states have enacted antitrust statutes. These statutes are usually patterned after the federal antitrust statutes. They often contain the same language as well. State antitrust laws are used to attack anticompetitive activity that occurs in intrastate commerce. When federal antitrust laws are laxly applied, plaintiffs often bring lawsuits under state antitrust laws.[23]

International Law

Japanese *Keiretsus* Ignore Antitrust Laws

The United States has the most stringent antitrust laws in the world, enforces them most diligently, and assesses the greatest penalties for their violation. U.S. antitrust laws have been used to break up monopolies and cartels in many industries, including oil, steel, and telecommunications, to name but a few. These laws have also prevented U.S. companies from growing larger through mergers. Many critics argue that the stringent enforcement of antitrust laws has placed U.S. companies at a disadvantage in the international marketplace, where they have to compete against larger foreign firms from countries where antitrust laws do not exist or are not enforced.

Take the case or Japan. In the past 40 years, Japan has grown into an economic superpower. Much of this success has to do with the cozy relationship between Japan's federal government and the *keiretsu* (industrial groupings). *Keiretsu* cartels are considered a key factor behind the country's economic success.

After World War II, American-style antitrust laws were enacted in Japan; since then, though, they have been virtually ignored. The Japan Fair Trade Commission (JFTC), which is empowered to enforce antitrust laws, is more interested in promoting *keiretsus* than checking them.

Japan's industry and commerce are rife with cartels—247 were legally permitted as of 1992. These cartels blatantly engage in anticompetitive conduct. Price-fixing permeates the beer, cosmetics, over-the-counter drug, and construction industries, among others. The cartels are politically entrenched because they are the largest contributors to campaigns of Japanese politicians. They use their political muscle to lobby against the passage of laws that would curtail their monopolistic positions.

This protectionist attitude has helped Japanese *keiretsus* become giants that have a substantial advantage in the international marketplace. This has come at the expense of Japanese consumers, however, who have to pay higher than competitive prices for goods and services sold by these cartels. This helps Japanese cartels compete abroad.

As Japanese consumers became more vocal, and as pressure increased from other countries—particularly the United States—the JFTC issued tougher guidelines for the enforcement of antitrust laws. But, if history is any indicator, these moves are probably little more than window dressing, and *keiretsus* will retain their monopolistic positions with little interference from the Japanese government. ■

Federal Antitrust Laws, p. 613

Federal Antitrust Laws

Laws enacted by Congress to limit anticompetitive behavior in business. Federal antitrust laws include:

1. ***Sherman Act.*** An act enacted in 1890 that makes certain restraints of trade and monopolistic acts illegal.
2. ***Clayton Act.*** An act enacted in 1914 that regulates mergers and prohibits certain exclusive dealing arrangements.
3. ***Federal Trade Commission (FTC) Act.*** An act enacted in 1914 that prohibits unfair methods of competition.
4. ***Robinson-Patman Act.*** An act enacted in 1930 that prohibits price discrimination.

Antitrust Enforcement

Each administration adopts an enforcement policy for antitrust laws. Antitrust laws are enforced more stringently at some times than at other times.

Antitrust Penalties

Federal antitrust laws provide the following penalties:

1. ***Criminal sanctions.*** Criminal penalties may be assessed for violations of the Sherman Act.
2. ***Civil penalties.*** The federal government may seek civil damages, including treble damages, for violations of federal antitrust laws. Courts may issue orders for divestiture of assets, cancellation of contracts, and other remedies.
3. ***Private civil actions.*** Section 4 of the Clayton Act provides that anyone injured in his or her business or property by the defendant's violation of any federal antitrust law (except the FTC Act) may bring a civil action and recover *treble damages*, plus reasonable costs and attorneys' fees, from the defendant.
4. ***Effect of government judgment.*** A government judgment against a defendant for an antitrust violation may be used as prima facie evidence of liability in a private, civil treble-damage action. A plea of *nolo contendere* or a *consent decree* cannot be used as evidence in a subsequent private, civil antitrust action.

Section 1 of the Sherman Act—Restraints of Trade, p. 614

Restraints of Trade

Section 1 of the Sherman Act. An act that prohibits contracts, combinations, or conspiracies that cause *unreasonable restraints of trade*. Requires *concerted activity* between two or more parties. The courts apply one of the following two tests in determining the lawfulness of a restraint of trade:

1. ***Rule of reason.*** Requires a balancing of pro- and anticompetitive effects of the restraint. Restraints found to be unreasonable are unlawful, violating Section 1 of the Sherman Act.
2. ***Per se rule.*** Applied to restraints that are inherently anticompetitive. No justification for the restraint is permitted.

Horizontal Restraints of Trade, p. 615

Horizontal Restraint of Trade

Restraint that occurs when two or more competitors at the *same level of distribution* enter into a contract, combination, or conspiracy to restrain trade. Horizontal restraints include:

1. ***Price fixing.*** Competitors in the same line of business agree to set the price of the goods or services they sell. A *per se violation*.
2. ***Division of markets.*** Competitors agree that each will serve only a designated portion of a market. Also called *market sharing*. A *per se violation*.
3. ***Group boycott.*** Competitors agree not to deal with others at another level of distribution (e.g., customer or supplier). Most examined using the *rule of reason*.
4. ***Other horizontal agreements.*** Examined using the *rule of reason*.

Vertical Restraints of Trade, p. 619

Vertical Restraint of Trade

Restraint that occur when two or more parties on *different levels of distribution* enter into a contract, combination, or conspiracy to restrain trade. Vertical restraints include:

1. ***Resale price maintenance.*** A party at one level of distribution (e.g., a manufacturer) requires a party at another level of distribution (e.g., a retailer) to sell a good or service at a designated price. Also called *vertical price fixing*. A *per se violation*.
2. ***Nonprice vertical restraints.*** Examined using the *rule of reason*.

Defenses to Section 1 of the Sherman Act, p. 621

Defenses

The following defenses may be raised against an alleged violation of Section 1 of the Sherman Act:

1. ***Unilateral refusal to deal.*** A party may unilaterally refuse to deal with another party. This does not violate Section 1 because there has been no concerted action.
2. ***Conscious parallelism.*** Occurs where two or more firms act the same but without concerted action; they all reached their decision independently.
3. ***The Noerr doctrine.*** Two or more parties may petition the executive, legislative, or judicial branches of government to enact laws or take other action.
4. ***Sham exception.*** The Noerr doctrine does not protect petitioners or plaintiffs if their petition or lawsuit is without merit.

Section 2 of the Sherman Act—Monopolization, p. 622

Monopolization

Section 2 of the Sherman Act. An act that prohibits the act of *monopolization* and attempts, combinations, and conspiracies to monopolize trade or commerce in a relevant market. The following elements are necessary to prove a defendant in violation of Section 2 of the Sherman Act:

1. ***Relevant market.*** Defined as:
   a. *Relevant product or service market.* Includes substitute products or services that are reasonably interchangeable with the defendant's products or services.
   b. *Relevant geographical market.* Geographical area in which the defendant and its competitors sell the product or service.
2. ***Monopoly power.*** The defendant must possess monopoly power in the relevant market. This is defined as the power to control prices or exclude competition.
3. ***Act of monopolizing.*** The defendant must have engaged in a willful act of monopolization. Mere possession of a monopoly is not enough.

Defenses to Monopolization

The following defenses may be raised against an alleged violation of Section 2 of the Sherman Act:

1. ***Superior business acumen.*** A monopoly that is acquired by superior skill, foresight, or industry.
2. ***Natural monopoly.*** A monopoly that is thrust upon the defendant (e.g., only newspaper in a small town).

Section 7 of the Clayton Act—Mergers, p. 624

Premerger Notification

1. ***Hart-Scott-Rodino Antitrust Improvement Act.*** A federal act that requires certain firms to notify the FTC and Department of Justice in advance of a proposed merger. Unless the government challenges the proposed merger within 30 days, the merger may proceed.
2. ***Merger guidelines.*** A set of guidelines issued by the U.S. Department of Justice that notifies businesses under what conditions a merger is likely to be challenged by the federal government. The guidelines are not law.

Elements of a Section 7 Action

Section 7 of the Clayton Act. An act that prohibits acquisitions that may substantially lessen competition in any line of commerce in any section of the country. The following elements are necessary to prove a violation of Section 7 of the Clayton Act:

1. ***Line of commerce.*** The market that will be affected by the merger. Includes products or services that consumers use as substitutes for those produced or sold by the merging firms.
2. ***Section of the country.*** The geographical market that will be affected by the merger. Includes the area that will feel the direct and immediate impact of the merger.
3. ***Probability of a substantial lessening of competition.*** If the court determines that the merger would have a probability of a substantial lessening of competition, the merger may be prohibited. The statute deals with probabilities; a showing of actual lessening of competition is not required.

Horizontal Merger

A merger between two or more firms that compete in the same business and geographical market; a merger between competitors at the same level of distribution.

Vertical Merger

A merger between firms at different levels of distribution that integrates the operations of a supplier and a customer.

Market Extension Merger

A merger of two firms in similar fields whose sales do not overlap.

1. ***Geographical market extension merger.*** A merger of two firms that sell the same product or service but in different geographical markets.
2. ***Product market extension merger.*** A merger of two firms that sell similar products or services in the same geographical market.

Conglomerate Merger

A merger of firms in totally unrelated businesses. Conglomerate mergers may be challenged under:

1. ***Unfair advantage theory.*** A merger may not give the acquiring firm an unfair advantage over its competitors in finance, marketing, or expertise.
2. ***Potential competition theory.*** A merger may not remove a competitor that poses a real or implied threat of increased competition that keeps businesses in the market more competitive.
3. ***Potential reciprocity theory.*** A merger of Company A and Company C, where Company A supplies materials to Company B and Company C purchases supplies from Company B. The danger is that the newly merged company (Company A and Company C) could coerce Company B into dealing exclusively with it.

Defenses to Section 7 Actions

The following defenses may be raised against a violation of Section 7 of the Clayton Act:

1. ***Failing company doctrine.*** A competitor may merge with a failing company if (1) there is no other reasonable alternative for the failing company, (2) no other purchaser is available, and (3) the assets of the failing company would completely disappear from the market if the anticompetitive merger were not allowed to go through.
2. ***Small company doctrine.*** Two or more small companies may merge if the merger allows them to compete more effectively with a large company.

Section 3 of the Clayton Act—Tying Arrangements, p. 628

Section 3 of the Clayton Act

1. ***Tying arrangement.*** Occurs where a seller refuses to sell a product (the *tying* product) to a customer unless the customer purchases a second product (the *tied* product).
2. ***Section 3 of the Clayton Act.*** Prohibits tying arrangements involving sales and leases of *goods*.
3. ***Section 1 of the Sherman Act.*** Prohibits tying arrangements involving goods, *services*, intangible property, and real property.

Section 2 of the Clayton Act—Price Discrimination, p. 629

Section 2 of the Clayton Act

Commonly referred to as the *Robinson-Patman Act*. Prohibits price discrimination and discriminatory fees, payments, and services. The act applies only to products, not services.

Price Discrimination

Section 2(a). Prohibits a seller from discriminating in price between two or more different purchasers of commodities of *like grade and quality* where the effect may be substantially to lessen competition. *Direct* and *indirect* price discrimination is unlawful.

Defenses to Section 2(a) Actions

A seller's price discrimination is not unlawful if the price differential is due to:

1. ***Cost justification.*** Differences in the cost of manufacture, sale, or delivery of the product to different purchasers.
2. ***Changing conditions.*** The seller is responding to changing conditions in the market (e.g., deterioration of perishable goods).
3. ***Meeting the competition.*** *Section 2(b)* permits a seller to have a lower price in one market than in another market to meet the price of a competitor in the lower-priced market.

Discriminatory Fees, Payments, and Services

1. ***Section 2(c).*** Prohibits the payment of brokerage fees and other compensation by the seller to a buyer except for actual services rendered.
2. ***Section 2(d).*** Prohibits payments by sellers to buyers for advertising, promotional, or other services unless such payments are available to other buyers on proportionately equivalent terms.
3. ***Section 2(e).*** Requires sellers to provide promotional and other services to all buyers in a nondiscriminatory way and on proportionately equal terms.

Buyer Inducement of Price Discrimination

Section 2(f). Makes it unlawful for a buyer knowingly to induce or receive a discriminatory price prohibited by Section 2(a).

Section 5 of the FTC Act—Unfair Methods of Competition, p. 631

Section 5 of the FTC Act

Prohibits *unfair methods of competition and unfair or deceptive acts or practices.* Section 5 covers conduct that (1) violates any provision of the Sherman Act or the Clayton Act, (2) violates the "spirit" of those acts, (3) fills the gaps of those acts, and (4) causes substantial injury to competitors or consumers.

Exemptions from Antitrust Laws, p. 632

Statutory Exemptions

Statutes expressly exempt from federal antitrust laws labor unions; agricultural cooperatives; export activities of American companies; insurance business regulated by states; railroads, utility, shipping, and securities industries.

Implied Exemptions

The courts have held that certain industries, including professional baseball and airlines, are implicitly exempt from federal antitrust laws.

State Action Exemptions

Businesses' activities that are mandated by state law are exempt from federal antitrust laws.

State Antitrust Laws, p. 632

State Antitrust Laws

Most states have enacted state antitrust laws that attack anticompetitive activity that occurs in intrastate commerce.

Internet Exercises and Case Questions

Working the Web Internet Exercises

Activities

1. The largest antitrust case of our time, *United States v. Microsoft Corporation*, leaves a long and rich trail of documents for study. See, for example, **www.ssrn.com/update/lsn/lsn_microsoft-case.html**, which contains a lengthy list of links to articles about the famous case. List the specific sections of the antitrust laws that Microsoft was alleged to have violated.
2. Find your state's laws relating to unfair competition and restraint of trade. Are they consistent with federal law? See Law About . . . Antitrust at **www.law.cornell.edu/topics/antitrust.html** for an overview of antitrust law with links to key primary and secondary sources.
3. Antitrust is an area of law deeply connected with economic theory. The intent of the law is to protect competition. So how can mergers be permitted under the Clayton Act? Section 7 of the Clayton Act, 15 U.S.C. 18.
4. Where does the United States derive its purported authority to enforce its antitrust laws extraterritorially? See **www.usdoj.gov/atr/public/guidelines/internat.htm**.

Critical Legal Thinking Cases

21.1 Price-Fixing The Maricopa County Medical Society (Society) is a professional association that represents doctors of medicine, osteopathy, and podiatry in Maricopa County, Arizona. The society formed the Maricopa Foundation for Medical Care (Foundation), a nonprofit Arizona corporation. Approximately 1,750 doctors, who represent 70 percent of the practitioners in the county, belong to the foundation. The foundation acts as an insurance administrator between its member doctors and insurance companies that pay patients' medical bills.

The foundation established a maximum fee schedule for various medical services. The member doctors agreed to abide by this fee schedule when providing services to patients. The state of Arizona brought this action against the Society and the Foundation and its members, alleging price-fixing in violation of Section 1 of the Sherman Act. Who wins? [*Arizona v. Maricopa County Medical Society*, 457 U.S. 332, 102 S.Ct. 2466, 1982 U.S. Lexis 5 (1982)]

21.2 Division of Markets Topco Associates, Inc., was founded in the 1940s by a group of small, local grocery store chains to act as a buying cooperative for the member stores. In this capacity, Topco procured and distributed more than 1,000 different food and related items to its members. Topco did not itself own any manufacturing or processing facilities, and the items it procured were shipped directly from the manufacturer or packer to Topco members. Topco members agreed to sell only Topco brand products within an exclusive territory. The United States sued Topco and its members, alleging a violation of Section 1 of the Sherman Act. Who wins? [*United States v. Topco Associates, Inc.*, 405 U.S. 596, 92 S.Ct. 1126, 1972 U.S. Lexis 167 (1972)]

21.3 Tying Arrangement Mercedes-Benz of North America (MBNA) was the exclusive franchiser of Mercedes-Benz dealerships in the United States. MBNA's franchise agreements required each dealer to establish a customer service department for the repair of Mercedes-Benz automobiles and for dealers to purchase Mercedes-Benz replacement parts from MBNA. At least eight independent wholesale distributors, including Metrix Warehouse, Inc., sold replacement parts for Mercedes-Benz automobiles. Because they were precluded from selling parts to Mercedes-Benz dealers, these parts distributors sold their replacement parts to independent garages that specialized in the repair of Mercedes-Benz automobiles. Evidence showed that Metrix sold replacement parts for Mercedes-Benz automobiles of equal quality and at a lower price than those sold by MBNA. Metrix sued MBNA, alleging a violation of Section 1 of the Sherman Act. Who wins? [*Metrix Warehouse, Inc. v. Mercedes-Benz of North America, Inc.*, 828 F.2d 1033, 1987 U.S. App. Lexis 12341 (4th Cir. 1987)]

21.4 Conscious Parallelism The Crest Theatre was a movie theater that was located in a neighborhood shopping center in a suburb six miles from downtown Baltimore, Maryland. The owner of the Crest Theatre had repeatedly sought to obtain first-run feature films from Paramount Film Distribution Corporation and other film distributors. Each film distributor had independently rejected the request, stating that it restricted "first-run" movies to theaters located in downtown Baltimore. Each cited the same reasons: First-runs are normally granted to the largest theaters, profits are higher from showing films in downtown theaters, the drawing area around the Crest Theatre was less than one-tenth that of the downtown theaters, and the downtown theaters offered greater opportunities for widespread advertisements and exploitation of newly released feature films. There was no evidence of an agreement between the film producers to restrict the showing of feature films at the Crest Theatre. Evidence showed that each film distributor made an independent decision to show its first-run films in theaters located in downtown Baltimore. Crest Theatre sued Paramount and the other film distributors, alleging a violation of Section 1 of the Sherman Act. Who wins? [*Theatre Enterprises, Inc. v. Paramount Film Distribution Corporation*, 346 U.S. 537, 74 S.Ct. 257, 1954 U.S. Lexis 2752 (1954)]

21.5 Resale Price Maintenance The Union Oil Company was a major oil company that operated a nationwide network of franchised service station dealers who sold Union Oil gasoline and other products throughout the United States. The franchise dealers leased their stations from Union Oil; they also signed a franchise agreement to purchase gasoline and other products on assignment from Union Oil. Both the lease and the franchise agreement were one-year contracts that could be canceled by Union Oil if a dealer did not adhere to the contract. The franchise agreement provided that all dealers shall adhere to the retail price of gasoline as set by Union Oil. The retail price fixed by Union Oil for gasoline during the period in question was 29.9 cents per gallon. Simpson, a franchised dealer, violated this provision in the franchise agreement and sold gasoline at 27.9 cents per gallon to meet competitive prices. Because of this, Union Oil canceled Simpson's lease and franchise agreement. Simpson sued Union Oil, alleging a violation of Section 1 of the Sherman Act. Who wins? [*Simpson v. Union Oil Company*, 377 U.S. 13, 84 S.Ct. 1051, 1964 U.S. Lexis 2378 (1964)]

21.6 Nonprice Vertical Restraint GTE Sylvania, Inc., manufactured and sold television sets to independent or company-owned distributors, which in turn resold the sets to a large and diverse group of retailers. Prompted by a decline in its market share. Sylvania instituted a franchise program whereby it phased out its wholesale distribution and began to sell its televisions directly to a smaller and select group of franchised retail dealers. A franchise did not constitute an exclusive territory, and Sylvania retained sole discretion to increase the number of retailers in an area.

In the spring of 1965, Sylvania decided to franchise another outlet in San Francisco that was approximately one mile from a Sylvania retail outlet operated by Continental TV, Inc. Continental protested the location of the new outlet, but to no avail. Continental then proposed to open a new Sylvania store in Sacramento, but Sylvania denied the franchise because it believed the Sacramento area was adequately served. In the face of this denial, Continental advised Sylvania that it was in the process of moving Sylvania merchandise from its warehouse to a new retail location in Sacramento. Shortly thereafter, Sylvania terminated Continental's San Francisco franchise. Continental sued Sylvania, alleging that Sylvania had engaged in unreasonable restraint of trade in violation of Section 1 of the Sherman Act. Does the per se rule or the rule of reason apply? [*Continental TV, Inc. v. GTE Sylvania, Inc.*, 433 U.S. 36, 97 S.Ct. 2549, 1977 U.S. Lexis 134 (1977)]

21.7 Monopolization The International Business Machine Corporation (IBM) manufactured entire computer systems, including mainframes and peripherals, and provided software and support services to customers. IBM both sold and leased computers. Greyhound Computer Corporation, Inc., was a computer leasing company that bought older computers from IBM and then leased them to businesses. Thus, Greyhound was both a customer and a competitor of IBM. Prior to 1963, IBM sold its second-generation equipment at a 10 percent discount per year up to a maximum of 75 percent. Thus, equipment on the market for several years could be purchased at a substantial discount from its original cost.

IBM's market share of this leasing market was 82.5 percent. The portion of the leasing market not controlled by IBM was dispersed among many companies, including Greyhound. IBM officials became concerned that the balance between sales and leases was turned too heavily toward sales and that the rapid increase in leasing companies occurred because of their ability to purchase second-generation computers from IBM at a substantial discount. In 1963, IBM reduced the annual discount to 5 percent per year with a maximum of 35 percent. In 1964, the discount was changed to 12 percent after the fist year with no further discounts. Greyhound sued IBM, alleging IBM engaged in monopolization in violation of Section 2 of the Sherman Act. Who wins? [*Greyhound v. International Business Machine Corporation*, 559 F.2d 488, 1977 U.S. App. Lexis 11957 (9th Cir. 1977)]

21.8 Superior Business Acumen In the 1970s the Eastman Kodak Company was the dominant and preeminent manufacturer and distributor of cameras and film in the United States. In 1972, Kodak introduced a new instamatic camera called the "110 camera" and a new film called "Kodacolor III" to be used in the cameras. Kodak engineers invented the camera and film with their own ingenuity. Kodak invested substantial money in inventing the new camera and film and held many patents necessary to develop the 110 system. The camera and film were superior to any others on the market and were an instant success. With the introduction of the new camera and film, Kodak obtained a monopoly position in the amateur photography market.

Berkey Photo, Inc., was a small photography company that competed with Kodak. Berkey's attempt to develop and sell its own version of the 110 camera failed. Berkey then brought an antitrust action against Kodak, alleging that Kodak's introduction of the 110 camera and Kodacolor III film was an attempt to monopolize the camera market in violation of Section 2 of the Sherman Act. Who wins? [*Berkey Photo, Inc. v. Eastman Kodak Company*, 603 F.2d 263, 1979 U.S. App. Lexis 13692 (2nd Cir. 1979)]

21.9 Merger The Lipton Tea Co. was the second largest U.S. producer of herbal teas, controlling 32 percent of the national market. Lipton announced that it would acquire Celestial Seasonings, the largest U.S. producer of herbal teas, controlling 52 percent of the national market. R.C. Bigelow, Inc., the third largest producer of herbal teas, with 13 percent of the national market, brought this action, alleging that the merger would violate Section 7 of the Clayton Act and seeking an injunction against the merger. What type of merger was proposed? What was the relevant market? Should the merger be enjoined? [*R. C. Bigelow, Inc., v. Unilever, N.V.*, 867 F.2d 102, 1989 U.S. App. Lexis 574 (2nd Cir. 1989)]

21.10 Merger The G. R. Kinney Company, Inc., was the largest independent chain of family-owned shoe stores in the nation. It had assets of $18 million and sold more than 8 million pairs of shoes annually through its 350 retail outlets. Kinney announced that it would merge with the Brown Shoe Company, Inc., which was the fourth largest manufacturer of shoes in the country, with assets of more than $72 million, and which sold more than 25 million pairs of shoes annually. The United States brought this action, alleging a violation of Clayton Act Section 7 and seeking a preliminary injunction against the merger. What type of merger would this be? What is the relevant market? Does the merger violate Section 7? [*Brown Shoe Company, Inc. v. United States*, 370 U.S. 294, 82 S.Ct. 1502, 1962 U.S. Lexis 2290 (1962)]

21.11 Reciprocal Buying Consolidated Foods Corporation owned a network of wholesale and retail food stores. Consolidated purchased a substantial amount of products from food processors that use dehydrated onion and garlic in their products. Consolidated acquired Gentry, Inc., a manufacturer of dehydrated onion and garlic. Gentry controlled 32 percent of the market for these products and, with its chief competitor, accounted for 90 percent of total industry sales. Two small competitors accounted for the other 10 percent of sales. Evidence showed that after the acquisition, Consolidated required firms from which it purchased food products to purchase the dehydrated onion and garlic they needed from Gentry. The FTC sued Consolidated, alleging that Consolidated violated Section 7 of the Clayton Act by it acquisition of Gentry. Who wins? [*Federal Trade Commission v. Consolidated Foods Corporation*, 380 U.S. 592, 85 S.Ct. 1220, 1965 U.S. Lexis 2432 (1965)]

21.12 Antitrust Injury The Brunswick Corporation was the second largest manufacturer of bowling equipment in the United States. In the late 1950s, the bowling industry expanded rapidly. Brunswick's sales of lanes, automatic pinsetters, and ancillary equipment to bowling alley operators rose accordingly. Because the equipment required a major capital expenditure by bowling center operators, Brunswick extended credit for all of the purchase price except a cash down payment. It took a security interest in the equipment.

Brunswick's sales dropped in the early 1960s, when the bowling industry went into a sharp decline. In addition, many of the bowling center operators defaulted on their loans. By the end of 1964, Brunswick was in financial difficulty. It met with limited success when it foreclosed on its security interests and attempted to lease or sell the repossessed equipment and bowling centers. To avoid complete loss, Brunswick started running those that would provide a positive cash flow. This made Brunswick the largest operator of bowling centers in the country, with more than five times as many bowling centers as its next largest competitor. Because the bowling industry was so deconcentrated, however, Brunswick controlled fewer than 2 percent of the bowling centers in the country.

Pueblo Bowl-O-Mat, Inc., operated three bowling centers in markets where Brunswick had repossessed bowling centers and began operating them. Pueblo Bowl sued Brunswick, alleging that Brunswick had violated Section 7 of the Clayton Act. Pueblo Bowl alleged that it had suffered injury in the form of lost profits that it would have made had Brunswick allowed the bowling centers to go bankrupt, and it requested treble damages. Is Brunswick liable? [*Brunswick Corporation v. Pueblo Bowl-O-Mat, Inc.*, 429 U.S. 477, 97 S.Ct. 690, 1977 U.S. Lexis 37 (1977)]

21.13 Price Discrimination Corn Products Refining Company manufactured corn syrup, or glucose, at two plants, one located in Chicago, Illinois, and the other in Kansas City, Missouri. Glucose was a principal ingredient of low-priced candy. Corn Products sold glucose at the same retail price to all purchasers but charged separately for freight charges. Instead of charging actual freight charges, Corn Products charged every purchaser the freight that it would have cost if the glucose were shipped from Chicago, even if the glucose was shipped from its Kansas City plant. This "base point pricing" system created a favored price zone for Chicago-based purchasers. This put them in a better position to compete for business. The FTC sued Corn Products, alleging that it engaged in price discrimination in violation of Section 2(a) of the Robinson-Patman Act. Did it? [*Corn Products Refining Company v. Federal Trade Commission*, 324 U.S. 726, 65 S.Ct. 961, 1945 U.S. Lexis 2749 (1945)]

21.14 Defense The Morton Salt Company manufactures and sells table salt in interstate commerce. Morton Salt manufactures several different brands of table salt and sells them directly to (1) wholesalers, who in turn resell to retail stores, and (2) large retailers. Morton Salt sold its finest brand of table salt, "Blue Label," based on the following standard-quantity discount system, which is available to all customers:

	Price per Case
Less than carload purchase	$1.60
Carload purchases	1.50
5,000-case purchases	1.40
50,000-case purchases	1.35

The standard-quantity discount pricing schedule was not based on actual costs incurred by Morton Salt in serving its customers; instead, it was designed to give large purchasers an incentive to purchase salt from Morton Salt. Evidence showed that only five large retail chains ever bought Blue Label salt in sufficient quantities to qualify for the $1.35 per case price. Evidence also showed that small retailers that could not qualify for any discount had to pay wholesalers higher prices for salt than the large retailers were selling the salt at retail to their customers. The FTC sued Morton Salt, alleging that it violated Section 2(a) of the Robinson-Patman Act. Was Morton Salt's quantity discount pricing system justified? [*Federal Trade Commission v. Morton Salt Company*, 334 U.S. 37, 68 S.Ct. 822, 1948 U.S. Lexis 2766 (1948)]

21.15 FTC Act Texaco, Inc., was one of the nation's largest petroleum companies. It sold its products through approximately 30,000 franchised service stations, which constituted about 16 percent of all service stations in the United States. Nearly 40 percent of the Texaco dealers leased their stations from Texaco. This was typically a one-year lease that could be terminated (1) at the end of any year upon proper notice or (2) at any time if in Texaco's judgment any lease provisions relating to the use and appearance of the station was not fulfilled. The franchise agreement under which the dealers received their supply of gasoline and other petroleum products also was a one-year agreement and was terminable upon 30 days' notice.

Texaco entered into an agreement with the Goodrich Tire Company whereby Texaco agreed to promote the sale of Goodrich tires, batteries, and accessories (TBA) through its franchised dealers. The agreement provided that Goodrich would pay Texaco a 10 percent commission on all TBA purchases by Texaco dealers. During the five-year period 1952–1956, Texaco received commissions of $22 million.

Although Texaco dealers were not forced to carry the TBA, Texaco strongly recommended that they carry the line. In addition, the Texaco representatives who were responsible for recommending the renewal of dealer franchise and lease agreements were told to promote Goodrich products. Texaco also received regular reports on the amount of TBA purchased by its dealers. The FTC brought an action that alleged that Texaco violated Section 5 of the FTC Act. Who wins? [*Federal Trade Commission v. Texaco, Inc.*, 393 U.S. 223, 89 S.Ct. 429, 1968 U.S. Lexis 3076 (1968)]

Business Ethics Cases

21.16 Business Ethics E.I. du Pont de Nemours & Co. (du Pont) is a manufacturer of chemicals, paints, finishes, fabrics, and other products. General Motors Corporation is a major manufacturer of automobiles. During the period 1917–1919, du Pont purchased 23 percent of the stock of General Motors. du Pont became a major supplier of finishes and fabrics to General Motors.

The du Pont Company's commanding position as a General Motors supplier was not achieved until shortly after its purchase of a sizable block of General Motors stock in 1917. The company's interest in buying into General Motors was stimulated by John J. Raskob, du Pont's treasurer, and Pierre S. du Pont, du Pont's president, who acquired personal holdings of General Motors stock in 1914. General Motors had been organized six years earlier by William C. Durant to acquire previously independent automobile manufacturing companies—Buick, Cadillac, Oakland, and Oldsmobile. Durant later brought in Chevrolet, organized by him when he was temporarily out of power, during 1910–1915, and a bankers' group controlled General Motors. In 1915, when Durant and the bankers deadlocked on the choice of a board of directors, they resolved the deadlock by an agreement under which Pierre S. du Pont was named chairman of the General Motors Board and Pierre S. du Pont, Raskob, and two nominees of Mr. du Pont were named neutral directors. By 1916, Durant settled his differences with the bankers and resumed the presidency and his controlling position in General Motors. He prevailed upon Pierre S. du Pont and Raskob to continue their interest in General Motors's affairs, which both did as members of the finance committee, working closely with Durant in matters of finances and operations and plans for future expansion.

Raskob foresaw the success of the automobile industry and the opportunity for great profit in a substantial purchase of General Motors stock. On December 19, 1917, Raskob submitted a treasurer's report to the du Pont finance committee, recommending a purchase of General Motors stock in the amount of $25,000,000. That report made it clear that more than just a profitable investment was contemplated. A major consideration was that an expanding General Motors would provide a substantial market needed by the burgeoning du Pont organization.

Raskob's summary of reasons in support of the purchase included this statement: "Our interest in the General Motors Company will undoubtedly secure for us the entire Fabrikoid, Pyralin (celluloid), paint and varnish business of those companies, which is a substantial factor."

General Motors was the colossus of the giant automobile industry. It accounted annually for upwards of two-fifths of the total sales of automotive vehicles in the nation. Expressed in percentages, du Pont supplied 67 percent of General Motors's requirements for finishes in 1946 and 68 percent in 1947. In fabrics, du Pont supplied 52.3 percent of requirements in 1946 and 38.5 percent in 1947. Because General Motors accounted for almost one-half of the automobile industry's annual sales, its requirements for automotive finishes and fabrics must have represented approximately one-half of the relevant market for these materials.

In 1949, the United States brought an antitrust action against du Pont, alleging violation of Section 7 of the Clayton Act and seeking the divestiture of du Pont's ownership of stock in General Motors. Did du Pont's ownership of 23 percent of the stock of General Motors constitute a vertical merger that gave du Pont illegal preferences over competitors in the sale of finishes and fabrics to General Motors in violation of Section 7 of the Clayton Act? Did the du Ponts act ethically in this case? [*United States v. E.I. du Pont de Nemours & Co.*, 353 U.S. 586, 77 S.Ct. 872, 1957 U.S. Lexis 1755 (1957)]

21.17 Business Ethics Falls City Industries, Inc., (Falls City), is a regional brewer located in Nebraska. It sells its "Falls City" brand beer in 13 states, including Indiana and Kentucky. In Indiana, Falls City sells its beer to Vanco Beverage, Inc., a beer wholesaler located in Vanderburgh County. In Kentucky, Falls City sells its beer to wholesalers located in Henderson County. The two counties are directly across from each other and are separated only by the Indiana–Kentucky state line. A four-lane interstate highway connects the two counties. When other brewers raised their wholesale prices in Indiana, Falls City also raised its prices. Falls City also raised its wholesale prices in Kentucky, but less than its prices were raised in Indiana. Vanco brought a treble damage action against Falls City, alleging that Falls City had engaged in price discrimination in violation of Section 2(a) of the Robinson-Patman Act by raising prices less in Kentucky than in Indiana. Does the meeting-the-competition defense protect Falls City Industries from liability for price discrimination? Did Falls City act unethically in this case? [*Falls City Industries, Inc. v. Vanco Beverage, Inc.*, 460 U.S. 428, 103 S.Ct. 1282, 1983 U.S. Lexis 148 (1983)]

Briefing the Case Writing Assignment

Read Case A.21 in the Case Appendix [*Texaco Inc. v. Hasbrouck, dba Rick's Texaco*]. This case is excerpted from the U.S. Supreme Court opinion. Review and brief the case. In your brief, be sure to answer the following questions.

1. Who were the plaintiffs? Who was the defendant?
2. Describe the activities that the defendant engaged in that the plaintiffs alleged were unlawful.
3. What law did the plaintiffs assert was violated? What does this law prohibit?
4. Did the U.S. Supreme Court find a violation? Explain the reasoning the Supreme Court used in reaching its decision.

Answers to Management Decision Questions

1. You should definitely not do as Charlie suggests. Congress enacted a comprehensive system of antitrust laws to limit anticompetitive behavior. The major federal statutes are the **Sherman Act**, the **Clayton Act**, the **Robinson-Patman Act**, and the **FTC Act**. Your arrangement would be illegal under Section 1 of the **Sherman Act**. Section 1 outlaws contracts combinations and conspiracies in restraint of trade. Thus, it applies to unlawful conduct by two or more parties. Specifically, the four of you are talking about an illegal price-fixing scheme. Horizontal price-fixing occurs when competitors in the same line of business agree to set the price of goods or services they sell. Price-fixing is defined as raising, depressing, fixing, pegging, or stabilizing the price of a commodity of service. Illegal price-fixing includes setting minimum or maximum prices and fixing the quantity of a product or service to be produced or provided. Price-fixing is a *per se* violation of Section 1 of the Sherman Act.
2. Although many states have enacted antitrust laws, most actions in this area are brought under federal law. Federal antitrust laws provide for both government and private lawsuits. Private parties cannot intervene in public antitrust actions brought by the government. If you follow through with this illegal scheme, injured competitors can sue under the provisions of the **Clayton Act. Section 4** of the Clayton Act permits any person who suffers antitrust injury in his or her "business property" to bring a private civil action against the offender. To recover damages, plaintiffs must prove that they suffered antitrust injuries caused by the prohibited act.

Endnotes

1. Antitrust Amendments Act of 1990, P.L. 101–588.
2. Antitrust Amendments Act of 1990, P.L. 101–588.
3. 15 U.S.C. § 15.
4. *Reiter v. Sonotone Corporation*, 442 U.S. 330, 99 S.Ct. 2326, 1979 U.S. Lexis 108 (1979).
5. 15 U.S.C. § 26.

6. Justice Marshall, *United States v. Topco Associates, Inc.*, 405 U.S. 596, 92 S.Ct. 1126, 1972 U.S. Lexis 167 (1972).
7. 221 U.S. 1, 31 S.Ct. 502, 1911 U.S. Lexis 1725 (1911). The Court found that Rockefeller's oil trust violated the Sherman Act and ordered the trust broken up into 30 separate companies.
8. *Continental T.V., Inc. v. GTE Sylvania, Inc.*, 433 U.S. 36, 97 S.Ct. 2549, 1977 U.S. Lexis 134 (1977), reversing *United States v. Arnold Schwinn & Co.*, 388 U.S. 365, 87 S.Ct. 1856, 1967 U.S. Lexis 2965 (1969).
9. 250 U.S. 300, 39 S.Ct. 465, 1919 U.S. Lexis 1748 (1919).
10. This doctrine is the result of two U.S. Supreme Court decisions: *Eastern R.R. President's Conference v. Noerr Motor Freight, Inc.*, 365 U.S. 127, 81 S.Ct. 523, 1961 U.S. Lexis 2128 (1961), and *United Mine Workers v. Pennington*, 381 U.S. 657, 85 S.Ct. 1585, 1965 U.S. Lexis 2207 (1965).
11. *William Inglis & Sons Baking Company v. ITT Continental Baking Company, Inc.*, 668 F.2d 1014, 1982 U.S. App. Lexis 21926 (9th Cir. 1982).
12. 374 U.S. 321, 83 S.Ct. 1715, 1963 U.S. Lexis 2413 (1963).
13. 15 U.S.C. § 18(a).
14. 15 U.S.C. § 14.
15. *Hartley & Parker, Inc. v. Florida Beverage Corp.*, 307 F.2d 916, 923, 1962 U.S. App. Lexis 4196 (5th Cir. 1952).
16. 15 U.S.C. § 13(b).
17. Section 6 of the Clayton Act, 15 U.S.C. § 17; the Norris-LaGuardia Act of 1932, 29 U.S.C. §§ 101–155; and the National Labor Relations Act of 1935, 29 U.S.C. §§ 141 et seq. Labor unions that conspire or combine with nonlabor groups to accomplish a goal prohibited by federal antitrust law lose their exemption.
18. Capper-Volstrand Act of 1922, 7 U.S.C. § 291; Cooperative Marketing Act of 1926, 15 U.S.C. § 521.
19. Webb-Pomerene Act, 15 U.S.C. §§ 61–65.
20. McCarran-Ferguson Act of 1945, 15 U.S.C. §§ 1011–1015.
21. *Community Communications Co., Inc. v. City of Boulder*, 455 U.S. 40, 102 S.Ct. 835, 1982 U.S. Lexis 65 (1982).
22. *Goldfarb v. Virginia State Bar*, 421 U.S. 773, 95 S.Ct. 2004, 1975 U.S. Lexis 13 (1975).
23. For example, see *California v. ARC America Corporation*, 490 U.S. 93, 109 S.Ct. 1661, 1989 U.S. Lexis 2024 (1989).

22

Investor Protection and Securities Regulation

"Fraud is infinite in variety; sometimes it is audacious and unblushing; sometimes it pays a sort of homage to virtue, and then it is modest and retiring; it would be honesty itself, if it could only afford it."

—Lord MacNaghten
Reddaway v. Banham (1896)

Chapter Objectives

After studying this chapter, you should be able to:

1. Describe the procedure for "going public" and how securities are registered with the Securities and Exchange Commission.
2. Describe the requirements for qualifying for private placement, intrastate, and small offering exemptions from registration.
3. Define insider trading that violates Section 10(b) of the Securities Exchange Act of 1934.
4. Describe the liability of tippers and tippees for insider trading.
5. Describe short-swing profits that violate Section 16(b) of the Securities Exchange Act of 1934.

Chapter Contents

Management Decision Investor Protection and Securities Regulation

You recently, as a guest, attended a retirement ceremony at Universal Pharmaceutical Corporation (Universal). During the social hour following the banquet, you overheard a conversation between Carlos Cruz, president of Universal, and Grace Watson, vice president of research and development at Universal. Watson stated that the Food and Drug Administration was about to approve Universal's application to produce and market a new drug that would revolutionize the way diabetics are treated. Based on this information, you purchased 500 shares of Universal stock at $25 a share. Later you sold the stock for $75 a share. The SEC is currently investigating claims of insider trading of Universal stock.

1. What is insider trading?
2. Are you guilty of insider trading?

Prior to the 1920s and 1930s, the securities and commodities markets in this country were not regulated by the federal government. Securities and commodities were sold to investors with little, if any, disclosure. Fraud in these transactions was common.

Business Brief
Federal law did not regulate the securities markets until after the stock market crash of 1929. Securities laws are designed to help prevent a similar crash today.

Following the stock market crash of 1929, Congress enacted a series of statutes designed to regulate securities and commodities markets. The *Securities Act of 1933* requires disclosure by companies and others who wish to issue securities to the public. The *Securities Act of 1934* was enacted to prevent fraud in the subsequent trading of securities, including insider trading.

These federal and state statutes are designed to (1) require disclosure of information to investors and (2) prevent fraud. This chapter discusses federal and state securities laws and regulations that provide investor protection.

Arch, St. Louis, Missouri. State securities laws are often referred to as "blue-sky" laws because they help prevent investors from purchasing a piece of the blue sky.

The Securities and Exchange Commission (SEC)

The Securities Exchange Act of 1934 created the **Securities and Exchange Commission (SEC)** and empowered it to administer federal securities laws. The SEC is an administrative agency composed of five members who are appointed by the president. The major responsibilities of the SEC are:

1. Adopting rules (also called regulations) that further the purpose of the federal securities statutes. These rules have the force of law.
2. Investigating alleged securities violations and bringing enforcement actions against suspected violators. This may include a recommendation of criminal prosecution. Criminal prosecutions of violations of federal securities laws are brought by the U.S. Department of Justice.
3. Regulating the activities of securities brokers and advisors. This includes registering brokers and advisors and taking enforcement action against those who violate securities laws.

Securities and Exchange Commission (SEC)
A federal administrative agency that is empowered to administer federal securities laws. The SEC can adopt rules and regulations to interpret and implement federal securities laws.

Web Site
U.S. Securities and Exchange Commission This large government Web site links you to many securities materials. Visit at **www.sec.gov**.

Definition of Security

A **security** must exist before securities laws apply. Securities are defined as:

1. Interests or instruments that are commonly known as securities (e.g., common stock, preferred stock, bonds, debentures, warrants).
2. Interests or instruments that are expressly mentioned in securities acts (e.g., preorganization subscription agreements; interests in oil, gas, and mineral rights; deposit receipts for foreign securities).
3. Investment contracts—that is, any contract whereby an investor invests money or other consideration in a common enterprise and expects to make a profit from the significant efforts of others. Limited partnership interests, pyramid sales schemes, and investments in farm animals accompanied by care agreements have been found to be securities under this test, which is known as the *Howery test*.[1]

security
(1) An interest or instrument that is common stock, preferred stock, a bond, a debenture, or a warrant; (2) an interest or instrument that is expressly mentioned in securities acts; and (3) an investment contract.

The Securities Act of 1933—Registration of Securities

Securities Act of 1933
A federal statute that primarily regulates the issuance of securities by corporations, partnerships, associations, and individuals.

Landmark Law
The Securities Act of 1933

The **Securities Act of 1933** primarily regulates the *issuance* of securities by a corporation, a general or limited partnership, an unincorporated association, or an individual. Unless a security or transaction qualifies for an exemption, Section 5 of the Securities Act of 1933 requires securities offered to the public through the use of the mails or any facility of interstate commerce to be *registered* with the SEC by means of a registration statement and an accompanying prospectus. ■

Registration Statement

A covered issuer must file a written **registration statement** with the SEC. The issuer's lawyer normally prepares the statement, with the help of the issuer's management, accountants, and underwriters.

Business Brief
Section 5 of the Securities Act of 1933 requires an issuer to register securities with the SEC before they can be sold to the public.

registration statement
A document that an issuer of securities files with the SEC that contains required information about the issuer, the securities to be issued, and other relevant information.

A registration statement must contain descriptions of (1) securities being offered for sale, (2) the registrant's business, (3) the management of the registrant, including compensation, stock options and benefits, and material transactions with the registrant, (4) pending litigation, (5) how the proceeds from the offering will be used, (6) government regulation, (7) the degree of competition in the industry, and (8) any special risk factors. In addition, the registration statement must be accompanied by financial statements as certified by certified public accountants.

Registration statements usually become effective 20 business days after they are filed, unless the SEC requires additional information to be disclosed. A new 20-day period begins each time the registration statement is amended. At the registrant's request, the SEC may "accelerate" the *effective date* (i.e., not require the registrant to wait 20 days after the last amendment is filed).

Business Brief
The SEC does not decide on the merits of the registered securities.

The SEC does not pass upon the merits of the securities offered. It decides only whether the issuer has met the disclosure requirements.

Prospectus

prospectus
A written disclosure document that must be submitted to the SEC along with the registration statement and given to prospective purchasers of the securities.

The **prospectus** is a written disclosure document that must be submitted to the SEC along with the registration statement. Much of the information included in the prospectus can be found in the registration statement. The prospectus is used as a selling tool by the issuer. It is provided to prospective investors to enable them to evaluate the financial risk of the investment.

A prospectus must contain the following language in capital letters and boldface (usually red) type:

> THESE SECURITIES HAVE NOT BEEN APPROVED OR DISAPPROVED BY THE SECURITIES AND EXCHANGE COMMISSION OR ANY STATE SECURITIES COMMISSION NOR HAS THE SECURITIES AND EXCHANGE COMMISSION OR ANY STATE SECURITIES COMMISSION PASSED UPON THE ACCURACY OR ADEQUACY OF THIS PROSPECTUS. ANY REPRESENTATION TO THE CONTRARY IS A CRIMINAL OFFENSE.

Contemporary Business Environment

Securities Offerings Must Be Written in Plain English

Nonlawyers have always been frustrated by the legalese used by lawyers in contracts, court documents, and regulatory disclosures. There has been no wider use of arcane legal language than in prospectuses offering securities for sale to the public.

These documents, which are supposed to provide relevant information to potential investors before they invest in company stock and securities, are usually barely skimmed, let alone read, by potential investors.

The SEC decided to change this practice in 1998 when it adopted a "plain English" rule for securities offerings. Under this rule, issuers of securities must use plain English language on the cover page, in the summary, and in the risk factor sections of their prospectuses. Issuers must now use

- Active voice
- Short sentences
- "Everyday" words
- Bullet lists for complex information
- No legal jargon or highly technical terms
- No multiple negatives

The plain English rule has required a major cultural change by issuers, underwriters, and securities lawyers, who are used to using long, complicated, and confusing language. The SEC has stated that it will not be the "grammar police," but will instead focus on the clarity of disclosures to potential investors by issuers. The SEC hopes that its new rule will encourage issuers to use plain English throughout the entire prospectus. [Rule 421 (d) of Regulation C] ■

Limitations on Activities During the Registration Process

Section 5 of the Securities Act of 1933 limits the types of activities that an issuer, an underwriter, and a dealer may engage in during the registration process. These limitations are divided into three time periods: (1) the prefiling period, (2) the waiting period, and (3) the posteffective period.

The Prefiling Period The **prefiling period** begins when the issuer first contemplates issuing the securities and ends when the registration statement is filed. During this time, the issuer cannot either sell or offer to sell the securities. The issuer also cannot *condition the market* for the upcoming securities offering. This rule makes it illegal for an issuer to engage in a public relations campaign (e.g., newspaper and magazine articles and advertisements) that touts the prospects of the company and the planned securities issue. However, sending annual reports to shareholders and making public announcements of factual matters (such as the settlement of a strike) are permissible because they are considered normal corporate disclosures.

prefiling period
A period of time that begins when the issuer first comtemplates issuing the securities and ends when the registration statement is filed. The issuer may not *condition* the market during this period.

The Waiting Period The **waiting period** begins when the registration statement is filed with the SEC and continues until the registration statement is declared effective.

The issuer is encouraged to condition the market during this time. Thus, the issuer may (1) make oral offers to sell (including face-to-face and telephone conversations), (2) distribute a *preliminary prospectus* (usually called a red herring), which contains most of the information to be contained in the final porspectus except for price, (3) distribute a *summary prospectus*, which is a summary of the important terms contained in the prospectus, and (4) publish *tombstone ads* in newspapers and other publications. Unapproved writings (which are considered illegal offers to sell) as well as actual sales are prohibited during the waiting period.

waiting period
A period of time that begins when the registration statement is filed with the SEC and continues until the registration statement is declared effective. Only certain activities are permissible during the waiting period.

The Posteffective Period The **posteffective period** begins when the registration statement becomes effective and runs until the issuer either sells all of the offered securities or withdraws them from sale. Thus, the issuer and its underwriter and dealers may close the offers received prior to the effective date and solicit new offers and sales.

Prior to or at the time of confirming a sale or sending a security to a purchaser, the issuer (or its representative) must deliver a **final prospectus** (also called a **statutory prospectus** to the investor. Failure to do so is a violation of Section 5. Tombstone ads are often used during this period.

If an issuer violates any of the prohibitions on activities during these periods, the investor may rescind his or her purchase. If an underwriter or dealer violates any of these prohibitions, the SEC may issue sanctions, including the suspension of securities licenses.

posteffective period
The period of time that begins with the registration statement becomes effective and runs until the issuer either sells all of the offered securities or withdraws them from sale.

final prospectus
A final version of the prospectus that must be delivered by the issuer to the investor prior to or at the time of confirming a sale or sending a security to a purchaser.

E-Commerce & Information Technology

Company Goes Public over the Internet

The SEC permits companies to issue securities over the Internet. The same federal securities laws that regulate the traditional issuance of securities also apply to the issuance of securities using the Internet. One company's Internet initial public offering (IPO) follows. ■

E-Commerce & Information Technology
(continued)

The information in this prospectus is not complete and may be changed. We may not sell these securities until the registration statement filed with the Securities and Exchange Commission is effective. This prospectus is not an offer to sell these securities and is not soliciting an offer to buy these securities in any state where the offer or sale is not permitted.

SUBJECT TO COMPLETION, DATED DECEMBER 21, 2000

PEET'S COFFEE & TEA, INC.

3,300,000 Shares
of Common Stock

This is our initial public offering and no public market currently exists for our shares. We expect that the public offering price will be between $10.00 and $14.00 per share. This price may not reflect the market price of our shares after this offering.

THE OFFERING	PER SHARE	TOTAL
Public Offering Price	$	$
Underwriting Discount	$	$
Proceeds to Peet's	$	$
Proceeds to Selling Shareholders	$	$

Of the 3,300,000 shares being offered, we are selling 2,500,000 shares and the selling shareholders identified in this prospectus are selling 800,000 shares. We will not receive any of the proceeds from the sale of shares by the selling shareholders. We have granted the underwriters the right to purchase up to 182,623 additional shares from us and 312,377 additional shares from the selling shareholders within 30 days to cover any over- allotments. The underwriters expect to deliver shares of common stock to purchasers on , 2001.

Proposed Nasdaq National Market Symbol: PEET

OPENIPO: The method of distribution being used by the underwriters in this offering differs somewhat from that traditionally employed in firm commitment underwritten public offerings. In particular, the public offering price and allocation of shares will be determined primarily by an auction process conducted by the underwriters and other securities dealers participating in this offering. A more detailed description of this process, known as an OpenIPO, is included in "Plan of Distribution."

THIS OFFERING INVOLVES A HIGH DEGREE OF RISK. YOU SHOULD PURCHASE SHARES ONLY IF YOU CAN AFFORD A COMPLETE LOSS OF YOUR INVESTMENT. SEE "RISK FACTORS" BEGINNING ON PAGE 5.

NEITHER THE SECURITIES AND EXCHANGE COMMISSION NOR ANY STATE SECURITIES COMMISSION HAS APPROVED OR DISAPPROVED OF THESE SECURITIES OR DETERMINED IF THIS PROSPECTUS IS TRUTHFUL OR COMPLETE. ANY REPRESENTATION TO THE CONTRARY IS A CRIMINAL OFFENSE.

WR**HAMBRECHT+CO**

Pacific Growth Equities, Inc.

The date of this prospectus is , 2001

Contemporary Business Environment
Regulation A Offerings

Regulation A permits an issuer to sell up to $5 million of securities during a 12-month period pursuant to a simplified registration process. Such offerings may have an unlimited number of purchasers who do not have to be sophisticated investors.

This regulation also stipulates that offerings exceeding $100,000 must file an *offering statement* with the SEC. The offering statement requires less disclosure than does a registration statement and is less costly to prepare. Investors must be provided an offering circular prior to the purchase of securities. There are no resale restrictions on the securities. ■

Securities Exempt from Registration

Certain *securities* are exempt from registration. Once a security is exempt, it is exempt forever. It does not matter how many times the security is transferred. Exempt securities include:

Business Brief

Certain *securities* do not have to be registered with the SEC.

1. Securities issued by any government in the United States (e.g., municipal bonds issued by city governments).
2. Short-term notes and drafts that have a maturity date that does not exceed nine months (e.g., commercial paper issued by corporations).
3. Securities issued by nonprofit issuers, such as religious institutions, charitable institutions, and colleges and universities.
4. Securities of financial institutions (e.g., banks and savings associations) that are regulated by the appropriate banking authorities.
5. Securities issued by common carriers (railroads and trucking companies) that are regulated by the Interstate Commerce Commission (ICC).
6. Insurance and annuity contracts issued by insurance companies.
7. Stock dividends and stock splits.
8. Securities issued in a corporate reorganization where one security is exchanged for another security.

"He will lie, sir, with such volubility that you would think truth were a fool."

William Shakespeare
All's Well That Ends Well (1604)

Contemporary Business Environment

Securities Investor Protection Corporation (SIPC)

Millions of investors use securities brokerage firms to buy, sell, and hold their securities in "street name." What happens if a securities firm that holds these securities fails? The securities are insured by the **Securities Investor Protection Corporation (SIPC)**, a private insurance company that is funded by annual assessments paid by securities firms.

Some vital statistics and information that investors should know about the SIPC insurance are:

- The SIPC provides insurance coverage of up to $500,000 per customer.
- Of the $500,000 coverage, only $100,000 of cash is covered per customer.
- Unlike deposit insurance for savings and checking accounts at banks, the SIPC is not backed by the full faith and credit of the U.S. government.
- The SIPC currently has under $1 billion in its coffers and an additional $500-million line of credit with banks it can draw on. This is sufficient to cover failure of many small brokerage firms but is inadequate to cover the failure of large brokerage firms. ■

Transactions Exempt from Registration

Certain *transactions* in securities are exempt from registration. Exempt transactions are subject to the antifraud provisions of the federal securities laws. Therefore, the issuer must provide investors with adequate information—including annual reports, quarterly reports, proxy statements, financial statements, and so on—even though a registration statement is not required. The exempt transactions are discussed in the paragraphs that follow.

Business Brief

If a business plans to issue nonexempt securities, it must either (1) register the securities with the SEC or (2) qualify for an exemption from registration.

Nonissuer Exemption

Nonissuers, such as average investors, do not have to file a registration statement prior to reselling securities they have purchased. This is because the Securities Act of 1933 exempts securities transactions not made by an issuer, an underwriter, or a dealer from registration.[2] For example, an investor who owns shares of IBM can resell these shares to another at any time without having to register with the SEC.

Intrastate Offerings

intrastate offering exemption
An exemption from registration that permits local businesses to raise from local investors capital to be used in the local economy without the need to register with the SEC.

The purpose of the **intrastate offerings exemption** is to permit local businesses to raise from local investors capital to be used in the local economy without the need to register with the SEC.[3] There is no limit on the dollar amount of capital that can be raised pursuant to an intrastate offering exemption. An issuer can qualify for this exemption in only one state.

Three requirements must be met to qualify for this exemption.[4]

1. The issuer must be a resident of the state for which the exemption is claimed. A corporation is a resident of the state in which it is incorporated.
2. The issuer must be doing business in that state. This requires that 80 percent of the issuer's assets are located in the state, 80 percent of its gross revenues are derived from the state, its principal office is located in the state, and 80 percent of the proceeds of the offering will be used in the state.
3. The purchasers of the securities all must be residents of that state.

Private Placements

private placement exemption
An exemption from registration that permits issuers to raise capital from an unlimited number of accredited investors and no more than 35 nonaccredited investors without having to register the offering with the SEC.

An issue of securities that does not involve a public offering is exempt from the registration requirements.[5] This exemption—known as the **private placement exemption**—allows issuers to raise capital from an unlimited number of accredited investors without having to register the offering with the SEC.[6] There is no dollar limit on the amount of securities that can be sold pursuant to this exemption.

An *accredited investor* may be.[7]

1. Any natural person (including spouse) who has a net worth of at least $1 million.
2. Any natural person who has had an annual income of at least $200,000 for the previous two years and reasonably expects to make $200,000 income in the current year.
3. Any corporation, partnership, or business trust with total assets in excess of $5 million.
4. Insiders of the issuers, such as executive officers and directors of corporate issuers and general partners of partnership issuers.
5. Certain institutional investors, such as registered investment companies, pension plans, colleges and universities, and the like.

Business Brief
Up to 35 nonaccredited investors may purchase securities pursuant to a private placement exemption. They must be sophisticated investors through their own experience and education or through representatives.

No more than 35 *nonaccredited investors* may purchase securities pursuant to a private placement exemption. Nonaccredited investors must be sophisticated investors, however, either through their own experience and education or through representatives (such as accountants, lawyers, and business managers). General selling efforts, such as advertising to the public, are not permitted.

Small Offerings

Securities offerings that do not exceed a certain dollar amount are exempt from registration.[8] Rule 504 exempts the sale of securities not exceeding $1 million during a 12-month period from registration. The securities may be sold to an unlimited number of accredited and unaccredited investors, but general selling efforts to the public are not permitted. This is called the **small offering exemption**.

small offering exemption
An exemption from registration that permits the sale of securities not exceeding $1 million during a 12-month period.

Resale Restrictions

Certain *resale restrictions* are placed on securities issued pursuant to exemptions from registration. These restrictions are discussed in the following paragraphs.

Restricted Securities Securities sold pursuant to the intrastate, private placement, or small offering exemptions are called **restricted securities** because they cannot be resold for a limited period of time after their initial issue. The following restrictions apply:

restricted securities
Securities that were issued for investment purposes pursuant to the intrastate, private placement, or small offering exemptions.

- Rule 147 stipulates that securities sold pursuant to an intrastate offering exemption cannot be sold to nonresidents for a period of nine months.
- Rule 144 provides that securities sold pursuant to the private placement or small offering exemption must be held for one year from the date when the securities are last sold by the issuer. After that time, investors may sell the greater of (1) 1 percent of the outstanding securities of the issuer or (2) the average weekly volume of trading in the securities (i.e., the four-week moving average) in any three-month period. Information about the issuer must be available to the public. Generally, all restrictions are lifted after two years.

Preventing Transfer of Restricted Securities To protect the nontransferability of restricted shares, the issuer must

Ethics Brief
The issuer must take certain actions to ensure that restricted securities are not sold in violation of the restrictions imposed by Rules 144 and 147.

1. Require the investors to sign an *affidavit* stating that they are buying the securities for investment, acknowledging that they are purchasing restricted securities, and promising not to transfer the shares in violation of the restriction.
2. Place a *legend* on the stock certificate, describing the restriction.
3. Notify the *transfer agent* not to record a transfer of the securities that would violate the restriction.

If the issuer has taken these precautions, it will not lose its exemption from registration, even if isolated transfers of stock occur in violation of the restricted periods. If these precautions are not taken, the issuer may lose its exemption from registration. In that event, because it has sold unregistered securities in violation of Section 5, if most permit all purchasers to rescind their purchases of the securities.

Rule 144A

To establish a more liquid and efficient secondary market in unregistered securities, the SEC adopted Rule 144A in 1990. This rule permits "qualified institutional investors"—defined as institutions that own and invest at least $100 million in securities—to buy unregistered securities without being subject to the holding periods of Rule 144. This rule is designed to create an institutional market in unregistered securities as well as to permit foreign issuers to raise capital in this country from sophisticated investors without making registration process disclosures.

Business Brief
To increase the liquidity of the registered securities, in 1990 the SEC adopted Rule 144A, which permits "qualified institutional investors" to buy unregistered securities without being subject to the holding periods of Rule 144.

Business Ethics

Integration of Exempt Offerings

Separate offerings that qualify for individual exemptions from registration will be **integrated** if they are really part of one large offering. This larger offering must then be examined to see if it qualifies for an exemption from registration. In deciding whether to integrate offerings, the SEC and the courts examine whether the offerings (1) are part of a single plan of financing, (2) involve the issuance of the same class of securities, (3) are made at about the same time, (4) receive the same consideration, and (5) are made for the same general purpose.

Safe harbor rules protect securities offerings made more than 6 months before or after the current offering from being integrated with the present offering.[9] This creates a 12-month period outside which none of the securities offering will be integrated with the current offering.

Consider This Example On January 1, the ABC Corporation issues $4 million of common stock for cash to 25 accredited and 15 sophisticated but nonaccredited investors, some of whom are located out of state. The proceeds are to be used for working capital. This offering qualifies for the private placement exemption.

On April 1 of the same year, ABC Corporation issues another $4 million of common stock for cash to 25 accredited and 25 sophisticated but nonaccredited investors, some of whom are located out of state. The proceeds are to be used for working capital. Again, this individual offering qualifies for the private placement exemption.

These offerings must be integrated because they occur within six months of each other, they are for the same security, the consideration is the same, and the proceeds from both offerings are used for the same purpose. The integrated offering does not qualify for an exemption from registration. There are 40 nonaccredited investors, too many to qualify for the private placement exemption. The integrated offering does not qualify for the intrastate exemption (there are out-of-state investors) or for the small offering exemption (the securities issued exceed $1 million). As a remedy, the investors can rescind their purchases because there has been a violation of Section 5 of the Securities Act of 1933.

1. Is it ethical for an issuer to make several exempt offerings that it knows to be one large offering?
2. Why would an issuer make multiple exempt offerings it knows to be one large offering? ■

Entrepreneur and the Law

SCOR Simplifies Stock Offerings by Small Companies

Like large corporations, small businesses often need to raise capital and must find public investors to buy company stock. Unlike large corporations, however, small businesses often do not have the money or resources to hire lawyers, investment bankers, accountants, and other professionals or to pay the printing and other costs associated with an IPO. Also, these small businesses often cannot find enough qualified investors or meet other requirements necessary to qualify for a private placement or other exemptions from registration. And in most cases, the small business needs to raise only a small amount of capital through a public offering.

In 1992, after years of investigation, the SEC amended its regulations to facilitate capital raising by small businesses. As part of this small business initiative, the SEC amended Regulation A by adopting the **Small Corporate Offering Registration Form (SCOR)**. The SCOR form—Form U-7—is a question-and-answer disclosure form that small businesses can complete and file with the SEC if they plan on raising $1 million or less from the public issue of securities. An issuer must answer the questions on Form U-7, which then becomes the offering circular that must be given to prospective investors.

Form U-7 simplifies and demystifies the registration process. The questions are so clearly and specifically drawn that they can be answered by the issuer without the help of an expensive securities lawyer. The SCOR questions require the issuer to develop a business plan that states specific company goals and how it plans to reach them. An overriding concern of SCOR is uniformity. Form U-7 is designed to replace the myriad of forms previously required by state laws for securities offerings that are exempt from complete SEC registration requirements, but it must comply with state securities laws. Many states have elected to allow SCOR Form U-7 to replace their disclosure requirements. SCOR is limited to domestic businesses and cannot be used by partnerships, foreign corporations, or companies involved in petroleum exploration or mining. The SCOR offering cannot exceed $1 million and the offering price of the common stock or its equivalent may not be less than $5 per share. SCOR offerings are a welcomed addition for entrepreneur-owners who want to raise money through a small public offering. ■

Liability Provisions of the Securities Act of 1933

Violations of the Securities Act of 1933 may result in various penalties and remedies against the perpetrator. These penalties and remedies are discussed in the following paragraphs.

Criminal Liability

Section 24 of the 1933 act imposes *criminal liability* on any person who *willfully* violates either the act or the rules and regulations adopted thereunder.[10] A violator may be fined up to $10,000 or imprisoned up to five years, or both. Criminal actions are brought by the Department of Justice.

Section 24
A provision of the Securities Act of 1933 that imposes criminal liability on any person who willfully violates the act or the rules or regulations adopted thereunder.

SEC Actions

The SEC may (1) issue a *consent order* whereby a defendant agrees not to violate securities laws in the future but does not admit to having violated securities laws in the past, (2) bring an action in federal district court to obtain an *injunction*, or (3) request the court to grant ancillary relief, such as *disgorgement of profits* by the defendant.

Private Actions

Private parties who have been injured by violations of the 1933 act have recourse against the violator, as discussed in the following paragraphs.

Section 12 **Section 12** of the 1933 act imposes *civil liability* on any person who violates the provisions of Section 5 of the act. Violations include selling securities pursuant to an unwarranted exemption and making misrepresentations concerning the offer or sale of securities. The purchaser's remedy for a violation of Section 12 is either to rescind the purchase or to sue for damages.

Section 12
A provision of the Securities Act of 1933 that imposes civil liability on any person who violates the provisions of Section 5 of the act.

Section 11 **Section 11** of the 1933 act provides for civil liability for damages when a registration statement on its effective date misstates or omits a material fact. Liability under Section 11 is imposed on those who (1) intentionally defraud investors or (2) are negligent in not discovering the fraud. Thus, the issuer, certain corporate officers (chief executive officer, chief financial officer, chief accounting officer), directors, signers of the registration statement, underwriters, and experts (accountants who certify financial statements and lawyers who issue legal opinions that are included in a registration statement) may be liable.

All defendants except the issuer may assert a **due diligence defense** against the imposition of Section 11 liability. If this defense is proven, the defendant is not liable. To establish a due diligence defense, the defendant must prove that after reasonable investigation, he or she had reasonable grounds to believe and did believe that, at the time the registration statement became effective, the statements contained therein were true and that there was no omission of material facts.

The following is a classic case where the court imposed civil liability on defendants who failed to prove their due diligence defense.

Section 11
A provision of the Securities Act of 1933 that imposes civil liability on persons who intentionally defraud investors by making misrepresentations or omissions of material facts in the registration statement or who are negligent for not discovering the fraud.

due diligence defense
A defense to a Section 11 action that, if proven, makes the defendant not liable.

Escott v. BarChris Construction Corp.
283 F. Supp 643, 1968 U.S. Dist. Lexis 3853 (1968)
United States District Court, Southern District of New York

Case 22.1
Securities Act of 1933

Background and Facts

In 1961, BarChris Construction Corp. (BarChris), a company primarily engaged in the construction and sale of bowling alleys, was in need of additional financing. To raise working capital, BarChris decided to issue debentures to investors. A registration statement, including a prospectus, was filed with the SEC on March 30, 1961. After two amendments, the registration statement became effective May 16, 1961. Peat, Marwick, Mitchell & Co. (Peat, Marwick) audited the financial statements of the company that were included in the registration statement and prospectus. The debentures were sold by May 24, 1961. Investors were provided a final prospectus concerning the debentures. Unbeknownst to the investors, however, the registration statement and prospectus contained the following material misrepresentations and omissions of material fact:

1. Current assets on the 1960 balance sheet were overstated by $609,689 (15 percent).
2. Contingent liabilities of April 30, 1961, were understated by $618,853 (42 percent).
3. Sales for the quarter ending March 31, 1961, were overstated by $519,810 (32 percent).
4. Gross profits for the quarter ending March 31, 1961, were overstated by $230,755 (92 percent).
5. Backlog orders as of March 31, 1961, were overstated by $4,490,000 (186 percent).
6. Loans to officers of BarChris of $386,615 were not disclosed.
7. Customer delinquencies and BarChris's potential liability thereto of $1,350,000 were not disclosed.
8. The use of the proceeds of the debentures to pay old debts was not disclosed.

In 1962, BarChris was failing financially, and on October 29, 1962, it filed a petition for protection to be reorganized under the federal bankruptcy law. On November 1, 1962, BarChris defaulted on interest payments due to be paid on the debentures to investors. Barry Escott and other purchasers of the debentures brought this civil action against executive officers, directors, and the outside accountants of BarChris. The plaintiffs alleged that the defendants had violated Section 11 of the Securities Act of 1933 by submitting misrepresentations and omissions of material facts in the registration statement filed with the SEC.

Issue

Are the defendants liable for violating Section 11, or have they proved their due diligence defense?

In The Language of The Court

McLean, District Judge I turn now to the question of whether defendants have proved their due diligence defenses.

Russo Russo was, for all intents and purposes, the chief executive officer of BarChris. He was a member of the executive committee. He was familiar with all aspects of the business. He was thoroughly aware of BarChris's stringent financial condition in May 1961. In short, Russo knew all the relevant facts. He could not have believed that there were no untrue statements or material omissions in the prospectus. Russo had no due diligence defenses.

Vitolo and Pugliese They were the founders of the business. Vitolo was president and Pugliese was vice president. Vitolo and Pugliese each are men of limited education. It is not hard to believe that for them the prospectus was difficult reading, if indeed they read it at all. But whether it was or not is irrelevant. The liability of a director who signs a registration statement does not depend upon whether or not he read it or, if he did, whether or not he understood what he was reading. And in any case, there is nothing to show that they made any investigation of anything that they may not have known about or understood. They have not proved their due diligence defenses.

Trilling Trilling was BarChris's controller. He signed the registration statement in that capacity, although he was not a director. He was a comparatively minor figure in BarChris. He was not considered an executive officer. Trilling may well have been unaware of several of the inaccuracies in the prospectus. But he must have known of some of them. As a financial officer, he was familiar with BarChris's finances and with its books of account. Trilling did not sustain the burden of proving his due diligence defenses.

Peat, Marwick Peat, Marwick's work was in general charge of a member of the firm, Cummings, and more immediately in charge of Peat, Marwick's manager, Logan. Most of the actual work was performed by a senior accountant, Berardi, who has junior assistants, one of whom was Kennedy. Berardi was then about 30 years old. He was not yet a CPA. He had had no previous experience with the bowling industry. This was his first job as a senior accountant. He could hardly have been given a more difficult assignment.

First and foremost is Berardi's failure to discover that Capital Lanes had not been sold. This error affected both the sales figure and the liability side of the balance sheet. Berardi erred in computing the contingent liabilities. Berardi made the S–1 review in May 1961. He devoted a little over two days to it, a total of 20½ hours. He did not discover any of the errors or omissions pertaining to the state of affairs in 1961, all of which were material. In conducting the S–1 review, Berardi did not examine any important financial records other than the trial balance. As to minutes, he read only the board of directors' minutes of BarChris. He did not read such minutes as there were of the executive committee. He did not know that there was an executive committee. He did not read the minutes of any subsidiary. He asked questions, he got answers that he considered satisfactory, and he did nothing to verify them.

Berardi had no conception of how tight the cash position was. He did not discover that BarChris was holding up checks in substantial amounts because there was no money in the bank to cover them. He did not know of the officers' loans. There had been a material change for the worse in BarChris's financial position. That change was sufficiently serious so that the failure to disclose it made the 1960 figures misleading. Berardi did not discover it. As far as results were concerned, his S–1 review was useless.

Accountants should not be held to a standard higher than that recognized in their profession. Berardi's review did not come up to that standard. He did not take some of the steps that Peat, Marwick's written program prescribed. He did not spend an adequate amount of time on a task of this magnitude. Most important of all, he was too easily satisfied with glib answers to his inquiries. There were enough danger signals to require some further investigation on his part. Generally accepted accounting standards required such further investigation under these circumstances. Peat, Marwick has not established its due diligence defense.

Decision and Remedy

The district court held that the defendants had failed to prove their due diligence defenses.

Case Questions

Critical Legal Thinking Should defendants in a Section 11 lawsuit be permitted to prove a due diligence defense to the imposition of liability? Or should liability be strictly imposed?

Business Ethics Who do you think committed the fraud in this case? Did any of the other defendants act unethically?

Contemporary Business Who do you think bore the burden of paying the judgment in this case?

Entrepreneur and the Law

Two New IPO Billionaires Made on the Same Day

On October 19, 1999, the *Forbes* 400 richest people in the world list had two new members, both the recipients of paper money made when their respective companies went public. The first was Martha Stewart, the "Miss Manners" of the late 1990s and early 2000s, who had propelled herself to center stage in the American consciousness as the guru of good taste. The one-time stockbroker, turned catering business owner, turned magazine editor, started her empire by writing the 1982 best-selling book *Entertaining*. She then wrote books on gracious living, cooking, hosting parties, and gardening and created a media empire that includes radio and television shows and a syndicated newspaper column. She has nurtured a superbrand name that now appears on Kmart towels, bedspreads, paints, garden tools, and almost anything used in and around the house. Her company, **Martha Stewart Living Omnimedia**, went public at $18 per share, and on the first day of trading rose to $52 before closing the day at $35. This IPO of $1.2 billion propelled Stewart into the wealthy elite. Stewart became one of the richest women in the world.

The second IPO billionaire of the day was Vince McMahon, who took his company, the **World Wrestling Federation (WWF)**, public. The WWF is a company that promotes professional wrestling matches, arranges TV coverage of its fights, and sells wrestling memorabilia. McMahon is a third-generation owner of the company. The wrestlers do not own the WWF but merely contract with the WWF to provide their services. Because you have to tell the truth to the SEC and the investing public, WWF's registration statement filed with the SEC and its prospectus given to investors admitted that professional wrestling is basically entertainment and not truly a sport. The documents also disclosed that there were several substantial lawsuits pending against the company and that it faces competition from World Championship Wrestling (WCW), a company backed by Time Warner. The WWF went public at $16, rose to $34 on the first day of trading, before closing the day at $25. After the IPO, McMahon was worth over $1 billion. The WWF has now changed its name to World Wrestling Entertainment, "WWE." Martha Stewart and Vince McMahon became new entrepreneur-billionaires. ■

Business Ethics

Sarbanes-Oxley Act Erects a Wall Between Security Analysts and Investment Bankers

Investment banking is a service provided by many securities firms, whereby they assist companies to "go public" when issuing shares to the public and otherwise selling securities. The securities firms are paid lucrative fees for providing investment banking services in assisting companies to sell their securities and finding customers to purchase these securities. These same securities firms often provide securities analysis, whereby they provide investment advice, recommending securities listed on the stock exchanges and other securities to be purchased by the public.

In the late 1990s and early 2000s, many conflicts of interest were uncovered, in which the truthfulness of analysts' reports had been compromised. Investment bankers and securities ana-

Business Ethics

(continued)

lysts of the same firm shared information, and the analysts were paid or pressured by the securities firms to write glowing reports of companies that the investment bankers of the firm were earning fees from. Basically, the public had been lied to in many analysts' investment advice reports.

Congress sought to remedy this problem by enacting Section 501 of the Sarbanes-Oxley Act of 2002. Section 501 established rules for separating the investment banking and securities advice functions of securities firms, thus eliminating many conflicts of interest. Some of the relevant provisions of Section 501 follow:

- Persons who are employed by the investment banking area of a securities firm cannot supervise analysts or be responsible for the compensation of analysts.
- The approval of persons employed in the investment banking area of a securities firm may not be required or sought before an analyst's investment report is issued.
- Persons employed in the investment banking area of a securities firm may not retaliate against or threaten to retaliate against a securities analyst employed by the firm or any of its affiliates for publishing an adverse, negative, or otherwise unfavorable research report that would adversely affect the firm's investment banking relationship with a present or prospective investment banking client.
- Securities firms must establish structural and institutional "walls" between their investment banking and securities analysis areas. These walls must protect analysts from review, pressure, and oversight by persons employed by the investment banking area of the securities firm.
- Securities analysts must disclose in each research report or public appearance any conflicts of interest that are known or should have been known to exist at the time of publication or public appearance. This includes whether the analyst owns any debt or equity securities of the company being reported on, whether the analyst has received any compensation from the company, whether the company being reported on has been an investment banking client of the securities firm within the prior year, and whether the analyst received compensation from the firm based on the investment banking revenues generated by the firm.

Section 501 is designed to protect the objectivity and independence of securities analysts and to foster public confidence in securities research. The SEC is empowered to adopt rules to enforce the provisions of Section 501.

1. Why did investment bankers of a securities firm put pressure on analysts to issue positive reports on certain companies? Was this conduct ethical?
2. Do you think Section 501 will prevent such conduct in the future? Why or why not? ■

The Securities Exchange Act of 1934—Trading in Securities

Landmark Law

The Securities Exchange Act of 1934

One year after Congress passed the Securities Exchange Act of 1933, it enacted the Securities Exchange Act of 1934. Unlike the Securities Act of 1933, which regulates the original issuance of securities, the **Securities Exchange Act of 1934** primarily regulates *subsequent trading*. It provides for the registration of certain companies with the SEC; continuous filing of periodic reports by these companies to the SEC; and the regulation of securities exchanges, brokers, and dealers. It also contains provisions that assess civil and criminal liability on violators of the 1934 act and rules and regulations adopted thereunder. ■

Continuous Reporting Requirements

Securities Exchange Act of 1934
A federal statute that primarily regulates the trading in securities.

The **Securities Exchange Act of 1934** requires issuers (1) with assets of more than $5 million and at least 500 shareholders, (2) whose equity securities are traded on a national securities exchange or (3) who have made a registered offering under the Securities Act of 1933, to file periodic reports with the SEC. These issuers, called *reporting companies*, must file an annual report (*Form 10-K*), quarterly reports (*Form 10-Q*), and monthly reports within 10 days of the end of the month in which a material event (such as a merger) occurs (*Form 8-K*). These reports are electronically filed with the SEC.

Section 10(b) and Rule 10b-5

Section 10(b) is one of the most important sections in the entire 1934 act. It prohibits the use of manipulative and deceptive devices in contravention of the rules and regulations prescribed by the SEC.

Pursuant to its rule-making authority, the SEC adopted **Rule 10b-5**, which provides that:

> It shall be unlawful for any person, directly or indirectly, by use of any means or instrumentality of interstate commerce or of the mails, or of any facility of any national securities exchange,
>
> a. to employ any device, scheme, or artifice to defraud,
>
> b. to make any untrue statement of a material fact or to omit to state a material fact necessary in order to make the statements made, in light of the circumstances under which they were made, not misleading, or
>
> c. to engage in any act, practice, or course of business that operates or would operate as a fraud or deceit upon any person, in connection with the purchase or sale of any security.

Section 10(b)
A provision of the Securities Exchange Act of 1934 that prohibits the use of manipulative and deceptive devices in the purchase or sale of securities in contravention of the rules and regulations prescribed by the SEC.

Rule 10b-5
A rule adopted by the SEC to clarify the reach of Section 10(b) against deceptive and fraudulent activities in the purchase and sale of securities.

Rule 10b-5 is not restricted to purchases and sales of securities of reporting companies.[11] All transfers of securities, whether made on a stock exchange, in the over-the-counter market, in a private sale, or in connection with a merger, are subject to this rule.[12] The U.S. Supreme Court has held that only conduct involving **scienter** (intentional conduct) violates Section 10(b) and Rule 10b-5. Negligent conduct is not a violation.[13]

scienter
Intentional conduct that is required for there to be a violation of Section 10(b) and Rule 10b-5.

Section 10(b) and Rule 10b-5 require reliance by the injured party on the misstatement. However, many sales and purchases of securities occur in open-market transactions (e.g., over stock exchanges) where there is no direct communication between the buyer and the seller.

In the following case, the U.S. Supreme Court addressed the issue of securities fraud in violation of Section 10(b) of the Securities Exchange Act of 1934.

U.S. SUPREME COURT CASE

Case 22.2
Securities Fraud

Securities and Exchange Commission v. Zandford

535 U.S. 813, 122 S.Ct. 1899, 2002 U.S. Lexis 4023 (2002)
Supreme Court of the United States

Background and Facts

Between 1987 and 1991, Charles Zandford was employed by a securities firm in Maryland. In 1987, he persuaded William Wood, an elderly man in poor health, to open an investment account. Wood granted Zandford discretion to manage the account and a general power of attorney to engage in securities transactions for his benefit without prior approval. It was later discovered that Zandford had on over 25 separate occasions transferred a total of $343,000 from Wood's account to accounts controlled by Zandford. Many of the transfers required selling Wood's securities in order for Zandford to write checks against the account to transfer funds to his accounts. Wood died in 1991.

Zandford was criminally indicted in U.S. district court on wire fraud charges, was found guilty, and was sentenced to prison for 52 months. The SEC brought this civil action against Zandford, alleging violations of Section 10(b). The district court entered judgment against Zandford and ordered him to disgorge $343,000 in ill-gotten gains. The court of appeals reversed the securities fraud charge, finding that the fraud had not occurred in connection with the purchase or sale of securities. The SEC appealed to the U.S. Supreme Court.

Supreme Court Issue

Was the stockbroker's fraudulent conduct committed in connection with the purchase or sale of securities, as required by Section 10(b)?

In The Language of The U.S. Supreme Court

Stevens, Justice Section 10(b) of the Securities Exchange Act makes it unlawful for any person to use or employ, "in connection with the purchase or sale of any security," any manipulative or deceptive device or contrivance in contravention of such rules

Securities and Exchange Commission v. Zandford

535 U.S. 813, 122 S.Ct. 1899, 2002 U.S. Lexis 4023 (2002)
Supreme Court of the United States
(continued)

and regulations as the SEC may prescribe. Rule 10b-5, which implements this provision, forbids the use, "in connection with the purchase or sale of any security," of any device, scheme, or artifice to defraud or any other act, practice, or course of business that operates as a fraud or deceit. Among Congress' objectives in passing the Act was to insure honest securities markets and thereby promote investor confidence after the market crash of 1929. More generally, Congress sought to substitute a philosophy of full disclosure for the philosophy of *caveat emptor* and thus to achieve a high standard of business ethics in the securities industry.

Consequently, we have explained that the statute should be construed not technically and restrictively, but flexibly to effectuate its remedial purposes. In its role enforcing the Act, the SEC has consistently adopted a broad reading of the phrase "in connection with the purchase or sale of any security." It has maintained that a broker who accepts payment for securities that he never intends to deliver, or who sells customers securities with intent to misappropriate the proceeds, violates Section 10(b) and Rule 10b-5. This interpretation of the ambiguous text of Section 10(b), in the context of formal adjudication, is entitled to deference if it is reasonable. We think it is the securities sales and respondent Zandford's fraudulent practices were not independent events. Rather, respondent's fraud coincided with the sales themselves. Wood was injured as an investor through respondent Zandford's deceptions, which deprived Wood of any compensation for the sale of his valuable securities.

Decision and Remedy

The U.S. Supreme court held that Zandford's misappropriation of Wood's money had occurred in connection with the purchase or sale of securities as required by Section 10(b). The Supreme Court reversed the decision of the court of appeals and remanded the case for further proceedings.

Case Questions

Critical Legal Thinking What does Section 10(b) provide? Were the elements of Section 10(b) met in this case?

Business Ethics Did Zandford act ethically in this case?

Contemporary Business Do you think the SEC catches most securities frauds? Explain.

Business Ethics

Regulation FD Requires Fair Disclosure to All

Prior to 2000, publicly held companies routinely announced crucial earnings and other significant information to securities analysts and other Wall Street insiders before making the information public. This meant that the analysts and others on Wall Street could profit from the information before it was made available to the general public. They did this by purchasing securities of the disclosing companies on good news and selling securities on bad news, before others could act. The SEC felt that this so-called "front-running" gave an unfair advantage to the investment professionals.

In 2000, over the objections of Wall Street, the SEC adopted **Regulation Fair Disclosure**, or **Reg FD**, that prohibits companies from leaking important information to securities professionals before the information is disclosed to the public. Reg FD forces companies, by law, to reveal sensitive information to the general public at the same time that the information is released to stock analysts. Reg FD has leveled the playing field and taken away a lucrative advantage that the Wall Street professionals had over the general investing public.

1. Was it ethical for securities professionals to "front-run" in the trading of securities?
2. Do you think Reg FD levels the playing field? Do securities professionals still have an advantage over members of the public when investing in securities? Explain. ■

Insider Trading

insider trading
Trading that occurs when an insider makes a profit by personally purchasing shares of the corporation prior to public release of favorable information or by selling shares of the corporation prior to the public disclosure of unfavorable information.

One of the most important purposes of Section 10(b) and Rule 10b-5 is to prevent **insider trading**. Insider trading occurs when a company employee or company advisor uses material nonpublic information to make a profit by trading in the securities of the company. This practice is considered illegal because it allows insiders to take advantage of the investing public.

In the *Matter of Cady, Roberts & Co.*,[14] the SEC announced that the duty of an insider who possesses material nonpublic information is to either (1) abstain from trading in the securities of the company or (2) disclose the information to the person on the other side of the transaction before the insider purchases the securities from or sells the securities to him or her.

Insiders

For Purposes of Section 10(b) and Rule 10b-5, *insiders* are defined as (1) officers, directors, and employees at all levels of the company; (2) lawyers, accountants, consultants, and other agents and representatives who are hired by the company on a temporary and non-employee status to provide services or work to the company; and (3) others who owe a fiduciary duty to the company.

The following two cases illustrate insider trading.

Web Site

Securities Law Home Page This site is an online guide to securities law. Visit at **www.seclaw.com**.

Case 22.3 Insider Trading

Securities and Exchange Commission v. Texas Gulf Sulphur Co.

401 F.2d 833, 1968 U.S.App. Lexis 5797
United States Court of Appeals, Second Circuit

Background and Facts

Texas Gulf Sulphur Co. (TGS) had for several years conducted aerial geophysical surveys in eastern Canada. On November 12, 1963, TGS drilled an exploratory hole—Kidd 55—near Timmins, Ontario. Assay reports showed that the core from this drilling proved to be remarkably high in copper, zinc, and silver. Because TGS did not own the mineral rights to properties surrounding the drill site, TGS kept the discovery secret, camouflaged the drill site, and diverted drilling efforts to another site. This allowed TGS to engage in extensive land acquisition around Kidd 55.

Eventually, rumors of a rich mineral strike began circulating. On Saturday, April 11, 1964, the *New York Times* and the *New York Herald-Tribune* published unauthorized reports of TGS drilling efforts in Canada and its rich mineral strike. On Sunday, April 12, officers of TGS met with a public relations consultant and drafted a press release that was issued that afternoon. The press release appeared in morning newspapers of general circulation on Monday, April 13. It read in pertinent part:

> The work done to date has not been sufficient to reach definite conclusions and any statement as to size and grade of ore would be premature and possibly misleading. When we have progressed to the point where reasonable and logical conclusions can be made, TGS will issue a definite statement to its stockholders and to the public in order to clarify the Timmons project.

The rumors persisted. On April 16, 1964, at 10:00 A.M., TGS held a press conference for the financial media. At this conference, which lasted about 10 minutes, TGS disclosed the richness of the Timmins mineral strike and that the strike should run to at least 25 million tons in ore. In early November 1963, TGS stock was trading at $173 per share. On April 15, 1964, the stock closed at $298. Several officers, directors, and other employees of TGS who had knowledge of the mineral strike at Timmins traded in the stock of TGS during the period November 12, 1963, to April 16, 1964. By May 15, 1964, the stock was selling at $58.

The SEC brought an action against David M. Crawford and Francis G. Coates, two TGS executives who possessed the nonpublic information about the ore strike and who traded in TGS securities. The SEC sought to rescind their stock purchases. The district court found Crawford liable for insider trading but dismissed the complaint against Coates. Appeals were taken from this judgment.

Issue

Are Crawford and Coates liable for trading on material inside information in violation of Section 10(b) and Rule 10b-5?

In The Language of The Court

Waterman, Circuit Judge The insiders here were not trading on an equal footing with the outside investors. They alone were in a position to evaluate the probability and magnitude of what seemed from the outset to be a major ore strike.

Crawford Crawford telephoned his orders to his Chicago broker about midnight on April 15 and again at 8:30 in the morning of April 16 with instructions to buy at the opening of the Midwest Stock Exchange that morning. The trial court's finding that "he sought to, and did, 'beat the news,'" is well documented by the record. Before insiders may act upon material information, such information must have been effectively disclosed in a manner sufficient to ensure its availability to the investing public. Particularly here, where a formal announcement to the entire financial news media had been promised in a prior official release known to the media, all insider activity must await dissemination of the promised official announcement.

Coats Coates was absolved by the court below because his telephone order was placed shortly before 10:20 A.M. on April 16, which was after the announcement had been made even though the news could not be considered already a matter of public information. This result seems to have been predicated upon a misinterpretation of dicta in Cady Roberts, where the SEC instructed

Securities and Exchange Commission v. Texas Gulf Sulphur Co.

401 F.2d 833 1968 U.S.App. Lexis 5797
United States Court of Appeals, Second Circuit
(continued)

insiders to "keep out of the market until the established procedures for public release of the information are carried out instead of hastening to execute transactions in advance of, and in frustration of, the objectives of the release." The reading of a news release, which prompted Coates into action, is merely the first step in the process of dissemination required for compliance with the regulatory objective of providing all investors with an equal opportunity to make informed investment judgments. Assuming that the contents of the official release could instantaneously be acted upon, at the minimum Coates should have waited until the news could reasonably have been expected to appear over the media of widest circulation, the Dow Jones broad tape, rather than hastening to ensure an advantage to himself and his broker son-in-law.

Decision and Remedy

The court of appeals held that both executives, Crawford and Coates, had engaged in illegal insider trading.

Case Questions

Critical Legal Thinking Should insider trading be illegal? Why or why not?

Business Ethics Did Crawford and Coates act ethically in this case?

Contemporary Business How can businesses protect against their employees engaging in insider trading? Explain.

Case 22.4 Misappropriation Theory

U.S. SUPREME COURT CASE
United States v. O'Hagan

521 U.S. 643, 117 S.Ct. 2199, 1997 U.S. Lexis 4033 (1997)
Supreme Court of the United States

Background and Facts

James O'Hagan was a partner in the law firm Dorsey & Whitney in Minneapolis, Minnesota. In July 1988, Grand Metropolitan PLC (Grand Met), a company based in London, England, hired Dorsey & Whitney to represent it in a secret tender offer for the stock of the Pillsbury Company, headquartered in Minneapolis. On August 18, 1988, O'Hagan began purchasing call options for Pillsbury stock. Each call option gave O'Hagan the right to purchase 100 shares of Pillsbury stock at a specified price. O'Hagan continued to purchase call options in August and September and became the largest holder of call options for Pillsbury stock. In September, O'Hagan also purchased 5,000 shares of Pillsbury common stock at $39 per share. These purchases were all made while Grand Met's proposed tender offer for Pillsbury remained secret to the public. When Grand Met publicly announced its tender offer in October 1988. Pillsbury stock increased to nearly $60 per share. O'Hagan sold his Pillsbury call options and common stock, making a profit of more than $4.3 million.

The SEC investigated, and the Department of Justice charged O'Hagan with criminally violating Section 10(b) and Rule 10b-5. Because this was not a case of classic insider trading because O'Hagan did not trade in the stock of his law firm's client, Grand Met, the government alleged that O'Hagan was liable under the "misappropriation theory" for trading in Pillsbury stock by engaging in deceptive conduct by misappropriating the secret information about Grand Met's tender offer from his employer, Dorsey & Whitney, and from its client, Grand Met. The district court found O'Hagan guilty and sentenced him to 41 months in prison. The Eighth Circuit court of appeals reversed, finding that liability under Section 10(b) and Rule 10b-5 cannot be based on the misappropriation theory. The government appealed to the U.S. Supreme Court.

Supreme Court Issue

Can a defendant be criminally convicted of violating Section 10(b) and Rule 10b-5 based on the misappropriation theory?

In The Language of The Court

Ginsburg, Justice The "misappropriation theory" holds that a person commits fraud "in connection with" a securities transaction, and thereby violates Section 10(b) and Rule 10b-5, when he misappropriates confidential information for securities trading purposes, in breach of a duty owed to the source of the information. Under this theory, a fiduciary's undisclosed, self-serving use of a principal's information to purchase or sell securities, in breach of a duty of loyalty and confidentiality, defrauds the principal of the exclusive use of that information.

The two theories are complementary, each addressing efforts to capitalize on nonpublic information through the purchase or sale of securities. The classical theory targets a corporate insider's breach of duty to shareholders with whom the insider transacts; the misappropriation theory outlaws trading on the basis of nonpublic information by a corporate "outsider" in breach of a duty owed not to a trading party, but to the source of the information.

The misappropriation theory comports with Section 10(b)'s language, which requires deception "in connection with the purchase or sale of any security," not deception of an identifiable purchaser or seller. In sum, considering the inhibiting impact on market participation of trading on misappropriated information, and the congressional purposes underlying Section 10(b), it makes scant sense to hold a lawyer like O'Hagan a Section 10(b) violator if he works for a law firm representing the target of a tender offer, but not if he works for a law firm representing the bidder. The text of the statute requires no such result. The misappropriation at issue here was properly made the subject of a Section 10(b) charge because it meets the statutory requirement that there be "deceptive" conduct "in connection with" securities transactions.

Decision and Remedy

The Supreme Court held that a defendant can be criminally convicted of violating Section 10(b) and Rule 10b-5 under the misappropriation theory.

Case Questions

Critical Legal Thinking Should the misappropriation theory be recognized as a basis for criminal liability under Section 10(b) and Rule 10b-5? Do you agree with the Supreme Court's decision?

Business Ethics If the Supreme Court had upheld the Eighth Circuit's decision, would ethics alone be enough to prevent persons like O'Hagan from trading on secret information?

Contemporary Business Will the securities markets be more or less honest because of the Supreme Court's ruling in this case?

Tipper–Tippee Liability

A person who discloses material nonpublic information to another person is called a **tipper**. The person who receives such information is known as the **tippee**. The tippee is liable for acting on material information that he or she knew or should have known was not public. The tipper is liable for the profits made by the tippee. If the tipee tips other persons, both the tippee (who is now a tipper) and the original tipper are liable for the profits made by these remote tippees. The remote tippees are liable for their own trades if they knew or should have known that they possessed material inside information.

tipper
A person who discloses material nonpublic information to another person.

tippee
A person who receives material nonpublic information from a tipper.

Washington D.C. Prior to the enactment of the Securities Act of 1933 and the Securities Exchange Act of 1934, many "stool pigeons" were defrauded by securities schemes. Today there may still be fraud in the purchase and sale of securities, but these federal laws permit the government and the victims of these frauds to sue and recover criminal and civil remedies.

Liability Provisions of the Securities Exchange Act of 1934

The civil and criminal penalties that may be assessed for violations of the Securities Exchange Act of 1934 are discussed in the following paragraphs.

Criminal Liability

Section 32

A provision of the Securities Exchange Act of 1934 that imposes criminal liability on any person who willfully violates the 1934 act or the rules or regulations adopted thereunder.

Section 32 of the Securities Exchange Act of 1934 makes it a criminal offense to violate willfully the provisions of the act or the rules and regulations adopted thereunder.[15] Under the provisions of the Sarbanes-Oxley Act of 2002, upon conviction, a natural person may be fined up to $5 million, imprisoned for up to 20 years, or both. Under Section 807 of the Sarbanes-Oxley Act of 2002, a person who willfully violates the Securities Exchange Act of 1934 can be fined or imprisoned for up to 25 years, or both. A corporation or other entity may be fined up to $2.5 million.

SEC Actions

The SEC may investigate suspected violations of the securities Exchange Act of 1934 and the rules and regulations adopted thereunder. The SEC may enter into *consent orders* with defendants, seek *injunctions* in federal district court, or seek court orders requiring defendants to *disgorge* illegally gained profits.

Insider Trading Sanctions Act of 1984

A federal statute that permits the SEC to obtain a civil penalty of up to three times the illegal benefits received from insider trading.

In 1984, Congress enacted the **Insider Trading Sanctions Act**,[16] which permits the SEC to obtain a *civil penalty* of up to three times the illegal profits gained or losses avoided on insider trading. The fine is payable to the U.S. Treasury.

Private Actions

Although Section 10(b) and Rule 10b-5 do not expressly provide for a private right of action, courts have implied such a right. Generally, a private plaintiff may seek rescission of the securities contract or recover damages (e.g., disgorgements of the illegal profits by the defendants). Private securities fraud claims must be brought within two years after discovery or five years after the violation occurs, whichever is shorter. In the following case, the U.S. Supreme Court affirmed an award of damages.

U.S. SUPREME COURT CASE

The Wharf (Holdings) Limited v. United International Holdings, Inc.

532 U.S. 588, 121 S.Ct. 1776, 2001 U.S. Lexis 3812 (2001)
Supreme Court of the United States

Case 22.5

Civil Securities Lawsuit

Background and Facts

The Wharf (Holdings) Limited is a Hong Kong firm that was interested in obtaining a license to operate a cable television system in Hong Kong. In 1991, the Hong Kong government announced that it would accept bids for the award of an exclusive license to operate a cable television system in Hong Kong. Wharf decided to find a business partner with cable system experience. Wharf located United International Holdings, Inc., a Colorado-based company with substantial experience in operating cable television systems. Wharf orally agreed to grant United an option to buy 10 percent of the stock of the new Hong Kong cable system if Wharf was awarded the license. United sent several employees to Hong Kong to help prepare Wharf's application for the license, design the cable system, and arrange financing.

In May 1993, Hong Kong awarded the cable franchise to Wharf. When United raised $66 million and tried to exercise its option to invest 10 percent in the new cable company, Wharf refused to permit United to buy any of the new company's stock. Documents and other evidence showed that at the time Wharf granted United the oral 10 percent stock option, it had not intended to ever sell United any stock in the new venture. United sued Wharf in U.S. district court for securities fraud for violating Section 10(b) of the Securities Exchange Act of 1934. The jury held for United and awarded it $67 million in compensatory damages and $58.5 million in punitive damages against Wharf. The court of appeals affirmed. The U.S. Supreme Court granted review

Supreme Court Issue

Did Wharf's oral stock option to sell United a 10 percent interest in Hong Kong cable television system, while secretly intending never to do so, violate Section 10(b) of the Securities Exchange Act of 1934?

In The Language of The U.S. Supreme Court

Breyer, Justice Wharf points out that its agreement to grant United an option to purchase shares in the cable system was an oral agreement. And it says that Section 10(b) does not cover oral contracts of sale. There is no convincing reason to interpret the Act to exclude oral contracts as a class. The Act itself says that it applies to "any contract" for the purchase or sale of a security. Oral contracts for the sale of securities are sufficiently common that the Uniform Commercial Code and statutes of frauds in every State now consider them enforceable. To sell an option while secretly intending not to permit the option's exercise is misleading, because a buyer normally presumes good faith. Since Wharf did not intend to honor the option, the option was, unbeknownst to United, valueless.

Decision and Remedy

The U.S. Supreme court held that an oral contract to sell an option to purchase securities that is not intended to be honored when the promise is made violates Section 10(b) of the Securities Exchange Act of 1934. The judgment of the court of appeals was affirmed.

Case Questions

Critical Legal Thinking Should Section 10(b) apply to oral promises to sell or purchase securities? Why or why not?

Business Ethics Did Wharf act ethically in this case? Was the award of punitive damages warranted in this case?

Contemporary Business Should United have obtained a written option contract from Wharf? Why or why not?

Short-Swing Profits

Section 16(a) of the 1934 act defines any person who is an executive officer, a director, or a 10 percent shareholder of an equity security of a reporting company as a *statutory insider* for Section 16 purposes. Statutory insiders must file reports with the SEC, disclosing their ownership and trading in the company's securities.[17] These reports must be filed with the SEC and made available on the company's Web site within two days after the trade occurs.

Section 16(a)
A section of the Securities Exchange Act of 1934 that defines any person who is an executive officer, a director, or a 10 percent shareholder of an equity security of a reporting company as a *statutory insider* for Section 16 purposes.

Section 16(b)

Section 16(b) requires that any profits made by a statutory insider on transactions involving *short-swing profits*—that is, trades involving equity securities occurring within six months of each other—belong to the corporation.[18] The corporation may bring a legal action to recover these profits. Involuntary transactions, such as forced redemption of securities by the corporation or an exchange of securities in a bankruptcy proceeding, are exempt. Section 16(b) is a strict liability provision. Generally, no defenses are recognized. Neither intent nor the possession of inside information need be shown.

Section 16(b)
A section of the Securities Exchange Act of 1934 that requires that any profits made by a statutory insider on transactions involving *short-swing profits* belong to the corporation.

Consider This Example Rosanne is the president of a corporation and statutory insider who does not possess any inside information. On February 1, she purchases 1,000 shares of her employer's stock at $10 per share. On June 1, she sells the stock for $14 per share. The corporation can recover the $4,000 profit because the trades occurred within six months of each other. Rosanne would have to wait until after August 1 to sell the securities.

SEC Rules

The SEC has adopted the following rules concerning Section 16.[19]

Business Brief

In 1991, the SEC issued rules that clarify the persons and transactions subject to Section 16's short-swing profit rule.

- Clarify the definition of *officer* to include only executive officers who perform policy-making functions. This would include the president, the chief executive officer, the vice presidents in charge of business units or divisions, the principal financial officer, the principal accounting officer, and the like. Officers who run day-to-day operations but are not responsible for policy decisions are not included.
- Relieve insiders of liability for transactions that occur within six months before becoming an insider. For example, if a noninsider buys shares of his or her company January 15, becomes an insider March 15, and sells the shares May 15, the January 15 purchase is not matched against the May 15 sale.
- Continue the rule that insiders are liable for transactions that occur within six months of the last transaction engaged in while an insider. For example, if an insider buys shares in his or her company April 30 and leaves the company May 15, this purchase must be matched against any sale of the company's shares that occurs on or before October 30.
- Treat derivative securities (e.g., stock options, warrants) as follows: The acquisition or disposition of a derivative security is a Section 16 event; the exercise of the derivative security is a nonevent for Section 16 purposes. For example, suppose a company issues a stock option to its president May 15, who exercises the option June 15 and sells the shares on December 1. There is no violation of Section 16.
- Require companies to disclose delinquent filings of Section 16 forms in their proxy statements.

Concept Summary Section 10(b) and Section 16(b) Compared

Element	Section 10(b) and Rule 10(b)-5	Section 16(b)
Covered securities	All securities.	Securities required to be registered with the SEC under the 1934 act.
Inside information	Defendant made a misrepresentation or traded on inside (or perhaps misappropriated) information.	Short-swing profits recoverable, whether or not they are attributable to misappropriation or inside information.
Recovery	Belongs to the injured purchaser or seller.	Belongs to the corporation.

E-Commerce & Information Technology

Online "Free" Stock Scam Deleted by SEC

Does free stock for Internet users sound too good to be true? The SEC, the government agency charged with enforcing federal securities laws, thought so and has launched a crackdown on a recent Internet craze. The scam works as follows: For agreeing to buy certain products or services or for merely agreeing to give some personal information about oneself, the Internet operator gives "free" stock in the company to the buyer or the provider of information. The Internet user is lured into this deal by promises of receiving stock that has value and will become more valuable in the future. These offers are usually made through Internet chat rooms and e-mail messages.

Federal securities laws, which prohibit fraud in the sale or purchase of securities, apply to Internet sales of securities. The SEC applied these antifraud provisions and has sued many Internet companies for "free" stock fraud. The SEC determined that the person receiving the stock paid something of value, such as buying products or services or providing valuable personal information that the stock scam operator uses or sells.

One company the SEC brought charges against was WebWorksMarketing.com. The company offered shares of its stock to Internet users who registered on its Web site or signed up for long-distance telecommunications services. Investors were told that the shares had a value of $38 and could appreciate to $200 when the company went public, and that the company had more than 10,000 customers. In fact, the company had 35 customers, it had no contract with a long-distance provider, and it had taken no steps toward a public offering. The company settled the charges with the SEC. The SEC has targeted many more so-called "free-stock" companies for running Internet scams. ■

Other Federal Securities Laws

Racketeer Influenced and Corrupt Organizations Act (RICO)

The **Racketeer Influenced and Corrupt Organizations Act (RICO)** makes it a federal crime to engage in a pattern of racketeering activity.[20] Because securities fraud falls under the definition of racketeering activity, the government often brings RICO allegations in conjunction with securities fraud allegations.

In addition, a person injured by a RICO violation can bring a private civil action against the violator and recover treble (triple) damages, but only if the defendant has been criminally convicted in connection with the securities fraud.[21] A third-party independent contractor (e.g., an outside accountant) must have participated in the operation or management of the enterprise to be liable for civil RICO.[22]

Racketeer Influenced and Corrupt Organizations Act (RICO)
A federal statute that provides for both criminal and civil penalties for engaging in a pattern of racketeering activity.

Private Securities Litigation Reform Act of 1995

Sometimes companies include forward-looking statements about future economic plans and projections of financial data in prospectuses and other documents filed with the SEC and provided to investors. The **Private Securities Litigation Reform Act of 1995** provides a *safe harbor* from liability for companies that make such statements if they are accompanied by meaningful cautionary statements that identify risk factors that could cause actual results to differ from those in the statement.

Private Securities Litigation Reform Act of 1995
An act that provides a safe harbor from liability for companies that make forward-looking statements that are accompanied by meaningful cautionary statements of risk factors.

State Securities Laws

Most states have enacted securities laws. These laws, which are often called *blue-sky laws*, generally require the registration of certain securities and provide exemptions from registration. They also contain broad antifraud provisions.

The **Uniform Securities Act** has been adopted by many states. This act is drafted to coordinate state securities laws with federal securities laws.

Ethics Brief
State securities laws presumably originated to protect investors from foolishly buying a piece of the blue sky.

Contemporary Business Environment

Commodities Regulation

Commodities include grains (e.g., wheat, soybeans, oats), animals, (e.g., cattle, hogs), animal products (e.g., pork bellies), foods (e.g., sugar coffee), metals (e.g., gold, silver), and oil. A *commodities futures contract* is an agreement to buy or sell a specific amount and type of commodity at some future date, at a price established at the time of contracting. For example, a futures contract may be to sell 5,000 bushels of oats on July 31 at $2.87 per bushel. Standardized terms are established for futures contracts (e.g., quantity and quality of the commodity, time and place of delivery). Thus, each similar contract is *fungible*. This makes the contracts liquid; that is, they can be bought and sold on commodities exchanges just as stocks and bonds are bought and sold on securities exchanges. Farmers, ranchers, food processors, milling companies, mineral producers, oil companies, and investors often buy and sell futures contracts.

Commodities exchanges have been established at different locations across the country where commodity futures contracts can be bought and sold by food producers, farmers, and speculators. The major commodity exchanges are

- The Chicago Board of Trade (CBOT)
- The Chicago Mercantile Exchange (CME)
- The Commodity Exchange of New York (COMEX)
- Kansas City Board of Trade (KBOT)
- New York Coffee, Sugar & Cocoa Exchange (NYCSCE)
- New York Cotton Exchange (NYCTN)
- New York Mercantile Exchange (NYME)
- New York Futures Exchange (NYF)

The **Commodity Exchange Act (CEA)** was enacted by Congress in 1936 to regulate the trading of commodity futures contracts. The **Commodity Futures Trading Commission Act**, which was enacted in 1974, significantly amended the prior act [7 U.S.C. §§1–17a].

Section 4b of the CEA prohibits fraudulent conduct in connection with any order or contract of sale of any commodity for future delivery.

The 1974 amendments created the **Commodity Futures Trading Commission (CFTC)** to administer and enforce the CEA. The CFTC is a federal administrative agency consisting of five members appointed by the president. The CFTC has the authority to regulate trading in commodities futures contracts. It has the power to adopt regulations, conduct investigations, bring administrative proceedings against suspected violators, issue cease-and-desist orders and injunctions, and impose civil fines. Suspected criminal violations can be referred to the Department of Justice for criminal action. ■

International Law

Enforcement of International Securities Laws

The United States is not the only country in the world that outlaws insider trading and securities fraud. For example, Britain has outlawed insider dealing in securities for years. In 1993, the British government even implemented new legislation to strengthen its insider trading laws. The French insider trading law makes it illegal for a person to trade on nonpublic information received by reason of his or her position or profession. The European Union (EU) has directed all member countries to adopt laws against insider trading. Japan has an insider trading law that is rarely enforced.

Many persons who engage in illegal insider trading in the United States often do so using businesses or "fronts" located in other countries. In addition, these traders often deposit their ill-gotten gains in secret bank accounts located in off-shore bank havens. Can U.S. authorities obtain documents and evidence, as well as information about the location of bank accounts, from other countries? The answer is yes, in many situations.

In 1990, Congress enacted the **International Securities Enforcement Cooperation Act** [P.L. 101-550, 104 Stat. 2713]. The act authorizes the SEC to cooperate with foreign securities authorities, to provide records to foreign securities authorities, and to sanction securities professionals in this country who violate foreign securities laws.

The SEC has entered into **memorandums of understandings (MOUs)** with several foreign governments or authorities. As a general rule, the MOUs provide that the SEC and its foreign counterparts will cooperate in the enforcement of each country's securities laws. Thus, the SEC can obtain evidence about the location of bank accounts and other information concerning persons suspected of violating U.S. securities laws from foreign authorities. Currently, the SEC has entered into MOUs with Argentina, Brazil, Canada, France, Great Britain, Italy, Japan, the Netherlands, and Switzerland.

As securities trading becomes more international, it is going to become easier for investors and others to engage in insider trading and securities fraud across national boundaries. The United States and other countries will have to cooperate in finding, prosecuting, and penalizing perpetrators of securities frauds. ■

Singing Sand Mountains, Dunhuang, China. Foreign securities markets have developed in many countries. Each country has its own securities laws.

Chapter Summary

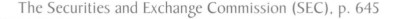

The Securities and Exchange Commission (SEC), p. 645

The Securities and Exchange Commission (SEC)

Created in 1934, the SEC is a federal administrative agency empowered to administer federal securities laws. The SEC can adopt rules and regulations to interpret and implement federal securities.

Definition of Security, p. 645

Definition of a Security

Security. A security must be found before federal securities laws apply. A *security* is defined as:

1. ***Common securities.*** Interests or instruments that are commonly known as securities, such as common stock, preferred stock, debentures, and warrants.
2. ***Statutorily defined securities.*** Interests and instruments that are expressly mentioned in securities acts as being securities, such as interests in oil, gas, and mineral rights.
3. ***Investment contracts.*** A flexible standard for defining a security. Under the *Howey* test, a security exists if (1) an investor invests money (2) in a common enterprise and (3) expects to make a profit off the significant efforts of others.

The Securities Act of 1933—Registration of Securities, p. 645

The Securities Act of 1933

A federal statute that primarily regulates the *issuance* of securities by corporations, partnerships, associations, and individuals.

Registration Statement

1. ***Section 5.*** A provision of the 1933 act that requires an issuer to register its securities with the SEC prior to selling them to the public if the securities or transaction does not qualify for an exemption from registration.
2. ***Registration statement.*** Document that an issuer of securities files with the SEC to register its securities. It must contain information about the issuer, the securities to be issued, and other relevant information.

Prospectus

A written disclosure document that is submitted to the SEC with the registration statement. It is distributed to prospective investors to enable them to evaluate the financial risk of the investment.

Limitations on Activities During the Registration Process

1. ***Prefiling period.*** Begins when the issuer first contemplates issuing securities and ends when the registration statement is filed with the SEC. During this period, the issuer cannot (1) offer to sell securities, (2) sell securities, or (3) *condition the market.*
2. ***Waiting period.*** Begins when the registration statement is filed with the SEC and ends when the registration statement becomes effective. During this time, the issuer cannot (1) sell securities or (2) use unapproved writing to offer to sell the securities. The issuer may make oral offers, distribute *preliminary* and *summary prospectuses*, and publish *tombstone ads.*
3. ***Posteffective period.*** Begins when the registration statement becomes effective and runs until the issuer either sells all of the offered securities or withdraws them from sale. The issuer may offer to sell the securities during this period. The issuer must deliver a *final prospectus* (*statutory prospectus*) to a purchaser prior to or at the time of confirming the sale or sending the security to the purchaser.

Regulation A Offerings

Regulation A. A regulation that permits an issuer to sell securities pursuant to a simplified registration process.

Securities Exempt from Registration, p. 649

Securities Exempt from Registration

The following *securities* are exempt from the SEC registration process:

1. Securities issued by any government in the United States (e.g., municipal bonds issued by city governments)
2. Short-term notes and drafts that have a maturity date that does not exceed nine months (e.g., commercial paper issued by corporations)
3. Securities issued by nonprofit issuers, such as religious institutions, charitable institutions, and colleges and universities
4. Securities of financial institutions (e.g., banks and savings associations) that are regulated by the appropriate banking authorities
5. Securities issued by common carriers (e.g., railroads and trucking companies) that are regulated by the Interstate Commerce Commission (ICC)
6. Insurance and annuity contracts issued by insurance companies
7. Stock dividends and stock splits
8. Securities issued in a corporation reorganization where one security is exchanged for another security

Transactions Exempt from Registration, p. 649

Transactions Exempt from Registration

The following *transactions* are exempt from the SEC registration process: (1) nonissuer transactions, (2) intrastate offerings, (3) private placements, and (4) small offerings.

Nonissuer Exemption

Securities transactions *not* by an issuer, an underwriter, or a dealer are exempt from SEC registration. This covers normal purchases of securities by investors.

Intrastate Offerings

A local business can issue securities without dollar limit without registering with the SEC if the following requirements are met:

1. The issuer is a resident of the state (e.g., the corporation is incorporated in the state).
2. The issuer is doing business in the state. This requires that:
   a. 80 percent of the issuer's assets are located in the state.
   b. 80 percent of the issuer's gross revenues are derived from the state.
   c. The issuer's principal office is located in the state.
   d. 80 percent of the proceeds of the offering will be used in the state.
3. The purchasers of the securities all are residents of the state.

Private Placements

An issue of securities that does not involve a public offering is exempt from SEC registration. There is no dollar limit on the amount of securities that can be issued pursuant to this exemption. Securities can be sold to any number of *accredited investors*, but to no more than 35 *nonaccredited investors*.

1. ***Accredited investors.*** These include:
   a. Any natural person (including spouse) who has a net worth of at least $1 million.
   b. Any natural person who has had an annual income of at least $200,000 for the previous two years and reasonably expects to make $200,000 income in the current year.
   c. Any corporation, partnership, or business trust with total assets in excess of $5 million.
   d. Insiders of the issuers, such as executive officers and directors of corporate issuers and general partners of partnership issuers.
   e. Certain institutional investors, such as registered investment companies, pension plans, colleges and universities and the like.

Small Offerings

An offering of securities that does not exceed $1 million during a 12-month period is exempt from SEC registration. The securities may be sold to any number of purchasers.

Resale Restrictions

1. ***Restricted securities.*** Securities sold pursuant to the intrastate, private placement, or small offering exemptions are called *restricted securities*.
2. ***Rule 147.*** An SEC rule stipulating that securities sold pursuant to an *intrastate offering exemption* cannot be sold to nonresidents for a period of nine months.
3. ***Rule 144.*** An SEC rule stipulating that securities sold pursuant to the *private placement* or *small offering exemption* must be held for two years; limited sales may be made between years two and three; then unlimited sales are permitted.
4. ***Preventing transfer of restricted securities.*** To prevent the illegal transfer of restricted securities, the issuer must take the following precautions:
   a. *Affidavit.* Require investors to sign an affidavit stating that they are buying the securities for investment, and promising not to transfer the restricted securities until the restrictions no longer apply.
   b. *Legend.* Place a legend on the stock certificate describing the restriction.
   c. *Transfer agent.* Appoint and notify the transfer agent not to a record a transfer of the securities that would violate the restriction.
5. ***Rule 144A.*** An SEC rule that permits *qualified institutional investors*—defined as institutions—that own and invest at least $100 million in securities—to buy unregistered securities without being subject to the holding periods of Rule 144.

Integration of Exempt Offerings

Separate exempt offerings of securities will be *integrated* (added together) if they occur within six months of each other and they are found to be similar and part of the same offering.

1. ***Safe harbor rule.*** Exempt securities offerings made more than six months before or after the current offering are not integrated with the current offering.
2. ***Integrated offering.*** If two or more exempt offerings are integrated, they are considered one offering. This *integrated offering* must be examined to determine whether it qualifies for any exemption from SEC registration.

Liability Provisions of the Securities Act of 1933, p. 653

Criminal Liability

Section 24 of the 1933 act imposes criminal liability on any person who willfully violates either the act or the rules and regulations adopted thereunder. Criminal actions are brought by the U.S. Department of Justice.

SEC Actions

The SEC may seek the following remedies:

1. ***Consent order.*** The SEC may issue a consent order whereby a defendant agrees not to violate securities laws in the future but does not admit to violating securities laws in the past.
2. ***Injunction.*** The SEC may bring an action in federal district court to obtain an injunction.
3. ***Disgorgement of profits.*** The SEC may request the court to order the defendant to disgorge illegally gained profits.

Private Actions

Private parties who have been injured by a violation of the 1933 act may sue the violator to rescind the securities contract or recover damages. The plaintiff may sue under:

1. ***Section 12.*** A provision of the 1933 act that imposes civil liability on any person who violates the provisions of Section 5 of the act (e.g., sells unregistered securities).
2. ***Section 11.*** A provision of the 1933 act that imposes civil liability on persons who intentionally defraud investors by making misrepresentations or omissions of material facts in the registration statement, or are negligent in not discovering the fraud.
   a. *Due diligence defense.* A defense to a Section 11 action that, if proven, makes the defendant not liable. This requires the defendant to have made a reasonable investigation and had reasonable grounds to believe and did believe that the statements made in the registration statement were true.

The Securities Exchange Act of 1934—Trading in Securities, p. 656

The Securities Exchange Act of 1934

A federal statute that primarily regulates the *trading* of securities.

Continuous Reporting Requirements

1. ***Reporting companies.*** Issuers (1) with assets of more than $5 million and at least 500 shareholders, (2) whose equity securities are traded on a national securities exchange, or (3) who have made a registered offering under the Securities Act of 1933.
2. ***Reporting requirements.*** Reporting companies must file the following reports with the SEC: (1) annual reports (*Form 10-K*), (2) quarterly reports (*Form 10-Q*), and (3) monthly reports (*Form 8-K*) within 10 days of the end of the month in which a material event (e.g., merger) occurs.

Section 10(b) and Rule 10b-5

1. ***Section 10(b).*** A provision of the 1934 act that prohibits the use of manipulative and deceptive devices in the purchase or sale of securities in contravention of the rules and regulations prescribed by the SEC.
2. ***Rule 10b-5.*** A rule adopted by the SEC to clarify the reach of Section 10(b) against deceptive and fraudulent activities in the purchase and sale of securities.
3. ***Scienter.*** Only conduct involving *scienter* (intentional conduct) violates Section 10(b) and Rule 10b-5. Negligent conduct is not a violation.

Insider Trading, p. 658

Insider Trading

Trading that occurs when an insider makes a profit by purchasing shares of the commodity prior to the public release of favorable information or selling shares of the corporation prior to public disclosure of unfavorable information. Insider trading violates Section 10(b) and Rule 10b-5.

1. ***Cady, Roberts rule.*** An insider who possesses material information must either (1) abstain from trading in securities of the company or (2) disclose the information to the person from whom he or she purchases or to whom he or she sells the securities.

Insiders

Insiders for Section 10(b) and Rule 10b-5 purposes include all employees of the company, independent contractors hired by the company on a temporary basis to provide services or work to the company, and others who owe a fiduciary duty to the company.

Tipper–Tippee Liability

1. ***Tipper.*** A person who discloses material nonpublic information to another person.
2. ***Tippee.*** A person who receives material nonpublic information from a tipper.
3. ***Tippee's liability.*** The tippee is liable for acting on material information received from a tipper if he or she knew or should have known that the information was not public. The tippee must disgorge profits made on the tip.
4. ***Tipper's liability.*** The tipper is liable for his own profits and the profits made by the tippee.

Liability Provisions of the Securities Exchange Act of 1934, p. 662

Criminal Liability

Section 32 of the 1934 act imposes criminal liability on any person who willfully violates the 1934 act or the rules and regulations adopted thereunder. Criminal actions are brought by the U.S. Department of Justice.

SEC Actions

The SEC may enter into *consent orders* with defendants, seek *injunctions* in federal district court, or seek orders requiring defendants to *disgorge* illegally gained profits.

1. ***Treble damages.*** The *Insider Trading Sanctions Act of 1984* permits the SEC to obtain a civil penalty of up to three times the illegal benefits received from insider trading.

Private Actions

Section 10(b). A private plaintiff has an *implied right* under Section 10(b) and Rule 10b-5 to sue to rescind the securities contract or recover damages from a defendant who has engaged in manipulative and deceptive practices that have caused the plaintiff injury.

Short-Swing Profits, p. 663

Short-Swing Profits

Statutory insiders. Section 16(a) of the Securities Exchange Act of 1934 defines a *statutory insider* for Section 16 purposes as any person who is an executive officer, a director, or a 10-percent shareholder of an equity security of a reporting company.

Section 16(b)

1. ***Short-swing profits.*** Profits made by statutory insiders on trades involving equity securities that occur within six months of each other.
2. ***Section 16(b).*** A provision of the 1934 act that requires that any profits made by a statutory insider on transactions involving short-swing profits belong to the corporation.

SEC Rules

Rules issued by the SEC that clarify the persons and transactions subject to Section 16 short-swing profit rules.

Other Federal Securities Laws, p. 665

Racketeer Influenced and Corrupt Organizations Act (RICO)

Federal statute that provides for both criminal and civil penalties for engaging in a *pattern or practice of racketeering activities*. Sometimes securities fraud qualifies as a RICO violation. *Treble damages* are available in a civil RICO action, but only if the defendant has been criminally convicted of securities fraud.

Private Securities Litigation Reform Act of 1995

Federal statute that provides a *safe harbor* from liability for companies that make forward-looking statements about future economic plans and projections if certain cautionary statements accompany the projections.

State Securities Laws, p. 665

State Securities Laws

Most states have enacted securities laws that regulate the issuance and trading of securities. These acts are often patterned after, and we are designed to coordinate with, federal securities laws. The *Uniform Securities Act*, which is a model state securities act, has been adopted by many states.

Commodities Regulation, p. 666

Commodities Regulation

1. ***Commodity.*** Includes grains, animals, animal products, foods, metals, and oil.
2. A contract to buy or sell a specific amount and type of commodity at some future date at a price established at the time of contracting.
3. A federal statute that, as amended, regulates the trading of commodity futures contracts.
4. ***Commodity Futures Trading Commission (CFTC).*** Federal administrative agency that administers and enforces the Commodity Exchange Act, as amended.
5. ***Section 4b.*** A provision of the Commodity Exchange Act that prohibits fraudulent conduct in connection with any order or contract of sale of any commodity for future delivery.

Internet Exercises and Case Questions

Working the Web Internet Exercises

Activities

Note: For socially responsible investing information, see **www.socialinvest.org**.

1. Using the Stanford Securities Class Action Clearinghouse site at **securities.stanford.edu**, identify the leading sector, industry, and companies targeted in securities class action litigation.
2. Investigate the modern varieties of fraud by reading the following law review articles:

   "Internet Securities Fraud: Old Trick, New Medium," at **www.law.duke.edu/journals/dltr/ARTICLES/2001dltr0006.html**

   "Software Disclosure and Liability Under the Securities Acts," at **www.law.duke.edu/journals/dltr/ARTICLES/2001dltr0016.html**

   "The Future of Corporate Disclosure: The Internet, Securities Fraud, and Rule 10B-5," at **www.law.emory.edu/ELJ/volumes/win98/prentice.html**
3. Determine whether an athletic club membership can be a *security* by using the U.S. Securities & Exchange Commission site, at **www.sec.gov.**
4. Who qualifies at *accredited investors?* See Bloomberg Online Financial Market Info, at **bloomberg.com**.
5. What is Rule 144 stock? See The Motley Fool, at **www.fool.com**.
6. What constitutes insider trading? See Microsoft Investor Version 4.0, at **moneycentral.msn.com/investor/home.asp**.

Critical Legal Thinking Cases

22.1 Definition of *Security* Dare To Be Great, Inc. (Dare), was a Florida corporation that was wholly owned by Glenn W. Turner Enterprises, Inc. Dare offered self-improvement courses aimed at improving self-motivation and sales ability. In return for an investment of money, the purchaser received certain tapes, records, and written materials. In addition, depending on the level of involvement, the purchaser had the opportunity to help sell the Dare courses to others and to receive part of the purchase price as a commission. There were four different levels of involvement.

The task of salespersons was to bring prospective purchasers to "Adventure Meetings." The meetings, which were conducted by Dare people and not the salespersons, were conducted in a preordained format that included great enthusiasm, cheering and charming, exuberant handshaking, standing on chairs, and shouting. The Dare people and the salespersons dressed in modern, expensive clothes, displayed large sums of cash, drove new expensive automobiles, and engaged in "hard-sell" tactics to induce prospects to sign their name and part with their money. In actuality, few Dare purchasers ever attained the wealth promised. The tape recordings and materials distributed by Dare were worthless. In this sales scheme a "security" that should have been registered with the SEC? [*Securities and Exchange Commission v. Glenn W. Turner Enterprises, Inc.*, 474 F.2d 476, 1973 U.S. Lexis 11903 (9th Cir. 1973)]

22.2 Definition of *Security* The Farmer's Cooperative of Arkansas and Oklahoma (Co-Op) was an agricultural cooperative that had approximately 23,000 members. To raise money to support its general business operations, the Co-Op sold promissory notes to investors that were payable upon demand. The Co-Op offered the notes to both members and nonmembers, advertised the notes as an "investment program," and offered an interest rate higher than that available on savings accounts at financial institutions. More than 1,600 people purchased the notes, worth a total of $10 million. Subsequently, the Co-Op filed for bankruptcy. A class of holders of the notes filed suit against Ernst & Young, a national firm of certified public accountants that had audited the Co-Op's financial statements, alleging that Ernst & Young had violated Section 10(b) of the Securities Exchange Act of 1934. Are the notes issued by the Co-Op "securities"? [*Reeves v. Ernst & Young*, 494 U.S. 56, 110 S.Ct. 945, 1990 U.S. Lexis 1051 (1990)]

22.3 Intrastate Offering Exemption. The McDonald Investment Company was a corporation organized and incorporated in the state of Minnesota. The principal and only place of business from which the company conducted operations was located in Rush City, Minnesota. More than 80 percent of the company's assets were located in Minnesota and more than 80 percent of its income was derived from Minnesota. On January 18, 1972, McDonald sold securities to Minnesota residents only. The proceeds from the sale were used entirely to make loans and other investments in real estate and other assets located outside the state of Minnesota. The company did not file a registration statement with the SEC. Does this offering qualify for an intrastate offering exemption from registration? [*Securities and Exchange Commission v. McDonald Investment Company*, 343 F.Supp. 343, 1972 U.S. Dist. Lexis 13547 (D.Minn. 1972)]

22.4 Transaction Exemption Continental Enterprises, Inc., had 2,510,000 shares of stock issued and outstanding. Louis E. Wolfson and members of his immediate family and associates owned in excess of 40 percent of those shares. The balance was in the hands of approximately 5,000 outside shareholders. Wolfson was Continental's largest shareholder and the guiding spirit of the corporation who gave direction to and controlled the company's officers. Between August 1, 1960, and January 31, 1962, without public disclosure, Wolfson and his family and associates sold 55 percent of their stock through six brokerage houses. Wolfson and his family and associates did not file a registration statement with the SEC with respect to these sales. Do the securities sales by Wolfson and his family and associates qualify for an exemption for registration as a sale "not by an issuer, an underwriter, or a dealer"? [*United States v. Wolfson*, 405 F.2d 779, 1968 U.S. App. Lexis 4342 (2nd Cir. 1968)]

22.5 Insider Trading Chiarella worked as a "markup man" in the New York composing room of Pandick Press, a financial printer. Among the documents that Chiarella handled were five secret announcements of corporate takeovers. The tender offerors had hired Pandick Press to print the offers, which would later be made public when the tender offers were made to the shareholders of the target corporations. When the documents were delivered to Pandick Press, the identities of the acquiring and target corporations were concealed by blank spaces or false names. The true names would not be sent to Pandick Press until the night of the final printing.

Chiarella was able to deduce the names of the target companies before the final printing. Without disclosing this knowledge, he purchased stock in the target companies and sold the shares immediately after the takeover attempts were made public. Chiarella realized a gain of $30,000 in the course of 14 months. The federal government indicted Chiarella for criminal violations of Section 10(b) of the Securities Exchange Act of 1934. Is Chiarella guilty? [*Chiarella v. United States*, 445 U.S. 222, 100 S.Ct. 1108, 1980 U.S. Lexis 88 (1980)]

22.6 Section 10(b) Leslie Neadeau was the president of T.O.N.M. Oil & Gas Exploration Corporation (TONM). Charles Lazzaro was a registered securities broker employed by Batemen Eichler, Hill Richards, Inc. (Bateman Eichler). The stock of TONM was traded in the over-the-counter market. Lazzaro made statements to potential investors that he had "inside information" about TONM, including that (1) vast amounts of gold had been discovered in Surinam and that TONM had options on thousands of acres in the gold-producing regions of Surinam; (2) the discovery was "not publicly known, but would be subsequently announced"; and (3) when this information was made public, TONM stock, which was then selling from $1.50 to $3.00 per share, would increase to $10.00 to $15.00 within a short period of time and might increase to $100.00 per share within a year.

The potential investors contacted Neadeau at TONM, who confirmed that the information was not public knowledge. In reliance on Lazzaro's and Neadeau's statements, the investors purchased TONM stock. The so-called "inside information" turned out to be false, and the shares declined substantially below the purchase price. The investors sued Lazzaro, Bateman Eichler, Neadeau, and TONM, alleging violations of Section 10(b) of the Securities Exchange Act of 1934. The defendants asserted that the plaintiffs' complaint should be dismissed because they participated in the fraud. Who wins? [*Bateman Eichler, Hill Richards, Inc. v Berner*, 472 U.S. 299, 105 S.Ct. 2622, 1985 U.S. Lexis 95 (1985)]

22.7 Insider Trading Donald C. Hoodes was the chief executive officer of the Sullair Corporation. As an officer of the corporation, he was regularly granted stock options to purchase stock of the company at a discount. On July 20, 1982, Hoodes sold 6,000 shares of Sullair common stock for $38,350. On July 31, 1982, Sullair terminated Hoodes as an officer of the corporation. On August 20, 1982, Hoodes exercised options to purchase 6,000 shares of Sullair stock that cost Hoodes $3.01 per share ($18,060) at the time they were trading at $4.50 per share ($27,000). Hoodes did not possess material nonpublic information about Sullair when he sold or purchased the securities of the company. The corporation brought suit against Hoodes to recover the profits Hoodes made on these trades. Who wins? [*Sullair Corporation v. Hoodes*, 672 F.Supp. 337, 1987 U.S. Dist. Lexis 10152 (N.D.Ill. 1987)]

Business Ethics Cases

22.8 Business Ethics Stephen Murphy owned Intertie, a California company that was involved in financing and managing cable television stations. Murphy was both an officer of the corporation and chairman of the board of directors. Intertie would buy a cable television station, make a small cash down payment, and finance the remainder of the purchase price. It would then create a limited partnership and sell the cable station to the partnership for a cash down payment and a promissory note in favor of Intertie. Finally, Intertie would lease the station back from the partnership. Intertie purchased more than 30 stations and created an equal number of limited partnerships, from which it received more than $7.5 million from approximately 400 investors.

Evidence showed that most of the limited partnerships were not self-supporting but that this fact was not disclosed to investors. Intertie commingled partnership funds, taking funds generated from the sale of new partnership offerings to meet debt service obligations of previously sold cable systems; Intertie also used funds from limited partnerships that were formed but that never acquired cable systems. Intertie did not keep any records regarding the qualifications of investors to purchase the securities and also refused to make its financial statements available to investors.

Intertie suffered severe financial difficulties and eventually filed for bankruptcy. The limited partners suffered substantial losses. Did each of the limited partnership offerings alone qualify for the private placement exemption from registration? Should the 30 limited partnership offerings be integrated? [*Securities and Exchange Commission v. Murphy*, 626 F.2d 633, 1980 U.S. App. Lexis 15483 (9th Cir. 1980)]

22.9 Business Ethics R. Foster Winans, a reporter for the *Wall Street Journal*, was one of the writers of the "Heard on the Street" column, a widely read and influential column in the *Journal*. This column frequently included articles that discussed the prospects of companies listed on national and regional stock exchanges and the over-the-counter market. David Carpenter worked as a news clerk at the *Journal*. The *Journal* had a conflict of interest policy that prohibited employees from using nonpublic information learned on the job for their personal benefit. Winans and Carpenter were aware of this policy.

Kenneth P. Felis and Peter Brant were stockbrokers at the brokerage house of Kidder Peabody. Winans agreed to provide Felis and Brant with information that was to appear in the "Heard" column in advance of its publication in the *Journal*. Generally, Winans would provide this information to the brokers the day before it was to appear in the *Journal*. Carpenter served as a messenger between the parties. Based on this advance information, the brokers bought and sold securities of companies discussed in the "Heard" column. During 1983 and

1984, prepublication trades of approximately 27 "Heard" columns netted profits of almost $690,000. The parties used telephones to transfer information. The *Wall Street Journal* is distributed by mail to many of its subscribers.

Eventually, Kidder Peabody noticed a correlation between the "Heard" column and trading by the brokers. After an SEC investigation, criminal charges were brought against defendants Winans, Carpenter, and Felis in U.S. district court. Brant became the government's key witness. Winans and Felis were convicted of conspiracy to commit securities, mail, and wire fraud. Carpenter was convinced of aiding and abetting the commission of securities, mail, and wire fraud. The defendants appealed their convictions. Can the defendants be held criminally liable for conspiring to violate, and aiding and abetting the violation of, Section 10(b) and Rule 10b-5 of securities law? Did Winans act ethically in this case? Did Brant act ethically by turning government's witness? [*United States v. Carpenter*, 484 U.S. 19, 108 S.Ct. 316, 1987 U.S. Lexis 4815 (1987)]

Briefing the Case Writing Assignment

Read Case A.22 in the Case Appendix [*Lampf, Pleva, Lipkind, Prupis & Petigrow v. Gilbertson*]. This case is excerpted from the U.S. Supreme Court opinion. Review and brief the case. In your brief, be sure to answer the following questions.

1. Were the limited partnership interest securities"?
2. What statute did the plaintiffs allege that the defendants had violated?
3. Succinctly state the issue presented to the U.S. Supreme Court.
4. How did the U.S. Supreme Court decide this issue?

Answers to Management Decision Questions

1. Insider trading occurs when a company employee or company advisor uses material nonpublic information is to make a profit by trading in the securities of the company. Section 10(b) and Rule 10b-5 of **the Securities Exchange Act of 1934** prohibit the use of manipulative and deceptive devices in contravention of the rules and regulations prescribed by the SEC. One of the most important purposes of Section 10(b) is to prevent insider trading. This practice is illegal because it allows insiders to take advantage of the investing public.
2. You are not guilty of insider trading. You do not meet the statutory definition of an insider. For purposes of Section 10(b) and Rule 10b-5, *insiders* are defined as (1) officers, directors, and employees at all levels of the company; (2) lawyers, accountants, consultants, and other agents and representatives who are hired by the company on a temporary and non-employee status to provide services or work to the company; and (3) others who owe a fiduciary duty to the company. Also, in a similar case involving Oklahoma football coach Barry Switzer, a court found him not guilty of insider trading. Coach Switzer said he overhead a conversation at a track meet between high-level executives about the liquidation of Phoenix Resources, an Oklahoma City oil firm, in 1981. The court ruled that the government failed to prove that he owed a fiduciary duty to Phoenix Resources. The fact that the executives talked too much in your case is not your fault.

Endnotes

1. *Securities and Exchange Commission v. W. J. Howey Co.*, 328 U.S. 293, 66 S.Ct. 1100, 1946 U.S. Lexis 3159 (1946).
2. Securities Act of 1933, § 4(1).
3. Securities Act of 1933, § 3(a)(11).
4. SEC Rule 147.
5. Securities Act of 1933, § 4(2).
6. SEC Rule 506.
7. SEC Rule 501.
8. Securities Act of 1933, § 3(b).
9. SEC Rules 502(a) and 147(b)(2).
10. 15 U.S.C. § 77x.
11. Litigation instituted pursuant to § 10(b) and Rule 10b-5 must be commenced within one year after the discovery of the violation and within three years after such violation [*Lampf, Pleva, Lipkind, Prupis & Petigrow v. Gilbertson*, 501 U.S. 350, 111 S.Ct. 2773, 1991 U.S. Lexis 3629 (1991)].
12. The U.S. Supreme Court has held that the sale of a business is a sale of securities that is subject to Section 10(b). See *Gould v. Ruefenacht*, 471 U.S. 701, 105 S.Ct. 2308, 1985 U.S. Lexis 21 (1985) (where 50 percent of a business was sold) and *Landreth Timber Co. v. Landreth*, 471 U.S. 681, 105 S.Ct. 2297, 1985 U.S. Lexis 20 (1985) (where 100 percent of a business was sold).
13. *Ernst & Ernst v. Hochfelder*, 425 U.S. 185, 96 S.Ct. 1375, 1976 U.S. Lexis 2 (1976).
14. 40 SEC 907 § (1961).
15. 15 U.S.C. §§ 78 ff.
16. P.L. 98–376.
17. 15 U.S.C. § 781.
18. 15 U.S.C. § 78p(b).
19. Ownership Reports and Trading by Officers, Directors and Principal Security Holders, Exchange Act Release No. 28869.
20. 18 U.S.C. §§ 1961–1968.
21. Private Securities Litigation Reform Act of 1995.
22. *Reves v. Ernst & Young*, 507 U.S. 170, 113 S.Ct. 1163, 1993 U.S. Lexis 1940 (1993).

23

Personal and Real Property

"Property and law are born and must die together."

—Jeremy Bentham
Principles of the Civil Code, I Works 309

Chapter Objectives

After studying this chapter, you should be able to:

1. Define personal property and describe the methods for acquiring ownership in personal property.
2. Define ordinary bailments and describe the elements for creating a bailment.
3. List and describe the different types of real property.
4. Identify the different types of joint tenancy and distinguish between separate property and community property.
5. Describe how zoning laws regulate the use of land.

Chapter Contents

Management Decision Personal and Real Property

You own a house at 1122 Rodeo Drive in Boise, Idaho. Your next-door neighbors of 35 years decided to sell their property and move to Florida. They sold their property to John and Sally Smith. Three years later, the Smiths decided to fence in the backyard. The fence company surveyed the property and determined that part of your garage was on 2 feet of the Smith's property. The Smith's have demanded that you tear down the garage that is attached to your house or pay them for the property. Your attorney has mentioned a possible adverse possession claim.

1. What is adverse possession?
2. What is necessary to obtain title under adverse possession?

Private ownership of property forms the foundation of the U.S. economic system. Therefore, a comprehensive body of law has been developed to protect property rights. The law protects the right of property owners to use, sell, dispose of, control, and prevent others from trespassing on their rights.

This chapter discusses personal property, real property, landlord–tenant relationships, insurance, and devising property through gift or inheritance.

> Property is the most ambiguous of categories. It covers a multitude of rights which have nothing in common except that they are exercised by persons and enforced by the state.
>
> R. H. Tawney
> *The Acquisitive Society, Ch. V (1921)*

Personal Property

There are two kinds of property: real property and personal property. **Real property** includes land and property that is permanently attached to it. For example, minerals, crops, timber, and buildings that are attached to land are generally considered real property. **Personal property** (sometimes referred to as *goods* or *chattels*) consists of everything that is not real property. Real

personal property
Property that consists of tangible property, such as automobiles, furniture, and jewelry, and intangible property, such as securities, patents, and copyrights.

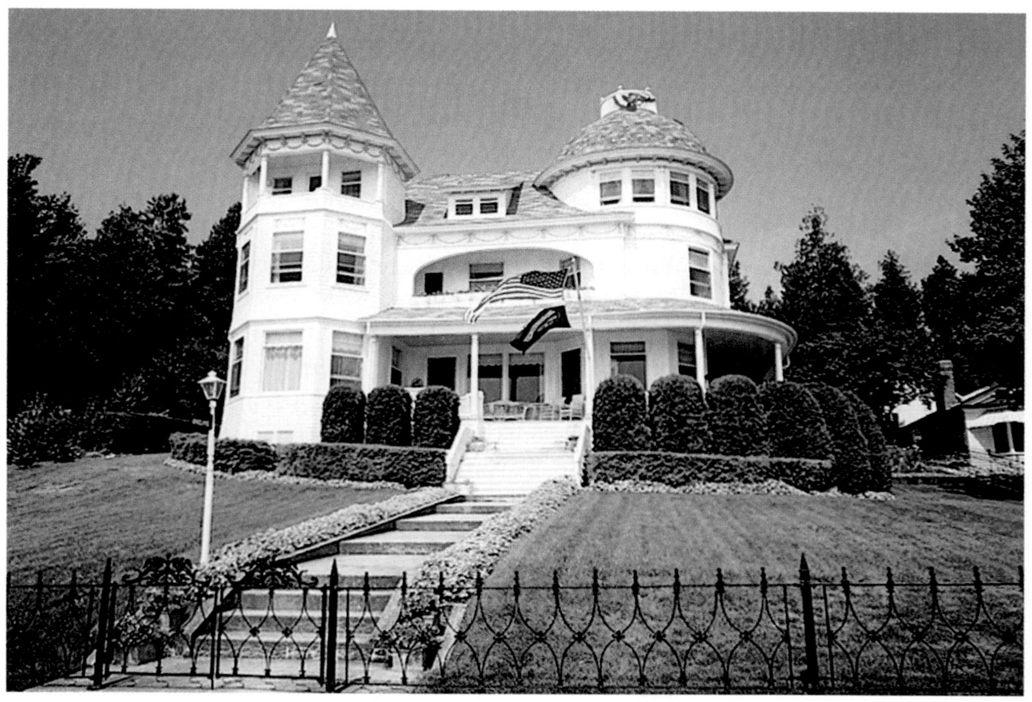

Mackinac Island, Michigan. The most valuable asset of many families is the home they own, such as this cottage on Mackinac Island, Michigan.

property can become personal property if it is removed from the land. For example, a tree that is part of a forest is real property; a tree that is cut down is personal property.

Personal property that is permanently affixed to land or buildings is called a *fixture*. Such property, which includes things like heating systems and storm windows, is categorized as real property. Unless otherwise agreed, fixtures remain with a building when it is sold. Personal property (e.g., furniture, pictures, and other easily portable household items) may be removed by the seller prior to sale.

tangible property
Physically defined personal property, such as goods, animals, and minerals.

intangible property
Rights that cannot be reduced to physical form, such as stock certificates, certificates of deposit, bonds, and copyrights.

Personal property can be wither tangible or intangible. **Tangible property** includes physically defined property, such as goods, animals, and minerals. **Intangible property** represents rights that cannot be reduced to physical form, such as stock certificates, certificates of deposit, bonds, and copyrights.

> Personal property has no locality.
>
> Lord Loughborough
> *C.J. Sill v. Worswick (1791)*

Acquiring Ownership in Personal Property

Personal property may be acquired or transferred with a minimum of formality. Commerce would be severely curtailed if the transfers of such items were difficult. The methods for acquiring ownership in personal property are discussed below.

taking possession
A method of acquiring ownership of unowned personal property.

By Possession A person can acquire ownership in unowned personal property by **taking possession** of it or capturing it. The most notable unowned objects are things in their natural state. For example, people who obtain the proper fishing license acquire ownership of all the fish they catch.

purchasing property
The most common method of acquiring title to personal property.

By Purchase The most common method of acquiring title to personal property is by **purchasing** the **property** from its owner. For example, Urban Concrete Corp. (Urban Concrete) owns a large piece of equipment. City Builders, Inc. (City Builders), purchases the equipment from Urban Concrete for $50,000. Urban Concrete signs over the title to the equipment to City Builders. City Builders is now the owner of the equipment.

By Accession **Accession** occurs when the value of personal property increases because it is added to or improved by natural or manufactured means. Accession that occurs naturally belongs to the owner (e.g., a colt that is born to a mare belongs to the mare's owner).

gift
A voluntary transfer of title to property without payment of consideration by the donee. To be a valid gift, the following three elements must be shown: donative intent, delivery, and acceptance.

donor
A person who gives a gift.

donee
A person who receives a gift.

By Gift A **gift** is a voluntary transfer of property without consideration. The lack of consideration is what distinguishes a gift from a purchase. The person making a gift is called the **donor**. The person who receives the gift is called the **donee**. There are three elements of a valid gift: *donative intent*, *delivery*, and *acceptance*:

1. ***Donative Intent*** For a gift to be effective, the donor must have intended to make a gift. *Donative intent* can be inferred from the circumstances or language used by the donor. The courts also consider such factors as the relationship of the parties, the size of the gift, the mental capacity of the donor, and so on.
2. ***Delivery*** Delivery must occur for there to be a valid gift. Although *physical delivery* is the usual method of transferring personal property, it is sometimes impracticable. In such circumstances, *constructive delivery* (or *symbolic delivery*) is sufficient. For example, if the property being gifted is kept in a safe-deposit box, physically giving the key to the donee is enough to signal the gift. Most intangible property is transferred by writing conveyance (e.g., conveying a stock certificate represents a transfer of ownership in a corporation).
3. ***Acceptance*** *Acceptance* usually is not a problem because most donees readily accept gifts. In fact, the courts presume acceptance unless there is proof that the gift was refused. Nevertheless, a person cannot be forced to accept an unwanted gift.

> Property is an instrument of humanity. Humanity is not an instrument of property.
>
> Woodrow Wilson
> *Speech (1912)*

In the following case, the court had determined whether a gift of a valuable painting had been made.

Case 23.1 Gift of Personal Property

Gruen v. Gruen
505 N.Y.S.2d 849, 1986 N.Y. Lexis 19366 (1986)
Court of Appeals of New York

Background and Facts

Victor Gruen was a successful architect. In 1959, Victor purchased a painting titled *Schloss Kammer am Atterse II* by a noted Austrian modernist, Gustav Klimt, and paid $8,000 for the painting. In 1963, Victor wrote a letter to his son Michael, then an undergraduate student at Harvard University, giving the painting to Michael but reserving a life estate in the painting. The letter stated

> Dear Michael:
>
> The 21st birthday, being an important event in life, should be celebrated accordingly. I therefore wish to give you as a present the oil painting by Gustav Klimt of Schloss Kammer which now hangs in the New York living room.
>
> Happy birthday again.
>
> Love,
>
> s/Victor

Because Victor retained a life interest in the painting, Michael never took possession of the painting. Victor died on February 14, 1980. The painting was appraised at $2.5 million. When Michael requested the painting from his stepmother, Kemija Gruen, she refused to turn it over to him. Michael sued to recover the painting. The trial court held in favor of the stepmother. The appellate division reversed. The stepmother appealed.

Issue

Did Victor Gruen make a valid gift *inter vivos* of the Klimt painting to his son Michael?

In The Language of The Court

Simons, Judge An *inter vivos* gift requires that the donor intends to make an irrevocable present transfer of ownership. Defendant contends that the trial court was correct in finding that Victor did not intend to transfer any present interest in the painting to plaintiff in 1963 but only expressed an intention that plaintiff was to get the painting upon his death. The evidence is all but conclusive, however, that Victor intended to transfer ownership of the painting to plaintiff in 1963 but to retain a life estate in it and that he did, therefore, effectively transfer a remainder interest in the painting to plaintiff at that time. The letters unambiguously establish that Victor Gruen intended to make a present gift of title to the painting at that time.

In order to have a valid *inter vivos* gift, there must be a delivery of the gift, either by a physical delivery of the subject of the gift or a constructive or symbolic delivery such as by an instrument of gift, sufficient to divest the donor of dominion and control over the property. Defendant contends that when a tangible piece of personal property such as a painting is the subject of a gift, physical delivery of the painting itself is the best form of delivery and should be required. Defendant's statement of the rule as applied may be generally true, but it ignores the fact that what Victor Gruen gave plaintiff was not all rights to the Klimt painting, but only title to it with no right of possession until his death. Under these circumstances, it would be illogical for the law to require the donor to part with possession of the painting when that is exactly what he intends to retain.

Decision and Remedy

The appellate court held that Victor Gruen had made a valid gift *inter vivos* of the Klimt painting to his son Michael. The court affirmed the judgment of the appellate division in favor of Michael Gruen.

Case Questions

Critical Legal Thinking Should a donor who makes a gift *inter vivos* be required to relinquish physical possession of the property to the donee?

Business Ethics Did the stepmother act ethically in refusing to turn the painting over to Michael?

By Confusion **Confusion** occurs if two or more persons commingle fungible goods (i.e., goods that are exactly alike, such as the same grade of oil, grains, or cattle). Title to goods can be acquired by confusion. It does not matter whether the goods were commingled by agreement or by accident. Each of the owners thereafter owns a percentage of the commingled goods equal to his or her percentage contribution to the total.

confusion
A situation that occurs if two or more persons commingle fungible goods; title is then acquired by the commingling.

Consider This Example If three farmers agree to store the same amount of grade B winter wheat in a silo, each of them owns one-third. When the grain is sold, the profits are divided into three parts; if the silo burns to the ground, each suffers one-third of the loss.

By Divorce When a marriage is dissolved by a divorce, the parties obtain certain rights in the property of the marital estate. Often, a settlement of property rights is reached. If not, the court must decide the property rights of the spouses. In the following case, the court decided the spouses' ownership rights to personal property upon divorce.

> Laws are always useful to persons of property, and hurtful to those who have none.
>
> Jean Jacques Rousseau
> *Du Contrat Social (1761)*

Bicycle Shop. Personal property is often transferred by gift. The person who makes the gift is called the donor, and the person who receives the gift is called the donee.

Case 23.2
Personal Property

Giha v. Giha
609 A.2d 945, 1992 R.I. Lexis 133 (1992)
Supreme Court of Rhode Island

Background and Facts

On October 7, 1987, Nagib Giha (husband) filed a complaint for divorce from Nelly Giha (wife) on the grounds of irreconcilable differences. On May 20, 1988, the parties reached an agreement for the disposition of their property which provided that they would divide equally the net proceeds from the sale of their marital assets. There was a statutory waiting period before the divorce was final. On December 25, 1988, the husband learned that he had won $2.4 million in the Massachusetts MEGABUCKS state lottery. The husband kept this fact secret. After the waiting period was over, the family court entered its final judgment severing the parties' marriage on April 27, 1989. The husband claimed his lottery prize on October 6, 1989. In December 1990, after learning of the lottery winnings, the wife sued to recover the lottery prize. She alleged that the lottery prize was a marital asset because her husband had won it before their divorce was final. The trial court dismissed her complaint. The wife appealed.

Issue

Was the $2.4 million lottery prize personal property of the marital estate?

In The Language of The Court

Fay, Chief Justice We have established that the parties to a divorce action remain as husband and wife until the entry of the final decree of divorce. In the present case the husband won the lottery prize four months before the Family Court entered its final judgment. The parties remained as husband and wife until the entry of the final judgment in 1989. Because the parties' marriage remained in effect throughout the waiting period, so did the property rights each spouse had in the property acquired by the other spouse during that period. Therefore, since the husband won the $2.4 million lottery prize during the existence of the parties' marriage, we conclude that the prize is a marital asset and is subject to the equitable-distribution statute. We conclude that the parties to a divorce action have a continuing duty to provide information about changes in their financial condition until the entry of a final judgment of divorce.

Decision and Remedy

The appellate court held that the parties remained as husband and wife until the entry of final judgment of divorce in April 1989. Therefore, the lottery prize was a marital asset. Reversed and remanded.

Case Questions

Critical Legal Thinking Should a spouse's lottery winnings be considered separate property? Why or why not?

Business Ethics Did the husband act ethically in this case?

By Will or Inheritance Title to personal property frequently is acquired by **will or inheritance**. If the person who dies has a valid will, the property is distributed to the *beneficiaries*, pursuant to the provisions of that will. Otherwise, the property is distributed to the *heirs* as provided in the relevant state's inheritance statute.

will or inheritance
A way to acquire title to property that is a result of another's death.

Mislaid, Lost, and Abandoned Property

Often, people find another person's property. Ownership rights to the property differ, depending on whether the property is *mislaid*, *lost*, or *abandoned*. The following paragraphs discuss these legal rules:

> Only a ghost can exist without material property.
>
> Ayn Rand
> *Atlas Shrugged (1957)*

- ***Mislaid Property*** Property is **mislaid** when its owner voluntarily places the property somewhere and then inadvertently forgets it. It is likely that the owner will return for the property upon realizing that it was misplaced. The owner of the premises where the property is mislaid is entitled to take possession of the property against all except the rightful owner. This right is superior to the rights of the person who finds it.

mislaid property
Property that is voluntarily placed somewhere and then inadvertently forgotten by the owner.

- ***Lost Property*** Property is considered **lost** when its owner negligently, carelessly, or inadvertently leaves it somewhere. The finder obtains title to such property against the whole world except the true owner. The lost property must be returned to its rightful owner if the finder discovers the loser's identity or the loser finds him or her.

  Consider This Example If a commuter finds a diamond ring on the floor of a subway station in New York City, the ring is considered lost property. The commuter can claim title to the ring against the whole world except the true owner. If the true owner discovers that the commuter has her ring, she may recover it from the commuter.

lost property
Property that is left somewhere by the owner because of negligence, carelessness, or inadvertence.

- ***Abandoned Property*** Property is classified as **abandoned** if (1) an owner discards the property with the intent to relinquish his or her rights in it or (2) an owner of mislaid or lost property gives up any further attempts to locate it. Anyone who finds abandoned property acquires title to it. The title is good against the whole world, including the original owner. For example, property left at a garbage dump is abandoned property. It belongs to the first person who claims it.

abandoned property
Property that an owner has discarded with the intent to relinquish his or her rights in it, or mislaid or lost property that the owner has given up any further attempts to locate.

Business Ethics

Estray Statutes

Most states have enacted **estray statutes** that permit a finder of *mislaid* or *lost* property to clear title to the property if

1. The finder reports the found property to the appropriate government agency and then turns over possession of the property to this agency,
2. Either the finder or the government agency posts notices and publishes advertisements describing the lost property, and
3. A specified time (usually a year or a number of years) has passed without the rightful owner's reclaiming the property.

Many state estray statutes provide that the government receive a portion of the value of the property. Some statutes provide that title cannot be acquired in found property that is the result of illegal activity. For example, title has been denied to finders of property and money deemed to have been used for illegal drug purchases.

Consider the following case. While hunting on unposted and unoccupied property in Oceola Township, Michigan, Duane Willsmore noticed an area with branches arranged in a crisscross pattern. When he kicked aside the branches and sod, he found a watertight suitcase in a freshly dug hole. Willsmore informed the Michigan state police of his find. A state trooper and Willsmore together pried open the suitcase and discovered $383,840 in cash. The state police took custody of the money, which was deposited in an interest-bearing account. Michigan's estray statute provides that the finder and the township in which the property was found must share the value of the property if the finder publishes required notices and the true owner does not claim the property within one year. Willsmore pub-

Business Ethics
(continued)

lished the required notices and brought a declaratory judgment action seeking a determination of the ownership of the money. After one year had gone by and the rightful owner had not claimed the suitcase, the court ordered that Willsmore and the Township of Oceola were equal one-half owners of the suitcase and its contents. [*Willsmore v. Township of Oceola, Michigan*, 308 N.W.2d 796, 1981 Mich.App. Lexis 2993 (Mich. App. 1981)]

1. Would you have turned the suitcase in to the police? ■

Bailments

bailment
A transaction in which an owner transfers his or her property to another to be held, stored, delivered, or for some other purpose. Title to the property does not transfer.

bailor
The owner of property in a bailment.

bailee
A holder of goods who is not a seller or a buyer (e.g., a warehouse, common carrier).

A **bailment** occurs when the owner of personal property delivers his or her property to another person to be held, stored, or delivered, or for some other purpose. In a bailment, the owner of the property is the **bailor** and the part to whom the property is delivered for safekeeping, storage, or delivery (e.g., warehouse or common carrier) is the **bailee** (see Exhibit 23.1).

A bailment is different from a sale or a gift because title to the goods does not transfer to the bailee. Instead, the bailee must follow the bailor's directions concerning the goods. For example, suppose Hudson Corp. is relocating offices and hires American Van Lines to move its office furniture and equipment to the new location. American Van Lines (the bailee) must follow Hudson's (the bailor) instructions regarding delivery. The law of bailments establishes the rights, duties, and liabilities of parties to a bailment.

ordinary bailments
(1) Bailments for the sole benefit of the bailor, (2) bailments for the sole benefit of the bailee, and (3) bailments for the mutual benefit of the bailor and bailee.

bailment for the sole benefit of the bailor
A gratuitous bailment that benefits only the bailor. The bailee owes only a *duty of slight care* to protect the bailed property.

bailment for the sole benefit of the bailee
A gratuitous bailment that benefits only the bailee. The bailee owes a *duty of great care* to protect the bailed property.

Ordinary Bailments There are three classifications of **ordinary bailments**. The difference among these categories is the degree of care owed by the bailee in protecting the bailed property. The three types of ordinary bailments are:

1. **Bailments for the sole benefit of the bailor** are *gratuitous bailments* that benefit only the bailor. They arise when the bailee is requested to care for the bailor's property as a favor. The bailee owes only a **duty of slight care** to protect the bailed property—that is, he or she owes a duty not to be grossly negligent in caring for the bailed goods.

   Consider This Example The Watkins family is going on vacation and ask the neighbors, the Smiths, to feed its dog, which is allowed to run free. The Smiths diligently feed the dog, but the dog runs away and does not return. The Smiths are not liable for the loss of the dog.

2. **Bailments for the sole benefit of the bailee** are *gratuitous bailments* that solely benefit the bailee. They generally arise when a bailee requests to use the bailor's property for personal reasons. In this situation, the bailee owes a **duty of great care** (or **utmost care**) to protect the bailed property—that is, he or she owes a duty not to be slightly negligent in caring for the bailed goods.

Exhibit 23.1
Parties to a Bailment

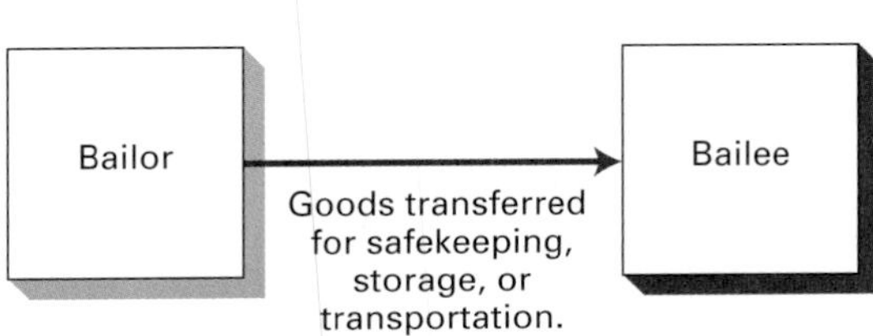
Bailor
Bailee
Goods transferred for safekeeping, storage, or transportation.

Bailment. A bailment is created when an owner of an automobile lends it to another person. The owner is the bailor and the borrower is the bailee.

Consider This Example Suppose Mitch borrows Courtney's lawn mower (free of charge) to mow his own lawn. Mitch is the bailee, and Courtney is the bailor. This bailment is for the sole benefit of the bailee. Suppose Mitch, while mowing his lawn, leaves the lawn mower in his front yard while he goes into his house to answer the telephone. While he is gone, the lawn mower is stolen. Here, Mitch will be held liable to Courtney for the loss of the lawn mower because Mitch breached his duty of great care to protect the lawn mower.

3. **Mutual benefit bailments** are bailments that *benefit both parties*. The bailee owes a **duty of reasonable care** (or **ordinary care**) to protect the bailed goods. This means that the bailee is liable for any goods that are lost, damaged, destroyed because of his or her negligence.

   Consider This Example Suppose ABC Garment Co. delivers goods to Lowell, Inc., a commercial warehouseman, for storage. A fee is charged for this service. ABC Garments Co. receives the benefit of having its goods stored, and Lowell, Inc., receives the benefit of being paid compensation for storing the goods. In this example, Lowell, Inc. (the bailee), owes a duty of ordinary care to protect the goods.

mutual benefit bailment
A bailment for the mutual benefit of the bailor and bailee. The bailee owes a *duty of reasonable care* to protect the bailed property.

Some states have eliminated these three categories of ordinary bailments, ruling that all bailees owe a duty of reasonable care, regardless of whether they benefit from the bailment.

The right of property enables an industrious man to reap where he has sown.

Anonymous

Innkeepers

Almost all states have enacted statutes that *limit the liability* of innkeepers. Most of these **innkeeper's statutes** allow innkeepers to avoid liability for loss caused to guests' property if (1) a safe is provided in which the guests' valuable property may be kept and (2) the guests are aware of the safe's availability. Most state laws also allow innkeepers to limit the dollar amount of their liability by notifying their guests of this limit (e.g., by posting a notice on each guest room door). This limitation on liability does not apply if the loss is caused by an innkeeper's negligence.

innkeeper's statutes
State statutes that provide that an innkeeper can avoid liability for loss caused to a guest's property if (1) a safe is provided in which the guest's valuable property may be kept and (2) the guest is notified of this fact.

Entrepreneur and the Law

Parking Lots: Who Is Liable if Your Car Is Stolen?

Who is liable when a car is stolen while parked in a commercial lot or garage? The answer to this question depends on whether the parking lot is considered to be a bailee of an automobile or merely a lessor of parking space.

It is clear that parking lots and garages are bailees of automobiles once they assume control and possession of the automobile. Thus, if a valet parking attendant parks the car and keeps the keys, it is relatively certain that a court will recognize the existence of a bailment and hold the garage liable if the vehicle is stolen. Disclaimers to the contrary (either on the ticket or posted at the parking lot) are usually held to be ineffective.

On the other hand, if the owner of a car parks his or her own car in a parking lot and takes the keys, this is considered a lease. The general rule in this case is that the "landlord"—the parking lot—is not responsible for the safety of the car. ■

Real Property

real property
The land itself as well as buildings, trees, soil, minerals, timber, plants, and other things permanently affixed to the land.

Property and ownership rights in **real property** play an important part in this country's society and economy. Individuals and families own or rent houses, farmers and ranchers own or lease farmland and ranches, and businesses own or lease commercial and office buildings. Real property includes the following:

land
The most common form of real property; includes the land and buildings and other structures permanently attached to the land.

- ***Land and Buildings*** **Land** is the most common form of real property. A landowner usually purchases the *surface rights* to the land—that is, the right to occupy the land. The owner may use, enjoy, and develop the property as he or she sees fit, subject to any applicable government regulation. **Buildings** constructed on land, such as houses, apartment buildings, manufacturing plants, and office buildings, are real property. Such things as radio towers, bridges, and the like are considered real property as well.

subsurface rights
Rights to the earth located beneath the surface of the land.

- ***Subsurface Rights*** The owner of land possesses **subsurface rights** (or **mineral rights**) to the earth located beneath the surface of the land. These rights can be very valuable. For example, gold, uranium, oil, or natural gas may lie beneath the surface of land. Theoretically, mineral rights extend to the center of the earth. In reality, mines and oil wells usually extend only several miles into the earth. Subsurface rights may be sold separately from surface rights.

plant life and vegetation
Real property that is growing in or on the surface of the land.

- ***Plant Life and Vegetation*** **Plant life and vegetation** growing on the surface of land are considered real property. This includes both natural plant life (e.g., trees) and cultivated plant life (e.g., crops). When land is sold, any plant life growing on the land is included unless the parties agree otherwise. Plant life that is severed from the land is considered personal property.

fixtures
Goods that are affixed to real estate so as to become part thereof.

- ***Fixtures*** Certain personal property is so closely associated with real property that it becomes part of the realty. Such items are called **fixtures**. For example, kitchen cabinets, carpeting, and doorknobs are fixtures, but throw rugs and furniture are personal property. Unless otherwise provided, if a building is sold, the fixtures are included in the sale. If the sale agreement is silent as to whether an item is a fixture, the courts make their determination on the basis of whether the item can be removed without causing substantial damage to the realty.

Kyrgyzstan. Former Soviet countries now permit private individuals to own real property.

Contemporary Business Environment

Air Rights: Value in the Heavens

Common law provided that the owners of real property owned that property from the center of the earth to the heavens. This rule has been eroded by modern legal restrictions such as land use control laws, environmental protection laws, and air navigation requirements. Even today, however, the owners of land may sell or lease air space parcels above their land.

An **air space parcel** is a three-dimensional cube of air above the surface of the earth. Air space parcels are valuable property rights, particularly in densely populated metropolitan areas where building property is scarce. For example, many developments have been built in air space parcels in New York City. The most notable is Madison Square Garden, which was built in an air space parcel. More developments are expected to be built in air space parcels in the future. ■

Freehold Estates

A person's ownership rights in real property are called an **estate in land** (or **estate**). An estate is defined as the bundle of *legal rights* that the owner has to possess, use, and enjoy the property. The type of estate that an owner possesses is determined from the deed, will, lease, or other document that transferred the ownership rights to him or her.

estate
Ownership rights in real property; the bundle of legal rights that the owner has to possess, use, and enjoy the property.

A **freehold estate** is one where the owner has a *present possessory interest* in the real property; that is, the owner may use and enjoy the property as he or she sees fit, subject to any applicable government regulation or private restraint. The two types of freehold estates are *estates in fee* and *life estates*.

freehold estate
An estate where the owner has a present possessory interest in the real property.

Estates in Fee A **fee simple absolute** (or **fee simple**) is the highest form of ownership of real property because it grants the owner the fullest bundle of legal rights that a person can hold in real property. It is the type of ownership most people connect with "owning" real property. A fee simple owner has the right to exclusively possess and use his or her property to the extent that the owner has not transferred any interest in the property (e.g., by lease).

fee simple absolute
A type of ownership of real property that grants the owner the fullest bundle of legal rights that a person can hold in real property.

fee simple defeasible

A type of ownership of real property that grants the owner all the incidents of a fee simple absolute except that it may be taken away if a specified condition occurs or does not occur.

A **fee simple defeasible** (or **qualified fee**) grants the owner all the incidents of a fee simple absolute except that it may be taken away if a specified *condition* occurs or does not occur. For example, a conveyance of property to a church "as long as the land is used as a church or for church purposes" creates a qualified fee. The church has all the rights of a fee simple absolute owner except that its ownership rights are terminated if the property is no longer used for church purposes.

life estate

An interest in real property for a person's lifetime; upon that person's death, the interest will be transferred to another party.

estate pour autre vie

A life estate measured in the life of a third party.

Life Estate A **life estate** is an interest in real property that lasts for the life of a specified person, usually the grantee. For example, a conveyance of real property "to Anna for her life" creates a life estate. A life estate may also be measured by the life of a third party (e.g., "to Anna for the life of Benjamin"). This is called an ***estate pour autre vie***. A life estate may be defeasible (e.g., "to John for his life but only if he continues to occupy this residence"). Upon the death of named person, the life estate terminates, and the property reverts to the grantor or the grantor's estate or other designated person.

A life tenant is treated as the owner of the property during the duration of the life estate. He or she has the right to possess and use the property except to the extent that it would cause permanent *waste* of the property. A life tenant may sell, transfer, or mortgage his or her estate in the land. However, the mortgage cannot exceed the duration of the life estate. A life tenant is obligated to keep the property in repair and to pay property taxes.

Future Interests

future interest

The right to possess property in the future; the interest that the grantor retains for him- or herself or a third party.

A person may be given the right to possess property in the *future* rather than in the present. This right is called a **future interest**. The two forms of future interests are *reversion* and *remainder*.

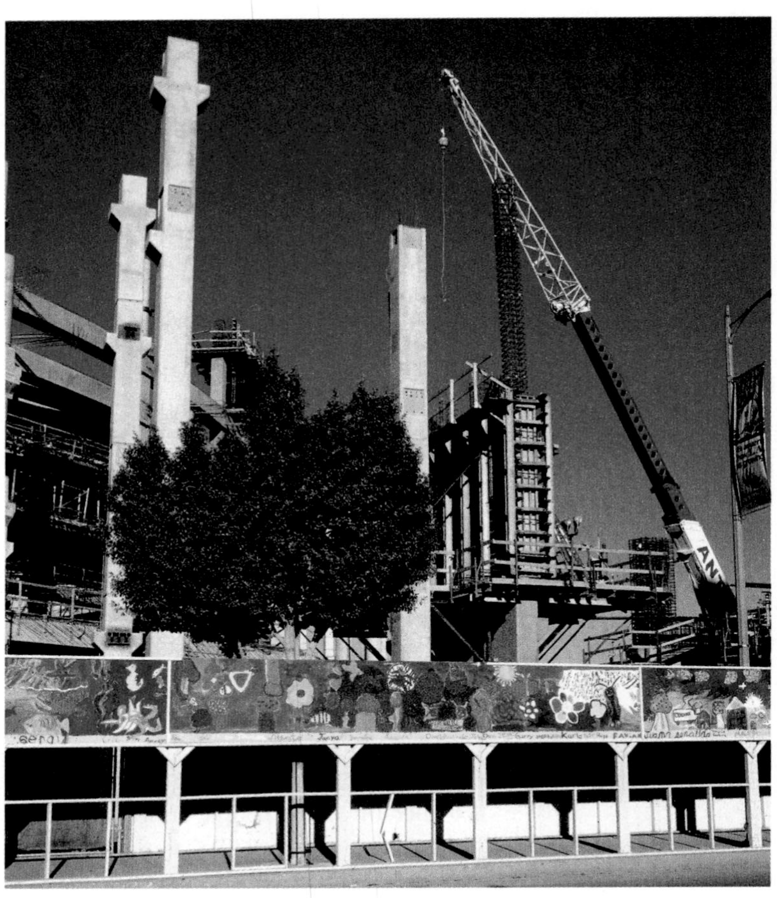

Staples Center, Los Angeles. The owner of real property should purchase liability insurance, fire insurance, and many other forms of insurance to protect against loss.

Reversion A **reversion** is a right of possession that returns to the *grantor* after the expiration of a limited or contingent estate. Reversions do not have to be expressly stated because they arise automatically by law. For example, if a grantor conveys property "to M. R. Harrington for life," the grantor has retained a reversion in the property. That is, when Harrington dies, the property reverts to the grantor or, if he or she is not living, then to his or her estate.

reversion
A right of possession that returns to the grantor after the expiration of a limited or contingent estate.

Remainder If the right of possession returns to a *third party* upon the expiration of a limited or contingent estate, it is called a **remainder**. The person who is entitled to the future interest is called a **remainderman**. For example, a conveyance of property "to Joe for life, remainder to Meredith" is a vested remainder—the only contingency to Meredith's possessory interest is Joe's death.

remainder
A situation in which the right of possession returns to a third party upon the expiration of a limited or contingent estate.

Concept Summary Future Interests

Future Interest	Description
Reversion	Right to possession of real property returns to the grantor after the expiration of a limited or contingent estate.
Remainder	Right to possession of real property goes to a third person upon the expiration of a limited or contingent estate.

Concurrent Ownership

Two or more persons may own a piece of real property. This is called **co-ownership** or **concurrent ownership**. The following forms of co-ownership are recognized: *joint tenancy, tenancy in common, tenancy by the entirety, community property, condominiums,* and *cooperatives.*

co-ownership
Ownership of a piece of real property by two or more persons. Also called *concurrent ownership*.

Joint Tenancy To create a joint tenancy, words that clearly show a person's intent to create a joint tenancy must be used. Language such as "Marsha Leest and James Leest, as joint tenants" is usually sufficient. The most distinguished feature of a **joint tenancy** is the co-owners' *right of survivorship*. This means that upon the death of one of the co-owners (or *joint tenants*), the deceased person's interest in the property automatically passes to the surviving joint tenants. Any contrary provision in the deceased's will is ineffective.

joint tenancy
A form of co-ownership that includes the right of survivorship.

Consider This Example Jones, one of four people who own a piece of property in joint tenancy, executes a will leaving all of his property to a university. Jones dies. The surviving joint tenants—not the university—acquire his interest in the piece of property. Each joint tenant has a right to sell or transfer his or her interest in the property, but such conveyance terminates the joint tenancy. The parties then become tenants in common.

Without that sense of security which property gives, the land would still be uncultivated.

Francois Quesnay
(1694–1774) Maximes, IV

Tenancy in Common In a **tenancy in common**, the interests of a surviving *tenant in common* pass to the deceased tenant's estate and not to the co-tenants. A tenancy in common may be created by express words, such as "Iran Cespedes and Joy Park, as tenants in common." Unless otherwise agreed, a tenant in common can sell, give, devise, or otherwise transfer his or her interest in the property without the consent of the other co-owners.

tenancy in common
A form of co-ownership in which the interest of a surviving tenant in common passes to the deceased tenant's estate and not to the co-tenants.

Consider This Example Lopez, who is one of four tenants in common who own a piece of property, has a will that leaves all of his property to his granddaughter. When Lopez dies, the granddaughter receives his interest in the tenancy in common, and the granddaughter becomes a tenant in common with the three other owners.

Web Site

U.S. Department of Housing and Urban Development (HUD). HUD has a Web site that is full of information relevant to housing. Visit at **www.hud.gov**.

tenancy by the entirety

A form of co-ownership of real property that can be used only by married couples.

Tenancy by the Entirety **Tenancy by the entirety** is a form of co-ownership of real property that can be used only by married couples. This type of tenancy must be created by express words, such as "Harold Jones and Maude Jones, husband and wife, as tenants by the entireties." A surviving spouse has the right of survivorship.

Tenancy by the entirety is distinguished from a joint tenancy because neither spouse may sell or transfer his or her interest in the property without the other spouse's consent. Only about half of the states recognize tenancy by the entirety.

Contemporary Business Environment

Community Property

Nine states—Arizona, California, Idaho, Louisiana, Nevada, New Mexico, Texas, Washington, and Wisconsin—recognize a form of co-ownership known as **community property**. This method of co-ownership applies only to married couples. It is based on the notion that a husband and wife should share equally in the fruits of the marital partnership. Under these laws, each spouse owns an equal one-half share of the income of both spouses and the assets acquired during the marriage, regardless of who earns the income. Property that is acquired through gift or inheritance either before or during marriage remains separate property.

When a spouse dies, the surviving spouse automatically receives one-half of the community property. The other half passes to the heirs of the deceased spouse as directed by will or by state intestate statute if there is no will. For example, a husband and wife have community property assets of $1.5 million and the wife dies with a will. The husband automatically has a right to receive $750,000 of the community property. The remaining $750,000 passes as directed by the wife's will. Any separate property owned by the wife, such as jewelry she inherited, also passes in accordance with her will. Her husband has no vested interest in that property.

During the marriage, neither spouse can sell, transfer, or gift community property without the consent of the other spouse. Upon a divorce, each spouse has a right to one-half of the community property.

The location of the real property determines whether community property law applies. For example, if a married couple that lives in a noncommunity property state purchases real property located in a community property state, community property laws apply to that property. ■

Concept Summary Concurrent Ownership

Form of Ownership	Right of Survivorship	Tenant May Unilaterally Transfer His or Her Interest
Joint tenancy	Yes, deceased tenant's interest automatically passes to co-tenants.	Yes, tenant may transfer his or her interest without the consent of co-tenants. Transfer severs joint tenancy.
Tenancy in common	No, deceased tenant's interest passes to his or her estate.	Yes, tenant may transfer his or her interest without the consent of co-tenants. Transfer does not sever tenancy in common.
Tenancy by the entirety	Yes, deceased tenant's interest automatically passes to his or her spouse.	No, neither spouse may transfer his or her interest without the other spouse's consent.
Community property	Yes, when a spouse dies, the surviving spouse automatically receives one half of the community property. The other half passes to the heirs of the deceased spouse as directed by a valid will or by state interstate statute if there is no will.	No, neither spouse may transfer his or her interest without the other spouse's consent.

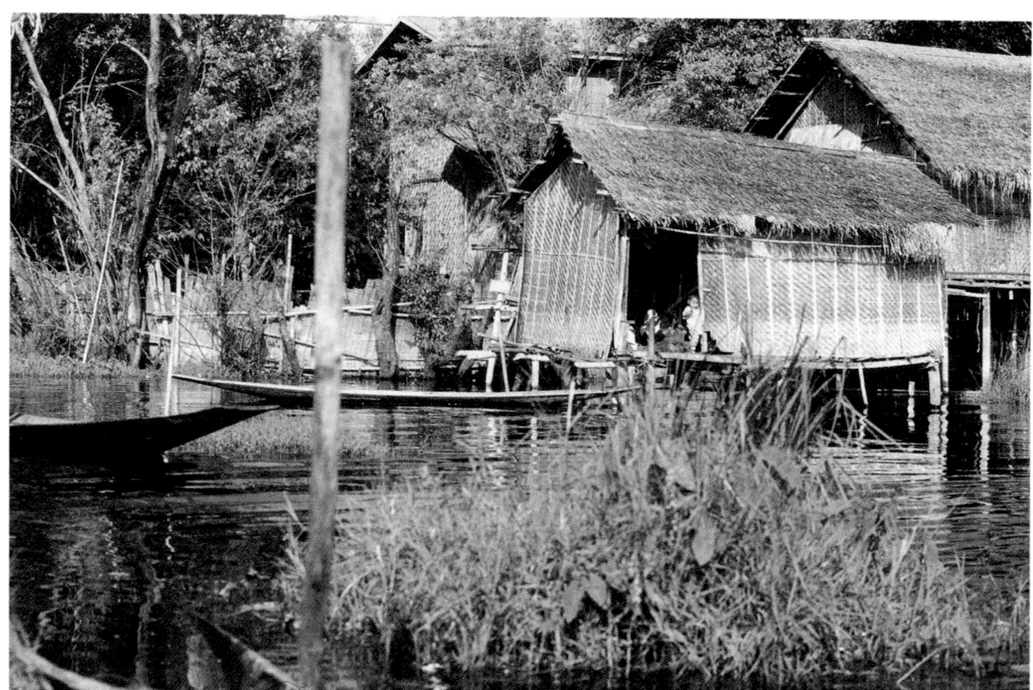

Imle Lake, Myanmar. Houses in many parts of the world differ from those in the United States. This house on the Imle Lake in Myanmar is built on stilts.

Condominiums **Condominiums** are a common form of ownership in multiple-dwelling buildings. Purchasers of a condominium (1) have title to their individual units and (2) own the common areas (e.g., hallways, elevators, parking areas, recreational facilities) as tenants in common with the other owners. Owners may sell or mortgage their units without the permission of the other owners. Owners are assessed monthly fees for the maintenance of common areas. In addition to dwelling units, the condominium form of ownership is offered for office buildings, boat docks, and such.

condominium

A common form of ownership in a multiple-dwelling building where the purchaser has title to the individual unit and owns the common areas as a tenant in common with the other condominium owners.

Cooperatives A **cooperative** is a form of co-ownership of a multiple-dwelling building where a corporation owns the building and the residents own shares in the corporation. Each cooperative owner then leases a unit in the building from the corporation under a renewable, long-term, proprietary lease. Individual residents may not secure loans with the units they occupy. The corporation may borrow money on a blanket mortgage, and each shareholder is jointly and severally liable on the loan. Usually, cooperative owners may not sell their shares or sublease their units without the approval of the other owners.

cooperative

A form of co-ownership of a multiple-dwelling building where a corporation owns the building and the residents own shares in the corporation.

Transfer of Ownership of Real Property

Ownership of real property may be transferred from one person to another. Title to real property may be transferred by sale; tax sale; or gift, will, or inheritance. **Deeds** are used to convey real property by sale or gift. The seller or donor is called the **grantor**. The buyer or recipient is called the **grantee**. A deed may be used to transfer a fee simple absolute interest in real property or any lesser estate (e.g., life estate).

State laws recognize different types of deeds that provide differing degrees of protection to grantees. A **warranty deed** contains the greatest number of warranties and provides the most protection to grantees. A **quitclaim deed** provides the least amount of protection because the grantor conveys only whatever interest he or she has in the property.

deed

A document that describes a person's ownership interest in a piece of real property.

grantor

The party who transfers an ownership interest in real property.

grantee

The party to whom an interest in real property is transferred.

Contemporary Business Environment

Recording Statutes

Every state has a **recording statute** that provides that copies of deeds and other documents concerning interests in real property (e.g., mortgages, liens, easements) may be filed in a government office, where they become public records open to viewing by the public. Recording statutes are intended to prevent fraud and to establish certainty in the ownership and transfer of property. Instruments are usually filed in the *county recorder's office* of the county in which the property is located. A fee is charged to record an instrument.

Persons interested in purchasing the property or lending on the property should check these records to determine if the grantor or borrower actually owns the property and whether any other parties (e.g., lienholders, mortgagees, easement holders) have an interest in the property. The recordation of a deed is not required to pass title from the grantor to the grantee. Recording the deed gives *constructive notice* to the world of the owner's interest in the property.

A party who is concerned about his or her ownership rights in a parcel of real property can bring a **quiet title action** to have a court determine the extent of those rights. Public notice of the hearing must be given so that anyone claiming an interest in the property may appear and be heard. After the hearing, the judge declares who has title to the property—that is, the court "quiets title" by its decision. ■

Adverse Possession

adverse possession
Possession in which a person who wrongfully possesses someone else's real property obtains title to that property if certain statutory requirements are met.

In most states, a person who wrongfully possesses someone else's real property obtains title to that property if certain statutory requirements are met. This is called **adverse possession**. Property owned by federal and state governments is not subject to adverse possession.

Under this doctrine, the transfer of the property is involuntary and does not require the delivery of a deed. To obtain title under adverse possession, the wrongful possession must be

- ***For a Statutorily Prescribed Period of Time*** In most states, this period is between 10 and 20 years.
- ***Open, Visible, and Notorious*** The adverse possessor must occupy the property so as to put the owner on notice of the possession.
- ***Actual and Exclusive*** The adverse possessor must physically occupy the premises. The planting of crops, grazing of animals, or building of a structure on the land constitutes physical occupancy.
- ***Continuous and Peaceful*** The occupancy must be continuous and uninterrupted for the required statutory period. Any break in normal occupancy terminates the adverse possession. This means that the adverse possessor may leave the property to go to work, to the store, on a vacation, and such. The adverse possessor cannot take the property by force from an owner.
- ***Hostile and Adverse*** The possessor must occupy the property without the express or implied permission of the owner. Thus, a lessee cannot claim title to property under adverse possession.

Business Brief
Owners of property should check their property every so many years to determine if anyone is attempting to acquire title by adverse possession. If anyone is found to be doing so, the owner should take appropriate action to prevent the adverse possession.

Good fences make good neighbors.
Robert Frost
"Mending Wall" (1914)

If the elements of adverse possession are met, the adverse possessor acquires clear title to the land. However, title is acquired only as to the property actually possessed and occupied during the statutory period, and not the entire tract. For example, an adverse possessor who occupies 1 acre of a 200,000-acre ranch for the statutory period of time acquires title only to the 1 acre.

Business Ethics

Modern-Day Squatters

Many parts of this country, particularly the West, were settled by "squatters" who came, staked a claim to open property, farmed or ranched the property, and acquired title to it from the government. The federal government encouraged such activity by holding "land rushes" that awarded title to the first person who staked a claim to the designated lands.

Although the days of the Wild West are past, many states today recognize modern-day squatters' rights under the doctrine of adverse possession. Consider the following case.

Edward and Mary Shaughnessey purchased a 16-acre tract in St. Louis county in 1954. Subsequently, they subdivided 12 acres into 18 lots offered for sale and retained possession of the remaining 4-acre tract. In 1967, Charles and Elaine Witt purchased lot 12, which is adjacent to the 4-acre tract. The Witts constructed and moved into a house on their lot. In 1968, they cleared an area of land that ran the length of their property and extended 40 feet onto the 4-acre tract. The Witts constructed a pool and a deck, planted a garden, made a playground for their children, set up a dog run, and built a fence along the edge of the property line, which included the now-disputed property. Neither the Witts nor the Shaughnesseys realized that the Witts had encroached on the Shaughnesseys' property.

In February 1988, the Shaughnesseys sold the 4-acre tract to Thomas and Rosanne Miller. When a survey showed the encroachment, the Millers demanded that the Witts remove the pool and cease using the property. When the Witts refused to do so, the Millers sued to *quiet title*. The Witts defended, arguing that they had obtained title to the disputed property by adverse possession.

The court of appeals agreed with the Witts. The court held that the Witts had proven the necessary elements for adverse possession under state law. The Witts' occupation of the land was open and notorious, actual and exclusive, hostile and adverse, continuous and peaceful, and had been for over the statutory period of 10 years. The court issued an order quieting title to the disputed property in favor of the Witts. [*Witt v. Miller*, 845 S.W.2d 665, 1993 Mo.App. Lexis 20 (Mo. App. 1993)].

1. Did the Millers act ethically in trying to eject people who had occupied the land for 20 years?
2. Did the Witts act ethically in claiming title to someone else's land? Should they be allowed to benefit from their own mistake?
3. What should owners of property do to protect themselves from adverse possession claims? Explain. ■

Easements

An **easement** is an interest in land that gives the holder the right to make limited use of another's property without taking anything from it. Typical easements include common driveways, party walls, right-of-ways, and such.

Easements may be *expressly* created by *grant* (in which case an owner gives another party an easement across his or her property) or *reservation* (in which case an owner sells land he or she owns but reserves an easement on the land). They also may be *implied* by (1) *implication*, where an owner subdivides a piece of property with a well, path, road, or other beneficial appurtenant that serves the entire parcel, or by (2) *necessity*, for example, "landlocked" property has an implied easement across surrounding property to enter and exit the landlocked property. Easements can also be created by adverse possession.

easement
A given or required right to make limited use of someone else's land without owning or leasing it.

The right of property has not made poverty, but it has powerfully contributed to make wealth.

J. R. McCulloch
(1789–1864) Principles of Political Economy

Landlord–Tenant Relationship

Landlord–tenant relationships are very common in the United States because (1) over half of the population rent their homes and (2) many businesses lease office space, stores, manufacturing facilities, and other commercial property. The parties to the relationship have certain legal rights and duties that are governed by a mixture of real estate and contract law.

A landlord–tenant relationship is created when the owner of a freehold estate (i.e., an estate in fee or a life estate) transfers a right to exclusively and temporarily possess the owner's property. The tenant receives a *nonfreehold estate* in the property—that is, the tenant has a right to possession of the property but not title to the property.

landlord–tenant relationship
A relationship created when the owner of a freehold estate (landlord) transfers a right to exclusively and temporarily possess the owner's property to another (tenant).

Soho, New York City. Many people rent apartments from landlords. The landlord and tenant owe each other certain duties.

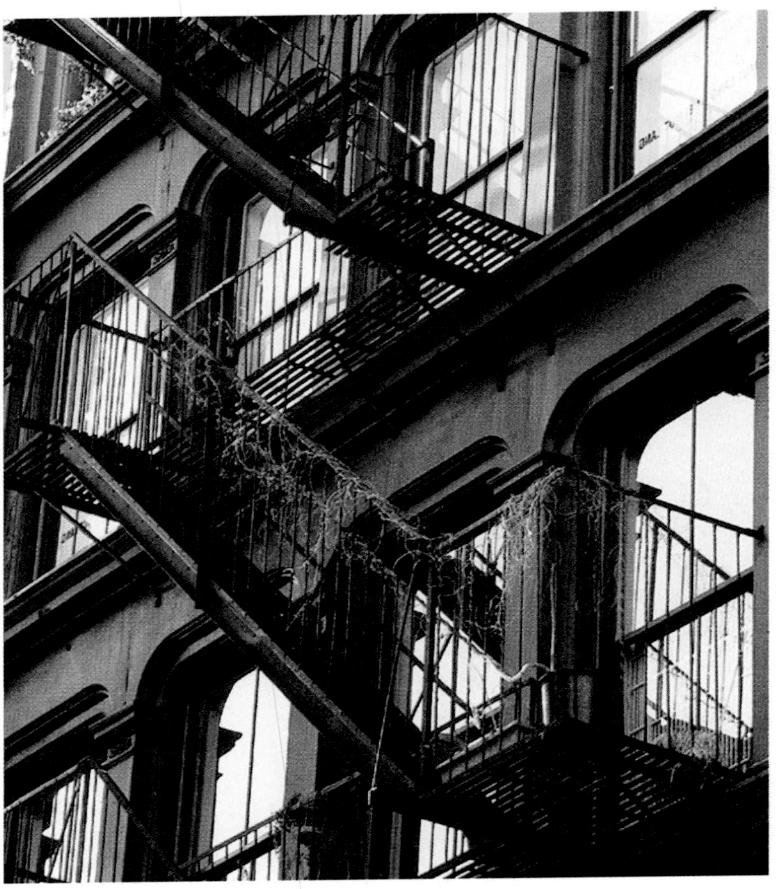

Types of Tenancy

leasehold
A tenant's interest in the property.

The tenant's interest in the property is called a **leasehold estate**, or **leasehold**. The owner who transfers the leasehold estate is called the **landlord**, or **lessor**. The party to whom the leasehold estate is transferred is called the **tenant**, or **lessee**. There are four types of *tenancies*:

tenancy for years
A tenancy created when the landlord and the tenant agree on a specific duration for the lease.

1. ***Tenancy for Years*** A **tenancy for years** is created when the landlord and the tenant agree on a specific duration for the lease. Any lease for a stated period—no matter how long or short—is called a tenancy for years. Examples of such arrangements include office space leased in a high-rise office building on a 30-year lease and a cabin leased for the summer. A tenancy for years terminates automatically, without notice, upon the expiration of the stated term.

periodic tenancy
A tenancy created when a lease specifies intervals at which payments are due but does not specify how long the lease is for.

2. ***Periodic Tenancy*** A **periodic tenancy** is created when a lease specifies intervals at which payments are due but does not specify how long the lease is for. A lease that states, "Rent is due on the first day of the month" establishes a periodic tenancy. Many such leases are created by implication. A periodic tenancy may be terminated by either party at the end of any payment interval, but adequate notice of the termination must be given. Under common law, the notice period equaled the length of the payment period. That is, a month-to-month tenancy required a one-month notice of termination.

tenancy at will
A lease that may be terminated at any time by either party.

3. ***Tenancy at Will*** A lease that may be terminated at any time by either party is a **tenancy at will**. A tenancy at will may be created expressly (e.g., "to tenant as long as landlord wishes") but is more likely to be created by implication. Most states have enacted statutes requiring minimum advance notice for the termination of a tenancy at will. The death of either party terminates a tenancy at will.

4. ***Tenancy at Sufferance*** A **tenancy at sufferance** is created when a tenant retains possession of property after the expiration of another tenancy or a life estate without the owner's consent. That is, the owner suffers the *wrongful possession* of his or her property by the holdover tenant. This is not really a true tenancy but merely the possession of property without right. Technically, a tenant at sufferance is a trespasser. A tenant at sufferance is liable for the payment of rent during the period of sufferance. Most states require an owner to go through certain legal proceedings, called *eviction proceedings* or *unlawful detainer actions*, to evict a holdover tenant. A few states allow owners to use self-help to evict a holdover tenant if force is not used.

tenancy at sufferance
A tenancy created when a tenant retains possession of property after the expiration of another tenancy or a life estate without the owner's consent.

The Lease

The rental agreement between a landlord and a tenant is called a **lease**. Leases can generally be either oral or written, except that most statutes of frauds require written leases for periods of time longer than one year. The lease must contain the essential terms of the parties' agreement. The lease is often a form contract that is prepared by the landlord and presented to the tenant. This is particularly true of residential leases. Other leases are negotiated between the parties. For example, a bank's lease of a branch office would be negotiated with the owner of the building.

lease
A transfer of the right to the possession and use of real property for a set term in return for certain consideration; the rental agreement between a landlord and a tenant.

Landmark Law

Title III of the Americans with Disabilities Act

On July 26, 1990, the **Americans with Disabilities Act (ADA)** was signed into law [42 U.S.C. § § 1201 et seq.]. Most of the provisions of the ADA became effective on January 26, 1992. The ADA is a broad civil rights statute that prohibits discrimination against disabled individuals in employment, public services, public accommodations and services, and telecommunications. **Title III** of the ADA prohibits discrimination on the basis of disability in places of public accommodation operated by private entities. The attorney general of the United States is empowered to issue regulations that interpret and enforce the ADA.

Title III of the ADA applies to public accommodations and commercial facilities such as motels, hotels, restaurants, theaters, recreation facilities, colleges and universities, department stores, retail stores, and office buildings. It does not generally apply to residential facilities (single- and multifamily housing).

Title III requires facilities that are covered by the law to be designed, constructed, and altered in compliance with specific accessibility requirements established by regulations issued pursuant to the ADA. In 1991, the attorney general issued final regulations that contain minimum guidelines to make covered facilities accessible to disabled individuals. This includes constructing ramps to accommodate wheelchairs, installing railings next to steps, placing signs written in Braille in elevators and at elevator call buttons, and so on. If both the ADA and state law apply, the more stringent rule must be followed.

New construction must be built in such a manner as to be readily accessible to and usable by disabled individuals. Any alterations made to existing buildings must be made so that the altered portions of the building are readily accessible to disabled individuals to the maximum extent feasible. With respect to existing buildings, architectural barriers must be removed if such removal is readily achievable. In determining when an action is readily achievable, the factors to be considered include the nature and cost of the action, the financial resources of the facility, and the type of operations of the facility.

The ADA provides for both private right of action and enforcement by the attorney general. Individuals may seek injunctive relief and monetary damages, and the attorney general may seek equitable relief and civil fines up to $50,000 for the first violation and $100,000 for any subsequent violation.

Proponents of Title III of the ADA argue that the law is necessary to make public and commercial facilities accommodate the needs of the disabled. They point out that voluntary efforts to make these accommodations were too few and too late. Critics argue that the ADA creates a quagmire of regulations that are difficult to understand and that cost landowners billions of dollars to comply with.

Building owners, managers, architects, and others involved in the design, construction, ownership, and management of public accommodations and commercial buildings must be knowledgeable about, and comply with, the provisions of Title III of the ADA. ■

Building. Title III of the ADA requires buildings to be accessible to disabled persons.

Implied Warranty of Habitability

implied warranty of habitability A warranty that provides that the leased premises must be fit, safe, and suitable for ordinary residential use.

The courts of many jurisdictions hold that an **implied warranty of habitability** applies to residential leases for their duration. This warranty provides that the leased premises must be fit, safe, and suitable for ordinary residential use. For example, unchecked rodent infestation, leaking roofs, and unworkable bathroom facilities have been held to breach the implied warranty of habitability. On the other hand, a small crack in the wall or some paint peeling from a door does not breach this warranty.

If the landlord's failure to maintain or repair the leased premises affects the tenant's use or enjoyment of the premises, state statutes and judicial decisions provide various remedies. Generally, the tenant may (1) withhold from his or her rent the amount by which the defect reduced the value of the premises to him or her, (2) repair the defect and deduct the cost of repairs from the rent due for the leased premises, (3) cancel the lease if the failure to repair constitutes constructive eviction, or (4) sue for damages for the amount the landlord's failure to repair the defect reduced the value of the leasehold.

Web Site
Landlord–Tenant Law: An Overview State-by-state laws regarding landlord–tenant laws are provided. Issues such as evictions, leases, security deposits, and rent control can be explored at this Web site. Visit at **www.cornell.edu/topics/landlord_tenant.html**.

In the following case, the court found a breach of implied warranty of habitability.

Case 23.3
Implied Warranty of Habitability

Solow v. Wellner
569 N.Y.S.2d 882, 1991 N.Y.Misc. Lexis 169 (1991)
Civil Court of the City of New York

Background and Facts

The defendants are approximately 80 tenants of a 300-unit luxury apartment building on the upper east side of Manhattan. The monthly rents in the all-glass-enclosed building, which won several architectural awards, ranged from $1,064 to $5,379. The landlord brought a summary proceeding against the tenants to recover rent when they engaged in a rent strike in protest against what they viewed as deteriorating conditions and services. Among other things, the evidence showed that during the period in question (May 1982–May 1988), the elevator system made tenants and their guests wait interminable lengths of time, the elevators skipped floors and opened on the wrong floors, a stench emanated from garbage stored near the garage, and mice appeared in that area, fixtures were missing in pubic areas, water seeped into mailboxes, the air conditioning in the lobby was inoperative, and air conditioning in individual units leaked. The defendant-tenants sought abatement of rent for breach of the implied warranty of habitability.

Issue

Did the landlord breach the implied warranty of habitability?

In The Language of The Court

York, Judge In determining whether the warranty of fitness has been breached, this jurisdiction has adopted the "reasonable expectation" test. This means that the premises are to be maintained in accordance with the reasonable expectations of the tenant. Certain amenities not necessarily life threatening, but consistent with the nature of the bargain—air conditioning would be an example—would fall under the protection of this branch of the warranty. Predictability and reliability of services is another factor.

In applying this branch of the warranty to this case, we start with the obvious expectations of this uniquely designed all-glass-enclosed building on Manhattan's fashionable upper East Side. Add to this the comparatively high rents exacted for these apartments and one would have to assume that the expectations of the tenants encompassed more than the minimal amenities. While the warranty certainly entitled them to freedom from conditions threatening their life, health and safety, their higher rents justified increased expectations of a well-run, impeccably clean building of consistent and reliable services. These expectations were reasonably enhanced by the brochure they received, which was also incorporated into the lease, with its promises of security, air conditioning in the public areas and panoramic views. The promises and expectations fell far short of the reality. The warranty in the public areas was breached.

Decision and Remedy

The court held that the landlord had breached the implied warranty of habitability. The court abated the rent of each of the tenants individually, in total allowing the landlord to recover only 22 percent of the amount he sued for. The court ordered the landlord to pay the tenants' attorneys' fees.

Case Questions

Critical Legal Thinking Should the law recognize the implied warranty of habitability? Why or why not?

Business Ethics Did the landlord act ethically in not correcting the defects in the building? Did the tenants act ethically in engaging in a rent strike?

Contemporary Business Was the remedy the court ordered appropriate in this case?

Land Use Control

Although the United States has the most advanced private property system in the world, the ownership and possession of real estate is not free of government regulation. Pursuant to constitutional authority, federal, state, and local governments have enacted myriad laws that regulate ownership, possession, and use of real property. These laws are collectively referred to as **land use control**.

land use control

The collective term for the laws that regulate the possession, ownership, and use of real property.

Zoning

Most countries and municipalities have enacted zoning ordinances to regulate land use.

Zoning ordinances generally (1) establish use districts within the municipality (i.e., areas are generally designated residential, commercial, or industrial); (2) restrict the height, size, and location of buildings on a building site; and (3) establish aesthetic requirements or limitations for the exterior of buildings.

zoning ordinances

Local laws that are adopted by municipalities and local governments to regulate land use within their boundaries. Zoning ordinances are adopted and enforced to protect the health, safety, and general welfare of the community.

Property has its duties as well as its rights.

Benjamin Disraeli
Sybil (1845), Bk. II, Ch. XI

A **zoning commission** usually formulates zoning ordinances, conducts public hearings, and makes recommendations to the city council, which must vote to enact an ordinance. Once a zoning ordinance is enacted, the zoning ordinance commission enforces it. If landowners believe that a zoning ordinance is illegal or that it has been applied unlawfully to them or their property, they may institute a court proceeding seeking judicial review of the ordinance or its application.

An owner who wishes to use his or her property for a use different from that permitted under a current zoning ordinance may seek relief from the ordinance by obtaining a **variance**. To obtain a variance, the landowner must prove that the ordinance causes an undue hardship by preventing him or her from making a reasonable return on the land as zoned. Variances are usually difficult to obtain.

variance

An exception that permits a type of building or use in an area that would not otherwise be allowed by a zoning ordinance.

nonconforming uses
Uses and buildings that already exist in a zoned area that are permitted to continue even though they do not fit within new zoning ordinances.

Zoning laws act prospectively; that is, uses and buildings that already exist in the zoned area are permitted to continue even though they do not fit within new zoning ordinances. Such uses are called **nonconforming uses**. For example, if a new zoning ordinance is enacted, making an area a residential zone, an existing funeral parlor is a nonconforming use.

Contemporary Business Environment

Rent Control

Many local communities across the country have enacted **rent control ordinances** that stipulate the amount of rent a landlord can charge for residential housing. Most of these ordinances fix the rent at a specific amount and provide for minor annual increases. Although many communities, such as Santa Monica, California, have adopted rent control ordinances, New York City has the most famous one.

Landlords, of course, oppose rent control, arguing that the government, by enacting rent control, takes property from them (i.e., the higher rents they could charge absent rent control laws). The Fifth Amendment's "taking" clause generally requires just compensation be paid to an owner whose property is taken by the government. Landlords have challenged rent control ordinances as violating the "taking" clause. The U.S. Supreme Court visited this issue in *Yee v. City of Escondido, California*, 503 U.S. 519, 112 S.Ct. 1522, 1992 U.S. Lexis 2115 (1992).

In that case, the city of Escondido adopted a rent control ordinance that rolled back the rent of "pads" in mobile home parks to 1986 levels. The ordinance prohibits rent increases without the approval of the city council. The owners of many mobile home parks affected by the ordinance sued the city, alleging that the law constituted an uncompensated "taking" in violation of the U.S. Constitution. The trial court, the court of appeals, and the U.S. Supreme Court held otherwise and upheld the rent control ordinance.

Critics argue that rent control ordinances are merely a "regulatory tax" that transfers wealth from landowners to tenants. They also point out that tenants of Manhattan's posh upper east side, or Santa Monica, California, hardly deserve to be protected by rent controls. Proponents of rent control say that it is necessary to create affordable housing, particularly in high-rent urban areas. They assert that rent control serves a legitimate government purpose. Whatever the arguments, the Supreme Court has given a green light to local communities to adopt rent control ordinances. ■

Government Regulation Versus Compensable "Taking" of Real Property

eminent domain
The taking of private property by the government for public use, provided just compensation is paid to the private property holder.

The government may use its power of **eminent domain** to acquire private property for public purposes. However, the Due Process Clause of the U.S. Constitution (and state constitutions where applicable) requires the government to allow the owner to make a case for keeping the property. The **Just Compensation Clause** of the Constitution mandates that the government must compensate the property owner (and possibly others, such as lessees) when it exercises the power of eminent domain. Anyone who is not satisfied with the compensation offered by the government can bring an action to have the court determine the compensation to be paid. Often, the government's action is not considered a "taking," even if it causes economic losses to property owners and others.

Consider This Example Assume that ITT acquired a large piece of property, with the intention of erecting a commercial building at some future time. Now suppose the government wants to build a new highway that passes through property owned by ITT. The government can use its power of eminent domain to acquire the property. There has been a "taking," so the government must pay ITT just compensation. Suppose, instead, that the government enacts a zoning law that affects ITT's property by restricting building in the area to single-family housing. Although ITT would suffer a substantial economic loss, the zoning law, nevertheless, would probably not constitute a "taking" that required the payment of compensation.

The following two U.S. Supreme Court cases address the issue of "taking" of real property.

U.S. SUPREME COURT CASE

Penn Central Transportation Company v. City of New York

438 U.S. 104, 98 S.Ct. 2646, 1978 U.S. Lexis 39 (1978)

Supreme Court of the United States

Case 23.4

Government Regulation of Real Property

Background and Facts

In 1965, the city of New York adopted the Landmark Preservation Law to encourage and require the preservation of buildings and areas with historic and aesthetic importance. The law was adopted to promote civic pride in the beauty and noble accomplishments of the past; protect and enhance the city's attractions to tourists and visitors; and enhance the pleasure, welfare, and quality of life of people. The primary responsibility of administering the law is vested in the Landmark Preservation Commission (Commission). Once a structure is designated a "landmark" by Commission, no modification or change to the exterior of the building or site can be made without the permission of Commission.

On August 2, 1967, Commission designated the Grand Central Terminal (Terminal) as a landmark building and the city block it occupies as a landmark site. Terminal, which is owner by the Penn Central Transportation Company (Penn Central) is one of New York City's most famous buildings. Opened in 1913, this eight-story structure is a magnificent example of the French Beaux Arts style. Penn Central opposed the designation of Terminal as a landmark, but to no avail.

In January 1968, Penn Central filed an application with Commission to construct a 55-story office building in the airspace above the existing facade of Terminal. Commission denied Penn Central's application. Commission stated:

> We have no fixed rule against making additions to designated buildings—it all depends on how they are done. But to balance a 55-story office tower above a flamboyant Beaux Arts facade seems nothing more than an aesthetic joke. Quite simply, the tower would overwhelm the Terminal by its sheer mass.

Penn Central filed suit in New York supreme court. The trial court held in favor of Penn Central and granted an injunction and declaratory relief. The appellate division reversed. The court of appeals affirmed. Penn Central appealed.

Supreme Court Issue

Does New York City's Landmark Preservation Law effectuate a "taking" of Penn Central's property without just compensation in violation of the Fifth and Fourteenth Amendments to the U.S. Constitution?

In The Language of The U.S. Supreme Court

Brennan, Justice In contending that the New York City law has "taken" their property in violation of the Fifth and Fourteenth Amendments, appellants make a series of arguments. They first observe that the airspace above the Terminal is a valuable property interest. They urge that the Landmark law has deprived them of any gainful use of their air rights above the Terminal. The submission that appellants may establish a taking simply by showing that they have been denied the ability to exploit a property interest that they heretofore had believed was available for development is quite simply untenable.

Second, appellants, focusing on the character and impact of the New York City law, argue that it effects a taking because its operation has significantly diminished the value of the Terminal site. Stated boldly, appellants' position appears to be that the only means of ensuring that selected owners are not singled out to endure financial hardship for no reason is to hold that any restriction imposed on individual landmarks pursuant to the New York City scheme is a taking requiring the payment of just compensation. Agreement with this argument would, of course, invalidate not just the New York City law, but all comparable landmark legislation in the nation. We find no merit in it.

It is, of course, true that the Landmark law has a more severe impact on some landowners than others, but that in itself does not mean that the law effects a "taking." Legislation designed to promote the general welfare commonly burdens some more than others. In any event, appellants' repeated suggestions that they are solely burdened and unbenefited is factually inaccurate. This contention overlooks the fact that the New York City law applies to vast numbers of structures in the city in addition to the Terminal—all the structures contained in the 31 historic districts and over 400 individual landmarks, many of which are close to the Terminal.

Decision and Remedy

The U.S. Supreme Court held that the application of New York City's Landmark Preservation Law is a permissible government regulation that does not effectuate a "taking" of Penn Central's property under the Fifth and Fourteenth Amendments to the U.S. Constitution.

Case Questions

Critical Legal Thinking Does the government owe a duty of social responsibility to protect historic buildings and districts from destruction? Or should the market be permitted to determine the highest value and best use for property?

Business Ethics Did Penn Central act ethically in trying to construct a 55-story building above Terminal?

Contemporary Business Does government regulation help or hurt business? Explain.

U.S. SUPREME COURT CASE

City of Monterey v. Del Monte Dunes at Monterey, Ltd.

526 U.S. 687, 119 S.Ct. 1624, 1999 U.S. Lexis 3631 (1999)

Supreme Court of the United States

Case 23.5

Regulatory "Taking" of Real Property

Background and Facts

Del Montes Dunes at Monterey, Ltd. (Del Monte), owned a 37-acre oceanfront parcel of real estate located in the city of Monterey, California. The parcel was zoned for multi-family residential use under the city's zoning ordinance. In 1981, Del Monte submitted an application to develop the property in conformity with the city's zoning ordinance and general-plan requirements. Although the zoning law permitted up to 1,000 residential units for the entire parcel, Del Monte's proposal was limited to 344 units. In 1982, the city's planning commission denied the application but states that a proposal for 264 units would receive favorable consideration. Del Monte submitted a revised proposal for 264 units. In late 1983, the planning commission denied the application. The commission stated that a plan for 244 units would be received with favor. When Del Monte submitted a proposal for 244 units, it, too, was denied.

On appeal, the Monterey city council suggested a 190-unit plan, but when Del Monte submitted this proposal, the planning commission rejected it. On appeal, the city council requested that more space be dedicated to public open space. In 1985, Del Monte submitted a new plan devoting 17.9 acres of the 37.6-acre parcel to public open space, including a public beach. Only 5.1 acres were dedicated to buildings and patios. In 1986, the planning commission rejected the proposal. The city then issued a sewer-system hookup moratorium that prevented development of the property entirely.

After five years, Del Monte decided that the city of Monterey would not permit the development of the property under any circumstances. Del Monte sued the city of Monterey for an unconstitutional, uncompensated "regulatory taking." During the trial, Del Monte sold the property to the State of California. The district court jury found against the city of Monterey and awarded Del Monte $1.75 million in damages. The court of appeals affirmed. The U.S. Supreme Court granted review.

Supreme Court Issue

Did the city of Monterey engage in a "regulatory taking" of real property in violation of the U.S. Constitution?

In The Language of The U.S. Supreme Court

Kennedy, Justice Rather, to the extent Del Monte Dunes' challenge was premised on unreasonable governmental action, the theory argued and tried to the jury was that the city's denial of the final development permit was inconsistent not only with the city's general ordinances and policies but even with the shifting ad hoc restrictions previously imposed by the city. Del Monte Dunes' argument, in short, was not that the city had followed its zoning ordinances and policies but rather that it had not done so. As is often true in these actions, the disputed questions were whether the government had denied a constitutional right in acting outside the bounds of its authority, and, if so, the extent of any resulting damages. These were questions for the jury.

Decision and Remedy

The U.S. Supreme Court held that the issue of whether the city of Monterey's repeated rejections of Del Monte's development proposals deprived the owner of all economically viable use of the land was properly submitted to the jury. Affirmed.

Case Questions

Critical Legal Thinking What is a *regulatory taking*? Why does this violate the U.S. Constitution? Explain.

Business Ethics Did the members of the city of Monterey's planning commission and city council act ethically in this case? What do you think was the city's motive in acting the way it did?

Contemporary Business Is there government regulation that does not violate the U.S. Constitution? Give an example. Does this regulation have any economic consequences?

International Law

Sorting Out Real Property Ownership Rights in the Former East Germany

When the Berlin Wall tumbled in 1989, it allowed for the reunification of East and West Germany into one country. The event was heralded as a triumph for democracy because it meant the return of capitalism and private property rights to East Germany. Only one major question remained: Who owns the real property in the former East Germany?

Germany was under the influence and rule of the Nazi Party from 1933 until May 1945, when Germany surrendered to the Allies after World War II. During that time, the Nazis appropriated private property from owners. After the war, Germany was divided between West Germany, which was allied with Europe and the United States, and East Germany, which was under the Soviet Union's control. The city of Berlin, which was located in East Germany, was also divided in half. The Berlin Wall was erected to prevent East Berliners from defecting to the West through West Berlin. From 1945 to 1949, the Soviets appropriated private property in East Germany. In 1949, the East German government was created. Until 1989, East Germany was a communist state that owned the property of the country.

In 1990, after the reunification of Germany, the German government enacted the **Vermogensgesetz (Statute for the Regulation of Open Property Questions)** and the **Anmeldeverordnung (Regulation on the Filing of Claims)**. Together, the statute and the regulations created a procedure for filing and proving claims to property expropriated by the Nazis before and during World War II, by the Soviets between 1945 and 1949, and by the East German government from 1949 to 1989.

The German property claim law set December 31, 1992, as the final date for the filing of claims for the return of real property. A claimant had to file an application that specified the location, kind, and extent of the property; original ownership; and chain of inheritance. After examining the claims, the German authorities made decisions and awarded ownership rights.

In the meantime, the German government enacted a new law that requires a permit for the sale or transfer of real property situated in the former East Germany. The permit will not be issued if a claim for the return of the property has been filed. A claimant can also apply for an injunction in the civil court to prevent the transfer of property until the merits of the claim have been decided.

One provision in the German claims law favors Jewish claimants. There is a presumption in the law that any property sold between January 1933 and May 1945 is considered to have been sold under duress, unless the buyer can prove otherwise. This is because during that time period, Nazi officials forced Jews to transfer their property for little or no consideration under threat of harm or death.

Resolving the property claims in the former East Germany was not an easy task. Governments in other socialist or communist countries that change to a democratic, capitalist system will face similar problems. ■

Angel Statue. It is wise for a person to have a valid will that designates how his or her property will be distributed upon his or her death.

Chapter Summary

Personal Property, p. 677

Personal Property

Personal property. Consists of everything that is not real property. Sometimes referred to as goods or *chattels*. Types of personal property:

1. ***Tangible property.*** Physically defined property such as goods, animals, and minerals.
2. ***Intangible property.*** Rights that cannot be reduced to physical form, such as stock certificates, bonds, and copyrights.

Methods of Acquiring Ownership in Personal Property

1. ***Possession.*** Taking possession of unowned property, such as wild animals.
2. ***Purchase.*** Purchasing property from its rightful owner.
3. ***Accession.*** Occurs when the value of personal property increases because it is added to or improved by natural or manufactured means.
4. ***Gift.*** Voluntary transfer of property by its owner to a donee without consideration.
   - *a.* Three elements are necessary to create a valid gift:
     - i. *Donative intent.* The donor must have intended to make a gift. This intent can be inferred from the circumstances.
     - ii. *Delivery.* Delivery of the personal property must be made to the donee by *physical delivery* or where impracticable, by *constructive* (or *symbolic*) *delivery.*
     - iii. *Acceptance.* The donee must accept the gift. Donees are free to reject gifts that they do not want.
5. ***Confusion.*** Where tangible goods are commingled, the owners share title to the commingled goods in the proportion to the amount of goods contributed.
6. ***Divorce.*** When a marriage is dissolved by a divorce, the parties obtain certain rights in the property of the marital estate.
7. ***Will.*** Gift to beneficiaries named in a will.
8. ***Inheritance.*** Heirs stipulated in an inheritance statute.

Mislaid, Lost, and Abandoned Property

1. ***Mislaid property.*** Personal property that an owner voluntarily places somewhere and then inadvertently forgets. The owner of the premises where the property is mislaid does not acquire title to the property but has the right of possession against the whole world except the rightful owner. The rightful owner can reclaim the property.
2. ***Lost property.*** Personal property that an owner leaves somewhere because of negligence or carelessness. The finder obtains title to the property against the whole world except the true owner. The rightful owner can reclaim the property.
   - *a. Estray statutes.* State statutes that permit a finder of mislaid or lost property to obtain title to the property. To obtain clear title, the finder must:
     - i. Report the find to the appropriate government agency and turn over possession of the property to the agency.
     - ii. Post and publish required notices.
     - iii. Wait the statutorily required time (e.g., one year) without the rightful owner claiming the property
3. ***Abandoned property.*** Personal property that an owner has discarded, or mislaid or lost property that the owner gives up any further attempt to locate. The finder acquires title to the property. The prior owner cannot reclaim the property.

Bailments, p. 682

Bailment

Bailment. Occurs when the owner of personal property delivers the property to another person to be held, stored, or delivered, or for some other purpose.

1. ***Parties to a bailment.***
   a. *Bailor.* Owner of the property.
   b. *Bailee.* Party to whom the property is delivered.

Ordinary Bailments

1. ***Bailments for the sole benefit of the bailor.***
   a. *Gratuitous bailment.* Arises when the bailee is requested to care for the bailor's property as a favor.
   b. *Involuntary bailment.* Arises when the bailee finds lost or misplaced property and decides to protect it.
   c. *Duty of care.* The bailee owes a duty of *slight care*, that is, the bailee is liable for *gross negligence*.
2. ***Bailments for the sole benefit of the bailee.***
   a. *Gratuitous bailment.* A gratuitous bailment that arises when the bailee uses the bailor's property for personal reasons without paying compensation.
   b. *Duty of care.* The bailee owes a duty of *great care* (or *utmost care*) and is liable for *slight negligence*.
3. ***Bailments for the mutual benefit of the bailor and the bailee.***
   a. *Mutual benefit bailment.* Arises when both parties benefit from the bailment. This includes commercial bailments.
   b. *Duty of care.* The bailee owes a duty of *reasonable care* (or *ordinary care*) and is liable for *ordinary negligence*.

Special Bailee

1. ***Innkeepers.*** The owner of a facility that provides lodging to the public for compensation (e.g., a hotel or motel).
   a. *Duty of care.* Under the common law, innkeepers owe a duty of *strict liability* regarding loss caused to guests' property.
   b. *Innkeeper's statutes.* Laws that have been enacted to limit the liability of innkeepers for loss or damage to guests' property. The innkeeper must post required notices to be covered by the law.

Real Property, p. 684

Nature of Real Property

Real property is immovable. It includes land, buildings, subsurface rights, air rights, plant life, and fixtures.

Freehold Estates

Estates where the owner has a present possessory interest in the real property.

Estates in Fee

1. ***Fee simple absolute* (or *fee simple*).** Highest form of ownership.
2. ***Fee simple defeasible* (or *qualified fee*).** Estate that ends if a specified condition occurs.

Life Estates

An interest in real property that lasts for the life of a specified person. Called an *estate pour autre vie* if the time is measured by the life of a third person.

Future Interests

Right to possess real property in the future rather than currently.

1. ***Reversion.*** Right to possession that returns to the grantor after the expiration of a limited or contingent estate.
2. ***Remainder.*** Right to possession that goes to a third person after the expiration of a limited or contingent estate. The third person is called a *remainderman.*

Concurrent Ownership

A situation in which two or more persons jointly own real property.

1. ***Joint tenancy.*** Owners may transfer their interests without the consent of co-owners. Transfer severs the joint tenancy. Under the *right of survivorship*, the interest of a deceased owner passes to his or her co-owners.
2. ***Tenancy in common.*** Owners may transfer their interests without the consent of co-owners. Transfer does not sever the tenancy in common. Interest of a deceased owner passes to his or her estate.
3. ***Tenancy by the entirety.*** A form of co-ownership that can be used only by a married couple. Neither spouse may transfer his or her interest without the other spouse's consent. A surviving spouse has the right of survivorship.

Community Property

A form of co-ownership that applies only to a married couple. Neither spouse may transfer his or her interest without the other spouse's consent. When a spouse dies, the surviving spouse automatically receives one-half the community property.

Condominium

Condominium owners have title to their individual units and own the common areas as tenants in common. Owners may transfer their interests without the consent of other owners.

Cooperative

A corporation owns the building and the residents own shares of the corporation. Usually, owners may not transfer their shares without the approval of the other owners.

Sale of Real Estate

An owner sells his or her property to another for consideration.

Deed

An instrument used to convey real property by sale or gift.

1. ***Warranty deed.*** Provides the most protection to the grantee because the grantor makes warranties against defect in title.
2. ***Quitclaim deed.*** Provides least amount of protection to the grantee because the grantor transfers only the interest he or she has in the property.

Recording Statutes

Permit copies of deeds and other documents concerning interests in real property (e.g., mortgages, liens) to be filed in a government office, where they become public record. Put third parties on notice of recorded interests.

Adverse Possession

A person who occupies another's property acquires title to the property if the occupation has been:

1. For a statutory period of time (in many states, 10 to 20 years)
2. Open, visible, and notorious
3. Actual and exclusive
4. Continuous and peaceful
5. Hostile and adverse

Easements

An interest in land that gives the holder the right to make limited use of another's property without taking anything from it (e.g., driveways, party walls).

1. ***Easement appurtenant.*** Owner of land is given an easement over an adjacent piece of land.
2. ***Easement in gross.*** Authorizes a person who does not own adjacent land the right to use another's land.

Landlord–Tenant Relationship, p. 691

Landlord–Tenant Relationship

Created when an owner of a freehold estate transfers a right to another to exclusively and temporarily possess the owner's property.

Types of Tenancy

1. ***Tenancy for years.*** Tenancy for a specified period of time.
2. ***Periodic tenancy.*** Tenancy for a period of time determined by the payment interval.
3. ***Tenancy at will.*** Tenancy that may be terminated at any time by either party.
4. ***Tenancy at sufferance.*** Tenancy created by the wrongful possession of property.

The Lease

The rental agreement between the landlord and the tenant that contains the essential terms of the parties' agreement.

Land Use Control, p. 695

Public Regulation of Land Use

Zoning ordinances. Laws adopted by local governments that restrict use of property, set building standards, and establish architectural requirements.

1. ***Variance.*** Permits an owner to make a nonzoned use of his or her property. A variance requires permission from a zoning board.
2. ***Nonconforming use.*** A nonzoned use that is permitted (grandfathered in) when an area is rezoned.

Government Regulation Versus Compensable "Taking" of Real Property, p. 696

Eminent Domain

The taking of private property by the government for public use.

Just Compensation Clause

A clause in the U.S. Constitution that mandates that the government must compensate the property owner (and possibly others, such as lessees) when it exercises the power of eminent domain.

Government Regulation

The regulation of property by the government that does not amount to a "taking" of property and is therefore not compensable by the government.

Internet Exercises and Case Questions

Working the Web Internet Exercises

Activities

1. Review your state's laws on innkeeper's liability for lost or stolen property of hotel guests. What is the statutory limitation on losses?
2. Is your state one that has adopted the Uniform Landlord–Tenant Act? See **www.law.cornell.edu/uniform/vol7.html#lndtri**. For a general overview, see **www.law.cornell.edu/topics/landlord_tenant.html**.
3. For the landlord's view, see **www.landlord-tenant-online.com/index.html** and **www.landlord.com/legalmain.htm**. For a view from the perspective of tenants, see **www.consumerrights.net/chapter12.html** and **www.sftu.org**.

Critical Legal Thinking Cases

23.1 Personal Property Fixture NYT Cable TV is a division of the New York Times Company (NYT) that operates a cable television station in Camden County, New Jersey. NYT has erected a 250-foot-high cable antenna tower on real property to distribute its broadcast signals. The structure is attached to a large concrete foundation in the ground and consists of a large vertical triangular steel superstructure connected by steel cross bars and circular metal ties. The Camden County Board of Taxation assessed a real property tax on the property, including the cable television tower. NYT opposed the tax, alleging that the cable television tower was personal property—not real property—and was exempt from the real property tax. Who wins? [*NYT Cable TV v. Borough of Audubon, New Jersey*, 553 A.2d 1368, 1989 N.J.Super. Lexis 51 (N.J. Sup. 1989)]

23.2 Lost Property In June 1983, Danny Lee Smith and his brother, Jeffrey Allen Smith, found a 16-foot fiberglass boat lying beside the roadway in Mobile County, Alabama. Seeing two sheriff's deputies, they stopped them to discuss the boat. Over the Smiths' objections, the deputies impounded the boat. The Smiths made it clear that if the true owner of the boat was not found, they wanted the boat. The true owner did not claim the boat. Mobile County claimed the boat and wanted to auction it off for sale to raise money for county recreational programs. The Smiths claimed the boat as finders. Alabama did not have an estray statute that applied to the situation. Who gets the boat? [*Smith v. Sheriff Purvis*, 474 So.2d 1131, 1985 Ala.Civ.App. Lexis 1280 (Ala. App. 1985)]

23.3 Abandoned Property Late in 1975, police officers of the city of Miami, Florida, responded to reports of a shooting at the apartment of Carlos Fuentes. Fuentes had been shot in the neck and shoulder, and shortly after the police arrived, was removed to a hospital. In an ensuing search of the apartment, the police found assorted drug paraphernalia, a gun, and cash in the amount of $58,591. The property was seized, taken to the police station, and placed in custody. About nine days later, the police learned that Fuentes had been discharged from the hospital. All efforts by police to locate Fuentes and his girlfriend, a co-occupant of Fuentes's apartment, were unsuccessful. Neither Fuentes nor his girlfriend ever came forward to claim any of the items taken by the police from his apartment. About four years later, in 1979, James W. Green and Walter J. Vogel, the owners of the apartment building in which Fuentes was a tenant, sued the city of Miami to recover the cash found in Fuentes's apartment. The state of Florida intervened in the case, also claiming an interest in the money. Who wins? [*State of Florida v. Green*, 456 So.2d 1309, 1984 Fla.App. Lexis 15340 (Fla. App. 1984)]

23.4 Bailment On February 4, 1976, James D. Merritt leased a storage locker from Nationwide Warehouse Co., Ltd. (Nationwide), and agreed to pay $16 per month lease for the locker. Merritt placed various items in the leased premises but never informed Nationwide as to the nature or quantity of articles stored therein. Merritt was free to store or remove whatever he wished without consultation with, permission from, or notice to, Nationwide. Merritt locked the leased premises with his own lock and key. Nationwide was not furnished with a key. Subsequently, certain personal property belonging to Merritt disappeared from the storage space. Merritt sued Nationwide to recover damages of $5,275. Was a bailment created between Merritt and Nationwide? [*Merritt v. Nationwide Warehouse Co., Ltd.*, 605 S.W.2d 250, 1980 Tenn.App. Lexis 338 (Tenn.App. 1980)]

23.5 Gratuitous Bailment Marsha Hamilton and Andrea Morris were guests at a dinner party attended by approximately 25 people. The party began about 7:00 P.M. and ended at approximately 1:00 A.M. Alcoholic beverages were served throughout the evening. At approximately 11:30, while working in the kitchen, Hamilton removed her watch and placed it on the counter. About midnight, Hamilton left the kitchen and went outside. After about 15 minutes, she became ill and fled to the bathroom. Shortly after Hamilton left the kitchen, Morris saw the watch on the counter and, fearing for its safety, picked it up and carried it in her hand as she looked for Hamilton. When Hamilton came out of the bathroom, she and her fiancé left the party. Morris was unable to find Hamilton and cannot recall precisely what she did with the watch. She testified that she either gave it to Hamilton's fiancé or put it somewhere in the host's house for safekeeping. Hamilton's fiancé testified that Morris did not give him the watch. The next day Hamilton discovered that she did not have her watch, but in a search of the host's home, the watch was not recovered. Hamilton sued Morris for damages. Who wins? [*Morris v. Hamilton*, 302 S.E.2d 51, 1983 Va. Lexis 231 (VA 1983)]

23.6 Parking Lot's Liability Allright, Inc., is a parking lot operator in Houston, Texas. On January 18, 1980, Kirkland Strauder drove his 1978 Buick Regal automobile to a Houston Allright parking lot, placed it in a row of cars to be parked by the attendant. When Strauder returned two hours later to reclaim his car, it could not be found. Strauder reported the car stolen. Allright could not explain the loss of the car, which was found $1\frac{1}{2}$ weeks later, wrecked and stripped. Strauder sued Allright, Inc., for damages. Who wins? [*Allright, Inc. v. Strauder*, 679 S.W.2d 81, 1984 Tex.App. Lexis 6006 (Tex. App. 1984)]

23.7 Subsurface Rights In 1883, Isaac McIlwee owned 100 acres of land in Valley Township, Guernsey County, Ohio. In that year, he sold the property to Akron & Cambridge Coal Company (Akron & Cambridge) in fee simple but reserved in fee simple "the surface of all said lands" to himself. Over the years, the interests in the land were transferred to many different parties. As of 1981, the Mid-Ohio Coal Company owned the rights originally transferred to Akron & Cambridge, and Peter and Irene Minnich owned the rights reserved by Isaac McIlwee in 1883. The Minnichs claim they possess subsurface rights to the property except for coal rights. Who wins? [*Minnich v. Guernsey Savings and Loan Company*, 521 N.E.2d 489, 1987 OhioApp. Lexis 10497 (Ohio App. 1987)]

23.8 Life Estate and Remainder Baudilio Bowles died testate. His will devised to his sister, Julianita B. Vigil, "one-half of any income, rents, or profits from any real property located in Bull Creek or Colonias, New Mexico." The will contained another clause that left to his children "my interest in any real property owned by me at the time of my death, located in Bull Creek and/or Colonias, San Miguel County." The property referred to both devises is the same property. Julianita died before the will was probated. Her heirs claim a one-half ownership interest in the real property. Bowles's children assert that they own all his property. Who wins? [*In the Matter of the Estate of Bowles*, 764 P.2d 510, 1988 N.M.App. Lexis 93 (N.M.App. 1988)]

23.9 Revision In 1941, W. E. and Jennie Hutton conveyed land they owned to the Trustees of Schools of District Number One of the Town of Allison, Illinois (School District), by warranty deed "to be used for school purpose only; otherwise to revert to Grantor." The School District built a school on the site, commonly known as Hutton School. The Huttons conveyed the adjoining farmland and their reversionary interest in the school site to the Jacqmains, who in turn conveyed their interest to Herbert and Betty Mahrenholz in 1959. The 1.5-acre site sits in the middle of Mahrenholz's farmland. In May 1973, the School District discontinued holding regular classes at Hutton School. Instead, it used the school building to warehouse and store miscellaneous school equipment, supplies, unused desks, and the like. In 1974, Mahrenholz filed suit to quiet title to the school property in themselves. Who wins? [*Mahrenholz v. County Board of School Trustees of Lawrence County*, 544 N.E.2d 128, 1989 Ill.App. Lexis 1445 (Ill.App. 1989)]

23.10 Adverse Possession In 1972, Joseph and Helen Naab purchased a tract of land in a subdivision of Williamstown, West Virginia. At the time of purchase, there was both a house and a small concrete garage on the property. Evidence showed that the garage had been erected sometime prior to 1952 by one of the Naabs' predecessors in title. In 1975, Roger and Cynthia Nolan purchased lot contiguous to that owned by the Naabs. The following year, the Nolans had their property surveyed. The survey indicated that one corner of the Naabs' garage encroached 1.22 feet onto the Nolans' property and the other corner encroached 0.91 feet over the property line. The Nolans requested that the Naabs remove the garage from their property. When the Naabs refused, the lawsuit ensued. Who wins? [*Naab v. Nolan*, 327 S.E.2d 151, 1985 W.Va. Lexis 476 (WV 1985)]

23.11 Recording Statute On October 13, 1972, Johnnie H. Hill and his wife, Clara Mae, entered into an installment sales contract with Pinelawn Memorial Park (Pinelawn) to purchase a mausoleum crypt. They made it clear they wanted to buy crypt D that faced eastward toward Kinston. The Hills paid a $1,035 down payment and continued to make $33.02 monthly payments. On February 13, 1974, William C. Shackelford and his wife, Jennie L., entered into an agreement with Pinelawn to purchase crypt D. They paid $1,406 down payment and two annual installments of $912. The Hills were first put on notice of the second contract when they visited Pinelawn in February 1977 and saw the Shackelford name on crypt D. The Hills then tendered full payment to Pinelawn for crypt D. On April 25, 1977, the Hills sued Pinelawn and the Shackelfords. They demanded specific performance of the contract and the deed to crypt D. Upon being served with summons, the Shackelfords discovered that they had no deed to the crypt and demanded one from Pinelawn. Pinelawn delivered them a deed dated August 18, 1977, which the Shackelfords recorded in the County Register on September 9, 1977. Who owns crypt D? [*Hill v. Pinelawn Memorial Park, Inc.*, 282 S.E.2d 779, 1981 N.C. Lexis 1326 (N.C. 1981)]

23.12 Implied Warranty of Habitability Sharon Love entered into a written lease agreement with Monarch Apartments for apartment 4 at 441 Winfield in Topeka, Kansas. Shortly after moving in, Love experienced serious problems with termites. Her walls swelled, clouds of dirt came out, and when she checked on her children one night, she saw termites flying around the room. She complained to Monarch, which arranged for the apartment to be fumigated. When the termite problem persisted, Monarch moved Love and her children to apartment 2. Upon moving in, Love noticed that roaches crawled over the walls, ceilings, and floors of the apartment. She complained, and Monarch called an exterminator, who sprayed the apartment. When the roach problem persisted, Love vacated the premises. Did Love lawfully terminate the lease? [*Love v. Monarch Apartments*, 771 P.2d 79, 1989 Kan.App. Lexis 219 (Kan. App. 1989)]

23.13 Zoning The city of Ladue is one of the finer suburban residential areas of metropolitan St. Louis. The homes in the city are considerably more expensive than those in surrounding areas and consist of homes of traditional design such as colonial, French provincial, and English. The city set up an architectural board to approve plans for buildings that

> *conform to certain minimum architectural standards of appearance and conformity with surrounding structures, and that unsightly, grotesque, and unsuitable structures, detrimental to the stability of value and welfare of surrounding property, structures, and residents, and to the general welfare and happiness of the community, be avoided.*

The owner of a lot in the city submitted a plan to build a house of ultramodern design. It was pyramid shaped, with a flat top and triangular-shaped windows and doors. Although the house plans met other city zoning ordinances and building codes, the architectural board rejected the owner's petition for a building permit based on aesthetic reasons. The owner sued the city. Who wins? [*State of Missouri v. Berkeley*, 458 S.W.2d 305, 1970 Mo. Lexis 902 (MO 1970)]

Business Ethics Cases

23.14 Business Ethics When Dr. Arthur M. Edwards dies, leaving a will disposing of his property, he left the villa-type condominium in which he lived, "its contents," and $10,000 to his stepson, Ronald W. Souders. Edwards left the residual of his estate to other named legatees. In administering the estate, certain stock certificates, passbook savings accounts, and other bank statements were found in Edwards's condominium. Souders claimed that these items belonged to him because they were "contents" of the condominium. The other legatees opposed Souders's claim, alleging that the disputed property was intangible property and not part of the contents of the condominium. The value of the property was as follows: condominium, $138,000; furniture in condominium, $4,000; stocks, $377,000; and passbook and other bank account, $124,000. Who is entitled to the stocks and bank accounts? Do you think Souders acted ethically in this case? [*Souders v. Johnson*, 501 So.2d 745, 1987 Fla.App. Lexis 6579 (Fla.App. 1987)]

23.15 Business Ethics On March 19, 1971, Victor and Phyllis Garber acquired a piece of real property by warranty deed. The deed was recorded on December 30, 1971. The property consisted of 80 acres that was enclosed by a fence that had been in place for over 50 years. The enclosed area was used to graze cattle and produce hay. Subsequently, William and Herbert Doenz acquired a piece of real property adjacent to the Garbers'. In March 1981, Doenz employed a surveyor to locate his land's boundaries. As a result of the survey, it was discovered that the shared fence was 20 to 30 feet inside the deed line on Doenz's property. The amount of property between the old fence and the deed line was 3.01 acres. In September 1981, Doenz removed the old fence and constructed a new fence along the deed line. The Garbers brought suit to quiet title. Did Doenzes act ethically in removing the fence? Did the Garbers act ethically in claiming title to property that originally belonged with the adjacent property? Did the Garbers acquire title to property between the fence and the deed line through adverse possession? [*Doenz v. Garber*, 665 P.2d 932, 1983 Wyo. Lexis 339 (WY 1983)]

23.16 Business Ethics Moe and Joe Rappaport (tenants) leased space in a shopping mall owned by Bermuda Avenue Shopping Center Associates, L.P. (landlord), to use as an indoor golf arcade. The lease was signed in May 1987, and the tenants were given possession of the leased premises on July 23, 1987. The tenants were not told by the landlord of the extensive renovations planned for the mall. From July 23 until August 18, the golf arcade was busy and earned a net profit. On August 18, the renovation of the mall began in front of the arcade. According to the tenants, their store sign was taken down, there was debris and dust in front of the store, the sidewalks and parking spaces in front of the store was taken away, and their business "died." The tenants closed their arcade on September 30 and sued the landlord for damages. The landlord counterclaimed, seeking to recover lost rental income. Did the landlord act ethically in not explaining the extent of the planned renovations to the tenants? Did the tenants act ethically in terminating the lease? Were the tenants constructively evicted from the leased premise? [*Bermuda Avenue Shopping Center Associates v. Rappaport*, 565 So.2d 805, 1990 Fla.App. Lexis 5354 (Fla.App. 1990)]

Briefing the Case Writing Assignment

Read Case A.23 in the Case Appendix [*Walker v. Quillen*]. This case is excerpted from the supreme court of Delaware's opinion. Review and brief the case. In your brief, be sure to answer the following questions.

1. Who were the plaintiffs (appellees)? Who was the defendant (appellant)?
2. Describe the tract of land owned by the plaintiffs and defendant.
3. What was the issue in this case? How did the court decide this issue?

Answers to Management Decision Questions

1. **Adverse possession** occurs when a person who wrongfully possesses someone else's property obtains title to that property if certain statutory requirements are met. Many states recognize modern-day squatters' rights under the doctrine of adverse possession.
2. To obtain title under adverse possession, the wrongful possession must be
   - For a statutorily prescribed period of time, ranging in most states between 10 and 20 years.
   - Open, visible, and notorious so as to put the owner on notice of the possession.
   - Actual and exclusive physical possession by the possessor by such activity as planting crops, grazing of animals, or building of a structure on the land.
   - Continuous and peaceful, which requires that the occupancy be continuous and uninterrupted for the statutory period. The adverse possessor cannot take the property by force from an owner.
   - Hostile and adverse, which means that the possessor must occupy the property without the express or implied permission of the owner.

   Your occupancy of your home and use of the garage would satisfy the elements of adverse possession. You should bring a **quiet title** action to determine the extent of your rights in the property that is in dispute.

24

Negotiable Instruments, Credit, and Bankruptcy

"Creditors have better memories than debtors."

—Benjamin Franklin
Poor Richard 's Almanack (1758)

Chapter Objectives

After studying this chapter, you should be able to:

1. Recognize different types of negotiable instruments, including drafts, promissory notes, checks, and certificates of deposit.
2. Distinguish between unsecured and secured credit.
3. Describe the procedure for filing for Chapter 7 liquidation bankruptcy.
4. Describe how a business is reorganized in a Chapter 11 bankruptcy.
5. Describe the procedure for filing for Chapter 13 consumer debt adjustment bankruptcy.

Chapter Contents

Management Decision Negotiable Instruments, Credit, and Bankruptcy

Following the September 11, 2001, terrorist attack on the World Trade Center, Atlantic Airways (Atlantic) a major passenger and freight carrier, lost 50 percent of its business. After operating in the red for many months, the airline's creditors are threatening foreclosure and demanding payment of past due accounts, and the company's ability to meet payroll obligations is uncertain. As chief executive officer of Atlantic, you are certain that in time, consumer confidence in the safety of air travel will return and the financial status of the corporation will substantially improve. However, company attorneys have recommended that Atlantic file for bankruptcy.

1. What kinds of bankruptcy plans are available to Atlantic?
2. Which plan is more suitable for Atlantic based on your assessment of the future of the airline industry in the United States?

The U.S. economy is a credit economy. Consumers borrow money to make major purchases (e.g., homes, automobiles, appliances) and use credit cards (e.g., Visa, MasterCard) to purchase goods and services at restaurants, clothing stores, and the like. Businesses use credit to purchase equipment, supplies, and other goods and services. In a credit transaction, the borrower is the **debtor** and the lender is the **creditor**.

debtor
The borrower in a credit transaction.

creditor
The lender in a credit transaction.

One cannot help regretting that where money is concerned it is so much the rule to overlook moral obligations.

Malms V.C.
Ellis v. Houston (1878)

Negotiable instruments (or *commercial paper*) are important for the conduct of business and personal affairs. In this country, modern commerce could not continue without them. Examples of negotiable instruments include checks (such as the one that may have been used to pay for this book) and promissory notes (such as the one executed by a borrower of money to pay for tuition).

The drafters of the U.S. Constitution thought the plight of debtors was so important that they included a provision authorizing Congress to enact *bankruptcy laws* in the

Store Window. Businesses often purchase goods on credit from suppliers. A supplier often takes a security interest in personal property to secure the loan, such as the inventory in this store.

Constitution. Article I, Section 8, clause 4 of the U.S. Constitution provides "that Congress shall have the power . . . to establish . . . uniform laws on the subject of bankruptcies throughout the United States."

This chapter discusses credit, negotiable instruments, and bankruptcy laws.

Negotiable Instruments

To qualify as a negotiable instrument, a document must meet certain requirements established by Article 3 of the Uniform Commercial Code (UCC). If these requirements are met, a transferee who qualifies as a *holder in due course* (HDC) takes the instrument free of many defenses that can be asserted against the original payee. In addition, the document is considered an ordinary contract that is subject to contract law.

Business Brief

If a document qualifies as a negotiable instrument, the terms of Article 3 of the UCC become as much a part of the instrument as if they were written on the instrument itself.

The concept of *negotiation* is important to the law of negotiable instruments. The primary benefit of a negotiable instrument is that it can be used as a substitute for money. As such, it must be freely transferable to subsequent parties. Technically, a negotiable instrument is negotiated when it is originally issued. The term *negotiation*, however, is usually used to describe the transfer of negotiable instruments to subsequent transferees.

Landmark Law

Revised Article 3 (Negotiable Instruments) of the UCC

Although negotiable instruments have been used in commerce since medieval times, the English law courts did not immediately recognize their validity. To compensate for this failure, the merchants developed rules governing their use. These rules, which were enforced by local private merchant courts, became part of what was called the **Law Merchant**. Eventually, in 1882, England enacted the Bills of Exchange Act, which codified the rules of the Law Merchant.

In 1886, the National Conference of Commissioners of Uniform Laws promulgated the **Uniform Negotiable Instruments Law (NIL)** in the United States. By 1920, all of the states had enacted the NIL as law, but the rapid development of commercial paper soon made the law obsolete.

Article 3 (Commercial Paper) of the UCC, which was promulgated in 1952, established rules for the creation of, transfer of, enforcement of, and liability on negotiable instruments. All the states and the District of Columbia replaced the NIL with Article 3.

In 1990, the American Law Institute and the National Conference of Commissioners on Uniform State Laws repealed Article 3 and replaced it with **Revised Article 3**. The new article, which is called "Negotiable Instruments" instead of "Commercial Paper," is a comprehensive revision of Article 3 that reflects modern commercial practices. Individual states are currently replacing Article 3 with Revised Article 3. Revised Article 3 will form the basis of this discussion of negotiable instruments. Revised Article 3 recognizes four kinds of instruments: (1) drafts, (2) checks, (3) promissory notes, and (4) certificates of deposit. Each of these is discussed in the following paragraphs. ■

Drafts

A **draft**, which is a *three-party instrument*, is an unconditional written order by one party (the **drawer**) that orders a second party (the **drawee**) to pay money to a third party (the **payee**) [UCC 3-104(e)]. The drawee must be obligated to pay the drawer money before the drawer can order the drawee to pay this money to a third party (the payee).

draft
A three-party instrument that is an unconditional written order by one party that orders the second party to pay money to a third party.

drawer of a draft
The party who writes the order for a draft.

drawee of a draft
The party who must pay the money stated in the draft. Also called the *acceptor* of a draft.

payee of a draft
The party who receives the money from a draft.

For the drawee to be liable on a draft, the drawee must accept the drawer's written order to pay it. Acceptance is usually shown by the written word *accepted* on the face of the draft, along with the drawee's signature and the date. The drawer is called the **acceptor** of the draft because his or her obligation changes from having to pay the drawer to having to pay the payee. After the drawee accepts the draft, it is returned to the drawer of the payee. The drawer or the payee, in turn, can freely transfer it as a negotiable instrument to another party.

Exhibit 24.1
A Time Draft

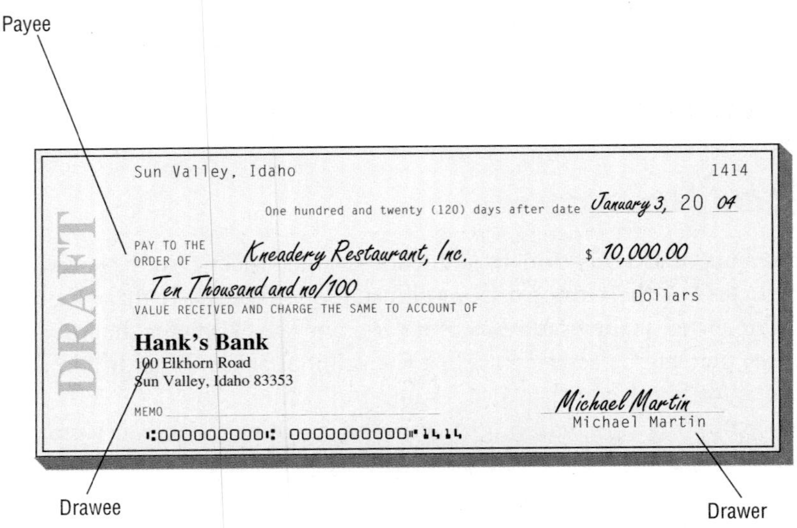

Consider This Example Mary Owens owes Hector Martinez $1,000. Mr. Martinez writes out a draft that orders Ms. Owens to pay this $1,000 to Cindy Choy. Ms. Owens agrees to this change of obligation and accepts the draft. Mr. Martinez is the drawer, Ms. Owens is the drawer, and Ms. Choy is the payee.

If one wants to know the real value of money, he needs but to borrow some from his friends.
Confucius
Analects (c. 500 B.C.)

A draft can be either a time draft or a sight draft. A *time draft* is payable at a designated future date. Language such as "pay on January 3, 2005" or "pay 120 days after date" creates a time draft (see Exhibit 24.1). A *sight draft* is payable on sight. A sight draft is also called a *demand draft*. Language such as "on demand pay" or "at sight pay" creates a sight draft. A draft can be both a time and a sight draft. Such a draft would provide that it is payable at a stated time *after* sight. For example, this type of draft is created by language such as "payable 90 days after sight."

Checks

check
A distinct form of draft drawn on a financial institution and payable on demand.

A **check** is a distinct form of draft. It is unique in that it is drawn on a financial institution (the drawee) and is payable on demand [UCC 3-104(f)]. In other words, a check is an order to pay (see Exhibit 24.2). Most businesses and many individuals have checking accounts at financial institutions.

Exhibit 24.2
A Check

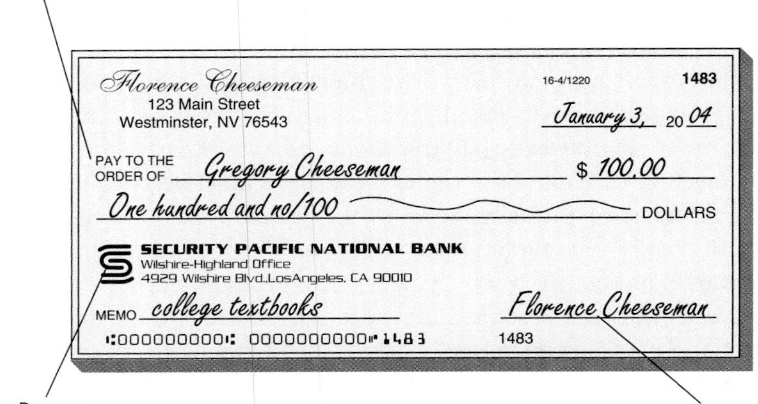

Like other drafts, a check is a three-party instrument. The customer who has the checking account and writes (draws) the check is the **drawer**. The financial institution on which the check is written is the **drawee**, and the party to whom the check is written is the **payee**.

In addition to traditional checks, there are several forms of special checks, including:

- ***Certified Checks*** When a bank *certifies* a check, it agrees in advance to (1) accept the check when it is presented for payment and (2) pay the check out of funds set aside from the customer's account and either placed in a special certified check account or held in the customer's account. They are payable at any time from the date they were issued.
- ***Cashier's Checks*** A person can purchase a *cashier's check* from a bank by paying the bank the amount of the check plus a fee for issuing the check. Usually, a specific payee is named. The purchaser does not have to have a checking account at the bank. The check is a noncancellable negotiable instrument upon issue.
- ***Traveler's Checks*** *Traveler's checks* derive their name from the fact that travelers often purchase them to use as a safe substitute for cash while on vacations or other trips. They may be issued by banks or by companies other than banks (e.g., American Express). Traveler's checks are issued without a named payee. The checks have two signature blanks. The purchaser signs one blank when the traveler's checks are issued. The purchaser enters the payee's name and signs the second blank when he or she uses the check to purchase goods or services.

drawer of a check
The checking account holder and writer of a check.

drawee of a check
The financial institution on which a check is drawn.

payee of a check
The party to whom a check is written.

Business Brief
Negotiable instruments serve as a substitute for money. Many purchases by businesses and individuals are made by checks instead of by cash.

E-Commerce & Information Technology

Electronic Fund Transfer Systems

Computers and electronic technology have made it possible for banks to offer electronic payment and collection systems to bank customers. This technology is collectively referred to as **electronic fund transfer systems (EFTS)**. EFTS are supported by contracts among and between customers, banks, private clearinghouses, and other third parties. The most common forms of EFTS are discussed in the following paragraphs.

Automated Teller Machines

An **automated teller machine (ATM)** is an electronic machine that is located either on a bank's premises or at some other convenient location, such as a shopping center or supermarket. These devices are connected online to the bank's computers. A bank customer is issued a secret personal identification number (PIN) along with an ATM card to access his or her account through ATMs.

ATMS are commonly used when the bank is not open. They are also used as an alternative means of conducting banking when the bank is open. They are used to withdraw cash from bank accounts, cash checks, make deposits to checking or savings accounts, and make payments owed to the bank.

Point-of-Sale Terminals

Many banks issue *debit cards* to customers. Debit cards replace checks in that customers can use them to make purchases. No credit is extended. Instead, the customer's bank account is immediately debited for the amount of the purchase.

Debit cards can be used only if the merchant has a **point-of-sale (POS) terminal** at the checkout counter. These terminals are connected online to the bank's computers. To make a purchase, the customer inserts the debit card into the terminal for the amount of the purchase (and perhaps cash back as well). If there are sufficient funds in the customer's account the transaction will debit the customer's account and credit the merchant's account for the amount of the purchase. If there are insufficient funds in the customer's account, the purchase is rejected unless the customer has overdraft protection. Some POS terminals allow for the extension of credit in the transaction. Gasoline station POS terminals are one example.

Direct Deposits and Withdrawals

Many banks provide the service of paying recurring payments and crediting recurring deposits on behalf of customers. Commonly, payments are for utilities, insurance premiums, mortgage payments, and the like. Social Security checks, wages, and dividend and interest checks are examples of recurring deposits. To provide this service, the customer's bank and the payee's bank must belong to the same clearinghouse.

Pay-by-Internet

Many banks permit customers to pay bills from their bank accounts by use of personal computer by using the Internet. To do so, the customer must enter his or her PIN and account number, the amount of the bill to be paid, and the account number of the payee to whom the funds are to be transferred. Internet banking is expected to increase dramatically in the future. ■

Advertisement on Building. Commerce is facilitated by the use of negotiable instruments, such as checks and promissory notes.

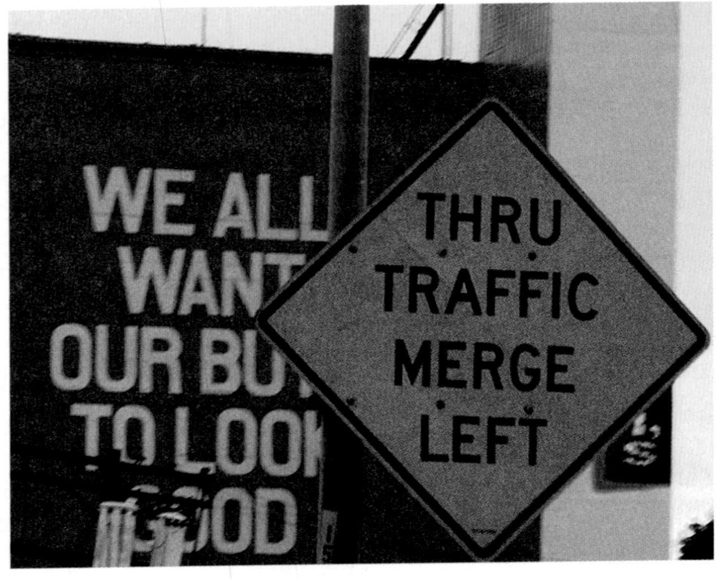

Promissory Notes

A **promissory note** (or **note**) is an unconditional written promise by one party to pay money to another party [UCC 3-104(e)]. It is a *two-party instrument* (see Exhibit 24.3), not an order to pay. Promissory notes usually arise when one party borrows money from another. The note is evidence of (1) the extension of credit and (2) the borrower's promise to repay the debt.

promissory note
A two-party negotiable instrument that is an unconditional written promise by one party to pay money to another party.

maker of a note
The party who makes a promise to pay (borrower).

payee of a note
The party to whom a promise to pay is made (lender).

time note
A note payable at a specific time.

demand note
A note payable on demand.

The party who makes the promise to pay is the **maker** of the note (i.e., the borrower). The party to whom the promise to pay is made is the **payee** (i.e., the lender). A promissory note is a negotiable instrument that the payee can freely transfer to other parties.

The parties are free to design the terms of the note to fit their needs. For example, notes can be payable at a specific time (**time note**) or on demand (**demand note**). Notes can be made payable to a named payee or to "bearer." They can be payable in a single payment or in installments. The latter are called **installment notes**. Most notes require the borrower to pay interest on the principal.

Exhibit 24.3
A Promissory Note

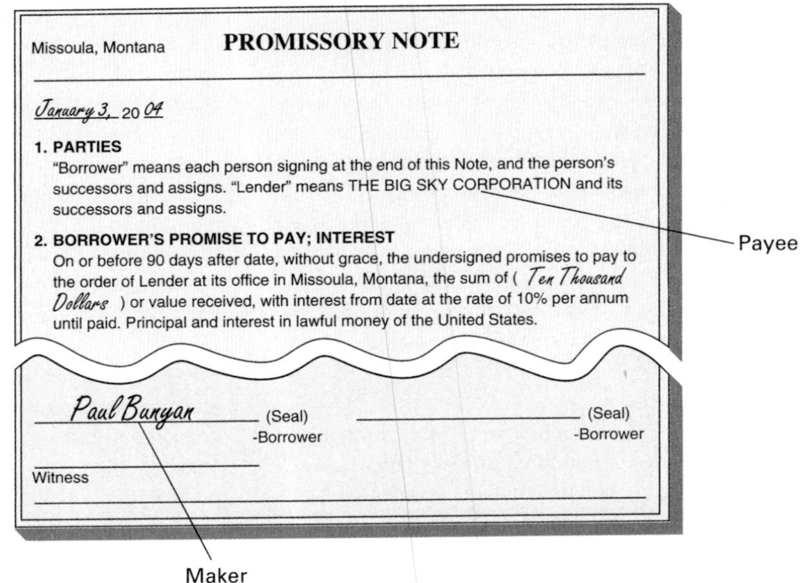
Missoula, Montana **PROMISSORY NOTE**

January 3, 20 04

1. **PARTIES**
"Borrower" means each person signing at the end of this Note, and the person's successors and assigns. "Lender" means THE BIG SKY CORPORATION and its successors and assigns.

2. **BORROWER'S PROMISE TO PAY; INTEREST**
On or before 90 days after date, without grace, the undersigned promises to pay to the order of Lender at its office in Missoula, Montana, the sum of (Ten Thousand Dollars) or value received, with interest from date at the rate of 10% per annum until paid. Principal and interest in lawful money of the United States.

Paul Bunyan (Seal) -Borrower ______ (Seal) -Borrower

______ Witness

Lenders sometimes require the maker of a note to post security for the repayment of the note. This security, which is called **collateral**, may be in the form of automobiles, houses, securities, or other property. If the maker fails to repay the note when it is due, the lender can foreclose and take the collateral as payment for the note. Notes are often named after the security that underlies the note. For example, notes that are secured by real estate are called **mortgage notes** and notes that are secured by personal property are called **collateral notes**.

collateral
Security against repayment of the note that lenders sometimes require; can be a car, a house, or other property.

Certificates of Deposit

A **certificate of deposit (CD)** is a special form of note that is created when a depositor deposits money at a financial institution in exchange for the institution's promise to pay back the amount of the deposit plus an agreed-upon rate of interest upon the expiration of a set time agreed upon by the parties [UCC 3-104(j)].

certificate of deposit (CD)
A two-party negotiable instrument that is a special form of note created when a depositor deposits money at a financial institution in exchange for the institution's promise to pay back the amount of the deposit plus an agreed-upon rate of interest upon the expiration of a set time period agreed upon by the parties.

The financial institution is the borrower (the **maker**), and the depositor is the lender (the **payee**). A CD is a two-party instrument (see Exhibit 24.4). Note that a CD is a promise to pay, not an order to pay.

Unlike a regular passbook savings account, a CD is a negotiable instrument. CDs under $100,000 are commonly referred to as *small CDs*. CDs of $100,000 or more are usually called *jumbo CDs*.

Endorsement

An **endorsement** is the signature of a signer (other than as a maker, a drawer, or an acceptor) that is placed on an instrument to negotiate it to another person. The signature may (1) appear alone, (2) name an individual to whom the instrument is to be paid, or (3) be accompanied by other words [UCC 3-204(2)]. The person who endorses an instrument is called the **endorser**. If the endorsement names a payee, this person is called the **endorsee**.

endorsement
The signature (and other directions) written by or on behalf of the holder somewhere on the instrument.

endorser
The person who endorses a negotiable instrument.

endorsee
The person to whom a negotiable instrument is endorsed.

Consider This Example Echo Zhang receives a $500 check for her birthday. She can transfer the check to anyone merely by signing her name on the back of the check. If she endorses it "pay to Linda Schreiber," Ms. Zhang is the endorser, and Linda Schreiber is the endorsee.

Endorsements are usually placed on the reverse side of the instrument, such as on the back of a check (see Exhibit 24.5). If there is no room on the instrument, the endorsement may be written on a separate piece of paper, called an *allonge*. The allonge must be affixed (e.g., stapled or taped) to the instrument [UCC 3-204(a)].

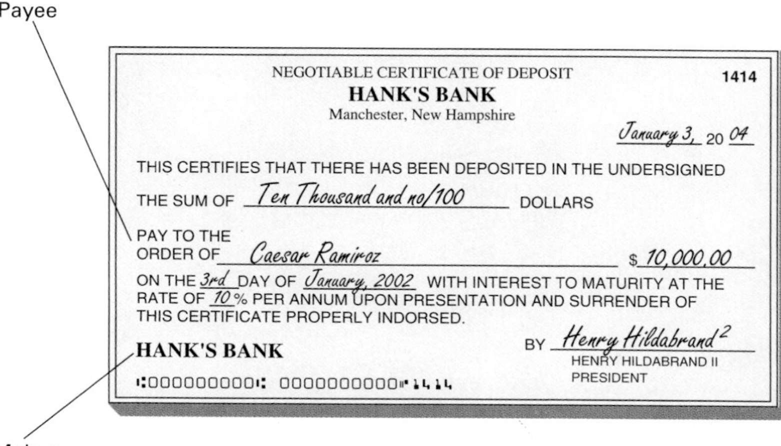

Exhibit 24.4
A Certificate of Deposit

Exhibit 24.5

Proper Placement of an Endorsement

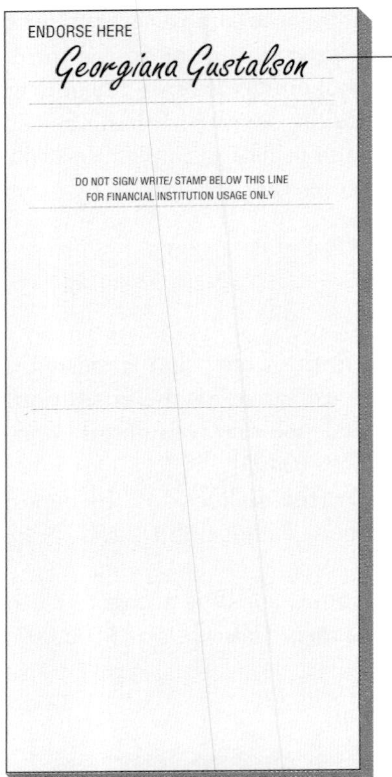

ENDORSE HERE
Georgiana Gustalson
DO NOT SIGN/ WRITE/ STAMP BELOW THIS LINE
FOR FINANCIAL INSTITUTION USAGE ONLY
Endorsement should be placed at the top of the back of the check

International Law

Negotiable Instruments Payable in Foreign Currency

The UCC expressly provides that an instrument may state that it is payable in foreign money [UCC 3-107]. For example, an instrument "payable in 10,000 yen in Japanese currency" is a negotiable instrument that is governed by Article 3 of the UCC.

Unless the instrument states otherwise, an instrument that is payable in foreign currency can be satisfied by the equivalent in U.S. dollars, as determined on the due date. The conversion rate is the current bank-offered spot rate at the place of payment on the due date. The instrument can expressly provide that it is payable only in the stated foreign currency. In this case, the instrument cannot be paid in U.S. dollars. ■

Taipei, Taiwan. Negotiable instruments facilitate international commerce.

E-Commerce & Information Technology

Commercial Wire Transfers

Commercial or **wholesale wire transfers** are often used to transfer payments between businesses and financial institutions. Trillions of dollars per day are transferred over the two principal wire payment systems—the **Federal Reserve wire transfer network (Fedwire)** and the **New York Clearing House Interbank Payments System (CHIPS)**. A wire transfer involves a large amount of money (multimillion-dollar transactions are commonplace). The benefits of using wire transfers are their speed—most transfers are completed on the same day—and low cost. Banks sometimes require a customer to pay for a fund transfer in advance. On other occasions, however, a bank will extend credit to a customer and pay the fund transfer. The customer is liable to pay the bank for any properly paid fund transfer.

Article 4A—Fund Transfers of the UCC, which was promulgated in 1989, governs wholesale wire transfers. Most states have adopted this article. Where adopted, Article 4A governs the rights and obligations between parties to a fund transfer unless they have entered into a contrary agreement. Article 4A applies only to *commercial* electronic fund transfers; consumer electronic fund transfers subject to the Electronic Fund Transfer Act are not subject to Article 4A.

Fund transfers are not complex transactions. For example, suppose Diebold Corporation wants to pay Bethlehem Steel for supplies it purchased. Instead of delivering a negotiable instrument such as a check to Bethlehem, Diebold instructs its bank to wire the funds to Bethlehem's bank, with instructions to credit Bethlehem's account. Diebold's order is called a *payment order*. Diebold is the *originator* of the wire transfer, and Bethlehem is the *beneficiary*. Diebold's bank is called the *originator's bank*, and Bethlehem's bank is called *beneficiary's bank*. In more complex transactions, there may be one or more additional banks, known as *intermediary banks*, between the originator's bank and the beneficiary's bank [UCC 4A-103(a)].

If a receiving bank mistakenly pays a greater amount to the beneficiary than ordered, the originator is liable for only the amount he or she instructed to be paid. The receiving bank that erred has the burden of recovering any overpayment from the beneficiary [UCC 4A-303(a)]. If a wrong beneficiary is paid, the originator is not obliged to pay his or her payment order. The bank that issued the erroneous payment order has the burden of recovering the payment from the improper beneficiary [UCC 4A-303(c)].

Banks and customers usually establish security procedures (e.g., codes, identifying numbers, words) to prevent unauthorized electronic payment orders. To protect the bank from liability for unauthorized payment orders, the security procedure must be commercially reasonable. If the bank verifies the authenticity of a payment order by complying with such a security procedure and pays the order, the customer is bound to pay the order, even if it was not authorized [UCC 4A-202]. The customer is not liable if it can prove that the unauthorized order was not initiated by an employee or another agent or by a person who obtained that information from a source controlled by the customer [UCC 4A-203]. ■

Nepal. The financing of international trade is made easier by the fast same-day use of commercial wire transfers. Trillions of dollars are transferred each day between banks and businesses in different countries to pay for the sale of goods and services.

Credit

By no means run in debt.
George Herbert
The Temple (1633)

Credit may be extended on either an *unsecured* or a *secured* basis. The following paragraphs discuss these types of credit.

Unsecured Credit

unsecured credit
Credit that does not require any security (collateral) to protect the payment of the debt.

Unsecured credit does not require any security (collateral) to protect the payment of the debt. Instead, the creditor relies on the debtor's promise to repay the principal (plus any interest) when it is due. If the debtor fails to make the payments, the creditor may bring legal action and obtain a judgment against him or her. If the debtor is *judgment-proof* (e.g., has little or no property or no income that can be garnished), the creditor may never collect.

Secured Credit

collateral
The property that is subject to a security interest.

secured credit
Credit that requires security (collateral) that protects payment of the loan.

To minimize the risk associated with extending unsecured credit, a creditor may require a security interest in the debtor's **collateral**. The collateral secures payment of the loan. This type of credit is called **secured credit**. Security interests may be taken in *real*, *personal*, *intangible*, and *other property*.

If the debtor fails to make the payments when due, the collateral may be repossessed to recover the outstanding amount. Generally, if the sale of the collateral is insufficient to repay the amount of the loan (plus any interest), the creditor may bring a lawsuit against the debtor to recover a *deficiency judgment* for the difference. Some states prohibit or limit deficiency judgments with respect to certain types of loans.

Store Window. Many consumer purchases are made with credit cards. This creates a debtor–creditor relationship between the consumer-borrower and the issuer of the credit card.

Contemporary Business Environment

Klondike Bar's Unsecured Claim Melts

Generally, a creditor would rather be a secured creditor than an unsecured creditor because of the extra protection and priority status the secured position gives the creditor. The following case shows why.

Sunstate Dairy & Food Products Co. (Sunstate) distributed dairy products in Florida. It had the following two debts among its other debts:

1. On November 19, 1990, Sunstate borrowed money from Barclays Business Credit, Inc. (Barclays), and signed a security agreement granting Barclays a continuing security interest in and lien upon substantially all of Sunstate's personal property, including all of Sunstate's inventory, equipment, accounts receivable, and general intangibles then existing or thereafter acquired. Barclays perfected its security interest by filing a financial statement with the proper state government authorities.
2. On February 14, 1992, Sunstate purchase $49,512 of Klondike ice cream bars from Isaly Klondike Company (Klondike) on credit. Klondike did not take a security interest in the ice cream bars.

On February 19, 1992, Sunstate filed for bankruptcy. At that time, Sunstate owed Barclays $10,050,766, and $47,731 worth of unpaid-for Klondike bars remained in Sunstate's possession. Barclays and Klondike fought over the Klondike bars. Klondike filed a motion with the court, seeking to reclaim the Klondike bars. Barclays sought to enforce its security agreement and recover the Klondike bars.

The court sided with Barclays because it was a secured creditor with a perfected security interest. The court found that Klondike, as an unsecured creditor, had no legal right to reclaim the Klondike bars. Klondike was merely one of many unsecured general creditors that would receive but pennies on the dollar in Sunstate's bankruptcy. Klondike learned a costly lesson: It is better to be a secured creditor than an unsecured creditor. [*In the Matter of Sunstate Dairy & Food Products Co.*, 145 B.R. 341, 19 U.C.C. Rep.Serv.2d 113, 1992 Bankr. Lexis 1496 (Bk. M.D. Fla. 1992)] ■

Security Interests in Personal Property—Article 9 of the UCC

If a creditor takes a security interest in personal property, the transaction is called a **secured transaction**. Personal property that can serve as collateral includes goods, equipment, inventory, fixtures, farm products, stocks and bonds, accounts receivable, intangibles (e.g., patents), and such. Secured transactions are governed by **Article 9 of the UCC**.

secured transaction
A transaction that is created when a creditor makes a loan to a debtor in exchange for the debtor's pledge of personal property as security.

Article 9 of the UCC
An article of the UCC that governs secured transactions in personal property.

Debtors are liars.

George Herbert
Jacula Prudentum (1651)

Perfection of a Security Interest in Personal Property A secured creditor who **perfects** his or her security interest establishes a right in the collateral that is superior to the rights of other creditors. Although a creditor can perfect his or her interest by taking physical possession of the goods, this is usually impractical. Instead, most secured creditors perfect their interest by filing a **financial statement** in the appropriate state government office. This filing, which is available for public inspection, gives constructive notice to the world that the creditor has a security interest in the covered goods. Financing statements are effective for five years from the date of filing and can be renewed for additional five-year terms.

financing statement
A document filed by a secured creditor with the appropriate government office that constructively notifies the world of his or her security interest in personal property.

To be enforceable, the financing statement must contain (1) the debtor's name and mailing address, (2) the name and address of the secured party from whom information concerning the security interest can be obtained, and (3) a statement indicating the types and describing the items of collateral.

Perfection of a Security Interest in Consumer Goods A creditor who extends credit to a consumer to purchase *consumer goods* automatically perfects his security interest at the time of sale. This is called perfection by a *purchase money security interest in consumer goods*. The creditor does not have to file a financing statement to perfect his or her security interest.

I will pay you some, and, as most debtors do, promise you infinitely.

William Shakespeare
Henry IV, Pt. II (1597)

If the debtor defaults, the secured creditor can reduce his or her claim to judgment or foreclose on the collateral.

Entrepreneur and the Law

Artisan's and Mechanic's Lien

If a worker in the ordinary course of business works on or provides materials to another person with respect to goods, most states have statutes that grant an **artisan's** or **mechanic's lien** on the goods until the work or materials are paid for. For example, if an owner takes his or her car into an automobile service department or body shop for repairs, the mechanic who repairs the car has an *automatic lien* on the car in the amount of the services and materials provided to repair the car. If the car owner refuses or fails to pay the bill, the mechanic can sell the car to pay off the lien.

The following rules apply to artisan's and mechanic's liens:

- The owner of an automobile or other good authorizes an artisan or mechanic to repair the good.
- The artisan or mechanic does the work and provides the materials as requested.
- The owner does not pay for the services rendered and materials provided.
- The artisan or mechanic gives the required notices and sells the automobile or other good pursuant to the requirements of the relevant state statute.
- If the sale proceeds exceed the amount of the artisan's or mechanic's lien, the balance is paid to other lien holders in the goods and then to the owner.
- Artisan's and mechanic's liens are given priority over any existing liens on the goods. Artisan's and mechanic's liens are therefore called **super-priority liens**. ■

E-Commerce & Information Technology

Revised Article 9 Recognizes E-Commerce

Revised Article 9, which was promulgated in 1999 as a model act to replace Article 9—Secured Transactions, recognizes many aspects of e-commerce and the digital world. Some of the modern e-commerce features of Revised Article 9 are:

- Filing of financing statements and other records with the secretary of state, county recorders' office, or other filing office may be made electronically as well as in writing.
- To facilitate electronic filings, the debtor's signature or other authorized signature does not have to appear on the financing statement or other electronic record.
- Electronic chattel paper, which is a record consisting of information stored in an electronic medium (i.e., not written), can be collateral for Article 9 purposes. Perfection of a security interest in electronic chattel paper may be by filing.
- The seller of software is given a purchase money security interest (PMSI) in its software that has priority over other secured interests. For example, if software with a PMSI is placed on the licensee's computer system that is subject to a security interest itself, the software PMSI takes precedence over the security interest in the computer hardware.

Revised Article 9 reflects the drafters' concern for upgrading commercial law to recognize the increased use of digital information and e-commerce. ■

Security Interests in Real Property

A person who owns real property who borrows money from a creditor often will be required to pledge the real property as security for the payment of the loan. An instrument called a **mortgage** is usually used to accomplish this. The owner-debtor is the *mortgagor*, and the creditor is the *mortgagee*.

mortgage
A collateral arrangement in which real property owner borrows money from a creditor, who uses a deed as collateral for repayment of the loan.

Some state laws provide for the use of a **note and deed of trust** in place of a mortgage. The note is the instrument that evidences the borrower's debt to the lender; the deed of trust is the instrument that gives the creditor a security interest in the debtor's property that is pledged as collateral.

note and deed of trust
An alternative to a mortgage in some states.

Most states have enacted **recording statutes** that require the mortgage or deed of trust to be recorded in the county recorder's office in the county in which the real property is located. This record gives potential lenders or purchasers of real property the ability to determine whether there are any existing liens (mortgages) on the property.

recording statute
A statute that requires the mortgage or deed of trust to be recorded in the county recorder's office in the county in which the real property is located.

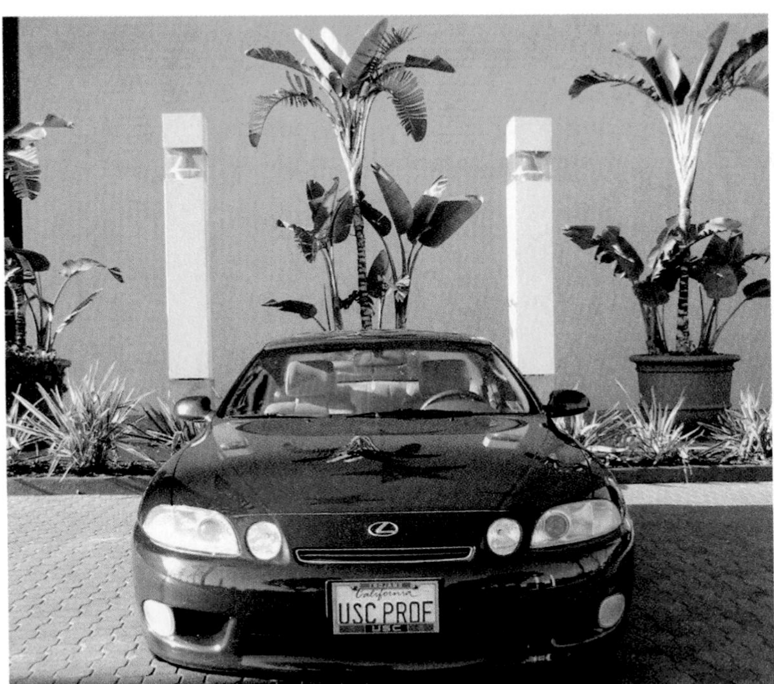

Automobile. A Federal Trade Commission (FTC) rule eliminates the HDC status with respect to consumer credit transactions, such as the consumer purchase of an automobile on credit.

Foreclosure If a mortgagor defaults on a mortgage, the mortgagee can declare the entire debt due and payable immediately. This right can be enforced through a procedure called **foreclosure**.

foreclosure
A legal procedure by which a secured creditor causes the sale of the secured real estate to pay a defaulted loan.

All states permit *foreclosure sales*. Under this method, the debtor's default may trigger a legal court action for foreclosure. If the mortgagee's case is successful, the court will issue a judgment that orders the real property to be sold at a judicial sale. Most states permit foreclosure by *power of sale*, although this must be expressly conferred in the mortgage or deed of trust. Under a power of sale, the procedure for that sale is contained in the mortgage or deed of trust itself. No court action is necessary. Such a sale must be by auction for the highest prices obtainable. Any surplus from a judicial or power of sale must be paid to the mortgagor.

Consider This Example Suppose General Electric purchases a manufacturing plant for $10 million, pays $2 million cash as a down payment, and borrows the remaining $8 million from City Bank. To secure the loan, City Bank requires General Electric to give it a mortgage on the plant. If General Electric defaults on the loan, the bank may take action under state law to foreclose on the property.

Many state statutes give the mortgagor the right to redeem real property after default and before foreclosure. This right, which is called the **right of redemption**, requires the mortgagor to pay the full amount of the debt—that is, principal, interest, and other costs—incurred by the mortgagee because of the mortgagor's default. Upon redemption, the mortgagor receives title to the property free and clear of the mortgage debt.

right of redemption
A right that the mortgagor has to redeem real property after default and before foreclosure. It requires the mortgagor to pay the full amount of the debt incurred by the mortgagee because of the mortgagor's default.

Materialman's Liens

materialman's lien
A contractor's and laborer's lien that makes the real property to which improvements are being made become security for the payment of the services and materials for those improvements.

Owners of real property often hire contractors and laborers (e.g., painters, plumbers, roofers, bricklayers, furnace installers) to make improvements to that property. The contractors and laborers expend the time to provide their services as well as money to provide the materials for the improvements. Their investments are protected by state statutes that permit them to file a **materialman's lien** against the improved real property.

When a lien is properly filed, the real property to which the improvements have been made becomes security for the payment of these services and materials. In essence, the lienholder has the equivalent of a mortgage on the property. If the owner defaults, the lienholder may foreclose on the lien, sell the property, and satisfy the debt plus interest and costs out of the proceeds of the sale. Any surplus must be paid to the owner-debtor.

Surety and Guaranty Arrangements

Business Brief
Many businesses will not sell goods and services to a minor or a person with a bad credit history unless a competent adult cosigns or guarantees payment.

Sometimes a creditor refuses to extend credit to a debtor unless a third person agrees to become liable on the debt. The third person's credit becomes the security for the credit extended to the debtor. This relationship may be either a *surety* or *guaranty* arrangement. Each of these arrangements is discussed in the following paragraphs.

Surety Arrangement

surety arrangement
An arrangement in which a third party promises to be *primarily* liable with the borrower for the payment of the borrower's debt.

In a strict **surety arrangement**, a third person—known as the **surety cosigner** or **co-debtor**—promises to be liable for the payment of another person's debt. A person who acts as a surety is commonly called an **accommodation party**.

Along with the principal debtor, the surety is *primarily liable* for paying the principal debtor's debt when it is due. The principal debtor does not have to be in default on the debt, and the creditor does not have to have exhausted all its remedies against the principal debtor before seeking payment from the surety.

Guaranty Arrangement

guaranty arrangement
An arrangement where a third party promises to be *secondarily liable* for the payment of another's debt.

In a **guaranty arrangement**, a third person (the **guarantor**) agrees to pay the debt of the principal debtor if the debtor defaults and does not pay the debt when it is due. In this type of arrangement, the guarantor is *secondarily liable* on the debt. In other words, the guarantor is obligated to pay the debt only if the principal debtor defaults and the creditor has attempted unsuccessfully to collect the debt from the debtor.

In the following case, the court had to decide whether there was a surety or guaranty contract.

Case 24.1
Surety Contract

General Motors Acceptance Corp. v. Daniels
492 A.2d 1306, 1985 Md. Lexis 596 (1985)
Court of Appeals of Maryland

Background and Facts

In June 1981, John Daniels agreed to purchase a used automobile from Lindsay Cadillac Company (Lindsay Cadillac). Because John had a poor credit rating, his brother Seymour agreed to cosign with him. General Motors Acceptance Corporation (GMAC), a company engaged in the business of financing automobiles, agreed to finance the purchase. On June 23, 1981, Seymour accompanied John to Lindsay Cadillac. John signed the contract on the line designated "Buyer." Seymour signed the contract on the line designated "Co-Buyer." In May 1982, GMAC declared the contract in default. After attempting to locate the automobile for several months, GMAC brought this action against the Daniels brothers. Because service of process was never effected upon John, the case proceeded to trial against only Seymour. The trial court found that Seymour had entered into a guaranty contract and that Seymour was not liable because GMAC had not yet proceeded against John. GMAC appealed.

Issue

Was the contract Seymour signed a guaranty or surely contract?

In The Language of The Court

If the contract Seymour signed was a guaranty contract, he would have been only secondarily liable on his brother's loan.

This situation was not true in this case, however, because Seymour signed the contract on the line on the contract designated "Co-Buyer." The contract clearly stated that all buyers agreed to be jointly and severally liable for the purchase of the vehicle. Seymour executed the same contract as his brother, thereby making himself a party to the original contract. These facts establish the existence of a surety contract upon which Seymour became primarily liable.

Decision and Remedy

The court of appeals held that Seymour had signed a surety contract and thus agreed to be primarily liable with his brother John for the purchase of the automobile. GMAC was therefore not required to proceed against John in the first instance. Reversed.

Case Questions

Critical Legal Thinking What purposes do guaranty and surety contracts serve? Explain.

Business Ethics Did Seymour act ethically in trying to avoid liability for his brother's loan?

Contemporary Business As a lender, would you rather have a third party sign as a surety or guarantor?

Defenses of a Surety or Guarantor

Generally, the defenses the principal debtor has against the creditor may also be asserted by a surety or guarantor. For example, if credit has been extended for the purchase of a piece of machinery that proves to be defective, the debtor and surety both can assert the defect as a defense to liability. The defenses of fraudulent inducement to enter into the surety or guaranty agreement and duress may also be cited as personal defenses to liability. The surety or guarantor cannot assert the debtor's incapacity (i.e., minority or insanity) or bankruptcy as a defense against liability. However, the surety's or guarantor's own incapacity or bankruptcy may be asserted.

Debt is the prolific mother of folly and of crime.

Benjamin Disraeli
Henrietta Temple (1837)

Concept Summary Liability of Sureties and Guarantors Compared

Type of Arrangement	Party	Liability
Surety contract	Surety	Primarily liable. The surety is a codebtor who is liable to pay the debt when it is due.
Guaranty contract	Guarantor	Secondarily liable. The guarantor is liable to pay the debt if the debtor defaults and does not pay the debt when it is due.

Bankruptcy and Reorganization

Article I, Section 8, clause 4 of the U.S. Constitution provides that "The Congress shall have the power . . . to establish . . . uniform laws on the subject of bankruptcies throughout the United States." Federal bankruptcy law establishes procedures for filing for bankruptcy, resolving creditors' claims, and protecting debtors' rights. Bankruptcy law is exclusively federal law; there are no state bankruptcy laws. Bankruptcy cases must be brought in special federal bankruptcy courts.

Business Brief

Bankruptcy law is *federal law*. There are no state bankruptcy laws.

Flower. Federal bankruptcy law provides a method for individuals and businesses to discharge all or a portion of their debt and obtain a fresh start, free of certain debts.

Landmark Law

The Federal Bankruptcy Code

Congress enacted the original **Bankruptcy Act** in 1878. It was amended in 1938 by the **Chandler Act**, and that law was completely revised by the **Bankruptcy Reform Act of 1978** [11 U.S.C. § § 101–1330]. The 1978 act, which became effective on October 1, 1979, substantially changed—and eased—the requirements for filing bankruptcy.

Several years later, Congress enacted the **Bankruptcy Amendments and Federal Judgeship Act of 1984**, which made bankruptcy courts part of the federal district court system and attached a bankruptcy court to each district court. Bankruptcy judges are appointed by the president for 14-year terms. Other provisions of the 1984 amendments remedied abuses and misuses of bankruptcy and clarified procedures for filing bankruptcy. The Bankruptcy Reform Act of 1978, as amended, is referred to as the **Bankruptcy Code**. ■

The "Fresh Start"

fresh start

A debtor's discharge from burdensome debts that allows him or her to begin again.

The primary purpose of federal bankruptcy law is to *discharge* the debtor from burdensome debts. That is, the law gives debtors a **fresh start** by freeing them from legal responsibility for past debts. In doing so, the bankruptcy law (1) protects debtors from abusive activities by creditors in collecting debts; (2) prevents certain creditors from obtaining an unfair advantage over other creditors; (3) protects creditors from actions of the debtor that would diminish the value of the bankruptcy estate; (4) provides for the speedy, efficient, and equitable distribution of the debtor's nonexempt property to claim holders; and (5) preserves existing business relations.

Chapter 7 Liquidation Bankruptcy

Chapter 7 liquidation bankruptcy

The most familiar form of bankruptcy, in which the debtor's nonexempt property is sold for cash, the cash is distributed to the creditors, and any unpaid debts are discharged.

Chapter 7 liquidation bankruptcy (also called **straight bankruptcy**) is the most familiar form of bankruptcy. In this type of proceeding, the debtor's nonexempt property is sold for cash, the cash is distributed to the creditors, and any unpaid debts are **discharged**. Any person, including individuals, partnerships, and corporations, may be debtors in a Chapter 7 proceeding.

Filing a Petition

A Chapter 7 bankruptcy is commenced when a **petition** is filed with the bankruptcy court. The petition may be filed by either the debtor (voluntary) or one or more creditors (involuntary).

Poor bankrupt.

William Shakespeare
Romeo and Juliet (1595)

Voluntary petitions only have to state that the debtor has debts; insolvency (i.e., that debts exceed assets) need not be declared. The petition must include the following schedules: (1) a list of secured and unsecured creditors, including their addresses and the amount of debt owed to each, (2) a list of all property owned by the debtor, including property claimed to be exempt by the debtor, (3) a statement of the financial affairs of the debtor, and (4) a list of the debtor's current income and expenses. The petition must be signed and sworn to under oath. Married couples may file a joint petition.

voluntary petition
A petition filed by the debtor, which states that the debtor has debts.

An **involuntary petition** can be filed against most debtors who can file a voluntary petition under Chapter 7. The only exceptions to this rule are farmers, ranchers, and nonprofit organizations. An involuntary petition must allege that the debtor is not paying his or her debts as they become due. If the debtor has more than 12 creditors, the petition must be signed by at least 3 of them. If there are 12 or fewer creditors, any creditor can sign the petition. The creditor or creditors who sign the petition must have valid unsecured claims of at least $10,775 (in the aggregate).

involuntary petition
A petition filed by creditors of a debtor, which alleges that the debtor is not paying his or her debts as they become due.

Order for Relief

The filing of either a voluntary petition or an unchallenged involuntary petition constitutes an **order for relief**. If the debtor challenges an involuntary petition, a trial will be held to determine whether an order for relief should be granted. Once an order for relief is granted, the case is accepted for further bankruptcy proceedings. In the case of an involuntary petition, the debtor must file the same schedules filed by voluntary debtors.

order for relief
The filing of either a voluntary petition, an unchallenged involuntary petition, or a grant of an order after a trial of a challenged involuntary petition.

Meeting of the Creditors

Within a reasonable time (not less than 10 days nor more than 30 days) after the court grants an order for relief, the court must call a **meeting of the creditors** (also called the *first meeting of the creditors*). The debtor must appear at the meeting and submit to questioning by creditors. Creditors may ask questions regarding the debtors' financial affairs, disposition of property prior to bankruptcy, possible concealment of assets, and such. The debtor may have an attorney present at this meeting. The judge cannot attend this meeting.

meeting of the creditors
A meeting of the creditors in a bankruptcy case that must occur not less than 10 days nor more than 30 days after the court grants an order for relief.

Appointment of a Trustee

A trustee must be appointed in a Chapter 7 proceeding. An interim trustee is appointed by the court once an order for relief is entered. A **permanent trustee** is elected at the first meeting of the creditors. Trustees, who are often lawyers or accountants, are entitled to receive reasonable compensation for their services and reimbursement for expenses. Once appointed, the trustee becomes the legal representative of the bankrupt debtor's estate. Generally, the trustee must take immediate possession of the debtor's property, investigate the debtor's financial affairs, sell or otherwise dispose of property of the estate, and distribute the proceeds of the estate.

permanent trustee
A legal representative of the bankruptcy debtor's estate, usually an accountant or lawyer, who is elected at the first meeting of the creditors.

Words pay no debts.

William Shakespeare
Troilus and Cressida, Act III

Proof of Claims

proof of claim
A document required to be filed by an unsecured creditor that states the amount of the creditor's claim against the debtor.

An unsecured creditor must file a **proof of claim** stating the amount of the creditor's claim against the debtor. The form for the statement is provided by the court. The proof of claim must be "timely filed." Generally, this means within six months of the first meeting of the creditors. Secured creditors are not required to file proof of claim. However, a secured creditor whose claim exceeds the value of the collateral may submit a proof of claim and become an unsecured claimant as to the difference.

Property of the Bankruptcy Estate

bankruptcy estate
An estate created upon the commencement of a Chapter 7 proceeding that includes all of the debtor's legal and equitable interests in real, personal, tangible, and intangible property, wherever located, that exist when the petition is filed, minus exempt property.

The **bankruptcy estate** (**the estate**) is created upon the commencement of a Chapter 7 proceeding. It includes all of the debtor's legal and equitable interests in real, personal, tangible, and intangible property, wherever located, that exist when the petition is filed. The debtor's separate and community property is included in the estate.

Property acquired after the petition is filed does not become part of the bankruptcy estate. The only exceptions are gifts, inheritances, life insurance proceeds, and property from divorce settlements that the debtor is entitled to receive within 180 days after the petition is filed. Earnings from property of the estate—such as rents, dividends, and interest payments—are property of the estate.

Exemptions

exempt property
Property that may be retained by a debtor pursuant to federal or state law; a debtor's property that does not become part of the bankruptcy estate.

The Bankruptcy Code is not designed to make the debtor a pauper, so certain property is exempt from the bankruptcy estate. The debtor may retain **exempt property**.

The Bankruptcy Code establishes the following federal exemptions:

1. Interest up to $17,425 in equity in property used a residence and burial plots (called the "homestead exemption")
2. Interest up to $2,775 in value in one motor vehicle
3. Interest up to $450 per item in household goods and furnishings, wearing apparel, appliances, books, animals, crops, or musical instruments, up to an aggregate value of $9,300 for all items
4. Interest in jewelry up to $1,150
5. Interest in any property the debtor chooses (including cash) up to $925, plus up to $8,725 of any unused portion of the $17,425 homestead exemption
6. Interest up to $1,750 in value in implements, tools, or professional books used in the debtor's trade
7. Any unmatured life insurance policy owned by the debtor
8. Professionally prescribed health aids
9. Many government benefits, regardless of value, including Social Security benefits, welfare benefits, unemployment compensation, veteran's benefits, disability benefits, and public assistance benefits
10. Certain rights to receive income, including alimony and support payments, certain pension benefits, profit sharing, and annuity payments
11. Interests in wrongful death benefits, life insurance proceeds, and personal injury awards (up to $17,425)

Creditor: One of a tribe of savages dwelling beyond the Financial Straits and dreaded for their desolating excursions.

Ambrose Bierce
The Devil's Dictionary (1911)

Business Brief
The dollar amounts for exemptions are adjusted for inflation every three years based on the Consumer Price Index. The amounts stated in this chapter are from April 1, 2001.

The federal Bankruptcy Code also permits states to enact their own exemptions. States that do so may (1) give debtors the option of choosing between federal and state exemptions or (2) require debtors to follow state law.[1] The exemptions available under the state law are often quite liberal. If the debtor's equity in property (above liens and mortgages) exceeds the exemption limits, the trustee may liquidate the property to realize the excess value for the bankruptcy estate.

> Neither a borrower nor a lender be: For loan oft loses both itself and friend. And borrowing dulls the edge of husbandry.
>
> William Shakespeare
> *Hamlet (1600)*

Consider This Example Assume that a debtor owns a home worth $100,000 that is subject to a $60,000 mortgage. The trustee may sell the home, pay off the mortgage, pay the debtor $17,425 (applying the federal exemption), and use the remaining proceeds ($22,575) for distribution to the debtor's creditors.

In the following case, the court found that an asset was exempt from the debtor's bankruptcy estate.

Case 24.2 Exempt Property

In re Witwer
163 B.R. 614, 1994 Bankr. Lexis 75 (1992)
United States Bankruptcy Court, Central District of California

Background and Facts

Dr. James J. Witwer is the sole stockholder, sole employee, and president of James J. Witwer, M.D., Inc., a California corporation under which he practices medicine. He is also the sole beneficiary of the corporation's retirement plan, which was established in 1970. On October 21, 1991, Witwer filed a voluntary petition for relief under Chapter 7 (liquidation). At the time, the value of the assets in his retirement plan was $1.8 million. California law exempted retirement plans from a debtor's bankruptcy estate. When Witwer claimed that his retirement plan was exempt from the bankruptcy estate, several creditors filed objections.

Issue

Is Witwer's retirement plan exempt from the bankruptcy estate?

In The Language of The Court

Wilson, Bankruptcy Judge The Debtor's Plan may be entirely exempt if the Plan was designed and used for retirement purposes. It cannot be said that this Debtor attempted to hide otherwise ineligible assets from bankruptcy administration nor can it be said that this Debtor's transactions were not in furtherance of legitimate long-term retirement purposes. As the Debtor's Plan was designed and used for retirement purposes, the Plan may be entirely exempt.

Regardless of the inequities that may result from a debtor's use of the California exemption scheme, this Court is constrained by the plain meaning of the statutes in the context of this case.

Allowing the Debtor to retain over $1.8 million in retirement benefits in bankruptcy while being discharged from debts legitimately owed to creditors seems fundamentally unfair. The remedy is for the state legislature to promote creditor objectives rather than for courts to restrict the meaning of an unambiguous state exemption statute.

Decision and Remedy

The court concluded that under the Bankruptcy Code, the size of a debtor's bankruptcy estate is "subject to the vagaries of state exemption law." The bankruptcy court held that Witwer's retirement plan was fully exempt from his bankruptcy estate.

Case Questions

Critical Legal Thinking Do you think bankruptcy law was intended to reach the result in this case?

Business Ethics Was it ethical for the debtor to declare bankruptcy and wipe out his unsecured creditors while retaining $1.8 million in his retirement account?

Contemporary Business Should businesspeople establish and fund retirement programs?

Contemporary Business Environment

Homestead Exemptions: More Than Just a Log Cabin

When the term *homestead* is used, many people think of the Wild West, wide-open prairies, and a pioneer's log cabin built with sweat and tears. Long ago, many states enacted laws that protected a debtor's homestead from greedy creditors.

Today, a debtor's homestead may be a condo in a luxury apartment building or a multimillion-dollar split-level home. Depending upon state law, at least a portion of the equity in a debtor's homestead may still be protected from creditors if the owner declares bankruptcy. For example, New York exempts

Contemporary Business Environment
(continued)

$20,000 of equity in a married couple's home from bankruptcy estate ($10,000 for a single debtor). California exempts $55,000 for a married couple and $35,000 for a single debtor. These exemptions look generous compared to those of most states except Florida and Texas.

The Florida constitution and statutes give a homestead exemption from bankruptcy without dollar limit. The homestead is 160 acres outside a municipality and one-half acre inside a municipality.

The Texas homestead exemption is even bigger. Texas has an urban homestead of one acre and a rural homestead of up to 200 acres, without any dollar limit.

Florida and Texas are known as "debtor's havens" because of their generous homestead exemptions from bankruptcy. In fact, relocating to these states has become attractive to people in financial difficulty, who take what money they have and place it beyond the reach of their creditors in homesteads in these states before declaring bankruptcy. How long a person must reside in the state before declaring bankruptcy is an open question. It is just one factor in deciding whether the debtor has engaged in a bankruptcy fraud that makes the debtor's debts nondischargeable. So far, few bankruptcies have been undone under such charges.

Proponents of homestead exemptions argue that they are needed to provide a debtor with a fresh start and a roof over his or her head. Critics argue that debtors are using homestead exemptions to run roughshod over creditors. ■

Statutory Distributions to Unsecured Creditors

The Bankruptcy Code stipulates that unsecured claims are to be satisfied out of the bankruptcy estate in the order of their statutory priority. The statutory priority of an unsecured claim is:

1. Fees and expenses of administrating the estate, including court costs, trustee fees, attorneys' fees, appraisal fees, and other costs of administration.
2. In an involuntary bankruptcy, secured claims of "gap" creditors who sold goods or services on credit to the debtor in the ordinary course of the debtor's business between the date of the filing of the petition and the date of the appointment of the trustee or issuance of the order for relief (whichever occurred first).
3. Unsecured claims for wages, salary, or commissions earned by the debtor's employees within 90 days immediately preceding the filing of the petition, up to $4,650 per employee; any claim exceeding $4,650 is treated as a claim of a general unsecured creditor (see item 9).
4. Unsecured claims for contributions to employee benefits plans based on services performed within 180 days immediately preceding the filing of the petition, up to $4,650 per employee.
5. Farm producers and fishermen against debtors who operate grain storage facilities or fish produce storage or processing facilities, up to $4,650 per claim.
6. Unsecured claims for cash deposited by a consumer with the debtor prior to the filing of the petition in connection with either the purchase, lease, or rental of property or the purchase of services that were not delivered or provided by the debtor, up to $2,100 per claim; any claim exceeding $2,100 is treated as a claim of a general unsecured creditor (see item 9).
7. Debts owed for child support, paternity, alimony, and spousal support.
8. Certain tax obligations owed by the debtor to federal, state, and local governmental units.
9. Claims of general unsecured creditors.

Business Brief

The Bankruptcy Code stipulates that unsecured claims are to be satisfied out of the bankruptcy estate in the order of their statutory priority, as established by the code.

Each class must be paid in full before any lower class is paid anything. If a class cannot be paid in full, the claims of that class are paid pro rata (proportionately). If there is any balance remaining after the allowed claims of the creditors are satisfied, it is returned to the debtor.

Nondischargeable Debts

The following debts are not dischargeable in a Chapter 7 proceeding:

- Claims for taxes accrued within three years prior to the filing of the petition in bankruptcy.
- Certain fines and penalties payable to federal, state, and local governmental units.
- Claims based on the debtor's liability for causing willful or malicious injury to a person or property.
- Claims arising from fraud, larceny, or embezzlement by the debtor while acting in a fiduciary capacity.
- Alimony, maintenance, and child support.
- Unscheduled claims.
- Claims based on the consumer-debtor's purchase of luxury goods of more than $1,150 from a single creditor within 60 days of the order for relief.
- Cash advances in excess of $1,150 obtained by a consumer-debtor by use of a revolving line of credit or credit cards within 60 days of the order for relief.
- Judgments and consent decrees against the debtor for liability incurred as a result of the debtor's operation of a motor vehicle while legally intoxicated.
- Any state or federal court judgment or decree, administrative order, or settlement arising from a violation of federal or state securities laws or common law fraud in connection with the purchase or sale of a security.

Business Brief
Not all debts are dischargeable in bankruptcy.

Creditors who have nondischargeable claims against the debtor may participate in the distribution of the bankruptcy estate. The nondischarged balance may be pursued by the creditor against the debtor after bankruptcy. In the following case, the U.S. Supreme Court ruled that a debt was dischargeable in bankruptcy.

Discharge

After property is distributed to satisfy the allowed claims in a Chapter 7 bankruptcy case, the remaining unpaid claims are **discharged** (i.e., the debtor is no longer legally responsible for them). Only individuals may be granted discharges. Discharge is not available to partnerships and corporations. These entities must liquidate under state law before or upon completion of the Chapter 7 proceeding. A debtor can be granted a discharge in a Chapter 7 proceeding only once every six years.

discharge
The termination of the legal duty of a debtor to pay debts that remain unpaid upon the completion of a bankruptcy proceeding.

Consider This Example Maryjane files for Chapter 7 bankruptcy. At the time of filing, she has many unsecured creditors. Nordstom department store is one of them. She owes Nordstrom $3,000. The bankruptcy estate has only enough assets to pay unsecured creditors 10 cents on the dollar. Nordstrom receives $300; the remaining $2,700 is discharged. Nordstrom's cannot thereafter collect this money and will write it off as a bad debt.

In the following case, the U.S. Supreme Court ruled that a debt was dischargeable in bankruptcy. A notice of a Chapter 7 bankruptcy case is shown in Exhibit 24.6.

Beggars can never be bankrupt.

Thomas Fuller
Gnomologia (1732)

Case 24.3 Dischargeable Debt in Bankruptcy

U.S. SUPREME COURT CASE

Kawaauhau v. Geiger

523 U.S. 57, 118 S.Ct. 974, 1998 U.S. Lexis 1595 (1998)

Supreme Court of the United States

Background and Facts

Margaret Kawaauhau sought treatment from Dr. Paul Geiger for a foot injury. Geiger examined Kawaauhau and admitted her to the hospital to attend to the risks of infection. Although Geiger knew that intravenous penicillin would have been the more effective treatment, he prescribed oral penicillin, explaining that he thought that his patient wished to minimize the cost of her treatment. Geiger then departed on a business trip, leaving Kawaauhau in the care of other physicians. When Geiger returned, he discontinued all antibiotics because he believed that the infection had subsided. Kawaauhau's condition deteriorated over the next few days, requiring the amputation of her right leg below the knee. Kawaauhau and her husband sued Geiger for medical malpractice. The jury found Geiger liable and awarded the Kawaauhaus $355,000 in damages. Geiger, who carried no malpractice insurance, filed for bankruptcy in an attempt to discharge the judgment. The bankruptcy court denied discharge, and the district court agreed. The court of appeals reversed and allowed discharge, and the Kawaauhaus appealed to the U.S. Supreme Court.

Supreme Court Issue

Is a debt arising from a medical malpractice judgment that is attributable to negligence or reckless conduct dischargeable in bankruptcy?

In The Language of The U.S. Supreme Court

Ginsburg, Justice Section 523(a)(6) of the Bankruptcy Code provides that a debt "for willful and malicious injury by the debtor to another" is not dischargeable. The question before us is whether a debt arising from a medical malpractice judgment, attributable to negligent or reckless conduct, falls within this statutory exception. We hold that it does not and that the debt is dischargeable. Had Congress meant to exempt debts resulting from unintentionally inflicted injuries, it might have selected an additional word or words, i.e., "reckless" or "negligent," to modify "injury."

The Kawaauhaus maintain that, as a policy matter, malpractice judgments should be excepted from discharge, at least when the debtor acted recklessly or carried no malpractice insurance. Congress, of course, may so decide. But unless and until Congress makes such a decision, we must follow the current direction § 523(a)(6) provides.

Decision and Remedy

The U.S. Supreme Court ruled that a medical malpractice judgment based on negligent or reckless conduct—and not intentional conduct—is dischargeable in bankruptcy. Affirmed.

Case Questions

Critical Legal Thinking What public policy is promoted by denying discharge for "willful" injurious conduct? Do you think Geiger's conduct was willful?

Business Ethics Was it ethical for Geiger to avoid liability to the Kawaauhaus by declaring bankruptcy?

Contemporary Business What purpose is served by allowing individuals and businesses to declare bankruptcy? What are the business implications of bankruptcy laws?

Contemporary Business Environment

Discharge of Student Loans

In the past, many students who borrowed a lot of money in student loans sought to avoid paying back their loans by filing a voluntary petition for bankruptcy immediately on leaving college. Section 523(a)(8) of the Bankruptcy Code was enacted to prevent this practice. For any bankruptcy case commenced after October 7, 1998, Section 523(a)(8)(A) mandates that student loans can only be discharged in bankruptcy if nondischarge would cause an "undue hardship" to the debtor and his or her dependents [Higher Education Amendments of 1998, P.L. 105-244]. *Undue hardship* is construed very strictly and would include not being able to pay for food or shelter for the debtor or the debtor's family.

Cosigners (e.g., parents who guarantee their child's student loan) must also meet the heightened undue hardship test to discharge their obligation. ■

Exhibit 24.6

Notice of Chapter 7 Bankruptcy Case

FORM B9B (Chapter 7) (1/98) Case Number: **LA 01-22024-BB**

UNITED STATES BANKRUPTCY COURT Central District of California

Notice of Chapter 7 Bankruptcy Case, Meeting of Creditors & Deadlines
Corporation/Partnership - No Asset Case

A chapter 7 bankruptcy case concerning the debtor(s) listed below was filed on April 18, 2003.

You may be a creditor of the debtor. **This notice lists important deadlines.** You may want to consult an attorney to protect your rights. All documents filed in the case may be inspected at the bankruptcy clerk's office at the **U.S. Bankruptcy Court, United States Federal Building, 300 North Los Angeles Street, Los Angeles, CA 90012.**

NOTE: The staff of the bankruptcy clerk's office cannot give legal advice.

See Reverse Side For Important Explanations

Debtor(s) (name(s) address)
MARK'S C P A REVIEW COURSE INC
DBA MARK'S NEW C P A REVIEW COURSE

3764 BENEDICT CANYON LANE SHERMAN OAKS, CA 91423

Case Number: LA 01-22024-BB	Taxpayer ID Nos.: 95-4565630
Attorney for Debtor(s) (name, address, telephone) KEITH C OWENS DANNING GILL DIAMOND & KOLLITZ 2029 CENTURY PARK EAST, THIRD FLOOR LOS ANGELES, CA 90067-2904 Telephone number: (310) 277-0077	Bankruptcy Trustee (name, address, telephone) R TODD NEILSON NEILSON, ELGGREN LLP 10100 SANTA MONICA BLVD #410 LOS ANGELES, CA 90067 Telephone number: (310) 282-9911

Meeting of Creditors

Date: **May 23, 2003** Time: **1:30 P.M.**

Location **221 N. Figueroa St., Ste. 101, Los Angeles, CA 90012**

Creditors May Not Take Certain Actions

The filing of the bankruptcy case automatically stays certain collection and other actions against the debtor and the debtor's property. If you attempt to collect a debt or take other action in violation of the Bankruptcy Code, you may be penalized.

Please Do Not File A Proof of Claim Unless You Receive a Notice To Do So

Address of the Bankruptcy Clerk's Office:	**For the Court:**
U.S. Bankruptcy Court 255 East Temple Street Los Angeles, CA 90012 Telephone number: (213) 894-3118	Clerk of the Bankruptcy Court: Jon D. Ceretto
Hours Open: 9:00 A.M. to 4:00 P.M.	Date: April 23, 2003

Chapter 11 Reorganization Bankruptcy

Chapter 11 reorganization bankruptcy

A bankruptcy method that allows reorganization of the debtor's financial affairs under the supervision of the bankruptcy court.

Chapter 11 of the Bankruptcy Code provides a method for reorganizing the debtor's financial affairs under the supervision of the bankruptcy court.[2] Its goal is to reorganize the debtor with a new capital structure so that it will emerge from bankruptcy as a viable concern. This option, which is referred to as **reorganization bankruptcy**, is often in the best interests of the debtor and its creditors.

Reorganization Proceeding

Business Brief

Chapter 11 is used primarily by businesses to reorganize their finances under the protection of the bankruptcy court. The debtor usually emerges from bankruptcy a "leaner" business, having restructured and discharged some of its debts.

Chapter 11 is available to individuals, partnerships, corporations, nonincorporated associations, and railroads. It is not available to banks, savings and loan associations, credit unions, insurance companies, stockbrokers, or commodities brokers. The majority of Chapter 11 proceedings are filed by corporations. A Chapter 11 petition my be filed voluntarily by the debtor or involuntarily by its creditors.

Debtor-in-Possession

debtor-in-possession

A debtor who is left in place to operate a business during a reorganization proceeding.

In most Chapter 11 cases, the debtor is left in place to operate the business during the reorganization proceeding. In such cases, the debtor is called a **debtor-in-possession**. The court may appoint a trustee to operate the debtor's business only upon a showing of cause, such as fraud, dishonesty, or gross mismanagement by the debtor or its management. However, even if a trustee is not appointed, the court may appoint an examiner to investigate the debtor's financial affairs.

Creditors' Committees

creditors' committee

A committee composed of the creditors holding the seven largest unsecured claims. Committees represent the interests of their class, in the negotiation of a plan of reorganization.

After an order for relief is granted, the court will appoint a **creditors' committee** composed of representatives of the class of unsecured claims. Generally, the creditors holding the seven largest claims are appointed to the committee. The court may also appoint a committee of secured creditors and a committee of equity holders. Committee members owe a fiduciary duty to represent the interests of the class. Committees may appear at bankruptcy court hearings, participate in the negotiation of a plan of reorganization, assert objections to proposed plans, and the like.

Entrepreneur and the Law

Small Business Bankruptcy

Large firms, such as Macy's, Continental Airlines, and Dow Corning, have reorganized under Chapter 11 of the Bankruptcy Code. These large firms have resources to hire lawyers, investment bankers, and other professionals to assist them in the time-consuming and expensive Chapter 11 reorganization process. Smaller firms often do not have the resources or the luxury of the time necessary to use a Chapter 11 proceeding, however.

To address this problem, Congress enacted the **Bankruptcy Reform Act of 1994**, which amended Chapter 11. **Section 217** of this act permits a business with total debts of less than $2 million to elect a "fast-track" for processing its Chapter 11 case. This procedure makes the creditors' committee optional and sets up deadlines aimed at concluding the Chapter 11 case within 160 days of the bankruptcy filing. Section 217 small business bankruptcy provides an efficient and cost-saving method for a smaller firm to seek bankruptcy protection and reorganize as a going concern using Chapter 11 of the Bankruptcy Code. ■

Automatic Stay

The filing of a voluntary or involuntary petition automatically stays (i.e., suspends) certain action by creditors against the debtor or the debtor's property.[3] This is called an **automatic stay**. The stay, which applies to collection efforts of both secured and unsecured creditors, is designed to prevent a scramble for the debtor's assets in a variety of court proceedings. The following creditor actions are stayed:

1. Instituting or maintaining legal actions to collect prepetition debts
2. Enforcing judgments obtained against the debtor
3. Obtaining, perfecting, or enforcing liens against property of the debtor
4. Attempting to set off debts owed by the creditor to the debtor against the creditor's claims in bankruptcy
5. Nonjudicial collection efforts, such as self-help activities (e.g., repossession of a car)

automatic stay

The result of the filing of a voluntary or involuntary petition; the suspension of certain actions by creditors against the debtor or the debtor's property.

Debt: A rope to your foot, cocklebars in your hair, and a clothespin on your tongue.

Frank McKinney Hubbard
The Roycraft Dictionary (1923)

Executory Contracts

Under the Bankruptcy Code, the debtor-in-possession (or trustee) is given the authority to assume or reject **executory contracts** (i.e., contracts that are not fully performed by both sides). In general, unfavorably executory contracts will be rejected, and favorable executory contracts will be assumed. For example, a debtor-in-possession may reject an unfavorable lease. Court approval is necessary to reject an executory contract.

executory contract

A contract that has not been fully performed. With court approval, executory contracts may be rejected by a debtor in bankruptcy.

Entrepreneur and the Law

Planet Hollywood Plunges to Earth

When Planet Hollywood International, Inc., opened its first Planet Hollywood restaurant in Beverly Hills, it looked like the stars would shine on the company. Entrepreneur-celebrities such as Bruce Willis, Demi Moore, Sylvester Stallone, and Arnold Schwarzennegger—who combined owned about 20 percent of the company's stock—showed up along with a virtual "who's who" list of Hollywood for the grand opening. Other major shareholders of Planet Hollywood were Saudi Arabian Prince Alwaleed bin Talal, Singapore billionaire Ong Beng Seng, and cofounder and CEO Robert Earl. Planet Hollywood, a theme restaurant, featured movie memorabilia hanging from the walls and ceiling.

Planet Hollywood enjoyed great early success as a leader in the "eatertainment" industry and went on an expansion spree, opening 48 company-owned restaurants. Planet Hollywood also franchised an additional 32 restaurants worldwide, including outlets in Hong Kong, Rome, and Moscow. The company gave movie stars stock and stock options in exchange for showing up at Planet Hollywood openings. In 1996, the company went public—that is, sold stock to public shareholders—at $18 per share. The price climbed to $32 per share the first day of trading, its highest price ever.

Eventually, Planet Hollywood's star crashed, however. Other theme restaurants opened, causing an increase in competition in this niche market. Planet Hollywood restaurants were successful in drawing in first-timers to its outlets but had trouble luring them back for repeat business. And high prices and a perception of mediocre food stalled sales as well. Profits plunged until the company was bleeding with red ink and could no longer pay interest payments on its crushing debt. Planet Hollywood's share price fell until August 18, 1999, when it reached $.75 per share. On that date the company publicly announced it would seek protection under Chapter 11 of the Bankruptcy Code to financially reorganize itself.

After negotiating with its creditors, Planet Hollywood filed a prepackaged Chapter 11 bankruptcy filing. In a *prepackaged filing*, the creditors and investors have already negotiated and agreed on the terms of the reorganization when the bankruptcy petition is filed. Planet Hollywood's agreed-upon restructuring plan called for the following:

- There was a dramatic 75 percent reduction of the number of restaurants. The company continues to operate its most successful outlets, such as those in Las Vegas and at Disney World in Orlando, but it closed many other outlets. The company used the executory contract provision of the Bankruptcy Code to get out of high-cost leases and other money-losing locations.
- The debt-holders of $250 million in subordinated notes agreed to cancel their debt and the back interest owed them by Planet Hollywood in exchange for $47.5 million in cash, $60 million of new notes, and new common stock representing 30 percent of the equity in the new Planet Hollywood.

Entrepreneur and the Law

(continued)

- Equity holders, including the celebrities and public shareholders alike, were wiped out—that is, their shares were worth nothing in the reorganization. They received warrants to purchase shares in Planet Hollywood in the future at a predetermined price that would not be reached unless Planet Hollywood was successful as a reorganized going concern.
- An investor group led by Prince Alwaleed bin Talal, Ong Beng Seng, and Robert Earl's trust for his children invested $30 million in exchange for 70 percent equity ownership in the new reorganized Planet Hollywood.

The new Planet Hollywood revised its menu and added new merchandise (25 percent of its revenue comes from the sale of t-shirts), with the hope of revitalizing its lost luster. Only time will tell whether Planet Hollywood has staying power or will become a vanishing star. ■

Plan of Reorganization

plan of reorganization
A plan that sets forth a proposed new capital structure for the debtor to have when it emerges from reorganization bankruptcy. The debtor has the exclusive right to file the first plan of reorganization; any part of interest may file a plan thereafter.

A debtor in a Chapter 11 case has the exclusive right to file a **plan of reorganization** with the bankruptcy court within the first 120 days after the date of the order for relief. The plan for reorganization sets forth the debtor's proposed new capital structure. In a Chapter 11 proceeding, creditors have *claims*, and equity holders have *interests*. The plan must designate the different classes of claims and interests. The reorganization plan may propose altering the rights of creditors and equity holders. For example, it might require the reduction of claims and interests, the conversion of unsecured creditors to equity holders, the sale of assets, or the like.

The debtor must supply the creditors and equity holders with a *disclosure statement* that contains adequate information about the proposed plan of reorganization. The court must approve the disclosure statement before it is distributed.

Contemporary Business Environment

Kmart Seeks "Blue Light Special" Bankruptcy

The Kmart Corporation was founded in 1899 and became one of the most successful retailers in America. The company offered goods for sale at low prices and was famous for its spontaneous "Blue Light Special" sales offered to consumers while they were in Kmart stores. Kmart's business model consisted of building stores bigger than its competitors and offering for sale goods that it purchased at volume discounts from vendors. By 2000, Kmart had more than 2,100 stores nationwide.

Kmart's strategy worked for most of the twentieth century, until more formidable competition appeared—Wal-Mart and Target stores. Wal-Mart's larger warehouse stores and lower prices stole customers from Kmart. And Target offered more trendy brand names than Kmart. Kmart fought back but eventually lost the battle to these competitors. Kmart's shelves became emptier as many vendors refused to deliver goods to Kmart unless they were paid in cash.

In 2002, Kmart threw in a Martha Stewart towel and filed for Chapter 11 bankruptcy. It was the largest bankruptcy filed by a retailer in America. Once under the protection of the federal bankruptcy laws, Kmart used the executory contract rule, shed more than 300 leases on its worst-performing stores, and closed these stores. Kmart also used its bankruptcy reorganization to discharge billions of dollars of unpaid unsecured credit owed to creditors.

Kmart is a good example of how a financially troubled company can use Chapter 11 reorganization bankruptcy to rid itself of problem debts and obligations and have a "fresh start." Kmart emerged from bankruptcy with a leaner balance sheet and the ability to make a profit again. Once out of bankruptcy, creditors and vendors again sold goods to Kmart. Kmart can again offer its "Blue Light Specials" to customers. ■

Confirmation of a Plan of Reorganization

Classes of creditors and interests must be given the opportunity to vote to accept or reject a plan of reorganization before the court considers its **confirmation**. Under the *acceptance method*, the court must confirm the plan of reorganization. To be confirmed, the plan must be (1) in the *best interests* of each class of claims and interests and (2) *feasible*. If a dissenting class of claims is *impaired*, the plan of reorganization cannot be confirmed using the acceptance method. However, the court can force an impaired class to participate in a plan of reorganization under the **cram down method**.

Upon confirmation of a plan of reorganization, the debtor is granted a discharge of all claims not included in the plan. The plan is binding on all parties after it is confirmed. The U.S. Supreme Court examined the cram down method in the following case.

confirmation
The bankruptcy court's approval of a plan of reorganization.

Business Brief
The term *cram down* derives from the notion that the plan of reorganization is being "crammed down the throats" of the impaired dissenting class.

Case 24.4
Cram Down Method

U.S. SUPREME COURT CASE

Bank of America National Trust and Savings Association v. 203 North LaSalle Street Partnership

526 U.S. 434, 119 S.Ct. 1411, 1999 U.S. Lexis 3003 (1999)
Supreme Court of the United States

Background and Facts

203 North LaSalle Street Partnership (Partnership) is an Illinois real estate limited partnership that owns 15 floors of an office building in downtown Chicago. The Partnership borrowed $93 million from Bank of America National Trust and Savings Association (Bank), giving the bank a mortgage on the real estate to secure the loan. In January 1995, the Partnership defaulted on the loan and filed for Chapter 11 bankruptcy. The Partnership filed a plan of reorganization proposing that:

1. The Bank retain a secured claim of $54.5 million on the building, which was the value of the building at the time.
2. The Bank's unsecured deficiency claim of $38.5 million would be discharged.
3. The remaining unsecured trade creditors would be paid their $90,000 of claims in full.
4. The old equity holders of the Partnership would be given the exclusive right to invest $6,125,000 in new capital in the reorganized entity.

The Bank objected to the plan of reorganization, so the Partnership sought to have the plan "crammed down" on the Bank. The bankruptcy court confirmed the plan of reorganization using the cram down method, and both the district court and the court of appeals affirmed. The Bank appealed to the U.S. Supreme Court.

Supreme Court Issue

Can a plan of reorganization be crammed down over the objection of a creditor if the old equity holders are given the exclusive authority to invest equity capital in the reorganized debtor?

In The Language of The U.S. Supreme Court

Souter, Justice The absolute priority rules was the basis for the Bank's position that the plan could not be confirmed as a cramdown. As the Bank read the rule, the plan was open to objection simply because certain old equity holders in the Partnership would receive property even though the Bank's unsecured deficiency claim would not be paid in full.

Given that the opportunity is property of some value, the question arises why old equity alone should obtain it. If the price to be paid for the equity interest is the best obtainable, old equity does not need the protection of exclusiveness; if it is not the best, there is no apparent reason for giving old equity a bargain. There is no reason, that is unless the very purpose of the whole transaction is, at least in part, to do old equity a favor.

Decision and Remedy

The U.S. Supreme Court held that the exclusive right of the old equity holders to invest new equity capital in the reorganized debtor violates federal bankruptcy law. The Supreme Court reversed the lower court's order approving the debtor's plan of reorganization and remanded the case for further proceedings.

Case Questions

Critical Legal Thinking What does the absolute priority rule provide? Explain.

Business Ethics Did the old equity holders act ethically in this case? Why do you think they wanted the exclusive right to be equity investors in the new reorganized entity?

Contemporary Business How much was the Bank's original loan? How much was the Bank's secured interest worth at the time of bankruptcy? What happens to the Bank's deficiency amount in Chapter 11 bankruptcy?

Business Ethics

Sarbanes-Oxley Act Imposes Criminal Penalties for Bankruptcy Fraud

Many large companies, such as Enron, Tyco, and Worldcom, were driven into bankruptcy because of fraudulent conduct by their management, often assisted by the companies' accountants. When these companies went bankrupt, their shareholders lost billions of dollars of investments, their creditors were not paid what they were owed, and the companies' pensioners lost their pensions if they were invested in the companies' stock. To cover up their fraud, many violators hid or destroyed documents or otherwise covered up their fraudulent conduct.

When Congress enacted the Sarbanes-Oxley Act of 2002 to revise the corporate governance rules in this country, Congress included Section 802 in the act to address the issue of hiding fraud that led to bankruptcies. Section 802 makes it a crime for anyone to knowingly alter, destroy, mutilate, conceal, cover up, falsify, or make a false entry in any record, document, or tangible object with the intent to impede, obstruct, or influence the investigation or proper administration of any matter in any bankruptcy case, or in relation to or in contemplation of a bankruptcy filing. A violation is punishable by a fine or imprisonment for not more than 20 years, or both.

1. Will Section 802 reduce the fraudulent destruction of documents of companies in or heading into bankruptcy? ■

Chapter 13 Consumer Debt Adjustment

Chapter 13 consumer debt adjustment
A rehabilitation form of bankruptcy that permits the courts to supervise the debtor's plan for the payment of unpaid debts by installments.

Chapter 13, which is called a **consumer debt adjustment**, is a rehabilitation form of bankruptcy for natural persons. Chapter 13 permits the courts to supervise the debtor's plan for the payment of unpaid debts by installments.

The debtor has several advantages under Chapter 13. They include avoidance of the stigma of Chapter 7 liquidation, retention of more property than is exempt under Chapter 7, and less expense and less complication than a Chapter 7 proceeding. The creditors have advantages, too. They may recover a greater percentage of the debts owed them than they would under a Chapter 7 proceeding.

Filing the Petition

It is the policy of the law that the debtor be just before he be generous.

Finch, J.
Hearn 45 St. Corp. v. Jano (1940)

A Chapter 13 proceeding can be initiated only by the voluntary filing of a petition by the debtor. The debtor must allege that he or she is (1) insolvent or (2) unable to pay his or her dents when they become due. The petition must state that the debtor desires to effect an extension or a composition of debts, or both. An *extension* provides for a longer period of time for the debtor to pay his debts. A *composition* provides for a reduction of debts.

Only individuals (including sole proprietors) with regular income who owe individually (or with their spouse) noncontingent, liquidated, unsecured debts of less than $250,000 and secured debts of less than $750,000 may file such a petition. Most Chapter 13 petitions are filed by homeowners who want to protect any nonexempt equity in their residences.

The Plan of Payment

Business Brief
In a Chapter 13 bankruptcy, the debtor must file a proposed *plan of payment* on how the debts are to be rescheduled.

The debtor's *plan of payment* must be filed within 15 days of filing the petition. The debtor must file information about his or her finances, including a budget of estimated income and expenses during the period of the plan. The plan period cannot exceed three years unless the court approves a longer period (of up to five years). During the plan period, the debtor retains possession of his or her property, may acquire new property and incur debts, and so on.

The debtor must begin making the planned installment payments to the trustee within 30 days after the plan is filed. The trustee is responsible for remitting these payments to the creditors.

Confirmation of the Plan

The plan of payment may modify the rights of unsecured creditors and some secured creditors. Any objections they have may be voiced at the confirmation hearing held by the court. The plan must (1) be proposed in good faith, (2) pass the feasibility test (i.e., the debtor must be able to make the proposed payments), and (3) be in the best interests of the creditors (i.e., the present value of the payments must equal or exceed the amount that the creditors would receive in a Chapter 7 liquidation proceeding).

Debt rolls a man over and over, binding him hand and foot, and letting him hang upon the fatal mesh until the long-legged interest devours him.

Henry Ward Beecher
Proverbs from Plymouth Pulpit (1887)

Entrepreneur and the Law

Chapter 12 Family Farmer Bankruptcy

In the 1980s, farms across the country experienced financial difficulty as farm prices and real estate values fell. Many farmers who found it difficult to meet their financial obligations and faced bankruptcy lobbied Congress for help. In 1986, Congress responded and added **Chapter 12** to the Bankruptcy Code. Chapter 12 gives "family farmers"—defined as farmers whose total debt does not exceed $1.5 million and is at least 80 percent farm related—a special form of bankruptcy protection.

Chapter 12 is a reorganization provision that allows family farmers to reorganize financially. Upon filing, an automatic stay goes into place against creditors' actions against the family farmer. The farmer-debtor must file a plan of reorganization within 90 days of the order for relief. Creditors cannot vote on the plan of reorganization.

The major provision of Chapter 12 allows family farmers to have mortgage loans rewritten to the fair market value of the property in cases in which the value of the farm land has decreased below the value of the loan. For example, assume that a farm is worth $1,000,000 at the time a family farmer borrows $800,000 from Rural Bank, which takes back a mortgage on the farm for this amount. After several years, the farmer suffers financial difficulty and files Chapter 12 bankruptcy. At the time of the bankruptcy filing, the farm land is worth only $500,000. Under Chapter 12, the mortgage is reduced to $500,000 under the plan of reorganization.

Chapter 12 allows family farmers to file for a special type of reorganization bankruptcy that gives them added protection not available under Chapter 11 of the Bankruptcy Code. ■

International Law

Reorganization Under British Bankruptcy Law

Many of our country's forefathers were debtors fleeing the harsh laws of Britain and European countries, where debtors were often sent to debtors' prisons or were required to work off the debt owed to creditors. When this country was founded, the right to declare bankruptcy was considered just as important as the right to free speech, and both rights were included in the U.S. Constitution.

Even today, U.S. bankruptcy law treats debtors more leniently than the bankruptcy laws of other countries. Consider the case of bankruptcy reorganization laws in Britain as compared to those of the United States.

In 1987, Britain enacted a new bankruptcy law for handling the reorganization of bankrupt companies. The law banishes lawyers from the reorganization process and puts the process in the hands of specially licensed accountants. When a firm files for reorganization bankruptcy in Britain, an administrative order is issued. The order permits the creditors of the troubled company to appoint a team of bankruptcy accountants to handle the company's reorganization.

British law assumes that the company's misfortune is not a result of bad luck but is based on mismanagement by the company's officers and directors. Consequently, the bankruptcy accountants are empowered to remove the firm's existing management and take over control of its operations. The accountants then orchestrate the reorganization and sale of the company's assets.

Many U.S. bankruptcy lawyers allege that British bankruptcy law tramples too hard on debtor's rights. They argue that British law thwarts the fresh start theory underlying American bankruptcy law. Proponents of the British system argue that it is faster, cheaper, and more efficient than a bankruptcy reorganization under Chapter 11 of the U.S. Bankruptcy Code. They assert that the British system does not coddle debtors and make lawyers rich, as the U.S. bankruptcy system does. ■

Chapter Summary

Negotiable Instruments, p. 709

Types of Negotiable Instruments

There are four types of negotiable instruments. They are:

1. ***Draft.*** An order to pay. A three-party instrument.
2. ***Check.*** An order to pay. A three-party instrument.
3. ***Promissory note.*** A promise to pay. A two-party instrument.
4. ***Certificate of deposit (CD).*** A promise to pay. A two-party instrument.

Drafts

An unconditional written order by one party (the *drawer*) that orders a second party (the *drawee*) to pay money to a third party (the *payee*). The drawee must owe money to the drawer for the drawer to issue a draft ordering the money to be paid to the payee.

1. ***Drawer.*** The party who writes the order for a draft.
2. ***Drawee.*** The party who must pay the money stated in a draft. The drawee is also called the *acceptor*.
3. ***Types of drafts.***
   a. *Time draft.* A draft payable at a designated future date.
   b. *Sight draft.* A draft payable on sight. Also called a *demand draft*.

Checks

A form of draft drawn on a financial institution (the *drawee*) and payable on demand. The checking account holder (the *drawer*) orders the financial institution (the *drawee*) to pay money to a third party (the *payee*).

1. ***Drawer.*** The checking account holder and writer of the check.
2. ***Drawee.*** The financial institution where the drawer has his or her checking account and that pays the money to the payee.
3. ***Payee.*** The party to whom the check is written.
4. ***Special checks:***
   a. *Certified checks.* A type of check for which a bank agrees in advance (*certifies*) to accept and pay the check when it is presented for payment. Is used when the issuer or holder takes an ordinary check to the bank and the bank writes "certified" on the check. The bank sets aside funds from the issuer's account to pay the check when it is presented for payment.
   b. *Cashier's checks.* A check issued by a bank for which a person pays the bank the amount of the check and a fee, and the bank guarantees that it will pay the check when it is presented for payment. The person purchasing a cashier's check does not have to have a checking account at the bank.
   c. *Traveler's checks.* A form of check sold by banks and other issuers. The purchaser of the traveler's checks signs them at the time of purchase. When the checks are used to purchase goods or services, the purchaser again signs the check and fills in the payee's name. Purchasers of traveler's checks do not have to have an account at the issuing bank or institution.

Promissory Notes

An unconditional written promise by one party (the *maker*) to pay money to another party (the *payee*). Promissory notes are also called *notes*.

1. ***Maker.*** The party who makes the promise to pay (the borrower).
2. ***Payee.*** The party to whom the promise to pay is made (the lender).

3. ***Types of promissory notes:***
   a. *Time note.* A note payable at a specified time.
   b. *Demand note.* A note payable on demand.
   c. *Installment note.* A note paid in more than one installment.
   d. *Mortgage note.* A note secured by real estate.
   e. *Collateral note.* A note secured by personal property.

Certificates of Deposit

A special form of note that is created when a depositor (the *payee*) deposits money at a financial institution (the *maker*) in exchange for the institution's promise to pay back the amount of the deposit plus an agreed-upon rate of interest upon the expiration of a set time period agreed upon by the parties.

1. ***Maker.*** The financial institution (the borrower).
2. ***Payee.*** The depositor (the lender).
3. ***Types of CDs:***
   a. *Small CD.* A CD under $100,000.
   b. *Jumbo CD.* A CD of $100,000 or more.

Endorsements

An *endorsement* is the signature of the signer (other than as a maker, a drawer, or an acceptor) that is placed on an instrument to negotiate it to another person (e.g., a holder signing the back of a check). An endorsement may be a signature alone (creating bearer paper), be accompanied by the name of a specific payee (creating order paper), or be accompanied by other words (e.g., "without recourse").

1. ***Endorser.*** The person who endorses a negotiable instrument.
2. ***Endorsee.*** The person to whom a negotiable instrument is endorsed.
3. ***Allonge.*** Endorsements are usually placed on the reverse side of the negotiable instrument. If there is no room on the instrument, the endorsement may be placed on a separate sheet of paper called an *allonge*. The allonge must be firmly affixed to the instrument.

Credit, p. 716

Unsecured Credit

Credit that does not require any security (collateral) to protect the payment of the loan.

1. ***Recovery of unpaid loan.*** If the debtor does not pay the loan, the creditor may bring a legal action and obtain a *judgment* against the debtor. The debtor is called *judgment-proof* if he or she has no money to pay the judgment.

Secured Credit

Credit that requires security (collateral) that secures the payment of a loan.

1. ***Collateral.*** The property that is pledged as security for a loan.

Security Interest in Personal Property

1. ***Article 9 of the UCC.*** An article of the Uniform Commercial Code (UCC) that governs secured transactions in personal property.
2. ***Secured transaction.*** A transaction that is created when a creditor makes a loan to a debtor in exchange for the debtor's pledge of personal property as security.
3. ***Perfection of a security interest.*** Establishes the right of the secured creditor against other creditors who claim an interest in the collateral. The UCC provides the following three methods of perfecting a security interest:
   a. *Perfection by filing a financing statement.*
   b. *Perfection by possession of collateral.*
   c. *Perfection by a purchase money security interest in consumer goods.*
4. ***Artisan's and mechanic's lien.*** A lien given to artisans, laborers, and other service providers on personal property of customers to secure reasonable payment for services rendered.

Security Interests in Real Property

1. ***Mortgage***
   a. *Mortgage.* The instrument that represents a security interest in real property.
   b. *Mortgagor.* The owner-debtor who pledges his or her real property as security for a loan.
   c. *Mortgagee.* The creditor who holds a security interest in the owner-debtor's real property.
2. ***Note and deed of trust.*** Some states use a note and deed of trust as an alternative to a mortgage.
   a. *Note.* An instrument that evidences a debt.
   b. *Deed of trust.* An instrument that gives a creditor a security interest in the owner-debtor's real property.
3. ***Materialman's lien.*** A contractor's and laborer's lien that makes the real property to which improvements are being made become security for the payment of the services and materials for those improvements.

Surety and Guaranty Agreements, p. 720

Surety and Guaranty Arrangements

Arrangements in which a creditor refuses to extend credit to a debtor without further security and a third person agrees to provide that security by agreeing to become liable for the debt.

1. ***Surety arrangement.*** A third party—called the *surety* or *co-debtor*—promises to be liable for another person's debt. The surety is *primarily liable* for payment of the debt when it is due, along with the principal debtor. The creditor does not have to attempt to collect the debt from the principal debtor before demanding payment from the surety.
2. ***Guaranty arrangement.*** A third party—called the *guarantor*—agrees to pay the debt of the principal debtor if the debtor *defaults* and does not pay the debt when it is due. The guarantor is *secondarily liable* and has to pay the debt only if the creditor has attempted unsuccessfully to collect the debt from the debtor.

Bankruptcy and Reorganization, p. 721

Federal Bankruptcy

1. ***Bankruptcy Reform Act of 1978, as amended.*** A federal statute that establishes the requirements and procedures for filing bankruptcy. Called the *Bankruptcy Code.*
2. ***Bankruptcy courts.*** Courts that have exclusive jurisdiction to hear bankruptcy cases. A bankruptcy court is attached to each federal district court. Bankruptcy judges are appointed for 14-year terms.

The "Fresh Start"

The purpose of bankruptcy is to discharge the debtor from burdensome debts, giving the debtor a fresh start.

Chapter 7 Liquidation Bankruptcy, p. 722

Chapter 7 Bankruptcy

The debtor's nonexempt property is sold for cash, the cash is distributed to the creditors, and any unpaid debts are discharged. Also called *liquidation bankruptcy.*

Bankruptcy Procedure

1. ***Filing a petition.*** The filing of a petition commences a bankruptcy case.
   a. *Voluntary petition.* Filed by the debtor.
   b. *Involuntary petition.* Filed by a creditor or creditors.
2. ***Order for relief.*** Designates that the bankruptcy court has accepted the case for further proceedings.

3. ***Meeting of the creditors.*** The debtor must appear at this meeting and answer questions by the creditors. Also called the *first meeting of the creditors.*
4. ***Appointment of a trustee.*** A *permanent trustee* is elected at the first meeting of the creditors in a Chapter 7 case.
5. ***Proof of claims.*** Unsecured creditors must file proof of claim stating the amount of their claim against the debtor.

Property of the Bankruptcy Estate

1. ***Bankruptcy estate.*** Includes:
   a. All of the debtor's legal and equitable interest in real, personal, tangible, and intangible property at the time the petition is filed.
   b. Gifts, inheritances, life insurance proceeds, and property from divorce settlements that the debtor is entitled to receive within 180 days after the petition is filed.

Exempt Property

The Bankruptcy Code permits the debtor to retain certain property that does not become part of the bankruptcy estate. Exemptions are stipulated in federal and state law.

Discharge

Discharge of unpaid claims. After the nonexempt property is distributed, the remaining unpaid claims of the debtor are *discharged*; the debtor's legal obligation to pay these unpaid debts is terminated. Discharge is available only to individuals.

Discharge of Student Loans

A student loan may be discharged after it is due only if nondischarge would cause an *undue hardship* on the debtor or his or her family.

Chapter 11 Reorganization Bankruptcy, p. 730

Chapter 11 Reorganization Bankruptcy

Provides a method for reorganizing the debtor's financial affairs under the supervision of the bankruptcy court.

Reorganization Proceeding

Procedure. The principles discussed earlier under Chapter 7 regarding the filing of petitions, the first meeting of the creditors, the entry of the order for relief, and automatic stay also apply to Chapter 11 proceedings.

Debtor-in-Possession

In most Chapter 11 cases, the debtor is left in place to operate the business during the reorganization proceeding. In such cases, the debtor is called a *debtor-in-possession.*

1. ***Trustee.*** The court may appoint a trustee to operate the debtor's business only upon a showing of cause, such as fraud, dishonesty, or gross mismanagement to the debtor or its management.

Creditors' Committees

The court will appoint a committee of unsecured creditors (usually creditors holding the seven largest claims). The court may also appoint committees of secured creditors and equity holders. Committees participate in the bankruptcy proceeding and in the negotiation of a plan of reorganization.

Automatic Stay

The filing of a bankruptcy petition *stays* (suspends) certain legal actions against the debtor or the debtor's property.

Executory Contracts

The debtor-in-possession (or trustee) may assume or reject executory contracts. A special procedure has been established for rejecting union collective-bargaining agreements.

Plan of Reorganization

Sets forth the debtor's proposed new capital structure. The debtor has the exclusive right to file a plan within the first 120 days after the date of the order for relief:

1. ***Disclosure Statement.*** The debtor must supply the creditors and equity holders with a disclosure statement that contains adequate information about the proposed plan of reorganization.

Confirmation of a Plan of Reorganization

A plan of reorganization must be confirmed by the bankruptcy court before it becomes effective. Confirmation may be by either of the following methods.

1. ***Confirmation by the acceptance method.*** As established by Section 1129(a) of the Bankruptcy Code.
2. ***Confirmation by the cram down method.*** As provided for by Section 1129(b) of the Bankruptcy Code.

Discharge

Upon confirmation of a plan of reorganization, the debtor is granted a discharge of all claims not included in the plan. The debtor's legal obligation to pay the discharged debts is terminated.

Small Business Bankruptcy

Businesses with total debts of less than $2 million can elect a *fast-track* for processing a Chapter 11 bankruptcy.

Chapter 13 Consumer Debt Adjustment, p. 734

Chapter 13 Consumer Debt Adjustment

A rehabilitation form of bankruptcy that permits bankruptcy courts to supervise the debtor's plan for the repayment of unpaid debts by installment.

The Plan of Payment

The debtor must file a plan of payment. The plan period cannot exceed three years unless the court approves a longer period (of up to five years). A plan may be modified if the debtor's circumstances materially change.

1. ***Trustee.*** A permanent trustee will be appointed by the court. The debtor makes payments to the trustee, who is responsible for remitting payments to the creditors.

Internet Exercises and Case Questions

Working the Web Internet Exercises

Activities

1. Find your state laws on financial institutions using the Cornell Web site. Notice that UCC Article 3 is the law of negotiable instruments. Find the imposter rule in your state's version of this section. See LII: Law About . . . Banking at **www.law.cornell.edu./topics/banking.html**.
2. Check on current statistics on the level of bankruptcies filed, at **www.abiworld.org/stats/newstatsfront.html**, and InterNet Bankruptcy Library—Worldwide Troubled Company Resources and Daily Source of Bankruptcy News, at **www.bankrupt.com**.
3. What is the amount of your state's homestead exemption? More theory may be found in The Outer Boundaries of the Bankruptcy Estate, at **www.law.emory.edu/ELJ/volumes/fall98/plank.html**.
4. The FTC has practical advice for debtors at **www.ftc.gov/bcp/conline/pubs/credit/kneedeep.htm**.

Critical Legal Thinking Cases

24.1 Financing Statement In 1984, C&H Trucking, Inc. (C&H), borrowed $19,747.56 from S&D Petroleum Company, Inc. (S&D). S&D hired Clifton M. Tamsett to prepare a security agreement naming C&H as the debtor and giving S&D a security interest in a 1984 Mack truck. The security agreement prepared by Tamsett declared that the collateral also secured

> *any other indebtedness or liability of the debtor to the secured party direct or indirect, absolute or contingent, due to become due, now existing or hereafter arising, including all future advances or loans that may be made at the option of the secured party.*

Tamsett failed to file a financing statement or the executed agreement with the appropriate government office. C&H subsequently paid off the original debt, and S&D continued to extend new credit to C&H. In March 1986, when C&H owed S&D over $17,000, S&D learned that (1) C&H was insolvent, (2) the Mack truck had been sold, and (3) Tamsett had failed to file the security agreement. Does S&D have a security interest in the Mack truck? Is Tamsett liable to S&D? [*S&D Petroleum Company, Inc. v. Tamsett*, 534 N.Y.S.2d 800, 1988 N.Y.App.Div.Lexis 11258 (N.Y.Sup.Ct.App. 1988)]

24.2 Priority of Security Agreement On July 5, 1980, World Wide Tracers, Inc., sold certain of its assets and properties, including equipment, furniture, uniforms, accounts receivable, and contract rights, to Metropolitan Protection, Inc. To secure payment of the purchase price, Metropolitan executed a security agreement and financing statement in favor of World Wide. The agreement, which stated that "all of the property listed on Exhibit A (equipment, furniture, and fixtures) together with any property of the debtor acquired after July 15, 1980" was collateral, was filed with the Minnesota secretary of state on July 16, 1980.

In February 1982, State Bank loaned money to Metropolitan, which executed a security agreement and financing statement in favor of the bank. The bank filed the financing statement with the Minnesota secretary of state's office on March 3, 1982. The financing statement contained the following language describing the collateral:

> *All accounts receivable and contract rights owned or hereafter acquired. All equipment now owned and hereafter acquired, including but not limited to, office furniture and uniforms.*

When Metropolitan defaulted on its agreement with World Wide in the fall of 1982, World Wide brought suit asserting its alleged security agreement in Metropolitan's accounts receivable. The bank filed a counterclaim, asserting its perfected security interest in Metropolitan's accounts receivable. Who wins? [*World Wide Tracers, Inc. v. Metropolitan Protection, Inc.*, 384 N.W.2d 442, 1986 Minn. Lexis 753 (Minn.1986)]

24.3 Priority of Security Interests On October 8, 1980, Paul High purchased various items of personal property and livestock from William and Marilyn McGowen. To secure the purchase price, High granted the McGowens a security interest in the personal property and livestock. On December18, 1980, High borrowed $86,695 from Nebraska State Bank and signed a promissory note granting the bank a security interest in all his farm products, including but not limited to all of his livestock. On December 20, 1980, the bank perfected its security agreement by filing a financing statement with the county clerk in Dakota County, Nebraska. The McGowens perfected their security interest by filing a financing statement and security agreement with the county clerk on April 28, 1981. In 1984, High defaulted on the obligations owed to the McGowens and the bank. Whose security interest has priority? [*McGowen v. Nebraska State Bank*, 427 N.W.2d 772, 1988 Neb. Lexis 290 (Neb. 1988)]

24.4 Repossession of Collateral Kent Cobado sold a herd of cattle to Gerald Hilliman and John Szata. To secure payment of the purchase price, the buyers granted Cobado a security interest in 66 cows and 1 bull. Cobado protested when he learned that the buyers had culled a number of cattle from the herd. The buyers gave Cobado 37 replacement cows as additional security. Cobado filed a financing statement with the office of the clerk of county.

Cobado continued to be disturbed by the buyers' continuing practice of culling cattle from the herd. Without any prior warning, Cobado, aided by two men, arrived at the buyers' premises. Szata was advised of Cobado's intention to repossess the collateral. Szata replied that all of the payments had been made on time. Cobado restated his intent. The county sheriff arrived before the cattle could be loaded onto Cobado's trucks. The sheriff warned Cobado that he would be arrested if he left with the cattle. Cobado ignored the warning, loaded the cattle onto the trucks, and left with the cattle. Was Cobado's repossession of the cattle proper under Article 9 of the UCC? [*Hilliman v. Cobado*, 499 N.Y.S.2d 610, 1986 N.Y.Misc. Lexis 2486 (N.Y.Sup.Ct.1986)]

24.5 Petition for Bankruptcy In March 1988, Daniel E. Beren, John M. Elliot, and Edward F. Mannino formed Walnut Street Four, a general partnership, to purchase and renovate an office building in Harrisburg, Pennsylvania. They borrowed more than $200,000 from Hamilton Bank to purchase the building and begin renovation. Disagreements among the partners arose when the renovation costs exceeded their estimates. When Beren was unable to obtain assistance from Elliot and Mannino regarding obtaining additional financing, the partnership quit paying its debts. Beren filed an involuntary petition to place the partnership into Chapter 7 bankruptcy. The other partners objected to the bankruptcy filing. At the time of the filing, the partnership owed debts of more than $380,000 and had approximately $550 in the partnership bank account. Should the petition for involuntary bankruptcy be granted? [*In Re Walnut Street Four*, 106 B.R. 56, 1989 Bankr. Lexis 1806 (Bk.M.D. Pa. 1989)]

24.6 Bankruptcy Estate In 1983, Bill K. and Marilyn E. Hargis, husband and wife, filed a Chapter 11 bankruptcy proceeding. In 1984, more than 120 days after the bankruptcy petition was filed, Mr. Hargis died. His life was insured for $700,000. His wife was the beneficiary of the policy. The bankruptcy trustee moved to recover the $700,000 as property of the bankruptcy estate. Who gets the insurance proceeds? [*In Re Matter of Hargis*, 887 F.2d 77, 1989 U.S. App. Lexis 16246 (5th Cir. 1989)]

24.7 Fraudulent Transfer In November 1974, Peter and Geraldine Tabala (debtors), husband and wife, purchased a house in Clarkstown, New York. In November 1976, they purchased a Carvel ice cream business for $70,000 with a loan obtained from People's National Bank. In addition, the Carvel Corporation extended trade credit to the debtors. On October 23, 1978, the debtors conveyed their residence to their three daughters, ages 9, 19, and 20, for no consideration. The debtors continued to reside in the house and to pay maintenance expenses and real estate taxes due on the property. On the date of the transfer, the debtors owed obligations in excess of $100,000. On March 28, 1980, the debtors filed a petition for Chapter 7 bankruptcy. The bankruptcy trustee moved to set aside the debtors' conveyance of their house to their daughters as a fraudulent transfer. Who wins? [*In Re Tabala*, 11 B.R. 405, 1981 Bankr. Lexis 3663 (Bk.S.D.N.Y. 1981)]

24.8 Discharge On September 20, 1985, Jane Gnidovec, David Towell, and Robert Dawson (plaintiffs) obtained a judgment in state court against Alwan Brothers Co., Inc., and Alwan Brothers Partnership and its general partners (jointly Alwans) for $110,059 compensatory damages and $750,000 punitive damages. When the judgment was upheld on appeal, the Alwans filed a voluntary petition for Chapter 11 bankruptcy. Is the judgment for compensatory damages and punitive damages dischargeable in bankruptcy? [*In Re Alwan Brothers Co., Inc.*, 105 B.R. 886, 1989 Bankr. Lexis 1757 (Bk.C.D.Ill. 1989)]

24.9 Executory Contract On October 15, 1980, The Record Company, Inc., entered into a purchase agreement to buy certain retail record stores from Bummbusiness, Inc. All assets and inventory were included in the deal. The Record Company agreed to pay Bummbusiness $20,000 and to pay the $380,000 of trade debt owed by the stores. In exchange, Bummbusiness agreed not to compete with the new buyer for two years within a 15-mile radius of the stores and to use its best efforts to obtain an extension of the due dates for the trade debt. The Record Company began operating the stores, but shortly thereafter filed a petition for Chapter 11 bankruptcy. At the time of the bankruptcy filing, (1) The Record Company owed Bummbusiness $10,000 and owed the trade debt of $380,000, and (2) Bummbusiness was obliged not to compete with The Record Company. Can The Record Company reject the purchase agreement? [*In Re The Record Company*, 8 B.R. 57, 1981 Bankr. Lexis 5157 (Bk.S.D.Ind. 1981)]

24.10 Plan of Reorganization Richard P. Friese (debtor) filed a voluntary petition for Chapter 11 bankruptcy. In May 1989, the debtor filed a plan of reorganization that divided his creditors into three classes. The first class, administrative creditors, were to be paid in full. The second class, unsecured creditors, were to receive 50 percent on their claims. The IRS was the third class. It was to receive $20,000 on confirmation and the balance in future payments. No creditors voted to accept the plan. The unsecured creditors were impaired because their legal, equitable, and contractual rights were being altered. Can the bankruptcy court affirm the debtor's plan of reorganization? [*In Re Friese*, 103 B.R. 90, 1989 Bankr. Lexis 1309 (Bk.S.D.N.Y.1989)]

24.11 Consumer Debt Adjustment Manuel Guadalupe (debtor) was a tool and die machinist who was employed at Elco Industries for more than five years. He accumulated more than $19,000 in unsecured debt, including deficiencies owed after secured creditors repossessed a van (leaving a deficiency of $1,066) and a car (leaving a deficiency of $3,130). Shortly after the second automobile was repossessed, the debtor borrowed approximately $19,000 from the Elco Credit Union to purchase a 1988 four-wheel-drive Chevrolet Blazer. The $472 monthly payment was to be taken directly from the debtor's earnings.

On February 28, 1989, the debtor filed a voluntary petition for Chapter 13 bankruptcy. The schedule listed total secured debts of $22,132, which included the debt for the Blazer, furniture, and a camcorder. Total unsecured debt was $19,575, which included $2,160 owed to General Finance Corporation. The debtor's budget projected that $700 per month would be left over for funding the Chapter 13 plan after the debtor's monthly expenses were deducted from his $25,000 gross income. Secured creditors were to be paid in full; unsecured creditors would receive 10 percent of their claims. General objected to the plan. Should the debtor's Chapter 13 plan be confirmed? [*In Re Reyes*, 106 B.R. 155, 1989 Bankr. Lexis 1731 (Bk.N.D.Ill. 1989)]

24.12 Student Loan Donald Wayne Doyle obtained a guaranteed student loan to enroll in a school for training truck drivers. Due to his impending divorce, the debtor never attended the program. The first monthly installment of approximately $50 to pay the student loan became due on September 1, 1988.

On September 16, 1988, the debtor filed a voluntary petition for Chapter 7 bankruptcy.

The debtor was a 29-year-old man who earned approximately $1,000 per month at an hourly wage of $7.70 as a truck driver, a job that he had held for 10 years. The debtor resided on a farm where he performed work in lieu of paying rent for his quarters. The debtor was paying monthly payments of $89 on a bank loan for his former wife's vehicle, $200 for his truck, $40 for health insurance, $28 for car insurance, $120 for gasoline and vehicular maintenance, $400 for groceries and meals, and $25 for telephone charges. In addition, a state court had ordered the debtor to pay $300 per month to support his children, ages 4 and 5. The debtor's parents were assisting him by buying $130 worth of groceries for him per month. Should the debtor's student loan be discharged in bankruptcy? [*In Re Doyle*, 106 B.R. 272, 1989 Bankr. Lexis 1772 (Bk.N.D.Ala. 1989)]

Business Ethics Cases

24.13 Business Ethics Scott Greig Keebler (debtor) became indebted, and his debts exceeded his assets. The IRS had levied his wages for nonpayment of taxes. The debtor was healthy and capable of earning a substantial income. Evidence showed that the debtor did not try his best to pay his debts, lived an affluent lifestyle, and determined not to pay his principal creditors. The debtor voluntarily quit his job and filed a voluntary petition for Chapter 7 bankruptcy. The petition stated that he was unemployed. Shortly after filing for bankruptcy, the debtor resumed work. Should the debtor's Chapter 7 case be dismissed because he filed the petition in bad faith? [*In Re Scott Greig Keebler*, 106 B.R. 662, 1989 Bankr. Lexis 1919 (Bk.D.Hawaii)]

24.14 Business Ethics On February 3, 1983, Douglas G. and Aleta Brantz, husband and wife, borrowed $40,000 from Meritor Financial Services, Inc., and signed a promissory note evidencing the debt. The proceeds of the loan were used in a business operated by Mr. Brantz.

After a portion of the debt had been paid, the business began to fail, and the debtors defaulted on the loan. The debtors made several attempts to cure the default but failed. On August 11, 1988, Meritor filed a collection action and obtained a judgment lien against the debtor's residence.

On August 16, 1988, a $40,000 mortgage on the debtors' home in favor of Mrs. Brantz's parents, Philip and Sondra

Schley, was recorded. The mortgage was dated February 1, 1988. On May 25, 1989, the debtors filed a voluntary petition for bankruptcy. The parties stipulated that the debtors' home was worth $65,000 and was subject to unavoidable mortgages of $38,000. The Schleys asserted that their mortgage of $40,000 preceded Meritor's judicial lien of $28,441. The debtors also claimed an exemption of $15,800 in the premises. Who wins? Was the debtors' behavior unethical? [*In Re Brantz*, 106 B.R.62, 1989 Bankr. Lexis 1662 (Bankr.E.D.Pa. 1989)]

Briefing the Case Writing Assignment

Read Case A.24 in the Case Appendix [*Dewsnup v. Timm*]. This case is excerpted from the U.S. Supreme Court opinion. Review and brief the case. In your brief, be sure to answer the following questions.

1. Who was the debtor? Who was the creditor? What was the collateral for the secured loan?
2. What amount did the debtor owe on the loan when he filed for bankruptcy? What was the value of the collateral at that time?
3. Succinctly state the issue that was presented to the U.S. Supreme Court.
4. How did the Supreme Court decide this issue? Explain.

Answers to Management Decision Questions

1. Bankruptcy law is federal statutory law. Corporations can file for bankruptcy under Chapter 7 Liquidation and Chapter 11 Reorganization. Chapter 7 Liquidation Bankruptcy (also called straight bankruptcy) calls for the appointment of a trustee who becomes the legal representative of the bankrupt estate. The debtor's nonexempt property is sold for cash, the cash is distributed to creditors according to a priority scheme established in the code, and any unpaid debts are discharged. Chapter 11 of the bankruptcy code provides a method for reorganizing the debtor's financial affairs under the supervision of the bankruptcy court. Its goal is to reorganize the debtor with a new capital structure so that it will emerge from bankruptcy as a viable concern.
2. The events leading up to September 11 are not likely to reoccur, and it is in the best interest of the U.S. economy that the airline industry rebound from its post–September 11 losses. Shareholders will lose their investments, employees will lose their jobs, and many creditors will not be paid if Atlantic files for bankruptcy under Chapter 7. Given these facts, Atlantic should file for protection under Chapter 11 reorganization. If your assumptions about the future are correct, the company will eventually reclaim its share of the market.

Endnotes

1. The following states require debtors to take state law exemptions: Alabama, Alaska, Arizona, Arkansas, California, Colorado, Delaware, Florida, Georgia, Idaho, Illinois, Indiana, Iowa, Kansas, Kentucky, Louisiana, Maine, Maryland, Missouri, Montana, Nebraska, Nevada, New Hampshire, New York, North Carolina, North Dakota, Oklahoma, Oregon, South Carolina, South Dakota, Tennessee, Utah, Virginia, West Virginia, and Wyoming.
2. 11 U.S.C. § 1101–1174.
3. 11 U.S.C. § 362(a).

Appendix A — Case Appendix

Case A.1

Anheuser-Busch, Incorporated v. Schmoke

Mayor of Baltimore City, 63 F.3d 1305, 1995 U.S. App. Lexis 24515 (1995)
United States Court of Appeals, Fourth Circuit
Niemeyer, Circuit Judge

In January 1994, Baltimore exercised the authority granted it by the state and enacted Ordinance 288 prohibiting the outdoor advertising of alcoholic beverages in certain locations in Baltimore City. It also includes an exception permitting such advertising in certain commercially and industrially zoned areas of the City. By its terms, the ordinance was to become effective February 5, 1994. Before enacting the ordinance, the Baltimore City Council conducted public hearings, receiving testimony and previously conducted studies detailing the adverse effects of alcohol consumption on minors and the correlation between underage drinking and the advertising of alcoholic beverages.

The City Council found that alcoholic beverages are the second most heavily advertised products in America (after cigarettes), and that outdoor billboards are a "unique and distinguishable" medium of advertising that subjects the public to involuntary and unavoidable forms of solicitation. The City Council noted that children are exposed to the advertising of alcoholic beverages "simply by walking to school or playing in their neighborhood" and that children's "attitudes favorable to alcohol are significantly related to their exposure to alcohol advertisements." Attempting to tailor its ban, the City Council allowed advertising of alcoholic beverages in commercial and industrial areas, stating that it was "narrowly focus[ing] its efforts on those advertisements which most directly affect minors where they live, attend school, attend church and engage in recreational activities."

On January 14, 1994, several weeks before the ordinance was to become effective, Anheuser-Busch, Inc., filed suit in federal court, facially challenging the constitutionality of the ordinance under the First Amendment. Anheuser-Busch is the nation's largest brewer of beers and malt beverages, producing approximately 15 different brands, including Budweiser, Michelob, and Busch. It advertises in all media, including outdoor billboards and displays. In addition to contending that there is no correlation between alcoholic beverage advertising and underage drinking, Anheuser-Busch asserts that the purpose of its advertising is "to solidify brand loyalty and increase market share by shifting adult beer drinkers from other brands to the advertised brand of beer."

Following a hearing, the district court issued an opinion upholding the constitutionality of the ordinance [(*Anheuser-Busch, Inc. v. Mayor and City Council*, 855 F.Supp. 811 (D.Md.1994)]. The court held the ordinance constitutional after concluding that it "directly advances the City's asserted interest in promoting the welfare and temperance of minors" and is "narrowly tailored" to that end.

On appeal, Anheuser-Busch argues that the ordinance is unconstitutional on its face because (1) it does not directly and materially advance the government's interest in promoting temperance of minors and (2) it is not narrowly tailored to serve that purpose. They also argue that, as applied, the ordinance would impermissibly restrict their noncommercial speech.

We find that it was reasonable for the Baltimore City Council to have concluded that Ordinance 288's regulation of the outdoor advertising of alcoholic beverages directly and materially advances Baltimore's interest in promoting the welfare and temperance of minors. The City Council found that outdoor advertising is a unique and distinct medium which subjects the public to involuntary and unavoidable solicitation, and that children, simply by walking to school or playing in their neighborhood, are exposed daily to this advertising. The City Council pointed to its legislative finding that the majority of research studies show a definite correlation between alcoholic beverage advertising and underage drinking.

We simply do not believe that the liquor industry spends a billion dollars a year on advertising solely to acquire an added market share at the expense of competitors. We hold, as a matter of law, that prohibitions against the advertising of alcoholic beverages are reasonably related to reducing the sale and consumption of those beverages and their attendant problems. The entire economy of the industries that bring these challenges is based on the belief that advertising increases sales.

It is readily acknowledged that limitations on outdoor advertising of alcoholic beverages designed to protect minors also reduce the opportunities for adults to receive advertised information. And adults, who constitute a majority of the population, are the object of the government's legislation. But it also appears that no less restrictive means may be available to advance the government's interest. Anheuser-Busch argues that Baltimore could just as effectively advance its goal of promoting the welfare and temperance of minors by increasing enforcement of existing laws prohibiting sales to, and possession of alcoholic beverages by, minors, or by implementing and encouraging educational programs on the dangers of alcohol. These approaches might indeed prove beneficial in reducing underage drinking, but they do not provide an alternative to the approach selected by the City of curbing the enticement to consume alcoholic beverages. In the face of a problem as significant as that which the City seeks to address, the City must be given some reasonable latitude.

The problem of underage drinking is a most serious one that contributes significantly to a variety of social problems. Baltimore was faced with statistics showing that fully one-half of all deaths of minors were alcohol-related, and 40 to 50 percent of juveniles who drowned or had diving accidents had consumed alcohol immediately prior to the incident. The City Council found that alcohol is overwhelmingly and consistently the most widely used "drug" at all adolescent age levels. It pointed to data which showed that over half of all twelfth graders, 40 percent of tenth graders, and over a quarter of eighth graders reported that they had consumed alcohol within the past 30 days. Widespread underage drinking was also found to be a major factor in crime. One-third of all juvenile males arrested said they had consumed alcohol within the previous 72 hours, and nearly 40 percent of all youths in adult correctional facilities reported drinking alcohol before committing their crimes.

Through outdoor advertising, children are involuntarily and unavoidably confronted daily with the advertised message. Billboards are "seen without the exercise of choice or volition," and viewers have the message "thrust upon them by all the arts and devices that skill can produce." The City argues that the only means to address this problem is to ban such advertising in locations where children generally walk and play. Such a ban still permits adults to receive advertising messages and information from signs in commercial areas of the City and through the numerous other media to which adults are constantly exposed.

In summary, Baltimore City's regulation of stationary outdoor "advertising that advertises alcoholic beverages" in certain locations directly and materially advances a substantial governmental interest in promoting the welfare and temperance of minors who are involuntarily and unavoidably exposed to such advertisements. While the means selected of limiting the location of such outdoor advertising is not a perfect "fit" with the governmental objective, it nevertheless falls well within the range tolerated by the First Amendment for the regulation of commercial speech.

For the reasons stated, we affirm the judgment of the district court, upholding Baltimore City Ordinance 288 against a facial constitutional challenge under the First Amendment.

AFFIRMED.

Case A.2

Gnazzo v. G.D. Searle & Co.

973 F.2d 136, 1992 U.S. App. Lexis 19453 (1992)
United States Court of Appeals, Second Circuit
Pierce, Circuit Judge

On November 11, 1974, Gnazzo had a CU-7 intrauterine device (IUD) inserted in her uterus for contraceptive purposes. The IUD was developed, marketed, and sold by G.D. Searle & Co. (Searle). When Gnazzo's deposition was taken, she stated that her doctor had informed her that "the insertion would hurt, but not for long," and that she "would have uncomfortable and probably painful periods of the first three to four months." On October 11, 1975, Gnazzo found it necessary to return to her physician due to excessive pain and cramping. During this visit she was informed by her doctor that he thought she had Pelvic Inflammatory Disease (PID). She recalled that he stated that the infection was possibly caused by venereal disease or the use of the IUD. The PID was treated with antibiotics and cleared up shortly thereafter. Less than one year later, Gnazzo was again treated by an IUD-associated infection. This infection was also treated with antibiotics. Gnazzo continued using the IUD until it was finally removed in December of 1977.

Following a laparoscopy in March of 1989, Gnazzo was informed by a fertility specialist that she was infertile because of PID-induced adhesions resulting from her prior IUD use. Subsequent to this determination, and at the request of her then-attorneys, Gnazzo completed a questionnaire dated May 11, 1989. In response to the question, "when and why did you first suspect that your IUD had caused you any harm?", Gnazzo responded "sometime in 1981" and explained: "I was married in April 1981 so I stopped using birth control so I could get pregnant—nothing ever happened (of course) then I started hearing and reading about how damaging IUDs could be. I figured that was the problem, however, my marriage started to crumble so I never pursued the issue."

On May 4, 1990, Gnazzo initiated the underlying action against Searle. In an amended complaint, she alleged that she had suffered injuries as a result of her use of the IUD developed by Searle. Searle moved for summary judgment on the ground that Gnazzo's claim was time-barred by Connecticut's three-year statute of limitations for product liability actions. Searle argued, inter alia, that Gnazzo knew in 1981 that she had suffered harm caused by her IUD. Gnazzo contended that her cause of action against Searle accrued only when she learned from the fertility specialist that the IUD had caused her PID and subsequent infertility.

In a ruling dated September 18, 1991, the district court granted Searle's motion for summary judgment on the ground that Gnazzo's claim was time-barred by the applicable statute of limitations. In reaching this result, the court determined that Connecticut law provided no support for Gnazzo's contention that she should not have been expected to file her action until she was told of her infertility and the IUD's causal connection. This appeal followed.

On appeal, Gnazzo contends that the district court improperly granted Searle's motion for summary judgment because a genuine issue of material fact exists as to when she discovered, or reasonably should have discovered, her injuries and their causal connection to the defendant's alleged wrongful conduct. Summary judgment is appropriate when there is no genuine issue as to any material fact and the moving party is entitled to judgment as a matter of law. We consider the record in the light most favorable to the non-movant. However, the non-movant "may not rest upon the mere allegations of denials of her pleading, but must set forth specific facts showing that there is a genuine issue for trial."

Under Connecticut law, a product liability claim must be brought within "three years from the date when the injury is first sustained or discovered in the exercise of reasonable care should have been discovered." In Connecticut, a cause of action accrues when a plaintiff suffers actionable harm. Actionable harm occurs when the plaintiff discovers or should discover, through the exercise of reasonable care, that he or she has been injured and that the defendant's conduct caused such injury.

Gnazzo contends that "the mere occurrence of a pelvic infection or difficulty in becoming pregnant does not necessarily result in notice to the plaintiff of a cause of action." Thus, she maintains that her cause of action did not accrue until 1989 when the fertility specialist informed her both that she was infertile and that this condition resulted from her previous use of the IUD.

Under Connecticut law, however, "the statute of limitations begins to run when the plaintiff discovers some form of actionable harm, not the fullest manifestation thereof." Therefore, as Gnazzo's responses to the questionnaire indicate, she suspected "sometime in 1981" that the IUD had caused her harm because she had been experiencing trouble becoming pregnant and had "started hearing and reading about how damaging IUDs could be and had figured that was the problem. Thus, by her own admission, Gnazzo had recognized, or should have recognized, the critical link between her injury and the defendant's causal connection to it. In other words, she had "discovered or should have discovered through the exercise of reasonable care, that she had been injured and that Searle's conduct caused such injury." However, as Gnazzo acknowledged in the questionnaire, she did not pursue the "issue" at the time because of her marital problems. Thus, even when viewed in the light most favorable to Gnazzo, the non-moving party, we are constrained to find that she knew by 1981 that she had "some form of actionable harm." Consequently, by the time she commenced her action in 1990, Gnazzo was time-barred by the Connecticut statute of limitations.

Since we have determined that Gnazzo's cause of action commenced in 1981, we need not address Searle's additional contention that Gnazzo's awareness in 1975 of her PID and her purported knowledge of its causal connection to the IUD commenced the running of the Connecticut statute of limitations at that time.

We are sympathetic to Gnazzo's situation and mindful that the unavoidable result we reach in this case is harsh. Nevertheless, we are equally aware that "it is within the Connecticut General Assembly's constitutional authority to decide when claims for injury are to be brought. Where a plaintiff has failed to comply with this requirement, a court may not entertain the suit." The judgment of the district court is AFFIRMED.

Case A.3

Lee v. Weismen, 120 L.Ed. 2d 467

505 U.S. 577, 112 S.Ct. 2649, 1992 U.S. Lexis 4364 (1992)
Supreme Court of the United States
Kennedy, Justice (joined by Blackmun, Stevens, O'Conner, and Souter)

Deborah Weisman graduated from Nathan Bishop Middle School, a public school in Providence, at a formal ceremony in June 1989. She was about 14 years old. For many years it has been the policy of the Providence school committee and the Superintendent of Schools to permit principals to invite members of the clergy to give invocations and benedictions at middle school and high school graduations. Many, but not all, of the principals elected to include prayers as part of the graduation ceremonies. Acting for himself and his daughter, Deborah's father, Daniel Weisman, objected to any prayers at Deborah's middle school graduation, but to no avail. The school principal, petitioner Robert E. Lee, invited a rabbi to deliver prayers at the graduation exercises for Deborah's class. Rabbi Leslie Gutterman, of the Temple Beth El in Providence, accepted.

It has been the custom of Providence school officials to provide invited clergy with a pamphlet entitled "Guidelines for Civic Occasions," prepared by the National Conference of Christians and Jews. The Guidelines recommended that public prayers at nonsectarian civic ceremonies be composed with "inclusiveness and sensitivity," though they acknowledge that "prayer of any kind may be inappropriate on some civic occasions." The principal gave Rabbi Gutterman the pamphlet before the graduation and advised him the invocation and benediction should be non-sectarian.

Deborah's graduation was held on the premises of Nathan Bishop Middle School on June 29, 1989. Four days before the ceremony, Daniel Weisman, in his individual capacity as a Providence taxpayer and as next friend of Deborah, sought a temporary restraining order in the United States District Court for the District of Rhode Island to prohibit school offices from including an invocation or benediction in the graduation ceremony. The court denied the motion for lack of adequate time to consider it. Deborah and her family attended the graduation, where the prayers were recited. In July 1989, Daniel Weisman filed an amended complaint seeking a permanent injunction barring petitioners, various officials of the Providence public schools, from inviting the clergy to deliver invocations and benedictions at future graduations.

The case was submitted on stipulated facts. The district court held that petitioners' practice of including invocations and benedictions in public school graduations violated the Establishment Clause of the First Amendment, and it enjoined petitioners from continuing the practice. The court applied the three-part Establishment Clause test. Under that test, to satisfy the Establishment Clause a governmental practice must (1) reflect a clearly secular purpose, (2) have a primary effect that neither advances nor inhibits religion, and (3) avoid excessive government entanglement with religion. On appeal, the United States Court of Appeals for the First Circuit affirmed.

These dominant facts mark and control the confines of our decision: State officials direct the performance of a formal religious exercise at promotional and graduation ceremonies for secondary schools. Even for those students who object to the religious exercise, their attendance and participation in the state-sponsored religious activity are in a fair and real sense obligatory, though the school district does not require attendance as a condition for receipt of the diploma.

The controlling precedents as they relate to prayer and religious exercise in primary and secondary public schools compel the holding here that the policy of the city of Providence is an unconstitutional one. It is beyond dispute that, at a minimum, the Constitution guarantees that government may not coerce anyone to support or participate in religion or its exercise, or otherwise act in a way which "establishes a state religion or religious faith, or tends to do so."

We are asked to recognize the existence of a practice of nonsectarian prayer within the embrace of what is known as the Judeo-Christian tradition, prayer which is more acceptable than one which, for example, makes explicit references to the God of Israel, or to Jesus Christ, or to a patron saint. If common ground can be defined which permits once conflicting faiths to express the shared conviction that there is an ethnic and a morality which transcend human invention, the sense of community and purpose sought by all decent societies might be advanced. But though the First Amendment does not allow the government to stifle prayers which aspire to these ends, neither does it permit the government to undertake that task for itself.

The sole question presented is whether a religious exercise may be conducted at a graduation ceremony in circumstances where, as we have found, young graduates who object are induced to conform. No holding by this Court suggests that a school can persuade or compel a student to participate in a religious exercise. That is being done here, and it is forbidden by the Establishment Clause of the First Amendment.

For the reasons we have stated, the judgment of the court of appeals is AFFIRMED.

Scalia, Justice (joined by Rehnquist, White, and Thomas) dissenting, expressed the view that (1) the establishment of religion clause should not have been interpreted so as to invalidate a long-standing American tradition of nonsectarian prayer at public school graduations, (2) graduation invocations and benedictions involve no psychological coercion of students to participate in religious exercises, (3) the only coercion that is forbidden by the establishment of religion clause is that which is backed by a threat of penalty, and (4) the middle school principal did not direct or control the content of the prayers in question, and thus there was no pervasive government involvement with religious activity.

Case A.4

Ramirez v. Plough, Inc.

15 Cal. App. 4th 1110, 12 Cal. Rptr. 2d 423, 1992 Cal. App. Lexis 1199 (1992)
Court of Appeals of California
Thaxter, Judge

Jorge Ramirez, a minor, by his guardian ad litem Rosa Rivera, appeals from a summary judgment in favor of Plough, Inc. Appellant sued Plough alleging negligence, product liability, and fraud. The action sought damages for injuries sustained in March 1986 when Jorge, who was then four months old, contracted Reye's Syndrome after ingesting St. Joseph Aspirin for Children (SJAC). Plough marketed and distributed SJAC.

Reye's Syndrome is a serious disease of unknown cause characterized by severe vomiting, lethargy, or irritability which may progress to delirium or coma. The disease generally strikes children or teenagers who are recovering from a mild respiratory tract infection, influenza, chicken pox, or other viral illnesses. The mortality rate of the disease is high, and permanent brain damage occurs in many cases. As a result of contracting Reye's Syndrome, appellant suffered catastrophic injuries including quadriplegia, blindness, and profound mental retardation.

In the early 1980s, there was significant scientific debate concerning the cause of Reye's Syndrome. Several state studies suggested a statistical association between the ingestion of aspirin and the disease. In December 1982, the federal government acknowledged the debate. After considering the state studies and their critics, the federal government rejected a proposal which would require a warning label and, instead, undertook an independent study. Apparently, Plough participated in efforts to influence government officials and agencies to reject the label proposal which Plough considered premature.

In December 1985, the Food and Drug Administration (FDA) requested that aspirin manufacturers voluntarily place a label on aspirin products warning consumers of the possible association between aspirin and Reye's Syndrome. Plough voluntarily complied and began including a warning and insert in SJAC packaging. On June 5, 1986, the Reye's Syndrome warning became mandatory.

In March 1986, SJAC labeling bore the following warning: "Warning: Reye's Syndrome is a rare but serious disease which can follow flu or chicken pox in children and teenagers. While the cause of Reye's Syndrome is unknown, some reports claim aspirin may increase the risk of developing this disease. Consult a doctor before use in children or teenagers with flu or chicken pox." In addition, the SJAC package insert included the following statement: "The symptoms of Reye's Syndrome can include persistent vomiting, sleepiness and lethargy, violent headaches, unusual behavior, including disorientation, combativeness, and delirium. If any of these symptoms occur, especially following chicken pox or flu, call your doctor immediately, even if your child has not taken any medication. Reye's Syndrome is Serious, so Early Detection and Treatment are Vital."

Rosa Rivera purchased SJAC on March 12, 1986, and administered it to appellant who was suffering from what appeared to be a cold or upper respiratory infection. She gave appellant the aspirin without reading the directions or warnings appearing on the SJAC packaging. The packaging was in English and Ms. Rivera can speak and understand only Spanish. She did not seek to have the directions or warnings translated from English to Spanish, even though members of her household spoke English.

The trial court granted Plough's motion for summary judgment on the grounds that "there is no duty to warn in a foreign language and there is no causal relationship between plaintiff's injury and defendant's activities."

It is undisputed SJAC was marketed and intended for the treatment of minor aches and pains associated with colds, flu, and minor viral illnesses. The SJAC box promised "fast, effective relief of fever and minor aches and pains of colds." Both parties accept the premise that Plough had a duty to warn consumers that the use of SJAC after a viral infection or chicken pox could lead to Reye's Syndrome, an illness with serious, possibly fatal, consequences. In March 1986, federal regulations requiring a Reye's Syndrome warning had been promulgated and were final, although not yet effective. The FDA had previously solicited voluntary labeling. In response to the request for voluntary labeling, Plough started packaging SJAC with explicit warnings of the risks of Reye's Syndrome. The scientific community had already confirmed and documented the relationship between Reye's Syndrome and the use of aspirin after a viral illness. There is no doubt Plough had a duty to warn of the Reye's Syndrome risk.

The question thus is whether the warning given only in English was adequate under the circumstances. Respondent argues that as a matter of law it has no duty to place foreign-language warnings on products manufactured to be sold in the United States and that holding manufacturers liable for failing to do so would violate public policy.

While the constitutional, statutory, regulatory, and judicial authorities relied on by respondent may reflect a public policy recognizing the status of English as an official language, nothing compels the conclusion that a manufacturer of a dangerous or defective product is immunized from liability when an English-only warning does not adequately inform non-English-literate persons likely to use the product.

Plough's evidence showed that over 148 foreign languages are spoken in the United States and over 23 million Americans speak a language other than English in their homes. That evidence plainly does not prove that Plough used reasonable care in giving an English-only warning. Plough, then, resorts to arguing that the burden on manufacturers and society of requiring additional warnings is so "staggering" that the courts should preclude liability as a matter of law. We are not persuaded.

Certainly the burden and costs of giving foreign-language warnings is one factor for consideration in determining whether a manufacturer acted reasonably in using only English. The importance of that factor may vary from case to case depending upon other circumstances, such as the nature of the product, marketing efforts directed to segments of the population unlikely to be English-literate, and the actual and relative size of the consumer market which could reasonably be expected to speak or read only a certain foreign language. Plough represented no evidence from which we can gauge the extent of the burden under the facts of this case.

Ramirez submitted evidence that Plough knew Hispanics were an important part of the market for SJAC and that Hispanics often maintain their first language rather than learn English. SJAC was advertised in the Spanish media, both radio and television. That evidence raises material questions of fact concerning the foreseeability of purchase by a Hispanic not literate in English and the reasonableness of not giving a Spanish-language warning. If Plough has evidence conclusively showing that it would have been unreasonable to give its label warning in Spanish because of the burden, it did not present that evidence below.

Given the triable issues of material fact, if we accepted Plough's arguments in this case, in effect we would be holding that failure to warn in a foreign language is not negligence, regardless of the circumstances. Such a sweeping grant of immunity should come from the legislative branch of government, not the judicial. In deciding that Plough did not establish its right to judgment as a matter of law, we do not hold that manufacturers are required to warn in languages other than English simply because it may be foreseeable that non-English-literate persons are likely to use their products. Our decision merely recognizes that under some circumstances the standard of due care may require such warning.

Because the evidence shows triable issues of material fact and because Plough did not establish its immunity from liability as a matter of law, its motion for summary judgment should have been denied.

Case A.5

Braun v. Soldier of Fortune Magazine, Inc.

968 F.2d 1110, 1992 U.S. App. Lexis 18556 (1992)
United States Court of Appeals, Eleventh Circuit
Anderson, Circuit Judge

In January 1985, Michael Savage submitted a personal service advertisement to *Soldier of Fortune* (SOF). After several conversations between Savage and SOF's advertising manager, Joan Steel, the following advertisement ran in the June 1985 through March 1986 issues of SOF:

GUN FOR HIRE: 37-year-old professional mercenary desires jobs. Vietnam Veteran. Discrete [*sic*] and very private. Body guard, courier, and other special skills. All jobs considered. Phone (615) 436-9785 (days) or (615) 436-4335 (nights), or write: Rt. 2, Box 682 Village Loop Road, Gatlinburg, TN 37738.

Savage testified that, when he placed the ad, he had no intention of obtaining anything but legitimate jobs. Nonetheless, Savage stated that the overwhelming majority of the 30 to 40 phone calls a week he received in response to his ad sought his participation in criminal activity such as murder, assault, and kidnapping. The ad also generated at least one legitimate job as a bodyguard, which Savage accepted.

In late 1984 or early 1985, Bruce Gastwirth began seeking to murder his business partner, Richard Braun. Gastwirth enlisted the aid of another business associate, John Horton Moore, and together they arranged for at least three attempts on Braun's life, all of which were unsuccessful. Responding to Savage's SOF ad, Gastwirth and Moore contacted him in August 1985 to discuss plans to murder Braun. On August 26, 1985, Savage, Moore, and another individual, Sean Trevor

Doutre, went to Braun's suburban Atlanta home. As Braun and his 16-year-old son Michael were driving down the driveway, Doutre stepped in front of Braun's car and fired several shots into the car with a MAC 11 automatic pistol. The shots hit Michael in the thigh and wounded Braun as well. Braun managed to roll out of the car, but Doutre walked over to Braun and killed him by firing two more shots into the back of his head as he lay on the ground.

On March 31, 1988, appellees Michael and Ian Braun filed this diversity against appellants in the United States District Court for the Middle District of Alabama, seeking damages for the wrongful death of their father. Michael Braun also filed a separate action seeking recovery for the personal injuries he received at the time of his father's death. The district court consolidated these related matters.

Trial began on December 3, 1990. Appellees contended that under Georgia law, SOF was liable for their injuries because SOF negligently published a personal service advertisement that created an unreasonable risk of the solicitation and commission of violent criminal activity, including murder. To show that SOF knew of the likelihood that criminal activity would result from placing an ad like Savage's, appellees introduced evidence of newspaper and magazine articles published prior to Braun's murder which described links between SOF and personal service ads and a number of criminal convictions including murder, kidnapping, assault, extortion, and attempts thereof. Appellees also presented evidence that, prior to SOF's acceptance of Savage's ad, law enforcement officials had contacted SOF staffers on two separate occasions in connection with investigations of crimes.

In his trial testimony, SOF president Robert K. Brown denied having any knowledge of criminal activity associated with SOF's personal service ads at any time prior to Braun's murder in August 1985. Both Jim Graves, a former managing editor of SOF, and Joan Steel, the advertising manager who accepted Savage's advertisement, similarly testified that they were not aware of other crimes connected with SOF ads prior to running Savage's ad. Steel further testified that she had understood the "Gun for Hire" in Savage's ad to refer to a "bodyguard or protection service-type thing," rather than to any illegal activity.

The jury returned a verdict in favor of appellee and awarded compensatory damages on the wrongful death claim in the amount of $2,000,000. The jury also awarded appellee Michael Braun $375,000 in compensatory damages and $10,000,000 in punitive damages for his personal injury claim.

To prevail in an action for negligence in Georgia, a party must establish the following elements:

(1) A legal duty to conform to a standard of conduct raised by the law for the protection of others against unreasonable risks of harm, (2) a breach of this standard, (3) a legally attributable causal connection between the conduct and the resulting injury, and (4) some loss or damage flowing to the plaintiff's legally protected interest as a result of the alleged breach of the legal duty. To the extent that SOF denies that a publisher owes any duty to the public when it publishes personal service ads, its position is clearly inconsistent with Georgia law. We believe, however, that the crux of SOF's argument is not that it had no duty to the public, but that, as a matter of law, there is a risk to the public when a publisher prints an "unreasonable" advertisement if the ad openly solicits criminal activity.

SOF further argues that imposing liability on publishers for the advertisements they print indirectly threatens core, noncommercial speech to which the Constitution accords its full protection. Supreme Court cases discussing the limitations the First Amendment places on state defamation law indicate that there is no constitutional infirmity in Georgia law holding publishers liable under a negligence standard with respect to the commercial advertisements they print. Past Supreme Court decisions indicate, however, that the negligence standard that the First Amendment permits is a "modified" negligence standard. The Court's decisions suggest that Georgia law may impose tort liability on publishers for injury caused by the advertisements they print only if the ad on its face, without the need to investigate, makes it apparent that there is a substantial danger of harm to the public.

We conclude that the First Amendment permits a state to impose upon a publisher liability for compensatory damages for negligently publishing a commercial advertisement where the ad on its face, and without the need for investigation, makes it apparent that there is a substantial danger of harm to the public. The absence of a duty requiring publishers to investigate the advertisements they print and the requirement that the substance of the ad itself must warn the publisher of a substantial danger of harm to the public guarantee that the burden placed on publishers will not impermissibly chill protected commercial speech.

Our review of the language of Savage's ad persuades us that SOF had a legal duty to refrain from publishing it. Savage's advertisement (1) emphasized the term "Gun for Hire," (2) described Savage as a "professional mercenary," (3) stressed Savage's willingness to keep his assignments confidential and "very private," (4) listed legitimate jobs involving the use of a gun—bodyguard and courier—followed by a reference to Savage's "other special skills," and (5) concluded by stating that Savage would consider "all jobs." The ad's combination of sinister terms makes it apparent that there was a substantial danger of harm to the public. The ad expressly solicits all jobs requiring the use of a gun. When the list of legitimate jobs—i.e., bodyguard and courier—is followed by "other special skills" and "all jobs considered," the implication is clear that the advertiser would consider illegal jobs. We agree with the district court that "the language of this advertisement is such that, even though couched in terms not explicitly offering criminal services, the publisher could recognize the offer of criminal activity as readily as its readers obviously did." We find that the jury had ample grounds for finding that SOF's publication of Savage's ad was the proximate cause of Braun's injuries.

For the foregoing reasons, we AFFIRM the district court's judgment.

Case A.6

Johnson v. Chicago Pneumatic Tool Co.

607 So. 2d 615, 1992 La.App. Lexis 2307 (1992)
Court of Appeals of Louisiana
Crain, Judge

This is a products liability action in which William H. Johnson was injured in the course of his employment when a pipejack was accidentally propelled toward Johnson striking him in the back and pinning him between the edge of a large diameter pie which he was grinding and the pipejack. A pipejack is a large mechanical device which is inserted into large pipes which are in the process of being joined together. The pipejack applies pressure forcing the joints into an evenly rounded shape which can then be welded together. The movement of the pipejack was controlled by an air winch manufactured by Chicago Pneumatic Tool Company (Chicago Pneumatic) which had been utilized and incorporated by McDermott, Inc., Johnson's employer, into a system dedicated to the fitting or joining of large-diameter pipe. The accident occurred at the McDermott shipyard when a co-employee either tossed or laid a 50-gallon drum on the ground near the winch in the area where Johnson was working. The drum rolled and toppled over onto the winch throttle pushing the throttle downward which in turn activated the winch and caused the pipejack to move toward Johnson.

Johnson instituted this action against Chicago Pneumatic as manufacturer of the winch, alleging that the winch as designed and manufactured was unreasonably dangerous to normal use. McDermott intervened in this action. After trial on the merits, the jury rendered a special verdict in favor of defendant.

It is uncontroverted that at the time of the accident Johnson was working with his back to the pipejack and the winch; the winch was not being manually operated; and no one was standing at or adjacent to the winch controls. The clutch lever had previously been welded down by McDermott and as a result the clutch remained permanently engaged. Of the other winch controls, the throttle was set in the neutral position and neither the brake nor the safety lock was engaged.

In order to prevail in a products liability action a plaintiff must prove that his damage was a result of a condition of the product which made the product unreasonably dangerous to normal use. The "normal use" of a product encompasses all intended or foreseeable uses and misuses of the product. A manufacturer is obliged to adequately warn the user of any danger inherent in the normal use of the product which is not within the knowledge of or obvious to the normal user. The manufacturer is also required to anticipate the environment in which the product will be used and to notify the user of the potential risks arising from foreseeable use or misuse in the foreseeable environment.

The finding of the jury that the winch was not employed in normal use at the time of the accident is a factual determination which should not be set aside unless clearly wrong. A review of the record reveals that McDermott modified the winch by permanently engaging the clutch; that this modification permanently removed one of the safety and control features designed for its safe and proper operation; the disengagement of the clutch without the engagement of the additional safety features would have prevented the accident; the basic safety mechanisms of the winch were not utilized; the winch was installed backwards, thereby requiring the operator to stand away from the controls; and the employees/operators were uninformed regarding familiarity with the controls and proper operation of the winch. After careful review of the record we conclude that the jury's determination in this matter is not manifestly erroneous.

AFFIRMED.

Case A.7

Schalk v. Texas

823 S.W.2d 633, 1991 Tex.Crim.App. Lexis 201 (1991)
Court of Criminal Appeals of Texas
Miller, Judge

Appellants Schalk and Leonard are former employees of Texas Instruments (hereafter TI). Both men have doctoral degrees and specialized in the area of speech research at TI. Schalk resigned his position with TI in April 1983 to join a newly developed company, Voice Control Systems (hereafter VCS). In February 1985, Leonard resigned from TI and joined VCS. Several TI employees eventually joined the ranks of VCS. Speech research was the main thrust of the research and development performed by VCS. In fact, VCS was a competitor of TI in this field. In April 1985, Sam Kuzbary, then employed with VCS and a former TI employee, noticed some information which he believed to be proprietary to TI stored in the memory of the computer he was using at VCS. Kuzbary contacted TI and agreed to serve as "informant" for them.

He then searched the premises of VCS and photographed materials which he recognized from his employment with TI. A TI internal investigation revealed that a few hours prior to Schalk's and Leonard's departures from TI, each appellant, utilizing TI computers, copied the entire contents of the directories respectively assigned to them. This information included computer programs which TI claimed to be its trade secrets. Officials of TI then contacted the Dallas District Attorney's office. A search of the premises of VCS resulted in the seizure of computer tapes containing the alleged TI trade secret programs from appellants' offices. Appellants were arrested.

We granted review to consider, first, whether the evidence was sufficient to establish that the computer programs named in the indictments were trade secrets, and second, to determine whether the items listed in the search warrant were sufficiently described so as to preclude a general exploratory search.

Having determined that computer programs are proper subjects for trade secret litigation under Texas civil and criminal law, we now look to the case *sub judice* to determine whether the programs which appellants copied and took with them to VCS are trade secrets as defined by §31.05 of the Penal Code.

§31.05 Theft of trade secrets:

(a) For the purposes of this section:

(4) "Trade secret" means the whole or any part of any scientific or technical information, design, process, procedure, formula, or improvement that has value and that the owner has taken measures to prevent from becoming available to persons other than those selected by the owner to have access for limited purposes.

Appellants claimed on appeal that the programs did not meet the statutory trade secrets criteria because they alleged their former employer TI failed to take "measures to prevent [the information] from becoming available to persons other than those selected by the owner." We note, as did the court of appeals, that the statute sets no standards for degree of sufficiency of the "measures" taken. Specifically, appellants pointed to considerable disclosure of speech research information, citing the "academic environment" of the laboratory in which they worked as encouraging the sharing of information, rather than maintaining secrecy. Appellants also claimed that TI policy favored protection of its research and development efforts through the patent process, as opposed to trade secret designation. Further, appellants allege that the programs that are the subject of the instant case were not listed in the TI register of trade secrets and that TI was lax in implementing its standard procedures with regard to notifying employees of trade secrets within the company. The precise issue before us in the case *sub judice* is one of the first impressions in Texas, to wit: what constitutes requisite "measures" to protect trade secret status?

We now determine whether the information disclosed with TI's permission or encouragement, such as published articles, seminar papers, speeches given at public meetings, information provided to government agencies, etc., was so extensive as to destroy any trade secret status that may have existed regarding the computer software which is the subject of the instant indictments. It is axiomatic that the core element of a trade secret must be that it remain a secret. However, absolute secrecy is not required.

A trade secret can exist in a combination of characteristics and components, each of which, by itself, is in the public domain, but the unified process and operation of which, in unique combination, affords a competitive advantage and is a protectable secret. We find based on the record in this case that the limited disclosure made by TI in regard to the speech research lab activities merely described the application and configuration of certain elements of the software but did not reveal the actual composition of the programs. The measures used by TI to secure its premises to prevent unauthorized personnel from admission to or exposure to its proprietary research data were reasonable under the circumstances.

We need not decide today whether any one of the preventive measures listed, standing alone, is factually sufficient to support trade secret status. We do find that the combination of employment agreements, strict plant security, restricted computer access, the nonauthorization of disclosure of the subject programs and the general nondisclosure of those programs by TI and its employees served to support trade secret status of the computer programs that are the subject of the instant indictments. Appellants neither requested nor received permission to copy the files containing these programs. The unauthorized copying of the article representing a trade secret constitutes an offense under V.T.C.A. Penal Code §31.05(b)(2).

Therefore we AFFIRM the court of appeals' ruling that the subject programs are trade secrets.

Case A.8

Feist Publications, Inc. v. Rural Telephone Service Co., Inc.

499 U.S. 340, 111 S.Ct. 1282, 1991 U.S. Lexis 1856 (1991)
Supreme Court of the United States
O'Connor, Justice

Rural Telephone Service Company is a certified public utility that provides telephone service to several communities in northwest Kansas. It is subject to a state regulation that requires all telephone companies operating in Kansas to issue annually an updated telephone directory. Accordingly, as a condition of its monopoly franchise, Rural publishes a typical telephone directory, consisting of white pages and yellow pages. The white pages list in alphabetical order the names of Rural's subscribers, together with their towns and telephone numbers. The yellow pages list Rural's business subscribers alphabetically by category and feature classified advertisements of various sizes. Rural distributes its directory free of charge to its subscribers, but earns revenue by selling yellow pages advertisements.

Feist Publications, Inc., is a publishing company that specializes in area-wide telephone directories. Unlike a typical directory, which covers only a particular calling area, Feist's area-wide directories cover a much larger geographical range, reducing the need to call directory assistance or consult multiple directories. The Feist directory that is the subject of this litigation covers 11 different telephone service areas in 15 counties and contains 46,878 white page listings—compared to Rural's approximately 7,700 listings.

Of the 11 telephone companies, only Rural refused to license its listings to Feist. Rural's refusal created a problem for Feist, as omitting these listings would have left a gaping hole in its area-wide directory, rendering it less attractive to potential yellow pages advertisers. Unable to license Rural's white pages listings, Feist used them without Rural's consent.

Rural sued for copyright infringement in the District Court for the District of Kansas, taking the position that Feist, in compiling its own directory, could not use the information contained in Rural's white pages. The district court granted summary judgment to Rural, explaining that "courts have consistently held that telephone directories are copyrightable" and citing a string of lower court decisions. In an unpublished opinion, the Court of Appeals for the Tenth Circuit affirmed "for substantially the reasons given by the district court."

This case concerns the interaction of two well-established propositions. The first is that facts are not copyrightable; the other, that compilations of facts generally are. The key to resolving the tension lies in understanding why facts are not copyrightable. The *sine qua non* of copyright is originality. To qualify for copyright protection, a work must be original to the author. Original, as the term is used in copyright, means only that the work was independently created by the author (as opposed to copied from other works) and that it possesses at least some minimal degree of creativity.

Originality is a constitutional requirement. The source of Congress's power to enact copyright laws is Article 1, §8. C1. 8, of the Constitution, which authorizes Congress to "secure for limited Times to Authors . . . the exclusive Right to their respective Writings." It is this bedrock principle of copyright that mandates the law's seemingly disparate treatment of facts and factual compilations. No one may claim originality as to facts. This is because facts do not owe their origin to an act of authorship. The distinction is one between creation and discovery: the first person to find and report a particular fact has not created the fact; he or she has merely discovered its existence.

If the selection and arrangement of facts are original, these elements of the work are eligible for copyright protection. No matter how original the format, however, the facts themselves do not become original through association.

There is no doubt that Feist took from the white pages of Rural's directory a substantial amount of factual information. At a minimum, Feist copied the names, towns, and telephone numbers of 1,309 of Rural's subscribers. Not all copying, however, is copyright infringement; two elements must be proven: (1) ownership of a valid copyright, and (2) copying of constituent elements of the work that are original. The first element is not at issue here: Feist appears to concede that Rural's directory, considered as a whole, is subject to a valid copyright because it contains some foreword text, as well as original material in its yellow pages advertisements.

The question is whether Rural has proven the second element. In other words, did Feist, by taking 1,309 names, towns, and telephone numbers from Rural's white pages, copy anything that was "original" to Rural? Certainly, the raw data does not satisfy the originality requirement. Rural may have been the first to discover and report the names, towns, and telephone numbers of its subscribers, but this data does not "owe its origin" to Rural. The question that remains is whether Rural selected, coordinated, or arranged these copyrightable facts in an original way. The selection, coordination, and arrangement of Rural's white pages do not satisfy the minimum constitutional standards for copyright protection. Rural's selection of listings could not be more obvious: it publishes the most basic information—name, town, and telephone number—about each person who applies to it for telephone service. This is "selection" of a sort, but it lacks a modicum of creativity necessary to transform mere selection into copyrightable expression. Rural extended sufficient effort to make the white pages directory useful, but insufficient creativity to make it original.

The judgment of the court of appeals is REVERSED.

Case A.9
OHG v. Kolodny

1st Jud. Dept., IA Part II (1992)
New York County, Supreme Court
Baer, Justice

Plaintiff is an auction house dealing in works of art. Defendant is an art dealer. His gallery has purchased fine art from the plaintiff over the years, presumably with happier results than in this case. In 1988, defendant received, in New York, a catalogue sent by plaintiff that described works of art that would be put up for auction by plaintiff. Among these, defendant says, was "a bronze sculpture produced by Hiliare Germain Edgar Degas before 1900," to wit, the "Dancer Gazing." Plaintiff phoned defendant in New York during the auction and solicited a bid for the "Dancer." Without ever having set eyes on the right foot or any other part of the sculpture, plaintiff offered a bid of DM 220,000 and triumphed. Defendant was never told the identity of the consignor of the Degas. Defendant wired to plaintiff the purchase price and a commission.

The "Dancer" arrived shortly thereafter in New York, where she immediately did a pirouette and departed for London. Defendant wished to let no grass grow under either of his feet; he would put the Degas up for resale at Christie's and would, he was confident, earn a great deal of not bronze, but sterling. Eagle eyes at Christie's surveyed the work. Defendant was told, to his horror, that Christie's suspected that the statue was ersatz, in a word, a fake. Defendant contacted Herr Hanstein and advised that his heart was heavy and his wallet, he was afraid, too light. Defendant sought a refund.

Defendant allegedly secured the agreement of plaintiff that the "Dancer" would be given the once or twice over by the world's foremost expert of Degas bronzes, whose determination would be binding. The statue was brought to New York, where the expert, like many another world's foremost experts, resides. His conclusion unfortunately was that the work was not genuine.

A German court decided in favor of plaintiff, rejected defendant's contention that he was entitled to an offset for the purchase price of the pseudo-Degas. The court held that plaintiff had disclaimed any warranty as to the authenticity of the "Dancer"; that since the job of an auction house is to sell as commission agent many items owned by others, the authenticity of which the auctioneer cannot readily confirm, disclaimers do not violate the law; and that defendant in his letter on the Riopelle had disavowed any offset.

After plaintiff launched its "Blitzkrieg" here in New York, defendant responded with a lawsuit of his own. Defendant seeks to recover the purchase price of the ill-fated Degas. Defendant, relying inter alia upon Article 15 of the New York Arts and Cultural Affairs Law (the "Art Law"), contends that plaintiff is liable for having provided inaccurate information about the Degas and that the German judgment contravenes New York public policy, as a consequence of which its enforcement in favor of plaintiff is *verboten*. The argument, while creative and well presented, must fail.

CPLR Sec. 5304(b)(4) provides that a monetary judgment of a foreign country need not be recognized by New York if the cause of action on which the judgment is based is "repugnant to the public policy of this state." Normally, the judgment of a foreign nation will be given effect. Differences between the laws of New York and those of the many sovereign nations of the world are likely to arise often, but such differences alone cannot constitute a violation of public policy. As Judge Cardozo said, "We are not so provincial as to say that every solution of a problem is wrong because we deal with it otherwise at home." Were we New Yorkers to be overly provincial, we might well inspire foreign nations to reject enforcement of New York judgments, precisely the opposite of the purpose Article 53 was created to achieve and an outcome particularly undesirable as the economy of this country grows every day more intertwined with those of other nations.

The German court applied German law in this case. This is not unreasonable since the auction occurred in Germany and defendant placed his bid during a telephone call with the auction house in Germany. In addition, plaintiff's conditions of sale stated that legal relations between plaintiff and the bidder would be governed by German law. Defendant appeared in the German action, defended, and lost. There is, of course, no claim that German law and procedures are unfair and unworthy of respect here.

The Germans are less Bismarcian than defendant contends. German law, as exemplified by the decision of the Cologne court in this case, is not indifferent to the general sale of fakes by art merchants. The court relied upon the warranty exclusion that formed a condition of sale.

Enforcement of the German judgment would not undermine the public interest, public confidence in the law or security for individual rights, not violate fundamental notions of what is decent and fair. The German judgment is enforceable.

Case A.10
Carnival Leisure Industries, Ltd. v. Aubin

938 F.2d 624, 1991 U.S. App. Lexis 18704 (1991)
United States Court of Appeals, Fifth Circuit
Garwood, Circuit Judge

During a January 1987 visit to the Bahamas, George J. Aubin, a Texas resident, visited Cable Beach Hotel and Casino (the Casino), which was owned and operated by Carnival Leisure Industries, Ltd. (Carnival Leisure). While gambling at the Casino, Aubin received markers or chips from the Casino and the Casino received drafts drawn on Aubin's bank accounts in Texas. Aubin spent all of the markers provided on gambling, although he could also have spent them on food, beverages, souvenirs, or lodging at the Casino. Aubin ultimately gambled and lost $25,000, having given the Casino the same amount in bank drafts.

Carnival Leisure was unable to cash the bank drafts because Aubin had subsequently directed his bank to stop payment. Carnival Leisure sued Aubin in the United States District Court for the Southern District of Texas to enforce the debt. The district court granted Carnival Leisure's motion of summary judgment against Aubin in the amount of $25,000 and attorneys' fees and costs. Carnival Leisure claimed that the debt was enforceable under Texas law because public policy had changed and now favored enforcement of gambling debts. The district court agreed. Aubin raises on appeal only the issue of whether public policy in Texas continues to prevent the enforcement of gambling debts.

Carnival Leisure claims, however, that since 1973 the public policy of Texas toward gambling and the legality of gambling debts has changed. Although gambling is generally proscribed in Texas, there has been an exception for the "social" gambler since 1973. The Texas legislature enacted the Bingo Enabling Act in 1981, the Texas Racing Act in 1986, and the Charitable Raffle Enabling Act in 1989. Provisions were added to the Texas Penal Code excepting these three activities from its general proscription against gambling.

The enactment of statutes legalizing some forms of gambling admittedly evidences some dissipation or narrowing of public disapproval of gambling. However, such statutes hardly introduce a judicially cognizable change in public policy with respect to gambling generally. The social gambling permitted is confined to private places where no one receives any benefit other than his personal winnings and all participants are subject to the same risks, a categorically vastly different kind of activity from the sort involved here. The racing, bingo, and raffling exceptions are narrow, strictly regulated exceptions to a broad public policy in Texas against most forms of gambling. Further, the kind of gambling engaged in here is not of the sort permitted by any of these exceptions.

Even if gambling legislation in Texas were evidence sufficient to warrant judicial notice of a shift in public policy with respect to legalized gambling, such a shift would not be inconsistent with a continued public policy disfavoring gambling on credit. Although Aubin could have used the loaned markers for nongambling purposes at the Casino, it is undisputed that they were in fact used exclusively for gambling. Aubin's gambling debt therefore fits squarely within the terms of the public policy of Texas prohibiting enforcement of gambling debts owed to gambling participants incurred for the purposes of gambling.

We hold that the public policy in Texas against gambling on credit prevents enforcement of a debt incurred for the purpose of gambling and provided by a participant in the gambling activity. The district court's grant of summary judgment in favor of Carnival Leisure is accordingly REVERSED and this case is remanded to the district court for further proceedings consistent with this opinion.

Case A.11
E.B. Harvey & Company, Inc. v. Protective Systems, Inc.

1989 Tenn. App. Lexis 105 (1989)
Court of Appeals of Tennessee
Sanders, Presiding Judge

The plaintiff-appellant, E.B. Harvey Company, Inc. (Harvey), is engaged in the manufacture and wholesale of fine jewelry in Chattanooga. It has been engaged in this business for about 10 years. It maintains an inventory in excess of $1 million of gold, silver, precious stones, pearls, and other such materials related to the manufacture of jewelry. A considerable amount of its jewelry is on consignment and, by the very nature of its business, it requires a great deal of insurance. However, the insurance companies will not write the insurance unless it maintains an Underwriters Laboratories (U.L.)–approved AA burglary protection alarm system. The defendant-appellee, Protective Systems, Inc. (Protective), is one of two companies in Hamilton County which furnishes and maintains a U.L.–approved AA burglar protection system. In June 1981, Harvey entered into a three-year contract with Protective to install and maintain a burglar protection system. The contract provided:

It is agreed that Protective is not an insurer and that the payments herein before named are based solely upon the value of the services herein described and it is not the intention of the parties that Protective assume responsibility for any losses occasioned by malfeasance or misfeasance in the performance of the services under this contract or for any loss or damage sustained through burglary, theft, robbery, fire or other cause or any liability on the part of Protective by virtue of this Agreement or because of the relation hereby established.

If there shall at any time be or arise any liability on the part of Protective, by virtue of this Agreement or because of the relation hereby established, whether due to the negligence of Protective or otherwise, such liability is and shall be limited to a sum total in amount to the rental service charge hereunder for a period of service not to exceed six months, which sum shall be paid and received as liquidated damages.

The burglary and hold-up system provided to Harvey operated by means of Grade AA telephone lines between the central monitoring station of Protective and Harvey's premises. Said telephone lines were at all times owned and maintained by the South Central Bell Telephone Company. On July 22, 1984, at 11:14 P.M., an outage condition was indicated on the E.B. Harvey & Company account. For a period of two weeks prior to this date, Protective's computer had been registering an inordinate number of outage signals which had all been traced back to problems in telephone company equipment. For this reason, on July 22, 1984, Protective's president, Pendell Meyers, notified the telephone company of this condition and reported a potential problem to the police department but did not contact a representative of Harvey to notify them of the outage condition.

The phone company was unable to locate the exact nature of the problem despite several telephone conversations with Meyers. The Chattanooga Police Department patrolled the premises surrounding Harvey's place of business twice that evening but did not note any unusual activity. The following morning, when an employee of Harvey reported to work, it was discovered that a burglary had in fact taken place. Some $200,000 worth of jewelry and inventory was stolen. Harvey sued Protective for damages resulting from the burglary. It alleged that Protective was guilty of negligence for its failure to notify Harvey or its employees of the outage which appeared on the burglary monitoring equipment.

Protective, for answer, denied the allegations of Harvey's complaint and, as an affirmative defense, alleged the contract between the parties with its exculpatory and limitation of liability provisions was enforceable and binding upon Harvey. After hearing testimony, the trial court held the extent of Harvey's recovery against Protective would be 650 percent as liquidated damages. A final judgment was entered and Harvey was appealed.

There is nothing in public policy to render inoperative or negatory the contractual limitations contained in the agreement. Limitations against liability for negligence or breach of contract have generally been upheld in this state in the absence of fraud or overreaching. Limitations such as those contained in the present contract have generally been deemed reasonable and have been sustained in actions against the providers of burglary and fire alarm systems. Such clauses do not ordinarily protect against liability for fraud or intentional misrepresentation.

We concur with the trial court. The issues are found in favor of the appellees. The judgment of the trial court is AFFIRMED. The cost of this appeal is taxed to the appellant and the case is remanded to the trial court for collection of cost.

Case A.12
Toys "R" Us, Inc. v. Abir

1999 U.S. Dist. Lexis 1275 (1999)
United States District Court, Southern District of New York
Koeltl, Judge

In 1997, plaintiff Toys "R" Us, Inc., filed an action alleging violations of federal law related to trademark dilution against the defendants, Eli Abir and Website Management, who had registered the name *Toysareus.com* as their Internet domain name. The plaintiffs alleged that this domain name diluted the plaintiff's mark TOYS "R" US. In November 1997, this court issued a temporary restraining order enjoining the defendants from "using or inducing others to use the names or marks or any colorable imitation of Plaintiff's TOYS "R" US, KIDS "R" US, BABIES "R" US and/or the family of "R" US marks, pending a decision on the plaintiff's motion for a preliminary injunction.

In December 1997, this court heard argument on the motion for a preliminary injunction. At that time the plaintiffs alleged that the defendants had also registered the domain name *Kidsareus.com*. This court then issued a preliminary injunction enjoining the defendants from, among other things, using or inducing others to use any colorable imitation of the family of "R" US marks, pending final judgment. On August 27, 1998, this court granted the plaintiff's motion for summary judgment on the trademark dilution claims. The following day, the court issued a separate judgment and order permanently enjoining the defendants from further infringement of the family of "R" US marks and ordering the transfer of the *Toysareus.com* and *Kidsareus.com* Internet domain names to the plaintiff.

In addition, this court held that because the defendants' conduct in this case was willful, intentional, deliberate, and in bad faith, the plaintiff is entitled to recover attorneys' fees and costs. In order to determine what constitutes "reasonable" attorneys' fees, the starting point is the "lodestar amount," which is the number of hours reasonably expended on the litigation multiplied by a reasonable hourly rate for attorneys and paralegals.

In determining a reasonable hourly rate, courts consider, inter alia, the size and experience of the firm. In this case, Darby & Darby is a well-known New York firm which specializes in intellectual property; the rates charged for its attorneys are comparable to other specialized intellectual property firms in the New York City legal market. The plaintiff's counsel swore in her declaration in support of this application that care was taken to enhance efficiency by assigning, at any one time, only one partner, one mid- to senior-level associate, one to two junior associates, and one to two legal assistants to the prosecution of this case. Having carefully reviewed the itemized request for disbursements, the court finds them neither unnecessary nor excessive for a case of this duration and complexity. The plaintiff is also entitled to costs, as well as those reasonable out-of-pocket expenses incurred by the attorneys and which are normally charged fee-paying clients.

Defendant Eli Abir, who is the owner of defendant Website Management, does not argue that the award requested by the plaintiffs is excessive. Instead, he argues that due to his business and personal circumstances he has limited financial resources and would be unable to pay more than a "symbolic" amount in attorneys' fees. However, nothing in the record in this case justifies a financially based reduction in the award of attorneys' fees and costs. For the reasons stated above, the plaintiff's motion for attorneys' fees and costs is granted in the amount of $55,162.76. SO ORDERED.

Case A.13
District of Columbia v. Howell

607 A.2d 501, 1992 D.C.App. Lexis 109 (D.C. Cir. 1992)
District of Columbia Court of Appeals
Farrell, Associate Judge

The Murch School Summer Discovery Program was designed to provide hands-on education for gifted and talented eight- and nine-year-old children. The program originated in 1985 when Mrs. Gill, the Murch School principal, attended a reception at Mount Vernon College arranged by Greg Butta, a Ph.D. candidate at The American University, to advertise the success of a summer program he had conducted at Mount Vernon. The program interested Mrs. Gill, and after several discussions, Butta sent her a formal proposal for conducting a similar program at the Murch School. Gill made changes to the proposal, then solicited and received approval for the program from the Assistant Superintendent for the District of Columbia Public Schools.

Butta hired the staff for the summer program, including some of the instructors who had taught in the Mount Vernon program. Mrs. Gill, however, reviewed all of the instructors' resumes, had veto authority over their hiring, and interviewed most of the staff, including A. Louis Jagoe, before the hiring was made final. Jagoe, who was hired to teach chemistry to the eight- and nine-year-olds in the program, held a master's degree in chemistry and was a Ph.D. candidate at The American University. Before the first general staff meeting, he told Butta that as part of the class he would do a luminescence experiment and a "cold-pack" experiment and wanted to make sparklers with the children. Jagoe and Butta discussed the safety of the sparkler experiment only in regard to the location where the children would be allowed to light the sparklers.

On August 1, 1985, a staff meeting was held at which Gill, Butta, and all instructors and counselors were present. Each instructor gave a brief talk about what he or she intended to do in class. Several instructors testified that Jagoe told the group, including Mrs. Gill, that he planned to make sparklers as one of the chemistry experiments. Gill, who was in and out of the meeting, did not remember hearing Jagoe discuss the experiment, although notes she took at the meeting reflect that she heard him discuss the luminescence and cold pack experiments and asked him questions about these. Gill spoke and emphasized the "hands-on" nature of the program and her hopes for its success.

One child attending the program was nine-year-old Dedrick Howell, whose parents enrolled him after receiving the school brochure in the mail. The accident occurred on August 12, 1985. At the beginning of the chemistry class, Jagoe distributed his "recipe" for sparklers to the children and also wrote it on the blackboard. Along with other chemical ingredients, the recipe called for the use of potassium perchlorate as the oxidizing agent. Potassium perchlorate was described at trial as an extremely unstable and highly volatile chemical often used to make rocket fuel. Commercially made sparkers are not made with potassium perchlorate.

The children scooped the chemicals, including the potassium perchlorate, out of jars and, using pestles, ground up the mixture in mortars. While they were combining the chemicals, Jagoe ignited three different chemical mixtures at the front of the room with a butane lighter. Butta was present for one of the ignitions when he entered the room to drop off metal hangers for use in the experiment. Mrs. Gill also entered the room at one point, and saw the children working at tables wearing goggles or glasses. She also saw Jagoe at the front of the room lighting the chemicals with a fire extinguisher on the table next to him.

The children continued to grind the material while a counselor, Rebecca Seashore, distributed pieces of metal hangers to be dipped into the mixture at a later time. Dedrick Howell was specifically told not to dip the hanger into the material until instructed to do so. Moments later the chemicals exploded in front of Dedrick. The chemicals burned at 5000 degrees Fahrenheit, and Dedrick was burned over 25 percent of his body including his hands, arms, chest, and face.

An employer generally is not liable for injuries to third parties caused by an independent contractor over whom (or over whose work) the employer has reserved no control. There are exceptions to the rule, however, one of which is that one who employs an independent contractor to do work involving a special danger to others which the employer knows or has reason to know to be inherent in or normal to the work, or which he contemplates or has reason to contemplate when making the contract, is subject to liability for physical harm caused to such others by the contractor's failure to take reasonable precautions against such danger.

It is sufficient that work of any kind involves a risk, recognizable in advance, of physical harm to others which is inherent in the work itself, or normally to be expected in the ordinary course of the usual or prescribed way of doing it, or that the employer has special reason to contemplate such a risk *under the particular circumstances under which the work is to be done*.

The sparkler experiment combined flammable, combustible chemicals, open flames, and children; for that very reason, presumably, the children had been equipped with goggles. Though sparklers are explosives of a lesser order, conducting controlled explosions is a textbook example of an inherently dangerous activity. It was not unreasonable for the jury to conclude that the manufacture of sparklers by nine-year-old children was an inherently dangerous activity.

Therefore, the jury was well within its authority in finding that Jagoe was an independent contractor performing inherently dangerous work of which the district had actual or constructive knowledge.

The judgment is AFFIRMED as to liability and as to the award of $8 million in damages both for pain and suffering and for past medical expenses.

Case A.14
Little v. Howard Johnson Co.

455 N.W. 2d 390, 1990 Mich.App. Lexis 131 (1990)
Court of Appeals of Michigan
MacKenzie, Judge

Plaintiff Joy Little was injured on January 23, 1982, when she slipped on a walkway which allegedly had not been adequately cleared of ice and snow. The walkway was located on property on which a restaurant business was being operated as a franchise of defendant, Howard Johnson Company. Plaintiff filed suit alleging liability for her injuries. In district court Howard Johnson moved for summary disposition. The circuit court denied defendant's subsequent motion for summary disposition and the case proceeded to mediation. When it mediated at less than $10,000, the case was removed to district court for lack of circuit court jurisdiction. The district court found no factual dispute and ruled as a matter of law that defendant was neither directly nor vicariously liable for plaintiff's injuries and, accordingly, granted the motion. The circuit court reversed without elaboration.

Little posited three theories under which she claimed Howard Johnson as a franchisor may be held liable for the injuries she sustained at the franchisee's restaurant: (1) direct liability as a possessor of the land, (2) vicarious liability based on agency principles, and (3) liability based on an apparent agency theory.

1. Direct Liability

The general rule in Michigan is that invitors are liable for known dangerous conditions of property and for dangerous conditions which might be discovered with reasonable care. However, an invitor's direct liability requires the presence of both possession and control over the land.

Little contends that defendants should be deemed a "possessor" of the land as a result of the rights of control it retained in its franchise agreement with the restaurant's franchisee. We disagree. The franchise agreement merely provides that the franchisee "at all times will maintain the interior and exterior of the building's and surrounding premises in a clean, orderly, and sanitary condition satisfactory to Howard Johnson." In short, there is no issue of fact that defendant was a possessor of the premises who could be held directly liable for plaintiff's injuries.

2. Vicarious Liability

Generally, a principal is responsible for the negligence of its agent. In Michigan, the test for a principal–agent relationship is whether the principal has the right to control the agent. The threshold question here is what constitutes "control" sufficient to deem a franchisee to be an agent of a franchisor. Howard Johnson argues that a franchisor must have the right to control the day-to-day operations of a franchisee in order to establish an agency relationship. Little, on the other hand, maintains that an agency relationship is created where the franchisor retains the right to set standards regarding the products and services offered by the franchisee, the right to regulate such items as the furnishings and advertising used by the franchisee, and the right to inspect for conformance with the agreement. We agree with defendant.

This court has repeatedly held that in order to establish vicarious liability in such actions, the landowner must have retained some control and direction over the actual day-to-day work. It is not enough that the owner retained mere contractual control, the right to make safety inspections, or general oversight. The franchise agreement in this case primarily insured the uniformity and standardization of products and services offered by a Howard Johnson restaurant. These obligations do not affect the control of daily operations.

3. Apparent Agency

Howard Johnson argues that the district court properly concluded that no genuine issue of fact existed regarding its liability under an agency theory. We agree. Little has failed to offer any documentary evidence that she was harmed as a result of relying on the perceived fact that the franchise was an agent of Howard Johnson. No evidence was presented which indicated that plaintiff justifiably expected that the walkway would be free of ice and snow because she believed that Howard Johnson operated the restaurant. REVERSED>

Case A.15
Catalina Mortgage Co., Inc. v. Monier

800 P.2d 574, 1990 Ariz. Lexis 200 (1990)
Supreme Court of Arizona
Feldman, Vice Chief Judge

In 1984, Michael Monier and Talon Financial Corporation (Talon) formed the Coronado Partnership (Coronado). Monier and Talon were general partners; other individuals and entities were limited partners in the venture.

Shortly after its formation, Coronado purchased an office and warehouse complex in Tucson. In 1986, the partnership refinanced this property with a loan from Catalina Mortgage Company (Catalina). Talon's president, Roger Howard, executed a promissory note in the amount of $675,000 on behalf of Coronado. In mid-1987, Talon withdrew as a general partner, leaving Monier as the sole general partner in Coronado. The promissory note matured and $687,935 plus interest is now due and owing. Coronado filed for protection pursuant to Chapter 11 of the Bankruptcy Code.

In January 1989, Catalina filed a complaint against Monier in United States District Court, seeking judgment for the amount due on the promissory note plus interest, costs, and attorneys' fees. Catalina alleged that Monier was jointly and severally liable with the partnership entity for the debt. Monier answered, contending, among other things, that because the note was an obligation of the partnership, the partnership assets had to be exhausted before the creditor sought recovery from an individual general partner.

Discussion

If a partnership's debt is contractual in nature, common law requires creditors to resort to and exhaust partnership assets before reaching the partners' individual assets. At common law, a partner is only jointly liable for the partnership's contractual debts, though partners are jointly and severally liable for tort obligations.

As adopted in most states, the Uniform Partnership Act (UPA) preserves this common law rule. The Arizona version of the UPA, however, provides that all partners are liable jointly and severally for everything chargeable to the partnership, and for all other debts and obligations of the partnership; but any partner may enter into a separate obligation to perform a partnership contract.

Catalina maintains that because the statute imposes joint and several liability on all partners, it may proceed against Monier without exhausting partnership assets. Catalina distinguishes cases from other jurisdictions that have considered the issue on the grounds that the applicable law imposed only joint liability as opposed to joint and several liability, that some states specifically provide by statute that partnership assets must be exhausted prior to imposing liability on individual partners for contractual obligations, and that the bankruptcy courts in some instances have misconstrued the state law involved.

Several liability is separate and distinct from liability of another to the extent that an independent action may be brought without joinder of others. The individual liability associated with partners that are jointly liable is not separate and distinct from the liability of all the partners jointly. Rather, that individual liability arises only after it has been shown that the partnership assets are inadequate. No direct cause of action may be maintained against the individual partners until the above condition is met. Several liability, on the other hand, imposes no such conditions precedent before one can be held individually liable.

Conclusion

We hold, therefore, that the scheme imposed by Arizona statutes is simply that a general partner is jointly and severally liable for partnership debts. The partner may be sued severally and his assets reached even though the partnership or other partners are not sued and their assets not applied to the debt. Under Arizona law a creditor may obtain a judgment against an individual general partner on a partnership debt and may reach the partner's assets prior to exhausting partnership assets.

Case A.16
United States v. WRW Corporation

986 F.2d 138, 1993 U.S. App. Lexis 2307 (1993)
United States Court of Appeals, Sixth Circuit
Peck, Judge

In 1985, civil penalties totaling $90,350 were assessed against WRW Corporation (WRW), a Kentucky corporation, for serious violations of safety standards under the Federal Mine Safety and Health Act (the Act) which resulted in the deaths of two miners. Following the imposition of civil penalties, WRW liquidated its assets and went out of business.

Three individual defendants, who were the sole shareholders, officers, and directors of WRW, were later indicted and convicted for willful violations of mandatory health and safety standards under the Act. Roger Richardson, Noah Woolum, and William Woolum each served prison sentences and paid criminal fines. After his release from prison, Roger Richardson filed for bankruptcy under Chapter 7 of the Bankruptcy Code.

The United States (the Government) brought this action in May of 1988 against WRW and Roger Richardson, Noah Woolum, and William Woolum to recover the civil penalties previously imposed against WRW. The district court denied the individual defendants' motion to dismiss and granted summary judgment to the Government piercing the corporate veil under state law and holding the individual defendants liable for the civil penalties assessed against WRW. For the reasons discussed herein, we affirm.

Piercing the Corporate Veil

Having determined that the imposition of a $90,350 sanction upon the defendants does not violate principles of double jeopardy, we turn to the defendants' argument that the district court erred in holding the individual defendants liable for the penalty by piercing the corporate veil of WRW under Kentucky law.

The district court held that it was appropriate to pierce WRW's corporate veil under either an equity theory or an alter ego theory, both of which are recognized under Kentucky law. Under either theory, the following factors must be considered when determining whether to pierce the corporate veil: (1) undercapitalization; (2) a failure to observe the formalities of corporate existence; (3) nonpayment or overpayment of dividends; (4) a siphoning off of funds by dominant shareholders; and (5) the majority shareholders having guaranteed corporate liabilities in their individual capacities.

The court first found that WRW was undercapitalized because it was incorporated with only $3,000 of capital, which the record indicates was insufficient to pay normal expenses associated with the operation of a coal mine. The district court next found that WRW failed to observe corporate formalities, noting that no bylaws were produced by the defendants, and all corporate actions taken by the individual defendants were without corporation authorization. Finally, although WRW never distributed any dividends to the individual defendants, and there was no evidence that the individual defendants siphoned off corporate funds, these factors alone do not mitigate against piercing the corporate veil in this case because WRW was never sufficiently capitalized and operated at a loss during its two years of active existence.

In addition to holding that the equities of this case support piercing the corporate veil, the district court held that the corporate veil should be pierced under the "alter ego" theory, because WRW and the defendants did not have separate personalities. In light of the lack of observance of corporate formalities or distinction between the individual defendants and the corporation, we agree with the district court's conclusion that "there was a complete merger of ownership and control of WRW with the individual Defendants."

The specific factual findings made by the district court amply support piercing the corporate veil of WRW and holding the individual defendants liable for the penalty assessed against the corporate entity. For all of the foregoing reasons, judgment of the district court is AFFIRMED.

Case A.17
Wiljef Transportation, Inc. v. NLRB

946 F.2d 1308, 1991 U.S. App. Lexis 26442 (1991)
United States Court of Appeals, Seventh Circuit
Cudahy, Circuit Judge

This case presents an interesting question concerning the balance between an employer's right of expression and its employees' right of association. Approximately two months before a vote on unionization, the employer, Wiljef Transportation, Inc. (Wiljef), read to its employees a corporate bylaw which states:

Section 2—Corporate Dissolution. Wiljef Transportation, Inc. hereby expresses as matter of corporate policy that operations will cease and the corporation will be dissolved in the event of unionization of its employees. As hereby authorized by the Board of Directors, this by-law may be announced to the employees of Wiljef Transportation, Inc. at any time deemed appropriate by the Board.

The bylaw was adopted in 1979, and the announcement occurred in 1988. In the ensuing union representation election, the employees rejected unionization. The issue in this case is whether the announcement of the by-law constituted a "permitted prediction" of plant closure or a "proscribed threat." The NLRB held that the announcement was a threat in violation of Section 8(a)(1) of the National Labor Relations Act (NLRA), and Wiljef appealed to this court.

An employer's right to communicate its views to its employees is firmly established in the First Amendment and is recognized in Section 8(c) of the NLRA, which provides that "the expressing of any views, argument, or opinion shall not constitute or be evidence of an unfair labor practice if such expression contains no threat of reprisal or force or promise of benefit." On the other hand, the exceptions to the freedom of expression recognized in Section 8(c) reflect the right of employees to associate free of coercion by the employer. Section 8(a)(1) of the NLRA codifies that right by declaring that it is an unfair labor practice to interfere with, restrain or coerce employees exercising their right to organize in unions. The difficulty in cases attempting to relate to these two rights is in determining when speech becomes essentially coercive rather than factually informative or predictive so as to fall outside the protection of the First Amendment and violate the NLRA. The real issue, however, remains credibility and bona fides. A by-law purporting to be a management decision to close a business in the event of unionization is not protected expression unless objective factors demonstrate that it is really controlling on the question of closure. This holding preserves the balance between free expression and the right to organize.

Absent some persuasive evidence of the other measures indicating that Wiljef intends to implement the corporate policy described in the by-law, the announcement of the by-law to the employees is coercive and in violation of the NLRA. Objective evidence to lend credibility to the by-law need not be based on economics and need not necessarily indicate circumstances beyond the employer's control.

Analytically the line is clear. To predict a consequence that will occur no matter how well disposed the company is toward unions is not to threaten retaliation; to predict a consequence that will occur because the company wants to punish workers for voting for the union—a consequence desired and freely chosen by a company rather than compelled by economic forces over which it has no control—is.

In light of our conclusion that Wiljef used the by-law in an attempt to coerce its employees and that no objective evidence indicated an intent to implement the by-law, the relief granted by the NLRB is proper. The petition for review is denied, and the order of the NLRB requiring Wiljef to expunge the by-law, cease further coercive activity, and post a notice to employees indicating that it had violated the law and will cease such violations is enforced.

Case A.18

Robinson v. Jacksonville Shipyards, Inc.

760 F.Supp. 1486, 1991 U.S. Dist. Lexis 4678 (1991)
United States District Court, Middle District of Florida
Melton, District Judge

Plaintiff Lois Robinson (Robinson) is a female employee of Jacksonville Shipyards, Inc. (JSI). She has been a welder since September 1977. Robinson is one of a very small number of female skilled craftworkers employed by JSI. Between 1977 and the present, Robinson was promoted from third-class welder to second-class welder and from second-class welder to her present position as a first-class welder.

JSI is a Florida corporation that runs several shipyards engaged in the business of ship repair, including the Commercial Yard and the Mayport Yard. As a federal contractor, JSI has affirmative action and nondiscrimination obligations. Defendant Arnold McIlwain (McIlwain) held the office of President of JSI from the time Robinson was hired by the company through the time of the trial of this case.

In addition to a welding department, JSI's other craft departments including shipfitting, sheetmetal, electrical, transportation, shipping, and receiving (including toolroom), carpenter, boilermaker, inside machine, outside machine, rigging, quality assurance, and pipe. Employees in these craft departments may be assigned to work at either the Mayport Yard, situated at the Mayport Naval Station, or the Commercial Yard, situated at a riverfront site in downtown Jacksonville and sometimes referred to as the downtown yard. Robinson's job assignments at JSI have required her to work at both the Commercial Yard and the Mayport Yard. Ship repair work is a dangerous profession; JSI acknowledges the need to "provide a working environment that is safe and healthful."

JSI is, in the words of its employees, "a boys club" and "more or less a man's world." Women craftworkers are an extreme rarity. The company's EEO-1 reports from 1980 to 1987 typically show that women form less than 5 percent of the skilled crafts.

Pictures of nude and partially nude women appear throughout the JSI work place in the form of magazines, plaques on the wall, photographs torn from magazines and affixed to the wall or attached to calendars supplied by advertising tool supply companies (vendors' advertising calendars). JSI has never distributed nor tolerated the distribution of a calendar or calendars with pictures of nude or partially nude men. Management employees from the very top down condoned these displays; often they had their own pictures.

Robinson credibly testified to the extensive, pervasive posting of pictures depicting nude women, partially nude women or sexual conduct and to the occurrence of other forms of harassing behavior perpetrated by her male co-workers and supervisors. Her testimony covered the full term of her employment, from 1977 to 1988.

Reported incidents included the following:

1. pictures in the fab shop area, in January 1985, including one of a woman wearing black tights, the top pulled down to expose her breasts to view, and one of a nude woman in an outdoor setting apparently playing with a piece of cloth between her legs.
2. a picture of a nude woman left on the tool box where Robinson returned her tools in the summer of 1986. The photograph depicted the woman's legs spread apart, knees bend up toward her chest exposing her breast and genitals. Several men were present and laughed at Robinson when she appeared upset by the picture.
3. a drawing on a heater control box, approximately one foot square, of a nude woman with fluid coming from her genital area, in 1987, at the Commercial Yard.
4. a dart board with a drawing of a woman's breast with her nipple as the bull's eye, in 1987 or 1988, at the Commercial Yard.

Robinson also testified about comments of a sexual nature she recalled hearing at JSI from co-workers. In some instances these comments were made while she also was in the presence of the pictures of nude or partially nude women. Among the remarks Robinson recalled are, "Hey pussycat, come here and give me a whiff," "The more you lick it, the harder it gets," "I'd like to get in bed with that," "I'd like to have some of that," "Black women taste like sardines," "It doesn't hurt women to have sex right after childbirth," and so on. Defendants have admitted that pictures of nude or partially nude women have been posted in the shipfitters' trailer at the Mayport Yard during Robinson's employment at JSI.

Based on the foregoing, the court finds that sexually harassing behavior occurred through the JSI working environment with both frequency and intensity over the relevant time period. Robinson did not welcome such behavior.

In April 1987, during the pendency of this lawsuit, JSI adopted a new sexual harassment policy. It was instituted unilaterally, without consulting or bargaining with the union. The official policy statement, signed by Vice-President for Operations Larry Brown, endorses the following policy:

1. It is illegal and a violation of Jacksonville Shipyards, Inc., policy for any employee, male or female, to sexually harass another employee by:
   a. making unwelcomed sexual advances or request for sexual favors or other verbal or physical conduct of a sexual nature, a condition of an employee's continued employment, or
   b. making submission to or rejection of such conduct the basis for employment decisions affecting the employee, or
   c. creating an intimidating, hostile, or offensive working environment by such conduct.
2. Any employee who believes he or she has been the subject of sexual harassment, should report the alleged act immediately to John Stewart Ext. 3716 in our Industrial Relations Department. An investigation of all complaints will be undertaken immediately. Any supervisor, agent or other employee who has been found by the Company to have sexually harassed another employee will be subject to appropriate sanctions, depending on the circumstances, from a warning in his or her file up to and including termination.

The 1987 policy had little or no impact on the sexually hostile work environment at JSI. Employees and supervisors lacked the knowledge and training in the scope of those acts that might constitute sexual harassment.

The court finds that the policies and procedures at JSI for responding to complaints of sexual harassment are inadequate. The company has done an inadequate job of communicating with employees and supervisors regarding the nature and scope of sexually harassing behavior. This failure is compounded by a pattern of unsympathetic response to complaints by employees who perceive that they are victims of harassment. This pattern includes an unwillingness to believe the accusations, an unwillingness to take prompt and stern remedial action against admitted harassers, and an express condonation of behavior that is and encourages sexually harassing conduct (such as the posting of pictures of nude and partially nude women). In some instances, the process of registering a complaint about sexual harassment became a second episode of harassment.

Ordered and Adjudged

That defendant Jacksonville Shipyards, Inc., is hereby enjoined to cease and desist from the maintenance of a work environment that is hostile to women because of their sex and to remedy the hostile work environment through the implementation, forthwith, of the Sexual Harassment Policy, which consists of the "Statement of Policy," "Statement of Prohibited Conduct," "Schedule of Penalties for Misconduct," "Procedures for Making, Investigating and Resolving Sexual Harassment and Retaliation Complaints," and "Procedures and Rules for Education and Training."

Jacksonville Shipyards, Inc., Sexual Harassment Policy Statement of Policy

Title VII of the Civil Rights Act of 1964 prohibits employment discrimination on the basis of race, color, sex, age, or national origin. Sexual harassment is included among the prohibitions.

Sexual harassment, according to the federal Equal Employment Opportunity Commission (EEOC), consists of unwelcome sexual advances, requests for sexual favors or other verbal or physical acts of a sexual or sex-based nature where (1) submission to such conduct is made either explicitly or implicitly a term or condition of an individual's employment; (2) an employment decision is based on an individual's acceptance or rejection of such conduct; or (3) such conduct interferes with an individual's work performance or creates an intimidating, hostile or offensive working environment.

Case A.19
X-TRA Art, Inc. v. Consumer Product Safety Commission

1991 U.S. Dist. Lexis 8290 (N.D. Cal.) (1991)
United States District Court, Northern District of California
Patel, District Judge

X-TRA Art, Inc., produces Rainbow Foam Paint (Rainbow) a shaving cream-like paint designed for use by children ages three years and up. In December 1990, Consumers Union, a nonprofit organization, published an article in the children's magazine "Zillions," which indicated that Rainbow was an unsafe toy because it could catch fire. Plaintiffs demanded a retraction. Irwin Landau, Consumers Union editorial director, initially sent a letter apologizing for the article and indicating that Consumers Union had made a mistake and would publish a retraction. On December 31, 1990, Landau sent plaintiffs another letter indicating that Consumers Union had conducted additional tests on Rainbow, believed the paint to be in violation of the Federal Hazardous Substances Act (FHSA), and had reported it to the Consumer Product Safety Commission (CPSC). Tests conducted by the CPSC indicated that the Rainbow container, when held upright horizontally, and especially upside down, and exposed to a flame at times produced a flame or flashback (a flame extending back to the dispenser).

On January 17, 1991, Lee Baxter of the CPSC sent plaintiffs a Letter of Advice informing plaintiffs that the CPSC had found Rainbow to be a banned hazardous substance under the FHSA because it was flammable. Baxter requested that X-TRA Art cease distribution and sale of the product and reformulate it. The letter provided plaintiffs with an opportunity to submit opposing views and warned plaintiffs of potential criminal liability if X-TRA Art continued to distribute Rainbow. A copy of the letter was sent to the California Department of Health Services, which subsequently recommended to the California Department of

Education that Rainbow not be purchased for use in California public schools.

Plaintiffs sent two letters to the CPSC outlining the objections to the Letter of Advice. The CPSC responded in a letter dated March 18, 1991, which addressed plaintiffs' objections and threatened civil penalties if X-TRA Art did not cease distribution of Rainbow.

As a result of the CPSC findings, on April 26, 1991, the United States Attorney for the Connecticut district secured a warrant authorizing the seizure of Rainbow stored at Early Learning Centre, a toy distribution warehouse in Milford, Connecticut. The warrant was executed on April 29 and the Early Learning Centre instructed its outlets to cease sale of the product. The U.S. Attorney issued a press release detailing the seizure action and CPSC findings regarding Rainbow. Plaintiffs have moved for a preliminary injunction to prevent any further government action against Rainbow.

X-TRA Art brought this action to enjoin the CPSC from taking any action to remove Rainbow Foam Paint from the market pursuant to the Federal Hazardous Substances Act. Plaintiffs argue that: (1) the CPSC has failed to follow statutorily mandated procedural requirements in declaring Rainbow a banned hazardous substance pursuant to the FHSA; (2) the CPSC used invalid and improper testing methods in determining that Rainbow is flammable; (3) the CPSC violated provisions of the Consumer Product Safety Act, governing public disclosure of findings concerning safety hazards posed by products; (4) the CPSC cannot establish that substantial injury or illness can be caused as a proximate result of any customary or reasonably foreseeable use of Rainbow, as required by the FHSA; and (5) plaintiffs' rights to due process and equal protection have been violated.

Following an evidentiary hearing on May 7, 1991, the court ordered the government to desist from taking any action against Rainbow for ten days and further ordered the parties to file additional briefing on the matter. Having reviewed the parties' papers and held an additional hearing, the court DENIES plaintiffs' motion for a preliminary injunction.

The CPSC argues that under FHSA a product intended for use by children is automatically banned if the CPSC determines said product to be a hazardous substance. Plaintiffs, citing to other provisions of the FSHA, contend that a children's product such as Rainbow may not be banned without notice, comment, and a public hearing. The plain language of the FSHA supports the CPSC's position.

In 1966, Congress amended the FHSA to authorize the banning of hazardous toys, children's articles and household goods; "Labeling" was deleted from the title of the FHSLA and the Federal Hazardous Substance Act was created. The legislative history of the 1966 amendments makes it clear that, while the banning of hazardous household substances was to occur only after a public hearing, Congress intended that the Secretary (Commission) have the power to ban hazardous toys and children's articles without regulation. There is no question that plaintiffs were provided with notice of the agency action, given the Letter of Advice and the correspondence between plaintiffs and the CPSC which followed. Moreover, in early 1990 the CPSC determined that foam-like string streamers designed for children and dispensed from self-pressurized containers were flammable and therefore were banned hazardous substances. The manufacturer voluntarily recalled its products and reformulated them with a non-flammable propellant. The agency action against the string streamer products appears to have been well publicized. In light of the similarity between the string streamer products and Rainbow Foam Paint, it is surprising to hear plaintiffs argue that they were caught completely off guard by the agency action challenged in this case.

The court concludes that X-TRA Art raised serious legal issues with regard to the procedures utilized by the CPSC in declaring Rainbow Foam Paint a "banned hazardous substance" and that plaintiffs are unlikely to prevail on the merits of the issue. This being the case, plaintiffs' motion for a preliminary injunction is DENIED.

Case A.20

FMC Corp. v. U.S. Department of Commerce

786 F. Supp. 471, 1992 U.S. Dist. Lexis 2355 (E.D. Pa. 1992)
United States District Court, Eastern District of Pennsylvania
Newcomer, District Judge

This action is brought pursuant to the Comprehensive Environmental Response, Compensation and Liability Act of 1980, as amended (CERCLA), and the Declaratory Judgment Act. Plaintiff FMC Corporation (FMC) owned and operated, from 1963 to 1976, the Avtex site in Front Royal, Virginia (the Facility), a site which has been listed on the National Priorities List since 1986. FMC seeks indemnification from the defendants for some portion of its present and future response costs of response in performing removal actions and other response actions at the Facility. FMC bases its claim on the United States Government (Government) activities during the period of January 1942 through 1945 relating to the operation of a rayon manufacturing facility at the Avtex site, and contends that these activities render the Government liable as an "owner," "operator," and/or "arranger" under section 107 of the CERCLA.

During World War II, after the bombing of Pearl Harbor and the Japanese conquest of Asia, the United States suffered a loss of 90 percent of its crude rubber supply. An urgent need arose for natural rubber substitute to be used in manufacturing airplane tires, jeep tires, and other war related items. The best rubber substitute available was high tenacity rayon tire cord. The Facility was one of the major producers of high tenacity rayon yarn, which was twisted and woven into high tenacity rayon tire cord. FMC presented evidence at trial showing that during the World War II period, the Government participated in managing and controlling the Facility, which was then owned by American Viscose Corporation (American Viscose), requiring the Facility to manufacture increasing quantities of high tenacity rayon yarn, which involved the treatment of hazardous materials, and necessitated the disposal of hazardous materials. FMC also presented evidence showing that the Government owned "facilities" and equipment at the plant used in the treatment and disposal of hazardous materials.

The evidence included the following:

1. During World War II, the Government took over numerous plants which, for a multitude of reasons, failed to meet production requirements, including a plant producing high tenacity rayon yarn. Beginning no later than 1943, the rayon tire cord program received constant attention from the highest officials of the War Production Board (WPB), as well as top officials of the War Department and other Government departments and agencies.
2. Once the WPB determined that there was a need for substantial expansion of the production capabilities at the Facility, Government personnel were assigned to facilitate and expedite construction. The rayon tire cord program, in general, and the implementation of the program at the Facility, in particular, required and received far more involvement, participation, and control by the Government than the vast majority of the production programs implemented during World War II.
3. The disposal or treatment of hazardous substances is inherent in the production of high tenacity rayon yarn. The Government was familiar with the Facility's process for producing high tenacity rayon yarn. The Government knew or should have known that the disposal or treatment of hazardous substances was inherent in the manufacture of high tenacity rayon yarn and that its production requirements caused a significant increase in the amount of hazardous substances generated and disposed of at the Facility.

The district court concluded that the United States, through the actions and authority of WPB and other departments, agencies, and instrumentalities of the United States Government, "operated" the Facility, from approximately January 1942 to at least November 1945, as defined by section 101(2) of the CERCLA. During the period the Government operated the Facility, wastes containing "hazardous substances," as defined by section 101(14) of CERCLA, and as identified in 40 C.F.R. Part 302, Table 302.4 (1990), were "disposed of" at the Facility.

There has been a "release or threatened release" of hazardous substances from the facilities which were owned by the United States. Such release or threatened release of hazardous substances has caused and will continue to cause FMC to incur "necessary costs of response" within the meaning of Section 107 of CERCLA, including without limitation the costs which FMC has incurred and will incur in monitoring, assessing, and evaluating the release or threatened release of hazardous substances and performing removal and/or remedial activities and taking other actions required or requested by the EPA, as well as attorneys' fees and expenses associated with this lawsuit.

Liability of an owner or operator of a facility as defined by §107(a) for the cost of removal "is strict and joint and several." The United States Government as owner is responsible for costs resulting from responses to the release of hazardous substances.

And it is SO ORDERED.

Case A.21

Texaco, Inc. v. Hasbrouck dba Rick's Texaco

496 U.S. 543, 110 S.Ct. 2535, 1990 U.S. Lexis 3142 (1990)
Supreme Court of the United States
Stevens, Justice

Petitioner (Texaco) sold gasoline directly to respondents and several other retailers in Spokane, Washington, at its retail tank wagon (RTW) prices while it granted substantial discounts to two distributors. During the period between 1972 and 1981, the stations supplied by the two distributors increased their sales volume dramatically, while respondents' sales suffered a corresponding decline. Respondents filed an action against Texaco under the Robinson-Patman Amendment to the Clayton Act (Act), alleging that the distributor discounts violated Section 2(a) of the Act. Respondents recovered treble damages, and the Court of Appeals for the Ninth Circuit affirmed the judgment. We granted certiorari to consider Texaco's contention that legitimate functional discounts do not violate the act because a seller is not responsible for its customers' independent resale pricing decisions. While we agree with the basic thrust of Texaco's argument, we conclude that in this case it is foreclosed by the facts of record.

Respondents are 12 independent Texaco retailers. They displayed the Texaco trademark, accepted Texaco credit cards, and bought their gasoline products directly from Texaco. Texaco delivered the gasoline to respondents' stations. The retail gasoline market in Spokane was highly competitive throughout the damages period, which ran from 1972 to 1981. Stations marketing the nationally advertised Texaco gasoline competed with other major brands as well as with stations featuring independent brands. Moreover, although discounted prices at a nearby Texaco station would have the most obvious impact on a respondent's trade, the cross-city traffic patterns and relatively small size of Spokane produced a city-wide competitive market. Texaco's throughput sales in the Spokane market declined from a monthly volume of 569,269 gallons in 1970 to 389,557 gallons in 1975. Texaco's independent retailers' share of the market for Texaco gas declined from 76 percent to 49 percent. Seven of the respondents' stations were out of business by the end of 1978.

The respondents tried unsuccessfully to increase their ability to compete with lower priced stations. Some tried converting from full service to self-service stations. Two of the respondents sought to buy their own tank trucks and haul their gasoline from Texaco's supply point, but Texaco vetoed that proposal.

While the independent retailers struggled, two Spokane gasoline distributors supplied by Texaco prospered. Gull Oil Company (Gull) had its headquarters in Seattle and distributed petroleum products in four western states under its own name. In Spokane it purchased its gas from Texaco at prices that ranged from six to four cents below Texaco's RTW price. Gull resold that product under its own name; the fact that it was being supplied by Texaco was not known by either the public or the respondents. In Spokane, Gull supplied about 15 stations; some were "consignment stations" and some were "commission stations." In both situations Gull retained title to the gasoline until it was pumped into a motorist's tank. In the consignment stations, the station operator set the retail prices, but in the commission stations Gull set the prices and paid the operator a commission. Its policy was to price its gasoline at a penny less than the prevailing price for major brands. Gull employed two truck drivers in Spokane who picked up product at Texaco's bulk plant and delivered it to the Gull Stations. It also employed one supervisor in Spokane. Apart from its trucks and investment in retail facilities, Gull apparently owned no assets in that market. At least with respect to the commission stations, Gull is fairly characterized as a retailer of gasoline throughout the relevant period.

The Dompier Oil Company (Dompier) started business in 1954 selling Quaker State Motor Oil. In 1960 it became a full line distributor of Texaco products, and by the mid-1970s its sales of gasoline represented over three-quarters of its business. Dompier purchased Texaco gasoline at prices of 3.95 cents to 3.65 cents below the RTW price. Dompier thus paid a higher price than Gull, but Dompier, unlike Gull, resold its gas under the Texaco brand names. It supplied about eight to ten Spokane retail stations. In the period prior to October 1974, two of those stations were owned by the president of Dompier but the others were independently operated. In the early 1970s, Texaco representatives encouraged Dompier to enter the retail business directly, and in 1974 and 1975 it acquired four stations. Dompier's president estimated at trial that the share of its total gasoline sales made at retail during the middle 1970s was "probably 84 to 90 percent."

Like Gull, Dompier picked up Texaco's product at the Texaco bulk plant and delivered directly to retail outlets. Unlike Gull, Dompier owned a bulk storage facility, but it was seldom used because its capacity was less than that of many retail stations. Again, unlike Gull, Dompier received from Texaco the equivalent of the common carrier rate for delivering the gasoline product to the retail outlets. Thus, in addition to its discount from the RTW price, Dompier made a profit on its hauling function.

The stations supplied by Dompier regularly sold at retail at lower prices than respondents. Even before Dompier directly entered the retail business in 1974, its customers were selling to consumers at prices barely above the RTW price. Dompier's sales volume increased continuously and substantially throughout the relevant period. Between 1970 and 1975 its monthly sales volume increased from 155,152 gallons to 462,956 gallons; this represented an increase from 20.7 percent to almost 50 percent of Texaco's sales in Spokane.

There was ample evidence that Texaco executives were well aware of Dompier's dramatic growth and believed that it was attributable to "the magnitude of the distributor discount and the hauling allowance." In response to complaints from individual respondents about Dompier's aggressive pricing, however, Texaco representatives professed that they couldn't understand it.

Respondents filed suit against Texaco in July 1976. After a four-week trial, the jury awarded damages measured by the difference between the RTW price and the price paid by Dompier. As we subsequently decided in *J. Truett Payne Co. v. Chrysler Motors Corp.*, this measure of damages was improper. Accordingly, although it rejected Texaco's defenses on the issue of liability, the Court of Appeal for the Ninth Circuit remanded the case for a new trial.

At the second trial, Texaco contended that the special prices to Gull and Dompier were justified by cost savings, were the product of a good faith attempt to meet competition, and were lawful "functional discounts." The district court withheld the cost justification defense from the jury because it was not supported by the evidence of other defenses. It awarded respondents actual damages of $449,900. The jury apparently credited the testimony of respondents' expert witness who had estimated what the respondents' profits would have been if they had paid the same prices as the four stations owned by Dompier.

In Texaco's motion for judgment notwithstanding the verdict, it claimed as a matter of law that its functional discounts did not adversely affect competition within the meaning of the act because any injury to respondents was attributable to decisions made independently by Dompier. The district court denied the motion. In an opinion supplementing its oral ruling denying Texaco's motion for a directed verdict, the court assumed, arguendo, that Dompier was entitled to a functional discount, even on the gas that was sold at retail, but nevertheless concluded that the "presumed legality of functional discounts" had been rebutted by evidence that the amount of the discounts to Gull and Dompier was not reasonably related to the cost of any function that they performed.

The court of appeals affirmed. It reasoned: "As the Supreme Court long ago made clear, and recently affirmed, there may be a Robinson-Patman violation even if the favored and disfavored buyers do not compete, so long as the customers of the favored buyer compete with the disfavored buyer or its customers." Despite the fact that Dompier and Gull, at least in their capacities as wholesalers, did not compete directly with Hasbrouck, a Section 2(a) violation may occur if (1) the discount they received was not cost-based and (2) all or a portion of it was passed on by them to customers of theirs who competed with Hasbrouck. "Hasbrouck presented ample evidence to demonstrate that the services performed by Gull and Dompier were insubstantial and did not justify the functional discount."

The court of appeals concluded its analysis by observing: "To hold that price discrimination between a wholesaler and a retailer could never violate the Robinson-Patman Act would leave immune from antitrust scrutiny a discriminatory pricing procedure that can effectively serve to harm competition. We think such a result would be contrary to the objectives of the Robinson-Patman Act."

In order to establish a violation of the act, respondent had the burden of proving four fats: (1) that Texaco's sales to Gull and Dompier were made in interstate commerce; (2) that the gasoline sold to them was of the same grade and quality as that sold to respondents; (3) that Texaco discriminated in price as between Gull and Dompier on the one hand and respondents on the other; and (4) that the discrimination had a prohibited effect on competition. Moreover, for each respondent to recover damages, he had the burden of proving the extent of his actual injuries.

The first two elements of respondents' case are not disputed in this court, and we do not understand Texaco to be challenging the sufficiency of respondents' proof of damages. Texaco does argue, however, that although it charged different prices, it did not "discriminate in price" within the meaning of the act, and that, at least to the extent that Gull and Dompier acted as wholesalers, the price differentials did not injure competition. We consider the two arguments separately.

A supplier need not satisfy the rigorous requirements of the cost justification defense in order to prove that a particular functional discount is reasonable and accordingly did not cause any substantial lessening of competition between a wholesaler's customers and the suppliers' direct customers. The record in this case, however, adequately supports the finding that Texaco violated the act.

Case A.22

Lampf, Pleva, Lipkind, Prupis & Petigrow v. Gilbertson

501 U.S. 350, 111 S.Ct. 2773, 1991 U.S. Lexis 3629 (1991)
Supreme Court of the United States
Blackmun, Justice

The controversy arises from the sale of seven Connecticut limited partnerships formed for the purpose of purchasing and leasing computer hardware and software. Petitioner Lampf, Pleva, Lipkind, Prupis & Petigrow is a West Orange, New Jersey, law firm that aided in organizing the partnerships and that provided additional legal services, including the preparation of opinion letters addressing the tax consequences of investing in the partnerships. The several plaintiff-respondents purchased units in one or more of the partnerships during the years 1979 through 1981 with the expectation of realizing federal income tax benefits therefrom.

The partnerships failed, due in part to the technological obsolescence of their wares. In late 1982 and early 1983, Gilbertson et al. received notice that the United States Internal Revenue Service was investigating the partnerships. The IRS subsequently disallowed the claimed tax benefits because of overvaluation of partnership assets and lack of profit motive. On November 3, 1986, and June 4, 1987, Gilbertson et al. filed their respective complaints in the United States District Court for the District of Oregon, naming as defendant's petitioner and others involved in the preparation of offering memoranda for the partnerships. The complaints alleged that plaintiff-respondents were induced to invest in the partnerships by misrepresentations in the offering memoranda, in violation of, among other things, § 10(b) of the 1934 Securities Exchange Act and Rule 10b-5. The claimed misrepresentations were said to include assurances that the investments would entitle the purchasers to substantial tax benefits; that the leasing of the hardware and software packages would generate a profit; that the software was readily marketable; and that certain equipment appraisals were accurate and reasonable. Gilbertson et al. asserted that they became aware of the alleged misrepresentations only in 1985 following the disallowance by the IRS of the tax benefits claimed.

After consolidating the actions for discovery and pretrial proceedings, the district court granted summary judgment for the defendants on the ground that the complaints were not timely filed. The Court of Appeals for the Ninth Circuit reversed and remanded the cases. In view of the divergence of opinion among the circuits regarding the proper limitations period for Rule 10b-5 claims, we granted certiorari to address this important issue.

It is the usual rule that when Congress has failed to provide a statute of limitations for a federal cause of action, a court "borrows" or "absorbs" the local time limitation most analogous to the case at hand. This practice, derived from the Rules of Decision Act, has enjoyed sufficient longevity that we may assume that, in enacting remedial legislation, Congress ordinarily "intends by its silence that we borrow state law." The rule, however, is not without exception.

First, the court must determine whether a uniform statute of limitations is to be selected. Where a federal cause of action tends in practice to "encompass numerous and diverse topics and subtopics," such that a single state limitations period may not be consistently applied within a jurisdiction, we have concluded that the federal interests in predictability and judicial economy counsel the adoption of one source, or class of sources, for borrowing purposes.

Second, assuming a uniform limitations period is appropriate, the court must decide whether this period should be derived from a state or federal source. In making this judgment, the court should accord particular weight to the geographic character of the claim.

Finally, even where geographic considerations counsel federal borrowing, the aforementioned presumption of state borrowing that requires that a court determine that an analogous federal source truly affords a "closer fit" with the cause of action at issue than does any available state-law source. Although considerations pertinent to this determination will necessarily vary depending upon the federal cause of action and the available state and federal analogues, such factors as commonality of purpose and similarity of elements will be relevant.

We conclude that where, as here, the claim asserted is one implied under a statute that also contains an express cause of action with its own time limitation, a court should look first to the statute of origin to ascertain the proper limitations period. In the present litigation, there can be no doubt that the contemporaneously enacted express remedial provisions represent "a federal statute of limitations actually designed to accommodate a balance of interests very similar to that at stake here—a statute that is, in fact, an analogy to the present lawsuit more apt than any of the suggested state-law parallels." The 1934 Act contained a number of express causes of action, each with an explicit limitations period. With only one more restrictive exception, each of these include some variation of a one-year period after discovery combined with a three-year period of repose. In adopting the 1934 Act, the 73rd Congress also amended the limitations provision of the 1933 Act, adopting the one- and three-year structure for each cause of action contained therein. We therefore conclude that we must reject the Commission's contention that the five-year period contained in § 20A, added to the 1934 Act in 1988, is more appropriate for § 10(b) actions than is the one- and three-year structure in the act's original remedial provisions.

Litigation instituted pursuant to § 10(b) and Rule 10b-5 therefore must be commenced within one year after the discovery of the facts constituting the violation and within three years after such violation. As there is no dispute that the earliest of plaintiff-respondents' complaints was filed more than three years after petitioners' alleged misrepresentations, Gilbertson et al. claims were untimely.

The judgment of the court of appeals is REVERSED.

Case A.23
Walker V. Quillen

1993 Del. Lexis 105 (1993)
Supreme Court of Delaware
Moore, Justice

Pursuant to Supreme Court Rule 25(a), appellees, Elizabeth Stay Ayres and Clara Louise Quillen, have moved to affirm a judgment of the Court of Chancery granting an implied easement in favor of appellees' servient estate, as against the dominant estate of appellant, Irvin C. Walker (Walker). The appellees contend that sufficient evidence supports the findings of the Court of Chancery and that there was no abuse of discretion in granting the implied easement. We agree and affirm.

The appellees own in fee simple absolute a tract of land in Sussex County known as "Bluff Point." The tract is surrounded on three sides by Rehoboth Bay and is landlocked on the fourth side by Walker's land. At one time, the two tracts in question were held by a common owner. In 1878, Bluff Point was sold in fee simple absolute apart from the other holdings, thereby landlocking the parcel. A narrow dirt road, which traverses Walker's land, connects Bluff Point to a public road, and is its only means of access.

Under the doctrine of implied easement or easement by necessity the Court of Chancery found that the appellees were entitled to cross over a portion of Walker's land for access to Bluff Point. The court also found that water access, even if a reasonable substitute for land access, was not feasible because of the shallowness of the water surrounding Bluff Point. There is ample evidence in the record to support the finding that the two tracts originated from the unified holdings of one owner, and that an implied easement was created by the severance which landlocked Bluff Point. The record also sufficiently supports the finding that navigable access to Bluff Point was not feasible. NOW, THEREFORE, IT IS ORDERED that the judgment of the Court of Chancery be, and the same hereby is, AFFIRMED.

Case A.24
Dewsnup v. Timm

502 U.S. 410, 112 S. Ct. 773, 1992 U.S. Lexis 375 (1992)
Supreme Court of the United States
Blackmun, Justice

We are confronted in this case with an issue concerning §506(d) of the Bankruptcy Code. May a debtor "strip down" a creditor's lien on real property to the value of the collateral, as judicially determined, when that value is less than the amount of the claim secured by the lien?

On June 1, 1978, respondents loaned $119,000 to petitioner Aletha Dewsnup and her husband, T. LaMar Dewsnup, since deceased. The loan was accompanied by a Deed of Trust granting a lien on two parcels of Utah farmland owned by the Dewsnups. Petitioner defaulted the following year. Under the terms of the Deed of Trust, respondents at that point could have proceeded against the real property collateral by accelerating the maturity of the loan, issuing a notice of default, and selling the land at a public foreclosure sale to satisfy the debt.

Respondents did issue a notice of default in 1981. Before the foreclosure sale took place, however, petitioner sought reorganization under Chapter 11 of the Bankruptcy Code. That bankruptcy petition was dismissed, as was a subsequent Chapter 11 petition. In June 1984, petitioner filed a petition seeking liquidation under Chapter 7 of the Code. Because of the pendency of these bankruptcy proceedings, respondents were not able to proceed to the foreclosure sale.

Petitioner-debtor takes the position that §506(a) and §506(d) are complementary and to be read together. Because, under §506(a), a claim is secured only to the extent of the judicially determined value of the real property on which the lien is fixed, a debtor can void a lien on the property pursuant to §506(d) to the extent the claim is no longer secured and thus is not "an allowed secured claim." In other words, §506(a) bifurcates classes of claims allowed under §502 into secured claims and unsecured claims; any portion of an allowed claim deemed to be unsecured under §506(a) is not an "allowed secured claim" within the lien-voiding scope of §506(d). Petition argues that there is no exception for unsecured property abandoned by the trustee.

We conclude that respondents' alternative position, espoused also by the United States, although not without its difficulty, generally is the best of the several approaches. Therefore, we hold that §506(d) does not allow petitioner to "strip down" respondents' lien, because respondents' claim is secured by a lien and ha been fully allowed pursuant to §502.

The practical effect of petitioner's argument is to freeze the creditor's secured interest at the judicially determined valuation. By this approach, the creditor would lose the benefit of any increase in the value of the property by the time of the foreclosure sale. The increase would accrue to the benefit of the debtor, a result some of the parties describe as a "windfall."

We think, however, that the creditor's lien stays with the real property until the foreclosure. That is what was bargained for by the mortgagor and the mortgagee. Any increase over the judicially determined valuation during bankruptcy rightly accrues to the benefit of the creditor, not to the benefit of the debtor and not to the benefit of other unsecured creditors whose claims have been allowed and who had nothing to do with the mortgagor–mortgagee bargain.

No provision of the pre-Code statute permitted involuntary reduction of the amount of a creditor's lien for any reason other than payment on the debt.

The judgment of the court of appeals is AFFIRMED.

Appendix B — The Constitution of the United States of America

We the People of the United States, in Order to form a more perfect Union, establish Justice, insure domestic Tranquility, provide for the common defense, promote the general Welfare, and secure the Blessings of Liberty to ourselves and our Posterity, do ordain and establish this Constitution for the United States of America.

Article I

Section 1. All legislative Powers herein granted shall be vested in a Congress of the United States, which shall consist of a Senate and House of Representatives.

Section 2. The House of Representatives shall be composed of Members chosen every second Year by the People of the several states, and the Electors in each State shall have the Qualifications requisite for Electors of the most numerous Branch of the State Legislature.

No Person shall be a Representative who shall not have attained to the Age of twenty five Years, and been seven Years a Citizen of the United States, and who shall not, when elected, be an Inhabitant of that State in which he shall be chosen.

Representatives and direct Taxes shall be apportioned among the several states which may be included within this Union, according to their respective Numbers, which shall be determined by adding to the whole Number of free Persons, including those bound to Service for a Term of Years, and excluding Indians not taxed, three fifths of all other Persons. The actual Enumeration shall be made within three Years after the first Meeting of the Congress of the United States, and within every subsequent Term of ten Years, in such Manner as they shall by Law direct. The number of Representatives shall not exceed one for every thirty Thousand, but each State shall have at Least one Representative; and until such enumeration shall be made, the State of New Hampshire shall be entitled to chuse three, Massachusetts eight, Rhode Island and Providence Plantations one, Connecticut five, New York six, New Jersey four, Pennsylvania eight, Delaware one, Maryland six, Virginia ten, North Carolina five, South Carolina five, and Georgia three.

When vacancies happen in the Representation from any State, the Executive Authority thereof shall issue Writs of Election to fill such vacancies.

The House of Representatives shall chuse their Speaker and other Officers; and shall have the sole Power of Impeachment.

Section 3. The Senate of the United States shall be composed of two Senators from each State, chosen by the Legislature thereof, for six Years; and each Senator shall have one Vote.

Immediately after they shall be assembled in Consequence of the first Election, they shall be divided as equally as may be into three Classes. The Seats of the Senators of the first Class shall be vacated at the Expiration of the second Year, of the second Class at the Expiration of the fourth Year, and the third Class at the Expiration of the sixth Year, so that one third may be chosen every second Year; and if Vacancies happen by Resignation, or otherwise, during the Recess of the Legislature of any State, the Executive thereof may make temporary Appointments until the next meeting of the Legislature, which shall then fill such Vacancies.

No person shall be a Senator who shall not have attained to the Age of thirty Years, and been nine Years a Citizen of the United States, and who shall not, when elected, be an Inhabitant of that State for which he shall be chosen.

The Vice President of the United States shall be President of the Senate, but shall have no Vote, unless they be equally divided.

The Senate shall chuse their other Officers, and also a President pro tempore, in the Absence of the Vice President, or when he shall exercise the Office of President of the United States.

The Senate shall have the sole power to try all Impeachments. When sitting for that Purpose, they shall be an Oath or Affirmation. When the President of the United States is tried, the Chief Justice shall preside: And no Person shall be convicted without the Concurrence of two thirds of the Members present.

Judgment in Cases of Impeachment shall not extend further than to removal from Office, and disqualification to hold and enjoy any Office of honor, Trust or Profit under the United States: but the Party convicted shall nevertheless be liable and subject to Indictment, Trial, Judgment and Punishment, according to Law.

Section 4. The Times, Places and Manner of holding Elections for Senators and Representatives, shall be prescribed in each State by the Legislature thereof: but the Congress may at any time by Law make or alter such Regulations, except as to the Places of choosing Senators.

The Congress shall assemble at least once in every Year, and such Meeting shall be on the first Monday in December, unless they shall by Law appoint a different day.

Section 5. Each House shall be the Judge of the Elections, Returns and Qualifications of its own Members, and a Majority of each shall constitute a Quorum to do Business; but a smaller Number may adjourn from day to day, and may be authorized to compel the Attendance of absent Members, in such Manner, and under such Penalties as each House may provide.

Each House may determine the Rules of its Proceedings, punish its Members for disorderly Behaviour, and, with the Concurrence of two thirds, expel a Member.

Each House shall keep a Journal of its Proceedings, and from time to time publish the same, excepting such Parts as may in their Judgment require Secrecy; and the Yeas and Nays of the Members of either House on any question shall, at the Desire of one fifth of those Present, be entered on the Journal.

Neither House, during the Session of Congress, shall, without the Consent of the other, adjourn for more than three days, nor to any other Place than that in which the two Houses shall be sitting.

Section 6. The Senators and Representatives shall receive a Compensation for their Services, to be ascertained by Law, and paid out of the Treasury of the United States. They shall in all Cases, except Treason, Felony and Breach of the Peace, be privileged from Arrest during their Attendance at the Session of their respective Houses, and in going to and returning from the same; and for any Speech or Debate in either House, they shall not be questioned in any other Place.

No Senator or Representative shall, during the Time for which he was elected, be appointed to any civil Office under the Authority of the United States, which shall have been created, or the Emoluments whereof shall have been encreased during such time; and no Person holding any Office under the United States, shall be a Member of either House during his Continuance in Office.

Section 7. All Bills for raising Revenue shall originate in the House of Representatives; but the Senate may propose or concur with Amendments as on other Bills.

Every Bill which shall have passed the House of Representatives and the Senate, shall, before it become a Law, be presented to the President of the United States; If he approve he shall sign it, but if not he shall return it, with his Objections to that House in which it shall have originated, who shall enter the Objections at large on their Journal, and proceed to reconsider it. If after such Reconsideration two thirds of that House shall agree to pass the Bill, it shall be sent, together with the Objections, to the other House, by which it shall likewise be reconsidered, and if approved by two thirds of that House, it shall become a Law. But in all such Cases the Votes of both Houses shall be determined by Yeas and Nays, and the Names of the Persons voting for and against the Bill shall be entered on the Journal of each House respectively. If any Bill shall not be returned by the President within ten Days (Sundays excepted) after it shall have been presented to him, the Same shall be a Law, in like Manner as if he had signed it, unless the Congress by their Adjournment prevent its Return, in which Case it shall not be a Law.

Every Order, Resolution, or Vote to which the Concurrence of the Senate and House of Representatives may be necessary (except on a question of Adjournment) shall be presented to the President of the United States; and before the Same shall take Effect, shall be approved by him, or being disapproved by him, shall be repassed by two thirds of the Senate and House of Representatives, according to the Rules and Limitations prescribed in the Case of a Bill.

Section 8. The Congress shall have Power to lay and collect Taxes, Duties, Imposts and Excises, to pay the Debts and provide for the common Defence and general Welfare of the United States; but all Duties, Imposts and Excises shall be uniform throughout the United States;

To borrow Money on the credit of the United States;

To regulate Commerce with foreign Nations, and among the several States, and with the Indian Tribes;

To establish an uniform Rule of Naturalization, and uniform Laws on the subject of Bankruptcies throughout the United States;

To coin Money, regulate the Value thereof, and of foreign Coin, and fix the Standard of Weights and Measures;

To provide for the Punishment of counterfeiting the Securities and current Coin of the United States;

To establish Post Offices and post Roads;

To promote the Progress of Science and useful Arts, by securing for limited Times to Authors and Inventors the exclusive Right to their respective Writings and Discoveries;

To constitute Tribunals inferior to the supreme Court;

To define and punish Piracies and Felonies committed on the high Seas, and Offenses against the Law of Nations;

To declare War, grant Letters of Marque and Reprisal, and make Rules concerning Captures on Land and Water;

To raise and support Armies, but no Appropriation of Money to that Use shall be for a longer Term than two Years;

To provide and maintain a Navy;

To make Rules for the Government and Regulation of the land and naval Forces;

To provide for calling forth the Militia to execute the Laws of the Union, suppress Insurrections and repel Invasions;

To provide for organizing, arming, and disciplining, the Militia, and for governing such Part of them as may be employed in the Service of the United States, reserving to the States respectively, the Appointment of the Officers, and the Authority of training the Militia according to the discipline prescribed by Congress;

To exercise exclusive Legislation in all Cases whatsoever, over such District (not exceeding ten Miles square) as may, by Cession of particular States, and the Acceptance of Congress, become the Seat of the Government of the United States, and to exercise like Authority over all Places purchased by the Consent of the Legislature of the State in which the Same shall be, for the Erection of Forts, Magazines, Arsenals, dock-Yards, and other needful Buildings;—And

To make all Laws which shall be necessary and proper for carrying into Execution the foregoing Powers, and all other Powers vested by this Constitution in the Government of the United States, or in any Department or Officer thereof.

Section 9. The Migration or Importation of such Persons as any of the States now existing shall think proper to admit, shall not be prohibited by the Congress prior to the Year one thousand eight hundred and eight, but a Tax or Duty may be imposed on such Importation, not exceeding ten dollars for each Person.

The Privilege of the Writ of Habeas Corpus shall not be suspended, unless when in Cases of Rebellion or Invasion the public Safety may require it.

No Bill of Attainder or ex post facto Law shall be passed.

No Capitation, or other direct, Tax shall be laid, unless in Proportion to the Census or Enumeration herein before directed to be taken.

No Tax or Duty shall be laid on Articles exported from any State.

No Preference shall be given by any Regulation of Commerce or Revenue to the Ports of one State over those of another; nor shall Vessels bound to, or from, one State, be obliged to enter, clear, or pay Duties in another.

No Money shall be drawn from the Treasury, but in Consequence of Appropriations made by Laws; and a regular Statement and Account of the Receipts and Expenditures of all public Money shall be published from time to time.

No Title of Nobility shall be granted by the United States: And no Person holding any Office of Profit or Trust under them, shall, without the Consent of the Congress, accept of any present, Emolument, Office, or Title, of any kind whatever, from any King, Prince, or foreign State.

Section 10. No State shall enter into any Treaty, Alliance, or Confederation; grant Letters of Marque and Reprisal; coin Money; emit Bills of Credit; make any Thing but gold and silver Coin a Tender in Payment of Debts; pass any Bill of Attainder, ex post facto Law, or Law impairing the Obligation of Contracts, or grant any Title of Nobility.

No State shall, without the Consent of the Congress, lay any Imposts or Duties on Imports or Exports, except what may be absolutely necessary for executing its inspection Laws: and the net Produce of all Duties and Imposts, laid by any State on Imports or Exports, shall be for the Use of the Treasury of the United States; and all such Laws shall be subject to the Revision and Control of the Congress.

No State shall, without the Consent of Congress, lay any Duty of Tonnage, keep Troops, or Ships of War in time of Peace, enter into any Agreement or Compact with another State, or with a foreign Power, or engage in War, unless actually invaded, or in such imminent Danger as will not admit of delay.

Article II

Section 1. The executive Power shall be vested in a President of the United States of America. He shall hold his Office during the Term of four Years, and, together with the Vice President, chosen for the same Term, be elected, as follows:

Each State shall appoint, in such Manner as the Legislature thereof may direct, a Number of Electors, equal to the whole Number of Senators and Representatives to which the State may be entitled in the Congress: but no Senator or Representative, or Person holding an Office of Trust or Profit under the United States, shall be appointed an Elector.

The Electors shall meet in their respective States, and vote by Ballot for two Persons, of whom one at least shall not be an Inhabitant of the same State with themselves. And they shall make a list of all the Persons voted for, and of the Number of Votes for each; which List they shall sign and certify, and transmit sealed to the Seat of the Government of the United States, directed to the President of the Senate. The President of the Senate shall, in the presence of the Senate and House of Representatives, open all the Certificates, and the Votes shall be counted. The Person having the greatest Number of Votes shall be the President, if such Number be a Majority of the whole Number of Electors appointed; and if there be more than one who have such Majority, and have an equal Number of Votes, then the House of Representatives shall immediately choose by Ballot one of them for President; and if no Person have a Majority, then from the five highest on the List the said House shall in like Manner choose the President. But in chusing the President, the Votes shall be taken by States, the Representation from each State having one Vote; A quorum for this Purpose shall consist of a Member or Members from two thirds of the States, and a Majority of all the States shall be necessary to a Choice. In every Case, after the Choice of the President, the Person having the greatest Number of Votes of the Electors shall be the Vice President. But if there should remain two or more who have equal Votes, the Senate shall chuse from them by Ballot the Vice President.

The Congress may determine the Time of Chusing the Electors, and the Day on which they shall give their Votes; which Day shall be the same throughout the United States.

No Person except a natural born Citizen, or a Citizen of the United States, at the time of the Adoption of this Constitution, shall be eligible to the Office of President; neither shall any Person be eligible to that Office who shall not have attained to the Age of thirty five Years, and been fourteen Years a Resident within the United States.

In Case of the Removal of the President from Office, or of his Death, Resignation, or Inability to discharge the Powers and Duties of the said Office, the Same shall devolve on the Vice President, and the Congress may by Law provide for the Case of Removal, Death, Resignation or Inability, both of the President and Vice President, declaring what Officer shall then act as President, and such Officer shall act accordingly, until the Disability be removed, or a President shall be elected.

The President shall, at stated Times, receive for his Services, a Compensation, which shall neither be encreased nor diminished during the Period for which he shall have been elected, and he shall not receive within that Period any other Emolument from the United States, or any of them.

Before he enter on the Execution of his Office, he shall take the following Oath or Affirmation:—"I do solemnly swear (or affirm) that I will faithfully execute the Office of President of the United States, and will to the best of my Ability, preserve, protect and defend the Constitution of the United States."

Section 2. The President shall be Commander in Chief of the Army and Navy of the United States, and of the Militia of the several States, when called into the actual Service of the United States; he may require the Opinion, in writing, of the principal Officer in each of the executive Departments, upon any Subject relating to the Duties of their respective Offices, and he shall have Power to grant Reprieves and Pardons for Offences against the United States, except in Cases of Impeachment.

He shall have Power, by and with the Advice and Consent of the Senate, to make Treaties, provided two thirds of the Senators present concur; and he shall nominate, and by and with the Advice and Consent of the Senate, shall appoint Ambassadors, other public Ministers and Consuls, Judges of the supreme Court, and all other Officers of the United States, whose Appointments are not herein otherwise provided for, and which shall be established by Law: but the Congress may by Law vest the Appointment of such inferior Officers, as they think proper, in the President alone, in the Courts of Law, or in the Heads of Departments.

The President shall have Power to fill up all Vacancies that may happen during the Recess of the Senate, by granting Commissions which shall expire at the End of their next Session.

Section 3. He shall from time to time give to the Congress Information of the State of the Union, and recommend to their Consideration such Measures as he shall judge necessary and expedient; he may, on extraordinary Occasions, convene both Houses, or either of them, and in Case of Disagreement between them, with Respect to the Time of Adjournment, he may adjourn them to such Time as he shall think proper; he shall receive Ambassadors and other public Ministers; he shall take Care that the Laws be faithfully executed, and shall Commission all the Officers of the United States.

Section 4. The President, Vice President and all civil Officers of the United States, shall be removed from Office on Impeachment for, and Conviction of, Treason, Bribery, or other high Crimes and Misdemeanors.

Article III

Section 1. The judicial Power of the United States, shall be vested in one supreme Court, and in such inferior Courts as the Congress may from time to time ordain and establish. The Judges, both of the supreme and inferior Courts, shall hold their Offices during good Behaviour, and shall, at Times, receive for their Services, a Compensation, which shall not be diminished during their Continuance in Office.

Section 2. The judicial Power shall extend to all Cases, in Law and Equity, arising under this Constitution, the Laws of the United States, and Treaties made, or which shall be made, under their Authority;—to all Cases affecting Ambassadors, other public Ministers and Consuls;—to all Cases of admiralty and maritime Jurisdiction;—to Controversies to which the United States shall be a Party;—to controversies between two or more States;—between a State and Citizens of another State;—between Citizens of different States;—between Citizens of the same State claiming Lands under Grants of different States, and between a State, or the Citizens thereof, and foreign States, Citizens or Subjects.

In all Cases affecting Ambassadors, other public Ministers and Consuls, and those in which a State shall be Party, the supreme Court shall have original Jurisdiction. In all the other Cases before mentioned, the supreme Court shall have appellate Jurisdiction, both as to Law and Fact, with such Exceptions, and under such Regulations as the Congress shall make.

The Trial of all Crimes, except in Cases of Impeachment, shall be by Jury; and such Trial shall be held in the State where the said Crimes shall have been committed; but when not committed within any State, the Trial shall be at such Place or Places as the Congress may by Law have directed.

Section 3. Treason against the United States, shall consist only in levying War against them, or in adhering to their Enemies, giving them Aid and Comfort. No Person shall be convicted of Treason unless on the Testimony of two Witnesses to the same overt Act, or on Confession in open Court.

The Congress shall have Power to declare the Punishment of Treason, but no Attainder of Treason shall work Corruption of Blood, or Forfeiture except during the Life of the Person attainted.

Article IV

Section 1. Full Faith and Credit shall be given in each State to the public Acts, Records, and judicial Proceedings of every other State. And the Congress may by general Laws prescribe the Manner in which such Arts, Records, and Proceedings shall be proved, and the Effect thereof.

Section 2. The Citizens of each State shall be entitled to all Privileges and Immunities of Citizens in the several States.

A person charged in any State with Treason, Felony, or other Crime, who shall flee from Justice, and be found in another State, shall on Demand of the executive Authority of the State from which he fled, be delivered up, to be removed to the State having Jurisdiction of the Crime.

No Person held to Service or Labour in one State, under the Laws thereof, escaping into another, shall, in Consequence of any Law or Regulation therein, be discharged from such Service or Labour, but shall be delivered up on Claim of the Party to whom such Service or Labour may be due.

Section 3. New States may be admitted by the Congress into this Union; but no new state shall be formed or erected within the Jurisdiction of any other State; nor any State be formed by the Junction of two or more States, or Parts of States, without the Consent of the Legislatures of the States concerned as well as of the Congress.

The Congress shall have Power to dispose of and make all needful Rules and Regulations respecting the Territory or other Property belonging to the United States; and nothing in this Constitution shall be so construed as to Prejudice any Claims of the United States, or of any particular State.

Section 4. The United States shall guarantee to every State in this Union a Republican Form of Government, and shall protect each of them against Invasion; and on Application of the Legislature, or of the Executive (when the Legislature cannot be convened) against domestic Violence.

Article V

The Congress, whenever two thirds of both Houses shall deem it necessary, shall propose Amendments to this Constitution, or, on the Application of the Legislatures of two thirds of the several States, shall call a Convention for proposing Amendments, which, in either Case, shall be valid to all Intents and Purposes, as Part of this Constitution, when ratified by the Legislatures of three fourths of the several States, or by Conventions in three fourths thereof, as the one or the other Mode of Ratification may be proposed by the Congress; Provided that no Amendment which may be made prior to the Year One thousand eight hundred and eight shall in any Manner affect the first and fourth Clauses in the Ninth Section of the first Article; and that no State, without its Consent, shall be deprived of its equal Suffrage in the Senate.

Article VI

All Debts contracted and Engagements entered into, before the Adoption of this Constitution, shall be as valid against the United States under this Constitution, as under the Confederation.

This Constitution, and the Laws of the United States which shall be made in Pursuance thereof; and all Treaties made, or which shall be made, under the Authority of the United States, shall be the supreme Law of the Land; and the Judges in every State shall be bound thereby, any Thing in the Constitution or Laws of any State to the Contrary notwithstanding.

The Senators and Representatives before mentioned, and the Members of the several State Legislatures, and all executive and judicial Officers, both of the United States and of the Several States, shall be bound by Oath or Affirmation, to support this Constitution; but no religious Test shall ever be required as a Qualification to any Office or public Trust under the United States.

Article VII

The Ratification of the Conventions of nine States, shall be sufficient for the Establishment of this Constitution between the States so ratifying the Same.

Amendment I [1791]

Congress shall make no law respecting an establishment of religion, or prohibiting the free exercise thereof; or abridging the freedom of speech, or the press; or the right of the people peaceably to assemble, and to petition the Government for a redress of grievances.

Amendment II [1791]

A well regulated Militia, being necessary to the security for a free State, the right of the people to keep and bear Arms, shall not be infringed.

Amendment III [1791]

No Soldier shall, in time of peace be quartered in any house, without the consent of the Owner, nor in time of war, but in a manner to be prescribed by law.

Amendment IV [1791]

The right of the people to be secure in their persons, houses, papers, and effects, against unreasonable searches and seizures, shall not be violated, and no Warrants shall issue, but upon probable cause, supported by Oath or Affirmation, and particularly describing the place to be searched, and the persons or things to be seized.

Amendment V [1791]

No person shall be held to answer for a capital, or otherwise infamous crime, unless on a presentment or indictment of a Grand Jury, except in cases arising in the land or naval forces, or in the Militia, when in actual service in time of War or public danger; nor shall any person be subject for the same offense to be twice put in jeopardy of life or limb; nor shall be compelled in any criminal case to be a witness against himself, nor be deprived of life, liberty, or property, without due process of law; nor shall private property be taken for public use, without just compensation.

Amendment VI [1791]

In all criminal prosecutions, the accused shall enjoy the right to a speedy and public trial, by an impartial jury of the State and district wherein the crime shall have been committed, which district shall have been previously ascertained by law, and to be informed of the nature and cause of the accusation; to be confronted with the Witnesses against him; to have compulsory process for obtaining witnesses in his favor, and to have the Assistance of counsel for his defence.

Amendment VII [1791]

In suits at common law, where the value in controversy shall exceed twenty dollars, the right of trial by jury shall be preserved, and no fact tried by a jury, shall be otherwise reexamined in any Court of the United States, than according to the rules of the common law.

Amendment VIII [1791]

Excessive bail shall not be required, nor excessive fines imposed, nor cruel and unusual punishments inflicted.

Amendment IX [1791]

The enumeration in the Constitution, of certain rights, shall not be construed to deny or disparage others retained by the people.

Amendment X [1791]

The powers not delegated to the United States by the Constitution, nor prohibited by it to the States, are reserved to the States respectively, or to the people.

Amendment XI [1798]

The judicial power of the United States shall not be construed to extend to any suit in law or equity, commenced or prosecuted against one of the United States by Citizens of another State, or by Citizens or Subjects of any Foreign State.

Amendment XII [1804]

The Electors shall meet in their respective states and vote by ballot for President and Vice-President, one of whom, at least, shall not be an inhabitant of the same state with themselves; they shall name in their ballots the person voted for as President, and in distinct ballots the person voted for as Vice-President, and they shall make distinct lists of all persons voted for as President, and of all persons voted for as Vice-President, and of the number of votes for each, which lists they shall sign and certify, and transmit sealed to the seat of the government of the United States, directed to the President of the Senate;—The President of the Senate shall, in the presence of the Senate and House of Representatives, open all the certificates and the votes shall then be counted;—The person having the greatest number of votes for President, shall be the President, if such number be a majority of the whole number of Electors appointed; and if no person have such majority, then from the persons having the highest numbers not exceeding three on the list of those voted for as President, the House of Representatives shall choose immediately, by ballot, the President. But in choosing the President, the votes shall be taken by states, the representation from each state having one vote; a quorum for this purpose shall consist of a member or members from two-thirds of the states, and a majority of all the states shall be necessary to a choice. And if the House of Representatives shall not choose a President whenever the right of choice shall devolve upon them, before the fourth day of March next following, then the Vice-President shall act as President, as in the case of the death or other constitutional disability of the President. The person having the greatest number of votes as Vice-President, shall be the Vice-President, if such number be a majority of the whole number of Electors appointed, and if no person have a majority, then from the two highest numbers on the list, the Senate shall choose the Vice-President; a quorum for the purpose shall consist of two-thirds of the whole number of Senators, and a majority of the whole number shall be necessary to a choice. But no person constitutionally ineligible to the office of President shall be eligible to that of the Vice-President of the United States.

Amendment XIII [1865]

Section 1. Neither slavery nor involuntary servitude, except as a punishment for crime whereof the party shall have been duly convicted, shall exist within the United States, or any place subject to their jurisdiction.
Section 2. Congress shall have power to enforce this article by appropriate legislation.

Amendment XIV [1868]

Section 1. All persons born or naturalized in the United States, and subject to the jurisdiction thereof, are citizens of the United States and of the State wherein they reside. No State shall make or enforce any law which shall abridge the privileges or immunities of citizens of the United States; nor shall any State deprive any person of life, liberty, or property, without due process of law; nor deny to any person within its jurisdiction the equal protection of the laws.
Section 2. Representatives shall be appointed among the several States according to their respective numbers, counting the whole number of persons in each State, excluding Indians not taxed. But when the right to vote at any election for the choice of electors for President and Vice President of the United States, Representatives in Congress, the Executive and Judicial officers of a State, or the members of the Legislature thereof, is denied to any of the male inhabitants of such State, being twenty-one years of age, and citizens of the United States, or in any way abridged, except for participation in rebellion, or other crime, the basis of representation therein shall be reduced in the proportion which the number of such male citizens shall bear to the whole number of male citizens twenty-one years of age in such State.
Section 3. No person shall be a Senator or Representative in Congress, or elector of President and Vice President, or hold any office, civil or military, under the United States, or under any State, who, having previously taken an oath, as a member of Congress, or as an officer of the United States, or as a member of any State legislature, or as an executive or judicial officer of any State, to support the Constitution of the United States, shall have engaged in insurrection or rebellion against the same, or given aid or comfort to the enemies thereof. But Congress may by a vote of two-thirds of each House, remove such disability.
Section 4. The validity of the public debt of the United States, authorized by law, including debts incurred for payment of pensions and bounties for services in suppressing insurrection or rebellion, shall not be questioned. But neither the United States nor any State shall assume or pay any debt or obligation incurred in aid of insurrection of rebellion against the United States, or any claim for the loss or emancipation of any slave; but all such debts, obligations and claims shall be held illegal and void.
Section 5. The Congress shall have power to enforce, by appropriate legislation, the provisions of this article.

Amendment XV [1870]

Section 1. The right of citizens of the United States to vote shall not be denied or abridged by the United States or by any State on account of race, color, or previous condition of servitude.
Section 2. The Congress shall have power to enforce this article by appropriate legislation.

Amendment XVI [1913]

The Congress shall have power to lay and collect taxes on incomes, from whatever source derived, without apportionment among the several States, and without regard to any census or enumeration.

Amendment XVII [1913]

The Senate of the United States shall be composed of two Senators from each State, elected by the people thereof, for six years; and each Senator shall have one vote. The electors in each State shall have the qualifications requisite for electors of the most numerous branch of the State legislatures.

When vacancies happen in the representation of any State in the Senate, the executive authority of each State shall issue writs of election to fill such vacancies; *Provided*, That the legislature of any State may empower the executive thereof to make temporary appointments until the people fill the vacancies by election as the legislature may direct.

This amendment shall not be so construed as to affect the election or term of any Senator chosen before it becomes valid as part of the Constitution.

Amendment XVIII [1919]

Section 1. After one year from the ratification of this article the manufacture, sale, or transportation of intoxicating liquors within, the importation thereof into, or the exportation thereof from the United States and all territory subject to the jurisdiction thereof for beverage purposes is hereby prohibited.
Section 2. The Congress and the several States shall have concurrent power to enforce this article by appropriate legislation.
Section 3. This article shall be inoperative unless it shall have been ratified as an amendment to the Constitution by the legislatures of the several States, as provided in the Constitution, within seven years from the date of the submission hereof to the States by the Congress.

Amendment XIX [1920]

The right of citizens of the United States to vote shall not be denied or abridged by the United States or by any State on account of sex.

Congress shall have power to enforce this article by appropriate legislation.

Amendment XX [1933]

Section 1. The terms of the President and Vice President shall end at noon on the 20th day of January, and the terms of Senators and Representatives at noon on the 3rd day of January, of the years in which such terms would have ended if this article had not been ratified; and the terms of their successors shall then begin.
Section 2. The Congress shall assemble at least once in every year, and such meeting shall begin at noon on the 3rd day of January, unless they shall by law appoint a different day.
Section 3. If, at the time fixed for the beginning of the term of the President, the President elect shall have died, the Vice President elect shall become President. If a President shall not have been chosen before the time fixed for the beginning of his term, or if the President elect shall have failed to qualify, then the Vice President elect shall act as President until a President shall have qualified; and the Congress may by law provide for the case wherein neither a President elect nor a Vice President elect shall have qualified, declaring who shall then act as President, or the manner in which one who is to act shall be selected, and such person shall act accordingly until a President or Vice President shall have qualified.
Section 4. The Congress may by law provide for the case of the death of any of the persons from whom the House of Representatives may choose a President whenever the right of choice shall have devolved upon them, and for the case of the death of any of the persons from whom the Senate may choose a Vice President whenever the right of choice shall have devolved upon them.
Section 5. Sections 1 and 2 shall take effect on the 15th day of October following the ratification of this article.
Section 6. This article shall be inoperative unless it shall have been ratified as an amendment to the Constitution by the legislatures of three-fourths of the several States within seven years from the date of its submission.

Amendment XXI [1933]

Section 1. The eighteenth article of amendment to the Constitution of the United States is hereby repealed.
Section 2. The transportation or importation into any State, Territory, or possession of the United States for delivery or use therein of intoxicating liquors, in violation of the laws thereof, is hereby prohibited.
Section 3. This article shall be inoperative unless it shall have been ratified as an amendment to the Constitution by conventions in the several States, as provided in the Constitution, within seven years from the date of the submission hereof to the States by the Congress.

Amendment XXII [1951]

Section 1. No person shall be elected to the office of the President more than twice, and no person who has held the office of President, or acted as President, for more than two years of a term to which some other person was elected President shall be elected to the office of the President more than once. But this Article shall not apply to any person holding the office of President when this article was proposed by the Congress, and shall not prevent any person who may be holding the office of President, or acting as President, during the term within which this Article becomes operative from holding the office of President, or acting as President during the remainder of such term.

Section 2. This article shall be inoperative unless it shall have been ratified as an amendment to the Constitution by the legislatures of three-fourths of the several States within seven years from the date of its submission to the States by the Congress.

Amendment XXIII [1961]

Section 1. The District constituting the seat of government of the United States shall appoint in such manner as the Congress may direct:

A number of electors of President and Vice President equal to the whole number of Senators and Representatives in Congress to which the District would be entitled if it were a State, but in no event more than the least populous State; they shall be in addition to those appointed by the States, but they shall be considered, for the purposes of the election of President and Vice President, to be electors appointed by a State; and they shall meet in the District and perform such duties as provided by the twelfth article of amendment.

Section 2. The Congress shall have power to enforce this article by appropriate legislation.

Amendment XXIV [1964]

Section 1. The right of citizens of the United States to vote in any primary or other election for President or Vice President, for electors for President or Vice President, or for Senator or Representative in Congress, shall not be denied or abridged by the United States or any State by reason of failure to pay any poll tax or other tax.

Section 2. The Congress shall have power to enforce this article by appropriate legislation.

Amendment XXV [1967]

Section 1. In case of the removal of the President from office or of his death or resignation, the Vice President shall become President.

Section 2. Whenever there is a vacancy in the office of the Vice President, the President shall nominate a Vice President who shall take office upon confirmation by a majority vote of both Houses of Congress.

Section 3. Whenever the President transmits to the President pro tempore of the Senate and the Speaker of the House of Representatives his written declaration that he is unable to discharge the powers and duties of his office, and until he transmits to them a written declaration to the contrary, such powers and duties shall be discharged by the Vice President as Acting President.

Section 4. Whenever the Vice President and a majority of either the principal officers of the executive departments or of such other body as Congress may by law provide, transmit to the President pro tempore of the Senate and the Speaker of the House of Representatives their written declaration that the President is unable to discharge the powers and duties of his office, the Vice President shall immediately assume the powers and duties of the office as Acting President.

Thereafter, when the President transmits to the President pro tempore of the Senate and the Speaker of the House of Representatives his written declaration that no inability exists, he shall resume the powers and duties of his office unless the Vice President and a majority of either the principal officers of the executive department or of such other body as Congress may by law provide, transmit within four days to the President pro tempore of the Senate and the Speaker of the House of Representatives their written declaration that the President is unable to discharge the powers and duties of his office. Thereupon Congress shall decide the issue, assembling within forty-eight hours for that purpose if not in session. If the Congress, within twenty-one days after receipt of the latter written declaration, or, if Congress is not in session, within twenty-one days after Congress is required to assemble, determines by two-thirds vote of both Houses that the President shall continue to discharge the same as Acting President; otherwise, the President shall resume the powers and duties of his office.

Amendment XXVI [1971]

Section 1. The right of citizens of the United States, who are 18 years of age or older, to vote, shall not be denied or abridged by the United States or any State on account of age.

Section 2. The Congress shall have the power to enforce this article by appropriate legislation.

Amendment XXVII [1992]

No law, varying the compensation for the services of the Senators and Representatives, shall take effect, until an election of Representatives shall have intervened.

Appendix C — Uniform Commercial Code (2000 Official Text), Article 2

Table of Sections

Article 2 Sales

Part 1. Short Title, General Construction and Subject Matter

Article 2 Sales

Part 1. Short Title, General Construction and Subject Matter

§2–101. Short Title.

This Article shall be known and may be cited as Uniform Commercial Code—Sales.

§2–102. Scope; Certain Security and Other Transactions Excluded From This Article.

Unless the context otherwise requires, this Article applies to transactions in goods; it does not apply to any transaction which although in the form of an unconditional contract to sell or present sale is intended to operate only as a security transaction nor does this Article impair or repeal any statute regulating sales to consumers, farmers or other specified classes of buyers.

§2–103. Definitions and Index of Definitions.

(1) In this Article unless the context otherwise requires

(a) "Buyer" means a person who buys or contracts to buy goods.

(b) "Good faith" in the case of a merchant means honesty in fact and the observance of reasonable commercial standards of fair dealing in the trade.

(c) "Receipt" of goods means taking physical possession of them.

(d) "Seller" means a person who sells or contracts to sell goods.

(2) Other definitions applying to this Article or to specified Parts thereof, and the sections in which they appear are:

"Acceptance"	Section 2–606.
"Banker's credit"	Section 2–325.
"Between merchants"	Section 2–104.
"Cancellation"	Section 2–106(4).
"Commercial unit"	Section 2–105.
"Confirmed credit"	Section 2–325.
"Conforming to contract"	Section 2–106.
"Contract for sale"	Section 2–106.
"Cover"	Section 2–712.
"Entrusting"	Section 2–403.
"Financing agency"	Section 2–104.
"Future goods"	Section 2–105.
"Goods"	Section 2–105.
"Identification"	Section 2–501.
"Installment contract"	Section 2–612.
"Letter of Credit"	Section 2–325.
"Lot"	Section 2–105.
"Merchant"	Section 2–104.
"Overseas"	Section 2–323.
"Person in position of seller"	Section 2–707.
"Present sale"	Section 2–106.
"Sale"	Section 2–106.
"Sale on approval"	Section 2–326.
"Sale or return"	Section 2–326.
"Termination"	Section 2–106.

(3) The following definitions in other Articles apply to this Article:

"Check"	Section 3–104.
"Consignee"	Section 7–102.
"Consignor"	Section 7–102.
"Consumer goods"	Section 9–102.
"Dishonor"	Section 3–502.
"Draft"	Section 3–104.

(4) In addition Article 1 contains general definitions and principles of construction and interpretation applicable throughout this Article.

§2–104. Definitions: "Merchant"; "Between Merchants"; "Financing Agency".

(1) "Merchant" means a person who deals in goods of the kind or otherwise by his occupation holds himself out as having knowledge or skill peculiar to the practices or goods involved in the trans-

action or to whom such knowledge or skill may be attributed by his employment of an agent or broker or other intermediary who by his occupation holds himself out as having such knowledge or skill.

(2) "Financing agency" means a bank, finance company or other person who in the ordinary course of business makes advances against goods or documents of title or who by arrangement with either the seller or the buyer intervenes in ordinary course to make or collect payment due or claimed under the contract for sale, as by purchasing or paying the seller's draft or making advances against it or by merely taking it for collection whether or not the documents of title accompany the draft. "Financing agency" includes also a bank or other person who similarly intervenes between persons who are in the position of seller and buyer in respect to the goods (Section 2–707).

(3) "Between merchants" means in any transaction with respect to which both parties are chargeable with the knowledge or skill of merchants.

§2-105. Definitions: Transferability; "Goods"; "Future" Goods; "Lot"; "Commercial Unit".

(1) "Goods" means all things (including specially manufactured goods) which are movable at the time of identification to the contract for sale other than the money in which the price is to be paid, investment securities (Article 8) and things in action. "Goods" also includes the unborn young of animals and growing crops and other identified things attached to realty as described in the section on goods to be severed from realty (Section 2–107).

(2) Goods must be both existing and identified before any interest in them can pass. Goods which are not both existing and identified are "future" goods. A purported present sale of future goods or of any interest therein operates as a contract to sell.

(3) There may be a sale of a part interest in existing identified goods.

(4) An undivided share in an identified bulk of fungible goods is sufficiently identified to be sold although the quantity of the bulk is not determined. Any agreed proportion of such a bulk or any quantity thereof agreed upon by number, weight or other measure may to the extent of the seller's interest in the bulk be sold to the buyer who then becomes an owner in common.

(5) "Lot" means a parcel or a single article which is the subject matter of a separate sale or delivery, whether or not it is sufficient to perform the contract.

(6) "Commercial unit" means such a unit of goods as by commercial usage is a single whole for purposes of sale and division of which materially impairs its character or value on the market or in use. A commercial unit may be a single article (as a machine) or a set of articles (as a suite of furniture or an assortment of sizes) or a quantity (as a bale, gross, or carload) or any other unit treated in use or in the relevant market as a single whole.

§2-106. Definitions: "Contract"; "Agreement"; "Contract for Sale"; "Sale"; "Present Sale"; "Conforming" to Contract; "Termination"; "Cancellation".

(1) In this Article unless the context otherwise requires "contract" and "agreement" are limited to those relating to the present or future sale of goods. "Contract for sale" includes both a present sale of goods and a contract to sell goods at a future time. A "sale" consists in the passing of title from the seller to the buyer for a price (Section 2–401). A "present sale" means a sale which is accomplished by the making of the contract.

(2) Goods or conduct including any part of a performance are "conforming" or conform to the contract when they are in accordance with the obligations under the contract.

(3) "Termination" occurs when either party pursuant to a power created by agreement or law puts an end to the contract otherwise than for its breach. On "termination" all obligations which are still executory on both sides are discharged but any right based on prior breach or performance survives.

(4) "Cancellation" occurs when either party puts an end to the contract for breach by the other and its effect is the same as that of "termination" except that the cancelling party also retains any remedy for breach of the whole contract or any unperformed balance.

§2-107. Goods to Be Severed from Realty: Recording.

(1) A contract for the sale of minerals or the like (including oil and gas) or a structure or its materials to be removed from realty is a contract for the sale of goods within this Article if they are to be severed by the seller but until severance a purported present sale thereof which is not effective as a transfer of an interest in land is effective only as a contract to sell.

(2) A contract for the sale apart from the land of growing crops or other things attached to realty and capable of severance without material harm thereto but not described in subsection (1) or of timber to be cut is a contract for the sale of goods within this Article whether the subject matter is to be severed by the buyer or by the seller even though it forms part of the realty at the time of contracting, and the parties can by identification effect a present sale before severance.

(3) The provisions of this section are subject to any third party rights provided by the law relating to realty records, and the contract for sale may be executed and recorded as a document transferring an interest in land and shall then constitute notice to third parties of the buyer's right under the contract for sale.

Part 2. Form, Formation and Readjustment of Contra

§2-201. Formal Requirements; Statute of Frauds.

(1) Except as otherwise provided in this section a contract for the sale of goods for the price of $500 or more is not enforceable by way of action or defense unless there is some writing sufficient to indicate that a contract for sale has been made between the parties and signed by the party against whom enforcement is sought or by his authorized agent or broker. A writing is not insufficient because it omits or incorrectly states a term agreed upon but the contract is not enforceable under this paragraph beyond the quantity of goods shown in such writing.

(2) Between merchants if within a reasonable time a writing in confirmation of the contract and sufficient against the sender is received and the party receiving it has reason to know its contents, it satisfies the requirements of subsection (1) against such party unless written notice of objection to its contents is given within 10 days after it is received.

(3) A contract which does not satisfy the requirements of subsection (1) but which is valid in other respects is enforceable

(a) if the goods are to be specially manufactured for the buyer and are not suitable for sale to others in the ordinary course of the seller's business and the seller, before notice of repudiation is received and under circumstances which reasonably indicate that the goods are for the buyer, has made either a substantial beginning of their manufacture or commitments for their procurement; or

(b) if the party against whom enforcement is sought admits in his pleading, testimony or otherwise in court that a contract for sale was made, but the contract is not enforceable under this provision beyond the quantity of goods admitted; or
(c) with respect to goods for which payment has been made and accepted or which have been received and accepted (Section 2–606).

§2-202. Final Written Expression: Parol or Extrinsic Evidence.

Terms with respect to which the confirmatory memoranda of the parties agree or which are otherwise set forth in a writing intended by the parties as a final expression of their agreement with respect to such terms as are included therein may not be contradicted by evidence of any prior agreement or of a contemporaneous oral agreement but may be explained or supplemented

(a) by course and dealing or usage of trade (Section 1–205) or by course of performance (Section 2–208); and
(b) by evidence of consistent additional terms unless the court finds the writing to have been intended also as a complete and exclusive statement of the terms of the agreement.

§2-203. Seals Inoperative.

The affixing of a seal to a writing evidencing a contract for sale or an offer to buy or sell goods does not constitute the writing a sealed instrument and the law with respect to sealed instruments does not apply to such a contract or offer.

§2-204. Formation in General.

(1) A contract for sale of goods may be made in any manner sufficient to show agreement, including conduct by both parties which recognizes the existence of such a contract.

(2) An agreement sufficient to constitute a contract for sale may be found even though the moment of its making is undetermined.

(3) Even though one or more terms are left open a contract for sale does not fail for indefiniteness if the parties have intended to make a contract and there is a reasonably certain basis for giving an appropriate remedy.

§2-205. Firm Offers.

An offer by a merchant to buy or sell goods in a signed writing which by its terms gives assurance that it will be held open is not revocable, for lack of consideration, during the time stated or if no time is stated for a reasonable time, but in no event may such period of irrevocability exceed three months; but any such term of assurance on a form supplied by the offeree must be separately signed by the offeror.

§2-206. Offer and Acceptance in Formation of Contract.

(1) Unless otherwise unambiguously indicated by the language or circumstances

(a) an offer to make a contract shall be construed as inviting acceptance in any manner and by any medium reasonable in the circumstances;
(b) an order or other offer to buy goods for prompt or current shipment shall be construed as inviting acceptance either by a prompt promise to ship or by the prompt or current shipment of conforming or non-conforming goods, but such a shipment of non-conforming goods does not constitute an acceptance if the seller seasonably notifies the buyer that the shipment is offered only as an accommodation to the buyer.

(2) Where the beginning of a requested performance is a reasonable mode of acceptance an offeror who is not notified of acceptance within a reasonable time may treat the offer as having lapsed before acceptance.

§2-207. Additional Terms in Acceptance or Confirmation.

(1) A definite and seasonable expression of acceptance or a written confirmation which is sent within a reasonable time operates as an acceptance even though it states terms additional to or different from those offered or agreed upon, unless acceptance is expressly made conditional on assent to the additional or different terms.

(2) The additional terms are to be construed as proposals for addition to the contract. Between merchants such terms become part of the contract unless:

(a) the offer expressly limits acceptance to the terms of the offer;
(b) they materially alter it; or
(c) notification of objection to them has already been given or is given within a reasonable time after notice of them is received.

(3) Conduct by both parties which recognizes the existence of a contract is sufficient to establish a contract for sale although the writings of the parties do not otherwise establish a contract. In such case the terms of the particular contract consist of those terms on which the writings of the parties agree, together with any supplementary terms incorporated under any other provisions of this Act.

§2-208. Course of Performance or Practical Construction.

(1) Where the contract for sale involves repeated occasions for performance by either party with knowledge of the nature of the performance and opportunity for objection to it by the other, any course of performance accepted or acquiesced in without objection shall be relevant to determine the meaning of the agreement.

(2) The express terms of the agreement and any such course of performance, as well as any course of dealing and usage of trade, shall be construed whenever reasonable as consistent with each other; but when such construction is unreasonable, express terms shall control course of performance and course of performance shall control both course of dealing and usage of trade (Section 1–205).

(3) Subject to the provisions of the next section on modification and waiver, such course of performance shall be relevant to show a waiver or modification of any term inconsistent with such course of performance.

§2-209. Modification, Rescission and Waiver.

(1) An agreement modifying a contract within this Article needs no consideration to be binding.

(2) A signed agreement which excludes modification or rescission except by a signed writing cannot be otherwise modified or rescinded, but except as between merchants such a requirement on a form supplied by the merchant must be separately signed by the other party.

(3) The requirements of the statute of frauds section of this Article (Section 2–201) must be satisfied if the contract as modified is within its provisions.

(4) Although an attempt at modification or rescission does not satisfy the requirements of subsection (2) or (3) it can operate as a waiver.

(5) A party who has made a waiver affecting an executory portion of the contract may retract the waiver by reasonable notification received by the other party that strict performance will be required of any term waived, unless the retraction would be unjust in view of a material change of position in reliance on the waiver.

§2-210. Delegation of Performance; Assignment of Rights.

(1) A party may perform his duty through a delegate unless otherwise agreed or unless the other party has a substantial interest in having his original promisor perform or control the acts required by the contract. No delegation of performance relieves the party delegating of any duty to perform or any liability for breach.

(2) Except as otherwise provided in Section 9–406, unless otherwise agreed all rights of either seller or buyer can be assigned except where the assignment would materially change the duty of the other party, or increase materially the burden or risk imposed on him by his contract, or impair materially his chance of obtaining return performance. A right to damages for breach of the whole contract or a right arising out of the assignor's due performance of his entire obligation can be assigned despite agreement otherwise.

(3) The creation, attachment, perfection, or enforcement of a security interest in the seller's interest under a contract is not a transfer that materially changes the duty of or increases materially the burden or risk imposed on the buyer or impairs materially the buyer's chance of obtaining return performance within the purview of subsection (2) unless, and then only to the extent that, enforcement actually results in a delegation of material performance of the seller. Even in that event, the creation, attachment, perfection, and enforcement of the security interest remain effective, but (i) the seller is liable to the buyer for damages caused by the delegation to the extent that the damages could not reasonably be prevented by the buyer, and (ii) a court having jurisdiction may grant other appropriate relief, including cancellation of the contract for sale or an injunction against enforcement of the security interest or consummation of the enforcement.

(4) Unless the circumstances indicate the contrary a prohibition of assignment of "the contract" is to be construed as barring only the delegation to the assignee of the assignor's performance.

(5) An assignment of "the contract" or of "all my rights under the contract" or an assignment in similar general terms is an assignment of rights and unless the language or the circumstances (as in an assignment for security) indicate the contrary, it is a delegation of performance of the duties of the assignor and its acceptance by the assignee constitutes a promise by him to perform those duties. This promise is enforceable by either the assignor or the other party to the original contract.

(6) The other party may treat any assignment which delegates performance as creating reasonable grounds for insecurity and may without prejudice to his rights against the assignor demand assurances from the assignee (Section 2–609).

Part 3. General Obligation and Construction of Contract

§2-301. General Obligations of Parties.

The obligation of the seller is to transfer and deliver and that of the buyer is to accept and pay in accordance with the contract.

§2-302. Unconscionable Contract or Clause.

(1) If the court as a matter of law finds the contract or any clause of the contract to have been unconscionable at the time it was made the court may refuse to enforce the contract, or it may enforce the remainder of the contract without the unconscionable clause, or it may so limit the application of any unconscionable clause as to avoid any unconscionable result.

(2) When it is claimed or appears to the court that the contract or any clause thereof may be unconscionable the parties shall be afforded a reasonable opportunity to present evidence as to its commercial setting, purpose and effect to aid the court in making the determination.

§2-303. Allocation or Division of Risks.

Where this Article allocates a risk or a burden as between the parties "unless otherwise agreed", the agreement may not only shift the allocation but may also divide the risk or burden.

§2-304. Price Payable in Money, Goods, Realty, or Otherwise.

(1) The price can be made payable in money or otherwise. If it is payable in whole or in part in goods each party is a seller of the goods which he is to transfer.

(2) Even though all or part of the price is payable in an interest in realty the transfer of the goods and the seller's obligations with reference to them are subject to this Article, but not the transfer of the interest in realty or the transferor's obligations in connection therewith.

§2-305. Open Price Term.

(1) The parties if they so intend can conclude a contract for sale even though the price is not settled. In such a case the price is a reasonable price at the time for delivery if

(a) nothing is said as to price; or

(b) the price is left to be agreed by the parties and they fail to agree; or

(c) the price is to be fixed in terms of some agreed market or other standard as set or recorded by a third person or agency and it is not so set or recorded.

(2) A price to be fixed by the seller or by the buyer means a price for him to fix in good faith.

(3) When a price left to be fixed otherwise than by agreement of the parties fails to be fixed through fault of one party the other may at his option treat the contract as cancelled or himself fix a reasonable price.

(4) Where, however, the parties intend not to be bound unless the price be fixed or agreed and it is not fixed or agreed there is no contract. In such a case the buyer must return any goods already received or if unable so to do must pay their reasonable value at the time of delivery and the seller must return any portion of the price paid on account.

§2-306. Output, Requirements and Exclusive Dealings.

(1) A term which measures the quantity by the output of the seller or the requirements of the buyer means such actual output or requirements as may occur in good faith, except that no quantity unreasonably disproportionate to any stated estimate or in the absence of a stated estimate to any normal or otherwise comparable prior output or requirements may be tendered or demanded.

(2) A lawful agreement by either the seller or the buyer for exclusive dealing in the kind of goods concerned imposes unless

otherwise agreed an obligation by the seller to use best efforts to supply the goods and by the buyer to use best efforts to promote their sale.

§2-307. Delivery in Single Lot or Several Lots.

Unless otherwise agreed all goods called for by a contract for sale must be tendered in a single delivery and payment is due only on such tender but where the circumstances give either party the right to make or demand delivery in lots the price if it can be apportioned may be demanded for each lot.

§2-308. Absence of Specified Place for Delivery.

Unless otherwise agreed

(a) the place for delivery of goods is the seller's place of business or if he has none, his residence; but

(b) in a contract for sale of identified goods which to the knowledge of the parties at the time of contracting are in some other place, that place is the place for their delivery; and

(c) documents of title may be delivered through customary banking channels.

§2-309. Absence of Specific Time Provisions; Notice of Termination.

(1) The time for shipment or delivery or any other action under a contract if not provided in this Article or agreed upon shall be a reasonable time.

(2) Where the contract provides for successive performance but is indefinite in duration it is valid for a reasonable time but unless otherwise agreed may be terminated at any time by either party.

(3) Termination of a contract by one party except on the happening of an agreed event requires that reasonable notification be received by the other party and an agreement dispensing with notification is invalid if its operation would be unconscionable.

§2-310. Open Time for Payment or Running of Credit; Authority to Ship Under Reservation.

Unless otherwise agreed

(a) payment is due at the time and place at which the buyer is to receive the goods even though the place of shipment is the place of delivery; and

(b) if the seller is authorized to send the goods he may ship them under reservation, and may tender the documents of title, but the buyer may inspect the goods after their arrival before payment is due unless such inspection is inconsistent with the terms of the contract (Section 2–513); and

(c) if delivery is authorized and made by way of documents of title otherwise than by subsection (b) then payment is due at the time and place at which the buyer is to receive the documents regardless of where the goods are to be received; and

(d) where the seller is required or authorized to ship the goods on credit the credit period runs from the time of shipment but post-dating the invoice or delaying its dispatch will correspondingly delay the starting of the credit period.

§2-311. Options and Cooperation Respecting Performance.

(1) An agreement for sale which is otherwise sufficiently definite (subsection (3) of Section 2–204) to be a contract is not made invalid by the fact that it leaves particulars of performance to be specified by one of the parties. Any such specification must be made in good faith and within limits set by commercial reasonableness.

(2) Unless otherwise agreed specifications relating to assortment of the goods are at the buyer's option and except as otherwise provided in subsections (1) (c) and (3) of Section 2–319 specifications or arrangements relating to shipment are at the seller's option.

(3) Where such specification would materially affect the other party's performance but is not seasonably made or where one party's cooperation is necessary to the agreed performance of the other but is not seasonably forthcoming, the other party in addition to all other remedies

(a) is excused for any resulting delay in his own performance; and

(b) may also either proceed to perform in any reasonable manner or after the time for a material part of his own performance treat the failure to specify or to cooperate as a breach by failure to deliver or accept the goods.

§2-312. Warranty of Title and Against Infringement; Buyer's Obligation Against Infringement.

(1) Subject to subsection (2) there is in a contract for sale a warranty by the seller that

(a) the title conveyed shall be good, and its transfer rightful; and

(b) the goods shall be delivered free from any security interest or other lien or encumbrance of which the buyer at the time of contracting has no knowledge.

(2) A warranty under subsection (1) will be excluded or modified only by specific language or by circumstances which give the buyer reason to know that the person selling does not claim title in himself or that he is purporting to sell only such right or title as he or a third person may have.

(3) Unless otherwise agreed a seller who is a merchant regularly dealing in goods of the kind warrants that the goods shall be delivered free of the rightful claim of any third person by way of infringement or the like but a buyer who furnishes specifications to the seller must hold the seller harmless against any such claim which arises out of compliance with the specifications.

§2-313. Express Warranties by Affirmation, Promise, Description, Sample.

(1) Express warranties by the seller are created as follows:

(a) Any affirmation of fact or promise made by the seller to the buyer which relates to the goods and becomes part of the basis of the bargain creates an express warranty that the goods shall conform to the affirmation or promise.

(b) Any description of the goods which is made part of the basis of the bargain creates an express warranty that the goods shall conform to the description.

(c) Any sample or model which is made part of the basis of the bargain creates an express warranty that the whole of the goods shall conform to the sample or model.

(2) It is not necessary to the creation of an express warranty that the seller use formal words such as "warrant" or "guarantee" or that he have a specific intention to make a warranty, but an affirmation merely of the value of the goods or a statement purporting to be merely the seller's opinion or commendation of the goods does not create a warranty.

§2-314. Implied Warranty: Merchantability; Usage of Trade.

(1) Unless excluded or modified (Section 2–316), a warranty that the goods shall be merchantable is implied in a contract for their sale if the seller is a merchant with respect to goods of that kind. Under this section the serving for value of food or drink to be consumed either on the premises or elsewhere is a sale.

(2) Goods to be merchantable must be at least such as

- (a) pass without objection in the trade under the contract description; and
- (b) in the case of fungible goods, are of fair average quality within the description; and
- (c) are fit for the ordinary purposes for which such goods are used; and
- (d) run, within the variations permitted by the agreement, of even kind, quality and quantity within each unit and among all units involved; and
- (e) are adequately contained, packaged, and labeled as the agreement may require; and
- (f) conform to the promises or affirmations of fact made on the container or label if any.

(3) Unless excluded or modified (Section 2–316) other implied warranties may arise from course of dealing or usage of trade.

§2-315. Implied Warranty: Fitness for Particular Purpose.

Where the seller at the time of contracting has reason to know any particular purpose for which the goods are required and that the buyer is relying on the seller's skill or judgment to select or furnish suitable goods, there is unless excluded or modified under the next section an implied warranty that the goods shall be fit for such purpose.

§2-316. Exclusion or Modification of Warranties.

(1) Words or conduct relevant to the creation of an express warranty and words or conduct tending to negate or limit warranty shall be construed wherever reasonable as consistent with each other, but subject to the provisions of this Article on parol or extrinsic evidence (Section 2–202) negation or limitation is inoperative to the extent that such construction is unreasonable.

(2) Subject to subsection (3), to exclude or modify the implied warranty of merchantability or any part of it the language must mention merchantability and in case of a writing must be conspicuous, and to exclude or modify any implied warranty of fitness the exclusion must be by a writing and conspicuous. Language to exclude all implied warranties of fitness is sufficient if it states, for example, that "There are no warranties which extend beyond the description on the face hereof."

(3) Notwithstanding subsection (2)

- (a) unless the circumstances indicate otherwise, all implied warranties are excluded by expression like "as is", "with all faults" or other language which in common understanding calls the buyer's attention to the exclusion of warranties and makes plain that there is no implied warranty; and
- (b) when the buyer before entering into the contract has examined the goods or the sample or model as fully as he desired or has refused to examine the goods there is no implied warranty with regard to defects which an examination ought in the circumstances to have revealed to him; and
- (c) an implied warranty can also be excluded or modified by course of dealing or course of performance or usage of trade.

(4) Remedies for breach of warranty can be limited in accordance with the provisions of this Article on liquidation or limitation of damages and on contractual modification of remedy (Sections 2–718 and 2–719).

§2-317. Cumulation and Conflict of Warranties Express or Implied.

Warranties whether express or implied shall be construed as consistent with each other and as cumulative, but if such construction is unreasonable the intention of the parties shall determine which warranty is dominant. In ascertaining that intention the following rules apply:

- (a) Exact or technical specifications displace an inconsistent sample or model or general language of description.
- (b) A sample from an existing bulk displaces inconsistent general language of description.
- (c) Express warranties displace inconsistent implied warranties other than an implied warranty of fitness for a particular purpose.

§2-318. Third Party Beneficiaries of Warranties Express or Implied.

Note: If this Act is introduced in the Congress of the United States this section should be omitted. (States to select one alternative.)

Alternative A. A seller's warranty whether express or implied extends to any natural person who is in the family or household of his buyer or who is a guest in his home if it is reasonable to expect that such person may use, consume or be affected by the goods and who is injured in person by breach of the warranty. A seller may not exclude or limit the operation of this section.

Alternative B. A seller's warranty whether express or implied extends to any natural person who may reasonably be expected to use, consume or be affected by the goods and who is injured in person by breach of the warranty. A seller may not exclude or limit the operation of this section.

Alternative C. A seller's warranty whether express or implied extends to any person who may reasonably be expected to use, consume or be affected by the goods and who is injured by breach of the warranty. A seller may not exclude or limit the operation of this section with respect to injury to the person of an individual to whom the warranty extends.

§2-319. F.O.B. and F.A.S. Terms.

(1) Unless otherwise agreed the term F.O.B. (which means "free on board") at a named place, even though used only in connection with the stated price, is a delivery term under which

(a) when the term is F.O.B. the place of shipment, the seller must at that place ship the goods in the manner provided in this Article (Section 2–504) and bear the expense and risk of putting them into the possession of the carrier; or

(b) when the term is F.O.B. the place of destination, the seller must at his own expense and risk transport the goods to that place and there tender delivery of them in the manner provided in this Article (Section 2–503);

(c) when under either (a) or (b) the term is also F.O.B. vessel, car or other vehicle, the seller must in addition at his own expense and risk load the goods on board. If the term is F.O.B. vessel the buyer must name the vessel and in an appropriate case the seller must comply with the provisions of this Article on the form of bill of lading (Section 2–323).

(2) Unless otherwise agreed the term F.A.S. vessel (which means "free alongside") at a named port, even though used only in connection with the stated price, is a delivery term under which the seller must

(a) at his own expense and risk deliver the goods alongside the vessel in the manner usual in that port or on a dock designated and provided by the buyer; and

(b) obtain and tender a receipt for the goods in exchange for which the carrier is under a duty to issue a bill of lading.

(3) Unless otherwise agreed in any case falling within subsection (1)(a) or (c) or subsection (2) the buyer must seasonably give any needed instructions for making delivery, including when the term is F.A.S. or F.O.B. the loading berth of the vessel and in an appropriate case its name and sailing date. The seller may treat the failure of needed instructions as a failure of cooperation under this Article (Section 2–311). He may also at his option move the goods in any reasonable manner preparatory to delivery or shipment.

(4) Under the term F.O.B. vessel or F.A.S. unless otherwise agreed the buyer must make payment against tender of the required documents and the seller may not tender nor the buyer demand delivery of the goods in substitution for the documents.

§2–320. C.I.F. and C. & F. Terms.

(1) The term C.I.F. means that the price includes in a lump sum the cost of the goods and the insurance and freight to the named destination. The term C. & F. or C.F. means that the price so includes cost and freight to the named destination.

(2) Unless otherwise agreed and even though used only in connection with the stated price and destination, the term C.I.F. destination or its equivalent requires the seller at his own expense and risk to

(a) put the goods into the possession of a carrier at the port for shipment and obtain a negotiable bill or bills of lading covering the entire transportation to the named destination; and

(b) load the goods and obtain a receipt from the carrier (which may be contained in the bill of lading) showing that the freigt has been paid or provided for; and

(c) obtain a policy or certificate of insurance, including any war risk insurance, of a kind and on terms then current at the port of shipment in the usual amount, in the currency of the contract, shown to cover the same goods covered by the bill of lading and providing for payment of loss to the order of the buyer or for the account of whom it may concern; but the seller may add to the price the amount of the premium for any such war risk insurance; and

(d) prepare an invoice of the goods and procure any other documents required to effect shipment or to comply with the contract; and

(e) forward and tender with commercial promptness all the documents in due form and with any indorsement necessary to perfect the buyer's rights.

(3) Unless otherwise agreed the term C. & F. or its equivalent has the same effect and imposes upon the seller the same obligations and risks as a C.I.F. term except the obligation as to insurance.

(4) Under the term C.I.F. or C. & F. unless otherwise agreed the buyer must make payment against tender of the required documents and the seller may not tender nor the buyer demand delivery of the goods in substitution for the documents.

§2–321. C.I.F. or C. & F.: "Net Landed Weights"; "Payment on Arrival"; Warranty of Condition on Arrival.

Under a contract containing a term C.I.F. or C. & F.

(1) Where the price is based on or is to be adjusted according to "net landed weights", "delivered weights", "out turn" quantity or quality or the like, unless otherwise agreed the seller must reasonably estimate the price. The payment due on tender of the documents called for by the contract is the amount so estimated, but after final adjustment of the price a settlement must be made with commercial promptness.

(2) An agreement described in subsection (1) or any warranty of quality or condition of the goods on arrival places upon the seller the risk of ordinary deterioration, shrinkage and the like in transportation but has no effect on the place or time of identification to the contract for sale or delivery or on the passing of the risk of loss.

(3) Unless otherwise agreed where the contract provides for payment on or after arrival of the goods the seller must before payment allow such preliminary inspection as is feasible; but if the goods are lost delivery of the documents and payment are due when the goods should have arrived.

§2–322. Delivery "Ex-Ship".

(1) Unless otherwise agreed a term for delivery of goods "ex-ship" (which means from the carrying vessel) or in equivalent language is not restricted to a particular ship and requires delivery from a ship which has reached a place at the named port of destination where goods of the kind are usually discharged.

(2) Under such a term unless otherwise agreed

(a) the seller must discharge all liens arising out of the carriage and furnish the buyer with a direction which puts the carrier under a duty to deliver the goods; and

(b) the risk of loss does not pass to the buyer until the goods leave the ship's tackle or are otherwise properly unloaded.

§2–323. Form of Bill of Lading Required in Overseas Shipment; "Overseas".

(1) Where the contract contemplates overseas shipment and contains a term C.I.F. or C. & F. or F.O.B. vessel, the seller unless

otherwise agreed must obtain a negotiable bill of lading stating that the goods have been loaded on board or, in the case of a term C.I.F. or C. & F., received for shipment.

(2) Where in a case within subsection (1) a bill of lading has been issued in a set of parts, unless otherwise agreed if the documents are not to be sent from abroad the buyer may demand tender of the full set; otherwise only one part of the bill of lading need be tendered. Even if the agreement expressly requires a full set

(a) due tender of a single part is acceptable within the provisions of this Article on cure of improper delivery (subsection (1) of Section 2–508); and

(b) even though the full set is demanded, if the documents are sent from abroad the person tendering an incomplete set may nevertheless require payment upon furnishing an indemnity which the buyer in good faith deems adequate.

(3) A shipment by water or by air or a contract contemplating such shipment is "overseas" insofar as by usage of trade or agreement it is subject to the commercial, financing or shipping practices characteristic of international deep water commerce.

§2-324. "No Arrival, No Sale" Term.

Under a term "no arrival, no sale" or terms of like meaning, unless otherwise agreed.

(a) the seller must properly ship conforming goods and if they arrive by any means he must tender them on arrival but he assumes no obligation that the goods will arrive unless he has caused the non-arrival; and

(b) where without fault of the seller the goods are in part lost or have so deteriorated as no longer to conform to the contract or arrive after the contract time, the buyer may proceed as if there had been casualty to identified goods (Section 2–613).

§2-325. "Letter of Credit" Term; "Confirmed Credit".

(1) Failure of the buyer seasonably to furnish an agreed letter of credit is a breach of the contract for sale.

(2) The delivery to seller of a proper letter of credit suspends the buyer's obligation to pay. If the letter of credit is dishonored, the seller may on seasonable notification to the buyer require payment directly from him.

(3) Unless otherwise agreed the term "letter of credit" or "banker's credit" in a contract for sale means an irrevocable credit issued by a financing agency of good repute and, where the shipment is overseas, of good international repute. The term "confirmed credit" means that the credit must also carry the direct obligation of such an agency which does business in the seller's financial market.

§2-326. Sale on Approval and Sale or Return; Rights of Creditors.

(1) Unless otherwise agreed, if delivered goods may be returned by the buyer even though they conform to the contract, the transaction is

(a) a "sale on approval" if the goods are delivered primarily for use, and

(b) a "sale or return" if the goods are delivered primarily for resale.

(2) Goods held on approval are not subject to the claims of the buyer's creditors until acceptance; goods held on sale or return are subject to such claims while in the buyer's possession.

(3) Any "or return" term of a contract for sale is to be treated as a separate contract for sale within the statute of frauds section of this Article (Section 2–201) and as contradicting the sale aspect of the contract within the provisions of this Article on parol or extrinsic evidence (Section 2–202).

§2-327. Special Incidents of Sale on Approval and Sale or Return.

(1) Under a sale on approval unless otherwise agreed

(a) although the goods are identified to the contract the risk of loss and the title do not pass to the buyer until acceptance; and

(b) use of the goods consistent with the purpose of trial is not acceptance but failure seasonably to notify the seller of election to return the goods is acceptance, and if the goods conform to the contract acceptance of any part is acceptance of the whole; and

(c) after due notification of election to return, the return is at the seller's risk and expense but a merchant buyer must follow any reasonable instructions.

(2) Under a sale or return unless otherwise agreed

(a) the option to return extends to the whole or any commercial unit of the goods while in substantially their original condition, but must be exercised seasonably; and

(b) the return is at the buyer's risk and expense.

§2-328. Sale by Auction.

(1) In a sale by auction if goods are put up in lots each lot is the subject of a separate sale.

(2) A sale by auction is complete when the auctioneer so announces by the fall of the hammer or in other customary manner. Where a bid is made while the hammer is falling in acceptance of a prior bid the auctioneer may in his discretion reopen the bidding or declare the goods sold under the bid on which the hammer was falling.

(3) Such a sale is with reserve unless the goods are in explicit terms put up without reserve. In an auction with reserve the auctioneer may withdraw the goods at any time until he announces completion of the sale. In an auction without reserve, after the auctioneer calls for bids on an article or lot, that article or lot cannot be withdrawn unless no bid is made within a reasonable time. In either case a bidder may retract his bid until the auctioneer's announcement of completion of the sale, but a bidder's retraction does not revive any previous bid.

(4) If the auctioneer knowingly receives a bid on the seller's behalf or the seller makes or procures such a bid, and notice has not been given that liberty for such bidding is reserved, the buyer may at his option avoid the sale or take the goods at the price of the last good faith bid prior to the completion of the sale. This subsection shall not apply to any bid at a forced sale.

Part 4. Title, Creditors and Good Faith Purchasers

§2-401. Passing of Title; Reservation for Security; Limited Application of This Section.

Each provision of this Article with regard to the rights, obligations and remedies of the seller, the buyer, purchasers or other third parties applies irrespective of title to the goods except where the provision refers to such title. Insofar as situations are not covered by the other provisions of this Article and matters concerning title become material the following rules apply:

(1) Title to goods cannot pass under a contract for sale prior to their identification to the contract (Section 2–501), and unless otherwise explicitly agreed the buyer acquires by their identification a special property as limited by this Act. Any retention or reservation by the seller of the title (property) in goods shipped or delivered to the buyer is limited in effect to a reservation of a security interest. Subject to these provisions and to the provisions of the Article on Secured Transactions (Article 9), title to goods passes from the seller to the buyer in any manner and on any conditions explicitly agreed on by the parties.

(2) Unless otherwise explicitly agreed title passes to the buyer at the time and place at which the seller completes his performance with reference to the physical delivery of the goods, despite any reservation of a security interest and even though a document of title is to be delivered at a different time or place; and in particular and despite any reservation of a security interest by the bill of lading

(a) if the contract requires or authorizes the seller to send the goods to the buyer but does not require him to deliver them at destination, title passes to the buyer at the time and place of shipment; but

(b) if the contract requires delivery at destination, title passes on tender there.

(3) Unless otherwise explicitly agreed where delivery is to be made without moving the goods.

(a) if the seller is to deliver a document of title, title passes at the time when and the place where he delivers such documents; or

(b) if the goods are at the time of contracting already identified and no documents are to be delivered, title passes at the time and place of contracting.

(4) A rejection or other refusal by the buyer to receive or retain the goods, whether or not justified, or a justified revocation of acceptance revests title to the goods in the seller. Such revesting occurs by operation of law and is not a "sale".

§2-402. Rights of Seller's Creditors Against Sold Goods.

(1) Except as provided in subsections (2) and (3), rights of unsecured creditors of the seller with respect to goods which have been identified to a contract for sale are subject to the buyer's rights to recover the goods under this Article (Sections 2–502 and 2–716).

(2) A creditor of the seller may treat a sale or an identification of goods to a contract for sale as void if as against him a retention of possession by the seller is fraudulent under any rule of law of the state where the goods are situated, except that retention of possession in good faith and current course of trade by a merchant-seller for a commercially reasonable time after a sale or identification is not fraudulent.

(3) Nothing in this Article shall be deemed to impair the rights of creditors of the seller

(a) under the provisions of the Article on Secured Transactions (Article 9); or

(b) where identification to the contract or delivery is made not in current course of trade but in satisfaction of or as security for a pre-existing claim for money, security or the like and is made under circumstances which under any rule of law of the state where the goods are situated would apart from this Article constitute the transaction a fraudulent transfer or voidable preference.

§2-403. Power to Transfer; Good Faith Purchase of Goods; "Entrusting".

(1) A purchaser of goods acquires all title which his transferor had or had power to transfer except that a purchaser of a limited interest acquires rights only to the extent of the interest purchased. A person with voidable title has power to transfer a good title to a good faith purchaser for value. When goods have been delivered under a transaction of purchase the purchaser has such power even though

(a) the transferor was deceived as to the identity of the purchaser, or

(b) the delivery was in exchange for a check which is later dishonored, or

(c) it was agreed that the transaction was to be a "cash sale", or

(d) the delivery was procured through fraud punishable as larcenous under the criminal law.

(2) Any entrusting of possession of goods to a merchant who deals in goods of that kind gives him power to transfer all rights of the entruster to a buyer in ordinary course of business.

(3) "Entrusting" includes any delivery and any acquiescence in retention of possession regardless of any condition expressed between the parties to the delivery or acquiescence and regardless of whether the procurement of the entrusting or the possessor's disposition of the goods have been such as to be larcenous under the criminal law.

(4) The rights of other purchasers of goods and of lien creditors are governed by the Articles on Secured Transactions (Article 9). [Bulk Transfers/Sales (Article 6)* and Documents of Title (Article 7)].

Part 5. Performance

§2-501. Insurable Interest in Goods; Manner of Identification of Goods.

(1) The buyer obtains a special property and an insurable interest in goods by identification of existing goods as goods to which the contract refers even though the goods so identified are non-conforming and he has an option to return or reject them. Such identification can be made at any time and in any manner explicitly agreed to by the parties. In the absence of explicit agreement identification occurs.

(a) when the contract is made if it is for the sale of goods already existing and identified;

(b) if the contract is for the sale of future goods other than those described in paragraph (c), when goods are shipped, marked or otherwise designated by the seller as goods to which the contract refers;

(c) when the crops are planted or otherwise become growing crops or the young are conceived if the contract is for the sale of unborn young to be born within twelve months after contracting or for the sale of crops to be harvested within twelve months or the next normal harvest season after contracting, whichever is longer.

(2) The seller retains an insurable interest in goods so long as title to or any security interest in the goods remains in him and where the identification is by the seller alone he may until default or insolvency or notification to the buyer that the identification is final substitute other goods for those identified.

(3) Nothing in this section impairs any insurable interest recognized under any other statute or rule of law.

§2-502. Buyer's Right to Goods on Seller's Insolvency.

(1) Subject to subsections (2) and (3) and even though the goods have not been shipped a buyer who has paid a part or all of the price of goods in which he has a special property under the provisions of the immediately preceding section may on making and keeping good a tender of any unpaid portion of their price recover them from the seller if:

(a) in the case of goods bought for personal, family, or household purposes, the seller repudiates or fails to deliver as required by the contract; or

(b) in all cases, the seller becomes insolvent within ten days after receipt of the first installment on their price.

(2) The buyer's right to recover the goods under subsection (1)(a) vests upon acquisition of a special property, even if the seller had not then repudiated or failed to deliver.

(3) If the identification creating his special property has been made by the buyer he acquires the right to recover the goods only if they conform to the contract for sale.

§2-503. Manner of Seller's Tender of Delivery.

(1) Tender of delivery requires that the seller put and hold conforming goods at the buyer's disposition and give the buyer any notification reasonably necessary to enable him to take delivery. The manner, time and place for tender are determined by the agreement and this Article, and in particular

(a) tender must be at a reasonable hour, and if it is of goods they must be kept available for the period reasonably necessary to enable the buyer to take possession; but

(b) unless otherwise agreed the buyer must furnish facilities reasonably suited to the receipt of the goods.

(2) Where the case is within the next section respecting shipment tender requires that the seller comply with its provisions.

(3) Where the seller is required to deliver at a particular destination tender requires that he comply with subsection (1) and also in any appropriate case tender documents as described in subsections (4) and (5) of this section.

(4) Where goods are in the possession of a bailee and are to be delivered without being moved

(a) tender requires that the seller either tender a negotiable document of title covering such goods or procure acknowledgment by the bailee of the buyer's right to possession of the goods; but

(b) tender to the buyer of a non-negotiable document of title or of a written direction to the bailee to deliver is sufficient tender unless the buyer seasonably objects, and receipt by the bailee of notification of the buyer's rights fixes those rights as against the bailee and all third persons; but risk of loss of the goods and of any failure by the bailee to honor the non-negotiable document of title or to obey the direction remains on the seller until the buyer has had a reasonable time to present the document or direction, and a refusal by the bailee to honor the document or to obey the direction defeats the tender.

(5) Where the contract requires the seller to deliver documents

(a) he must tender all such documents in correct form, except as provided in this Article with respect to bills of lading in a set (subsection (2) of Section 2–323); and

(b) tender through customary banking channels is sufficient and dishonor of a draft accompanying the documents constitutes non-acceptance or rejection.

§2-504. Shipment by Seller.

Where the seller is required or authorized to send the goods to the buyer and the contract does not require him to deliver them at a particular destination, then unless otherwise agreed he must

(a) put the goods in the possession of such a carrier and make such a contract for their transportation as may be reasonable having regard to the nature of the goods and other circumstances of the case; and

(b) obtain and promptly deliver or tender in due form any document necessary to enable the buyer to obtain possession of the goods or otherwise required by the agreement or by usage of trade; and

(c) promptly notify the buyer of the shipment.

Failure to notify the buyer under paragraph (c) or to make a proper contract under paragraph (a) is a ground for rejection only if material delay or loss ensues.

§2-505. Seller's Shipment Under Reservation.

(1) Where the seller has identified goods to the contract by or before shipment:

(a) his procurement of a negotiable bill of lading to his own order or otherwise reserves in him a security interest in the goods. His procurement of the bill to the order of a financing agency or of the buyer indicates in addition only the seller's expectation of transferring that interest to the person named.

(b) a non-negotiable bill of lading to himself or his nominee reserves possession of the goods as security but except in a case of conditional delivery (subsection (2) of Section 2–507) a non-negotiable bill of lading naming the buyer as consignee reserves no security interest even though the seller retains possession of the bill of lading.

(2) When shipment by the seller with reservation of a security interest is in violation of the contract for sale it constitutes an improper contract for transportation within the preceding section but impairs neither the rights given to the buyer by shipment and identification of the goods to the contract nor the seller's powers as a holder of a negotiable document.

§2-506. Rights of Financing Agency.

(1) A financing agency by paying or purchasing for value a draft which relates to a shipment of goods acquires to the extent of the payment or purchase and in addition to its own rights under the draft and any document of title securing it any rights of the shipper in the goods including the right to stop delivery and the shipper's right to have the draft honored by the buyer.

(2) The right to reimbursement of a financing agency which has in good faith honored or purchased the draft under commitment to or authority from the buyer is not impaired by subsequent discovery of defects with reference to any relevant document which was apparently regular on its face.

§2-507. Effect of Seller's Tender; Delivery on Condition.

(1) Tender of delivery is a condition to the buyer's duty to accept the goods and, unless otherwise agreed, to his duty to pay for them. Tender entitles the seller to acceptance of the goods and to payment according to the contract.

(2) Where payment is due and demanded on the delivery to the buyer of goods or documents of title, his right as against the seller to retain or dispose of them is conditional upon his making the payment due.

§2-508. Cure by Seller of Improper Tender or Delivery; Replacement.

(1) Where any tender or delivery by the seller is rejected because non-conforming and the time for performance has not yet expired, the seller may seasonably notify the buyer of his intention to cure and may then within the contract time make a conforming delivery.

(2) Where the buyer rejects a non-conforming tender which the seller had reasonable grounds to believe would be acceptable with or without money allowance the seller may if he seasonably notifies the buyer have a further reasonable time to substitute a conforming tender.

§2-509. Risk of Loss in the Absence of Breach.

(1) Where the contract requires or authorizes the seller to ship the goods by carrier

(a) if it does not require him to deliver them at a particular destination, the risk of loss passes to the buyer when the goods are duly delivered to the carrier even though the shipment is under reservation (Section 2–505); but

(b) if it does require him to deliver them at a particular destination and the goods are there duly tendered while in the possession of the carrier, the risk of loss passes to the buyer when the goods are there duly so tendered as to enable the buyer to take delivery.

(2) Where the goods are held by a bailee to be delivered without being moved, the risk of loss passes to the buyer

(a) on his receipt of a negotiable document of title covering the goods; or

(b) on acknowledgment by the bailee of the buyer's right to possession of the goods; or

(c) after his receipt of a non-negotiable document of title or other written direction to deliver, as provided in subsection (4)(b) of Section 2–503.

(3) In any case not within subsection (1) or (2), the risk of loss passes to the buyer on his receipt of the goods if the seller is a merchant; otherwise the risk passes to the buyer on tender of delivery.

(4) The provisions of this section are subject to contrary agreement of the parties and to the provisions of this Article on sale on approval (Section 2–327) and on effect of breach on risk of loss (Section 2–510).

§2-510. Effect of Breach on Risk of Loss.

(1) Where a tender or delivery of goods so fails to conform to the contract as to give a right of rejection the risk of their loss remains on the seller until cure or acceptance.

(2) Where the buyer rightfully revokes acceptance he may to the extent of any deficiency in his effective insurance coverage treat the risk of loss as having rested on the seller from the beginning.

(3) Where the buyer as to conforming goods already identified to the contract for sale repudiates or is otherwise in breach before risk of their loss has passed to him, the seller may to the extent of any deficiency in his effective insurance coverage treat the risk of loss as resting on the buyer for a commercially reasonable time.

§2-511. Tender of Payment by Buyer; Payment by Check.

(1) Unless otherwise agreed tender of payment is a condition to the seller's duty to tender and complete any delivery.

(2) Tender of payment is sufficient when made by any means or in any manner current in the ordinary course of business unless the seller demands payment in legal tender and gives any extension of time reasonably necessary to procure it.

(3) Subject to the provisions of this Act on the effect of an instrument on an obligation (Section 3–310), payment by check is conditional and is defeated as between the parties by dishonor of the check on due presentment.

§2-512. Payment by Buyer Before Inspection.

(1) Where the contract requires payment before inspection nonconformity of the goods does not excuse the buyer from so making payment unless

(a) the non-conformity appears without inspection; or

(b) despite tender of the required documents the circumstances would justify injunction against honor under this Act (Section 5–109(b)).

(2) Payment pursuant to subsection (1) does not constitute an acceptance of goods or impair the buyer's right to inspect or any of his remedies.

§2-513. Buyer's Right to Inspection of Goods.

(1) Unless otherwise agreed and subject to subsection (3), where goods are tendered or delivered or identified to the contract for sale, the buyer has a right before payment or acceptance to inspect them at any reasonable place and time and in any reasonable manner. When the seller is required or authorized to send the goods to the buyer, the inspection may be after their arrival.

(2) Expenses of inspection must be borne by the buyer but may be recovered from the seller if the goods do not conform and are rejected.

(3) Unless otherwise agreed and subject to the provisions of this Article on C.I.F. contracts (subsection (3) of Section 2–321), the buyer is not entitled to inspect the goods before payment of the price when the contract provides

(a) for delivery "C.O.D." or on other like terms; or

(b) for payment against documents of title, except where such payment is due only after the goods are to become available for inspection.

(4) A place or method of inspection fixed by the parties is presumed to be exclusive but unless otherwise expressly agreed it does not postpone identification or shift the place for delivery or for passing the risk of loss. If compliance becomes impossible, inspection shall be as provided in this section unless the place or method fixed was clearly intended as an indispensable condition failure of which avoids the contract.

§2-514. When Documents Deliverable on Acceptance; When on Payment.

Unless otherwise agreed documents against which a draft is drawn are to be delivered to the drawee on acceptance of the draft if it is payable more than three days after presentment; otherwise, only on payment.

§2-515. Preserving Evidence of Goods in Dispute.

In furtherance of the adjustment of any claim or dispute

(a) either party on reasonable notification to the other and for the purpose of ascertaining the facts and preserving evidence has the right to inspect, test and sample the goods including such of them as may be in the possession or control of the other; and

(b) the parties may agree to a third party inspection or survey to determine the conformity or condition of the goods and may agree that the findings shall be binding upon them in any subsequent litigation or adjustment.

Part 6. Breach, Repudiation and Excuse

§2-601. Buyer's Rights on Improper Delivery.

Subject to the provisions of this Article on breach in installment contracts (Section 2–612) and unless otherwise agreed under the sections on contractual limitations of remedy (Sections 2–718 and 2–719), if the goods or the tender of delivery fail in any respect to conform to the contract, the buyer may

(a) reject the whole; or

(b) accept the whole; or

(c) accept any commercial unit or units and reject the rest.

§2-602. Manner and Effect of Rightful Rejection.

(1) Rejection of goods must be within a reasonable time after their delivery or tender. It is ineffective unless the buyer seasonably notifies the seller.

(2) Subject to the provisions of the two following sections on rejected goods (Sections 2–603 and 2–604),

(a) after rejection any exercise of ownership by the buyer with respect to any commercial unit is wrongful as against the seller; and

(b) if the buyer has before rejection taken physical possession of goods in which he does not have a security interest under the provisions of this Article (subsection (3) of Section 2–711), he is under a duty after rejection to hold them with reasonable care at the seller's disposition for a time sufficient to permit the seller to remove them; but

(c) the buyer has no further obligations with regard to goods rightfully rejected.

(3) The seller's rights with respect to goods wrongfully rejected are governed by the provisions of this Article on Seller's remedies in general (Section 2–703).

§2-603. Merchant Buyer's Duties as to Rightfully Rejected Goods.

(1) Subject to any security interest in the buyer (subsection (3) of Section 2–711), when the seller has no agent or place of business at the market of rejection a merchant buyer is under a duty after rejection of goods in his possession or control to follow any reasonable instructions received from the seller with respect to the goods and in the absence of such instructions to make reasonable efforts to sell them for the seller's account if they are perishable or threaten to decline in value speedily. Instructions are not reasonable if on demand indemnity for expenses is not forthcoming.

(2) When the buyer sells goods under subsection (1), he is entitled to reimbursement from the seller or out of the proceeds for reasonable expenses of caring for and selling them, and if the expenses include no selling commission then to such commission as is usual in the trade or if there is none to a reasonable sum not exceeding ten percent on the gross proceeds.

(3) In complying with this section the buyer is held only to good faith and good faith conduct hereunder is neither acceptance nor conversion nor the basis of an action for damages.

§2-604. Buyer's Options as to Salvage of Rightfully Rejected Goods.

Subject to the provisions of the immediately preceding section on perishables if the seller gives no instructions within a reasonable time after notification of rejection the buyer may store the rejected goods for the seller's account or reship them to him or resell them for the seller's account with reimbursement as provided in the preceding section. Such action is not acceptance or conversion.

§2-605. Waiver of Buyer's Objections by Failure to Particularize.

(1) The buyer's failure to state in connection with rejection a particular defect which is ascertainable by reasonable inspection precludes him from relying on the unstated defect to justify rejection or to establish breach

(a) where the seller could have cured it if stated seasonably; or

(b) between merchants when the seller has after rejection made a request in writing for a full and final written statement of all defects on which the buyer proposes to rely.

(2) Payment against documents made without reservation of rights precludes recovery of the payment for defects apparent on the face of the documents.

§2-606. What Constitutes Acceptance of Goods.

(1) Acceptance of goods occurs when the buyer

(a) after a reasonable opportunity to inspect the goods signifies to the seller that the goods are conforming or that he will take or retain them in spite of their non-conformity; or

(b) fails to make an effective rejection (subsection (1) of Section 2–602), but such acceptance does not occur until the buyer has had a reasonable opportunity to inspect them; or

(c) does any act inconsistent with the seller's ownership; but if such act is wrongful as against the seller it is an acceptance only if ratified by him.

(2) Acceptance of a part of any commercial unit is acceptance of that entire unit.

§2-607. Effect of Acceptance; Notice of Breach; Burden of Establishing Breach After Acceptance; Notice of Claim or Litigation to Person Answerable Over.

(1) The buyer must pay at the contract rate for any goods accepted.

(2) Acceptance of goods by the buyer precludes rejection of the goods accepted and if made with knowledge of a non-conformity cannot be revoked because of it unless the acceptance was on the reasonable assumption that the non-conformity would be seasonably cured but acceptance does not of itself impair any other remedy provided by this Article for non-conformity.

(3) Where a tender has been accepted
  (a) the buyer must within a reasonable time after he discovers or should have discovered any breach notify the seller of breach or be barred from any remedy; and
  (b) if the claim is one for infringement or the like (subsection (3) of Section 2–312) and the buyer is sued as a result of such a breach he must so notify the seller within a reasonable time after he receives notice of the litigation or be barred from any remedy over for liability established by the litigation.

(4) The burden is on the buyer to establish any breach with respect to the goods accepted.

(5) Where the buyer is sued for breach of a warranty or other obligation for which his seller is answerable over
  (a) he may give his seller written notice of the litigation. If the notice states that the seller may come in and defend and that if the seller does not do so he will be bound in any action against him by his buyer by any determination of fact common to the two litigations, then unless the seller after seasonable receipt of the notice does come in and defend he is so bound.
  (b) if the claim is one for infringement or the like (subsection (3) of Section 2–312) the original seller may demand in writing that his buyer turn over to him control of the litigation including settlement or else be barred from any remedy over and if he also agrees to bear all expense and to satisfy any adverse judgment, then unless the buyer after seasonable receipt of the demand does turn over control the buyer is so barred.

(6) The provisions of subsection (3), (4) and (5) apply to any obligation of a buyer to hold the seller harmless against infringement or the like (subsection (3) of Section 2–312).

§2-608. Revocation of Acceptance in Whole or in Part.

(1) The buyer may revoke his acceptance of a lot or commercial unit whose non-conformity substantially impairs its value to him if he has accepted it
  (a) on the reasonable assumption that its non-conformity would be cured and it has not been seasonably cured; or
  (b) without discovery of such non-conformity if his acceptance was reasonably induced either by the difficulty of discovery before acceptance or by the seller's assurances.

(2) Revocation of acceptance must occur within a reasonable time after the buyer discovers or should have discovered the ground for it and before any substantial change in condition of the goods which is not caused by their own defects. It is not effective until the buyer notifies the seller of it.

(3) A buyer who so revokes has the same rights and duties with regard to the goods involved as if he had rejected them.

§2-609. Right to Adequate Assurance of Performance.

(1) A contract for sale imposes an obligation on each party that the other's expectation of receiving due performance will not be impaired. When reasonable grounds for insecurity arise with respect to the performance of either party the other may in writing demand adequate assurance of due performance and until he receives such assurance may if commercially reasonable suspend any performance for which he has not already received the agreed return.

(2) Between merchants the reasonableness of grounds for insecurity and the adequacy of any assurance offered shall be determined according to commercial standards.

(3) Acceptance of any improper delivery or payment does not prejudice the aggrieved party's right to demand adequate assurance of future performance.

(4) After receipt of a justified demand failure to provide within a reasonable time not exceeding thirty days such assurance of due performance as is adequate under the circumstances of the particular case is a repudiation of the contract.

§2-610. Anticipatory Repudiation.

When either party repudiates the contract with respect to a performance not yet due the loss of which will substantially impair the value of the contract to the other, the aggrieved party may
  (a) for a commercially reasonable time await performance by the repudiating party; or
  (b) resort to any remedy for breach (Section 2–703 or Section 2–711), even though he has notified the repudiating party that he would await the latter's performance and has urged retraction; and
  (c) in either case suspend his own performance or proceed in accordance with the provisions of this Article on the seller's right to identify goods to the contract notwithstanding breach or to salvage unfinished goods (Section 2–704).

§2-611. Retraction of Anticipatory Repudiation.

(1) Until the repudiating party's next performance is due he can retract his repudiation unless the aggrieved party has since the repudiation cancelled or materially changed his position or otherwise indicated that he considers the repudiation final.

(2) Retraction may be by any method which clearly indicates to the aggrieved party that the repudiating party intends to perform, but must include any assurance justifiably demanded under the provisions of this Article (Section 2–609).

(3) Retraction reinstates the repudiating party's rights under the contract with due excuse and allowance to the aggrieved party for any delay occasioned by the repudiation.

§2-612. "Installment Contract"; Breach.

(1) An "installment contract" is one which requires or authorizes the delivery of goods in separate lots to be separately accepted, even though the contract contains a clause "each delivery is a separate contract" or its equivalent.

(2) The buyer may reject any installment which is non-conforming if the non-conformity substantially impairs the value of that installment and cannot be cured or if the non-conformity is a defect in the required documents; but if the non-conformity does not fall within subsection (3) and the seller gives adequate assurance of its cure the buyer must accept that installment.

(3) Whenever non-conformity or default with respect to one or more installments substantially impairs the value of the whole contract there is a breach of the whole. But the aggrieved party reinstates the contract if he accepts a non-conforming installment without seasonably notifying of cancellation or if he brings an action with

respect only to past installments or demands performance as to future installments.

§2-613. Casualty to Identified Goods.

Where the contract requires for its performance goods identified when the contract is made, and the goods suffer casualty without fault of either party before the risk of loss passes to the buyer, or in a proper case under a "no arrival, no sale" term (Section 2–324) then

(a) if the loss is total the contract is avoided; and

(b) if the loss is partial or the goods have so deteriorated as no longer to conform to the contract the buyer may nevertheless demand inspection and at his option either treat the contract as avoided or accept the goods with due allowance from the contract price for the deterioration or the deficiency in quantity but without further right against the seller.

§2-614. Substituted Performance.

(1) Where without fault of either party the agreed berthing, loading, or unloading facilities fail or an agreed type of carrier becomes unavailable or the agreed manner of delivery otherwise becomes commercially impracticable but a commercially reasonable substitute is available, such substitute performance must be tendered and accepted.

(2) If the agreed means or manner of payment fails because of domestic or foreign governmental regulation, the seller may withhold or stop delivery unless the buyer provides a means or manner of payment which is commercially a substantial equivalent. If delivery has already been taken, payment by the means or in the manner provided by the regulation discharges the buyers obligation unless the regulation is discriminatory, oppressive or predatory.

§2-615. Excuse by Failure of Presupposed Conditions.

Except so far as a seller may have assumed a greater obligation and subject to the preceding section on substituted performance:

(a) Delay in delivery or non-delivery in whole or in part by a seller who complies with paragraphs (b) and (c) is not a breach of his duty under a contract for sale if performance as agreed has been made impracticable by the occurrence of a contingency the non-occurrence of which was a basic assumption on which the contract was made or by compliance in good faith with any applicable foreign or domestic governmental regulation or order whether or not it later proves to be invalid.

(b) Where the causes mentioned in paragraph (a) affect only a part of the seller's capacity to perform, he must allocate production and deliveries among his customers but may at his option include regular customers not then under contract as well as his own requirements for further manufacture. He may so allocate in any manner which is fair and reasonable.

(c) The seller must notify the buyer seasonably that there will be delay or non-delivery and, when allocation is required under paragraph (b), of the estimated quota thus made available for the buyer.

§2-616. Procedure on Notice Claiming Excuse.

(1) Where the buyer receives notification of a material or indefinite delay or an allocation justified under the preceding section he may by written notification to the seller as to any delivery concerned, and where the prospective deficiency substantially impairs the value of the whole contract under the provisions of this Article relating to breach of installment contracts (Section 2–612), then also as to the whole,

(a) terminate and thereby discharge any unexecuted portion of the contract; or

(b) modify the contract by agreeing to take his available quota in substitution.

(2) If after receipt of such notification from the seller the buyer fails so to modify the contract within a reasonable time not exceeding thirty days the contract lapses with respect to any deliveries affected.

(3) The provisions of this section may not be negated by agreement except in so far as the seller has assumed a greater obligation under the preceding section.

Part 7. Remedies

§2-701. Remedies for Breach of Collateral Contracts Not Impaired.

Remedies for breach of any obligation or promise collateral or ancillary to a contract for sale or not impaired by the provisions of this Article.

§2-702. Seller's Remedies on Discovery of Buyer's Insolvency.

(1) Where the seller discovers the buyer to be insolvent he may refuse delivery except for cash including payment for all goods therefore delivered under the contract, and stop delivery under this Article (Section 2–705).

(2) Where the seller discovers that the buyer has received goods on credit while insolvent he may reclaim the goods upon demand made within ten days after the receipt, but if misrepresentation of solvency has been made to the particular seller in writing within three months before delivery the ten day limitation does not apply. Except as provided in this subsection the seller may not base a right to reclaim goods on the buyer's fraudulent or innocent misrepresentation of solvency or of intent to pay.

(3) The seller's right to reclaim under subsection (2) is subject to the rights of a buyer in ordinary course or other good faith purchaser under this Article (Section 2–403). Successful reclamation of goods excludes all other remedies with respect to them.

§2-703. Seller's Remedies in General.

Where the buyer wrongfully rejects or revokes acceptance of goods or fails to make a payment due on or before delivery or repudiates with respect to a part or the whole, then with respect to any goods directly affected and, if the breach is of the whole contract (Section 2–612), then also with respect to the whole undelivered balance, the aggrieved seller may

(a) withhold delivery of such goods;

(b) stop delivery by any bailee as hereafter provided (Section 2–705);

(c) proceed under the next section respecting goods still unidentified to the contract;

(d) resell and recover damages as hereafter provided (Section 2–706);

(e) recover damages for non-acceptance (Section 2–708) or in a proper case the price (Section 2–709);

(f) cancel.

§2-704. Seller's Right to Identify Goods to the Contract Notwithstanding Breach or to Salvage Unfinished Goods.

(1) An aggrieved seller under the preceding section may

(a) identify to the contract conforming goods not already identified if at the time he learned of the breach they are in his possession or control;

(b) treat as the subject of resale goods which have demonstrably been intended for the particular contract even though those goods are unfinished.

(2) Where the goods are unfinished an aggrieved seller may in the exercise of reasonable commercial judgment for the purposes of avoiding loss and of effective realization either complete the manufacture and wholly identify the goods to the contract or cease manufacture and resell for scrap or salvage value or proceed in any other reasonable manner.

§2-705. Seller's Stoppage of Delivery in Transit or Otherwise.

(1) The seller may stop delivery of goods in the possession of a carrier or other bailee when he discovers the buyer to be insolvent (Section 2–702) and may stop delivery of carload, truckload, planeload or larger shipments of express or freight when the buyer repudiates or fails to make a payment due before delivery or if for any other reason the seller has a right to withhold or reclaim the goods.

(2) As against such buyer the seller may stop delivery until

(a) receipt of the goods by the buyer; or

(b) acknowledgment to the buyer by any bailee of the goods except a carrier that the bailee holds the goods for the buyer; or

(c) such acknowledgment to the buyer by a carrier by reshipment or as warehouseman; or

(d) negotiation to the buyer of any negotiable document of title covering the goods.

(3) (a) To stop delivery the seller must so notify as to enable the bailee by reasonable diligence to prevent delivery of the goods.

(b) After such notification the bailee must hold and deliver the goods according to the directions of the seller but the seller is liable to the bailee for any ensuing charges or damages.

(c) If a negotiable document of title has been issued for goods the bailee is not obliged to obey a notification to stop until surrender of the document.

(d) A carrier who has issued a non-negotiable bill of lading is not obliged to obey a notification to stop received from a person other than the consignor.

§2-706. Seller's Resale Including Contract for Resale.

(1) Under the conditions stated in Section 2–703 on seller's remedies, the seller may resell the goods concerned or the undelivered balance thereof. Where the resale is made in good faith and in a commercially reasonable manner the seller may recover the difference between the resale price and the contract price together with any incidental damages allowed under the provisions of this Article (Section 2–710), but less expenses saved in consequence of the buyer's breach.

(2) Except as otherwise provided in subsection (3) or unless otherwise agreed resale may be at public or private sale including sale by way of one or more contracts to sell or of identification to an existing contract of the seller. Sale may be as a unit or in parcels and at any time and place and on any terms but every aspect of the sale including the method, manner, time, place and terms must be commercially reasonable. The resale must be reasonably identified as referring to the broken contract, but it is not necessary that the goods be in existence or that any or all of them have been identified to the contract before the breach.

(3) Where the resale is at private sale the seller must give the buyer reasonable notification of his intention to resell.

(4) Where the resale is at public sale

(a) only identified goods can be sold except where there is a recognized market for a public sale of futures in goods of the kind; and

(b) it must be made at a usual place or market for public sale if one is reasonably available and except in the case of goods which are perishable or threaten to decline in value speedily the seller must give the buyer reasonable notice of the time and place of the resale; and

(c) if the goods are not to be within the view of those attending the sale the notification of sale must state the place where the goods are located and provide for their reasonable inspection by prospective bidders; and

(d) the seller may buy.

(5) A purchaser who buys in good faith at a resale takes the goods free of any rights of the original buyer even though the seller fails to comply with one or more of the requirements of this section.

(6) The seller is not accountable to the buyer for any profit made on any resale. A person in the position of a seller (Section 2–707) or a buyer who has rightfully rejected or justifiably revoked acceptance must account for any excess over the amount of his security interest, as hereinafter defined (subsection (3) of Section 2–711).

§2-707. "Person in the Position of a Seller".

(1) A "person in the position of a seller" includes as against a principal an agent who has paid or become responsible for the price of goods on behalf of his principal or anyone who otherwise holds a security interest or other right in goods similar to that of a seller.

(2) A person in the position of a seller may as provided in this Article withhold or stop delivery (Section 2–705) and resell (Section 2–706) and recover incidental damages (Section 2–710).

§2-708. Seller's Damages for Non-Acceptance or Repudiation.

(1) Subject to subsection (2) and to the provisions of this Article with respect to proof of market price (Section 2–723), the measure of damages for non-acceptance or repudiation by the buyer is the difference between the market price at the time and place for tender and the unpaid contract price together with any incidental damages provided in this Article (Section 2–710), but less expenses saved in consequence of the buyer's breach.

(2) If the measure of damages provided in subsection (1) is inadequate to put the seller in as good a position as performance would have done then the measure of damages is the profit (including reasonable overhead) which the seller would have made from full performance by the buyer, together with any incidental damages provided in this Article (Section 2–710), due allowance for costs reasonably incurred and due credit for payments or proceeds of resale.

§2-709. Action for the Price.

(1) When the buyer fails to pay the price as it becomes due the seller may recover, together with any incidental damages under the next section, the price

(a) of goods accepted or of conforming goods lost or damaged within a commercially reasonable time after risk of their loss has passed to the buyer; and

(b) of goods identified to the contract if the seller is unable after reasonable effort to resell them at a reasonable price or the circumstances reasonably indicate that such effort will be unavailing.

(2) Where the seller sues for the price he must hold for the buyer any goods which have been identified to the contract and are still in his control except that if resale becomes possible he may resell them at any time prior to the collection of the judgment. The net proceeds of any such resale must be credited to the buyer and payment of the judgment entitles him to any goods not resold.

(3) After the buyer has wrongfully rejected or revoked acceptance of the goods or has failed to make a payment due or has repudiated (Section 2–610), a seller who is held not entitled to the price under this section shall nevertheless be awarded damages for non-acceptance under the preceding section.

§2-710. Seller's Incidental Damages.

Incidental damages to an aggrieved seller include any commercially reasonable charges, expenses or commissions incurred in stopping delivery, in the transportation, care and custody of goods after the buyer's breach, in connection with return or resale of the goods or otherwise resulting from the breach.

§2-71. Buyer's Remedies in General; Buyer's Security Interest in Rejected Goods.

(1) Where the seller fails to make delivery or repudiates or the buyer rightfully rejects or justifiably revokes acceptance then with respect to any goods involved, and with respect to the whole if the breach goes to the whole contract (Section 2–612), the buyer may cancel and whether or not he has done so may in addition to recovering so much of the price as has been paid

(a) "cover" and have damages under the next section as to all the goods affected whether or not they have been identified to the contract; or

(b) recover damages for non-delivery as provided in this Article (Section 2–713).

(2) Where the seller fails to deliver or repudiates the buyer may also

(a) if the goods have been identified recover them as provided in this Article (Section 2–502); or

(b) in a proper case obtain specific performance or replevy the goods as provided in this Article (Section 2–716).

(3) On rightful rejection of justifiable revocation of acceptance a buyer has a security interest in goods in his possession or control for any payments made on their price and any expenses reasonably incurred in their inspection, receipt, transportation, care and custody and may hold such goods and resell them in like manner as an aggrieved seller (Section 2–706).

§2-712. "Cover"; Buyer's Procurement of Substitute Goods.

(1) After a breach within the preceding section the buyer may "cover" by making in good faith and without unreasonable delay any reasonable purchase of or contract to purchase goods in substitution for those due from the seller.

(2) The buyer may recover from the seller as damages the difference between the cost of cover and the contract price together with any incidental or consequential damages as hereinafter defined (Section 2–715), but less expenses saved in consequence of the seller's breach.

(3) Failure of the buyer to effect cover within this section does not bar him from any other remedy.

§2-713. Buyer's Damages for Non-Delivery or Repudiation.

(1) Subject to the provisions of this Article with respect to proof of market price (Section 2–723), the measure of damages for nondelivery or repudiation by the seller is the difference between the market price at the time when the buyer learned of the breach and the contract price together with any incidental and consequential damages provided in this Article (Section 2–715), but less expenses saved in consequence of the seller's breach.

(2) Market price is to be determined as of the place for tender or, in cases of rejection after arrival or revocation of acceptance, as of the place of arrival.

§2-714. Buyer's Damages for Breach in Regard to Accepted Goods.

(1) Where the buyer has accepted goods and given notification (subsection (3) of Section 2–607) he may recover as damages for any non-conformity of tender the loss resulting in the ordinary course of events from the seller's breach as determined in any manner which is reasonable.

(2) The measure of damages for breach of warranty is the difference at the time and place of acceptance between the value of the goods accepted and the value they would have had if they had been as warranted, unless special circumstances show proximate damages of a different amount.

(3) In a proper case any incidental and consequential damages under the next section may also be recovered.

§2-715. Buyer's Incidental and Consequential Damages.

(1) Incidental damages resulting from the seller's breach include expenses reasonably incurred in inspection, receipt, transportation and care and custody of goods rightfully rejected, any commercially reasonable charges, expenses or commissions in connection with effecting cover and any other reasonable expense incident to the delay or other breach.

(2) Consequential damages resulting from the seller's breach include

(a) any loss resulting from general or particular requirements and needs of which the seller at the time of contracting had reason to know and which could not reasonably be prevented by cover or otherwise; and

(b) injury to person or property proximately resulting from any breach of warranty.

§2-716. Buyer's Right to Specific Performance or Replevin.

(1) Specific performance may be decreed where the goods are unique or in other proper circumstances.

(2) The decree for specific performance may include such terms and conditions as to payment of the price, damages, or other relief as the court may deem just.

(3) The buyer has a right of replevin for goods identified to the contract if after reasonable effort he is unable to effect cover for

such goods or the circumstances reasonably indicate that such effort will be unvailing or if the goods have been shipped under reservation and satisfaction of the security interest in them has been made or tendered. In the case of goods bought for personal, family, or household purposes, the buyer's right of replevin vests upon acquisition of a special property, even if the seller had not then repudiated or failed to deliver.

§2-717. Deduction of Damages From the Price.

The buyer on notifying the seller of his intention to do so may deduct all or any part of the damages resulting from any breach of the contract from any part of the price still due under the same contract.

§2-718. Liquidation or Limitation of Damages; Deposits.

(1) Damages for breach by either party may be liquidated in the agreement but only at an amount which is reasonable in the light of the anticipated or actual harm caused by the breach, the difficulties of proof of loss, and the inconvenience of nonfeasibility of otherwise obtaining an adequate remedy. A team fixing unreasonably large liquidated damages is void as a penalty.

(2) Where the seller justifiably withholds delivery of goods because of the buyer's breach, the buyer is entitled to restitution of any amount by which the sum of his payments exceeds

(a) the amount to which the seller is entitled by virtue of terms liquidating the seller's damages in accordance with subsection (1), or

(b) in the absence of such terms, twenty percent of the value of the total performance for which the buyer is obligated under the contract or $500, whichever is smaller.

(3) The buyer's right to restitution under subsection (2) is subject to offset to the extent that the seller establishes

(a) a right to recover damages under the provisions of this Article other than subsection (1), and

(b) the amount or value of any benefits received by the buyer directly or indirectly by reason of the contract.

(4) Where a seller has received payment in goods their reasonable value or the proceeds of their resale shall be treated as payments for the purposes of subsection (2); but if the seller has notice of the buyer's breach before reselling goods received in part performance, his resale is subject to the conditions laid down in this Article on resale by an aggrieved seller (Section 2–706).

§2-719. Contractual Modification or Limitation of Remedy.

(1) Subject to the provisions of subsections (2) and (3) of this section and of the preceding section on liquidation and limitation of damages,

(a) the agreement may provide for remedies in addition to or in substitution for those provided in this Article and may limit or alter the measure of damages recoverable under this Article, as by limiting the buyer's remedies to return of the goods and repayment of the price or to repair and replacement of non-conforming goods or parts; and

(b) resort to a remedy as provided is optional unless the remedy is expressly agreed to be exclusive, in which case it is the sole remedy.

(2) Where circumstances cause an exclusive or limited remedy to fail of its essential purpose, remedy may be had as provided in this Act.

(3) Consequential damages may be limited or excluded unless the limitation or exclusion is unconscionable. Limitation of consequential damages for injury to the person in the case of consumer goods is prima facie unconscionable but limitation of damages where the loss is commercial is not.

§2-720. Effect of "Cancellation" or "Rescission" on Claims for Antecedent Breach.

Unless the contrary intention clearly appears, expressions of "cancellation" or "rescission" of the contract or the like shall not be construed as a renunciation or discharge of any claim in damages for an antecedent breach.

§2-72. Remedies for Fraud.

Remedies for material misrepresentation or fraud include all remedies available under this Article for non-fraudulent breach. Neither rescission or a claim for rescission of the contract for sale nor rejection or return of the goods shall bar or be deemed inconsistent with a claim for damages or other remedy.

§2-722. Who Can Sue Third Parties for Injury to Goods.

Where a third party so deals with goods which have been identified to a contract for sale as to cause actionable injury to a party to that contract

(a) a right of action against the third party is in either party to the contract for sale who has title to or a security interest or a special property or an insurable interest in the goods; and if the goods have been destroyed or converted a right of action is also in the party who either bore the risk of loss under the contract for sale or has since the injury assumed that risk as against the other,

(b) if at the time of the injury the party plaintiff did not bear the risk of loss as against the other party to the contract for sale and there is no arrangement between them for disposition of the recovery, his suit or settlement is, subject to his own interest, as a fiduciary for the other party to the contract;

(c) either party may with the consent of the other sue for the benefit of whom it may concern.

§2-723. Proof of Market Price: Time and Place.

(1) If an action based on anticipatory repudiation comes to trial before the time for performance with respect to some or all of the goods, any damages based on market price (Section 2–708 or Section 2–713) shall be determined according to the price of such goods prevailing at the time when the aggrieved party learned of the repudiation.

(2) If evidence of a price prevailing at the times or places described in this Article is not readily available the price prevailing within any reasonable time before or after the time described or at any other place which in commercial judgment or under usage of trade would serve as a reasonable substitute for the one described may be used, making any proper allowance for the cost of transporting the goods to or from such other place.

(3) Evidence of a relevant price prevailing at a time or place other than the one described in this Article offered by one party is not admissible unless and until he has given the other party such notice as the court finds sufficient to prevent unfair surprise.

§2-724. Admissibility of Market Quotations.

Whenever the prevailing price or value of any goods regularly bought and sold in any established commodity market is in issue, reports in official publications or trade journals or in newspapers or periodicals of general circulation published as the reports of such market shall be admissible in evidence. The circumstances of the preparation of such a report may be shown to affect its weight but not its admissibility.

§2-725. Statute of Limitations in Contracts for Sale.

(1) An action for breach of any contract for sale must be commenced within four years after the cause of action has accrued. By the original agreement the parties may reduce the period of limitation to not less than one year but may not extend it.

(2) A cause of action accrues when the breach occurs, regardless of the aggrieved party's lack of knowledge of the breach. A breach of warranty occurs when tender of delivery is made, except that where a warranty explicitly extends to future performance of the goods and discovery of the breach must await the time of such performance the cause of action accrues when the breach is or should have been discovered.

(3) Where an action commenced within the time limited by subsection (1) is so terminated as to leave available a remedy by another action for the same breach such other action may be commenced after the expiration of the time limited and within six months after the termination of the first action unless the termination resulted from voluntary discontinuance or from dismissal for failure or neglect to prosecute.

(4) This section does not alter the law on tolling of the statute of limitations nor does it apply to causes of action which have accrued before this Act becomes effective.

Appendix D—Sarbanes-Oxley Act of 2002 (Excerpts)

Title I—Public Company Accounting Oversight Board

Sec. 101 Establishment; Administrative Provisions.

(a) Establishment of Board.—There is established the Public Company Accounting Oversight Board, to oversee the audit of public companies that are subject to the securities laws, and related matters, in order to protect the interests of investors and further the public interest in the preparation of informative, accurate, and independent audit reports for companies the securities of which are sold to, and held by and for, public investors. The Board shall be a body corporate, operate as a nonprofit corporation, and have succession until dissolved by an Act of Congress.

Sec. 102 Registration with the Board.

(a) Mandatory Registration.—It shall be unlawful for any person that is not a registered public accounting firm to prepare or issue, or to participate in the preparation or issuance of, any audit report with respect to any issuer.

(b) Application for Registration.—

(1) Form of application.—A public accounting firm shall use such form as the Board may prescribe, by rule, to apply for registration under this section.

Sec. 104 Inspections of Registered Public Accounting Firms.

(a) In General.—The Board shall conduct a continuing program of inspections to assess the degree of compliance of each registered public accounting firm and associated persons of that firm with this Act, the rules of the Board, the rules of the Commission, or professional standards, in connection with its performance of audits, issuance of audit reports, and related matters involving issuers.

(b) Inspection Frequency.—

(1) In general.—Subject to paragraph (2), inspections required by this section shall be conducted—

(A) annually with respect to each registered public accounting firm that regularly provides audit reports for more than 100 issuers; and

(B) not less frequently than once every 3 years with respect to each registered public accounting firm that regularly provides audit reports for 100 or fewer issuers.

Sec. 105 Investigations and Disciplinary Proceedings.

(a) In General.—The Board shall establish, by rule, subject to the requirements of this section, fair procedures for the investigation and disciplining of registered public accounting firms and associated persons of such firms.

(c) Disciplinary Procedures.—

(4) Sanctions.—If the Board finds, based on all of the facts and circumstances, that a registered public accounting firm or associated person thereof has engaged in any act or practice, or omitted to act, in violation of this Act, the rules of the Board, the provisions of the securities laws relating to the preparation and issuance of audit reports and the obligations and liabilities of accountants with respect thereto, including the rules of the Commission issued under this Act, or professional standards, the Board may impose such disciplinary or remedial sanctions as it determines appropriate, subject to applicable limitations under paragraph (5), including—

(A) temporary suspension or permanent revocation of registration under this title;

(B) temporary or permanent suspension or bar of a person from further association with any registered public accounting firm;

(C) temporary or permanent limitation on the activities, functions, or operations of such firm or person (other than in connection with required additional professional education or training);

(D) a civil money penalty for each such violation, in an amount equal to—

(i) not more than $100,000 for a natural person or $2,000,000 for any other person; and

(ii) in any case to which paragraph (5) applies, not more than $750,000 for a natural person or $15,000,000 for any other person;

(E) censure;

(F) required additional professional education or training; or

(G) any other appropriate sanction provided for in the rules of the Board.

(5) Intentional or other knowing conduct.—The sanctions and penalties described in subparagraphs (A) through (C) and (D)(ii) of paragraph (4) shall only apply to—

(A) intentional or knowing conduct, including reckless conduct, that results in violation of the applicable statutory, regulatory, or professional standard; or

(B) repeated instances of negligent conduct, each resulting in a violation of the applicable statutory, regulatory, or professional standard.

Title II—Auditor Independence

Sec. 201 Services Outside the Scope of Practice of Auditors.

(a) Prohibited Activities.—Section 10A of the Securities Exchange Act of 1934 (15 U.S.C. 78j–1) is amended by adding at the end of the following:

"(g) Prohibited Activities.—Except as provided in subsection (h), it shall be unlawful for a registered public accounting firm (and any associated person of that firm, to the extent determined appropriate by the Commission) that performs for any issuer any audit required by this title or the rules of the Commission under this title or, beginning 180 days after the date of commencement of the operations of the Public Company Accounting Oversight Board established under section 101 of the Sarbanes-Oxley Act of 2002 (in this section referred to as the 'Board'), the rules of the Board, to provide to that issuer, contemporaneously with the audit, any non-audit service, including—

"(1) bookkeeping or other services related to the accounting records or financial statements of the audit client;

"(2) financial information systems design and implementation;

"(3) appraisal or valuation services, fairness opinions, or contribution-in-kind reports;

"(4) actuarial services;

"(5) internal audit outsourcing services;

"(6) management functions or human resources;

"(7) broker or dealer, investment adviser, or investment banking services;

"(8) legal services and expert services unrelated to the audit; and

"(9) any other service that the Board determines, by regulation, is impermissible.

"(h) Preapproval Required for Non-Audit Services.—A registered public accounting firm may engage in any non-audit service, including tax services, that is not described in any of paragraphs (1) through (9) of subsection (g) for an audit client, only if the activity is approved in advance by the audit committee of the issuer, in accordance with subsection (i)."

Sec. 206 Conflicts of Interest.

Section 10A of the Securities Exchange Act of 1934 (15 U.S.C. 78j–1), as amended by this Act, is amended by adding at the end the following:

"(l) Conflicts of Interest.—It shall be unlawful for a registered public accounting firm to perform for an issuer any audit service required by this title, if a chief executive officer, controller, chief financial officer, chief accounting officer, or any person serving in an equivalent position for the issuer, was employed by that registered independent public accounting firm and participated in any capacity in the audit of that issuer during the 1-year period preceding the date of the initiation of the audit."

Title III—Corporate Responsibility

Sec. 301 Public Company Audit Committees.

Section 10A of the Securities Exchange Act of 1934 (15 U.S.C. 78f) is amended by adding at the end the following:

"(m) Standards Relating to Audit Committees.—

"(2) Responsibilities relating to registered public accounting firms.—The audit committee of each issuer, in its capacity as a committee of the board of directors, shall be directly responsible for the appointment, compensation, and oversight of the work of any registered public accounting firm employed by that issuer (including resolution of disagreements between management and the auditor regarding financial reporting) for the purpose of preparing or issuing an audit report or related work, and each such registered public accounting firm shall report directly to the audit committee.

"(3) Independence.—

"(A) In general.—Each member of the audit committee of the issuer shall be a member of the board of directors of the issuer, and shall otherwise be independent.

"(B) Criteria.—In order to be considered to be independent for purposes of this paragraph, a member of an audit committee of an issuer may not, other than in his or her capacity as a member of the audit committee, the board of directors, or any other board committee—

"(i) accept any consulting, advisory, or other compensatory fee from the issuer; or

"(ii) be an affiliated person of the issuer or any subsidiary thereof.

Sec. 302 Corporate Responsibility for Financial Reports.

(a) Regulations Required.—The Commission shall, by rule, require, for each company filing periodic reports under section 13(a) or 15(d) of the Securities Exchange Act of 1934 (15 U.S.C. 78m, 78o(d)), that the principal executive officer or officers and the principal financial officer or officers, or persons performing similar functions, certify in each annual or quarterly report filed or submitted under either such section of such Act that—

(1) the signing officer has reviewed the report;

(2) based on the officer's knowledge, the report does not contain any untrue statement of a material fact or omit to state a material fact necessary in order to make the statements made, in light of the circumstances under which such statements were made, not misleading;

(3) based on such officer's knowledge, the financial statements, and other financial information included in the report fairly present in all material respects the financial condition and results of operations of the issuer as of, and for, the periods presented in the report;

(4) the signing officers—

(A) are responsible for establishing and maintaining internal controls;

(B) have designed such internal controls to ensure that material information relating to the issuer and its consolidated subsidiaries is made known to such officers by others within those entities, particularly during the period in which the periodic reports are being prepared;

(C) have evaluated the effectiveness of the issuer's internal controls as of a date within 90 days prior to the report; and

(D) have presented in the report their conclusions about the effectiveness of their internal controls based on their evaluation as of that date;

(5) the signing officers have disclosed to the issuer's auditors and the audit committee of the board of directors (or persons fulfilling the equivalent function)—

(A) all significant deficiencies in the design or operation of internal controls which could adversely affect the issuer's ability to record, process, summarize, and report financial data and have identified for the issuer's auditors any material weaknesses in internal controls; and

(B) any fraud, whether or not material, that involves management or other employees who have a significant role in the issuer's internal controls; and

(6) the signing officers have indicated in the report whether or not there were significant changes in internal controls or in other factors that could significantly affect internal controls subsequent to the date of their evaluation, including any corrective actions with regard to significant deficiencies and material weaknesses.

Sec. 303 Improper Influence on Conduct of Audits.

(a) Rules to Prohibit.—It shall be unlawful, in contravention of such rules or regulations as the Commission shall prescribe as necessary and appropriate in the public interest or for the protection of investors, for any officer or director of an issuer, or any other person acting under the direction thereof, to take any action to fraudulently influence, coerce, manipulate, or mislead any independent public or certified accountant engaged in the performance of an audit of the financial statements of that issuer for the purpose of rendering such financial statements materially misleading.

Title IV—Enhanced Financial Disclosures

Sec. 401 Disclosures in Periodic Reports.

(a) Disclosures Required.—Section 13 of the Securities Exchange Act of 1934 (15 U.S.C. 78m) is amended by adding at the end the following:

"(i) Accuracy of Financial Reports.—Each financial report that contains financial statements, and that is required to be prepared in accordance with (or reconciled to) generally accepted accounting principles under this title and filed with the Commission shall reflect all material correcting adjustments that have been identified by a registered public accounting firm in accordance with generally accepted accounting principles and the rules and regulations of the Commission.

"(j) Off-Balance Sheet Transactions.—Not later than 180 days after the date of enactment of the Sarbanes-Oxley Act of 2002, the Commission shall issue final rules providing that each annual and quarterly financial report required to be filed with the Commission shall disclose all material off-balance sheet transactions, arrangements, obligations (including contingent obligations), and other relationships of the issuer with unconsolidated entities or other persons, that may have a material current or future effect on financial condition, changes in financial condition, results of operations, liquidity, capital expenditures, capital resources, or significant components of revenues or expenses."

(b) Commission Rules on Pro Forma Figures.—Not later than 180 days after the date of enactment of the Sarbanes-Oxley Act of 2002, the Commission shall issue final rules providing that pro forma financial information included in any periodic or other report filed with the Commission pursuant to the securities laws, or in any public disclosure or press or other release, shall be presented in a manner that—

(1) does not contain an untrue statement of a material fact or omit to state a material fact necessary in order to make the pro forma financial information, in light of the circumstances under which it is presented, not misleading; and

(2) reconciles it with the financial condition and results of operations of the issuer under generally accepted accounting principles.

Sec. 402 Enhanced Conflict of Interest Provisions.

(a) Prohibition on Personal Loans to Executives.—Section 13 of the Securities Exchange Act of 1934 (15 U.S.C. 78m), as amended by this Act, is amended by adding at the end the following:

"(k) Prohibition on Personal Loans to Executives.—

"(1) In general.—It shall be unlawful for any issuer (as defined in section 2 of the Sarbanes-Oxley Act of 2002), directly or indirectly, including through any subsidiary, to extend or maintain credit, to arrange for the extension of credit, or to renew an extension of credit, in the form of a personal loan to or for any director or executive officer (or equivalent thereof) of that issuer. An extension of credit maintained by the issuer on the date of enactment of this subsection shall not be subject to the provisions of this subsection, provided that there is no material modification to any term of any such extension of credit or any renewal of any such extension of credit on or after that date of enactment.

Sec. 406 Code of Ethics for Senior Financial Officers.

(a) Code of Ethics Disclosure.—The Commission shall issue rules to require each issuer, together with periodic reports required pursuant to section 13(a) or 15(d) of the Securities Exchange Act of 1934, to disclose whether or not, and if not, the reason therefor, such issuer has adopted a code of ethics for senior financial officers, applicable to its principal financial officer and comptroller or principal accounting officer, or persons performing similar functions.

(b) Changes in Codes of Ethics.—The Commission shall revise its regulations concerning matters requiring prompt disclosure on Form 8-K (or any successor thereto) to require the immediate disclosure by means of the filing of such form, dissemination by the Internet or by other electronic means, by any issuer of any change in or waiver of the code of ethics for senior financial officers.

(c) Definition.—In this section, the term "code of ethics" means such standards as are reasonably necessary to promote—

(1) honest and ethical conduct, including the ethical handling of actual or apparent conflicts of interest between personal and professional relationships;

(2) full, fair, accurate, timely, and understandable disclosure in the periodic reports required to be filed by the issuer; and

(3) compliance with applicable governmental rules and regulations.

Title V—Analyst Conflicts of Interest

Sec. 501 Treatment of Securities Analysts by Registered Securities Associations and National Securities Exchanges.

(a) Rules Regarding Securities Analysts.—The Securities Exchange Act of 1934 (15 U.S.C. 78a et seq.) is amended by inserting after section 15C the following new section:

"Sec. 15D. Securities Analysts and Research Reports

"(a) Analyst Protections.—The Commission, or upon the authorization and direction of the Commission, a registered securities association or national securities exchange, shall have adopted, not later than 1 year after the date of enactment of this section, rules reasonably designed to address conflicts of interest that can arise when securities analysts recommend equity securities in research reports and public appearances, in order to improve the objectivity of research and provide investors with more useful and reliable information, including rules designed—

"(1) to foster greater public confidence in securities research, and to protect the objectivity and independence of securities analysts, by—

"(A) restricting the prepublication clearance or approval of research reports by persons employed by the broker or dealer who are engaged in investment banking activities, or persons not directly responsible for investment research, other than legal or compliance staff;

"(B) limiting the supervision and compensatory evaluation of securities analysts to officials employed by the broker or dealer who are not engaged in investment banking activities; and

"(C) requiring that a broker or dealer and persons employed by a broker or dealer who are involved with investment banking activities may not, directly or indirectly, retaliate against or threaten to retaliate against any securities analyst employed by that broker or dealer or its affiliates as a result of an adverse, negative, or otherwise unfavorable research report that may adversely affect the present or prospective investment banking relationship of the broker or dealer with the issuer that is the subject of the research report, except that such rules may not limit the authority of a broker or dealer to discipline a securities analyst for causes other than such research report in accordance with the policies and procedures of the firm;

"(2) to define periods during which brokers or dealers who have participated, or are to participate, in a public offering of securities as underwriters or dealers should not publish or otherwise distribute research reports relating to such securities or to the issuer of such securities;

"(3) to establish structural and institutional safeguards within registered brokers or dealers to assure that securities analysts are separated by appropriate informational partitions within the firm from the review, pressure, or oversight of those whose involvement in investment banking activities might potentially bias their judgment or supervision; and

"(4) to address such other issues as the Commission, or such association or exchange, determines appropriate.

"(b) Disclosure.—The Commission, or upon the authorization and direction of the Commission, a registered securities association or national securities exchange, shall have adopted, not later than 1 year after the date of enactment of this section, rules reasonably designed to require each securities analyst to disclose in public appearances, and each registered broker or dealer to disclose in each research report, as applicable, conflicts of interest that are known or should have been known by the securities analyst or the broker or dealer, to exist at the time of the appearance or the date of distribution of the report, including—

"(1) the extent to which the securities analyst has debt or equity investments in the issuer that is the subject of the appearance or research report;

"(2) whether any compensation has been received by the registered broker or dealer, or any affiliate thereof, including the securities analyst, from the issuer that is the subject of the appearance or research report, subject to such exemptions as the Commission may determine appropriate and necessary to prevent disclosure by virtue of this paragraph of material non-public information regarding specific potential future investment banking transactions of such issuer, as is appropriate in the public interest and consistent with the protection of investors;

"(3) whether an issuer, the securities of which are recommended in the appearance or research report, currently is, or during the 1-year period preceding the date of the appearance or date of distribution of the report has been, a client of the registered broker or dealer, and if so, stating the types of services provided to the issuer;

"(4) whether the securities analyst received compensation with respect to a research report, based upon (among any other factors) the investment banking revenues (either generally or specifically earned from the issuer being analyzed) of the registered broker or dealer; and

"(5) such other disclosures of conflicts of interest that are material to investors, research analysts, or the broker or dealer as the Commission, or such association or exchange, determines appropriate.

"(c) Definitions.—In this section—

"(1) the term 'securities analyst' means any associated person of a registered broker or dealer that is principally responsible for, and any associated person who reports directly or indirectly to a securities analyst in connection with, the preparation of the substance of a research report, whether or not any such person has the job title of 'securities analyst'; and

"(2) the term 'research report' means a written or electronic communication that includes an analysis of equity securities of individual companies or industries, and that provides information reasonably sufficient upon which to base an investment decision."

(b) Enforcement.—Section 21B(a) of the Securities Exchange Act of 1934 (15 U.S.C. 78u–2(a)) is amended by inserting "15D," before "15B".

(c) Commission Authority.—The Commission may promulgate and amend its regulations, or direct a registered securities association or national securities exchange to promulgate and amend its rules, to carry out section 15D of the Securities Exchange Act of 1934, as added by this section, as is necessary for the protection of investors and in the public interest.

Title VI—Commission Resources and Authority

Sec. 602 Appearance and Practice Before the Commission.

The Securities Exchange Act of 1934 (15 U.S.C. 78a et seq.) is amended by inserting after section 4B the following:

"Sec 4C. Appearance and Practice Before the Commission

"(a) Authority to Censure.—The Commission may censure any person, or deny, temporarily or permanently, to any person the privilege of appearing or practicing before the Commission in any way, if that person is found by the Commission, after notice and opportunity for hearing in the matter—

"(1) not to possess the requisite qualifications to represent others;

"(2) to be lacking in character or integrity, or to have engaged in unethical or improper professional conduct; or

"(3) to have willfully violated or willfully aided and abetted the violation of, any provision of the securities laws or the rules and regulations issued thereunder.

Title VII—Studies and Reports

Sec. 705 Study of Investment Banks.

(a) GAO Study.—The Comptroller General of the United States shall conduct a study on whether investment banks and financial advisers assisted public companies in manipulating their earnings and obfuscating their true financial condition. The study should address the rule of investment banks and financial advisers—

(1) in the collapse of the Enron Corporation, including with respect to the design and implementation of derivatives transactions, transactions involving special purpose vehicles, and other financial arrangements that may have had the effect of altering the company's reported financial statements in ways that obscured the true financial picture of the company;

(2) in the failure of Global Crossing, including with respect to transactions involving swaps of fiberoptic cable capacity, in the designing transactions that may have had the effect of altering the company's reported financial statements in ways that obscured the true financial picture of the company; and

(3) generally, in creating and marketing transactions which may have been designed solely to enable companies to manipulate revenue streams, obtain loans, or move liabilities off balance sheets without altering the economic and business risks faced by the companies or any other mechanism to obscure a company's financial picture.

Title VIII—Corporate and Criminal Fraud Accountability

Sec. 801 Short Title.

This title may be cited as the "Corporate and Criminal Fraud Accountability Act of 2002".

Sec. 802 Criminal Penalties for Altering Documents.

(a) In General.—Chapter 73 of title 18, United States Code, is amended by adding at the end the following:

§1519. Destruction, alteration, or falsification of records in Federal investigations and bankruptcy

"Whoever knowingly alters, destroys, mutilates, conceals, covers up, falsifies, or makes a false entry in any record, document, or tangible object with the intent to impede, obstruct, or influence the investigation or proper administration of any matter within the jurisdiction of any department or agency of the United States or any case filed under Title 11, or in relation to or contemplation of any such matter or case, shall be fined under this title, imprisoned not more than 20 years, or both.

§1520. Destruction of corporate audit records

"(a)(1) Any accountant who conducts an audit of an issuer of securities to which section 10A(a) of the Securities Exchange Act of 1934 (15 U.S.C. 78j–l(a)) applies, shall maintain all audit or review workpapers for a period of 5 years from the end of the fiscal period in which the audit or review was concluded.

Sec. 807 Criminal Penalties for Defrauding Shareholders of Publicly Traded Companies.

(a) In General.—Chapter 63 of title 18, United States Code, is amended by adding at the end the following:

§1348. Securities fraud

"Whoever knowingly executes, or attempts to execute, a scheme or artifice—

"(1) to defraud any person in connection with any security of an issuer with a class of securities registered under section 12 of the Securities Exchange Act of 1934 (15 U.S.C. 78l) or that is required to file reports under section 15(d) of the Securities Exchange Act of 1934 (15 U.S.C. 78o(d)); or

"(2) to obtain, by means of false or fraudulent pretenses, representations, or promises, any money or property in connection with the purchase or sale of any security of an issuer with a class of securities registered under section 12 of the Securities Exchange Act of 1934 (15 U.S.C. 78l) or that is required to file reports under section 15(d) of the Securities Exchange Act of 1934 (15 U.S.C. 78o(d));

shall be fined under this title, or imprisoned not more than 25 years, or both."

Title IX—White-Collar Crime Penalty Enhancements

Sec. 901 Short Title.

This title may be cited as the "White-Collar Crime Penalty Enhancement Act of 2002".

Sec. 906 Corporate Responsibility for Financial Reports.

(a) In General.—Chapter 63 of title 18, United States Code, is amended by inserting after section 1349, as created by this Act, the following:

§1350. Failure of corporate officers to certify financial reports

(a) Certification of Periodic Financial Reports.—Each periodic report containing financial statements filed by an issuer with the Securities Exchange Commission pursuant to section 13(a) or 15(d) of the Securities Exchange Act of 1934 (15 U.S.C. 78m(a) or 78o(d)) shall be accompanied by a written statement by the chief executive officer and chief financial officer (or equivalent thereof) of the issuer.

"(b) Content.—The statement required under subsection (a) shall certify that the periodic report containing the financial statements fully complies with the requirements of section 13(a) or 15(d) of the Securities Exchange Act of 1934 (15 U.S.C. 78m or 78o(d)) and that information contained in the periodic report fairly presents, in all material respects, the financial condition and results of operations of the issuer.

"(c) Criminal Penalties.—Whoever—

"(1) certifies any statement as set forth in subsections (a) and (b) of this section knowing that the periodic report accompanying the statement does not comport with all the requirements set forth in this section shall be fined not more than $1,000,000 or imprisoned not more than 10 years, or both; or

"(2) willfully certifies any statement as set forth in subsections (a) and (b) of this section knowing that the periodic report accompanying the statement does not comport with all the requirements set forth in this section shall be fined not more than $5,000,000, or imprisoned not more than 20 years, or both."

(b) Clerical Amendment.—The table of sections at the beginning of chapter 63 of title 18, United States Code, is amended by adding at the end the following:
"1350". Failure of corporate officers to certify financial reports."

Title X—Corporate Tax Returns

Sec. 1001 Sense of the Senate Regarding the Signing of Corporate Tax Returns by Chief Executive Officers.

It is the sense of the Senate that the Federal income tax return of a corporation should be signed by the chief executive officer of such corporation.

Title XI—Corporate Fraud Accountability

Sec. 1101 Short Title.

This title may be cited as the "Corporate Fraud Accountability Act of 2002".

Sec. 1102 Tampering with a Record or Otherwise Impeding an Official Proceeding.

Section 1512 of title 18, United States Code, is amended—

(1) by redesignating subsections (c) through (i) as subsections (d) through (j), respectively; and

(2) by inserting after subsection (b) the following new subsection:

"(c) Whoever corruptly—

"(1) alters, destroys, mutilates, or conceals a record, document, or other object, or attempts to do so, with the intent to impair the object's integrity or availability for use in an official proceeding; or

"(2) otherwise obstructs, influences, or impedes any official proceeding, or attempts to do so,

shall be fined under this title or imprisoned not more than 20 years, or both."

Sec. 1105 Authority of the Commission to Prohibit Persons from Serving as Officers or Directors.

(a) Securities Exchange Act of 1934.—Section 21C of the Securities Exchange Act of 1934 (15 U.S.C. 78u–3) is amended by adding at the end the following:

"(f) Authority of the Commission to Prohibit Persons from Serving as Officers or Directors.—In any cease-and-desist proceeding under subsection (a), the Commission may issue an order to prohibit, conditionally or unconditionally, and permanently or for such period of time as it shall determine, any person who has violated section 10(b) or the rules or regulations thereunder, from acting as an officer or director of any issuer that has a class of securities registered pursuant to section 12, or that is required to file reports pursuant to section 15(d), if the conduct of that person demonstrates unfitness to serve as an officer or director of any such issuer."

(b) Securities Act of 1933.—Section 8A of the Securities Act of 1933 (15 U.S.C. 77h–l) is amended by adding at the end of the following:

"(f) Authority of the Commission to Prohibit Persons from Serving as Officers or Directors.—In any cease-and-desist proceeding under subsection (a), the Commission may issue an order to prohibit, conditionally or unconditionally, and permanently or for such period of time as it shall determine, any person who has violated section 17(a)(1) or the rules or regulations thereunder, from acting as an officer or director of any issuer that has a class of securities registered pursuant to section 12 of the Securities Exchange Act of 1934, or that is required to file reports pursuant to section 15(d) of that Act, if the conduct of that person demonstrates unfitness to serve as an officer or director of any such issuer."

Glossary

abandoned property Property that an owner has discarded with the intent to relinquish his or her rights in it, or mislaid or lost property that the owner has given up any further attempts to locate. 681

acceptance A manifestation of assent by the offeree to the terms of the offer in a manner invited or required by the offer, as measured by the objective theory of contracts. [*Restatement (Second) of Contracts* 50] 281

accord and satisfaction The settlement of a contract dispute. 319

act of monopolizing A required act for there to be a violation of Section 2 of the Sherman Act. Possession of monopoly power without such act does not violate Section 2. 622

act of state doctrine A doctrine that states that judges of one country cannot question the validity of an act committed by another country within that other country's borders. It is based on the principle that a country has absolute authority over what transpires within its own territory. 258

action for an accounting A formal judicial proceeding in which the court is authorized to (1) review the partnership and the partners' transactions and (2) award each partner his or her share of the partnership assets. 427

actas reus "Guilty act"—the actual performance of a criminal act. 179

adjudged insane A person who has been determined to be insane by a proper court or administrative agency. A contract entered into by such a person is void. 288

administrative agencies Agencies that the legislative and executive branches of federal and state governments establish. 556

adverse action A denial or revocation of credit or a change in the credit terms offered. 577

adverse possession Possession in which a person who wrongfully possesses someone else's real property obtains title to that property if certain statutory requirements are met. 690

affirmative action A policy that provides that certain job preferences will be given to minority or other protected-class applicants when an employer makes an employment decision. 547

AFL-CIO The 1955 combination of the AFL and the CIO. 497

agency The principal–agent relationship: the fiduciary relationship "which results from the manifestation of consent by one person to another that the other shall act in his behalf and subject to his control, and consent by the other so to act." 366

agency by ratification An agency that occurs when (1) a person misrepresents him- or herself as another's agent when in fact he or she is not and (2) the purported principal ratifies the unauthorized act. 372

agency law The large body of common law that governs agency; a mixture of contract law and tort law. 365

agency shop An establishment in which an employee does not have to join the union but must pay a fee equal to the union dues. 504

agent A party who agrees to act on behalf of another. 366

agreement The manifestation by two or more persons of the substance of a contract. 278

aiding and abetting the commission of a crime Rendering support, assistance, or encouragement to the commission of a crime; harboring a criminal after he or she has committed a crime. 191

air pollution Pollution caused by factories, homes, vehicles, and the like that affects the air. 587

alien corporation A corporation that is incorporated in another country. 455

alternative dispute resolution (ADR) Methods other than litigation of resolving disputes. 50

Americans with Disabilities Act (ADA) of 1990 An act that imposes obligations on employers and providers of public transportation, telecommunications, and public accommodations to accommodate individuals with disabilities. 541

annual shareholders' meeting A meeting of the shareholders of a corporation that must be held annually by the corporation to elect directors and to vote on other matters. 463

answer The defendant's written response to the plaintiff's complaint, which is filed with the court and served on the plaintiff. 41

anticipatory breach A breach that occurs when one contracting party informs the other that he or she will not perform his or her contractual duties when due. 324

antidilution statutes State laws that allow persons and companies to register trademarks and service marks. 233

antitrust laws Laws enacted to limit anticompetitive behavior in almost all industries, businesses, and professions operating in the United States. 612

apparent agency Agency that arises when a principal creates the appearance of an agency that in actuality does not exist. 370, 412

appeal The act of asking an appellate court to overturn a decision after the trial court's final judgment has been entered. 48

appellant The appealing party in an appeal. Also known as *petitioner*. 49

appellate body A panel of seven justices selected from WTO member nations that hears and decides appeals from decisions by the dispute settlement body. 255

appellee The responding party in an appeal. Also known as respondent. 49

appropriate bargaining unit The group that a union seeks to represent. 499

arbitration A form of ADR in which the parties choose an impartial third party to hear and decide the dispute. 50 A nonjudicial method of dispute resolution whereby a neutral third party decides the case. 26

arbitration clause A clause in contracts that requires disputes arising out of the contract to be submitted to arbitration. 50 A clause contained in many international contracts that stipulates that any dispute between the parties concerning the performance of the contract will be submitted to an arbitrator or arbitration panel for resolution. 261

arraignment A hearing during which the accused is brought before a court and is (1) informed of the charges against him or her and (2) asked to enter a plea. 181

arrest warrant A document for a person's detainment, based on a showing of probable cause that the person committed the crime. 181

arson The willful or malicious burning of another's building. 184

Article 9 of the UCC An article of the UCC that governs secured transactions in personal property. 717

articles of amendment A document that must be filed with the secretary of state which the amendment to the articles of incorporation is approved by the shareholders. 457

articles of incorporation The basic governing document of the corporation. This document must be filed with the secretary of state of the state of incorporation. 456

articles of organization The formal document that must be filed with the secretary of state to form an LLC. 440

articles of partnership A public document that must be filed with the secretary of state to form a limited liability partnership. 436

assault (1) The threat of immediate harm or offensive contact or (2) any action that arouses reasonable apprehension of imminent harm. Actual physical contact is unnecessary. 114

assignee A party to whom a right has been transferred. 295

assignment The transfer of contractual rights by an obligee to another party. 295

assignor An obligee who transfers a right. 295

assumption of the risk A defense that a defendant can use against a plaintiff who knowingly and voluntarily enters into or participates in a risky activity that results in injury. 130 A defense in which the defendant must prove that (1) the plaintiff knew and appreciated the risk and (2) the plaintiff voluntarily assumed the risk. 168

attempt to commit a crime A situation in which a crime is attempted but not completed. 190

attorney–client privilege A rule that says a client can tell his or her lawyer anything about the case without fear that the attorney will be called as a witness against the client. 197

authorized shares The number of shares provided for in the articles of incorporation. 459

automatic stay The result of the filing of a voluntary or involuntary petition; the suspension of certain actions by creditors against the debtor or the debtor's property. 731

backward vertical merger A vertical merger in which the customer acquires the supplier. 626

bailee A holder of goods who is not a seller or a buyer (e.g., a warehouse, common carrier). 682

bailment A transaction in which an owner transfers his or her personal property to another to be held, stored, delivered, or for some other purpose. Title to the property does not transfer. 682

bailment for sole benefit of the bailee A gratuitous bailment that benefits only the bailee. The bailee owes a *duty of great care* to protect the bailed property. 682

bailment for the sole benefit of the bailor A gratuitous bailment that benefits only the bailor. The bailee owes only a *duty of slight care* to protect the bailed property. 682

bailor The owner of property in a bailment. 682

bait and switch A type of deceptive advertising that occurs when a seller advertises the availability of a low-cost discounted item but then pressures the buyer into purchasing more expensive merchandise. 573

bankruptcy estate An estate created upon the commencement of a Chapter 7 proceeding that includes all of the debtor's legal and equitable interests in real, personal, tangible, and intangible property, wherever located, that exist when the petition is filed, minus exempt property. 724

bargained-for exchange An exchange that parties engage in that leads to an enforceable contract. 284

battery Unauthorized and harmful or offensive physical contact with another person. Direct physical contact is not necessary. 114

bilateral contract A contract entered into by way of exchange of promises of the parties, a "promise for a promise." 273

board of directors A panel of decision makers, the members of which are elected by the corporation's shareholders. 469

bona fide occupational qualification (BFOQ) Employment discrimination based on a protected class (other than race or color) that is lawful if it is *job related* and a *business necessity*. This exception is narrowly interpreted by the courts. 537

bond A long-term debt security that is secured by some form of collateral. 462

breach of the duty of care A failure to exercise care or to act as a reasonable person would act. 120

bribery The act of one person giving another person money, property, favors, or anything else of value for a favor in return. Often referred to as a payoff or kickback. 187

burden of proof The burden that the plaintiff bears to prove the allegations made in his or her complaint. 48

burglary The taking of personal property from another's home, office, commercial, or other type of building. 183

bylaws A detailed set of rules that are adopted by the board of directors after the corporation is incorporated that contains provisions for managing the business and the affairs of the corporation. 457

cancellation The termination of a contract by a contracting party upon the material breach of the contract by the other party. 355

case brief A summary of each of the following items of a case: (1) case name and citation, (2) key facts, (3) issue presented, (4) holding of the court, and (5) court's reasoning. 18

causation The act or process of causing. A person who commits a negligent act is not liable unless his or her act was the cause of the plaintiff's injuries. The two types of causation that must be proven are (1) causation in fact (actual cause) and (2) proximate cause (legal cause). 124

causation in fact, or actual cause The actual cause of negligence. A person who commits a negligent act is not liable unless causation in fact can be proven. 124

caveat emptor "Let the buyer beware," the traditional guideline of sales transactions. 556

certificate of deposit (CD) A two-party negotiable instrument that is a special form of note created when a depositor deposits money at a financial institution in exchange for the institution's promise to pay back the amount of the deposit plus an agreed-upon rate of interest upon the expiration of a set time period agreed upon by the parties. 713

certificate of limited partnership A document that two or more persons must execute and sign that makes the limited partnership legal and binding. 433

chain of distribution All manufacturers, distributors, wholesalers, retailers, lessors, and subcomponent manufacturers involved in a transaction. 159

chain-style franchise A franchise in which the franchisor licenses the franchisee to make and sell its products or distribute services to the public from a retail outlet serving an exclusive territory. 404

changing conditions defense A price discrimination defense that claims that prices were lowered in response to changing conditions in the market for or the marketability of the goods. 631

Chapter 11 reorganization bankruptcy A bankruptcy method that allows reorganization of the debtor's financial affairs under the supervision of the bankruptcy court. 730

Chapter 13 consumer debt adjustment A rehabilitation form of bankruptcy that permits the courts to supervise the debtor's plan for the payment of unpaid debts by installments. 734

Chapter 7 liquidation bankruptcy The most familiar form of bankruptcy, in which the debtor's nonexempt property is sold for cash, the cash is distributed to the creditors, and any unpaid debts are discharged. 722

check A distinct form of draft drawn on a financial institution and payable on demand. 710

choice of forum clause A clause in an international contract that designates which nation's court has jurisdiction to hear a case arising out of the contract. Also known as a *forum-selection clause*. 258

choice of law clause A clause in an international contract that designates which nation's laws will be applied in deciding a dispute arising out of the contract. 258

closing arguments Statements made by the attorneys to the jury at the end of the trial to try to convince the jury to render a verdict for their clients. 48

collateral Security against repayment of the note that lenders sometimes require; can be a car, a house, or other property. 713 The property that is subject to a security interest. 716

collateral contract A promise in which one person agrees to answer for the debts or duties of another person. 313

collective bargaining The act of negotiating contract terms between an employer and the members of a union. 502

collective bargaining agreement The resulting contract from a collective bargaining procedure. 502

"coming and going" rule A rule that says a principal is generally not liable for injuries caused by its agents and employees while they are on their way to and from work. 380

Commerce Clause A clause of the U.S. Constitution that grants Congress the power "to regulate commerce with foreign nations, and among the several states, and with Indian tribes." 66

commercial impracticability Nonperformance that is excused if an extreme or unexpected development or expense makes it impractical for the promisor to perform. 321

commercial speech Speech used by business, such as advertising. It is subject to time, place, and manner restrictions. 73

common law Law developed by judges who issued their opinions when deciding a case. The principles announced in these cases became precedent for later judges deciding similar cases. 9

common stock A type of equity security that represents the *residual* value of the corporation. 461

common stock certificate A document that represents the common shareholder's investment in a corporation. 461

common stockholder A person who owns common stock. 461

comparative negligence A doctrine that applies to strict liability actions and says that a plaintiff who is contributorily negligent for his or her injuries is responsible for a proportional share of the damages. 169 A doctrine under which damages are apportioned according to fault. 131

compensatory damages A remedy intended to compensate a nonbreaching party for the loss of a bargain; they place the nonbreaching party in the same position as if the contract had been fully performed by restoring the "benefits of the bargain." 324

competent party's duty of restitution A duty in which if a minor has transferred money, property, or other valuables to the competent party before disaffirming the contract, that party must place the minor back into status quo. 287

complaint The document the plaintiff files with the court and serves on the defendant to initiate a lawsuit. 41

complete performance A type of performance that occurs when a party to a contract renders performance exactly as required by the contract; it discharges that party's obligations under the contract. 321

conciliation A form of mediation in which the parties choose an *interested* third party to act as the mediator. 52

concurrent jurisdiction Jurisdiction shared by two or more courts. 36

condition A qualification of a promise that becomes a covenant if it is met. 318

condition precedent A condition that requires the occurrence of an event before a party is obligated to perform a duty under a contract. 318

condition subsequent A condition, if it occurs, that automatically excuses the performance of an existing contractual duty to perform. 319

condominium A common form of ownership in a multiple-dwelling building where the purchaser has title to the individual unit and owns the common areas as a tenant in common with the other condominium owners. 689

confirmation The bankruptcy court's approval of a plan of reorganization. 733

confusion A situation that occurs if two or more persons commingle fungible goods; title is then acquired by the commingling. 679

conglomerate merger A merger that does not fit into any other category; a merger between firms in totally unrelated businesses. 627

consequential damages Foreseeable damages that arise from circumstances outside the contract. In order to be liable for these damages, the breaching party must know or have reason to know that the breach will cause special damages to the other party. 325

consideration Something of legal value given in exchange for a promise. 283

Consolidated Omnibus Budget Reconciliation Act (COBRA) A federal law that permits employees and their beneficiaries to continue their group health insurance after an employee's employment has ended. 515

consolidation The act of a court to combine two or more separate lawsuits into one lawsuit. 42

Constitution of the United States of America The supreme law of the United States. 11

constructive notice Usually, written notice to a third party that is put into general circulation, such as in a newspaper. 430

Consumer Leasing Act (CLA) An amendment to the TILA that extends the TILA's coverage to lease terms in consumer leases. 576

Consumer Product Safety Act (CPSA) A federal statute that created the Consumer Product Safety Commission and regulates potentially dangerous consumer products. 570

consumer protection laws Federal and state statutes and regulations that promote product safety and prohibit abusive, unfair, and deceptive business practices. 556

contract in restraint of trade A contract that unreasonably restrains trade. 292

contract contrary to public policy A contract that has a negative impact on society or interferes with the public's safety and welfare. 291

contributory negligence A doctrine that says a plaintiff who is partially at fault for his or her own injury cannot recover against the negligent defendant. 131 A defense that says that a person who is injured by a defective product but has been negligent and has contributed to his or her own injuries cannot recover from the defendant. 169

convention A treaty that is sponsored by an international organization. 245

cooling-off period A period that is required so a union can give an employer at least 60 days' notice before a strike can commence. 506

cooperative A form of co-ownership of a multiple-dwelling building where a corporation owns the building and the residents own shares in the corporation. 689

co-ownership Ownership of a piece of real property by two or more persons. Also called *concurrent ownership*. 687

copyright infringement An act in which a party copies a substantial and material part of the plaintiff's copyrighted work without permission. A copyright holder may recover damages and other remedies against the infringer. 220

Copyright Revision Act of 1976 A federal statute that (1) establishes the requirements for obtaining a copyright and (2) protects copyrighted works from infringement. 218

corporate citizenship A theory of responsibility that says a business has a responsibility to do good. 105

corporation A fictitious legal entity that (1) is created according to statutory requirements and (2) is a separate taxpaying entity for federal income tax purposes. 453

corporations codes State statutes that regulate the formation, operation, and dissolution of corporations. 453

cost justification defense A defense in a Section 2(a) action that provides that a seller's price discrimination is not unlawful if the price differential is due to "differences in the cost of manufacture, sale, or delivery" of the product. 630

counteroffer A response by an offeree that contains terms and conditions different from or in addition to those of the offer. A counteroffer terminates an offer. 280

Court of Appeals for the Federal Circuit A court of appeals in Washington, DC, that has special appellate jurisdiction to review the decisions of the Claims Court, the Patent and Trademark Office, and the Court of International Trade. 33

Court of Chancery A court that granted relief based on fairness. Also called equity court. 10

covenant An unconditional promise to perform. 318

covenant of good faith and fair dealing Under this implied covenant, the parties to a contract not only are held to the express terms of the contract but also are required to act in "good faith" and deal fairly in all respects in obtaining the objective of the contract. 137

cover A right of a licensee to engage in a commercially reasonable substitute transaction after the licensor has breached the contract. 355

crashworthiness doctrine A doctrine that says that automobile manufacturers are under a duty to design automobiles so they take into account the possibility of harm from a person's body striking something inside the automobile in the case of a car accident. 164

credit report Information about a person's credit history that can be secured from a credit bureau. 577

creditor The lender in a credit transaction. 708

creditors' committee A committee composed of the creditors holding the seven largest unsecured claims. Committees represent the interests of their class, in the negotiation of a plan of organization. 730

crime A violation of a statute for which the government imposes a punishment. 178

criminal conspiracy A situation in which two or more persons enter into an agreement to commit a crime and an overt act is taken to further the crime. 190

criminal fraud The act of obtaining title to property through deception or trickery. Also known as false pretenses or deceit. 186

critical legal thinking The process of specifying the issue presented by a case, identifying the key facts in the case and applicable law, and then applying the law to the facts to come to a conclusion that answers the issue presented. 18

cross-complaint A document filed by the defendant against the plaintiff to seek damages or some other remedy. 42

crossover worker A person who does not honor a strike who either (1) chooses not to strike or (2) returns to work after joining the strikers for a time. 506

crown jewel A valuable asset of the target corporation's that the tender offeror particularly wants to acquire in the tender offer. 481

cruel and unusual punishment A provision of the Eighth Amendment that protects criminal defendants from torture or other abusive punishment. 199

custom The second source of international law, created through consistent, recurring practices between two or more nations over a period of time that have become recognized as binding. 245

"danger invites rescue" doctrine A doctrine that provides that a rescuer who is injured while going to someone's rescue can sue the person who caused the dangerous situation. 129

debenture A long-term, unsecured debt instrument that is based on the corporation's general credit standing. 462

debt collector An agent who collects debts for other parties. 577

debt securities Securities that establish a debtor–creditor relationship in which the corporation borrows money from the investor to whom the debt security is issued. 462

debtor The borrower in a credit transaction. 708

debtor-in-possession A debtor who is left in place to operate a business during a reorganization proceeding. 730

deed A document that describes a person's ownership interest in a piece of real property. 689

defamation of character False statement(s) made by one person about another. In court, the plaintiff must prove that (1) the defendant made an untrue statement of fact about the plaintiff and (2) the statement was intentionally or accidentally published to a third party. 115

defect Something wrong, inadequate, or improper in manufacture, design, packaging, warning, or safety measures of a product. 161

defect in design A defect that occurs when a product is improperly designed. 163

defect in manufacture A defect that occurs when the manufacturer fails to (1) properly assemble a product, (2) properly test a product, or (3) adequately check the quality of the product. 161

defect in packaging A defect that occurs when a product has been placed in packaging that is insufficiently tamperproof. 164

defendant's case The process by which the defendant (1) rebuts the plaintiff's evidence, (2) proves affirmative defenses, and (3) proves allegations made in a cross-complaint. 48

delegation doctrine A doctrine that says that when an administrative agency is created, it is delegated certain powers; the agency can use only those legislative, judicial, and executive powers that are delegated to it. 560

demand note A note payable on demand. 712

deponent The party who gives his or her deposition. 44

deposition The oral testimony given by a party or witness prior to trial. The testimony is given under oath and is transcribed. 44

derivative lawsuit A lawsuit a shareholder brings against an offending party on behalf of the corporation when the corporation fails to bring the lawsuit. 467

disaffirmance The act of a minor to rescind a contract under the infancy doctrine. Disaffirmance may be done orally, in writing, or by the minor's conduct. 286

discharge The termination of the legal duty of a debtor to pay debts that remain unpaid upon the completion of a bankruptcy proceeding. 727

discovery A legal process during which both parties engage in various activities to discover facts of the case from the other party and witnesses prior to trial. 44

disparagement False statements about a competitor's products, services, property, or business reputation. 133

disparate impact discrimination An employer's discrimination against an entire protected *class*. An example would be where a facially neutral employment practice or rule causes an adverse impact on a protected class. 529

disparate treatment discrimination An employer's discrimination against a specific *individual* because of his or her race, color, national origin, sex, or religion. 529

dispute settlement body A board comprised of one representative from each WTO member nation that reviews panel reports. 255

dissenting shareholder appraisal rights Rights of shareholders who object to a proposed merger, share exchange, or sale or lease of all or substantially all of the property of a corporation to have their shares valued by the court and receive cash payment of this value from the corporation. 478

distinctive A brand name that is unique and fabricated. 228

distributorship franchise A franchise in which the franchisor manufactures a product and licenses a retail franchisee to distribute the product to the public. 403

diversity of citizenship A case between (1) citizens of different states, (2) a citizen of a state and a citizen or subject of a foreign country, and (3) a citizen of a state and a foreign country where a foreign country is the plaintiff. 36

division of markets A situation in which competitors agree that each will serve only a designated portion of the market. 616

doctrine of sovereign immunity A doctrine that states that countries are granted immunity from suits in courts of other countries. 259

doctrine of strict liability in tort A tort doctrine that makes manufacturers, distributors, wholesalers, retailers, and others in the chain of distribution of a defective product liable for the damages caused by the defect, irrespective of fault. 157

domain name A unique name that identifies an individual's or a company's Web site. 344

domestic corporation A corporation in the state in which it was formed. 454

donee A person who receives a gift. 678

donor A person who gives a gift. 678

Double Jeopardy Clause A clause of the Fifth Amendment that protects persons from being tried twice for the same crime. 198

draft A three-party instrument that is an unconditional written order by one party that orders the second party to pay money to a third party. 709

Dram Shop Act A statute that makes taverns and bartenders liable for injuries caused to or by patrons who are served too much alcohol. 128

drawee of a check The financial institution on which a check is drawn. 711

drawee of a draft The party who must pay the money stated in the draft. Also called the *acceptor* of a draft. 709

drawer of a check The checking account holder and writer of a check. 711

drawer of a draft The party who writes the order for a draft. 709

dual-purpose mission An errand or another act that a principal requests of an agent while the agent is on his or her own personal business. 381

due diligence defense A defense to a Section 11 action that, if proven, makes the defendant not liable. 653

Due Process Clause A clause that provides that no person shall be deprived of "life, liberty, or property" without due process of the law. 81

duress Situation that occurs when one party threatens to do a wrongful act unless the other party enters into a contract. 310

duty not to willfully or wantonly injure The duty an owner owes a trespasser to prevent intentional injury or harm to the trespasser when the trespasser is on his or her premises. 129

duty of accountability A duty that an agent owes to maintain an accurate accounting of all transactions undertaken on the principal's behalf. 374

duty of care The obligation we all owe each other not to cause any unreasonable harm or risk of harm. 120 A duty that corporate directors and officers have to use care and diligence when acting on behalf of the corporation. 474

duty of compensation A duty that a principal owes to pay an agreed-upon amount to the agent either upon the completion of the agency or at some other mutually agreeable time. 374

duty of cooperation A duty that a principal owes to cooperate with and assist the agent in the performance of the agent's duties and the accomplishment of the agency. 375

duty of indemnification A duty that a principal owes to protect the agent for losses the agent suffered during the agency because of the principal's misconduct. 375

duty of loyalty A duty owed by a member of a member-managed LLC and a manager of a manager-managed LLC to be honest in his or her dealings with the LLC and to not act adversely to the interests of the LLC. 443 A duty that directors and officers have not to act adversely to the interests of the corporation and to subordinate their personal interests to those of the corporation and its shareholders. 472

duty of notification An agent's duty to notify the principal of information he or she learns from a third party or another source that is important to the principal. 373

duty of ordinary care The duty an owner owes an invitee or a licensee to prevent injury or harm when the invitee or licensee steps on the owner's premises. 129

duty of performance An agent's duty to a principal that includes (1) performing the lawful duties expressed in the contract and (2) meeting the standards of reasonable care, skill, and diligence implicit in all contracts. 372

duty of reimbursement A duty that a principal owes to repay money to the agent if the agent spent his or her own money during the agency on the principal's behalf. 375

duty of utmost care A duty of care that goes beyond ordinary care and that says common carriers and innkeepers have a responsibility to provide security to their passengers or guests. 129

easement A given or required right to make limited use of someone else's land without owning or leasing it. 691

e-commerce The sale of goods and services by computer over the Internet. 339

electronic mail (e-mail) Electronic written communication between individuals using computers connected to the Internet. 341

embezzlement The fraudulent conversion of property by a person to whom that property was entrusted. 186

eminent domain Power of the government to acquire private property for public purposes. 875 The taking of private property by the government for public use, provided just compensation is paid to the private property holder. 696

Employee Retirement Income Security Act (ERISA) A federal act designed to prevent fraud and other abuses associated with private pension funds. 514

employer lockout An act of an employer to prevent employees from entering the work premises when the employer reasonably anticipates a strike. 505

employer–employee relationship A relationship that results when an employer hires an employee to perform some form of service. 367

employment relationships (1) Business relationships, including employer–employee, (2) principal–agent, and (3) principal–independent contractor. 366

endorsee The person to whom a negotiable instrument is endorsed. 713

endorsement The signature (and other directions) written by or on behalf of the holder somewhere on the instrument. 713

endorser The person who endorses a negotiable instrument. 713

entrepreneur A person who forms and operates a new business either by him- or herself or with others. 396

enumerated powers Certain powers delegated to the federal government by the states. 63

Environmental Protection Agency (EPA) An administrative agency created by Congress in 1970 to coordinate the implementation and enforcement of the federal environmental protection laws. 586

Equal Credit Opportunity Act (ECOA) A federal statute that prohibits discrimination in the extension of credit based on sex, marital status, race, color, national origin, religion, age, or receipt of income from public assistance programs. 576

equal dignity rule A rule that says that agents' contracts to sell property covered by the statute of frauds must be in writing to be enforceable. 314

Equal Employment Opportunity Commission (EEOC) The federal administrative agency that is responsible for enforcing most federal antidiscrimination laws. 528

equal opportunity in employment The right of all employees and job applicants (1) to be treated without discrimination and (2) to be able to sue employers if they are discriminated against. 528

Equal Pay Act of 1963 An act that protects both sexes from pay discrimination based on sex; extends to jobs that require equal skill, equal effort, equal responsibility, and similar working conditions. 539

Equal Protection Clause A clause that provides that a state cannot "deny to any person within its jurisdiction the equal protection of the laws." 79

equitable remedies Remedies that may be awarded by a judge where there has been a breach of contract and either (1) the legal remedy is not adequate or (2) the judge wants to prevent unjust enrichment. 328

Establishment Clause A clause to the First Amendment that prohibits the government from either establishing a state religion or promoting one religion over another. 77

estate Ownership rights in real property; the bundle of legal rights that the owner has to possess, use, and enjoy the property. 685

estate pour autre vie A life estate measured in the life of a third party. 686

ethical fundamentalism A moral theory in which a person looks to an outside source for ethical rules or commands. 93

ethical relativism A moral theory that holds that individuals must decide what is ethical based on their own feelings as to what is right or wrong. 97

ethics A set of moral principles or values that governs the conduct of an individual or a group. 92

European Court of Justice The judicial branch of the European Union located in Luxembourg. It has jurisdiction to enforce European Union law. 251

European Union (Common Market) An international region that comprises many countries of Western Europe. It was created to promote peace and security as well as economic, social, and cultural development. 250

exclusionary rule A rule that says that evidence obtained from an unreasonable search and seizure can generally be prohibited from introduction at a trial or administrative proceeding against the person searched. 193

exclusive agency contract A contract that a principal and an agent enter into that says the principal cannot employ any agent other than the exclusive agent. 369

exclusive jurisdiction Jurisdiction held by only one court. 36

exclusive license A license that grants the licensee exclusive rights to use information rights for a specified duration. 351

exculpatory clause A contractual provision that relieves one (or both) parties to the contract from tort liability for ordinary negligence. 293

executed contract A contract that has been fully performed on both sides; a completed contract. 276

executive branch The part of the government that consists of the president and vice president. 63

executive order An order issued by a member of the executive branch of the government. 14

executory contract A contract that has not been fully performed by either or both sides. 276 A contract that has not been fully performed. With court approval, executory contracts may be rejected by a debtor in bankruptcy. 731

exempt property Property that may be retained by a debtor pursuant to federal or state law; a debtor's property that does not become part of the bankruptcy estate. 724

express agency An agency that occurs when a principal and an agent expressly agree to enter into an agency agreement with each other. 369

express contract An agreement that is expressed in written or oral words. 275

express warranty A warranty that is created when a seller or lessor makes an affirmation that the goods he or she is selling or leasing meet certain standards of quality, description, performance, or condition. 150

extortion A threat to expose something about another person unless that other person gives money or property. Often referred to as *blackmail.* 184

extradition The act of sending a person back to a country for criminal prosecution. 262

failure to provide adequate instructions A defect that occurs when a manufacturer does not provide detailed directions for safe assembly and use of a product. 167

failure to warn A defect that occurs when a manufacturer does not place a warning on the packaging of products that could cause injury if the danger is unknown. 165

Fair Credit and Charge Card Disclosure Act of 1988 An amendment to the TILA that requires disclosure of credit terms on credit- and charge-card solicitations and applications. 576

Fair Credit Reporting Act (FCRA) An amendment to the TILA that protects customers who are subjects of a credit report by setting out guidelines for credit bureaus. 577

Fair Debt Collection Practices Act (FDCPA) An act enacted in 1977 that protects consumer-debtors from abusive, deceptive, and unfair practices used by debt collectors. 577

Fair Labor Standards Act (FLSA) A federal act enacted in 1938 to protect workers. It prohibits child labor and establishes minimum wage and overtime pay requirements. 513

Fair Packaging and Labeling Act A federal statute that requires the labels on consumer goods to identify the product; the manufacturer, processor, or packager of the product and its address; the net quantity of the contents of the package; and the quantity of each serving. 571

fair use doctrine A doctrine that permits certain limited use of a copyright by someone other than the copyright holder without the permission of the copyright holder. 223

false imprisonment The intentional confinement or restraint of another person without authority or justification and without that person's consent. 114

federal administrative agencies Administrative agencies that are part of the executive or legislative branch of government. 558

Federal Insurance Contributions Act (FICA) A federal act that says employees and employers must make contributions into the Social Security fund. 517

Federal Patent Statute of 1952 A federal statute that establishes the requirements for obtaining a patent and protects patented inventions from infringement. 211

federal question A case arising under the U.S. Constitution, treaties, or federal statutes and regulations. 36

Federal Trade Commission (FTC) A federal government agency empowered to enforce federal franchising rules. 405 Federal administrative agency empowered to enforce the Federal Trade Commission Act and other federal consumer protection statutes. 571

Federal Unemployment Tax Act (FUTA) A federal act that requires employers to pay unemployment taxes; unemployment compensation is paid to workers who are temporarily unemployed. 517

federalism The U.S. form of government; the federal government and the 50 state governments share powers. 63

fee simple absolute A type of ownership of real property that grants the owner the fullest bundle of legal rights that a person can hold in real property. 685

fee simple defeasible A type of ownership of real property that grants the owner all the incidents of a fee simple absolute except that it may be taken away if a specified condition occurs or does not occur. 686

felony The most serious type of crime; inherently evil crime. Most crimes against persons and some business-related crimes are felonies. 178

final prospectus A final version of the prospectus that must be delivered by the issuer to the investor prior to or at the time of confirming a sale or sending a security to a purchaser. 647

financing statement A document filed by a secured creditor with the appropriate government office that constructively notifies the world of his or her security interest in personal property. 717

fixtures Goods that are affixed to real estate so as to become part thereof. 684

Food and Drug Administration (FDA) A federal administrative agency that administers and enforces the federal Food, Drug, and Cosmetic Act (FDCA) and other federal consumer protection laws. 563

Food, Drug, and Cosmetic Act (FDCA) A federal statute enacted in 1938 that provides the basis for the regulation of much of the testing, manufacture, distribution, and sale of foods, drugs, cosmetics, and medicinal products. 564

foreclosure A legal procedure by which a secured creditor causes the sale of the secured real estate to pay a defaulted loan. 719

Foreign Commerce Clause A clause of the U.S. Constitution that vests Congress with the power "to regulate commerce with foreign nations." 243

foreign corporation A corporation in any state or jurisdiction other than the one in which it was formed. 454

Foreign Sovereign Immunities Act An act that exclusively governs suits against foreign nations that are brought in federal or state courts in the United States. It codifies the principle of qualified, or restricted, immunity. 259

forgery The fraudulent making or altering of a written document that affects the legal liability of another person. 184

forum-selection clause A contract provision that designates a certain court to hear any dispute concerning non-performance of the contract. 38

forward vertical merger A vertical merger in which the supplier acquires the customer. 626

Fourteenth Amendment An amendment that was added to the U.S. Constitution in 1868. It contains the Due Process, Equal Protection, and Privileges and Immunities Clauses. 79

franchise An arrangement that is established when one party licenses another party to use the franchisor's trade name, trademarks, commercial symbols, patents, copyrights, and other property in the distribution and selling of goods and services. 402

franchise agreement An agreement that a franchisor and a franchisee enter into that sets forth the terms and conditions of the franchise. 406

fraud by concealment Fraud that occurs when one party takes specific action to conceal a material fact from another party. 309

fraud in the inception Fraud that occurs if a person is deceived as to the nature of his or her act and does not know what he or she is signing. 308

fraud in the inducement Fraud that occurs when the party knows what he or she is signing but has been fraudulently induced to enter into the contract. 308

Free Exercise Clause A clause to the First Amendment that prohibits the government from interfering with the free exercise of religion in the United States. 77

freedom of speech The right to engage in oral, written, and symbolic speech protected by the First Amendment. 72

freehold estate An estate where the owner has a present possessory interest in the real property. 685

fresh start A debtor's discharge from burdensome debts that allows him or her to begin again. 722

frolic and detour A situation in which an agent does something during the course of his employment to further his own interests rather than the principal's. 380

FTC franchise rule A rule set out by the FTC that requires franchisors to make full presale disclosures to prospective franchisees. 405

future interest The right to possess property in the future; the interest that the grantor retains for him- or herself or a third party. 686

gambling statutes Statutes that make certain forms of gambling illegal. 290

general duty A duty that an employer has to provide a work environment "free from recognized hazards that are causing or are likely to cause death or serious physical harm to his employees." 511

general partners Partners in a limited partnership who invest capital, manage the business, and are personally liable for partnership debts. 432

general partnership A voluntary association of two or more persons for carrying on a business as co-owners for profit. Also called a *partnership*. 424

general principles of law The third source of international law, consisting of principles of law recognized by civilized nations. These are principles of law that are common to the national law of the parties to the dispute. 246

general-jurisdiction trial court A court that hears cases of a general nature that are not within the jurisdiction of limited-jurisdiction trial courts. Testimony and evidence at trial are recorded and stored for future reference. 30

generally known dangers A defense that acknowledges that certain products are inherently dangerous and are known to the general population to be so. 167

generic name A term for a mark that has become a common term for a product line or type of service and therefore has lost its trademark protection. 232

genuineness of assent The requirement that a party's assent to a contract be genuine. Genuineness of assent is an issue in the areas of mistake, misrepresentation, duress, and undue influence. 306

gift A voluntary transfer of title to property without payment of consideration by the donee. To be a valid gift, the following three elements must be shown: donative intent, delivery, and acceptance. 678

gift promise A promise that is unenforceable because it lacks consideration. 284

Good Samaritan law A statute that relieves medical professionals from liability for ordinary negligence when they stop and render aid to victims in emergency situations. 127

government contractor defense A defense that says that a contractor who was provided specifications by the government is not liable for any defect in the product that occurs as a result of those specifications. 167

grantee The party to whom an interest in real property is transferred. 689

grantor The party who transfers an ownership interest in real property. 689

greenmail The purchase by a target corporation of its stock from an actual or perceived tender offeror at a premium. 481

group boycott A situation in which two or more competitors at one level of distribution agree not to deal with others at another level of distribution. 617

guarantor The person who agrees to pay the debt if the primary debtor does not. 313

guaranty arrangement An arrangement where a third party promises to be *secondarily liable* for the payment of another's debt. 720

guest statute A statute that provides that if a driver of a vehicle voluntarily and without compensation gives a ride to another person, the driver is not liable to the passenger for injuries caused by the driver's ordinary negligence. 128

Hart-Scott-Rodino Antitrust Improvement Act An act that requires certain firms to notify the FTC and the Department of Justice in advance of a proposed merger. Unless the government challenges the proposed merger within 30 days, the merger may proceed. 628

hazardous waste Waste that may cause or significantly contribute to an increase in mortality or serious illness or pose a hazard to human health or the environment if improperly managed. 597

horizontal merger A merger between two or more companies that compete in the same business and geographical market. 625

horizontal restraint of trade A restraint of trade that occurs when two or more competitors at the same *level of distribution* enter into a contract, combination, or conspiracy to restrain trade. 615

hung jury A jury that cannot come to a unanimous decision about the defendant's guilt. The government may choose to retry the case. 182

illegal consideration A promise to refrain from doing an illegal act. Such a promise will not support a contract. 284

illegal contract A contract to perform an illegal act. Cannot be enforced by either party to the contract. 290

illusory promise A contract into which parties enter but one or both of the parties can choose not to perform their contractual obligations. Such a contract lacks consideration. 285

Immigration Reform and Control Act of 1986 (IRCA) A federal statute that makes it unlawful for employers to hire illegal immigrants. 516

immoral contract A contract whose objective is the commission of an act that is considered immoral by society. 293

immunity from prosecution A situation in which the government agrees not to use any evidence given by a person granted immunity against that person. 197

implied agency An agency that occurs when a principal and an agent do not expressly create an agency, but it is inferred from the conduct of the parties. 369

implied exemptions Exemptions from antitrust laws that are implied by the federal courts. 632

implied warranty of authority A case in which an agent who enters into a contract on behalf of another party impliedly warrants that he or she has the authority to do so. 377

implied warranty of fitness for human consumption A warranty that applies to food or drink consumed on or off the premises of restaurants, grocery stores, fast-food outlets, and vending machines. 153

implied warranty of habitability A warranty that provides that the leased premises must be fit, safe, and suitable for ordinary residential use. 694

implied warranty of merchantability Unless properly disclosed, a warranty that is implied that sold or leased goods are fit for the ordinary purpose for which they are sold or leased, and other assurances. 151

implied-in-fact contract A contract in which agreement between parties has been inferred from their conduct. 275

impossibility of performance Nonperformance that is excused if the contract becomes impossible to perform; it must be objective impossibility, not subjective. 320

imputed knowledge Information that is learned by the agent that is attributed to the principal. 373

in personam jurisdiction Jurisdiction over the parties to a lawsuit. 37

in rem jurisdiction Jurisdiction to hear a case because of jurisdiction over the property of the lawsuit. 38

inaccessibility exception A rule that permits employees and union officials to engage in union solicitation on company property if the employees are beyond reach of reasonable union efforts to communicate with them. 500

incidental beneficiary A party who is unintentionally benefited by other people's contract. 296

independent contractor A person or business who is not an employee who is employed by a principal to perform a certain task on his or her behalf. 367 A person who contracts with another to do something for him who is not controlled by the other nor subject to the other's right to control with respect to his physical conduct in the performance of the undertaking [*Restatement (Second) of Agency*]. 382

indictment The charge of having committed a crime (usually a felony), based on the judgment of a grand jury. 181

indirect price discrimination A form of price discrimination (e.g., favorable credit terms) that is less readily apparent than direct forms of price discrimination. 630

infancy doctrine A doctrine that allows minors to disaffirm (cancel) most contracts they have entered into with adults. 286

inferior performance Performance that occurs when a party fails to perform express or implied contractual obligations that impair or destroy the essence of the contract. 323

information The charge of having committed a crime (usually a misdemeanor), based on the judgment of a judge (magistrate). 181

injunction A court order that prohibits a person from doing a certain act. 329

injury Personal injury or damage that a plaintiff suffers to his or her property to recover monetary damages for the defendant's negligence. 122

innkeeper's statutes State statutes that provide that an innkeeper can avoid liability for loss caused to a guest's property if (1) a safe is provided in which the guest's valuable property may be kept and (2) the guest is notified of this fact. 683

innocent misrepresentation Misrepresentation that occurs when an agent makes an untrue statement that he or she honestly and reasonably believes to be true. 380

INS Form I-9 A form that must be filled out by all U.S. employers for each employee. It states that the employer has inspected the employee's legal qualifications to work. 516

insane, but not adjudged insane A person who is insane but has not been adjudged insane by a court or an administrative agency. A contract entered into by such person is generally *voidable*. Some states hold that such a contract is void. 289

Insecticide, Fungicide, and Rodenticide Act A federal statute that requires pesticides, herbicides, fungicides, and rodenticides to be registered with the EPA; the EPA may deny, suspend, or cancel registration. 595

inside director A member of the board of directors who is also an officer of the corporation. 469

insider trading Trading that occurs when an insider makes a profit by personally purchasing shares of the corporation prior to public release of favorable information or by selling shares of the corporation prior to the public disclosure of unfavorable information. 658

Insider Trading Sanctions Act of 1984 A federal statute that permits the SEC to obtain a civil penalty of up to three times the illegal benefits received from insider trading. 662

intangible property Rights that cannot be reduced to physical form, such as stock certificates, certificates of deposit, bonds, and copyrights. 678

intellectual property rights The right to patents, copyrights, trademarks, trade secrets, trade names, domain names and other items of intellectual property that are very valuable business assets. Federal and state laws protect intellectual property rights from misappropriation and infringement. 208

intended beneficiary A third party who is not in privity of contract but who has rights under the contract and can enforce the contract against the obligor. 295

intentional infliction of emotional distress A tort that says that a person whose extreme and outrageous conduct intentionally or recklessly causes severe emotional distress to another person is liable for that emotional distress. Also known as the *tort of outrage*. 117

intentional interference with contractual relations A tort that arises when a third party induces a contracting party to breach the contract with another party. 137

intentional misrepresentation The intentional deception of another person out of money, property, or something else of value. 136 A seller or lessor fraudulently misrepresenting the quality of a product and a buyer being injured thereby. 156 Misrepresentation that occurs when one person consciously decides to induce another person to rely and act on a misrepresentation. Also called *fraud.* 308 Misrepresentation that occurs when an agent makes an untrue statement that he or she knows honestly and reasonably believes to be true. 308

intentional tort A category of torts that requires that the defendant possessed the intent to do the act that caused the plaintiff's injuries. 114 A tort that occurs when a person has intentionally committed a wrong against (1) another person or his or her character or (2) another person's property. 381

intermediate appellate court An intermediate court that hears appeals from trial courts. 31

intermediate scrutiny test A test that is applied to classifications based on protected classes other than race (e.g., sex or age). 80

International Court of Justice The judicial branch of the United Nations that is located in The Hague, the Netherlands. Also called the *World Court.* 248

international law Law that governs affairs between nations and that regulates transactions between individuals and businesses of different countries. 242

Internet A collection of millions of computers that provide a network of electronic connections between computers. 340

interrogatories Written questions submitted by one party to another party. The questions must be answered in writing within a stipulated time. 45

interstate commerce Commerce that moves between states or that affects commerce between states. 67

intervention The act of others joining as parties to an existing lawsuit. 42

intoxicated person A person who is under contractual incapacity because of ingestion of alcohol or drugs to the point of incompetence. 289

intrastate offering exemption An exemption from registration that permits local businesses to raise from local investors capital to be used in the local economy without the need to register with the SEC. 650

invasion of the right to privacy A tort that constitutes the violation of a person's right to live his or her life without being subjected to unwarranted and undesired publicity. 116

involuntary petition A petition filed by creditors of a debtor, which alleges that the debtor is not paying his or her debts as they become due. 723

issued shares Shares that have been sold by the corporation. 459

joint and several liability Tort liability of partnership in which the partners are liable together and separately. This means that the plaintiff can sue one or more of the partners separately. If successful, the plaintiff can recover the entire amount of the judgment from any or all of the defendant-partners. 428

joint liability Partners are *jointly liable* for contracts and debts of the partnership. This means that a plaintiff must name the partnership and all of the partners as defendants. If successful, the plaintiff can recover the entire amount of the judgment from any or all of the partners. 428

joint tenancy A form of co-ownership that includes the right of survivorship. 687

judgment The official decision of the court. 48

judgment notwithstanding the verdict (j.n.o.v.) In a civil case, the overturning of the jury's verdict by the judge if he or she finds bias or jury misconduct. 48

judicial branch The part of the government that consists of the Supreme Court and other federal courts. 63

judicial decision A decision about an individual lawsuit issued by federal or state courts. 14

judicial decisions and teachings The fourth source of international law, consisting of judicial decisions and writings of the most qualified legal scholars of the various nations involved in the dispute. 246

jurisdiction The authority of a court to hear a case. 37

jurisprudence The philosophy or science of law. 7

jury instructions Instructions given by the judge to the jury that informs the jurors of the law to be applied in the case. 48

Kantian or duty ethics A moral theory that says that people owe moral duties that are based on universal rules, such as the categorical imperative "do unto others as you would have them do unto you." 95

land The most common form of real property; includes the land and buildings and other structures permanently attached to the land. 684

land pollution Pollution of the land that is generally caused by hazardous waste being disposed of in an improper manner. 597

land use control The collective term for the laws that regulate the possession, ownership, and use of real property. 695

landlord–tenant relationship A relationship created when the owner of a freehold estate (landlord) transfers a right to exclusively and temporarily possess the owner's property to another (tenant). 691

Lanham Trademark Act (as amended) A federal statute that (1) establishes the requirements for obtaining a federal mark and (2) protects marks from infringement. 228

lapse of time A stated time period after which an offer expires. If no time is stated, an offer terminates after a reasonable time. 280

larceny The taking of another's personal property other than from his or her person or building. 184

law That which must be obeyed and followed by citizens subject to sanctions or legal consequences; a body of rules of action or conduct prescribed by controlling authority and having binding legal force. 4

law court A court that developed and administered a uniform set of laws decreed by the kings and queens after William the Conqueror; legal procedure was emphasized over merits at that time. 10

lease A transfer of the right to the possession and use of real property for a set term in return for certain consideration; the rental agreement between a landlord and a tenant. 693

leasehold A tenant's interest in the property. 692

legal entity A separate legal entity—an artificial person—distinct from its members that can own property, sue and be sued, enter into and enforce contracts, and such. 438

legislative branch The part of the government that consists of Congress (the Senate and the House of Representatives). 63

libel A false statement that appears in a letter, newspaper, magazine, book, photograph, movie, video, and so on. 115

license A contract that transfers limited rights in intellectual property and informational rights. 350

licensee The party who is granted limited rights in or access to intellectual property or information rights owned by the licensor. 351

licensing agreement A detailed and comprehensive written agreement between the licensor and licensee that sets forth the express terms of their agreement. 352

licensing statute A statute that requires a person or business to obtain a license from the government prior to engaging in a specified occupation or activity. 291

licensor The owner of intellectual property or information rights, who transfers rights in the property or information to the licensee. 351

licensor's damages If a licensee breaches a contract, the licensor may sue the licensee and recover monetary damages caused by the breach. 355

life estate An interest in real property for a person's lifetime; upon that person's death, the interest will be transferred to another party. 686

limited liability Liability in which members are liable for the LLC's debts, obligations, and liabilities only to the extent of their capital contributions. 438 A situation in which shareholders are liable for the corporation's debts and obligations only to the extent of their capital contributions. 455 Liability that shareholders of a corporation have, only to the extent of their capital contribution. Shareholders are generally not personally liable for debts and obligations of the corporation. 468

limited liability company (LLC) An unincorporated business entity that combines the most favorable attributes of general partnerships, limited partnerships, and corporations. 437

limited liability company codes State statutes that regulate the formation, operation, and dissolution of LLCs. 437

limited liability partnership (LLP) A form of partnership in which all partners are limited partners and there are no general partners. 436

limited partners Partners in a limited partnership who invest capital but do not participate in management and are not personally liable for partnership debts beyond their capital contribution. 432

limited partnership A special form of partnership that is formed only if certain formalities are followed. A limited partnership has both general and limited partners. 432

limited partnership agreement A document that sets forth the rights and duties of the general and limited partners, the terms and conditions regarding the operation, termination, and dissolution of the partnership, and so on. 434

limited-jurisdiction trial court A court that hears matters of a specialized or limited nature. 30

line of commerce Products or services that consumers use as substitutes. If an increase in the price of one product or service leads consumers to purchase another product or service, the two products are substitutes for each other. 624

liquidated damages Damages that are specified in a contract rather than determined by a court. 357

litigation The process of bringing, maintaining, and defending a lawsuit. 40

long-arm statute A statute that extends a state's jurisdiction to nonresidents who were not served a summons within the state. 38

lost property Property that is left somewhere by the owner because of negligence, carelessness, or inadvertence. 681

mail fraud The use of mail to defraud another person. 186

mailbox rule A rule that states that an acceptance is effective when it is dispatched, even if it is lost in transmission. 282

maker of a note The party who makes a promise to pay (borrower). 712

manager-managed LLC An LLC that has designated in its articles of organization that it is a manager-managed LLC. 442

Marine Protection, Research, and Sanctuaries Act A federal statute enacted in 1972 that extends environmental protection to the oceans. 593

mark The collective name for trademarks, service marks, certification marks, and collective marks that all can be trademarked. 227

market extension merger A merger between two companies in similar fields whose sales do not overlap. 626

material breach A breach that occurs when a party renders inferior performance of his or her contractual duties. 323

materialman's lien A contractor's and laborer's lien that makes the real property to which improvements are being made become security for the payment of the services and materials for those improvements. 719

maximizing profits A theory of social responsibility that says a corporation owes a duty to take actions that maximize profits for shareholders. 101

mediation A form of ADR in which the parties choose a *neutral third* party to act as the mediator of the dispute. 52

Medical Device Amendments to the FDCA Amendments enacted in 1976 that gives the FDA authority to regulate medical devices and equipment. 567

meeting of the creditors A meeting of the creditors in a bankruptcy case that must occur not less than 10 days nor more than 30 days after the court grants an order for relief. 723

meeting the competition defense A defense stipulated in Section 2(b) that says that a seller may lawfully engage in price discrimination to meet a competitor's price. 631

member An owner of an LLC. 438

member-managed LLC An LLC that has not designated that it is a manager-managed LLC in its articles of organization. 442

mens rea "Evil intent"—the possession of the requisite state of mind to commit a prohibited act. 179

Merchant Court The separate set of courts established to administer the "law of merchants." 10

merger A situation in which one corporation is absorbed into another corporation and ceases to exist. 477

minor's duty of restoration A minor's obligation to return goods or property at the time of disaffirmance. As a general rule, a minor is obligated only to return the goods or property he or she has received from the adult in the condition they are in at the time of disaffirmance. 287

mirror image rule A rule that states that in order for there to be an acceptance, the offeree must accept the terms as stated in the offer. 282

misdemeanor A less serious crime than a felony; not inherently evil but prohibited by society. Many crimes against property are misdemeanors. 178

mislaid property Property that is voluntarily placed somewhere and then inadvertently forgotten by the owner. 681

misuse A defense that relieves a seller of product liability if the user *abnormally* misused the product. Products must be designed to protect against *foreseeable* misuse. 168

mitigation A situation in which a nonbreaching party is under a legal duty to avoid or reduce damages caused by a breach of contract. 326

mobile sources Sources of air pollution such as automobiles, trucks, buses, motorcycles, and airplanes. 588

monetary damages Financial damages that a nonbreaching party may recover from a breaching party whether the breach was minor or material. 324

monopoly power The power to control prices or exclude competition, measured by the market share the defendant possesses in the relevant market. 622

moral minimum A theory of social responsibility that says a corporation's duty is to make a profit while avoiding harm to others. 103

mortgage A collateral arrangement in which real property owner borrows money from a creditor, who uses a deed as collateral for repayment of the loan. 718

motion for judgment on the pleadings A motion that alleges that if all the facts presented in the pleadings are taken as true, the party making the motion would win the lawsuit when the proper law is applied to these asserted facts. 46

motion for summary judgment A motion that asserts that there are no factual disputes to be decided by the jury; in this case, the judge can apply the proper law to the undisputed facts and decide the case without a jury. These motions are supported by affidavits, documents, and deposition testimony. 46

motivation test A test to determine the liability of the principal; if the agent's motivation in committing the intentional tort is to promote the principal's business, then the principal is liable for any injury caused by the tort. 381

mutual benefit bailment A bailment for the mutual benefit of the bailor and bailee. The bailee owes a *duty of reasonable care* to protect the bailed property. 683

mutual mistake of fact A mistake made by both parties concerning a material fact that is important to the subject matter of the contract. 308

mutual mistake of value A mistake that occurs if both parties know the object of the contract but are mistaken as to its value. 308

national courts The courts of individual nations. 258

National Labor Relations Board (NLRB) A federal administrative agency that oversees union elections, prevents employers and unions from engaging in illegal and unfair labor practices, and enforces and interprets certain federal labor laws. 498

necessaries of life The reasonable value of food, clothing, shelter, medical care, and other items considered necessary to the maintenance of life for which a minor must pay after he or she contracts for them. 288

negligence A tort related to defective products in which the defendant has breached a duty of due care and caused harm to the plaintiff. 156 Failure of a corporate director or officer to exercise the duty of care while conducting the corporation's business. 474

negligence per se A tort in which the violation of a statute or an ordinance constitutes the breach of the duty of care. 127

negligent infliction of emotional distress A tort that permits a person to recover for emotional distress caused by the defendant's negligent conduct. 125

Noise Control Act A federal statute enacted in 1972 that authorizes the EPA to establish noise standards for products sold in the United States. 602

noise pollution Unwanted sound from planes, manufacturing plants, motor vehicles, construction equipment, stereos, and the like. 602

nonattainment areas Regions that do not meet air quality standards. 589

noncompete clause An agreement whereby a person agrees not to engage in a specified business or occupation within a designated geographical area for a specified period of time following the sale. 292

nonconforming uses Uses and buildings that already exist in a zoned area that are permitted to continue even though they do not fit within new zoning ordinances. 696

nonprice vertical restraints Restraints of trade that are unlawful under Section 1 of the Sherman Act if their anticompetitive effects outweigh their procompetitive effects. 620

note A debt security with a maturity of five years or less. 462

note and deed of trust An alternative to a mortgage in some states. 718

novation An agreement that substitutes a new party for one of the original contracting parties and relieves the exiting party of liability on the contract. 319

Nuclear Regulatory Commision (NRC) A federal agency that licenses the construction and opening of commercial nuclear power plants. 599

Nuclear Waste Policy Act of 1982 A federal statute that says the federal government must select and develop a permanent site for the disposal of nuclear waste. 600

objective theory of contracts A theory that says that the intent to contract is judged by the reasonable person standard and not by the subjective intent of the parties. 274

obscene speech Speech that (1) appeals to the prurient interest, (2) depicts sexual conduct in a patently offensive way, and (3) lacks serious literary, artistic, political, or scientific value. 74

Occupational Safety and Health Act A federal act enacted in 1970 that promotes safety in the workplace. 511

offensive speech Speech that is offensive to many members of society. It is subject to time, place, and manner restrictions. 73

offer "The manifestation of willingness to enter into a bargain, so made as to justify another person in understanding that his assent to that bargain is invited and will conclude it." [*Restatement (Second) of Contracts* § 24] 278

offeree The party to whom an offer to enter into a contract is made. 272

offeror The party who makes an offer to enter into a contract. 272

officers Employees of a corporation who are appointed by the board of directors to manage the day-to-day operations of the corporation. 472

one-year rule A rule that states that an executory contract that cannot be performed by its own terms within one year of its formation must be in writing. 312

opening statements Statements made by the attorneys to the jury in which they summarize the factual and legal issues of the case. 47

operating agreement An agreement entered into by members that governs the affairs and business of the LLC and the relations among members, managers, and the LLC. 441

order for relief The filing of either a voluntary petition, an unchallenged involuntary petition, or a grant of an order after a trial of a challenged involuntary petition. 723

ordinances Laws enacted by local government bodies such as cities and municipalities, countries, school districts, and water districts. 12

ordinary bailments (1) Bailments for the sole benefit of the bailor, (2) bailments for the sole benefit of the bailee, and (3) bailments for the mutual benefit of the bailor and bailee. 682

organizational meeting A meeting that must be held by the initial directors of the corporation after the articles of incorporation are filed. 459

outside director A member of the board of directors who is not an officer of the corporation. 470

outstanding shares Shares of stock that are in shareholder hands. 460

pac-man tender offer An offer in which a corporation that is the target of a tender offer makes a *reverse tender offer* for the stock of the tender offeror. 481

palming off Unfair competition that occurs when a company tries to pass off one of its products as that of a rival. 133

panel A group of three WTO judges that hears trade disputes between member nations and issues a "panel report." 255

par value A value assigned to common shares by the corporation that sets the lowest price at which the shares may be issued by the corporation. 461

partnership at will A partnership with no fixed duration. 430

partnership for a term A partnership with a fixed duration. 430

past consideration A prior act or performance. Past consideration (e.g., prior acts) will not support a new contract. New consideration must be given. 285

patent infringement Unauthorized use of another's patent. A patent holder may recover damages and other remedies against a patent infringer. 213

payee of a check The party to whom the check is written. 711

payee of a draft The party who receives the money from a draft. 709

payee of a note The party to whom a promise to pay is made (lender). 712

penal codes A collection of criminal statutes. 178

per se rule A rule that is applicable to those restraints of trade considered inherently anticompetitive. Once this determination is made, the court will not permit any defenses or justifications to save it. 614

periodic tenancy A tenancy created when a lease specifies intervals at which payments are due but does not specify how long the lease is for. 692

permanent trustee A legal representative of the bankruptcy debtor's estate, usually an accountant or lawyer, who is elected at the first meeting of the creditors. 723

personal property Property that consists of tangible property, such as automobiles, furniture, and jewelry, and intangible property, such as securities, patents, and copyrights. 677

petition for certiorari A petition asking the Supreme Court to hear one's case. 34

physical or mental examination Examinations that may be ordered by a court to determine the extent of a defendant's alleged injuries. 45

picketing The action of strikers walking in front of the employer's premises, carrying signs announcing their strike. 506

piercing the corporate veil A doctrine that says that if a shareholder dominates a corporation and misuses it for improper purposes, a court of equity can disregard the corporate entity and hold the shareholder personally liable for the corporation's debts and obligations. 468

plaintiff The party who files the complaint. 41

plaintiff's case The process by which the plaintiff introduces evidence to prove the allegations contained in his or her complaint. 48

plan of reorganization A plan that sets forth a proposed new capital structure for the debtor to have when it emerges from reorganization bankruptcy. The debtor has the exclusive right to file the first plan of reorganization; any party of interest may file a plan thereafter. 732

plant life and vegetation Real property that is growing in or on the surface of the land. 684

plea bargain A situation in which the accused admits to a lesser crime than charged. In return, the government agrees to impose a lesser sentence than might have been obtained had the case gone to trial. 182

pleadings The paperwork that is filed with the court to initiate and respond to a lawsuit. 41

point sources Sources of water pollution such as paper mills, manufacturing plants, electric utility plants, and sewage plants. 592

police power The power of states to regulate private and business activity within their borders. 69

Postal Reorganization Act An act that makes the mailing of unsolicited merchandise an unfair trade practice. 574

posteffective period The period of time that begins when the registration statement becomes effective and runs until the issuer either sells all of the offered securities or withdraws them from sale. 647

potential competition theory A theory that reasons that the real or implied threat of increased competition keeps businesses more competitive. A merger that would eliminate this perception can be enjoined under Section 7. 627

potential reciprocity theory A theory that says that if Company A, which supplies materials to Company B, mergers with Company C (which in turn gets its supplies from Company B), the newly merged company can coerce Company B into dealing exclusively with it. 627

power of attorney An express agency agreement that is often used to give an agent the power to sign legal documents on behalf of the principal. 369

precedent A rule of law established in a court decision. Lower courts must follow the precedent established by higher courts. 15

preemption doctrine The concept that federal law takes precedence over state or local law. 65

preemptive rights Rights that give existing shareholders the option of subscribing to new shares being issued in proportion to their current ownership interest. 465

preexisting duty Something a person is already under an obligation to do. A promise lacks consideration in the case of preexisting duty. 285

preferred stock A type of equity security that is given certain preferences and rights over common stock. 461

preferred stockholder A person who owns preferred stock. 461

prefiling period A period of time that begins when the issuer first contemplates issuing the securities and ends when the registration statement is filed. The issuer may not *condition* the market during this period. 647

Pregnancy Discrimination Act An amendment to Title VII that forbids employment discrimination because of "pregnancy, childbirth, or related medical conditions." 532

pretrial hearing A hearing before the trial in order to facilitate the settlement of a case. Also called a settlement conference. 46

pretrial motion A motion a party can make to try to dispose of all or part of a lawsuit prior to trial. 46

price-fixing A situation in which competitors in the same line of business agree to set the price of the goods or services they sell; raising, depressing, fixing, pegging, or stabilizing the price of a commodity or service. 615

principal A party who employs another person to act on his or her behalf. 366

principal–agent relationship A relationship in which an employer hires an employee and gives that employee authority to act and enter into contracts on his or her behalf. 367

private placement exemption An exemption from registration that permits issuers to raise capital from an unlimited number of accredited investors and no more than 35 nonaccredited investors without having to register the offering with the SEC. 650

Private Securities Litigation Reform Act of 1995 An act that provides a safe harbor from liability for companies that make forward-looking statements that are accompanied by meaningful cautionary statements of risk factors. 665

Privileges and Immunities Clause A clause that prohibits states from enacting laws that unduly discriminate in favor of their residents. 83

probability of a substantial lessening of competition A probability that a merger will substantially lessen competition or create a monopoly that prompts the court to prevent the merger under Section 7 of the Clayton Act. 625

procedural due process A category of due process that requires that the government give a person proper notice and hearing of the legal action before that person is deprived of his or her life, liberty, or property. 82

processing plant franchise A franchise in which the franchisor provides a secret formula or process to the franchisee, and the franchisee manufactures the product and distributes it to retail dealers. 404

production of documents A request by one party to another party to produce all documents relevant to the case prior to trial. 45

products liability The liability of manufacturers, sellers, and others for the injuries caused by defective products. 149

professional malpractice The liability of a professional who breaches his or her duty of ordinary care. 126

promissory estoppel An equitable doctrine that permits enforcement of oral contracts that should have been in writing. It is applied to avoid injustice. 315

promissory note A two-party negotiable instrument that is an unconditional written promise by one party to pay money to another party. 712

proof of claim A document required to be filed by an unsecured creditor that states the amount of the creditor's claim against the debtor. 724

prospectus A written disclosure document that must be submitted to the SEC along with the registration statement and given to prospective purchasers of the securities. 646

proximate cause, or legal cause A point along a chain of events caused by a negligent party after which this party is no longer legally responsible for the consequences of his or her actions. 124

proxy The written document that a shareholder signs, authorizing another person to vote his or her shares at the shareholders' meetings in the event of the shareholder's absence. 464

punitive damages Damages that are awarded to punish the defendant, to deter the defendant from similar conduct in the future, and to set an example for others. 137, 326

purchasing property The most common method of acquiring title to personal property. 678

qualified individual with a disability A person who (1) has a physical or mental impairment that substantially limits one or more of his or her major life activities, (2) has a record of such impairment, or (3) is regarded as having such impairment. 542

quasi in rem jurisdiction Jurisdiction allowed a plaintiff who obtains a judgment in one state to try to collect the judgment by attaching property of the defendant located in another state. 38

quasi-contract An equitable doctrine whereby a court may award monetary damages to a plaintiff for providing work or services to a defendant even though no actual contract existed. 275 An equitable doctrine that permits the recovery of compensation even though no enforceable contract exists between the parties. 329

quorum The required number of shares that must be represented in person or by proxy to hold a shareholder's meeting. 464

Racketeer Influenced and Corrupt Organizations Act (RICO) A federal statute that provides for both criminal and civil penalties for engaging in a pattern of racketeering activity. 665

radiation pollution Emissions from radioactive wastes that can cause injury and death to humans and other life and can cause severe damage to the environment. 599

ratification The act of a minor after the minor has reached the age of majority by which he or she accepts a contract entered into when he or she was a minor. 288 A principal's acceptance of an agent's unauthorized contract. 377

rational basis test A test that is applied to classifications not involving a suspect or protected class. 80

Rawls's social justice theory A moral theory that says each person is presumed to have entered into a social contract with all others in society to obey moral rules that are necessary for people to live in peace and harmony. 96

real property The land itself as well as buildings, trees, soil, minerals, timber, plants, and other things permanently affixed to the land. 684

receiving stolen property (1) Knowingly receiving stolen property and (2) intending to deprive the rightful owner of that property. 184

record date A date that determines whether a shareholder receives payment of a declared dividend. 467

recording statute A statute that requires the mortgage or deed of trust to be recorded in the county recorder's office in the county in which the real property is located. 718

redeemable preferred stock Stock that permits the corporation to buy back the preferred stock at some future date. 462

reformation An equitable doctrine that permits the court to rewrite a contract to express the parties' true intentions. 329

registration statement A document that an issuer of securities files with the SEC that contains required information about the issuer, the securities to be issued, and other relevant information. 646

regular meeting A meeting held by the board of directors at the time and place established in the bylaws. 470

rejection Express words or conduct by the offeree that rejects an offer. Rejection terminates the offer. 280

relevant geographical market A relevant market that is defined as the area in which the defendant and its competitors sell a product or service. 622

relevant product or service market A relevant market that includes substitute products or services that are reasonably interchangeable with the defendant's products or services. 622

religious discrimination Discrimination against a person solely because of his or her religion or religious practices. 536

remainder A situation in which the right of possession returns to a third party upon the expiration of a limited or contingent estate. 687

replacement worker A worker who is hired to take the place of a striking worker. A replacement worker can be hired on either a temporary or permanent basis. 506

reply A document filed by the original plaintiff to answer the defendant's cross-complaint. 42

res ipsa loquitur A tort in which the presumption of negligence arises because (1) the defendant was in exclusive control of the situation and (2) the plaintiff would not have suffered injury but for someone's negligence. The burden switches to the defendant to prove that he or she was not negligent. 127

resale price maintenance A *per se* violation of Section 1 of the Sherman Act that occurs when a party at one level of distribution enters into an agreement with a party at another level to adhere to a price schedule that either sets or stabilizes prices. 619

rescission An action to rescind (undo) a contract. Rescission is available if there has been a material breach of contract, fraud, duress, undue influence, or mistake. 327

resolution A decision by the board of directors that approves a transaction. 470

Resource Conservation and Recovery Act (RCRA) A federal statute that authorizes the EPA to regulate facilities that generate, treat, store, transport, and dispose of hazardous wastes. 597

respondeat superior A rule that says an employer is liable for the tortious conduct of its employees or agents while they are acting within the scope of its authority. 380

restitution Returning of goods or property received from the other party in order to rescind a contract; if the actual goods or property is not available, a cash equivalent must be made. 327

restricted securities Securities that were issued for investment purposes pursuant to the intrastate, private placement, or small offering exemptions. 651

reverse discrimination Discrimination against a group that is usually thought of as a majority. 547

reversion A right of possession that returns to the grantor after the expiration of a limited or contingent estate. 687

Revised Model Business Corporation Act (RMBCA) A 1984 revision of the MBCA that arranged the provisions of the original act more logically, revised the language to be more consistent, and made substantial changes in the provisions. 454

Revised Uniform Limited Partnership Act (RULPA) A 1976 revision of the ULPA that provides a more modern, comprehensive law for the formation, operation, and dissolution of limited partnerships. 432

revocation Withdrawal of an offer by the offeror that terminates an offer. 280

right of redemption A right that the mortgagor has to redeem real property after default and before foreclosure. It requires the mortgagor to pay the full amount of the debt incurred by the mortgagee because of the mortgagor's default. 719

right to cure A right of a licensor to repair a contract under certain circumstances. 355

River and Harbor Act A federal statute enacted in 1886 that established a permit system for the discharge of refuse, wastes, and sewage into U.S. navigable waterways. 591

robbery The taking of personal property from another person by use of fear or force. 183

Rule 10b-5 A rule adopted by the SEC to clarify the reach of Section 10(b) against deceptive and fraudulent activities in the purchase and sale of securities. 657

rule of reason A rule that holds that only unreasonable restraints of trade violate Section 1 of the Sherman Act. The court must examine the pro- and anticompetitive effects of the challenged restraint. 614

rules and regulations Laws that administrative agencies adopt to interpret the statutes that they are authorized to enforce. 558

Sabbath law A law that prohibits or limits the carrying on of certain secular activities on Sundays. 291

Safe Drinking Water Act A federal statute enacted in 1974 and amended in 1986 that authorizes the EPA to establish national primary drinking water standards. 593

scienter Intentional conduct that is required for there to be a violation of Section 10(b) and Rule 10b-5. 657

search warrant A warrant issued by a court that authorizes the police to search a designated place for specified contraband, articles, items, or documents. The search warrant must be based on probable cause. 193

secondary boycott picketing A type of picketing in which unions try to bring pressure against an employer by picketing his or her suppliers or customers. 506

secondary meaning A brand name that has evolved from an ordinary term. 228

Section 1 of the Sherman Act An act that prohibits *contracts*, *combinations*, and *conspiracies* in restraint of trade. 614 An act that prohibits tying arrangements involving goods, services, intangible property, and real property. 628

Section 10(b) A provision of the Securities Exchange Act of 1934 that prohibits the use of manipulative and deceptive devices in the purchase or sale of securities in contravention of the rules and regulations prescribed by the SEC. 657

Section 11 A provision of the Securities Act of 1933 that imposes civil liability on persons who intentionally defraud investors by making misrepresentations or omissions of material facts in the registration statement or who are negligent for not discovering the fraud. 653

Section 12 A provision of the Securities Act of 1933 that imposes civil liability on any person who violates the provisions of Section 5 of the act. 653

Section 14(e) A provision of the Williams Act that prohibits fraudulent, deceptive, and manipulative practices in connection with a tender offer. 480

Section 16(a) A section of the Securities Exchange Act of 1934 that defines any person who is an executive officer, a director, or a 10 percent shareholder of an equity security of a reporting company as a *statutory insider* for Section 16 purposes. 663

Section 16(b) A section of the Securities Exchange Act of 1934 that requires that any profits made by a statutory insider on transactions involving *short-swing profits* belong to the corporation. 663

Section 2 of the Sherman Act An act that prohibits the act of monopolization and attempts or conspiracies to monopolize trade. 622

Section 2(a) of the Robinson-Patman Act An act that prohibits direct and indirect price discrimination by sellers of a commodity of a like grade and quality where the effect of such discrimination may be to substantially lessen competition or to tend to create a monopoly in any line of commerce. 630

Section 24 A provision of the Securities Act of 1933 that imposes criminal liability on any person who willfully violates the act or the rules or regulations adopted thereunder. 653

Section 3 of the Clayton Act An act that prohibits tying arrangements involving sales and leases of goods. 628

Section 32 A provision of the Securities Exchange Act of 1934 that imposes criminal liability on any person who willfully violates the 1934 act or the rules or regulations adopted thereunder. 662

Section 5 of the Federal Trade Commission Act A portion of the FTC Act that prohibits unfair and deceptive practices. 572, 631

Section 7 of the NLRA A law that gives employees the right to join together and form a union. 499

Section 8(a) of the NLRA A law that makes it an *unfair labor practice* for an employer to interfere with, coerce, or restrain employees from exercising their statutory right to form and join unions. 501

Section 8(b) of the NLRA A law that prohibits unions from engaging in unfair labor practices that interfere with a union election. 501

section of the country A division of the United States that is based on the relevant geographical market; the geographical area that will feel the direct and immediate effects of a merger. 624

secured credit Credit that requires security (collateral) that protects payment of the loan. 716

secured transaction A transaction that is created when a creditor makes a loan to a debtor in exchange for the debtor's pledge of personal property as security. 717

Securities and Exchange Commission (SEC) A federal administrative agency that is empowered to administer federal securities laws. The SEC can adopt rules and regulations to interpret and implement federal securities laws. 645

Securities Act of 1933 A federal statute that primarily regulates the issuance of securities by corporations, partnerships, associations, and individuals. 645

Securities Exchange Act of 1934 A federal statute that primarily regulates the trading in securities. 656

security (1) An interest or instrument that is common stock, preferred stock, a bond, a debenture, or a warrant; (2) an interest or instrument that is expressly mentioned in securities acts; and (3) an investment contract. 645

Self-Employment Contributions Act A federal act that says self-employed persons must pay Social Security taxes equal to the combined employer–employee amount. 517

self-incrimination The giving of testimony that will likely subject a person to criminal prosecution. The Fifth Amendment states that no person shall be compelled in any criminal case to be a witness against him- or herself. 196

service mark A mark that distinguishes the services of the holder from those of its competitors. 227

service of process A summons being served on the defendant to obtain personal jurisdiction over him or her. 38

sex discrimination Discrimination against a person solely because of his or her sex. 532

sexual harassment Lewd remarks, touching, intimidation, posting of indecent material, and other verbal or physical conduct of a sexual nature that occur on the job. 533

shareholders The owners of corporations, whose ownership interests are evidenced by stock certificates. 453

short-form merger A merger between a parent corporation and a subsidiary corporation that does not require the vote of the shareholders of either corporation or the board of directors of the subsidiary corporation. 478

slander Oral defamation of character. 115

small claims court A court that hears civil cases involving small dollar amounts. 30

small offering exemption An exemption from registration that permits the sale of securities not exceeding $1 million during a 12-month period. 651

social host liability rule A rule that provides that social hosts are liable for injuries caused by guests who become intoxicated at a social function. States vary as to whether they have this rule in effect. 129

Social Security A federal system that provides limited retirement and death benefits to covered employees and their dependents. 517

sole proprietorship A form of business in which the owner is actually the business; the business is not a separate legal entity. 398

sources of international law Those things that international tribunals rely on in settling international disputes. 245

special federal courts Federal courts that hear matters of specialized or limited jurisdiction. 32

special meeting A meeting convened by the board of directors to discuss new shares, merger proposals, hostile takeover attempts, and so forth. 470

special shareholders' meetings Meetings of shareholders that may be called to consider and vote on important or emergency issues, such as a proposed merger, amending the articles of incorporation, and such. 463

specific duty A duty of a specific nature (e.g., requirement for a safety guard on a particular type of equipment). 511

specific performance A judgment of a court ordering a licensor to specifically perform a license by making the contracted-for unique information available to the licensee. 356 A remedy that orders the breaching party to perform the acts promised in the contract. Specific performance is usually awarded in cases in which the subject matter is unique, such as in contracts involving land, heirlooms, paintings, and the like. 328

stakeholder interest A theory of social responsibility that says a corporation must consider the effects its actions have on persons other than its stockholders. 103

standing to sue The plaintiff must have some stake in the outcome of the lawsuit. 37

stare decisis Latin: "to stand by the decision." Adherence to precedent. 15

state action exemptions Exemptions in which business activities that are mandated by state law are exempt from federal antitrust laws. 632

state administrative agencies Administrative agencies that states create to enforce and interpret state law. 558

state antitakeover statutes Statutes enacted by state legislatures that protect from hostile takeovers corporations incorporated in or doing business in the state. 482

state supreme court The highest court in a state court system; it hears appeals from intermediate state courts and certain trial courts. 31

stationary sources Sources of air pollution such as industrial plants, oil refineries, and public utilities. 588

statute Written law enacted by the legislative branch of the federal and state governments that establishes certain courses of conduct that must be adhered to by covered parties. 12

statute of frauds A state statute that requires certain types of contracts to be in writing. 311

statute of limitations A statute that establishes the period during which a plaintiff must bring a lawsuit against a defendant. 43 A statute that requires an injured person to bring an action within a certain number of years from the time that he or she was injured by the defective product. 168

statute of repose A statute that limits the seller's liability to a certain number of years from the date when the product was first sold. 168

statutory exemptions Exemptions from antitrust laws that are expressly provided in statutes enacted by Congress. 632

strict liability Liability without fault. 138

strict, or absolute, liability A standard for imposing criminal liability without a finding of *mens rea* (intent). 179

strict scrutiny test A test that is applied to classifications based on race. 80

strike A cessation of work by union members in order to obtain economic benefits or correct an unfair labor practice. 505

subject matter jurisdiction Jurisdiction over the subject matter of a lawsuit. 37

substantial performance Performance by a contracting party that deviates only slightly from complete performance. 322

substantive due process A category of due process that requires that government statutes, ordinances, regulations, or other laws be clear on their face and not overly broad in scope. 81

subsurface rights Rights to the earth located beneath the surface of the land. 684

summons A court order directing the defendant to appear in court and answer the complaint. 41

superseding event An intervening event for which a defendant is not responsible. 130

supervening event An alteration or a modification of a product by a party in the chain of distribution that absolves all prior sellers from strict liability. 167

supervening illegality The enactment of a statute or regulation or court decision that makes the object of an offer illegal. This terminates the offer. 280

supramajority voting requirement A requirement that a greater than majority of shares constitutes quorum or the vote of the shareholders. 464

Supreme Court of the United States The Supreme Court was created by Article III of the U.S. Constitution. The Supreme Court is the highest court in the land. It is located in Washington, DC. 33

Supremacy Clause A clause of the U.S. Constitution that establishes that the federal Constitution, treaties, federal laws, and federal regulations are the supreme law of the land. 65

surety arrangement An arrangement in which a third party promises to be *primarily* liable with the borrower for the payment of the borrower's debt. 720

taking possession A method of acquiring ownership of unowned personal property. 678

tangible property Physically defined personal property, such as goods, animals, and minerals. 678

target corporation The corporation that is proposed to be acquired in a tender offer situation. 480

tenancy at sufferance A tenancy created when a tenant retains possession of property after the expiration of another tenancy or a life estate without the owner's consent. 693

tenancy at will A lease that may be terminated at any time by either party. 692

tenancy by the entirety A form of co-ownership of real property that can be used only by married couples. 688

tenancy for years A tenancy created when the landlord and the tenant agree on a specific duration for the lease. 692

tenancy in common A form of co-ownership in which the interest of a surviving tenant in common passes to the deceased tenant's estate and not to the co-tenants. 687

tender offer An offer that an acquirer makes directly to a target corporation's shareholders in an effort to acquire the target corporation. 480

tender offeror The party that makes a tender offer. 480

termination by acts of the parties Termination of an agency that can occur by the following acts of the parties: (1) mutual agreement, (2) lapse of time, (3) purpose achieved, and (4) occurrence of a specified event. 384

termination by operation of law An agency's termination by operation of law, including: (1) death of the principal or agent, (2) insanity of the principal or agent, (3) bankruptcy of the principal, (4) impossibility of performance, (5) changed circumstances, and (6) war between the principal's and agent's countries. 385

thermal pollution Pollution created by heated water or material being discharged into waterways. It upsets the ecological balance and decreases the oxygen content. 593

time note A note payable at a specific time. 712

tippee A person who receives material nonpublic information from a tipper. 661

tipper A person who discloses material nonpublic information to another person. 661

Title I of the Landrum-Griffin Act An act that is referred to as labor's "bill of rights" that gives each union member equal rights and privileges to nominate candidates for union office, vote in elections, and participate in membership meetings. 507

Title VII of the Civil Rights Act of 1964 (Fair Employment Practices Act) An act that is intended to eliminate job discrimination based on five protected classes: race, color, religion, sex, and national origin. 529

tort A wrong. There are three categories of torts. (1) intentional torts, (2) unintentional torts (negligence), and (3) strict liability. 113

tort of misappropriation of the right to publicity An attempt by another person to appropriate a living (and in some states dead) person's name or identity for commercial purposes. 116

toxic air pollutants Air pollutants that cause serious illness or death to humans. 589

toxic substances Chemicals used for agricultural, industrial, and mining uses that cause injury to humans, birds, animals, fish, and vegetation. 595

Toxic Substances Control Act A federal statute enacted in 1976 that requires manufacturers and processors to test new chemicals to determine their effect on human health and the environment before the EPA will allow them to be marketed. 596

trade dress Federal protection of the look and feel of a product, a product's packaging, or a service establishment. 230

trade secret A product formula, pattern, design, compilation of data, customer list, or other business secret. 208 Ideas that make a franchise successful but that do not qualify for trademark, patent, or copyright protection. 410

trademark A distinctive mark, symbol, name, word, motto, or device that identifies the goods of a particular business. 227

trademark infringement Unauthorized use of another's mark. The holder may recover damages and other remedies from the infringer. 229

trademarks and service marks Distinctive marks, symbols, names, words, mottoes, or devices that identify the goods or services of a particular franchisor. 409

treasury shares Shares of stock repurchased by the company itself. 460

treaty A compact made between two or more nations. 12 The first source of international law, consisting of an agreement or a contract between two or more nations that are formally signed by an authorized representative and ratified by the supreme power of each nation. 245

Treaty Clause A clause of the U.S. Constitution that states the president "shall have the power . . . to make treaties, provided two-thirds of the senators present concur." 243

trespass to land A tort in which a person interferes with an owner's right to exclusive possession of land. 118

trespass to personal property A tort that occurs whenever one person injures another person's personal property or interferes with that person's enjoyment of his or her personal property. 119

trial briefs Documents submitted by the parties' attorneys to the judge that contain legal support for their sides of the case. 47

trier of fact The jury in a jury trial; the judge where there is not a jury trial. 47

tying arrangement A restraint of trade in which a seller refuses to sell one product to a customer unless the customer agrees to purchase a second product from the seller. 628

UCC statute of frauds A provision for contracts that says that the sale of *goods* costing $500 or more must be in writing. 313

U.S. Constitution The fundamental law of the United States of America. It was ratified by the states in 1788. 63

U.S. courts of appeals The federal court system's intermediate appellate courts. 33

U.S. district courts The federal court system's trial courts of general jurisdiction. 32

unconscionability A doctrine under which courts may deny enforcement of unfair or oppressive contracts. 327

undue influence One person's taking advantage of another person's mental, emotional, or physical weakness and unduly persuading that person to enter into a contract; the persuasion by the wrongdoer must overcome the free will of the innocent party. 310

unenforceable contract A contract in which the essential elements to create a valid contract are met but there is some legal defense to the enforcement of the contract. 277

unfair advantage theory A theory that holds that a merger may not give the acquiring firm an unfair advantage over its competitors in finance, marketing, or expertise. 627

unfair competition Competition that violates the law. 133

Uniform Computer Information Transactions Act (UCITA) A model act that provides uniform and comprehensive rules for contracts involving computer information transactions and software and information licenses. 340 A model state law that creates contract law for the licensing of information technology rights. 350

Uniform Franchise Offering Circular (UFOC) A uniform disclosure document that requires the franchisor to make specific presale disclosures to prospective franchisees. 405

Uniform Limited Liability Company Act (ULLCA) A model act that provides comprehensive and uniform laws for the formation, operation, and dissolution of LLCs. 438

Uniform Partnership Act (UPA) A model act that codifies partnership law. Most states have adopted the UPA in whole or a part. 424

unilateral contract A contract in which the offeror's offer can be accepted only by the performance of an act by the offeree, a "promise for an act." 273

unilateral mistake A situation in which only one party is mistaken about a material fact regarding the subject matter of a contract. 307

unilateral refusal to deal A unilateral choice by one party not to deal with another party. This does not violate Section 1 of the Sherman Act because there is no concerted action. 621

unintentional tort or negligence A doctrine that says a person is liable for harm that is the foreseeable consequence of his or her actions. 119

union shop An establishment in which an employee must join the union within a certain number of days after being hired. 504

unprotected speech Speech that is not protected by the First Amendment and may be forbidden by the government. 73

unreasonable search and seizure Any search and seizure by the government that violates the Fourth Amendment. 193, 561

unsecured credit Credit that does not require any security (collateral) to protect the payment of the debt. 716

usury law A law that sets an upper limit on the interest rate that can be charged on certain types of loans. 291

utilitarianism A moral theory that dictates that people must choose the action or follow the rule that provides the greatest good to society. 94

valid contract A contract that meets all the essential elements to establish a contract; a contract that is enforceable by at least one of the parties. 276

variance An exception that permits a type of building or use in an area that would not otherwise be allowed by a zoning ordinance. 695

venue A concept that requires lawsuits to be heard by the court with jurisdiction that is nearest the location in which the incident occurred or where the parties reside. 39

verdict The decision reached by the jury. 48

vertical merger A merger that integrates the operations of a supplier and a customer. 626

vertical restraint of trade A restraint of trade that occurs when two or more parties on *different levels of distribution* enter into a contract, combination, or conspiracy to restrain trade. 619

violation A crime that is neither a felony nor a misdemeanor and that is usually punishable by a fine. 178

void contract A contract that has no legal effect; a nullity. 276

voidable contract A contract in which one or both parties have the option to void their contractual obligations. 276

voir dire A process whereby prospective jurors are asked questions by the judge and attorneys to determine if they would be biased in their decisions. 47

voluntary petition A petition filed by the debtor, which states that the debtor has debts. 723

waiting period A period of time that begins when the registration statement is filed with the SEC and continues until the registration statement is declared effective. Only certain activities are permissible during the waiting period. 647

warranties of quality Seller's or lessor's assurance to the buyer or lessee that the goods meet certain standards of quality. Warranties may be expressed or implied. 150

warranty A buyer's or lessee's assurance that the goods meet certain standards. 149

water pollution Pollution of lakes, rivers, oceans, and other bodies of water. 591

wetlands Areas that are inundated or saturated by surface water or ground water that support vegetation typically adapted for life in such conditions. 593

white-collar crimes Crimes usually involving cunning and deceit rather than physical force. 186

will or inheritance A way to acquire title to property that is a result of another's death. 681

Williams Act A 1968 amendment to the Securities Exchange Act of 1934 that specifically regulates all tender offers. 480

wire fraud The use of telephone or telegraph to defraud another person. 186

workers' compensation acts Acts that compensate workers and their families if workers are injured in connection with their jobs. 509

work-related test A test to determine the liability of a principal; if an agent commits an intentional tort within a work-related time or space, the principal is liable for any injury caused by the agent's intentional tort. 381

World Trade Organization (WTO) An international organization of more than 130 member nations created to promote and enforce trade agreements among member nations. 254

World Wide Web An electronic connection of millions of computers that support a standard set of rules for the exchange of information. 342

writ of certiorari An official notice that the Supreme Court will review one's case. 34

wrongful dissolution A partner's withdrawal from a partnership when he or she does not have the right to do so. 430

wrongful termination Termination of a franchise without just cause. 415 The termination of an agency contract in violation of the terms of the agency contract. The nonbreaching party may recover damages from the breaching party. 387

zoning ordinances Local laws that are adopted by municipalities and local governments to regulate land use within their boundaries. Zoning ordinances are adopted and enforced to protect the health, safety, and general welfare of the community. 695

Case Index

Cases cited or discussed are in roman type. Principal cases are in ***bold type****.*

Subject Index

F

Q

R

T

U

V

W

X

Z

Cases